PANDORA PRESS

A

FEMINIST

DICTIONARY

A
FEMINIST
DICTIONARY

**CHERIS KRAMARAE
AND PAULA A. TREICHLER**

WITH ASSISTANCE FROM ANN RUSSO

P A N D O R A   P R E S S

Boston, London and Henley

First published in 1985 by Pandora Press
(Routledge & Kegan Paul plc)

9 Park Street, Boston, Mass. 02108, USA

14 Leicester Square, London WC2H 7PH, England and

Broadway House, Newtown Road,
Henley on Thames, Oxon RG9 1EN, England

Set in Baskerville 8 point on 9
by Columns of Reading
and printed in Great Britain

Library of Congress Cataloging in Publication Data

Kramarae, Cheris.

A feminist dictionary.
Bibliography: P.
1. Feminism—Dictionaries. I. Treichler,
Paula A. II. Title
HQ1115.K73   1985   305.4'2'0321   85—9278

ISBN 0-86358-060-2 (c)
*   0-86358-015-7 (p)*

Contents

A living language must keep pace with improvements in knowledge and with the multiplication of ideas.

(Noah Webster 1817)

Our Earthly Possessions are truly enough called a Patrimony, as derived to us by the industry of our FATHERS; but the Language that we speak is our MOTHER-TONGUE; And who so proper to play the Criticks in this as the FEMALES.

(Quoted in Elizabeth Elstob 1715)

You must know who is the object and who is the subject of a sentence in order to know if you are the object or the subject of history.

(Nélida Piñon 1982)

The dictionary is, however, only a rough draft.

(Monique Wittig and Sande Zeig 1976)

For
Brinlee Kramer and Jana Kramer
Cora Davis Cambron and Jessie Cambron Treichler

Acknowledgments

We want to thank all who contributed to this project, many of whom are listed in the internal citations. Philippa Brewster originated the idea of a feminist dictionary and provided advice and support throughout. Research assistants at various stages of the project were Karen Lee Cole, Sally Green, Robin Johnston, Chandra Talpade Mohanty, and Lana Rakow. We give special thanks to Jane Cook who typed the original manuscript and the bibliography with speed and good will.

Others who provided technical assistance, contributed ideas or material, or critiqued the manuscript include Laura Battle, Phyllis Barkhurst, Evelyn Torton Beck, Shari Benstock, Sid Berger, Daniel K. Bloomfield, Audrey Cermak, Berenice A. Carroll, Patricia Cramer, Jesse Delia, Priscilla Diaz-Dorr, Pat Donze, Renate Duelli-Klein, Thomas W. Filardo, Francine Frank, Diane Friedmann, Gail Glende-Rost, Steve Goldman, Larry Grossberg, Mona Howard, Mary Jacobus, Dale Kramer, Sylvia A. Law, Shelly Levy, Howard Maclay, Marilyn Malina, Sally McConnell-Ginet, Bridget McGill, Carol Thomas Neely, Cary Nelson, Laura O'Banion, Sandra Panici, Joan Patchen, Pamela Patton, Constance Penley, William M. Plater, Suzanne Poirier, Heidi Reindl-Scheuering, Andrew Ross, Pam Salela, Joan Schultz, Muriel Schulz, Ailbhe Smyth, Dale Spender, Jack Stillinger, Edward P. Sullivan Jr., Harold M. Swartz, Meg Sweet, Barrie Thorne, Lourdes Torres, Ellen Wartella, Sarah Wasserman, Sandra Watanabe, Denice Wells, Patricia Wenzel, Cheryl West, Linda S. Wilson, and Pamela Yates.

We received valuable help from many librarians and curators, including Fran Allegri and Phyllis Self, University of Illinois Library of the Health Sciences; Maryann Bamberger, University of Illinois at Chicago; Nan Becker, Printed Matter; Butler Library, Columbia University; Chicago Historical Society; Joclyn Cohen, Helaine/

Acknowledgments

Victoria; Priscilla Diaz-Dorr, University of Tulsa; Duke University Archives; Equal Opportunities Commission, Manchester; Catherine Ireland and David Doughan, Fawcett Library; Diana Lachatanere, Schomburg Center for Research in Black Culture; Edith P. Mayo, Smithsonian Division of Political History; Republic of Ireland Council for the Status of Women; Sarah Sherman, North-western University Library; Beth Stafford, University of Illinois at Urbana-Champaign; Tulsa Center for the Study of Women's Literature; Women in Publishing, Dublin; Women's Studies Center, Dublin.

We also received important material support from the University of Illinois at Urbana-Champaign Graduate College Research Board, School of Humanities, Department of Speech Communication, Institute of Communications Research, Office of Women's Studies, and Unit for Criticism and Interpretive Theory; from the College of Medicine at Urbana-Champaign and the College of Medicine's Word Processing Center; and from the National Council of Teachers of English.

Finally, we were also supported by the wit and wisdom of the thousands of women whose words we encountered and enjoyed.

Words on a Feminist Dictionary

This is a word-book with several purposes: to document words, definitions, and conceptualizations that illustrate women's linguistic contributions; to illuminate forms of expression through which women have sought to describe, reflect upon, and theorize about women, language, and the world; to identify issues of language theory, research, usage, and institutionalized practice that bear on the relationship between women and language; to demonstrate ways in which women are seizing the language; to broaden knowledge of the feminist lexicon; and to stimulate research on women and language. Like many other dictionaries, it is a compendium of words arranged in alphabetical order together with definitions, quoted citations and illustrations, and other forms of commentary. Yet in some respects, it is different from what many people expect a "dictionary" to be. In this introduction, we will briefly elaborate on our goals for this book in relation to those of other lexicographic projects by women and men and suggest what future dictionary-making might include. (See also the dictionary entries under AUTHORITY, DICTIONARY, LANGUAGE, and LEXICOGRAPHER.)

Lexicography (the writing or compiling of dictionaries), as we note below, may have a variety of aims and encompass many different sorts of projects. Though *A Feminist Dictionary* shares some of the aims and characteristics of other dictionaries, several important points should be noted:

(1) We recognize women as linguistically creative speakers – that is, as originators of spoken or written language forms. The identification, documentation, and celebration of *women's* words and definitions depart from traditional lexicographic practice. Though dictionary editors claim (often militantly) to collect words and definitions from diverse sources, their criteria and procedures (both explicit and implicit) for identification and preservation nearly always

preclude the gathering of women's definitions. Definitions for many dictionaries, for example, are constructed from usages found in works of the "best authors"; though the equation has been challenged in recent years, this designation usually means "male authors." Similarly, one criterion for the inclusion in a dictionary of a "new word" is the number of times it is found cited in print; given current cultural practices, not only are men's words more likely to be cited in the mainstream press, but also few dictionary editors seek out print media where women's words would predominate (such as feminist periodicals). Thus despite whatever usage practices may actually exist in the world, multiple mechanisms act to exclude women's usages from dictionaries.[1]

Sexism is also at work. H. Lee Gershuny (1973), examining sentences in the *Random House Dictionary* that illustrated word usage, argued that a dictionary not merely reflects sexist social attitudes but acts in a variety of ways to preserve and recreate stereotypes as well – thus perpetuating notions of women as particular kinds of speakers (to illustrate usage for the word *nerves*, the *RHD* used "Women with shrill voices get on his *nerves*." As Meaghan Morris (1982) notes, a dictionary may also render women invisible; the Australian *Macquarie Dictionary* obliterates women's linguistic and political achievements through the way in which it constructs definitions and thus achieves what Morris calls "code control": *sexism* is defined as "the upholding or propagation of sexist attitudes," a *sexist attitude* as one which "stereotypes a person according to gender or sexual preference, etc.," and *feminism* as an "advocacy of equal rights and opportunities for women." As Morris points out, *sexism* was originally used by *women* attempting to construct a theory of patriarchy; the notion of stereotyping a "person" by virtue of holding certain "attitudes" obscures and almost makes nonsense of its original political meaning; by defining *feminism* in terms of its lowest common denominator, both current and historical distinctions among different feminist positions are eliminated. "While it is true," writes Morris, "that the usages accepted by the *Macquarie* are standard liberal currency today, the point is that the concepts developed by feminists are not even marginalised into second place, but rather omitted entirely" (89). For another example, one might point to the *Doublespeak Dictionary* (William Lambdin 1979) which cites a small number of feminist linguistic innovations – largely, it would appear, to ridicule them;

though one of the dictionary's stated aims is to identify deceptive, distorted, or ambiguous language, the nonsexist usage *him/her* [or her/him], designed to reduce the ambiguity of the so-called generic *he*, is castigated as a "clumsy," "legal," and "neutered" style (109-10). Dictionaries are, in fact, a prime example of discourse in which the generic *he* has evidently seemed adequate to represent the whole of humankind.[2]

In short, the systematic – even when inadvertent – exclusion of one sex replicates and preserves the linguistic and cultural rule of the other. The traditional focus on "literary," "newsworthy," or "authoritative" sources obscures women's very existence as speaking subjects. Interestingly, women's documented reputation for speaking more "correctly" than men do does not help them here: for they are interpreted to be mere receivers and transmitters of the code and hence incapable of making original contributions to the language. While men's definitions have been preserved in hundreds of dictionaries, this view of women's speech has excluded their words; in producing this dictionary, it is this view that we most wish to challenge and subvert. Accordingly, *A Feminist Dictionary* insists upon the significance of women as speaking subjects and documents their linguistic contributions.

(2) We acknowledge the sociopolitical aspects of dictionary-making. While we see this dictionary as a balance to the weight of other dictionaries in men's favor, we have tried as well to be self-conscious and explicit about our decisions and procedures. A recurrent difficulty in creating a "feminist" dictionary concerns *whose* feminism an entry represents. Our 1980s feminism has inevitably pulled us toward the material that seems most useful and enriching to us. Though citations from earlier periods perform the valuable task of making women's names and words visible and attesting to the existence of women's rebellious words through the years, we are especially aware as we make selections from archival materials that we may be disturbing somewhat the links between the words of our foresisters and their times. Forms of domination and the texture of feminist discussions have changed over the years in ways our selection process and the structure of the dictionary may obscure. The dictionary format can only hint at the complexities involved in feminist discussions.

As feminist lexicographers, we do not claim objectivity nor believe that simply by offering a dictionary of "women's words" we can reverse the profound structural inequities of history and culture. The dictionary is also therefore a critique of current and past practices; collectively, the entries provide commentary on the institutionalized processes and politics through which some forms of language are privileged over others – how words get into print, why they go out of print, the politics of bibliography and archival storage, the politics of silence, of speech, of what can be said, of who can speak and who listen.

(3) We preserve women's *own* words. *A Feminist Dictionary* is subtitled *In Our Own Words*. Though *our* words – as scholars and writers – figure in many of the entries, the core of the book lies in the verbatim citation of other women's words. These citations are intended not only to illustrate word usage or illuminate a particular perspective but also to encourage a reading of the original source in its entirety. As we initially talked about this project, we thought it might be a book of key words – that is, a set of short essays about words or concepts that have had special significance for feminism.[3] But such synthesizing articles would have hidden the diversity we found as well as obscured both the problematics and pleasures of feminist talk and writing. We have tried to provide narrative entries at certain key points to create a framework for the book as a whole but these are not forced on the reader; rather they are offered as background, interpretation, and allusion. Accordingly, as we note below, entries take a variety of shapes including short aphorisms, longer citations, dialogues and trialogues, etymologies, and narrative text.

(4) We are not seeking to set forth a linguistic norm for a given community of speakers. In practical terms, the fact that we forsake this traditional theoretical grounding for lexicography means that with few exceptions we do not specify "part of speech" (noun, verb, etc.) nor label entries according to their linguistic status (obsolete, rare, visionary, neologism, etymologically incorrect, politically incorrect, etc.).[4] The entry for HERSTORY, for example, labels it neither as a coinage (all words are coinages) nor as folk linguistics; such labels have meaning only in reference to a "real" body of "authorized" words, and as we have already noted there are many reasons why we should be dubious of this authorization process. At the same time, the dictionary draws words and definitions from such utopian works as Monique Wittig's and Sande Zeig's *Lesbian Peoples:*

Material for a Dictionary (1976), Sally Miller Gearhart's *Wanderground*, and Suzette Haden Elgin's *Native Tongue* (1984), thereby suggesting not only what is or has been but what might be.

(5) Though *A Feminist Dictionary* is not intended to be a guide to women's intellectual thought, individual entries (see for example FARKSOO, GIRL, MARRIAGE, TRAFFIC IN WOMEN) are intended to stimulate research or theoretical development; collectively, the dictionary's entries should work to illuminate many lines of feminist thinking and debate. At the same time, by tracing a word or idea through a series of cross-references, the reader may begin to explore a particular line of theoretical thinking and see links between particular words and ideas. Our dictionary does not spell out all those links nor attempt to fashion contemporary feminisms into a seemingly codified and interpreted body of thought. We hope that *A Feminist Dictionary* will be used as women work to name and analyze specific structural oppressions and work for revolutionary change.

A NOTE ON MALE DICTIONARY-MAKING

We have suggested ways in which *A Feminist Dictionary* is different from many other dictionaries. But it is also important to note that our project addresses many of the same theoretical questions and practical problems that other dictionary-makers have had to address. Further, the term *dictionary* itself encompasses projects of striking diversity – many of which, like this one, depart from the practices characteristic of the "standard" American dictionary with its familiar claims to authority, comprehensiveness, legislative value, and scientific objectivity.

Under the rubric "dictionary" go the *Oxford English Dictionary*, *Webster's Third International*, the *Random House Dictionary*, the *American Heritage Dictionary*, and other standard contributions to lexicography. But the term also includes a range of individual, often quirky, projects. These include Gustave Flaubert's *Dictionary of Accepted Ideas*, published in 1881 (See ACTRESS) and Ambrose Bierce's 1911 *The Devil's Dictionary* (See MUSH); even Raymond Williams' *Keywords* (1976) can in some sense be called a dictionary. A number of influential dictionaries explicate and analyze subsets of the lexicon: J. Laplanche and J.-B. Pontalis' *Dictionary of Psychoanalysis* (1973), Thomas Bottomore's *Dictionary of Marxist Thought* (1983), and Oswald Ducrot and Tzvetan Todorov's *Encyclopedic Dictionary of the Sciences of*

Language are examples. There have also been hundreds of man-made dictionaries produced to explicate even more specialized subsets of the lexicon, virtually all oriented toward traditionally masculine occupations, interests, or values. Dictionaries vary as to organizational arrangement (some, like *Roget's Thesaurus* or David Wallechinsky and Irving Wallace's *The People's Almanac* (1975), are arranged by semantic category as opposed to alphabetical format, for example), purpose (some dictionaries are essentially glossaries of "hard words"), accessibility, influence, and methodology (e.g., whether the data are primarily qualitative or quantitative – the latter an important feature of linguistic atlases and many dialect dictionaries). Finally, dictionaries vary enormously in terms of resources. Some are products of one person alone in a room with books. In contrast, the *Oxford English Dictionary* took 70 years to complete. *Webster's Third* was estimated to have required 757 "editor years" and to have cost more than $3,500,000 to produce.

The 1612 Italian *Vocabolario degli Accademici della Crusca* was the first big dictionary of a modern standard language; based almost exclusively on citations from classical Florentine writers like Dante, it did not claim to describe or prescribe general speech norms but did establish the tradition of drawing meanings from the "best authors." The disjunction between spoken and written language continually complicates the task of specifying what a given language consists of.[5] Many countries established academies, language boards, or commissions to legislate upon this question; in France, most notoriously, the Académie Française officially determines what *the code* is to be. Despite attempts to establish similar bodies as keepers of the code in Britain and the United States, a generally anti-authoritarian tradition has prevailed, with dictionaries – beginning with Samuel Johnson's very influential *Dictionary* of 1755 – taking on this codifying role. When the final volume of James Murray's *Oxford English Dictionary* was published in 1928 (seventy years after the British Philological Society initiated the project), the Oxford University Press expounded upon its "superiority to all other English dictionaries, in accuracy and completeness . . . [It] is the supreme authority, and without a rival" (K. M. Elisabeth Murray 1977, 312). Most other English and American dictionaries have been directed toward the documentation of existing language forms; a tradition of lexicographic positivism leads editors to claim "scientific objectivity." In contrast, dictionary editors in other languages have often inserted themselves much more forcefully into the codification process; one German lexicographer, for example, invented an elaborate system for labelling entries which among other things distinguished between obsolete words "recently introduced by good writers or deserving re-introduction" and those "incapable of re-introduction" (Ladislav Zgusta ed. 1980, 9).

In contemporary linguistics, attempts to define "the lexicon"[6] are linked to various theoretical questions: How is our internal knowledge of a language – its "internalized norm" – to be externally and explicitly represented? What is the source of our knowledge of these norms (e.g., introspection, experience, empirical research)? How do dictionary entries relate to each other and to objects in the world?[7] What is the status of cultural knowledge in our understanding of the meaning of a word? What is the relation of word usage to conditions for speaking? How is it possible to represent anything in language when in representing or interpreting one text, we inevitably create another? These questions are relevant as we explore the relationship between women and language: How is a concept like *woman* to be explicitly specified in a definition? (See BLACK WOMEN, DICTIONARY, ETYMOLOGY, WHITE WOMEN, WOMAN, WOMEN OF COLOR) Whose data will be used to formulate such a definition? (See OBJECTIVITY) What kind of "research" is deemed necessary (and by whom) for the construction of dictionary definitions? (See WOMEN AND LANGUAGE RESEARCH) Whose purposes will particular definitions serve? (See LANGUAGE) What consequences (e.g. legal) might a given definition have for women in the "real world"? (See RAPE, PROSTITUTION, WOMAN) From what stance or perspective does one present "new" definitions of women without inscribing authority and universality upon the definition by its very construction and publication? (See AUTHOR, AUTHORITY, DICTIONARY).

There is no doubt that the "male" dictionaries, constructed almost entirely by men with male readers and users in mind, offer useful information about words and about the world. Yet their exclusion of women, together with their pervasive claims to authority, is profoundly disturbing. The authority inherent in dictionary-making, and the strange arrogance toward language it may generate, is explicitly articulated by some lexicographers:

To me, making a dictionary has seemed much like building a sizable house singlehanded; and, having built it, wiring, plumbing, painting and furnishing it. Moreover, it takes about as long. But there can be no question that there is great satisfaction in the labor. When at last you survey the bundles of manuscript ready for the press you have the pardonable but, alas, fleeting illusion that now you know everything; that at last you are in the position to justify the ways of man to God. (J. A. Cuddon 1977)

Thus despite the immense achievements that some of these dictionaries represent and their unique contributions to scholarship, they have been created within the context of social arrangements where hostility toward and exclusion of women have thrived.

As H. Lee Gershuny (1977) has pointed out, the dictionary's significant role as the cultural authority for meaning and usage makes it an important site for feminist analysis. As the review above suggests, lexicography is a complex enterprise that encompasses many kinds of projects. It is all the more striking then that for women, no matter what the project, the ultimate outcome is the same: whether descriptive or prescriptive, authoritarian or democratic, massive or minimal, systematic or quixotic, these dictionaries have systematically excluded any notion of women as speakers, as linguistic innovators, or as definers of words. Women in their pages have been rendered invisible, reduced to stereotypes, ridiculed, trivialized, or demeaned.[8] Whatever their intentions, then, dictionaries have functioned as linguistic legislators which perpetuate the stereotypes and prejudices of their writers and editors, who are almost exclusively male.

WOMEN'S DICTIONARIES, FEMINIST DICTIONARIES

But there is another tradition. In 1892, Anna Julia Cooper in her essay "The Higher Education of Women" wrote:

In the very first year of our century, the year 1801, there appeared in Paris a book by Silvain Marechal, entitled 'Shall Woman Learn the Alphabet.' The book proposes a law prohibiting the alphabet to women, and quotes authorities weighty and various, to prove that the woman who knows the alphabet has already lost part of her womanliness. The author declares that woman can use the alphabet only as Moliere predicted they would, in spelling out the verb *amo*; that they have no occasion to peruse Ovid's *Ars Amoris*, since that is already the ground and limit of their intuitive furnishing; that Madame Guion would have been far more adorable had she remained a beautiful ignoramus as nature made her; that Ruth, Naomi, the Spartan woman, the Amazons, Penelope, Andromache, Lucretia, Joan of Arc, Petrarch's Laura, the daughters of Charlemagne, could not spell their names; while Sappho, Aspasia, Madame de Maintenon, and Madame de Staël could read altogether too well for their good; finally, that if women were once permitted to read Sophocles and work with logarithms, or to nibble at any side of the apple of knowledge, there would be an end forever to their sewing on buttons and embroidering slippers. (Anna Julia Cooper 1892; in Bert James Loewenberg and Ruth Bogin, eds 1976, 318)

But women were not to be kept from the alphabet. While N.H.'s *The Ladies Dictionary* (1694), was not a sisterly effort but a male effort which offered ladies some definitions of women's names and essays on topics such as love and religion, several eighteenth-century dictionaries suggested the growth of more genuine interest in women as readers; they were dedicated not only to "scholars" but also to "the Female sex" (Shirley Morahan 1981, 55). Women became writers as well. Elizabeth Elstob produced the first grammar of Anglo-Saxon in 1715; her dedication to the Princess of Wales noted that her royal highness had probably never before received a book written by a member of the female sex.

With the feminist movement, certainly by the time of Mary Wollstonecraft's *Vindication of the Rights of Women* in 1789, came increasing self-conscious attention to the meaning of words. Not only have feminists been concerned with women's access to words – through reading, education, writing, and publication – but also they write about how words like WOMAN, RIGHTS, JUSTICE, MARRIAGE, and EQUALITY are to be defined (see the dictionary entries under these words). They critique existing definitions (see WILL) and propose new ones (see HOME, CHIVALRY, WOMEN). They point to words and concepts in the cultural mainstream that undermine our ability even to articulate women's condition (see ANGEL); the so-called "generic" use of *he* and *man* was challenged (e.g., by Charlotte Carmichael Stopes 1908; and see entries under HE and MAN). They challenge existing language and originate new language (see -ESS, BIBLE, OBEY, PRAYER). With the organization of the suffrage movement, this engagement with language grew even more intense, with women beginning the process of reclaiming male-defined negative words about women (see RECLAMATION, SUFFRAGETTE). Suffragists and suffragettes published their own ABCs ("N is for NOW, Mr. Putoff, M. P., The day after no-time Will not do for me"). In 1941 Mary Ritter Beard undertook a feminist critique of the *Encyclopaedia Britannica*; though the editors who had commissioned the 42-page report did not act on her suggestions, she recommended redefining many entries and adding material on the contributions and concerns of women (Ann J. Lane 1977).

In the modern feminist movement, beginning in the late 1960s, feminists have addressed language issues in relation to feminist theory, scholarship, action, and policy. A central problem is the relationship of women to a male-oriented symbolic system: what the writer Varda One called "Manglish" in her language columns in the early 1970s and what Dale Spender identifies as "man-made language" (1980). Examination of the processes of cultural authorization has led feminists to the institution where language and authority most dramatically intersect: the dictionary. Gershuny, mentioned above, undertook a systematic study of the dictionary in the early 1970s. At the same time, Varda One's columns inspired the *New Feminist English Dictionary*, subtitled "An Intelligent Woman's Guide to Dirty Words" (1974). Ruth Todasco and her colleagues began their project as they "sat around with an unabridged dictionary and started shouting out dirty words," a process that yielded six types of "patriarchal epithets: Woman as Whore, as Whorish, as Body, as Animal, as -ess, and as -ette" (Ruth Todasco 1974). This demonstration of men's myths about women and their sexuality was drawn primarily from the established dictionaries of the English language which, Todasco wrote, "are museum pieces of an archaic culture," but also a "powerful reinforcing expression of men's prejudice against women." Julia Penelope Stanley (1977b) also used standard dictionaries and grammars to identify words designating males and females, pointing out both structural and political exclusions of females; Muriel Schulz (1975), examining pairs of words like dog and bitch, proposed a process that she called the SEMANTIC DEROGATION OF WOMEN to account for the repeated "sliding" of the female term toward negative meanings, usually associated with sexuality or prostitution. Many other projects during the last fifteen years have sought to illuminate the implications for women of the received male standard and of the semantic and social space in which words and their meanings come to life. (E.g., Alice Molloy c.1973, Alleen Pace Nilsen, Jenny R. Snider 1975, Una Stannard 1977; and see references in Casey Miller and Kate Swift 1976, Dale Spender 1980, Barrie Thorne and Nancy Henley eds 1975, Barrie Thorne, Cheris Kramarae, and Nancy Henley eds 1983, and the journal *Women and Language*).

A different approach is taken in the "Woman's New Word Dictionary," an issue of a feminist journal edited by Midge Lennert and Norma Willson (1973). Feminist definitions replace man-made ones; *construction*, for example, is defined as "a well-paying field of human endeavor not open to women" and *tipping* as "a fantasy that allows our society to justify less than minimum wages for waitresses." In the 1976 *Lesbian Peoples: Material for a Dictionary*, published first in French, Monique Wittig and Sande Zeig offer their work as a corrective to what they call the "lacunary" — the empty spaces of our history as represented by most dictionaries and fables. More recently Suzette Haden Elgin, a linguist, has created a women's language to incorporate women's concerns; the Láadan lexicon includes many words about, for example, the complexities of and feelings toward pregnancy, menstruation, the failure of published histories to record accomplishments of women, the varieties of love – concepts which exist at present only through lengthy explanations. (Begun in 1982, the Láadan language project is the subject of Elgin's 1984 science fiction novel *Native Tongue*.) Other projects, similarly, seek not merely to challenge the male lexicon but to offer radical new interpretations of it (Barbara G. Walker 1983), to change what the lexicon of the English language is to consist of (Bina Goldfield 1983, Judy Grahn 1984) and how it is organized (Joan Marshall 1977), and in doing so to challenge the processes and institutions which create and codify language use. Thus Liz Mackie's "Socialist Feminist Dictionary (59th edition)" defines CAREER WOMAN as

an archaic term which correlates strongly with the meritocratic phase of British monopoly capitalism. It became obsolete in the twenty-first century when the entry of large numbers of women into the workforce reduced the working day, improved conditions at the workplace and eventually brought about universal 'part-time' working and shared childrearing. (Liz Mackie 1984, 8)

Thus a "dictionary" is created not to authorize but to challenge and envision.

While different in scope and format, all these projects are companions to *A Feminist Dictionary* and signal the continuing and intense interest women have had in finding, creating, and using alternatives to male lexicographic traditions.

A FEMINIST DICTIONARY

We have called this book "a feminist dictionary" to capture the multiple meanings that those words convey. It is at once a dictionary of feminist thinking and word-making; a conceptual guide to that subset of the lexicon concerned with feminism; a documentation of feminist perspectives, interpretations of words, and contributions to linguistic creativity and scholarship; and a dictionary itself made by feminists (See DICTIONARY). Though this book is concerned with *women*, we have called it a feminist dictionary rather than a women's dictionary because we are particularly interested in the words of writers and speakers who have taken a self-conscious stand in opposition to male definition, defamation, and ignorance of women and their lives. All women are subject to masculine laws and linguistic forms, but not all women have the same resources, opportunities, or desires to challenge words and meanings and to explore the theoretical and transformative powers of language. Thus while we are interested in commentary that illuminates all women's lives and experiences, we find that "feminist" commentary does this in the most linguistically conscious and challenging ways.

We also seek to signal our attempt to build feminist values into the process of dictionary-making itself. The OED was called "a dictionary not of *our* English, but of *all* English: the English of Chaucer, of the Bible, and of Shakespeare" (Murray 1977, 312, our emphasis). This feminist dictionary includes the English of many of the women who did not fit into that exclusive *all*. Yet we acknowledge from the outset that this project is partial and incomplete. Theoretically, there are many reasons why it will always be. Through conception, selection, and methodology, every dictionary is of necessity partial and incomplete. Yet the failure to acknowledge this results in impaired lawgiving – in Manglish dictionaries which, despite their bias and incompleteness, are presented as authoritative works by masters of language who set proprietory standards about what is proper, correct, expert, respectable, reputable, standard and prescriptive.

No one is more aware than we are of the problems with our own project. In working on it, we have had many different responses to the notion of a "feminist dictionary." We share some of these to clarify, perhaps, the nature of this book. Our first request to the University of Illinois for research support was reviewed by a microbiologist; to our great joy, he recommended funding for the project. We heard that his evaluation was based not only on the positive recommendations he had obtained from feminist scholars on campus but also because he felt the dictionary would help "clean up the pronoun mess." His comment made clear that he expected a "dictionary" to prescribe word usage authoritatively. On the same grounds, several linguistics students to whom the project was presented objected to our calling it a "dictionary." Because we were claiming to be neither definitively authoritative nor comprehensive, they felt a more neutral designation such as "word-book" would be preferable (of course a dictionary *is*, precisely, a word-book). A related response was that "feminism" and "dictionary" were somehow incompatible. A woman friend sent this account of a conversation she had with a male colleague:

Pat: This week has been real exciting. Got to hear a mentor of mine give a paper on making a feminist dictionary.

David: Oh no (groan). That's scary.

Pat: What's scary about it?

David: Feminist dictionaries and such always remind me of a friend who once informed me that history means *his story*, and that in order for it to include women it must be called *herstory*.

Pat: Well, that may not be the right etymology, but that *has* been the effect of male historians on the writing of history.

David: Yes, but she really believed that was the etymology.

Pat: You're missing the point. Though she may not have performed the simple task of using a dictionary, the distinction between history and herstory is a rhetorical one; therein lies its importance. The making of a feminist dictionary is central to redefining our language.

Feminist friends and colleagues wondered how to reconcile feminist pluralism and diversity with a dictionary's traditions of hierarchy and privileging. At the same time, some women commended the dictionary's authoritative potential and hoped that its scholarly goals would not obscure or compromise its value and visibility as a political document: if a dictionary has authority, then let *our* dictionary authorize feminist linguistic change; if a dictionary is prescriptive, then let it prescribe nonsexist language.

This response moves to the heart of the matter: is a "feminist dictionary" a *feminist* dictionary, a nonsexist dictionary, or a women's dictionary? We suggest that a *feminist* dictionary cannot merely celebrate women's words: rather it must offer us descriptions which point at what is functional in a patriarchal society and so help us criticize and oppose patriarchal structures. Meaghan Morris (1982) and others argue similarly that feminist linguistic innovations do not confront "conditions of speaking" – the larger discourse patterns as well as the social and economic inequities within which patriarchal words arise and have meaning.

Meanwhile, a news release about the feminist dictionary appeared in the local newspaper. "POPCORN!" a male colleague shouted as he rode by us on his bike. "What!!??" we asked. "POPCORN! SPINSTERS!" he shouted back. "Those hard kernels left at the bottom of the popcorn bowl: spinsters!"

A friend phoned. "May I ask you a frank and personal question?" she asked. "WHY a feminist dictionary?" Given a fairly long and detailed rationale, she said, "Oh – sort of like a women's *Joys of Yiddish*. But *women's* language isn't a *language*; I still don't see what there is to write a *book* about."

More recently, we presented the project, with slides, at the University of Illinois. Despite positive responses, we were told we had (1) excluded the language of women athletes, and (2) displayed "inappropriate levity."

But the response of one of the women archivists who helped us was more heartening: "Oh!" she said with delight, after we had explained our project, "Sort of a cross between the OED and the Whole Earth Catalogue!"

In our view, this is a feminist dictionary, and a nonsexist dictionary, and a dictionary for women. It seeks both to elucidate and complicate the terms of feminist discourse. In doing so, we have no illusion that we have achieved equal representation (women athletes are one group among many who are underrepresented) nor that we have included everything. This should very much be seen as a first edition, and we are depending upon the responses of readers to make subsequent editions more systematically complete. We are resigned to the fact that some readers will perceive "inappropriate levity" while others will no doubt perceive "inappropriate solemnity." We have used *The Joys of Yiddish* and many other books about language as useful source materials for our book; we hope that *A Feminist Dictionary* will now, in turn, become a useful source for the work of others. Yet the crucial point is that it places *women* at the center and rethinks language from that crucially different perspective.

STRUCTURE, FORMAT, AND EDITORIAL CONVENTIONS

We have tried to be attentive to our own procedures. We began this project with a commitment to feminism and to collaborative scholarship and with a wish to create a reference book that would be both an accessible work for general readers and a useful resource for other researchers. From the outset, we have attempted to inform people of this project and have invited their suggestions and contributions (many of which are embodied or included). We have read widely, though not widely enough, and have worked for accurate and plentiful citations in order to make the book a resource which will serve a variety of purposes. This dictionary primarily includes the terminology of people who are concerned about women's exclusion from the creation of meaning and from accounts of that creation, and who identify and comment upon the ways in which language has impact on our lives. In general, we have not included replications of standard male definitions even if they are also held by some or many women. Rather, we have included many of the coinages, explanations, and definitions which explore possible reformations, renouncements, reversions, or revelations. In including the *self-defining* of feminists we work toward a recognition and respect for *all* female experience – politically, culturally, economically, spiritually – not only that which has been approved by patriarchal authorization. For example, some women may think of home as a comfortable, safe shelter where one can be at ease and can relax from work – that is, some perhaps accept the types of definitions offered frequently by men in their dictionaries. What we have included in this dictionary are those definitions which challenge such descriptions and which offer other ways of conceptualizing and expressing women's experiences. So we include Betty Friedan's (1963) definition of home as a comfortable concentration camp as well as definitions which indicate that for many women it is not even comfortable (See HOME).

This volume is suggestive, certainly not comprehensive. We chose for inclusion, out of the centuries of women's explanations of the world, those statements which have been especially important for the women's movement and which seem best to articulate new ways of understanding and speaking about our experiences. We chose words and definitions for their controversial nature, and for their ability to undermine, unmask, and overturn ruling definitions and paradigms. We attempted to provide balance on controversial issues, knowing that we did not always succeed. We do not "agree with" all the definitions included but we do appreciate the discoveries and shrewdness they embody.

In making this volume a reference work which will also stimulate further work by others, we have included precise references whenever possible. There are many coined words and phrases whose complete histories we have not had the time or knowledge to trace; doing so would entail a different kind of research, though it is a much needed project. We anticipate that readers will be able to make many corrections and additions for subsequent editions. In other cases, there are special feminist issues to be considered. A given word or definition may not be original with the person cited – words are repeated and shared, after all, through multiple readings, conversations, presentations, and publications – and it is very difficult without extensive research to trace linguistic creativity through these kinds of interactions (see HERSTORY, FEMINISM IS THE THEORY AND LESBIANISM IS THE PRACTICE). In many cases (e.g. SEXUAL HARASSMENT) definitions have been collectively created and promoted; by giving a single citation to one printed source we obscure this collaborative effort. Because we could not trace each word ourselves, however, we offer a starting point whenever possible for further research.

Individual entries are organized in a variety of ways, often dependent upon the nature of the entry but always with some attention to readability. For some words for which we have multiple definitions we have organized the citations somewhat chronologically to highlight continuities or changes in meaning (See GOD); elsewhere we have organized the entries in other ways to show contrasts in how speakers and authors have used words (See FEMINIST). Other entries include information on how words have changed in meaning – either in the way a word has been shaped and changed in the past and present by men (see Muriel Schulz's work on WOMAN), or in the way male definitions of a word have been reshaped over the years by women's use (See LESBIAN). These types of definitions often highlight changes in social attitudes. Some entries stipulate usage, calling attention to what the authors state are common misuses of words and women (e.g. PRINCESS, JEWISH). Some entries are formed by stating what a word does *not* mean to the author of the definition. Because men's representation of experience has for so many years been presented as the only representation of the world, many of the women quoted in *A Feminist Dictionary* begin their explanations by pointing out how their understandings and visions differ from men's, by stating what is the traditional and non-acceptable definition, or by otherwise commenting on the understood traditional definitions (REALITY, WITCH). In this sense the book is a meta-dictionary, discussing the discourse of other dictionaries. Use of a flexible format is a conscious effort to honor the words and arguments of women, to liberate our thinking about what can be said about language, and to guard against lexicographical ownership of words and definitions.

We have used many sources for this book, some of them unconventional. Feminist critics suggest that we must look for women's language and communication in new ways and in new places. We must look beneath the surface orthodoxy, to find the female sub-version. We need to look in such places as gynecological handbooks passed between women for centuries; in women's art; in folklore and oral histories; in graffiti and gossip; in journals; in letters and diaries; in songs, billboards and posters; in the cant and chant of witchcraft and voodoo; in slogans; in parodies and humor; in poetry; in graphics; in comics and symbols; and in the mass of work by "noncanonized" writers whose richness and diversity we are only just beginning to comprehend.

The problem has not been in finding enough material for many women's dictionaries, but in selecting material to be put in *this* dictionary. A number of problems of identification and documentation should be noted. Most of our entries come from written or printed sources. This means that we are inevitably missing many of the important words of women whose color, class, age, disabilities, resources and circumstances have made them particularly marginal.

As one woman discussing this project said, "How can we know what women's definitions have been ignored and gone unrecorded since women's definitions *have* been ignored and gone unrecorded?" This project is intended as one effort to interrupt this process of centuries, but we recognize that much of the silencing of women is irreparable, particularly the erasure of women's unwritten words. Many men are also silenced, of course, but all men as a class have had power over the actions, including the speech, of women. For each race and class the voices of women have been repressed with impressive fervor. Men have selected their own voices, excluding women's, and then have called their selections culture. We have tried to note many modes of expression women have used through the years, but here also the words of those women who are most marginal are likely to be in archives.

We have, except in a few illustrative cases, limited our search to English speakers and writers, or to women whose words have been translated into English. While we have had the assistance of women from several cultures and countries, we are aware of some of the limitations of our own experiences, and know that it is important that, for example, we not base our assumptions about women of color on what we ourselves know of white women. Maritcha Rémond Lyons (1848-1929), for example, was only one of hundreds of noted Black women speakers (Sojourner Truth was not alone) – foresisters of Black women today like Shirley Chisholm or Barbara Jordan – for whom verbal argumentation and public speaking do *not* seem to be the same sort of language problems they have been for some white women.

We are also aware of the need to pay close attention to the words of disabled women, some of whom call others TABS – "temporarily able-bodied." One question is whether we make an effort to expunge phrases from our language like "stand up for what you believe" or "blind as a bat" that exclude or reflect negatively on those who are physically different from "the norm"; or whether we attempt to "reclaim naming" – and revisit these words, changing our usage to yield such affirmative possibilities as "sensitive as a blind woman." This is an issue among disabled women themselves, though for many, perhaps, a more pressing problem is their lack of access to writings which discuss these issues (see WOMYN'S BRAILLE PRESS).

Language is everywhere and nowhere. Out of 10,000 references in the Library Guide to Women's Collections (Andrea Hinding ed. 1980), only ten are on language. Yet in every collection we looked, we found material we could use for this book. Our selections have been both by choice and by necessity: on the one hand we have wanted to portray a diversity of issues and ideas and thus read widely in unconventional and often unfamiliar material; on the other hand, we did not undertake this dictionary as a lifelong project and thus had to limit what we could do. In addition, though many dictionaries are funded by continuing financial support from publishers, academic societies, or national governments, the feminist dictionary project is not thus institutionalized. The single most useful and used library was the Fawcett Library at the City of London Polytechnic which has thousands of feminist publications and writings from both sides of the Atlantic. The Femina Collection at Northwestern University was also helpful. We have also worked with private collections of feminist materials, and in archives in Chicago and Urbana; the University of Tulsa; New York City; the Smithsonian Institution; and Manchester and Dublin. The "we" has included Ann Russo, who has worked on the dictionary since its inception four years ago, Sally Green, Karen Lee Cole, Chandra Talpade Mohanty, Robin Johnston, Lana Rakow, Shelly Levy, and other women at the University of Illinois, curators (particularly David Doughan) and many others who have sent us letters, photocopies and postcards telling us about women's linguistic creativity in other places. We are much more aware of these rich resources at the end of this project than we were when we started, and can state fervently that we have only begun to touch the breadth and depth of available materials for this work.

In preparing final entries, we have adopted a number of conventions:

(1) An entry followed by a citation indicates a summary or paraphrase of that work; verbatim quotations are in quotation marks; an entry without an author's name indicates that it was written by us. Omitted words are marked by ellipses [. . .]; omitted words at the beginning and end of citations are not indicated.

(2) Most citations give author's name followed without punctuation by date of publication; this guides the reader to the appropriate entry in the bibliography, where date immediately follows author's name. A page number is also given in the citation where this was available. In

order to convey most accurately chronological information about citations, the date of publication given internally is usually that when the piece was written or first published; if we used a subsequent edition, reprint, or other later source, this is noted in the bibliography.

(3) In some cases the internal citation includes the later source in which the piece is reprinted; in most cases, this means that the later source is the one cited in the bibliography (example: letters reprinted in Alice Rossi ed., *The Feminist Papers*).

(4) Material taken from magazines, newspapers, and journals, particular pieces with no author's name, are cited internally with the entry; these items do not appear in the bibliography.

(5) Several dictionaries are cited by the names by which they are generally known (e.g., the *Oxford English Dictionary* edited by James Murray); most, however, are cited by author or editor's name, like other citations. Full citations are given in the bibliography.

(6) In reproducing quoted material, we have been guided by considerations of readability, space, and loyalty to the spirit of the original text. Punctuation has in general been made uniform (e.g., commas and periods inside quotation marks); the original spelling has in virtually all cases been preserved. Obvious typographical errors were corrected if they seemed irrelevant to the spirit of the entry. To save space, the paragraphing of the original was not preserved. Line spacing for poetry is preserved, but space between lines is sometimes omitted. Italics in the original text were not always reproduced (for example, when the entire original was in italics and thus provided no contrast).

(7) Documentation to unpublished material in archival collections varies in precision, depending upon available information.

(8) *Word order*: We have placed MEN before WOMEN, but HOUSEWORK before WAR. Our order does not imply a value judgment. We have used alphabetical order to organize the definitions. *Variants*: We include many variant definitions without specifying which one is more variant than others. Readers are capable of determining their preferred definitions for particular situations. *Inflected forms*: The dictionary has a noun bias. In this we follow the conventions of most English speakers who have been more attuned to things than to processes or qualifications. We encourage experimenta-tion. *Pronunciation and stress*: We do not offer syllabification, pronuncia-

tion, or stress symbols for most of the words. We encourage experimentation, such as that which is mentioned for CIVIL RIGHTS.

(9) A critical feature of the dictionary are the cross references. Many entries refer the reader to other entries in the dictionary where related material may be found. Sometimes this consists of related content, or to further work by the same author. In other cases, the cross reference provides a contradiction, qualification, or challenge to the first entry. A cross reference may be a reminder of a recurrent omission, for example to WOMEN OF COLOR or DISABLED WOMEN, or a repeated acknowledgment|that all knowledge is partial and flawed (for example to ETYMOLOGY). In some cases (e.g., a reference to FEMINIST DICTIONARY), this is intended as a deliberately self-subverting process, to remind readers (and ourselves) that this dictionary is a constructed product, not a law. The reproduction of text inevitably creates another text; this cross referencing is also a way of providing interpretation and commentary without forcing this upon the reader.

(10) Finally, the blank pages at the end of *A Feminist Dictionary* invite you to keep a record of your own contributions to the dictionary, and of women's words from conversations, diaries, letters, novels, and other sources. We plan to continue the compiling of this inventory of insights and interpretations and, with your help, to revise the dictionary in future editions. Comments and contributions will be very welcomed by us at 244 Lincoln Hall, University of Illinois, 702 South Wright Street, Urbana, Illinois 61801, U.S.A. or by our publishers at Pandora Press, 14 Leicester Square, London WC2H 7PH

NOTES

1 Though many sources might be acceptable as historical evidence for word usage, the rule for most dictionaries has been (even when as in the case of the OED the rule has been made for largely pragmatic reasons) that "where choice is possible, preference should, of course, be given to quotations from the best writers" (*Encyclopedia Britannica* entry for Dictionary, Univ. of Chicago 1943).

2 Sexism in dictionaries has been documented in terms of the sources of definitions, definitional stereotypes, illustrative examples, and historical evidence. See, for example, Dennis E. Baron forthcoming; H. Lee Gershuny 1973; and Barrie Thorne, Cheris Kramarae, and Nancy Henley, eds, 1983, 166-73.

3 An early stimulus for the creation of a feminist dictionary was a reading (by CK) of Raymond Williams' illuminating book *Keywords: A Vocabulary of Culture and Society* (1976); out of 111 "key" words considered, only one (Family) reflects traditionally "female" interests or concerns, few women writers or thinkers are cited (e.g., Jane Austen), and feminism is barely mentioned (e.g., the problem of "sexual specialization" is mentioned briefly under the word Man). This is not to say that the 110 other words (Communication, Culture, Revolution, etc.) are not relevant for women but rather to ask questions that Williams himself would not find unreasonable: Whose words? Key to whom? Vocabulary for what purpose? Which culture? Which society? Meanwhile, *Feminist Keywords* remains a book to be written.

4 *Webster's Third New International Dictionary* (Phillip Gove ed. 1961) was denounced (especially by the literary, journalistic, and educational establishment) as "a scandal" because, following modern descriptive (rather than prescriptive) linguistic principles, it not only lexicalized many "non-standard" forms that were in widespread use but also failed to label them appropriately. Gove took as his epigram a quotation from Noah Webster in 1817: "A living language must keep pace with improvements in knowledge and with the multiplication of ideas." It thus failed in its expected task as keeper of the code: to legislate what English was to consist of and adjudicate "correct usage." (See Sheridan Baker 1972, James Sledd and Wilma A. Ebbitt 1962.)

5 The term *diglossia* refers to the disjunction in all languages between spoken forms and written codification, especially writing in its "best forms" – classical grammars, the literary canon, etc.

6 Defining "the lexicon" for the purposes of providing a complete grammar of a language is different from "lexicography," or the actual making of dictionaries. Ladislav Zgusta ed., *Theory and Method in Lexicography* (1980), offers a good introductory discussion of this point and includes a number of relevant essays.

7 One distinction claims that dictionaries relate words to words while encyclopedias relate words to things; a useful contrast is given in John Haimann (1980) and Umberto Eco (1984). Douglas Medin and Edward Smith (1984) discuss problematic issues in the formation and codification of concepts (and definitions).

8 Not all "male" dictionaries ignore feminist concerns. Flaubert's *Dictionary of Accepted Ideas* was open to clichés about women as well as to those about men. A number of recent dictionaries include lexical items generated by the feminist movement (though often it would seem in order to ridicule them, as in the *Barnhart Dictionary of Contemporary Usage*), discuss issues of concern to women (e.g., Wallechinsky and Wallace's *The People's Almanac*), or include entries on feminism (e.g., Michèle Barrett's entry in the *Dictionary of Marxist Thought*, Tom Bottomore ed., 1983).

A

The letter in sacred alphabets of the ancient world to signify birth and beginning. "This letter meant the Creatress, who invented alphabets and gave them to mankind – though most traditions said womankind had them first." (Barbara G. Walker 1983, 2)

A-

Prefix meaning without, not, or opposite to. Used to suggest states of being opposite to existing reality for which there are not yet words.

(See A-MAZING)

ABBESS

Female superior of a convent of nuns. In slang usage, the keeper of a house of ill-fame, a procuress. "The analogy was carried still further, by the inmates being termed 'nuns' and 'sisters of charity.' This depravation in the meaning of words, usually applied only to the holders of sacred offices, may . . . be regarded as resulting from the mockery born of the degradation, in the popular mind, of the priestly office" (J. S. Farmer and W. E. Henley 1890-1904). According to Muriel Schulz (1975b, 66), these terms "illustrate the most frequent course followed by pejorated terms designating women. In their downhill slide, they slip past respectable women and settle upon prostitutes and mistresses. . . . [But] here, at last, one male title also pejorated. *Abbott* at the same time came to mean 'the husband, or preferred male of a brothel keeper.' "

(See -ESS, SEMANTIC DEROGATION OF WOMEN)

ABLEISM

"Systematic oppression of a group of people because of what they can or cannot do with their bodies or minds. It is the result of too little awareness of the experience of those with disabilities." (Arachne Rae 1981, 39)

(See DISABLED, TAB)

ABILITY

"Is sexless." (Christabel Pankhurst, *Calling All Women*, February 2, 1957)

ABOLITION

Movement in nineteenth century U.S. to abolish slavery. Many feminists learned organizing strategies and public speaking in the abolition movement, and saw certain parallels between the struggle for the liberation of Black people from slavery and that for the liberation of women from male domination. As in the 20th century, the movement for civil rights preceded a strong feminist movement. The term also designates movement among European prostitutes to abolish laws that persecute prostitutes. The U.S. term is usually *decriminalization*. Both are distinct from *legalization* (i.e., the State taking charge of the sex industry). Different groups organize around different approaches to abolition. (Claude Jaget ed. 1980, 17-18)

ABOMINABLE SNOWMEN OF ANDROCRATIC ACADEMIA

Scholars dominated by male-centered traditions. (Mary Daly 1978, 8)

(See ACADEMIA)

ABORIGINAL

A name applied to the Ancients (Black, Yellow, Brown, or Red) "in South Africa and Australia and other lands, invaded, expropriated and occupied by whites." Yet the word derives from Latin *ab origine* 'from the source, from the beginning' (Alice Walker 1982c, 264).

ABORTION

Termination of pregnancy prior to about twenty weeks gestation, or before the point when the fetus could be expected to live on its own (be "viable." Varda One in *Everywoman*, Sept. 10, 1971, 17, compares alternative definitions as to when "viability" begins). It can be spontaneous (miscarriage) or induced (result of deliberate termination of pregnancy). The *Oxford English Dictionary* cites "the act of giving untimely birth to offspring," from L *abortus* "an untimely birth," and gives a 1547 citation: "Aborsion is when a woman is delyvered of her chylde before her tyme." Types of induced abortion in Western medicine include *D & C* (dilation and curettage), where the cervix is dilated and the uterus scraped with a sharp instrument; *suction abortion*, where the cervix is dilated and a suction hose used to remove its contents; *saline abortion*, where a salt solution is injected through the abdomen into the uterus, triggering labor and abortion within 24 hours; and *prostaglandin abortion*, where a hormone suppository is placed in the vagina and induces labor and abortion within 24 to 36 hours (Michelle Harrison 1982, 260). The right to obtain an abortion under some circumstances is a key issue in the women's health movement; for many feminists in the West, this right to abortion is symbolic of women's right to control their own bodies. "For women, the right to abort often seems a necessary condition for the free exercise of all other human rights, since there is not and never has been a fully reliable method of contraception (other than celibacy), and since bearing an unwanted child can be disastrous for a woman's health, happiness, personal life and career aspirations,

and may even be fatal" (Mary Anne Warren 1980, 2). Despite this central tenet of self-determination, women take many positions on abortion. For some women, in the U.S. and elsewhere, self-determination involves the right to have children and not, for example, undergo involuntary sterilization. The public and political airing of these issues has been a crucial feature of the 1970s; the *Manifesto of the 343*, for example, was a public petition presented by 343 French women, including Simone de Beauvoir, presented in April 1969 declaring that they had had illegal abortions. Such actions moved abortion issues from the private to the public sphere. The statements below suggest what abortion means to some feminists.

(See ACTION, BIRTH, CHILDREN, CHOICE, CONTRACEPTION, HEALTH, MIDWIFE, PRO-CHOICE, TESTOSTERONE POISONING)

Is a form of punishment for the crime of wishing not to be pregnant. Judgments against women who choose to abort go back far into history. Like other acts that threaten male interests and male institutions, abortion is considered deviant or criminal. (Adrienne Rich 1976a, 265–9) Likewise, for poor women and women of color, a hospital abortion is sometimes a prelude to hysterectomy – a form of genocide and/or punishment for "immoral behavior." (Jane 1973)

Is, in masculinist terms, "an act of violence against the phallus itself. It is akin to chopping off a cock. Because a fetus is perceived of as having a phallic character, its so-called life is valued very highly, while the woman's actual life is worthless and invisible since she can make no claim to phallic potentiality." (Andrea Dworkin 1976, 55)

Is the death of a fertilized egg. (Oriana Fallaci 1975, 104)

Has often been carried out by women for women:

"Am I the only girl who ever spent the night in a young man's arms, my sister?

You're telling me, my sister, that such lovely nights are not worth the morning after.
Well, at least keep the secret, my sister.
Old Tamchoucha knows all about those plants, the plants which will soon deliver me from my trouble.
Nothing shows yet, you know.
Tamchoucha has already bought the alum and resin to make me a new virginity."

(Berber women's folk song; cited by Elizabeth Warnock Fernea and Basima Quattan Bezirgan eds 1977, 128)

Involves ancient methods. Those described in medieval women's health guides include anointing the cervix with a quill dipped in various herbal preparations, violent exercise, and being wound so tightly in a kind of whole-body tourniquet that the fetus is expelled. (Beryl Rowland 1981)

Was one of the seven demands of the British women's liberation movement, formulated from 1971 to 1978: "Free contraception and abortion on demand. . . . It is vital to remember that the underlying issue is one of reproductive freedom – freedom to have a child (against forced sterilization of Black and Third World women, against pressure on lesbians who want to have children) as well as not." (Sona Osman 1983, 27)

Has been a central issue in women's reform campaigns. The right to abortion, like campaigns for birth control, control of property, divorce, political rights, and access to the professions, "represent[s] an onslaught on the principle of the bourgeois married woman's dependence, and they suggest that the bourgeois family-household has been resisted with some strength by organizations of its female members." (Michèle Barrett 1980, 216)

Was, for the illegal abortion collective Jane, which operated in Chicago in the early 1970s, "only the best of two tragic choices" which necessarily involved "grappling with matters of life and death." Ultimately, "the life and freedom of choice of the woman took priority." (Jane 1973) "Abortions will not let you forget." (Gwendolyn Brooks 1944, "The Mother," in Florence Howe and Ellen Bass eds 1973, 116-17)

Has been a germinal topic in feminist philosophy. Arguing in favor of a woman's right to abortion in some circumstances, Judith Jarvis Thompson, for example, distinguished this from the right to secure the death of the unborn child. (Judith Jarvis Thompson 1971)

For the protagonist in the short story "Abortion," her first abortion, when she was in college, represented "a supreme coming of age and a seizing of the direction of her own life." (Alice Walker 1982, 67)

May be a necessary measure for some women, but is never the fulfillment of their highest dreams; a humiliating procedure, and hardly the embodiment of liberation. "Few if any feminists are deceived in this matter, although male proponents of the repeal of abortion laws tend often to be short-sighted in this respect, confusing the feminist revolution with the sexual revolution." (Mary Daly 1973, 112)

ABORTION, ILLEGAL

Self-abortion methods used by women who are unable to obtain legal, safe, or low-cost abortions include: "wire coat-hangers, knitting needles, goose quills dipped in turpentine, celery stalks, drenching the cervix with detergent, lye, soap, Ultra-Jel (a commercial preparation of castor oil, soap, and iodine), drinking purgatives or mercury, applying hot coals to the body." (Adrienne Rich 1976a, 267)

Protest slogan, 1970: "Women of the world unite, you have nothing to lose but your coat hangers!" "In most of the United States, the rich aborted by going abroad; the poor went to backroom butchers." (Claudia Dreifus; in Claudia Dreifus ed. 1978, 133)

Is a degrading ritual. When abortion in the U.S. was first legalized in some states, a woman could obtain a medical abortion only with a psychiatrist's testimony that failure to have an abortion would endanger her mental health. A cartoon by Patricia McGinnis, a pro-choice activist, showed a sobbing woman with a $500 check in front of "Mercy Hospital" saying, on her knees, "Please may I have a state-approved, politician-sanctioned, clergy-counselled, psychiatrist-rubber-stamped, residency-investigated, abortion committee-inspected, therapuked, public health dept.-statistized, contraceptive-failure, accredited hospital abortion?" (Cited in Pauline Bart 1981, 112)

ABORTIONIST

Originally, any man or woman who induced an abortion, including the woman whose fetus was aborted. Now generally refers to the practitioner. The illegal abortion collective Jane, which operated in Chicago in the early 1970's, paid tribute to the courage of those medical practitioners who would agree to perform illegal abortions under high risk conditions; at the same time, they expressed serious reservations about "these strange bedfellows whose purpose was so different from ours": "They each wanted the most possible money, the greatest possible anonymity and the fewest possible problems. They each also wanted the greatest possible freedom of action and the most possible freedom from responsibility. They all preferred to be called 'doctor.' " (Jane 1973)

"Often alcoholic, disenfranchised members of the medical profession [who] besides operating in septic surroundings and performing unnecessary curettages on poor women who cannot afford a pregnancy test, frequently rape or sexually molest their patients." (Adrienne Rich 1976a, 267)

ABSENTEEISM

Word used by nineteenth-century British School Boards to describe the absences of girls. The boys' absences were called *truancy*; the girls' absences were often explained in terms of having to care for siblings or to help in their homes. (Carol Dyhouse 1981, 102)

ABSTRACTION

"Often a tool to keep us from looking at the realities of oppression." (A Redstockings sister c. 1969; manuscript, Northwestern University Library, Evanston, Illinois)
(See CONSCIOUSNESS-RAISING, REALITY, THEORY, WOMEN'S STUDIES)

A mode of conceptualizing which may require time and resources. "Given . . . the history of women's studies; its origins in the women's movement; its dependence on faculty with marginal status in the academy; and its practical, opportunistic, and immensely successful method of growth, essential abstract questions have understandably received sustained attention only recently." (Marilyn J. Boxer 1982, 683)

ABUSE

Verbal: Terms of address or reference which denigrate women; in English, these are legion. Verbal abuse is a ubiquitous form of sexual harassment which renders the workplace, campus, or public setting inhospitable to women and interferes with their ability to carry out their responsibilities; it is defined as a form of sexual harassment.
(See DICTIONARY, NAMES, SEMANTIC DEROGATION OF WOMEN, SEXUAL HARASSMENT, TESTOSTERONE POISONING)

Physical: Actions which inflict bodily harm on women.
(See MARITAL RAPE, RAPE, WIFE-BATTERING, VIOLENCE AGAINST WOMEN)

Psychological: Interpersonal strategies in personal, social, or professional situations which serve to reinforce stereotypical views of women, disregard or erase evidence of their contributions, deny or fail to credit the reality of women's experience, and encourage women to analyze situations and problems as personal and individual rather than systemic and collective.
(See FEMINISM, GASLIGHTING, PERSONAL IS POLITICAL, PHRASEBOOK FOR THE

FOREIGN COUNTRY OF FEMIN-
ISM, YELLOW WALLPAPER)

ACADEMIA

A "chilly climate" for women that, according to statistics and verbal reports, many
women find profoundly alienating; this
alienation, in turn, may lead to lower self-
confidence, discourage intellectual participation, and jeopardize women's potential
for equal education and achievement.
(Roberta M. Hall with the assistance of
Bernice Sandler 1982)

A subculture "that women and men
experience and relate to differently. This
subculture typically fosters interaction
patterns more compatible with men's established interaction patterns than with
women's and it is this fundamental inhospitability to women's talk that helps
account for the continuing 'chilly climate'
that significant numbers of women on
campus experience." (Paula A. Treichler
and Cheris Kramarae 1983, 118)

A man's world. "The fact that women
are mainly trained by the male of the
species in his own modes and manners or
in his notions of her 'proper sphere' . . .
may unduly crush the initiative of the girl
student and force her to believe that she
must follow the masculine leadership or
authority without deviation and at all
costs." (Mary Ritter Beard 1942; in Ann J.
Lane 1977 ed. 149)

A hierarchy whose "purpose is the
production of prestige." (Jo Freeman 1979,
26)

"Offers survival and acceptance
(graduation, a job, prestige) to those who
will quietly take their place on the
assembly line or who are themselves
willing to be mutilated into professionals."
(Sally Miller Gearhart 1983, 4)

"What we [lesbian teachers] must
remember in order to survive is that we
cannot change our dress, or speech, or the
focus of our academic interests in order to
become acceptable. Hiding our anger will
not save us. If we cannot be who we are
and be acceptable, that is a political
reality we must recognize and consider in
every act of our day-to-day existence."
(Judith McDaniel 1982, 43)

ACADEMESE

"She spoke academese, a language that
springs like Athene from an intellectual
brow, and she spoke it with a non-
regional, 'good' accent." (May Sarton
1961, 55)

ACADEMIC FREEDOM

A fundamental principle of the modern
university which traditionalists sometimes
claim is jeopardized by affirmative action
policies, sexual harassment policies,
grievance procedures, open meetings laws,
and other measures designed to provide
due process to all members of the academic community.

ACCENT

In linguistics, the marking of a particular
syllable through stress (stress accent) or
pitch or tone (pitch accent). In English,
women's speech is typically more highly
accented than men's, displaying a greater
range of stress and pitch; this is one of the
few consistent differences between men's
and women's speech. Also refers to systematic regional variations in speech
production ("Southern accent"); research
indicates that the same accent is evaluated
differentially by hearers depending on
whether the speaker is male or female.
(See PITCH)

"A deviation from the norm, but a
deviation which is ascertained by an
increase in intensity in the use of certain
words and certain sounds, since accent is
an expressive sound." "This alien
language, which nonetheless inhabits us
intimately, is spoken by all of us women
with *an accent*. It is moreover by this
accent that we can recognize each other
even if we cannot always understand each
other." (Nicole Brossard 1984, 9)

ACCIDIE, ACEDIA

Spiritual torpor, ennui (AHD); profound
apathy. Ecclesiastical term for the acute
depression afflicting those in the monastic
life which made monks and nuns especially
susceptible to demonic possession. (Barbara G. Walker 1983, 7)

ACHIEVEMENT

For men, this means status, recognition, and positions of responsibility, and is "quite closely related to educational opportunity. . . . Yet for women the relationship between education and achievement is not at all clear. It may be that for able women higher education is a necessary condition, but not a sufficient condition for achievement. Some other factor, some X factor, has kept the number of women lower than their proportionate share of talent and education would lead us to expect. What is that X factor? We may find the missing ingredient in the attitudes toward women abroad in the land at any given time." (Anne Firor Scott 1974; rpt 1984, 299-300)

(See ACADEMIA, CLASS SYSTEM OF THE INTELLECT, ORIGINAL, X FACTOR)

ACKNOWLEDGMENTS

Before feminism, that portion of a book where authors acknowledged the ideas and intellectual contributions of males and the clerical and editorial assistance of females and where men thanked their wives for critically reading their manuscripts without asking for co-authorship. After feminism, the place where women authors often acknowledge the intellectual, emotional, editorial, and clerical contributions of women and sometimes of men. Some sample feminist acknowledgments follow.

(See PREFACE)

"To the dedicated sisters who have contributed their papers to this collection, I can say only *Venceremos!* Thank you all for your warm encouragement and help. Especially to The Group." (Leslie B. Tanner 1970, 15)

"The task of writing 'acknowledgments' becomes increasingly perplexing and ridiculous. There is no way that I can adequately name or measure the contributions of other Hags, Sisters, Spinsters, Crones, to the creation of this book." (Mary Daly 1978, xvi)

"I am extremely grateful to . . . my father who helped with some of the typing and the bibliography." (Rosalind Coward 1983, vii)

ACRONYM

Word formed from the initial letters of a name, or by combining initial letters or parts of a series of words. The women's movement has used acronyms creatively; some examples follow.

(See elsewhere in the dictionary for more information on some of these groups.)

ASP: Association of Seattle Prostitutes. (See COYOTE)

BWE: Black Women Enraged. U.S. group in Harlem first organized to aid the wife and children of assassinated leader Malcolm X and then involved in anti-war organizing. (Sara Evans 1980, 196)

CAT: California Advocates for Trollops. (See COYOTE)

CHICKS: Coalition for Harboring Indefinite Chastity and Kaffee-Klatsch Sentimentality. Organized by Akron's NOW chapter to protest anti-feminist leaders such as Phyllis Schlafly. (*Off Our Backs*, April 1982, 16)

CLUW: Coalition of Labor Union Women. U.S. group founded in 1974.

COYOTE: Call Off Your Old Tired Ethics. San Francisco group organized in 1973 by Margo St. James to fight for the decriminalization of prostitution. The group's annual fundraiser, The Hooker's Ball, remained a popular event. Groups with parallel names (PONY, PUMA) organized in other cities. (Claude Jaget ed. 1980)

DARE: Dykes Against Racism Everywhere. (*Sinister Wisdom* 16, 100)

FAST: "Stands for Feminists Against Sexual Terrorism and is a newsletter for all women struggling against male violence, in all its forms" in Manchester.

FATSO: Fat Sisters Organizing. Washington, D.C. Women's support group.

FIST: Philadelphia Women Insist on Safe Transit. (Rebecca Clay 1982, 7)

F.I.S.T.: Feminists in Self-Defense Training. Organization that trains women in the Korean martial art of Tae Kwon Do, focusing specifically on attack situations women may be faced with. (*Sojourner* 10:2, 1982, 7)

LACW: Latin American and Caribbean Women Collective.

LADIES: Life After Divorce Is Eventually Sane. A club formed by women married to famous men in Hollywood to help each other cope with the problems of being divorced from celebrity husbands. (*Daily Illini*, October 6, 1983, 17)

LAW: Ladies Against Women. U.S. groups organized in the early 1980's to satirize anti-feminist positions. Dress: suits, white gloves, pillbox hats. Motto: "I'd Rather Be Ironing."

LEAP: Lesbians for Empowerment, Action, and Politics (formerly the Southern Lesbian Conference). (*Telewoman* 1984, July, n.p.)

LUNA: Lesbians United in Non-Nuclear Action. (Gina Foglia and Dorit Wolffberg 1981, 451)

MALE: Males Against Linguistic Equality.

MAMA: March Against Media Arrogance on Mothers Day.

MAW: Mothers for Adequate Welfare. Interracial welfare rights group organized in Boston in 1965; demonstrated women's excellent talents for organizing around community issues. (Sara Evans 1980, 143)

NAWSA: National American Woman Suffrage Association. The mainstream U.S. women's suffrage organization of the nineteenth and early twentieth centuries.

NOW: National Organization for Women. U.S. organization founded in 1966 by Betty Friedan and others to work for equal rights and opportunities for women. Slogan: "Out of the mainstream – and into the revolution."

NWP: National Women's Party, an important U.S. suffrage organization.

OWL: Older Women's League.

PLAN: Prostitution Laws Are Nonsense. British group fighting for the abolition of laws persecuting prostitutes. (Claude Jaget ed. 1980)

PONY: Prostitutes of New York.
   (See COYOTE)

PUMA: Prostitutes Union of Massachusetts.
   (See COYOTE)

SAD: Sisters Against Disablement.

SASS: Sisters Against Sexual Slavery. (Ann Forfreedom 1970, 9)

SCUM: Society for Cutting Up Men. The SCUM Manifesto, by Valerie Solanas (1968), argues for the destruction of the male sex and defines SCUM as "dominant, secure, self-confident, nasty, violent, selfish, independent, proud, thrill-seeking, free-wheeling arrogant females, who consider themselves fit to rule the universe." (Valerie Solanas 1968, rpt 1983; also rpt Robin Morgan ed. 1970, 579)

SIN: Speak Its Name. A theatre company in Chicago, a democratic production company of lesbian/gay artists dedicated to promoting plays reflective of the lesbian/gay experience. The name is from Oscar Wilde's "love that dare not speak its name." (*Catalyst* May 1980)

S.O.W.: Salty Old Woman. Coined by Caroline Bird,

"Ageless S.O.W. are made, not born. You are one of us if you:
* have switched careers in mid-life.
* express your opinion even when outnumbered, and speak up in public.
* [are] always learning something new.
* wake up every morning wondering what's going to happen and looking forward to it.
* have always felt that you were different from your contemporaries."

S.O.W.: Salty Old Woman who "have respect, even affection for their bodies. They buy clothes that fit the way their bodies actually are instead of trying to make them fit into the clothes that the stores are showing. . . . [They] have the authority to stand up to macho military and economic policies that could destroy us. They have the historical perspective that can hold us together through a time of rapid change." (Caroline Bird 1983, 102)

SPAZM: Sofia Perovskaya and Andrei Zhelyabov Memorial Coeducational Society of Peoples' Freedom Through Women's Liberation. (Berkeley Women's

Liberation 1969; Northwestern University Library, Evanston, Illinois)

WAC: Women's Army Corps.

WAGE: Women's Alliance to Gain Equality.

WARN: Women of All Red Nations. South Dakota organization of American Indian women focused on issues affecting the Indian community (e.g., water pollution). (Winona LaDuke 1983, 53)

WE: Women Employed. Chicago organization of clerical employees concerned with employment conditions including sexism on the job. (Sara Evans 1980, 230)

WIND: Women in Distribution. (*Sinister Wisdom* 16, 100)

WITCH: Women's International Conspiracy from Hell. Founded in 1967 as a militantly activist branch of the U.S. women's liberation movement. One hex: "WITCH calls down destruction on Babylon. Oppressors: the curse of women is on you." Reborn in various cities as Women Incensed at Telephone Company Harassment, Women Inspired to Commit Herstory, etc. (Robin Morgan 1978)

WONT: Women Opposed to Nuclear Technology. (Gina Foglia and Dorit Wolffberg 1981, 451)

WOW: Women Office Workers.

WAP: Women Against Pornography.

WISE: Women for the Inclusion of Sexual Expression. (*WISE Newsletter* 1971, New York)

ACTING

The art of self-disguise. Creative study of people and their behavior and reactions; "second nature to many women who have learnt that to dissemble makes life very much easier in a world where they are subject to prejudice." (Edith Summerskill to her daughter Shirley 1955; quoted in Karen Payne 1983, 187)

ACTION

Strategic, often public, behaviour which functions practically or symbolically to challenge the conditions of women's oppression and other forms of injustice. Women's actions go back at least as far as Aristophanes' Lysistrata, who organized the women of ancient Greece to withhold sex from their husbands as an anti-war protest. Feminists in the U.S. have drawn upon additional traditions: the non-violent marches and demonstrations of the civil rights and anti-war movements, the picket lines of the labor movement, and the flamboyant consciousness-raising interventions of performance art and guerrilla theatre. When the action is interpreted as "a curiosity," newspapers report it under headlines like "Grandmother Is First Woman Mayor of Manville." When the action is more threatening, newspapers report it as a raging hormones or crime story, and it is seldom mentioned in subsequent histories. Below are a few examples of women's actions.

(See ABORTION, BREAST, GREENHAM COMMON, LYSISTRATA, MENSTRUAL STRIKE, MISS AMERICA PROTEST, MISS WORLD ACTION, OGLE-IN, SUFFRAGE MOVEMENT, VITRIFRAGISTS)

"In 1600, Iroquois women organized a successful 'Lysistrata' action, refusing sex or childbearing until unregulated warfare ceased. Last year, thousands of women circled the Pentagon to mourn and defy the \$500,000,000-a-day war machine. This is the legacy of women as peacemakers." (New Society Publishers flyer 1982; from Pam McAllister 1982)

In the U.S., "the new feminist movement made its explosive debut in the Miss America demonstration of August 1968. With a sharp eye for flamboyant guerrilla theater, young women crowned a live sheep to symbolize the beauty pageant's objectification of female bodies, and filled a 'freedom trashcan' with objects of female torture – girdles, bras, curlers, issues of *Ladies' Home Journal*. Peggy Dobbins, dressed as a stockbroker, auctioned off an effigy of Miss America: 'Gentlemen, I offer you the 1969 model. She's better every year. She walks. She talks. She smiles on cue. *And* she does housework.' Even though the coverage of such events was likely to be derogatory – in reports of the Miss America demonstration the media coined the term 'bra-burner' – the dramatic rise in media coverage in 1969 and 1970 provoked a massive influx of new members into all branches of the feminist movement." (Sara Evans 1980, 213-14)

A retrospective critique of the Miss America protest was written by one of its organizers: "At this point in our struggle, our actions should be aimed primarily at doing two inter-related things: 1) awakening the latent consciousness of women about their own oppression, and 2) building sisterhood." From this perspective, the Miss America protest reflected a "definite strain of anti-womanism" which "really harmed the cause of sisterhood. Miss America and all beautiful women came off as our enemy instead of as our sisters who suffer with us." (Carol Hanisch 1968; Special Collections, Northwestern University Library, Evanston, Illinois)

"At the end of the 19th century, during the great miners' strike in Chile, women organized themselves into women's committees to promote the 'unlit ovens' (*cocinas apagadas*) strike: when the strikers came home to eat, they were thus pressured into going back to the mine to continue the strike. The women thereby prevented the miners from giving in and actively stimulated the struggle." (LACW Collective 1977, 24-5)

"Long before the Civil War made relief work a practical necessity, Black women had formed organizations that directed attention to the needs of fugitives. The Female Benevolent Firm of Boston, Mass., was organized as early as 1848 to provide clothing and shoes to women and children who had been rescued by the Underground Railroad." (Erlene Stetson 1979, 45)

"The Combahee River Collective is a Black feminist group in Boston whose name comes from the guerrilla action conceptualized and led by Harriet Tubman on June 2, 1863, in the Port Royal region of South Carolina. This action freed more than 750 slaves and is the only military campaign in American history planned and led by a woman." (Combahee River Collective 1977; in Cherríe Moraga and Gloria Anzaldúa eds 1981, 210)

It became known as the "night of terror": November 14, 1917. About 30 women, including a young activist named Alice Paul [who later wrote the Equal Rights Amendment] had been picketing the White House. Women's struggle to win the right to vote in this country had gone on for nearly 70 years, and now some women had resorted to militant tactics to gain attention for their cause and to scorn President Wilson for his opposition. The women – some elderly – were attacked by guards and thrown into grimy prison cells. (Susan G. Butruille 1981)

Some other actions:

1913-present: Tens of thousands of women defy passlaws in South Africa.

Alabama 1955: Rosa Parks refuses to give up her bus seat to a white man, an act of defiance that inspires Montgomery Bus Boycott and sets civil rights movement in motion.

Little Rock, Arkansas, 1957: Elizabeth Eckford, facing a white mob screaming "Lynch her!" becomes the first Black student to attend Central High School.

1966-present: Delores Huerta leads United Farm Workers' boycotts.

1970-present: Women establish hundreds of Peace Encampments all over the world – Mt. Fuji, Greenham Common, Seneca Falls, Reckershausen.

Buenos Aires, 1976-present: Mothers of the Plaza de Mayo each Thursday put on white kerchiefs embroidered with the names of their missing children and march to Government House protesting the "disappearance" of 6,000-15,000 persons.

Rochester, N.Y., 1977: Four women spray-paint, chain shut doors, and glue locks of porno theater.

Seattle, 1978: Two women pour blood on financial records of Save Our Moral Ethics, a group working to deny civil rights to lesbians and gay men.

Washington, D.C., 1981: Women's Pentagon Action Group weaves web around Pentagon.

June 1980: Native American women lead

the 'Longest Walk' from California to Washington D.C. to protest forced sterilization.

Berkeley, 1980: Disabled women demonstrate for bus accessibility.

Springfield, Illinois, 1982: Grassroots Group of Second Class Citizens chains to Illinois Senate doors, for 4 days takes over House floor, blocks doors of Governor's office, and conducts sit-ins and bloodwriting for Equal Rights Amendment.

New Bedford, Massachusetts, 1983: Feminists organize candlelight vigil to protest gang rape in a local bar.

Venice, California, 1983: Sisters of Survival and L.A. Artists for Survival hold a Torongashi ceremony (floating lanterns with names of victims attached) to commemorate bombings of Hiroshima and Nagasaki

(Actions listed in "Women Rising in Resistance" brochure, Champaign, Illinois)

France, 1919: Nelly Roussel proclaims "strike of the wombs" against forced maternity and natalist propaganda of the postwar government.

France, 1970: A group of prominent feminists place on the tomb of the unknown soldier a wreath dedicated to "the unknown wife of the soldier."

France, 1971: *Manifesto of the 343.* Women stage a protest of the laws prohibiting abortion by presenting a public petition signed by 343 women (including prominent writers and public figures like Simone De Beauvoir), declaring that they have had illegal abortions. (Elaine Marks and Isabel De Courtivron eds 1981)

"Dressed in costumes that parodied today's standards of beauty, and wearing banners that bore titles such as 'Miss-Informed,' 'Mi$$-Used,' 'Miss-Fortunate,' ['Miss Anna-Rexia'], and 'Miss-Ogyne,' more than 500 participants in this year's Myth California protest parade gathered on July 25 to demonstrate against the use of women's bodies for profit in the annual Miss California Beauty Pageant." (*Off Our Backs* 1983, October, 13)

Advice about action: "One of the steps necessary for effective action is to stop concentrating on everything that is wrong with what we consider doing and to admit to ourselves as revolutionaries, that all activities are reform – only a partial strategy working toward a larger goal. Then we will be able to risk change, experimentation, making mistakes, creating hope, and a vision." (Jackie St. Joan 1975; rpt. 1983, 118)

In February 1982 the anti-feminist leader Phyllis Schlafly spoke in Cleveland. "To challenge Schlafly's characterization of her opponents as bitter, disillusioned career women, the Pro-Choice Action Committee, a member of the Reproductive Rights National Network, transformed itself into 'Ladies Against Women' (acronym: LAW; motto: I'd Rather be Ironing). Members of LAW and CHICKS (Coalition for Harboring Indefinite Chastity and Kaffee-klatsch Sentimentality, aka Akron National Organization for Women) waved signs that read 'Suffer Not Suffrage,' 'Sperm Are People Too,' and 'You're Nobody Till You're Mrs. Somebody' and chanted 'Hit us again! Hit us again! Harder! Harder!' and 'Fifty-nine cents is to-o-o much!' " (Deborah van Klef 1982, 16)

A group called the Wimmin's Fire Brigade, finding the legal route ineffective in closing a pornographic video chain, decided that illegal action was necessary; the stores stocked videos depicting incest, rape, and other forms of sexual violence against women. On November 22, the group firebombed three Red Hot Video outlets in the lower mainland of British Columbia. (*Off Our Backs*, April 1983, 4)

The testicular approach to action: "There's a little story I've been telling about strategy, and it applies to the church, to the media, to the police, the government, business, everyone. It's the story of a woman who's at the dentist, and she's leaning back in the chair. She's a very square lady, and I don't mean Kimberley knit square, I mean housedress square. So she's leaning back in the chair and the dentist has worked on her for about three minutes, and all of a sudden he realizes that she has managed to obtain a very tight grip on his testicles, and she's squeezing just short of agony. So he stops and says, 'What is this?' And she says, 'We are not going to hurt each other, are we, doctor?' " (Florynce Kennedy; in Gloria Kaufman and Mary Kay Blakely, eds 1980, 88)

Actions are sometimes subtle, quiet, undramatic. Discussing forms of address as signals of social change, Sally McConnell-Ginet (1978a) writes that "social and political structures are created and maintained or destroyed through the operation of countless individual communicative acts. The woman who returns [a first name form of address] to her gynecologist has fired a small but significant shot in the battle for sexual egalitarianism" (34). Even the indexing of a book may constitute a subversive feminist action. An index entry in the 1976 edition of *Williams' Obstetrics*, a medical "bible" edited by Jack A. Pritchard and Paul C. MacDonald, reads "CHAUVINISM, MALE, variable amounts, 1-923"; the 1980 edition reads "CHAUVINISM, MALE, voluminous amounts, 1-1102." The preface thanks Signe Pritchard for her indexing skills.

ACTIVISM

Theory or practice based on the view that militant action will cause or initiate change. Often involves "direct action tactics" which have ranged from "letter writing to fire-bombing depending on the women's (emphasis on plural, solidarity provides strength) values and their own personal situations for doing confrontive action. . . . Historically, activism has been implemented into almost every major social change movement: the U.S. and British suffrage movements, the labor movement, the struggle for Indian independence, the anti-war movement, the Civil Rights movement. . . . The use of direct action tactics brings issues that have been trivialized, passed over, and neglected into direct and immediate importance." (Lee Smith 1984)

ACTIVIST APPROACH TO LANGUAGE CHANGE

One view holds that language "reflects" social practices and attitudes and that language change must therefore follow social change. In contrast, an activist view holds that language shapes rather than reflects social realities and that changing language is therefore a source of social change.

Approach of the National Organization for Women: "In any social movement, when changes are effected, the language sooner or later reflects the change. Our approach is different. Instead of passively noting the change, we are changing language patterns to actively effect the changes." (Wilma Scott Heide; quoted in Casey Miller and Kate Swift 1976, xi)

"Linguists are said to be amused at partisan efforts to influence language just as doctors are amused at the joke about the man who, since he had no money for an operation, offered his physician a small fee to touch up the X-ray. The analogy, from our point of view, is not persuasive. Sexist words and usage reveal sexist assumptions much as an X-ray reveals a tumor, but there the similarity stops: to paint out the tumor on the X-ray film cannot affect the body, but to consciously discard semantic symbols of deeply rooted cultural assumptions will, we think, help in time to free us from their power." (Casey Miller and Kate Swift 1976, xii)

Few feminists believe linguistic activism – coinages, for example – will magically eradicate sexist language and sexist social practices. Their objective is often to educate. Varda One called words like *manglish* and *herstory* "reality-violators and consciousness-raisers," designed "to make us realize that language is the basis of our thought and that our thought patterns are steeped in sexism-racism, class snobbery, adult chauvinism, and other lousy values." (Varda One, *Everywoman*, October 23, 1970)

ACTRESS

A term that at first seems valid, since in the theater men customarily play male roles and women female roles. H. W. Fowler (1950, 176) promoting feminine designations like *-ess*, commented that "if there is one profession in which more than in others the woman is the man's equal it is acting; & the actress is not known to resent the indication of her sex." But the term still assumes a male norm, for *actor* is the generic term for a theater professional (as in Actors Equity, Actors Playhouse, etc.). "The distinction between *actor* and *actress* is not a distinction between male and female; it is the difference between the standard and a deviation." (Casey Miller and Kate Swift 1980, 50)

(See DICTIONARY OF ACCEPTED IDEAS, -ESS, MARKEDNESS)

The term *actor* was originally used for both women and men. Women began acting on the English stage in 1656; in 1666 Samuel Pepys wrote of a woman that she "will be an excellent actor, I think." According to the OED, *actress* was first used around 1700. (Casey Miller and Kate Swift 1980, 173)

Flaubert's *Dictionary of Accepted Ideas* caustically summarized clichés about actresses as follows: "The ruin of young men of good family. Are fearfully lascivious; engage in 'nameless' orgies; run through fortunes; end in the poorhouse. 'I beg to differ, sir: some are excellent mothers!' " (Gustave Flaubert 1881, 13)

A.D.

After Defiance: "There we were, feministically aware of the problem (sexism) and able to exchange grown-up names for how it worked (objectification, socialization, commercialization, internalization, and various other -ations." (Robin Morgan 1982, 49)

ADA

A computer language (pronounced AYda) developed for and sponsored by the U.S. Dept. of Defense for widespread government use. The language was named after Ada Augusta (1816-52), Countess of Lovelace (and daughter of the poet George Byron), mathematician and assist-

ant to Charles Babbage, whose computer design in 1834 contained many of the concepts of modern computers. Progressively more powerful ADA software packages were called Strawman, Woodenman, Tinman, Ironman, and finally, Steelman. (*Datamation* 25:8, July 1979, 147; Mary Zajicek 1983, 27; the *Barnhart Dictionary Companion* 1982, 1:3, 34)

ADAM

"Mate of Eve; alleged father of two; an easily led male. History's first nonfunctioning head of household." (Midge Lennert and Norma Willson eds 1973, 1)

"Literally, a man made of blood; in pre-biblical myths, a creature formed by the Goddess of Earth from her own clay (*adamah*), given life by her blood." (Barbara G. Walker 1983, 8-9)

"Ate the apple and attempted to pass on the blame." (John A. Phillips 1984, 77)

(See EVE)

AD FEMINAM

Arguments against the woman; appealing to anti-feminist interests, prejudices, or emotions. (Julia Penelope Stanley 1981, and 1984, correspondence)

Argument to the woman. An argument *ad feminam* appeals to a reader's special interests rather than to her intellect. Used by Jane Sunderland (1978, 21). A useful word *if* a person believes that a division separates prejudice and intellect in the argument *ad hominem*.

ADJECTIVE

Any of a class of words that modify a noun, thus a key space in language where attributions can occur. In some languages, adjectives (like nouns and pronouns) are grammatically marked for gender: thus in French *nouveau* and *beau* are the masculine forms of "new" and "beautiful," respectively, while *nouvelle* and *belle* are the feminine forms. There is normally "concord" with the grammatical gender of the noun: thus "the new professor" is rendered as *le nouveau professeur* because *professeur* is grammatically classified as a masculine noun, though it may refer to a man or a woman. But if it does refer to a woman, problems arise when the adjective appears in the predicate, as in the construction "The new professor [female] is beautiful":

Neither the masculine form of the adjective (e.g., *beau*) nor its feminine form (*belle*) can be used appropriately in these circumstances without resolving, as it were the "conflict" between "grammatical" and "natural" gender. Neither *Le nouveau professeur est beau* (which necessarily refers to a man) nor *Le nouveau professeur est belle* (which is ungrammatical) is possible. The "conflict" is resolved with a sentence like *Elle est belle, le nouveau professeur* (John Lyons 1969, 286).

Julia P. Stanley (1977) notes that in English, adjectives often function to connote behaviours which are "appropriate" for or expected of women and men in our culture. Thus masculinist values are often attached to such words as *feminine* (weak, gentle, delicate), *masculine* (virile, strong, bold), *hysterical* (characterizing women's raging hormones), and so on. Feminist critiques have caused some dictionary-makers to define adjectives in a less biased way.

(See GENDER-MARKING, SPEAKING SUBJECT)

"The most of women are, in their youth, at least, by both habit and temperament . . . decidedly 'adjective.' Few of them have ever had the chance of becoming a 'noun substantive' – (whether or not that be a natural or enviable position). They have been accustomed all their lives hitherto to be governed, if not guarded; protected or unprotected, as may be; but rarely placed in circumstances where they had actively to assume the guardianship or rule of others." (Dinah Maria (Mulock) Craik 1858, 96)

ADOLESCENCE

When persons are considered inadequate adults. Defined for men "in terms of economic and occupational independence . . . If adolescence is identified as a transitional phase between childhood and the assumption of 'adult' tasks, a hiatus institutionalised to some extent as a period of liberty and choice, then adolescence for girls had relatively little meaning" since girls – especially working-class girls – are unlikely to have a period of time removed from adult surveillance and free from responsibility for domestic chores. (Carol Dyhouse 1981, 119)

ADORNMENT

"Sound business instinct" for a marriageable girl since "what else will her future husband will demand of her is more or less guesswork . . . [and since] the one branch of women's work which is likely to bring her a material reward in the shape of an economically desirable husband is cultivation of a pleasing exterior and attractive manners." (Cicely Hamilton 1909, 90, 91)

(See APPEARANCE)

Topic for discussion and experimentation. During the nineteenth century and more recently, young Indian women explored many forms of adornment, often incorporating items that were foreign or unusual with traditions, women in some clans and tribes showing more variety and experimentation than others. They experimented, for example, with a variety of materials, including jewelry, clothing, beads, body paints, perfume, feathers, claws, belts, armlets, garters, and aprons. In contrast, hair was generally worn in a traditional style according to tribe and region, with little fluctuation. (John Upton Terrell and Donna M. Terrell 1974, 101-12)

Opportunity for drama. Elspeth Huxley, in her account of her childhood, tells of a woman "who wore a live snake instead of a necklace at dinner parties; she said it kept her neck cool. That sounds a tall story but it's true." (Elspeth Huxley 1959, 70)

ADULTERY

Voluntary sexual intercourse of a married person with a person other than a spouse. In many societies, a widespread practice; in virtually all societies, more generally and severely punished in women than in men, sometimes by death.

"In early history adultery had a definition made by men and for men. Adultery was committed *only* when a married woman had sexual intercourse with a man who was not her husband. A married man could cheat freely: adultery didn't apply to him. . . . When adultery was finally applied to both men and women, there were several court cases questioning whether a man could be guilty of committing adultery with a female slave. [Even today] adultery is objectionable in a man [and] odious in a woman." (Barbara B. Hirsch 1973, 25, 35)

"I read this somewhere, I wasn't there: In feudal Europe, if a woman committed adultery her husband would sometimes tie her down, catch a mouse and trap it under a cup on her bare belly, until it gnawed itself out, now are you afraid of mice?" (Judy Grahn 1977, 15)

The Bible commands stoning to death an adulterous wife or a bride suspected of premarital affairs (Deut. 22:21). In Hebrew law, widows who remarried "unto a stranger" (outside the dead husband's family) were also considered adulterous.

From *ad alterum se conferre*, 'to confer (property) upon another.' "In the age of matrilineal inheritance, female property owners could leave cast-off husbands destitute by conferring their 'matrimony' (wealth) upon another. Patriarchal societies therefore sought to insure wives' sexual fidelity for economic reasons." (Barbara G. Walker 1983, 11)

ADVERB

As modifiers of verbs, adverbs offer a linguistic space where cultural values about actions may be marked. Stereotypical notions about who may perform certain kinds of actions and how those actions are performed may promote sexist adverbial usages. "She sat daintily on the step" links the feminine subject with traditionally "appropriate" feminine behavior; "She stepped boldly up to the podium" suggests other behavioral options. Adverbs can also modify the

speaker's expressed attitude toward her own speech action. This makes them important indicators of the speaker's assessment of what she is doing and its significance for her relation to the hearer. Adverbs intensify, qualify, and sometimes mollify: "She's *incredibly* talented," "You *definitely* need a vacation," "I'm *kinda* tired," "*Unfortunately*, Athena, we had to give that job to a family man" (Penelope Brown and Stephen Levinson 1978; Penelope Brown 1980). In addition, adverbs can bring in covert assumptions of a false universality or function to obscure the absence of explicit reasoning and the presence of suspect assumptions: "*Obviously*, women are less reliable employees than men" [obvious to whom?], "*Biologically*, heterosexuality is inevitable." More positively (to shift adverbs), adverbs are tools for a woman-centered discourse that recognizes the many-faceted nature of our experience: "She is *sexually* adventurous, *personally* compassionate, and *intellectually* fearless." (Sally McConnell-Ginet 1984, correspondence)

(See ADVERTISING, AGENT-DELETION, AMBIGUITY, MEANING, POLITENESS)

ADVERTISING

"A permanent consciousness-raising mechanism, constantly reminding [aware women] of their position in American life, constantly dredging up insulting and demeaning images that anger them and make them reflect upon the condition of all women today." (Lucy Komisar 1971, 317)

(See MADISON AVENUE'S WOMAN, MAGAZINE MENSTRUATION, REPRESENTATION)

Frequently plays on ambiguity and implicit sexist assumptions. "As long as feminist opposition . . . is focussed solely on the level of the ad's sexist content, it falls prey to the efficiency of the ad itself. . . . Instead, we must work at the level of the discourse within which the ad does its communicating. We must point to the presuppositions for its effectiveness . . . We need to expose its ambiguity and its implicit dependence on our internalization of sexism as 'second nature.' " (Terry R. Winant 1983, 618)

"Sample comments from women respondents to an advertising monitoring project conducted by the Ontario Status of Women Council in 1974:

- In my opinion, almost all TV ads make women appear as fools, interested only in their wash or their breath.
- I realize 'ad men' believe it doesn't matter if their ads aggravate the buyer so long as they remember the name of the product. 'Taint so!
- That wife could use an extra pair of hands to share the work-load – not hand lotion.
- I'm fed up with these sultry male voices telling me what to buy and why. They don't know.
- If she can't be trusted to purchase dog food, God help the rest of the family.
- The wife has apparently had a frontal lobotomy and cannot read, understand print, or feed the dog without male help.
- Advertisers must have a low opinion about women to put this garbage on the air."

(in Dorothy Aaron 1975)

Salesmanship, whose prime medium is a woman's "autonomy, her dignity, her sexuality, her body and her mind." (Mary MacNamara c. 1978, 1)

"Is an incredibly powerful agent of male supremacy, a fact which the ASA [Advertising Standards Authority] glosses over with platitudes like 'You have your views and other people have theirs.' Of course we have our views but the advertisers have the power and pay a fortune to buy space to push their products. The rest of us are left speechless." (Jill Nicholls and Pat Moan 1978; in Marsha Rowe 1982, 65)

ADVICE

"An incessant drip of exhortation to be feminine (as if women were by nature unwomanly) according to some male standard of the female." (H. M. Swanwick 1935, 167)

(See CONVERSATION, FEMININITY, POLITENESS, WOMEN'S LANGUAGE, WOMEN'S MAGAZINES)

AFFIRMATIVE ACTION

"Referred originally to the policy adopted by the federal government on the basis of Executive Order 11246 (as amended by Executive Order 11375), by President Johnson. This order requires that all companies, universities and other institutions which do business with the government, or receive federal funding, shall not only refrain from racial, sexual, or religious discrimination in hiring, promotion and admissions, but also 'take affirmative action to ensure that applicants are employed, and that employees are treated during their employment, without regard to their race, color, religion, sex, or national origin.' The term has since come to refer to any such institutional policy designed to open up white-male-dominated fields to larger numbers of women, blacks, Chicanos and other minority persons." (Mary Anne Warren 1980, 10)

As constituted in 1977, the structure of the National Women's Studies Association (NWSA) enables individual special interest groups (e.g., lesbians, Third World women) to form "caucuses" which are officially sanctioned, structured on a quota system, and given special voting rights by the organization. Because individual caucuses are formed *with regard* to such characteristics as race, color, and ethnicity, the caucus structure reverses the "without regard" philosophy of the affirmative action directive. A Constitutional Review Task Force in 1981 debated the implications of this language, noting that " 'without regard' presumably leads to 'indiscriminate' behaviour which is compatible with NWSA's constitution and 'with regard' leads to 'indiscriminative' behavior which is incompatible with our constitution." The Task Force concluded that "with regard" implied *a priori* decisions as to the criteria for oppression and was not a practical and fair way to ensure full recognition and participation of all oppressed groups. (National Women's Studies Association 1981; "Text of Proposed Constitutional Revision," printed flyer dated February)

"Requires an employer or educational institution to tip evenly balanced scales in favor of a candidate from an underrepresented group. If two persons are similarly qualified, affirmative action requires that the candidate from the underrepresented group should be hired or admitted. Preferential hiring and quota admission . . . are stronger programs. The employer or educational institution must use different criteria in accepting persons from underrepresented groups." Problems in carrying out affirmative action programs include the fact that "(1) a person's own sense (real or imagined) of his or her inadequacies significantly limit his or her opportunities; (2) even when two persons are equally qualified, the person who makes the choices, because of discrimination, may believe that the oppressed person is less qualified; and (3) the nature of the qualifications required might not adequately reflect the job to be filled." (Mary Lou Kendrigan 1984, 80-1)

AFRO-AMERICANS

Identify roots in Africa.
    (See BLACK)

AGE

"Old age is not an illness, it is a timeless ascent. As power diminishes, we grow toward the light." (May Sarton 1982, 56)

AGEISM

A term popularized by Robert Butler, M.D., former director of the national Institute of Aging, to refer to discrimination against older persons. Many writers (Susan Sontag, Marilyn Block, Jane Porcino, Maggie Kuhn, Ruth Harriet Jacobs, Lillian Rubin, Elissa Melamed, and others) have pointed out that ageism is much more frequently experienced by women, because of what Sontag terms the double standard of aging. Ageism assumes "that older people are not real people; not only are their needs fewer, and in some important areas such as sexuality, nonexistent; but it is considered that their experience is of little account and is to be avoided." Nobody knows what "to do" with older people, especially older women (Pauline Long 1979; in Marsha Rowe 1982, 61, 62). Ageism is also, however, "reproduced (or created) by older people [who] perpetuate prejudices about, and discriminate against young people." (Helen Blackhouse 1984, 5)

AGENT-DELETION

A method discussed by Julia P. Stanley (1971, 1974, 1976) of erasing responsibility in linguistic structures, especially characteristic of professional languages (scientific jargon, medical jargon, technological writing, bureaucratese, advertising, among others): "The passive and its related constructions theoretically permit the deletion of the agent in contexts where the reader can ascertain the deleted agent from the context. However . . . the agent may be deleted or never surfaces, and this deletion has the effect of creating an appeal to a universal consensus . . . so that the major proposition of the sentence appears to have more weight than it actually does [e.g. 'Women are said to be especially sensitive to others' needs' – Who says? On what basis?]. In other contexts, the agent is deleted in order to protect the agents responsible for the action [e.g., 'Mary was sexually abused as a young child' obscures the fact that she was abused *by her father*]." (Julia P. Stanley 1974) The phrase *untreated menopause*, for example, implies a need for treatment. "Again, gynecologists apply the term *necessary* to a forceps delivery which becomes 'necessary' only within the context of anti-woman ob/gyn practices. They also deceptively use constructions such as the passive voice. Thus the physician who proclaims that 'estrogen replacement therapy is required' neglects to explain *by whom* it is required." (Mary Daly 1978, 257-8)

AGGRESSIVITY

"Means many different things to different people; it is not value-free, objective, or uniquely defined, and when used with reference to people, it is not synonymous only with fighting behavior. In primate research, the word has often been used synonymously with dominance. With respect to humans, I believe the inordinate amount of scientific and popular interest in a biological basis for sex differences in 'aggressivity' does not have to do with explaining why women so seldom fight in bars, but rather with explaining differences in achievement in the public world. In such a contest, the word is invested with qualities that remain unexpressed and unspecified, such as assertiveness, independence, intelligence, creativity and imagination, which are usually associated with men who are leaders; that is, aggressive. So, by means of semantic flim-flam, such animal experiments are used to 'prove' that men are naturally, hence inevitably, dominant or superior to women because of hormonal differences. Thus, however exemplary the work itself may be, it lends itself to misuse and misinterpretation when it uses language in ways that are both imprecise and laden with ill-defined anthropomorphic values and meanings." (Ruth Bleier 1984, 95)
(See ESSENTIALISM, NATURAL, NATURE, NORMAL, OBJEC-TIVITY, SCIENCE, SOCIO-BIOLOGY)

AGING

A life-spanning process of growth and development running from birth to death. Old age is an integral part of the whole, which can bring fulfillment and self-actualization. (Gray Panthers Fact Sheet 1980)
(See ACRONYMS, AGEISM, GRAY PANTHERS)
Is a period when "influence for an African woman often really begins as her children get older and as she reaches menopause. Aging, therefore, is in fact a positive factor for African women, unlike aging for women in some Western cultures." (Pala Okeyo; cited in Martha Lagace (1984, 4)

AGORAPHILIA

Love of the marketplace; opposite of agoraphobia. (Julia P. Stanley 1984, correspondence)
(See AGORAPHOBIA)

AGORAPHOBIA

Intense fear of open spaces. "Commonly known as a morbid fear of public places. Sufferers often prefer to define it as a fear of any situation in which they feel trapped. Neither definition gives any indication of the true misery of people made prisoners by their fears. Isolated, they live in a twilight world of panic and apprehension, where a train journey is total impossibility and the corner shop might as well be on the other side of the world." (Hilary Wilce 1972; in Marsha Rowe 1982, 393-4)

AGRICULTURE

The planting, harvesting, and management of food, accomplishments of many women in ancient times and today.
(See FARMER)
Food production which in some parts of the world is managed primarily by women. In Africa, women are 60-80% of the agriculture labor force. (World Conference of the United Nations Decade for Women: Equality, Development and Peace 1980; UN document)
"One of women's oldest occupations." (Margaret Hamlin 1931, 152)

A.I.D.

Artificial Insemination by [anonymous] Donor. "The development of A.I.D. has, in many cases, met the needs of women who desire their own children and who, for a variety of reasons, have not become pregnant." Considerable legal and financial problems are attached to the practice: the quality of the sperm remains minimally specified; growing commercialism has the potential for exploiting women financially; and "women must petition the medical profession (a notoriously conservative and male dominated institution) for A.I.D. Women may also encounter legal strictures, as when the male sperm donor wins legal visitation rights to the child." Men, however, can become parents without being required to make any special commitments (legal, financial, social, emotional) to the women who bear the children. (Joanne Finkelstein and Patricia Clough 1983, 398)

AIDS

Acquired Immune Deficiency Syndrome. A serious and often fatal disease first identified in 1980 which involves the total breakdown of the human auto-immune system; this in turn leaves the body open to infection and other problems, some of which may cause death. Though current research suggests a viral agent of some kind is responsible, there is currently no known cause for the disease and no known cure. Populations whose members are most likely to contract AIDS are hemophiliacs, Haitian immigrants, and sexually-active homosexual males; because the disease is such a mystery and because little can at present be done for its victims, AIDS is an intense social and political as well as a medical problem. Fear of AIDS within and outside of the homosexual community, in particular, has led to attacks and actions against male homosexuals and, more recently, lesbians.

AIM

American Indian Movement. Activist organization concerned with the rights and interests of American Indians.

A.I.M.

Action, Information, Motivation. The first pressure group (1972) of the Irish Women's Liberation Movement, with a goal of law reform in areas related to women and the family. (June Levine 1982, 236)

AIN'T I A WOMAN

Famous speech of Sojourner Truth to the Akron Convention on Women's Rights 1851; has been used to name feminist books, bookstores, newsletters, conferences.

"Well, children, where there is so much racket there must be something out of kilter. I think that 'twixt the negroes of the South and the women at the North, all talking about rights, the white men will be in a fix pretty soon. But what's all this here talking about? That man over there says women need to be helped into carriages, and lifted over ditches, and to have the best place everywhere. Nobody ever helps me into carriages, or over mud-puddles, or gives me any best place! And ain't I a woman? Look at me! Look at my arm! I have ploughed, and planted, and gathered into barns, and no man could head me! And ain't I a woman? I could work as much and eat as much as a man – when I could get it – and bear the lash as well! And ain't I a woman? I have borne thirteen children, and seen them most all sold off to slavery, and when I cried out with my mother's grief, none but Jesus heard me! And ain't I a woman?" (Sojourner Truth 1851; in Bert James Loewenberg and Ruth Bogin ed. 1976, 235). Sojourner Truth (originally Isabella Van Wagener) is often presented as speaking a substandard southern dialect – most implausibly, since she grew up in the northern U.S. speaking Dutch and did not learn English until she was ten.

"A collective of eight women functioning as a world wide conspiracy of Radical Lesbians." (Ain't I A Woman Collective 1971; *Ain't I A Woman*, 17 February, 9)

ALICE DOESN'T

Title of a book on feminist film theory by Teresa De Lauretis taken from a protest sign she picked up in 1975 and posted near her desk throughout the writing process. The book, like the placard, are both "signs of the same struggle, both are texts of the women's movement." Not only does the title suggest the many associations with the name "Alice." "For me it is important to acknowledge, in this title, the unqualified opposition of feminism to existing social relations, its refusal of given definitions and cultural values, and at the same time to affirm the political and personal ties of shared experience that join women in the movement and are the condition of feminist work, theory, and practice." (Teresa De Lauretis 1984, vii)

ALICE IN WONDERLAND

Children's book by Lewis Carroll (Charles Dodson) whose paradoxes, absurdities, conundrums, and jokes about language and its arbitrary nature have furnished countless epigrams for feminists analyzing language within patriarchal structures and advocating linguistic change (e.g., Sally McConnell-Ginet 1984).

ALIMONY

Back salary; reparation. From L. *alimonia* "nutriment," "support," from *alere* 'to nourish.' But "for all the magic of the word, for all the fabulous tabloid stories, alimony is simply an allowance to pay for the support of a spouse unable to provide for herself after the marriage is washed up. Alimony isn't an automatic benefit. Unlike child support . . . alimony is decreed only under certain circumstances. It can be waived, denied, forgotten. Sometimes, the court decrees so little that it's forgettable. Alimony most resembles a pension . . . Many states consider alimony a reward for services rendered and earned only by the ideal little woman." (Barbara B. Hisrch 1973, 138-9)

ALMA MATER

From the Latin, "bounteous mother," the term originally applied to a number of Roman goddesses; during the medieval period, it came to be used by male students to refer to their universities. For many women, the spirit of a nurturing female figure sometimes seems to be rarely in evidence in modern colleges and universities: "The Alma Mater is a woman of ill repute. At least she is so for the women . . . who were educated in the

1950's and early 1960's." (Joanne Spencer Kantrowitz 1981, 15)

ALONGSIDE-OUR-MAN-KNEE-JERK-PHENOMENON

According to Cherríe Moraga this is the weakness of much Chicana theory about women's lives and conditions. (Cherríe Moraga 1983, 107)

ALPHABET

Invented by women in many of the myths through which people have ordered their sense of reality: Carmenta created a Latin alphabet from the Greek; Medusa, a beautiful Libyan warrior queen, gave the alphabet to Hercules; Queen Isis, a refugee from Greece in Egypt, gave the alphabet to the Egyptians; Samothea, possibly a Briton, invented letters, astronomy and science and, according to some stories, conducted the Hyperborean University where Pythagoras is rumored to have studied. Pythagoras is also said to have learned ancient alphabets from priestesses at a Minoan-Cretan college, who turned the older hieroglyphics into an alphabet-syllabary. The priestess-goddess Kali invented the Sanskrit alphabet. The goddess Safekh-Aabut was acknowledged as the source of the alphabet in Egypt, alternately with Isis, and was the "recording angel," in charge of literature and libraries. (Elise Boulding 1976, 193-4) "Hindu scriptures say the Goddess invented alphabets, pictographs, mandalas and other magical signs, hence her title of Samjna (sign, name, image). . . . As Great Mother Kali Ma, she wore on her necklace of skulls the sacred Sanskrit letters, which she invented, and invested with such magic power that she could create things simply by pronouncing their names in this language." (Barbara G. Walker 1983, 685)

"Ought women to learn the alphabet? There lies the whole question. Concede this little fulcrum, and Archimedea will move the world before she has done with it: it becomes merely a question of time." (Thomas Wentworth Higginson 1859; in Sandra M. Gilbert and Susan Gubar

1982, 1. See also Anna Julia Cooper, cited in the introduction to this dictionary)

"I sit with my cup
To catch the crazy falling alphabet.
It crashes, it gravels down,
a fault in the hemispheres.
High rise L's, without windows –
buckling in slow motion;
subway G's, Y's, twisted, collapsing
    underground:
screams of passengers
buried in the terrible phonemes,
arms and legs paralyzed,
And no one, no one at all,
Is sifting through the rubble."

(Ruth Stone, "Poetry"; cited by Sandra M. Gilbert and Susan Gubar 1982, 1)
    "Alphabet" is the nickname of the protagonist in a Zora Neale Hurston novel, "a magical female protagonist . . . who recovers the black magic of what she calls 'de maiden language' over and over again." "Can it be that women writers must look beyond the traditional alphabetizings of history, with its masculinist syntax of subordination, to discover and recover woman as the Alpha and Omega of both the life of letters and the letters of life? For not only have women always articulated the sounds of the alphabet, women have inscribed the symbols of the alphabet in elegant, intelligent ways." (Sandra M. Gilbert and Susan Gubar 1982, 9, 17)

ALUMNAE
Plural of the feminine-gender word *alumna*, used to describe women who graduate from an institution. The plural of the masculine-gender word *alumnus* is *alumni*. These English words, from classical Latin, have no generic form. Men who graduate from previously all-female institutions object to being called *alumnae*; women who graduate from any institution attended by males are expected to accept being called *alumni*. Alternatives to the false generic *alumni*: *alumnae and alumni* (or the other way around, or *alumnae/i* (or the other way around). An individual woman is an *alumna*, and a woman who is a

retired professor is a *professor emerita*. (Casey Miller and Kate Swift 1980, 106)

A.M.
Ante Marriage. As reflected in newspaper stories, one of the two great stages in a woman's life, the other being Post Marriage (P.M.). (Jean Ward 1980, 38)

AMANUENSES
Persons employed to take dictation or to copy manuscripts. Much of our knowledge of the language and narratives of people who cannot write themselves – including American Indian myths and stories and African slave narratives – comes by way of amanuenses whose role, theoretically, is merely to "transcribe" yet whose procedures, inevitably, are determined by social, cultural, and ideological structures which act together to reshape the original narrative into something with a different form. Thus we have inherited a body of American Indian literature transcribed by missionaries and other white folk whose reshaped narratives yield what Patricia Clark Smith (1983) calls "eagle feather poetry" (110). Many slave narratives were taken down by white women and changed in the process (Alice Deck 1984, correspondence). Mrs Frances D. Gage, for example, transcribed Sojourner Truth's famous "Ain't I A Woman" speech, rendering it into southern "Black" dialect although Sojourner Truth's original language was Dutch.
    (See AIN'T I A WOMAN)

A-MAZING
"Within a culture possessed by the myth of feminine evil, the naming, describing, and theorizing about good and evil has constituted a maze/haze of deception. The journey of women becoming is breaking through this maze – springing into free space, which is an a-mazing process." (Mary Daly 1978, 2)

A-MAZING FEMALE MIND
"Is the labrys that cuts through the double binds and doublebinding words that block our breakthrough to under-

standing radical feminist friendship and sisterhood." (Mary Daly 1978, 369)

AMAZON

Powerful female. According to some scholars, archeological and linguistic evidence suggests that the Indo-Europeans were once a matriarchal culture that worshipped the powerful female; the social structure was probably that of the matrifocal clan or tribe; males were probably nomadic; and the Amazons were the last of the original Indo-Europeans to remain in their homeland; "their slaughter well into recorded history was simply the last of many violent battles fought between the matriarchal warriors and the patriarchs of the 'new age.' " (Susan J. Wolfe and Julia Penelope Stanley 1980, 236-7)

(See ETYMOLOGY, MATRIARCHY)

The etymology of *amazon* is controversial. Carol F. Justus, who has studied questions of cultural and linguistic change involving women in Hittite (1983), notes that the hypothesized root **magh-* for *amazon* is very problematic and is probably not of Indo-European origin. A non-Indo-European root *mag-* may be responsible not only for Gothic *magan* "have power, be able" (to which *amazon* is sometimes linked) but also to Gothic *magus* "son." In contrast to the Indo-European word *sunus*, which meant the "son" in the paternal line, the non-Indo-European *magus* and its relatives refer to the son in the maternal line. These non-Indo-European words suggest the linguistic traces of a pre-patriarchal social organization. (Carol Justus 1984, correspondence)

She who guards the harmony. "In the beginning, if there ever was such a time, all the companion lovers called themselves amazons. Living together, loving, celebrating one another, playing, in a time when work was still a game, the companion lovers in the terrestrial garden continued to call themselves amazons throughout the entire Golden Age. Then, with the settlement of the first cities, many companion lovers disrupted the original harmony and called themselves

mothers. Thereafter, amazon meant, for them, daughter, eternal child, she who does not assume her destiny. Amazons were banished from the cities of the mothers. At the time they became the violent ones and fought to defend harmony. For them the ancient name amazon had retained its full meaning. From now on it signified something more, she who guards the harmony. From then on, there were amazons in every age, on every continent, island, ice bank. To the amazons of all these times, we owe having been able to enter the Glorious Age." (Monique Wittig and Sande Zeig 1976, 5)

The African Amazons of Dahomey "were highly prized, well-trained, and ferocious women warriors who guarded, and fought under the direction of, the Panther Kings of Dahomey." (Audre Lorde 1978, 119)

"The black female was depicted by whites as an Amazon because they saw her ability to endure hardships no 'lady' was supposedly capable of enduring as a sign that she possessed an animalistic sub-human strength." (bell hooks 1981, 81-2)

A 15-year-old's fantasy: "When the starships returned, they would all be driven by black women, seven feet tall, landing and reducing to rubbish all the earth's ammunition and the bishop of our church to fly shit. I imagined . . . all of the church women getting naughty winks from Amazons." (Pat Suncircle 1981, 4) Young white women meanwhile learned about amazons from Wonder Woman, a comic book hero of the 1940s and 1950s.

"Ritual for the Integrity of the Body," written by a woman who has had a mastectomy, derives a vision of wholeness from the Amazons. In the ritual, "each womon of the group bares her chest, puts her hand – outstretched in a gesture of acceptance – on the scarred or flattened area where breast had been." (J. Wattles 1980; rpt 1982, 47)

An epithet used to scorn women working for voting rights. (Teresa Billington-Greig 1911b, 43)

Greek name for goddess-worshipping

tribes in North Africa, Anatolia, and the Black Sea area. Disputed etymology from Gk. *a-* "not, without" + *mazos* "breast," based on the erroneous belief that Amazons cut off their right breasts so as not to impede the drawing of a bow. Some scholars now believe the word meant "moon-woman." Women warriors are mentioned, in many myths. "Again and again, legends mention the women's magic battle-cries, which made their enemies helpless." (Barbara G. Walker 1983, 24-7)

"Collective name for belligerent hordes of women with self-government, whose aversion to any kind of permanent, matrimonial ties varies in graduation. The mildest form of this aversion caused them to engage in a quick assignation with their male neighbors, totally indiscriminate as a matter of principle, every spring. Female offspring was retained; the male was sent to its distant fathers." (Helen Diner 1973, 98)

"Amazons: The Universal Male Nightmare." (Phyllis Chesler 1972a, 97)

"Ancient separatists who got it right the first time." (Jackie Urbanovic and Susie Day 1983, #35)

AMBIGUITY

Both lexical and structural linguistic ambiguity – open to more than one interpretation – have been of concern to feminists. The so-called "generic" pronoun *he* illustrates lexical ambiguity: it is an individual word which is variously employed to mean both 'human being' and 'male human being.' The slogan/grafitti "If you think women are revolting, you're right!" illustrates structural ambiguity. Up to the comma, you're encouraged to read it as "women are revolting (people)," with "revolting" as a predicate adjective; the exclamation after the comma encourages a re-reading of "revolting" as a verb to mean "women are in the process of revolting." The saying plays upon a negative stereotype about women and suddenly transforms it into something positive and formidable, thus using the ambiguous structure to point out that

things are not always what they seem. Ambiguity often requires us to "disambiguate" or "deconstruct" what words and sentences actually mean in context; but as Sally McConnell-Ginet points out, "language users can play with the multiply available meanings (this is sometimes used in defense of *he*). Indeed, this possibility of deliberate ambiguity underlies both positive (the effective humor of good political slogans, evocative titles, subtle literary constructions) and harmful language uses (exploitative ads, evasion of responsibility for one's actions, etc.). There are many cases where a single form has alternative and sometimes overlapping interpretations – e.g., the general overlay of power and solidarity which surfaces in analysis of endearments, compliments, etc. A related multiplicity underlies devices like tags and rising intonations: interactiveness vs. deference and insecurity. The politics of ambiguity is vitally important: who interprets and evaluates? It is in such ambiguous situations that we find different interpretations for the language and behavior of males and females. More generally, differential evaluation and ranking is easiest where alternative analyses are plausible." (Sally McConnell-Ginet 1984, correspondence)

(See AGENT DELETION, GENERICS, PRONOUNS)

AMEN

Not a God-given ritual. "January 25, 1971. 'Women's Lib Adds Church to List' was the headline on a UPI story by Patricia McCormack. She cited the ending of a prayer at a Women's Strike for Equality, where those assembled didn't say 'amen,' but rather 'Ah-woman.' They did this to make the point that discrimination against women by organized religion is one of the wrongs they want to right." (Alleen Pace Nilsen et al. 1977, 4)

AMERICAN

A term to be used with care. "Many people in the United States refer to themselves as Americans, as if America and the United States were synonymous.

We forget that we are one of the North American countries, and the people from Central and South America are also Americans" (Jo Delaplaine 1978, 11). "I do not equate 'American' with imperialist/racist, but I do equate American people who do not transform their ignorance about 'non-dominant' cultures and their relationship to these cultures, with imperialism and racism" (Judit Moschkovich 1981, 81).

(See AFRO-AMERICAN, ASIAN-AMERICAN, EURO-AMERICAN)

AMERICAN FRONTIER

A place for Anglo men only, an adventure of settlement and conquest that women (according to most histories) were only peripherally involved in. Men use female imagery to describe the frontier: it required masculine mastery over a feminine realm. As more and more accounts by women came to light, we learn not only of their presence at the frontier but also that for them it is a gender-neutral landscape, with gardens which are neither virginal nor maternal. (Annette Kolodny 1975 and 1978; Elizabeth Hampsten 1982)

AMERICAN HERITAGE DICTIONARY

The *American Heritage Dictionary* (William Morris ed. 1969) sought to be not only an authoritative guide to "grace and precision" in language but also an unforbidding treasury of information, "an agreeable companion," that would illuminate many dimensions of language and communication. In addition to prescriptive information, the dictionary provides "usage notes" as a guide to actual current usage. Its scholarly information (e.g., history of English, linguistic structure, compendium of Indo-European roots) is accessible and relatively easy to use. As Casey Miller and Kate Swift (1980) point out, the dictionary contains many instances of sexist usage; the recent edition improves on this (but some find the scholarly information less satisfactorily presented).

AMERICAN HERITAGE SCHOOL DICTIONARY

First published in 1972, this dictionary was the first whose editors consciously tried to correct sexist biases. Designed to define the words U.S. school children most frequently encounter in grades 3 through 9, the dictionary was based on a computerized study which also provided "impeccable evidence that the language of American school books mirrors the sexist assumptions of society" (Casey Miller and Kate Swift 1980, 142-3). Alma Graham, one of the editors, wrote that if the dictionary "were to serve elementary students without showing favoritism to one sex or the other, an effort would have to be made to restore the gender balance. We would need more examples featuring females, and the examples would have to ascribe to girls and women the active, inventive, and adventurous human traits traditionally reserved for men and boys." The *American Heritage School Dictionary* was the first to include the entry *Ms.*

AMERICANIZATION

Process by which cultural and ethnic subgroups are encouraged to adopt behaviors and attitudes of U.S. mainstream culture. With the passage of the 19th amendment, concern mounted that immigrant girls and women would be Americanized before it was in their best interests. "It is better in my judgment not to take away language and customs and traditions until we are sure we have something better to take their place. It is better not to get young Italian girls to go to night schools unless the neighborhoods are safe for them to go and come." (Frances A. Kellor 1918)

AMNIOCENTESIS

Sampling the fluid surrounding the fetus in the womb, drawn through a needle inserted under local anaesthetic. Can be used to determine the sex of the fetus and to detect some fetal problems.

ANARCHA-FEMINIST MOVEMENT

"The first English anarcha-feminist groups

appeared in 1977 and soon grew to a national [and international] network with its own bulletins and newspaper, with two national and several regional conferences." It promoted a critique of the feminist movement which – the anarcha-feminists claimed – was forgetting many of the early principles: absence of leaders, decentralism, federalism, lack of dogma. "By 1980 the anarcha-feminist movement had to all intents and purposes ceased to function. It seems, looking back, rather short-lived. For one thing it faced opposition not only from marxist and reformist feminists but also from the traditional, and male-dominated, anarchist movement, which regarded anarcha-feminists as some kind of threat to its position." (*Quiet Rumours: An Anarcha-Feminist Anthology* c.1983, 3)

ANARCHISM

"From the Greek *anarchos* – without ruler. Is the affirmation of human freedom and dignity expressed in a negative, cautionary term signifying that no person should rule or dominate another person by force or threat of force . . . We consider Anarcho-Feminism to be the ultimate and necessary radical stance at this time in world history, far more radical than any form of Marxism." (*Siren* c.1983, 4-5)

(See ANARCHIST-FEMINIST)

"Really stands for the liberation of the human mind from the dominion of religion; the liberation of the human body from the dominion of property; liberation from the shackles and restrictions of government. Anarchism stands for a social order based on the free grouping of individuals for the purpose of producing real social wealth, an order that will guarantee to every human being free access to the earth and full enjoyment of the necessities of life, according to individual desires, tastes, and inclinations." (Emma Goldman; in Peggy Kornegger 1979, 237)

ANARCHIST-FEMINIST

A woman who insists that female subordination is rooted in an obsolete system of sexual and familial relationships, who insists on both economic and psychological independence, who argues that personal autonomy is an essential component of sexual equality and that political and legal rights can not of themselves provide such equality. Except for Emma Goldman, anarchist-feminists have been largely forgotten or ignored by historians. (Margaret S. Marsh 1981, 5)

(See ANARCHA-FEMINISM, ANARCHISM)

ANATOMY

"Is creativity." Men's physiology is their fate. Women labor reproductively and men do not. (Mary O'Brien 1981, 116-39) If women sometimes feel that anatomy is used as a weapon against them, their perceptions have a linguistic basis: the Greek elements analyze as "Tomy cutting Ana up," an ancient joke much beloved of male Greek teachers. (David Doughan 1985, correspondence)

ANATOMY IS DESTINY

"These are Freud's words, and they have become almost as famous as his name itself. But ah, fame is not truth; and destiny is precisely what anatomy is *not*. A hole is not destiny. A protuberance is not destiny. Even two protuberances – a pair of legs, nearly half the human body – are not destiny. If anatomy were destiny, the wheel could not have been invented: we would have been limited by legs. . . ." "Reduce woman to her anatomy – to Womb – and it is death, death, death, all the way; death and death and death, always endlessly, gluttonously death. The destiny of anatomy is death." (Cynthia Ozick 1972, 153, 161)

"Anatomy may, at its point of hypothetical normality, give us two opposite but equal sexes (with the atrophied sex organs of the other present in each) but Freudian psychoanalytic theory does not . . . Freud was concerned over and over again to establish that there was no one-to-one correlation between biology and psychology, that, for example, in psychological terms masculinity and femininity really reduced themselves to activity and passivity and that neither of the sexes held an absolute prerogative over either." (Juliet Mitchell 1974, 30-1) For Freud, "the biological female is destined to become a woman, but the question to which psychoanalysis must address itself, is *how*, if she does manage this, is it to happen?" Anatomy, then, is *not* destiny, in the sense that a biological sex, given at the outset, automatically yields a "male" or "female" person; rather, sexual differentiation occurs only when the child experiences a key external event – in Freud's view, the castration complex, which ushers in a symbolic and historical order embodying human law. "To Freud the castration complex divided the sexes and thus made the human being, human." It was Freud's colleagues and followers, resisting the theoretical importance he gave the castration complex, who explained sexual differentiation in terms of "biological predisposition." (Juliet Mitchell; in Juliet Mitchell and Jacqueline Rose ed. 1982, 24, 18-19)

"Is anatomy linguistic destiny? Is a womb a metaphorical mouth, a pen a metaphorical penis?" Sandra M. Gilbert and Susan Gubar critique speculations (usually French) "which would translate a long-silenced female anatomical reality into a new linguistic destiny." (Sandra M. Gilbert and Susan Gubar 1982, 1, 3)

ANDREW PHENOMENON

Label given the observation that "gay men may be close to, love and respect, women, but as soon as another man walks in the room it seems to go straight to their crotch. . . . Perhaps gay men too have a double vision of reality, but this is for them to explore and not us." (Liz Stanley and Sue Wise 1983, 76)

ANDROCENTRISM

Male-centeredness. Men's greater power to control words, and to represent and preserve in language their interests and ideologies, has many consequences, including some specific ones for women and language research. Despite the increased

publication of women's words generated by the feminist movements of the nineteenth and twentieth centuries, it remains difficult to find information on what women have talked and written about, and the ways they have talked and written.

First, women's words often occur in non-traditional publications which are difficult for libraries to find, catalogue, and store. Many underground publications are ephemeral and unless a library inherits an existing collection of such materials, they will only be identified and collected through unflagging detective work on the part of a committed librarian or archivist. Archivists, in turn, use their own training, their own understanding of the wisdom of the ages, to decide what to keep, catalogue, and care for. Women's memoirs, diaries, personal essays, notes, letters, broadsides, and graphics are sometimes considered less serious or useful to researchers than men's comparable productions. In the Chicago Historical Society, for example, there are preserved hundreds of letters from women who wrote to Elizabeth Cady Stanton in 1880, at her request, to support a women's suffrage plank in the Republican platform. These eloquent letters, which graphically express the frustration and anger of the suffrage battle, might not exist today had not a contemporary archivist, a woman, considered them important historical documents and arranged with Stanton to preserve them in the Chicago collection. On a smaller scale, a woman who found a 1915 suffrage publication among her mother's papers wrote: "I suspect that had my brother found this rather than me he would have thrown it away because he would not have seen any reason to keep it. I wonder how much significant material has been lost in this way" (Betty Hembrough 1982, correspondence).

A related problem is that women's writing *about* language is often not indexed as such and is thus not often cited by traditional researchers. It is a topic that is everywhere and nowhere. Andrea Hinding's (1980) invaluable guide to the more than 18,000 library collections on women in the U.S. contains a mere ten entries on *language* (e.g., linguistic field notes); yet material pertinent to the study of women and language exists in a large number of these collections. An artificial prominence is therefore given, by default, to citations which are easy to find and/or which are categorized in accepted (and often androcentric) ways. Scholars untrained in what Germaine Greer (1982) calls the excavation methods of scholarship may find themselves at a particular disadvantage; the continued citation of Otto Jespersen's 1922 sexist but visible work on women and language speaks to this fact.

Women produce fewer words than men, publish fewer, and their books remain in print for fewer years. Tillie Olsen (1979) notes that four to five books by men are published for every one by a woman. Women's silences are often the direct consequence of social, racial, sexual, or economic oppression. And when women do write, much of their writing remains unknown, untaught, unrecognized. The representation of white women writers in college textbooks is one in twelve; for Black women, working class women, and lesbians, it is even more marginal (Bonnie Zimmerman 1982, for example, calculates one in 30 for lesbian writers).

Another challenge is to make audible the inaudible. Thus Nina Baym (1978) describes the hundreds of novels by 19th-century women writers whom critics have ignored; Erlene Stetson (1982) documents the politics of publication for Black women; Marlene Dixon (1976) publishes the documents of her confrontation with McGill University in the early 1970's ("this book," she writes, "is one long breach of confidentiality"); Cheryl Clarke and her colleagues (1983) engage in a pentalog on Black feminist criticism and the politics and aesthetics of lesbian writing; Evelyn Torton Beck ed. (1982) describes *Nice Jewish Girls: A Lesbian Anthology* as a "book written by people who do not exist."

Without self-conscious attention to the processes of production and preservation, women themselves are at risk of reproducing the same biased structures that have excluded them. A U.S. newsletter published by women prisoners charges that "accessibility to print has been dominated by those with material privilege (money). The women's presses and publications are often a reflection of the hierarchies (power relationships) of the dominant (enemy) culture. In other words, white women with money write to white women with money about whatever it is that concerns white women with money. So where do women behind bars fit in with all this?" (*No More Cages* December 1982, 16)

Finally, though women's written words have some hope of retrieval, their spoken language is known to us chiefly through the written words of men whose comments are often based – like Jespersen's – on stereotyping rather than observation or – more typically – on the pervasive view that women make no contributions to language. To find wheat (useful ideas and information) within the chaff is often difficult.

To remedy androcentrism, women can share information about promising research material in library collections; encourage archivists to save women's documents; press for information retrieval mechanisms (computer files, card catalogues, bibliographies, library finder's guides) that cite women's words and works; insist upon a more thorough understanding of the processes through which words are produced and preserved; and in short, identify androcentrism wherever it occurs in language study as well as create and maintain gynocentric alternatives.

(See ANONYMOUS, AUTHOR, AUTHORITY, DICTIONARY, FEMINIST DICTIONARY, PATRIARCHY, PEN NAMES, PRINT, WIRING)

ANDROCENTRIC CULTURE

"A man-made world . . . a masculine culture in excess. . . . That one sex should have monopolized all human activities, called them 'man's work,' and managed them as such, is what is meant by the phrase 'Androcentric Culture.' " (Charlotte Perkins Gilman 1911, 27)

ANDROCRACY

Governance by a group of males. (Charlotte Perkins Gilman 1911, 229)

ANDROGYNE

The absolute androgyne: Jesus. He is "the unisex model, whose sex is male . . . Male femininity incarnate." (Mary Daly 1978, 88)

(See ANDROGYNY, RELIGION, PRAYER)

ANDROGYNY

From Greek *anêr/andros* "man, male," and *gyne* "woman." Used by contemporary feminists "to refer to the state of a single individual, male or female, who possesses both traditionally masculine and traditionally feminine virtues. By *virtues* they mean morally – and generally also personally – desirable character traits, such as honesty, loyalty and compassion. Androgyny is thus a *psychological* condition or characteristic, not to be confused with physical hermaphroditism – the anomalous biological condition in which an individual has primary and secondary sexual characteristics of both the masculine or feminine sort (or lacks them to an equal extent). (*Webster's Third*, for example, confuses the two.) . . . There is a paradox inherent in the ideal of androgyny, namely that, while it calls for the elimination of the sexual stereotyping of human virtues, it is itself formulated in terms of the discredited concepts of masculinity and femininity which it ultimately rejects." (Mary Anne Warren 1980, 17, 23)

(See ANDROGYNE, SEX DIFFER-ENCES, SEX ROLE)

A concept which "has enabled many people, in many disciplines and ways of life, to question the veracity of sex differences, their immutability and their ultimate power to affect our lives." "It seeks to suggest that sex roles are societal constructs which ought to be abandoned.

I am willing enough to let the word androgyny go since I seek the ends, not the work. But I think we might as well recognize that it began what is a wonderfully liberating process and . . . can we not at least recognize 'androgyny' as a step along a path that may be the most important, and is certainly the most revolutionary, traveled by humanity?" (Carolyn G. Heilbrun 1980, 258, 265)

A concept in psychology which called into question the largely unquestioned assumptions that it is desirable for males to be "masculine" and females "feminine." Sandra Bem instead proposed a view of the healthy individual as an androgynous person who can react appropriately in a wide variety of situations. The Bem Sex-Role Inventory (BSRI) overturned traditional scales for testing so-called sex differences by allowing for two separate dimensions of Masculine and Feminine, thus enabling respondents to be categorized as strong in both masculine *and* feminine attributes or low on both, thus introducing the concept of androgyny. According to Bem, individuals "might be both masculine and feminine, both assertive and yielding, both instrumental and expressive – depending on the situational appropriateness of these various behaviors." Although the measurement of androgyny has "become an industry" in psychological research on sex roles and has been criticized for a number of reasons (primarily because the BSRI itself ignores situational context, so important to Bem's definition), it does offer an alternative to the moribund polarization of masculinity and femininity that characterized previous sex role research. (Sandra Bem 1974; Beverly M. Walker 1981)

"Describes those persons, men and women, who possess in high degree the socially desirable traits, or virtues, of both the so-called 'masculine' and 'feminine' personalities. . . . The term androgyny is derived from the Greek andro (male) and gyne (female). It may not be the most felicitous choice of term, since it has connotations of the hermaphrodite (physiologically half male and half female) and of the hormone androgen, which is secreted in males in greater quantities than in females." "It is now clear that psychological variation, both between and within men and women, cannot be represented by dichotomous, either/or categories, nor can it be based on a one dimensional scale, with the end points being defined as masculine and feminine." (Norma Grieve 1981, 247, 256)

"Not sexual hermaphroditism but spiritual bisexuality." (Cheryl Walker 1974, letter to *Off Our Backs*, August-September)

"Gender-merged androgyny is a tempting vision. It breathes justice and reconciliation; it demands no wrenching changes in society; there is an easy plausibility about it. The trouble with it . . . is that the very constructs 'masculine' and 'feminine' are intrinsic to patriarchal ideology . . . they are not, in short, two cleanly split halves of a whole person waiting to be reunited. . . . Merger does not correct the distortion." (Isabel Knight 1981, 30)

"There are words I cannot choose again;
 humanism androgyny
Such words have no shame in them, no
 diffidence before the raging stoic grandmothers:
their glint is too shallow, like a dye that
 does not permeate
the fibers of actual life as we live it, now"

(Adrienne Rich 1977a, 66)

Is a perfect blend of the female and male cultures into the ideal person. "As a concept, it . . . raise[s] anxiety levels by conjuring up a conformist, unisex vision, the very opposite of the individuality and uniqueness that feminism actually has in mind." (Gloria Steinem 1983, 158)

"Not and was not meant to be the answer to sexual politics. Freedom from repression and dominance is. Freedom of choice is. Freedom of contact with and expression of our feelings and needs was not meant to be construed as riding shod over others or an exchange of roles." (Suzanne Harris 1980, 3)

A "semantic abomination." "Feminist

theorists have gone through frustrating attempts to describe our integrity by such terms as *androgyny*. Experience proved that this word, which we now recognize as expressing pseudowholeness in its combination of distorted gender descriptions, failed and betrayed our thought. The deceptive word was a trap. . . . [It] is a vacuous term which not only fails to represent richness of be-ing. It also functions as a vacuum that sucks its spellbound victims into itself." (Mary Daly 1978, xi, 387-8)

ANDROGYNOUS FUCKING

The one relationship possible between "men" and "women" in the face of the increasing impossibility of heterosexuality. "Requires the destruction of all conventional role-playing, of genital sexuality as the primary focus and value, of couple formations, and of the personality structures dominant-active ('male') and submissive-passive ('female')." (Andrea Dworkin 1974, 184-5)

(See HETEROSEXUALITY)

ANDROLOGY

Non-existent medical specialty for the study of the male reproductive system, non-existent in part because males were more protective toward experimentation on bodies of their own sex. Urology developed slowly as a specialty and its early period was marked by an effort "to protect patients from unprepared practitioners and to raise standards of education," concerns that did not mark the development of gynecology. (Mary Roth Walsh 1977, 114)

ANGEL

A widely used allegorical figure in the iconography of the U.S. women's suffrage movement. The original was created by Sylvia Pankhurst for the British movement, but blended in the U.S. with the idealized goddesses of Liberty and Justice familiar since the early Republic. The angel was paired with the theme of enlightenment to represent women's exalted role as culture-bearer and culture-preserver for western civilization. (Edith P. Mayo 1981) Also the moral ideal; women are supposed to be angels. "If you happen to have human failings, as most of us do, especially if you display any kind of strength or power, creative or otherwise, then you are . . . a witch, a Medusa, a destructive, powerful, scary monster. An angel with pimples and flaws is not seen as a human being but as a devil." (Margaret Atwood 1982, 226-7)

(See ENLIGHTENMENT, ICONOGRAPHY)

ANGEL IN THE HOUSE

"It was she who used to come between me and my paper when I was writing reviews. It was she who bothered me and wasted my time and so tormented me that at last I killed her. You who come of a younger and happier generation may not have heard of her – you may not know what I mean by the Angel in the House. I will describe her as shortly as I can. She was intensely sympathetic. She was immensely charming. She was utterly unselfish. She excelled in the difficult arts of family life. She sacrificed herself daily. If there was chicken, she took the leg; if there was a draught she sat in it – in short she was so constituted that she never had a mind or a wish of her own, but preferred to sympathize always with the minds and wishes of others. Above all – I need not say it – she was pure. Her purity was supposed to be her chief beauty – her blushes, her great grace. In those days – the last of Queen Victoria – every house had its Angel. And when I came to write I encountered her with the very first words. The shadow of her wings fell on my page; I heard the rustling of her skirts in the room." (Virginia Woolf 1931; in Michèle Barrett 1979, 58-9) The phrase seems to have been first used in the title of an 1858 poem by Coventry Patmore. (David Doughan 1985; correspondence)

ANGER

"A human emotion whose needed expression has been denied the 'feminine' woman. Subverted anger in women may appear as migraine headaches, menstrual cramps, menopausal fears, nagging, screaming, child beating, and other self-defeating distortions. Honest anger in a woman can be magnificent." (Midge Lennert and Norma Willson eds 1973, 1)

"A well-stocked arsenal . . . potentially useful against those oppressions, personal and institutional, which brought that anger into being. . . . Anger is loaded with information and energy." Anger and racism: "My response to racism is anger. I have lived with that anger, on that anger, beneath that anger, on top of that anger, ignoring that anger, feeding upon that anger, learning to use that anger before it laid my visions to waste, for most of my life. . . . Women responding to racism means women responding to anger, the anger of exclusion, of unquestioned privilege, of racial distortions, of silence, ill-use, stereotyping, defensiveness, misnaming, betrayal, and coopting." "Black women are expected to use our anger only in the service of other people's salvation, other people's learning. But that time is over. My anger has meant pain to me but it has also meant survival, and before I give it up I'm going to be sure that there is something at least as powerful to replace it on the road to clarity." (Audre Lorde 1981c, 8, 7, 9)

An emotion whose analysis has been transformed by the feminist movement. "Consider women and anger. Part of what makes it true that a woman is angry today is that her vague and unfocused feelings are apt to crystallize in the future as she becomes clearer about the nature of sexism and its role in her life." We identify her anger because *we* credit the political views she now holds as being *true*. In the past, "there was then neither the likelihood of future crystallization nor any way of thinking that would have made it appropriate to gather together some odd jumble of feeling and behavior and call it 'anger.' The meaning that the jumble has for us today is the product of social change; it has acquired a way to organize itself and grow . . . What counts as anger has changed. We have given a meaning to what previously had none; it had none because there was no future for it within the social, political, and economic reality of earlier times." (Naomi Scheman 1980, 184-5)

"Anger as well as pain can mislead us. Across the fear barrier, a woman sees for the first time what she opposes; and once she starts to fight, she finds more and more targets of rage.

Surrounded by enemies who have suddenly been revealed, unconstrained by false modesty, she strikes back wildly. She no longer cares what happens to her. . . . Subordinated to the movement, rage may be disciplined into effective [strategy]; uncontrolled, it becomes catatonia or ritual." (Ann Fury c.1970)

ANGLO

Term used by members of several ethnic groups to designate people of non-color, particularly white Anglo-Saxon protestants. (See Carol Lee Sanchez 1983, 14)

(See AMERICAN, EURO-AMERICAN, WHITE)

ANKH

Important women's symbol. The Egyptian ankh, the knotted sign of life, is a hieroglyphic representation of the womb and a symbol of protection. It's one of many symbols, rituals, stories, and artistic practices that link women to the sacred arts of spinning and weaving. (Buffie Johnson and Tracy Boyd 1982, 66)

ANLU

A female social action practiced among the Kom of West Cameroon whereby women punish such offences as beating or insulting a parent, incest, abusing an old or pregnant woman, and seizing the sex organs during a fight. According to a Kom informant, "Anlu is started off by a woman who doubles up in an awful position and gives out a high-pitched shrill, breaking it by beating on the lips with the four fingers. Any woman recognizing the sound does the same and leaves whatever she is doing and runs in the direction of the first sound. The crowd quickly swells and soon there is a wild dance to the tune of impromptu stanzas informing the people of what offence has been committed, spelling it out in such a manner as to raise emotions and cause action." Additional rituals complete the punishment. (Shirley Ardener 1977, 36-7)

(See MIKIRI, NAMES, WOMEN'S WAR)

ANNE'S FAN, QUEEN ANNE'S FAN

Putting the tip of the thumb to the nose and then spreading the fingers in the shape of a fan. A gesture of triumph or glee.

ANONYMITY

In the view of some women, one of the real achievements of modern science. "Thank God for a [science] periodical like *Nature*. Thank God for the marvelous anonymity it provides so we can produce papers that are virtually identical. An anonymous paper in *Nature* is a very *good* thing for people who would otherwise be incapable of declaiming their results out loud. . . . Don't you see? Anonymity is an *achievement*, a real achievement, of the enterprise. It provides a comfortable framework in which we are all *equal* and our agonies are hidden from the public gaze. . . . There is no comparable framework . . . elsewhere, for the real world is very brutal." (Anna Brito; quoted in June Goodfield 1981, 236)

(See ANDROCENTRISM, ANONYMOUS, EPONYM, ORIGINAL, PEN NAMES)

A professional state not permitted to women when men desire to know their identity. Many scientific journals, for example, required women to provide their first names as authors of articles while men customarily needed only to supply their initials. Similarly, the tables of contents typically listed given name plus surname for women, initials plus surname for men. Individual women who achieved eminence were permitted to list initials only, a manglish initiation into the elite fraternity. (*Women and Language News* 1982, 6:1, 10)

A state, in contrast, sometimes enforced by publishers who, publishing "good" literature, wish their readers not to know a woman wrote it. Thus *Playboy*, reprinting an Ursula K. LeGuin short story, suppressed her first name and therefore her gender. (David Doughan 1985; correspondence)

A mechanism that obscures women's achievements. "Why is the pioneering legal research technique worked out by Josephine Clara Goldmark universally known as the Brandeis brief?" (Anne Firor Scott 1972; rpt 1984, 156)

ANONYMOUS

Prolific female author. Has written hundreds of thousands of books, articles, poems, essays, memos, broadsides, and treatises. Under this name many women for centuries have written, published, or produced art, either deliberately to avoid the problems and punishments awaiting the woman artist or by default because their names were lost or forgotten. Pen names, used by women to protect their anonymity for a variety of reasons ("Anonymous was a woman"), often add to their invisibility: Deborah Rosenfeld (1982) counts 25 pages in the British Museum Catalogue headed simply "A Lady"; an 1880 pamphlet lists 151 works by English writers published under that name. Other women used male pen names or initials to reduce problems of publication. Making these invisible authors visible is a challenging task. Anonymous also names the composite ordinary woman who would not call her productions "art" yet "who ornamented every phase of her experience from girlhood through old age with handiwork of startling power and invention." (Mirra Bank 1979, 9)

(See AMANUENSES, ANDRO-CENTRISM, AUTHOR, PEN NAMES, WRITING)

ANOREXIA NERVOSA

"A psychosomatic disease entity named in the late 1870s by physicians William Gull (Great Britain) and Charles Lasegue (France) almost simultaneously. The first clinical reports described adolescent girls whose refusal of food was unrelated to either organic causes or religious belief (food asceticism). Among doctors, *anorexy* or *anorexia* denoted loss of appetite but did not specify the cause. *Anorexia mirabilis* was a term used to describe religiously inspired fasting. *Anorexia nervosa*, however, was commonly regarded as a gastrointestinal disorder associated with female hysteria. In the 19th century, doctors still saw cases of both *anorexia mirabilis* and *anorexia nervosa*. *Anorexia nervosa* may be seen as an expression of continuity in female experience – that is, it points to the links in women's experience between religious and secular fasting." (Joan Jacobs Brumberg 1984, correspondence)

(See FASTING, HYSTERIA, NORMAL, OBESITY)

"A self-starvation disease characterized by an obsession with food to the exclusion of other developmental tasks. Predominantly seen in women (average age of onset 13-15 years). It's an escape from the traditional definition of woman: a desire for the non-sexual look of an adolescent boy; the purposeful starvation of the intelligent creative woman within us all; a way for a woman to manipulate those around her to meet her needs as opposed to her regularly assigned role of woman as caregiver; a means of maintaining an identity; a process by which a woman is encouraged to lose weight or maintain a low body weight and then is told that she is ill and needs expensive treatment." (Mary Ellen Shanesey 1984, correspondence)

A self-perpetuating eating disorder which may result in starvation even to death. Anorexia is an illness, a social disease, which has an exhibitionistic quality. The young women "afflicted with it know full well that they can win respect through their ability to display triumph over their bodies. ... If our will were sufficient to accomplish our desire, many of us would begin to look like our anorexic sister. The anorexic girl has become our present cultural heroine."

(Kim Chernin 1981, 48) "It is now a glamorous cross between two Victorian favorites, consumption and hysteria, but updated for a modern audience." (Sandra M. Gilbert; quoted in Kim Chernin 1981, 48)

ANTAGONIST

"To the male mind an antagonist is essential to progress, to all achievement." (Charlotte Perkins Gilman 1911, 244)

ANTENNA

"Invisible organ that one has at birth which allows for instantaneous perception of the possible alliances between lesbians." (Monique Wittig and Sande Zeig 1976, 8)

ANTHROPOLOGY

"Anthropologists looking at women's language use have focused on two central concerns that parallel those in the anthropology of women. First, they have asked how a woman's social position in any particular community or institution affects her speech. Second, they have asked how the cultural ideas and models of language, of gender and of power and status give meaning to language use and shape linguistic behavior." (Ruth Borker 1980, 26)

ANTI

Label for an opponent of women's suffrage in the U.S. suffrage movement.

"IMPRESSIONS AT A RECENT ANTI MEETING.

One Male Speaker   A Chorus of Lady-Antis

Speaker: I am Cleverer than you.
Chorus: Very true, very true.
Speaker: I am braver, too, by far.
Chorus: So you are, so you are.
Speaker: I can use my mind a lot.
Chorus: We cannot, we cannot.
Speaker: Men adore your lack of mind.
Chorus: Oh, how kind; oh, how kind!
Speaker: You do very well without.
Chorus: Not a doubt, not a doubt.
Speaker: You have hardly any sense.
Chorus: What eloquence, what eloquence!

Speaker: Yet your moral sense is weaker.
Chorus: Isn't he a charming speaker!"

(Alice Duer Miller, *The Woman Voter* October 1915, 6:10, 19)
   (See ANTI-FEMINISM, EQUAL RIGHTS AMENDMENT)

In the opinion of suffragist leader Carrie Chapman Catt, the "antis" were essentially a front for more potent forces working against women's suffrage, specifically the liquor interests. "A trail led from the women's organizations into the liquor camp and it was traveled by the men the antis employed . . . These men were observed in counsel with the liquor political managers too often to doubt that they laid their respective plans before each other so far as cooperation could be of advantage." (Carrie Chapman Catt 1923; cited in Eleanor Flexner 1968, 296)

ANTI-ACADEMIC

Opposed to the orthodoxies of the male-dominated academy but not necessarily opposed to thinking. "The Amazon Voyager can be anti-academic. Only at her greatest peril can she be anti-intellectual." (Mary Daly 1978, xiii)

ANTI-FEMINISM

The conviction that women are not entitled to the same moral and legal rights as men, or to the same social status and opportunities. "All antifeminist thinkers hold in common the thesis that there are innate and unalterable psychological differences between women and men, differences which make it in the interests of both sexes for women to play a subordinate, private role, destined for wife-and-motherhood. Aristotle is one of the earliest antifeminists, and one whose influence has permeated much of later Western thought. The Christian tradition, as represented by Paul, Augustine, and Aquinas, has been almost uniformly antifeminist, if not misogynous." (Mary Anne Warren 1980, 28-9) Involves "the idea that women ought to sacrifice the development of their own personalities for the sake of men and children." (Rebecca

West, *The Clarion*, December 12, 1913)
(See FEMINISM)

ANTI-FEMINIST

"The man who is convinced that his mother was a fool." (Rebecca West, *The Clarion*, October 24, 1913)

The woman who claims the only place for woman is in the home and who has come out of the home to prove it.

ANTI-FLIRT CLUB

Was formed by female office workers to combat street harassment of women, Washington D.C., in the 1920s. (*New Directions for Women* 1984, September/October, 15)

ANTI-MALE

Term used to dismiss many feminist thoughts, ideas, and writings. "Even the most cautious and circumspect feminist writings are described in this way. The cliché is not only unimaginative but deadeningly, deafeningly, deceptive – making real hearing of what radical feminists are saying difficult, at times even for ourselves." (Mary Daly 1978, 27-8)

ANTI-MASCULINIST

"One who is opposed to androcentric or male-supremacist ideas, actions, and institutions." (Mary Anne Warren 1980, 661)
(See MASCULINIST)

ANTIMONY

Against marriage. (Fanny Fern 1853)
(See MATRIMONY)

ANTI-SEMITISM

(See JEW-HATING)

APARTHEID

Pronounced aPARtite or aPARtate (the standard Afrikaans pronunciation actually sounds like 'abart-hate'— David Doughan 1985, correspondence); an official policy of racial segregation enforced in the Republic of South Africa for the purpose of maintaining white supremacy. From Afrikaans 'apartness.' Males of color working in cities are frequently separated from their families who live on special compounds in arid and desolate areas; "passlaws" require that all employed people carry papers at all times, curtailing free movement around the country. Women have played a leading role in fighting apartheid.

APHRA

Feminist periodical of the late 1960s and early 1970s. Named in honor of Aphra Behn, 17th century adventurer, spy, debtor, feminist, sexual pioneer, political activist, abolitionist, novelist, playwright, and poet whose accomplishments were all but completely erased by a series of male "de-biographers" after her death (Dale Spender 1982b, 24-31). "All women together ought to let flowers fall upon the tomb of Aphra Behn ... for it was she who earned them the right to speak their minds." (Virginia Woolf 1929, 69)
(See ANDROCENTRISM, APHRA-ISM, DE-BIOGRAPHER, WRITING)

APHRA-ISM

Aphorism from the journal *Aphra*, usually combining feminist politics with linguistic creativity. For example: "Love, usually spelled s-e-x, has replaced religion as the opiate of the masses" (Fall 1969).
(See APHRA)

APOLITICAL WOMEN

A term used in the early years of the women's movement to describe women who did not identify themselves with women's liberation and were not involved in movement activities – in contrast to "political women." The term was questioned by some women because it seemed to identify being "political" with familiar leftist politics rather than with women's own experiences and concerns: "I think we must listen to what so-called apolitical women have to say – not so we can do a better job of organizing them but because together we *are* a mass movement. . . . I think 'apolitical' women are not in the movement for very good reasons, and as long as we say 'You have to think like us and live like us to join the charmed circle,' we will fail. What I am trying to say is that there are things in the consciousness of 'apolitical' women (I find them very political) that are as valid as any political consciousness we think we have." (Carol Hanisch 1969, 205)

APPEARANCE

"A woman's appearance is her work uniform. If she shows up to work without the proper uniform her boss (or husband) can harass her or find a replacement.... A woman's concern with her appearance is not a result of brainwashing; it is a reaction to necessity – one which, incidentally, requires more skill than we've been given credit for." (A Redstockings Sister c. 1969)
   (See ADORNMENT)

APPROPRIATION

A power play whereby the class of women is appropriated by the class of men through the following means: the labor market; spatial confinement; show of force; sexual constraint; and the arsenal of the law and customary rights. (Collette Guillaumin 1981, 5, 19-20)

APPROVAL

"Depending less and less upon male approval, recognizing that such approval is more often than not a reward for weakness, we approve of our Selves. We prove our Selves. Such Self-approval attracts, and attracting Hags bond." (Mary Daly 1978, 341-2)

APRON-STRINGS, TO BE TIED TO A WOMAN'S

Dependence on or subservience to women; an expression attributed to women. First said of children who continue to depend upon women, then of all who follow a woman subserviently. "The fair sex . . . heartily despise [a man] who, to use their own expression, is always hanging at their apron-strings." Hence, *apron-string tenure*, an estate held by a man during his wife's life or by virtue of her inheritance; considered a weak position from which to govern. (1712, cited in J. S. Farmer and W. E. Henley, 1890-1904)

ARCHITECTURE

Traditional schools: "Most tend to graduate white, middle-class male designers regardless of whether you were Third World and/or a woman when you entered!" (Phyllis from the Women's School of Planning and Architecture; quoted in Leslie Kanes Weisman and Noel Phyllis Birkby 1983, 234)

ARETAEGNOSIS

Excellent ignorance. (Julia P. Stanley 1984, correspondence)

ARGOT

Specialized vocabulary or idiomatic expressions used by a particular class or group, especially by a professional and/or underworld subculture; functions to establish and maintain the group's solidarity, often by playing off a dominant mainstream culture. Writing some 30 years ago of prostitution, a subculture consisting almost exclusively of women, David W. Maurer (1939) noted the relative lack of argot among prostitutes in contrast to many other underworld groups. Arguing that "argots originate in tightly closed cliques, in groups where there is a strong sense of camaraderie and highly developed group solidarity," he hypothesized that the economic structure and internal organization of prostitution prevented prostitutes from developing the professional pride and solidarity necessary for the creation of argot. Maurer's account suggests that he held sexist views of prostitutes (in sharp contrast to his delight in other underworld groups) which may have prevented his perceiving their language usage accurately; further, the prostitutes he talked with may have identified a male investigator as an enemy who could not be trusted with professional secrets. There is growing evidence that many female communities and subcultures do demonstrate considerable linguistic creativity. For example, some of the so-called "women's" vocabulary items in

Japanese were apparently deliberately created by nineteenth-century court women to give themselves distinctive forms of talk (Sally McConnell-Ginet 1984, correspondence).

(See ACRONYMS, SLANG, TESTOSTERONE POISONING)

ARMS

Anti-war slogan: Arms Are for Linking.

ARPILLERA

"The *arpilleras* are social statements sewn from factory remnants by friends and relatives of political prisoners, 'disappeared' persons, and the unemployed in the *junta*'s Chile. They are not only concrete expressions of the women's daily and political lives, their environment, struggles, and visions for a better life, but also a means of livelihood." (*Heresies* 1980, 3:1 (Issue 9), 21)

ARROGANT

Unjustifiably convinced of one's own importance. From the Latin *arrogare* "to appropriate for oneself presumptuously; claim, take, or assume without right; to claim for oneself."

ARROGANT EYE

"That eye [which] gives all things meaning by connecting all things to each other by way of their references to one point – Man. We fear that if we are not in that web of meaning there will be no meaning: our work will be meaningless, our lives of no value, our accomplishments empty, our identities illusory. The reason for this dread, I suggest, is that for most of us, including the exceptional, a woman existing outside the field of vision of man's arrogant eye is really inconceivable." (Marilyn Frye 1983, 80)

(See LOVING EYE)

ART

For women as for men, the skilled, creative production or expression of what is significant or appealing. In Manglish, women's art has been labelled by such terms as stitchery, craft, and accomplishments. Some androcentric definitions of art do not include women at all. In its forms, themes, and reception, art is always, in part, a political act. Some feminist comments follow.

Art "represents a high grade of social service, of extreme value; but . . . art, like economics, is prevented by individualism and is even considered by many artists as a mere means of self-expression. . . . The world suffers and starves for lack of beauty, while the artist is engaged in exhibiting to us his own interior – which is not always beautiful." (Charlotte Perkins Gilman 1916, November, 290)

"The art world is a neolithic, loose association of clans within a larger tribe. The clan chiefs are the dealers. The critics are the bards who sing the praises of the clan and its leaders. Artists are the shamans whose talents are sold through the chief, achieved through strategies dependent on the buddy system and nepotism. White males hold most of the prominent positions . . . white females may be elevated to a position of prominence through personal financial status, ties of kinship or temporary bonds of affection. The 'mongrel' hordes represent the taboos and negative fantasies of the tribe. The 'mongrel' hordes, or alternate clans, are made up of men *and* women, shamans and bards who are non-white or whites who have been outlawed by the main clan." (Howardena Pindell 1979, 3)

Alice Walker reflects upon the difficulties faced by a Black woman in the U.S. with artistic ambition: "What did it mean for a black woman to be an artist in our grandmothers' time? In our great-grandmothers' day? It is a question with an answer cruel enough to stop the blood." (Alice Walker 1977; quoted in Michelle Cliff 1982, 35)

Though twentieth-century art historians have multiple sources to show that women artists have always existed, they ignore them. Their silence on the subject of women is absolute. The organizers of a 1972 exhibition of the work of women painters titled it *Old Mistresses: Women*

Artists of the Past to point out the implications of that silence:

"The title of this exhibition alludes to the unspoken assumption in our language that art is created by men. The reverential term 'Old Master' has no meaningful equivalent; when cast in its feminine form, 'Old Mistress,' the connotation is altogether different, to say the least." (A. Gabhart and E. Broun 1972, *Walters Art Gallery Bulletin* 24:7)

Taking the term further, Rozsika Parker and Griselda Pollock (1981) titled their book *Old Mistresses: Women, Art and Ideology* to point not only to the evidence but to the processes and practices whereby women's art has been systematically devalued and effaced.

"Art, as we know it, is a masculine product, wrought by the hands and conceived by the brains of men; the works of art that have forced themselves into the enduring life of the world have been shaped, written, builded, painted by men. They have achieved and we have imitated – on the whole, pitifully." (Cicely Hamilton 1909, 107)

Often takes the form of ceramics, embroidery, lacemaking, jewelry, metalworking, woodcarving, and interior design. (Ann Oakley 1982, 321)

"The lines drawn between work designated art and work downgraded as craft have long militated against women who have by choice and circumstances made art with thread, not paint." (Rosie Parker, *Spare Rib*, October 1982, 46)

"Art, in my terms, is like a basket, and a basket is useful." "Women's art . . . must be useful to women, must work in our interest. Must not work to divide us, must not lie about us to each other, must not give false information which would fall apart when people try to make use of it." (Judy Grahn 1978c, 12, 13)

"True art, art that comes from the centre of a people, from their very core, is inherently political. The stuff you see on Sixth Avenue in New York is dead art, art that the patriarchy wants to buy, a terrible self-indulgence and insidious . . .

creativity is about change." (Beverly Smith 1982, 8)

"Early feminist art, particularly as it developed on the West Coast, began with a consideration of women's personal experience. Work took the form of autobiography, exploration of self, and affirmation of female experience. Some audiences used 'autobiographical' in a pejorative sense; 'self-indulgent' and 'narcissistic' were dismissals of feminist work. However, within the women's community such work was seen within the context of the then-common process of consciousness-raising and the oft-repeated slogan, 'the personal is political.' Feminists viewing autobiographical work could readily locate an individual woman's experience within an emerging analysis of women's oppression. For this audience, feminist art was not narcissistic but profoundly political." (Mici McGee 1981, 88)

Feminist artists work "with the raw materials of the construction of femininity. Their subject matter has ranged from childbirth and pregnancy to make-up, advertising, cooking, menstruation, shopping, and the sexual division of labour in industry." (Rozsika Parker 1983, 90)

"Only recently have women begun to portray the male body in terms of their own unabashed sexuality or dealt explicitly with phallic imagery . . . an art that celebrates as well as explores women's sexuality through the use of the male image is so revolutionary and carries such a powerful threat that it has provoked considerable suppression from the male establishment." "[In my art] I used the 'male landscape' theme to depict our bombardment by phallic imagery. . . . I also wanted to explore the 'phallacy' of that power – its vulnerability to and dependence on a female audience." (Eunice Golden 1981, 40-2)

"In myths about the invention of art, the first artist is sometimes named as Kora, the daughter of the potter Dubutade, a young maiden who was moved to sketch the shadow outline of her lover before he went off to war . . . Art may well have been invented by women for the purpose of sketching their *own* shadow-selves rather than those of their lovers. Self-portrait as self-identity: like diaries, one of the few ways women have to leave their side of the story." (Karen Petersen and J. J. Wilson 1976, 1)

ARTICULATE
A characteristic of working-class women who "are more articulate than middle-class women in using a combination of language, anger, and emotion in order to be understood." (Marlene Packwood 1983, 7)

ARTIST
A professional whose work is evaluated by the grant system, the gallery system, and other validating cultural institutions, through the identification of the work of art by the name of its individual author. "The failure of institutions to approach the work of artists in terms of materials, labour, organization and community renders the *work* of art abstract, both as a product and as a functional meaning. . . . [We] work with no guaranteed income, no benefits, no job security, in short, as an economically exploited producer." (Editorial 1984, *Incite* [published by the Canadian Cultural Workers Network] 1:4 (March/April), backcover and frontcover)

ASDF
The position of the left hand of the secretary in front of a typewriter. In the U.K. "three million women, nearly a third of the total female labour force, work in clerical and secretarial work." (Hazel Downing 1981, 82, 83)
   (See OFFICE, SECRETARY, TYPEWRITER)

ASIAN AMERICAN
A controversial term. "Like its predecessor, 'Oriental,' it was created in the West from the need to make racial categorizations in a racially divided or, at least, a racially diverse society. It has always been difficult for me to accept being called Oriental, since 'Oriental' denotes east of somewhere, east of some other-defined center. Oriental is such an imprecise term: what is an Oriental flavor? an Oriental atmosphere or look? Asian American is a bit more precise. At least this term connotes an American identity for Asians, and it sounds more objective than Oriental. But Asian American and Asian Pacific American, while convenient for census count purposes, are also terms created and used to differentiate us from non-Asian and Pacific Americans. I would venture that the vast majority of persons of Chinese, Vietnamese, or Samoan ancestry would not, if asked, describe themselves as Asian and Pacific Americans but as Chinese, Vietnamese, or Samoan Americans, or indeed as Chinese, Vietnamese, and Samoans. To Asians all Orientals do not 'look alike.' " (Elaine H. Kim 1982, xii)

ASSERTIVENESS TRAINING
A process designed to enable women to revise some of the limiting and habitual patterns of their interactions. Directed primarily toward middle-class women, the training programs and self-help books have been embraced by thousands of women who have received guidance and support in relieving or resolving interpersonal problems. While acknowledging the value of such guidance and support, critics point out that assertiveness training is largely cosmetic: it helps individuals at the expense of others who need help, and by addressing the problems of individual women necessarily minimizes the pervasive economic and social oppression of women; it thus treats symptoms without acknowledging the underlying disease.
   The "ultimate effect is a re-education process for victims rather than oppressors. . . . To focus on women's own minds and interaction styles as the source of their oppression is the most vicious sort of blaming the victim, right up there with curfews for women to save them from attack." (Nancy Henley 1977, 201)

ASTEROID SOROMUNDI
Asteroid 2682 was discovered in 1979 by planetary scientist Eleanor Helin, who

named it Soromundi (sisters of the world) in honor of the Los Angeles YWCA. (*Ms*, August 1983, 20)

ASTROLOGICAL COMPUTATION

"A method of birth control which works on the principle of determining when a woman will be fertile based on the angular relationship of the sun and moon at the time of her birth. The effectiveness of this method is fairly high because there are relatively few times of the month when unprotected coitus is allowed." (Federation of Feminist Women's Health Centers 1981, 163)

ATOM BOMB

Bomb with an extremely violent explosion attended by great heat, blinding light and strong gamma-ray radiation. "The atom bomb was in manufacture before the first automatic washing machine." (Tillie Olsen 1979, 38)

ATOMIC WIDOWS

"A group of women whose lives have already been dramatically altered by nuclear weapons. . . . They call themselves 'atomic widows' – widows who believe that their husbands died from delayed effects of exposure to radiation at nuclear bomb tests in Nevada and the Pacific in the 1940s, 50s, and 60s." (*Ms*, August, 1983, 84)

ATTITUDES

"Are deeply ingrained however progressive the political ideas may be." (Fahimah, pseudonym of a Palestinian woman; conversation with Soraya Antonius 1983, 76)

AUNT

Title of respect and affection given to older females in many cultures.

AUNT JEMIMA

(See MAMMY, RECLAMATION)

AUTHOR

From Latin *auctor* "creator" and *augere* "to create, increase"; means specifically "to write or author" but more generally "to create, originate." *Authority* comes from the same root, suggesting the power and influence that comes with the power to create. As Virgina Woolf and other feminist writers have argued, we live within a system of social arrangements which offer women less access to the resources, opportunities, education, and social support for becoming authors than is afforded to men. When women do become authors, they sometimes author works anonymously or under pen names; when their sex is known, critics have, historically, denied that women were the authors of particular works or judged those works differently and more negatively. When large numbers of women achieve success as authors, other means are found to dismiss their work (thus Hawthorne's famous attack on the "damned mob of scribbling women" whose sales so dramatically exceeded his own). In similar fashion, writings by women of color – surely a field of great excitement today – are categorized and marginalized by many white male academics and critics as "ethnic literature," with the implication that the product is less original and creative than that of a "real author." This complex subject obviously cannot be treated in a brief dictionary entry: it is enough to say here that the feminist movement and particularly feminist criticism has called into question the whole process of authoring and of evaluating authors and authored works. This took the form of action when Adrienne Rich, Audre Lorde, and Alice Walker collectively accepted the National Book Award for Rich's *Diving Into the Wreck*: "We . . . together accept in the name of all the women whose voices have gone and still go unheard in a patriarchal world, and in the name of those who, like us, have been tolerated as token women in this culture, often at great cost and in great pain. . . . We dedicate this occasion to . . . the women who will understand what we are doing here and those who will not understand yet; the silent women whose voices have been denied us, the articulate women who have given us strength to do our work." (Adrienne Rich, with Audre Lorde and Alice Walker; cited in Barbara Charlesworth Gelpi and Albert Gelpi eds 1975, 204) In the study of language, too, there is the same reluctance to recognize women as authors – of words, of sentences, of original discourse: "To construct a voice, to have authority, to author a text, to tell a story, to give birth to the word. To author is to have the power to originate, to name. Women who seek to produce natural knowledge, like our sisters who learned to write and speak, also must decipher a text, the book of nature, authored legitimately by men" (Donna J. Haraway 1981, 471). This dictionary seeks to show that women – both as speakers and writers – are significant authors of language. By quoting disparate sources we wish to show that authoring is not the province of a small number of (relatively) privileged women but rather a process occurring everywhere, individually and collectively, and stimulated tremendously by the discoveries and empowering potential of the feminist movement. Yet in publication there is always a politics of visibility: the citations or recurrence of some names more than others should be taken as a sign that *our* research procedures, sources, and resources were limited and not that women authors do not exist everywhere.

(See ANONYMOUS, AUTHORITY, CLASS SYSTEM OF THE INTELLECT, LANGUAGE, PEN NAMES, ROOM OF ONE'S OWN, WRITING)

AUTHORIALITY

"A penis-tic lineage from father to son." (Domna Stanton 1983, 1)

AUTHORITY

The word *authority* has the same root as *author* and thus includes the notion of creation and empowerment as well as that of expertise and control. This is important for women, who often must author their own authority. Where language is concerned, this may require setting aside much of what constitutes authority on the subject of women, words, and language. This is not always easy to do. When researchers in the early 1970s sought earlier scholarship on language and sex, they turned up very little besides Otto Jespersen's 1922 chapter on women and language; though his work is shot through with sexist and racist assumptions, he was eminent, male, and orthodox in his views of women and men. He thus qualified as an authority, worthy of citation in numerous bibliographies. In contrast, Elsie Clews Parsons' 1913a feminist work on language and sex remains largely unread, though she later became well-known for her more traditional descriptive linguistics. Citations take on a life of their own: each year Jespersen's authority increases while Parsons' work becomes harder and harder to find. (As feminists have noted, "authority" often consists of persuasion by the rhetorical strategy of patrilineal naming: "Harvard biologist X, the great physicist Y, the leading evolutionary biologist Z, and so on." (Donna J. Haraway 1981, 472)

Authority is the key credential for many dictionaries. Webster's 1864 unabridged edition was held, prior to publication of the *Oxford English Dictionary*, "to be superior to every other dictionary and taken as the leading authority on the meaning of words" (K. M. Elisabeth Murray 1977, 133). The *Harper Dictionary of Contemporary Usage* (William Morris and Mary Morris eds 1975) describes itself as "the most authoritative and comprehensive reference book on the state of the language today" and invokes the "piercing, perceptive, and witty comments" of its distinguished panel of 136 experts. The *Harper Dictionary of Modern Thought* offers "expert entries." The new *Dictionary of Bahamian English* (John A. Holm and Alison Watt Shilling eds 1982) is "an authoritative guide." *Webster's New Word Dictionary* (1982) offers "clear, precise definitions" and is promoted in a recent flyer simply as "*The Authority.*" In their role as authoritative legislators, dictionaries, in H. Lee Gershuny's words, "perpetuate the stereotypes and prejudices of their editors, who traditionally have been male"; to challenge this authority, Gershuny (1973) demonstrated statistically how dictionary-makers select or create exemplary sentences to illustrate meaning that reflect gender stereotypes prejudicial to women. In the *Random House Dictionary*, masculine gender sentences occurred three times more often than female; when female did occur, seven out of ten usages were likely to reflect a stereotype. This was true not only for stereotypically "feminine" entries like *delicate, emotional, passive, vain*, but also for "neutral" entries: "His mother-in-law was no *bargain*"; "Women with shrill voices get on his *nerves*."

The 1970s were characterized by increasing attention to the relationship between language and authority. Some women critiqued Biblical language (the word of God); most challenges were directed toward man-made language (Dale Spender) or Manglish (Varda One). A number of feminist dictionaries were created. These critiques were part of a much broader challenge by women to authority in general. In the U.S. women's movement, such processes as consciousness-raising identified the value of one's own experience as a valid source of truth and upheld the authority of experience and "conscious subjectivity" as grounds for determining truth and making decisions. Many feminists expressed a need to turn from the hierarchical and authoritarian structures that characterized many masculine practices and evolve woman-centered ways. Thus women's words and experiences were no longer to be devalued (Ruth Borker's example: Men share news; women gossip. In Sally McConnell-Ginet, Ruth Borker, and Nelly Furman eds 1980, 31). Accordingly, a collection of feminist scholarship essays called *The Authority of Experience* (Arlyn Diamond and Lee R. Edwards eds 1977) took its epigram from Chaucer's Wife of Bath: "Experience, though noon auctoritee/ Were in this world, is right ynogh for me/ To speke." In their feminist dictionary, Monique Wittig and Sande Zeig (1976) authorize their own words, blending "facts" with

truths; thus one poem fragment is said to have been "found in the *Bibliotec*, assemblage of books and fragments from the past, salvaged by the companion lovers in the last chaotic period" (15). Another example is the word *herstory*, a feminist creation of the late 1960s that has frequently been attacked for its "etymological incorrectness." From the standpoint of traditional authority, *herstory* will never be more than folk-etymology. But the feminist view asserts that this is beside the point. *Her story*, in structure and usage, effectively unmasks and counters *his story*, a male-centered narrative in which women have traditionally been invisible. By preempting the word itself, *herstory* "seizes the language," asserting its right to exist precisely in its unauthorized incorrectness. For herstory is not just a feminist version of history: it is a different narrative altogether, told in a new voice. It proclaims women's power to create their own words and, in doing so, to (literally) change history (Robin Morgan 1978).

(See AUTHOR, DICTIONARY, ENGLISH, FEMINIST DICTIONARY, HERSTORY, INTRODUCTION, LANGUAGE, MATRIARCHY, ORIGINAL, OXFORD ENGLISH DICTIONARY, WOMANISM)

AUTONOMY

"Autonomy and separatism are fundamentally different. Whereas autonomy comes from a position of strength, separatism comes from a position of fear. When we're truly autonomous we can deal with other kinds of people, a multiplicity of issues, and with differences, because we have formed a solid base of strength with those with whom we share identity and/or political commitment." (Barbara Smith 1983, xl-xli)

AUXILIARY

A submissive role: "men always regarded women as allies or auxiliaries at most – but not leaders." For example, women are encouraged "in their religious careers as long as these could be conceived as extensions of traditional womanly functions or attributes" and as aids to men's activities. (Dorothy P. Ludlow 1978, 346)

AVIATRIX

"This term, like its correlative, *aviator*, is now used chiefly in the context of the early history of aviation." The *Oxford English Dictionary* Supplement records usage between 1910 and 1927. (*Barnhart Dictionary Companion* 1982, 1:3, 35)

AXE

"The double-headed axe was the first known weapon of the ancient amazons. This axe, famous above all others, never left their side. After the time of the amazons, the double-headed axe in the form of a cross with equal arms was retained as a symbol for numerous goddesses." (Monique Wittig and Sande Zeig 1976, 13)

(See LABRYS)

AZTLAN

"The mythical/historical place, in the area of present-day northern New Mexico, from where the Aztecs were to have migrated before settling in what is now Mexico City. It is the mythical homeland of the present-day Chicano people." (Cherríe Moraga 1983, 44)

BABE

Used by men as a "term of endearment" or as a general descriptive label, which indicates the subordinate place men wish for women. As the *American Heritage Dictionary* says: "1. *Archaic*. A baby; an infant. 2. *Slang*. An innocent or naive person. 3. *Slang*. A girl or young man – babe in the woods. Slang. A naive or easily victimized person in an unfamiliar or dangerous situation."
(See FORMS OF ADDRESS)

BABY

Is a female in more than half the cribs despite the linguistic presumption of maleness in baby-care books.
(See CHILDREN)

BACHELOR

An unmarried man who often relies on women (mother, waitress, cleaning woman, etc.) for help with his food preparation, housecleaning and laundry. He is not a match, semantically or otherwise, for *spinster*.
(See SPINSTER)

BAG LADY

A woman, generally past forty, who lives on the streets and carries her few possessions in bags, a homeless casualty of a sexist, ageist society which rejects and gives no good roles to her. (Ruth Harriet Jacobs 1984, correspondence)

BALLS

Accolades hung on critically acclaimed men's writing. "Work by a male writer is often spoken of by critics admiring it as having 'balls'; ever hear anyone speak admiringly of work by a woman as having 'tits?' " (Margaret Atwood 1982, 198)

BANK

Usually a storage place for what men call their money. However, it can mean economic cooperation. "In many of Cairo's old lower- and lower-middle-class neighborhoods . . . women run co-ops, where a few of their members go to the market to buy and sell for the whole group, thus saving one another considerable time and money. Their most interesting money-saving project is their informal bank . . . a typical one works something like this: the group decides to save so much per week or month and give the entire sum to each member in turn. The bank tries to time the cash gift according to each woman's needs." (Naila Minai 1981, 180)
(See CLOTHING)

BANK TELLER

A clerical position with variable status. Before WWII, the tellers who dealt with people coming to the bank to deposit or obtain their money "were almost exclusively white men. The job had high prestige and was a step toward bank officer. Since that time, banks have been hiring women and minorities as tellers. Tellers' pay has not kept pace with that of other, predominantly male jobs. In addition, the promotion ladder has been sawed off. Today future bank officers are more likely to be hired from among recent college or MBA graduates than from among the tellers." (Mary Lou Kendrigan 1984, 54–5)

BANNERS

A large, visual, often attractive, public announcement. Used in many suffrage and civil rights campaigns. "A banner is not a literary affair, it is not a placard: leave such to boards and sandwichmen. A banner is a thing to float in the wind, to flicker in the breeze, to flirt its colours for your pleasure, to half show and half conceal a device you long to unravel; you do not want to read it, you want to worship it. Choose purple and gold for ambition, red for courage, green for long-cherished hopes. . . . Avoid any tendency to think favourably of the bedclothes; a sheet between two poles is a poor ideal. I know it has its conveniences for street processions, but after all we do not make and carry banners, for our convenience – it is indisputably more convenient to walk about without them." Banners are associated with women's political activities. In all ages it has been women's task to make the banners. However, the nineteenth- and twentieth-century women working for women's rights produced beautiful banners for their own political societies and public activities. (Mary Lowndes 1910, 174, 175, 172; Fawcett Library has a catalogue of some of the designs and fabrics of the U.K. suffrage banners)

(See COLOURS)

BAPTISM

A ritual designed by men to purify a human child. "In 418 A.D., a Catholic church council decided that every human child is born demonic as a result of its sexual conception. . . . The Oedipal jealousies of men apparently developed these ideas, since few women would have pictured babies screaming in an eternity of torture in hellfire, simply because no priest had sprinkled them with water before they perished. . . . The primitive notion of the public name-giving ritual seems to be all that is left to justify the formalities." (Barbara G. Walker 1983, 90-1)

BAREFOOT & PREGNANT AWARD

An "award" given by the Media Evalu-ation Committee of the National Organiz-ation for Women "for advertising degrading to women."

BASKET

"The idea of a basket, of something constructed to carry things, is certainly useful. You could say that a basket is an idea (a form) made of straw (which is the content). Or you could say that the idea of a basket (a portable container) is the content, and the woven straw is the *form*, as an egg is another kind of form, and a clay jar is another and so on to containers (ideas) such as houses, trains, ships – and stories." (Judy Grahn 1978c, 12)

BASKETRY

A clear and well-documented continuation of African cultural practices and preser-vation of African artistic forms in the U.S., especially in the coil basketry tradition of South Carolina. Both basket-making as a form of cultural expression and the baskets themselves as symbolic objects have long been associated with women (for example, the baskets' holding capacity is equated with women's carrying children). "Other information as well is passed on within the aesthetic community formed by the basketmakers, including family and regional histories relating to basket sewing, jokes, legends, tales, and a wide variety of folkloristic materials and commentaries." With quilting, basketry is a key feature in a system of cultural expression and shares, along with other Afro-American expressive traditions, a marked degree of improvisation and innovation. (Nancy Faires Conklin, Brenda McCallum, and Marcia Wade 1983, 48-9)

BASTARD

The term used to be one of honor; "men boasted of being bastards." There was a "mysterious glamour of having an un-known father who might be a hero." However, the Anglo-Saxon synod decided in 786 that "the son of a meretricious union shall be debarred from legally inheriting" and gradually it became a disgrace to be a bastard. "A bastard was not a son because his father was unknown, the law recognizing no physical relationship to the mother. Once it became a sin for a woman to have a baby without a certified father, women were required to be virgins before marriage and sexually faithful after marriage; otherwise a woman might bear a child not her husband's and thus cheat him of his posterity."

Illegitimate children are sometimes called "nameless." Legitimate children (i.e., father known) are given the father's name. (Una Stannard 1977, 300-1)

(See CHASTITY BELT)

BATTERED WOMEN

A phrase that uncovered a major kind of violence that had been long hidden. "It helped us to reveal the fact that most violence in America takes place in our homes, not in the streets." (Gloria Steinem 1980b, 23)

(See WIFE BEATING)

Wife and woman battering: "Sexual violence. It usually occurs in the kitchen or bedroom where most murders of women by husbands and lovers also occur, and it is usually precipitated by the . . . perceived failure of some domestic responsibility. It is often followed by rape." An estimated three to four million women are brutally beaten each year in the U.S. (Ruth Bleier 1984, 188)

BATTLE-AXE

"One of the American male's favorite putdown words for the strong, fist-shaking, foot-stomping, rights-demanding woman. . . . [F]eminists should consider it a compliment. The battle-axe was the characteristic weapon carried by the Amazons." (Barbara Miles 1971, 5)

(See LABRYS)

"Slang. Aggressive woman, harridan, virago, amazon, lesbian – all those women who don't comply with conventional ideas of femininity." (Sona Osman 1983, 27)

BATTLE NAME

New name given to a woman when she begins work in a brothel. "You couldn't work calling yourself Jeannine, Jacqueline or Marie-Louise. They immediately stuck a name on you like Nathalie, Sophie, Clara. As snobby and fashionable as possible. I think that's really also part of the apprenticeship, giving up your old name for a new one. It's rather like a woman getting married and taking on the man's name. There, they gave us a name that all the clients would like. A universal Christian name. There are some nuns, too, who give up their real name when they go into a convent." (prostitute quoted in Claude Jaget ed. 1980, 145-6)

BC

Before Consciousness. Prefeminism. A time when we were "denying there was any problem, solitarily certain that each of us was herself The Problem." (Robin Morgan 1982, 49)

(See BF)

BEAR

To support. To be patient with. To give birth to. Women are given "the duty of bearing everything, children included." (Sarah Ida Rowler [Morgan] Dawson, nineteenth century)

BEAUTY

A standard of personal appearance which changes somewhat from decade to decade but is continually applied to women in all occupations and conditions. At present, men are not thought to have beauty and are the richer for it. As Shirley Morahan writes, "The exclusive identification of women with beauty occurred at the same time that men stopped being sex objects. Around the end of the 1830s men gave up wearing bright colors, silks, laces, earrings, and perfumes and stopped setting their hair. [Men do continue some of these practices but usually do not let many others know.] Men became modest; they now conceal everything and signify their maleness only by a symbol – the necktie." (Shirley Morahan 1981, 91)

"A highly normative cult message,"

which posits the *duty* to beauty for women. "It is a social, cultural and economic fact that for some women their facial contours or body shape can determine their income and status more than their life chance situation, enabling us to posit 'tit' and 'cheekbone' determinism. This is possible because it concerns the distribution of a scarce resource. To be born beautiful is to be born a rarity, yet female beauty is a generalised cultural ideal." (Marjorie Ferguson 1983, 58-9)

"The concept of beauty for women is based on White male values. It is highly questionable to downright ridiculous for any woman to measure her physical features against a contrived set of standards designed to please the male imagination and desires. . . . White males created the values; White women strive for the image; and Black women have to strive even harder." "For a Black woman to be beautiful does not mean that she has skin and hair and features that closely resemble the White woman. . . . The beauty of Blackness is historical and should be defined by Blacks along lines that are germane to their African heritage and genealogy and their Afro-American culture." (Gloria I. Joseph; in Gloria I. Joseph and Jill Lewis 1981, 159, 161)

"Much of what man calls beauty in woman is not human beauty at all, but gross over-development of certain points which appeal to him as a male." (Charlotte Perkins Gilman 1911, 57)

"Beauty ought, besides all else, to bring extension of dignity, to give a wider sweep to human splendour. Hitherto, the most beautiful woman of all have been most the slaves of their beauty. That their servitude should not be too rudely emphasised, the most beautiful women have been called mistresses." (Anonymous [Elizabeth Robins] 1924, 68)

It is exemplified by the "countless Black grandmothers with aged features, rheumatic bones, and distant memories, who raise the spirits and lighten the burdens of others with their encouraging, comforting words and selfless deeds. The beauty was in the heritage of communal struggle and cultural collaboration – both to survive and to challenge oppression." (Gloria I. Joseph; in Gloria I. Joseph and Jill Lewis 1981, 161)

"It is rare in either sex. In most species in the animal kingdom, one sex *is* more colorful or attractive than the other; more often than not it is the male. But in the human species neither sex, *au naturel*, is more attractive than the other." (Una Stannard 1971, 193)

"The beauty of strong, creative women is 'ugly' by misogynistic standards of 'beauty' to those who fear us." (Mary Daly 1978, 15)

An idea which is "cultural, social, ethnic, racial, changeable, and disputable." It is also an idea that people *do* respond to and that response is "real, measurable, and indisputable." (Letty Cottin Pogrebin 1983b, 75)

BEAUTY-CONTEST

An event in which exploited women compete against one another as men's beauty objects. ("Plastic Men for Plastic Women" n.d., *Women Now*, No. 4, 3)

"The exhibition and parade of young women before judges, turning beautiful young women into prize cattle. Beauty defined and judged as bust, waist, hip measurements and the 'classic' little girl virginal face." (Midge Lennert and Norma Willson eds 1973, 1)

Presented in the magazine *Jackie* (U.K. sales approx. 600,000 weekly) as an everyday event, "the ideal 'hobby' for a girl. It relates both to the notion of securing a boyfriend and in its repetition it prefigures the housework which is the eventual outcome of love, romance and boy-friends." (Angela McRobbie 1981, 124)

An event which does not solve women's poverty. Feminists protesting the Miss Universe pageant in Lima, Peru, July 1982, denounced the debasing character of the beauty contests and demanded a new civil code, adequate medical services, jobs and equal pay, access to information, and birth control. (*Spare Rib*, Oct. 1982, 17)

BEAUTY PARLORS

Places for obtaining hair and body treatments, and information. They have "long been a stronghold for the dissemination of facts about men and about women's involvements with men. Comments about mistreatment from men, the sweetness of men, two-timing men and faithful women are topics that typically elicit animated conversations." (Gloria I. Joseph; in Gloria I Joseph and Jill Lewis 1981, 182)

BE-FRIENDING

The patriarchal definition is: show kindness, sympathy, and understanding to, as in "befriend a helpless person." Mary Daly considers this action ungenuine and patronizing. She uses *be-friending* to mean the creation of a context in which female friendship, Gyn/affection, can flourish. (Mary Daly 1984, 373)
   (See GYN/AFFECTION)

BEGET

This English word fails to convey, in the translations of the Hebrew Scriptures, the full sense of the original Hebrew verb, which means either the begetting of a father or the bearing of a mother. (Casey Miller and Kate Swift 1976, 73)

BEGINNING

"In the beginning was not the word. In the beginning is the hearing." (Mary Daly 1978, 424)

BELCHING

A disruption which – along with yawns and farts – can be seen "as jolly shows of power against authority. However, this form of 'power' is as much a sign of powerlessness as bowing and scraping. . . . It may be a peculiarly male type of aggressiveness and hostility toward authority. If it should ever come into women's repertoire, however, it will carry great power, since it directly undermines the sacredness of women's bodies, a cornerstone of their suppression; and it will consequently command greater retaliation." (Nancy Henley 1977, 83, 91)

BERDACHE

Institution among certain tribes of Plains Indians. The berdaches were male transvestites; a similar female tradition evidently existed. An example cited in anthropological and other literature to complicate the notion of "being a man" or "being a woman" in any given culture. (Sue-Ellen Jacobs 1977)

BF

Before feminism. (Michelene Wandor 1980, 135)

BIA

"The Bureau of Indian Affairs, part of the U.S. Department of the Interior, developed out of the old War Department. It was specifically mandated to maintain the trust relationship, specified by treaties, between the United States government and federally recognized Indian Tribes (that is, tribes who negotiated treaties with the government). Generally the subject of jokes and the object of ridicule by many Indian people, the Bureau remains the major agency within which the government-to-government relationships between the United States and the Tribes are maintained." (Rayna Green 1984, 306)

THE BIBLE

"One of the greatest anthologies of all time, spanning over a thousand years of Hebrew writings, both religious and political. . . . Certain passages from the Bible – particularly from Genesis and the Pauline epistles – have been quoted *ad nauseam* for (more or less) two thousand years as evidence that God intended women to be subordinate to men. For the most part the authors of the Bible *presume*, rather than *defend*, the propriety of male domination. There is some, but relatively little, overt misogyny, and almost no explicit or other argument for the severely patriarchal institutions and attitudes of the ancient Hebrews." (Mary Anne Warren 1980, 68)

   The first feminist bible and the first English translation of the whole bible by a woman was produced by Julia Smith, who taught herself Latin, Greek, and Hebrew in order to work on the translation. Known as the "Alderney Edition" (named for the cows claimed by the town in lieu of the taxes Julia Smith and her sisters refused to pay on the grounds that they couldn't vote), the book was likely typeset and proof-read by women as well. (Julia Smith 1876)

Another feminist interpretation, *The Woman's Bible*, was published in 1895 and 1898. The General Editor was Elizabeth Cady Stanton who wrote that the Bible inaccurately "teaches that woman brought sin and death into the world, that she precipitated the fall of the race, that she was arraigned before the judgment seat of Heaven, tried, condemned and sentenced. Marriage for her was to be a condition of bondage, maternity a period of suffering and anguish, and in silence and subjection, she was to play the role of a dependent on man's bounty for all her material wants, and for all the information she might desire on the vital questions of the hour, she was commanded to ask her husband at home. Here is the Bible position of woman briefly summed up." (Elizabeth Cady Stanton 1898, 13)

"A sexist document. . . . To say that the Bible only reflects a culture of the times ignores the power of the word that legitimates continuance of these attitudes." (*National Coalition of American Nuns Newsletter* 1978, 9:1)

A book with many words on women. "Although only about ten percent of the bible even mentions women . . . it manages to deal with every possible feminine issue," even bowel movements, flat chests, women's periods, childbirth, confinement, hair styles, housewifely duties. These are described "usually with scorn, over-familiarity, frequently with loathing and fear." (Annie Laurie Gaylor 1981, 6)

A book which "deals in implicit sex, disgusting violence, rape, even advocates family planning, and encourages revolution. It is on open sales everywhere and *six-year-old children* can get their hands on it easily." (*Banshee: Journal of Irishwomen United* c. 1981, 84)

BICYCLE

A mode of exercise and physical freedom which in the late nineteenth century was for women an instrument and a symbol of newly discovered freedom. In 1895 Elizabeth Cady Stanton declared that "Many a woman is riding to the suffrage on a bicycle." Cycling contributed to dress reform for women. (Paul Atkinson 1978, 120-3)

"Until I rode a bicycle I had been considered quite a nice, well-behaved girl, but when my parents allowed me to ride about the streets and park with my brother [in 1891], I was supposed to have gone absolutely to the bad. People called dreadful names at me, and even tried to pull me off the machine." (E. Heuchner 1937, *Daily Telegraph*, 5 May)

BILINGUALISM

A language situation where "language is not merely a medium for content, but is itself a referent, a source of meaning and group identity." (A. Aguirre 1976; quoted in Pedro Pedraza, Jr. et al. 1980, 34-5)

BI-MORALISM

A two-tiered evaluation system such as that active in mid-19th century, when "it was comparatively common for medical men to recommend vice to their men patients [while declaring] it was highly reprehensible in a woman to try to acquire knowledge of physical facts and the consequences of vice." (W. Lyon Blease 1913b, 145)

(See DOUBLE STANDARD)

BIOLOGICAL DETERMINISM

Hard: "The thesis that certain (real or alleged) social and psychological differences between the sexes – e.g. the greater aggressiveness of males – are the result of biology and not (just) culture, and that these differences make male supremacy and the patriarchal social system inevitable. . . . All hard biological determinists are *ipso facto* antifeminists, or at least nonfeminists."

Soft: "*Soft* biological determinism may be a useful term to describe the view that biological factors cause but do not (necessarily) justify sex-role differences." (Mary Anne Warren 1980, 71-2)

The modern version is Sociobiology which "attempt(s) to validate the belief that genes determine behaviors and that social relationships and cultures have evolved through the genetic transmissions of behavioral traits and characteristics. Of central importance in Sociobiological theory, in keeping with the biological determinist tradition, are its efforts to explain in terms of *biology* the origins of the gender-differentiated roles and positions held by women and by men in modern as well as past civilizations. In so doing, Sociobiologists attempt to assign natural causes to phenomena of social origin." (Ruth Bleier 1984, 46)

(See SOCIOBIOLOGY)

BIOLOGY

"The science of life, conceived and authored by a word from the father. Feminists have inherited knowledge through the paternal line. The word was Aristotle's, Galileo's, Bacon's, Newton's, Linnaeus's, Darwin's; the flesh was woman's. And the word was made flesh, naturally. We have been engendered." (Donna J. Haraway 1981, 470)

"Does not mean 'genetically determined' or 'inevitable.' It means 'of the animal.'" Our bodies are molded by socialization, so that "by the time we are gendered adults, masculinity and femininity *are* 'biological.'" (Marilyn Frye 1983, 37)

BIOLOGY IS DESTINY

"If the phrase . . . has any meaning for a woman right now it has to be the urgent project of woman reclaiming her self, her own biology in her own image, and this is why the lesbian is *the* revolutionary feminist and every other feminist is a woman who wants a better deal from her old man." (Jill Johnston 1973, 156)

(See ANATOMY IS DESTINY)

BIRTH

Not a natural event, but always mediated by beliefs about creation and dangers to the mother and child, and by the practices of those attending. In 1958 a registered nurse sent a note to the *Ladies Home Journal* "reporting abuses she had witnessed in delivery rooms and demanding an investigation of 'the tortures' that were going on there. That brief note brought a greater response from readers than almost any full-length feature article the *Journal* had ever printed. Many hundreds of women from all over the country wrote letters and most of them confirmed the nurse's charges." (Gena Corea 1977, 201)

(See BIRTHING)

An experience which differs a great deal for women even within the same culture. Joan Patchen writes, "In 1960 when I had my first child I did not know there was a choice. The doctor gave me drugs and I ended up black and blue from thrashing against the sides of the bed when my contractions woke me. Two years later when my second was born I found out about the Lamaze Method and Natural Childbirth. They educated me and my husband about the process my body would be going through and gave me exercises that enabled me to be in full control. It changed what had previously been a painful experience into one of overwhelming beauty, sensuality, and harmony. For doctors to continue to perpetuate the idea that childbirth has to be painful is ridiculous and perhaps a lackadaisical sadism as well." (Joan Patchen 1984, correspondence).

"Natural childbirth, without complications, is an expansion of the orgasmic experience. This is quite logical because the same physiological mechanisms are operating, namely vaginal distension and total genital stimulation." (Elaine C. Pierson; quoted in Gena Corea 1977, 207)

"The birth itself is an epitome of de-sexualisation and infantilisation for many women. Making love and giving birth ideally and intrinsically have much in common, but the link between sexuality and birth has been completely broken down – it is obvious at once that making love in the sort of conditions we are customarily expected to give birth in would be quite a perverse and alienating act." (Lesley Saunders 1983, 94)

Giving Birth: "Who gives it? And to whom is it given? Certainly it doesn't feel like giving, which implies a flow, a gently handing over, no coercion. . . . Maybe the phrase was made by someone viewing the result only. . . . [Y]et one more thing that needs to be re-named." (Margaret Atwood 1977, 225)

BIRTH CERTIFICATE

An "ideological instrument" which forces one model of family relationships. Assumes married parents with the father the socially significant parent. (Bob Hodge 1979, 175)

(See FAMILY PLANNING)

BIRTH CONTROL

Control of the number of children conceived. The Christian tradition "from Paul, Augustine, and Aquinas to the contemporary Catholic Church, has generally viewed any method of birth prevention other than total abstinence (or, now, the 'rhythm' method) as an abominable crime against nature. . . . It was Margaret Sanger who . . . led the struggle for legal, effective and available contraceptive methods in this country." (Mary Anne Warren 1980, 74-5)

(See CONTRACEPTION, PILL, STERILIZATON)

"The expression 'birth control' was devised [a decade ago in New York] in my little paper of advanced feminism, *The Woman Rebel*, as one of the fundamental rights of the emancipation of working women. The response to this idea of birth control was so immediate and so overwhelming that a league was formed – the first birth control league in the world." (Margaret Sanger 1923; rpt. 1973, 123)

Use of contraception which "means acknowledging and planning and taking direction of intercourse, accepting one's sexual availability and appearing non-spontaneous. It means appearing available to male incursions. A good user of contraception is a bad girl. She can be presumed sexually available, among other consequences; she can be raped with relative impunity. (If you think this isn't true, you should consider those rape cases in which the fact that a woman had a diaphragm in is taken as an indication that what happened to her was intercourse, not rape.)" (Catharine MacKinnon 1983b)

"Was initially publicized as a middle-class prescription to alleviate the economic hardships of the working class." (Sylvia Strauss 1982, 76) "What was demanded as a 'right' for the privileged came to be interpreted as a 'duty' for the poor." (Angela Davis 1981, 210)

Some massive campaigns for so-called "birth control" in underdeveloped non-white areas of the world and in Black communities in the U.S. are "in fact nothing but a method of outright surgical genocide." (Frances Beale 1970, 96)

"Has *always* been women's obsession. Whatever the burden of excess births represents either for a father or for a nation, their experience never comes close to that experienced by the female Atlas, this weak body that carries the entire weight of the world." (Françoise d'Eaubonne 1974, 65)

Methods: "It is frivolous to advocate the continence of men; it simply doesn't work." (Anonymous nurse; cited by Genevieve Grandcourt 1919, 7)

Methods: "Few gynecologists recommend to their heterosexual patients the most foolproof of solutions, namely Misterectomy." (Mary Daly 1978, 239)

BIRTHING

"Another of the archetypal experiences exclusive to the female." (Midge Lennert and Norma Willson eds 1983, 1)

(See BIRTH)

A consequence, frequently, of women's fears "of being called old maids." (Cicely Hamilton 1909, 29)

An experience which knocks the ego out of a woman. "its the heaviest experience, you become a common denominator with the soil. i remember i was like a wolf, it goes into another realm because the pain is so excruciating that you no longer feel like a hot-shit guitar player or a great artist in the middle of that." (Dusty Roach 1979, 24)

"That woman come and, in just the time we've been talking, I had the baby. I had the baby and she covered me and that's that." (Zahrah Muhammad 1977, 208)

"Like shitting a pumpkin." (Shulamith Firestone 1970, 227)

A natural event "that the medical establishment now treats as pathological." (Marilyn Grossman and Pauline B. Bart 1979, 165)

An unspeakable pain. "My mother [only] said that I would have to work hard, and my friend who had a baby a month or so before had just said it wasn't all that it was cracked up to be. I was so angry afterwards. . . . I've been told I am a social disaster now because I always tell women what it was like for *me* so they can have a more realistic picture of what to expect. . . . There seems to be a conspiracy to stop women from getting information on what happens, on what it feels like . . . to be out of control." (Lou Bachan 1978; cited by Dale Spender 1980, 55)

BIRTH NAME

A term used by feminists as a more accurate label for the name received at birth than the older term *maiden name* which has sexual double standard implications. (Gloria Steinem 1983, 154)

(See MAIDEN NAME, NAME, NAMING)

BISEXUAL

"A person of either sex who enjoys and willingly engages in both heterosexual and homosexual eroticism. As a category, bisexuals have received less attention than have homosexuals (male and female), even though there may in fact be many more bisexuals than exclusive homosexuals." (Mary Anne Warren 1980, 75)

BISEXUALITY

"I think for males, bisexuality is just another form of phallic imperialism – just another adventure in the quest for assist-ance in masturbation – and just another escalation in masculinist sexual aggression. The man who can bang away to orgasm in the vagina of a woman is just going to bang away in my ass. The woman whose sense of herself depends on male approval is just going to expect me 'to be a man to her' in a way that would be wholly dishonest for both of us. So I don't want to talk about bisexuality. I don't like what it means when it refers to male sexual activity and response. I don't believe in bisexuality. I reject it as a word. I reject it as a way of life." (John Stoltenberg 1977; rpt. 1984, 26)

BITCH

"In technical use, a bitch is a female dog or other canine capable of estrus and gestation. . . . A dog in heat actively seeks insemination. . . . judged by our cultural standards, the dog is 'lewd,' and according to standard dictionaries that is one of the meanings the word bitch is assigned when applied to a woman. . . . Bitch should not be regarded as a derogatory word, but a complimentary one . . . John may think Mary is a bitch because she is aggressive, but since he would praise the same quality in James, his use of bitch is in fact a compliment." (Casey Miller and Kate Swift 1976, 118-19)

(See BITCH MANIFESTO)

The main term used by a member of the (male) oppressor group to a member of the (female) oppressed group who challenges the oppressor on his use of oppressive tactics. Woman to rapist: "You're hurting me." Rapist: "Shut up, you bitch, and do as I say." Woman to partner: "Honey, do you think you could empty your own ashtrays – I don't smoke." Honey answers: "Will you quit bitching at me?" (Batya Weinbaum 1983, correspondence)

"Has certain phonetic qualities that make it an unlikely candidate for rehabilitation. It can be spat out in such a way that anyone within earshot whose native tongue is English will recognize it as an epithet of disgust . . ." (Casey Miller and Kate Swift 1976, 120)

"Has taken on such negative connotations – children are taught it is a swear word – that in everyday American English, speakers are hesitant to call a female dog a *bitch*. Most of us feel that we would be insulting the dog." (Alleen Pace Nilsen 1977, 28)

"This became a naughty word in Christian Europe because it was one of the most sacred titles of the Goddess, Artemis-Diana, leader of the . . . hunting dogs." (Barbara Walker 1983, 109)

A female character introduced on television in lieu of female villains. Strong-willed, selfish, destructive, a sneak and a cheat. The crimes of this character have been minor; she has lacked the vision and the power to be truly evil. She is related to "the wicked stepmother of fairy tale fame and to the wicked witch of myth and lore," except she does not have their force or power. (Diana M. Meehan 1983, 57-63)

BITCH MANIFESTO

A feminist tract which argues that "bitch" is a word used to put down uppity women but that it is also a synonym for a special woman: "Bitches are good examples of how women can be strong enough to survive even the rigid, punitive socialization of our society. As young girls it never quite penetrated their consciousness that women were supposed to be inferior to men in any but the mother/helpmate role. They asserted themselves as children and never really internalized the slave style of wheedling and cajolery which is called feminine." (Joreen c.1970, 3)

BLACK

"Is defined by blacks themselves not only by skin color and hair but also through a specific configuration of life experiences that are distinctly different from those of all other racial and ethnic groups. Surviving and prospering in a hostile milieu, blacks having these life experiences require psychological skill." (Faye Gary-Harris 1982, 99, 100)

(See BROWN, CHICANA, WHITE, WOMEN OF COLOR)

"We use the term black to refer to the two main groups of black people in this country [U.K.], namely those people who came originally from India, Pakistan, Bangladesh, many via East Africa, and those people who have their origins in Africa or who as a result of slavery now have their immediate origins in a number of Caribbean countries." (Valerie Amos and Pratibha Parmar 1981, 130)

Is a word which, like Afro-American, is ambiguous and does not identify roots in Africa as *African-American* does. (Brenda Verner 1983, Common Differences Conference, University of Illinois)

A dynamic color. "Sammy Lou [character in Walker's poem "Revolutionary Petunias"] is so 'incorrect' she names her children after Presidents and their wives; she names one of them after the founder of the Methodist church. To her, this does not mean a limitation of her blackness; it means she is so black she can absorb – and change – all things, since everybody knows that a black-skinned Jackie Kennedy still bears resemblance only to her great-aunt Sadie Mae Johnson." (Alice Walker 1973; rpt. 1983, 267)

Some blacks argue that the word should not be capitalized until the label white is also capitalized; otherwise the effect is, once again, the special and prejudicial setting aside of blacks as Other. However, some Blacks argue that it should be capitalized because, as Geneva Smitherman says, Black has become the designation for race (replacing the former designation for race, Negro), unlike *white* which does not designate race. (Most whites would designate themselves as Italian, Polish, British, etc.) The ethnicity/race label for Blacks in North America, especially, no longer holds since the ethnicities of Ibo, Yoruba, Mandingo, etc. have long since been lumped together as Negro and now Black. (Geneva Smitherman 1981, correspondence)

"I capitalize 'Black' because I regard it not simply as a color but as a cultural, personal, and political identity." (Gloria I. Joseph 1983, 134)

BLACK-COATS/BLACK ROBES

"Catholic priests. In spite of the acceptance of Christianity by many Native people, the presence of the Black-Coats always symbolized the changes in cultures brought by the European way of life." (Rayna Green 1984, 306)

BLACK FEMINISM

"Is not white feminism in blackface. Black women have particular and legitimate issues which affect our lives as Black women, and addressing those issues does not make us any less Black." (Audre Lorde 1979, rpt. 1984, 60)

Is "the unstoppable combination because we know about everybody's emptinesses and wrongs – white men's, white women's, black men's, our own – and will not hesitate to tell them, change them, and finally purify." (Barbara Smith 1974, *Ms.*, 3:2 (August), 4)

"Is the context for the development of Black-defined sexual-political struggles, examining the sexual tensions and conflict in the terms of Black culture and its shaping within and against the White dominant culture. It has to seek ways that Black women and men can politically negotiate sexual-political tension and abuse in a way that reinforces their collaboration against racism and the capitalist formulations that embody and sustain that racism." (Gloria I. Joseph and Jill Lewis 1981, 281)

" 'Womanist' encompasses 'feminist' as it is defined in Webster's, but also means *instinctively* pro-woman. It is not in the dictionary at all. Nonetheless, it has a strong root in Black women's culture. It comes (to me) from the word 'womanish,' a word our mothers used to describe, and attempt to inhibit, strong, outrageous or outspoken behavior when we were children: 'You're acting *womanish*!' A labeling that failed, for the most part, to keep us from acting 'womanish' whenever we could, that is to say, like our mothers themselves, and like other women we admired.... An advantage of using 'womanist' is that, because it is from my own culture, I needn't preface it with the word 'Black' (an awkward necessity and a problem I have with the word 'feminist'), since Blackness is implicit in the term; just as for white women there is apparently no felt need to preface 'feminist' with the word 'white,' since the word 'feminist' is accepted as coming out of white women's culture." (Alice Walker 1980b, 100fn.)

(See WOMANIST)

BLACK HISTORY MONTH

Month set aside in the U.S. for study, commemoration, and celebration of Black history; many communities and universities include programs on Black women's history and Afro-American historians.

(See VALENTINE'S DAY)

BLACK IS BEAUTIFUL

A popular statement of Blacks in 1960s, 1970s, 1980s. It "meant not simply a particular shade, but to have pride in one's ancestry, one's race, one's history. It meant developing a world view of humanity based on equality and marked by an absence of personal greed or the desire to exploit others." (Gloria I. Joseph; in Gloria I. Joseph and Jill Lewis 1981, 160)

BLACK WOMAN

" . . . I
am a black woman
tall as a cypress
strong
beyond all definition still
defying place
and time
and circumstance
     assailed
          impervious
               indestructible
Look
     on me and be
renewed."

(Mari Evans 1970; quoted in Gloria I. Joseph; in Gloria I. Joseph and Jill Lewis 1981, 229)

A term which in the mouths of whites assumes a white norm. "Can justly be described as a 'slave of a slave, . . . used in some cases as the scapegoat for the evils that this horrendous system has perpetrated on Black men . . . It is the depth of degradation to be socially manipulated, physically raped, used to undermine your own household, and to be powerless to reverse this syndrome." (Frances Beale 1970, 92)

Was not dehumanized under slavery but in white minds. (Michelle Cliff 1982, 39)

Euro-American slang includes the following terms for "Negress" or Black female: Black doll, -mama, -skirt, brown-skin baby, charcoal blossom, chocolate drop, culled gal, dusky dame, femmoke, jit, laundry queen, nigger gal, piece of dark meat, shady lady, sugar-brown, fox, mink, fine fryer, redbone, spotlight, high yaller, pinky, and yola. These are terms coined by men and largely related to Black women's color and appearance. No terms are synonymous with "beautiful" sister – i.e., they do not describe the historical persistence or political strength of Black women. (Patricia Bell Scott 1974, 219-21)

A definition usually "formulated by others to serve out their fantasies, a definition we have to combat at an unconscionable cost to the self and even use, at times, in order to survive; the cause of so much shame and rage as well as, oddly enough, a source of pride . . ." (Paule Marshall 1962, rpt 1970, 21)

(See WHITE)

She is a woman, gap-toothed and full of herself, who has a smile with gold ornaments peeking out. A woman sporting sweat and rolls of flesh earned over years of giving herself by her own volition. Her beauty is unique and only for those with a seeing eye who can see it, appreciate it, and then revel in it – if they are lucky. (Cheryl West 1985, correspondence)

Her life is a story about "being torn up, ground down, turned around, borne backwards, but blossoming and bearing anyhow." (Michele Russell 1979, 99)

Black Women: "Are rarely recognized as a group separate and distinct from black men, or as a present part of the larger group 'women'. . . . [W]hen black people are talked about the focus tends to be on black *men*; and when women are talked about the focus tends to be on *white* women." (bell hooks 1981, 7)

(See WOMANIST)

BLACK WOMEN'S STUDIES

A growing movement in the 1980s. It has developed because Black Studies tend to focus on Black men, Women's Studies, white women. This problem is titled and addressed in *All the Women are White, All the Blacks are Men, BUT SOME OF US ARE BRAVE*, edited by Gloria T. Hull, Patricia Bell Scott, and Barbara Smith.

"To use the term [Black Women's Studies] and to act on it in a white-male world is an act of political courage." (Gloria T. Hull and Barbara Smith 1983, 19)

BLAMING MOM

"The long-running American serial. . . . The Woman-as-Nature-as-magic-as-powerful-as-bad-Mom package has gone the rounds . . . sometimes accompanied by the smell of burning." (Margaret Atwood 1984, 1)

BLAMING THE VICTIM

A process which locates the problem with the one who is suffering. The victims are viewed as having faulty attitudes and destructive lifestyles. "Victim blaming is essential for a social order in which women are valued chiefly as wives and mothers. . . . Victim blaming becomes a weapon in the intense conflict over a woman's place that goes on at both the individual and impersonal levels. It is used not only against traditional wives, but also against those in conscious or unconscious revolt." (Dorie Klein 1982, 91)

BLAZING STAR

The name of a feminist newsletter and of a lavender-colored wildflower that grows throughout the Midwestern, Southern, and Eastern United States. "Because of their 'feathery' appearance, Blazing Star has two very appropriate common-names, 'Gayfeather' and 'Fairy Wand'!! We also felt that Blazing Star was a good name because the Lesbian liberation/pride movement is taking-off like a 'blazing star' across the heavens!!!" (Chicago Women's Liberation Union 1975; in Special Collection, Northwestern University Library, Evanston, Illinois)

BLEED-IN

A ritual of female culture, first created Friday, July 13, 1973, by 13 women. The decorative signs and symbols were of menstruation and the women told anecdotes of their first periods and the feelings of helplessness and embarrassment. The purpose was to gain self-awareness, hold an irreverent but solemn celebration of women's "mysteries," and to attempt to honor what is generally defiled and repressed. (Janice Delaney, Mary Jane Lupton and Emily Toth 1977, 225)

BLEEDS, THE

(See CURES, MENSTRUATION)

BLOND/BLONDE

"When English took over the masculine-gender French words *blond* and *brunet*, it also annexed their feminine-gender counterparts *blonde* and *brunette* and acquired in the process . . . nonstandard English nouns to use of females: 'He is a blond. She is a blonde'. . . . [T]he seemingly innocuous difference between *blond* and *blonde* becomes in English the difference between the standard (male) and the deviation (female). Why not *blond* for both women and men?" (Casey Miller and Kate Swift 1980, 106)

BLOOD PRINTS

Art work in which the body is the instrument and menstrual blood is the medium. Donna Berry writes: "At first, I would simply sit on the paper and make images. Then I learned to scoot backwards in two ways: one going straight back and the other moving from side to side. I sometimes sit on the same piece of paper several times. This gives me a repeat of a

similar image. I catch my blood with a sponge or a menstrual cup and use the blood as ink. I write some of the work that I've written about blood right on the blood print. I also use the caught blood to drip or fling lines onto the paper and to finger paint with . . . I recently started doing blood prints on cloth. The way cloth combines with blood is entirely different than the way blood and paper combine. It feels like a whole new art form to me. I have shown my blood prints in two art shows." (*WomanSpirit* May 1980, 6:24, 35)

"BLOOMER GIRLS"

An early musical about the textile industry (1936), it caused a stir because the chorus line of women wore bloomers.

BLOOMERS

Nineteenth-century pantsuit, designed by Elizabeth Smith Miller. Loose trousers, gathered at the ankles and worn under a skirt. They were designed in 1850, and promoted by Amelia Bloomer, editor of the women's temperance and women's suffrage paper, *The Lily*, and other women who campaigned for "rational dress" for women. "Between 1850 and 1860 feminists enjoyed freedom from long, heavy, hampering skirts that swept the ground. Wearers of the bloomer became the butt of jokes, cartoons, and ridiculing comment." (Mary Stetson Clark, n.d.) The costume was so ridiculed by press and pulpit that Elizabeth Cady Stanton reported "that to escape constant observation, criticism, ridicule, and persecution, one after another [of the women] gladly went back to the old [clothing], and sacrificed freedom of movement. . . . I have never wondered since that Chinese women allow their daughters' feet to be encased in iron shoes, nor that the Hindoo widows walk calmly to the funeral pyre." The name *bloomers* has survived to be used as a label for any loose-fitting knickers. (Lisa Tickner 1976; in Marsha Rowe 1982, 41, 42)

BLUES, THE

Songs which help record Black women's history and struggle. "The topics and words in [female blues singers'] songs, combined with their personality and expressive deliveries, created an idiom that has helped Black women remember the past and live the present." Many of the songs deal with the ways and means for Black women to deal with their sex and sexuality vis-à-vis men. Songs such as "Mean Mistreater Blues" by Memphis Minnie; "All Fed Up" and "Ain't No Fool" by Big Mama Thornton; "Yellow Dog Blues" by Lizzie Miles; "Tricks Ain't Walkin' No More" by Bessie Jackson and "Empty Bed Blues" by Bessie Smith. (Gloria I. Joseph; in Gloria I. Joseph and Jill Lewis 1981, 183) "The Black female blues aesthetic [is] the very direct use to which Black women put language and song, in order, as critic Joanne Braxton states, to 'transcend the most brutal, painful and personal of disasters in daily life and go on fighting – strong and alive.' The blues, according to Ralph Ellison 'does not skirt the painful facts of human experience, but works through them to an artistic transcendence.' " (Lorraine Bethel 1982, 180)

(See MUSIC)

BLUESTOCKINGS

Viewy women who gather for artistic, literary, intellectual and witty exchanges. Critics have used the term to refer to learned, and thus in their minds, unfeminine and pretentious women. The origin of the term is in dispute but was evidently first used in 1750s to refer to women and men in London who gathered for conversation; one of the people attending wore blue worsted instead of black silk stockings. The women who attended were first derisively called *bluestockingers* and *Blue Stocking Ladies* and later *Bluestockings* and *Blues*. The terms were thus first used to denote informal or homely dress and then to refer to intellectual, literary, or learned women. To "wear your blues" became a metaphor for evenings of intellectual and witty conversation. As the term *bluestocking*

became associated with the women who held salons and who put their energies and emotions into work with each other, it became a term of abuse, with connotations of snob and misfit. The bluestockings, excluded from politics, law, education and employment because they were female, formed an alternative, knowledgeable, supportive, competent and intellectually self-sufficient group. There are many bluestockings today, learning, reading, writing, and exchanging ideas in women's groups. (Susan Conrad 1976; Seon Manley and Susan Belcher 1972; Barbara Schnorrenberg and Jean E. Hunter 1980; Dale Spender 1982b; Edith Rolt Wheeler 1919b)

(See REDSTOCKINGS, VIEWY)

"He has left off his old friends and his blue stockings." (Lady Mary Wortley Montague 1757, *Oxford English Dictionary*)

BOARDING SCHOOL

Places of education for middle- and upper-class boys and girls marked by "forms of separation from urban, culture, from other social classes, from family and home, and from the opposite sex." Girls in a boarding school are also "separated from the vision of political power." (Judith Okely 1978, 113, 119)

Created, along with reservations, by the U.S. Government to educate Indians in white ways. The schools were so far from the reservations that the children were often separated from their families for years with the result that the children lost fluency in their own language and familiarity with their culture.

BOARDROOM

A white room where decisions affecting many other people of all colors are made. Women and minorities are rarely seen in the boardroom, except as secretaries.

BODY

Our most basic "land" – which has been regarded as an exploitable resource for sex and children and has been mystified in the process. "Our campaign for 'home rules' . . . is still being met with passive callousness, sentimental and cooptative 'adoration,' and, when all else fails, active severity. . . . [Our bodies] are defined, possessed, abused, veiled, exposed, air-brushed, or metaphorized by men. Men are hardly immune from the body-mind split, of course. They have constructed entire philosophical, poetic, religious, and political systems around this predicament (which they claim as unique to them)." (Robin Morgan 1982, 53)

"[Man] thinks of his body as a direct and normal connection with the world, which he believes he apprehends objectively, whereas he regards the body of woman as a hindrance, a prison, weighed down by everything peculiar to it." (Simone de Beauvoir 1970, xvi)

Physical substance that is both to be ravishing, and (more often than the woman or official law can prevent) ravished. (Julie Feldman 1984, correspondence)

BOMFOG

The Brotherhood Of Man and the Fatherhood Of God. Reporters covering political campaigns have heard the phrase so often they record it in their notes only as BOMFOG. As shorthand for all the false generic terms and expressions that define women as nonhuman, BOMFOG "continues to engulf our language and distort our thinking." (Eve Merriam; cited by Casey Miller and Kate Swift 1980, 34)

BONDING

"As it applied to Hags/Harpies/Furies/Crones is as thoroughly Other from 'male bonding' as Hags are the Other in relation to patriarchy. Male comradeship/bonding depends upon energy drained from women (its secret glue), since women are generators of energy. The bonding of Hags in friendship *for* women is not draining but rather energizing/gynergizing." (Mary Daly 1978, 319)

(See BE-FRIENDING, HAG, FRIENDSHIP, GYNERGY, WOMAN-IDENTIFIED WOMAN)

BOOKS

Published volumes which mostly portray women writers and characters as adjuncts to the men. What men write and think of women has been considered more important than what women write and think. (W. Lyon Blease 1913a, 202)

" 'Yes, yes, if you please, no reference to examples in books. Men have had every advantage of us in telling their own story. Education has been theirs in so much higher a degree; the pen has been in their hands. I will not allow books to prove anything.' " (Jane Austen 1818, 237)

BORDWEAL

"An artificial barrier raised to keep women out of things, such as an irrelevant height requirement. From *Oxford English Dictionary* 'bord-weal,' 'a wall of shields.' " (Suzette Haden Elgin 1981, 2)

BORN OUT OF WEDLOCK

An expression which sounds "like thumbscrews hanging in a medieval museum." (Naomi Weisstein 1981, 38)

(See ILLEGITIMATE)

BOTTLE

Container with a nipple on the top used for feeding liquids to young children. Some women use bottles and formula from choice or because they are a necessary substitution for breastfeeding. Some, because of aggressive marketing of infant formulas in Third World countries, use it because they have been deviously led to believe it is better for the health of their babies.

BOURGEOIS

A label constantly thrown at white, radical feminists by white upper-middle-class marxist men. (Ann Russo 1984)

BOY

A male youth (cared for primarily by women) who is in training to support the institutions which state that his caretakers are kindly but otherwise inferior beings.

Defined in an essay on sex differences

in education as a late starter but an easy winner in The Educational Stakes. ("The Education of Women" c.1972, *Women Now*)

A term seldom used for men "except to impart a tone of frivolousness of purpose, as in 'going out with the boys.' " One dictionary notes "that the word 'boy,' when applied to a young adult, suggests that the person in question lacks maturity and judgment, or is considered by the speaker to be an inferior individual." (Harriet E. Lerner 1976b, 295, 296)

(See GIRL)

A term used by whites to refer to Black and so-called minority men.

Boy, like "girl," is a "term that undoes any implications of status, authority, and true seriousness of purpose . . . An exception . . . occurs in wartime, when we speak of our fighting men as 'boys' (e.g. 'the boys in Vietnam'). As with the term girl, the use of the diminutive term boy in this context may reflect an unconscious attempt to deny or minimize the destructiveness and sadism (in this case real rather than fantasied) associated with men at war." (Harriet E. Lerner 1976a, 296)

Old Boy: A British term meaning a graduate of a preparatory school. "This usage has been imported to the United States in *the old-boy network*, an expression that describes the exclusive, informal system long used by upper-class men to help their old school buddies into positions of power." (Casey Miller and Kate Swift 1980, 72)

BOYCOTT

An attack, through withdrawal of support and, often, a redistribution of money. A turn of century example: "Until women have the Vote, not only can the State be deprived of a considerable revenue by concerted action on the part of women who have capital, but money in increasingly large sums can be, and is being, diverted from the ordinary trade channels into new ones from which the male electorate will derive little or no benefit. . . . Money will still be in circulation; but only openly avowed friends of the Women's cause will get it." (Gwynneth Chapman c.1912)

BPBP

Barefoot-Pregnant-and-Behind-the-Plow. "Although the BPBP status of peasant days now translates into various updated versions, there is little doubt that sex and the female ability to bear children is a frequent rationalization for ever so many of the (at least) fifty-seven varieties of rationales for oppressing women." (Florynce Kennedy; quoted in Robin Morgan ed. 1970, 494)

BRA

"The breast binding undergarment that symbolizes woman's readiness to misshape her natural body to suit the current mode of fashion to gain male approval." (Midge Lennert and Norma Willson eds 1973, 2)

BRA-BURNING

A media-created label for women's liberation. "Well into the 1970s, on both sides of the Atlantic, this remained the image which was most widely associated with feminism. So farcical did it seem that it laid to rest any serious questions being asked (outside the movement) about *why* women wore bras, or why some women now chose to stop wearing them. . . . Just as the scale and coherence of suffragette militancy had been hidden from view, so the smokescreen of the 'burning bra' helped to obscure the real nature of the women's liberation movement." (Anna Coote and Beatrix Campbell 1982, 12)

BRAILLE

System of printing and writing for blind people in which letters, numerals, and punctuation are made of raised dots distinguishable by the fingers.

(See WOMYN'S BRAILLE PRESS)

BRAIN

"The softest, freest, most pliable and changeful living substance . . . the hardest and most iron-bound as well." (Charlotte

Perkins Gilman 1904, 6)

Is "that great and sole true Androgyne, that can mate indifferently with male or female and beget offspring upon itself." (Dorothy Sayers 1947; in Betty Roszak and Theodore Roszak eds 1969, 120)

BRAINWASHING

A "justification" or "explanation" sometimes used for women's oppression or behavior. "This view makes it convenient to ignore the political realities a woman must deal with every day of her life due to male supremacy." (A Redstockings Sister, c.1969) "Women's submission is not the result of brainwashing, mental illness or stupidity, but of continual, daily pressure from men. We do not need to change ourselves, but to change men." (Redstockings Manifesto 1970) "My own suspicions [about the charge of being brainwashed] were first raised when I found it being used against me whenever I wouldn't have sex on demand. Suddenly men became concerned with my hangups and insistent that I accept their offers of instant emancipation." (A Redstockings Sister, c.1969)

BREAD AND ROSES

The slogan comes from the historic strike of 20,000 textile workers in Lawrence, Mass., in 1912. The strikers – most of them women and children immigrants – struck against intolerable wages and working conditions. Their banners proclaimed, "We Want Bread and Roses, Too." The strike and slogan were later commemorated in a song still popular today. As one version of the song has it, "Yes, it is Bread we fight for, but we fight for Roses too." (Moe Foner; in Diana Scott ed. 1982) One recording (words by James Oppenheim and music by Caroline Kohlsaat) is on the record "Honor Thy Womanself: Songs of Liberation" by the Arlington Street Women's Caucus, c.1975, available in the Fawcett Library, London.

BREAD-WINNER

" 'We men are the bread-winners,' we hear said, not seldom, in the face of all the female teachers, artists, operatives, dress-makers, shopkeepers, authors, and domestics in the United Kingdom. 'We men are the bread-winners,' say the sentimentalists, who are ashamed of their female relatives appearing to work, though female earnings usually drop into men's pockets. But the fact is, and has long been, that a vast proportion . . . of the women of the kingdom work for their bread . . ." (excerpt from *Daily News*; in *Englishwomen's Journal* 1:5 [July 1, 1858], 340)

BREAST

"The human mammary gland, similar in function to the bovine udder but with a lower nipple to breast ratio." (Brinlee Kramer 1984, conversation)

The superior ventral surface of the body, bared by pornography "for profit and entertainment . . . In our society, pornographers have the legal right to strip women, expose them, and make a profit for themselves. Yet, women don't even have the legal right to bare their *own* breasts" (as Nikki Craft, a feminist activist from California has pointed out). This phenomenon was explored by another feminist: "Recently i called the Champaign, Illinois, University of Illinois, and Urbana, Illinois, police departments. i was trying to find out whether it was actually illegal for a woman to take off her shirt in public. It was surely not illegal for a man to do the same thing. When i called the Urbana Police they were stumped. They didn't know what to think of such a question. It had never occurred to them before. So they looked and looked and couldn't seem to come up with anything. i think they're still looking. Then, i called the Champaign Police Department and was immediately told by a male officer that of course it was illegal. So i asked if there was anything actually written down saying that it was illegal. So he looked and didn't seem to come up with anything particular, except he felt for sure that it would be an arrestable offense under the public indecency code. Then i called the University Police who referred me to the State's Attorney's Office who referred me to the Student's

Legal Services Office who told me that they don't give legal advice over the phone. Well, i started to get the feeling that people really didn't want to talk abut this." (Lee Smith 1984)

"A rich source of allusion. It nourishes, comforts, cares." (Anna Coote 1983; "All You Need is Balls," *New Statesman*, 16 September)

According to the *American Heritage Dictionary*: As a noun: "1. The human mammary gland." As a verb: "To encounter or advance against manfully; confront boldly."

(See AMAZON, MASTECTOMY, WOMEN'S HEALTH MOVEMENT)

BREASTFEEDING

Providing a baby with milk from the breast. A nurturing task which if done openly in public provokes sniggers and jokes from some men who see such activity as the most private part of the private sphere moving into the public, "a rejection of and a challenge to the validity of the boundaries" they have set up for women and men. (Linda Imray and Audrey Middleton 1983, 20)

BREEDERS

A term used in the Chicago lesbian community to label heterosexuals. (Elizabeth Snyder 1983, correspondence)

BRIDE OF FRANKENSTEIN

"We have chosen the 'Bride of Frankenstein' as our symbol of Women's Liberation. The plot of this movie runs as follows: The Mad Doctor resurrects Elsa Lanchester from the dead to be the mate of his Frankenstein monster, but she takes one look at her intended husband and won't have any of it. Because of her rebellion, the mad doctor's castle comes tumbling down. We see a parallel between this story and the growth of the Women's Liberation movement within the New Left. Radical men who have treated their women as mindless subordinates now find themselves confronted by a storm of female anger and militancy. Soon the phallic castle of male supremacy will

tumble too." (*It Ain't Me Babe* [editorial statement about the cover] 1971, 6)

BRIDGES

Needed to cover the world – the bridge of love, of friendship, of dream, etc. (Nelida Piñon 1982, 73)

" . . . I must be the bridge to nowhere
But my true self
And then
I will be useful."

(Donna Kate Ruskin 1981, xxii)

BROAD

A woman who is liberal, tolerant, unconfined, and not limited or narrow in scope.

BROADSIDE

"Means either a dead-centre attack on the enemy, an advertising flyer, or a political poster (as in the Xi Dan Democracy Wall in Beijing)." (Editorial note 1984, *Broadside* 6:1 (October), 3)

BROOM

"For several centuries up to the end of the Steam Age, there were rebels called witches. The broom was supposed to have been their means of locomotion for going to the festivals or sabbaths. Their opponents always described them riding brooms . . . Though traveling by broom is a pleasant idea, it seems that in reality witches could move without transportation, as described in the writings of Maria Feiticeira (*Acts of the Witches*, Iberia, Iron Age). According to her, witches knew how to reach a state which permitted them to go to the sabbath and, at the same time, remain materially in their prisons. From which come the expressions 'second sight' and 'second state.' " (Monique Wittig and Sande Zeig 1976, 22)

BROOMSTICK

The long handle of a brush used for sweeping and the name of a feminist journal by and for women more than 40 years old. "We repossess the BROOM-

STICK as a symbol of our strength and unity. It stands for many aspects of our lives and interests: SKILLS – homemaking and paid jobs; CHANGE – the new broom sweeps clean; POWER – the witch flies on the broom; HEALING – witches were ancient healers; CONFRONTATION – exposing what society calls ugliness." (Mickey Spencer and Polly Taylor 1982, 2)

BROTHER

A male who has a close relationship to another. A term which is not a symbol of universal human kinship, when it ignores generations of sisters.

BROWN

"While I know and identify black, my first knowing of myself before I knew much about skin color and its effects was as a brown baby girl looking in the mirror of my mother's face. Brown is my color, the very shade of which colors my existence both inside the black community and outside of it." (Andrea Canaan 1981, 232)

(See BLACK, WOMEN OF COLOR)

BRUSH ARBORS

"Structures made of small branches with leaves, put up by many Southeastern Indian peoples for the purposes of worship, shelter, ceremony, and escape from the heat. Like the Seminole 'chickee,' it keeps people cool with its open sides and loosely thatched roof. Choctaws, among others, make them in the twentieth century for singing songs, often Christian hymns in Choctaw." (Rayna Green 1984, 306)

BUDDY

A member of the brotherhood.

BUFFER LANGUAGE

"We have coined the term 'buffer' language to characterize what has been called 'empty language,' because such words and phrases serve a purpose . . . and therefore are not empty." Examples of terms which are sometimes used as buffer language: "I may be wrong, but . . ."

"or anything like that". (Deborah Tannen and Cynthia Wallat 1982, 47)

BULL DAGGER

Butch lesbian considered extremely masculine. The term has been used to demean lesbians.

(See BUTCH, LESBIAN)

BULIMIA

Binge-Purge Syndrome. "An expression of anger at society, an anger which is taken out on oneself. A woman overeats (for some a carrot, for another three carrot cakes), feels bloated, guilty and angry at self so she self-induces vomiting, or fasts for a while, or uses laxatives. It's a method to disguise one's discontent with her treatment by others. It's a purging of creativity, frustration and intelligence in a world where a heavy price is asked of creative women; it's a way to feel guilty and bad about oneself when things may be going too well. It's an ambivalent rejection of the traditional definition of woman." (Mary Ellen Shanesey 1984, correspondence)

BUNNY

One of many kinds of living meat which men associate with women. Small game hunted for their pelts and for sport, or domesticated. *Bunny* has been enshrined by Hugh Hefner who dresses women with rabbit ears and tail in order to provide men with an evening's chase. (Julie Belle White 1980)

Men's use of this term for women illustrates a principle about the use of animal metaphors. "If both the animal and the woman are young, the connotation is positive, but if the animal and the woman are old, the connotation is negative. Hugh Hefner might never have made it to the big time if he had called his girls *rabbits* instead of *bunnies*. He probably chose *bunny* because he wanted something close to, but not quite so obvious as, *kitten* or *cat* – the all-time winners for connotating female sexuality." (Alleen Pace Nilsen 1977, 29)

BUNNY BOSOMS
Playboy Bunny breasts which are often formed in part by: tissue paper, plastic dry cleaner's bags, absorbent cotton, cut-up Bunny tails, foam rubber, lamb's wool, sanitary napkin halves, silk scarves, gym socks. (Gloria Steinem 1983, 64)

BURNOUT
"Sense of emotional numbness [which] reduces stress by reducing access to the feelings through which stress introduces itself. It provides an exit from overwhelming distress that allows a person to remain physically present on the job. Burnout spares the person in the short term, but it may have a serious long-term cost." Many women have emotional labor jobs which can lead to this estrangement, an occupational hazard. (Arlie Russell Hochschild 1983a, 188)

BUTCH
Term used to describe an assertive and strongminded lesbian, and sometimes to describe the counterpart to the "Fem" of a lesbian couple.
(See DIKE, DYKE)
"A tough companion lover is called a butch. This word was used to designate lesbians at the end of the Concrete Age. In spite of the fact that butch was not a friendly designation, it was, for the most part adopted by the lesbian peoples. At present it is often said of a little companion lover who goes travelling alone." (Monique Wittig and Sande Zeig 1976, 23)

BUTTERFLY
"Symbol of the clitoris." (Midge Lennert and Norma Willson, eds, 1973, 2)

BUTTON
Small disks, attached to lapel, shirt, back pack and coat, bearing statements such as "We've Been Nice Too Long," "*Ms*chief," "Mean Mother," "Now You Have Touched The Women, You Have Struck A Rock!" (S. African women's slogan), "Lesbians Ignite," "Sexism Is A Social Disease," "If You Begin To Sink Into His Arms, You'll End In The Sink," "How Dare You Presume I'm A Stereotype," "How Dare You Presume I'm Heterosexual," "If We Can Send One Man To The Moon, Why Not Send Them All?" "Pray to God She Will Hear You," "Trust in God She Will Provide," "When God Made Man She Was Only Kidding."
(See SLOGAN)

CABLE ACT
The legislation which in 1922 declared that a U.S. woman who married an alien no longer became one in citizenship with her husband; she was allowed to retain her own citizenship. The introduction of the Equal Rights Amendment into Congress in 1923 was also part of the women's movement to force the law to treat wives as separate from and equal to their husbands. (Una Stannard 1977, 219)
(See ERA, LUCY STONER)

CAESAREAN/C-SECTION
Surgical delivery which has reached epidemic proportions in the United States. The caesarean knife is the ultimate symbol of technocratic interference in the process of hospital childbirth which now includes many invasive procedures. (Nancy Wainer Cohen and Lois J. Estner 1983)

CALCULATING FEMALES
A term used by men to describe women. It is inaccurately applied to most women because men have worked to keep math in their exclusive domain. (Laura Jane Fraser 1984, letter to editor, *Plexus*, March, 6)

CALIFIA COMMUNITY
An alternative feminist educational space for women created in Los Angeles, Calif., in 1976. Named after "the legendary Black Amazon/Goddess for whom California was originally named." (Marilyn Murphy 1983, 139)

CALL AND RESPONSE
A concept from Black folklore that implies participation, collectivism. "I can best describe it by musical example, the arena with which it is most closely associated. Take a lyric like that found in the old spiritual 'Have You Got Good Religion?' A lead voice sings a first line:

Have you got good religion?

A chorus of voices – say a church congregation – will answer the lead singer:

Certainly Lord.
Leader (Call): Have you been baptized?
Congregation (Response): Certainly Lord.

When I use this format in the classroom, it helps to defuse some of the 'authority' invested exclusively in the 'professor.' I try to get students to see the importance – no, necessity – of trusting the authority of their own and their classmates' voices. By the middle of the term, it works marvelously." (Deborah McDowell 1984, correspondence)

CALL OUT OF ONE'S NAME
Insult. (John Langston Gwaltney 1980, xv)
(See NAME)

CAMARADERIE
A bonding such as that boys and men enjoy on the playing field, for example. Camaraderie among women is often labelled *lesbianism*. "Apparently the kinds of things [men learn through camaraderie] help them maintain their place as rulers of the world, and it would prove a real threat if women experienced the same kind of 'bonding.' Well, obviously we do –

we call it sisterhood, and we learn it on playing fields as well as in political organization." (Helen Lensky 1984, letter to editor, *Broadside*, 6:1 [October], 2)

CAMEL

A humped, often domesticated, mammal used by political cartoonist Lou Rogers as the suffrage symbol because of its reputation for carrying enormous burdens and being the water wagon of the animal world. Rogers' work was published in *The Woman's Journal*, a weekly which was published by the National American Women's Suffrage Association, and first edited by Lucy Stone and Henry Blackwell. (Alice Sheppard, in press)

CAMP

Public behavior which is for practicing males "a combination of anti-woman mimicry and self-mockery." A subculture offered to "effeminate men" by the patriarchy in order to "keep us oppressed and also increase the oppression of women." This subculture "would deny us any chance of awakening to our own suffering, the expression of which is called madness by the patriarchy, but which can be recognized as revolutionary sanity by the oppressed." (Steven Dansky, John Knoebel, and Kenneth Pitchford 1973; in Susan Rennie and Kirsten Grimstad 1975, 222)

(See EFFEMINISM)

CAMPFIRE GIRLS

"Like the Girl Scouts, only we had prettier uniforms, our ceremonies echoed Native American rituals, and we took Indian names for ourselves. The organization was founded by American feminists to encourage self-reliance, friendship, a passion for the out of doors, and respect for Native American traditions among girls. During the resurgence of feminism in the 1970s, the organization changed its name [to Campfire, Inc.] and admitted boys to its groups and camps, in the interests of equal rights and keeping itself afloat financially." (Harriet Ellenberger 1984, 56)

CANDOUR

"Is a virtue [of frankness] which has been assumed by so many who have it not that it has become rather a disguise than a livery." ("Problems of the Day" 1914, *The Englishwoman*, 21:63 (March), 258)

CAP

Verbal retort to Black speech event known as *rapping*. "In response to a rap, black women are not only as sexually assertive as black men; they are often equally verbally skilled, frequently *capping* a male rap with an effective retort of their own. In one example, a man coming from the bathroom forgot to zip his pants. An unescorted party of women kept watching him and laughing among themselves. The man's friends 'hipped' him to what was going on. He then approached one woman and said, 'Hey, baby, did you see that big black Cadillac with full tires – ready for action with nobody but you?' She responded, 'No, motherfucker, but I saw a little gray Volkswagen with two flat tires.' " (Thomas Kochman 1981, 78)

A barrier method of birth control that caps the cervix; smaller than the diaphragm.

CAPITALISM

"The first mode of economy with the weapon of propaganda, a mode which tends to engulf the entire globe and stamp out all other economies, tolerating no rival at its side. Yet at the same time it is also the first mode of economy which is unable to exist by itself, which needs other economic systems as a medium and a soil." (Rosa Luxemburg 1963; cited by Sheila Rowbotham 1973a, 103)

(See IMPERIALISM)

"An advanced stage of patriarchy." (Azizah Al-Hibri 1981, 167)

CAPITALIST

Someone "who treats us as property. Socialists treat us like men." (June Levine 1982, 184)

CAPITALIST PATRIARCHY

"Patriarchy (as male supremacy) provides

the sexual hierarchical ordering of society for political control and as a political system cannot be reduced to its economic structure, while capitalism as an economic class system driven by the pursuit of profit feeds off the patriarchal ordering. Together they form the political economy of the society, not merely one or another, but a particular blending of the two." (Zillah Eisenstein 1979b, 28)

CARE

"What women are 'meant' to do for others – for anyone but themselves. This is one part of 'femininity' we want to redefine and keep, not throw away: caring for ourselves, caring for other women, caring what happens." (Sona Osman 1983, 27)

(See CARING)

CAREER-GIRL

"That term is a double fraud, since most women who work are at least a generation past girlhood . . . and they do not have the opportunities for advancement or personal satisfaction that a career affords. By career I mean women in the professions, in the arts and sciences, and at quasi-responsible levels of government, business, and industry which is the closest to the top they have come . . . Today the archetype of the career woman has come to replace the adulteress, and a scarlet A (for Absenteeism-from-home) may yet be branded upon her forehead." (Eve Merriam 1958; rpt 1964, 63)

CAREER-WOMAN

"An epithet conveying [a] judgment of feminine abnormality and calling up a familiar spectre of illegitimately wielded authority." (Ann Oakley 1982, 91)

"A derogatory term for unmarried middle-class woman with fulltime job and career prospects. Career woman is sometimes married but childless; or, more rarely, a married mother with au pair or able to afford private nursery and home help while she careers outside the home." (Liz Mackie 1984, 8)

There is no analogous term, *career-man*.

If a woman "enters on an active career, she should be as free from criticism as under similar conditions a man would be." (Helen Leah Reed 1891, 342)

(See INTRODUCTION to this book, NEW WOMAN)

CARING

Has two elements. In one sense it means "caring about" while in another "it describes the direct work which is performed in looking after those who, temporarily or permanently, cannot do so for themselves. It comprises such things as feeding, washing, lifting, protecting, representing, and comforting. It is the active and personalised manifestation of care." The word *tending* can be used to distinguish this task-oriented concept of *caring for* from the *caring about* concept. (Roy Parker 1980; quoted in Clare Ungerson 1983, 63)

CARL

Used to be the English unambiguous word for a male (and *wif* was the word for a female). Another word for male was *wer*. *Waepman* and *carlman* both meant an adult male person, and *wifman*, an adult female person. (*Mann* meant a human being.)

(See MAN, WIFE)

CASANOVA

An Italian (1725-98) named in traditional dictionaries as an "amorous adventurer," "romantic" and "libertine." In writing about his sex life Casanova boasted of seducing children, suggesting that a child could be most easily seduced in the presence of someone she trusted – such as an older sister. (Florence Rush 1980a, 76)

(See INCEST)

CASSANDRA

A woman in mythology texts, endowed with the gift of prophecy but fated by Apollo never to be believed. Many of us feel a close kinship with her trouble, at least in our dealings with men in positions of authority. CASSANDRA is the name of the radical feminist nurses network which seeks to provide a strong feminist voice in nursing. The name is a tribute to Florence Nightingale who wrote an essay titled "Cassandra" in 1852: "Why have women passion, intellect, moral activity – these three – and a place in society where only one of three can be exercised?" The group is dedicated to providing a place where all three can be voiced and heard and to providing an alternative to traditional hierarchical structures.

CASTRATION

One of the surgical methods, mythologies suggest, that men used (before they understood their reproductive role) to try to "make women" of themselves in the hope of achieving womanlike fertility. (Barbara G. Walker 1983, 142)

In the literary past, a diminishing of the male by a shrew, usually a challenging, ill-tempered wife. Now castration is seen in male literature "as a daily and entirely domestic occurrence, less dramatic than emptying the ash trays." (Mary Ellmann 1968, 138-9)

"Mary Daly has called for the *castration* of language. She means 'precisely in the sense of cutting away the phallus centered value system imposed by patriarchy, in its subtle as well as its more manifest expressions.' " (Mary Daly 1974; cited by Dale Spender 1980, 183)

CASTRATION COMPLEX

One traditional dictionary defines this as "the often unconscious fear or feeling of bodily injury or loss of power at the hands of authority." Casey Miller and Kate Swift ask "Why, then, is castration more often associated with male loss of power than female? Why do we not refer to 'castrating males' in connection with the losses women have suffered under a system that renders them impotent? Can it be because Authority is male? Because the Establishment is male? To admit women to full human membership is a threat to male prerogatives, and women who challenge this 'natural' order are called castrating women. We forget, or refuse to acknowledge, the reality that men are more often the castraters of each other and of women. Used carelessly, the word assumes the warp our culture imposes, just as, used carelessly, language castrates thought." (Casey Miller and Kate Swift 1976, 151)

CASTRATION FEAR

"Inevitable in a species that has knock-offable external dangling genitalia. . . . [When castration] does happen in real life, it is *men* who castrate men: men in wars and men in courts where eunuchs are required." (Beata Bishop 1977, 16)

CATHOLIC CHURCH

"Is an obscenity – an all-male hierarchy, celibate or not, that presumes to rule on the lives and bodies of millions of women." (Robin Morgan ed. 1970, xxii)
(See RELIGION)

CATHOLIC MARY

A saint of the Catholic church whose "only contact with divinity is through her 'servicing' of men: be it the Holy Father or her own son. . . . The Madonna often grows younger as her son grows older until, in Michelangelo's sculpture of the Rome 'Pietà', she is idealized as the eternal Virgin Mother, and looks young enough to be her son's bride. The Madonna is the primary role-model for women in our culture." (Phyllis Chesler 1972a, 168 c,e) [sic]

CAUCASIAN

Only correctly applied to people from the area of the Caucasus mountains, i.e. Armenia (Soviet) Georgia, Aserbaijan. Its common use derives from the (probably inaccurate) supposition of some nineteenth century philologists that "racially pure" (i.e. white) Indo-European speakers originated in that area. (David Doughan 1985, correspondence) "Most people on this planet are *not* Caucasion and have no reason to either love or respect Caucasians." (Angela Carter 1983, 72)
(See RACE, WHITE SOLIPSISM, WHITE)

CAUDLE

Any sloppy mess, especially that sweet mixture of gruel and wine or spirits given by nurses to recently confined women and their "gossips" who call to see the baby during the first month. The word simply means something warm (Latin *calidus*). (*Brewer's Dictionary* 1962, 189)
(See GOSSIP)

CAUGHT

"The use of 'caught' (rather than 'delivered') means the midwife does not use forceps or perform episiotomy. . . . Instead, she prefers to massage the perineum and apply hot compresses to encourage stretching without tearing." (Shirley Streshinsky 1973, 24)

CELIBACY

Sexual singleness which can mean "an affirmation of autonomy and independence." (Sona Osman 1983, 28)

CELLULITE

"A term which means, in fact, *fat*, but which is privileged by many doctors as being a 'special kind' of fat which is particularly unsightly (on women) and which can be specifically eradicated from a woman's body by the use of special creams, exercises, surgery, diets, pills, etc. – if she is willing to pay a price. A purely economic construction." (Elizabeth Nelson 1984, conversation)

CHAIR

A label which is an obvious solution to the problem caused by *chairman*, a sex-specific word. Other sex-inclusive words which have been used are *chairperson*, *chairer*, *presider*, *coordinator*, *president*, and *convener*. (Casey Miller and Kate Swift 1980, 25)

CHAIRMAN

A man who heads an academic department or chairs a committee or meeting. "According to the Oxford English Dictionary, *chairman* has been used since at least 1654 and *chairwoman* since 1699. In each of the seventeenth-century quotations the dictionary provides to illustrate the use of *chairman*, the person referred to was clearly male, and none of the citations from later periods shows the use of this word for a female." (Casey Miller and Kate Swift 1980, 25)

CHAIRONE/CHAIR-ONE

A neutral alternative to *chairman*.
(See CHAIR)

CHAIRPERSON

A term coined as a gender-neutral alternative to *chairman* that was widely adopted in the U.S. during the 1970s when it appeared that the Equal Rights Amendment would be ratified – making sexism in legislative language unconstitutional.
(See CHAIRMAN, M.A.L.E., MAN AS FALSE GENERIC, -MAN IN COMPOUNDS, NONSEXIST LANGUAGE)

CHALKING-THE-PAVEMENTS

Announcing, on [British and U.S.] sidewalks, the time and place of a suffrage meeting or a demanding of the vote. An act of courage since some women were arrested, and many more ridiculed, for this action. (H. M. Swanwick 1935, 201) Feminists chalk-the-pavements now to mark, with an outline of a woman, the locations where men have raped women.

CHANA

Translates in English as *cunt*. According to a feminist group in Brazil, "The word 'chana' cannot be merely defined as the female sexual organ; it is much broader. To some it sounds like 'chance' (opportunity), to other like 'chama' (flame). The important thing is to free yourself from previous connotations." A lesbian experimental journal by the group was named *Chana con Chana*. (Groupe de Acao Lesbico-Feminista 1982, 2)
(See CUNT)

CHANGE

A word associated primarily with men's actions except as in "to change a baby." Actually, women have been a very real (if unrecognized) force in society, responsible for many powerful and creative alterations in all aspects of life (Mary Ritter Beard 1946). Yet they have been put in charge of continuity rather than change. They are supposed to "keep the office going," write the letters which maintain family and friendship networks, and do volunteer work to support institutions men consider desirable to continue but not at a heavy cost to themselves. Men rely upon women for social wisdom, perseverance, and tact to "keep things going smoothly." Women have done well and have found satisfaction in some of their social work activities and are not eager for changes in all the arts of social living. Yet women, organized and unorganized, have worked for many social improvements and have been forceful in their demands for changes in public and private affairs.

(See ACTION)

"Men always want to change things, and women probably don't. I don't think it has much to do with women's powerlessness. Change could be death. You don't have to change everything. Some things should be just the way they are. Change in itself is not important." (Toni Morrison; cited in Michele Wallace 1983, 8)

"It is difficult to think of changing things when you have so many children, and you can't even give them enough to eat. It doesn't make sense to talk about a better life, unless your children are eating well, have shoes, and are getting an education." (Felipe, Peruvian peasant woman; cited in Audrey Bronstein 1982, 253)

"Neither passive acceptance nor stoic endurance lead to change. Change occurs when there is action, movement, revolution." (bell hooks 1981, 193)

"If what we change does not change us/we are playing with blocks." (Marge Piercy 1973, 17)

"When I speak of change, I do not mean a simple switch of positions or a temporary lessening of tensions, nor the ability to smile or feel good. I am speaking of a basic and radical alteration in all those assumptions underlining our lives." (Audre Lorde 1981c, 8)

CHAOS

"Chaos is not brought about by rebellion; it is brought about by the absence of political struggle." (Susan Sherman 1983, 137)

CHAP. RULES

The strict chaperonage regulations for women of pre-war Oxford were "always disrespectfully referred to as 'chap. rules'." (Vera Brittain 1933, 111)

CHARITY

Is a duty "which a mistress owes to herself as well as to her fellow-creatures." (Elizabeth Robins 1861, 5)

"Is an ugly trick. It is a virtue grown by the rich on the graves of the poor. Unless it is accompanied by sincere revolt against the present social system, it is cheap moral swagger." (Rebecca West 1912, *The Clarion*, Dec. 13)

CHARM

A word used to describe and praise women who are modest, pleasing, agreeable and deferential. Contrast words used for those women who do not talk to men in the terms men desire are *unfeminine, impolite, impertinent.* (Dale Spender 1982b; summarizing an analysis of Aphra Behn, 17th century)

CHASTITY

Refers to complete sexual abstinence, or to virginity before marriage with sexual fidelity thereafter. "However it is defined, chastity is a virtue which has usually been demanded of women more than men. The Old Testament mandated death by stoning for a female adulteress, but recommended no particular penalty for the man involved." (Mary Anne Warren 1980, 95)

A sexual innocence demanded of young women but not of young men who "are expected to chase women, and if they can to seduce them; the women being classed as 'fair game.' " (Shirley Ardener 1978, 36)

CHASTITY BELT

"Medieval device [its use continued in Europe from twelfth to sixteenth or seventeenth centuries] for locking a woman's potential lovers out of her body, while her husband was away from home at wars, pilgrimages, or crusades. The pelvic fetter had small spike holes through which urine, feces, and menstrual effluents might pass – in theory. In practice, it would have been impossible to keep clean. Vaginal infections, skin eruptions, and ulcers would have been inevitable after wearing such a device for only a short time, let alone months or years." (Barbara G. Walker 1983, 162-3)

(See CLITORIDECTOMY)

The sexual double standard is the newer invisible chastity belt for women. (Una Stannard 1977, 301)

CHAUVINISM/MALE CHAUVINISM

From the name of Nicolas Chauvin, a Napoleonic super-patriot. A term initially applied to U.S. aggression in South-East Asia, it has become a useful way to describe men's efforts to subjugate half the world's population. (Anna Coote and Beatrix Campbell 1982, 14)

(See MALE CHAUVINIST PIG)

CHERRY

"Like many slang expressions, the use of 'cherry' for 'virginity' may be traced to a mythic past. Like other red fruits, such as the apple and pomegranate, the cherry symbolized the Virgin Goddess: bearing her sacred blood color and bearing its seed within, like a womb." (Barbara G. Walker 1983, 163)

CHICANA

"We will use the term 'Chicana' to denote a woman of Mexican ancestry living in the United States, whether she refers to herself as Mexican, Mexican-American, latina, hispana, or whatever." Despite their diversity (of language, identification, demographic circumstances, and relationship to traditional female roles), the Chicana is also a woman who is "culturally neither Mexican nor American but influenced by both societies," and is "from a colonized minority. An overriding characteristic shared by Chicanas, in addition to their Mexican heritage, is a sense of marginality in an Anglo-dominated society . . . Perhaps the unique characteristic of the Chicana is in the nature of her triple oppression." This involves her membership in Chicana culture, her sex, and, finally, "the additional burden of internal oppression by a cultural heritage that tends to be dominated by males and exaggerates male domination over women." (Alfredo Mirandé and Evangelina Enriquez 1979, 12-14)

A designation for women is subsumed, and lost, in the male term *Chicano*. "In a quest for identity and an affirmation that brown is beautiful, the Chicana has sought refuge in the image of the indigenous mother. Some Chicanas view the Indian mother as Mother Earth; some identify with the bronze reality in religious themes of the Virgin of Guadalupe, the spiritual mother, and still others identify directly with the Mexican Eve, the historical mother, La Malinche." (Marcella Trujillo 1979, 6)

A woman with many tasks. "She must keep the cultural home-fires burning while going out and making a living. She must fight racism alongside her man, but challenge sexism single-handedly, all while retaining her 'femininity' so as not to offend or threaten her man." (Cherríe Moraga 1983, 107)

(See HISPANIC, LATINA, (LA) MALINCHE)

CHILD

Once meant a young person of either sex, but especially a female. . . . By the seventeenth century *girl* which had meant a young person of either sex was increasingly used to mean female and eventually replaced the special *female* meaning of child.

(See CHILDREN)

A being and an event which "changes the lives of most women, opening up previously unimaginable new selves, new areas of responsibility, delight, exhaustion, anxiety, ambivalence, and physiological change. It could be said that, in this sense, 'The child is mother of the woman.' The proverbial Wordsworth line, however, is 'The Child is father of the Man' – one of the senses of which contains a premature prophecy that won't come true until men are as intimately and committedly engaged in the raising of children as women have been." (Robin Morgan 1982, 223)

CHILD/CHILE
Form of address like *man*, *girl*, mostly used to and among children and females in the Virgin Islands English Creole. (Lito Valls 1981, 23)
(See GIRL)

CHILD ABUSE
(See CHILD-MOLESTATION, INCEST)

CHILDBIRTH
(See BIRTHING)

CHILDHOOD ENRICHMENT CENTERS
Called Day-Care Centers now. Our present terminology suggests that we "mean no more than places to dump children." Other terms which could help adjust our thinking and expectations: Youth Environments, or Assemblies for Educational Opportunities. (Elizabeth Janeway 1972; rpt. Elizabeth Janeway ed. 1973a, 529)

CHILD-MOLESTATION
Sexual abuse of children. In most cases, this type of child-assault is perpetrated by adult heterosexual males on female children. (Robin Morgan 1982, 221)
(See INCEST)

CHILDREN
"Use up the same part of my head as poetry does. To deal with children is a matter of terrific imaginative identification. And the children have to come first. It's no use putting off their evening meal for two months." (Libby Houston; cited in Bristol Women's Study Group 1979, 231)
Are often "selfish, autocratic, demand-

ing," boring companions. (Sara Maitland 1980, 87)
"Are not a medicine or a vaccine which stamps out loneliness or isolation, but . . . people, subject to the same weaknesses as friends and lovers." (Irena Klepfisz 1980, 18-19)
Are property, in patriarchal terms. "Property may, properly, be handed only from one man to another, even if a female channel is used. A woman alone cannot make legitimate her 'property'/child." (Stephanie Dowrick 1980, 68)
(See ILLEGITIMATE CHILD)
Often unwanted, especially if they are female. "I don't want to have a baby girl . . . I want a boy. Women lead such terrible lives. They suffer and are treated badly by the men. Things are bad enough in this country with the government the way it is. I don't want my daughter to have to fight all her life to make simple choices." (Maria, Guatemalan teacher; cited in Audrey Bronstein 1982, 259)
A term used by the anti-abortion movement to label teenagers who are past puberty. The goal "is to deny teenagers access to abortion and to put daughters back under the control of the patriarchal father." (*Diary of a Conference* 1982, 14)
Are "the least represented group in our society." (Rachel 1983, one of the workers at Children's Legal Centre; quoted in *City Limits*, Oct. 7-13, 62)
As defined by "women's magazines," before the feminist movement encouraged a re-assessment, children "were the expected outcome, not only of imperfect contraception, but also of the perfect union-providing emotional and sexual fulfilment within marriage." Children were an important element in "the happy family" as exemplified by the royal family, a "regal myth." (Marjorie Ferguson 1983, 49)

CHILD SUPPORT
A serious issue for single parents and their children, but not a major concern for many absentee fathers or for the legal system. "Apparently, trying to collect money from a recalcitrant husband is a

really antisocial act entitling you to parole without benefit of trial." (Joanna Clark 1970, 67)

CHINGADA, LA

Octavio Paz says that every woman, even if she gives herself willingly, is torn open (violated) by men – she is La Chingada. "Our 'feminine condition,' according to him, dooms us by nature to being 'open' and 'violated' by 'penetration' (I suppose virgin-mother/mother-saints are the only females exempt from such a fate." (Adelaida R. Del Castillo 1978, 144)

CHIVALRY

From Fr. *cheval* <Latin *caballas*. Originally meant a collection of men who rode horses. Women have had a lot to say about the intent of the actions traditionally included in the definitions of this word because far from representing altruistic bravery, courtesy and protection – as men have pretended – the actions work to hold women in subordinate positions. In 1694 Mary Astell called chivalry a praise of women's incompetence and ignorance by those "who under pretence of loving and admiring you, really serve their *own* base ends." (cited in Dale Spender 1982, 44)

Other, twentieth-century definitions of chivalry:

Goes "no further than the door!" "No chivalry prevents men from getting women at the very lowest possible wage." (A public speaker in Elizabeth Robins' 1907 novel, 119, 118)

A form of "condescension to an inferior. . . . A code of deferential behaviour affecting such matters and contingencies as the opening of doors, the lifting of hats, and the handing of teacups; but not touching or affecting the pre-eminence and predominance of man in the more important interests of life." (Cicely Hamilton 1909, 80, 84)

"A word which lends itself to many interpretations, and its definitions appear to vary with custom, country, and climate. The general idea concerning chivalry, of course, is that . . . it embodies something fine and heroic – a protective, courtly,

magnanimous spirit, peculiarly belonging to the male species, and exercised chiefly for the benefit of women and all who are weak and helpless. It is supposed to have taken its birth in the eleventh century, and was originally a military institution, carrying with it the dignity of knighthood. . . . In spite of the vows of chivalry, the persons of women seem to have been very insufficiently protected . . . exposed to dangers of all kinds." (Louisa Thomson-Price 1910)

A sometimes phenomenon, not there when you need it. "So long as you fold your hands and smile when your husband comes in, it is all right; but the moment the chivalry is put to the test, bang it goes." (Cicely Hamilton 1911, 140, 141)

"If it means anything at all save a superficial veneer of politeness, [it] is not limited to an abstention from inflicting physical pain, but also from wounding a human being's most tender susceptibilities and self-respect. Threats of the withdrawal of men's chivalrous feelings of respect for women have been made at every step taken by women towards independence." (E. Palliser 1913, 138)

"Is but the courteous exterior of a bigot." (Max Eastman 1914, 6)

"It is a very fine thing – what there is of it. The trouble is, there is not enough to go around. Nearly all the opportunities educational and political, that woman has acquired, have been gained by a march of conquest with a skirmish at every post. . . . Masculine chivalry has failed us." (Helen Keller 1915; quoted in Karen Payne ed. 1983, 153)

Behavior which seeks to soften the injustice of women's social position and is also a technique for disguising it. "One must acknowledge that the chivalrous stance is a game the master group plays in elevating its subject to pedestal level." (Kate Millett 1971, 37)

CHOICE

"The salt of life which makes much rough fare palatable. . . . [It's] generally withheld from women. . . . Choice is a duty which we have no right to evade or to delegate to another." ("Problems of the Day" 1913, *The Englishwoman*, 20:58 (Oct.), 21)

Involves consent. "True consent requires that one's agreement not be prearranged. Patriarchal ideology, which prohibits and prescribes sexual behavior, overdetermines some kinds of behavior and underdetermines other forms. . . . [C]onsent requires that neither party be dependent upon the other, a situation that cannot exist when patriarchal institutions make women economically, psychologically, and socially dependent upon men." (Sally Roesch Wagner 1982, 31)

Involves the freedom to have and freedom to refuse to have.

(See PRO-CHOICE)

CHRIST

"A psychic healer and visionary (even if somewhat patronising); an anarchist who caused mass hysteria wherever he went. As with the hippie movement of the 60s, this movement was ultimately absorbed and distorted by the men in power. Orthodox Christianity had a 400 year battle before it was finally established as the ultimate authority. There were the gnostic christians who believed that to know God you must know yourself at the deepest level . . . they rejected hierarchies . . . they ridiculed early christian martyrs who were killed and thus 'saved,' saying that if God sanctioned such actions he was a cannibal. But the orthodox christians developed a strong hierarchical structure and found great support in the middle classes." (Susan Paxton 1982, 4)

CHRISTENED

"I have always found it offensive when the word 'christened' is used to mean named. It's like saying that non-Christians don't have a name, don't have an identity. I can't think of anything much more symbolic of compulsory Christianity than that." (Hilary Saltburn 1984, letter to editor, *Trouble and Strife*, 2 [Spring], 5)

CHRISTIAN

Has been used "as a synonym for virtuous, just, peace-loving, generous, etc. etc. (In a similar way the phrase 'that's white of you' implied that you were behaving with the superior decency and morality expected of white, but not of Black people.) . . . Anti-Semitism was so intrinsic as to not have a name. . . . The Jews had actually allowed *moneylenders in the Temple* (again, the unexplained obsession with Jews and money). They were of the past, archaic, primitive as older (and darker) cultures are supposed to be primitive: Christianity was lightness, fairness, peace on earth, and combined the feminine appeal of 'the meek shall inherit the earth' with the masculine stride of 'Onward, Christian Soldiers.' " (Adrienne Rich 1983, 175)

CHRISTIANITY

"Emerged from the patriarchal Greek and Hebrew traditions, is devoted to a divinity conceptualized as masculine, and has for the most part lent its support to patriarchal ideas and institutions. Christ himself, as reported in the New Testament, seems to have little or nothing to say about the equality or inequality of the sexes, although he also seems to have behaved as if he considered women at least the spiritual equals of men." (Mary Anne Warren 1980, 97)

(See CATHOLIC CHURCH, CHURCH, JUDAISM, RELIGION, SPIRITUALITY)

Male: Composed of "Desire – to save one's own soul. Combat – with the devil. Self-expression – the whole gorgeous outpouring of pageant and display, from the jewels of the high priest's breast plate to the choir of mutilated men to praise a male deity no woman may so serve." (Charlotte Perkins Gilman 1911, 209)

CHRISTIANS

Purveyors of Christianity which has "destroyed the history and cultures of the peoples of Africa and North and South America – wherever values were transmitted via an oral tradition. They have almost totally stamped out a diversity of heritages and it is only with difficulty that we can learn scraps about what has been lost. . . . Whether or not Christianity is presently a comfort to women of any color, it is my enemy. I may understand or forgive women for their continued association with the church but particularly spiritual, 'holy' depictions . . . are revolting to me. They are, to me, inherently anti-Semitic." (Selma Miriam 1982b, 117)

CHRISTMAS

An annual celebration of the birth of Jesus which is, in Western countries, both wide spread and exclusive. "The very existence of Jewish and other non-Christian cultures is totally denied by the media, stores, and people who *sellebrate*. People who don't celebrate are ignored at best, hated, mistrusted, and made to feel guilty for being a Scrooge. . . . People who don't do the straight family lifestyle have more self-hatred and loneliness causing the most suicides of the year; and Jewish and other non-Christians are made even more invisible and oppressed." (Kathie Bailey 1979; quoted in Selma Miriam 1982a, 50)

CHURCH

The religious institution where "the preachers perform and the men sanction and pay [while] the women fill the pews, maintain the Sunday schools, the church societies and missions, and place their stamp increasingly upon them." (John W. Herring 1931, 183)

The institution with the most power in the Black community. "We no longer have our schools. We never did have 'town hall.' All we ever really had was the black church, and thank God it hasn't been integrated out of existence. It was my *church* that sponsors the day-center I run. There was no other black institution that could take the responsibility." (Faye, a preacher; quoted in Alice Walker 1977; rpt. 1983, 184)

CHUTZPAH

"Something that in this society sprouts more commonly from the egos of men than from the more shattered and battered egos of women. Women are not encouraged toward professionalism in general, and we are certainly not in the [New Left] Movement encouraged to give ourselves too many airs." (Marge Piercy 1969, 426)

CINDERELLA

"The fairy tale of the cinder-maid originated as an anti-ecclesiastical allegory repeated by real 'fairies' – that is, pagans. Ella was Hel, or Helle, daughter of Mother Earth, the Goddess with her regenerative fires reduced to cinders. Her ugly stepmother was the new church. Her ugly stepsisters were the church's darlings, the military aristocracy and the clergy." (Barbara G. Walker 1983, 168)

"Prototype of the passive maiden who becomes a prince's footnote instead of stepping out with her own imprint." (Eve Merriam 1975, 11)

CIRCLE

A curved structure, a ring which can be used to break down "the fragmentation and linear thinking of patriarchy." In a circle "every womon sits in the same relation to each other." (Eileen O'Laura 1978, 3-4)

CIRCLE OF MEN

An enclosure which excludes women. The philosophers, politicians, poets and policy-makers who for centuries have been talking to each other about the things of significance to them; each generation is given instruction in the particular and partial record of this circle from which women are excluded. (Dorothy Smith 1978)

CIRCUMCISION

Usually refers to the surgical removal of the loose fold of skin, the foreskin, that covers the glans of the penis. Sometimes done as a religious ceremony, or, when the penis is slit the whole length of the urethra, as an attempt to make male genitals more like females. (Una Stannard 1977, 290)

(See CLITORIDECTOMY)

CIRCUMSPECTION

A carefulness which, along with tightness "are the signals we offer up to superiors, or exhibit in public, to indicate our subordinate position." (Nancy Henley 1977, 85)

CITY

A collection of dwelling and interdependent lives, a place which has different meanings for women and men. From someone who has experienced life as both a woman and a man: "It would never have occurred to me, Anders, to give familiar objects the same names I had used for them when I was a woman, if only I could have come up with other words. True, I remembered what 'city' meant for her: an abundance of constantly disappointed hope constantly renewing itself. For him – that is, for me, Anders – it was a tight cluster of inexhaustible opportunities. He – that is, I – felt intoxicated by a city which was ready to teach me that my duty was to make conquests, whereas the woman in me had not yet unlearned the technique of presenting herself and, if the situation required, acquiescing timidly." (Christa Wolf 1978, 122)

CIVILIZATION

Western: "The history of genderic *struggle* that has been presented and viewed (obscured and mystified) as a history of male deeds and thoughts, from which women have been absent as a result of the constraints of reproduction and motherhood." Accounts which "in fact trace the chronology of the historical development of *patriarchy*, a coincidence that appears to escape scholarly attention." (Ruth Bleier 1984, 198, 199)

"You see we have built the world's seminal thought and knowledge system – the rationale for western civilization. This system combines all scientific and philosophical knowledge into a single poly-knowledge known formally as histro-sociopolecoanthropaterdickology. The informal name is poly/to/uni. In layman's terms what all these long words mean is 'the beauty of nothingness.' Yes folks. Those four little words summarize the sum total of western man's thought from the beginning of time. Amazing isn't it?" (Hattie Gossett 1981, 15)

CIVIL RIGHTS

Collective social action which, along with the Black Power movement, was "transforming for all kinds of people – Black, white, male and female. These movements were the political training ground for thousands who would later be active in anti-war, anti-nuclear, women's and continuing Black community organizing." (Linda C. Powell 1983, 285)

A term which "could never adequately express black people's revolutionary goals, because it could never adequately describe our longings and our dreams, or those of the nonblack people who stood among us. And because, as a term, it is totally lacking in color. . . . Older black country people did their best to instill what *accurate* poetry they could into this essentially white civil servants' term . . . by saying the words with a comprehending passion, irony, and insight, so that what one *heard* was '*Silver writes.*' " (Alice Walker 1983, 336)

CIVIL RIGHTS MOVEMENT

Group activity "based upon the concept of love and deep spirituality. It was a movement with a transcendent vision. *A movement whose very goal was to change the impossible, what people thought could not be changed.*" (Barbara Smith; quoted in Cherríe Moraga 1983, 131)

CLANS

All people belong to clans, some determined through the male, others through the female, line. Usually smaller than a tribe, the clans are related by blood and by some ceremonial relationship to spirits and the natural universe. One ordinarily marries outside one's own clan, no matter what the tribe, and inter- and intra-clan relationships impose specific rules of individual behavior. (Rayna Green 1984, 307)

CLAPPING-MILITANTS
"Those [feminists] who applauded but never joined in militancy." (H. M. Swanwick 1935, 225)

CLASS
A social and economic hierarchy and division which sets one woman against another, "in the past creating a lively antagonism between whore and matron, and in the present between career woman and housewife. One envies the other her 'security' and prestige, while the envied yearns beyond the confines of respectability for what she takes to be the other's freedom, adventure and contact with the great world . . . Women are a dependency class who live on surplus. And their marginal life frequently renders them conservative, for like all persons in their situation they identify their own survival with the prosperity of those who feed them." (Kate Millett 1971, 62)

"Is not defined by our relationship to the mode of production in the simple sense that if we sell our labor power (for a day or a lifetime), or are part of the family of someone (presumably male) who does, we are working-class. Being working-class is a mode of life, a way of living life based on, but not exclusively defined by, the simple fact that we must sell our labor power to stay alive. Class distinctions in capitalist society are part of a totality, a mode of life structured as well by sexism and racism. Class distinctions . . . affect the everyday lives of women and men, whites or black or Third World people, in different ways." (Nancy Hartsock 1976-7; rpt. 1981, 40)

In Marxist theory, is both race- and sex-blind.

"Presently class categories are primarily male-defined, and a woman is assigned to a class on the basis of her husband's relation to the means of production; woman is not viewed as an autonomous being. . . . A feminist class analysis must begin with distinctions drawn among women in terms of the work they do within the economy as a whole . . . among working women outside the home . . . , among houseworkers (houseworkers who do not work outside the home and women who are houseworkers and also work outside), welfare women, unemployed women, and wealthy women who do not work at all." (Zillah R. Eisenstein 1979b, 31, 32)

CLASSISM
"Represents a specific oppression where the rules, values, mores, and ideals of one class are imposed upon another, within the hierarchy of class values. Within feminism it filters through from middle class to working class women, denying them a language, banning them from self-expression, labelling them ignorant, stupid, coarse, bombastic, rough, uneducated, ineffectual." (Marlene Packwood 1983, 11)

CLASSROOM INTERACTION
Traditionally, "interaction patterns more compatible with men's established interaction patterns than with women's. . . . It is this fundamental inhospitability to women's talk that helps account for the continuing 'chilly climate' . . . that significant numbers of women on campus experience." (Paula A. Treichler and Cheris Kramarae 1983, 118)

(See CONVERSATION)

CLASS SYSTEM OF THE INTELLECT
A male determined, male glorified hierarchy of mental powers. "Women plough, harrow, reap, dig, make hay, rake, bind grain, thrash, chop wood, milk, churn, do anything that is hard work, physical labor, and who says anything against it? But let one presume to use her mental powers – let her aspire to turn editor, public speaker, doctor, lawyer – take up any profession or avocation which is deemed honorable and requires talent, and O! bring cologne, get a cambric kerchief and feather fan, unloose his corsets and take off his cravat! What a

fainting fit Mr. Propriety has taken! Just to think that 'one of the deah creathures' – the heavenly angels, should forsake the sphere – woman's sphere – to mix with the wicked strife of this wicked world!" (Jane Grey Swisshelm 1853; in Marion Marzolf 1977, 15; see also Berenice A. Carroll 1981)

CLEANING
Sanitation work; a great national service carried out primarily by women. Men *can* clean, of course, but women *do* clean. (Mary Lowndes 1914b, 131)

CLERK
A sex-segregated office job. While in the 1870s men held almost all clerical jobs, which offered them a career and possibilities of advancement, with increased bureaucracy the clerical job became a dead-end job held almost entirely by women.

(See SECRETARY)

CLICK
"A way of describing that instant of recognizing the sexual politics of a situation; any moment of feminist truth. (As in 'May you have sons to take care of you in old age.' *Click!*)" (Gloria Steinem 1980b, 19)

"That parenthesis of truth around a little thing that completes the puzzle of reality in women's minds – the moment that brings a gleam to our eyes and means the revolution has begun." (Jane O'Reilly 1972, 12)

CLITORIDECTOMY
Physical removal of the clitoris. "Female circumcision is the remnant of the chastity belt, it's trying to diminish female sexuality to fit it into monogamous marriage." (Nawal el Saadawi interviewed by Jill Nicholls 1979; in Marsha Rowe 1982, 455)

(See CHASTITY BELT, CLITORIS)

Has several forms: " 'sunna' circumcision, where the tip of the clitoris is removed; excision/clitoridectomy, where the entire clitoris and labia minora are removed, and sometimes part of the labia majora; and infibulation, where the two sides of the vulva are sewn up after excision." (Jill Nicholls 1979; in Marsha Rowe 1982, 455)

In the U.S., the last recorded clitoridectomy for curing masturbation was performed in 1948 on a five-year-old girl; there appear to be no references in medical literature for amputation of the penis or testes to stop masturbation.

CLITORIS
A small organ of erectile tissue that is composed of shaft (from root to top) and glans; it has hollow areas (cirpora cavernosa) which during sexual arousal fill with blood making the clitoris become stiff or erect. . . . The clitoris is merely the visible tip of a vast and complicated internal system of highly responsive sexual tissue. During sexual excitement, the blood vessel engorgement of the male is obvious but the engorgement of the female is less obvious, being mainly subterranean, but it is probably greater." (Midge Lennert and Norma Willson eds 1973, 2)

The word *clitoris* is derived from Greek *kleitoris*, originally, e.g., by the *Oxford English Dictionary*) glossed as "to shut" but more recently (e.g., by the *American Heritage Dictionary*) as "little hill." Based on its Greek origin, the correct pronunciation is [KLYteris], with the accent on the first syllable and a long *i* (to rhyme with "kite"). The more common pronunciation is [KLIToris], with the first syllable accented but a short *i* (to rhyme with "kit"). Another common pronunciation is [klitORis], with the accent on the second syllable, again with a short *i* on the first syllable. "Perhaps the persistent soft *i*," writes Ruth Herschberger in support of the original strong, long *i* pronunciation "can be traced to a subconscious desire on the part of scholars to reduce by phonetic magic the actual frequency of the organ! . . . A Greek formulation with *kleit-* in it always receives a strong vowel from scholars. It is significant that in this one word, however, the imperishable rules of scholarship gave way to a more irresistible psychological need: that of suppressing the pronunciatory gusto of an organ which never did quite fit in with woman's subordinate role in society." (Ruth Herschberger 1948, 36)

"A complex structure which includes the inner lips, hood, glans, shaft and legs, muscles, urethral sponge, bulbs, networks of nerves and blood vessels, the suspensory ligaments and pelvic diaphragm." (Federation of Feminist Women's Health Centers 1981, 156)

"From Greek *kleitoris*, 'divine, famous, goddess-like.' Greek myth personified the phallus as Priapus and the clitoris as an Amazon queen named Kleite, ancestral mother of the Kleitae, a tribe of warrior women who founded a city in Italy.... Later patriarchal society managed to ignore the clitoris.... Even physicians came to believe that no clitoris would be found on a virtuous woman." (Barbara G. Walker 1983, 170-1)

"The organ of pleasure ... the only organ in the body to have pleasure as its function." (Monique Wittig and Sande Zeig 1976, 33)

The center of women's erotic pleasure. It "remains – like the mad woman locked in the attic – an awkward half-secret." (Anna Coote and Beatrix Campbell 1982, 212)

"Plays a fundamental role in all women's orgasms, no matter *where* a woman likes to be stimulated, or stimulates herself, or ultimately where she experiences the most pleasure." (Sona Osman 1983, 28)

CLITORIA-WORSHIP

A celebration not well represented (as is phallus-worship) in myth, painting, sculpture, and modern bedroom practices. (Phyllis Chesler 1972b, 46)

CLOTHES

The "rich and powerful dress more expensively and exclusively, both because they can afford to and because dress is a primary indicator of their class status.... The super-rich have more freedom to dress in ratty old clothes if they wish, being under no compulsion to indicate wealth that is everywhere self-evident. The ill fit of mass-produced clothes, the shabbiness of clothes one can't afford to replace, and the inappropriateness of clothes for some occasions because of limited wardrobe all proclaim low social status." (Nancy Henley 1977, 87)

(See CROSS-DRESSING, DRESS, DUNGAREES, FASHION)

"Clothes represent occasions: women's clothes, anyway ... I folded a life." (Jessamyn West 1979, 473)

CLOTHING

Wearing apparel, which is sharply gender differentiated. "On the girls' racks are princess dresses, granny gowns, pink satin pantsuits, and bikinis; on the boys' ... are baseball uniforms, tweed suits ... astronaut pajamas and starched white dress shirts" (L. Walum 1977; quoted in Sara Delamont 1980, 14). For people with enough money, clothing can provide aesthetic choices involving color, textures and shapes. Yet women are very conscious that their "character" is continually judged by the clothing they wear, by their knowledge of what is fashionable, and by the fit of their bodies into what is presented by designers. While the general restrictions of what women are allowed to wear are dictated by men (see BLOOMERS and DRESS FOR SUCCESS), yet in the home and in industry women are in charge of cutting out, sewing, buying, laundering, folding, mending and ironing most clothing – their own, children's and men's.

"I think woman's dress, as at present arranged, is liable to the objections of dirt, danger, discomfort, and ... indelicacy. Woman has two legs as well as any man, and it is essential to have them as closely and as separately clothed to insure from cold and undue exposure.... It is my opinion that woman's walking robe should be independent of drenched flagstones and filthy puddles. She ought to be able to walk without devoting her sole attention to the bottom of her dress ... I am mentally convinced that woman might be invested with a freer and safer style of attire, without being disqualified for any of her important relations, either as a mother, wife, sister, or citizen." (*The Lily* 1852, 4:3, 24)

"I am seized with an angry resentment against the conventions of twenty years ago, which wrapped up my comely adolescent body in woollen combinations, black cashmere stockings, 'liberty' bodice, dark stockinette knickers, flannel petticoat and often, in addition, a long-sleeved, high-necked, knitted woollen 'spencer.' " (Vera Brittain 1933, 34)

"The school coat had stopped one thinking of her as a woman, just as a nun's habit would. A whole treatise could probably be written . . . on the protective quality of school coats. Protective in both senses: armour and camouflage." (Josephine Tey 1949, 58)

"As an artist I have always thought of clothing in terms of color and form, as costume. The idea that by clothing our bodies we could effectively hide our nakedness and therefore our sex (a la the fig leaf) implies that we have no imagination and is entirely laughable. Is there anyone who does not know that we are all born with the same basic parts?" (Joan Patchen 1984, correspondence)

CLUB

A word with strong masculine connotations. The New England Women's Club was the first organization to call itself openly a "women's club," after much discussion of whether the term "club" was strictly masculine. Though a number of male intellectuals participated, women were the group's leaders and decision-makers.

A type of organization that assumed an importance and a context quite different in white and Negro communities. Southern Negro women were responsible for social benefits which were civic responsibilities in the white community (care of the sick, homeless and aged, and concern with health and education). The early Negro women's organized clubs were less often

related to the literary and educational societies of white women's clubs and more concerned with reforms. The National Federation of Afro-American Women was organized in 1895; within a year it affiliated or merged with many other groups and became the National Association of Colored Women. (Eleanor Flexner 1968, 186; see also Angela Davis 1981)

CLUNK

"KlƏnk [noun] 1: a sharp stab of disappointment or frustration that negates previous visions of idealism and independence; a feminist word. 2: a backsliding attack that arouses fantasies of a simpler, more protected time for women. See 'Click': the reverse state of clunk." (Jane O'Reilly 1977, 66)

(See CLICK)

CND

Campaign for Nuclear Disarmament. In 1955 "two women in a North London branch of the Co-operative Women's Guild, both of whom were on the left and one of whom has been a suffragette, took up the issue of radiation and were instrumental in getting what became CND off the ground." (Elizabeth Wilson 1980, 177)

CO

A common gender pronoun, proposed by Mary Orovan, now being used in everyday speech and writing by members of several alternative-life-style communities in Virginia and Missouri. *Co* is used in a book on radical therapy published in 1973. (Casey Miller and Kate Swift 1977, 116)

COALITION

Collective activity which depends upon the recognition of differences. For example, "when Black and White women coalesce around an issue, it is important for both groups to recognize the crucial differences in the ways in which the oppression each suffers is manifested." (Gloria I. Joseph; in Gloria I. Joseph and Jill Lewis 1981, 40)

"Most of the time you feel threatened to the core and if you don't, you're not really doing no coalescing. . . . You don't go into coalition because you just *like* it. The only reason you would consider trying to team up with somebody who could possibly kill you, is because that's the only way you can figure you can stay alive." (Bernice Johnson Reagon 1983, 356)

"You don't necessarily have to like or love the people you're in coalition with. . . . What *I* really feel is radical is trying to make coalitions with people who are different from you." (Barbara Smith; in Barbara Smith and Beverly Smith 1981, 126)

"Without the political autonomy of oppressed groups, coalition politics are a bankrupt notion." (Cherríe Moraga 1983, 134)

COCAINE

An addictive drug, the valium of the 1980s. Provides women with the types of control demanded of them: loss of appetite and therefore weight loss; the feeling that being super woman is possible in home and other jobs; increased libido so genitals and feelings can be separated. Can also cause poverty, crime, and loss of job and life. Help groups are available for the addicted.

COEDUCATION

Has usually meant the admission of women to academic institutions planned for men. M. Carey Thomas called it a "fiery ordeal," but the only means available in the 19th century for women to prepare for serious scholarly endeavors. (Charlotte Williams Conable 1977, 20)

COIL

(See INTRAUTERINE DEVICE)

COLLABORATIVE FLOOR

Periods of talk when formal turn-taking gives way to participation not character-ized by a hierarchy of speakers but rather by a free-for-all interaction. In mixed-sex interaction women have a greater chance to talk during periods of collaborative floor. (Carole Edelsky 1982)

COLLABORATIVE TALK

Patterns of talk frequently heard among women – "drawing out other speakers, supportive listening and head nods, mutual sharing of emotions and personal knowledge, respect for one another's con-versational space." This differs from patterns of talk which more sharply distinguish speaker from audience. (Barrie Thorne, Cheris Kramarae and Nancy Henley 1983, 18-19)

COLONEL BLESSINGTON

Title of a mystery story by Pamela Frankau in which sexual identity forms the main theme; the denouement hinges on the sex of a personal pronoun. (Pamela Frankau 1970)

COLOR

(See BLACK, BROWN, RED, WHITE, WOMEN OF COLOR)

COLORBLINDNESS

Seemingly, the ignoring, or inability to notice, the color of people's skin. "I no longer believe that 'colorblindness' – if it even exists – is the opposite of racism; I think it is . . . a form of naivete and moral stupidity. It implies that I would look at a black woman and see her as white, thus engaging in white solipsism to the utter erasure of her particular reality." (Adrienne Rich 1978; rpt. 1979, 300)

COLORISM

"Prejudicial or preferential treatment of same-race people based solely on their color. . . . There is probably as much difference between the life of a black black woman and a 'high yellow' black woman as between a 'high yellow' woman and a white woman. . . . To me, the black black woman is our essential mother – the blacker she is the more us she is – and to see the hatred that is turned on her is enough to make me despair." (Alice Walker 1983, 290-1)

COLORS

Colors were important in the iconography of the suffrage movement. The use of the color *gold* began with Elizabeth Cady Stanton and Susan B. Anthony's campaign in Kansas in 1867 and derived from the color of the sunflower, the Kansas state symbol. Suffragists used gold pins, ribbons, sashes, and yellow roses to symbolize their cause. In 1876, during the U.S. Centennial, women wore yellow ribbons and sang the song "The Yellow Ribbon." In 1916, suffragists staged "The Golden Lane" and the national Democratic convention; to reach the convention hall, all delegates had to walk through a line of women stretching several blocks long, dressed in white with gold sashes, carrying yellow umbrellas, and accompanied by hundreds of yards of draped gold bunting. Gold also signified enlightenment, the professed goal of the mainstream U.S. suffrage movement. A second color theme was the use of the tricolors *purple, white, and green*, and later, when the National Woman's Party (NWP) was created and its colors selected, *purple, white, and gold*. These colors originated with the Women's Suffrage and Political Union (WSPU) in England; symbolizing loyalty, purity, and hope, they were brought to the U.S. by women who had worked in the British suffrage movement. The purple, white, and gold of the modern women's movement have their origins with the NWP. (Edith P. Mayo 1981) The nearly 100,000 women who marched in Washington, D.C., in 1978, in support of the Equal Rights Amendment, wore white, with pins, sashes, and ribbons of green, purple and gold. Green and white are the colors of the National Organization for Women. Lavender is a color associated with lesbians, and other woman-identified-women.

(See WEARING THE COLOURS)

COLOR-STRUCK

Is a term used within Black culture to denote the identification by people of color with Euro-American aesthetic and racial values. Black females sometimes make this charge of Black males who appear to have internalized, via work and personal relationships, white values. (John Langston Gwaltney 1980, xv)

COMBAHEE RIVER COLLECTIVE

A Black feminist group formed in 1974. The name comes from "the guerilla action conceptualized and led by Harriet Tubman on June 2, 1863, in the Port Royal region of South Carolina. This action freed more than 750 slaves and is the only military campaign in American history planned and led by a woman." (Combahee River Collective 1977; rpt. 1981, 210)

COMBAT

"Intended to improve the species by elimination of the unfit. Amusingly enough, or absurdly enough, when applied to society it eliminates the fit, and leaves the unfit to perpetuate the race! . . . The pick of the country, physically, is sent off to oppose the pick of another country, and kill – kill – kill! . . . It is a minor incident of life, belonging to low levels, and not of a developing influence socially." (Charlotte Perkins Gilman 1911, 223, 228)

COME OUT, TO

1. A young woman comes out when she is presented formally to society as a debutante; after this point, she may have social engagements with men. 2. A woman comes out [of the closet] when she openly acknowledges that she is a lesbian. She might come out in all settings, or only to selected groups (e.g., to friends but not at work).

COMING OUT

A process which involves naming oneself. "I did not have the word for lesbian when I was nine years old in 1951 . . . I did not know that I was coming out." (Janet Cooper) "The day I accepted my label I still didn't know the word lesbian. The label I accepted was homosexual." (C. J. Martin) "Gay-Lesbian-Dyke. These terms represent the changing self-image I ex-

perienced in the process of coming out."
(Patricia E. Hand; quoted in Julia
Penelope Stanley and Susan J. Wolfe
1980, xvix)

"To this day I wonder why it is not
called, 'coming home'. . . . It was the
most natural thing in the world. I wondered where I had been all my life."
(Sarah Lucia Hoagland 1980, 147)

"Gay people have a special kind of
loosening up; an act of self-affirmation we
call 'coming out.' Philosophically speaking, 'coming out' means Free To Be I and
Thou. It means the promise of Freedom,
Justice, and Dignity. . . . So I was
wondering, Mr. President [Reagan]: why
don't you 'come out'? Come out of
Central America. Come out of the
Caribbean. Yes, and while you're at it,
why don't you try coming out of the Arms
Race?" (Susie Day 1984a)

COMMANDMENT
An edict demanding obedience. If Moses
is to be believed there are ten basic
commandments. Isabella Beecher Hooker
pointed out that the fifth commandment
"Honor thy father and thy mother" can
not be obeyed as long as boys "are taught
by our laws and constitutions to hold all
women in contempt." (Isabella Beecher
Hooker 1870; quoted in Carol McPhee
and Ann Fitzgerald eds 1979, 32)

COMMITTEE OF TWELVE
A scheme outlined by Fanny Smart in
1915 for British women in each district to
organize, through committees, their own
protection from men during wartime.
(Fanny Smart 1915)

COMMON DIFFERENCES
Defined and applied by Gloria I. Joseph
and Jill Lewis in their groundbreaking
book, *Common Differences: Conflicts in Black
and White Feminist Perspectives* (1981). It
refers to the issues and themes that may
be common across racial, national, and
economic contexts for women, but which
simultaneously are very different in their
definition, impact and implications within
those contexts.

COMMON-LAW WIFE
Is the "veiled description employed by
newspaper columnists to describe a movie
actor's mistress, a gangster's moll, or any
other woman who is openly shacking up.
From a legal standpoint, the description
is totally incorrect." A common-law wife
is a legally married woman in those states
in the U.S. which recognize marriages
without a license, blood test or any third
person making the pronouncement, if the
woman and man consider themselves
married and live together as married.
(Barbara B. Hirsch 1973, 2)

COMMON WOMAN
"What is 'common' in and to women is
the intersection of oppression and strength,
damage and beauty. It is, quite simply,
the *ordinary* in women which will 'rise' in
every sense of the word – spiritually and
in activism. For us, to be 'extraordinary'
or 'uncommon' is to fail. . . . The 'common
woman' is in fact the embodiment of the
extraordinary will-to-survival in millions
of obscure women, a life-force which
transcends childbearing: unquenchable,
chromosomatic reality." (Adrienne Rich
1977; rpt. 1979, 255)

COMMUNICATIONS REVOLUTION
Is in fact an electronic era term that turns
the very word *communication* into a euphemism. It has promised something for
every constituency – every group that can
pay the cable bills, that is. "The main
effect of the new technologies is a growing
information gap – between the information
haves and the *have nots*." (Dee Dee Halleck
1983, 26)

Developments such as radio, communication satellites which are hailed as the
dawn of new eras in the nature of
communication. "But in fact, far from
entering a brave new world, many women
find themselves in a false dawn, facing
new and unfamiliar forms of old stereotypes about women's language and communication and, as new fields develop,
struggling not only to gain a foothold but
even to hold their own." (Cheris Kramarae
and Paula Treichler 1982)

COMMUNITY

"Community is simply the way people live a life together. And they're doing it all over the world. The only way to write for la comunidad is to write so completely from your heart what is your own personal truth. This is what touches people." (Friend of Cherríe Moraga; quoted in Cherríe Moraga 1983, vi)

Has collectivity at its core. The women's movement often stresses struggles for individualism, more than collectivity; this emphasis threatens Third World women, since collectivity is vital to Third World survival, and their biggest issue is survival of their communities. (Francisca James-Hernandez 1982, classroom discussion; reported by Barrie Thorne, correspondence)

COMPARABLE WORTH

Usually refers to a standard to eliminate discriminatory compensation systems, and to provide equal pay for equal work or equal pay for different jobs of comparable value. A term used in discussions of job segregation by gender and the resultant pay inequities, as well as efforts to change current salary structures to reflect real job value in the marketplace. (Jo Whitney, correspondence 1984, Durham, N.C.) Equitable job evaluation techniques could be used to eliminate discriminatory wage differentials within the [U.S.] federal civil service system. For example, in 1982, more than "62% of all women employed in white collar government jobs were in grades one through six, which pay less than $15,000 per year, while fewer than 20% of men held jobs in these lower-paying categories." (*National NOW Times* 1984, 17:3 [May/June], 1)

Shorthand for the following: "Women should get the same pay as men, not only when they are doing the same jobs as men, but when they are doing jobs of 'comparable worth' — jobs roughly equivalent in terms of skills, education and work conditions." (Ruth Walker 1984, *Champaign-Urbana News-Gazette*, Feb. 12, A-6)

(See EQUAL PAY)

COMPLACENCY

An ease. "A far more dangerous attitude than outrage." (Naomi Littlebear 1977; quoted by Gloria Anzaldúa 1981b)

COMPLETION COMPLEX

Dale Spender's term for the obsessive concern and argument of men that a woman is incomplete without a man. While it is possible for women to accept themselves as complete entities, the average man seems to believe that without a definite and physical relation to a man, a woman is merely raw material of womanhood — underdeveloped and unfinished. Scorn for this complex is found in the work of many feminists, including Cicely Hamilton and Charlotte Perkins Gilman. (Dale Spender 1982b *passim*)

(See PHALLOPANACEA)

COMPLIMENT

A statement of social judgment. Higher status speakers give most of the compliments, in non-reciprocal fashion. "You are looking very pretty today, Jane," says the boss. The great majority of compliments of appearance and possession (including children, friends) are directed to women. In these cases, the status of the women seems not to matter for they can be complimented in this way by virtually anyone. (Nessa Wolfson in press; in *Applied Linguistics*, special issue ed. by Elite Olshtain and Shoshana Blum-Kulka)

COMPROMISE

"Is commonly praised as an expedient pre-eminently British, almost exclusively masculine and . . . as the oil that makes the wheels go around and saves us from the violent rocking-horse movements by means of which nations unable to 'settle disputes by mutual concessions' achieve disturbance without making progress. The willingness to compromise is regarded rather than an heroic virtue. . . . [It means] almost any course of conduct from refraining from abuse of opponents to justifiable homicide. . . . The housemother of moderate means arranges enough compromises while her children are growing up to make a diplomatist's reputation for life." ("Problems of the Day" 1914, *The Englishwoman* 23:67 (July), 7, 9, 13)

COMPULSORY HETEROSEXUALITY

Refers to "the enforcement of heterosexuality for women as a means of assuring male right of physical, economical, and emotional access. One of the many means of enforcement is, of course, the rendering invisible of the lesbian possibility, an engulfed continent which rises fragmentedly to view from time to time only to become submerged again." (Adrienne Rich 1980, 647)

COMPUTER LITERACY

"A catchphrase that implies as a universal goal some knowledge or skill in analogy with literacy itself. But only rarely does anyone try to say what this might mean in practice.... It is [the] issue of *control* that is central to our understanding the limitations of the notion of computer literacy." Computer literacy programs "give the illusion of control but in reality present the technology as a given and ask people to learn to adjust to it. In none of its manifestations does computer literacy imply an examination of why the technology is being introduced and by whom. Nor do such programs explore the ways in which the technology itself could or should be changed. . . . Overall, computer literacy simply supports the status quo." (Margaret Lowe Benston 1984, 20-1)

A term that "bullies people into thinking that they are obsolete human beings if they do not admit to the incontrovertible necessity of the computer's eventual ubiquity." (Sharon LeBell 1983, *Women and Language News* 7:1, 9)

CONCLUSION

A final summary, usually made by men. An exception is the conclusion of the 1739 book *Woman Not Inferior to Man*: "[T]he worst of us deserve much better treatment than the best of us receive." (Sophia 1739, 62)

CONFESSIONAL WRITING

"There is no such *thing* as confessional poetry. Anne Sexton gets branded with that and it's absurd. I think it's a putdown term for women, a sexist label for women's poetry. People who use the term are falling into the subject-matter fallacy. Subject matter doesn't make a poem. And so a critic who uses that term is showing his total ignorance of what poetry is about." (Erica Jong 1975, 26) Julia [Penelope] Stanley adds that the label is "handy for dismissing art that the critic wishes to trivialize." (1976, 62)

"For centuries, women have written in a style which has been termed 'confessional,' using it for describing our own lives in private [in diaries and journals]; now we are bringing it forth as our art, as a dynamic affirmation of our newly acquired identities as whole women." (Julie Penelope (Stanley) and Susan J. Wolfe 1983, 135)

CONFLICT

A needed struggle for growth, inherent in all of life. Conflict is also one of the emotions women – in their work as mothers, daughters, wives, sisters and general helpmates – are made to feel guilty about experiencing. So we try to disguise it as depression, inadequacy, helplessness and other feelings, and if it seems to threaten the public presentation of sisterhood, we often deny its existence. Jean Baker Miller suggests an integrative approach to the concept: "We can think of conflict as a process between that which is beginning or new, and that which is old, or from which we are moving on. This conflict has been made difficult to perceive because we have been living within a structure which seeks to suppress all conflict in order to maintain a *status quo*. Such a structure has kept us from awareness of this most basic conflict, because it has to keep down all conflict." (Jean Baker Miller 1983, 8)

CONGRESSMAN

(See -MAN IN COMPOUNDS, WOMAN, Shirley Morahan)

CONQUEST

"Is not civilization, nor any part of it." (Charlotte Perkins Gilman 1911, 226)

(See COMBAT, WAR)

CONSCIOUSNESS

Feminist: Awareness and insightfulness "rooted in the concrete, practical, and everyday experiences of being, and being treated as *a woman*." (Liz Stanley and Sue Wise 1983, 18)

"Once experienced, cannot be denied." (Andrea Dworkin 1974, 18)

(See FEMINISM)

CONSCIOUSNESS-RAISING (CR)

Talk in small, supportive groups about women's experiences. Kathie Sarachild outlined the original program for "Radical Feminist Consciousness-Raising," presented at the First National Women's Liberation Conference near Chicago, November 27, 1968. (Redstockings 1975, 144). It is "the major technique of analysis, structure of organization, method of practice, and theory of social change of the women's movement. In consciousness raising, often in groups, the impact of male dominance is concretely uncovered and analyzed through the collective speaking of women's experience, from the perspective of that experience. (Catharine MacKinnon 1982, 519-20) It "is a valuable cornerstone of feminist theory and practice. But as a verbal exercise in self-examination and group sharing, it is also an approach with a class and race bias. White middle-class women are comfortable with a form that relies mainly on verbal skills. Women of other races and classes are not as comfortable in situations that stress group process . . . the formality of using CR as a technique for communication is stifling and intimidating to women who are accustomed to expressing themselves in many less defined and directed forms." (Beverly Fisher-Manick 1977; rpt. 1981, 158)

It is what happens when women translate their personal feelings into political awareness. (Anna Coote and Beatrix Campbell 1982, 14)

It is a process rooted in the belief that the theory we develop must come from our real, lived experience. (Terry Wolverton 1983, 188)

It was "one of the main ways to get involved in the women's liberation movement [in the late 1960s and early 1970s], and it's still as good a way as any. It was in these groups that 'the personal is political' slogan took on real meaning. Through talking together in a situation of mutual trust, women learned that what they had believed was a personal problem was in fact shared or understood by many other women." (Sona Osman 1983, 28)

(See PERSONAL IS POLITICAL)

It "is the permanent struggle against an ever impinging bourgeois ideology that attacks us not only in the form of political doctrine but also as fears, ambitions, resentments, feelings: the stuff of everyday political practice. Under its more congenial name of criticism and self-criticism, its universalization is recognized as one of the great achievements of the Chinese cultural revolution." (Rosario Morales 1973; rpt. 1975, 199)

In the nineteenth century an activity related to consciousness-raising took place as some women tried to spread messages counter to those spread by male governed institutions: "We had to adopt the method which physicians sometimes use, when they are called to a patient who is so hopelessly sick that he is unconscious of his pain and suffering. We had to describe to women their own position, to explain to them the burdens that rested so heavily upon them, and through these means, as a wholesome irritant, we roused public opinion on the subject, and through public opinion, we acted upon the Legislature." (Ernestine Rose 1860; quoted in Kathie Sarachild 1973; rpt. 1975, 146)

CONSUMPTION

In common usage it is the purchasing and usage of materials produced by industries: "For advertisers, that is why women exist." (Alice Embree 1970, 183)

CONSTITUTION

U.S. Constitution and Bill of Rights: Documents whose basic framework, structure and egalitarian ideals "were quite liberally 'borrowed' from a group of northeastern 'heathen savages' known as The Iroquois Confederacy. The complex system of self-government called *The Law of the Great Peace* practiced by a league of six tribal nations dates back to 950 A.D. . . . Can you imagine the outraged cries of protest that would ensue if, from tomorrow on, *every* fourth-, fifth-, and sixth-grader in this country were taught that the Constitution of the United States is a direct descendant of *The Great Law* of the Iroquois Indians?" (Carol Lee Sanchez 1983, 14)

CONTENTMENT

A state of considered well-being seldom experienced by most women. Christabel Pankhurst's answer to critics who ask when it is that women will settle down and be content: "Happily and mercifully there is no such thing. . . . If there were, no doubt we should all of us have remained as it is said we once were, primeval apes." (Christabel Pankhurst 1911; quoted in *Votes for Women*, Oct. 27, 53)

CONTINGENT LIFE

The existence experienced by those who "are more ambitious for brother, husband, or boss than for personal success." (Elizabeth J. Sherwood, September 1931b, 408)

CONTRACEPTION

Hazardous but often necessary birth control devices and techniques. "[B]arrier methods combined with abortion if the method fails are *on the average* safest. . . . Vasectomies and condoms are as safe for women as anything based on men's behavior can be. . . . To be reasonably sure of not conceiving, some women find they must abstain from heterosexual intercourse almost all of the time!" (Sona Osman 1983, 28)

CONTRACEPTIVE SPONGE

A contraceptive which "is just a way of making sex seem more like doing the dishes." (Elayne Boosler 1984; quoted in *Newsweek*, April 30, 59)

CONTRACEPTIVE TRAIN

The carriages taken by approximately 50 Dublin women, on May 22, 1971, to Belfast where they purchased contraceptives (banned in the Irish Republic), and returned home to a supporting crowd and customs men who tried to ignore the display of purchases. (June Levine 1982)

CONVENT

An institution which implies a reason for woman's existence other than sexual intercourse and reproduction and, with all its defects, has stood for the advancement of women. (Cicely Hamilton 1909, 87)

(See NUN)

CONVERSATION

Social interaction which constructs reality. Women's same-sex conversations often serve as a satisfying, cooperative expression of affiliation, a state which may seem a danger to men. (Pamela Fishman 1977; Cheris Kramarae 1981) Men have more say in mixed-sex interaction; they are more likely to treat women as conversation pieces rather than as conversationalists. Because women spend more time listening and observing than do men who control, women hear and see things men do not.

(See GOSSIP, INTUITION)

Social interaction which requires at least two people. "Conversation is produced not simply by their presence, but also by the display of their continuing agreement to pay attention to one another. That is, all interactions are potentially problematic and occur only through the continual, turn-by-turn, efforts of the participants. Conversation is work." "Women are more actively engaged in insuring interaction than are the men. They ask more questions and use more attention beginnings [such as 'This is really interesting']. Women do support work while the men are talking and it is the women who generally do active maintenance and continuation work in conversations. The men . . . do much less active work when they begin or participate in interactions. They rely on statements, which they assume will get responses. They much more often discourage interactions initiated by women than vice versa." (Pamela Fishman 1983, 90, 98)

Is a complex process of communication in mixed-sex groups when women find that even being as neutral as possible, offering neither support nor rebuff, "can be seen as an unfriendly gesture by many men who in a patriarchal order are accustomed to conversational deference, who are used to having their topics taken up with interest by women, [and] who are used to being given the floor – and undivided attention." (Dale Spender 1980, 45)

Informal talk which has its own norms about leaving of spaces and interruptions. Jewish women are sometimes told 'You talk like a man.' It's not 'male' it's Jewish – talking at the same time, interrupting, 4 people and 5 opinions. A kind of talk that's devalued in the women's movement when it comes up against some other modes of talk. (Sharon Silverstein 1982, classroom discussion; reported by Barrie Thorne, correspondence)

"Men tend to give you a speech, whereas women will ask a question and then listen for the answer and make another contribution to the dialogue. In countless situations I have a male in my audience stand up and in effect say I don't know what you're arguing about, here's the answer to this thing. And then proceed to give a mini-speech that I feel he wants written in granite. If you're in a social situation and women are gathered talking to each other, and one woman says, 'I was hit by a car today,' all the other women will say, 'You're kidding! What happened? Where? Are you all right?' The same situation with males, and one male says, 'I was hit by a car today.' I guarantee you there will be another male in that group who will say,

Wait until I tell you what happened to *me*." (Phil Donahue 1982; in an interview with Gloria Steinem, 1982 *Ms.*, October, 36)

(See COLLABORATIVE TALK)

COOKIES

"1. Combustibles. The amount and frequency of their appearance (if homemade) is directly proportional to a mother's love for her children and husband, as perceived by them. Absence of homemade cookies has been documented as a cause of guilt in working parents (females are afflicted 99 times more often than males), even though the store-bought kind is often preferred by their offspring. 2. One of the many food metaphors for women (sweetie, creampuff, dish, cheesecake, tomato, pumpkin, cupcake, plum, peach, cheesecake) exemplifying the oral fixation men are subject to." (Brinlee Kramer 1984, manuscript)

COOKING

Producing meals to be consumed, a task done primarily by women although husbands/boyfriends/fathers may be "very good really" helping the cooks with carrying heavy shopping bags, preparing vegetables, switching on the oven when told, doing the dishes afterwards. Even if this help is offered on a regular basis, it is not regarded as men doing the cooking; for a man, competence in the kitchen may be suspect. (Anne Murcott 1983, 82)

A reassuringly predictable activity. "What I love about cooking is that after a hard day, there is something comforting about the fact that if you melt butter and add flour and then hot stock, *it will get thick*! It's a sure thing! It's a sure thing in a world where nothing is sure." (Nora Ephron 1983, 167)

COOKS

People who prepare food for eating; they are usually female except for the cooks in prestigious restaurants. We are told that women who are good cooks can win love and admiration from men. Charlotte Perkins Gilman advised that "This is one of the roaring jokes of history. The breakers of hearts, the queens of romance, the goddesses of a thousand devotees, have not been cooks." (Charlotte Perkins Gilman 1903; quoted in Carol McPhee and Ann Fitzgerald eds 1979, 53)

COOK-UP

A dish hastily prepared, usually by males, consisting of rice, meat, vegetables, and other left-overs. Virgin Islands English Creole. (Lito Valls 1981, 29)

CORN WOMAN/CORN MOTHER

"Corn Mother gave the people life in some tribes' emergence tales. She is part of the first stories because she taught the people how to grow corn, how to domesticate it in many varieties, how to preserve life. She is the essential female symbol." (Rayna Green 1984, 307)

CORRECTNESS

Women are said to be more correct in their speech than men. In this exchange, male and female twins embody this stereotype as they argue about slang:

"There are lots of things you wouldn't dare say before everybody," averred Dora.
"No, there isn't."
"There is, too. Would you," demanded Dora gravely, "would you say 'tomcat' before the minister?"
This was a staggerer. Davy was not prepared to supply a concrete example of the freedom of speech. But one did not have to be consistent with Dora.
"Of course not," he admitted sulkily.
" 'Tomcat' isn't a holy word. I wouldn't mention such an animal before a minister at all."
"But if you had to?" persisted Dora.
"I'd call it a Thomas pussy," said Davy.
"I think 'gentleman cat' would be more polite," reflected Dora
"*You* thinking!" retorted Davy with withering scorn.

(L. M. Montgomery 1915, 132)
Traditional proper behavior. Especially demanded of but seldom accredited to mothers.

"Once my mother phoned me and said, 'Oh, why did the mother in your story have to be so slangy?' "
" 'It's not you, Mama.' "
" 'But why the mother? Since it's all fiction anyway, the mother didn't have to be the slipshod speaker, did she?' " (Jessamyn West 1979, 11)
(See ENGLISH/CORRECT, MISS FIDDITCH)

COSMETICS

A mask, used primarily by women, which can be an aid for performances of various kinds, even for appearing a conventional woman. (*Banshee: Journal of Irishwomen United* c.1980, 1:2, 14)
(See MASK)
Method of changing appearance. Make-up may not have identical meanings in different cultures. For example, it may be used to challenge notions of pure and natural womanhood. (Jayne Egerton 1983, 30)
1. "Man-made chemicals that clog your pores and make your eyelashes fall out; 2. Sweet-smelling potions and decorations for the face and body, which help a woman transform herself into the exotic gypsy or shy wood nymph she desires to be that day." (Brinlee Kramer 1984, notebook)
"Modern war paint." (Mary Ellen Shanesey 1984, conversation)
"The persistent need I have to make myself 'attractive,' to fix my hair and put on lipstick – is it the false need of a chauvinized woman, encouraged since infancy to identify her values as a person with her attractiveness in the eyes of men? Or does it express a wholesome need to express love for one's own body by adoring it, a behaviour common in primitive societies, allowed us but denied to men in our own still-puritan culture?" (Sandra Lee Bartky 1975, 29)

COUNTRY

Is an entity personified by a woman (Marianne, Germania, Britannia, Columbia) whereas male national figures (John Bull, Uncle Sam, even the Russian

Bear) represent national governments (matters of taxation, diplomacy, war) rather than countries – an important distinction. In other words, the country is romanticized as a love object, a woman, to fight for, while the serious work of fighting is done by man. (Wolfgang Lederer; cited by Varda One 1971b, 12)

(See AMERICAN FRONTIER)

" 'For,' the outsider will say, 'in fact, as a woman, I have no country. As a woman I want no country. As a woman my country is the whole world.' " (Virginia Woolf 1938, 109)

(See OUTSIDERS SOCIETY)

COURAGE

"To be courageous, means to be afraid but to go a little step forward anyway. If you say, 'I'm not afraid of anything,' that's white boy bullshit." (Beverly Smith; cited in Jill Clark 1981, 14)

COURTESY

"The name given to such practices as a man helping a woman into her coat, leading her through crowded places or into a restaurant, opening her doors – the same as mothers do for their children. See it this way and you know how men look on women." (Heidi Reindl-Scheuering 1984, correspondence)

COURTESY TITLES

"1. A news media term for the prerogative that news editors assume to label and name women, through terms designating gender and marital status and choices about first and last names. 2. A misnomer for a practice that pretends women should be shown special politeness but that actually impolitely appropriates women's right to name themselves. 3. A site of struggle between feminists and the news media over the power to name." (Lana Rakow 1984, correspondence)

(See FORMS OF ADDRESS)

COURTLY LOVE

A male preoccupation with love and courtesy which made an appearance in European languages in 12th century po-

etry. One theory holds that the concept of courtly love originated in the Islamic culture. The term was introduced in the 19th century by Gaston Paris. In the typical courtly love situation, the poet expresses his adoration and desire for a Fair Maiden of indescribable beauty and perfection. "Transformed by the power of love into her faithful vassal, the self-effacing lover hopes for some sign of her affection. But, being cold of heart, she ordinarily fails to respond to his entreaties . . . she is never portrayed as a flesh-and-blood human being, with the emotions and cares of real life. . . . [She] is the creation of a set of powerful feminine stereotypes, which typecast women as beautiful, morally superior, pure, youthful, and delicate – but also as fickle, even treacherous. . . . It is not uncommon to find that the beloved is described in extremely hostile, obscene language." (Elizabeth Judd, in press)

(See CHIVALRY)

COURTSHIP

In traditional terms this means male pursuit of a woman who is considered the passive courted. This tradition "is still very much a ruling factor and pervades not only the relationship in courtship, but in obvious or subtle forms invades the majority of the relationships between men and women." (John W. Herring 1931, 151)

COUVADE

From French *couver*, to hatch, sit on (eggs) and Latin *cubâre*, to lie down (on). A practice in which men pretend they are having a baby at the time their mates *are* giving birth.

CRAFT

A term used by men to demote, from fine art, the work of women who use fabric and stitches rather than paint. (Marsha Rowe 1982, 259)

(See ART)

CRAMPS

A male-dominated religion that keeps

women out of decision-making processes; a problem once thought to be located in the head, now located in the prostaglandin release which causes uterine contractions. This was so ordained by the *New England Journal of Medicine* in 1971 (yes, 1971) after centuries of women's suffering. (Mary Ellen Shanesey 1983, correspondence)

"An abdomenable pain." (Jana Kramer 1984, personal reminiscence)

"Pain caused by a rudimentary third fist in the abdomen which squeezes your uterus." (Brinlee Kramer 1984, "Blood, Blood," unpublished manuscript)

CRAZY LADIES

Warriors rather than victims. " 'Crazy ladies' and 'wasted women' hold particular appeal to some Asian American women writers because they are often strong and creative women who are both rebels and seers, despite the fact that they are not appreciated fully by those around them." "It is the memory of them that lingers on to challenge the smug complacency of those who consider themselves normal." (Elaine H. Kim 1982, 253, 255)

"I thought every house had to have its crazy woman or crazy girl, every village its idiot. Who would it be at our house? Probably me. . . . I was messy, my hair tangled and dusty. My dirty hands broke things: . . . And there were adventurous people inside my head to whom I talked whenever I was frivolous, violent, orphaned." (Maxine Hong Kingston 1977, 220-1)

CREATION

Creation of the universe was envisioned by polytheistic religions "as a process and product of sexual unions between goddesses and gods. . . . The primary divine source of life was presented as female." (Judith Ochshorn 1981, 139)

CREATIVE

A political term, closely aligned with "original," "innovative," "first rank" and "excellent," used to maintain and justify a male monopoly on intelligence. A "term used by the gatekeepers to exclude women

from entry in the 'worthwhile' records of our society." (Dale Spender 1982b, 21)

CRECHE

A nursery where children can associate with other children. Caretaking supported by the state only when women are wanted in the work force.

CREEDS

Interpretations and symbols "built up by men – generally of no great education or enlightenment – at times of hot controversy . . ." (Winifred Holtby to her mother Alice 1923; quoted in Karen Payne 1983, 167)

CRICKET

A game: "Male idleness elevated into religion." (Zoë Fairbairns 1979, 44)
(See FOOTBALL)

CRIME

The "tragic" and gruesome stories reported by "middle-class reporters employed by upper-class media owners entertaining/shocking their listeners. . . . When one realizes that tragedy is used only to be exploited, to sell aspirin, tranquilizers and burglar alarms, and to blame the poor for their situation of unemployment and poverty, one begins to understand the classism and racism pervading the U.S. criminal 'justice' system. For the 'justice' system, as practiced today, is truly *criminal*." (Marianne Stewart 1984, 20)

CRITIC, ART

"Has today assumed an unprecedented importance, reconsidering and assessing the theories and premises upon which modern art is based. Her or his voice is that of authority, though nevertheless dependent upon and considered secondary to the artist, who in turn needs critical notice to survive professionally." (Rozsika Parker 1983, 88)
(See ART)

CRITICISM, LITERARY

"A radical critique of literature, feminist in its impulse, would take the work first of all as a clue to how we live, how we have been living, how we have been led to imagine ourselves, how our language has trapped as well as liberated us, how the very act of naming has been till now a male prerogative, and how we can begin to see and name – and therefore live – afresh. . . . We need to know the writing of the past, and know it differently than we have ever known it; not to pass on a tradition but to break its hold over us." (Adrienne Rich 1972; rpt. 1979, 35)

CRITICS, LITERARY

Usually males who are the judges of the "moral sex values which are contained in Literature [and] exert an influence so pervasive that there can be little change in moral estimates as long as such implied standards remain unquestioned. . . . Women have been almost exclusively readers and portrayers, and very rarely [accepted by males] as critics." ("The Freewoman" 1911, *Votes for Women*, Nov. 17, 103, 104)

CRITIQUE

In masculinist strategy: "Starts off with a positive definition of the self and opposes to it a negatively defined 'other.' " Feminist model: Begins with an effort to understand the 'other,' an effort to avoid self-righteous comparison. (Marvat Hatem 1984, 5)

CRONES

"The Great Hags of history, when their lives have not been prematurely terminated, have lived to be Crones. . . . They are the Survivors of the perpetual witch-craze of patriarchy, the Survivors of The Burning Times." (Mary Daly 1978, 16)
   (See HAG)

CRONE'S NEST

A Community for Older Women, sponsored by the women of the Pagoda Temple of Love, a spiritual and cultural center for all women, located since July 7, 1977, in St. Augustine, Florida. The Crone's Nest is a project which hopes to provide a place for women to grow old

and die together. It is described as "a place affirming in its processes the self-determination of each woman within . . . a place where the wisdom of elder women is celebrated; wherein an elder woman may lead as active, as purposeful, as vocal – or as quiet and contemplative – a life as she wills." (*Matrices* 1983, 6:2, 18-19)

CROSS

"Now the primary symbol of Christianity, [it] was not shown in Christian art until six centuries after Christ. But long before the Christian era it was a pagan religious symbol throughout Europe and western Asia. . . . The cross was also a male symbol of the phallic Tree of Life; therefore it often appeared in conjunction with the female-genital circle or oval, to signify the sacred marriage." (Barbara G. Walker 1983, 188)

CROSS-DRESSING

Wearing clothing that is associated with the other sex in such quantity and detail to make it possible to be mistaken for a member of the other sex. Women and men have been cross-dressing for centuries, sometimes in order to participate in activities otherwise closed to them. "In my opinion there was nothing essentially improper in my putting on the uniform of a Confederate officer for the purpose of taking an active part in the war; and, as when on the field of battle, in camp, and during long and toilsome marches, I endeavored, not without success, to display a courage and fortitude not inferior to the most courageous of the men around me, and as I never did aught to disgrace the uniform I wore, but, on the contrary, won the hearty commendation of my comrades, I feel that I have nothing to be ashamed of." (Loreta Janeta Velasquez 1876, 6)

CUCKOLD

The husband of an unfaithful wife. The wife of an unfaithful husband is just called *wife*.

CULT OF TRUE WOMANHOOD

A concept governing women's activities in

the 19th and 20th centuries. "A compound of four ideas: a sharp dichotomy between the home and the economic world outside that paralleled a sharp contrast between female and male natures, the designation of the home as the female's only proper sphere, the moral superiority of women, and the idealization of her function as mother." (Barbara Harris 1978, 33)

CULTURAL FEMINISM

"Changes the focus of the women's movement from winning our freedom to being a 'good person.' It promotes the therapy model of liberation . . . and replaces political organizing with moral rearmament." (Brooke 1975; in Sara Scott 1983, 25)

"In 1973, I defined cultural feminism as 'the belief that women will be freed via an alternate women's culture.' The definition still applies and cultural feminism still controls the movement, but it is far less benign than it was then. The matriarchal tendency has grown much stronger and spread throughout the women's movement. . . . Cultural feminism has evolved into spirituality and goddess-worshipping cults, disruptive 'dyketactics' groups and – more peacefully – academic cultural feminism, the main activity of which seems to be reading novels by women. Cultural feminism is an ideology. . . . As a radical feminist I base my politics on the fact that men oppress women; this is a *basic* oppression common to all economic systems and classes, races, countries and other groups throughout history, The only historically effective way of *mitigating*, much less *ending*, the situation is a strong independent mass movement of women whose goal is women's liberation from male supremacy. I would add that the solution to male supremacy lies in revolutionary feminist change and to accomplish this a movement must be political and radical." (Brooke 1980, 70)

(See WOMEN'S MOVEMENT)

CULTURAL FEMINISTS

Women who "emphasize building a powerful female culture with all the necessary accouterments: music, art, poetry, films, religion, science, medicine – all female based. . . . They are often outspokenly antiauthoritarian, antileadership, and antistructure." (Lucia Valeska 1975; rpt. 1981, 25)

(See FEMINISM, WOMEN'S MOVEMENT, WOMANIST)

CULTURAL SADISM

"An ideology that permeates thinking and attitudes so deeply that its consequences (in the practice of sadism or masochism, for example) are assumed to be to some degree normal if not biologically determined.)" (Kathleen Barry 1980, 308)

CULTURE

"No longer organically reflects us, it is not our sum total, it is not the collective phenomenology of our creative possibilities – it possesses and rules us, reduces us, obstructs the flow of sexual and creative energy and activity, penetrates even into what Freud called the id, gives nightmare shape to natural desire." (Andrea Dworkin 1974, 157)

"Is not really something I have a choice in keeping or discarding. It is in me and of me. Without it I would be an empty shell and so would anyone else. There was a psychology experiment carried out once in which someone was hypnotized and first told they had no future; the subject became happy and careless as a child. When they were told they had no past they became catatonic." (Judit Moschkovich 1981, 82)

Western: "Is based on Judaeo-Christianity, a bit of Greek transcendentalism via the father of lies, Plato, and . . . other bits and pieces." (Angela Carter 1983, 72-3)

Western: "Is in love with death, in which the powerful and the privileged – be it class, race, or sex – cling onto their topdog status by fashioning their rapacity and greed into Romance." (Noel Greig 1983, 79)

CUNNILINGUS

Oral-genital stimulation, "something that is done *to* a woman – an act not requiring her active engagement as fellatio does; and one, therefore, not quite so incongruent with her socialization to passivity." (Lillian Rubin 1976, 140)

A tonguetwister. (graffiti cited by Rachel Bartlett 1982)

CUNNING STUNTS

A London-based theatre group.

CUNT

"In ancient writings, the word for 'cunt' was synonymous with 'woman,' though not in the insulting modern sense." "From the same root came county, kin, and kind . . . Other cognates are 'cunabula,' a cradle, or earliest abode; 'Cunina,' a Roman Goddess who protected children in the cradle; 'cunctipotent,' all powerful (i.e., having cunt-magic); 'cunicle,' a hole or passage; 'cuniculate,' penetrated by a passage; 'cundy,' a covered culvert; also cunning, kenning, and ken: knowledge, learning, insight, remembrance, wisdom." (Barbara G. Walker 1983, 197)

(See CHANA)

Given in Eric Partridge as *c*nt*, the word dates back at least to Middle English and is from the same root as *cuneiform*, from *cuneus* "wedge." Partridge writes that "owing to its powerful sexuality, the term has, since the 15th century, been avoided in written and in polite spoken English," and has been held to be obscene since about 1700, making it a legal offence to print it in full. Even playwrights and dictionary-makers courageous where other language was concerned, found ways of avoiding the word. J. S. Farmer and W. E. Henley (1890-1904) provide a brief entry under *cunt* but place their major entry for the word under the heading *monosyllable*, where hundreds of synonyms are listed. Partridge notes that even James Murray of the *Oxford English Dictionary* did not include it, though he included *prick*: "Why this further injustice to women?" (Eric Partridge 1961, 198)

CUNT ART

A term used by some women artists to describe their new female imagery, "in celebration of the discovery that not all sexual symbols are phallic." (Gloria Steinem 1983, 154)

(See BLOOD PRINTS)

CUNTIONARY

An alternative to dic-tionary. (Suggested by a post-graduate anthropology student at University of Sussex for the title of this dictionary, 1983)

CURSE

One of the flood of menstrual expressions. Others are "falling off the roof," "on the rag," "riding the rag," "have the rag on," and "ride the cotton pony" or "the cotton bicycle." Women may have "a red-letter day," say "I'm Bloody Mary today," or "the Red Sea's out." Except for "time of flower" (American Indian) and "Eve's blessing" most of the expressions are negative, intended either to hide the subject or be overly gross. The terminology reflects the historically widely circulated patriarchal idea that menstruation is an offense against God and Man. (Janice Delaney, Mary Jane Lupton and Emily Troth 1977)

(See MENSTRUATION)

Slang words for periods and for news-reporting are combined in the titles of several feminist publications such as *Red Rag* (a women's communist periodical), *Big Mama Rag*, *Women's Monthly*, and *Monthly Cycle* (from Lawrence, Kansas). A related title is *Hot Flash* (a newsletter for midlife and older women).

CUSTOM

"That merciless torrent that carries all before it. . . . [T]he grand motive to all those irrational choices which we daily see made in the World, so very contrary to our *present* interest and pleasure, as well as to our Future." "An unaccountable Authority, that she who would endeavor to put a stop to its Arbitrary Sway and reduce it to Reason, is in a fair way to render her self the Butt for all of the Fops in Town to shoot their impertinent Censures at." (Mary Astell 1694, 30-1, 82)

Practice linked to prejudice. "It is enough for the Men to find a thing establish'd to make them believe it well grounded." (Sophia 1739, 35)

CUSTOM-MADE WOMAN BLUES

The lament of women "trying to find some sense and meaning to our lives after such long years of working to find it through our men or through society's definition of womanhood." The title of a song by Alice Gerrard. (Alice Gerrard; quoted in Sheila Rowbotham 1975, in Rowbotham 1983, 262)

(See BLUES)

CUTESIPATE

"To trivialize the concerns of women by seeming to indulge them, 'poking gentle fun' at them." (Suzette Haden Elgin 1981, 3)

CYCLICITY

Usually refers to the monthly changes of the lining of the uterus, the endometrium, which ordinarily culminates in menstruation. "Some diurnal as well as larger interval cyclicity has been reported in males in a variety of species, including humans. The differences in patterns of cyclicity between females and males have been shown by measuring blood levels of the (so called, sex) hormones in various species, though information in this area is far from complete. Most of the information, however, concerning the mechanisms of the regulations of cyclicity in females comes from investigation of rodents." (Ruth Bleier 1984, 83-4)

(See SEX HORMONES)

DADDY

(See FATHER)

DALKON SHIELD

A tiny piece of plastic manufactured by A. H. Robins, the largest-selling and most dangerous intrauterine device ever marketed. It can cause infection, infertility, hysterectomy, and death. The longer it stays in, the greater the chance of development of pelvic inflammatory disease. A. H. Robins has announced a recall of the Dalkon Shield. (Sybil Shainwald 1984, 6)

DANCE

1. A skill at which women have excelled.
2. Complex social events. "Those dances [in 1912] were by no means the mere gay functions they seemed; they were supposed to test out the marriageable qualities of the young women on the basis of their popularity as dancing partners." (Vera Brittain 1933, 50-1)

"An important activity of the Old Religion. It represented a reunion with nature. It was a rite, an act of adoration to the Goddess. On the great Sabbats when whole villages met together to celebrate, there was ritual dancing and feasting. The church recognized dance as an integral part of the Old Religion, so they condemned it as an invention of the devil. In 589 the third council of Toledo forbade people to dance in churches on saints days, but dancing in churchyards continued throughout the Middle Ages." (Susan Paxton 1982, 8)

A swing through history. "If I can't dance, I don't want to be part of your revolution." (Emma Goldman)

D & C

"Divide and conquer – that's what they try to do to any group trying to make social change. I call it D & C. Black people are supposed to turn against Puerto Ricans. Women are supposed to turn against their mothers and mothers-in-law. We're all supposed to compete with each other for the favors of the ruling class." (Florynce Kennedy; in Gloria Steinem 1973, 89)

DANGEROUS DRUGS

Includes the barbituates and tranquilizers Valium and Librium prescribed by doctors to help women "cope." Drugs that in western countries would only be prescribed as a last resort, or that have been declared unsafe, are dumped in the Third World by drug companies in search of quick profits. (Sona Osman 1983, 29)

DARK AGES

What men call the "Dark Ages" appears almost enlightened for some people. At least the upper-class women depicted in historical documents had rights, alternatives, and power which those living in the late medieval or early modern period did not. (Sheila C. Dietrick 1980, 32, 43)

DATA

"Everything is data. But data isn't everything." (Pauline Bart, in press)

DATE/DATING

A ritual of western culture in which a female and a male make appointments to meet at a specified time. In those societies which practice compulsory heterosexuality, girls and boys are supposed to show interest in dating during their teenage years.

(See COMPULSORY HETERO-SEXUALITY)

DAUGHTER

A female in a relationship to a parent. "Women of every race, ethnicity, religion, region, and historical period write stories about mothers and daughters, and the similarities among the stories are greater than the differences because what we share as women, at least in terms of this primary relationship, is more than whatever else divides us." (Susan Koppelman ed. 1985, xv)

"Todavía soy la hija de mi mamá. Keep thinking, *it's the daughters.* It's the daughters who remain loyal to the mother. She is the only woman we stand by. It is not always reciprocated. To be free means on some level to cut that painful loyalty when it begins to punish us . . . Free the daughter to love her own daughter. It is the daughters who are my audience." (Cherríe Moraga 1983, vii)

DAUGHTER-RIGHT

A term coined by Janice Raymond in response to the chasm between mothers and daughters created by patriarchy. Mary Daly uses the word this way: "Daughter-Right names the right to re-claim our original movement, to re-call our Selves. . . . When we reach the Daughter within the mother we break the bindings of our false inheritance; we cut our ties to the institution of patriarchal motherhood. . . . When a woman comes to recognize the Daughter in her Self, in the mother, she comes into touch with her true tradition." *Daughterhood* has a universality which *motherhood* lacks; *all* mothers are daughters. (Mary Daly 1978, 347)

DAWN

Emergence, the beginning. The name of an Australian equal rights periodical.

DAY CARE

Institutions which "buy women off. They ease the immediate pressure without asking why that pressure is on WOMEN." (Shulamith Firestone 1970, 233)

DEAR

One of the so-called terms of endearment used primarily in addressing females. It carries "the implication that the addressee is in some way subordinate to the speaker. It is extremely interesting that there are cases in which women are addressed by these 'intimate' forms while men are not, but that we do not find the opposite occurring. It is perhaps this which so many women find irritating about the form *dear.*" (Nessa Wolfson and Joan Manes 1980, 91)

(See FORMS OF ADDRESS, HONEY)

"Nobody really likes to be called a dear. There is something so very faint and dull about it." (Barbara Pym 1952, 128)

DEAR READER

Was the winning entry in the 1982 contest to find a nonsexist, natural substitute for *Gentlemen* (*Dear Sir or Madam*, etc.) as a salutation in a letter to someone in an organization whose name and title you don't know. (Albert Joseph 1983, 14)

DEATH

An important part of the historical experience of women since so much of the actual care of those sick and dying has fallen to women. Historian Gerda Lerner points out the very different relationships women and men have toward death: "Men experienced death by seeking it out or confronting it alone or in a predominantly male context: on sea voyages, in Indian fighting, in wars. Women encountered death in the home or went out to bring home their wounded and dying men during wartime. . . . There was, of course, one particularly female mode of the death experience: in pregnancies, abortions, and during and after childbirth. . . . One can only guess at the effect upon the psychology of women exerted by the inevitable connection between sexual activity and consequent pregnancy, at a time when it was much more likely for a woman to die in childbirth than it was for a man to die violently in war. In the centuries before soldiers were drafted, a man meeting death on the battlefield or in Indian warfare usually had made a choice in the matter. Women's way of death, like women's lives, was cast in a passive mold" (1977, 147-9).

The theme of death, especially the death of children, appears in women's embroidery samples, in needlepoint paintings, in diaries and in correspondence among women friends and between husbands and wives. In general, though, women of the past did not write very freely of their feelings; they were taught to think of others, not themselves. This is one reason that Dorothy Parker's obsession with death, embedded in the mechanics of her verbal style, seems unusual. When she worked for *Vanity Fair* she subscribed to two trade magazines for undertakers. Her books have funeral titles: *Sunset Gun*, *Enough Rope*, *Laments for the Living*, *Death and Taxes*, *Not so Deep as a Well*, *Here Lies*. She claimed to have named her characters from phone books and obituary columns. Her verses are filled with bones, shrouds, weeds, graves, linen, ghosts, worms. "People ought to be one of two things," she wrote, "young or old. No; what's the good of fooling? People ought to be one of two things, young or dead" (Parker 1973, 596). She attempted suicide. Death is a crucial element in many of her stories, including the humorous ones. Likewise, humor was for her a not unthinkable element of death.

When Parker was at her husband's funeral, a woman who didn't much like her came up and asked if there were anything she could do. "Get me a new husband," said Parker. After a stunned silence, the woman retorted: " 'I think that is the most callous and disgusting remark I ever heard in my life.' Dottie turned to look at her, sighed, and said gently, 'So sorry. Then run down to the corner and get me a ham and cheese on rye and tell them to hold the mayo.' " (Lillian Hellman 1970; quoted in Paula Treichler 1980, 55-6)

DE-BIOGRAPHER

An historian who proves that any claims made about remarkable women are really only myths and who returns women to the silence he thinks proper for a woman. (Angeline Goreau 1980; in Dale Spender 1982, 26)

DECENCY

"Is a rather dirty thing. It is responsible for more indecency than anything else in the world. It is a string of taboos. You must not mention this: you must not appear conscious of that: you must not meddle with the other – at least, not in public. And the consequence is that everything that must not be mentioned in public [such as the possibility of women serving in important governmental positions] is mentioned in private as a naughty joke." (George Bernard Shaw 1909, 112)

DE-DIKING THE APARTMENT

Is what lesbians do before the visit of parents or a friend who don't yet know. (Kate Clinton 1982a)

DEFINITION

The statement of the explicit, distant significance of a word, phrase or term. Making definitions is a powerful act expressing confidence in one's perceptions; women and children are not encouraged in this activity.

Traditionally, a definition "takes precedence of experience. A certain uniform type is assumed, varying doubtless in individuals, but basically recognisable, independently of race, period and environment; and any divergence from this accepted and restricted type is regarded as abnormal, undesirable, and even dangerous." (Catherine Osler 1913, 52) *A Feminist Dictionary* is a protest of, and a beginning correction of, this state of affairs.

"Is a process as various and capable of change and 're-vision' as the process of language. We know that to judge a 'correct' definition, we need first to decide what purpose we have for defining, then to evaluate what method would most aptly meet that purpose, and finally to consider the site and audience for the definition. When I ask which definition is correct, we know that 'the correct answer' must be 'that all depends.' " (Shirley Morahan 1981, 53)

DEPENDENCY

Is more accurately called *subordination* if it is not reciprocal. Women are often inaccurately called the excessively dependent sex. "It's true that we learn to fear the 'destructive' consequences of our strivings for autonomy and self-determination. But the problem is not, nor has it ever been, our 'excessive dependency.' " (Harriet E. Lerner 1982, *Ms.* Nov., 9)

DEPO-PROVERA

"An injectible birth control method which suppresses ovulation. Because of its effects, which can include permanent infertility, irregular bleeding, and possible cancer, it has, until now, not been approved by the FDA for use in the United States, but has been used extensively in other countries" especially imposed on women of Third World countries. (Nancy Breeze 1984, 48)

(See BIRTH CONTROL)

DEPRECIATION

Belittling. One of the many devices to deny/resist/ignore the sexual caste system. "It is intended to make gynocide seem less important than the other atrocities of phallocracy." "The device of depreciation basically is the deceptive minimizing of gynocide and the cutting down of women's hopes and ambitions. Feminists are well aware of the condoning of rape and woman-battering that prevails in patriarchy. Less obvious is the disparagement of our powers and aspirations, and the seduction of women into cooperation in this Self-belittling." (Mary Daly 1984, 320)

DEPRESSION

An illness which is caused by a variety of physical and environmental factors. A lowness often produced by a pressing down from "superior" forces. Sometimes also an addiction – "the most acceptable way of living out a female existence, since the depressed cannot be held responsible, doctors will prescribe us pills, alcohol offer its blanket of blankness." (Adrienne Rich 1974; rpt. 1979, 122)

Is a stone at the bottom of the throat that in no way hampers speech or action; it makes all speech appear useless. (Jessamyn West 1979, 451)

"A psychiatric label that . . . hides the social fact of the housewife's loneliness, low self-esteem, and work dissatisfaction." (Ann Oakley 1982, 176)

Unexpressed anger. For example, "The media culture engenders in women a lot of unexpressed anger [and depression]. We need to work with the empowerment which can come from women's anger." (Julia Lesage 1982)

"A condition called in Victorian times *melancholy* which seemed to be more peculiar to middle- and upper-class women, or it could be that their melancholy was recorded whereas the condition of the working class women was not considered." (Roisin Boyd c.1982, 6)

DESPAIR

"The worst betrayal, the coldest seduction: to believe at last that the enemy will prevail." (Marge Piercy; in Peggy Kornegger 1979, 248)

DEVELOPMENT

A term used frequently to describe the changes in the countries in Africa, Asia and Latin America. The term is inadequate in describing how changes develop in quite different ways for women and men. For example: "While economic development of a sort has been taking place [in India] the discrepancy between the conditions for males and females has been widening. Among infants, females die at higher rates than males." "In India, and globally, women are displaced from income-earning opportunities with technological progress or other forms of 'modernization.' " A wide gap between males and females occurs in literacy rates in India and elsewhere. According to the 1981 Pakistan census, 35% of all men and

16% of all women can read and write.
(*Asian Monitor* Jan. 6, 1984)

DEVIL

A necessary component in male religion
because a God without an adversary is
inconceivable to the masculine mind.
(Charlotte Perkins Gilman 1911, 142)

DEXTERITY, MANUAL

"Is strategically called a woman's talent.
Such explanations are used to restrict the
work available to women, to classify this
work as women's work and, as such, to
rationalize paying women less." (Marsha
Rowe 1982, 151)

DIALECT

A variety of a language, distinguished
from other varieties by, especially, pronunciation, grammar or vocabulary. Many
accounts of Black women's speech which
use "dialect writing" (e.g., Harriet
Tubman [See FREEDOM]) make it
appear that only Blacks have a dialect.
(See STANDARD ENGLISH)

DIALECTIC OF SEX, THE

The title of a book by Shulamith Firestone
(1970) in which she argues that the
primary cause of conflict between women
and men is located in the relations of
reproduction. The material base of patriarchy is the work women do reproducing
the species. Pregnancy and the dependency
of small children on their mothers put
them at a disadvantage and lead to men's
domination of women. To free themselves
they will have to seize control of reproduction; she proposes the development of
artificial means of reproduction.

DIAPERS

(See NAPPIES)

DIARY

A private chronicle, at least for women,
who seldom publish them. A document of
a person's life. Historically, a high proportion of diary writers have been young
women who have had more time to write
than older married women; however,
many women continue to try to find time
to write all their lives for a variety of
reasons including self-improvement, self-
examination, societal examination, and
self-protection. (Vera Brittain [1933]
wrote that her diary, at eighteen, kept her
"from dying of spontaneous combustion"
[54].) Some diary writing has been religiously inspired, an exercise in self-
examination and self-improvement. Some
writing has been inspired by loneliness.
For some women this private writing has
been a (sometimes secret) way to record
events which are important to them but
seemingly to no one else ("merely daily
events"), a way of arranging and ordering
the events of life. Describing the diaries
of working-class women, Elizabeth
Hampsten (1982) suggests that they write
"to assert a pattern and to blur distinctions between recurring and unique
events . . . keeping the pattern intact day
after day is the mark of a well regulated
and successful life. Their effort is not, I
think, to belittle their own value. . . .
Rather, their writing emphasizes patterns
because patterns compose their days, and
they do not see time as a succession of
discrete or climactic events [as do male
diary writers]" (68-9). Most diaries of
women have been considered worthless,
except perhaps to immediate family; most
diaries of women have been thrown away.
Yet the diaries and letters of our predecessors provide one way, sometimes the
only way, that we can hear their voices.
(Nancy F. Cott 1977; Annette Kolodny
1975)

DICTIONARY

A dictionary is a word-book which collects
somebody's words into somebody's book.
Whose words are collected, how they are
collected, and who collects them all
influence what kind of book a given
dictionary turns out to be and, in turn,
whose purpose it can best serve. Though
thousands of dictionaries exist for many
different purposes, men have edited or
written virtually all of them; and the
words they have collected have, in large
measure, been from the speech or writing

of men. Women's invisibility as language-producers is closely bound to the scholarly practices of dictionary-producers. Oxford University Press promoted the finally-completed *Oxford English Dictionary* (the OED) as "a Dictionary not of our English, but of all English: the English of Chaucer, of the Bible, and of Shakespeare" (*Periodical* 13:143 (19 Feb. 1928) 1). Though many dictionaries explicitly and even militantly reject this equation of "all English" with the Anglo-American literary canon, dictionary-makers have nevertheless been as one in their failure to explore seriously the reality of women as language users. It has been through chance rather than editor's choice that women's contributions have been included. One example: Marghanita Laski, an erudite journalist and book reviewer, responded to a 1958 appeal from the Oxford University Press for help with the histories of individual words. She began on *alley cat* but went on to contribute more than 100,000 citations to the supplement, primarily from contemporary authors but also from particular subject areas including fashion, food, social life, sewing, embroidery, gardening, and cooking. In this instance, what constituted "the lexicon" was enlarged by a woman's contributions from traditionally women's areas of interest. (Israel Shenker 1979)

A growing interest in semantics has rekindled interest in theoretical aspects of dictionary-making. One question involves how we arrive at the conceptualization which we represent in dictionaries as linguistic entities (see Douglas L. Medin and Edward E. Smith 1984, Charles J. Fillmore 1975, and Linda Coleman and Paul Kay 1981). Other questions involve the pragmatics of meaning in particular discourse settings (Sally McConnell-Ginet 1984), the relation of linguistic knowledge to cultural knowledge (Herbert H. Clark and Eve V. Clark 1979, Mark Aronoff 1980, John Haiman 1980, Umberto Eco 1984), the nature of the processes by which words are formed and acquire meaning (John Lyons 1977, Laurie Bauer 1983), the relation between linguistic

knowledge and conceptualization during language acquisition (Eve V. Clark 1983, Susan J. Wolfe 1984), and the role of authority and/or expertise in the creation, specification, and authorization of meaning (Hilary Putnam 1973, Paula A. Treichler 1984, and Gregory L. Murphy and Douglas L. Medin in press). Much of this work challenges any sharp division between meaning and usage and between the theory and the actual practices of dictionary-making.

Feminists have pointed out that a dominant group often exercises its power over other groups by controlling words and language. It is, according to H. Lee Gershuny (1973, 1974), the dictionary's role as arbiter of meaning and usage that led feminists to detail the myriad ways in which most dictionary-making selects, preserves, and authorizes sexist discourse. The recent *Macquarie Dictionary*, writes Meaghan Morris (1982), "provides a wealth of instances of linguistic anti-feminism through code control. . . . The concepts developed by women [e.g., *sexism*, *feminism*] are not even marginalised in second place, but rather omitted entirely." Women's dictionaries offer more than an alternative lexicon; they call attention to the social and political ways that language functions in the world.

(See AMERICAN HERITAGE DICTIONARY, AMERICAN HERITAGE SCHOOL DICTIONARY, DICTIONARY OF MAN-MADE.CONCERNS, DOUBLESPEAK DICTIONARY, INTRODUCTION to this dictionary, MEANING, OXFORD ENGLISH DICTIONARY, OBSOLETE, SEMANTICS, SEXIST LANGUAGE, WOMEN AND LANGUAGE RESEARCH)

A record of some words and some usages of speakers. "Because language changes constantly, dictionaries can never record all the possible ways of using words. The written word always lags behind the spoken word and the dictionary always lags behind contemporary usage. Moreover, dictionaries are prepared by fallible humans who can make mistakes of fact and judgment. They might select words for entry while wearing lenses which filter real usage through personal and societal biases. Dictionaries are not value-free and can't offer absolute accuracy or truth. In fact, by describing the language conventions of the majority speakers of English, they might affirm and perpetuate inhuman behaviors of racism, sexism, and ageism practiced by those majority speakers." (Shirley Morahan 1981, 54)

"A self-referring system. Words in dictionaries do not 'refer' to anything except all the other words in the dictionary; and to understand the definition of one item, it is necessary to understand the code of which the item is a part. That is why it is impossible to learn a foreign language using nothing but the dictionary of that language . . . and that is also why the attempt to be both accessible and consistent in a technical discourse often fails in spite of the best intentions." (Meaghan Morris 1982, 76)

DICTIONARY, FEMINIST

A feminist dictionary seeks more gynocentric processes of dictionary-making. Earlier feminist dictionaries collected and critiqued many words from androcentric dictionaries. The 19th-century *Woman's Bible* Elizabeth Cady Stanton) was in large part an attack on male-oriented language. More recently, Midge Lennert and Norma Willson's *A Woman's New Word Dictionary* (1973) defines *construction* as "a well-paying field of human endeavor not open to women" and *supermom* as "a do-it-all woman, male chauvinist approved; takes care of the kids and manages the house and brings home an income too; a nervous wreck, an obnoxious and guilt-ridden person." The 1973 *Intelligent Woman's Guide to Dirty Words*, ed. Ruth Todasco, categorized the "patriarchal epithets" for women authorized by *Webster's New World Dictionary*. Ingrid Bengis' *Woman's New World Dictionary* put into print some of the newly-created words of the women's liberation move-

ment. Varda One's columns in *Everywoman* (1971) called attention to women's linguistic contributions as well as to what she called "Manglish."

More recently, feminists have sought to "seize the language" – use language creatively to put forth new ideas and visions about the world and to conceptualize women's relationship to language differently. Women's dictionaries, as one expression of this larger project, offer more than an alternative lexicon; they call attention to the ways language functions in the world.

Women's dictionaries have depended upon women's ideas and labor, and have been created with limited resources. Monique Wittig and Sande Zeig (1976) created *Lesbian Peoples: Material for a Dictionary* as "a lacunary" which "allows us to eliminate those elements which have distorted our history"; their dictionary is, they add, "only a rough draft." The *Oxford English Dictionary* (OED) was from the beginning conceived as an immensely ambitious project; seventy years in the making, it depended upon a vast number of readers all over the world (including "many very intelligent ladies, lonely widows or spinsters living at home" (K. M. Elisabeth Murray 1977, 185). The controversial *Webster's Third New International Dictionary* cost $3,500,000 over 757 "editor-years" (Philip Gove 1961, preface). Women will probably not be able to carry out such large-scale projects for some time (though see Barbara G. Walker 1983 for inspiration). It thus behoves us to make good use of existing dictionaries. Some of these, like the OED, have much to offer us in *our* interpretations. Others are shallow, careless or incorrigibly misogynistic maledictionaries of Manglish in which we will never find ourselves.

Can a dictionary explore theoretical questions and tell us anything about women as language-users? In general, dictionary-making is thought to be a kind of pedestrian cataloguing activity, and is accordingly devalued by language scholars in other areas. A linguistic discussion of gender in English, for example, concluded that "this is not a matter of grammar and should be dealt with in the lexicon or dictionary" (Frank Palmer 1971, 37). It is true that many dictionaries are created with little theoretical coherence or self-conscious attention to the significance of the lexicon for language structure and language use; this marginalizes the lexicon, separating it from the study of "discourse," the production of language.

But more than a decade of research on women and language argues against this dichotomy, and suggests some of the ways in which traditional dictionaries may help us explore the question of women's relationship to language. For examples in this dictionary, see ANDROCENTRISM, AMAZON, CLITORIS, -ESS, ETYMOLOGY, HUSSY, INVISIBILITY, MEDICA, PRONOUNS, SPINSTER. Feminist dictionaries are part of an important and collective effort to discover these words, illuminate their function, and place women language-users at the center.

(See AUTHORITY, DICTIONARY-FEMINIST, INTRODUCTION to this dictionary, LANGUAGE AND GENDER RESEARCH, MEANING, SEMANTICS, WOMEN AND LANGUAGE RESEARCH)

DICTIONARY OF MAN-MADE CONCERNS

Generic term describing virtually every dictionary published and sold to date. Includes the dictionaries of Battles, of Barley, Malting, and Brewing, of Weapons and Military Terms, of Maritime and Shipbuilding Terms, of Otho-Rhino-Laryngology (in 5 languages), of Foundries, and of Insults; they include the Nautical dictionary, the Polygraph dictionary, the Rubber dictionary (in 10 languages), the Technical Dictionary of High Polymers, and the dictionary of Surface Coating, Plating Products, Finishing, Corrosion, Plastics, and Rubber.

(See INTRODUCTION to this dictionary, DICTIONARY, DICTIONARY/FEMINIST)

DICTIONARY ON LEGS

Metaphor for sterile and moribund ideas and scholarship. Or, the male scholar. Fanny Fern was one of several 19th century American women writers who "deliberately and even proudly disavowed membership in an artistic fraternity." (Nina Baym 1978, 32) Dedicating her *Rose Clark* to a female and family readership and picturing a cozy reading setting round the fire, she added: "Should any *dictionary on legs* rap inopportunely at the door for admittance, send him away to the groaning shelves of some musty library, where 'literature' lies embalmed, with its stony eyes, fleshless joints, and ossified heart, in faultless preservation." (Fanny Fern c.1850; quoted in Nina Baym 1978, 33)

DIETING

Weight-watching and appetite controlling techniques directed primarily at women and designed to reduce the body, to make smaller, narrow, lightweight, lose gravity, be-little, shrink, confine, contract, lessen. The emphasis is on restraint, prohibition, confining and controlling the hungers of the self. (Kim Chernin 1981, 101)

(See CELLULITE, FAT, OBESITY, SLIMMING)

DIFFERENCE

This word has a bad name – and for good reasons. Malestream culture focuses on dissimilarity, stressing distinctions and discord between sexes, races, and nations. Difference *can* mean illumination (as Audre Lorde and Mary Daly state below), but usually it has been promoted as meaning hierarchical distinctions, as in *sex differences* where, as Colette Guillaumin suggests below, females are too often assumed to be more different than males. The word is also important in terms of race and class issues.

(See COALITION, IDEOLOGY)

Comes "from *education, exercise,* and the *impressions* of those external objects which surround us in different Circumstances." "There can be no real difference pointed out between the inward or outward constitution of Men and Women, excepting what merely tends to giving birth to posterity." (Sophia 1739, 23, 50)

A man-made gulf. "When we meet in the flesh we speak with the same accent; use knives and forks in the same way, expect maids to cook dinner and wash up after dinner . . . moveover, we both earn our livings. . . . But . . . those three dots mark a precipice, a gulf so deeply cut between us that for three years and more I have been sitting on my side of it wondering whether it is any use to try to speak across it." (Virginia Woolf 1938, 4)

"Because of our social circumstances, male and female are really two different cultures, and their life experiences are utterly different – and this is crucial." (Kate Millett 1971, 53)

Is a vital concept for our understanding. "To simplify differences would be to settle for a less than Dreadful judgment of the multiple horrors of gynocide. It would also impoverish our imaginations, limiting our vision to the Otherworld Journey's dimensions . . . would blind us to the necessity for separating at times even from sisters in order to allow our Selves the freedom and space of our own unique discoveries." (Mary Daly 1978, 381-2)

A diversity present among women as well as between women and men. "There is no logical comparison between the oppression of Third World women on welfare and the suppression of the suburban wife and her protests about housework. This is exemplified in the situation of the welfare mother who does not know where the next meal is coming from and the suburbanite who complains about preparing and serving meals." (Dorothy; interviewed by Gloria I. Joseph; in Gloria I. Joseph and Jill Lewis 1981, 22)

Is "a fund of necessary polarities between which our creativity can spark like a dialectic. . . . Only within that interdependency of different strengths, acknowledged and equal, can the power to seek new ways to actively 'be' in the world generate, as well as the courage and sustenance to act where there are no charters. . . . Difference is that raw and powerful connection from which our personal power is forged." (Audre Lorde 1981a, 99)

"Difference produces great anxiety. Polarization, which is a theatrical representation of difference, tames and binds that anxiety." (Jane Gallop 1981, 93)

Belongs to a political order not sexual categories. "The ideology of sexual difference functions as censorship in our culture by masking, on the ground of nature, the social opposition between men and women. Masculine/feminine, male/female are the categories which serve to conceal the fact that social differences always belong to an economic, political, ideological order." (Monique Wittig 1982, 64)

"The ideological significance of difference is the distance from the Referent [white, middle-class, male]. To speak of 'differences' is to articulate a rule, a law, a Norm – briefly, an absolute, which would be the measure, the origin, the fixed point of a relationship, by which the 'rest' would be defined." (Colette Guillaumin 1982, 45)

(See DOMINATED PEOPLE)

DIFFERENCES BETWEEN WOMEN AND MEN

The clitoris missing in men. (Ruth Herschberger 1948; rpt. 1970, 31)

DIKE

Judy Grahn alternates spellings: "A dike learns much of her social function from other dykes, even those so firmly in the closet as to never have heard the word *dike*. . . . A dyke, especially if she is young and rebellious, may notice that most progressive women in her society clip their hair, wear plain faces and 'man'-tailored clothes, and do work traditionally assigned to men. And so she may redesign herself with lavish, even garish hair and brilliant makeup to make the statement 'Here's still *another* way of being a woman.' And that's a dykish thing to do, a balancing thing. That's literally what *dike* means – balance, the path." (Judy Grahn 1984, 46-7)

(See DYKE)

DINING ROOM

A room in middle- and upper-class homes which is used for eating and, historically, for women's writing. Men write in their libraries and studies. Jane Austen wrote in the drawing room. Elizabeth Gaskell wrote in the dining room, which had three doors leading from it and from which she could supervise the household. In a letter to a friend she wrote: "If I had a library like yours all undisturbed for hours, how I would write. . . . But you see everybody comes to me perpetually. Now in this hour since breakfast I have had to decide on the following variety of important questions. Boiled beef – how to boil? What perennials will do in Manchester smoke, and what colours our garden wants. Length of skirt for a gown. Salary of a nursery governess and stipulations for a certain quantity of time to be left to herself. Settle twenty questions of dress for the girls . . . and it's not half past ten yet." (Elizabeth Gaskell; quoted in Dale Spender 1980, 220)

DINNER

An activity which precedes washing the dishes. "You eat your dinner only to face the washing up. Even as we munch, delight turns into a dirty plate." (Sheila Rowbotham 1983, 162)

DINNER PARTY

A collective work of five years and 400 people, the art work was initiated and organized by Judy Chicago. It opened in 1979 at the San Francisco Museum of Modern Art. It's a triangular table, set with embroidered runners and 39 ceramic plates, 13 place settings on each of the three wings. "The number thirteen refers to the number of guests present at the Last Supper and to the number of members in a witches' coven. The fact that the number thirteen had both a positive and a negative meaning – i.e., the 'holy' table of men versus the 'demonic' coven of witches – seemed consistent with the dual meaning of The Dinner Party." The plates represent a period of time in western civilization and some [mostly white] women who exemplify that period. The table rests on a floor inscribed with the names of 999 women of achievement. (Judy Chicago with Susan Hill 1980, 8-9)

DIRT

Pollution delegated to women who are "assigned the role of *controlling* dirt [and are] also seen as being, in some sense, the *cause* of it." (Juliet Mitchell and Ann Oakley 1976, 40-1)

DIRTY WORDS

Words and expressions which are taboo for women's use; many of the words are derogatory words for women's bodies. Dirty words have a power because they have belonged to men. "I think a female's use of words abusive to females *defuses* them. *Our* use takes away the power of the words to damage us. They are no longer tools with which to shock and humiliate. And it's fun, after all these years of proper servitude to a restrictive language code, to bounce them all over the walls and hear not only their echoes but the shock waves from men." (Roz Wolbarsht 1977, letter to editor *Ms.* 6:2 (August), 9)

DISABLED

The older term for differently abled women; physically challenged women. Sisters Against Disablement (SAD) are concerned with the common assumption that disability is an individual tragedy and are showing it for what it really is, a political designation. "We are dis-abled by society not by ourselves or our 'dis-abilities.' " (*Spare Rib*, Oct. 1982, 13)

(See ABLEISM, TAB)

A term which "now just maintains the status quo. By whose standards is someone 'disabled' if she is doing the best she can with what she's got? Certainly not mine. The only 'disabled' people in my book are those who do not try to see through the prejudice." (sheila zakre 1984, 20)

DISCIPLINE, ACADEMIC

"A particular body of knowledge which has its own ways of finding out what it wants to know" and is committed to a secret sign system. (Gloria Bowles; quoted in Taly Rutenberg 1983, 73)

DISCONTENT

Women's discontent, radical feminists argue, "is not the neurotic lament of the maladjusted, but a response to a social structure in which women are systematically dominated, exploited, and oppressed." (Heidi Hartmann 1979; revised 1981, 13)
(See DEPRESSION)

DISCOURSE

For women, this usually means conversation, not the written work. "It happens on the back porch." (Gail Scott 1984; quoted in Tessera Editorial Discussion, 17)

DISCOVERY

Critical knowledge which occurs in the eye of the beholder. Women are from time to time "discovered." "For instance, the realization that women habitually have sustained themselves by friendships with other women in spite of scorn from both women and men – that 'fact' may be new to some observers who now, at long last, are being persuaded by the sheer quantity of information made public to that effect. There is a store of knowledge that women have always 'known' about themselves, obvious to them, but not said aloud. Now to speak of discoveries gives public credence to these old truths." (Elizabeth Hampsten 1982, 3)

DISPLACED HOMEMAKER

A term coined in 1974 by Tish Sommers and others in California to refer to a woman "who has, for a substantial number of years, provided unpaid service to her family, has been dependent on her spouse for her income but who loses that income through death, divorce, separation, desertion, or the disablement of her husband." (Laurie Shields 1981, ix) She is often rejected by employers and others. (Ruth Harriet Jacobs 1979)

DISTAFF

The staff from which the flax was drawn in spinning; hence, figuratively, women's work, and a woman herself, the allusion being to the old custom of women, who spun from morning to night. (*Brewer's Dictionary* 1962, 290) Now a cutesy term for women used in after-dinner speech and such.
(See SPINDLE, SPINSTER)

DIVIDE AND CONQUER

(See D & C)

DIVIDED BEINGS

The presentation of women as divided beings has been and continues to be an important theme in women's writing and use of language. Kate Chopin, in *The Awakening*, first published in 1899, writes of her heroine that "at a very early period she had apprehended instinctively the dual life – that outward existence which conforms, the inward life which questions" (Chopin 1964, 35). "In interaction with men," writes Simone de Beauvoir (1953, 605), "woman is always play-acting; she lies when she makes believe that she accepts her status as the inessential other; she lies when she presents to him an imaginary personage through mimicry, costumery, studied phrases. These histrionics require a constant tension: when with her husband, or with her lover, every woman is more or less conscious of the thought: 'I am not being myself.'" Women of color are asked to identify exclusively with race or sex, which is asking them to divide themselves.

DIVISION

Separation which can cause alienation. When divisions are insisted upon, interdependence is denied. Dualism destroys us – the dualism of superior/inferior, ruler/ruled, owner/owned, user/used. Divisions are not as healthy as integration and integrity are. (Ursula K. LeGuin; in Susan Wood 1979a, 169)
(See DIFFERENCE)

DIVORCE

A legal end to a marriage; many times a woman's entry into poverty. "A recent

California study found that in the first year after a divorce, the standard of living for women plunged by 73 percent while the former husbands experienced a rise in living standard of 42 percent." (Karin Stallard, Barbara Ehrenreich and Holly Sklar 1983, 10)

(See EQUALITY, NO-FAULT DIVORCE, PATRIARCHY)

A valuable legal aid. Divorce "is just as much a refuge for women married to brutal men as Canada was once a refuge [for slaves] from brutal masters." (Susan B. Anthony 1905; quoted in Elizabeth Janeway, ed. 1973, 25)

"Is the state's act to restore husband and wife to the status of single people. Divorce proceedings fix the care, support, and visitation of the spouses' offspring. Divorce divides up the family wealth. Divorce makes it possible for each to marry again. The right and the power to do all of these things is in the state and it is only the state that may declare when and how a marriage becomes an un-marriage. It may seem presumptuous, nervy, and nosey for the legislators to sit down in the assembly hall in your state capitol and decide the terms under which you are entitled to divorce your husband. Yet that is exactly what happens." (Barbara B. Hirsch 1973, 13)

"The significant *rite de passage* of our society and, as such, it is sadly without ceremony. There are no special garments worn for divorce, no announcements traditionally sent out, no patterns to follow to help us through the change. Even a small ritual, such as walking around in a circle three times or publicly burning the joint books and records, would ease the sense of isolation and confusion everyone feels when they get divorced." (Jane O'Reilly 1976, 38)

In androcentric terms, divorce is a failure in women's only business, married life. (Elizabeth Miller Walsh 1981, 213)

Bill of divorce: A *get* which is handed by the husband to the wife along with a formal declaration in the presence of witnesses. Requires the sanction of a court consisting of three men well versed

in the Jewish laws of marriage and divorce. The husband is allowed to remarry immediately, but the wife must wait three months – to establish for everyone else the paternity of any child she has after her remarriage. (Elana Rubinstein 1984, correspondence)

DOCTOR

Originally from Latin *docere* "to teach." As early as the 15th century, it was a form of address. The *Oxford English Dictionary* cites a 13th century use of a "doctour of deth" as well as George Eliot's use in *Middlemarch* of "a common country doctor." The term also came to be applied to various mechanical appliances used for curing or removing defects: *lint-doctor', cleaning-doctor', rug-doctor'*. In popular British usage, to castrate a male cat.

(See HEALTH, MEDICA, MEDICINE, MIDWIFE, NURSE)

A name for a male physician but frequently withheld from a female physician on the grounds that her sex, scientific training, clinical training, temperament, physical make-up, brain-size, beauty, sensibility, courage, ability to act quickly, ability to think quickly, stamina, experience, or technical credentials disqualified her. One female physician wrote that her exclusion made her "a traitor, outlaw, felon" who was beyond the laws of the male medical world. (Harriot K. Hunt 1856; cited in Mary Roth Walsh 1977, 2) Historically, women were the healers, until in the modern age when men entered this field and tried to drive women out. (Mary Ritter Beard 1942; rpt. in Ann J. Lane, ed. 1977, 221)

An old occupation for women. "It may be a new thing for a woman to hold a diploma, but she has been a doctor, for ages . . . and no prospect of any pay beyond a string of onions . . . and the reputation of a witch." ("Our Grand-mothers" 1876, *The New Century for Women* July 29, 92)

A title that was not willingly given to Elizabeth Blackwell when she received her medical degree at the General Medical

College in New York in 1849. Her formal diploma granted her the title of "Domina," the only feminine form the Senate could find for "Doctor." "The President taking off his hat, rose, and addressing her in the same formula, substituting *domina* for *Domine*, presented her the diploma" ran her sister's account of the commencement ceremony (cited in Elizabeth Blackwell 1895, 90). The *Medical Times* offered this alternative in a congratulatory verse (cited in Elizabeth Blackwell 1895, 261):

For Doctrix Blackwell – that's the way
    To dub in rightful gender –
In her profession, ever may
    Prosperity attend her!

She wrote about the title: "I have been asked by physicians again and again if they shall call me doctor – they fully recognize my right. I always answer this question in the affirmative, as a matter of principle." (Elizabeth Blackwell 1895, 109)

"Miss Doctor" was a nineteenth-century form of professional address and reference as evidenced by an 1874 usage of "Miss Doctor Kilpam" and an 1847 use (by Oliver Wendell Holmes) of "Madam le Docteur Boivin." (Mary Roth Walsh 1977, 28, 136)

DOCTORESS

A term for female healer common in the U.S. colonial period. It applied to women doctors, nurses, midwives, and witches (Mary Roth Walsh 1977, 4). This term for woman teacher and woman physician probably came from French *doctoresse* (fifteenth century) or by way of Latin *doctrissa*. The term was sometimes applied to things personified as feminine; the *Oxford English Dictionary* cites "doctrice of discipline" (1450) and "that long tongd doctresse Dame Law" (1580). The term applied generally to medical practitioners: "The women . . . take upon them to be great doctresses in physicke" (i.e. medical doctors, 1577); "bird and dog doctress" (1879). By the late nineteenth century, the OED noted that the term was used only "when sex is emphasized," and even then *woman-doctor* or *lady-doctor* were more

common. Jokingly, the title was also used for a doctor's wife and daughters: "The doctor . . . came accompanied by his lady Mrs. Doctoress Savage" (1810).

(See DOCTOR, -ESS, GENDER MARKING, MEDICA)

DOLL

A toy playmate given to, or made by children. Some adult males continue their childhood by labelling adult female companions "dolls."

DOLLANITY

A population of children's dolls, from *doll* + *humanity*. "One forlorn fragment of *dollanity* had belonged to Jo and, having led a tempestuous life, was left . . . in the rag bag, from which dreary poorhouse it was rescued by Beth and taken to her refuge." (Louisa May Alcott 1869; rpt. 1962, 51)

DOMINANCE

The sexual geography in the way people use space. "Public places like the village square, the cafes, and the mayor's house are the domain of men, while private places such as houses and the back streets that connect them into residential neighborhoods belong to women." (Rayna R. Reiter 1975; quoted in Kathryn S. March and Rachelle Taqqu 1982, 21)

DOMESTIC DUTIES

"High-sounding words, which, for the most part, are bad habits (which [a woman] has not the courage to enfranchise herself from, the strength to break through) . . ." (Florence Nightingale 1952; rpt. in Ray Strachey 1978, 404)

DOMESTIC FEMINISTS

"Social scientists [at the end of the nineteenth century] who saw women primarily as sexual beings whose biology was their destiny. They believed that women could improve their status and enhance their value to society by performing more expertly in their traditional sphere." (Sylvia Strauss 1982, xi)

DOMESTICITY
"A cage that the state sees as the natural habit of women." (Mary Evans 1983b, 2)

DOMESTIC METAPHOR
"The image of a beautifully articulated, patriarchal society in which every southerner, black or white, male or female, rich or poor, had an appropriate place and was happy in it." The domestic metaphor gave a presentation of slavery as "an admirable educational system as well as an ideal society." (Anne Firor Scott 1984, 175-6)

DOMESTIC SCIENCE
"The name has progressed [in England] from Domestic Economy, which was intended to teach managing in the kitchen, to Domestic Science, to Domestic Studies, to Housecraft, and finally to Home Economics. The trend today is back towards Domestic Science because current thinking is that the subject should be seen as a science. One other possibility is Home Economics, with 'Home' enclosed in brackets, because the word makes people think of *women* in the home implying that that is her place and where she should be. If [Home] Economics became used, I think the subject would take on a wider meaning and a more corect one, namely management." (Ruth Powell; cited by Mary Buchanan 1980, 23) [In Ireland the title is Domestic Science and has not gone through these changes.]

DOMESTIC SERVANTS
"The only class of female manual workers (except wives) whose hours of labour are unregulated." (Margaret G. Bondfield c.1910, 13)

DOMESTIC VIOLENCE
  (See WIFE BATTERING)

DOMINANCE
A control that "is not merely technological or economic or military, it is also emotional, cultural, and psychological, producing in the dominated a pervasive sense of inferiority and insecurity." (Kay Boals 1974; in Carol Ehrlich 1981, 123)

DOMINATED PEOPLE
Defined (collectively) as incomplete, "while the dominant are singularized and defined as the incarnation of achieved human nature. Dominant speech certainly assigns each one her or his place, but only the dominant individuals have the place of singular beings, and apart from the collection of unique individuals to which they belong, only masses of undifferentiated elements are distinguished: 'the people' or 'Blacks' or 'women.' Indeed, in the world 'order' created and articulated by the dominant, the dominated have no individuality or singularity, and particularities attributed to their group suffice to define them completely." (Nöelle Bisseret Moreau 1984, 46)
  (See UNIVERSALIZATION)

DOMINATION
A lust which perhaps "becomes more shrill as the physical means of domination decline.... The most naked modern exponent of this lust of domination, D. H. Lawrence, may be observed as a specimen under a microscope; immensely magnified, we perhaps see in him what lies hidden in the hearts of many weak men." (H. M. Swanwick 1935, 168-9)
  Power exercised by many men, not all.
  "A destructive behavior which is in the patriarchal blood; it passes from man to man as blood bond and blood victory. Domination in sexual terms demands a victim and a willing victim, therefore an ignorant victim, one who is younger, smaller, weaker, softer, in effect, helpless, choiceless, powerless . . . the abuse of children, specifically girl children, is the means and the end of the patriarchy and male supremacy as we know it, live it and breathe it every moment of our lives." (Julia O'Faolain 1983, 156)

DOROLEDIM
A Láadan word which "has no English equivalent. Say you have an average woman, with little control over her life. She has little or nothing in the way of a

resource for being good to herself. . . . She has family and animals and friends and associates that depend on her for sustenance of all kinds. She rarely has adequate sleep or rest; she has no time for herself, no space of her own, little or no money to buy things for herself, no opportunity to consider her own emotional needs. . . . For such a woman, the one and only thing she is likely to have a little control over for indulging her own self is FOOD. When such a woman overeats, the verb for that is *doroledim*." (Suzette Elgin 1984, correspondence)

(See LÁADAN)

DOUBLE-BIND

A very familiar story which goes like this: If we try to be "human" we are punished for not being "women"; if we try to be "women" we are punished for not being "human." (Jeanette Silveira 1980, 167)

DOUBLE CROSTIC

A sophisticated word game (based on nineteenth-century word game designs) invented by Elizabeth Seelman Kingsley in 1933 or 1934 as a method of reviving interest in the classics. Her puzzles were printed in the *Saturday Review of Literature* for 19 years. Answers are words divined from definitions. Letters from the correct words, placed in a diagram, form a British or American literary quotation; the first letters of the answers spell out the author and title of the work. (Jean England 1974, 119)

DOUBLE-DOUBLE UNTHINK

A phrase of Andrea Dworkin's which means to see through "the obvious level of male-made reversals and find the underlying Lie. . . . It is a pitfall simply to reverse 'penis envy' into 'womb envy,' for such theories trick women into fixating upon the womb, female genitals, and breasts as our ultimately most valuable endowments" rather than "focusing upon the real 'object' of male envy, which is female creative energy in *all* of its dimensions." (Mary Daly 1978, 60)

DOUBLE-F

A magazine of effeminism started in 1973. "The name, *Double-F*, was chosen to suggest that 'effeminist' better describes an anti-sexist man than 'feminist,' which women now reserve for themselves. *Double-F* also affirms those unmanly men ('flaming faggots') persecuted in medieval times: 'When a woman was to be burned as a witch, men accused of homosexuality were bound and mixed with bundles of kindling (faggots) at the feet of the witch, and set on fire "to kindle a flame foul enough for a witch to burn in." ' So the enemy has always seen that strong women and gentle men are a real threat to masculine domination." (Steven Dansky, John Knoebel, and Kenneth Pitchford 1973; in Susan Rennie and Kirsten Grimstad 1975, 223)

(See EFFEMINATE)

DOUBLE SHIFT

Working in the public realm all day, and then working the rest of the day and night in the home and with the family.

DOUBLESPEAK DICTIONARY

The entry in this dictionary (ed. William Lambdin 1979) under CHANGE acknowledges the inevitability of language change and the arbitrariness of what we know as "English." "There is no real connection between the meanings of words and their physical appearance. Spoken usage will dictate some changes whether we want them or not. The only accurate label that can be placed on English is one similar to that found on some commercial products: 'Warning – Man-Made Materials.' " (21) Yet this dictionary is itself a good example of "doublespeak" because it consistently attacks those changes in language recommended by feminists and ridicules their observations (see, for example, the comments on *The Woman's New World Dictionary*, 302-3). By "man-made," he really *does* mean *man*.

(See AUTHORITY, DICTIONARY, ENGLISH)

DOUBLE STANDARD

Crime has no sex and yet today
  I wear the band of shame
Whilst he and the gay and proud
  Still bears an honored name.

Can you blame if I've learned to think
  Your hate of vice a sham,
When you so coldly crushed me down
  And then excused the man.

(Frances Harper n.d. [mid-nineteenth century], 13; in Rennie Simson 1983, 234)
  A principle that gets us all into trouble. It works like this: "Women considering themselves very pure and very moral, will sneer at the street-walker, yet admit to their homes the very man who victimized the street-walker. Men at their best, will pity the prostitute, while they themselves are the worst kind of prostitutes." (Voltairine de Cleyre 1914b, 354)
  "Excuses all in the male and accuses all in the female." (Rennie Simson 1983, 234)

DOWAGER'S HUMP

A curvature of the upper spine caused by osteoporosis ("light bones"). Vertebral bones collapse more at the front causing a forward curve in the spine. Osteoporosis is much more common in older women than in men. It is a condition which can be avoided or retarded if a woman receives enough calcium in her adult diet. (Patricia Mirwaldt 1984, 44)

DOWNPRESSION

To press down, in contrast to *oppression* (to press against). "The downpression of native people is linked to the subjugation and exploitation of the Earth." (Winona LaDuke 1983, 54)

DOWN THERE

Reality works as a word of our own for *Down There*. Many have already used it. For example: "Dr. Seymour Fisher is so out of touch with *reality* that he sincerely thinks menstrual cramps occur in the vagina" – Barbara Seaman. Playing bridge "is a substitute . . . for the pleasures one should be receiving from *reality* – Sidney J. Harris. "To make a precise scientific description of *reality* out of words is like trying to build a rigid structure out of pure quicksilver" – Dorothy Sayers. (Sue Held 1980, 184)

DOZENS, THE

"A Black game of supposedly friendly rivalry and name-calling; in reality, a crucial exercise in learning how to absorb verbal abuse without faltering." (Audre Lorde 1984, 171)

DRAFT

Compulsory assignments. We are drafts.

" . . . .
incomplete roughcopy
onionskin foolscap
manifold carboncopy
throwaway getanother
tissuetypewriter
womansecretary
officewife."

(Chris Llewellyn 1978, 99)
  A military institution which provides a ready force of soldiers to go out and kill. (Karen Lindsey 1982, 323)

DRAGON

The basic meaning is "to see." "A woman who watches vigilantly and fiercely over the welfare of her charges." (*Heresies Great Goddess Collective* 1982, 129)
  "A mythical monster, usually represented with wings and breathing out fire. It has come to describe a fierce older woman. Something to be proud about, sisters!" (Sona Osman 1983, 29)

DRESS

Clothing. "A form of social expression of the highest importance; . . . at present the dress of both men and women largely fails of its functions, while that of women is pitiful, grotesque and injurious along many lines . . . The clothing of women, and their slavish submission to the constant changes dictated to them by tradesmen, seriously affects the race, owning to the close connection between soul, body and dress. No noble body can endure in the costume of an idiot pet monkey, no noble soul can exist in such a contemptible exterior." (Charlotte Perkins Gilman November 1916f, 289)

(See CLOTHES)

DRESS FOR SUCCESS

A sad joke which suggests that if women dress in a manner acceptable to men, career success will follow. In the 1970s John T. Molloy, the author of *Dress for Success*, wrote a sequel *The Women's Dress for Success*. The titles and the order of publication tell us part of the story; this "wardrobe engineering" for women is a very second class affair. Wearing dark suits and white blouses with soft bows at the neck may be required of women in some jobs, but it has not been demonstrated that this clothing leads women toward their goals. Neither will Molloy's "principle" of "Always carry an executive gold pen." Of more practical use: The "proper" clothing bank which some London feminists have established to cover situations when one of them feels she has to temporarily pass as a "proper" woman.

DRUGS

Substances which have been linked with women and their dangerous allure; drugs have always been associated with "the mystical, intuitive dimension – the forbidden, the mystery of woman." (Cynthia Palmer and Michael Horowitz 1982, 21)

(See DANGEROUS DRUGS)

DRYLONGSO

Ordinary, everyday. This is the title of John Langston Gwaltney's anthropological book of first-person narratives by Black men and women. One of his informants, Harriet Jones, furnishes an epigram: "Since I don't see myself or most people I know in most things I see or read about black people, I can't be bothered with that. I wish you could read something or see a movie that would show the people just, well, as my grandmother would say, drylongso." (Harriet Jones; quoted in John Langston Gwaltney 1980, 1)

DUALISM

The construction of the world in binary oppositions: male/female; white/black; rational/emotional; good/bad. A construction "crucial to masculinism – the realm of spirit, God, and eternal life, and the realm of Earth, the Devil, and death . . . From it follows the hostility, the bravado and the show of disregard for the living of life, for the Earth, for Nature and for her carrier, Woman." (Sheila Ruth 1983, 351)

(See DIVISION)

DULLNESS, MALE

Is labelled "by the specious Names of Judgment and Solidarity." (A Lady 1721, 17)

DUNGAREES

[In the U.S., overalls.] "The straight media's stereotype of what feminists always wear – preferably baggy and shapeless. Some of us have never pulled on a pair. (But nevertheless the issue of comfortable, practical clothing remains an important issue.)" (Sona Osman 1983, 29)

(See CLOTHING)

DUVELSE KRING

Women's devils' circle in The Netherlands. A group which recently took the Playboy magazines from two Communist bookshops, and threw them in the Amsterdam canals. (*Women of Europe* 1984)

D'YA KNOW WHAT

A device children use as a partial solution to their problem of insuring rights to speak. If the adult replies "What?" then the children may say what they wanted to say in the first place. Use of this device "informs us both about the work of guaranteeing interaction and the differential rights of the participants. [In one study] this device was used twice as often by the women." (Pamela Fishman 1983, 95)

(See CONVERSATION)

DYEING

The coloring of fabrics and other materials. "An early performance of women" which has been as important as weaving. (Mary Ritter Beard 1942; rpt. in Ann J. Lane ed. 1977, 221)

DYKE

"Unfortunately, the etymology of the word DYKE remains clouded. Nowhere in dictionaries which laboriously define DIKE (spelled alternately in Dutch, DYKE) as 'a barrier of stones designed to prevent lowland inundation by waters,' 'ditch' (English), TICH (German), pond, dike, etc., have I found any plausible connection between those meanings of the word and its contemporary American slang usage, 'a female homosexual who plays the male role, especially a large masculine looking woman.' Speculating that the term DYKE perhaps was once part of a larger word, conversations with older lesbians revealed the folklore belief that the root word of DYKE was once HERMAPHRODITE. According to Greek mythology, Hermes, the god of roads, commerce, invention, eloquence, and cunning, once on an escapade accosted Aphrodite (goddess of love and beauty) and became joined in one body with her. Today the word hermaphrodite is defined as (1) an animal or plant having both male and female reproductive organs, (2) homosexual, and (3) possessing both male and female principles, androgynous.

"In pre-liberation lesbian subculture, the terms BUTCH and DYKE were both used to define women who adopted masculine roles. Though sometimes used synonymously, colloquial speech often delineated the BUTCH as the woman who prefers to play the male role and a DYKE as one who thinks of herself as male, to the extent of binding her breasts and/or wearing a dildo. While the former was much more numerically common, the word DYKE has come to be used as an ultimate threat hurled at women who say "NO" to men.

"The contemporary redefinition of a DYKE as 'a strong, independent, aggressive, self-defined woman' recaptures much of the original double-principled (androgynous) meaning of the word 'hermaphrodite.' DYKE is a term proudly used by lesbian and radical feminists today." (Jeanne Cordova 1974, 22)

"An American word of abuse reclaimed by lesbians as in, for example, 'dynamite dykes.' " (Sona Osman 1983, 29)

"If you're poor / then you're a dyke / if you're rich / you're sapphic // but if you're neither one nor the other / a lesbian, a lesbian is what you'll have to be // if you're strong / then you're a dyke / and if you're weak / you're sapphic // but if you're neither one nor the other / a lesbian, a lesbian is what you'll have to be // if you're earthy / then you're a dyke / and if you're aesthetic / you're sapphic / but if you're neither end round the middle / a lesbian, a lesbian is what you'll have to be." (Monique Wittig and Sande Zeig 1976, 47)

(See LESBIAN)

"Lesbians are 'dykes,' not 'dikes.' We are not dams, although some people consider us damned." (Margaret A. Robinson 1973, letter to editor) *Ms.* editor's note: "Since the dictionary-approved spelling we use is not preferred by many of our readers, we will adopt the alternate spelling in this and future issues." (*Ms.*, 1:8 (February), 4-8)

'E

Pronoun in Caribbean English Creole, "he, she, his, hers, its." (Lito Valls 1981, 39)

(See PRONOUNS)

EAGLE FEATHER POETRY

The translations and "renditions" of American Indian poetry by white missionaries, anthropologists, and various representatives of the Bureau of American Ethnology. The products of this process – dubbed "eagle feather poetry" by a contemporary Indian poet – is what many people equate with "Indian poetry." Some Indian poets are working to establish their own writing as distinct from and often subversive of this stereotypical mainstream tradition. (Patricia Clark Smith 1983)

(See AMANUENSES, INDIAN WAY)

EARLY AMERICAN

"The most popular decor for American kitchens . . . the maintenance of a fundamentally inefficient mode of household operation, requiring the full attention of the housewife for the better part of every single day, has been a crucial part of the symbolic quality of the individual American home." (Ruth Schwartz Cowan 1979, 39)

EARRINGS

Jewelry such as gold loops, worn on the ear and containing social information. In the fifteenth century, Christian rulers *required* all Jewish women in some northern Italian cities to wear long mantles over their heads when in public and – except for the widows – to wear earrings. In Bologna, a law of 1521 *prohibited* Jewish women from wearing earrings, which became a sign of honor and aristocracy, and Jews were marked with other, degrading signs. (Diane Hughes 1984, 1,5-6)

EASTER

(See EGG)

ECOLOGY

The study of the relationships of organisms and their environments. Ellen Swallow (1842-1911), chemist, environmentalist, the first woman to obtain a degree from the Massachusetts Institute of Technology, and the founder of consumer and environmental sciences, popularized the word "oekology" and devoted her life to studying and teaching about healthful environments. (Robert Clarke 1973)

ECONOMIC DEPRESSION

Period during which there is a decline in business and a rise in unemployment and anti-feminism. "Not only are women workers – especially married women – invited to retire from wealth-producing in favor of men, but by suggestion, in literature, the drama, and even in changing fashions of dress, they are artfully invited to return to older and softer ideals of living. . . Not that [men] propose to push women off the rafts, but they want to be sure that they are going to do most of the navigating themselves." (Rheta Childe Dorr 1931, 483)

ECONOMIC PROVIDER(S)

A needed term to substitute for the obsolete "head of household" which "assumes that being an economic supporter (and/or male) entitles men to authority prerogatives, implicitly devalues shared authority, and perpetuates unequal living arrangements." (Wilma Scott Heide 1976, 89)

ECONOMICS

Analyses which deal with production, distribution and consumption of commodities and wealth. It has its origin in a male frame of reference and is designed to explain men's experience. The analyses seldom count what women do as work. (Charlotte Perkins Gilman 1899)

The management of finances. Women are expected to be economical (they are the economy class) but their management of money is usually supervised by others.

Management which can not provide the solution to the problem of inequality between the sexes because "it only resolves one area of conflict. Economic independence and strength may be a necessary but is not a sufficient condition for assuring women's liberty." (Devaki Jain 1978, 13)

L'ECRITURE FEMININE

A term used by some French feminists to refer to women's writing. "Women must write through their bodies, they must invent the impregnable language that will wreck partitions, classes, and rhetorics, regulations and codes, they must submerge, cut through." "A feminine text cannot fail to be more than subversive. It is volcanic; as it is written it brings about an upheaval of the old property crust, carrier of masculine investments; there's no other way. There's no room for her if she's not a he. If she's a her-she, it's in order to smash everything, to shatter the framework of institutions, to blow up the law, to break up the 'truth' with laughter." (Hélène Cixous 1975b, 256, 258)

(See FEMALE)

EDEN

"Based on the Persian *Heden* or primal garden where the first couple were joined together as a bisexual being in the Golden Age." (Barbara G. Walker 1983, 269)

-EE

A suffix that marks the passive, the person to whom things are done.

(See –ESS)

EDITOR

One of the people who "function as filters between people's own stories (political & social stances) and the owners of patriarchal publishing companies. Editors 'clean up' or 'uplift' a story whose common English is considered 'dirty' or low. They rifle through it looking for eccentricities, soften its anger and outrage, take away what is aggressive, what is detailed, specific, physical – and instead substitute what is abstract, distant, objective, passive." (Judy Grahn 1978c, 10)

EDUCATION

An institution with a gate, which can open to some opportunities for some people. "The desire for education which is widely felt by English women . . . is a desire which springs from no conceit of cleverness, from no ambitions of the prizes of intellectual success as it is sometimes falsely imagined, but from the conviction that for many women to get knowledge is the only way to get bread, and still more from the instinctive craving for light which in many is stronger than the craving for bread." (Josephine Butler 1868, 7-8)

Usually refers to the *practices* of educational institutions which usually have systems of learning especially unsuited for girls. "The greatest and most universal error is, teaching girls to exaggerate the importance of getting married." This focus is unfortunate for everyone since "making the education of girls such a series of 'man-traps,' makes the whole system unhealthy." (Mrs Child 1832, 116, 119)

It "is a human process, and should

develop human qualities – not sex qualities. Surely our boys are sufficiently masculine without needing a special education to make them more so." The process of the education system now "is thwarted and hindered, not by . . . 'feminisation,' but by an overweening masculisation." (Charlotte Perkins Gilman 1911, 149, 159, 160)

An institution "which women had a large hand in creating. It is ironic that the sex which has so often been thought to need little formal education should have been responsible for so many educational institutions, but the record is clear. From colonial dame schools to Pestalozzian, Froebellian, and John Dewey-style kindergartens women have been largely responsible for the development of early childhood education, upon which we presume much else is built." (Anne Firor Scott 1972; rpt 1984, 152-3)

"I thought education was a means to an end, but I find for Black women that there is no end." (Young woman quoted by Julianne Malveaux 1979, 53)

What formal education now means to women: "Every day of our lives we are informed that women do not count, that we are wrong, that our different descriptions and explanations are ridiculous or unreal . . . We learn that we are wrong: we become educated." (Dale Spender 1982a, 34)

(See CLASSROOM INTERACTION)

EFFEMINATE

An expression used properly in the following: "When a Man is possest of our virtues he shou'd be call'd *effeminate* by way of the highest praise of his good nature and justice." (Sophia 1739, 51)

A word which, when defined by men, reveals much about the associations they make. The *American Heritage Dictionary* (1969) defines *effeminate*, which comes from the Latin *effeminare*, meaning "to make a woman out of" as: "Having the qualities associated with women; not characteristic of a man; unmanly" and "characterized by softness, weakness, or lack of force; not dynamic or vigorous."

For synonyms readers of the AHD are referred to *feminine*. (Cited in Casey Miller and Kate Swift 1976, 60)

EFFEMINISM

Revolutionary commitment to subverting and transcending the mentality and behavior of male supremacism. Effeminists are men (whether celibate, homosexual, or heterosexual) who have "become traitors to the class of men by uniting in a movement of Revolutionary Effeminism so that collectively we can struggle to change ourselves from non-masculinists into anti-masculinists and begin attacking those aspects of the patriarchal system that most directly oppress us." (Steven Dansky, John Knoebel, and Kenneth Pitchford 1973; in Susan Rennie and Kirsten Grimstad 1975, 222)

EGG

A symbol of fertility. Decorated eggs are used in the pagan custom of giving eggs at Eastertime. "The word Easter comes from Oestre, the Goddess of fertility, and Easter is celebrated close to Spring Equinox, March 22nd, when new life comes springing forth." (Susan Paxton 1982, 5)

EGG MONEY

Income from farmyard enterprises such as poultry raising. Prior to the industrial boom this money was often, for rural Irish women, an important psychological mainstay, the only "independence" they had. Daughters were often given a "start" in Dublin or London with some of the egg money. (*Banshee: Journal of Irishwomen United*, c.1980, 1:2, 8)

EGOISM, MALE

Produces the following: "God's in *His* Heaven; All's Well in the World." (Teresa Billington-Greig c.1955)

EGO–TESTICLE WORLDVIEW

Men's point of view on all issues. Places men and their interests as central: e.g. Octavio Paz's view that "a woman's nature (the physical condition of her body) is by its very essence always being 'violated.' " (Adelaida R. Del Castillo 1978, 143)

(See POINT OF VIEW)

EIGHT DEADLY SINS OF THE FATHERS

Processions, Professions, Possession, Aggression, Obsession, Assimilation, Elimination, Fragmentation. (Mary Daly 1978, 30-1)

ELITE

From Latin *eligere* and French *élite* "choice, selected, elected." In the early days of the U.S. women's movement, individual women or small groups of women were sometimes charged with elitism by their sisters, who perceived they were taking too much leadership upon themselves, gaining too much prominence (e.g., becoming known to the press as a spokesperson for the group or for women generally), or obtaining privileged knowledge about the workings of the larger women's liberation group. One proposal to guard against elitism was that "No member of Women's Liberation, so far as it is practicable, shall take on so much of a task or duty that no other member could take her place. This implies 'apprenticeship' in specialized tasks, with deliberate effort by skilled people to share their knowledge and deliberate effort by the membership to produce volunteers." At the same time, all individual members were urged to participate in meetings and take personal and moral responsibility for their own behavior and collectively for the organization as a whole. (Sheryn Kallaway n.d.; see also Joreen 1976). In recent years, concerns about elitists have shifted to the overall relationship of the women's movement to other revolutionary struggles and to the status and hierarchies within the women's movement (e.g., the place of white middle-class women, women of color, working-class women, etc., in terms of influence, voice and other issues).

(See HORIZONTAL HOSTILITY, PHANTOM ELITE)

ELITISTS

The label used by feminists, from 1969 to 1971, to denounce other feminists who acquired public notoriety. Since feminists had rejected overt structure and hierarchy, this labelling was one of the few methods available to control others.

(See CONSCIOUSNESS RAISING)

ELOQUENCE

"Is a talent so natural and peculiar to Woman, that no one can dispute it in her. . . . All the oratory of the schools is not able to give the Men that eloquence and ease of speech, which costs us nothing." (Sophia 1739, 39)

EMALFING

"Flame spelled backwards is Emalf. On this occasion of my 90th and last Flame [a newsletter concerning women and religion], I'd like to indulge in some looking backwards – emalfing, as it were." (Jo Haugerud, *The Flame*, March 8, 1983)

EMBEDDED RABBIT

Discrimination that exists but is not yet identified by feminist consciousness. Policy scholar Jean Lipman-Blumen says that before the women's movement she was not aware of discrimination. "I often think of this as the problem of the embedded rabbit," she says, referring to those drawings in children's books where the artist hides different animals. "Once I became aware of discrimination, it was hard for me not to see it. I couldn't go back to seeing the larger landscape without seeing all the pieces of the landscape." (Jean Lipman-Blumen in *Comment*, May 1984, 1-2)

EMOTION

"The word *emotion* originally meant strong feeling or agitation, but it has been modified by usage until it fits like a glove the mild unsatisfied longings of women. Emotion, to accommodate this nebulous feminine world, has taken on a meaning of diffuseness and internal vibration. It is, so to say, an Excitement from which the intensity and motor efficiency have been removed." (Ruth Herschberger 1948, 145)

EMPLOYMENT AGENCY
"An organization that does the dirty work for biased employers. Synonym: pimp." (Marie Shear 1984, correspondence)

EMPOWERMENT ADVOCACY
A feminist alternative to traditional models of therapy, consultation, and education, "empowerment has become our primary focus, which means, for us, acting as agents or advocates to the process of redefining, experiencing and realizing one's own power." (Donna M. Hawxhurst and Susan L. Rodekohr c1984)
   (See FOURTH WORLD)

ENCLOSURE
"A rose is a rose by any other name and so is penetration. . . . Enclosure, where an active vagina (helped by strengthening exercises) sucks in a penis, could only take place where a woman and a man were born fully formed, totally innocent, onto an uninhabited desert island (where they might well never discover fucking anyway). No act of penetration takes place in isolation. Each takes place in a system of relationships that is male supremacy. As no individual woman can be 'liberated' under male supremacy, so no act of penetration can escape its function and its symbolic power [the punishment and control of women]." (Leeds Revolutionary Feminist Group 1981, 7)

ENCODINGS
"New language shapes for concepts not yet lexicalized in any known language." An example of a concept which needs a word: "To refrain from asking, with evil intentions; especially when it's clear that someone badly wants you to ask – for example, when someone wants to be asked about their state of mind or health and clearly wants to talk about it." (Suzette Haden Elgin 1984, 25, 29) For examples of *encodings* see LÁADAN.

ENCYCLOPAEDIA
A category system which details the important elements of the world view of males, particularly scholarly males, but ignores many elements of the women's world view.

ENEMY
An opponent, often found at a woman's own hearth and board "ready to exploit her for his own selfish interest, to climb up on her shoulders to paths of pleasure and ambition and then to burn her soul with scorn for being what he himself has made her." (Lady McLaren 1908)
   Often, men are the enemy, it must be acknowledged. The countering phrase *men are not the enemy* "dismisses feminism and the reality of patriarchy in one breath and overlooks some major realities. If we cannot entertain the idea that some men *are* the enemy, especially white men and in a different sense Black men too, then we will never be able to figure out all the reasons why, for example, we are being beaten up every day, why we are sterilized against our wills, why we are being raped by our neighbors, why we are pregnant at age twelve and why we are at home on welfare with more children than we can support or care for." (Barbara Smith 1979a, 124)
   Is "Madison Avenue, Wall Street, the White House, the Church . . . legislators in the unratified states, appliance manufacturers." (Midge Lennert and Norma Willson eds 1973, 3)
   The "original enemy, the one who created all the splits amongst us [w]ho is exploiting all of us [is] imperialism and the patriarchal class system. Male domination *and* class domination." (Nawal el Saadawi 1980, 3)
   (See MAIN ENEMY, THE)
   "Each intelligent woman has millions of enemies: all stupid men." (Marie v. Ebner-Eschenbach, nineteenth-century poet and author; Heidi Rendl-Scheuering 1984, conversation)
   "The enemy is brownness and whiteness, maleness and femaleness. The enemy is our urgent need to stereotype and close off people, places, and events into isolated categories. Hatred, distrust, irre-

sponsibility, unloving, classism, sexism, and racism, in their myriad forms, cloud our vision and isolate us . . . . We close off avenues of communication and vision so that individual and communal trust, responsibility, loving, and knowing are impossible." (Andrea Canaan 1981, 236)

ENGLISH

A language which came to be a recognizable entity about 1500 years ago. English is a member of the Germanic branch of the Indo-European "family" of languages, one of many language families in the world today. As Casey Miller and Kate Swift (1976) point out, English has undergone continual change (more than many languages have). It "has been molded and modified, nudged toward change here and held intact there by people who have made their language the special province. Not coincidentally, these people were rarely female before the last few decades" (89). While in the time of the Anglo-Saxon king called Alfred the Great *man* meant a human of either sex (with *wif* and *wer* words for an adult female and an adult male) and women had strong personal, property and employment rights, by the end of the fifteenth century women had lost many of their personal, economic and linguistic options and rights. *Man* and *men* were used increasingly to refer to males only. Women's scholarship and interest in language and literature was discouraged (See SHAKESPEARE'S SISTER). As this dictionary declares, for centuries women have been expressing their ideas about the problem with the English language. A few have constructed other languages to illustrate and bypass problems with English (see FARK-SOO and LÁADAN). Thousands of other women have formed, repaired, modified and redefined words with little effect on what the masters of English said and recorded (Kramarae 1981, 33-51). The early grammarians of the sixteenth and seventeenth century made many rulings about English in books designed primarily for males, since few women were literate. Patriarchs of churches also had a strong influence on the language, calling upon the Godhead through use of *Father* and *He* and using female symbols for subordinate entities (Casey Miller and Kate Swift 1980); creation, for example, is glorified as both masculine and divine (H. Lee Gershuny 1977, 111). While men in courts and governments have debated whether a female is included in the term *person* (Haig Bosmajian 1977), literary critics have repeatedly decreed that women can certainly not be included in the phrase *writers* except with the qualification *woman* writer. For centuries men have told us that we fit uneasily in the English language; for centuries women have pointed out that the "women and language" problems posed and debated by men have been created by men. For some solutions see all entries above and below.

A foreign language for people of African heritage living in the "New World" and the Caribbean. The African is "to use a foreign language, expressive of an alien experiential life; a language comprised of word symbols that . . . had affirmed negative images about her . . . . This was to eventually become her only language, her only tool to create and express images about herself and her life experiences, past, present and future. The paradox of this acquisition is that the African learned both to speak and to be dumb at the same time. . . . The language has in fact to be destroyed, dislocated and acted upon so that it begins to serve our purposes. It is our only language, our mother tongue, or maybe it would be more accurate to say, ours is a father tongue." (Marlene I. Philip 1983, 25, 24. See also John Langston Gwaltney 1980)

An acquired language for Americans. In 1901 Zitkala-Sa, a Dakota Sioux woman wrote in her preface to *Old Indian Legends*: "I have tried to transplant the native spirit of these tales – roots and all – into the English language since America in the last few centuries has acquired a second tongue." Dexter Fisher (1980) adds, "At the time of Columbus's first contact with the New World, Native Americans spoke over four hundred different languages, which derived from at least seven language families, each as complex as Indo-European. Each language represented a distinct culture, and while contact existed between tribes, there was no common linguistic denominator. . . . With few exceptions, the language of American Indian literature is English because this is the first written language that Indians learned." (15)

A man-made language. (Dale Spender 1980)

Manglish. (Varda One, 1971)

"A subject which girls [who are native-speakers] are successful at, and usually enjoy; it's an academic subject which isn't directly connected with being a wife and mother, a haven, a refuge, where girls can work with boys on equal terms. . . . [It] is seen as an 'amateur' subject, connected with intuition and the emotions; a subject which doesn't involve learning a 'block of knowledge,' like history, or working things out, as in math or science, or making things, as in woodwork. In English, you can keep your hands clean and your clothes tidy. You don't have to compete as directly as in other subjects where there are clearly 'right' and 'wrong' answers." (Gill Frith 1981, 30-1)

ENGLISH, CORRECT

Is "nothing other than the blatant legitimation of the white middle-class code." (Dale Spender 1980, 13)

(See MISS FIDDITCH, STANDARD ENGLISH)

Is "full of subtleties and nuances which are available [only] to the middle classes. Certain words are totally out of our area of experience and the 'Queen's English' a foreign language, as divorced from us as the monarchy itself. It is another aspect of middle class lifestyles which reiterate the different world we were brought up in." (Marlene Packwood 1983, 12)

ENLIGHTENMENT

Was an important theme in the iconography of the U.S. women's suffrage movement. Mainstream suffragists emphasized not women's equality with men nor their right to vote but rather the "special" qualities of their traditional role as preserver of culture and morality and hence their *duty* to vote. The NAWSA (National American Women's Suffrage Association) showed a woman with a torch enlightening the nation; the NWP's (National Women's Party's) official motto was "Forward Out of Darkness, Forthward Into Light." (Edith P. Mayo 1981)

EPITHETS

Invective nouns and adjectives often used by men to publicly and privately humiliate women. Clare Booth [Luce] collected a partial list of epithets applied by the "Gentlemen of the Press" to the women in her play *The Women*; she published it in the foreword to the hardback edition. A few words from the long list: Cats, Tiger cats, Supercilious cats, Malignant cats, Hell cats, Jades, Sluts, Trollopes, Parasites, Poison-tongues, Tittle-tattlers, Gossip-peddlers, Slanderers, Fiendish liars, Insatiables, Cheats, False friends, Irrepressible interlopers, Cat o'nine tongues, Cobras, Female lice, Werewolves, Vixens, Acid, Adder-fanged, Bawdy, Carbolic, Dynical, Evil, Flashy, Flossy, Frightful, Filthy, Harlots, Odious harpies, Brazen hussies, Stalking hussies, Lewd hussies. . . . Clare Booth wrote, "Now, whether or not, this play is a good *play* is any man's business to say. But whether or not it is a true portrait of [mischievous, unlikeable] women is a matter which no man can adequately judge, for the good reason that all their actions and emotions are shown forth in places and times which no man has ever witnessed. . . . So all sentimental gentlemen, young and old, who read this book, are here warned that the fact that their mothers were women does not constitute them, ipso facto, able critics of Life in *The Women's* No-Man's Land." (Clare Booth, 1937, ix-x)

EPONYM

A real or mythical person from whose name the name of an invention, nation, epoch, institution, practice, etc. is derived, supposedly derived, or commonly associated. As Berenice A. Carroll points out, eponymous credit is much more often given to men than to women – not merely because men have been culturally placed in ways that give them greater access to the resources involved in invention, discovery, and so on, but because naming practices and cultural values act to devalue women's contributions. (Berenice A. Carroll 1981)

(See ANDROCENTRISM, NAMING)

EQUALITY

A principle and a practice which means the insurance of the same opportunities, expectations and support for all. It is a problematic term since the referent condition is that of the white male. It is impossible in a capitalist system which is based upon and can only be maintained through inequality.

"The basis of social philosophy" as announced by Christ's whole life and words. "Only in one case has (equality) been consistently ignored, and that is in the case of that half of the human race (women)." (Josephine Butler 1869, ix)

An insufficient slogan for women. "Equality may take the form of common hunger and want. Is that sufficient in its justice?" (Mary Beard 1931, 375)

Is an unfortunate goal since a commitment to sexual equality with males "is a commitment to becoming the rich instead of the poor, the rapist instead of the raped, the murderer instead of the murdered." Such a commitment does not work toward the abolition of poverty, rape and murder; what is needed is work toward the ending the male sexual model itself. (Andrea Dworkin 1976, 12)

"The right of the man and the women to have sound and healthy relations." (Ghadah al-Samman 1970, 393)

"Means everyone's having the same rights to vote, to work, to live where we choose, and to attend school." It is not as clear that people agree that equal opportunity is included in the definition. (Shirley Morahan 1981, 131)

"A major component of any conception of democracy. Feminists' demands can only be met if equality is understood as equality of results." (Mary Lou Kendrigan 1984, 112)

"Incompatible with capitalism. . . . I realize many women today must work for a bigger slice of the pie, but *I* will not do so – I prefer to work to change the recipe." (Jackie Lapidus to her mother 1975; quoted in Karen Payne 1983, 327)

EQUALITY RULE

The measurement of "our similarity with men to see if we are or can be men's equals. . . . It is considered gender-neutral, abstract, neutral, principled, essentially procedural and objective. I will argue that it substantively embraces masculinity, the male standard for men, and applies it to women." (Catharine MacKinnon 1983b; manuscript)

EQUAL PAY

An abbreviation for the feminist demand "Equal Pay for Equal Work" which "would mean that men and women would be paid equally if and only if they work equally well. . . . Skill and productivity could still be claimed as relevant and legitimate criteria – even if (or when) all the institutions operate so as to discourage such skill and productivity in women and encourage such in some men. Equal pay for equal work would undoubtedly be an advancement in the quest for more equality for women. . . . However, equal pay for equal work . . . will do little to provide the economic conditions necessary for women to become financially equal with men . . . (since) most demand for labor has been sex-specific." (Mary Lou Kendrigan 1984, 68-9)

(See COMPARABLE WORTH)

ERA

Equal Rights Amendment, proposed as the 27th U.S. Constitutional Amendment, reads: "Equality of rights under the law shall not be denied or abridged by the United States or by any State on account of sex." It was drafted by Alice Paul and adopted unanimously by the National Women's Party (NWP) convention in

Seneca Falls, New York, in July 1923. The NWP was formed in 1916 and 1917, a militant offshoot of the National American Woman Suffrage Association. The ERA was introduced into both houses of Congress in 1923. The U.S. Senate passed the ERA in 1949, 1953, and 1959, but with the "Hayden rider" which exempted all sex-specific legislation and thus made the Amendment meaningless. The House Judiciary Committee refused throughout the 1940s, 1950s and 1960s to hold hearings on the Amendment. In 1970 Representative Martha Griffiths presented a discharge petition in the House of Representatives, which approved the ERA the same day. The House approved the ERA again in 1971 and the Senate passed it in 1972. Almost half the state legislative bodies approved the Amendment almost immediately. A three year extension of the 1979 ratification deadline ended without the required three-fourths of the state legislatures, overwhelmingly male, having approved of the Amendment. (Susan D. Becker 1981)

"Twenty-four words have never been so misunderstood since the four words 'One size fits all.' " (Erma Bombeck 1978; quoted in Suzanne Levine and Harriet Lyons eds. 1980, 79)

"The ERA is the real social security amendment for every home with a daughter, a mother, a grandmother, any female who may ever have to depend on herself." (Ellen Goodman, in the AAUW publication *GRADUATE WOMAN*, October 1983)

ERECTION, MALE

A rigidity of the penis. Is usually a "tension artificially induced (I say 'usually' because I am discounting those rigid erections which occur naturally in males when the bladder is very full). The truth is that bone-hard erections aren't very comfortable. They stick out from your body and are painful if bent. And they feel a little dead. They function in fucking very well, in that they are good for rape. But the idea that they feel good – that they are sensate – is only a cultural

illusion. I believe that the culture reinforces stiff hardons as symbols of male aggression and power. And I believe that in order to fulfill that cultural expectation, a man growing up in this society learns how to make himself feel hard by certain muscle constructions and by certain fantasies of penetration and violation." (John Stoltenberg 1977; rpt. 1984, 27)

ER/ET

"Embryo replacement is the term used when the embryo is returned to the donor mother, and ET (embryo transfer) when it is implanted into a woman other than the donor of the ovum (egg)." (Diana Leonard 1984, 46)

EROTIC

"Comes from the Greek word *eros*, the personification of love in all its aspects . . . and personifying creative power and harmony. When I speak of the erotic, then, I speak of it as an assertion of the life force of women; of that creative energy empowered, the knowledge and use of which we are now reclaiming in our language, our history, our dancing, our loving, our work, our lives." The erotic, "those physical, emotional, and psychic expressions of what is deepest and strongest and richest within each of us, being shared" is the bridge which connects the spiritual and the political which are falsely declared as dichotomous. (Audre Lorde 1980b, 297)

"Exists at the very core of our being, in the materiality of our bodies. It informs in deeply important ways how we perceive others, the interests we bring to those others, the demands of our environment, the sensibility and care we give to others, our physiological response to others as well as our identity as sexually and emotionally resourceful and responsible human beings." (Jacqueline Zita 1981, 185)

EROTICA

"Contains the idea of love, positive choice, and the yearning for a particular person. Unlike pornography's reference to a harlot or prostitute, *erotica* leaves entirely open the question of gender." (Gloria Steinem 1983, 222)

EROTICISM

Is more a philosophy "than an art of pleasure. Because it is founded on the theorem that woman is an object, that love and pleasure are two distinct realities which are mutually harmful, eroticism can only be misogynous." (Francoise Parturier 1968a, 63)

Often used as a sentimental and euphemistic word involving beautiful, romantic, soft, nice love-making, with an "emphasis on *relationships*, not (yuck) *organs*. This goody-goody concept of eroticism is not feminist but feminine" and comes from the view that sexual excitement is "an aggressive, unladylike activity, an expression of violent and unpretty emotion, and a specifically genital experience that has been taboo for women." (Ellen Willis 1981, 224)

ESCALATOR

Constantly moving stairs, run by electricity, "dangerous to the nervous, the slightly infirm, or to the woman carrying or leading young children." (*The Englishwoman* 1914, 21:61 (Jan.), 110)

(See SEAT BELTS FOR AUTOMOBILES)

A method of transportation not to be trusted. "Watch the escalator. Someone told me a horror story of a child's wellington getting stuck down the side." (Sheila Rowbotham 1979; in Sheila Rowbotham 1983, 125)

ESQ.

(See FORMS OF ADDRESS)

-ESS

An ending which indicates "deviation from what is consciously or unconsciously considered the standard. Tacking an -ess ending onto a common gender English word because the person referred to is a woman is reasonably resented by most people so identified. When it is relevant to make a special point of someone's sex,

pronouns are useful and so are the adjectives male and female" (Casey Miller and Kate Swift 1976, 159). However, in some countries and in some languages, especially those such as Germany and German in which all nouns have a gender marker (e.g. der Professor), women make the argument that using a special suffix to job titles (e.g. der Professorin) calls attention to just how many (or how few) women have the jobs. (Marlis Hellinger 1984)

"An archaic word-ending which denotes female." (Midge Lennert and Norma Willson eds 1973, 3)

Examples include: Murderess, female wardress, executor/executrix, testatrix. (Dorothy L. Sayers 1930, 28)

"The habit of making the masculine primary and the feminine the appendage gives women the feeling they are an afterthought, a decoration while men are the substance. Is it possible, as some grammarians think, that the feminine form is primary and the masculine is the shortened version? Imagine the difference in feeling if we always put the feminine first." (Varda One, *Everywoman* January 2, 1971, 6)

(See GENDER-MARKING)

ESSENTIALISM

That set of assertions, classically challenged by feminism, designed to demonstrate that there is a "female nature" which is made manifest in all art by women. It assumes (1) a psychology and emotional temper peculiar to women, (2) a prose or verse style endemic in, and characteristic of, women; (3) a set of preoccupations appropriate, by nature, to female poets and novelists – e.g., female friendship, female madness, motherhood, love and romance, domestic conflict, duty, religiosity, etc.; (4) a natural social community grounded in biology and reproductive characteristics rather than in intellect or temperament or derivation or societal experience; (5) a difference between "male" writing and "female" writing by virtue of women's unique sensibility; and (6) a purely sexual base for intellect and imagination. Together these constitute the Great Multiple Lie. "Classical feminism – i.e. feminism at its origin, when it saw itself as justice and aspiration made universal, as mankind widened to humankind – rejected anatomy not only as destiny, but as any sort of governing force." (Cynthia Ozick 1977; rpt. in Ozick 1983, 288)

(See CULTURAL FEMINISM, FEMINISM, WOMAN)

ESTROGEN

"A hormone secreted by the cells of the follicle which aids the sperm's entrance to the uterus." (Midge Lennert and Norma Willson eds 1973, 3)

One "of the so-called sex hormones, estrogens and androgens, which are secreted in both sexes by ovaries, testes, and adrenal glands" though in different relative quantities, in females and males of all species. "The main difference between females and males is that the secretion of . . . hormones is considered to be constant (or tonic) in males rather than cyclic, though there are fluctuations in levels, and some diurnal as well as larger interval cyclicity has been reported in males in a variety of species, including humans." (Ruth Bleier 1984, 81, 84)

ETHICS

"Deals mainly with forbidding as does religion. . . . [Since our] recorded history begins in the patriarchal period, it is its ethics alone which we know." (Charlotte Parkins Gilman 1911, 133)

Has to do with the mysteries of good and evil, phallocratic categories which "no longer apply when women *honor* women, when we become honorable to ourselves. . . . In the name of our life/freedom, feminist metaethics O-mits seminal omissions." (Mary Daly 1978, 12-13)

ETHNIC

Refers to a speech group and to other groups of people historically connected by common descent or geographical heritage. *Ethnic* classification is for many people a sometimes-identification, unlike *race* which is often a more consuming distinguishing characteristic for those of minority groups.

ETHNOCENTRISM

Concern with one's own group, and assumption of its superiority.

(See ANDROCENTRISM)

ETHNOCIDE

The denying or neutralising of ethnic and cultural differences. For example, many West Indian women in the U.S. have been denied (by white design) cultural reference.

-ETTE

A suffix which "indicates feminine gender in French words and frequently has nothing to do with sex, as in *bicyclette*, which means "bicycle." In English the suffix has three functions: to indicate imitation, as in *flannelette*; to denote small size, as in *dinette*; and to suggest that females need not be taken seriously, as in *farmerette* and *astronette*. By implication an usherette is a frivolous little woman hired to replace a bona fide usher." (Casey Miller and Kate Swift 1976, 159)

(See SUFFRAGETTE)

ETYMOLOGY

Is from the Greek *etymon*, "the true meaning of a word according to its origin." Etymology is (1) the general process of tracing and describing word changes (both in form and meaning) over time and (2) the information about those changes for a given word. Etymology offers information for the study of language change, which remains one of the great mysteries in the study of language. What precise mechanisms bring about changes in sound, structure and meaning? How does "a definition" interact with the conditions of usage? How do the pervasive facts of male dominance and control affect change? How do women as language-users and linguistic creators figure in this equation? Could their asymmetrical influence in diverse speaking situations in fact constitute a force for language change?

One theme of women and language research has been the etymology of words related to women, men, and their relations; such research seeks not merely to document the evolution of negative language about women but rather to illuminate the linguistic and social processes that accompanied these changes, reclaim earlier positive meanings of words, and pinpoint bias against women in traditional scholarship. Knowing what a word was empowers us to envision what it might be.

(See AMAZON, HUSSY,
MATRIARCHY, SCHOLARSHIP,
SEMANTIC DEROGATION OF
WOMEN, SPINSTER)

The history of a word which "can never give us its definition," according to Max Müller (1865, OED). Müller, a philologist, was involved in the matriarchialist controversy of the 19th century, which, in considerably different form, continues today (see Elizabeth Gould Davis 1971, Charlene Spretnak, ed., 1982, and Rosalind Coward 1983). His statement refers to the disjunction between a word's history and its current range of usage. Some feminists would argue, however, that etymology offers more "truth" about women and their history than does any current language; earlier forms of words, particularly those which are said to predate patriarchal culture, are in this sense more "pure" and less corrupted by the forces of oppression.

The study of "Background meanings" in Mary Daly's *Gyn/Ecology*. Her strategy, Meaghan Morris writes, "is to warp the words of the patriarchal dictionary, to bend the code back against itself until it snaps to our shrieks of derision. . . . It's rather like a game of buried treasure, an illuminating search through the storehouse of signs. . . . But reworking 'words' as dictionary items (subverting the code) is not the same thing as paying attention to the ways that words work together in discourse, or *language in use*." (Meaghan Morris 1982, 72, 73)

A process that involves interpretation about the history of women. Susan J. Wolfe and Julia Penelope Stanley argue that Indo-European society (from which contemporary culture developed and whose language we reconstruct from the records of the Indo-European languages) may originally have been matriarchal. They point out many instances in which vocabulary items suggesting women's power and influence were given meanings by scholars that confirmed a patriarchal view. Thus marriage and the patrilinear household are projected historically through the lexicon of kinship and religion. The posited IE word *swesor* "sister," for example, is related to terms meaning "self," "blood relation," and "relative," and seems literally to mean "she who is one of us." Instead of placing the female sibling within this web of connection, scholars root her firmly within the immediate family unit; *bhrater* "brother," however, despite an etymology which is fuzzy, is linked to a broader "mystical" brotherhood. Viewed as a group, such instances "reflect the biases of those working within the patriarchal paradigm." A feminist reinterpretation positing a matriarchal culture is supported by both linguistic and historical evidence. (Susan J. Wolfe and Julia Penelope Stanley 1980, 233-6)

ETYMOLOGY, AMAZON

Language history which considers the evidence for the matriarchy. Research of linguists Susan Wolfe and Julia Penelope indicates that "historical linguists have been blind to semantic links to a matriarchy on the European continent. The patriarchs become his-sterical as a result of pro-matriarchal findings." (Susan J. Wolfe 1980, 18-20)

(See AMAZON, ETYMOLOGY,
MATRIARCHY)

EUCHARIST
(See FASTING)

EURO-AMERICAN WOMAN
A term for a woman whose European heritage places her within the white

"mainstream" of U.S. culture. In contrast to American women whose background routinely leads them to be designated by a hyphenated name (Afro-American, Asian-American, etc.), Euro-American women are often designated simply as "women." (Vickie M. Mays 1981, 76).
To people of other cultures within America, the Euro-American or white culture is one among many, and not necessarily "mainstream." (John Langston Gwaltney 1980, xxiii)

> (See MALESTREAM, NAME, WOMAN, WOMEN OF COLOR)

EUTHENICS

The science with the goal of educating a population to live in harmony with its environment. The application of scientific principles and knowledge to human living. A word coined by Ellen Swallow Richards, instructor of chemistry at the Massachusetts Institute of Technology 1884-1907. (c.1900; cited in Jessie Bernard 1964, 11)

EVE

The brave one in the biblical story. Perhaps "the serpent was Adam masquerading, in his intense desire for the forbidden fruit, and lacking the courage of his conviction!" (Mrs Harmon; cited by Emma W. Babcock 1891, 459)

> (See ADAM)

"The strong, courageous, innovative, curious, self-contained confident mate of Adam; mother of two; grandmother of the world. History's first dominant spouse." (Midge Lennert and Norma Willson eds 1973, 4)

The mythical woman of Genesis who "showed initiative and an interest in acquiring knowledge." Because of the results, church officials have "used the story to deny women education, . . . free speech and, in general, opportunity." (Annie Laurie Gaylor 1981, 10)

"In the biblical story, she is the dynamic, curious, anti-authoritative, active, courageous, powerful part of a couple, of which the man is timid, anxious and passive, doing what Eve orders. She was the first explorer in the world and didn't accept forbidding (not even by God). Our foremother." (Heidi Reindl-Scheuering 1984, correspondence)

"The most important character in the drama enacted in the Garden of Eden. Her actions precipitate the fall from unity and harmony with God into estrangement and sin; into the human condition of sexual consciousness and conscience, as well as the hard realities of birth, work, and death. . . . She is also Everywoman, the prototypical woman. . . . Her story . . . shapes a Western ideology of women." (John A. Phillips 1984, xiii)

"The biblical title of Eve, 'Mother of All Living,' was a translation of Kali Ma's title *Jaganmata*. She was also known in India as Jiva or Ieva, the Creatress of all manifested forms. In Assyrian scriptures she was entitled Mother-Womb, Creatress of Destiny, who made male and female human beings out of clay, 'in pairs she completed them.' The first of the Bible's two creation myths gives this Assyrian version, significantly changing 'she' to 'he' (Genesis 1:27). The original Eve had no spouse except the *serpent*, a living phallus she created for her own sexual pleasure. Some ancient peoples regarded the Goddess and her serpent as their first parents. Sacred icons showed the Goddess giving life to a man, while her serpent coiled around the apple tree behind her. Deliberate misinterpretation of such icons produced ideas for revised creation myths like the one in Genesis." (Barbara G. Walker 1983, 288)

EVERYBODY ELSE'S MOTHER

A person used frequently in the arguments of children, this is "a woman who likes live-in snakes, ice cream before dinner and unmade beds. . . . She's a myth, that's who she is." (Erma Bombeck 1984, 21)

EXCEPTIONAL WOMAN

A label which provides an illusion and which is used to isolate women from each other. Exceptional Woman "is one of our chief obstacles. . . . I can scarcely find one of my sex whom someone has not been ready to persuade of her Exceptionalness." (Elizabeth Robins 1913, 66)

EXHAUSTION

Weariness frequently caused by "male absenteeism in the home" and the resulting extra cooking, cleaning, and washing work on top of holding an outside job. (Harriet Harman 1983, 75)

EXORCISM

The process of "peeling off the layers of mindbindings and cosmetics . . . movement past the patriarchally imposed sense of reality and identity. This demystification process, a-mazing The Lies, *is* ecstasy." (Mary Daly 1978, 6)

EXPERIENCE

The accumulation of knowledge and skill, from personal participation in events. Men think that experience described by men is more valuable, yet it is often not "even in a language derived from *their* experience . . . it is removed from experience altogether by being cast in abstract and theoretical terms. We need a woman's language, a language of experience. And this must necessarily come from our exploration of the personal, the everyday, and what we experience – women's lived experience." (Liz Stanley and Sue Wise 1983, 146)

(See PERSONAL IS POLITICAL)

EXPERIENCED WOMAN

A term "frequently used by men as a pejorative to designate a woman who has had sexual experience and who, as a consequence, is no longer 'chaste.' " In a short story by Maul Haimson, "Hands," the phrase is used to designate a knowledgeable woman, an example of reworking language without creating new words. (Julia Penelope [Stanley] and Susan J. Wolfe 1983, 127-8)

EXPERT

A label often given to males who are allowed, publicly, to finish the statement: "Every Woman Ought . . ." ("Problems of the Day", 1912, *The Englishwoman*, 13:38 [Feb.], 129)

A person "always willing and sometimes able to give advice on the subject he has made his own. . . . [For example] The mother's work is to be superseded . . . [and] her opinions are considered to be trivial and profitless. The fact that she is likely to be familiar with every flaw and every perfection in [her child's] body and soul is nugatory beside the opinion of the expert who may know children in the mass and on paper." (Edith Macrosty 1913, 273)

A member of the "establishment" (physicians, philosophers, scientists and related professionals). He often addresses himself to "the Woman Question in a constant stream of books and articles." The increase in number and status of the experts in the nineteenth century was not clearly progressive. "It is true that the experts represented a less parochial vision than that of the individual woman, submerged in her family and household routines; the experts had studied; they were in a position to draw on a wider range of human experience than any one woman [was likely to know]. But too often the experts' theories were grossly unscientific, while the traditional lore of the women contained wisdom based on centuries of observation and experience. The rise of the experts was the inevitable triumph of right over wrong, fact over myth; it began with a bitter conflict which set women against men, class against class. Women did not learn to look to an external 'science' until after their old skills had been ripped away, and the 'wise woman' who preserved them had been silenced, or killed." (Barbara Ehrenreich and Deirdre English 1979, 3, 33)

(See WITCH)

EXPLOITATION

Using another for selfish, often economic, purposes. "An integral aspect of all exploitation. . . is that the exploited love their exploitation. It is precisely the mark of extreme exploitation or degradation that those who suffer from it the most do not see themselves differently from how their exploiters see them. Either they do not reflect upon their situation at all or else they acquiesce passively in the role in which they have been cast." (Carole E. Gregory 1980, 14-17)

EXTREMISM

Severe, intense behavior. The only form of extremism which discredits us before our children is "the acceptance of our present condition." (Lorraine Hansberry; quoted in Carole E. Gregory 1980, 16)

FACE

A body part which with all its features and expressions forms a site for sex differentiation. "Males tend to use their faces in power plays; females tend to use theirs in submissive acts." Many women perform such cosmetic acts on their face as "plucking eyebrows, adding artificial eyelashes, and wearing eye shadow, eyeliner, and mascara . . . because society defines so much of [women's] worth in terms of looks." (Bobbye D. Sorrels 1983, 109)

FACTORY

Sex- and class-segregated places of work which offer women work but seldom careers. The factory is often a place of labor-intensive methods of production which do not encourage women to expect job satisfaction. For women in the factory their work, domestic life, and financial situation are more tightly linked than they are for the relatively small number of women with professional careers. (Ruth Cavendish 1982, 163)

FACTS

Words treated as statements of actuality by those who agree with them. Facts "are theory laden; theories are value laden; values are history laden." (Donna J. Haraway 1981, 477)

(See METHODOLOGY, REALITY, THEORY)

FADED BEAUTIES

Women who are socialized to believe their only value is in their physical appearance, and who spend their later years trying to meet a cruel standard. (Ruth Harriet Jacobs 1979)

FAERIES

Originally the "pre-Celtic descendants of people from Northern Europe . . . feared by subsequent invaders because of their magical powers. They were short, Neolithic pastoral folk who lived in wild, uncultivated areas. They were herders, fleet-footed and able to take cover quickly; thus their reputation for vanishing into thin air. Their houses looked like small hills because they were sunk into the ground. . . They were spinners, weavers and dyers. They often wore green robes, for camouflage and a cape or a hood. . . The fairy Queen was the community's ruler; property was communal and marriage laws non-existent. They had knowledge of medicines, poisons and the power of hypnosis. They were builders, poets and musicians. In short, they lived as matriarchs whose Pagan ideas and sexual laxity were contrary to christian philosophy." (An adaptation of Margaret Murray's views by Susan Paxton 1982, 17)

FAGGOT

"Coming from the Italian word FOGOT-TO, the French derivation is spelled FAGGOT (pronounced with a silent T) and refers to a small bundle of kindling wood or twigs used for fueling a larger fire (i.e., 'a bundle of faggots'). Simultaneously, 15th and 16th century France was the hotbed of the Inquisition, the Roman Catholic tribunal which tried and executed hundreds of thousands for 'heresy.'

Most executions were by burning at the stake, and the great majority of Inquisition victims were the sexually 'deviant' (male homosexuals) and witches (often a guise for lesbianism). For the most part, small bundles of faggots were used to start the flames. Because the ignominy of depraved womanhood was more heinous than male homosexuality, it became common practice to save a number of convicted male homosexuals until the Inquisitors found a 'witch,' and then wrap the males around the convicted female and use them as faggots to start the flames. Hence, the term 'faggot' was applied to homosexual men." (Jeanne Cordova 1974, 22)

FAGHAG

"A woman, whether lesbian, bisexual, or heterosexual, who devotes an important part of her social, affectional, or sexual attention specifically to homosexual men and who finds them erotically interesting because of their homosexuality. This attention need not be overt, it can take the form of fantasies." ". . . the woman recognizes in the faggot a socio-erotic position she herself would like to hold, as the recognized peer *and* the lover of a male, a position impossible for women in sexist culture to secure." (Camilla Decarnin 1981, 10)

FAIR SEX, THE

A racist and "mock-complimentary label . . . . It has always been an ambiguous designation applied in contemptuous disregard of fact to all degrees of darkness . . . but to a certain type of mind it seemed to be a symbol, a presumption, at length even a proof of a kind of uniformity among women which no one would have predicted of men." ("Logic" 1914, *The Englishwoman*, 21:61 [Jan.], 5)

FAIR PRINCE, THE

A delightful illusion which "can hardly be accounted a complete solution of the woman problem, and only an unreal sentimentality would condemn the whole race of womankind to this long-drawn-out anguish of waiting for the impossible." (Ethel Rolt Wheeler 1910a, 17)

FAIRY TALE

A harmful, cross-cultural, educative story told to unsuspecting children that shows women as passive, opportunistic, or cruel. (Midge Lennert and Norma Willson eds 1973, 4)

(See CINDERELLA)

A story which is told not only in another place, another time: "They tell you fairy tales, too, you women of the West – fairy tales which, like ours, have all the appearance of truth." (Zeyneb Hanoum 1908: quoted in Naila Minai 1981, 225)

A tale which praises demure heroines. "Powerful female figures in fairy tales were either deprived of (verbal) power or their power was transformed into the wickedness of witchcraft." (Ruth Bottigheimer 1984; quoted in "Fairy tales 'unfair to women,' " ([*Michigan*] *State Journal*, March 5)

FAIRYTALE BRIGADE

"These are usually men who for some strange reason are attracted to the ideas of involvement in women's studies. They tell you fairytales. They offer you many marvelous visions of how they can help you, which they never back up and which never come true. They want to 'help' you to design and run the course, but in discussions they aim to manipulate and control, and do not understand the basis of feminism." (Robyn Rowland 1982, 490)

FALLEN WOMAN

A woman who has "failed in her vocation to guide men and to uplift society . . . thereby endangering not only national morality, but also male property and paternity rights." A convention of Victorian literature, she is a result of "the double standard of sexual ethics, reinforced by English laws and customs surrounding marriage, divorce, wife beating, women's property rights, and prostitution, and fostered by the belief in women's lack of sexual desires... Although the fallen, or unchaste, woman was not necessarily identical to the prostitute, she was believed to have taken the fatal first step toward a life of total degradation." (Kathleen Hickok 1984, 92-3)

FALLING IN LOVE

A passion. A "love choice" of sexual orientation or life partners "so complicated a thing, so tangled with other desires, sexual and social, that we must always be cynical about that magical [condition] which is supposed to justify the most preposterous social arrangements." (Sara Maitland 1980, 81)

"Falling carries with it a presupposition of having been in a stable position and at a higher point than before the fall occurred. Falling is unstable, uncontrolled movement from a higher to a lower place. In this hierarchical culture, up is positive and down is negative. The combined negative elements of Falling and In Love (as meaning captivated) make falling in love equal to falling in a trap. Furthermore, a fall is accidental." It loses as a positive term. (Debbie Alicen 1983, 18)

FALSE GENERICS

He and *Man*. "Elastic words. They function as rubber bands which can be stretched to include women when such weakness or deficiency is being discussed.... They can also be stretched to include women in a flattering and deceptive solidarity... Of course, the elastic 'we' and 'us' snaps back to normal whenever the planetary Men's Association shows its hand." (Mary Daly 1978, 326)

(See GENERICS, HE/MAN APPROACH, MAN AS FALSE GENERIC)

FAMILY

"The modern nuclear form, with a particular sexual division of labor, has been writ large as The Family and elevated as the only desirable and legitimate family form.... Women's subordination is linked to The Family as a specific household arrangement *and* as an ideology. Within households that resemble The Family in composition, boundedness, and division of labor, women are excluded from gaining direct access to valued resources such as income, recognized and status-giving work, and political authority. They are economically dependent on their husbands; their unpaid work at home is generally burdensome and devalued; and the work of mothering is done in relative isolation, to the detriment of both mother and child." (Barrie Thorne 1982, 4)

"Comes from the Latin *famulus*, meaning a servant or slave [which] is itself a reminder that wives and children, along with servants, were historically part of a man's property." The family is still considered man's institution. "Women are said to 'marry into' families, and families are said to 'die out' if an all-female generation occurs." (Casey Miller and Kate Swift 1976, 9)

"Simply an institution for the more complete subjugation and enslavement of women and children." (Frances Swiney 1918, 401)

The basic institution of sexism "with father at the head and mother and children in a lump together dependent on father's goodwill." (Stephanie Dowrick 1980, 72)

"Is both a mirror of and a connection with the larger society; a patriarchal unit within a patriarchal whole. Mediating between the individual and social structure, the family effects control and conformity where political and other authorities are insufficient... Serving as an agent of the larger society, the family not only encourages its own members to adjust and conform, but acts as a unit in the government of the patriarchal state which rules its citizens through its family heads." (Kate Millett 1971, 55)

"The Chicano family can be seen as a vehicle which incorporates those strengthening qualities that are necessary for social units to survive under exploitive conditions and paradoxically embodies those values which mitigate against the development and exercise of self-determination [particularly for women]." (Betty Garcia-Bahne 1978, 43)

"The family supports capitalism by providing a way for calm to be maintained amidst the disruption that is very much a part of capitalism. . . . It supports capitalist economy by providing a productive labor force and supplying a market for massive consumption. The family also performs an ideological role by cultivating the belief in individualism, freedom, and equality basic to the belief structure of society, although they are at odds with social and economic reality." (Zillah Eisenstein 1979b, 26)

"Is the basic unit of the community, and the vast increase in numbers of [white] women going out to work has made little difference to the division of labour in the family. home." (Anna Coote and Beatrix Campbell 1982, 81)

In its conventionalized, white form (2 parents, 2.4 children, father breadwinning and mother housekeeping) provides a model of gender and generation hierarchies "for the social relations of factories, schools, universities, business corporations, religious organizations, political parties, governments, armies, and hospitals." (Ann Oakley 1982, 242)

Seldom appears in its "typical" form: "According to the 1978 General Household Survey, out of the entire 'economically active' population [of the U.K.] *only five per cent* can be described as representative of the supposedly typical family unit (i.e. the breadwinning man with a wife and two children to support)." (Anna Coote and Beatrix Campbell 1982, 61)

White slave owners defined the Black *family* in another way. "Auction records and manifestos of slaves sent to New Orleans . . . prove that separation of families was the rule rather than the exception. When families were advertised for sale, they almost always included only the mother and her younger children, and often not even all of them. Youngsters of ten or twelve were generally considered

single." (August Meier and Elliott Rudwick 1966, 52)

Differs in history and function for whites and Blacks. "The family has been used by the white agency to perpetuate the state, and Blacks have been used as an extension of the white family, as the prisoners of war enslaved, to do the dirty work of the family, i.e., the state. If the family as an institution were destroyed, the state would be destroyed. If Black people were destroyed, but the family left intact, the basic structure of the state would allow for rebuilding. If all white institutions with the exception of the family were destroyed, the state could also rise again, but Black rather than white." (Kay Lindsey 1970, 87)

Is "the smallest organized, durable network of kin and non-kin who interact daily, providing the domestic needs of children, and assuring their survival. . . An arbitrary imposition of widely accepted definitions of the family . . . blocks the way to understanding how people in The Flats [a Black community] describe and order the world in which they live." (Carol B. Stack 1974, 31)

"A group of people who love each other, willingly share a common destiny, and nurture each other in an ongoing way. Marriage is not required in my definition; nor are children; nor is 'one-roof-ed-ness.' (If the sociologists can say 'female-head-ed-ness.')" (Susan Dworkin 1978, 95)

Sometimes *family* or *families* are code words in men's writing to mean women are present, as in "Men and families moved west across the plains." (Elizabeth Hampsten 1982, 5)

Groupings which have dramatically different compositions and resources. "Households headed by women – now 15 percent of all households – are the fastest growing type of family in the country." "In 1980 the median income of a female household head, with no husband present, was $10,408; for black women it was $7,425 and for Latinas, $7,031." "A woman over 60 years of age is almost twice as likely as her male counterpart to be impoverished. One-fifth of all elderly women are poor. For elderly black women the poverty rate in 1981 was 43.5 percent; for elderly Latina women 27.4 percent. Among black women over 65 living alone the 1982 poverty rate was about 82 percent." (cited in Karin Stallard, Barbara Ehrenreich and Holly Sklar 1983, 6-7, 9)

The white, nuclear form is built on women's unpaid work: "bearing and raising children, doing housework, providing sex and emotional support for men. There are a lot of other 'family' arrangements that similarly oppress women elsewhere in the world." (Sona Osman 1983, 29)

". . . uses people, *not* for what they are, nor for what they are intended to be, but for what it wants them for – its own uses. It thinks of them not as what God has made them but as the something which it has arranged that they shall be. If it wants someone to sit in the drawing room, *that* someone is supplied by the family. . . This system dooms some minds to incurable infancy, others to silent misery." (Florence Nightingale c.1855; quoted in Karen Payne 1983, 103)

"Is *not* by definition the man in a dominant position over women and children. Familia is cross-generational bonding, deep emotional ties between opposite sexes, and within our sex. It is sexuality, which involves, but is not limited to, intercourse or orgasm. It springs forth from touch, constant and daily. The ritual of kissing and the sign of the cross with every coming and going from the home. It is finding familia among friends where blood ties are formed through suffering and celebration shared." (Cherríe Moraga 1983, 111)

FAMILY MAN

Refers to a man who shows more concern with other members of the family than is normal. There is no label *family woman*, since that would be heard as a redundancy.

FAMILY OF MAN

"A mis-statement of biological fact."

(Midge Lennert and Norma Willson eds 1973, 4)

FAMILY PLANNING

"The very use of the term 'family planning' as a euphemism for birth control or contraception indicates a particular construction of heterosexual sexuality, with primacy given to reproductive functions within the family." (Helen Roberts 1981, 3)

FAMILY WAGE

Monetary support which is justification for keeping women out of the paid labor force and for maintaining lower wages for women. During depressions men are the ones to receive the Family Wage as they are considered *the* supporter of the family.

FANTASY

"An escape mechanism" especially for women. (bübül [Genny Pilgrim] July 1984, *off our backs*, 19)

FARKSOO

A language invented when she was a child by the U.S. writer Barbara Newhall Follet (1914-39) to be spoken on her imaginary planet Farksolia. A sample utterance from the *nairheen Farksoo* (farksoo grammar): *Na oparil* "the greatest dream of my life would be to go there." Follet married in the mid-1930s and worked as a secretary and stenographer. On Dec. 7, 1939, she walked out of her apartment in Brookline, Maine, taking with her thirty dollars and her stenographic notebook, and was never seen again. (manuscript in Columbia Univ. Manuscript Library)

FARMER

In most of Africa, usually female. (Barbara Rogers 1978; in Marsha Rowe 1982, 230)

(See AGRICULTURE)

FARMER'S WIFE

A hard worker:

"The farmer and his men came in at noon,

full of the open air's fresh vigorous life, and had an hour of rest: a blessed boon denied the farmer's wife."
(Elizabeth Akers 1891, 490)

Is also a farmer – one who shares the joys and problems associated with "the curse of the soil." (Edith Summers Kelley 1923)

FASHION

Restrictions on the independence of women. Because of the clothing a woman wears, men "must help her up stairs and down, in the carriage and out, on the horse, up the hills, over the ditch and fence, and thus teach her the poetry of dependence." (Elizabeth Cady Stanton 1857; cited by Lisa Tickner 1976; in Marsha Rowe 1982, 39)
(See CLOTHING, COSMETICS, PANTS)

An industry which invented the hobble skirt at exactly the same time that Suffragettes were marching toward freedom. (Elizabeth Robins 1907)

"Woman's striving after the ideal [which] may be a healthier sign than man's obstinate deference to established custom. But . . . why should the ideal silhouette for woman vary from that of an inflated balloon to that of a cod-fish or a stove-pipe?" ("The Tyranny of Fashion" 1909, *The Englishwoman*, 4:11 [December], 136)

A business which operates "to persuade women to spend more money than they can afford and to spend it on things that will not last." ("Problems of the Day" 1913, *The Englishwoman* 17:50 [Feb.], 129)

A mystery. "Why it is that a garment which is honestly attractive in, say, 1910 should be honestly ridiculous a few years later and honestly charming again a few years later . . . is one of those things which are not satisfactorily to be explained and are therefore jolly and exciting and an addition to the perennial interest of life." (Margery Allingham 1938, 5)

A set of routines which include washing your hair, shaving under your arms, using deodorant, polishing your nails, and obtaining new clothes. "They are feminine chores from which men and boys are more or less exempt. They depend on planning and forethought, they are time-consuming and often seem distinctly more like work than leisure. Although men and boys have become increasingly fashion-conscious in the last few years, they are not expected to place such importance on their daily beauty ritual, the day-to-day 'reproduction' of their looks" or on the "re-upholstery of the self." (Angela McRobbie 1981, 122-4)

An industry which creates an image of beauty few women are able to realize for themselves and which creates a longing to win approval, a longing which has a cost "to our health, our identity as women, our experience of pleasure in our bodies. But fashion also reflects hidden cultural intentions, as it did in China with the binding of women's feet. As it does in our own day, with pants so tight they serve as an adequate replacement for the girdle that binds us. Fashion . . . is a mirror in which we can read the responses of conventional culture to what is occurring, at the deepest levels of cultural change, among its people." (Kim Chernin 1981, 99)

FASTING

Non-eating, a behavior which in women and girls "has obviously been around for a very long time. Work by historian Caroline Walker Bynum demonstrates that in the High Middle Ages (thirteenth through sixteenth centuries) the lives of women saints were characterized by extensive fasting and passionate devotion to the eucharist (taking the wafer and the wine, a symbol of the body and blood of Christ). Moreover, where writings by these women survived, they contain pervasive images of eating, drinking, and food – much as the twentieth-century anorectic is food-obsessed, counting calories, and structuring her life around non-meals and strenuous exercise. Living with food deprivation was the particular skill of female saints; in fact, Bynum maintains that 'almost all saints who were completely unable to eat or who survived for years on the Eucharist alone were women.' . . . Just as the anorectic loses control of her behavior and oftentimes cannot eat even when she wants to, some of the medieval women occasionally claimed that their inability to eat was *not* a religious practice precisely because it became involuntary." (Joan Jacobs Brumberg 1983)

(See ANOREXIA NERVOSA)

FAT

"Noun: A substance in the form of energy stored; essential to the preservation of life and health among humans – but presented to contemporary Western women as a mortal enemy. Adjective: When used to discuss research, is generally a positive evaluative term, synonymous with 'rich' or 'full.' When used to describe young mammals, fat (until recently) carried the implication of 'good health,' 'cuddly', and 'cute.' When used to describe adult women, fat is an ultimate pejorative, meaning that they are larger than fashion dictates they ought to be, and implying that they are undisciplined, lazy, self-destructive, out of control, and morally weak." (Elizabeth Nelson 1984, correspondence)

A label given to people who weigh more than the fashion, entertainment, and health industries say is appropriate. "Since there is evidence that being fat is related to one's racial or class origins, this is one more way the system acts to grind down the poor." (Martha Courtot 1982, 15)

FATHER

The male who "makes the decisions which control the family's work, purchases, marriages." In the Old Order: "At home was the father, in church was the priest or minister, at the top were the 'town fathers,' the local nobility, or, as they put it in Puritan society 'the nursing fathers of the Commonwealth' and above all was 'God the Father' " (Barbara Ehrenreich and Deirdre English 1979, 7)

An elder male person who has a central role in our lives. Fathers "lay the basis subtly, coercively or violently of our fear of male anger, and therefore our fear of challenging men." (Liz Kelly 1984, 19)

In early cultures, meant merely elder man or provider (since people believed that women could procreate wthout men). (Una Stannard 1977, 292)

"[Trad.] Male parent. [New]. A psychologically involved male parent." (Midge Lennert and Norma Willson eds. 1973, 4)

"To a female of two, four, ten, thirteen years, a 'father' is any male who is in an omnipotent position while she remains utterly powerless under his influence." (Stella Chess and Jane Whitbread 1979; paraphrased by Elizabeth Denny 1984, 49)

To father. The meaning assigned to this term – to give life – is quite different from the traditional meaning given to to *mother* – to nurture. This use represents the classic seminal ideas of men about who is given credit for creation. Some feminists are using these verbs as equivalents, meaning *to parent.*

(See OVULAR, SEMINAL)

FATHERING

"Is a hobby. It may turn out to be a lifelong passion, but it is still a hobby, and fathers who want to alter this find no real model available to them. A father can choose his duties; there is no normal or essential behaviour which defines him as a father or predetermines the nature of his fathering. He can be attentive and cherishing or neglectful and violent, but he still remains simply a father. There is no such flexibility with mothering. The job is laid down, defined, set in cement." (Ursula Owen 1983, 13)

"Our concept of good fathering is almost nonexistent [while] our culture is top-heavy with images and indeed impossible ideals about what constitutes good *mothering*. . . . [At present] a good father is one who does *not* drink all the housekeep'ng, and does *not* scar the children." (Eileen Fairweather 1983, 195)

FEAR

"Is almost an inseparable attendant on virtue. The virtuous are ever timid more or less; their own inoffensive deposition and the knowledge they have how much vice abounds among Men, are sufficient to incline them to fear on every appearance of danger." (Sophia 1739, 53)

Is "a function of our so-called femininity. We are taught systematically to be afraid, and we are taught that to be afraid not only is congruent with femininity, but also inheres in it. We are taught to be afraid so that we will not be able to act, so that we will be passive, so that we will be women. . ." (Andrea Dworkin 1976, 55)

(See FEMININITY, PASSIVITY)

FEAR-OF-CRIME

The diffuse feeling of anxiety which accompanies women when they are alone after dark; U.S. and British government surveys indicate that women's fear is three times that of men's fear of crime. (This finding has led some researchers to conclude that women's feelings are "irrational" and "excessive." These researchers ignore statistics on battering and rape.) (Elizabeth A. Stanko 1984)

FELLOWSHIPS

We call them Scholarships. (Eve Merriam 1974, 22)

FEMALE

"A middle English variant of the Old French *femelle*, from the Latin diminutive of *femina*, meaning woman, *female* has no etymological connection with *male* at all; its present spelling and pronunciation evolved only because people mistakenly assumed it did." (Casey Miller and Kate Swift 1976, 89)

Designates the sex that produces ova or offspring; it is not a parallel term to *male* which is used less frequently. *Female* "might belong to any animal tribe, and . . . in our version of the Bible, is never used except of animals, or of the abstract, the sex in general. Why not call a man a 'male,' if a woman is to be a

'female'?" (Henry Alford 1864; cited in Dennis Baron 1982, 193-4)

A term which, along with *male*, has "become so loaded and politicized, so laden with old prejudices, that [it is] almost useless for purposes of communication." (Erica Jong 1972, 121)

Was the replacement "neutral" term when in the 19th century the word *woman* acquired the meaning of "paramour or mistress" or the sense of intercourse with women when used in the plural as in *Wine, Woman, and Song*. "It was replaced by *female*, but this term also came to be considered degrading and indelicate. . . The *OED* recorded *female* as a synonym 'avoided by writers,' and [*Webster's Third International*] identified it as a disparaging term when used for women. It was replaced in the 19th century by *lady*." *Lady* also become vulgarized and in the 20th century it was replaced by *woman*, newly rehabilitated. (Muriel Schulz 1975b, 71)

"The binary opposite of male, it describes a biological state. To oversimplify, feminine is to female as clothes and gestures are to the body. A profound quarrel among feminist critics now has to do with the ways in which the female body might influence a woman's consciousness, her language and her literature." (Catherine Stimpson 1981, 60)

(See L'ECRITURE FEMININE, WRITING)

"Primal power. [In the oldest artifacts] she is at the very center of what is sacred and necessary." Women were, in early religion, "linked with food not only because they cultivated and prepared it but also because their own bodies were a source of food and life." (Christine Downing 1984, 9-10)

(See AGRICULTURE)

THE FEMALE EUNUCH

A book by Germaine Greer, published in 1970, which argued that women should pull themselves together, stop loving the victors in violent encounters, and replace compulsiveness and compulsion by the pleasure principle. The book "dug a channel through to the women's movement from the Love Generation, and introduced many thousands of women to a new sense of themselves." (Anna Coote and Beatrix Campbell 1982, 20)

FEMALENESS

Presented in much literary criticism as a "congenital fault, rather like eczema or Original Sin. . . . But fortunately, some women can be saved. By good manners, they are translated from females into ladies; and by talent, into feminine creatures (or even into 'classical heroines')." (Mary Ellmann 1968, 34)

FEMALE PATRIOTISM

The title of a column published in the early 19th century by publisher, printer and editor Sara Hillhouse, under the name Dorothy Distaff. She declared that a "hundred thousand spinning wheels would be as effective as 10,000 of the best militia." (Marion Marzolf 1977, 10-11)

FEMALE PRINCIPLE

"Is, or at least historically has been, basically anarchic. It values order without constraint, rule by custom, not by force. It has been the male who enforces order, who constructs power-structures, who makes, enforces, and breaks laws." (Ursula K. Le Guin 1976, 134)

FEMALE SEXUAL SLAVERY

Refers to international traffic in women and forced street prostitution. Also the private practice by husbands and fathers who use battery and sexual abuse as a personal measure of their power over their wives and/or daughters. *Female sexual slavery is present in ALL situations where women or girls cannot change the immediate conditions of their existence; where regardless of how they got into those conditions they cannot get out; and where they are subject to sexual violence and exploitation.*" (Kathleen Barry 1979, 39-40)

"Once known by the nineteenth-century racist term *white slavery*, because for the most part it was the only form of slavery to which whites were also subjec-

ted . . . . We know now it flourishes in many of our own cities where prostitution and pornography are big business and a fact of international life." (Gloria Steinem 1983, 159)

(See WHITE SLAVERY)

FEMALE SOLIPSISM

The idea that the female self is the only reality. "There is no such thing as vicarious Manhood or Womanhood. What each soul is, that and that only it possesses." (Celia Burleigh 1873, 81)

(See WHITE, WHITE SOLIPSISM)

FEMICIDE

The murder of a woman by her husband. "The subordinate position of women in Bangladesh and their status as 'property of men' have been leading to a number of 'femicide' cases almost parallel to the bride-burning phenomenon in India. . . . Most of the murders, accomplished with the aid or collusion of in-laws, [are] due to dowry [disputes]." (Shahana Rahman 1984, 7)

FEMINA

Latin word for *woman*. Name of journal *Femina: A Magazine for Thinking Women*, edited 1914-16 by Jessie F. Atwater, published in Massachusetts, with a group of 30 "Femina Associates" who guided the policies of the magazine.

FEMINARY

"From O.A. [Old Amazon] *femi*: female, strong; *na*: person: she who is the first person + ry – noun. 1. a visionary guidebook containing the wisdom and information collected by our foremothers. 2. the new name of the formerly entitled FEMINIST NEWSLETTER; we hope that all women will read and contribute to this forum." (*A FEMINARY* 1974, 5:20 [October 6], cover)

A journal title (*Feminary: A Feminist Journal for the* [U.S.] *South*). The title comes from Monique Wittig's *Les Guerillères*: "The women are seen to have in their hands small books which they say are feminaries. . . . In one of them someone has written an inscription which they whisper in each other's ears and which provokes them to full-throated laughter. When it is leafed through, the feminary presents numerous blank pages in which they write from time to time." A member of the *Feminary* collective writes that the journal is a "symbol of personal disobedience and rebellion, a way of breaking down the silences that are very nearly as Southern as manner." (Cris South 1980, 5)

FEMININE

"An adjective, the binary opposite of masculine; it refers to a set of behaviors that are normatively powerful and empirically observable, to a cluster of characteristics that have ethical significance and social appearances." (Catharine Stimpson 1981, 59)

"Every quality which we regard as distinctively feminine, will, under conditions of greater freedom, develop more freely." (Josephine Butler, 1868, 18)

Is very different from *female*, just as masculine is different from *male*. Feminine and masculine are "perhaps the most culturally biased words in the language. Rarely employed in a biological sense, they are used instead to describe what a group or society has decided female and male persons should (or should not) be." (Casey Miller and Kate Swift 1976, 69)

What we are supposed to be. No necessary connection with what we are. (Sona Osman 1983, 30)

FEMININE MYSTIQUE

Betty Friedan's 1960s term for the identification of womanhood with the roles of wife and mother. The myth, conveyed to women by popular culture, that "the highest value and the only commitment for women is the fulfillment of their own femininity . . . The new mystique makes the housewife-mother, who never had a chance to be anything else, the model for all women." Interviewing American women in the early 1960s, Betty Friedan identified a "nameless aching dissatisfaction" produced by the split between the ideal of feminine fulfillment and the reality of isolation and despair in real life." (Betty Friedan 1963, 43, 33)

FEMININE PROTECTION
(See ADVERTISING, MENSTRUATION, REPRESENTATION, TAMPON)

FEMININITY

"Means attractiveness to men, which means sexual attractiveness, which means sexual availability on male terms." (Catharine A. MacKinnon 1982a, 530-1)

"Weak elegancy of mind, exquisite sensibility, and sweet docility of manner." (Mary Wollstonecraft 1789; rpt in Alice Rossi ed. 1973, 42)

A counterpart to the machismo stereotype of masculinity, developed by the patriarchal system, it is the "female object" or "female eunuch." (LACW Collective 1977, 7)

"A man-made mess." A paradox (madonna-whore) which has a high cost of living. (Joanna Russ 1979, 68-70)

Differs in function and effect for white and Black women. "Most Black women still do not receive the respect and treatment – mollycoddling and condescending as it sometimes is – afforded White women. So when these Black women complain about not wanting to lose their femininity, they are referring to something quite different." (Gloria I. Joseph; in Gloria I. Joseph and Jill Lewis 1981, 27)

"Femininity pleases men because it makes them appear more masculine by contrast; and, in truth, conferring an extra portion of unearned gender distinction on men, an unchallenged space in which to breathe freely and feel stronger, wiser, more competent, is femininity's special gift. One could say that masculinity is often an effort to please women, but masculinity is known to please by displays of mastery and competence while femininity pleases by suggesting that these concerns, except in small matters, are beyond its intent." (Susan Brownmiller 1984a, 16)

(See MASCULINITY)

FEMINISM

(See all entries above and below)

A movement with a long history. Three basic positions of feminism during 1400-1789: (1) a conscious stand in opposition to male defamation and mistreatment of women; a dialectical opposition to misogyny. (2) a belief that the sexes are culturally, and not just biologically, formed; a belief that women were a social group shaped to fit male notions about a defective sex. (3) an outlook that transcended the accepted value systems of the time by exposing and opposing the prejudice and narrowness; a desire for a truly general conception of humanity. (Joan Kelly 1982, 6-7)

Has as its goal to give every woman "the opportunity of becoming the best that her natural faculties make her capable of." (Millicent Garrett Fawcett 1878, 357)

Has as a goal: The liberation of women for women. "We don't have to have anything to do with men at all. They've taken excellent care of themselves." (Jill Johnston 1973a, 91)

"May be defined as a movement seeking the reorganization of the world upon a basis of sex-equality in all human relations; a movement which would reject every differentiation between individuals upon the ground of sex, would abolish all sex privileges and sex burdens, and would strive to set up the recognition of the common humanity of woman and man as the foundation of law and custom." (Teresa Billington-Greig 1911a, 694, 703)

". . . has as yet no defined creed. . . [Is] the articulate consciousness of mind in women . . . in its different forms of expression." ("The Freewoman" 1911, *Votes for Women*, 17 November, 103)

Is that part of the progress of democratic freedom which applies to women. (Beatrice Forbes-Robertson Hale 1914, 3)

"A many-headed monster which cannot be destroyed by singular decapitation. We spread and grow in ways that are incomprehensible to a hierarchical mentality." (Peggy Kornegger 1979, 243)

"Feminism at heart is a massive complaint. Lesbianism is the solution. . . . Until all women are lesbians there will be no true political revolution. No feminist per se has advanced a solution outside of accommodation to the man." (Jill Johnston 1973a, 166)

"An integration of various here-to-fore incompatible elements built on a collective base of thought-action-feeling. Feminism integrates the subjective, and objective, the rational and the intuitive, the mystical and the scientific, the abstract and concrete aspects of the universe and considers them harmonious parts of a whole rather than in opposition to one another." (Anne Kent Rush and Anica Vesel Mander 1974, 14-15)

"Begins but cannot end with the discovery by an individual of her self-consciousness as a woman. It is not, finally, even the recognition of her reasons for anger, or the decision to change her life, to go back to school, to leave a marriage. . . . Feminism means finally that we renounce our obedience to the fathers and recognize that the world they have described is not the whole world. . . . Feminism implies that we recognize fully the inadequacy for us, the distortion, of male-created ideologies, and that we proceed to think, and act, out of that recognition." (Adrienne Rich 1976; rpt. 1979, 207)

"A method of analysis as well as a discovery of new material. It asks new questions as well as coming up with new answers. Its central concern is with the social distinction between men and women, with the fact of this distinction, with its meanings, and with its causes and consequences." (Juliet Mitchell and Ann Oakley 1976, 14)

"We are actively committed to struggling against racial, sexual, heterosexual, and class oppression and see as our particular task the development of integrated analysis and practice based upon the fact that the major systems of oppression are interlocking. The synthesis of these oppressions creates the conditions of our lives. As Black women we see Black feminism as the logical political movement to combat the manifold and simultaneous oppressions that all women of color face." (Combahee River Collective 1977; rpt. in Cherríe Moraga and Gloria Anzaldúa eds 1981, 210)

Women uniting as women to generate "a force which presses society to accept and accommodate femaleness as equal, even if different, in its attributes." (Devaki Jain 1978, 9)

"Potentially the most threatening of movements to Black and other Third World people because it makes it absolutely essential that we examine the way we live, how we treat each other, and what we believe. It calls into question the most basic assumptions about our existence and this is the idea that biological, i.e., sexual identity, determines all, that it is the rationale for power relationships as well as for all levels of human identity and action." (Barbara Smith 1983, xxv-xxvi)

"Is a mode of analysis, a method of approaching life and politics, a way of asking questions and searching for answers, rather than a set of political conclusions about the oppression of women." (Nancy Hartsock 1979, 58-9)

"Feminism is the political theory and practice to free all women: women of color, working-class women, poor women, physically challenged women, lesbians, old women, as well as white economically privileged heterosexual women. Anything less than this is not feminism, but merely female self-aggrandizement." (Barbara Smith 1979; quoted in Cherríe Moraga and Gloria Anzaldúa eds 1981, 61)

(See BLACK FEMINISM)

Woman responding to question, "As an Asian American woman, do you consider yourself a feminist?": "There is feminism where all the problems of women in society are seen as caused by men. I don't believe in that. I don't believe men are the creators of the problems in society. . . . I do believe that men and women have to work together to solve the problems in society." (In Susie Ling's dissertation; quoted by Lucie Cheng 1984, 11)

"Feminism means you have to read a lot, to understand a lot, to feel a lot, and to be honest." "To me, real feminism means being revolutionary. To be revolutionary means that one examines the problems of women from all aspects: historically, sociologically, economically, and psychologically. . . . And as a radical feminist, I think you should oppose imperialism, Zionism, feudalism, and inequality between nations, sexes, and classes." (Nawal el Saadawi 1980, 3)

A philosophy "based on the recognition that we live in a male dominated culture in which women remain unacknowledged, and where women are forced into sex roles which demand that they be dependent, passive, nurturant, etc. Men too must assume sex roles [but these] are not nearly as crippling as women's." (*Banshee: Journal of Irishwomen United* 1981, 8:10)

"Is a commitment to eradicating the ideology of domination that permeates Western culture on various levels – sex, race, and class, to name a few – and a commitment to reorganizing U.S. society, so that the self-development of people can take precedence over imperialism, economic expansion, and material desires." (bell hooks 1981, 194-5)

"Means to me the movement towards creating a society where women can live a full, self-determined life. This may seem a bland statement but in terms of the changes we need to achieve this, it is revolutionary." (Mary MacNamara c.1982, 6)

Is "the desire and struggle for freedom," which is the same for each of us – Black, Latina, Native American, etc. – "even though our methods may differ." (Deborah Aslan Jamieson 1982, 6)

"Is an entire world view or *gestalt*, not just a laundry list of 'women's issues.' Feminist theory provides a basis for understanding every area of our lives, and a feminist perspective can affect the world politically, culturally, economically, and spiritually." (Charlotte Bunch 1983, 250)

"Two elements constitute the discipline of feminism: political, ideological, and strategic confrontation with the sex-class system – with sex hierarchy and sex segregation – and a single standard of human dignity. Abandon either element and the sex-class system is unbreachable, indestructible; feminism loses its rigor, the toughness of its visionary heart. . . . One other discipline is essential both to the practice of feminism and to its theoretical integrity: the firm, unsentimental, continuous recognition that women are a class having a common condition." (Andrea Dworkin 1983, 200)

"Is a theory that calls for women's attainment of social, economic, and political rights and opportunities equal to those possessed by men. Feminism is also a model for a social state – an ideal, or a desired standard of perfection not yet attained in the world." (Rebecca Lewin 1983, 17)

Is the fairy godmother. "Do you remember the story of Cinderella? She is sitting at home rather pissed off, wanting to go to the ball, and not having a thing to wear, when the fairy godmother whizzes in and puts it all right. One of the most important things about the fairy godmother is that she transforms all the old stuff around Cinderella into new and useful equipment: the rags, the pumpkin, the rats, and so forth. This little girl's fairy godmother turned out to be called Feminism. As well as cheering the little girl up no end Feminism also transformed all the old things around her." (Sara Maitland 1983, 18)

"Third World feminism is about feeding people in all their hungers." (Cherríe Moraga 1983, 132) "[It] is bringing the strains together." (Barbara Smith; quoted in Cherríe Moraga 1983, 133)

Is a powerful homeopathic remedy which goes beyond the symptoms to the deeper causes of our troubles: the imbalance between masculine and feminine energies, manifested in the ills of patriarchy. (Jill Raymond and Janice Wilson 1983, 59)

Is neither original nor radical; women's ideas about the relationship of women and men are either coopted or lost by men and have to be recreated every fifty years or so. (Dale Spender 1982b)

A set of beliefs and "theoretical constructions about the nature of women's oppression and the part that this oppression plays within social reality more generally." (Liz Stanley and Sue Wise 1983, 55)

With a capital 'F' it is a theory, a position. With small 'f' it is an organic conviction based on experience. (Osha Davidson 1984, 11A)

FEMINISM IS THE THEORY; LESBIANISM IS THE PRACTICE

An aphorism attributed (by Anne Koedt 1971, 246) to radical feminist Ti-Grace Atkinson, 1970, and taken in the early 1970s to affirm a strong theoretical and practical connection between feminism and lesbianism. The affirmation was particularly important during a period in which some feminists expressed the view that the aims of women's liberation would be compromised by "the lesbian connection." Actually, Atkinson's paper, which she delivered to the New York Chapter of Daughters of Bilitis in 1970, questioned whether feminists and lesbians could work together in meaningful ways. "Feminism is a theory," she said, "but lesbianism is a practice." She later changed her position and spoke out against the oppression of lesbians within the women's movement and within society at large. (Sidney Abbott and Barbara Love 1972, 117)

(See AUTHORITY, LESBIANISM)

FEMINISSIMA

"Joyousness, the pride in my body and its abilities. . . . In order to claim the feminine power for my own, I gave it a name: *feminissima*." (Seph Weene 1981, 37)

FEMINIST

"I myself have never been able to find out precisely what feminism is: I only know that people call me a feminist whenever I express sentiments that differentiate me from a doormat . . ." (Rebecca West 1913, *The Clarion*, Nov 14)

"Mother, what is a Feminist?"
"A Feminist, my daughter,
Is any woman now who cares
To think about her own affairs
    As men don't think she oughter"
    (Alice Duer Miller 1915; in Red-
    stockings eds 1975, 52)

"Feminist is formed with the word 'femme,' 'woman,' and means: someone who fights for women. For many of us this means someone who fights for women as a class and for the disappearance of this class. For many others it means someone who fights for woman and her defense – for the myth, then, and its reinforcement." (Monique Wittig 1981, 50)

A person who knows that we hold up half the sky and who is going to make everyone else notice it. (Dawn Russell 1979, 75)

What is unique about the feminist mode of analysis: "(1) The focus on everyday life and experience makes action a necessity, not a moral choice or an option. We are not fighting other people's battles but our own. (2) The nature of our understanding of theory is altered and theory is brought into an integral and everyday relation with practice. (3) Theory leads directly to a transformation of social relations both in consciousness and in reality because of its close connection to real needs." (Nancy Hartsock 1979, 64)

A word that frightens some people. "For the feminist [literary] critic, however, it is less a bogey or a bugaboo than a badge of honor. . . . It refers to the conviction that our production of culture and meaning, like our consumption of culture and meaning, influences our sex/gender systems. In turn, our sex/gender systems influence our production and consumption of culture and meaning." (Catharine Stimpson 1981, 59)

"From the early generalizations about 'all women,' feminists are recognizing the need to understand the specific nature and conditions of women's oppression in differing cultures, societies, and economies." (Jill Lewis 1981; in Gloria I. Joseph and Jill Lewis 1981, 67)

"To be a feminist means recognizing that one is associated with all women not as an act of choice but as a matter of fact. . . . Feminists do not create this common condition by making alliances; feminists recognize this common condition because it exists as an intrinsic part of sex oppression. . . What is that common condition? Subordination to men, sexually colonized in a sexual system of dominance and submission, denied rights on the basis of sex, historically chattel, generally considered biologically inferior, confined to sex and reproduction; this is the general description of the social environment in which all women live." (Andrea Dworkin 1983, 221)

"Well, I'm convinced that many frustrated and crabby women are merely feminists in restraints." (Diane F. Germain 1983, 154)

"A person, female or male, whose worldview places the female in the center of life and society, and/or who is not prejudiced based on gender or sexual preference. Also, anyone in a male-dominated or patriarchal society who works toward the political, economic, spiritual, sexual, and social equality of women." (*The Wise Woman* 1982, 4:2 [June 21], 7)

When used by a man to refer to himself it is a "male appropriation of language no less stupidly defensive than a white man imagining myself a black radical." Profeminist is a term used to describe the male who works towards feminist goals. (Irving Weinman 1983, 133-4)

(See WOMANIST)

FEMINIST DICTIONARY

A word book which calls into question the androcentric nature of much "standard language usage" and problematizes many words and phrases in the light of feminist perspectives and commentary. *This* feminist dictionary (1) recognizes women as linguistically creative speakers, (2) explicitly acknowledges the socio-political aspects of dictionary-making, (3) draws heavily on excerpted material from feminist publications, (4) does not generally specify "parts of speech" (noun, verb, etc.) or linguistic status (coinage, obsolete, etc.) but rather provides commentary on the general cultural knowledge that the reader brings to this book, (5) assumes that a book about words is inevitably a book about the world as well, (6) emphasizes definitions by feminists without making continual reference to male authorities, (7) sometimes offers "contradictions" without resolving them. That this book is incomplete goes without saying. It is not intended to be the last word. We urge readers to make their own contributions using the blank pages at the back of the book and send them to us for the next edition.

(See INTRODUCTION to this book, AUTHOR, AUTHORITY, DICTIONARY, REPRESENTATION)

FEMINIST HUMORIST
(See FUMERIST)

FEMINIST LESBIANISM
"Consciously 'out of line' with the all-pervading 'normalities' of heterosexist prejudice, feminist lesbianism generates an imagining of different levels of challenge and terms in vision, which can nourish fundamental perspectives needed for the overthrow of male dominance." (Jill Lewis 1981; in Gloria I. Joseph and Jill Lewis 1981, 269)

FEMINIST MAN
"A man who has humour and sympathy is generally a feminist *sans le savoir*." ("The Maze of the Law" 1914, *The Englishwoman*, 25:73, 65)

The New Man: "the male member of the human species who is psychologically complete and is able to identify with a woman on her terms." (Midge Lennert and Norma Willson eds 1973, 7)

FEMINIST NETWORK
"Is the sum of innumerable one-to-one relationships expanding into the distance without being homogenized." (Lucy Lippard 1983, 120)

FEMINIST REALIZATION
The awareness that one's own position and the position of women in general is political. (Gloria Steinem 1983, 100)

FEMININE VISION
"Has to do with the abolition of all sex roles – the absolute transformation of human sexuality and the institutions derived from it." (Andrea Dworkin 1976, 12-13)

FEMINITUDE
"A term coined by Francoise d'Eaubonne to describe the state of servitude of women in a phallocratic world." (Mary Daly 1978, 53)

(See PHALLOCRACY)

FEMINIZATION OF POVERTY
"A structural feature of capitalism in the Third World. It is fast becoming so in the United States (and Europe) too where women are pushed into the permanent 'underclass' in larger and larger numbers as domestic work is subsumed by capitalism and the nuclear family weakens." (Asoka Bandarage 1983, 9)

In the U.S., the following condition: "Two out of three poor adults are women and one out of five children is poor. Women head half of all poor families and over half the children in female-headed households are poor: 50 per cent of white children; 68 per cent of black and Latin children." (In Karin Stallard, Barbara Ehrenreich and Holly Sklar 1983, 6)

FEMINOLOGY
A term coined by Nynne Koch, a Danish librarian, as a convenient catalog classification for women's studies. Josephine Donovan suggests that *women's studies* remains a more appropriate phrase in the U.S., considering its "hard-won currency," but that *feminology* may be better for international use. (Josephine Donovan 1978, 916)

(See WOMEN'S STUDIES)

"The science of women." (Suzette Haden Elgin 1981, 3)

FEMYNYE

Medieval designation for the kingdom of Amazons. (*Brewer's Dictionary of Phrase and Fable* 1962, 356)

FERTILITY

"Becoming pregnant and carrying a fetus to term is a problem for at least 15% of women of reproductive age, whether lesbian or heterosexual.... Social rules about fertility are at least as much a problem as physical problems. There is tremendous social pressure on women to have the 'right' number of children." (Sona Osman 1983, 30)

(See REPRODUCTION, STERILIZATION)

FERTILITY CULTS

The condescending labels for our oldest Earth Mother religions. (Susan Paxton 1982, 3)

FETCH

" 'Home again,' 'to fetch home,' expressions once used by the witches who effected passages and transformations, meaning 'return to one's own shape.' 'Yet I shall go into a bee / and flit to hive / ere I be fetched home.' " (Monique Wittig and Sande Zeig 1976, 55)

"Bending over, walking to, or getting on a mule, bicycle, bus, or getting into a car, carriage, or wagon to go after something you want. My great grandmother tells me to fetch things that she can no longer get easily for herself." (Cheryl West 1985, correspondence)

FICTION

Events and statements of imagination. Most published fiction deals with men's perspectives. Androcentric culture "has not given any true picture of woman's life." (Charlotte Perkins Gilman 1911, 105) [Charlotte Perkins Gilman's *Yellow Wallpaper* is a stunning portrayal of a woman's life in androcentric culture.]

Writing which "allows for the vagaries of life, the loose strands that refuse the tidying hand, the nonsequiturs, the unanswerable questions, the questionable answers, the sheer disorder of things that journalism does not permit, dealing as it does with beginnings, middles, and ends in a random world that has no perceptible beginning or middle, only the looming shadow of an end." (Jill Tweedie 1983, 115)

FIFTH WORLD

(See FOURTH WORLD)

FILM

(See FILM CRITICISM, MASS MEDIA, VISUAL PLEASURE)

FILM CRITICISM

Makes visible the invisible at several levels. "A feminist analysis may offer a reading of a film which starts out by exposing the absences of the text, or by pointing to the ways in which it constructs women through its images or its narrative structure ... at the level of film production itself, through an examination of the place of films within the context in which they are produced, by looking at the question of how films are put together in the ways they are, the kinds of social relations involved in that process, and the relationships between modes of production and the formation of textual structures and operations foregrounded by a feminist perspective." (Annette Kuhn 1982, 73)

Has an experimental glossary of terms, offered by B. Ruby Rich: *validative* (films which validate and legitimate women's culture and individual lives); *correspondence* (introspective missives sent out into the world); *reconstructive* (rebuilding of forms and genres); *medusan* (humor and sexuality); *corrective realism* (beyond just the "positive roles model"); *projectile* (men's films depicting male fantasies of women – men's projections of themselves and their fears onto female characters). (B. Ruby Rich 1980, 78-80)

FINISH

As in finishing school which smoothes and polishes and makes undone. Vera Brittain writes that the effect of finishing school was "to be shaped yet more definitely in the trivial feminine mould which every youthful instinct and ambition prompted me to repudiate." (Vera Brittain 1933, 52)

FIREMAN

(See WOMAN, Shirley Morahan)

FIREWEED

"A hardy perennial so called because it is the first growth to reappear in fire-scarred areas; a troublesome weed which spreads like wildfire invading and clearing bomb-sites, waste land and other disturbed areas." (Epigram of the journal collective *Fireweed*)

FIRST LADY

"A title that had probably been invented in 1877 by Mary Clemmer Ames to describe Mrs. Hayes . . . the adjective 'first' had democratic implications, for if the wife of the president was the 'first' lady of the land, then other wives were also ladies in their secondary spheres." (Una Stannard 1977, 24-5)

FIRST MANIFESTO

A frequently quoted document from Redstockings of New York, a feminist group, which includes the following: "Women are an oppressed class. . . . We are exploited as sex objects, breeders, domestic servants, and cheap labor. . . . Our prescribed behavior is enforced by threat of physical violence. Because we have lived so intimately wih our oppressors, in isolation from each other, we have been kept from seeing our personal suffering as a political condition. This creates the illusion that a woman's relationship with her man is a matter of interplay between two unique personalities, and can be worked out individually. In reality, every such relationship is a *class* relationship, and the conflicts between individual men and women are political conflicts that can only be solved collectively. We regard our personal experience, and our feelings about that experience, as the basis for an analysis of our common situation. We cannot rely on existing ideologies as they are all products of a male supremacist culture. We question every generalization and accept none that is not confirmed by our experience. We identify with all women. We define our best interest as that of the poorest, most brutally exploited woman. In fighting for our liberation we will always take the side of women against their oppressors. We will not ask what is 'revolutionary' or 'reformist,' only what is good for women." (Redstockings 1969; in Anna Coote and Beatrix Campbell 1982, 15)

(See REDSTOCKINGS)

FIRST NAME

Serves as a quick identifier of sex in most cultures. Girls are more likely to be given derivative, diminutive names such as Georgette, Georgina, Henrietta and Paulette; flower names such as Rose, Violet, Lily, Myrtle, Florence, and Iris, Holly, Ivy, Fern and Heather; seasons of the year names such as April, May, June; nurturing names such as Dawn and Sunny; and virginity names such as Chastity and Virginia. First names are used more for children, servants, and other supposed inferiors than for those who are older, richer and "superior"; women are first named more than are men. Women in high status jobs are more likely to greet and address colleagues on equal terms. (Casey Miller and Kate Swift 1976, 7-8; Julie Belle White 1980)

(See NAMING)

FIRST WAVE

Often assumed to have begun with the Seneca Falls, New York, convention of 1848. However, this is a short-sighted, ethnocentric view. Elizabeth Sarah asks: "What does the brutal murder of nine million *witches* suggest to us about the scale of *feminist* resistance [in the sixteenth and seventeenth century] . . . . Are we justified in fixing the 'first wave' between the mid-nineteenth century and the first two decades of the twentieth century? Timing the 'first wave' in this way, presupposes a particular political and economic context – the development of liberalism, capitalism, and socialist movements in this period – which is only relevant for the feminist movements which developed in the western world. India, for example, subjected to British colonial rule and characterized by a different set of political and economic factors, experienced the 'high point' of her 'first wave' later." (Elizabeth Sarah 1982, 521)

FLATTERY

Words of praise commonly given to women in substitution of money and occupational status. Flattery (e.g. concerning appearance) is often used to try to keep women happily in their traditional place.

Vague statements of approval which often "do not hide a low opinion of women's ability." (Christopher St John 1914, 92)

(See CHIVALRY, COMPLIMENT)

FLIGHT ATTENDANT

A woman's job (usually restricted to white women) in a highly competitive and volatile airline industry. Flight attendants are trained to handle oxygen masks, life rafts, frustrated passengers – and to smile and smile. They "manage their clients' feelings, and, in doing so, they manage their own." (Arlie Russell Hochschild 1983b, 38-40)

FOG

"A kind of white, transparent mist that forms at eye level when the companion lovers are in a state of love. A thick halo may likewise appear all around their bodies. The bearers of fables say that the ancient amazons called this their camouflage cloud when they were in a state of love outside in the forest or on the beaches. From which comes the expression 'to be in a fog.' " (Monique Wittig and Sande Zeig 1976, 57)

FOLKLORE

Is a "straightforward set of devices for making real life more exciting." Unlike myth, folklore is easy "to infiltrate with

different kinds of consciousness." (Angela Carter 1983, 71)

FOOD

"A feminist issue, from the millions of women who don't get enough to live, to the pressure on women in countries where there is food in abundance not to eat it. In most societies, even now, women (and children) get less food, and less of high status food, than men. . . . Women grow, harvest, and prepare most of the world's food; in our society, women do almost all the shopping for food, and many women work in the food processing industries, mostly in low paid, routine work." (Sona Osman 1983, 30)

FOOLISH

A descriptive term used in George Eliot's aphorism ". . . women are foolish. God made 'em to match the men." These two sentences were used frequently at British suffrage meetings: "If one's meetings were dull, or faintly hostile, one had only to utter the first sentence to get a round of delighted applause from the men." (H.M. Swanwick 1935, 175)

FOOTBALL

"The practical basis of football is the fact that young males love physical combat, the more violent the better, and that colleges gain cash and glory through this part of the curriculum. The theoretical basis is that these youthful struggles fit one for 'the battle of life.' . . . But is life a battle? Does a man's life-work consist in fighting other men? Is social service a process of trampling on one another? Does society as a whole advance by the successful efforts of one man to get ahead of, outwit, ruin if need be, his neighbors?. . . If life means mutual service it is far from useful – quite the contrary." (Charlotte Perkins Gilman 1916d, 269)

FOOTBINDING

"Strange erotic custom of medieval China, practiced for a thousand years, up to the beginning of the 20th century, even exerting some influence on western Eur-

ope where women were often praised in romantic literature for having the tiniest possible feet. Crippling of the Chinese girl began at the age of five or six. Footbinding was a lifelong torment that slowly broke bones and deformed the flesh until the full 'beauty' of the atrophied, three-inch 'lotus hook' was achieved. Many women died of suppuration and gangrene before the desired effect was complete." (Barbara G. Walker 1983, 319)
(See BEAUTY, BLOOMERS, FASHION, HIGH HEELS)

FORCE
The activities of women that keep the world moving. Men have a curious blindness to this force. (Lady McLaren 1908, 7)

FOREMOTHER
An ancestor. The word was used in the nineteenth century by Mrs. Charlotte Conrad who wrote an essay titled "Our Literary Foremother" about Hannah Adams (1755-1831), American historian and novelist who published with difficulty and fell into obscurity after her death. (Mrs Charlotte Conrad 1891, 528)

FOREPLAY
"A concept created for male purposes, but works to the disadvantage of many women, since as soon as the woman is aroused the man changes to vaginal stimulation, leaving her both aroused and unsatisfied." (Anne Koedt 1970; rpt. 1973, 201)

In patriarchal heterosexuality in which penetration is considered *the* sex act, it is "what men have to do to get women to open their legs voluntarily." ("The Heterosexual Fix" 1981, *Scarlet Women* 13:5)

FORMS OF ADDRESS
The names people call each other in direct address. How one person chooses to address another is a profound signal of, among other things, social, cultural or political affiliations, kinship relationship, equality or asymmetry of power, emotional intimacy or distance, length of relationship, individuality, approval or disapproval, respect or disrespect, love or hatred. Few forms of address are truly neutral. Females receive more "terms of endearment" from women and men, and females receive more obscenities from males. Males receive more formal and respect forms from everyone, and have a wider repertoire of socially accepted terms to use for both females and males. The asymmetry in address forms is one way that asymmetry in social rights is reflected and maintained. (Sally McConnell-Ginet 1978a; Cheris Kramer 1975; Nessa Wolfson and Joan Manes 1980)
(See BOY, CALL OUT OF ONE'S NAME, DOCTOR, FIRST NAME, GIRL, LUCY STONER, MISS, MISS ANNE, MISTRESS, MR, MRS, MS, MUSH, NAME, NAMING, OCCUPATIONAL TERMS)

Many terms of address label a married women as "wife of." From a brass in St Mary at the Tower, Ipswich (1506). "Of your charitie pray for the soull of Alys late the wyf of Thomas Baldry merchant somtyme the wyfe of Master Robert Wymbyll Notari. . ." (Cited in Una Stannard 1977, 1)

The Mrs John Jones or Mrs Lawyer Jones style came into common use in the eighteenth century in England and in the nineteenth century in the U.S. To a seventeenth century mind a Mrs John Jones "would have been not only incomprehensible, but once understood, sacrilegious." (Woman was an inferior sex and thus a woman's use of a man's name would have been regarded as an outrageous presumption.) "The old concept of the unity of husband and wife depended upon there being two persons – one who commanded and one who obeyed. The new concept depended upon their being one person, the husband, in whom the wife was totally merged and who therefore obeyed not because her husband was her ruler but because she was one with him." Only fathers' names are handed down to posterity. (Una Stannard 1971, 7-8)
(See MRS)

"It still remains to be seen how much

longer women will suffer themselves to live under the disability of having to put 'Mrs.' or 'Miss' before their names so that the world in general may know whether they are some man's property or still on sale, while men are always 'Mr.' It may be that we shall make a now meaningless term do double duty, and address an envelope to a lady as 'Jane Smith, Esq.' " (J. Beanland 1911, *The Vote*, 18 February, 207)

As defined by Elizabeth Cady Stanton to Rebecca R. Eyster, May 1, 1847: "My dear Friend, – Last evening we spoke of the propriety of women being called by the names which are used to designate their sex, not by those assigned to males. You differed with me on the ground that custom had established the rule that a woman must take the whole of her husband's name, particularly when public mention is made of her. But you are mistaken about this. It is the custom now, since women have commenced forming themselves into independent societies, to use names of the feminine gender... I have very serious objections, dear Rebecca, to being called Henry. There is a great deal in a name. Why are the slaves nameless unless they take that of their master? Simply because they have no independent existence. . . . The custom of calling women Mrs. John This and Mrs. Tom That, and colored men Sambo and Zip Coon, is founded on the principle that white men are lords of all. I cannot acknowledge this principle as just; therefore, I cannot bear the name of another." (Stanton and Blatch 1922: II, 15-16; citing Elizabeth Cady Stanton 1847; in Alice Rossi 1973, 244-5)

Names and titles which cause identity problems for women who are not able to hold onto their own name: "Because of her husband's matrimonial adventures and the fact that she was by no means the only Lady Selvedge she was usually known as Lady (Muriel) Selvedge. The parentheses gave her a sense of not existing, un-being perhaps was not too strong a word. She would have preferred Muriel, Lady Selvedge, with its dowager-like dignity. Sometimes people addressed

letters mistakenly to Lady Muriel Selvedge, and on these occasions she imagined herself as the daughter of an earl, a marquess, or even a duke, comfortably unmarried." (Barbara Pym 1982, 57-8)

"The purpose of a social title (or courtesy title, or honorific) is to indicate respect for the person addressed. Ironically, one often conveys more respect for a woman by avoiding the conventional courtesy titles than by using them, since the distinction they make is related to a woman's marital state rather than to the person herself. Therefore, unless a woman's preference in titles is known, courtesy and honor may be better served by addressing her, in either speech or writing, by her first and last names together." (Casey Miller and Kate Swift 1976, 160)

Sir is a respect title spoken to men customers during service encounters, while women customers receive such forms as *hon*, *honey*, or *dear*, which imply that no sign of respect is needed. While suggesting intimacy, this supposed friendliness is nonreciprocal. (Nessa Wolfson and Joan Manes 1980)

Madam signals a married woman, *Miss* an unmarried woman. In this passage, the physician tells the narrator she is pregnant. " 'Congratulations, Madam.' Automatically I corrected him: 'Miss.' It was as though I'd given him a slap. Solemnity and cheerfulness disappeared, and staring at me with calculated indifference, he replied, 'Ah!' Then he took his pen, crossed out *Mrs.*, and wrote *Miss*. . . I was surprised that my marital status should be emphasized and that a correction had to be made on a sheet of paper. It smacked of a warning, a complication for the future." (Oriana Fallaci 1975, 24-5)

FORMS OF EXPRESSION
(See ACRONYMS, ACTION, ANDROCENTRISM, ART, BASKETRY, FEMINIST DICTIONARY, GOSSIP, GRAFFITI, QUILT, and many other entries above and below)

FOUND WOMEN

"Brave women all over the country who are working to change their own lives, the lives of their sisters, and the world around them.... Often these women work in near obscurity." (*Ms.* 1973, 1:7 (January), 45)

FOUR

"The sacred number for most Native people (as opposed to three for European and Mediterranean people), though seven, nine, two, and three also have some currency. Four is the four directions, the four colors (red, black, yellow, and blue – or green), the four winds, the number of times that episodes in stories or lines in chants might be repeated." (Rayna Green 1984, 309)

4-F CLUB

The American macho club with the motto: "find 'em, feel 'em, fuck 'em, forget 'em." (Margo St James 1980; in Claude Jaget ed. 1980, 194)

FOURTEENTH AMENDMENT

Added to the U.S. Constitution in 1868, it states in part that "No State shall make or enforce any law which shall abridge the privileges or immunities of the citizens of the United States; nor shall any State deprive any person of life, liberty, or property, without due process of law; nor deny to any person within its jurisdiction the equal protection of the law." In 1872 Susan B. Anthony tried to vote under the Fourteenth Amendment and lost a court case. In 1953 the Lucy Stone League protested the Supreme Court's continued decisions that women were not persons under the Fourteenth Amendment and urged the passage of the Equal Rights Amendment. (Una Stannard 1977)

(See ERA)

FOURTH WORLD

Was used for a while "as a way of describing the commonality of *all* women in the patriarchal world, regardless of race, but that term was taken over in the late seventies as a label for the poorest, nonindustrialized countries. To continue this reference, women are now sometimes self-described as the *Fifth World* – the half of the population that tends to be used as cheap labor and to have the least control over capital or technology, wherever we are." (Gloria Steinem 1983, 157)

FOURTH WORLD: EMPOWERMENT ADVOCACY

"a new approach to the problems of oppression. we believe it is only as more people become conscious of where the privilege lies and how to deal with it that changes will be made. we are involved, then, in an interim tactic which is, first, to recognize how existing systems and traditions can lead us to give up our power and, second, to find a way to reclaim it." (Donna M. Hawxhurst and Susan L. Rodekohr c.1984)

(See THIRD WORLD)

FRAGILITY

"This worrying, hampering thing [in men's novels] – her fragility, by which is meant her womanhood – is inevitably there at all important crises of her life" in such novels as Arnold Bennett's *Hilda Lessways*. ("New Novels" 1911, *Votes for Women*, Nov. 17, 103)

(See FEMININITY)

FRAGMENTATION

Splits such as those associated with race and class divisions and "with the psychic dismemberment of the female in this culture: whore/madonna, you've got a body *or* a soul, you've got brains *or* beauty, you can't be a mother *and* an artist." (Michele Roberts 1983, 66)

FRANKNESS

A freedom of speech not encouraged in subordinates. One woman, a servant, wrote, "And I'm quite sure that being a servant all one's live [sic] takes off that nice free way o'talking." (*Hannah Cullwick, Victorian Maidservant*; in Liz Stanley ed. 1984, 177)

FREAK, THE

"It is the woman who sheds the paint and manifests her Original Moving Self who appears to be The Freak in the State of Total Tokenism. It is she who is attacked by the mutants of her own kind, the man-made woman. It is she who is threatened with ostracism and cruelty by those submerged in tokenism, those total women taken as tokens before they had a chance to be Selves." (Mary Daly 1978, 334)

FREEDOM

A concept of liberty which is much more problematic for women than for men. It is not the same as equality. "There is no *freedom* or *justice* in exchanging the female role, for the male role. . . There is no *freedom* or *justice* in using male language, the language of your oppressor, to describe sexuality. There is no *freedom* or *justice* or even common sense in developing a male sexual sensibility – a sexual sensibility which is aggressive, competitive, objectifying, quantity oriented. There is only equality." (Andrea Dworkin 1976, 12)

(See EQUALITY)

Is liberty from restraints of many types. What men call *rights* for themselves, they call *impertinence* when women push for them. Freedom remains, however, a commitment for women. "Lock up your libraries if you like; but there is no gate, no lock, no bolt that you can set upon the freedom of my mind." (Virginia Woolf 1928; quoted in Michèle Barrett 1979, 17)

Liberty from slavery. Former slave, abolitionist leader and rescuer of hundreds Harriet Tubman wrote: "I had crossed de line of which I had so long been dreaming. I was free; but dere was no one to welcome me to de land of freedom, I was a stranger in a strange land, and my home after all was down in de ole cabin quarter, wid de ole folks, and my brudders and sisters. But to dis solemn resolution I cam; I was free, and dey should be free also; I would make a home for dem in de North, and de Lord helping me, I would bring dem all dere." [Spelling of the original record; such

'dialectic writing' makes it appear that Blacks and other minority groups are the only people who talk in dialect.] (Harriet Tubman, n.d.; quoted by Michelle Cliff 1982, 36)

(See DIALECT)

"In this society the nearest any of us reach freedom, honesty, and spontaneity with others is in bed with a lover or in the street hurling beer cans at the police." (Letter to *The Levellers* 1982; cited by Lynne Segal 1983, 30)

FREE SPIRIT

" 'Free Spirit' has been branded into [women] as a brand name for girdles and bras rather than as the name of our verbing, be-ing Selves. Such brand names brand women 'Morons.' " (Mary Daly 1978, 5)

FRENCH REVOLUTION

A revolt against the monarchy designed to win rights for men, not women. Olympe de Gouges, who pointed this out on bulletins placed on the walls of Paris, was sentenced to death by Robespierre and guillotined. Before she was beheaded she demanded of the women in the crowd: "What are the advantages you have derived from the Revolution? Slights and contempt more plainly displayed." (Judy Chicago 1979, 177)

FRESCOED FEMININITY

"Haughty, huge ladies, several tons overweight [who] stroll on clouds, brandish swords and represent the Spirit of Freedom" on rotundas or on the ceilings of our State Capitols. "The titles of these ladies are as elegant as their men: Spirit of Peace, Spirit of War, Spirit of Night, Spirit of Weebaskus Public School, Number 899, Spirit of Electricity, Spirit of the Seesawkus Flour and Grain Industry, the Soul of Poesie, the Latin Soul, the Teuton Soul, the Spirit of the Alaskan Chamber of Commerce." They hold maps, globes, scrolls, chisels, shields, miniature models of houses or ships, books, harps and dynamos. "They hold, in brief, everything that Man, their creator, has objected to their using, professionally and in real life." (Miriam Beard 1927; rpt. in Elizabeth Janeway ed. 1973, 147)

FRESH START

A women's housing group in Leeds, England. The members provide housing for women like themselves who have left women's aid refuges and do not want to return to their violent husbands. (*Spare Rib*, Oct. 1982, 10)

FREUD

"The greater part of the feminist movement has identified Freud as the enemy. It is held that psychoanalysis claims women are inferior and that they can achieve true femininity only as wives and mothers. Psychoanalysis is seen as a justification for the status-quo, bourgeois and patriarchal, and Freud in his own person exemplifies these qualities. I would agree that popularized Freudianism must answer to this description; but . . . a rejection of psychoanalysis and of Freud's work is fatal for feminism. However it may have been used, psychoanalysis is not a recommendation *for* a patriarchal society, but an analysis *of* one. If we are interested in understanding and challenging the oppression of women, we cannot afford to neglect it." (Juliet Mitchell 1974, introduction)

"The great mind-shrinker." (Mary Daly 1978, 267)

FREUDIANISM

A theory of men's and women's thoughts and actions which have had pervasive influence in 20th century Euro-American culture. "It sought the source of female dissatisfaction in the individual rather than in the social situation. . . . Freud and his followers prescribed traditional roles for women and defended customary attitudes toward them in up-to-date scientific terminology." (Barbara J. Harris 1978, 157-8). Focusing on Freud's attention to language, a psychoanalytic approach which stresses symbolism has received a great deal of attention and criticism from feminists and others in France, Great Britain and the United States.

"Was the perfect foil for feminism, because, though it struck the same nerve, it had the safety catch that feminism didn't – it never questioned the given reality. . . . Thus Freudianism gained the ground that Feminism lost. It flourished at the expense of Feminism, to the extent that it acted as a container of its shattering force." (Shulamith Firestone 1970, 79)

FRIEND

"Derives from a word meaning 'free.' We generally consider a lover to be more important than a friend. . . . The fathers provide us with the phrase 'just friends' to indicate that it is 'someone I don't *have* (possess) sex with,' and that the absence of overt sexual behavior in a relationship makes it deficient and worth less than being 'lovers.' The culture does not supply a comparable phrase of 'just lovers'. . . . A friend is someone who allows us the space and freedom to be, while relationships with lovers often feel binding." (Debbie Alicen 1983, 22)

FRIENDSHIP

"Is derived from an Old English term meaning to love, and . . . is akin in its roots to an Old English word meaning free. The radical friendships of Hags means loving our own freedom, loving/encouraging the freedom of the other, the friend, and therefore *loving freely*." (Mary Daly 1978, 367)

FRIGID

A term used by men to label a woman who is cold (i.e. unresponsive to) men. "Has anyone considered that along with the Loch Ness monster and Piltdown man, the deep-freeze female may be something of a hoax? Quite possibly, the case of the frigid wife could be an ingenious alibi for the middle-aged husband." (Eve Merriam 1958; rpt 1964, 112)

FRIGIDITY

Has been defined by men as a sexual problem of individual women which causes men problems. For women the concept, if it is to have relevance in their life, needs to be defined in the context of sexuality in general. Phyllis Chesler writes: "Women have had to barter their sexuality (or their capacity for sexual pleasure) for economic survival and maternity. . . . Most women cannot be 'sexual' as long as prostitution, rape and patriarchal marriage exist, with such attendant concepts and practices as 'illegitimate' pregnancies, enforced maternity, 'non-maternal' paternity, and the sexual deprivation of 'aging' women." (Phyllis Chesler 1972a, 47)

"It could be [considered] a form of power against an oppressor, a form of passive resistance or unavailability." (Dale Spender 1980, 177)

LA FRONDE

"A newspaper owned, written, composed, set, and printed entirely by women" in France, its first issue appearing December 9, 1897. Marguerite Durand was owner and publisher. The daily newspaper worked against social injustices. "The name *La Fronde* originally meant a slingshot like the one David used to kill Goliath, and had once been applied to the short-lived nobles' revolt against Louis XIV." (Beatrice Braude 1973, 33)

FRUSTRATION

"The feeling of a sitting dog being told to sit." (Gloria Steinem 1981, xi)

FUCK

The men define it as "A Germanic verb originally meaning 'to strike, move quickly, penetrate (akin or perhaps borrowed from Middle Dutch *fokken*, to strike, copulate with)." (*American Heritage Dictionary* 1973)

An oral gesture of disgust which like most taboo epithets has a blowing sound and "can no more be cleaned up by open and high-minded usage than can the Bronx cheer or the symbolic gestures of spitting and hawking." The aggression and contempt expressed by the use of this

word betrays "facets of male attitudes toward women that civilized men prefer not to acknowledge." This word is more taboo for women than it is for men, even when women use it to describe what has happened to them. (Ethel Strainchamps 1972; cited in Casey Miller and Kate Swift 1976, 120)

"It is one of what etymologists sometimes call 'the sadistic group of words for the man's part in copulation.' " (Barbara Lawrence 1974, 33)

FUMERIST

Feminist humorist. "A feminist humorist makes light. She is a fumerist, a sparking incendiary with blazes of light and insight. Fumerists make whys cracks. We ask our own questions and they have the potential of splitting the world apart. Light shines through the whys cracks we make and illuminates all aspects of our oppression." (Kate Clinton 1982b, 38-9)

(See DE-DIKING, PENILE HUMOR)

FURIES

Dread goddesses (*OED*), as in The Furies Collective, Washington, D.C., 1971-4. This was an organization which articulated lesbian feminism as a political theory. (Brooke 1980, 71)

FUTURE

View of what is to come which determines the way we act to solve problems in the present. (Margrit Eichler and Hilda Scott 1981, v)

FW2

Shorthand for the media-created "First woman to. . ." story. "We are well into the age of the FW2 ('First woman to. . .'). By patronizing the continuing struggle of women and by minimizing the distance from FW2 to HW2 ('Hundredth woman to. . .'), these newspaper articles create an illusion of progress." (Matilda Butler and William Paisley 1980, 319)

(See PROGRESS)

GABACHA

Anglo woman. (Marcela Christine Lucero-Trujillo 1980, 401)

GABALASHING

A word used in quilting circles on the South Shore of Nova Scotia. Gabalashing is making the rough large stitching to sew the quilt into the frame so that the quilting stitches, tiny and fine, can be done. Hence, if you want to insult some one's stitching, you can say, "You're just gabalashing it." (Lewis J. Poteet 1983)

GALAH SESSION

A time set aside for women of isolated outback areas of Australia to talk with one another by radio. (Arthur Delbridge ed. 1982)

GAMINE

A good name for a daughter. "It means plucky. Ability to stick it out. To endure hardships or humiliation without complaint." (Red Acrobateau 1978, 108)

GARDENS

Forms of expression and sources of income for millions of women – as in vegetable patch, herb garden, rock garden, rose garden, kitchen garden, nursery, flower garden, hanging garden, floating garden, bed, Victory garden, greenhouse, back yard.

Cultivation which has been heavily influenced by Gertrude Jekyll, a "cultivated spinster" who through her landscape designing and her books revolutionized English (and by extension American) gardening by using indigenous trees, shrubs, and flowers; inventing the herbaceous border composed of hardy perennials; pioneering the rock garden; and using "flowering plants as if they were the paint on an Impressionist canvas." Her long collaboration with the architect Sir Edwin Lutyens established her as a professional. England's prestigious *Dictionary of National Biography* makes no mention of Miss Jekyll but gives a lengthy write-up to Lutyens. (Eleanor Perényi 1983)

Part of the title of Alice Walker's book, *In Search of Our Mothers' Gardens: Womanist Prose.* " 'Mama, why are we brown, pink, and yellow, and our cousins are white, beige, and black?' Ans.: 'Well, you know the colored race is just like a flower garden, with every color flower represented.' " (Alice Walker 1983, xi) Alice Walker's mother ordered her gardens into her personal conception of beauty: "Whatever she planted grew as if by magic. . . . Because of her creativity with her flowers, even my memories of poverty are seen through a screen of blooms – sunflowers, petunias, roses, dahlias, forsythia, spirea, delphiniums, verbena. . . ." (Alice Walker 1974; rpt. 1983, 241)

GARMENT INDUSTRY

Built with the labor of women who spent 60 hours a week in sweatshops where the doors were locked from the outside. (See TRIANGLE SHIRTWAIST COMPANY). In 1900, more than 53% of all employed Jewish women worked in the garment industry, on rented sewing machines with thread they paid for out of their small wages. (June Sochen 1981, 9)

GASLIGHTING

The denying of women's expression of reality. (The term stems from a play made into a 1944 movie in which a woman's account of her frightening experiences is denied by her husband, who causes the seemingly inexplicable happenings such as the swaying of gaslights.) "Women have been driven mad, 'gaslighted,' for centuries by the refutation of our experience and our instincts in a culture which validates only male experience. The truth of our bodies and our minds has been mystified to us. We therefore have a primary obligation to each other; not to undermine each others' sense of reality for the sake of expediency; not to gaslight each other." (Adrienne Rich 1975; rpt. 1979, 190)

GATEKEEPING

Systematic use of processes of selection and censorship to ensure perpetuation of male views of the world. For example, publishers have an effective gatekeeping system which has helped to ensure that women's understandings of the world do not receive wide circulation in print. (Dorothy Smith; in Dale Spender and Lynne Spender 1983, 467)

GATHERSTRETCHING

Mind-touching; non-verbal communication which, in Sally Gearhart's novel, allows women to establish and maintain contact over great distances. (Sally Gearhart 1978)

GAY

"Is a Middle English word derived from the Middle French term GAI (gai). It is defined in British dictionaries as 'joyful, akin to merry, frivolous, showy, given to dissipated or vicious pleasure.' GAI became popularized in the Middle French burlesque theatre's description of effeminate, pretentious male character roles. . . . English theatre began to use the word GAY to describe 'saucy, prostituting, or sexually promiscuous' characters. Since women were not at that time allowed on stage in either country, these mock feminine roles were always caricatured by men. The Scottish tradition of the word GAI (guy) was more distinctly used to describe someone different, i.e., an astrologer, forester, or recluse. (E.g., 'I say, he is a bit gai!') This tradition originally was not negative, but merely implied 'different or queer from the norm'. . . . It is interesting to note that the word GAY was not used to describe 'homosexual' women until it found its way to the Americas. Today the terms LESBIAN and SAPPHIC are still the tradition in Europe. In the 1920s and 1930s the word GAY surfaced in the underground homosexual subculture as a term of identification among homosexual men. Expressions such as 'You're looking gay tonight,' or 'That's a gay tie you have there' were used to establish mutual identity in social situations. Finally, in the late 1960s, the term GAY was taken up by the Gay Liberation Movement in its attempt to affirm 'a truly joyous alternative lifestyle' and throw off the sexually objectifying term 'homosexual.' " (Jeanne Cordova 1974, 21, 22, 23)

"For myself, I am 41, and have been 'bed gay' since the age of twenty-nine and 'head gay' forever." (Christine Pattee, Oct. 1982, letter to mailing list members of Independent Woman Books)

GENEALOGY

The study of ancestry and family history to trace a person's genetic and cultural heritage, which works particularly well for white paternal lines because women's and Blacks' last names are frequently lost or discarded in official and informal records.

GENDER

Is "often used as a synonym for *sex*, i.e. biological maleness or femaleness. However, it is also used, particularly by contemporary writers, to refer to the socially imposed dichotomy of masculine and feminine roles and character traits. Sex is physiological, while gender, in the latter usage, is cultural. The distinction is a crucial one, and one which is ignored by unreflective supporters of the status quo who assume that cultural norms of masculinity and femininity are 'natural,' i.e. directly and preponderantly determined by biology." (Mary Anne Warren 1980, 181)

(See SEX, SEXUALITY)

"Is a social construction of so thin a fabric as to demand continual enactment to support its fiction." (Nancy Henley 1980, 309)

"In late capitalist patriarchy . . . our ideology and practice of sex roles construct, out of what are only tendencies toward genital dimorphism, two mutually exclusive categories, that is, genders. The dress and behavior codes of our culture try to hide the full range of diversity in order to create an appearance of dimorphism." (Muriel Dimen 1981, 67)

A division of women and men caused "by the social requirements of heterosexuality, which institutionalizes male sexual dominance and female sexual submission. If this is true, sexuality is the linchpin of gender inequality." (Catharine A. MacKinnon 1982a, 533)

"Is not a unitary, or 'natural' fact, but takes shape in concrete, historically changing social relationships." The social regulation of sexuality "is closely intertwined with gender." (Barrie Thorne, Cheris Kramarae and Nancy Henley 1983, 16)

In Anglo-Saxon grammar: "The Substantive and the Adjective, must not only agree in Number, but they must accord in Gender, or Sex, and in Case, or Termination: For the Adjective being a proper Attendant upon the Substantive, it hath been thought decent that it should not only be of the same Sex, that is, a Male to wait upon a Male, and a Female upon a Female, but likewise to appear in a Dress, or Habit, by which it may easily be discern'd to which Sex they belong. The first of these Answers, the Grammatical Term of Gender, the other, of Case." (Elizabeth Elstob 1715, 58)

(See GENDER MARKING)

GENDER DIFFERENCES

"Different sets of social attributions – characteristics, behavior, appearance, dress, expectations, roles, etc. – made to individuals, according to their gender assignment at birth. . . . Science [incorrectly] views these gender attributions as *natural* categories for which biological explanations are appropriate and even necessary." (Ruth Bleier 1984, 80)

GENDER GAP

"The term 'gender gap,' meaning the difference in political vote and attitude between women and men, became part of the political vernacular during the 1982 [U.S.] election. Women provided margins for victory in the gubernatorial races of three major states: Michigan, New York, and Texas. Further, women favored Democrats over Republicans by 21 percentage points in Congressional races, according to network exit polls." (Marjorie Lansing 1984, 3)

Percentage difference between women and men voting on issues and candidates.

GENDERIC

An adjective relating to gender, as in: The genderic split [i.e., female/male] is a basic social problem. (Mary O'Brien 1981)

GENDER IDENTITY

"Is the sex you *feel* yourself to be, regardless of your physical sex. It differs from gender role in that it is not actively expressed. *Gender role* is the male or female role performed in the real world." (Lesley J. Rogers 1981, 48)

GENDERIZATION

A linguistic marking of sex which is nearly obligatory while using the English language. "For example, English pronominal reference to a definite individual is (necessarily) sex-marked. It would therefore be extraordinarily difficult to do something like write a letter of recommendation with no mention, if only implicit through use of *she* or *he*, of the candidate's sex." Genderization works towards making sex central to self-identity and to our views of others. (Elizabeth Beardsley 1977; cited in Sally McConnell-Ginet 1980, 8)

GENDERLECT

A notion invented in the early 1970s to suggest overall characterizations of sex differences in speech. "The 'genderlect' portrayal now seems too abstract and overdrawn" stressing more homogeneity among women, and among men, and more differences between the sexes, than exists. Instead of conceptualizing speech in terms of an abstracted code, more attention is now on how words are used within contexts of actual use. (Barrie Thorne, Cheris Kramarae, and Nancy Henley 1983, 14)

GENDER MARKING

The linguistic noting of the presence of a female or male. Because of *false generics* and other problems the females often are made to disappear in our historical records. For example, the history of women in medicine has not been accurately preserved, in part because copyists or printers didn't recognize women's feminine names or mistook feminine nouns and adjectives for masculine. "Many a change of an '*a*' to an '*e*' or an '*us*' has made a profound difference in our medical history. When in the eleventh century some careless calligrapher wrote 'Trottus' for 'Trotula' he . . . deprived a woman of her identity." Yet, preservation on tombstones of the term MEDICA [with the feminine ending -*a*] tells us that women physicians lived and practiced in ancient times. (Kate Campbell Hurd-Mead 1938, v., 66f)

GENERIC ASSUMPTION

"Is the assumption that *he* consistently refers to generic or sex-indefinite antecedents (as recommended in prescriptive grammars), a usage that has been called 'generic he.' In fact, however, generic he is not used consistently to mean 'he or she' and is more accurately labeled 'prescrip-

tive *he*.' " (Donald G. MacKay 1983, 39) (See HE, HE/MAN APPROACH, PRESCRIPTIVE HE)

GENERICS

Words which pertain to an entire group or class.
(See HE, MAN, FALSE GENERICS)
" 'Words [*he* and *man*] importing the masculine gender' [have been held in court] to include women in the clauses imposing burdens, and to exclude them in the clauses conferring privileges, in one and the same Act of Parliament." (The Political Disabilities of Women 1872; tract in the Fawcett Library, London)

GENITALIA

An attractive name for a girl child. (Brinlee Kramer, conversation)
(See LABIA)

GENITALS

Reproductive organs usually inaccurately and incompletely labeled in the case of females. Girls are told that they have a vagina, but they are seldom told that they have a vulva which includes the clitoris and labia. "Neither sex is informed that the clitoris is part of 'what girls have.' " (Harriet E. Lerner 1976, 276)

GENIUS

A label given most often to men who "have been either depraved egomaniacs or people who led the most distressing lives." (Angela Carter 1983, 75)

GENTLEMAN

A contradiction in terms (Laura X 1984, correspondence)
(See DEAR READER)

GEORGE

"Pseudonym of the famous women novelists George Eliot and George Sand; hence, a term of admiration for something very well done: 'By George.' " (Eve Merriam 1975, 11)

GERMINAL

Earliest stages of development; significant; stimulating subsequent thinking by others. Used by some feminist writers in place of *seminal*.

(See OVULAR)

GERM THEORY OF DISEASE

An explanation of disease, contributed by biological sciences in mid-nineteenth century, which made a disease "look like a natural event which depended less on God than on the growth rates of what appeared to be fairly amoral species of microbes." This change moved responsibility for health to the housewife who was to establish sanitary regimes in every room of the house. (Barbara Ehrenreich and Deirdre English 1979, 73, 158)

GETHENIANS

The human inhabitants of the fictional planet called Gethen. "Instead of our continuous sexuality, the Gethenians have an oestrus period, called *kemmer*. When they are not in *kemmer*, they are sexually inactive and impotent; they are also androgynous." (Ursula K. LeGuin; in Susan Wood 1979a, 162)

GIGGLE

A laughter from girls "at the moment of taboo. It is a way at once of making a point and of avoiding the issue. It precludes criticism and does not give the game away. A guerrilla tactic rather than a head-on encounter." (Sheila Rowbotham 1983, 11)

(See LAUGHTER)

GIRDLE

A body binding undergarment which inhibits body building and muscular control.

GIRL

A word used to imply childishness, dependency, conformity, purity, delicacy, nonaggressiveness, and noncompetitiveness. Used to label young females. Also used to label women, by people who have a need to see women "in narrow, nonthreatening, or diminutive terms." "*Girl*, like *boy*, is a term that undoes any

implications of status, authority, and true seriousness of purpose." (Harriet E. Lerner 1976a, 296, 299)

"1. A female person under 12 years of age or pre-puberty. 2. A [demeaning] epitaph for women used by men who foolishly think they are being complimentary." (Midge Lennert and Norma Willson eds 1973, 5)

"In recalling youth, frivolity, and immaturity, *girl*, as used by whites, brings to mind irresponsibility: you don't send a girl to do a woman's errand. . . . It seems that again, by appeal to feminine vanity . . . the users of English have assigned women to a very unflattering place in their minds." (Robin Lakoff 1975, 25-6)

"A person may appropriately be called a 'girl' until her middle or late teens. After that, although her family and close friends may go on calling her a girl with impunity, most red-blooded women find the term offensive. Just as *boy* can be blatantly offensive to minority men, arousing feelings of helplessness and rage, so *girl* can have comparable patronizing and demeaning implications for women." (Casey Miller and Kate Swift 1980, 70-1)

For a woman to be called a girl "is not so offensive on the surface as to be called a pig, yet the harm done may be deeper and longer-lasting." (Eve Merriam 1974)

"When applied to women in the dominant culture the word 'girl' is regarded either as a term of contempt or of disrespect. . . . However, judging by my contacts with women of color and by my readings, I have come to believe that the word 'girl' is often used in the Black community to address a woman in a familiar manner, sometimes for emphasis, sometimes to show affection, not as a sign of inequality or disrespect." The following gives an example taken from *Sula* by Toni Morrison: "Suddenly Nel stopped. Her eye twitched and burned a little. 'Sula?' she whispered, gazing at the tops of trees, 'Sula?' Leaves stirred; mud shifted; there was the smell of overripe green things. A soft ball of fur broke and scattered like dandelion spores in the breeze. 'All that time, I thought I was missing Jude.' And the loss pressed down on her chest and came up into her throat. 'We was girls together,' she said as though explaining some thing. 'O Lord, Sula,' she cried, 'girl, girl, girlgirlgirl.' " (Marthe Rosenfeld 1973; quoting Toni Morrison 1973)

GIRLFRIEND

A special friend who has many friendship responsibilities as well as privileges.
(See FRIEND, FRIENDSHIP, HOME GIRLS)

GIRL GUIDES

A scouting movement initially organized in 1909 to keep girl scouts well separated from the boy scouts, in name and activities. The 1909 "Scheme" for Girl Guides indicated that the training for girls "has to be administered with great discrimination; you do not want to make tomboys of refined girls, yet you want to attract, and thus raise, the slum girl from the gutter. The main object is to give them *all* the ability to be better mothers and Guides to the next generation." (Carol Dyhouse 1981, 110). In fact, the Girl Guides and, in the U.S., the Girl Scouts and Campfire Girls, have provided many adolescents with many skills and with female companionship.
(See CAMPFIRE GIRLS)

GIVEN NAME

The first name assigned at birth. Also the last name for many women who are given a surname at birth and are given new surnames at times of marriage.
(See BIRTH NAMES)

GLAMOUR

One definition given in Merriam-Webster is "a magic spell." It was once believed that witches possessed the power of glamour; according to the authors of *Malleus Maleficarum*, witches by their glamour "could cause the male 'member' to disappear." (Mary Daly 1978, 4)
(See BEAUTY)

GLORIOUS AGE

"There have been the Golden Age, the Silver Age, the Stone Age, the Bronze Age, the Iron Age, the Concrete Age or the High-Speed Steel Age. We have now entered the Glorious Age. For almost two millenniums lesbians had been represented with glories around their heads. This was mistaken for a sign of sanctity and was not yet recognized as a form of energy. When the companion lovers appeared to one another in their brilliance and were able to stand the sight, they caught and used this energy that they immediately called 'glorious.' From which comes the 'Glorious Age.' " (Monique Wittig and Sande Zeig 1976, 63-4)

GLOTOLOG

Intergalactic colloquialism: information control without direct censorship; *Glotologgish* refers to "ridiculous self-deception bolstered by widespread and elaborate social fictions leading to the massive distortion of information." Thus: "When the female weevil displays unusual competence in climbing the tree, you avert your eyes and claim it is a male weevil; how disgustingly Glotologgish of you!" (Joanna Russ 1983, 3, 4)

GOD

A noble idea, a "superior, general, providence." "Were we to express our conceptions of God, it would never enter into the heads of any one of us to describe him as a venerable old man." (Sophia 1739, 42-3)

"Parent of Good, Almighty. We have had enough of *man's* thoughts of God – of God first as the King, the 'Man of War,' the Demiurge, the Mover of all things, and then, at last, since Christian times, of God as the Father of the World." (Frances Power Cobbe 1861, 81)

Is still called, "manfully, . . . King, Father, Master, Shepherd and Lord in the language of the Sunday hymns." (Andrew Moncur 1981, 8:2)

The notion of God as an all-powerful judge, male supreme being is rejected by Mary Daly. She suggested in 1973 that we consider god as a verb, a complete "participation in being." She writes "God the Verb cannot be broken down simply into past, present, and future times, since God is form-destroying, form-creating, transforming power that makes all things new." God, however, becomes obsolete in Daly's next work *Gyn/Ecology*. She argues that the word cannot be stripped of its patriarchal meanings and mythology. (Mary Daly 1978)

A member of the patriarchy. "Even after I am dead, I am told, a father in heaven will decide whether to take me in or toss me out. The judgments of the patriarchy are harsh, and unfit to shape my reality." (Stephanie Dowrick 1980, 70)

An image that "is female as well as male. By reestablishing the notion that women's experience can be a source of knowledge about God, we are righting the centuries-old wrong that associates women with the malevolent powers of earth, darkness, and sexuality, and man with reason, light, and God." (Linda Clark *et al.* 1981, 5)

Although usually presented to us as a man-shaped deity, according to Flora MacDonald Denison, "Spirit is free, not personality." (Flora MacDonald Denison c.1916; in Carol Lee Bacci 1983, 67)

A secret concealed by Christian history, "the many-named Goddess [was] the original Holy Trinity who created and governed the world, gave birth to its Saviors, sent her tablets of divine law to the prophets, and watched over every life from womb to tomb, according to pre-Christian belief. . . . If women's religion had continued, today's world might be less troubled by violence and alienation. Gods, including Yahweh, tended to order their followers to make war; whereas the great mother Goddesses advocated peaceful evolution of civilized skills." (Barbara G. Walker 1983, x, xi)

(See SPIRITUALITY)

The goddesses are called upon for inspiration, guidance and brightness in many feminist journal titles: The *Aurora* (journal of Prism of Feminism, Rockland County Feminists, 1971) is goddess of the dawn. *Cassandra* (another journal title) was gifted with powers of prophecy; her predictions were not believed although they were invariably correct. A *Sibyl-Child* (a woman's arts and culture quarterly) possesses powers of prophecy or divination (and is also described in some dictionaries as a witch). *Hecate* (an Australian interdisciplinary journal focusing on Marxist and radical methodology) was adept at sorcery and is the mother of witches. *Bright Medusa* has a bright reflection which turns into stone men who look at her. *ISIS* (International Bulletin) was the principal goddess of ancient Egypt and is identified with the moon.

(See CURSE, PERIODICALS, for other feminist titles)

GODFATHERS

The Godfathers: Freudians, Marxists, and the Scientific and Political Protection Societies. A 1976 book by Naomi Weisstein, Virginia Blaisdell, and Jesse Lemisch (published in New Haven, Conn.: Belladonna Publishing).

GOING TOO FAR

Some vague something females are supposed to avoid doing. "One [London woman] I well remember saying to me, just after she 'came out,' that she was always afraid of going too far with men, because she really didn't know what 'too far' was. I was quite unable to enlighten her." (Vera Brittain 1933, 45)

A frequent accusation of opponents of women, used when women try to transform their lives. "They said we [people in the Women's Movement in the 1970s] were 'going too far.' Perhaps this has been their most frequent and basic accusation, phrased in a thousand different ways. Never mind that we are forced to act, or react, by the pain of our status itself. . . . No, it's our fault, always. . . . More recently, perhaps: "Well, equal pay for equal work, yes, but a woman learning karate, a woman raising a child with her lesbian lover, a woman brain surgeon or priest or astronaut or architect or President – now *that's* going too far." (Robin Morgan 1978, 8)

GOLDEN RULE

"He (or she) who has the gold, rules." (Elizabeth Nickles with Laura Ashcraft 1981, 7)

GOOD-OLD-DAYS

A fiction for most people. "Nine children Hory gave me. One dies in the war. Twenty-five he were. I've had a hard life. A very hard life. I don't want them days back no more. People say 'Oh them good old days.' But what was good about them? You tell me." (Alice Rushmer; in Mary Chamberlain 1983, 81)

GOODWIFE

A paragon in the home whose only interest is family and house. On prime-time television shows "her sphere of influence [is] limited to domestic concerns, but within the home the goodwife exercise[s] considerable personal power, making decisions, advising, and chastising family members. In interpersonal relationships among family members, her contribution [is] wise counsel and moral guidance." (Diana M. Meehan 1983, 34)

GORGONS

In traditional mythology, the snakey-haired sisters of Greek mythology who turned beholders to stone. According to Barbara Deming, they are "those very untidy women who don't hold back any of the truths they experience.... We women become our natural selves as we allow ourselves to be gorgons – to acknowledge the anger we feel at what has been asked of us, done to us. The gorgons have healing energy to turn us all to flesh and blood, not stone as patriarchs have claimed." (Barbara Deming; quoted by Mab Segrest 1982, 51)

GOSPEL SINGERS

Artists without formal training who sing "in the spirit" – not for fame or fortune, but to move, sustain, and bring joy to black people. Singers such as Eva Hill

Roundtree and Mattie Shannon "raised up in the church" carry on a powerful, traditional black cultural art. (Emily Herring Wilson 1983)

GOSSIP

"A way of talking between women in the roles as women, intimate in style, personal and domestic in topic and setting, a female cultural event which springs from and perpetuates the restrictions of the female role, but also gives the comfort of validation." (Deborah Jones 1980, 194)

"Is not only about people; it communicates information about both tradition and change. It is a uniquely powerful form of communication since it not only transmits ideas, but also consolidates opinions about those ideas." (Kathryn S. March and Rachelle Taqqu 1982)

Is an "important way of perceiving and describing the world. In an underground and rather subversive way it communicates through anecdote. In a more reflective and elaborate form it has become the novel. For the women dependent on men it provides also a powerful form of social control over the behavior of other women. Gossip can determine who is within the protection of society and restrict other women from moving over into self-determination and giving the game away. It is specifically directed against any manifestation of liberation, sexual or otherwise, and is designed to prevent women scabs taking on some of the power of the men." (Sheila Rowbotham 1983, 11)

"An indispensable feminist weapon." (Sona Osman 1983, 30)

The name of the new Women's Studies newsletter at Worcester Polytechnic. (Cynthia Enloe 1983, correspondence)

GOSSIP/GODSIB/GODSYB

"A woman's female friend invited to be present at a birth; to be a sponsor; Gossiphood: A spiritual relationship, a body of gossips. Gossipred: the relationship of gossips; spiritual affinity." (*Oxford English Dictionary*) In the word's original sense: " 'Godsib' meant godparent, then sponsor and advocate; then it became a relative, then a woman friend, then a woman 'who delights in idle talk,' 'groundless rumor' and 'tattle.' Now it means malicious and unfounded tales told by women about other people.... Thus, in the old sense, spoken propaganda, or gossip, means *relating* – a feminized style of communication either way." (Lucy R. Lippard 1980, 37)

GOTHIC NOVEL

Has the following text: A young woman marries, is taken to an isolated castle or estate, and learns she must fear the man she's married. Is perhaps truthful in that marriage may cause women to be fearful and suspicious. (Tania Modleski 1982)

GOVERNESS

A symbol of status incongruity: "She was a lady and wage-earner, living in the home but neither a servant nor a member of the family. The employment of a governess was a form of conspicuous consumption for the middle-class and upper-class family, because she was a symbol of the wife/mother emancipation from . . . teaching children – and of the [wife/mother's] adoption of a totally ornamental role. The governess had to be a lady to live in the family, yet ladies did not earn money, so all governesses were people whose father or brother had failed to support them." (M. Jeanne Peterson 1972; cited by Sara Delamont 1978, 137)

GRACE

"A free shift away from the vicious circle of god and man's 'regeneration or sanctification'; a Spiraling. Metamorphic leap of Be-Witching." *Webster's First New Intergalactic Wickedary of the English Language.* (Mary Daly 1984, 387)
(See WICKEDARY)

GRAFFITI

A silent political discourse, often on toilet walls, about the distribution of power in society. (Edward M. Bruner and Jane Paige Kelso 1980, 239)
"A popular feminist sport. Easy to learn; equipment cheap and readily available; pitches all over the place." (Sona Osman 1983, 30)

GRAMMAR

The system of rules about morphologic, syntactic, and semantic language usage. Seldom deals with language as a powerful social and political force. (See Sally McConnell-Ginet 1983)
(See ENGLISH, LANGUAGE, MEANING, WOMEN AND LANGUAGE RESEARCH)
Grammar is sometimes equated with language and separated from behavior: "It doesn't matter if a man's grammar is askew, so long as he doesn't swear at you." (L. M. Montgomery 1912, 294)
"Grammar is the Art of Speaking and Writing, truly and properly. In speaking we use certain Signs, which are necessary to discover our Thoughts to one another. These Signs, are Sound, and Voice. But besides, Sound, and Voice, by which we are able to converse with one another when present; there are other Signs that have been invented, where these Sounds cannot be heard, to supply the want of them in such a manner, as that we may both converse with one another at a distance, and communicate our Thoughts to future Ages. The first of these Signs belongs properly to Speech, or unwritten Discourse. The latter are made use of in Writing." (Elizabeth Elstob 1715, 1)
"The ultimate arena of sexist brainwashing." (Susan Sontag 1973, 186)

GRANDMOTHER

"Grandmother Turtle, Grandmother Spider, or just Grandma. She brought the people to earth and gave them the rules and knowledge they needed to live. Indian peoples have many grandmothers, real and mythic. Some are biological relatives, some adopted ones. Grandmothers raise children; they tell stories in the winter and teach children the skills they need for survival. Grandmothers are the central characters in the daily and symbolic lives of Native women – indeed, of Native people." (Rayna Green 1984, 310)

A woman "little lower than the angels in the poet's song, yet in the hard world of fact [she was] treated as little higher than domestic animals." (Teresa Billington-Greig 1911b, 1)

Represented in histories by "pages from fashion books! . . . [A] travesty of our countrywomen." (H. M. Swanwick 1935, 196-7)

(See DIARY, HISTORY)

GRANDMOTHER TURTLE

"In the Iroquoian world view, the world sits on her back. Many believe she brought the world into existence, and her representation, quite common to many tribes, reminds people of her persistence and support." (Rayna Green 1984, 310)

GRAY PANTHERS

An intergenerational coalition of people working together for social *change* rather than social service. This primarily women's organization, founded in 1970 by Margaret E. Kuhn, has task forces in the U.S. and Europe working in the areas of health, housing, youth, media watch, economics, access, poverty and older women. (Gray Panthers 1980; Fact Sheet, 3635 Chestnut St., Philadelphia, Penn. 19104)

GREAT ARTIST

A myth, the "godlike subject of a hundred monographs – bearing within his person since birth a mysterious essence, called genius or talent, which must always out, no matter how unlikely or unpromising the circumstances. . . . What is stressed in all these stories is the apparently miraculous, nondetermined, and asocial nature of artistic achievement." (Linda Nochlin; cited in Bristol Women's Study Group 1979, 244)

GREAT HAGS

"Our foresisters . . . whom the institutionally powerful but privately impotent patriarchs found too threatening for co-existence, and whom historians erase." (Mary Daly 1978, 14)

GREAT MEN

"Great men!! Yes, here and there one; but a gardener would think he [sic] had tended his hot house in vain, did not more than half of the plants send forth full blown beautiful flowers and fruits. All that we can say is that the result is not what, from the mighty flourish of trumpets that has so long sounded in our ears, we have a right to expect." ("Sun Flower" [Elizabeth Cady Stanton] 1850, 12)

GREECE

A country with an ancient society which in most histories consists of free and slave men "although women had been involved in all aspects of ancient Greek society, as members of all the Greek schools of philosophy, as teachers, healers, writers, and heads of philosophic academies." (Mary Ritter Beard 1942; in Ann J. Lane ed. 1977, 47)

GREENHAM COMMON

A peace camp in England, near a U.S. military base, which has been for many women a home without physical security but with purpose, patience, sacrifice and courage.

Women have changed that name from the sign of a missile base to the sign of peace. (Wendy Mulford 1983, 39)

(See SENECA FALLS)

GREENS

To have, get or give one's greens was a slang phrase for heterosexual intercourse meaning "to enjoy, procure, or confer sexual favour." It was used for both sexes. J. S. Farmer and W. E. Henley cite a number of other terms under this heading which were used by or applied to women only. These include: to catch an oyster; to do the naughty; to do a spread, a tumble, a backfall, what mother did before me; a turn on one's back, what Eve did with Adam; to hold, or turn up one's tail, to get one's leg lifted, one's kettle mended, one's chimney swept out, one's leather stretched; to lift one's leg; to open up to; to get shot in the tail; to get a shove in one's blind eye; to get a wet bottom; to suck the sugar-stick; to take in beef; to look at the ceiling over a man's shoulder; to play one's ace; to take in cream; to feed one's pussy; to take the starch out of; to get a green gown; to have a hot pudding (or live sausage) for supper; to give mutton for beef, juice for jelly, soft for hard, a cure for the horn; to take off one's stays. (J. S. Farmer and W. E. Henley 1890-1904, 208-9)

(See SEXUAL INTERCOURSE, SLANG)

GREY HAIRS

Women of experience and knowledge, recognized as such in some cultures. "Women who are returned pilgrims or ceremonial cooks become the core figures of influence, power, and authority among Shahsevan women; they come to be called *ag birchek* (literally 'grey hairs')." (Nancy Tapper 1978; cited by Kathryn S. March and Rachelle Taqqu 1982, 32)

GRILLE, THE

One divider which *has* been removed. On Oct. 28, 1908, Muriel Matters took her place in the London Gallery of the House of Commons in the front row next to the grille behind which all women visitors had to sit so as not to distract the members. She chained herself to the grille and proceeded to address the House on the subject of Votes for Women. In order to remove her, the grille had to be removed also. It was never replaced and women now take places in all galleries and The Grille is part of the Suffragette collection in the London Museum. (M. L. *Calling All Women*, Feb. 1970, 19)

GROONBLID

A word without a concept, available to fit a concept which does not yet have an adequate word. "The word I'd like to suggest for males and females in a relationship (hetero- or homosexual) which involves love, sex, and usually shared living space, is 'groonblid.' Though 'groonblid' may seem strange at first, it does have a few advantages. It is spelled simply. It has no negative connotation

that I can see. It is totally devoid of etymology, sexist or otherwise, having been created to compensate for missing letters in a Scrabble set." (Lynne Derus 1975, letter to the editor, *Ms.* 54:4 (Oct. 1975), 10, 14)

GUERILLA ACTION

"A dramatic form of confrontational direct action. i looked up guerilla action in the *American Heritage Dictionary* and this is what i came up with: 'A member of the military forces of a patriotic or revolutionary movement that seeks to immobilize and isolate the superior forces of an occupying enemy, strategically by means of the political mobilization of the local peasant population and tactically by means of sudden acts of harassment executed by small bands recruited in part from the able-bodied section of the population.' Well, needless to say, i didn't feel very included in this so i wrote my own: 'A group of radical women of a militant wing of the Revolutionary Women's Movement that seeks to immobilize and isolate the superior forces of the patriarchal enemy, strategically by means of the political mobilization of the local women and tactically, by means of sudden acts of harassment executed by small and large bands of women motivated and mobilized from the able-minded section of the majority of the population.' " (Lee Smith 1984, manuscript)

GUIDELINES, LANGUAGE

Suggested or required ways of writing or speaking. A type of language planning practiced by publishers and teachers and others interested in changing or regulating language usage. Guidelines of suggested ways of avoiding sexist language are listed in Cheris Kramarae, Barrie Thorne and Nancy Henley 1983, 200-4; and in Casey Miller and Kate Swift 1980.

GUILT

1. A brainwashing process used by many religious, societal, and educational institutions to make women feel bad about being alive and taking up space. 2. The

G

emotion that stops women from doing what they may need to do to take care of themselves as opposed to everyone else. (Mary Ellen Shanesey 1984, correspondence)

"Is *not* a feeling. It is an intellectual mask to a feeling." (Cherríe Moraga and Gloria Anzaldúa eds 1981, 62)

"Guilt is only another way of avoiding informed action, of buying time out of the pressing need to make clear choices, out of the approaching storm that can feed the earth as well as bend the trees." (Audre Lorde 1981c, 9)

"Guilt does not move, guilt does not look you in the eye, guilt does not speak a personal language. I would like to ask every white woman who feels that her guilt is being provoked in discussions of racism to consider what uses she has for this guilt and how it uses her; and to decide for herself if a guilt-ridden feminism, a guilt-ridden rebellion, sounds like a viable way of life." (Adrienne Rich 1981a, 6)

GUMPTION

"Anyone who has gumption knows what it is, and any one who hasn't can never know what it is. So there is no need of defining it." (L. M. Montgomery 1914, 291)

GYMNASTICS

Physical training developed in the late nineteenth century into a science and art by Madame Osterberg, a Swedish teacher working in England. She "led the way for a new profession for men." (L. R. Taylor 1919, 67)

GYNAECOCRACY

"A government wholly in the hands of women." (Charlotte Perkins Gilman 1911, 231)

(See GYNARCHY)

GYNAESTHESIA

"A kind of multidimensional/multiform power of sensing/understanding her environment . . . a Self-identified *synaesthesia*: it is woman-identified *gynaesthesia* . . . a complex way of perceiving the interrelatedness of seemingly disparate phenomena." (Mary Daly 1978, 316)

(See EUTHENICS)

GYN/AFFECTION

"Personal and political movement of women toward each other." (Janice Raymond 1982, 8)

(See BE-FRIENDING)

GYNANDRY

Sometimes referred to as *androgyny*. (Hester Eisenstein 1980, xiii)

(See ANDROGYNY)

GYNARCHISM

The belief "that women will seize power from the patriarchy and, thereby, totally change life on this planet as we know it." (Steven Dansky, John Knoebel, and Kenneth Pitchford 1973; in Susan Rennie and Kirsten Grimstad 1975, 222)

GYNARCHY

"(Greek gyn + archy) Government by women." (Heresies Great Goddess Collective 1982, 129)

Women-centred government and organization embodied in American Indian tribes and devastated by white invaders. "The destruction of the tribes was not simply a fight for land and wealth, but . . . was a continuation of the European wars that ended in the destruction of Britain's, Ireland's, and Europe's tribal peoples. . . . The same war that devastated American Indian tribes devastated African tribal peoples as well. It is my profound conviction that those wars are about the supremacy of industrial patriarchies over the tribal gynarchies they supplant. The destruction of tribal social systems has not been confined to physical warfare; it has been equally waged within the minds of the people, all the people, who are carefully taught versions of our past(s) that erase those pasts, that make them into something they never were." (Paula Gunn Allen; quoted in Carol Lee Sanchez 1983, 15-16)

GYNECOLOGY

A medical specialty, dealing with women's reproductive systems, which was developed by men during the last century. In the U.S., in 1900, 50 percent of babies were still being delivered by midwives. By 1930 public campaigns against midwives were almost totally eliminated, "*female* assistance at births was in effect being turned into a crime," and "the day of the totally medicalized childbirth – hazardously overdrugged and overtreated – was on its way." (Barbara Ehrenreich and Deirdre English 1979, 93-8)

(See MIDWIFE)

A military science. "In reading the history of gynecology and plowing through endless descriptions of 'bold,' 'daring' surgeons possessed of 'ruthless courage' who 'attack' and 'tackle' ailments by cutting out most of the female sex organs, doctors began to sound like warriors to me, and women's bodies, like conquered lands. Might women, who come from the gentler female culture, bring a less military approach to healing? Perhaps they would emphasize the maintenance of health rather than the defeat of disease." (Gena Corea 1977, 19)

GYN/ECOLOGY

"The title *Gyn/Ecology* is a way of wrenching back some wordpower. The fact that most gynecologists are males is in itself a colossal comment on 'our' society. . . . Gyn/Ecology is by and about women a-mazing all the male-authored 'sciences of womankind,' and weaving world tapestries *of our own kind*. That is, it is about dis-covering, de-veloping the complex web of living/loving relationships *of our own kind*. . . . It *is* dis-possessing our Selves, enspiriting our Selves, hearing the call of the wild, naming our wisdom, spinning and weaving world tapestries out of genesis and demise." (Mary Daly 1978, 9-11)

GYNEPHOBIA/GYNOPHOBIA

"The age-old, cross-cultural male fear and hatred of women, which women too inhale like poisonous fumes from the air we breathe daily." (Adrienne Rich 1979, 289)

"Literally, fear of women; defined as hatred of women." (Heresies Great Goddess Collective 1982, 129)

"*Internalized gynephobia*: if I despise myself as woman I must despise you even more, for you are my rejected part, my antiself." (Adrienne Rich, 1979, 300)

GYNERGY

"Is a new word invented by Emily Culpepper in 1975. It stands for that female energy which 'both comprehends and creates who we are. It is woman-identified be-ing.' . . . This word has passed into common usage in many areas." (Mary Daly 1983, 59)

GYNOCIDE

The murder of women, especially mass murder.

(See WITCH)

"Is the systematic crippling, raping, and/or killing of women by men. . . . We must finally understand that under patriarchy gynocide is the ongoing reality of life lived by women. And then we must look to each other – for the courage to bear it and for the courage to change it." (Andrea Dworkin 1976, 19)

GYNOCRITICS

Is an analysis which "begins at the point when we free ourselves from the linear absolutes of male literary history, stop trying to fit women between the lines of the male tradition, and focus instead on the newly visible world of female culture." (Elaine Showalter 1979, 22)

HAG

Originally "Holy Woman," a cognate of Egyptian *heg*, a predynastic matriarchal ruler who knew words of power, or *hekua*. (*Book of the Dead*, E. A. Wallis Budge, trans. 1960, 351). Old English *haegtesse*, Old High German, *hagzissa*, which meant "harpy, witch," or Female demon, an ugly repulsive old woman. (*Heresies Great Goddess Issue* 1982, 129) It also formerly meant "an evil or frightening spirit" or "nightmare." One must ask though " 'Evil' by whose definition? 'Frightening' to whom? Whose nightmare?" (Mary Daly 1978, 14-15) Feminist contemporary definition derives from this archaic past. Hags may now be considered wise women of independent spirit.

(See HAGGARD WOMEN)

Hag, hedge, hex – all related to a root meaning "wood." A hag was a woman of the woods, hence a witch, hence an independent woman. (Varda One 1971)

HAGGARD

"Although *haggard* is commonly used to describe one who has a worn or emaciated appearance, this was not its original or primary meaning. Applied to a hawk, it means 'untamed.' So-called obsolete meanings given in Merriam-Webster include 'intractable,' 'willful,' 'wanton,' and 'unchaste.' The second meaning is 'wild in appearance: as a) *of the eyes*: wild and staring, b) *of a person*: WILD-EYED.' ... As a noun, *haggard* has an 'obsolete meaning: an intractable person, especially: a woman reluctant to yield to wooing.' " (Mary Daly 1978, 15)

(See HAG, HAGGARD WOMEN)

HAGGARD WOMEN

"Those who refuse to assume the woes of wooed women, who cast off these woes as unworthy of Hags, of Harpies. Haggard women are not man-wooed. As Furies, women in the tradition of the Great Hags reject the curse of the compromise." (Mary Daly 1978, 15-16)

HAG-OCRACY

"The background into which feminist journeying spins ... the wild realm of Hags and Crones." (Mary Daly 1978, 3)

HAG-OGRAPHY

The history of "women who are on the journey of radical be-ing, the lives of the witches, of the Great Hags [a hidden history which is] deeply intertwined with our own process. As we write/live our own story, we are uncovering their history, creating Hag-ography and Hag-ology." (Mary Daly 1978, 15)

HAIRLESSNESS

"Under the male definition of femininity there is the notion of female 'hairlessness.' The feminine woman has no facial hair, no hair on arms or legs or under arms, and women who wish to conform to this definition of femininity will constantly present themselves to males without a hint of hair [on these places]." (Dale Spender 1980, 92)

HALLOWEEN

Old English *hallow* (holy) + e'en (eve). In the old Celtic calendar the year began on Nov. 1, with Oct. 31 being "Old Year's Night," the night of all witches. (*Heresies Great Goddess Collective* 1982, 199)

(See WICCE, WITCH)

"Was/is a remnant of one of the great Sabbats, or feasts of Wicce, the old Religion." (Mary Daly 1978, 462n)

HANDBAGS
Containers which get bigger and bigger when mothers take care of young children, and smaller when the children become teenagers. (Michelene Wandor 1980, 134)

HANDICAPIST LANGUAGE
Use of statements such as "I see what you mean," "What is your view on this point," "Thatcher deaf to union," "Turn a blind eye," instead of "I understand what you mean" or "What is your opinion," etc. (Kirsten Hearn 1983, letter to *Spare Rib*, Nov. 5)

(See ABLEISM, DISABLED)

HANDS
Palm and fingers which can "take away, obstruct, refuse to build the walls and bombs and jails. And then they give, stretch out, open, gesture a return, offer not rejection but solace." (Pam McAllister 1982, 2)

HANDSHAKE
"As a [U.S. and U.K.] masculine ritual of recognition and affirmation, it serves to perpetuate male clubbiness and to exclude women from the club. The handshake is a gesture rare between two women, and optional between a man and a woman.... Handshaking between women, or between women and men, is more likely to take place in a group containing men (who are likely to shake hands)." (Nancy Henley 1977, 110) In France and Germany women now use the handshake as their own action of recognition and friendship.

HAPPILY EVER AFTER
"Is a BF (before feminism) concept." (Michelene Wandor 1980, 135)

HARASSMENT, CLASSROOM
"Runs through the whole familiar spectrum, from the uncomfortable feeling you are being eyed up, through suggestive remarks, jokes, groping, to 'serious' propositions of sex." (Deborah Cameron 1980; in Marsha Rowe 1982, 257)

(See SEXUAL HARASSMENT)

HARDSELF
The material body. (Sally Gearhart 1978)

HAREM
"The harem was a powerful decision-making, social welfare, and public relations center. Not only were marriages made there, help for neighbors in need was organized with remarkable speed. The support was psychological as often as it was material. For example, harem pressure inspired many a mean husband and mother-in-law to shape up. It was also through the women that the latest aspect of oasis life was disseminated, as were new remedies and ideas. Men who ignored harem power risked their domestic tranquility and public dignity." (Naila Minai 1981, 114)

Primate harem: A single-male troop. "For a female, males are a resource in her environment which she may use to further the survival of herself and her offspring. If environmental conditions are such that the male role can be minimal, a one-male group is likely. Only one male is necessary for a group of females if his only role is to impregnate them." (Jane Lancaster 1975, 34)

HARLEQUIN ROMANCES
Romance novels. "The traditional Harlequin heroine is young, vulnerable, in a deadend job; the hero is ten years older, arrogant and moody, as well as being rich and powerful. Sometimes he's brutal as well, alternating between kissing and hitting. But in the end the heroine learns that he's mocked her because he really loves her: he feared she was just another 'scheming little adventuress,' but now respects her as true blue." The latest Harlequins show more equalization of the major characters. (Emily Toth 1984, 12; Tania Modleski 1982)

(See GOTHIC NOVEL, ROMANCE)

The "Harlequin world is inhabited by two species incapable of communicating with each other, male and female . . . these Pollyanna books have their own dream-like truth: our culture produces a pathological experience of sex differences. The sexes have different needs and interests, certainly different experiences. They find each other totally mystifying." "Harlequins may well be closer to describing women's hopes for love than the work of fine women novelists. Harlequins eschew irony; they take love straight. Harlequins eschew realism; they are serious about fantasy and escape." (Ann Barr Snitow 1983, 247, 261-2)

Pornography for women.

HARLOT

A term introduced from French in the 13th century, it signified *vagabond* or *rogue* and applied only to men; it received its present meaning of *prostitute* or *whore* in the late Middle Ages. It occurs most often in religious contexts and seems to reflect the exaggerated notion of feminine evil that is more typical of theological circles than of the courtly love tradition. (Elizabeth Judd, in press)

(See COURTLY LOVE)

HARPIE/HARPY

(See HAG)

HAT

A topper, as worn by, for example, Bella Abzug, known for her "advocacy of women's issues, her hard-hitting, 'unladylike' style, and her hats. . . . As Abzug has pointed out many times, though she usually wears a hat, she removed her gloves a long time ago." (Willa Young 1984, 4)

HATRED

(See ANGER, MAN-HATING)

HE

(See FALSE GENERICS, HE/MAN APPROACH, PRONOUN)

HEAD OF FAMILY

A role not needed for friendship, love or family. (Charlotte Perkins Gilman 1911, 46)

HEALTH

A state of well-being and freedom from disease and pain, which should be considered a "basic right and a high social priority. . . . We need to develop a planned decentralized system, funded by public money, that is responsible to the community." (Boston Women's Health Collective 1971, 1976, 343)

Condition of body and mind traditionally assigned to our care. "As mothers and wives we have been held responsible for the health (or illness) of children, men, and parents. As 'caring' nurses and auxiliaries in hospitals we have worked long hours for low pay. On the other hand our own health, in body and mind, has often been seen as flowing or blocked by our female biology, and as something to be controlled by doctors." (Sona Osman 1983, 30)

A word which is "one of the major bludgeons used against fat women. Isn't it really unhealthy to be fat? No, it is not more unhealthy to be fat. Many health problems that seem to be specific to fat people are actually caused by stress from oppression and constant dieting." (Martha Courtot 1982, 14)

(See FAT)

HEALTH-CURE

The restoring of health to the sick, often best accomplished by "an old woman's recipe, as it is term'd . . . ." However, women must yield to men "in the art of inventing hard names, and puzzling a cure with the number, as well as adding to a patient's grievance with the costliness, of remedies." (Sophia 1739, 41)

(See ILLNESS)

HEALTH MOVEMENT, WOMEN'S

"Composed of individuals and groups who are working to improve women's and infants' health care, women's reproductive and sexual freedom and the status and power of women health workers, both paid and unpaid.... Self-help is an approach to the solution of these and other problems, and is based on the idea that women have been controlled through the suppression of their sexuality, and the belief that if women can learn directly about their bodies through self-examination together, they can regain sexual and reproductive control." (Federation of Feminist Women's Health Centers 1981, 163)

(See SELF-HELP)

HEALTH SYSTEM

"Our present health system relies mainly on haphazardly distributed, crisis-oriented, expensive, hospital-based facilities for dispensing many health services.... [It] is disease rather than health oriented, and doctor and hospital dominated." (Boston Women's Health Collective 1971, 1976, 338)

HEAR

One meaning is *understand*. "I sometimes think men don't 'hear' very well, if I take your meaning to be 'understand what is going on in a person.' That's what makes them so restful. Women wear each other out with their everlasting touching of the nerve." (May Sarton 1961; rpt. 1976, 203-4)

HEARING

The beginning. "In the beginning was not the word. In the beginning is the hearing. Spinsters spin into the listening deep." (Mary Daly 1978, 424)

HEART

"The heart of a woman falls back with the night,
And enters some alien cage in its plight,
And tries to forget it has dreamed of the stars
While it breaks, breaks, breaks on the sheltering bars."

(Georgia Douglas Johnson 1918, 263)

HECATE

The ruler of life and death, fertility and infertility. "The Great Goddess Hecate is anathema to those who worship Western father gods, governing as she does the aspects of strong women who demand the exercise of choice and individuality.... Hecate was too fearful (to men) to be allotted a spouse and so she escaped the dreary fate of most other matriarchal goddesses.... Hecate is at once crone and virgin.... In the middle ages rebellious women worshipped Hecate as Diana ... the Queen of Elfin or Faerie, the Goddess of the Crossroads or the heath. She was the patroness of the midwives and the women healers whose traditional knowledge of medicine passed from woman to woman." (*Hecate: A Women's Interdisciplinary Journal* 1978, 4:1 (February) back cover)

A journal: "We have named our journal 'Hecate,' a symbolic gesture to all that is proud, untameable, autonomous, compassionate, angry, strong, creative, intelligent and brave in women that, although repressed and denied for thousands of years, has never been crushed, and now pushes towards the light like shooting blades of barley. Hecate is mythologically represented as a bitch and as the witches would have said 'So mote it be'. " (*Hecate* 1978, 4:1, back cover)

HEEBEE

Temper tantrum, in the vocabulary of a girls' school in northeast England. (Partridge 1961, rev. 1984)

HELL

A motherless place. (James Douglass; cited in Teresa Billington-Greig c. 1952)

Before Christianity gave the underworld the name of Goddess Hell, it was quite a different place. "The ancients didn't view the underworld as primarily a place of punishment. It was dark, mysterious, and awesome, but not the vast torture chamber the Christians made of it." (Barbara G. Walker 1983, 383)

HE/MAN
(See MAN AS FALSE GENERIC)

HE/MAN APPROACH
"Involves the use of male terms to refer both specifically to males and generically to human beings. The *he/man* approach has received most attention in current debates on sexist language, due not only to its ubiquity but also to its status as one of the least subtle of sexist forms." "[However,] studies of pronoun usage show striking sex differences in both the use and understanding of the generic masculine. Females use *he* less often than do males, and turn more frequently to alternatives such as *he or she* and *they*. Males have an easier time imagining themselves as members of the category referenced by generic *he*." (Wendy Martyna 1983, 25-6, 30)
(See FALSE GENERICS)

HEMBRISMO
Extreme female submission. (Anna Macias 1982, 3)
(See MACHISMO)
"A term coined by Maria Elvira Bermúdez (1955) to describe the traditional Hispanic female role, the counterpart of *machismo*. *Hembra* means female." This dichotomy can be compared to the masculinity/femininity dichotomy in the Anglo American culture. (Guadalupe Gibson 1983, 127-8)

HEN
"a hen
is useful to men
she lays eggs
between her legs"
(Anonymous 7-year-old wimmin 1979, *This Magazine Is For, About, and By Young Wimmin*, Aug. 3)

HERA
"Celebrated as Hera the Leader of War. Queen of the Mysian amazons who lived in Anatolia during the Bronze Age. The names of her companion lovers are unknown. . . The celebrants of Hera or those who accomplished feats in her name were called heraines or heroines." (Monique Wittig and Sande Zeig 1976, 71)
(See HERO)

HERESY
A free personal choice in act and thought which rejects traditional faiths and customs. "Only in an enemy's mouth did *heresy* become a negative thing." (Jane Ellen Harrison 1910, 10)

HERE TODAY AND GONE TOMORROW
First said by Aphra Behn in her play *The Lucky Chance*, first performed by Drury Lane Theatre 1686. The play ends with an understanding that capture and possession are not enough in marriage. (Fidelis Morgan 1981, 74)

HERLAND
A feminist utopia created by Charlotte Perkins Gilman in 1915. *Herland* is "like a pleasant family – an old, established, perfectly-run country place." The women in Herland have no enemies; the success of the society is due to "sister love" or "mother love." There is no illegitimacy because all children have mothers. All children are female. (Charlotte Perkins Gilman 1915)

HERO
According to male conception: "the strong, square, determined jaw. He may be cross-eyed, wide-eared, thick-necked, bandy-legged – what you please; but he must have a more or less [protruding] jaw." (Charlotte Perkins Gilman 1911, 62).

Rather than one who is superhuman and above the rest of society in strength and power, it is a woman who shares our conflicts and struggles in a contradictory world. "She shows us how to struggle more successfully. . . . The genuine hero helps her friends and comrades by teaching them directly or indirectly what she has learned from her experience, and how she has applied theoretical and practical knowledge to specific situations." (Berenice Fisher 1980, 13)
(See HERA)

HER SAY

A U.S. women's weekly news service, syndicated to radio stations, newspapers, and women's organizations throughout the world. (*womenews*, June 1983, 3)

(See PERIODICALS)

HERSTORY

"The human story as told by women about women (and, possibly, men); accounts of the human past and human activity that consider women as being at the center of society, not at the margins; women's history." (Anne Forfreedom 1983, personal communication, Sacramento)

(See AUTHOR, IDENTITY)

"1. The past as seen through the eyes of women. 2. The removal of male self-glorification from history." (Midge Lennert and Norma Willson, eds 1973)

"Alternative form: hystery (origin, womb)." (Jo Haugerud 1982)

(See HISTORY, PREHISTORY, HISTORIANS)

"When women in the movement use *herstory*, their purpose is to emphasize that women's lives, deeds, and participation in human affairs have been neglected or undervalued in standard histories." (Casey Miller and Kate Swift 1976, 135)

(See MANGLISH)

HES

A word proposed as a substitution or replacement of the phrase *her/his* or *her and his*. A word coined for a board game called Broadway by Ernie Permentier. ("Mid-Revolutionary Mores," 1984, *Ms.*, May, 22)

HETERODITES

Luncheon club for unorthodox women which flourished in Greenwich Village, New York City, from about 1910 through the 1930s, meeting every other week except in the summer. "It was a meeting place for women of widely divergent political views, from staunch members of the Democratic and Republican parties to Stella Coman Ballantine, anarchist sympathizer and Emma Goldman's niece; from admirers of Senator Robert LaFollett's Progressive Party such as his daughter Fola La Follette, Marie Jenny Howe, Netha Roe and Zona Gale, to the Socialists Elizabeth Gurley Flynn, Rose Pastor Stokes (both of whom eventually became active Communists) and Katharine Anthony; and from the pacifist founder of the American Union against Militarism, Crystal Eastman, to strong military advocates like Mary Logan Tucker of the Navy League and the pro-Wilson Daughters of the American Revolution. . . . The personal lives and relationships of the members ran the gamut from conventionally married heterosexual women . . . through scandalously divorced members and free-love advocates, to a rather large number of never married women, several of whom were lesbians involved in long-term relationships with each other or non-Heterodoxy women. All of the Heterodoxy club were ardently pro-women supporters who felt strong friendships and contacts with other women were vital to their lives. . . . For all the fame of some of its individual members, Heterodoxy barely rates a mention or a footnote in modern published sources . . . as if they had disappeared without a trace – not a remarkable or unusual fate for women, but damnably aggravating none the less." (Judith Schwarz 1982, 1, ii)

"A tribe of women living on the Island of Manhattan in the North Seas." (Florence Guy Woolson 1919; in Judith Swartz 1982, 95)

HETEROMAN

1. Easy to look at, pleasing to touch, but if you want caring you're asking too much. (Cherie Lyn, 1982, correspondence [written during her transition from bisexual to lesbian]) 2. A heterosexual, sexist man. (Cherie Lyn 1984, correspondence)

HETEROPHOBIA

Fear of and resistance to heterosexuals which sometimes surfaces in women's movements around the world. It relies on a "sexual-fundamentalist reduction of curiosity and desire." (Robin Morgan 1982, 145)

HETERO-RELATIONS

A term "used to express the wide range of affective, social, political, and economic relations that are ordained between men and women by men." (Janice Raymond 1982, 9)

(See HETEROSEXUALITY)

HETEROSEXISM

The "dominant perspective of patriarchal culture [which] defines wimmin as sexually, intellectually, and emotionally inferior to males, prescribes that the proper conduct for wimmin is passivity, servility, domesticity, and maintains social institutions which insure the economic dependence of wimmin on males, either through husbands or fathers." (Julia Penelope 1980, 1-3)

"The belief that heterosexuality is better, more 'natural' or 'normal' (both words no feminist should use without extreme caution) than homosexuality. Like sexism and racism, it ranges from the overt and violent ('queer bashing,' believing homosexual sex should be illegal) to the subtle (asking lesbians, but never oneself, 'how you got that way'; thinking that some lesbians and gay men are too 'blatant' even though displays of heterosexual sex are all around us.)" (Sona Osman 1983, 30)

"Is the view that heterosexuality is the 'norm' for all social/sexual relationships and as such the heterosexist imposes the model on all individuals through homophobia (fear of homosexuality). S/he supports and/or advocates this continued institutionalization of heterosexuality in all aspects of society – including legal and social discrimination against homosexuals and the denial of homosexual rights as a political concern." (Cherríe Moraga 1983, 105)

(See HETEROSEXUALITY, HOMOPHOBIA, LESBIANISM, SEXISM)

HETEROSEXUAL IMPERATIVE

The coercive social programming that produces heterosexuals. (Julia P. Stanley 1984, correspondence)

HETEROSEXUALITY

A sexual feeling for a person (or persons) of the opposite sex, a feeling experienced and enjoyed by some women and some men.

A bizarre mixture of myth and coercion which "is defended more vigorously than any other precept on which our society is supposed to be founded." Defended more than religion, equality, or freedom of expression. (Anna Coote and Beatrix Campbell 1982, 213)

"A compulsory set of relations produced not at the level of the body, but at the level of discourse and social practice, a compulsory sexuality which enables male dominance and refuses autonomy or solidarity among women." (Biddy Martin 1982, 12)

A political institution. Compulsory adherence is demanded in U.S. culture. Women are pressured into believing that marriage and sexual orientation towards men are inevitable, even if they are unsatisfying or oppressive. Forms of compulsion include "chastity belts, child marriage, erasure of lesbian existence . . . idealization of heterosexual romance and marriage." (Adrienne Rich 1980, 635-40)

"For women, heterosexual relations are always intense, frightening, high-risk situations which ought, if a woman has any sense of self-preservation, to be carefully calculated." (Linda Gordon 1976; cited in Adrienne Rich 1979, 196)

"Basically, heterosexuality means men first. That's what it's all about. It assumes that every woman is heterosexual; that every woman is defined by and is the property of men. Her body, her services, her children belong to men. If you don't accept that definition, you're a queer – no matter who you sleep with; if you do not accept that definition in this society, you're a queer." (Charlotte Bunch 1975; rpt. 1981, 69)

Seemingly the norm of our society

"because most men are fixated on women as sexual objects; but, in fact, we live in a homosexual society because all transactions of power, authority, and authenticity take place among men.... Heterosexuality, which can be defined as the sexual dominance of men over women, is like an acorn – from it grows the mighty oak of the male homosexual society." (Andrea Dworkin 1976, 104)

"A choice; respect from others for that choice demands that heterosexual feminists explain their choice as a reasonable choice." (Marilyn Frye 1980, 7)

(See COMPULSORY HETEROSEXUALITY, HOMOEROTICISM, HOMOSEXISM, LESBIAN, SEXUALITY)

HETEROSEXUALISE

The process of directing women into heterosexuality. "The making of women is like the making of eunuchs, the breeding of slaves, of animals." (Monique Wittig 1982, 67)

HETEROSEXUALLY IMPAIRED

Large group, often ignorant of their condition. (Term used by Kate Clinton 1982, album jacket)

HIDDEN CURRICULUM

Methods of education, seemingly neutral, which promote, maintain and perpetuate sexism and sexual inequality. Includes separating pupils by sex on registers, addressing boys and girls differently, expecting differences in achievements based on sex, using so-called generics, organizing curriculum so that men are directed toward prestige jobs and salaries, subsidising the materials for wood-work but not cookery, and advising students into sex segregated classes. ("Learning to be a Girl" 1980, 4)

(See CLASSROOM INTERACTION)

HIGH CLASS BURGLARS

The phrase used by Mother (Mary) Jones to describe capitalists who expressed opposition to union labor. (*New York Times* Dec. 1, 1930; rpt. Elizabeth Janeway ed. 1973, 166)

HIGH CULTURE

"A ruling class preoccupation." (Lillian Robinson 1978, 29)

"It is a male idea that to be 'high' and 'fine' both women and art should be beautiful, but not useful or functional." (Patricia Mainardi; in Suzanne Levine and Harriet Lyons eds 1980, 142)

HIGH HEELS

Shoes which throw the weight of the wearer on the balls of the feet. "Make walking, never mind running, a feat in itself; but more than this, *symbolically* they represent women's dependent fragile status. They summon up all sorts of ideas about male chivalry, female bondage; they have an immediate and unambiguous resonance as sexual signs." (Angela McRobbie 1981, 125)

"The abnormal heel." (Charlotte Perkins Gilman 1916c, 168)

HISPANIC

"A generic label for the diverse group of Spanish-speaking and/or Spanish-surnamed people in the United States, who reflect various histories, ethnic backgrounds and, therefore, a wide range of values. There is not only considerable inter-group diversity, but there is also marked and significant intra-group heterogeneity.... Included among the Hispanics are Puerto Ricans, Cubans, and Mexican Americans, the groups most readily identifiable; as well as Central and South Americans, Dominicans, and others. Chicanos, who constitute the largest sub-group, are primarily concentrated in the Southwest, the Puerto Ricans mostly in the Northeast, and the Cubans in the Southeast. Hispanics are now considered to be the second-largest minority group in the United States, but may constitute the largest minority group by the turn of the century.... Most Hispanic women in spite of the heterogeneity among them, share similar concerns about maintaining the language and

cultural identity and a commonality of experience as a 'minority' group within the dominant society, [particularly] racism, the most pernicious of which is generalized poverty... Hispanic women also share, as all American women do, their struggles with the issues of equity and their victimization due to sexism." (Guadalupe Gibson 1983, 113-14)
(See CHICANA, LATINA)

HISTORIANS
Black women historians "congregate – against granite.... The historians – like those who came before them – mean to survive.... They plant, weed, hoe, raise houses, sew, and wash – and continue their investigations ... opening the sutures, applying laundry soap and brown sugar, they draw out the poisons and purify the wounds. And maintain vigilance to lessen the possibility of reinfection." (Michelle Cliff 1979, 49)
(See HERSTORY, HISTORY)

HISTORIC INVISIBILITY TREATMENT
"Obscuring, over-simplifying, or deliberately misinterpreting feminist ideas; [it is] 'done' by academics, socialists, and even other feminists. It is usually directed at the most radical section of the WLM." (Kathie Sarachild 1975; quoted in Sara Scott 1983)

HISTORY
Stories written primarily by men about men's experience of the world. It is "largely a record of battles or of alliances in preparation for battles." (H.M. Swanwick 1935, 436) In other words, a "story of warfare and conquest." (Charlotte Perkins Gilman 1911, 94) Women's experience is largely left out or is a mere ornament tacked on to "real history." "Of our fathers we know always some fact, some distinction. They were soldiers or they were sailors; they filled that office or they made that law. But of our mothers, our grandmothers, our great-grandmothers, what remains? Nothing but a tradition. One was beautiful; one was red-haired; one was kissed by a Queen. We

know nothing of them except their names and the dates of their marriages, and the number of children they bore." (Virginia Woolf 1929; in Michele Barrett 1979, 44)
(See HERSTORY, HISTORIANS)

Is written from the perspective of the male city dweller and as an "as if" story: *as if* every household consisted of a husband, wife and children; *as if* every household must have a woman home at all times; *as if* all productive labor were carried out by men, and all significant civic arrangements created by men." (Elise Boulding 1976, 279, 690)

his story
history
my story
mystery
(adele aldridge 1972)

Not just past and finished time. "All History is current; all injustice continues on some level, somewhere in the world. 'Progress' affects few." (Alice Walker 1979; rpt. 1983, 370-1)

"Is not the word made finite but the culling and coaxing of available material." (Sheila Rowbotham 1983, 4)

Women's history is narrative "riddled with mysteries, inconsistencies, and unanswered questions. Even more damning than the unanswered questions are the questions that are never even asked." (Sara Maitland; quoted in Marsha Rowe 1982, 234)

HOLLOWAY PRISON
Bastille of the Women's movement in England. The Suffragette Wing has now been torn down, an event attended by some of the women who had been forcefed there. In London alone during the years 1905-14 the number of suffragettes imprisoned was 1,083.

HOLY TRINITY
Once was "the female Holy Trinity ruling all cycles of creation, birth, and death in her Virgin, Mother, and Crone forms." The concept "was destroyed by Christians' attacks on her temples, scriptures, rituals, and followers. The church de-

clared from the first that the Great Goddess 'whom Asia and all the world worshippeth' must be destroyed (Acts 19:27). This is virtually the only Gospel tenet that churches followed through all their centuries with no deviation or contradiction. It seemed necessary to hide the fact that Christianity itself was an offshoot of Middle-Eastern Goddess worship, skewed by the asceticism of Persia and India." (Barbara G. Walker 1983, viii)

HOLY WOMEN

Priestesses and female devotees of Ishtar, and her counterparts Kybele, Asherah, Aphrodite, or Astarte, in the Ancient Near East near the third to the first millenium. "They engaged in sacred rites that often included a free and active sexual life, in celebration of the active sexual aspect of the goddess they served, who was seen by people of those times as the source of fertility and abundance for the community." Masculinists refer to these women as "harlots" or "ritual prostitutes" but to their own communities they were *quadishtu*, "holy women." (Judith Ochshorn 1981, 127)

HOME

The location of both work and recreation for women with small children. "Women clean, prepare food, mend clothes, and generally put things in order for their husbands and children, for whom the home is more normally regarded as a place of rest and respite from work." In an increasing number of homes there is no husband or father. Yet for male sociologists the unit of analysis is the household, "headed" by a man. (Linda McDowell 1983, 142-3)

Called "the woman's place" by men "anxious to stamp out the enthusiasms of women political reformers." For poor women, it is often a poor place. (Mary Lowndes 1914a, 46) In the masculist tradition, it is idealized as "the appointed limit of [a woman's activity] to be exceeded only under the frown of society, and under many material disadvantages."

(A. B. T. 1919, 117) The "domestic sphere, inside enclosures." A restricted and restricting area. (Josephine Donovan 1981, 87)

Ideally should be: "to the child a place of happiness and true development; to the adult a place of happiness and that beautiful reinforcement of the spirit needed by the world's workers." (Charlotte Perkins Gilman 1904, 3) Ideally, "the location of known others and assumptions of shared values about social behaviour." (Jalna Hanmer and Sheila Saunders 1983, 32) "Has always meant a lot to people who are ostracized as racial outsiders in the public sphere. It is above all a place to be ourselves." (Barbara Smith 1983, li)

A comfortable concentration camp. (Betty Friedan 1963)

"Not where the heart is, but the house and the adjacent buildings." (Emily Dickinson; quoted in Adrienne Rich 1979, 158)

Where the revolution begins. (Cherríe Moraga and Gloria Anzaldúa eds 1981, xxvi)

HOME ECONOMICS
(See Domestic Science)

HOME GIRLS

"The girls from the neighborhood and from the block, the girls we grew up with." (Barbara Smith 1983, xxii)

HOMEMAKER

A role assigned to women by a society which at the same time devalues that role. "The mass media usually portray the homemaker as the helpless, sometimes giddy woman whose major concerns in life revolve about her embarrassed husband's ring around the collar, her dull floors, cooking for the family, and buying the right toilet paper." Most women work outside the home as well as doing much more than their share of the homemaking. Yet the mailboxes for the homes are often labelled "The George Smiths" which perpetuates the absorption of other people into the male. (Bobbye D. Sorrels 1983, 70, 82)

HOME-TRUTH
"Sound and sensible." ("Notices of Books" 1858, *The English Woman's Journal*, March 1, 68)

HOMEWORKERS
Women who are exploited as "mothers tied to the home with toddlers, as daughters left to care for the aged or as immigrants whose vulnerability makes them a cheap and malleable labour force.... They have few rights under the law. They are generally considered 'self-employed' and so are not covered by the Employment Protection Act ... they have no job security and get no holiday pay, sick pay, maternity leave, or redundancy pay." (Chris Poulter 1978; in Marsha Rowe 1982, 166-7)
(See HOUSEWIFE)

HOMODOXY
"English provides two terms, *orthodoxy* and *heterodoxy*, 'right-thinking' and 'deviant-thinking,' respectively. So, I argued that *homodoxy* is really the right word to denote what 'they' call 'orthodoxy,' since it names it accurately – conformity in ideology." (Julia P. Stanley 1984, correspondence)

HOMOEROTICISM
Man-loving in a "heterosexual male culture." Straight men, though they may fixate on women as sexual objects, reserve their real love for other men. "The people whom they admire, respect, adore, revere, honor, whom they imitate, idolize, and form profound attachments to, whom they are willing to teach and from whom they are willing to learn, and whose respect, admiration, recognition, honor, reverence, and love they desire ... are, overwhelmingly, other men." (Marilyn Frye 1983, 135)

HOMOPHOBIA
"The fear of feelings of love for members of one's own sex and therefore the hatred of those feelings in others." (Audre Lorde 1978; rpt. 1984, 45)
Heterosexual fear of homosexuals.

"The straight person's anger at being so confused." (Jeanne Cordova 1981, 77)

HOMOPHOBIC
A word "invented to describe the irrational fear of any sexual expression between people of the same gender, a fear so common in the past that it needed no name." (Gloria Steinem 1983, 153)

HOMOSEX
A concept produced by a "sexist society [which] lumped gay men and lesbian women together as 'homosexuals' because [researchers] never took their 'research' out of our bedrooms." (Jeanne Cordova 1974, 23)

HOMOSEXUAL
An outlaw. "Quite unknown to themselves they feared her; it was fear that aroused their antagonism. In her they instinctively sensed an outlaw, and theirs was the task of policing nature." (Radclyffe Hall 1928, 121)
(See GAY, HOMOPHOBIC, LESBIAN)

HOMOSOCIALITY
"The situation where people turn to one another for their primary social and political relationships, and personal respect and affection, strictly according to criteria of gender. Homosociality has no bearing on sexuality, or choice of sexual partner. In many of those societies where homosociality is most strongly developed heterosexuality is the only form of sexuality permitted legitimate expression. At the other extreme are those sub-societies where the homosocial and homosexual coincide exclusively, as in the gay ghettos of the modern city. There are also situations where the homosocial and homosexual coincide without ruling out heterosexual relations for reproductive and familial purposes." "The division of the world into 'public' and 'private' spheres makes it easy for adult homosocial relations to flourish in the public domain (in business, politics, etc.) while across the threshold of the domestic space

(whether it be a wife's, a mistress's, or a prostitute's), heterosexual relations predicate the nature of the interaction." (Annette Hamilton 1981, 82)
(See HOMOEROTICISM)

HONEY
A sweet thick name used especially to address females. In cases in which the same term does not seem appropriate in return address, the proper response is "Young Lad" if the male is younger than 30, and "Old Man" if he is older. (Mona Howard 1983, at "Feminists at Fawcett" meeting)

As an address label *Honey* is "inappropriate unless you are a bear talking to your lunch." (Alan Alda; quoted in Gloria Kaufman and Mary Kay Blakely, eds 1980, 175)
(See FORMS OF ADDRESS)

HONORARY WOMAN
"Any man who has the courage to come hear me speak." (Sonia Johnson 1983, 4)

HONOUR
"Truth-telling, independence of thought and action, self-reliance and courage . . . the qualities of a free people; and [thus] they have not been required of [a woman]." (Cicely Hamilton 1909, 63)

Male: "A man's 'word' sufficed – to other men – without guarantee . . . having something to do with killing . . . as something needing to be avenged; hence the duel." Female: "Honesty in women has not been considered important. We have been depicted as generically whimsical, deceitful, subtle, vacillating. And we have been rewarded for lying." (Adrienne Rich 1979, 186)

HONOURABLE THING, THE
A man's sometimes response which at least considers the impact of his behavior on a woman's life. An action which assumes he is the answer to the problems a woman experiences. Eileen Fairweather says that "the honorable thing" was expected of men in the past but is now rare. (1979, 33)

HOPE
Ability to see connections, to dream the present into the future. "Hope is women's most powerful revolutionary tool; it is what we give each other every time we share our lives, our work, and our love. It pulls us forward out of self-hatred, self-blame, and the fatalism which keeps us prisoners in separate cells." (Peggy Kornegger 1979, 248)

HORIZONTAL HOSTILITY
"In the name of elitism, we do a crabs-in-a-barrel number, and pull down any of our number who get public attention or a small success. As long as we're into piranha-ism and horizontal hostility, honey, we ain't going to get nowhere." (Florynce Kennedy; quoted in Gloria Steinem 1973, 89)
(See ELITISTS)

HORSE
The Woman on a Horse was an important symbol in the iconography of the suffrage movement. This originated in England as a relatively militant image associated with Joan of Arc, "the patron saint of suffragettes"; in the U.S., it retained this meaning of righteousness and redemption only for the National Women's Party; to suffragists at large the woman on a horse was a vaguely classical figure akin to the Herald/Angel. (Edith P. Mayo 1981)

HOSPITAL
Institutions in which sick and injured people are nursed by women. In the middle ages the great hospitals were in women's convents. Women were the first doctors and nurses until the modern age when "men entered this field of sick care, shut women [healers] out of the hospitals, and forced them to make their way back to their age-old responsibility." (Mary Ritter Beard 1942; in Ann J. Lane ed. 1977, 221)

Includes a (primarily) female nursing staff and a (primarily) female domestic staff for the catering, laundry, provision of beds and bedding, and all the minutiae of housekeeping. The management is largely male, even in hospitals exclusively for children or for maternity hospitals. ("Man's Sphere – The Hospital" 1914, *The Englishwoman*, 21-62 (Feb.), 137)

(See HEALTH)

HOST COUNTRY

In this phrase *host* is a euphemism for dominant. (Valerie Alia 1984a)

HOSTILITY

Can take the form of physical combat disguised as love. Women are "swung painfully dizzy at square dances, chased by playful gangs of men and thrown in water, carried, spanked, or dunked at a beach, all clearly against their will. The cheek- and hair-patting, chin-chucking, and bottom patting and pinching continue as part of many women's daily experience." Women are not encouraged to complain about such "teasing" because of its outward guise of affection. (Nancy Henley 1977, 122)

HOST WORLD

"To native peoples, there is no such thing as the first, second, and third worlds; there is only an exploiting world . . . and a host world. Native peoples, who occupy more land, make up the host world." (Winona LaDuke 1983, 55)

(See IMPERIALISM, THIRD WORLD)

HOUSEHOLD WORD

Could be used to refer to a word particular to or important to an individual family. In this sense, women coin and preserve (through usage) many household words. But usually it is an expression which means that almost everyone knows the term – and thus it is likely a term coined and disseminated by men. (Cheris Kramarae 1981, 37)

HOUSE LIFE

"Another day, another dolor." (Eve Merriam 1958; rpt 1964, 28)

As a long-time occupation, it "is not good for man, woman, or child." (Charlotte Perkins Gilman 1911, 67)

HOUSEMAID'S KNEE

A swelling resulting from kneeling while washing floors and cleaning grates. (Hannah Cullwick, Victorian maidservant; in Liz Stanley 1984, 232)

HOUSE OF COMMONS

A governing body which in principle is open to both women and men, but "women members have less than 3% of the space in this legislature. Nevertheless, women *are* allowed in this tiny piece of public space in what is constantly referred to by members as 'a men's Club' and . . . this is done by re-classifying women as men. This enables those women who are elected to the House to be absorbed into the political body, while preserving its masculinity." (S. Rogers 1981; cited by Linda Imray and Audrey Middleton 1983, 19)

HOUSEWIFE

In fourteenth-century England, the term meant the coordinator and organizer of an establishment and of a centre of production. At that time, the house had a different function in that there was not such a distinct separation between public and private life. (Catherine Hall 1974; in Marsha Rowe 1982, 134) Currently the term signifies the domestic service of wife to husband, children and house within the private (vs. the public) realm of society.

(See WORKING WOMAN)

"1. One of the acceptable roles for women. 2. The basic maintenance service unit for family, friends, and [husband's] friends. 3. Unpaid additional employee for company who hires husband. 4. Guilt-ridden wife. 5. Household worker who never reaches retirement age." (Midge Lennert and Norma Willson, eds 1973, 5)

According to patriarchal ideology, the role of housewife is supposed to be rewarding and inspiring to women. Yet, "for a woman to get a rewarding sense of total creation by way of the multiple monotonous chores that are her daily lot would be as irrational as for an assembly line worker to rejoice that he had created an automobile because he tightened a bolt." (Edith 'Mendel Stern 1949; in Elaine Partnow 1977, 39)

"You say being a housewife is the noblest calling in the world. . . . You remind me of those company executives who . . . praise the 'little guys' of their organizations in their speeches." (Françoise Parturier 1968; cited in Elaine Partnow 1977, 240)

One who is more married to a house than to the man she once thought it was all about. (*Banshee: Journal of Irishwomen United* c.1980, 1:2, 7)

"Their tables are set;
their children are scrubbed;
their worlds appear ordered, but
beneath the thinnest of skins
is chaos. Everyone who's read mythology
knows:

The women are made,
quite made. This explains everything."
(Sharon Nelson 1982, 70)

Some marxists and socialists equate the position of housewife with that of the bourgeoisie. However, some have argued that despite the fact that a housewife might be married to a man of the upper class, she does not have the same class as he.

"No housewife
is bourgeois any more than pets
are, just one owner away
from the streets and starvation."
(Marge Piercy 1983, 119)

HOUSEWIFERY

A home job for which there are no clear descriptions. "Housewives belong to no trade unions; they have no professional associations to define criteria of performance, establish standards of excellence and develop sanctions for those whose performance is inadequate or inefficient. No single organization exists to defend their interests and represent them on issues and in areas which affect the

performance of their role." (Ann Oakley 1976, 8)

HOUSEWIFING

An "occupation in which every single waking act is judged by the person who means the most to you in the world. Is the house clean? Is the food good? Was it too expensive? Are the children well behaved? A thousand times a day our contracts come up for renewal. No wonder our nerves are shot." (Kathleen Phillip Satz 1982, *Ms.*, Nov., 9)

HOUSEWORK

Child rearing and the provision of food, clothing and shelter. This essential work, though not recognized as productive labor, is "the number-one full-time occupation." (Clair [Vickery] Brown 1982, 151) It "includes shopping, preparing meals, washing up, cleaning, washing clothes, ironing, and mending, as well as emotional servicing . . . it is tied up with loving care and as such its frontiers are interminable." (Marsha Rowe 1982, 129)

An unpaid and thankless job that is relegated to women "from birth because they possess certain physical characteristics." "The most obvious reason that no attention has been given to the situation of the houseworker is simply the fact that men aren't engaged in this work." (Betsy Warrior 1971, 29, 33)

Is not a bad activity in itself. "The trouble with it is that it's inhumanely lonely." (Pat Loud 1974; cited in Elaine Partnow 1977, 304)

Receives no direct payment. "In 1970 . . . it was estimated by Chase Manhattan Bank in the USA that it would cost as much as $257 (about £200) a week to pay someone else for all the components of a housewife's job." (Marsha Rowe 1982, 129) *Wages for housework debate*: Some feminists have argued that housework is productive labor and should be paid as such. Others argue that payment would not challenge the most basic assumption that it is still "women's work." They argue that rather than stimulating change, wages for housework would "strengthen the traditional system of male-female relations, the structures of the patriarchal family and hence the capitalist system. It is not impossible that male demands on women could actually increase as a result . . . since women would be paid for doing it, men would expect them to put even more effort into it." (LACW Collective 1977, 57)

"If women were compensated for housework, it could cost between $500 billion and $650 billion annually – the government's total budget. This unpaid and underpaid labor of all women, especially Black women, sustains the economy." (Gloria I. Joseph 1981, 34)

"Unpaid housework is the single largest industry in Canada. An army of 5 million women work as full-time housewives in the nation's homes for no pay, no benefits, no holidays, and no pensions. Most housewives never retire, they just tire." (Judith Ramirez 1979; cited in Gloria I. Joseph and Jill Lewis 1981, 35)

"A worm eating away at one's ideas." (Peckham Rye Women's Liberation Group 1970; quoted in Ann Oakley 1982, 174)

"Rat-poison." Rebecca West wrote: "That simile has had a great success. It has been so widely quoted by a scandalized Press that I hope it will ultimately enter the language." (*The Freewoman*, June 6, 1912)

"My mother was always cleaning or scrubbing or washing and ironing. It seems like I can hardly remember her doing anything else. Oh yes, she cooked, too." (A working-class woman describing her mother's history; quoted in Lillian Rubin 1976, 32)

". . . a job without remuneration, [so] it must be camouflaged as much as possible. . . . There is a systematic attempt to substitute the word 'work' with 'domestic obligations' or 'domestic assignments.' " (Marielouise Janssen-Jurreit 1982, 167)

HOWEVERISM

Grammatical construction which allows what is given to be simultaneously taken away. "Unsaying what one says in the act of saying it." The major French legal texts dealing with women and public employment "which proclaim equality are actually constructed according to the same linguistic model. First of all comes the principle, proclaimed and reproclaimed as often as may be necessary, agreeable or useful to the brand-image of a government. Then comes a fresh paragraph, or simply a comma's pause, and at once the fragile bark springs a leak in every quarter. 'However, when the nature of the posts or the conditions of their exercise justify it. . .' etc. Every time the principle is proclaimed, what is in fact being reproclaimed is the indefeasible, inalienable right of the government to take no account of it." Thus such legal texts "are written down, argued over, amended, published, taught in law faculties, learned by budding jurists, all to no purpose; except that they accredit the sidelong implication that henceforth in France everything is duly resolved, and that moreover any outstanding difficulties are being actively worked on." (Michèle Le Doeuff 1984, 4)

HUBRIS

"Greek 'lechery,' or 'pride,' both words associated with penile erection; said to be the sin of Lucifer. Patriarchal gods especially punished *hubris*, the sin of any upstart who became – in both senses – 'too big for his breeches.' " (Barbara Walker 1983, 416)

HUMAN

"Of, relating to, or characteristic of man," according to the *American Heritage Dictionary of the English Language*, and to the male-ridden minds of the past four hundred years or more. The form, nature and qualities of white, western men are called *human* processes. Thus women, Dorothy Sayers argues, are considered by men to be "the human-not-quite-human." The "Are Women Human?" debate of the sixteenth century continues in the twentieth. Initially one of the arguments was that the word *homo* came from *humus*, the stuff of which man (but not rib-created woman) was made. Because she was not created of humus, she could not be human. In the nineteenth century poet Lady Caroline Norton discovered that in court she was not considered a person, and as a married woman she could neither sue nor be sued. The arguments change but women are still told that there is something funny about their nature which requires that some of the major human activities – religion, education, government and commerce, for example – are basically male functions. (Manfred P. Fleischer 1981; Charlotte Perkins Gilman 1912, cited in Ronald W. Hogeland and Aileen S. Kraditor, eds 1973; Dorothy Sayers 1947, cited in Betty Roszak and Theodore Roszak, eds 1969; Elizabeth Miller Walsh 1981)

HUMAN INTEREST

In journalism, considered women's province: "Love-affairs, sex crises and maternal self-indulgence [were] irreverently familiar in journalistic terminology under the comprehensive abbreviation of 'H.I.' " (Vera Brittain 1933, 72)

HUMANISM

(See ANDROCENTRISM, ANDROGYNY)

HUMANITY

Often used as meaning special but basic consideration for people, or as civilized behavior. However, "when any group sees itself as the bearer of civilization this very belief will betray it into behaving barbarously at the first opportunity." (Simone Weil 1940; cited in Elaine Partnow 1977, 145)

(See IMPERIALISM)

HUMAN RIGHTS

In reality, men's rights. Never do we hear included in discussions of human rights the sexual assault and torture of women and girls – rape, forced prostitution, polygamy, genital mutilation, pornography, the beating of girls and women. (Fran Hosken 1981, 15)

"Is a luxury I, being black, cannot always afford." (Morena to her mother 1977; quoted in Karen Payne 1983, 384)

"Is something more than a mere species: it is a historical development." (Simone de Beauvoir 1953; cited in Elaine Partnow 1977, 122)

As presented by males: Is a wobble "between two convictions – the one, that [a woman] exists for the entire benefit of contemporary mankind; the other, that she exists for the entire benefit of the next generation." (Cicely Hamilton 1909, 24)

Collective behavior of those around us. "Kay: Because it's just a question of plain humanity as to how people are treated. Terri: Honey, if everybody on the block is doing it *that's* humanity! That's your source of reference." (From an interview in Gloria I. Joseph and Jill Lewis 1981, 199)

HUMILITY

Submission. "When it is found in a woman who has to earn her own living, generally leads to an underevaluation of herself and the acceptance of starvation wages." (*The Vote* 1911, 3:66 (Jan. 28), 161)

HUMOR/HUMOUR

A verbal weapon in the social arsenal constructed to maintain caste, class, race and sex inequalities. (Naomi Wiesstein 1973; cited by Elaine Partnow 1977, 440)

A joke "used as a weapon and directed at objects the laugher considers out of line with his ideas of reason and correct behaviour." "Women do not tend to find sexist jokes funny, cripples don't respond well to 'sick' jokes about cripples, Blacks don't like 'nigger' jokes, and Jews aren't fond of anti-semitic jokes. There is no such thing as universal humour. . . . The funnybone, like other personality traits, is related to class, sex, colour, nationality and even age, as well as to individual character." (Margaret Atwood 1982, 183, 175)

"Generally double-edged . . . there's always something beyond just the laughing. . . . [It can] keep you from feeling that God had just dropped a rock on your head alone or that you had been singled out in some way.... The function of humor is very serious and very complex." (Leslie Marmon Silko 1980, 23)

Women's: Often ironic art form, developed as a coping mechanism, openly shared with women but seldom around men. (P. R. Mecking 1981, 18)

Feminist: Satirizes the silliness of our circumstances. E.g., "Isn't it incredible, for example, that 99 per cent of the 2,800 equal-employment officers in the state of Indiana are white males? And *they* are calling *us* the protected classes. How, I'd be grateful to know, did this happen?" ... "Our humor turns our anger into a fine art." (Mary Kay Blakely 1980, 11-12)

A form of verbal stitchery. "One must not wage war on man. That is his way of attaining value.... One must simply deflate his values with the needle of ridicule." (Annie Leclerc 1974, 79)

HUMORLESS

The cliché "She lacks a sense of humor" is applied by men to every threatening woman when she does not find the following funny: rape, big breasts, sex with little girls. On the other hand there is no imputation of humorlessness if she does not find impotence, castration and vaginas with teeth humorless. (Ellen Willis 1981, 147) The word when applied to women is "insidious. It is boring and predictable if seen through, devastating if believed." (Mary Daly 1978, 19)

HUNGER

Need of food and other necessities. Women in this world experience a disproportionate amount of hunger because they are more likely to be poor and are less likely to be perceived as needing food. Hunger for food is connected by feminists to other forms of hunger. "When we are not physically starving, we have the luxury to realize psychic and emotional starvation." (Cherríe Moraga 1981, 29)

"and he said: you pretty full of yourself
  ain't chu

so she replied: show me someone not full of herself and i'll show you a hungry person"
(Nikki Giovanni 1975c, n.p.)

(See POVERTY)

HURRICANE

Usually personified as female. After some public pressure in 1979, the U.S. National Weather Service decided to spread "responsibility" for the devastation by naming some hurricanes Bob, David, Fred and Henri. (Casey Miller and Kate Swift 1980, 64)

A feminist review chose the title *Hurricane Alice* to claim for themselves the image of a hurricane. "The origins of a hurricane suggests that it starts from a depression. Once formed, it is characterized by winds that move with great force in a counter-clockwise direction. Its shape is an elliptical circle which traces the beauty and energy of a spiral and which is marked at the center by a clear eye of calm." (*Hurricane Alice* 1983, [Spring] 3)

HUSBAND

A married man who has, by self-appointment, served as "the ultimate determinant of feminine worth." (Sally Brett 1982, 17)

(See FRIEND, LOVER, PARTNER, PHALLOPANACEA, POSSLQ, UM)

"Are like fires. They go out when unattended." (Zsa Zsa Gabor 1960; cited in Elaine Partnow 1977, 254)

HUSSY

A word with a complicated history. In Old English and Middle English *hussy* was a variant or shortened form of *housewife*: a woman, usually married, who directed the affairs of her household. The shortened form *hussy* came to have a sexual slur attached to it and eventually lost its original meaning altogether.

(See SEMANTIC DEROGATION OF WOMEN)

We can suggest the discourse conditions by which *hussy* came to be used as a sexual insult. "For some members of the speech community, a salient characteristic mutually believed to belong to the housewife was some kind of sexual wantonness. Such people could try to mean what we mean by *hussy* through saying *huswif* (or . . . *hussy*) and relying on the hearer to bring that characteristic to bear in interpreting the utterance. . . So long as the negative stereotype of housewives was widely known, even hearers who did not share belief in its accuracy could be counted on to recognize an appeal to it and thus to understand that an insult was intended in the reference to someone as a *hussy*." (Sally McConnell-Ginet 1982, manuscript)

HYMENOPLASTY

Surgical operation to "restore virginity" in women. A woman "loses her virginity" when the membrane which covers part of the vaginal opening is ruptured, in sexual contact or from other causes. The operation to fix up the woman is done in less than an hour under local anesthesia to, for example, Arab or Indian Muslim women who are victims of desertion by lovers, and who believe it critical to their future to have a conventional arranged marriage. (Priya Darshini 1984, 9)

HYPERCORRECTION

A speaker's attempt to shift to unfamiliar linguistic usage perceived as more "correct"; this may involve overusage in instances where the usage is not fully appropriate. Hypercorrection in pronoun usage generated this 1981 sentence by a male physician during an orientation of medical students to clinical work in hospitals: "Whether a medical student wears a coat and tie is really his or her own decision." Since he later described dress standards for female medical students, this sentence was directed toward male medical students only, yet used a hypercorrected pronoun form.

HYPHENATED NAMES

(See NAMES)

HYSTERIA

"The Greek *hystera*, or womb, is the root of *hysteria* because it was believed that the mental disorder, to which women were particularly subject (and small wonder, with such medical attendants), was caused by disorders of the womb. We have now made so much progress that a woman may be hysterical without being subjected to a hysterectomy – though one should notice that the hysterectomy remains a favorite among factitious operations. (Still, with a middle-aged woman patient, when the surgeon thinks, What should I take out? the word *uterus* darts through his mind first.)" (Mary Ellmann 1968, 12)

"*The* female disease . . . derived from the Greek *hysterikos*, which means uterus." The traditional interpretation of hysteria has focused on the emotional meaning of the bodily dysfunction. (Joanna Bunker Rohrbaugh 1979, 397)

" 'Womb,' the orgiastic religious festival of Aphrodite in Argos, where the Womb of the World was adored and symbolically fructified. Hysteria was given its present meaning by Renaissance doctors who explained women's diseases with a theory that the womb sometimes became detached from its place and wandered about inside the body, causing uncontrolled behavior." (Barbara G. Walker 1983, 421)

HYSTERICAL

An alternative role option for middle class Victorian women faced with conflicting expectations (to be a "lady," to manage a house, to endure frequent childbirth). (Carroll Smith Rosenberg 1972)

(See LADY)

HYSTERICAL WOMEN'S MOVEMENT

"We know this movement existed because reviewers frequently mention it in relation to women poets who appear to have reacted against it [and write calm, sane words]. . . But in none of [the reviews] are we given the names of the members of that movement, or titles of the books they wrote. All we know is that their voices were almost uniformly 'shrill' or 'strident'. Perhaps the time has come to set the record straight, and I should like to suggest that those who have documented the movement provide a list of the women who deserve our scorn." (Sylvia Kantaris 1982, 882)

HYSTERY

Alternative version of HERSTORY that emphasizes origin or womb. (*The Flame* 1982, 8:11, December)

ICONOGRAPHY

The conversion of ideas and perceptions into visual imagery. Prominent symbols in the U.S. women's movement in the early 20th century included the use of color, the slogan VOTES FOR WOMEN, the allegorical figure of the Herald/Angel, the theme of enlightenment and the figure of the woman on a horse. In general, this iconography, as well as the rhetoric of the National American Women's Suffrage Association reified women's traditional role (rather than their equality with men) and stressed that the vote would enhance this role and thus the moral good of the nation. An excellent example of this rhetorical strategy is the banner carried in a 1916 parade:

For the Safety of the Nation
To the Women Give the Vote
For the Hand that Rocks the Cradle
Will Never Rock the Boat!

The more militant National Women's Party, influenced by the British suffrage movement, drew on imagery of women breaking free and included a "Jailed for Freedom Pin" which was given to all NWP members who served prison sentences. (Edith P. Mayo 1981)
(See BANNERS, HORSE, WEARING THE COLOURS)

IDEA, FEMINIST

Arises out of the common condition of women and is not therefore the exclusive property of any individual. (The Feminists 1970)
(See ORIGINALITY)
An intellectual and creative resource.

"I would rather talk about women of ideas than women theorists. The word *theory* does not have a good feminist history. What theory has been a friend to women?" (Dale Spender 1984, lecture at University of Illinois, Urbana-Champaign)
(See THEORY)

IDEAL/IDEAL WOMAN

"Is defined by the Concise Oxford as 'answering to one's highest conception, perfect or supremely excellent.' Immediately I trip at this first hurdle in the attempt to describe an Ideal Woman because to put flesh on these words – 'highest,' 'perfect,' 'supremely excellent' – instantly conjures up for me only one female image: the Virgin Mary.... I [would rather] include two rather more conventional virtues.... Honesty; not the petty legal kind but the robust honesty that is frequently conditioned out of women as unsuitable and irrelevant to our lives. That honesty requires giving up the luxury of innocence, martyrdom and the whole silly sham of the world's ideas of femininity... To be honest is to renounce pretense and pretentions.... The second Ideal Woman virtue is courage ... the overcoming of fear. The courage to face the particular kind of hostility and insult directed at women who step out of line without faltering, without bitterness and without retreating into a female ghetto. And ... the courage to preserve in the outside world what is easy enough to keep in the shelter of the home: emotional vulnerability. . . . My Ideal Woman is not one of the boys." (Jill Tweedie 1984)

IDENTITY

One's conception of oneself as a woman is not an individual matter, but "part of the larger reality of one's definition as a member of the sex-class woman." It is racially, economically and sexually determined. (Zillah R. Eisenstein 1981, 188)

"One is not born, but rather becomes, a woman." (Simone de Beauvoir 1953; 1968, 267)

"Identity is what you can say you are according to what they say you can be." (Jill Johnston 1973a, 68)

"What I did is who I am." (Jessamyn West 1979, 12)

" 'Of course I'm not a woman's libber – I guess I should say feminist,' said a brilliant pioneer woman doctor to me a couple of years ago, in total contradiction of all she had been recounting of her own career. 'Yes, you are,' I said." (Elizabeth Janeway 1980, 96)

One's identity (and sexuality) "can only be understood . . . in terms of the complicated and often paradoxical ways in which pleasures, knowledges, and power are produced and disciplined in language, and institutionalized across multiple social fields." (Biddy Martin 1982, 9)

For women, "identity is defined in the context of a relationship and judged by a standard of responsibility and care. . . . Although the world of the self that men describe at times includes 'people' and 'deep attachments,' no particular person or relationship is mentioned, nor is the activity of relationship portrayed in the context of self-description. Replacing the women's verbs of attachment are adjectives of separation – 'intelligent,' 'logical,' 'imaginative,' 'honest,' sometimes even 'arrogant' and 'cocky.' Thus the male 'I' is defined in separation." (Carol Gilligan 1982, 160-1)

"The concept of the unconscious [does not] sit comfortably with the necessary attempt by feminism to claim a new sureness of identity for women. . . . But its

challenge to the concept of psychic identity is important for feminism in that it allows into the political arena problems of subjectivity (subjectivity *as* a problem) which tend to be suppressed from other forms of political debate." (Jacqueline Rose 1983, 19)

"I have not labeled myself yet. I would like to call myself revolutionary, for I am always changing, and growing, it is hoped for the good of more black people. I do call myself black when it seems necessary to call myself anything. . . . It seems necessary for me to forget all the titles, all the labels, and all the hours of talk and to concentrate on the mountain of work I find before me." (Alice Walker 1971; rpt. 1983, 133)

Male identity is thought to be produced through the annihilation of the female's. "Man establishes his 'manhood' in direct proportion to his ability to have his ego override woman's, and derives his strength and self esteem though this process." (New York Radical Feminists 1969, 380)

IDEOLOGICAL VENEREAL DISEASE

One of the symptoms "is one sex's use of the other as a commodity." (Ghadah al-Samman 1970, 394)

IDEOLOGY

"A set of ideas that help mystify reality. It has this potential because it reflects enough of reality to appear persuasive. . . . To the extent that ideology seems to describe some part of one's life correctly, it can pressure, direct, and affect people." (Zillah R. Eisenstein 1981, 10)

Ideological thought is "the presentation of error in a sincere and convincing way, an error which emerges from the particular position in time and space of the thinker and of the structure of thought itself. . . . The distortions are not dreamt up, but emerge from the situation and intention of the theorist. . ." (Mary O'Brien 1981, 7)

Some Marxist/Feminist theorists see ideology as more than a system of ideas or false consciousness. "Any analysis of ideology is an analysis of *social relations* themselves, not a reflection of social relations in the world of ideas." (Roisin McDonough and Rachel Harrison 1978, 17) Michèle Barrett argues that ideology "refers to those processes which have to do with consciousness, motive, emotionality; it can best be located in the category of *meaning*." (Michèle Barrett 1980, 97) It may be defined as "A practice of representation; it is the way an individual lives his or her role in the social totality. Ideology ... participates in the construction of that individual and it succeeds insofar as it can produce acceptance of existing power relations as 'natural.' " (Michèle Barrett 1980, 32; summarizing Rosalind Coward and John Ellis 1977, 69) The ideological construction of the sexed object is seen as the crucial place to situate the question of sexual difference and the struggle against women's oppression. (Biddy Martin 1982, 3)

(See IDENTITY)

The system by which power relationships are interpreted; social discourse about the world and about human beings. This system "is perpetually created by social agents through their practices, through unconscious – perceptive, motor and verbal – behavior as well as through systematized mental constructs (thought and values of the hierarchy). Although ideology often takes the form of a conscious and rational discourse on reality, it draws its dynamic strength from its unconscious dimension, its unstated assumptions. . . . In our culture, a definition of 'Man,' based on possession, is the hidden referent of social discourse." (Nöelle Bisseret Moreau 1984, 45-6)

Sexist: "serves the dual purpose of glorifying male characteristics/capitalist values, and denigrating female characteristics/social need." (Heidi Hartmann 1979; rpt. 1981, 28)

Patriarchal: The belief that men are superior to women, and that men have the right to control the life circumstances of women.

IGNORANCE

"Ignorance is not something simple: it is not a simple lack, absence or emptiness, and it is not a passive state. . . . The determined ignorance most white Americans have of American Indian tribes and clans, the ostrichlike ignorance most white Americans have of the histories of Asian peoples in this country, the impoverishing ignorance most white Americans have of Black language – ignorance of these sorts is a complex result of many acts and many negligences. To begin to appreciate this one need only hear the active verb 'to ignore' in the word 'ignorance.' " (Marilyn Frye 1983, 119)

ILLEGITIMATE CHILD

It has traditionally meant that the person was born incorrectly because the father is not known or the parents are not married. This word is maliciously used even though the mother is known, and knows that the child is hers.

(See BASTARD, BORN OUT OF WEDLOCK)

In many languages, including English creoles, a child is not simply "legitimate" or "illegitimate." Instead, a range of terms indicates the child's relationship to its parents, not necessarily in pejorative ways. Virgin Islands English creole, for example, includes *bush child* for a child born to a woman and a casual acquaintance; *inside child* for a child born within a marriage (i.e., the child's father is the mother's husband); *outside child* for a child born to a couple whose father is married to another woman; *spree child* for a child born of a (known) mother but unknown father; and *yard child* for a child fathered by a man other than the woman's husband. (Lito Valls 1981, 18, 61, 90, 117, 138)

ILLITERATE

Often incorrectly used as a synonym for "workingclass writing as workingclass people do it. . . . I'm talking about the use of forms of workingclass English which are much less acceptable in modern American literature than swearwords, class snobbery, racist and sexist portrayals of people, outright lies, etc. Worse than any of those things is to, for instance, spell a word differently than Mr. Webster, in a workingclass manner. . . . [Used to mean] not literate, not able to read and write, with an underlying implication that it also means not able to think." (Judy Grahn 1978c, 9)

ILLNESS

Sickness, which has had a different impact on women and men. "Gradually, the tubercular look, which symbolized an appealing vulnerability, a superior sensitivity, became more and more the ideal look for women – while great men of the mid- and late-nineteenth century grew fat, founded industrial empires, wrote hundreds of novels, made wars, and plundered continents." (Susan Sontag 1977, 29)

(See ANOREXIA NERVOSA, HEALTH, SICKNESS)

Sickening experience which can have ultimately healthful results. "Illness has always been of enormous benefit to me. It might even be said that I have learned little from anything that did not in some way make me sick." (Alice Walker 1979; rpt. 1983, 370)

IMMACULATE CONCEPTION

"The female fantasy of her own birth without the aid of the male." (Jill Johnston 1973a, 170)

IMMIGRANTS

People who have moved from one geographical location to another; includes some sense of voluntary action. (Most Blacks in the U.S. trace their ancestry through white slavery practices, not through immigration.) "American immigration policies have favored students, merchants, and diplomats [as immigrants] over common laborers from Asia." (Elaine H. Kim 1982, 307)

IMMORAL

Best defined through illustration: "Injustice is immoral; oppression is immoral; the sacrifice of the interests of the weaker for the stronger is immoral." (Josephine Butler 1871, 116)

IMMORALITY

Wrong-doing which brings scorn and condemnation to a woman, while the man is "smiled upon and forgiven." (Teresa Billington-Greig 1911b, 49)

I'M NOT A FEMINIST, BUT . . ."

The introduction to a sentence used by a woman who goes on to advocate one or more feminist practices.

"At once split and united by the conjunction 'but,' the words are a linguistic symptom of a tension between two very interrelated modern events: A special movement devoted to reform of our sex/gender arrangements, and the individual lives of people who are concretely experiencing that change. . . . Their suspicion is rooted in the true perception that the Women's Movement is radical and in the false perception that it is monolithic." (Catharine Stimpson 1979, 62)

IMPERIALISM

One group's rule over another group. Prevention of one group from self-determination. Rape, for instance, may be considered an imperialist attack upon the territory of women's bodies. (Barbara Burris 1971, 335) Erica Jong defines it as "man against nature and man against woman." (1972, 119) Barbara Burris explains: "In all the forms of dominant male culture – advertising, pornography, the underground press, literature, art, etc. female bodies are exploited as territory to demean, subject, control and mock." (Barbara Burris 1971, 335)

Cultural: A built-in system of conquest and control. "American women have been socialized, even brainwashed, to accept a version of American history that was created to uphold and maintain racial imperialism in the form of white supremacy and sexual imperialism in the form of patriarchy. One measure of the success of such indoctrination is that we perpetuate both consciously and unconsciously the very evils that oppress us." (bell hooks 1981, 120)

Economic: It "does not produce a series of little capitalisms which reproduce its own characteristics; it creates a curious kind of bastard society which is neither capitalist nor non-capitalist, but totally dependent on its continued exploitation by the capitalist mode of production." (Sheila Rowbotham 1973a, 107)

IMPOSING

"When used to describe a male, retains its customary English meaning [of impressive], but when used [by males] in reference to a female, it always means battle-ax." (John Leo 1984, 78)

IMPOTENCE

An "internalization of a perverse system of male-dominant cultural values. Men (and women) are taught to believe that a cock is either limp and disfunctional or erect and functional, and anything in between doesn't have any sense unless it's clearly on its way to erectness or legitimately on its way to limpness (a legitimacy which can be presumed only if ejaculation has been achieved)." (John Stoltenberg 1977; rpt. 1984, 26-7)

IN-CASES

The contents of the bags mothers and child minders carry. "A mac, in case it rains; nappies, in case Will wets the one he has on; trousers, in case it goes through," etc. (Sheila Rowbotham 1979; cited in Sheila Rowbotham 1983, 125)

(See HANDBAGS)

INCEST

"Is derived from the Latin 'incestum' which literally means 'impure.' One root of the word 'pure' is the Latin 'purus' which means 'to cleanse.' To purify, one cleanses. Inextricably woven into the etymology of the word incest is the concept of uncleanliness: in incest one is not pure, one does not cleanse oneself. The tradition of condemning daughters for incestuous acts performed and per-

petuated by fathers is as ancient as the Latin origin of the word. Women have for centuries been forced not only to yield to the sexual inclinations of fathers but also to become in a profound sense unclean and impure." (Elizabeth Denny 1984, 49)

The *Best Kept Secret*. The most muted crime, yet one of the most pervasive. "It is time we face the fact that the sexual abuse of children is not an occasional deviant act, but a devastating commonplace fact of everyday life." The offenders are usually male (80-90 percent) and from all social, economic and racial groups. (Florence Rush 1980b, xii, 2)

The legal definition of incest is changing because "1) the identification of incest with marriage prohibitions is breaking down; 2) the emphasis on preventing genetic defects is becoming less compelling; 3) the protection of children is increasingly constituting the focus of legislation. . . [A] more secular rationale, which espouses the protection of social actors who cannot protect themselves, is coming to replace moral, religious and pseudo-scientific justifications for prohibiting incestuous behavior." (Susan F. Hirsch 1984)

"The Red I". A brand that finally burnt the other way as women organized in the 1980s to publicize the issue, expose the myths, found refuges for girls and form self-help groups. (Julia O'Faolain 1983, 156-7)

INCEST TABOO

The only taboo on incest is the taboo on talking about it. (Sally Roesch Wagner 1982, 42, 14n)

"In a matriarchal or Amazonian Society, the incest taboo would have another purpose entirely, and *women* would not violate it. The taboo would function as a way of keeping sons and husbands away from daughters – who are their mothers' only heiresses." (Phyllis Chesler 1972a, 43)

(See INCEST)

INCLUSIVE LANGUAGE

Language which includes everyone involved or wishing to be involved. From a 1982 publication of the Wheadon United Methodist Church, Evanston, Illinois: "Wheadon makes every conscious effort to eliminate sexist terminology and to use inclusive language. It is our strong conviction that language shapes thought and action as well as the other way around. References to God or humanity in exclusively masculine terms belies the fullness of creation and God's identity. Whatever the accidents of scriptural transcription, language, or cultural tradition and history, we believe biblical faithfulness requires use of inclusive language."

(See FALSE GENERICS)

INDEPENDENCE
"Means autonomy, means aggressive control of one's own destiny." (Jill Johnston 1973a, 154)

Economic: "Goal of woman's hopes, sole guardian of her liberty, her one sure chance of safety! – it is for this and not for mastery that women strive. We want a world where every woman must be won and where there are no women to be bought." (Lady McLaren 1908, 42)

INDIAN PRINCESS
(See PRINCESS)

INDIAN WAY
"The Indian Way is a different way. It is a respectful way. The basic teachings in every Tribe that exists today as a Tribe in the western hemisphere are based on respect for all the things our Mother gave us. . . . We are raised to be cautious and concerned for the *future* of our people, and that is how we raise our children – because *they* are *our* future. Your 'civilization' has made all of us very sick and has made our mother earth sick and out of balance. Your kind of thinking and education has brought the whole world to the brink of total disaster." (Carol Lee Sanchez 1983, 152)

INDIVIDUALISM
"Posits the importance of self-sovereignty and independence as a universal claim and therefore can be used to justify women's independence from men." We need to be careful to distinguish this individualism from that which posits the isolated, competitive individual which would mitigate against women coalescing together. (Zillah R. Eisenstein 1981, 154)

INDUSTRY
"At its base . . . a feminine function. The surplus energy of the mother does not manifest itself in noise, or combat, or display, but in productive industry. Because of her mother-power she became the first inventor and labourer, being in truth the mother of all industry as well as of all people." (Charlotte Perkins Gilman 1911, 40)

INDIGESTION, FEMINIST
"Over-indulgence in good food causing temporary but painful heartburn and a need to avert the mind from the cause until the appetite returns." (Jill Tweedie 1983, 116)

(See BURNOUT)

INERTIA, LAW OF
"Bodies in power tend to stay in power, unless external forces disturb them." (Catharine R. Stimpson 1979a, 71)

INEXPEDIENT
A piece of administrative jargon which means inconvenient or repellent to men. Harriet K. Hunt was told with regard to her admission to Harvard Medical College in the 1850s that, despite her qualifications, it was "inexpedient" for the College to grant her request. This decision served to radicalize Hunt, who called it "semi-barbaric" to base a refusal on inexpediency: "Expedient for us to enter hospitals as patients, but inexpedient for women, however well qualified, to be there as a physician. . . That word *inexpedient* I had always abhorred – it is so shuffling, so shifting, so mean, so evasive – an apology for falsehood, a compromise of principle. . . . It has always been a *little* word in my lexicon, and it became still *littler*, when used by a medical conclave.

Any kind of reason might have been accepted, but this *inexpedient* aroused my risibles, my sarcasm, my indignation." (Harriet K. Hunt 1856; in Mary Roth Walsh 1977, 29) The word has also been used as an administrative answer to demands for voting rights and civil rights.

INEXPRESSIVENESS

"*Not* just a matter of inarticulateness nor even a deeply socialized inability to respond to the needs of others... In general, male inexpressiveness emerges as an intentional manipulation of a situation when threats to the male position occur." (Jack W. Sattell 1983, 122)

INFANTICIDE

The killing of infants, practiced primarily on females. Being born female can "be extremely dangerous. Jesuit missionaries reported in the 17th century that the Chinese killed infant daughters by the thousands. The British found female infanticide rampant in India in the late 18th century." The killing of baby girls at birth in India and China today is a grave social problem. "More common today, however, is relative neglect of girls – poorer nutrition and care. Mortality rates for infant females [who are hardier than boys at birth] exceed those for males in Bangladesh, Burma, Jordan, Pakistan, Sri Lanka, Thailand, Lebanon, and Syria. In parts of South America, mothers wean girls earlier than boys because they fear that nursing them too long will make the girls unfeminine. Less well nourished, the female children tend to succumb to fatal diseases." (Barbara Burke 1984, 30)

INFANT MORTALITY

The death of young children occurs more frequently among the poor. "A 'high rate of infant mortality among the poor' largely means 'a high rate of infant mortality among the improperly housed.' " ("Problems of the Day" 1912, *The English-woman* 14:42, (June 1912, 248)

INITIALS

Single letters used in place of first and middle names. Use of initials is a frequent practice of men. "Initials exasperate my patience to the last degree of endurance. They may properly answer for barrels of flour, kegs of fish, or spools of thread; but for immortal beings, made in the image of God, the custom is degrading." (Elizabeth Cady Stanton, October 22, 1898, 343)

(See FIRST NAMES, NAMING)

Used by some women writers who would hide their female identity in order to have their work read and reviewed seriously, as men's work is more likely to be.

"Are you bothered about something as seemingly inconsequential as the way you type initials at the end of business letters? If so, this could be due to the fact that unconsciously you realize you are subordinating yourself every time you type upper case initials for the person signing the letter (usually a man) and lower case initials for yourself (usually a woman)." (From an "open letter to all secretaries," Elsie Bradberry 1970, 2)

IN LOVE

A difficult condition to maintain "when you've got no money, no decent housing, no job." (Vera Brearly 1982, 23)

(See FALLING IN LOVE, LOVE)

IN MY DIRT

Body and clothing grimy from housekeeping work. "Dirty frock and striped apron and old bonnet and hands and arms and face begrimmed with dirt." (Hannah Cullwick, Victorian maidservant; in Liz Stanley 1984, 57)

INNOCENT

"Person whose principal quality is not to be harmful. During the Concrete Age, the word degenerated since no one could imagine not being harmful as a quality. It only applied to 'weak minds,' oppressed enslaved persons, to foolish persons or to children." (Monique Wittig and Sande Zeig 1976, 82)

(See GLORIOUS AGE)

Blameless, uncorrupted. "No politics

remains innocent of that which it contests." (Elizabeth Fox-Genovese 1979; in Alice Echols 1983, 440)

INSANITY
"Going crazy [an action which] has always been a personal solution in extremis to the unarticulated conflicts of political realities, a way of transcending these conflicts by going into orbit and settling the world." (Jill Johnston 1973a, 84)

(See MADNESS)

INSPIRE
"Is to draw air into the lungs – to be inspiring is to breathe life into dreams and have them become real." (Carmen Silva 1983, 167)

INSTITUTIONAL MOTHERHOOD
A role which "demands of women maternal 'instinct' rather than intelligence, selflessness rather than self-realization, relation to others rather than the creation of self." (Adrienne Rich 1976, 42)

(See MATERNAL INSTINCT)

INSULTS, SEXUAL
Powerful, potent weapons wielded against women. (Sally McConnell-Ginet 1980, 14)

(See FORMS OF ADDRESS, STREET HARASSMENT)

INTEGRITY
Responsibility in confronting the ultimate unity of discrete experiences. (Carole Walley [Birmingham] 1983, correspondence)

The process of integrity "enables us to begin seeing through mad reversals which have been our mindbindings. It empowers us to question the sacred and secular 'texts' which have numbed our brains by implanting 'answers' before we had a chance to question and to quest." (Mary Daly 1978, 21)

INTELLECTUALITY
Is *not* the collection of mental activities rewarded in academia – "qualities such as droning docility, obsequiousness, linear thinking, absence of passion and creativity, inability to challenge authority, et cetera.... Essentially, intellectuality involves a choice to use one's mind to its fullest capacity, questioning/questing under all circumstances, Realizing Reason." (Mary Daly 1984, 321)

INTELLIGENCE
A reasoning competence owned by men who assign to women "a much inferior, capricious and lucky process – intuition." (Dale Spender 1982b, 19)

(See INTUITION)

INTENTIONALITY
(See MEANING)

INTERMARRIAGE
Marriage between members of different racial, ethnic or religious groups, a threatening act in a society built on division. Often regulated by law. E.g., "Intermarriage between Chinese or 'Mongolians' and whites was prohibited [by white laws] in the fourteen states where most Chinese lived. Intermarriage was deemed a 'gross misdemeanor' in Nevada, subject to a $500 fine or one year in prison. In Maryland, it was an 'infamous crime' subject to ten years' imprisonment. Antimiscegenation legislation remained on the books in California until 1967." Currently, there are social restrictions against intermarriage from some minority groups. For example, "Intermarriage between whites and Asians has been seen in recent times by some Asian Americans as evidence of racial conquest and cultural genocide rather than social acceptance and success for the Asian minority." (Elaine H. Kim 1982, 97, 230)

INTERCOURSE, HETEROSEXUAL
An act of sexual pleasure for some women, a felt duty for others, and an event to be avoided for others. "It means remaining the victim, forever annihilating all self-respect. It means acting out the female role, incorporating the masochism,

self-hatred and passivity which are central to it." (Andrea Dworkin 1974, 184)

"A great exercise in communication when a woman acts on choice not necessity." (Cheryl West 1985, correspondence)

INTERNATIONAL WOMEN'S DAY

"In New York on March 8th, 1907, a long cortege of war-ravaged, widowed and poverty-stricken women garment workers carried picket signs demanding improved working conditions and the recognition of equal rights for women. 'Decent wages! A ten-hour day!' the women called as they walked through the cold. When they reached the rich districts, however, they were trampled and dispersed by police. Many [women] were arrested. On March 8, 1908, marking the date of this earlier revolt, women workers in the needle trades again demonstrated on the Lower East Side of New York for the right to vote and an end to sweat shops and child labor. They too met the police. In 1910 Clara Zetkin, a German Socialist leader, placed a resolution before the Second International. She proposed that March 8th be observed each year as International Women's Day in memory of these first struggles . . . each year since, March 8th has been celebrated by women the world over." (*off our backs* 1980, 14:3 [March], 1)

In the late 1960s, feminists in the West began, again, to celebrate IWD. By now, March 8 symbolized IWD for women in many countries, but not in all. South Africa's women's day, for example, is August 9. In 1956, on this day, 20,000 women marched on Pretoria to express their opposition to the extension of the iniquitous pass law system to women, a system aimed at controlling Black migrant labourers. (*Outwrite: Women's Newspaper*, March 1983, 1)

INTERNATIONAL WOMEN'S YEAR

1975, celebrating the United Nation's Decade of Women. Generated practical and symbolic outcomes – one example

was the Women's Declaration of Independence.

INTERRUPTION

A violation of a speaker's turn at talk. Females find themselves subject to interruptions more frequently than males in cross-sex conversations. The asymmetry in the initiation of interruption constitutes a power differential. "It is . . . a way of 'doing' power in face-to-face interaction . . . it is a way of 'doing' gender as well." (Candace West and Don. H. Zimmerman 1983, 103, 111)

One form of silencing. Women are "eminently interruptible. . .[and] are extremely unlikely to interrupt others (or if they do, are unlikely to be successful at it)." (Nancy M. Henley 1977, 74)

It is the "common lot of women in mixed sex groups describing what happened to them as women." (Julia Lesage, Oct. 5, 1982, lecture at the Univ of Illinois, Urbana-Champaign)

"There was such a thing as women's work and it consisted chiefly, Hilary sometimes thought, in being able to stand constant interruption and keep your temper." (May Sarton 1965; cited in Elaine Partnow 1977, 168)

A break in activity. Often leads to loss, diminishment of a woman's activities and to impediments to her writing and other expressions of creativity. "Motherhood means being instantly interruptible, responsive, responsible. Children need one *now* (and remember, in our society, the family must often try to be the center for love and health the outside world is not). The very fact that these are needs of love, not duty, that one feels them as one's self; *that there is no one else to be responsible for these needs*, gives them primacy. . . . Work interrupted, deferred, postponed makes blockage – at best, lesser accomplishment." (Tillie Olsen 1979, 33)

INTERVIEW

A face-to-face meeting with a formal discussion where women are often made uncomfortable by inappropriate questions.

"The men on [a medical school admissions committee] always asked of a woman applicant, 'Why should we give you this precious space when everyone knows you're going to take ten years off to raise children?' . . . I told them . . . they had to stop asking this question. That it was unfair, irrelevant, illegal, and cruel. But they wouldn't stop. Finally, I told them if they did not stop asking this question of women applicants, I was going to start asking male applicants why they should be considered when everyone knew they were going to die ten years earlier." (Woman physician, quoted in Vivian Gornick 1983, 98)

INTIMACY

Sharing confidences. Below, a conversation that reveals male-female differences about the definition:

"I've heard any number of guys confiding their problems to a workmate," he argued.

"What kinds of problems?" I asked.

"For example, they'll talk about the fact that their car is a lemon," he replied.

"You call that intimate talk?" I asked.

"Sure," he answered, "in the sense that the guy reveals something about himself and his lack of judgment in getting stuck like that. It threatens his manly image, the pose that he can always take care of himself, that nobody can get the best of him."

"Granted," I replied, "but does he tell his workmates that he's worried about his sexual performance; that he has nightmares that his wife might leave him; that he's just found out she's having a love affair with another man? That's the kind of sharing I'm talking about. It's of a different order than the things you call intimate." (Lillian Rubin 1976, 221)

INTRAUTERINE DEVICE (IUD)

Short plastic rods bent into different shapes and sometimes wound with copper wire. Inserted into the uterus for the purpose of birth control. It is not clear how the IUD works. The incidence of serious infection with the IUD is a concern for many women. (Federation of Feminist Women's Health Centers 1981, 106, 159)

(See DALKON SHIELD)

INTUITION

Sharp insight considered a natural trait in women, yet it has "probably been developed through default or male-imposed necessity, rather than through either biological predisposition or free choice." (Phyllis Chesler 1972, 263)

It is "largely an economic product. . . . As inferiors – dependents – the women of a household learned to study and anticipate the wishes of their lord and master . . . it would be strange, therefore, if they had not, in the course of ages, acquired a measure of that mental dexterity and rapid skill which, in any other business, would be dubbed mechanical." (Cicely Hamilton 1927, *Time and Tide*, Sept. 16, 817)

Although intuition in women is trivialized, men rely on women's intuition to make their decisions. "Women monitor the emotional temperature of existence. In any situation that lies outside the ordinary give-and-take of life, we're expected to weep or cry out in fear or shrink away in horror, and by these reactions to give a lead to others. Female intuition estimates that a reaction is required and supplies one that serves as a guide for men, for whom intuition is suspect and emotional expression inappropriate." (Elizabeth Janeway 1980, 273)

INVERT

The common term for homosexual, in the medical and psychoanalytic literature through the 1920s. "None knew better the terrible nerves of the invert, nerves that are always lying in wait. Super-nerves, whose response is only equalled by the strain that calls that response into being." (Radclyffe Hall 1928, 173-4)

(See HOMOPHOBIA, HOMOSEXUAL, LESBIAN)

INVISIBILITY

One of the problems of producing a feminist dictionary. How do you show that women's words and definitions have been lost when women's words and definitions *have* been lost? A starting point is to deduce presence from absence. The virtually complete absence of women's terms for males and male activities in most standard dictionaries defies common sense about the many centuries women have been in the world as speakers and writers. Thus one must conclude that these words and definitions (1) have been lost or suppressed, (2) have been expressed in subtexts or other subversions of conventional expression, (3) have been expressed orally but not written down, and (4) have been expressed in non-linguistic forms. Possible avenues of research thus include (1) the examination of "lost" works, unpublished writings by women, and the records of women's communities and activities, (2) the "close reading" of women's written work to discover its subversive meanings, (3) the use of oral histories to capture the language of women who do not read or write or are not likely to write themselves, and (4) the codes and symbols produced by women in non-print form. This dictionary includes examples of all these approaches.

(See ANONYMOUS, ART, CRAFT, DIARY, DICTIONARY, ENGLISH, FASTING, FORMS OF EXPRESSION, OEDIPUS, PEN NAME, POETRY, QUILT, TORAH, WOMAN'S BIBLE)

IRATE

A noun used by flight attendants to refer to the blaze-eyed client whose frustration with missed connections and anxiety about air travel erupts as complaints about food and service. As in "Irene, I had three irates on this morning's flight." (Arlie Russell Hochschild 1983, 37)

IRONY

"Is frequently the weapon of isolated people facing impossible odds." (Sheila Rowbotham 1972, 144)

(See HUMOR)

ISOLATION

Being set apart from others, the lot of many women. "Man has almost invariably reserved for himself . . . those particular occupations which brought him into frequent contact with his fellows." (Cicely Hamilton 1909, 94)

(See PRIVACY)

IYETIKO

"The Mother of the Pueblo people. Her home lies in the Underworld, reached through the shipapu, where The People used to live." (Rayna Green 1984, 310)

JANE EYRE-ITY

Independence. "Coming to her husband in economic independence and by her free choice, Jane [in *Jane Eyre* by Charlotte Brontë] can become a wife without sacrificing a grain of her Jane Eyre-ity." (Adrienne Rich 1973; rpt. 1979, 105)

JARGON

Nonsensical, or in-group talk. One way of closing out women. Feminist scholars "have to write and speak in plain and comprehensible language and avoid excesses of feminist esoteric jargon which would certainly be counter-productive to our aim of making our research accessible (and useful) to as many women as possible." (Renate Duelli Klein 1983a, 100)

Of the New Left: "With the professional comes his professional language. . . . The use of scholarly Marxist jargon is exactly analogous to the use of any other academic jargon. It is a way of indicating that you have put in your time, read the right texts and commentaries, that you are an expert. It is one thing to learn from the long line of revolutionaries who have come before us: we must learn that history or caricature it. . . . It is another thing to adopt the language of any of them, especially translated into lousy American. . . . Women in the Movement, with a few outstanding exceptions, have trouble talking jargon." (Marge Piercy 1969, 427-8)

JESUS

"A prophet and teacher who never nagged at [women], never flattered or coaxed or patronized; who never made arch jokes about them, never treated them either as 'The women, God help us!' or 'The ladies, God bless them!'; who rebuked without querulousness and praised without condescension; who took their questions and arguments seriously; who never mapped out their sphere for them, never urged them to be feminine or jeered at them for being female; who had no axe to grind and no uneasy male dignity to defend; who took them as he found them." (Dorothy Sayers 1947; in Betty Roszak and Theordore Roszak eds 1969, 121)

(See CHRIST, CHRISTMAS, RELIGION)

A prophet who never talked about ruling anyone but only of service to all. Yet he, who posed such a threat to church and state alike, is now elevated to the "position left vacant when he removed the false gods from the Temple, to look down for ever more as the ruler of a Jerusalem he once wept over." (*Banshee: Journal of Irishwomen United* c.1980, 10)

Is portrayed in Leonard Swidler's article "Jesus was a Feminist" (1971) as one who "disregarded the established conventions and taboos in his relationships with women . . . . he treated them with equality and respect." (Marilyn Warenski 1978, 261)

"Androcracy's Absolute Androgyne . . . male femininity incarnate. . . . He is the Supreme Swinging Single, forever freed from challenge by Forceful Furious Females." (Mary Daly 1978, 88)

Man-made. Males conceived of Mary as a hollow shell through which "god the father reproduces himself in the world. Jesus is not the son of Mary or of woman, nor is he ever named that way. He is the son of god, the son of man. In other words, he is a totally man-made product, a clone." (Anne G. Dellenbaugh 1982, 60)

JEW-HATING

"I use the term 'Jew-hating' because 'anti-Semitism' has become a euphemism, a nonword that is hardly commensurate with the feelings and realities behind it. (Some feminists are for similar reasons giving up the term 'sexism' in favor of the more explicit 'woman-hating.') There has also been some verbal jiujitsu surrounding the term 'anti-Semitism' in some feminist circles, which says that since Jews are not the only Semites, the term should not be used exclusively for them. The national Women's Studies Association itself succumbed to refusing to go on record in its recently changed Constitution as being against 'anti-Semitism' unless it read, as it now does, 'anti-Semitism, as directed against both Arabs and Jews.' Now, I certainly will not deny that anti-Arab racism exists and that it may at this point in time be necessary to list the different kinds of racism by name. But all common usage and every dictionary I have consulted will tell you that anti-Semitism means prejudice and hatred against *Jews*. . . . If it takes the term 'Jew-hating' to make the NWSA take a clear position, so be it." (Evelyn Torton Beck 1983, 13)

JEWISH PRINCESS

(See PRINCESS, JEWISH)

JEWISH WOMEN

The "Jewish Mother" and "Jewish American Princess" are stereotypes which "single out certain qualities in women, characterize them in the first place as unattractive and in the second, as specifically Jewish." Studies of Jewish women show that they "are not the matriarchal tyrants literature sets them up to be. The studies imply that Jewish families are not home breweries for neuroses, but all-American nests in which Jewish children are raised in the accepted middle-class fashion." (Charlotte Baum, Paula Hyman and Sonia Michel 1975, 239)

(See ANTI-SEMITISM, PORTNOY'S MOTHER'S COMPLAINT, PRINCESS, RECLAMATION, TORAH)

JOAN OF ARC

A 17-year-old peasant whose presence and activity changed the course of the Hundred Years' War between England and France. In 1429 she appeared at the borders of the duchy of Lorraine, introduced herself to the Dauphin Charles of France as his God-given saviour, guided by divine messengers. Captured by enemies during a battle, she was sold to the English, turned over to the Inquisition, tried and burned as a heretic. She is a heroine of history, she pursued goals with bravery, loyal to convictions in the face of a treacherous trial. "She is a universal figure who is female, but is neither a queen, nor a courtesan, nor a beauty, nor a mother, nor an artist of one kind or another, nor – until . . . 1920 when she was canonised – a saint. She eluded the categories in which women have normally achieved a higher status that gives them immortality. . . . Joan is instantly present in the mind's eye; a boyish stance, cropped hair, medievalised clothes, armour, an air of spiritual exaltation mixed with physical courage. . . . [She is] presented as an Amazon, or a knight of old, or a personification of virtue, because the history of individual women and of women's roles has been so thin." (Marina Warner 1982, 3,4,6,9)

"A virgin warrior who helps men . . . one of Christianity's prime remembrances of Amazonian cultures. . . . Although she is doomed (and women might identify with her on this ground alone), she is also physically and spiritually bold." (Phyllis Chesler 1972a, 49)

Her trial has recently been re-seen as "part of the War between Christianity and the Old Religion, or Ritual Witchcraft – an ancient religion of pre-Christian origins." Margaret Murray has gathered historical evidence to show that "Joan's accusers were aware of her connection with the Ancient religion." (Mary Daly 1973, 147) She was also attacked for her use of male attire. She stepped outside patriarchal boundaries and was killed for it.

JOB TITLES

In Anglo-Saxon England and through most of the Middle English period the ending *er* (or *-ere*) was used to denote male persons only and *-ster* (or *-estre*) was used to denote female persons and thus the women who did the weaving, baking and sewing. When some of the more lucrative jobs (such as huckster/peddler and brewster/maker of liquors) were taken over by men they also took the job titles. In the 11th century, with the Norman invasion of England, the French *-ess* suffix began to be used for feminine-gender compounds such as shepherdess and goddess. By the 19th century, the once-masculine *-er* suffix was being assigned to those holding jobs, as long as *only* women performed the job. The Latin feminine ending *-trix* as in *obstetrix* ("she who stands before" to catch the baby as the mother delivers it) caused some problems for the 18th century male barber-surgeons who began to "deliver" babies; their title was defeminized to *obstetrician*. "Words denoting occupations or professions could be and from time to time were used for females and males without distinction. But because males are . . . the norm, new feminine designations were introduced and accepted whenever the need was felt to assert male prerogatives. . . . Once certain occupations ceased to be women's work and became trades or vocations in which men predominated, the old feminine-gender words were annexed by men and became appropriate male designations. Then new endings were assigned to women." (Casey Miller and Kate Swift 1976, 46-9)

(See -ESS, OCCUPATIONAL TERMS)

JOCKOCRATIC SOCIETY

"In a jockocratic society, you can turn on the TV and find out the score of some basketball game in Alaska – but you can't find out how many states have ratified the Equal Rights Amendment. You can turn on the radio, and hear every score in the country repeated all day long – but you don't hear how many women died from illegal abortions." (Florynce Kennedy; quoted in Gloria Steinem 1973, 89)

JONAH AND THE WHALE
(See WOMB)

JOURNALISM

"A bastion of nepotism in the hands of the middle classes." (Marlene Packwood 1983, 9)

JOURNALISM, FEMINIST

"In the Women's Institute for Freedom of the Press and at *Media Report* we've devised some criteria for the selection and presentation of news information. We call these the Principles of Feminist Journalism, and we believe that journalism based on these standards is more respectful of people. Briefly, they are: First, no attacks on people. The public news media should work to widen the social, political or economic option for people, not inhibit them. Second, more factual information, with full texts and direct quotes where possible. Last, people should speak for themselves." (Donna Allen 1977, 27)

JOURNALISTS

Writers whose subject matter and salaries vary depending on sex. "Women journalists usually [end] up writing obituaries or wedding announcements for the women's page, in accordance with their ancient roles as goddesses of life and death, deckers of nuptial beds and washers of corpses." (Margaret Atwood 1982, 216)

(See WOMEN'S PAGE)

JUDAISM

"Is a religion (roughly divided into four sub-groupings: Orthodox, Conservative, Reform and Reconstruction), but even the naming of religious branches does not convey the true diversity simply within these groupings. Moreover, although Judaism has its roots in religion, Jews also embody a culture, a civilization, a people – and these are themselves both one and many – so it is entirely meaningful to speak of secular Judaism or to identify as a Jewish atheist who still chooses to attend services as an act of solidarity with the Jewish people." (Evelyn Torton Beck 1984, 10)

Is governed by Jewish law and tradition. "The role and image of females in Jewish law is very different from that of males.... In orthodox synagogues, women sit apart from men so as not to distract them. In synagogues in which this physical separation is not enforced, women are separated from men by the words of Talmud and Torah, which instruct females to be content with their subordinate roles in the Jewish community. The nature of the religion lies in interplay between a father-god and His sons. In such a religion, women will always be on the periphery. When Jewish women take a central place in their religion, they will no longer be practicing Judaism." (Naomi Goldenberg 1979, 7-8)

JUDGMENT
(See DULLNESS)

JUDITH
A fictional sister of Shakespeare, described by Virginia Woolf as one of the anonymous women whose genius in language and literature was thwarted by enforced illiteracy and domesticity, and by the ridicule of men. (Virginia Woolf 1929, 80-4)

(See PRINCESS, SHAKESPEARE'S SISTER)

JUSTICE
The spirit of justice was female in classical paganism. (Barbara Walker 1983, 485). During the past few centuries justice has meant moral rightness, symbolized by the figure of a handsome woman, blindfolded, holding a pair of scales in her outstretched hand. During most of those years the men who revered her kept her sisters from the bar and jury duty. (Miriam Beard 1927; rpt in Elizabeth Janeway ed. 1973a, 146)

(See FRESCOED FEMININITY)

"As long as we are under the shadow of a *kingdom*, real or symbolic, there will be no creative justice." (Mary Daly 1973, 128)

KIBBUTZ
The kibbutz (in-gathering) movement developed out of the early experience of second wave immigrants to Palestine who came after the failure of the 1905 Russian Revolution. Mostly young Jewish socialists, they became agriculturalists and tried to create a social structure based on equality and mutual aid. In 1907 the World Zionist Organization purchased land in the Jordan Valley and a new community Deganiah (God's wheat) was established as an extended family. Originally women's work was much the same as men's work. More than 255 kibbutzim have been founded since Deganiah. Now women are often assigned domestic roles although most still work outside the household also.

KING
The name for supreme men, in heaven and on earth. Also the name for a playing card and a chess piece. The kings are all involved in manly power plays.
"Most powerful court person, sometimes known familiarly as billiejean." (Eve Merriam 1980, 174)

KINGDOM
Masculine dominance. When the Queen reigns we are not allowed a Queendom. (Teresa Billington-Greig c.1949-60)

KINSHIP RELATIONS
"Men and women, and often different generations, in different, deferential and often antagonistic relations." (Rosalind Coward 1983, 124)
"Unlike many other societies, Black women in The Flats feel few if any restrictions about childbearing. . . . A girl who gives birth as a teen-ager frequently does not raise and nurture her first born child. While she may share the same room and household with her baby, her mother, her mother's sister, or her older sister will care for the child and become the child's 'mamma.' People show pride in all their kin, and particularly new babies born into their kinship network." (Carol Stack 1974; quoted in Gloria I. Joseph; in Gloria I. Joseph and Jill Lewis 1981, 181-2)

KITCHEN
Called, by exponents of the merits of the Co-operative Kitchen, " 'the enemy of women.' This saying is, doubtless, only an over-emphasized protest against the masculine heresy that to be a good cook is to be happy, virtuous, and beloved." ("Problems of the Day" 1912, *The English-woman*, 16:48 (December), 261)
National: Centralized kitchen established by the British Government as a WWI emergency measure to economize foodstuffs and fuel. Lightened women's drudgery. Discontinued by Government after the war. (C. Turner 1919)

KITCHEN THINGS
Household items of significance to women. In Susan Glaspell's 1917 short story "A Jury of Her Peers," a group of wives "read" domestic minutiae to discover that a goaded neighbor has murdered her husband; where the men see only insignificant "kitchen things," the women see life

and living death. (Annette Kolodny 1979-80)

KNITTING

An activity for the hands which helps keep women awake in between nightwork tasks. (Hannah Cullwick, Victorian maidservant; in Liz Stanley 1984, 237)

KNOWLEDGE

"If knowledge is power, power is also knowledge, and a large factor in [women's] subordinate position is the fairly systematic ignorance patriarchy imposes on women." (Kate Millett 1971, 66)

(See FEMINIST THEORY, METHODOLOGY, OBJECTIVITY, PERSONAL IS POLITICAL)

"Knowledge is power if it can be implemented." (Elizabeth Janeway 1980, 45)

"All knowledge which does not recognize, which does not take social oppression as its premise, denies it, and as a consequence objectively serves it. . . . Knowledge that would take as its point of departure the oppression of women would constitute an epistemological revolution." (Christine Delphy 1981, 73)

Perception. "Each of us is a barometer of social conditions which we observe through the perceptual screen of our needs." (Jill Johnston 1973a, 136)

KOINETOPOGRAPY

Study of the commonplace. (Julia Penelope 1984, correspondence)

KORE

"Greek Holy Virgin, inner soul of Mother Earth (Demeter); a name so widespread, that it must have been one of the earliest designations of the World Shakti or female spirit of the universe." (Barbara Walker 1983, 514)

(See GODDESS)

"The story of the rape of Kore is a late addition, an historical reference perhaps to the destruction of the early Goddess Culture, or a patriarchal attempt to subvert the power of the myth. The myth itself is a story strung together around the original experience, which was a ritual, the celebration of the Thesmophoria, in ancient Greece. The ritual was one of descent and rising. . . . The ancient Kore shows us that renewal cannot be separated from decay, that it is death that makes life fertile." (Starhawk 1982, 83)

KRAMER VS. KRAMER

A 1970s film with "the classic woman-in-search-of-fulfillment-leaves-husband-and-child story, with the overworked husband left to pick up the pieces of a broken home . . . [yet] only 2 percent of single parent households are headed by men and most men don't challenge their wives for custody." (Karin Stallard, Barbara Ehrenreich and Holly Sklar 1983, 10)

LÁADAN

The construction of Láadan, a language for women by a woman, was begun in June 1982 by Suzette Haden Elgin, who used it for her science fiction novel *Native Tongue* which takes as its premise that existing human languages are inadequate to express the perceptions of women. Láadan contains many "women-function" words not included in English. (See examples under MENSTRUATION, MENOPAUSE, PREGNANT) If there are words which you would like to have that require you to go on and on in English, and you need to express their meanings, the Láadan Group will be happy to supply you with a Láadan word for the purpose. (Write to Suzette Haden Elgin, Route 4, Box 192-E, Huntsville, AR 72740, sending the information you need and a stamped return envelope.)

Pronunciation of Láadan: Sound equivalents are given below with English examples. For Láadan vowels with an accent, pronounce them as if you were pronouncing a stressed syllable in an English word.

b	AS IN bed	h	AS IN help
d	did	zh	pleasure
s	set	lh	Put the tip of
sh	*sh*ip		your tongue
th	*th*ink		against the
m	may		back of your
n	now		upper teeth;
l	let		draw your lips
r	red		back as for a
w	will		smile, and say 'sh'

y	yes	a	c*a*lm
		e	b*e*ll
		i	b*i*d
		o	h*o*me
		u	d*u*ne

(Suzette Haden Elgin 1983, 1)

LABELS

Something which identifies. People "rope themselves off with labels They stand inside a box called their job, their clothes, their political and social opinions, the movies or books they read I've never believed those items which is why I was considered crazy I want to know the truth. I glimpse under that malarky called 'civilization' Maybe people have become so stupid as a result of having too many machines The company we keep." (Chrystos 1981, 243)

Epithets which are attached by others. "What am I? A *third world lesbian feminist with Marxist and mystic leanings*. They would chop me up into little fragments and tag each piece with a label.

You say my name is ambivalence? Think of me as Shiva, a many-armed and legged body with one foot on brown soil, one on white, one in straight society, one in the gay world, the man's world, the woman's, one limb in the literary world, another in the working class, the socialist, and the occult worlds. A sort of spider woman hanging by one thin strand of web.

Who, me confused? Ambivalent? Not so. Only your labels split me." (Gloria

Anzaldúa; in Cherríe Moraga and Gloria Anzaldúa eds 1981, 205)

(See IDENTITY)

LABIA

(1) Four lips protecting the inner sanctum of the female genitals. (2) The name of the leading character, the heraine, in the 1982 unpublished romance "The Red Lips of Labia" by Brinlee Kramer who suggests that Genitalia is another nice, proper name.

(See HERA)

LABOR

(See BIRTH, BIRTHING)

LABRYS

"Name given to the double-headed axe of the ancient amazons and to the representation of this arm as the emblem of amazon empires." (Monique Wittig and Sande Zeig 1976, 93)

(See AXE)

Used in contemporary times by radical and lesbian feminists to indicate woman-identification. Labryses represent "double axes" of our own Wild wisdom and wit, which cut through the mazes of man-made mystification, breaking the mind-bindings of master-minded doublethink." (Mary Daly 1984, xi)

LACK

What is missing and wanted. For women it often involves recognition of needed reproduction control, economic independence, and a share of control in the cultural institutions now dominated by men. These changes could make possible a freedom and richness lacking in most women's lives.

LADIES

Women who seem to stay in their male-defined place. Mary Widener, one of the women who in 1973 organized a picket in support of the miners in the union and who was imprisoned, said of the men in court who judged them: "They didn't call us ladies or mothers, they called us females. Ladies don't stand on picket lines." (Mary Widener; in Sheila Rowbotham 1983, 266)

LADIES AGAINST WOMEN

A nationwide [U.S.] ladies' auxiliary, begun in San Francisco, to satirically promote sexual inequality. Some ladies attend political events dressed in white gloves and appropriate accessories, while others wear cheerleading costumes and carry pom-poms. Some of their slogans: "Roses not Raises; Father Knows Best; I'd Rather be Ironing; Brooms, Not Basketballs; Gold Rings, Not Gold Medals; Pump Iron: Do His Shirts." One Ladies Against Women unit held a bake sale outside the 1984 Republican Convention, selling Twinkies at $9 million apiece to retire the national deficit.

LADY

Of Germanic origin, this term initially expressed a degree of rank equal to that of *Lord*. As its application was extended, as early as 900, *lady* was used to refer to the Virgin Mary, and was used as a general term for *woman* or *wife* about 1200. By the fourteenth century it had acquired courtly overtones which have been preserved down to the modern period. (Elizabeth Judd, in press)

(See CHIVALRY)

Has recently become the paragon for all American women. "As late as 1890, nearly half of all American women lived and worked in (the) immediate social environment of a farm family, providing many necessities for the farm through daily hard work. Yet the farm wife lost her cultural standing to a new sector of women: the wives and daughters of the rising entrepreneurs and merchant capitalists of the urban Northeast. This new sector remained a numerical minority, while its ethos became central to American Woman's self-definition . . . for all women this new ideal of femininity became the model, however unrealizable in their own lives." (Ann D. Gordon and Mari Jo Buhle 1976, 284)

A creature who overshadows the rest of her sex. "She is an anomaly to which the western nations of this planet have grown accustomed but which would require a great deal of explanation before a Martian could understand her. Economically she is supported by the toil of others; but while this is equally true of other classes of society, the oddity in her case consists in the acquiescence of those most concerned. . . . She is not a producer; in most communities productive labour is by consent unladylike. On the other hand she is the heaviest of consumers. . . In aristocratic societies she is required for dynastic reasons to produce offspring, but in democratic societies even this demand is often waived." (Emily James Putnam 1910; rpt. 1969, xxx, xxxi)

A condition created by men, to keep women's minds and actions away from labor matters. Mary Harris ("Mother") Jones said, "No matter what your fight . . . don't be ladylike!" ("Mother" Jones; quoted in W. E. Brownlee and M. Brownlee 1976, 242) "God almighty made the women and the Rockefeller gang of thieves made the ladies." (Mother Jones; epigraph in Kathy Kahn 1973, n.p.)

A term to describe the well-adjusted woman in a patriarchal society, i.e. "the well-repressed woman." (Rebecca West 1912, *The Clarion*, December 20)

"Lady doctor, lady poet, lady author, lady jockey, lady blackjack dealer, lady wrestler – all are putrid enough but when I saw lady revolutionary this week, THAT was too much!" (Varda One, October 23, 1970, 14)

"I ain't no lady. I'm a newspaperwoman." (Hazel Brannon Smith; cited in Elaine Partnow 1977, 187)

"A lady, that is an enlightened, cultivated liberal lady – the only kind to be in a time of increasing classlessness – could espouse any cause: wayward girls, social diseases, unmarried mothers, and/or birth control with impunity. But never by so much as the shadow of a look should she acknowledge her own experience with the Facts of Life." (Virgilia Peterson 1961; in Elaine Partnow 1977, 66)

"My mother's generation – my aunts and other relatives – wanted to be 'ladies.' They didn't find it especially gratifying to work in factories or stand there trimming tomatoes so that at 70-years-old all they've got out of their work is arthritis and very little Social Security. The title 'lady' meant something, and they wanted their daughters to be 'ladies.' That's why so many of them scrubbed floors and took other menial jobs to send their children to college. So when something came along that began to threaten that dream, it became a real problem." (Barbara Mikulski 1976, 37-8)

Hey Lady!
You, Gay Lady;
Will you play Lady?

Say Lady,
This way Lady,
I will PAY lady!

Hey Lady!
Don't go away Lady!
OH, please stay Lady. . .

O.K. Lady. . .
But *that's* no way, Lady
(*Time In* [Holloway Prison Education and Occupational Therapy Department] c.1980, *2,3*)

Treatment of: "In society it is etiquette for ladies to have the best chairs and get handed things. In the home the reverse is the case. That is why ladies are more sociable than gentlemen." (Virginia Graham 1949; cited in Elaine Partnow 1977, 162)

LADY WITH THE LAMP

Florence Nightingale. She was also known as "The Lady with the Hammer." During the Crimean War when she first arrived in Turkey where she was to have complete charge of the nursing in the military hospitals, she was refused the key to the store-room. With a hammer, she broke open the door. (*Votes for Women* 1912, April 9, 737)

LANGUAGE

Is a symbol system which is a basic problem and a brilliant possibility. Angela

Carter writes that language "is power, life, and the instrument of culture, the instrument of domination and liberation." (1983, 77) Dale Spender also notes this paradox: "It is both a creative and an inhibiting vehicle. On the one hand it offers immense freedom for it allows us to 'create' the world we live in;. . . . But on the other hand, we are restricted by that creation, limited to its confines, and, it appears, we resist, fear and dread any modifications to the structures we have initially created, even though they are 'arbitrary,' approximate ones." (Dale Spender 1980, 141-2) As this dictionary illustrates, we do not all speak the same language. This dictionary is a critical defining element of our identities. Below are some of our words about language:

Language is "that social and historical reality in and through which we have been assigned our social and personal identities since infancy." (Wendy Mulford 1983, 34)

"A living body we enter at birth, sustains and contains us. it does not stand in place of anything else, it does not replace the bodies around us. placental, our flat land, our sea, it is both place (where we are situated) and body (that contains us), that body of language we speak, our mothertongue. it bears us as we are born in it, into cognition." (Daphne Marlatt 1984, 53)

"The language is principally spoken by others. We come to it as borrowers or as servants who have stolen their master's clothing, in a way. We teach everyone to speak – women teach children to speak, but when it comes to establishing the language of a tribe, purifying it, defining it, women haven't traditionally done that. There are certain realms, I think, that are closed to women, which women struggle to open, only to find they are a sort of Pandora's box, because the language is even repulsive." (Germaine Greer 1983, 136-7; interviewed by Joseph Kestner)

"Is almost another sense, like sight or touch." (Rebecca Gordon 1983, 71)

"Is not only the vehicle of thought, it is also its faithful mirror, and the evolution of women's independence and equality is reflected in our current speech as one of the signs of the times. No longer is a word mangled [with, for example, an *-ess* ending] or a fresh one coined to tell us that women have invaded one more sphere of masculine privilege. A clerk is a clerk, though wearing a skirt, and the woman who 'pokes her nose' into the mill will have H.M. 'Inspector' on her card, not 'Inspectress.' The extension of the municipal franchise to women made them citizens and voters equal to men in name as in voting power." (J. Beanland 1911, *The Vote*, February 18, 207)

"Is magic. It makes people and things appear and disappear." (Nicole Brossard 1984; quoted by Sarah Sheard 1984)

"Is the medium through which the dominant and the dominated consciously and unconsciously perceive and interpret the appropriation by a small social group of the means of subsistence and of other human beings. Each class speaks itself, in other words, by taking on and shaping its historical identity according to the *same hidden referent*. This social referent is the dominant group whose identity is based on what it possesses (including knowledge and a validated verbal code). It is the group which legitimizes the material power by defining itself as a collection of individuals incarnating the perfection of 'humanity,' a collection of 'subjects,' of 'I's.' It is because the social referent is the same for all classes that language practices are efficient." (Noëlle Bisseret Moreau 1984, 59-60)

"The ability to destroy and recreate by Word-power belonged originally to the Goddess, who created languages, alphabets, and the secret mantras known as 'Words of Power.' " (Barbara G. Walker 1983, 546)

"There seems no reason to doubt that the baby-tending sex contributed at least equally with the history-making one to the most fundamental of all human inventions: Language." (Dorothy Dinnerstein 1976, 20)

"Is your culture, it determines your life. Latin people here [U.S.] are especially affected when we can't speak the official language. It affects what kinds of jobs we get which are now mostly as maids and dishwashers. The kinds of jobs . . . determine where we live." (Susanna Cepeda-Cidique; in Jo Delaplaine 1978, 9)

"Man Made." (Dale Spender 1980)

Represents "man's image of himself and of ourselves and the world as his creation." (Sheila Rowbotham 1983, 8)

"Attitudes are expressed in semantic equations that simply turn out to be two languages; one for men and another for women." (Jane O'Reilly 1972, 14)

"The most intense and stubborn fortress of sexist assumptions," one which "crudely enshrines the ancient bias against women." (Susan Sontag 1973, 186)

"Is inherited from a masculine society, and it contains many male prejudices. . . . Women simply have to steal the instrument; they don't have to break it, or try, a priori, to make of it something totally different. Steal it and use it for their own good." (Simone de Beauvoir; interview by Alice Jardine 1979, 229-30)

"Women's struggles against their confinement by the 'circles' of representative systems cannot be waged in isolation from their political struggles against material oppression. To assert that a women's language miraculously IS, and may be spoken by I – here – now, is to return to an imaginary closure, which is all the more dangerous because it closes itself *from* the multiple, diverse and diffused movements of women." (Meaghan Morris 1982, 88)

"The crucial signifying practice in and through which the human subject is constructed and becomes a social being."
"Women have a special difficulty with language; how can they subvert that language which is the instrument of the Law?" (Wendy Mulford 1983, 34)

(See SYNTAX)

"The wall that had separated John and herself was, she saw . . . the old old war which might in the last analysis be the war between men and women. By what language then might she and John have

knocked their message of love through it?" (May Sarton 1961, 63)

"If they [women] begin to speak and write *as men do*, they will enter history subdued and alienated; it is a history that, logically speaking, their speech should disrupt." (Xavière Gauthier 1974; rpt. 1981, 162-3)

"As Simone Weil says, those who suffer from injustice most are the least able to articulate their suffering; and that the silent majority, released into language, would not be content with a perpetuation of the conditions which have betrayed them." (Adrienne Rich 1979, 67)

"The language I learned was pretty, full of passivity and silence. I had no proper language for the issues of blood and anger, yet much of what went on when I was a child made me angry. There were no words a nice girl could use to describe anger; her options were to remain silent or to use indirect language, the kind that curls in the room like smoke and soon disappears. We girls were taught to speak safely and to bandage our anger with polite, pretty words. We might talk about the anger only in questions and sighs, unable to curse, yell, or break windows in the beautiful garden." (Beth Bagley 1984, 42)

"It is clear that among women we need a new ethics; as women, a new morality. The problem of speech, of language, continues to be primary." (Adrienne Rich 1979, 185)

"Women . . . are faced with the task of inventing a language of behavior that is based on authentic feeling; but for it to be a useful language, the fundamental requirement of a language has to be met. That is, it must deliver messages accurately over quite a wide range of meaning, and be comprehensible to its viewers and listeners . . . women. . . . But the general surrounding community ought to be able to follow them too, for it will only be supportive if it can do so." (Elizabeth Janeway 1980, 302)

"For those of us who write, it is necessary to scrutinize not only the truth of what we speak, but the truth of that language by which we speak it." (Audre Lorde 1980a, 22)

"We wish to develop a framework inclusive of all women's experience. (Sexuality must not be a code word for heterosexuality, or women a code word for white women.)" (Carole S. Vance 1982, 40)

"As long as our language is inadequate, our vision remains formless, our thinking and feeling are still running in the old cycles, our process may be 'revolutionary' but not transformative." (Adrienne Rich 1979, 248)

LANGUAGE AND GENDER RESEARCH
(See WOMEN AND LANGUAGE RESEARCH)

LANGUAGE OF THE BODY
"The body's language is stronger than sounds shaped by the tongues and teeth." (Jessamyn West 1979, 442)

"Censor the body and you censor breath and speech at the same time." (Hélène Cixous 1975b; rpt. in Elaine Marks and Isabelle de Courtivron 1981, 250)

LATIN/GREEK
Secret codes, supplied through an education traditionally denied women, which make men feel superior. (Aphra Behn 17th century; in Dale Spender 1982)

LATINA
Preferred term to *Hispanic, Spanish, Spanish-speaking* or *Spanish sur-named,* which imply identification with Spain (and its imperialistic conquest and exploitation of Latin America) and deny the diversity of roots in Indian, Mestizo, African, Caribbean and other cultures. (Jo Delaplaine 1978, 11)

(See HISPANIC)

LAUGHTER
A facial expression "exhibited to those higher in status: to laugh long and hard at the boss's jokes is a cliché, but at the same time a painful reality. . . . Both smiling and laughing are ostensibly ex-

pressions of pleasure and relaxation which, when coming from subordinates, belie the true nature of the situation. It is as if they are exhibited for the purpose of maintaining the myth of pleasant relations and equality between superior and subordinate." (Dale Spender 1980, 171-2)

"The roaring laughter of women is like the roaring of the eternal sea . . . more and more, one hears them [hags] roaring at the reversal that is patriarchy, that monstrous jock's joke, the Male Mothers Club that gives birth only to putrefaction and deception. One can hear pain and perhaps cynicism in the laughter. . . . But this laughter is the one true hope, for as long as it is audible there is evidence that someone is seeing through the Dirty Joke." (Mary Daly 1978, 17)

(See HAGS)

LAW
Is, along with habit, custom, and convention, a monument and sepulchre "of old thought and past feeling. They are the dead hand laid heavy upon the shoulder of life." (Teresa Billington-Greig 1908a, 109)

A profession which interprets the laws of man. An institution with a hierarchy involving federal and state bar associations which "exert substantial influence over judicial appointments. [It] is significant that women are largely excluded from the boards of governors of bar associations and from executive positions within these organizations. Further, political party leaders who slate judicial candidates tend to follow value systems that invariably favor the selection of male candidates." Women judges "are assigned mostly to matrimonial and juvenile courts rather than trial courts." (Edith Elisabeth Flynn 1982, 319)

(See FRESCOED FEMININITY)

LAWYER
"A power role" for the practice of law. "Being a lawyer is . . . substantially more consistent with the content of the male role, what men are taught to be in this society: ambitious, upwardly-mobile,

capable of hostility, aggressive not just assertive, not particularly receptive or set-off from the track of one's argument by what someone else might be saying or, god forbid, feeling." (Catharine Mac-Kinnon 1982b)

LEADERSHIP

"The simplest most down-to-earth defini-tion of leadership is actually chronologi-cal: in terms of history, she who goes first; in terms of hard work, she who paves the way; in terms of getting to one's destina-tion, she who guides. Often leadership was simply not recognized [in the con-temporary women's liberation movement] for what it was because it was coming from a woman or because it was so unfamiliar, so radical, so 'simple.' " (Kathie Sarachild 1975a, 26)

LEFT, THE

A movement dominated by white males, with the goals of destruction of capital-ism, imperialism, and patriarchy. The male Left has been "unable to understand the fundamental unity of theory and practice" which leads the male Left "to adopt the elitist assumptions of capitalist society." (Nancy Hartsock 1976-7; rpt. 1981, 33)

"The left has been criticized for having a prefabricated theory made up of nine-teenth century leftovers, a strategy built on scorn for innovation in politics or for expanding political issues. Too often leftist groups have held that the working class was incapable of working out its own future and that those who would lead the working class to freedom would be those who had memorized the sacred texts and were equipped with an all-inclusive theory that would help them organize the world." (Nancy Hartsock 1979, 56)

All myths agree that the right side was male, the left side female. (See Barbara G. Walker 1983, 530-4)

LESBIAN

"The word LESBIAN comes to us as a British word derived from the Greek 600 B.C. Isle of Lesbos and 'the reputed female homosexual band associated with Sappho of Lesbos.' (*Webster's Seventh New Collegiate Dictionary*). Etymologically speaking, the word LESBIAN, rather than the word 'gay,' is the more correct term when speaking of women-identified women." (Jeanne Cordova 1974, 21) Mary Daly makes the distinction between LESBIAN and GAY or HOMO-SEXUAL. She prefers "to reserve the term *Lesbian* to describe women who are woman-identified, having rejected false loyalties to men on all levels. The terms *gay* or *female homosexual* more accurately describe women who, although they relate genitally to women, give their allegiance to men and male myths, ideologies, styles, practices, institutions, and professions." (Mary Daly 1978, 26)

(See DYKE, LESBIAN CONTINUUM, OFFICE OF SECRET INVESTIGATION, PURGE)

A social identification of woman-identified woman. A concept which causes many people discomfort. "Fancy being able to upset the world by not minding being called a woman who loves people like herself! It's the world who's in trouble, not me." (Jackie Lapidus to her mother 1975; quoted in Karen Payne 1983, 328)

"A lesbian is the rage of all women condensed to the point of explosion." (Radicalesbians 1970, 1)

"A lesbian is a woman whose primary erotic, psychological, emotional, and social interest is in a member of her own sex, even though that interest may not be overtly expressed." (Del Martin and Phyllis Lyon 1972; rpt. 1973, 135)

"Most dictionary definitions refer to love between women, but by 'love' they only mean 'sexual practice'. And I mean so much more. . . . [The relationship with my lover] is moving, it is tender, it is fierce . . . the give and take, the fights, the reconciliations, the willingness to work it out . . . the realization of joy in our lives together, in each, in ourselves, the delight, the knowing of our cycles, of sexual passion, of abstinence, always the tenderness. . . Is unlearning what we have been taught to despise. It is learning that love of self and other women – it is essential to my survival and my capacity to be a self-determining person." (Susan Abbott to her mother Miriam 1980; quoted in Karen Payne 1983, 312, 321)

"Before the night of the vanishing powder, lesbian meant she who was interested in 'only' half of the population and had a violent desire for that half. A lesbian is a companion lover, or a companion lover is a lesbian. The lesbian peoples had been called such after Lesbos, the most beloved center of their culture. The word is still used in the Glorious Age, despite its geographical meaning." (Monique Wittig and Sande Zeig 1976, 97)

"The word 'lesbian' may not, in any case, be suitable (or comfortable) for black women, who surely would have begun their woman-bonding earlier than Sappho's residency on the Isle of Lesbos. . . . My own term for such women would be womanist.' " (Alice Walker 1981; rpt. 1983, 81)

(See WOMANIST)

"I, for one, identify a woman as a lesbian who says she is." (Cheryl Clarke 1981, 129)

"In the context of compulsory heterosexuality, lesbian existence, by definition, is an act of resistance." (Jacquelyn N. Zita 1981, 175)

"Of course I am a woman, but I belong to another geography as well and the two worlds are complicated and unique." (Joan Nestle 1981a, 23)

"Lesbian is the only concept I know of which is beyond the categories of sex (woman and man), because the designated subject (lesbian) is *not* a woman, either economically, or politically, or ideologically." (Monique Wittig 1981, 53)

Those who "have a history of perceiving them Selves as such, and the will to assume responsibility for Lesbian acts, erotic and political." (Janice Raymond 1982, 16)

"One who, by virtue of her focus, her attention, her attachment is disloyal to phallocratic reality. She is not committed to its maintenance and the maintenance of those who maintain it, and worse her mode of disloyalty threatens its utter dissolution in the mere flicker of the eye." (Marilyn Frye 1983, 172)

Ten years ago this "was a secret word, and *lesbian mother* was thought to be a contradiction in terms." (Gloria Steinem 1983, 151)

LESBIANISM CHAUVINISM

"The aggressive assertion of your sexual and sensual needs and interests." (Jill Johnston 1973a, 154)

LESBIAN CONSCIOUSNESS

" 'Lesbian consciousness' is really a point of view, a view from the boundary. And in a sense everytime a woman draws a circle around her psyche, saying 'this is a room of *my own*' and then writes from within that 'room' she's inhabiting 'lesbian consciousness.' " (Harriet Desmoines 1976; quoted by Bonnie Zimmerman 1982, 466)

LESBIAN CONTINUUM

Includes "a range – through each woman's life and throughout history – of woman-identified experience; not simply the fact that a woman has had or consciously desired genital sexual experience with another woman." Adrienne Rich wants to expand the concept of lesbian to "many more forms of primary intensity between and among women, including the sharing of a rich inner life, the bonding against male tyranny, the giving and receiving of practical and political support." If the concept is expanded, she suggests, then "we begin to grasp breadths of female history and psychology which have lain out of reach as a consequence of limited, mostly clinical, definitions of 'lesbianism.' " (Adrienne Rich 1980, 648, 649)

LESBIAN FEMINISM

"An imaginative identification with all women." (Adrienne Rich 1979, 228)

In the "deepest, most radical sense" is

"that love for ourselves and other women, that commitment to the freedom of all of us, which transcends the category of 'sexual preference' and the issue of civil rights, to become a politics of *asking women's* questions, demanding a world in which the integrity of all women – not a chosen few – shall be honored and validated in every aspect of culture." (Adrienne Rich 1979, 17)

"To claim our lesbianism, to take full advantage of its advantages. This is central to our feminism: that women can know their own bodies and desires, interpret their own erotic currents, create and choose environments which encourage chosen changes in all these; and that a female eroticism that is independent of males and of masculinity *is* possible and *can* be chosen." (Marilyn Frye 1983, 149)

"If radical lesbian-feminism purports an anti-racist, anti-classist, anti-woman-hating vision of bonding as mutual, reciprocal, as infinitely negotiable, as freedom from antiquated gender prescriptions and proscriptions, *then all people struggling to transform the character of relationships in this culture have something to learn from lesbians.*" (Cheryl Clark 1981, 135)

LESBIANISM

Means that "you forget the male power system, and that you give women primacy in your life – emotionally, personally, politically." (Rita Mae Brown 1976, 90)

"Feminism is the complaint, and lesbianism is the solution." (Jill Johnston 1975; cited in Sara Scott 1983, 26) Joan Nestle challenges this slogan, on the grounds that it invalidates lesbian herstory. Pre-Stonewall lesbians, though not lesbian feminists as currently defined, were nevertheless feminists. "Their feminism was not an articulated theory, it was a lived set of options based on erotic choice." (Joan Nestle 1981, 23) Further, the playing out of butch-fem roles, now considered oppressive, was actually a mode of adventuring produced by their social and sexual autonomy from mainstream culture. (Joan Nestle 1981, 23) Similarly, Chrystos points out that les-

bianism is not necessarily a "political" choice for many lesbians. "For most women – especially of my age – it is not a choice. Being attracted to women sexually is a unique and precious response." (Chrystos 1982, 26)

"Far more than a sexual preference; it is a political stance." (Sidney Abbott and Barbara J. Love 1972; quoted in Elaine Partnow 1977, 409)

"A remnant of self-love in a society that would otherwise have me hate myself." (Sally Gearheart 1974, 3)

"The subject of lesbianism
is very ordinary; it's the question
of male domination that makes everybody angry."
(Judy Grahn 1978a, 55)

"A recognition, an awakening, a reawakening of our passion for each (woman) other (woman) and for same (woman). This passion will ultimately reverse the heterosexual imperialism of male culture. Women, through the ages, have fought and died rather than deny that passion." (Cheryl Clarke 1981, 129)

Although it may not solve patriarchal dilemmas, "it is nonetheless unquestionable that the refusal – and lack of desire – to act out heterosexually reinforced roles of femininity and submission in the immediate presence of men suggests new dimensions in the struggle for women's liberation." (Jill Lewis 1981b, 269)

LESBIAN POLITICS OF NAMING

"The attempt to criminalize lesbianism through a clause in the 1921 [U.K.] Criminal Law Amendment Bill (to place it on a par with the 1885 criminalisation of male homosexuality) foundered on the conviction that drawing attention to the existence of a practice unknown to most women might itself incite the practice." (Lucy Bland 1983, 20)

"The denial of lesbians is literally Victorian. The Queen herself was appalled by the inclusion of a paragraph on lesbianism in the 1885 Criminal Law that sought to penalize private homosexual acts by two years' imprisonment. She expressed complete ignorance of female inversion or perversion and refused to sign the Bill, unless all reference to such practices was omitted." (Blanche Cook 1977)

A concept created by the ideology of heterosexism. (Gill Hanscombe; quoted in *Wiplash* [Women in Publishing newsletter], October 26, 1983)

"A label invented by the Man to throw at any woman who dares to be his equal, who dares to challenge his prerogatives (including that of all women as part of the exchange medium among men), who dares to assert the primacy of her own needs." (Radicalesbians 1970, 2)

Pejorative labels created to put down the Brazilian lesbian, such as "big shoe" (sapatao) in carioca (Rio) slang. We can recognize that this expression was created by men and reflects a 'macho' resentment, a frustration of the Brazilian man himself against what is seen as the dominant character in the lesbian pair." (Graca Maria Aires Montini 1978, 44)

"Like black men and women who refused to be the exceptional 'pet' Negro for whites, and who instead said they were 'niggers' too (the original 'crime' of 'niggers' and lesbians is that they prefer themselves), perhaps black women writers and nonwriters should say, simply, whenever black lesbians are being put down, held up, messed over, and generally told their lives should not be encouraged, *We are all lesbians*." (Alice Walker 1980; rpt. 1983, 288-9)

"I received a letter from the National Council of Teachers of English explaining that our Committee on Lesbian and Gay Male Concerns in the Profession ought to contain a representative number of 'declared heterosexuals.' " (Susan J. Wolfe and Julia Penelope 1980; in Gloria Kaufman and Mary Kay Blakely 1980, 119)

"To call oneself a lesbian now seems to be a 'new provincialism.' Excluding women who don't have your sexual preference is not feminist, and it is not ethical to call yourself a feminist when you mean lesbian, or to use those words interchangeably." (Thyme Siegel 1983, letter to *off our backs*, October, 27)

"Seven Letters"
haven't you heard

heard what?
she's a l-e-s-b-i-a-n!
Strange how seven letters
Can change one's world around
Turn it upside down
Inside out
Strange how seven letters
Can make Mothers cry
Fathers storm
Friends disappear
But isn't it strange
How those same seven letters
Can set one's life "straight"
Make one whole
Set one free?
(Cheryl Regina Miller 1980, 5)

LESBIAN SEPARATISM

"The logical extension of a separatist organization strategy, particularly given the [Women's Liberation Movement's] notion of the personal being political. Along with celibacy (also favoured by some first-wave feminists) it could be seen as the ultimate sign of repudiation of and withdrawal from male society. Lesbian separatism, however, had the added advantage of being able to be presented as a crucial ingredient of an alternative feminist culture. Its role led to conflict within the WLM. At the same time as heterosexual women expressed feelings of oppression by a lesbian orthodoxy, lesbian women could believe themselves to be as unfree within the movement as they were in the society outside." (Marian Simms 1981, 231)

LESBOPHOBIA

Similar to homophobia but more accurate for lesbians. Anti-lesbian attitudes and feelings (Doris Davenport 1981; and Margaret Cruikshank 1982, xiii)

"Misogyny directed specifically at lesbians." (Cherie Lyn 1984, correspondence)

LESBOS

"Amazons took this [Greek] isle of Lesbos and made it one of their 'isles of women,' a sacred colony dedicated to worship of the female principle. . . . In the 6th century B.C., Lesbos was ruled by a group of women devoted to the . . . practice of [the arts,] philosophy and romantic 'Lesbian' love." (Barbara G. Walker 1983, 535)

LESOPHOBIA
Fear of strong women. (Cherie Lyn 1984, correspondence)

LEXICOGRAPHER
Samuel Johnson was wrong; in his whimsical definition a lexicographer is "a harmless drudge." A lexicographer writes or compiles a dictionary by describing, correcting, or proscribing language usage. Some lexicographers work carefully to record words and their conventional usages, thus providing important and influential reference tools to language and culture, including aspects of racism, sexism, and ageism practiced by some speakers.
   (See DICTIONARY)

LIB
"When working toward our liberation
And basic change in civilization,
'Lib' is an abbreviation
In which we hear your condemnation."
   (Joann Haugerud 1978, 17)

LIBERAL
A political stance; a person. "The liberal fears and opposes clarity and effectiveness because she fears angering the powerful; she does not want to fight. In order to perserve peace, the liberal resists any idea that requires real change in the status quo, in action or theory." (Kathie Sarachild 1974, 58)

LIBERAL FEMINIST
Today, in our culture, "is one who advocates such reforms as legal equality between the sexes, equal pay for equal work, and equal employment opportunities, but who denies that complete equality requires radical alterations in basic social institutions e.g. the capitalist economic system, the biological family, monogamous marriage, biological motherhood . . . or in the presumption that most childrearing must be done by women. John Stuart Mill and Bertrand Russell remain the greatest philosophical proponents of liberal feminism, with Betty Friedan and (some of) the leadership of NOW representing the liberal wing of the [U.S.] women's movement today." (Mary Anne Warren 1980, 280)

LIBERALISM
"The essence of liberalism [is] to sit on the fence, avoid taking sides, to denounce polarization, confrontation and the use of force. It is the perfect tool for the oppressor's use." According to Kathie Sarachild, "Liberalism emerges whenever an oppressed group begins to move against the oppressor. It works to preserve the oppressor's power by avoiding and preventing exposure and confrontation." (Kathie Sarachild 1974, 58, 57)

LIBERATED WOMAN
"A contradiction in terms." (Susan Sontag 1973, 205) An impossibility in the present society. "Whether we live with or without a man, communally or in couples or alone, are married or unmarried, live with other women, go for free love, celibacy, or lesbianism, or any combination, there are only good and bad things about each bad situation. There is no 'more liberated' way; there are only bad alternatives." (Carol Hanisch 1969; rpt. 1975, 204)

LIBERATION
"Women's liberation is the liberation of the feminine in the man and the masculine in the woman." (Corita Kent; quoted by Lucie Kay Scheuer 1974; cited in Elaine Partnow 1977, 224)
   (See WOMEN'S LIBERATION)
   "Not an insular experience; it occurs in conjunction with other human beings. There are no individual 'liberated women.'" (Peggy Kornegger 1979, 244)
   (1) The freeing of one people who had

been in the possession of another. This was the primary meaning of liberation, referring to such events as the exodus of the Jews from Egypt and the civil rights movement of Americans of color. (2) Since the 1960s the word liberation has taken on a secondary meaning: the personal freedom to do whatever you want, with whomever you want to do it, freedom sought by people already in power. The (always male) proponents of the sexual revolution, members of the gay men's movement and sadomasochists have borrowed the rhetoric of the black and women's movement to assert their freedom of association and speech. (Judith Pasternak 1983, 5)

"*When we view liberation as a scarce resource, something only a precious few of us can have, we stifle our potential, our creativity, our genius for living, learning and growing.*" (Andrea Canaan 1981, 235)

"Women's liberationists, white and black, will always be at odds with one another as long as our idea of liberation is based on having the power white men have." (bell hooks 1981, 156)

"Just as women cannot trust men to 'liberate' them, Black women cannot trust white women to 'liberate' them during or 'after the revolution,' in part because there is little reason to think that they would know how; and in part because white women's immediate self-interest lies in continued racial oppression." (Gloria Joseph 1981, 104-5)

LIBERTY

Freedom which "was never won by pleading, and cannot be purchased.... The liberty of the subject, liberty of speech, and religious liberty are all harvested from the same field of human labour – the field of revolt. Existing authority has never hastened to extend freedom, and every franchise reform has been preceded by a greater or lesser degree of organised disorder." (Teresa Billington-Greig c.1908b, 8-9)

LIBERTY BONDS

Investments in continuing freedom. "You [women] who have aided in winning the war . . . were able to give your services because you were free – free through a knowledge of Birth Control. Will you not, for every child that you would have had, had you not known how to limit your family, purchase one $10 share of stock in The Birth Control Review? For every bond you purchase, I promise to free ten women from the bondage of ignorance. You have purchased Liberty Bonds for the men 'over there.' Why not 'Liberty Bonds' now for the women over here?" (Margaret Sanger 1919, 20)

LIFE

"My feeling about life is a curious kind of triumphant feeling about seeing it bleak, knowing it is so, and walking into it fearlessly because one has no choice." (Georgia O'Keefe, *Women Artists Calendar*, 1983)

Life perhaps is a lengthy street
where a woman walks
everyday with her basket.
(Furugh Farrukhzad 1970; rpt. 1977, 305)

For women, life is "living in a body defined as Body in a patriarchal world." (Betty Willis Brooks and Sharon L. Sievers 1983, 80)

"Life to the 'male mind' (we have heard enough of the 'female mind' to use the analogue!) *is* a fight, and his ancient military institutions and processes keep up the delusion." (Charlotte Perkins Gilman 1911, 228)
(See FOOTBALL)

"If patriarchal males loved life, the planet would be different." (Mary Daly 1978, 352)
(See EUTHENICS)

LILA

To do that which a woman does during the sexual act. Lover (not used of males) is called *lilahá*. (Suzette Haden Elgin 1983, 8)
See LÁADAN for pronunciation guide.

LILITH

"1. The first woman, made from the same dust and at the same time as Adam and therefore created his equal. 2. A mythological figure who, because of her independence, resistance to male supremacy, and sexual openness was transformed into a mother-creator-destroyer, a scapegoat for instinctual (and therefore evil) drives." (Midge Lennert and Norma Willson, eds 1973, 6)

LILY ON THE DUSTBIN

A woman waiting on a street corner for a friend who doesn't turn up. Australian slang. In using this phrase as the title for her collection of Australian women's and family slang, Nancy Keesing writes, " 'The lily on the dustbin' (or perhaps garbage tin, or dirt bin) was one phrase that early became, for me, a symbol of a whole range of women's speech and domestic language that I call 'Sheilaspeak' and 'Familyspeak,' and that has had an inexplicably small place in standard compilations of Australian slang and colloquialisms. The lily means different things to different people and sometimes several things to one person. Those who use it are most often women, but their sons and grandsons remember their words. Where the lily originally grew I know not, neither do I care. Much Australian slang has been imported, though it is adapted to our own speech needs. Consider the lily: sometimes it expresses incongruity, and some women liken an over-dressed person to the lily. But most often it means a person left languishing. Sheilaspeak and Familyspeak, too, have languished, forlornly disregarded by philologists and linguists." (Nancy Keesing 1982, 3-4)

LINE PARTY

Attendance at a social event as part of a female group (e.g., sisters in a sorority) rather than as a man's date ('queening'), University slang, 1920s. (Olive Deane Hormel 1926, 63)

LINGUISTIC CREATIVITY

A woman undergraduate asks, "Haven't I as good a right to make a word as any one else?" (L.M. Montgomery 1915, 288)

LINGUISTIC SEXISM

"English does not use gender extensively, but its linguistic sexism is intact because sexism is intact." (Arlene Raven 1973; quoted in Elaine Partnow 1977, 485)

(See FALSE GENERICS, LANGUAGE, NAMING, PRONOUNS, SEXISM)

LINGUISTIC TYRANNY

The process whereby, through "put downs" (such as giving titles which denote inferior status), interruptions, flattery, and an unwillingness to discuss things with women, men have generally paralyzed women into a kind of silence. Women do speak, but they have been discouraged from speaking publicly, authoritatively, argumentatively or at any length. (Mary Ritchie Key 1975; 127-32)

LINGUISTS

Scholars who treat language as subject and object. This dictionary illustrates the work of many linguists.

(See DICTIONARY, LÁADAN, LANGUAGE)

LISTENING

Is active hearing, something which women do more than men, something which is invisible, and "which has therefore (mistakenly) been associated with passivity? Is it coincidence that women are often considered to be the 'better' listeners, providing the understanding and sympathetic ear, being more inclined to 'hear someone out'? Is there any connection between the devaluation of women and the devaluation of listening? I suspect that there might be." (Dale Spender 1980, 121)

"Women aren't blessed with intuition. They just listen in a way that men don't, right? You know when I first joined [the staff] I was pretty intimidated, if the truth be known. Sort of didn't say a word, or anything. I was too frightened to open my mouth. . . . So I just shut up. . . . And you know what I found when I listened? All those little nuances, all those little things, underlying things that give you the complete picture. I knew who was *in* and who was *out*. The politics of it all . . . it was all there to see. . . . But when you start talking, now that's different. When I started talking, you don't get that kind of information. You're too concerned about getting into it, saying your piece at the next opportunity. . . . When you're *just* listening, you pick up all kinds of information. And when you *act* on it, you know, that's when people say how *intuitive* you are!" (Woman quoted in Dale Spender 1980, 123)

(See INTUITION)

LITERARY CRITICISM

(See CRITICISM)

LITERARY HISTORY

A record of choices, concerning which written works are recognized as worthy. "Which writers have survived their time and which have not depends upon who noticed them and chose to record the notice. Which works have become part of the 'canon' of literature, read, thought about, discussed and in which have disappeared depends, in the same way, on the process of selection and the power to select along the way." (Louise Bernikow ed. 1974, 3)

"The world did not say to her as it said to them, Write if you choose; it makes no difference to her. The world said with a guffaw, Write? What's the use of your writing?" (Virginia Woolf 1928; in Bristol Women's Studies Group 1979, 238)

LITERATURE

Is man-prejudiced writing. In male terms literature has only two branches of fiction – conflict or love which means to them mating. (Charlotte Perkins Gilman 1911, 221, 98)

LITTLE WOMEN

Title of best-known book by Louisa May Alcott, nineteenth-century writer who wrote "books for girls" as well as (under pen names) feminist mysteries and pot-boilers.

LIVELIHOOD

Wife's: "is a precarious dependence upon another person's life." (Cicely Hamilton 1909, 67-8)

(See MARRIAGE)

LOCKER-ROOMING

Telling stories about people and events to enhance one's macho image. (Emily Prager 1983, 145)

LOGIC

That which has been considered neutral and "uncontaminated" by human values, "may indeed be culture-specific, arbitrary and inappropriate. We may need to change our ideas of what constitutes logic if we are to come closer to making sense of the world." (Dale Spender 1980, 97)

LONELY

"I sure did live in this world."

"Really? What have you got to show for it?"

"Show? To Who? Girl, I got my mind. And what goes on in it. Which is to say, I got me."

"Lonely, ain't it?"

"Yes. But my lonely is *mine*. Now your lonely is somebody else's. Made by somebody else and handed to you. Ain't that something? A second hand lonely." (Toni Morrison 1973, 143)

LONGTHINK

Action by a kind of automatic pilot which relies on deeper brain structures. (Sally Gearhart 1978)

LOQUACITY

"Is only a readiness of ideas, and an ease of delivery, which [men] in vain labour, for years, to attain." (Sophia 1739, 39)

LORELEI

Famous rock in the Rhine, anciently identified with a Water-siren or River-goddess who lured men to death by drowning. Possibly it was once a shrine of the Water-Goddess. Early in the nineteenth century, a German writer transformed the Lorelei into the usual maiden disappointed in love. (Barbara G. Walker 1983, 549)

LOSERISM

"Is when oppressed people sit around and think up reasons why they can't do something. Well, just *do* it. Thinking up reasons why you can't is the Establishment's job." (Florynce Kennedy; quoted in Gloria Steinem 1973, 55)

LOSS

"An emptiness, filled with terrifying feelings: burning hate, sizzling despair, rage that tears you apart." (Michele Roberts 1983, 64)

LOST WOMEN

Often used as an adjective phrase preceding nouns normally reserved for men, such as "lost women writers" and "lost women artists," to indicate women have a history of their own to be recovered. (Lana Rakow 1984, correspondence) A section of *Ms.* magazine that recovers them.

LOVE

"1. [Trad.] The profoundly tender and passionate feelings one person may have for another person. 2. A deep personal experience no longer considered the viable foundation for a woman's existence. 3. To be cared for, thought of and valued, not abstractly, as men often value women, but in the accumulation of daily minutiae that make life dense and intricate and worthy." (Midge Lennert and Norma Willson, eds 1973, 7)

"Love is a space which is attracted
to energy and repelled by
vacuums.
does that say anything to you
about what irritates me
when you speak only of what you have to
need

and never what you need to have to
offer?"
(Judy Grahn, from "Confrontations with the Devil in the Form of Love"; quoted in Debbie Alicen 1983, 13-14)

"A wordless language by which the untutored body is taught." "I had given up trying to define love. 'Love to be with' didn't need definition. It was demonstrable." (Jessamyn West 1979, 145, 232)

"A refined degree of madness." (Dorothy Osborne; quoted in Teresa Billington-Greig c.1949-69)

"They never wanted us to feel like this. Killers beware! With love like this we can move mountains and break your prisons down. It is no hope to help us to forget, oh no. This love is dangerous." (Anonymous; quoted in Lucy Goodison 1983, 51)

Heterosexual romantic love has been reconceptualized as "delibitating dependency and selfishness." (Brook D'Abreu 1980, 95) Marilyn Frye suggests that "under the name of Love, a willing and unconditional servitude has been promoted as something ecstatic, noble, fulfilling, and even redemptive." (Marilyn Frye 1983, 72) Andrea Dworkin defines romantic love as the "mythic celebration of female negation. . . . For the female, the capacity to love is exactly synonymous with the capacity to sustain abuse and the appetite for it. . . . For the woman, love is always self-sacrifice, the sacrifice of identity, will and bodily integrity, in order to fulfill and redeem the masculinity of her lover." (Andrea Dworkin 1976, 105)

"Learning to love men sexually is a social process not a natural one . . . involves at least as much pain as joy, as much struggle as mutual support." (Sally Alexander and Barbara Taylor 1980; rpt. 1981, 79)

"A career . . . a means of livelihood" for a woman. (Cicely Hamilton 1909, 117)

A reaction to the threat of violence and economic deprivation. (Laura X 1969; correspondence 1984)

An ideology which is a primary means of keeping women in their place. "It is generally accepted that Western patriarchy has been much softened by the concepts of courtly and romantic love. While this is certainly true, such influence has also been vastly overestimated. In comparison with the candor of 'machismo' or oriental behavior, one realizes how much of a concession traditional chivalrous behavior represents a sporting kind of reparation to allow the subordinate female certain means of saving face." (Kate Millett 1971, 60)

(See CHIVALRY)

"The means by which women in our society resolve the contradiction between being sexually desirous but not sexually experienced. They sublimate their sexual feelings into a 'courtly love' mould . . . and thereby also ignore the passive, dominated role they must occupy in heterosexual courtship. And for both sexes, the near inevitability of entry into the labour contract of marriage is obscured by the process being seen as one of choice, attainment, love, sexual excitement, and individual development." (Diana Leonard 1982, 262)

"An emotion most men feel for their wives and children . . . but they love themselves also, and many love themselves best." If the loved wives "waste or perish from excessive child-birth, their husbands incur no legal responsibility." (Lady McLaren 1908, 36-7)

Françoise Parturier suggests that men do not really love the women they have access to, only those who are inaccessible, such as "dead women, exiled women, women prisoners, women saints, fiancees, angels, queens, heroines, stars, infidels, fugitives. It's not women you love, sir, but Woman; that is, an invention which 'real presence' doesn't live up to. . . . You fight for Isolde when it is forbidden to approach her, but as soon as she belongs to you, you place a sword between the two of you so you can sleep in peace." (Françoise Parturier 1968; rpt. 1981, 62)

Cake love: "This thing they've all got that's hurting them so and making us all feel they may blow up. Cake love as opposed to the bread-and-butter kind." (Margery Allingham 1938, 95)

"Really being in love means wanting to live in a different world." (Situationist Leaflet; quoted in Lucy Goodison 1983, 48)

Mother's: "The general underlying, world-lifting force. The 'life force,' now so glibly chattered about (in Love Stories), finds its fullest expression in motherhood; not in the emotions of an assistant in the preliminary stages." (Charlotte Perkins Gilman 1911, 101)

Below is a set of nouns from the women's language Láadan "to replace that maddeningly obscure four-letter word 'love' ":

áayá	mysterious love, not yet known to be either welcome or unwelcome
áazh	love for one sexually desired at one time, but not now
azh	love for one sexually desired now
ab	love for one liked but not respected
ad	love for one respected but not liked
éeme	love for one neither liked nor respected
am	love for one related by blood
ashon	love for one not related by blood, but kin of the heart
aye	love that is unwelcome and a burden
oham	love for that which is holy
sham	love for the child of one's body; neither liking nor respect is presupposed

See LÁADAN for pronunciation guide. (Suzette Haden Elgin 1983, 8)
(See HETEROSEXUALITY, LESBIAN, LESBIANISM, ROMANCES, SEX, SEXUALITY, LUST, MARRIAGE

LOVEMAKING

"Any activity between individuals which involves sexual pleasure and/or satisfaction. Sexual activity between caring people." (Nomadic Sisters 1976, 9) In Victorian England and U.S. the term was applied to courtship customs.

LOVE POTIONS

The celebrated love potions of ancient texts may actually have been poisons: women's last defense against patriarchal power. (Theodore Thass-Thienemann 1967)

LOVER

"One who loves; a sexual partner." (Nomadic Sisters 1976, 9)

"Ironically and unfortunately, 'lover' is considered a pejorative by some people. In its original meaning, 'someone who loves' (could be a lover of music, a lover of dance, a lover of a person. . .), it is useful, strong, and accurate." (Alice Walker 1982; rpt. 1983, 357)

". . . seems more active than 'wife.' One becomes a lover by loving and being loved. One hardly becomes a wife by wifing and being wifed." (Ida VSW Red 1981, 65)

LOVE STORY

Usually "the story of the pre-marital struggle. It is the Adventures of Him in Pursuit of Her – and it stops when he gets her. Story after story, age after age, over and over and over, this ceaseless repetition of the Preliminaries." (Charlotte Perkins Gilman 1911, 99)

LOVING EYE

"The contrary of the arrogant eye. The loving eye knows the independence of the other. . . . It is the eye of one who knows that to know the seen, one must consult something other than one's own will and interests and fears and imagination. . . . The loving eye is one that pays a certain sort of attention." (Marilyn Frye 1983, 75)

(See ARROGANT EYE)

LUCY STONER

A woman who refuses to be a name-dropper when she marries a man. As in "Will Lucy Stoners please note that among the Aleuts of Kodiak Island it is the practice for the husband to discard his own name and take that of the wife." (Elizabeth J. Sherwood, June 1931, 268)

The term Lucy Stoner appears in some pre-1960s U.S. dictionaries, defined as "a person who advocates the keeping of their own names by married women." Married in 1855 to Henry Blackwell, Lucy Stone continued to use her name. In 1879, when Massachusetts, U.S., women were allowed to vote in school district elections, Lucy Stone registered in her own name. The Board of Registrars scratched her name from the voting list. Ruth Hale in 1917 continued the fight when she refused to change her name after she married Heywood Broun, and organized the Lucy Stone League. Its motto (and Lucy Stone's words): "My name is the symbol of my identity which must not be lost." (Malanie Granfors, *her-self* 3 (3), 17; Una Stannard 1977)

LUNATECHS

A computer group organized in April 1983 by lesbians in Chicago whose work is in data processing and tele-communications. (*Matrices: A Lesbian-Feminist Research Newsletter*, 7:2 [March], 20)

LUST

Patriarchal: lechery, lasciviousness. Other meanings: "vigor, fertility"; an intense longing: craving; eagerness, enthusiasm. (Mary Daly 1984, 2)

An expression of sexual desire which represents "an affirmation of our collective right to unfettered, unguilty, undefined sexuality . . . an appreciation of another's – and one's own – sexual dynamism . . . an assertive statement of the positive virtues of sexual exploration." (J. Lee Lehman 1981, 81)

Pure: The term and title *Pure Lust* (1984), for Mary Daly, "Names the high humor, hope and cosmic accord/harmony of those women who choose to escape, to follow our hearts' deepest desire and bound out of the State of Bondage, Wanderlusting and Wonderlusting. . . . This Lust is in its essence astral. It is pure Passion: unadulterated, absolute, simple sheer striving for abundance of being. It is unlimited, unlimiting desire/fire." (Mary Daly 1984, 3)

LYING

By the time you swear you're his,
    Shivering and sighing,
And he vows his passion is
    Infinite, undying –
Lady, make a note of this:
    One of you is lying.
    (Dorothy Parker, "Unfortunate Coinci-
    dence," quoted in John Keats 1970,
    103)

"Patriarchal lying has manipulated
women both through falsehood and
through silence. Facts we needed have
been withheld from us. False witness has
been borne against us." (Adrienne Rich
1979, 189)

LYNCH

To kill, especially by hanging. The execution without due process of law of
American Black men, women, and children was intended to terrorize and intimidate the Black population and discourage
their economic and political development.
(Ida B. Wells-Burnett 1892; cited in Pam
McAllister 1982, 87)

LYSISTRATA

Greek, means "Army-disbander." An
early feminist plot.
    (See ACTION)

MA

"Basic mother-syllable of Indo-European languages, worshipped in itself as the fundamental name of the Goddess. The universality of the mother-word (not shared by words for 'father') indicated either that the human race carried the same word from its earliest source to all parts of the earth at a period previous to the discovery of fatherhood; or else that all human beings instinctively say something like 'ma' as the first verbal sound and associate it with the mother's breast, consequently with emotional dependence on a divinity perceived as a milk-giving mother." (Barbara G. Walker 1983, 560)

(See MATRIARCHY)

MACHO, MACHISMO

Terms borrowed from Spanish to connote extreme male-ness, masculinity, or male dominance. Though useful "to describe the supreme male chauvinist [the terms] reflect the Latin male stereotype. . . . The selection of words from one culture for the popular language of another [reflects] deep-rooted value judgments and cultural assumptions" which can have serious and even disastrous consequences for Latinas. (Lourdes Miranda King 1979, 124-5) Some ways the words are used in English follow.

Machismo "is the Latin-American word for the mystique of 'manliness.' It denotes a configuration of attitudes, values, and behaviors." Includes: breaking the rules, violence, sexual potency, contempt for women. (Sheila Ruth 1980, 48-9) Is "an expression – sometimes at the level of caricature – of the patriarchal system. It consists in establishing a certain superiority of men over women, by which men feel themselves to be privileged beings both in society and in the family." (LACW Collective 1977, 7) Means extreme male dominance. (Anna Macías 1982, 3) Leads to the "battering [of] women, the callous impregnation of women, the lack of emotional connection and the love of violence and death by men." (Brigitte Sutherland, 1984, 34)

Macho "in classical Nahuatl [Uto-Aztecan languages of central Mexico] means 'image,' 'reflection of myself.' " (Marcela Christine Lucero-Trujillo 1980a, 330). In the field of medicine the term *macho medicine* is a shorthand way of describing certain practices, including emphasis on "strong" rather than "weak" professional performance, willingness to "get tough" with patients and "keep them from pushing you around," territoriality, and competitiveness. (Perri Klass 1984, "Hers," *New York Times*, October 11)

(See HEMBRISMO, MARIANISMO)

MACQUARIE

Known as The Macquarie, the 1982 *Macquarie Dictionary* of Australian English (Arthur Delbridge ed.) was compiled over 11 years and represents "an important act of linguistic self-assertion, as part of an effort in [Australia] of 15 million people to build respect for their own version of the language." The dictionary cost more than $1 million to produce, most of it provided by a South Australian newspaper. Though copies cost $50 each, the first printing of 50,000 copies sold out in 3 months. A number of newspapers, broadcasting companies, and academic departments have adopted the Macquarie as the standard for English in Australia. (Richard Bernstein 1983) For a feminist perspective on the dictionary, see the Introduction to *A Feminist Dictionary* and Meaghan Morris 1982.

MADAM

Form of address and reference. "Derived from the French *ma dame* ("my lady") and cognate to the Italian *madonna*. Madam originally denoted high rank, but in the love poetry of the 14th and 15th centuries, this became a common form of address for the beloved. The modern sense of prostitute or head of a brothel acquired momentum in the late Middle Ages or early Renaissance. The sexualized sense won out over the high rank sense." (Elizabeth Judd, in press)
(See FORMS OF ADDRESS)

MADISON AVENUE'S WOMAN

The female as she is represented and constructed by the advertising industry. "We all know her and she's changed very little over the years. She's blond, white, blue-eyed and has no pores. She doesn't piss, shit, or swear and never gets dirty. Yet she's always in the tub, using deodorants under her arms and in her crotch and then covering the deodorant smell with lots of perfume." (Nedhera Landers 1980, 6)
(See ADVERTISING, MAGAZINE MENSTRUATION, REPRESENTATION)

MAD MONEY

Money taken on a date to cover emergencies. "The fellow was supposed to bring me home, lead me safely through the asphalt jungle, protect me from slithering snakes, rapists and the like. But my mother and I knew young men were apt to drink too much, to slosh down so many rye-and-gingers that some hero might well lead me in front of an oncoming bus, smash his daddy's car into Tiffany's window or, less gallantly, throw up on my new dress. Mad money was for getting

home on your own, no matter what form of insanity your date happened to evidence." (Anne Roiphe 1972; rpt. Shirley Morahan 1981, 252)
(See PIN MONEY, PUSHKE)

MADNESS

M-A-Dness is Male Approval Desire. "M-A-D is the filter through which we're pressed to see ourselves – if we don't, we won't get published, sold, or exhibited – I blame none of us for not challenging it except not challenging it may drive us mad. . . ." (Honor Moore, quoted in Mary Daly 1978, 68)
(See MENTAL HEALTH)

MADRIGAL

Women's song, an unaccompanied vocal composition for two or three voices. Probably from Latin *matricalis* (of the womb), *matrix* (womb), *mater* (mother).

MADWOMAN

In novels written by women, the mad or monstrous woman character who is often the author's double, an image of her anxiety and rage. (Sandra Gilbert and Susan Gubar 1979, 78)

MAGAZINE MENSTRUATION

Representation in magazine advertisements of the menstruating woman. "She can have Stayfree and run, like the black-haired beauty in gossamer dress, through green fields. In gossamer dress? Nowhere under that transparent material can Bea make out belts, pins, metal tips, wads of cotton batting. Bea, all of her life, has failed the menstrual ads. They were so discreet, they whispered. She would never, if she heeded them, be inconvenienced by bleeding, backaches, nausea, bad circulation in feet and hands, twitching of leg muscles, chills, or cracked lips. The girls in the Land of Magazine Menstruation, the girls with periods in the periodicals leap immediately into the water, wearing tight swimsuits or, in short, crisp, white, swinging tennis skirts, there they were out on the court!" (E. M. Broner 1978; in

Gloria Kaufman and Mary Kay Blakely 1980, 23)

(See ADVERTISING, MADISON AVENUE'S WOMAN, REPRESENTATION, TAMPON)

MAGAZINES, WOMEN'S

(See WOMEN'S MAGAZINES)

MAGIC

Is the art of changing consciousness at will. "Political acts, acts of protest and resistance, acts that speak truth to power, that push for change, are acts of magic." (Starhawk 1982, 13, 169)

MAHATMA

"Hindu sage, a word literally meaning 'Great Mother,' masculinized in much the same way as the Semitic *ima*, 'mother,' became *imam*, a male sage. The original *mahatmas* were the Primal Matriarchs, or *matrikadevis*." (Barbara G. Walker 1983, 571)

MAIDEN

"Of Germanic origin, this word began as a synonym for *girl* or *young woman* and soon came to include *maidservant* (as in *maid of honor*). Under Christian influence, *maiden* took on connotations of chastity or virginity. The feature of virginity has largely won out over that of youthfulness (*old maid* and *maiden aunt*)." (Elizabeth Judd, in press)

(See MAIDEN NAME)

MAIDEN NAME

The symbol of the independent, unbonded female self. Both name and self are relinquished in marriage. (Theodore Thass-Thienemann 1967) The term *birth name* is now often used instead.

(See MAIDEN, NAMES)

MAIN

"Newly coined neutral word . . . a contraction of man and maid which is intended for those awkward occasions when gender is irrelevant. Thus, the [U.K.] Equal Opportunities Commission turgidly suggests the use of the word 'mainpower' for manpower and 'main-made' for man-made." (*Glasgow Herald* c.1980)

MAIN ENEMY

Patriarchy – which historically enables men to enjoy material benefits from the subordination of women and is the most longstanding and primary form of oppression. Title of essay by Christine Delphy (1977, in Delphy 1984).

MAINSTREAM

How you define it depends on which river you're talking about. For example: "The notion that black culture is some kind of backwater or tributary of an American 'mainstream' is well established in much popular as well as standard social science literature. To the prudent black American masses, however, core black culture *is* the mainstream." (John Langston Gwaltney 1980, xxiii)

MAINSTREAMING

Integrates women's studies material into traditional curricula; also called transforming, revising, reconstructing, expanding, and balancing the curriculum.

"Problems with the word: it implies women have been outside of the Main Stream; it suggests that feminist scholarship is a tributary which, having entered the Main Stream, will go with the flow; it sounds like a quick fix; it suggests only one Main Stream rather than many streams of feminist scholarship and expression." (Peggy McIntosh 1983, 29-30)

MAJORITY

The majority of people do not question the conditions of their lives. "They come into the world, and they accept the world as they found it, dirt and all. They pass a life comfortable or uncomfortable, and they leave the world as they found it." (Mrs Cavendish Bentink 1911, *Votes for Women* December 15, 177)

MAKE-UP

A mask, used primarily by women, which can be an aid for performances of various kinds, even for appearing a conventional woman. (*Banshee: Journal of Irishwomen United* c.1980, 1:2, 14) Method of changing appearance. "Make-up may not have identical meanings in different cultures." For example, it may be used to challenge notions of pure and natural womanhood. (Jayne Egerton 1983, 30)

MAKE WAR NOT LOVE

MAKE LOVE NOT WAR was the U.S. antiwar slogan of the 1960s; drawn from the writings of Wilhelm Reich, it evoked the so-called sexual revolution. In reaction, MAKE WAR NOT LOVE was created in the late 1960s by The Feminists, an early radical feminist group based in New York City. (*off our backs* 1984, July, 13)

MAKE WAR ON

An Igbo term "derived from the pidgin English expression 'making war,' an institutionalized form of punishment employed by Igbo women and also known as 'sitting on a man.' To 'sit on' or 'make war on' a man involved gathering at his compound at a previously agreed-upon time, dancing, singing scurrilous songs detailing the women's grievances against him (and often insulting him along the way by calling his manhood into question), banging on his hut with the pestles used for pounding yams, and, in extreme cases, tearing up his hut. . . . This might be done to a man who particularly mistreated his wife, who violated the women's market rules, or who persistently let his cows eat the women's crops. The women would stay at his hut all night and day, if necessary, until he repented and promised to mend his ways." (Judith Van Allen 1976, 61-2)

MALAPROPISM

A form of linguistic creativity which has come to be regarded as the ludicrous misuse of a word, especially in mistake for one resembling it. It was the habit of Mrs Malaprop, a character in Sheridan's play *The Rivals* (originally acted at Covent Garden Theatre in London in 1775), to

deliver such error with great dignity: "Don't attempt to extirpate yourself from the matter" – "I would by no means wish a daughter of mine to be a progeny of learning" – "He is the very pineapple of politeness" – "She's as headstrong as an allegory on the banks of the Nile." (Cecil Hunt 1949, 102)

MALE

Adjective referring to the male in contrast to the female sex. Often includes the notion of a biological category; overlaps with *masculine* which emphasizes social and cultural characteristics. But like masculinity, is also a constructed, not a "natural," category: "A social and political concept, not a biological attribute." (Catharine MacKinnon 1983a, 636)

(See FEMALE, MAN, SEX/GENDER SYSTEMS)

As a word, has been explicitly or implicitly used to bar women from many areas of activity; women have consequently campaigned against it. "To get the word 'male' in effect out of the Constitution cost the women of the country fifty-two years of pauseless campaign. . . . During that time they were forced to conduct fifty-six campaigns of referenda to male voters; 480 campaigns to get Legislatures to submit suffrage amendments to voters; 47 campaigns to get State constitutional conventions to write woman suffrage into state constitutions; 277 campaigns to get State party conventions to include woman suffrage planks; 30 campaigns to get presidential party conventions to adopt woman suffrage planks in party platforms, and 19 campaigns with 19 successive Congresses." (Carrie Chapman Catt 1923; cited in Eleanor Flexner 1968, 173)

Represents a variant of or deviation from the category of female. "The first males were mutants, freaks produced by some damage to the genes caused perhaps by disease or a radiation bombardment from the sun. Maleness remains a recessive genetic trait like color-blindness and hemophilia with which it is linked. The suspicion that maleness is abnormal and that the Y chromosome is an accidental mutation boding no good for the race is strongly supported by the recent discovery by geneticists that congenital killers and criminals are possessed of not one but *two* Y chromosomes, bearing a double dose, as it were, of genetically undesirable maleness. If the Y chromosome is a degeneration and a deformity of the female X chromosome, then the male sex represents a degeneration and deformity of the female." (Elizabeth Gould Davis 1971, 35)

M.A.L.E.

Acronym for Men Against Linguistic Equality, "the English-speaking branch of an international secret brotherhood known to have existed since the third millennium B.C. Founded in Sumeria to combat the influence of the world's first poet, Enheduanna, who through her writing established the cultic primacy of the female deity Inanna, the organization is still dedicated to the belief, according to one member, 'that women should be seen and not heard.' . . . The 1966 plenary session of MALE, held at the Bohemian Grove, near Monte Rio, California, was the first meeting to receive publicity, a consequence, it is believed, of internal dissent over how to defuse the feminist countermovement which works openly in political, educational, and corporate spheres to expose MALE's previously concealed influence on the language. Stung by the growing acceptance of the social title Ms. and of changes in political and occupational nomenclature, as well as by 'nonsexist guidelines' issued by several major American publishing houses, a number of men believed to hold important leadership positions in MALE have adopted the tactic of open counter-attack through ridicule. The majority of members, however, are said to support the organization's traditional strategy of working behind the scenes to influence grammarians, usage experts, teachers, and others who mold the thinking of children. This so-called 'Schoolmasters' approach relies on the early inculcation of language habits, presumably in the belief

that once indoctrinated, future leaders in the arts, sciences, education, government, and industry will continue to employ language habits that work to exclude or downgrade women through subsuming and belittling terminology." (Casey Miller and Kate Swift 1976, 84-5)

(See LINGUISTIC SEXISM, PRESCRIPTIVISM)

MALE CHAUVINISM

Widely-used term especially in the U.S. women's movement c.1967-72 to designate actions, attitudes, language, policies, etc. that appear to reflect a belief in the inherent superiority of males over females. The term was "first used in the 1960s by women active in civil rights organizations and the Student Left who objected to the demeaning roles to which they were relegated by males in the movement." (Casey Miller and Kate Swift 1976, 141). But Harry Brod points to an earlier use: "In 1952, Herbert A. Philbrick published *I Led 3 Lives* (New York: Grosset & Dunlap), an account of his activities as an FBI infiltrator into the U.S. Communist Party from 1940-9. (Readers may form their own conclusion about the feminist consciousness of the book from the Dedication: 'To Eva, My Wife, Who proved that a woman can keep a secret.' The text reveals, however, that he did not entrust his secret to her.) The book's glossary of Communist Terms includes an entry for

'*White Chauvinism*: the private Communist expression for racial prejudice against the Negroes. The Communists have other uses, or misuses, of the word chauvinism; a man who tends to relegate women to a secondary role is a "male chauvinist." '

"This debt to the earlier left may have been unknown, or it may have been intentionally unacknowledged in the nascent women's movement for fear of provoking red-baiting tactics." (Harry Brod 1984, correspondence)

MALE CHAUVINIST CHAMELEON

Is "the proper term for someone who shuttles between bigotry and liberality, according to the situation." (Suzanne L. Clouthier; cited in Gloria Kaufman and Mary Kay Blakely 1980, 185)

MALE CHAUVINIST PIG

Not kosher. Widely-used term in early U.S. women's liberation movement; aka MCP. "A hybrid produced by trying to combine feminism with leftist rhetoric, which was often antifeminist in itself; in this case, a willingness to reduce adversaries to something less than human as a first step toward justifying violence against them. (Years of being *chicks*, *dogs*, and *cows* may have led to some understandable desire to turn the tables, but it also taught us what dehumanization feels like.) Police had been pigs in the sixties – as in 'Off the Pigs!' – so all prejudiced men became the same for a while; a period that has mercifully passed." (Gloria Steinem 1983, 158)

MALE DOMINANCE

(See MALE SUPREMACY)

MALE GENITALIA

(See PENIS)

MALE MIND

"Assumed to function primarily like a penis. Its fundamental character is seen to be aggression, and this quality is held essential [by men] to the highest or best working of the intellect." (Mary Ellmann 1968, 23)

MALENESS

Is implicitly equated with humanness in our language, which has led to legal, social, and psychological exclusion of women. (Wendy Martyna 1983, 32-3)
  (See LINGUISTIC SEXISM, MALE, M.A.L.E., MAN AS FALSE GENERIC)

MALE POINT OF VIEW

"Unfortunately, for all of us, man has always been the dictating force in determining what our female nature is really all about regardless of whether or not his impressions are true. His only criterion being that his definition of us be relevant to him and 'his world.'" (Adelaida R. Del Castillo 1978, 144)

MALE-RIDDEN

Adjective; synonym is *androcentric*. Both words were used by Charlotte Perkins Gilman who wrote that male-ridden minds believe that the freedoms women want are masculine things; in actuality, they are human things hitherto monopolized by men. (Charlotte Perkins Gilman 1912; cited in Ronald W. Hogeland and Aileen S. Kraditor 1973, 134)

MALESTREAM

Feminist designation (coined by Mary Daly) for that body of thought perceived and judged *by (white educated) males* to constitute the "mainstream."
  (See MAINSTREAM)

MALE SUPREMACY

Generic term meaning the doctrine – explicit or implicit set of beliefs, rules, and practices – that males are inherently superior to females and are justified in having power over them; designates the institutional, systemic power men have as a group over women which excludes women from power and devalues the roles and characteristics society assigns them. "Like other political creeds, does not finally reside in physical strength, but in the acceptance of a value system which is not biological." (Kate Millett 1971, 48) Is "perhaps the most pervasive and tenacious system of power in history." (Catharine A. MacKinnon 1983a, 638) "Stems from a bodily conformation which assigns to every human being an inescapable role, duty, and place in the world." (Elizabeth Janeway 1980, 8)

MALFUNCTION

Male-function. (Mary Daly 1978, 30)

MALINCHE, LA

The "Mexican Eve," Malintzen (or La Malinche) was an Aztec noble woman who was presented to Cortes when he landed in Veracruz in 1519 and became known in history as "the one who betrayed the country, the one who opened up the country to foreign invaders." (Marcella Trujillo 1979, 8) She was "translator and strategic advisor and mistress to the Spanish conqueror of Mexico"; in Mexican culture, "she is now slandered as La Chingada, meaning the 'fucked one,' or La Vendida, sell out to the white race." (Cherríe Moraga 1983, 99) She "became the maligned symbol of her country's fall to the Spanish, in spite of evidence that she tried to lessen the negative impact of colonization on her people." (Rayna Green ed. 1984, 312) "The myth of Malinche contains the following sexual possibilities woman is sexually passive, and hence at all times open to potential use by men whether it be seduction or rape. The possible use is double-edged: that is, the use of her as pawn may be intra-cultural – 'amongst us guys' or intercultural, which means if we are not using her then 'they' must be using her." (Norma Alarcón 1981: cited in Cherríe Moraga 1983, 113-14) Chicana feminists have researched and reinterpreted the myth of La Malinche. Sylvia Gonzales, for example, redefines her as "the feminine messiah who must return to redeem her forsaken daughters, born out of the violence of the Spanish and Aztec religions and cultures." (Marcella Trujillo 1979, 8)

(See VENDIDA)

MALISM

Malism is the opposite of feminism; malist society is the opposite of feminist society. "In Judaic-Christian malism we can see how the male sex first claims that men give man birth and then that man gives womon birth." (Mia Albright 1980, 52c)

MAMA-LOSHEN

Yiddish; literally mother language, mother's tongue (from *mama* + Hebrew *loshn* 'tongue'). Hebrew was the father's language, since the holy books were in Hebrew and only Jewish males were taught to read. Yiddish thus became known as the mother's tongue, the language of the home. "Can I talk *mama-loshen*? means "Will you understand if I speak Yiddish?" To say "Let's talk *mama-loshen*" means "Let's cut out the double-talk and get to the heart of the matter." (Leo Rosten 1968, 222-3)

(See YIDDISH)

MAMMY

A figure for Black women that is both stereotypical and mythical.

(See MATRIARCHY, RECLAMATION)

The myth: "Sapphire. Mammy. Tragic mulatto wench. Workhorse, can swing an ax, lift a load, pick cotton with any man. A wonderful housekeeper. Excellent with children. Very clean. Very religious. A terrific mother. A great little singer and dancer and a devoted teacher and social worker. She's always had more opportunities than the black man because she was no threat to the white man so he made it easy for her. But curiously enough, she frequently ends up on welfare. Nevertheless, she is more educated and makes more money than the black man. She is more likely to be employed and more likely to be a professional than the black man. And subsequently she provides the main support of the family. Not beautiful, rather hard looking unless she has white blood, but then *very* beautiful. The black ones are exotic though, great in bed, tigers. And very fertile. If she is middle class she tends to be uptight about sex, prudish. She is hard on and unsupportive of black men, domineering, castrating. She tends to wear the pants around her house. Very strong. Sorrow rolls right off her brow like so much rain. Tough, unfeminine. Opposed to women's rights movements, considers herself already liberated. Nevertheless, unworldly. Definitely not a dreamer, rigid, inflexibile, uncompassionate, lacking in goals any more imaginative than a basket of fried chicken and a good fuck." (Michele Wallace 1978, 106)

"She expresses an attitude of the white mind which is at once ludicrous, tragic, and fraught with future peril. . . . She deserves a funeral, bless her; and she certainly needs one – a competent, permanent funeral that will not have to be done over again every few days. Her removal will clear the atmosphere and enable us to see the old soul's granddaughters, to whom we must in justice pay something of the debt we so freely acknowledge to her." (L. H. Hammond 1917, 31, 32)

The artist Bettye Saar "understands the power of dolls and in fact has been collecting commercial (and derogatory) images of black women for some time, the better to use them in her own affirmative doll-house-type box constructions. . . ." Her work *The Liberation of Aunt Jemima* transforms the grinning image of a "mammy" doll into an aggressive warrior for black liberation. "The real Aunt Jemima will be free." (Karen Petersen and J. J. Wilson 1976, 142)

MAN

Adult male human being. Also (usually without *a* or *the*) may mean men as a group or class, the male sex. The definitions that follow challenge or subvert the ways the word is often used in traditional dictionaries and male writing.

> (See MALE, MALE CHAUVINISM, MALE SUPREMACY, MEN, MAN AS FALSE GENERIC, PATRIARCHY)

Originally in the prehistoric world dominated by the reptile and the dinosaur, man was an anomaly – a "two-legged, apposite-thumbed monster," "an alternative of suspicious origin." (Ruth Herschberger 1948, 3) Today he is an obsolete life form: "Like the tyrannosaurus, man is blocking evolution and sustaining his life at the expense of other better life forms." (Betsy Warrior 1969b) "Member of extinct species of the third planet which he did so befoul with his own wastes that he perished." (Gina 1970, *It Ain't Me, Babe*, May 21-June 10, 5)

"That sex which seems to pique itself with no other degree of equity, than that of never praising any of ours beyond their desert." Also "one whom no sacred ties can bind to the observation of just treaties, and whom no blood-shed can deter from the most cruential violence and rapin." (Sophia 1739, 47, 51) An individual who benefits from the subjugation of women. (Eileen Fairweather 1979, 28)

That sex that "has ever found its chief interest in war and commerce." (Lady McLaren 1908, 39) A sportsman who wants to hunt, seek, chase, and catch what he wants. (Charlotte Perkins Gilman 1911, 122)

"The Romancer" who speaks for women, clothing them with his words. (Beatrice Forbes-Robertson Hale 1914; quoted in Cheris Kramarae 1981, 44) "A person who is convinced that woman is a form of animated doll whereof the mechanism, when pressed on the right spot, squeaks out the two ejaculations of, 'I love you,' and 'Oh, my dear baby'." (Cicely Hamilton 1909, 113)

A contradictory baby-man.

> "why this baby, this boy, this baby man
> he's just a mass of contradictions
> claims reason for himself
> institutionalizes his hatred
> gives her his seat on the bus
> wages war on Indochina
> and nods off in front of the TV
> and dreams of mommy
> and dreams of power
> This baby will not grow up
> he thinks he can do what he wants
> he has fastened his mouth on my life"
> (Sondra Segal 1981, 9)

An ordinary creature who needs to be watched. "If he is left quite alone, he fancies he is alone." (Mrs Millicent Fawcett 1905)

"A one-eyed monster; he sees just what he wants to see." (R. L. Hine, "Confessions of An Uncommon Attorney," quoted in Teresa Billington-Greig c.1949-1960)

MAN AS FALSE GENERIC

Convention in English of using the word *man* to refer "generically" to people, both men and women. Though custom and convention are used to defend this and related usages, sound arguments based on research demonstrate that the claims of generic meaning are false: these words do not include everyone equally. "The use of *man* to refer to people in general or *he* to refer to sex-indefinite antecedents is a paramount example of the invisibility of women in language. Many grammarians and linguists claim that this form is innocuous in its omission of women and girls and that it includes the female in its meaning. However, there is ample research evidence that the masculine 'generic' does not really function as a generic." (Barrie Thorne, Cheris Kramarae, and Nancy Henley eds 1983, 10.) English has evolved historically as the result of both planned and unplanned language change. "Generic man" and the third person masculine pronoun *he* were legislated changes which have never been fully adopted in actual usage; it now seems time to acknowledge the failure and obsolescence of these forms and endorse inclusive alternatives. Some feminist comments follow.

(See FALSE GENERICS, HE/MAN APPROACH, LINGUISTIC SEXISM, M.A.L.E., MANGLISH, MARKEDNESS, NONSEXIST LANGUAGE, PRONOUNS)

Protest against false male generics is not new. "Arab women preceded the women of the world in resisting the patriarchal system based on male domination. Fourteen centuries ago, Arab women succeeded in opposing the unilateral use of the male gender in the Koran when its passages referred to both men and women. Their outspoken objection was couched in terms that have remained famous: 'We have proclaimed our belief in Islam, and done as you have done. How is it then that you men should be mentioned in the Koran while we are ignored!' At the time both men and women were referred to as Moslems, but, in response to the objections voiced by women, Allah henceforward said in the Koran: 'Al Mouslimeena Wal Mouslimat, wal Mou'mineena wal Mou'minat.' ('The Muslims, men and women, and the believers, men and women.')" (Nawal el Saadawi 1982, 212)

The history of the occurrence of the words *man* and *woman* in British legal documents reveals that nineteenth-century lawyers have determined the rules for how these terms are used. "The word *man* always includes *woman* when there is a penalty to be incurred, it never includes *women* when there is a privilege to be conferred." This was not the case in earlier centuries. (Charlotte Carmichael Stopes 1908, 5)

"*Man* in Manglish is used both specifically and generally. When obligations are meant such as taxation, women are included and considered equal; when rights are meant such as suffrage, they are excluded and must fight for each one. Imagine how convenient it would have been for racists to have a word that meant both white and white and black." (Varda One 1971, *Everywoman*, March 26, 6)

Pseudogeneric usage is (1) based on "an absurd assumption still accepted by some that both sexes are included when the word 'man' is used; (2) a misstatement of fact; (3) an egotistical male distortion, legitimized in the language, that 'man' could/should represent both sexes; (4) a false hope." (Midge Lennert and Norma Willson, eds, 1973, 7)

"The word 'man' has been making confusion in many respects for more than a thousand years. It was certainly used in the Anglo-Saxon language as early as 825 A.D. to mean specifically the human creature in general; but about the same time it was also used to mean an adult male person; while contemporaneously the word 'woman' was in use as meaning an adult female human being. And persons who have occasion to study Anglo-Saxon laws and literature, if they care anything at all about exactness, have to be constantly on guard as to whether 'man' means a human creature in general or an adult male. Of course if precision is no consideration, then the translation of the word *man* or *mann* from Anglo-Saxon into English may simply run riot at the will and pleasure of its repeater. . . So many uncertainties appeared in the administration of the law in England, as citizens, judges, and administrators wrestled with the terms *man* and *men* that Parliament tried in 1850 to clear some of them away by legislation. A law known as Lord Romilly's or Lord Brougham's Act provided that 'words importing the masculine gender shall always include women, except where otherwise stated.' England, respecting the use of the word *man* in statues and judicial decisions. . . . This problem of clarity of thought, or the lack of it, looms large in hundreds of thousands of printed pages where the words *man* and *men* appear in bewildering profusion, as well as in common and formal speech. . . . Freedom of speech allows for large liberties, but speech so free as to be inexact and unintelligible is markedly licentious – and dangerous – when such subjects as human nature, the emotions, education, science, art, democracy, government, society, literary values, history, progress, retrogression, barbarism, and civilization are brought under a discussion intended to be serious and informed." (Mary Ritter Beard 1946; in Ann J. Lane ed. 1977, 175-6)

"In Old English the word *man* meant 'person' or 'human being,' and when used of an individual was equally applicable to either sex. It was parallel to the Latin *homo*, 'a member of the human species,' not *vir*, 'an adult male of the species.' English at the time of Ercongota had separate words to distinguish the sexes: *wer* (equivalent to the Latin *vir*) meant 'adult male,' and *wif* meant 'adult female.' The combined forms *waepman* and *wifman* meant, respectively, 'adult male person' and 'adult female person.' In the course of time *wifman* evolved into the modern word *woman*, and *wif* narrowed in meaning to become *wife* as we use that word today. *Man* eventually ceased to be used of individual women and replaced *wer* and *waepman* as a specific term distinguishing an adult male from an adult female. But *man* continued to be used in generalizations about both sexes. As long as most generalizations about people were made

by men about men, the ambiguity nestling in this dual usage was either not noticed or thought not to matter." (Casey Miller and Kate Swift 1980, 9-10)

(See MANGLISH)

"In English the once truly generic word man has come to mean male, so that males are seen as representing the species in a way females are not. Humanity, divided against itself, becomes the norm and the deviation, the namer and the named." (Casey Miller and Kate Swift 1976, 17)

"One difficulty about using 'men' as a generic term for 'human' is that when it's applied to social circumstances it has the effect of making male experience appear to be the norm. Thus it blurs women's experience when it doesn't happen to match that of men." (Elizabeth Janeway 1980, 210)

"If a woman is swept off a ship into the water, the cry is 'Man overboard!' If she is killed by a hit-and-run driver, the charge is 'manslaughter.' If she is injured on the job, the coverage is 'workmen's compensation.' But if she arrives at a threshold marked 'Men Only,' she knows the admonition is not intended to bar animals or plants or inanimate objects. It is meant for her." (Alma Graham 1973, 16)

"Is one of the most overworked words in the English language." (Women in Publishing Industry Group c.1980)

MAN, FEMINIST

"A man who has humour and sympathy is generally a feminist *sans le savoir*." ("The Maze of the Law," 1914, *The Englishwoman* 25:73, 65)

"Any man who is your comrade will know in his gut the indignity, the demeaning indignity, of systematic exclusion from the rights and responsibilities of citizenship. Any man who is your true comrade will be committed to laying his body, his life, on the line so that you will be subjected to that indignity no longer. I ask you to look to your comrades on the left, and to determine whether they have made the commitment to you. If they have not, then they do not take your lives seriously, and as long as you work for and with them, you do not take your lives seriously either." (Andrea Dworkin 1976, 69)

-MAN IN COMPOUNDS

One focus of feminist language reform has been the form -*man* in such combined words as *chairman*, *policeman*, and *congressman*. Though it is sometimes argued that reform is unnecessary because the final syllable -*man*, typically unstressed in English, is really only a suffix and distinct from the stressed syllable of the noun *man*, proposals for change have been relatively successful and widespread. Many states in the U.S. as well as the federal government have officially established job titles unmarked for gender (thus *police officer*, *Congressional representative*, *Congressperson*, *firefighter*, etc.). Comparable movements for reform exist in many other countries.

(See GENERIC ASSUMPTION, MAN AS FALSE GENERIC, NON-SEXIST GUIDELINES, NON-SEXIST LANGUAGE)

According to Connecticut law, whenever the title of a public office denotes gender, the title shifts to suit the sex of the person holding the office. State Senator Betty Hudson, sponsor of the law, argues that an office holder's sex is irrelevant to the performance of the job, but where such titles exist, they should suit the office holder. "To call a woman a 'man' is not only unfair to the woman involved, but also denies to all women the recognition and regard which accrue from the achievements of members of their sex and attributes those achievements to the male sex." (Betty Hudson, quoted in Casey Miller and Kate Swift 1980, 128)

The term *chairperson* remains symbolic of disagreements over linguistic – and social – reform. For example, when the term *chairperson* was used in a university English department faculty meeting in the mid-1970s, an elderly male faculty member sitting at the back of the room set up a continuous mutter which lasted through the remainder of the meeting: "Chair-

person . . . chairperson . . . women's lib . . . women's lib . . . hate it . . . hate it . . . chairperson . . . women's lib . . . hate it. . . ." (Reported by Cary Nelson 1975) Some speakers use *chair* to avoid the sometimes politically-sensitive choice between *chairman* and *chairperson*. It's also been observed that *chairperson* is often used only to designate a woman chair (and sometimes only when she is a feminist).

MANA

"*Mana*, bread, was 'The food of the mother' in the old phraseology, the giver of the Staff of Life." (Frances Swiney 1918, 54) "Nearly all languages had a cognate of this word, the basic meaning of which was maternal power, moon-spirit, magic, supernatural force, and a title of the Goddess." It came back into English via anthropological studies in the South Pacific, which described it as the sacred stuff through which magic works. (Barbara G. Walker 1983, 575)

MAN AND WIFE

"A cliché which suggests that a man's identity remains intact when he marries while the woman's is redefined to be a part of him." (Midge Lennert and Norma Willson, eds, 1973, 7) Many guidelines for nonsexist writing recommend parallel usage: man and woman, husband and wife.

MANGLISH

The English language as it is used by men in perpetuation of male supremacy. Term coined by Varda One in the early 1970s, as the name of her column on language for the feminist publication *Everywoman*. Words like *manglish* (see HERSTORY) are "reality-violators" and "consciousness-raisers" which function "to make us realize that language is the basis of our thought and that our thought patterns are steeped in sexism-racism, class snobbery, adult chauvinism, and other lousy values." (Varda One 1970, *Everywoman*, October 23) Another Sample: "Woman means that which was taken out of man. (Yes, I know WOMEN give birth to MEN but in

Manglish everything is bassakwards.)"
(Varda One 1970, *Everywoman* June 19, 2)

MAN-HATING

"(1) A refusal to suppress the evidence of one's experience with men; (2) A woman's defense against fear and pain; (3) An affirmation of the cathartic effects of justifiable anger." (Ingrid Bengis; cited by Midge Lennert and Norma Willson, eds, 1973, 7) "Not a life philosophy built on destructiveness but the only healthy direct reaction to the patriarchal establishment." (*off our backs* 8, July 1974) "The program which is called 'Misogyny' has been criticized as 'Man-Hating.' " It seems interesting and worth exploring that a program on the woman-hating behavior of men becomes a program on man-hating in the minds of some women." (Marilyn Murphy 1983, 146)
  (See MISANDRY)

MANIC

"Of or like a man ('the profession of psychiatry is really manic')." (zana 1983, correspondence)

MANIC DEPRESSION

"Depression caused by having to live in a manic world." (zana 1983, correspondence)
  (See MANIC)

MAN JUNKY

"In order to make sure that we will see ourselves as half-people, with an addiction to getting our identity from serving others, society tries hard to convert us as young women into 'man junkies'; that is, into people who need regular shots of male-approval and presence, both professionally and personally." (Gloria Steinem 1979, 66)

MANKIND

Manglish for HUMANITY, PEOPLE, PERSONS, HUMANKIND, WOMEN AND MEN, EVERYONE, FOLK, OUR ANCESTORS, UPPERCLASS BRITISH GENTLEMEN, and so on. Usually means nonfemale and nonblack. A small group compared to humankind.

MAN-MADE

Generic label for the customs, practices, language, institutions, and ideals of patriarchal culture. (Charlotte Perkins Gilman 1911; Dale Spender 1980)

MANNISH

Adjective applied to women who appear to be usurping work and behavior claimed by men as theirs. Dr Anna Manning Comfort, an 1865 medical school graduate, writes, "As a physician there was nothing that I could do that satisfied people. If I wore square-toed shoes and swung my arms they said I was mannish, and if I carried a parasol and wore a ribbon in my hair they said I was too feminine. If I smiled they said I had too much levity, and if I sighed they said I had no sand." (Anna Manning Comfort 1916; quoted in the *New York Times*, April 9)

MAN IN THE STREET

"Is a term that is altogether too narrow. Why should it not be 'the man and woman in the street'? This may seem a trivial objection; but it touches a condition which is both important and historic, and, one might add, far too habitual and thoughtless." (James Haslam 1912, 135)

MARGINALIA

Productions on and from the margins, literal or metaphorical. "The authorship [of the Bayeux Tapestry] has always been the subject of speculation, but while people have usually assumed that the Bayeux designer must have been a man, no one has ever questioned that the incredible task of embroidering all of this huge vision on the toile was executed by the skillful needles of women workers. To whom then goes the credit or blame for the graphically portrayed nudes in the border? Were these the spontaneous contributions of a group of women bent over their embroidery frames and bent on mischief, or part of the official design?

What was the conversation in the workshop that day? There is no telling what kinds of doodles women might make in the margins of male history when given access to tools of expression." (Karen Petersen and J. J. Wilson 1976, 18)

MARGINALITY

"Opens the possibility of seeing structures of the dominant culture which are invisible from within it." "One of the privileges of being normal and ordinary is a certain unconsciousness. . . . If one is the norm, one does not have to know what one is. If one is marginal, one does not have the privilege of not noticing what one is. . . . This absence of privilege is a presence of knowledge. As such, it can be a great resource." (Marilyn Frye 1983, 148, 147)

MARIANISM

Worship of Mary, mother of Christ; particularly in Roman Catholic countries, some women feel this sets an impossible standard for all females. (Sheila Ruth 1980)
(See MARIANISMO)

MARIANISMO

The flip side of *machismo* (the cult of virility). "*Marianismo* is just as prevalent as *machismo* but it is less understood by Latin Americans themselves and almost unknown to foreigners. It is the cult of feminine spiritual superiority, which teaches that women are semi-divine, morally superior to and spiritually stronger than men . . . [Its] roots are both deep and widespread, springing apparently from primitive awe at women's ability to produce a live creature from inside her own body . . . Far from being an oppressive norm dictated by tyrannical males, *marianismo* has received considerable impetus from women themselves. This fact makes it possible to regard *marianismo* as part of a reciprocal arrangement, the other half of which is *machismo*." (Evelyn P. Stevens 1973, 91, 92, 99)
(See MACHO, MACHISMO, MARIANISM)

MARILYN MONROE

An American icon whose life and death seem to some to represent a feminine tragedy. "In her public image Marilyn is everything we're told we want to be; in her private life she's everything we fear we probably are." (Margaret Walters 1972; quoted in Marsha Rowe ed. 1982, 31)

MARITAL RAPE

Marital rape, or wife rape, remains a legal impossibility in many states of the U.S. "If you can't rape your wife," asked a California state senator, "Who can you rape?" It is estimated that 400,000 battered wives each year in the U.S. are forced by their husbands to have sex as part of a beating or as a sequel to it; if rape by intimidation (the threat of violence) is added, the figure would be more than a million. The California Marital Rape bill, which became law in 1980, altered the existing rape code to include sexual intercourse with one's spouse if accomplished under force or violence or threat of great and immediate bodily harm. (National Clearinghouse on Marital Rape brochure 1984, Women's History Research Center, Berkeley, California) Related to domestic violence; "rape with a domestic object." Also "sexual harassment on the job." (Laura X 1984, corespondence; and 1982, AEGIS, Summer, 36)

MARKEDNESS

Refers to differences between pairs of words that are formally "marked," for example by the different suffixes in *medico* 'male doctor' and *medica* 'female doctor' in Spanish. Often this marking is asymmetrical, with one member of the pair considered neutral, general, "the norm," – the unmarked term – and the marked member considered the "deviation." In many languages, the male term is considered unmarked, the female marked. Alma Graham spelled out the consequences of this asymmetry: "If you have a group half of whose members are A's and half of whose members are B's and if you call the group C, then A's and B's may be equal members of group C. But if you call the group A, there is no way that B's can be equal to A's within it. The A's will always be the rule and the B's will always be the exception – the subgroup, the subspecies, the outsiders." (Alma Graham 1974, Letter to the Editor, *The Columbia Forum*, Fall)

"Any pair of concepts, like masculine/feminine or male/female, that signifies sex-gender automatically constitutes a distinction of 'markedness'. . . . The unmarked is assumed to be desirable, expected, familiar, while the marked is considered undesirable, unexpected, unfamiliar. The unmarked form is usually shorter and therefore easier to say than the marked; for example, 'male' is shorter than 'female,' and 'man' is shorter than 'woman.' If a person crosses the sex-gender line in occupational roles, the unexpected situation must be 'marked' by an additional signifier. Marking may be carried out by suffixes like the '-ess' in 'poetess' or by qualifiers such as those in the expressions 'woman doctor' and 'male secretary.' It is the trace of this all too ubiquitous masculine 'presence' that must be erased." (Namascar Shaktini 1982, 32)

MARKS

"My husband gives me an A
for last night's supper,
an incomplete for my ironing,
a B plus in bed.
My Son says I am average,
an average mother, but if
I put my mind to it
I could improve.
My daughter believes
in Pass/Fail and tells me
I pass. Wait 'til they learn
I'm dropping out."
  (Linda Pastan 1978, "Marks," 19)

MARRIAGE

As defined (in interviews) by many mid-American marrieds, it means a lasting relationship in which another person helps meet needs, including those for "sex, love, companionship, shared experience, being comfortable with someone, being important to someone, trust, approval, moral support, help, emotional security, cooperation in attaining a common goal, closeness, affection, touching, feedback, understanding, feeling like a part of something, the need to do for others, the need for personal growth."
"There are frequent metaphors of marital difficulty as crisis, trial, struggle, trauma, problem, perilous journey over a rocky road." (Naomi Quinn 1984) Much feminist writing about marriage draws upon similar notions but also emphasizes marriage as an institution existing within patriarchy and serving men's interests more than women's. Within this system, individuals who strive for equality in the marriage union are constrained by larger social, political, and economic realities. Feminists have defined marriage in several ways, including (but not limited to): (1) as a woman's trade, (2) as a system of economic exchange, (3) as a system of legalized rape and/or prostitution, (4) as a union to be entered into for countless practical, economic, spiritual, legal, political, emotional, or other reasons, not necessarily between a man and a woman, with many possibilities for form and structure, (5) as the material appropriation of women by men, (6) as a social contract between individuals who have some freedom to determine its terms, (7) as slavery and servitude, (8) as freedom and escape from family, community, or class, (9) as a power struggle between two differently-sexed individuals whose power is unequal and whose conduct is judged differentially, (10) as a mutual negotiation of rights, needs, joys, and responsibilities, (11) as a trap which promotes both security and disability, and (12) as no longer required of women for economic support or social approval. Some illustrations of these meanings follow.
  (See FAMILY, LOVE, MARITAL RAPE, MATRIMONY, PATRIARCHY)
  (1) "Has always been not only a trade, but [for a woman] a trade that is

practically compulsory." "Woman's only trade." (Cicely Hamilton 1909, 28, 105)

"Both for the young women and their mothers, the potential occurrence that loomed largest on the horizon. . . . Almost every girl left school with only two ambitions – to return at the first possible moment to impress her school-fellows with the glory of a grown-up *toilette*, and to get engaged before everybody else." (Vera Brittain 1933, 33-4)

"Is woman's profession: and to this life her training – *that of dependence* – is modelled. Of course, by not getting a husband, or losing him, she may find that she is without resources. All that can be said of her is, she has failed in business and no social reform can prevent such failures." (*The Saturday Review* 1857; quoted in Evelyn Acworth 1965 and Eileen M. Byrne 1978, 56)

Was "a woman's vocation. She had only two choices: be an old maid or be a married woman. For a woman, spinsterhood was failure. . . . An old maid was a failure in the same way that hobos and bums were failures: she was unemployed. Housekeeping, having babies, taking care of a man – all this was her profession: a profession she couldn't practice without a partner. And if no one wanted her for a partner, she was jobless." (Jessamyn West 1979, 200)

(2) An exchange on the part of the woman "of her person for the means of subsistence." (Cicely Hamilton 1909, 36)

"A trade. . . . Girls are brought up with a view of getting a job in it." (H. M. Swanwick 1927, *Time and Tide*, November 18, 1930)

"It is clear that the sole business which legislation has with marriage is with the arrangement of property; to guard the reciprocal rights of the children of the marriage and the community." (Harriet Martineau 1837; in Alice Rossi ed. 1973, 132)

In a capitalistic system, involves economics, not sentiment. Such marriages seem "worse than prostitution. To call them sacred or moral is a desecration. . . ." (Eleanor Marx Aveling and Edward Aveling 1886)

Was "until a time well within living memory the only creditable occupation for a young lady (no ideals were set up for poor women). . . . Others might be as honest, but they were all of a meaner sort, there was an atmosphere of failure, a brand of the second-best attached to all of them." (W. Lyon Blease 1913a, 200)

A financial alliance in which "each household operates as an economic entity much like a corporation." (Kate Millett 1971, 59)

"Most women are only a husband away from welfare." (Toni Carabillo 1974; in Elaine Partnow 1977, 294)

"Is a labour relationship. . . . The marriage ceremony [has] parallels with the signing of indentures, or even more with the selling of oneself into personal, domestic slavery when one can see no other way to support oneself adequately. . . . Marriage, however, differs from these other labour relations in being shrouded in talk of love, companionship and sharing, and of 'making a life together,' so that the economic aspects of the agreement are more than usually occluded. It is therefore significant that the terms of the marriage contract are never spelled out." (Diane Leonard 1982, 261)

(3) Is "an institution which robs a woman of her individuality and reduces her to the level of a prostitute." (Mrs Flora Macdonald Denison 1914; in Carol Lee Bacchi 1983, 31)

" . . . is prostitution, definitely. Even worse, because you have to cater to his every bloody need." (A prostitute c.1980; in *Wicca* 4, 12-13)

In those cases where young women are encouraged to marry older, rich men, marriage is legal prostitution: "No environment of beauty or sentiment can deprive the fact of its coarseness." (Harriet Martineau 1837; in Alice Rossi ed. 1973, 133)

Legalized sanction for rape. "Marriage laws sanctified rape by reiterating the right of the rapist to ownership of the raped. Marriage laws protected the property rights of the first rapist by designating a second rapist as an adulterer, that is, a thief. Marriage laws also protected the father's ownership of the daughter. Marriage laws guaranteed the father's right to sell a daughter into marriage, to sell her to another man." (Andrea Dworkin 1976, 27)

Legal prostitution: phrase first applied to marriage by Mary Wollstonecraft. (Claire Tomalin 1977, 137)

(4) Marriage is called "tying the knot" because it used to be viewed as a binding of two life-threads by the goddess Aphrodite, or Juno. (Barbara G. Walker 1983, 511)

All-encompassing union. "To me, a sexual relationship cannot be complete unless it is a total relationship of human closeness which begins with the head and involves a mutual drowning in each other's depths. Thus, a complete sexual relationship such as I have described cannot take place either before or after marriage. For it is itself marriage." (Ghadah al-Samman 1970, 396)

"On the West Coast of Africa, the Fon of Dahomey still have twelve different kinds of marriage. One of them is known as 'giving the goat to the buck,' where a woman of independent means marries another woman who then may or may not bear children, all of whom will belong to the blood line of the first woman. Some marriages of this kind are arranged to provide heirs for women of means who wish to remain 'free,' and some are lesbian relationships. Marriages like these occur throughout Africa, in several different places among different peoples." (Audre Lorde 1978, rpt. 1984, 50)

"The home of the bridegroom is the center of activity in a Hopi wedding. When a couple decides to marry, the father of the groom takes over. He furnishes everything – cotton for the weaving and food to feed the [male weavers]. Each household keeps a supply of cotton on hand against the time when a son may marry." (Helen Sekaquaptewa 1980, 31)

In some societies in Africa, woman marriage is practiced; it functions as an avenue for women to exercise social influence and patronage. "Woman marriage is a political and social relationship, not a sexual one. The wife bears children by a male genitor chosen by herself or by her female husband. Although there are several forms of woman marriage. . . . [one] is that in which a woman marries another woman and takes on the status of female husband, head of household founded by the marriage. She becomes the legal and social father of all children born to the wife and has control over the domestic services of the wife. In many of these societies, a female husband can also be married to a man and thus be simultaneously husband and wife." (Karen Sacks 1982, 77-8)

(5) A practice designed to deprive women of their resources in order that men might have more. Men, instead of admitting what they have to gain from marriage, insist that it is an arrangement in women's interest, rather than their own. (Frances Power Cobbe 1868; in Dale Spender 1982)

Is not a union of two souls or a partnership of equals. It is not a highly developed form of relationship but the most degraded. "We are the only animal species in which the female depends on the male for food, the only animal species in which the sex relation is also an economic relation. With us an entire sex lives in a relation of economic dependence on the other sex." (Charlotte Perkins Gilman 1899, 5)

"A bastion of male power." (Caryl Rivers 1977, 40)

"A money-box (to guard possessions) with the male holding the master key." (Eve Merriam 1958; rpt 1964, 223)

"True to their role as symbols of the condition of the weak, women still customarily take their husbands' names when they marry." (Elizabeth Janeway 1980, 83)

"Chief vehicle for the perpetuation of the oppression of women (citing Marlene Dixon); A gift man gives to a woman for which she never forgives him (citing Thomas Szasz)." (Midge Lennert and

Norma Willson, eds, 1973, 7)

Marriage is "the only institutional (contractual) surface of a generalized relationship: the appropriation of one sex class by the other. It . . . concerns the entirety of two classes and not a part of each of them, as the consideration of the marriage contract alone might lead one to believe. . . . It legalizes and confirms a relationship which exists *before* it and *outside* of it: the material appropriation of the class of men − sexage." (Colette Guillaumin 1981, 17-18)

(6) When Lucy Stone and Henry Blackwell were married in 1855, they joined hands and read aloud a statement: "While we acknowledge our mutual affection by publicly assuming the relationship of husband and wife . . . we deem it a duty to declare that this act on our part implies no sanction of, nor promise of, voluntary obedience to such of the present laws of marriage as refuse to recognize the wife as an independent, rational being, while they confer upon the husband an injurious and unnatural superiority." They protested laws giving the husband custody of the wife's person, exclusive control of the children, sole ownership of the wife's property and real estate, absolute right to the product of her work, and giving the widower rights denied the widow. "Finally, [we protest] the whole system by which 'the legal existence of the wife is suspended during marriage' so that, in most States, she neither has a legal part in the choice of her residence, nor can she make a will, nor sue or be sued in her own name, nor inherit property." (Lucy Stone and Henry Blackwell, 1855; in Eleanor Flexner 1968, 64)

(7) "Someone coming from another planet and looking at a marriage contract and the semi-slavery it entails for the woman would think it insane that she should enter into it voluntarily." (Sue Bruley 1976, 64)

"Is slavery." (Nelly Ptaschkina 1918; in Elaine Partnow 1977, 57)

(8) Escape, if only a temporary one. "I left home to marry a man whom no one liked," says a woman character in a novel, "and after I married I didn't like him either." (Margery Allingham 1938, 11)

Means to an end. "I married him to change my name." (Dorothy Parker, quoted in John Keats 1970, 35)

(9) Analogous to the relationship between two tarantulas in a bell jar. "When one of these delightful creatures is placed under a glass with a companion of his own species, a little smaller than himself, he forthwith gobbles him up." (Frances Power Cobbe 1868, 789)

"What seems monstrous when a wife here and there does it to her husband seems simply male − normally, heedlessly male − when a husband as a matter of course does it to his wife." (Dorothy Dinnerstein 1976, 95)

"If our divorce laws were improved, we could at least say that if marriage does nobody much good it does nobody any harm." (Rebecca West 1913, *The Clarion*, January 24)

An "obscene travesty of a dance." (Dorothy Parker 1933, 12)

"A game of chess in which checkmate is the rule." (Ruth Herschberger 1948, 101)

(10) An institution that can be reclaimed. "Many of us who consider ourselves card-carrying feminists also believe in the possibilities of marriage. There is more to marriage, we believe, than its function as a mechanism to preserve male power. Change the politics, adjust that balance of power, many feminists now argue, and marriage will no longer be sexist. In other words, don't bulldoze the institution − rehab it instead." (Caryl Rivers 1977, 40)

(11) "A cage entered with the eyes open." "A short horse and soon curried." (Jessamyn West 1979, 494)

"One of the principal causes of the various disabilities, economic, and otherwise, under which [a woman] labours today." (Cicely Hamilton 1909, 22)

(12) "It is no longer obligatory upon a woman to give herself to one man to save herself from being torn to pieces by the rest." (Jennie June 1891, 540)

" 'How *can* you send your daughter to college, Mrs Brittain!' moaned one lugubrious lady. 'Don't you want her ever to get *married*?' " (Vera Brittain 1933, 73)

MARRIAGE, ARRANGED

Is a conventional social practice in many parts of the world in which marriage is arranged between a man and a woman (sometimes when they are children) by others, usually their parents. "Love" is not usually a priority, but it is a system within which attraction nevertheless eludes control: "Our family allowed some romance, paying adult brides' prices and providing dowries so that their sons and daughters could marry strangers. Marriage promises to turn strangers into friendly relatives – a nation of siblings." (Maxine Hong Kingston 1975, 14) While Asian parents thus decide whom their children will marry, white English girls are said to have "freedom" to "choose" their mates. But " 'choice,' 'arrangement' and 'freedom' are all relative concepts and often it is people's class which determines whom they meet, and whom they marry, more than any romantic or idealistic notions of falling in love with 'Mr Right' who happens to fatefully cross your path. For Asian girls, the amount of choice they have over whom they marry varies a lot from one Asian community to another, and from one Asian family to another. Some parents are more strict than others, just like some white English parents exercise more control over their children than others." (Valerie Amos and Pratibha Parmar 1981, 140-1)

MARRIAGE CEREMONY

At one time, a woman-centered event. During the transition from the pre-Christian to the Christian era, women ignored God in marriage and family matters and appealed to their own goddesses. "The idea that a male priest should preside alone over a marriage ceremony was unthinkable – which is one reason why Christians didn't think of it. For many years, marriage existed in a limbo without a deity to solemnize it . . . which is why marriage remained so long under the jurisdiction of common law." (Barbara G. Walker 1983, 589)

MARRIAGE CONTRACT

Not "quite the same as a Guild contract. The time clause is different." (Margery Allingham 1938, 177)

MARRIAGE CUSTOMS

Among the women of the New York club Heterodoxy, as described in Florence Guy Woolson's spoof on her friend Elsie Clews Parson's anthropological writings: "Marriage customs among the Heterodites are varied. Three types of sex relationships may be observed, practiced by those who call themselves *monotonists*, *varietists*, and *resistants*. Most of the *monotonists* were mated young and by pressure of habit and circumstance have remained mated. The *varietists* have never been ceremonially mated but have preferred a succession of matings. The *resistants* have not mated at all." (Florence Guy Woolson 1919; rpt. Judith Schwartz 1982, 95)

(See HETERODITES)

MARRIED LIFE

"It's too much like being a woman." (Hannah Cullwick, Victorian maidservant; quoted in Liz Stanley ed. 1984, 170)

MARTYRDOM, FEMALE

Involves "that womanly 'virtue' of self-sacrifice." (Kate 1979; quoted in Karen Payne 1983, 246)

MARXISM

Political and economic theories of Karl Marx and others. "Feminism stands in relation to marxism as marxism does to classical political economy: its final conclusion and ultimate critique. Compared with marxism, the place of thought and things in method and reality are reversed in a seizure of power that penetrates subject with object and theory with practice. In a dual motion, feminism turns marxism inside out and on its head." (Catharine A. MacKinnon 1982a, 544)

As a theoretical tool, is sex-blind. (Heidi Hartmann 1979)

Not clearly relevant to feminism, marxism is "a theory in search of a movement. Since it is . . . a theory which is largely incorrect, which was irrelevant to the needs and demands of the movement constituencies of the 'sixties' and is irrelevant to the needs and demands of feminism today, we must question why we are considering it at all." (Naomi Weisstein, Virginia Blaisdell, and Jesse Lemisch 1975, 36)

A more overarching basis for analysis than feminism. "Class oppression is stronger. . . . In my milieu – which is a workers' milieu – I have never known women who had emancipated themselves on the woman question before they had emancipated themselves on the political question." (Arlette Laguiller 1975, 123)

"A political theory which often reduces the world to a series of economic and social relations. There is little language on the Left to talk about illness, death, birth, animal life, the natural world, the place of our planet in the galaxies." (Lucy Goodison 1980, 38)

"Marxism will not liberate women simply because marxists are (generally) not feminists; they are not out to question the patriarchal principle of domination itself; but only some aspects of it." (Azizah al-Hibri 1981, 183)

"Not even Marx is more important to us than the truth." (Simone Weil 1933; in Elaine Partnow, 1977, 147)

A method of analysis which enables us to understand many aspects of capitalism but does not explain "why particular people fill particular places." "The blinkered nature of Marxist categories and the Marxist method of social analysis insist that the only valid analysis of women's oppression is one which is grounded in materialism. Thus we are prevented from asking questions about the enduring nature of patriarchal power. For example, although material bases may change from society to society, male violence against women is constant." (Linda Imray and Audrey Middleton 1983, 14)

MARXIST-FEMINIST

"As Marxist-feminists we straddle an uneasy horse. We have not worked out this means, this hyphen. . . . All too often all this has meant is that we are Marxists to our feminist sisters and feminists to our Marxist brothers. . . . The gravest danger . . . facing us right now is that we will settle for this hyphen, we will settle in with it comfortably as a self-explanation. It will become a counter, a cipher, instead of a project. . . . What intervenes in this relationship of two terms is desire, on every level. Hyphen is wish. We have heard its whisperings." (Mary Bailey; in Rosalind Petchesky 1979, 375)

"Presently class categories are primarily male-defined, and a woman is assigned to a class on the basis of her husband's relation to the means of production; woman is not viewed as an autonomous being . . . a feminist class analysis must begin with distinctions drawn among women in terms of the work they do within the economy as a whole – distinctions among working women outside the home (professional vs. nonprofessional), among houseworkers (houseworkers who do not work outside the home and women who are houseworkers and also work outside), welfare mothers, unemployed women, and wealthy women who do not work at all. These class distinctions need to be further defined in terms of race and marital status." (Zillah Eisenstein 1979b, 31-2)

"The 'marriage' of marxism and feminism has been like the marriage of husband and wife depicted in English common law; marxism and feminism are one, and that one is marxism." (Heidi Hartmann 1979, rpt. 1981, 2)

MARY

Males conceived (of) her, a hollow shell through which "god the father reproduces himself in the world. Jesus is not the son of Mary or of woman, nor is he ever named that way. He is the son of god, the son of man. In other words, he is a totally man-made product, a clone." (Anne G. Dellenbaugh 1982, 60) Men worship

Mary, mother of Jesus, "only because their inner being demands a mother-archetype, and she is the only one presented to them." (Barbara G. Walker 1983, 611) "Is certainly the good girl of Christianity. Absolutely obedient to the male God, she derives all her status from her son. Because of her absolute purity and obedience, she is the only pinup girl who has been permitted in monks' cells throughout the ages." (Naomi Goldenberg 1979, 75)

In the Victorian era, one of the stock names for female servants. (Liz Stanley ed. 1984, 32)

(See MARIANISM, MARIANISMO)

MARY AND MARTHA

Story in the New Testament (Luke 10:39-42) sometimes used to argue for Jesus Christ's feminism or at any rate for his ability to see women outside traditional domestic roles. Mary forsakes her domestic duties to sit at Christ's feet and hear his teaching; her sister Martha remains at home taking care of the house. She protests to Christ: "Lord, dost thou not care that my sister did leave me to serve alone? Bid her therefore that she help me." But Christ replies: "Martha, Martha, thou art anxious and troubled about many things: but one thing is needful: for Mary hath chosen the good part, which shall not be taken away from her."

MASCULINE

"Masculine – a word often appropriated to those qualities which ought to be the mutual possessions of the sexes – courage generosity trust activity magnanimity and other noble qualities. And how much is done in education to render the boy masculine the girl feminine. After years of training to this effect then because there is a difference it is referred to as organic – Yet every thing that is really strengthening elevating enlarging a woman wants a woman needs. Intellect is the same in one envelope that it is in another and its rights and duties are the same." (Harriet Farley 1850)

MASCULINIST

Used as early as 1912: "Mr Edgar takes the usual masculinist standpoint of regarding women as incompetent weaklings except for their maternal functions." (Rebecca West, *Manchester Daily Dispatch*, November 26, 1912) Male supremacist (not a symmetrical concept with feminist). (Mary Anne Warren 1980, 663)

MASCULINITY

"Is not the opposite of femininity. The starting point for understanding masculinity lies . . . in the asymmetrical dominance and prestige which accrue to males in this society. Male dominance takes shape in the positions of formal and informal *power* men hold in the social division of labor; greater male prestige includes, and is evidenced by, the greater *reward* which attaches to male than to female activities, as well as the codification or differential prestige in our language and customs. What our culture embodies, in other words, is not simply two stereotypes – one masculine, one feminine – but a set of power and prestige arrangements attached to gender." (Jack W. Sattel 1983, 119-20)

MASCULISM

"The form of sexism practiced in our culture. . . . [It] is in part the mistaking of male perspectives, beliefs, attitudes, standards, values, and perceptions for all human perceptions. Both the cause and result of women's social and intellectual disenfranchisement." "The guiding principle of patriachy; we have put names to it. On its most obvious level it is the lived expression of the Martial ideals – a lust for power and control over others and self; absorption by the abstract and unfelt, by duties, principles and behaviors legitimated only by rationalistic argument; the mystification of The Fight [Flight?] in all its aspects – war, competition, contention; a passion for order, the soldier's order; a belief in hierarchy, in the rights of the strong over the weak, in God over men, in men over nature and women, in winners over losers. . . . It rejects and diminishes anything relaxed, gentle, and easy, spontaneous, or wild." (Sheila Ruth 1983, 7, 350)

(See ANDROCENTRISM, MASCULINITY, SEX-GENDER SYSTEM, PATRIARCHY)

MASK

Self, identity, shield, costume, persona. The faces of the individual characters, created by ourselves and others, who inhabit our space. "She tore off mask after mask – Wonder Woman-Noble Martyr-Big Mama-Con Woman-Tough Broad-Sexy Kitten-Cold Bitch-Daddy's Girl-Frightened Child-Whiny Brat, and on and on. . . ." (Nancy Green 1978, 185) "No more masks! No more mythologies!" (Muriel Rukeyser 1971; in Florence Howe and Ellen Bass, eds 1973, 1)

(See COSMETICS)

MASOCHISM

Pleasure, usually sexual, derived from pain, dominance; submission to violence. Glorified in Church Art. "Christ is nailed to a phallic tree – crowned with thorns and his side pierced to propitiate a vengeful patriarchal God. His martyrs, helpless victims of brute male force, win glory by enduring the most bloody and sadistic tortures." (Margaret Walters 1978, 10) Term sometimes used to attempt to account for the fact that women remain in relationships that appear to cause them pain, humiliation, etc.

(See PATRIARCHY, SADO-MASOCHISM)

MASS MEDIA

"Is a curiously uniform product which comes to us daily from the cinema screen, the TV, and newspapers. We as women are consumers of this culture, but traditionally have not been its producers . . . Access to the new communication technology for women varies greatly across the world, but the same mass media span the globe and affect all our lives." (*ISIS [Women's International Bulletin]* 1983, 23, 3) Are "technology for male ends." (Mary Daly 1978, 5)

(See ADVERTISING, FILM, NEWSPAPERS, REPRESENTATION, TELEVISION, WOMEN'S MAGAZINES, WOMAN'S PAGE)

"Bloody cultural revolutions are prevented through the bloodless ones which are gradually fought in our mass media every day." (Madonna Marsden 1972, 78)

"What it does to everyone, it does to women even more. . . . Instead of liberating people through leisure time and real knowledge about the surrounding environment, the technology has been used to wage war on the domestic consumer." (Alice Embree 1970, 181, 190)

MASTECTOMY

Mammectomy, from *mamma-* 'breast' + Greek *ektome* 'excision,' amputation of the breast. The detection of breast cancer is the main reason for mastectomy. Controversy surrounding the procedure includes how much of the breast tissue and related muscle and lymph system needs to be removed, whether alternative treatments would be more effective (radiation, chemotherapy, removal of the malignant lump only, or some combination of these), and whether a woman has the right to choose whether and how soon to have a mastectomy after she learns the biopsy results (instead of having the surgeon perform the surgery immediately without consulting her).

(See AMAZON, BREAST, PROSTHESIS, WOMEN'S HEALTH MOVEMENT)

"Women with breast cancer are warriors, too. I have been to war, and still am. So has every woman who has had one or both breasts amputated because of the cancer that is becoming the primary physical scourge of our time. For me, my scars are an honorable reminder that I may be a casualty in the cosmic war against radiation, animal fat, air pollution, McDonald's hamburgers and Red Dye No. 2, but the fight is still going on, and I am still a part of it. . . . For me, the primary challenge at the core of mastectomy was the stark look at my own mortality, hinged upon the fear of a life-threatening cancer. This even called upon me to reexamine the quality and texture of my entire life, its priorities and commitments, as well as the possible alterations that might be required in the light of that reexamination." (Audre Lorde 1980a, 60, 61)

"Ritual for the Integrity of the Body" was written to affirm "a vision of wholeness related to our mothers, the Amazons." In the Ritual, "each womon of the group bares her chest, puts her hand – outstretched in a gesture of acceptance – on the scarred or flattened area where breast had been." "I would like to carry out a ritual like this wherever wimin gather and are free to share their pain and their support with one another." (J. Wattles 1980, rpt. 1982, 47)

MASTER'S TOOLS

Patriarchal skills, training, methodologies, perceptions, all of the above. Can such tools be used by feminists to fight patriarchal oppression, or are they inevitably compromised and indentured by their origins? *"The master's tools will never dismantle the master's house.* They may allow us temporarily to beat him at his own game, but they will never enable us to bring about genuine change. And this fact is only threatening to those women who still define the master's house as their only source of support." (Audre Lorde 1981a, 99)

MASTURBATION

A practice of the self-made woman. "One of the few acts going that can truly stand alone, and it requires only a quorum of one." (Mopsy Strange Kennedy 1976, 25)

"i learned how
to masturbate
through the new york times"
(Sonia Sanchez 1968, 252)

"While masturbating, or in my dreams at night, I often find solutions that eluded me before, or new ways of looking at my problems." (Sandra Whisler 1981, 27)

Reliable method that women use to achieve orgasm which does not depend on heterosexuality or penile penetration. *The Hite Report* (Shere Hite 1976) revealed that many women routinely masturbate and evolve elaborate routines, rituals, and fantasies for achieving pleasure. Interestingly, many reviews of the book noted its general findings about women's sexuality but omitted to mention Hite's important emphasis on masturbation.

"The primary sexual activity of humans." (Thomas Szasz; cited in Midge Lennert and Norma Willson, eds, 1973, 7)

MATCHGIRLS' STRIKE

A protest in 1888 of London Matchgirls who worked on benches covered in phospherous and in clothes which "shone at night when you took them off." Their strike (over fines being deducted from their pay) "was successful and provided the inspiration for gasworkers and dockers to organize." (Joan Rudder 1982, 12)

MATER

Mother. The root *ma* plus the suffix *-ter* yield *mater*, a very old linguistic form which is among the earliest words we can reconstruct historically. Its cognates are found across the Indo-European languages and include in English 'mother,' 'mama,' 'matriarchy,' 'maternal,' 'material,' 'matrix,' and 'matter.' The centrality of these words is one kind of evidence for the view that a matrilineal Indo-European culture and 'mother-tongue' antedate the patriarchal culture of more recent history. (See Susan J. Wolfe and Julia Penelope Stanley 1980)
(See AMAZON, MA, MATERIALISM, PIE)

"Here we have Mother Earth, the primitive goddess of fertility, symbolizing by her processes the productivity of every human mother as indicated in the relation of *mater* to *materia*. We are amid conceptions immensely more antique and far more universal than are involved in the mother of the Aryan household as she has been sketched for us by the philologists." (Karl Pearson 1897, 201)

MATERIAL FEMINIST

"Is a term I coined: it indicates an intellectual approach but doesn't define a particular group or even tendency within the movement." (Christine Delphy 1984a, 25)

MATERIALISM

Engels: "We have the certainty that *matter remains eternally the same in all its transformations, that none of its attributes can ever be lost.*" Materialism as a doctrine emphasizes the primacy of material reality; economically, it emphasizes the motivating and controlling force of material production, goods, needs, and profits. "The women's struggle, imprinting the word oppression on the domain of sexuality, annexes it to materialism." (Christine Delphy 1981, 74) "To answer the question of the individual subject in materialist terms is first to show, as the lesbians and feminists did that supposedly 'subjective,' 'individual,' 'private' problems are in fact social problems, class problems; that sexuality is not for women an individual and subjective expression, but a social institution of violence." (Monique Wittig 1981, 53) Barbara Deming notes the similarity of Engels' position to that of the Great Mother: "In the Mother, all things exist. The words 'matter' and 'mater' (mother) are of course very close. Something for materialists to muse about I think. Beyond all contradiction, female and male are matter and are also mater, flesh of their mother's flesh – the male as a fetus in the beginning female, too; then becoming a variation of the female. Until this truth is accepted, the so-called materialist is not really a materialist." (Barbara Deming 1977, 74)

(See MATER, PROLETARIAT)

MATERNAL INSTINCT

Concept invented by males "to ensure that we would fulfill our procreative duties as well as assuming full responsibility for children per se. 'Maternal instinct' is defined as follows: It is 'natural' for women to *want* to give birth and to go through any amount of pain and inconvenience in order to bear a child; it is 'natural' for women to love their children and to be willing to sacrifice anything for their benefit; therefore, women fulfill themselves through childbirth and raising children. This was solidified in the concept of maternal love." (Barbara Mehrhof and Sheila Cronan 1969, 4-5)

MATRIARCHY

Is a term used variously in feminist writings to mean (a) an actual society believed to be governed by women long before the current patriarchal epoch, (b) a hypothesized or visionary society in which the practices and values of 'women's culture' would prevail, (c) a myth created by men both to envision and contain the idea of governance by women, (d) a descriptive term (with matrifocal and matrilineal) for various female-centered social arrangements, and (e) a stereotypical construction of social scientists and others to characterize and disparage Black women and their strengths and contributions (held to have a weakening effect on Black men). The following comments illustrate these meanings.

(See CULTURAL FEMINISTS, MA, MYTH, PUBLIC ENEMY NUMBER ONE, WOMEN'S MOVEMENT)

Different from patriarchy with an M. New feminist research on female spirituality and matriarchy claims "that female deities, reflecting women's culture and women's power, were universally accepted by humankind until the modern era of immediate pre-industrial societies; that women's lives were not subordinate, and that women's values were indeed uppermost. Such values linked the physical with the spiritual, and were monist and holist rather than split and dualist." (Asphodel 1982, 103)

Named for its most significant legal characteristic: "This institution ignored the male's role in the child's procreation and traced descent solely from the maternal line. . . . Genealogy, therefore, was strictly feminine. There was no difference between children born inside or outside of wedlock, for all children inherited their mother's class and bore her name or that of her clan. Property also was inherited solely in the feminine line: it passed from the mother to her daughters, and so on." (Helen Diner 1973, 19-20)

"The over throw of mother-right (matriarchy) was the *world historical defeat of the female sex*. The man took command in the home also; the woman was degraded and reduced to servitude, she became the slave of his lust and a mere instrument for the production of children." (Frederick Engels 1884, 50; quoted in Heather M. Ferguson, 1982, 60)

"The period of woman's supremacy lasted through many centuries – undisputed, accepted as natural and proper wherever it existed, and was called the matriarchate, or mother-age." (Elizabeth Cady Stanton, 1891, 143)

"Matriarchy may have been a psychological reality in the world of fantasies, while the factual reality was ruled by men. Various stories exhibiting women as supreme might have grown up as utopian dreams in an age of female subservience." (Theodore Thass-Thienemann 1967, 322)

"The *idea* of matriarchy is powerful for women in itself." (Margot Adler 1979, 131)

"The whole question challenges women to imagine themselves with power. It is an idea about what society would be like where women are truly free." (Paula Webster and Esther Newton 1972; quoted by Margot Adler 1979, 131)

"Originally, a female oriented society led by women, with social values that operated in harmony with Nature and women's needs; a concept that has been attacked, distorted, or derided by misogynistic males and conservative scholars loath to believe that women ever had, or ever could have, political, religious, and social power." (Ann Forfreedom 1983, correspondence)

"Members of the matriarchy school . . . serve neither the status quo nor contemplate a return to earlier forms. The main force of their arguments is to challenge patriarchy's claims to eternal authority,

primeval or primordial origins, and biological or environmental necessity. They see patriarchy as but one era of human history and therefore, theoretically, as capable of dissolution as it was of institution." (Kate Millett 1971, 154)

" 'Matriarchy is a patriarchal myth' (Rosemary Ruether). Patriarchal progressivists (like Engels) of the Nineteenth Century created this myth, not necessarily consciously, out of fear, perhaps, that if women ever got any power, they would behave as men have done under patriarchy – oppress their oppressors." (Heather M. Ferguson 1982, 61)

"Matriarchy is no less heterosexual than patriarchy: it is only the sex of the oppressor that changes." (Monique Wittig 1981, 48)

Has an implied resemblance to patriarchy, "which refers to the dominance of one gender over the other in a social order based on close interdependence between men and women." (Dorothy Dinnerstein 1976, 192)

"Nancy Ward [Indian name Nanye'hi] was the last Beloved Woman (or Clan Mother) of the Cherokee people before Removal. She was a major decision-maker for the people, operating under the old matriarchal system so disrupted by the encroachment of European governmental forms and social values. She introduced commercial cattle-raising and banking to North Carolina and helped develop the valuable resources that unfortunately made the tribe the envy of all around. On her death, she became a kind of folk heroine to the Cherokee people, remembered even in the Oklahoma Cherokee tribal symbol taken from a sculpture carved by the Cherokee artist, Willard Stone." (Rayna Green 1984, 313)

"The myth of the black matriarch is a cruel one. The word matriarch connotes power, but the disproportionate number of black women on welfare who head their own households can hardly be powerful." (Kathryn Christensen 1975, 19)

"The paucity of literature on the Black woman is outrageous." What is published is often riddled with clichés and myths, foremost among them the myth of the Black matriarch, "repeatedly invoked as one of the fatal by-products of slavery. When the Moynihan Report consecrated this myth with Washington's stamp of approval, its propagandistic mission should have been apparent. Yet even outside establishment ideology and also among Black people, unfortunate references to the matriarchate can still be encountered. Occasionally, there is even acknowledgement of the 'tangle of pathology' supposedly engendered . . . Lingering beneath the notion of the Black matriarch is an unspoken indictment of our female forebears as having actively assented to slavery. The 'emasculating female' cliché has its roots in the fallacious inference that the Black woman related to the slaveholding class as collaborator. Nothing could be further from the truth. In the most fundamental sense, the slave system did not – and could not – engender and recognize a matriarchal family structure. Inherent in the very concept of the matriarchy is 'power.' It would have been exceedingly risky for the slaveholding class to openly acknowledge symbols of authority – female symbols no less than male." (Angela Davis 1971, 242)

"I first became acquainted with [the Moynihan Report,] Daniel P. Moynihan's popularization of the idea that Black women were matriarchs, i.e., all-powerful, domineering, sexually permissive, and aggressive women, when Angela Davis wrote her essay on the role of Black women in the community of slaves. Angela was still in jail at the time, and I was working with her, and was on the national staff of her defense committee. . . . [She] was charged with first-degree murder, kidnapping, and conspiracy to commit both . . . The evidence connecting Angela Davis to these events was circumstantial, and had she not been the subject of political controversy as a Black woman who was both [a university instructor] and a prominent member of the Communist Party, it is likely that the charges would never have been brought against her . . . Without direct evidence . . . the issue of her motive became a key one in the case. The Moynihan doctrine became the cornerstone of the prosecution's trial strategy. Angela was portrayed as the epitome of the Black matriarch – criminal, scheming, without morality. . . . [Her] motives were lust and the desire for power – precisely the images conjured by Moynihan's matriarch. It was a vicious brew to be endured and overcome. We saw it coming, of course, and when Angela Davis delivered her opening statement to the jury, she explicitly repudiated the ideological underpinnings of the prosecution's case. Angela endured. She was found 'not guilty' on all counts. . . . Some weeks after the trial I became friends with the foreperson of the Davis jury. Mary M. Timothy told me that the eight (white) women on the jury never bought the prosecution's main line." (Bettina Aptheker 1982, 129-30)

MATRIFOCAL

Cultural system "in which men are relatively peripheral to the domestic scene and women carry a relatively high degree of economic and social authority." (Dorothy Dinnerstein 1976, 192)

MATRIMONY

"Girls, leave matrimony alone; it's the hardest way on earth of getting a living." (Fanny Fern 1853) Is "a bad conduct prize." (Dorothy L. Sayers 1930, 37)
 (See ANTIMONY, MARRIAGE)

MATRIX

Originally womb, uterus; from *mater* 'mother.' From this derive the meaning of a center from within which something originates or takes form; also a mold, plate, or cast from which forms are created.
 (See MA, MATER)

MATRIX SISTERS

Women descended from the same matrilineage. (Anne Cameron 1981, 20)

MATRONYMY, METRONYMY

A matronymic is a name derived from the

name of the mother, foremother, or female ancestor. Many women have taken matronymics, e.g., by adopting their mother's birth name or by creating names that incorporate their mother's name with their own (Paula Mariesdaughter).

MAWULISA

The Dahomean female-male, sky-goddess-god principle. . . . "Mawu is [sometimes] regarded as the Creator of the Universe, and Lisa is either called her first son, or her twin brother." (Audre Lorde 1978, 120)

MCP

(See MALE CHAUVINIST PIG)

MDEITY

The doctor as god and father figure "whose omnipotence extends far beyond the performance of a specialized medical task. The MDeity has the power to withhold life-sustaining measures, to pronounce who is sane and who is insane, and who will be saved and who sacrificed. . . . The MDeity not only acts as a god, he actually believes he *is* one." Term coined by Belita H. Cowan for her collection *Death of the MDeity*. (Susan Rennie and Kirsten Grimstad 1975, 27)

MEANING

"Our understanding of the meaning process is still rudimentary, but recent work in the philosophy of language and in linguistic semantics and pragmatics suggests a useful framework. The basic idea is that to 'mean' to express thought A by utterance B is to intend to get your hearers to recognize thought A by virtue of their recognition that your utterance of B is intended to get them to recognize A. Using this sort of reflexive intentionality in talking about how a speaker 'means' is a strategy first suggested by Grice, and later developed and modified by others. . . . Oversimplifying, the standard or linguistically specified meaning can be thought of as what is recognizable solely on the basis of interlocutors' mutual knowledge of established practices of interpretation of the language system. Speakers can augment, modify, or 'fill in' standard meanings by drawing on what they assume to be extralinguistic mutual beliefs – either in the speech community at large or in the more local speech situation. Some of these beliefs are quite general ones about linguistic communication; others relate more directly to the topics of discourse. This general perspective provides a way to begin investigating the connection between language as a cognitive phenomenon, a system represented in the minds of individuals, and language as a social process through which individuals interact. It directs attention to MUTUAL knowledge and belief; it goes beyond individual intentions to the social web of interconnected aims, and recognitions thereof, on which a Gricean-type analysis relies, thus beginning to shed light on questions about gender-related content. This is because the complex gender system discussed above constitutes an important part of that web, supporting linguistic communication. . . . The sexual politics of discourse affects WHO can mean WHAT, and WHOSE meanings get established as community currency. Men, with superior extralinguistic resources and privileged discourse positions, are often less likely than women to treat perspectives different from their own as mutually available for communication, and are more likely to assume that their view is the only one. Their attitudes are thus more likely to leave a lasting imprint on the common semantic stock than women's . . . Investigations of gender-related content cannot go very far unless they grapple with basic questions of meaning – particularly with questions about how human thought and action enter into the assignment of interpretations to natural language systems." (Sally McConnell-Ginet 1983, 387-8)

MEANS OF PRODUCTION

"The repossession by women of our bodies will bring far more essential equality to human society than the seizing of the means of production by workers."

(Adrienne Rich 1976; quoted in Barbara Deming 1977, 74)

MEAT

"We are mad
mad as hatters, mad
as headless chickens, mad.
We will be cloaked in madness, wrapped
like butchers' packets in our own clean
sheets
and carted off like sides of meat."
   (Sharon H. Nelson 1982, 70)

MEAT AND BONES

The transient human body (North American Indian). "The arrangement of meat and bones doesn't mean anythin'." (Anne Cameron 1981, 119)

MEDEA

The Greek means 'wise woman.' "Magician queen who lived in Colchis during the Bronze age. She was the guardian of the Golden Fleece until wandering amazons came to take it away. They also took Medea with them. They learned magic from her. The bearers of fables say that later she joined Circe on her island Aeaea and there became her companion queen and lover." (Monique Wittig and Sande Zeig 1976, 105)

"Such a good suffrage play!" (Millicent Fawcett; quoted in H. M. Swanwick 1935, 186)

MEDICA

Woman physician, woman healer. The feminine gender marker -a in Latin enabled later scholars to establish the existence of women physicians in ancient Rome and thereafter because this term appeared on their tombstones. In the U.S., the feminine form gave way to the quasi-colloquial and sometimes derogatory *female medicos* or *hen medicos*.

   (See DOCTOR, DOCTORESS, GENDER MARKING, MARKEDNESS)

MEDICAL LUST

"There is such a thing as the 'medical lust of indecently handling women,' as well as the legislative lust of ruling them with an iron hand for the purpose of gratifying vicious propensities in men." (Josephine Butler 1872)

MEDICINE

In broadest sense, means doctoring, healing. "It seemed to me that doctoring was a form of mothering, the nurturing and healing came from the same energies, from the same center of my self that wanted to mother." (Michelle Harrison 1982, 5)

The
medicine
   is all
      in
her long
   un-
      braided
         hair.
   (Alice Walker 1968, "Medicine,"; in Florence Howe and Ellen Bass eds 1973, 326)

In this sense includes folk medicine, nursing, culturally-based traditional health systems, and other forms of healing. But the term also more specifically means western biomedical science and the medical profession – i.e., physicians – as well as the medical system of which they are a part. "Medicine, especially as it is practiced in the hospital, is a service industry that systematically and impersonally processes sick and healthy people. Physicians are trained and conditioned to see their patients as objects to be assembled and reassembled once they enter the system. If you are sick, or even if you are having a baby, you are presumed to be incapable of intelligent judgment, and therefore – quite properly – under the control of the experts." (Michelle Harrison 1982, 250) This means a male-dominated profession which has vigorously and rigorously resisted female participation or competition. (See Sandra Chaff et al eds 1978) "The result of this male monopolization of the practice of medicine has been not only a limitation of women's pro-

fessional opportunities, and not only much higher medical costs than were the rule earlier when most medical and obstetric care was provided by midwives and folk healers (many of them women); but also a distressing history of medical malpractice directed largely against women. The history of obstetrics and gynecology is replete with horror stories, from the surgical mutilations (ovaridectomy and clitoridectomy) practiced on women who were thought to have psychological problems, to the excessive and unsafe use of drugs, instruments and Caesarian sections to intervene in the birth processes – abuses which have by no means entirely ended. . . . The American Medical Association has campaigned for laws prohibiting abortion, and has never lent its full support to make safe and effective methods of contraception available to all women." (Mary Anne Warren 1980, 317)
    (See DOCTOR, DOCTORESS, HEALTH SYSTEM, WOMEN'S HEALTH MOVEMENT)

MEDICINE WOMAN

Term for female Indian healer. (Lynn V. Andrews 1981) "In 1818 there was a famous [Mohawk] Indian woman, the daughter of a chief and a noted medicine woman, who practiced the 'laying on of hands.' The sorceress was entitled to be called a chieftainess because chieftainship descended through the female line; she had learned all the lore and mysteries of medicine men and conjures . . . She was almost six feet in height and straight as a lance . . . She owned a beautiful canoe which no one else was permitted to touch; it was fantastically decorated and the Indians were afraid to go near it and the whites called it 'the devil's canoe.' " (Carolyn Thomas Foreman 1954, 56)

MEDUSA

Means in Greek 'Knowing Woman.' "You have only to look at the Medusa straight on to see her. And she's not deadly. She's beautiful and she's laughing." (Hélène Cixous 1975b, 255)

MEMORIES

"A bag of mending wools, not too carefully kept, when the first ball taken out is entangled with a second and that with half a dozen more." (H. M. Swanwick 1935, 15)

MEN

More than one man. "The term 'men' [in this book] should not be taken in its more comprehensive sense. Rather it was feared that a cumbersome use of qualifiers – such as some, many, several, eight, eighteen, eighteen hundred, a few men – would impair the flow of the narrative. These have been waived, therefore, and the reader left free to assume them according to her (or his) own observations. . . . If not otherwise specified, the term 'men' is best taken in the standard sense of the English plural, to wit, 'more than one.' " (Ruth Herschberger 1948, preface)
    (See MAN)
    "'One sex . . . quite capable of representing two.' (Teresa Billington-Greig 1911b, 19)

    Humans who as males have experienced unchecked supremacy which "has resulted in an abnormal predominance of masculine impulses in our human processes. . . . This predominance has been largely injurious." (Charlotte Perkins Gilman 1911, 244)

    The military sex. (Carrie Chapman Catt 1909, 12)

"Seldom make passes
At girls who wear glasses."
    (Dorothy Parker; in John Keats 1970, 10)

"For years I rebelled against men because of their demands and their contempt, because of the monopoly on their glory. But I have noticed that men happily accepted women's rebellion and delicately savored their bits: they perceived in our anger the expression of a supreme and sad devotion to those values of theirs to which we could never accede. . . . It was indeed on that occasion that laughter began to tickle me – I took to observing the men around me, Tom, Dick, and Harry, in the light of greatness and human dignity and honestly those men who could pass for the best in the business were simply not up to standard. Weaklings in the light of Strength. Cowards in the light of Courage. Blinkered in the light of Genius. Short-winded in the light of Inspiration. Stingy in the light of Generosity. It was pitiful to see them falling so short." (Annie Leclerc 1974, 79-80)

"How they struggle against the fact that they are born of woman and from the moment of their leaving our wombs, they begin to die!" (Pat Robinson and Group 1969, 198)

MEN ARE OPPRESSED TOO

"It may be said man does not have his fair play either; his energies are repressed and distorted by the interposition of artificial obstacles. Aye, but he himself has put them there; they have grown out of his own imperfections." (Margaret Fuller 1843; in Alice Rossi ed. 1973, 168)

MENDING

"Is a niggling, tedious business, by which the housewife ... succeeds merely in heartening worn-out fabrics for yet another visit to the washtub. Mending is, no doubt, a necessary ill, but it should be kept within narrow limits. At best a poor substitute for making, at worst it is a waste of time, a method of throwing good money after bad, and a cloak for busy idleness. Mending as an episode in the day, an occasional penance, a reminder of mortality, a guide to humility, has (as our great-aunts too often told us) its moral uses. But to take mending as a lifework is to sit voluntarily among dust and ashes. To spend one's life in the contemplation of holes is to renounce the impetus to goodness which comes of high spirits ... Excluding cobblers, plumbers, and riveters, the world's menders are mostly women ... It is the virtue of [the woman] whose time is of little value." ("Problems of the Day" 1913, *The Englishwoman* 20:59 (November), 137-41)

MENOPAUSE

"(1) The cessation of ovulation and menstruation; (2) an archetypal experience exclusive to the human female; (3) traditionally from the medical (male) point-of-view a debilitating trauma; in actuality a simple [although sometimes painful] life experience." (Midge Lennert and Norma Willson, eds 1973, 8)

"Menopause is as much a natural physiological characteristic of women as is menstruation, pregnancy, and lactation. Yet there is a veil of mystery surrounding this natural womanly function. At worst it is labelled a disease and shrouded in fear. At best menopause has become a catchall for all the physical and emotional problems of women between the ages of forty and fifty-five. Most doctors, therapists, and health-care givers are woefully uninformed about menopause and are neither interested nor motivated in researching this area. 'You're just in the menopause' is often the answer given to a patient who comes to a doctor reporting depression, anxiety, headaches, loss of libido, etc." (Judith Golden 1984, 74)

Is "the best form of birth control. Face it graciously and brag about it. It's great." (Questionnaire respondent, quoted in Paula Weideger 1977, 5)

"Is a convenient let-out label [to describe physical problems of the middle years], just as 'hysteria' is the tag put on to the younger woman with symptoms that don't interest her doctor." (Jane Robertson 1983, 50)

To menopause – *zháadin*; uneventfully – *azháadin*; when it's welcome – *elazháadin*. (See LÁADAN for pronunciation guide.) (Suzette Haden Elgin 1983, 9)

The time when for many women sexual desire is at its greatest. "Yet at menopause a husband often curtails sexual relations entirely, begs his wife to have breakfast in bed, and worst of all, professes an eternal love for her spirit no matter how withered her ovaries become." (Ruth Herschberger 1948, 58)

An aspect of feminine biology "which has been treated by medicine and psychology in an extremely negative way: it is generally presumed to mark the end of a woman's womanhood – her femininity, physical beauty and sexual desire. Yet the objective fact, [Ruth] Herschberger [1948] argues, is that menopause is of great biological value, since it relieves older women of the bother of menstruation and the danger of pregnancy. Contrary to the general belief, the ovaries do not suddenly cease to produce estrogen, and sexual desire – which is not dependent on this hormone anyway – often increases rather than decreases. Scientists generally ignore the fact that men also undergo a diminution of sexual functioning in middle age (a male climacteric), preferring to think of the 'change of life' as a purely feminine phenomenon." (Mary Anne Warren 1980, 213)

MENSH, MENCH

Yiddish for human being (from German *mensch* 'person'); an upright, honorable, decent person of either sex. "It is hard to convey the special sense of respect, dignity, approbation, that can be conveyed by calling someone 'a real *mensh*!' " Being a *mensh* is linked to character rather than to success, wealth, status, or sex; it involves rectitude, dignity, a sense of what is right and responsible. (Leo Rosten 1968, 237)

MEN'S ILLNESSES

Nonexistent category of disability. If a female-controlled medical system had developed instead of but parallel to the male-controlled system, the following statements might be common:

" – Man's supreme function in life is the impregnation of women. If he spends his energy in reading, writing or working outside the home, he will injure his reproductive capacity and therefore threaten the survival of the species.
– Woman's sex drive is much stronger than man's. Men who demonstrate an unnatural zest for intercourse or who maladjust to their housekeeping function can often be cured through castration.
– The monthly change in the man's

testosterone level so upsets his emotional equilibrium that he is unqualified for professional jobs.
– Failure to accept the male role causes many of men's abdominal pains."
(Gena Corea 1977, 18)

(See ANDROLOGY)

MEN'S LANGUAGE

"It is of interest to note that men's language is increasingly being used by women, but women's language is not being adopted by men, apart from those who reject the American masculine image [for example, homosexuals]. . . . The language of the favored group, the group that holds the power, along with its nonlinguistic behavior, is generally adopted by the other group, not vice versa." (Robin Lakoff 1975, 10)

Dorothy Parker satirized men's language as well as women's. Her short story "Too Bad" describes a boring husband: "Mr Weldon turned a page, and yawned aloud. 'Wah-huh-huh-huh-huh,' he went, on a descending scale. He yawned again, and this time climbed the scale." "The Lovely Leave" is about a woman married to and increasingly alienated from a soldier. "Hell," says the husband, searching for something to polish his belt buckle with, "I don't suppose you've got a Blitz Cloth, have you? Or a Shine-O?" The wife coldly replies: "If I had the faintest idea what you were talking about, I might be better company for you." (Dorothy Parker 1973, 180, 15; Paula A. Treichler 1981)

MEN'S STUDIES

"The academic curriculum." (Dale Spender ed. 1981, 1)

MENSTRUAL CALENDAR

The unofficial lunar calendar used by peasants in contrast to the Christian era's official solar calendar. Has thirteen 28-day months of four 7-day weeks each, yielding 364 days per year; one extra day is added to make 365. From this derives the refrain from fairy tales, nursery rhymes, charms, and elsewhere of "a year and a day." (Barbara G. Walker 1983)

MENSTRUAL STRIKE

Proposed monthly refusal of women to work in protest of the view that menstruation hampers women's abilities; the strike would demonstrate that women *do* work by dramatizing what would happen were they to stop. The strike idea was provoked by views like that of Dr Edward H. Clarke, whose 1883 book *Sex in Education; or, A Fair Chance for the Girls* held that female biology severely limited girls' ability to participate in education and advocated "a special and appropriate education, that shall produce a just and harmonious development of every part." (Edward H. Clarke 1883; in Mary Roth Walsh 1977, 129). Though vague on concrete proposals, Clarke did recommend that girls spend less time on their studies than boys and that they be given time off during their menstrual periods. Eliza Bisbee Duffey's *No Sex in Education; or, an equal chance for both girls and boys* (1874) was one of many publications refuting Clarke's views. Duffey pointed out that Clarke's plan could work only if all students had their menstrual periods at the same time; "but each girl has her own time; and if each were excused from attendance and study during this time, there could be neither system nor regularity in the classes." She noted that the teacher, who was probably also a woman, would need time off as well. Duffey went on to speculate that Clarke might include the home in his argument and argue that women should leave their work undone for three or four days each month. "I think a concerted action among women in this direction," she wrote, "would bring men who are inclined to agree with the doctor to their senses sooner than anything else." (Eliza Bisbee Duffey 1874; quoted in Mary Roth Walsh 1977, 129)

MENSTRUAL WEAR

Any loose-fitting, flowing clothing worn by women, especially before and during their menstrual period. Also any loose-fitting clothing of red, brown, purple, or other tones signifying blood, or black, signifying depression. (Pat Parker 1984, correspondence)

MENSTRUATION

"(1) The act of periodically discharging blood and mucosal tissue from the uterus, occurring approximately monthly from puberty to menopause; (2) mistaught simple body function that provides a reason for young girls to fear activity and to accept passivity." (Midge Lennert and Norma Willson, eds, 1973, 8) "A sign of the continued health of ovaries and uterus, and of the smooth functioning of the sex hormones." (Ruth Herschberger 1948, 49) For many women, not a severe disruption: "Menstrual days did not interrupt my training; I was as strong as on any other day. 'You're now an adult,' explained the old woman on the first one, '. . . You can have children.' " (Maxine Hong Kingston 1975, 36)

(See MENSTRUAL STRIKE, MENOPAUSE, PREMENSTRUAL SYNDROME, WOMEN'S HEALTH MOVEMENT)

Studies of menstruation by male scientists and physicians portray it not only as a symptom of a disease but itself "a morbid state fraught with danger" and "an infirmity" which severely limits women's activities. But the evidence is overwhelming that women in modern society have always performed physical and other kinds of labor. "From this brief glance at the actual condition of modern society, it is evident that its existing regulations are little prepared to 'yield to nature her inexorable demand for rest during one week out of four' in the adult life of women." (Mary Putnam Jacobi 1877, 14, 21)

"Is a factor in the control of women by men not only in ancient and primitive societies, where knowledge of physiology is rudimentary at best, but also in our post-industrial world. Women are physically and emotionally handicapped by menstruation, goes the argument, and therefore cannot and may not compete with men." It is a subject not talked about: "Even literature has been silent on menstruation, probably because most 'literature' has been written by men." (Janice Delaney, Mary Jane Lupton, and Emily Toth 1977, 1-2, 144)

"From the earliest human cultures, the mysterious magic of creation was thought to reside in the blood women gave forth in apparent harmony with the moon, and which was sometimes retained in the womb to 'coagulate' into a baby. Men regarded this blood with dread, as the life-essence, inexplicably shed without pain, wholly foreign to male experience." (Barbara G. Walker 1983, 635)

"In the old guerrilla war
between father and son
I am the no man's land.
When the moon shows
over my scorched breast
they fire across me.
If a bullet ricochets
and I bleed,
they say it is my time
of month."
(Linda Pastan 1978, "In the Old Guerrilla War," 15)

Though menstruation is often assumed in anthropological literature to be threatening and "polluting," among many cultures, including the Beng of the Ivory Coast, menstruation has positive associations with life and fertility. (Alma Gottlieb 1982)

Feminist graffiti: "War is menstruation envy!" (Rachel Bartlett, compiler, 1982)

In cultures "where the fact of menstruation is concealed and thus culturally occupies a covert position, as among the Irish, the vocabulary [for menstruation] is meager; where it is more overtly accepted, as in France or the present-day United States, the vocabulary is vivid and luxuriant, unless the society enforces highly formalized behavior toward menstruation as with Orthodox Jews." Women have many terms for menstruation. A selection: *in season, flowers* (Irish); *to read a book* (Polish); *a guest in the house, my package of troubles* (East European Jewish); *the red*

king, *Friederich Barbarossa* (German); *the magnificent marquis, the red road* (Italian); *to have the English* (i.e., redcoats), *I am going to see my relatives at Montrouge, I am going to see Sophie* (French); *on the rag, the hammock is swinging* (from the shape of a sanitary napkin), *Bloody Mary, the nuisance, My friend is here, After the manner of women, Grandma is here, falling off the roof* (U.S.).

"The most consistent term [for menstruation] used by women, which is largely age-typed, almost universally used by American women under thirty-five years of age, is *the curse*, while for men speaking it is *the rag* or *she's got the rag on*. This men's term, interestingly, reflects the material culture of over twenty-five years ago with regard to the type of sanitary protection characteristically used by women." (Natalie F. Joffe 1948, 181-3)

"A woman's 'sick time' is when she 'comes round,' which means that she is having her menses. So, for a woman to say, 'That makes me sick' was the same as to say, 'That makes me menstruate'; a perfectly normal happening but no more to be mentioned in public than urination." (Jessamyn West 1979, 204)

Called "my grandmother is visiting me" as part of puberty ceremonies in many Canadian Indian Nations. (Lenore Keeshig Tobias 1982)

To menstruate – osháana; for the first time – elasháana; early – desháana; late – wesháana; painfully – husháana; joyfully – ásháana. (See LÁADAN for pronunciation guide.) (Suzette Haden Elgin 1983, 9)

MENTAL HEALTH

"There is a double standard of mental health – one for men the other for women – existing among clinicians . . . For a woman to be healthy, she must 'adjust' to and accept the behavioral norms for her sex – passivity, acquiescence, self-sacrifice, and lack of ambition – even though these kinds of 'loser' behaviors are generally regarded as socially undesirable (i.e., nonmasculine)." (Phyllis Chesler 1972b; cited in Elaine Partnow 1977, 442)

(See GASLIGHTING, MADNESS,

MARRIAGE, PERSONALITY DISORDERS, YELLOW WALL-PAPER)

"Some clinicians are now seriously questioning whether the qualities that are associated with marital happiness for women may not themselves be contrary to good health. Is it possible that many women are 'happily married' *because* they have poor mental health?" (Jessie Bernard 1971, 11)

A selective concept, "incorporating only certain conditions as undesirable in matters of mental ill-health. . . . While extremes of hatred or ambition are not in themselves considered symptomatic of sickness, extremes of anxiety and fear are." (Joan Busfield 1983, 106)

"One of the more overtly political forms of disability. *Insanity* and *madness* are appropriate terms when used seriously, as is *psychiatrically disabled* when used in self-definition." (seamoon house 1981, 34)

"Masculine-biased assumptions about what behaviors are healthy and what behaviors are crazy are codified in diagnostic criteria [and specifically in the psychiatric manuals *DSM II* and *DSM III*]; these criteria then influence diagnosis and treatment rates and patterns . . . What does impairment in social or occupational functioning mean? I believe these criteria contain assumptions and then generate diagnoses accordingly. For instance, is a woman unemployed outside the home impaired in occupational functioning? Is a man who is employed outside the home and thus never there when his children come home from school impaired in social functioning? Evidently users of *DSM-III* assume not, or many 'healthy' individuals who assume traditional sex roles would have diagnoses; yet a woman who neglects her children and a man who can't hold down a job – perhaps healthy individuals who assume nontraditional roles – may be labeled *impaired* by a diagnostician." (Marcie Kaplan 1983, 786, 788-9)

MENTAL ILLNESS

For women, often a form of logical

resistance to a "kind and benevolent *enemy*" they are not permitted to openly fight. In a sick society, women who have difficulty fitting in are *not* ill but are demonstrating a healthy and positive response. (Charlotte Perkins Gilman; quoted in Dale Spender 1982b, 377)

"Going crazy has always been a personal solution in extremis to the unarticulated conflicts of political realities, a way of transcending these conflicts by going into orbit and settling the world." (Jill Johnston 1973a, 84)

(See MENTAL HEALTH)

METHOD

A way of doing anything; a set of procedures for carrying out an investigation. "One of the false Gods of theologians, philosophers, and other academics" whereby method determines the problem instead of the problems determining the method and women's questions are erased. (Mary Daly 1973, 11-12)

"Once a scholar showed me the sky.
He held up a grapefruit:
here is the sun.
He held up an orange:
this is the harvest moon . . .
But there is a star in my apple when I cut it
and some hungry traveler is paring the moon away."
(Nancy Willard 1971, "The Scholar Stumbles Upon the Astronomer's Orchard," n.p.)

METHODOCIDE

Killing the Methodolatry of the patriarchal disciplines so that creative thought can live. (Mary Daly 1978, 23)

METHODOLATRY

"Tyranny [which] hinders new discoveries. It prevents us from raising questions never asked before and from being illuminated by ideas that do not fit into pre-established boxes and forms. The worshippers of Method have an effective way of handling data that doesn't fit into the Respectable Categories of Questions and

Answers. They simply classify it as non-data, thereby rendering it invisible." (Mary Daly 1973, 11)

METHODOLOGY

Often equated in the modern academic world with positivism, which emphasizes induction from empirical, "scientific" data. Feminists argue that this paradigm helps to construct as well as identify and interpret the nature of social reality, and rules other kinds of exploration out of bounds. They sometimes propose alternatives: "Gynocentric Method requires not only the murder of misogynistic methods (intellectual and affective exorcism) but also ecstasy, which I have called *ludic cerebration*. This is 'the free play of intuition in our own space, giving rise to thinking that is vigorous, informed, multi-dimensional, independent, creative, tough.' " (Mary Daly 1978, 23) "[This] is not a scholarly book: It makes no effort to survey the relevant literature. Not only would that task be (for me) unmanageably huge. It would also be against my principles. I believe in reading unsystematically and taking notes erratically. Any effort to form a rational policy about what to take in, out of the inhumane flood of printed human utterance that pours over us daily, feels to me like a self-deluded exercise in pseudomastery." (Dorothy Dinnerstein 1976, ix)

(See ACADEMIA, FACTS, METHODOLATRY, METHODO-CIDE, REALITY, THEORY)

M/F

Abbreviation for male/female, marxist/feminist, and other socially constructed positions (cf. the British journal *m/f*); a new term used in business advertising to show a nonsexist, equal opportunity employer. (Midge Lennert and Norma Willson, eds, 1973, 8)

MICHAEL FIELD

Pen name of Katherine Badley and Edith Cooper who around 1880 made a mutual commitment to love and poetry. They blended their talents:

" . . . our souls so knit,
I leave a page half-writ –
The word begun
Will be to heaven's conception done,
If she come to it."
   (Michael Field; in Kathleen Hickok 1984, 144-5)

MIDDLE-AGE

"(1) The good years for a woman when the responsibility of children has waned and she is sexually and intellectually more alive; (2) for a feminist a time of increasing positive self-awareness and self-assurance – the peak years of sexual experience; (3) for the traditional woman the time 'she feels like a long-term prisoner who is going to have to face freedom in the morning' (Doris Lessing)." (Midge Lennert and Norma Willson, eds, 1973, 8)

MIDDLE-CLASS

"The first assertion is the parrot cry that the suffrage movement is a middle-class movement. Well, so it is, to a great extent. But . . . the only offense I can trace to the middle-class woman is the middle-class man . . . his attitude to working women was commonly so brutal. . . . [And] now that the hussies of Surbiton have taken to becoming suffragists the middle-class man is becoming a better employer of the working woman." (Rebecca West 1913, *Manchester Daily Dispatch*, January 23)

MIDWIFE

Healer, usually female, who assists women giving birth. "In alle my grete sorowe of my trauail of childe thou were to me a mydwife." (1400, *Oxford English Dictionary*) The word developed from Middle English *medewife* (among other forms). If *mid* is taken as an adjective, the historical meaning is "a woman by whose means the delivery is effected"; if taken as a preposition, the meaning is "a woman who is *with* the mother at the birth." Despite lack of evidence, the *Oxford English Dictionary* favors the latter (and lesser) meaning. Ample literature, however, supports the former (see Barbara G. Walker 1983, 654-7). Figuratively, also means one who brings anything to birth. "Jefferson . . . had acted as undertaker for the royal colonies and as midwife for the United States of America." (1883, *Oxford English Dictionary*)

Means 'wise-woman' or 'witch.' "Medieval Christianity detested midwives for their connections with pagan matriarchy and Goddess-worship. Churchmen viewed them as implacable enemies of the Catholic faith. Handbooks of the Inquisition stated: 'No one does more harm to the Catholic faith than midwives'. . . . The real reason for ecclesiastical hostility seems to have been the notion that midwives could help women control their own fate, learn secrets of sex and birth control, or procure abortions. The pagan women of antiquity had considerable knowledge of such matters, which were considered women's own business, not subject to male authority." (Barbara G. Walker 1983, 654-5)

"The word . . . comes from the Anglo-Saxon 'with woman.' There have always been women who have attended other women in childbirth, and down the ages these women have been under attack. At times they were classed as witches and put to death. Attempts have been made consistently by men in powerful positions, such as priests or medicine men, to destroy the midwife, and take control of the birth process – an essentially female process." (Jenny Spinks 1978; in Marsha Rowe ed. 1982, 375)

"When I came in 1936 the midwives were very important people in their villages, and they helped with many other things besides births. Lots of places they were called medicas. We might ask for the partera, the midwife, when we went into a village, and in the conversation the word medica would come out. The medica served all the medical needs and, often, whatever ailment they had, they went to the midwife. The midwives often dispensed herbs for different complaints and also played the part of a counselor to the villagers. The midwife was the only type of leader in a village community except for the men who were politically inclined, and, of course, except for the religious leaders. People would go to the midwife because there was no other woman leader . . . So, the midwife was a very special person, especially for the other women." (Edith Rackley; in Fran Leeper Buss 1980, 115-16)

" 'Midwife is translated from an ancient Greek term which means "attendant at birth," ' says Lt. Col. Beverly Dyches, who has been a midwife at the U.S. Air Force Hospital at Langley Air Force Base in Virginia since 1974. She explained that midwives are skilled in taking care of the emotional as well as the physical needs of pregnant women." (Champaign-Urbana [Illinois] *News-Gazette* 1982, April 11)

MIKIRI

Among the Igbo of Africa, "gatherings of women based on common residence . . . which [appear] to have performed the major role in daily self-rule among women and to have articulated women's interests as opposed to those of men. *Mikiri* provided women with a forum in which to develop their political talents and with a means for protecting their interests as traders, farmers, wives, and mothers." (Judith Van Allen 1976, 69)

(See ANLU, WOMEN'S WAR)

MILITANCE

"Why is it that men's blood-shedding militancy is applauded and women's symbolic militancy punished with a prison cell and the forcible feeding horror: . . . [Men] have decided that it is entirely right and proper for men to fight for their liberties and their rights, but that it is not right and proper for women to fight for theirs." (Emmeline Pankhurst 1914, 268-9)

"Alice Paul, militant suffragist and mother of the Equal Rights Amendment, expressed [the feeling of ERA activists in 1981]: 'It's like a mosaic. Each of us puts in one little stone and then you get a great mosaic at the end.' " " 'We're now taking off our white gloves, [says] Sonia Johnson. 'There's a recipe for justice of any kind,' in her view. 'The last ingredient you add is risk. After you've done everything else, then you risk your reputation, your fortune, physical damage, your life.' " (Susan G. Butruille 1981, B16)

"Is a strangely misleading term. Our so-called militant methods consist solely in having things done to us." (Katherine Roberts 1910, 17-18)

"They call us militants, but General Westmoreland, General Abrams, General Motors and General Dynamics – they're the real militants. We don't even have a helicopter." (Florynce R. Kennedy, quoted in Gloria Steinem 1973, 55)

"Militancy no longer means guns at high noon, if it ever did. It means actively working for change, sometimes in the absence of any surety that change is coming. It means doing the unromantic and tedious work necessary to forge meaningful coalitions, and it means recognizing which coalitions are possible and which coalitions are not ... It means fighting despair." (Audre Lorde 1984, 141-2)

MILITARISM
"Most usefully treated as pathology." (Elise Boulding 1976, xx)

"Is the most obvious product of patriarchy. For the same social and historic reasons, men have usually taken the lead in the Peace Movement, but when this leads to a confrontation situation, men confronting men, this becomes a microcosm of the original problem." (Greenham Common Peace Camp 1983)

MILK
"The first food which sustains human life. Milk signified rebirth to the initiates of Cybele in Rome. Numerous Goddesses, such as Hathor, were symbolized by a cow. . . . The nursing madonna was a favorite subject of Renaissance painters. The nipple and breast inspired dome architecture such as St. Sophia's Cathedral. And to the Slavs, the milk of Mother Mokosh has signified rain." (Rose-Ellen Hope 1982, 8)

MIND
"Lock up your libraries if you like; but there is no gate, no lock, no bolt that you can set upon the freedom of my mind." (Virginia Woolf 1929, 79) *Masculine*: "It will be noted that the masculine mind is prolific in titles, in designations, in definitions, in classifications, in names." (Frances Swiney 1918, 397) *Collective*: Composed of "certain timid minds which, believing themselves to be guided by a far-sighted prudence, are always in the rear of any advance in thought or deed." (Margaret J. Tuke 1919, 89)

MIND-SETS
"The limits of thought are not so much from outside, by the fullness or poverty of experiences that meet the mind, as from within, by the power of conception, the wealth of formulative notions with which the mind meets experiences." (Suzanne Langer 1951; cited in Mary Daly 1973, 11)

MIND-THE-BABY ARGUMENT
"A seeming concern that to allow women new freedoms will tax all their energies – and will detract from the care of the home and children. Other clauses are usually attached to make sure the spinster is included, to keep her out of Imperial politics also." (Robert F. Cholmeley 1908, 9)

MINISTRY
"Reaching back into our tradition, we can begin to appropriate that which is already ours – so great a ministry! How timidly women have said, 'I am minister!' How apologetically, 'I am theologian!' Yet by virtue of baptism, everyone of us is minister." (Nelle Morton n.d., 8)

MINORITY
Activist portion of the population. "They challenge all things, question customs, laws, superstitions, conventionalities, and woe betide those that do not give them a

satisfactory answer!" (Mrs Cavendish Bentinck 1911, *Votes for Women*, December 15, 177)

MISANDRY

Hatred of men, from Greek *misein* "to hate" + *aner/andros* "a man." "Note that the word *anthropos*, from which misanthropy derives, means mankind in general; *aner* means a specific man." "As of today, there is a word to express man-hating: misandrism; and if you are a man-hater, nameless one, you are now a misandrist. If there is any truth to the theory that the assignation of a name to an idea gives the idea validity, then misandrists now have a place in this sexist world and a name under which they can unite to dispel the male indoctrinated theory of perverted female behavior." (Marilyn Goldberg, n.d.) Means "(1) a refusal to suppress the evidence of one's experience with men; (2) a woman's defense against fear and pain; (3) an affirmation of the cathartic effects of justifiable anger." (Ingrid Bengis, n.d.) Means man-hating; is a companion word for misogyny. (Constance Rover; quoted in Dale Spender 1983a, 170) Should not be confused with *misanthropy*, a hatred of men and women, or with *misogyny*, woman-hating, a widely accepted social attitude in a sexist world.

(See ANDROCENTRISM, MALE SUPREMACY, MISOGYNY, PATRIARCHY)

MISOANDRY

(See MISANDRY)

MISOGYNY

Woman-hating. "Includes the beliefs that women are stupid, petty, manipulative, dishonest, silly, gossipy, irrational, incompetent, undependable, narcissistic, castrating, dirty, over-emotional, unable to make altruistic or moral judgments, oversexed, undersexed.... Such beliefs culminate in attitudes that demean our bodies, our abilities, our characters, and our efforts, and imply that we must be controlled, dominated, subdued, abused, and used, not only for male benefit but for our own." (Sheila Ruth 1980, 89) "Is the passion; antifeminism is its ideological defense; in the sex-based insult passion and ideology are united in an act of denigration and intimidation." (Andrea Dworkin 1983, 201) "There is no attraction without possible repulsion, and the fact of sexual antagonism can be denied no more than the far more obvious fact of sexual attraction . . . Too often [civilization] overstimulates sex attraction to the danger point, so rendering an increase in its corollary inevitable. Celibates and misogynists are most numerous in a licentious age; in fact one may say that a misogynist is almost always a reformed rake." (Beatrice Forbes-Robertson Hale 1914, 50) Includes antifeminist as well as antifemale attitudes. (Judy Page 1983, correspondence)

(See MISANDRY)

MISS

Form of address now used for unmarried women but used in earlier centuries as a marriage-neutral title for any adult woman; common in the 17th century and continued in the 18th and 19th, it has never entirely disappeared. "In 1914, the feminist Fola La Follette urged the formal extension of *Miss* to serve as the general feminine title both before and after marriage. By the mid-twentieth century, usage books acknowledged *Miss* as an appropriate title for a married woman to retain in business or public life. In addition, twentieth-century secretarial and etiquette handbooks often suggest that *Miss* could function exactly like *Mr.*, that it could be used as a safe generic title in addressing a letter to a woman whose marital status was unknown." (Dennis Baron 1984, 10)

(See FORMS OF ADDRESS, MS)

Form of address indicating respect. "I became suddenly conscious of a complete change in his manner from the easy familiarity of the morning before. Instead of the generic name of 'Sally,' or the Christian name which on better acquaintance he applied to the other girls, he had politely prefixed a 'Miss' to my surname.

There had come, too, a peculiar feeling of trust and confidence in him – a welcome sensation in this horrible, degraded place." (Dorothy Richardson 1905, 255)

Form of address with economic consequences. Examining why female civil servants in Great Britain were paid less than their male counterparts, Virginia Woolf quoted several letters to the newspaper that were anti-female in sentiment. "After considering the evidence contained in those three quotations, you will agree that there is good reason to think that the word 'Miss,' however delicious its scent in the private house, has a certain odor attached to it in Whitehall which is disagreeable to the noses on the other side of the partition; and that it is likely that a name to which 'Miss' is attached will, because of this odor, circle in the lower spheres where the salaries are small rather than mount to the higher spheres where the salaries are substantial. As for 'Mrs.,' it is a contaminated word; an obscene word. The less said about that word the better. Such is the smell of it, so rank does it stink in the nostrils of Whitehall, that Whitehall excludes it entirely. In Whitehall, as in heaven, there is neither marrying nor giving in marriage." (Virginia Woolf 1938; in Gloria Kaufman and Mary Kay Blakely eds 1980, 111)

MISS AMERICA PAGEANT

Most famous U.S. beauty pageant, held each year in Atlantic City. Contestants from all 50 states compete; the winner is crowned Miss America and "reigns" for a year, earning financial rewards and career opportunities. Contestants must meet both physical and moral standards; offenders are ousted. For many women, the pageant symbolizes many of the worst aspects of patriarchal culture.

(See MISS AMERICA PROTEST)

MISS AMERICA PROTEST

Important 1968 protest. "The Women's Liberation Movement surfaced with its first major militant demonstration on September 7, 1968, in Atlantic City, at the Miss America Pageant. . . . About two hundred women descended on this tacky town and staged an all-day demonstration on the boardwalk in front of Convention Hall (where the pageant was taking place), singing, chanting, and performing guerrilla theater nonstop throughout the day. The crowning of a live sheep as Miss America was relevant to where the society is at. . . . The demonstrators mock-auctioned off a dummy of Miss America and flung dishcloths, steno pads, girdles, and bras into a Freedom Trash Can. This last was translated by the male-controlled media into the totally invented act of 'bra-burning,' a nonevent upon which they have fixated constantly ever since, in order to avoid presenting the real reasons for the growing discontent of 'women, . . . The death of the concept of Miss America in Atlantic City (which was celebrated by a candlelight funeral dance on the boardwalk at midnight) was only the beginning. A sisterhood of free women is giving birth to a new life-style, and the throes of its labor are authentic stages in the Revolution." (Robin Morgan 1968; in Robin Morgan 1978, 64-7)

(See ACTIONS, BEAUTY, BRA-BURNING, COSMETICS, MISS WORLD ACTION)

Another participant's critique of the protest: "No action taken in the Women's Liberation Struggle will be all good or all bad. It is necessary that we analyze each step to see what we did that was effective, what was not, and what was downright destructive . . . One of the biggest mistakes of the whole pageant was our anti-womanism . . . Posters which read 'Up Against the Wall, Miss America,' 'Miss America Sells it,' and 'Miss America Is a Big Falsie,' hardly raised any women's consciousness and really harmed the cause of sisterhood. Miss America and all beautiful women came off as our enemy instead of as our sisters who suffer with us . . . We didn't say clearly enough that we women are all FORCED to play the Miss America role – not by beautiful women but by men who we have to act that way for and by a system that has so well institutionalized male supremacy for its own ends ... Also, crowning a live sheep Miss America sort of said that beautiful women are sheep. However ... the grandmother of one of the participants really began to understand the action when she was told about the sheep, and she ended up joining the protest." (Carol Hanisch 1968)

MISS ANNE

Is the mythical folk representation of all white women, except very young ones, in U.S. Black culture. It's also used for Black women who seem to be putting on the airs of white women (e.g., speaking pretentiously). (John Langston Gwaltney 1980, xvi, 50-2)

MISS FIDDITCH

Is a mythical schoolteacher to whom American usage critics attribute many stereotypes supposedly associated with women's language use, including prissiness and hyper-propriety. She was originally named by linguist Henry Lee Smith, Jr, but the stereotype had been described earlier by critic H. L. Mencken as one of those old-maid schoolteachers who would rather parse than eat; Martin Joos then used the character of Miss Fidditch to embody a fanatic obsession with "correct" usage in his book on stylistic variation, *The Five Clocks* (1961). Feminists have noted the sexism and condescension inherent in this (Margaret B. Fleming 1983), while research on women's supposed linguistic conservatism (e.g., William Labov 1972, Patricia Nichols 1976 and 1980) indicates that "correctness," like other linguistic phenomena, depends upon many social, cultural, and contextual factors and is not always the province of women.

(See POLITENESS, PRESCRIPTIV-ISM)

MISSIONARIES

Figures who carried Euro-American and European patriarchal culture to the rest of the world. "They stressed Christ's submission to humiliation, and so ...

conditioned the people of Africa to humiliation by the white man." (Nadine Gordimer 1965; cited in Elaine Partnow 1977, 274) From *Diary of an African Nun*: "For the drums will soon, one day, be silent. I will help muffle them forever. To assure life for my people in this world I must be among the lying ones and teach them how to die. I will turn their dances into prayers to an empty sky, and their lovers into dead men, and their babies into unsung chants that choke their throats each spring. In this way will the wife of a loveless, barren, hopeless Western marriage broadcast the joys of an enlightened religion to an imitative people." (Alice Walker 1968, 41)

MISSIONARY POSITION

Man on top face down/woman on bottom face up. A supposed "universal" position for sexual intercourse, unknown and unmissed in many parts of the world.

MISS WORLD ACTION

"The 1970 Miss World competition in Albert Hall was the occasion for an experiment with civil disobedience. In a carefully organized operation about 100 feminists infiltrated and disrupted the competition. They were charged with riotous behavior and throwing dangerous weapons – leaflets and plastic mice. They wrote later, 'We've been in the Miss World contest all our lives ... judging ourselves as the judges judge us.' " (Anna Coote and Beatrix Cambell 1982, 23)

(See ACTIONS, MISS AMERICA PROTEST)

Slogans from Miss World picketing banners, Fall 1969;

MIS FIT REFUSES TO CONFORM
MIS CONCEPTION DEMANDS
    FREE ABORTIONS FOR ALL
    WOMEN
MIS FORTUNE DEMANDS EQUAL
    PAY FOR ALL WOMEN
MIS JUDGED DEMANDS AN END
    TO BEAUTY CONTESTS
MIS DIRECTED DEMANDS
    EQUAL OPPORTUNITY

MIS LAID DEMANDS FREE
CONTRACEPTION
MIS GOVERNED DEMANDS
LIBERATION
MIS USED DEMANDS 24 HOUR
CHILD CARE CENTERS
MIS PLACED DEMANDS A
CHANCE TO GET OUT OF THE
HOUSE
MIS TREATED DEMANDS
SHARED HOUSEWORK
MIS NOMER DEMANDS A NAME
OF HER OWN
MIS QUOTED DEMANDS AN
UNBIASED PRESS
(*Shrew* 1971, Special Review Issue,
cover; Berkeley Women's History Collec-
tion)

MISTER-ECTOMY
"The most foolproof of contraceptives."
(Mary Daly 1978, 239)

MISTERHOOD
Slogan of Ladies Against Women:
"Misterhood is Powerful!"
(See ACRONYM, ACTION)

MISTRESS
Form of address and reference. "A term
introduced from French in the 14th
century, it originally denoted a woman
who rules or is in command. Almost from
the beginning, however, it was also used
in extended senses that implied little
power or authority, and it also acquired
sexual connotation. The literary evidence
suggests that this development took place
in the context of romantic love. In
modern usage, this term is almost devoid
of its original meaning of status and
power. The term survives in the forms of
address *Miss* and *Mrs.* (originally abbrevi-
ations of *mistress*), and in the sexual
sense." (Elizabeth Judd, in press) "One of
the acceptable roles for women." (Midge
Lennert and Norma Willson, eds, 1973,
8)
(See FORMS OF ADDRESS,
SEMANTIC DEROGATION)

MNGL
Courtesy title for single men. *Mngl.*
(pronounced "mingle") is the merging of
M and single. (Bobbye D. Sorrels 1983,
10)
(See FORMS OF ADDRESS)

MOBILE, DOWNWARDLY
A luxury of the rich. "Poor people don't
need to prove they're poor. . . . It's only
the rich in their guilt and denial who can
really afford to be downwardly mobile."
(Morena to her mother 1977, in Karen
Payne 1983, 386)

MODERN TIMES
For Western men, the fifteenth century.
For women, the eighteenth century when
"the death of women in childbirth and the
death of young infants are no longer
accepted as the workings of fate; there is
increasing interest in the techniques of
delivering babies, though the research is
still haphazard and naive; married couples
seek to have fewer children and begin to
practice coitus interruptus, which heretofore had been strictly forbidden by the
Church." (Evelyne Sullerot 1974, 143)

MOMIST
"Everything is all Mom's fault with her
dominating, unfeminine ways. Popular
attitude in late forties and fifties, and
sixties where it is more commonly known
as 'Jewish Momism' or Portnoyism."
(Marlene Dixon and Joreen 1970, 16)
(See PORTNOY'S MOTHER'S
COMPLAINT)

MONEY
A commodity controlled primarily by
men, and needed by women; a financial
resource which is mostly in the hands and
pockets of men. Barbara Bodichon pointed
out in the 19th century that "there is a
prejudice against women accepting money
for work." Men are not opposed to
women working, just against their being
paid for it. (Barbara Bodichon 1857) The
term "took its name from a title of Rome's
Great Mother, Juno Moneta . . . whose
Capitoline temple included the Roman

mint. Silver and gold coins were valuable not only by reason of their precious metal but also by the blessing of the Goddess herself." (Barbara G. Walker 1983, 667) It "is the only virtue recognized in many a Court of Justice." (Frances Swiney 1918, 405) It "dignifies what is frivolous if unpaid for." (Virginia Woolf 1929; in Michèle Barrett 1979, 90) "Without money, you are nothing. I keep the money I earn. I don't even let my husband smell it." (Latin American peasant woman; cited in Audrey Bronstein 1982, 253)

MONOPOLY

Of trade: Man's ideas about "what is becoming. . . . If women may not work in mines, why should men be allowed to paint teacups?" (Lady McLaren 1908, 40)

THE MONTHLY EXTRACT: AN IRREGULAR PERIODICAL

Newsletter of the gynecological self-help clinics of America in the mid-1970s.
(See PERIODICALS)

MOON

In much of mythology, "ruled the sexuality of women, and sometimes made them scornful of the male-dominated society's notions of hierarchy." In history, frequently a symbol of women's sexuality, spiritual strength, and other powers. (Barbara G. Walker 1983, 673) "The moon is my mother. She is not sweet like mary . . . /She is bald and wild." (Sylvia Plath 1961, 173) "For the uses of men we have been butchered and crippled and shut up and carved open under the moon that swells and shines and shrinks again into nothingness, pregnant and then waning towards its little monthly death. The moon is always female but the sun is female only in lands where females are let into the sun to rush and climb." (Marge Piercy; in Karen Lindsey 1981, 15)

MOON THINKING

"A profoundly important intuitive capacity that Western rationalistic traditions have

shunted to one side." (Elise Boulding 1976, 195)

MORALITY

"Morality has never concerned itself with the use of sexual coercion, force or violence for maintaining male power is precisely its function." (Sally Roesch Wagner 1982)

"you are what is female
you shall be called Eve.
and what is masculine shall be called God.
And from your name Eve we shall take the word Evil.
and from God's, the word Good.
now you understand patriarchal morality."
(Judy Grahn 1978a, 137)

MORALS

Laws used to regulate many primitive impulses but with "this little masculine exception: – 'All's fair in love and war.' " (Charlotte Perkins Gilman 1911, 144-5)

MOTHER

One who gives birth, originates, nurtures, has responsibility and authority, or heads a religious order. Feminists are exploring a number of issues concerning the figure of the mother, some of which are suggested by the comments below.
(See EVE, FAMILY, MA, MATER, MATRIARCHY, MATRONYMY, MOTHERHOOD, MOTHERING, MOTHERWORK, ORIGINAL, PATRIARCHY, POST-PARTUM DOCUMENT)
Definitions: a mother is "that which gives birth to something, is the origin or source of something or nurtures in the manner of a mother . . . Contrary to some stereotypical misinformation about the at-home work life of mothers, our role is the most expansive and outward-looking one in the world." (Marilyn D. Clancy 1984)
"(1) Womon who gives birth; (2) a prototype ('i rerecorded this tape from the mother copy'); (3) largest or more important ('agatha sleeps in the mother bed-

room').'' (zana 1983, correspondence) Mothers are "considered by sons to be less human than they are themselves." (Teresa Billington-Greig 1911b, 71) A mother "is a separate and imperfect individual who is not always available and who cannot and will not satisfy all of one's needs and expectations." (Karen Payne 1983, 333) "The most automated appliance in a household." (Beverly Jones 1970, 56; cited in Elaine Partnow 1977, 313)

Place of the mother in discourse: Mistress of the biological process of conception and gestation: "Cells combine, redouble, proliferate; size grows, tissue is distended, moods change their rhythm. . . . Motherhood has hitherto been addressed within two modes of discourse: science, whose 'objectivity' excludes the treatment of the subject, the matrix of its operations, and Christian theology, which valorizes motherhood as the receptacle of divinity. Instead, however, we may see the mother as the filter, the passage, the threshold on which nature and culture confront each other." (Julia Kristeva 1980, 158)

Place of the mother in society: "So central is the identity bestowed by the mother role that we can't get rid of it even when we are not fulfilling it. A childless woman does not become an honorary man, free to do the world's work. On the contrary, her condition has usually been seen as a defect." (Elizabeth Janeway 1980, 308) "I'm no more your mother/ Than the cloud that distills a mirror to reflect its own slow/Effacement at the wind's hand." (Sylvia Plath 1961, "Barren Woman," 157) "The harsh truth is that no societal compromise which changes other features of woman's conditioning while leaving her role as first parent intact will get at the roots of asymmetric sexual privilege." (Dorothy Dinnerstein 1976, 71)

On the qualities of being a mother: "If enforced wakefulness is the handmaiden and necessary precursor to serious brainwashing, a mother – after her first child – is ready for her final demise." (Beverly Jones 1970, 56) "Being a mother is a noble status, right? Right. So why does it change when you put 'unwed' or 'welfare' in front of it?" (Florynce Kennedy; cited in Elaine Partnow 197, 203) "Is the *official* good woman of the Western world. . . . Her converse, the Playmate." The wife is supposed to be both of these incompatible people. "It is schizophrenic." (Sheila Ruth 1980, 92-3)

On the mother-daughter relationship: "My mother and I work to unravel the knot. The task is daily: bloody, terrifying, and necessary, and filled with joy. The relationship between mother and daughter stands at the center of what I fear most in our culture. Heal that wound and we change the world. *A revolution capable of healing our wounds.*" (Aurora Levins Morales 1981, 56)

The mother in psychoanalysis: "Briefly, the concept of the Mother is completely organized in Freud by the theories of the Phallus, the Oedipus complex, and Castration. Before their introduction, what was there? The 'pregenital,' 'preoedipal,' dust, chaos, a 'prehistoric' continent: a time, in any case, which cannot threaten men. Aren't they guaranteed to be cut off from the Mother by Castration? . . . At the same time as the child, however, an imaginary Super-Mother entered into psychoanalysis. She rolled into France from across the Channel with good and bad breasts; her womb full of babies, her primary femininity, her incorporated-phallus-of-the-father. The mother as primordial system, source and place of the first psychological experiences of the child (Melanie Klein). That mother had a sacred fullness." (Monique Plaza 1982, 80-1)

The mother as metaphor: "the best of herself given to woman by another woman for her to be able to love herself and return in love the body that was 'born' to her . . . I don't mean the overbearing, clutchy 'mother' but, rather, what touches you, the equivoice that affects you, fills your breast with an urge to come to language and launches your forces; the rhythm that laughs you; the intimate recipient who makes all metaphors possible and desirable; body (body? bodies?), no more describable than god, the soul, or the Other; that part of you that leaves a space between yourself and urges you to inscribe in language your woman's style." (Hélène Cixous 1975b, 252)

Mother as stormtrooper for the patriarchy: "Mothers raise daughters to conform to the strictures of the conventional female life as defined by men, whatever the ideological values of the men. Mothers are the immediate enforcers of male will, the guards at the cell door, the flunkies who administer the electric shocks to punish rebellion . . . Most girls, however much they resent their mothers, do become very much like them. Rebellion can rarely survive the aversion therapy that passes for being brought up female." (Andrea Dworkin 1983, 15)

MOTHERHOOD

"During the early evolution of the human race, motherhood was the only recognized bond of relationship." Unlike paternity, maternity was a known biological fact and could serve as the basis for kinship relationships and other social arrangements. Motherhood and maternal relationships were recognized and documented on inscriptions on tombs, records of land ownership, inheritance and other documents, scriptures, and legends. Because women kept calendars, it is likely they who gave fathers the secret of fatherhood. Though "modern male scholars often tried to conceal or deny the evidence of the ancient matriarchate," evidence abounds that motherhood was of primary importance. (Barbara G. Walker 1983, 680-95)

A state of being that creates both pleasures and hardships. "Is not . . . a kind of malady." (Elizabeth Robins 1913, 197) "A calamity to be avoided if possible [at times when] it meant loss of work and wages as soon as it became known to authorities." (Ernestine Mills 1919, 10) "However natural it's very troublesome and after they grow up generally a great anxiety." (Hannah Cullwick, Victorian maidservant; in Liz Stanley ed. 1984,

238) "The most beautiful thing in my life. The wonder of it never ceases for me – to see you all developing from tiny helpless babies into big strong girls and boys, to see your minds changing with your years and to remember that some day you will be grown men and women. It is overwhelming." (Mrs Colbert to her daughter Jane 1930; quoted in Karen Payne 1983, 283)

"You see, they were Mothers, not in our sense of helpless involuntary fecundity, forced to fill and overfill the land, every land, and then see their children suffer, sin, and die, fighting horribly with one another; but in the sense of Conscious Makers of People. Motherlove with them was not a brute passion, a mere 'instinct,' a wholly personal feeling; it was – a religion. It included that limitless feeling of sisterhood, that wide unity in service which was so difficult for us to grasp. And it was National, Racial, Human – oh, I don't know how to say it." (Charlotte Perkins Gilman 1915, 68)

Motherhood lends itself to no simple analysis; socially and experientially, it is fraught with complexities and ambiguities. "It is very hard to disentangle the positive qualities [of motherhood] from the web of associations spun by social and economic facts which elevate and restrict our strength into a static role." (Lesley Saunders 1983, 95) "Is a matter with ambiguity built right in at the beginning. Even before the beginning. But the women's movement [like all other social movements] has yet to be very good about ambiguity." (Paula Weideger 1980, 205) Invokes frequent confusion including "painful, wonderful, destructive, liberating love that many of us feel for our children." Motherhood affects all other relationships in ways "impossible to analyze away into accepted modes of feminist orthodoxy." (Sara Maitland 1980, 79)

"Inside the patriarchy, is bound by institutional forms." That same patriarchy tells us that

" – we cannot be good mothers alone
 – every child must have [an acknowledged] father

– without a husband, a woman's child is not legitimate"
(Stephanie Dowrick 1980, 68)

"Is admirable . . . only so long as mother and child are attached to a legal father: motherhood out of wedlock, or under the welfare system, or lesbian motherhood, are harassed, humiliated, or neglected." (Adrienne Rich 1976, rpt. 1979, 196)

A form of service not recognized as an important job by many people on the political left who regard a mother "as handicapped or a drop-out from the real action of class struggle." (Lucy Goodison 1980, 39)

"Has been nothing as much as a long term routine of nurturance: allowing the growth of another at the same time as trying to make room for one's own growth. It has meant – above all – keeping in constant communication and providing meals (over one thousand a year)." (Jane Melnick 1980, 184)

MOTHERING

Caring processes and skills. Includes: "(1) Time available at short-notice and in flexible lumps; (2) high levels of skill in domestic tasks – e.g. cooking, cleaning, washing; (3) high levels of social skill in, for example, talking to their clients – be they very young or very old – and in listening to their clients in order to assess their present and future needs; (4) skills in information gathering about other services, and ability to manipulate other services on the client's behalf; (5) ability to act autonomously over a wide range of tasks of widely differing skill level; (6) punctuality and reliability; (7) ability to operate over long periods in fairly isolated circumstances, engaging in routine and often unpleasant tasks, with – particularly in the case of the very old, the mentally handicapped and mentally ill – very little measurable 'success,' let alone positive response from the client." (Clare Ungerson 1983, 63-4) Other definitions follow.
(See MOTHER, MOTHERHOOD)
"Is a job which not only demands a

unique combination of management responsibilities, manual labour, and skilled work, but also goes on seven days a week, twenty-four hours a day and is completely unpaid, unrewarded, and undervalued. Moreover it is a no-win arrangement nowadays: if you devote yourself entirely to the child, you are failing yourself in your duties to self-development, damaging your husband's frail ego, and probably 'over-mothering – or spoiling – ' your child. If you do not so devote yourself you are depriving your child of her/his emotional needs. Either way you are isolated and either way, whatever happens, it is *all your fault*." (Sara Maitland 1980, 88)

Is parental work which is not a personal, individual matter. "As single mothers, lesbian mothers, and co-parenting women continually remind us, there are many ways to provide children with examples of caring which do not incorporate the inequalities of power and privilege which so nicely prepare the next generation to find 'natural' a world in which they will either exploit or be exploited." (Sara Ruddick 1980, 262)

Is a complex task. "Being a mother is no piece of cake – and probably never was – especially if there's a father to deal with as well as the kids." (Jackie Page 1980; quoted in Karen Payne 1983, 37)

Means "claiming some power over who we choose to be, and knowing that such power is relative within the realities of our lives. Yet knowing that only through the use of that power can we effectively change those realities. Mothering means the laying to rest of what is weak, timid, and damaged – without despisal – the protection and support of what is useful for survival and change, and our joint explorations of the difference." (Audre Lorde 1984, 173-4)

MOTHERING SUNDAY

In England, mid-Lent Sunday, a day when children feast on mothering cakes and simnel cakes and customarily give small presents to their mothers. In earlier times, "going a-mothering" involved offering one's mother a simnel cake in exchange for her blessing; "the simnel was a manikin, Gingerbread Man, similitude, or Host: a god ceremonially eaten." (Barbara G. Walker 1983, 695; *Brewer's Dictionary of Phrase and Fable*)

MOTHER-IN-LAW

Mother of one's husband or wife. A female villain in the drama of marriage, documented in nasty quotations from as early as 1440 in the *Oxford English Dictionary*. "Quite nice women suddenly have to wear this title with the stigma on it and a crown of thorns. We're so frightened of it that we change our nature to avoid it and in doing so we end up the classical mother-in-law we feared in the first place; so gravely have we twisted ourselves." (Sylvia Ashton-Warner 1970; in Elaine Partnow 1977, 119)

MOTHER NATURE

Has been confounded with *women* throughout our civilization. Like Mother Nature, "we have been taken to be resources for men, supposed to provide for the necessary (needy) parts of their lives. . . . Woman, like nature, has been what man has fought for, and against, but not with. . . . We should remember that a translation is needed from what is found in nature to what is enforced by positive law or social sanction. Natural qualities and needs do not in themselves have anything at all to do with political and social roles and rights." (Elizabeth Kamarck Minnich 1982, 2)

MOTHER-RITE CULTURE

Specifically refers to the theory of "mother-right" developed by J. J. Bachofen and others in the 19th century (see Barbara G. Walker 1983, 680-95). Generally refers to matriarchal practices within cultures. "We still have Women's Societies and there are at least 30 active women-centered Mother-Rite Cultures existing and practicing their everyday life in that manner, on this continent." (Carol Lee Sanchez 1983b, 151)

MOTHER'S DAY

In the U.S., the second Sunday in May is an occasion for remembering one's mother; was originally intended by Julia Ward Howe as a day to protest war. Can be seen as an occasion for celebrating the potential role of mothers in the rebirth of society. "I do believe that the hand that rocks the cradle should rock the boat and the world as well." (Marilyn D. Clancy 1984)

MOTHER'S DAY POEM

M is for her menopausal problems
O is for her "masochistic" needs
T is for her terror as she ages
H is for the help for which she pleads
E is for the emptiness her life is
R is for the roles that she has lost
Put them all together: they spell
    MOTHER
The ones the culture's double-crossed.

  (Pauline B. Bart; in Gloria Kaufman and Mary Kay Blakely eds 1980, 147)

MOTHER TONGUE

First language. Original language. A vision of women inventing and producing language, of women talking, of mothering texts, of verbal play. (Daphne Marlatt 1984) The power to use language that women have always had through their role in teaching language to children. (Sandra Gilbert and Susan Gubar 1982) "Women struggling for words feel haunted by false feelings of personal inadequacy, by anger, frustration, and a kind of sadness/bereavement. For it is, after all, our 'mother tongue' that has been turned against us by the tongue-twisters. Learning to speak our Mothers' Tongue *is* exorcising the male 'mothers.'" (Mary Daly 1978, 330)

MOTHER-WIT

"'The cure for false theology is mother-wit,' says Emerson." (Frances Swiney 1918, 53)

MOTHERWORK

"The labor of birthing, raising, tending,

guiding and caring for children and families within the home, and the extension of this work into the community and the labor market. . . . Motherwork is one of the most intense and sophisticated forms of choreography in which one must plan and coordinate a series of often simultaneous or disparate movements in both a daily and lifelong pattern." (Editorial, *Woman: A Journal of Liberation* 1980, 7:2, 68)

MOTTO

From French *mot* 'word.' A word, phrase, or sentence inscribed on something, placed on a literary work, newspaper, etc., or taken up by an organization or movement as being expressive of its spirit. Some mottos are: "Think globally; act locally." (Gina Foglia and Dorit Wolffberg 1981, 449)

"I will not resign myself to the usual lot of women who bow their heads and become concubines." (Trieu Thi Trinh, 248 A.D., leader of thousands of Vietnamese in a campaign to get rid of the Chinese; cited in Arlene Eisen Bergman 1975, 31)

"Those Who Nurture Will Govern." (Motto of the newspaper *The Matriarchist*; cited in Carol Erlich 1981, 116)

"The only way to have a free press is to own one." (Motto of the Chicago newspaper *The Spark*)

"Do Everything." (Motto of the Women's Christian Temperance Union)

MOVEMENT

Series of organized activities by and for people working toward common goals; to the people within it, often "the movement" with no other identifier. The women's movement, historically and currently linked to other movements for liberation, seeks its own identity in part by examining women's role in other struggles, and whether other movements are addressed toward women's interests and goals.

(See FEMINISM, MARXIST-FEMINIST, WOMAN QUESTION, WOMEN'S LIBERATION MOVEMENT, WOMEN'S MOVEMENT)

"Women played a very important role in the Puerto Rican workers' movement. The bitterest struggles against North American military power and other capitalist interests were in fact wages by women, in the clothing and tobacco industries. Throughout the 1930's women took to the streets to organize strikes, trade unions, and political campaigns, both in the towns and in the countryside. These Puerto Rican women workers completely rejected the image of the fragile, weak, pure, and passive 'ideal woman.' " (LACW Collective 1977, 36)

"The Atlanta Congress of Colored Women [1895] was the first congress of Black women in the United States and possibly in the world. This little-known historical fact provides compelling evidence that the first grass-roots, all Black, mass-organized and mass-led movement for social and political good happened among Black women." (Erlene Stetson 1979, 46)

"Feminists may lose the Women's Movement, as we did almost 100 years ago, in the 1880's, through co-optation – and co-optation can be so easily made to look like debilitation. There is a theory, however, that the Movement will be born Feminist again and again. According to this theory, it is men who through rape father such an offspring upon women, so that as long as there is a phallocracy, there will be a breeding Feminist Women's Movement." (Grace Shinell 1982, 111)

MOYNIHAN REPORT

(See MATRIARCHY)

MR

"A form of address for men, marital status deemed not relevant, as for Mr. Clean, the detergent, and Mr. Ed, the horse." (Eve Merriam 1975, 11)

(See FORMS OF ADDRESS, MUSH)

MRD

Abbreviation for "married." *Mrd* (pronounced "murd") is the courtesy title for married men, as in Mrd Walter Jones. (Bobbye D. Sorrels 1983, 10)

(See FORMS OF ADDRESS)

MRS

Form of address for married women. "The use of desigations like 'Mrs John Jones' does not go back much before 1800. Martha Washington would have been mystified to receive a letter addressed to 'Mrs. George Washington,' for at that time the written abbreviation *Mrs.*, a social title applied to any adult woman, was used interchangeably with its spelled-out form *mistress* and was probably pronounced the same way. 'Mistress George' would have made little sense." (Casey Miller and Kate Swift 1976, 13)

(See FORMS OF ADDRESS, MRS, MAN, NAMES)

Title of dignity and honor. "In order to interpret accurately and critically the historical past of Black women, we must accept their definitions of themselves . . . It's the old argument of not calling Mrs. Booker T. Washington Mrs. Booker T. Washington when she wanted to be called Mrs. Booker T. Washington, because for a long time she couldn't use 'Mrs.' She wanted that. That was her definition for herself." (Bonnie Johnson; in Cheryl Clarke et al. 1983, 128)

Dedication of the novel *Tar Baby*:

"FOR
Mrs. Caroline Smith
Mrs. Millie McTyeire
Mrs. Ardelia Willis
Mrs. Ramah Wofford
Mrs. Lois Brooks
– and each of their sisters,
all of whom knew
their true and ancient
properties"
(Toni Morrison 1981)

Conveys respect and identity. " 'A nice young woman she was, and not stuck-up like some as I could name. 'Mrs Pettican,' she said to me, which I call it better manners than callin' you Cook as they mostly do, as though they paid your wages for the right of callin' you out of your name.' " (Dorothy L. Sayers 1930, 76)

Labels a woman as the property of a male. "The title *Mrs* and the abandonment of their father's name (a name which required no effort on their part and could not be construed as an achievement) for their husband's name, appears to confirm [for many women] their identity. In a patriarchal society it is not unrealistic to perceive that security lies in marriage – even if this is eventually revealed as a myth." (Dale Spender 1980, 28)

MRS BRYNE'S DICTIONARY

Collection of 6,000 unusual, obscure, difficult, unfamiliar, amusing, weird, or otherwise interesting English words compiled by Josefa Heifetz Byrne, who wrote clear and concise definitions and pronunciation guides after comparing other dictionaries. (Josefa Heifetz Byrne 1974)

MRS GODBLESS

The token woman. "When I would ask if there was a woman in the chemistry department the answer would often be: 'Yes, of course. Haven't you met our Mrs. Godbless? Wonderful woman. She's been with us for years.' Mrs. Godbless invariably proved to be a faculty wife who was employed by the year as an associate or a fellow or a visiting professor, and had been teaching freshman chemistry for twenty years." (Vivian Gornick 1983, 98)

(See TOKEN)

MRS MAN

Title of a study by Una Stannard which traces the practice, a few centuries old, of calling a married woman by her husband's first name and surname, as in "Mrs John Jones." It enables men to claim women as wombs which belong to men and to consider themselves as the only true parent. (Una Stannard 1977)

MRS M. E. STOTT

"Here is a woman who has filled an important office [station agent] for eighteen years, who presents herself to the public as the relict of Mr. Stott, who was laid under the sod long ago. When she is laid by his side, 'Mrs. M. E. Stott' will be inscribed on her tombstone. Her father and mother, from whom she inherited her noble qualities, are not recognized; all the glory of her remarkable executive ability redounds to the credit of Mr. Stott." (Elizabeth Cady Stanton 1898b, 343)

  (See INITIALS, NAMES, TOMB-STONE)

MS

Courtesy title for women which does not reflect marital status. Pronounced "miz." (Bobbye D. Sorrels 1983, 10) Title supported by more than a third of American women as well as "government publications, businesses, and most of the media." (Gloria Steinem 1983, 150) "(1) A form of address being adopted by women who want to be recognized as individuals, rather than being identified by their relationship with a man. The use of Ms. is not meant to protect either the married or the unmarried woman from social pressure – only to signify a female human being. (2) The form of address meaning whole person, female." (Midge Lennert and Norma Willson, eds, 1973, 8) "*Ms.* is being adopted as a standard form of address by women who want to be recognized as individuals, rather than being identified by their relationship with a man." (*Ms.* 1973) "Eliminating *Mrs.* and *Miss* in favor of *Ms.* allows the person to be seen as a woman in her own right rather than in relation to someone else." (Casey Miller and Kate Swift 1976, 120) "*Ms.* is the only serious twentieth-century addition to the system of titles, and the only one that has made some headway." (Dennis Baron 1984, 10)

Because it does not label a woman as the property of a male, subverts, patriarchal ideology and practices: "The (unstated) reason for the undesirability of *Ms* is that it is of no assistance in the maintenance of the patriarchal order and it can even be problematic for males. . . . This is why I think it extremely important that all women should make use of it as a title – if we are to persist with titles." (Dale Spender 1980, 28)

  (See FORMS OF ADDRESS)

"*Ms.* is at least forty years old. It appears to have originated in the 1940s,

though it may have been coined even earlier than that. The controversy surrounding its use [in the media, usage guides, etc.] is much more recent; it does not surface until the 1970s. *Ms.* does not, however, go as far back as 1767, as some have suggested. The *Ms* carved on the tombstone of Sarah Spooner, who died in that year and was buried in Plymouth, Massachusetts, is not an example of colonial feminism or a slip of the chisel, but an abbreviation for *Mistress.* . . . The earliest cite so far uncovered for marriage-neutral *Ms.* occurs in Mario Pei's *The Story of Language* (1949). Pei attributes its creation to the women's rights movement. . . . [This explanation and additional evidence connect] the title both to the women's movement of the nineteenth and early twentieth centuries, and [show] it to be an integral and logical part of the development of the feminine title paradigm of *Miss, Mrs.,* and *Mistress* from Middle English to the present." (Dennis Baron 1984, 10)

MS MAGAZINE

"The best known of any feminist publication, *Ms.* has come to define mainstream feminism. . . . *Ms.* is the most known, most controversial, most praised and most condemned publication in the women's movement. That must say something." (Polly Joan and Andrea Chesman 1978, 39) Sample fan letters:

"My daughter, a junior in medical school, introduced me to *Ms.* It is difficult to express the sense of exhilaration I experienced upon finding in print the ideas which have been smoldering in my semi-rebellious soul for some 40 years. It is comforting to know one is not alone." (Elaine Schramm 1972, letter to the editor, *Ms*, 1:2 [August], 7)

"I know I share my troubles with all women who are involved in any way with the Women's Movement – loneliness, frustration, isolation, and so on. Isolation is the worst enemy for me – that feeling that I am the only one in the world acting and feeling as I do. *Ms.* combats that enemy. Reading some of the articles in the July issue, I felt as though I were reading my own (hypothetical) diary. *Ms.* will give us all a chance for some healthy communication with each other." (Kathleen Salem 1972, letter to the editor, *Ms.* 1:3 [September] 4)

"I happened to need something to read during a recent visit to the beauty salon, and decided I'd see what *Ms.* was all about. There *I* was! On almost every page of the February issue, I found a piece of me: my thoughts, emotions, fears, and confidences. To discover a whole world of women like me . . . I was truly thrilled!" (Linda Clay 1979, letter to the editor, *Ms.* 8:12 [June], 8)

MULE OF THE WORLD

"So de white man throw down de load and tell de nigger man tuh pick it up. He pick it up because he have to, but he don't tote it. He hand it to his women-folks. De nigger woman is de mule uh de world so far as Ah can see. Ah been prayin' for it tuh be different wid you. Lawd, Lawd, Lawd!" (Zora Neale Hurston 1937, 29)

"There is not a Black woman in America who has not felt, at least once, like 'the mule of the world,' to use Zora Neale Hurston's still apt phrase." (Barbara Smith 1983, xxxiv)

MURDERING THE KING'S ENGLISH

"A crime only if you identify with the King." (Judy Grahn 1978c, 10)

MUSE

An archaic meaning is to become astonished; to wonder, marvel. Is "etymologically connected with the Greek *mnasthai*, meaning to remember. Unlike the muse-less/useless man-made 'memories' that mummify our minds, the Musings of Muses fly into the future." "Women who Lust for wisdom become astonished/astonishing, Wondering. As Muses of our own creation, Wonderlusters re-member our Original Powers." (Mary Daly 1984, 13, 26)

MUSH

Unmarried man. "Miss, Missis (Mrs.) and Mister (Mr.) are the three most distinctly disagreeable words in the language, in sound and sense. Two are corruptions of Mistress, the other of Master. In the general abolition of social titles in this our country they miraculously escaped to plague us. If we must have them let us be consistent and give one to the unmarried man. I venture to suggest Mush, abbreviated to Mh." (Ambrose Bierce 1911, 88)

(See FORMS OF ADDRESS, MRD)

MUSIC

Has been "closely associated with the Church, from which women were debarred and you should read Sophie Drinker's book Music and Women if you want to appreciate the struggle of women to establish themselves in this field. It has been impossible to quieten a naturally beautiful voice, even a woman's, because society has permitted her to sing to her children, and to express her joy and sorrow in life whether through lullabies to her children or laments for those she has lost. Consequently, the world has enjoyed the singing of many brilliant women." (Edith Summerskill to her daughter Shirley 1955; in Karen Payne 1983, 186)

"Many times songs were used to plot the escape, relay plans and alert the slaves that a conductor [on the underground railway] was in the area. Harriet Tubman, contributor to the liberation of Black People in many ways, was a leading conductor and always used a special song to disclose her presence. . . . These words indicated Harriet Tubman was in the area, and although the journey would be rough, preparation for leaving should be made." (Eleanor Smith 1979, 59)

"Is suffering made powerful." (Adrienne Rich 1974, 232)

Women's: "I want to see women's music as a definition dropped from our culture. . . . It's a big thing. Women's music is so big that it no longer should be called that. It's just music." (Ferron; interview with denise kulp 1984, 17)

MUTTER

"A girl's best friend is her mutter."
(Dorothy Parker, cited in John Keats
1970, 19)

MYSTIFICATION

"A-mazing Amazons must be aware of
the male methods of mystification. . . .
First, there is *erasure* of women. (The
massacre of millions of women as witches
is erased in patriarchal scholarship.)
(Second, there is *reversal*. (Adam gives
birth to Eve, Zeus to Athena, in patriarchal myth.) Third, there is *false polarization*. (Male-defined 'feminism' is set up
against male-defined 'sexism' in the patriarchal media.) Fourth, there is *divide and
conquer*. (Token women are trained to kill
off feminists in patriarchal professions.)"
(Mary Daly 1978, 8)

MYTH

From Greek *mythos* 'word, speech, story,
legend.' Used by feminists to mean: myth
as the true version of a classical or
popular myth, lost through androcentric
disguise; myth as vision; myth as illusion;
myth as cliché. See entries above and
below.

"Is quintessentially intimate material,
the stuff of dream life, forbidden desire,
inexplicable motivation – everything in
the psyche that to rational consciousness
is unreal, crazed, or abominable." (Alicia
Ostriker 1982, 72)

"Exists in a state of tension. It is not
really describing a situation, but trying by
means of this description *to bring about*
what it declares to exist." (Elizabeth
Janeway 1971, 37)

Its essential characteristics are "simplicity, as well as ambiguity, which
always supplies new excuses for oppression." (Marielouise Janssen-Jurreit
1982, 98)

"Something that never was but is
always happening." (Jean Houston;
quoted in Gloria Steinem 1984, xii)

"Myth, legend, and ritual . . . function
to maintain a status quo. That makes
them singularly bad in coping with
change, indeed counterproductive, for

change is the enemy of myth." (Elizabeth
Janeway 1980, 147)

Myths "are said to be stories that
express intuitive insights and relate the
activities of the gods. The mythical
figures are symbols. These, it is said, open
up depths of reality otherwise closed to
'us.' It is not usually suggested that they
close off depths of reality which would
otherwise be open to us." (Mary Daly
1978, 44)

Myths are "extraordinary lies designed
to make people unfree." (Angela Carter
1983, 71)

Amazon myths: "Tend to express more
about men's fears of women than about
women's aspirations towards independence." (Sheila Rowbotham 1983, 154)

Goddess myths: "If women allow themselves to be consoled for their culturally
determined lack of access to the modes of
intellectual debate by the invocation of
hypothetical great goddesses, they are
simply flattering themselves into submission (a technique often used on them
by men). All the mythic versions of
women, from the myth of the redeeming
purity of the virgin to that of the healing,
reconciling mother, are consolatory non-
senses; and consolatory nonsense seems to
me a fair definition of myth, anyway."
(Angela Carter 1978, 5)

MYTH OF THE BIRTH OF WESTERN CULTURE

"After Adam's rib became Eve and Eve
managed to turn herself into a wicked
woman, human society, so the myth goes,
was made up of archetypal outgoing male
heroes and submissive home(cave)-loving
women: men hunting while women endlessly gestated, lactated, and kept the
home fires burning." (Ann Oakley 1982,
329)

MYTH OF THE BLACK MATRIARCH

Black women are such strong, independent, and verbally abusive matriarchs
that each "is equipped with extraordinary
survival skills that enable her to single-
handedly manipulate her hostile environment." This stereotype, combined with

overt and covert prejudice and hostility, results in the denial to black women of many resources available to others. (Jacqueline Jordan Irvine 1982, 114-15)
  (See MATRIARCHY)

MYTH OF THE BURNING BRA

A story that never happened. (Anna Coote and Beatrix Campbell 1982, 10)
  (See BRA-BURNING, MISS AMERICA PROTEST)

MYTH OF EJACULATORY INEVITABILITY

"Sexual release is a biological necessity for men but not for women. Women but not men are said to need 'romantic love' before they can respond sexually." (Pat Whiting 1972, 189)

MYTH OF THE FALL OF MAN

"It represented women's permanent inferiority; without this myth the European witch trials, for example, are unimaginable. . . . The myth descended from the semitic herding culture, passing through very different social and economic conditions, and has been adjusted to show that the domination of man over woman in the family is God's will." (Marielouise Janssen-Jurreit 1982, 98) An essay titled 'Genesis Revisited' retells the genesis story in terms of male fear of female "power to create life." (Alene Staley 1971, 46-9)
  (See EVE)

MYTH OF THE FEMININE MYSTIQUE

"The women's movement arose because Betty Friedan and other witches came along and told women they were unhappy." (*Wicca: Wise Woman Irish Feminist Magazine* c.1982, 19)

MYTH OF MAN, GOD, AND DESTINY

"The man is making his way toward God, and suddenly the woman crosses the path of this self-denying pilgrimage. Sometimes she will aid him in his journey toward salvation; at other times she will turn him aside from his goal, distract him from it, tear him away from it. In either case it scarcely matters. The one important thing, the real drama, takes place between the man and his destiny as the image of God, or between the man and his idea of what man is, if he is a freethinker. The woman makes her appearance only after the story has already begun; she is the pretext for new twists in the plot." (Evelyne Sullerot 1974, 1-2)

MYTH OF THE VAGINAL ORGASM

Landmark essay for radical feminists in 1970, written by Anne Koedt. She suggested that "frigidity has generally been defined by men as the failure of women to have vaginal orgasms. Actually the vagina is not a highly sensitive area and is not constructed to achieve orgasm. It is the clitoris which is the center of sexual sensitivity and which is the female equivalent of the penis." (Anne Koedt 1970, rpt. 1973, 198)

MYTH OF THE WEAK FEMALE

"The society's (male) belief restated in law, religious codes, literature, art, business practices, that woman is weak though wicked and man must both protect and fear her." (Midge Lennert and Norma Willson eds 1973, 9)

MYTHICAL NORM

"Each of us within our hearts knows 'that is not me.' In America, this norm is usually defined as white, thin, male, young, heterosexual, christian, and financially secure. It is with this mythical norm that the trappings of power reside within this society," (Audre Lorde 1984, 116)

MYTHOLOGY

"Mythology comprises a significant fibre of our lives. Stories, like dreams, can serve to relieve unconscious pressures. Seeking the legacy of the warrior, women contribute to the creation and re-creation of a positive female mythology. The building of a vocabulary of images is an essential element in our political evolution. Imaging is a radical tool that can help us build inner confidence and dissipate crippling fears." (Siew Hwa Beh 1981, 125)

NAG

To gnaw, bite, nibble; to vex, irritate; to complain. Originally a dialect word, probably of Scandinavian origin (variants *nagg, knag, gnag*). Mary Daly suggests it means to affect "recurrent awareness, uncertainty, need for consideration, or concern; make recurrently aware of something (as a problem, solution, situation)." (Mary Daly 1984, 12) Though the term has come to be associated with female speech (e.g., "Man was formed to bully, as woman was formed to nag," *Saturday Review*, Oct. 3, 1863, cited in the *Oxford English Dictionary*), it has also been used to describe male behavior. Rebecca West defines it as a process in which men see what women are doing and tell them not to, in response to the following sequence: "Man, baffled and fatigued by his struggle to establish and perpetuate human life in the universe, becomes afraid of judging his progress by the standard of approach to the absolute good. He prefers a relative standard. He wants to feel that however badly he is doing someone else is doing worse." (Rebecca West, *Time and Tide*, October 21, 1052)

NAG-GNOSTIC ARCHEOLOGIANS

Those who "sense with certainty the reality of transcendental knowledge. At the same time, we never cease to Nag our Selves and others with recurrent awareness and uncertainty." (Mary Daly 1984, 12)

   (See NAG)

NAGS

"The following list will Name and summon forth a few. We are: Augurs, Brewsters, Dikes, Dragons, Dryads, Fates, Phoenixes, Gorgons, Maenads, Muses. We are Naiads, Nixes, Gnomes, Norns, Nymphs. We are Oceanids, Oreads, Orishas, Pixies. We are Prudes, Salamanders, Scolds, Shrews, Sibyls, Sirens. We are Sooth-sayers, Sprites, Stiffs, Sylphs, Undines. We are Viragos, Virgins, Vixens, Websters, Weirds." (Mary Daly 1978, 57)
   (See NAMES)

NAKEDNESS

Means liberation, a joyful and non-neurotic sexuality for some people; "for others, it stands for a licentiousness which threatens traditional moral standards. Both of these seemingly contradictory attitudes rest on a common assumption: that the exposed body is emotionally charged and potentially subversive." (Margaret Walters 1978, 11)
   (See NUDE, REPRESENTATION)

NAKED TRUTH

Plain, unvarnished truth. According to the fable, Truth and Falsehood went bathing; Falsehood came out of the water first and dressed herself in Truth's clothes. Truth, unwilling to put on the garments of Falsehood, went naked.

NAME

An ancient word, appearing in some form or other in all of the Indo-European languages; names are universal in language. The particular combination of sounds that makes reference to objects, classes of objects, concepts, or other names has complicated functions in human societies. Some of the meanings of names are noted below.

(See ANONYMITY, BIRTH NAME, FORMS OF ADDRESS, LUCY STONE LEAGUE, MAIDEN NAME, NOM DE LAIT, PEN NAME, OCCUPATIONAL TERMS, TITLE, WORD)

A form of power. "Denying people names is denying them power, denying others information. There is power in knowing the source of things, power for the oppressed. When names are withheld without need, the people lose political knowledge, and knowledge of themselves. Withholding names can also be a way of denying accountability. Names are actually anti-mystique. The proper name reveals the source of an idea, clarifies and demystifies the process of politics and political thinking. But there has also been an opposite task within revolutionary movements. There has been the 'class' question on names – an effort to present a solid front, to create complete egalitarianism, to eliminate leadership, to uphold an alleged anonymous tradition among the oppressed.... An examination of just a sampling of so-called anonymous forerunners revealed, however, that they did not choose anonymity. It was imposed on them by people who were willing to appreciate the work but not the people who did it. The women quiltmakers are an example of this." (Kathie Sarachild 1975b, 53). "Names give power to people and to those who know the names of others, animal or human. If we call spirits' names, they have to listen or come – good reason for many Indian peoples not to say a spirit's name out loud. Animals and humans may have many names and may change them according to the events or visions in their lives. Names may be mocking, given for silly or foolish behavior, but in general, they represent a kind of special power reserved for the person having the name." (Rayna Green 1984, 312)

Record of existence and accomplishment. Scientific explorer Fanny Workman appended this note to the published account of a journey to Eastern Karakoram: "The object of placing my full name in connection with the expedition on the map, is not because I wish to thrust myself forward, but solely that in the accomplishments of women, now and in the future, it should be known to them and stated in print that a woman was the initiator and special leader of this expedition. When later, a woman occupies her acknowledged position as an individual worker in all fields, as well as those of exploration, no such emphasis of her work will be needed; but that day has not fully arrived, and at present it behooves women, for the benefits of their sex, to put what they do, at least, on the record." (Fanny Workman and William Hunter Workman, n.d.)

Sanction of patrimony. "In the whole name game, it is society's sanction of patrimony that most diminishes the importance of women's names – and that sanction is social only, not legal. In the United States no state except Hawaii legally requires a woman to take her husband's name when she marries, although social pressures in the other states are almost as compelling. The very fact that until recently few women giving up their names realized they were not required to do so shows how universal the expectation is. Any married couple who agree that the wife will keep her own name are in for harassment, no matter how legal their stand: family, friends, the Internal Revenue Service, state and local agencies like motor vehicle departments and voter registers, hotels, credit agencies, insurance companies are all apt to exert pressure on them to conform. One judge is quoted as saying to a married woman who wanted to revert to her birth name, 'If you didn't want his name, why did you get married? Why didn't you live with him instead?' To thus equate marriage with the desire of some women to be called 'Mrs.' and the desire of some men to have 'a Mrs.' is insulting to both sexes; yet the equation is so widely accepted that few young people growing up in Western societies think in any different terms."

(Casey Miller and Kate Swift 1976, 8-9)

Marker of familial relationships, often paternal. "The patronymic affix in Irish, 'O' as in 'O'Hara,' means grandson, not son of. Also, the Irish used the word 'ni,' a matronymic affix, to mean daughter of as in Mary ni Hara so the poetess who took the name Barbara O'Mary would be incorrect since this would mean Barbara, grandson of Mary." (Gary Jennings 1965, *Personalities of Language*; cited by Varda One 1970, *Everywoman*, November 13, 15)

A designation of sex, often unasked for. "The minute a child is given a name he or she is forced into a classification system, which gives the baby a gender label . . . [and] carries messages about strength versus frivolity." The *Collins Gem Dictionary of First Names* (1976) has over 2000 names, all but 24 of them labelled either 'm' or 'f.' (Sara Delamont 1980, 13). Jo March in Louisa May Alcott's *Little Women* deplores being a girl and becoming a young lady. " 'I hate to think I've got to grow up, and be Miss March, and wear long gowns, and look as prim as a China aster!' " " 'Poor Jo!' " responds her sister Beth, " 'It's too bad, but it can't be helped. So you must try to be contented with making your name boyish, and playing brother to us girls.' " (Louisa May Alcott 1869, rpt. 1962, 13) "If women are ever to go to Congress or to command respect on starting in the career and professions to which they aspire, they must have something more substantial to append Honorable and Doctor and Reverend to, than the Tinnies and Mamies and Lulus to which now they so perniciously cling." (Abba Gould Woolson; quoted in Fuller Walker 1873, *The Woman's Journal*, April 5, 43) "Names like Georgette and Georgina, Josephine, Paulette and Pauline, beautiful as they may sound, are diminutives. They are copies, not originals, and like so many other words applied to women, they can be diminishing." (Casey Miller and Kate Swift 1976, 5)

A marker and symbol of identity. "My name is the symbol of my identity and must not be lost." (Lucy Stone; quoted in Casey Miller and Kate Swift 1976, 13) Genny Pligrim, the feminist cartoonist, bülbül, writes that "in Middle Eastern poetry a bülbül is a bird of protest. I took it as a pen name when my family suffered for my outspoken opinions." (bülbül, *off our backs*, July 1984, 18)

"Whether a name is self-chosen or bestowed at birth, making it one's own is an act of self-definition. . . . It is one of the things a little girl grows up knowing she will be expected to lose if she marries . . . [whereas] a man in most Western societies can not only keep his name for his lifetime but he can pass it on intact to his son, who in turn can pass it on to *his* son." (Casey Miller and Kate Swift 1976, 5-6)

"My mother . . . named me Orpha after Orpheus, the legendary Greek poet. . . . Perhaps the name affected me, I think names can. In any case, though the language of my story, let alone the events, remembered and reported, would probably not have my mother's approval, still she, by her naming, put a pen in my hand." (Jessamyn West 1979, 12)

"The Chinese I know hide their names; sojourners take new names when their lives change and guard their real names with silence." (Maxine Hong Kingston 1975, 6)

"She was a nameless woman, and so at home among all those who were never found and never missed, who were uncommemorated, whose deaths were not remarked, nor their begettings." (Marilynne Robinson 1981, 172)

A feminist statement. Throughout the 1970s, women have explored ways to name themselves. They have retained or retrieved birth names, taken their mothers' names, hyphenated their names with that of their husband, created entirely new names. See examples throughout this dictionary. "Why couldn't women keep their own surnames and name their daughters after themselves? Men, as they have always done, would give their last names to their sons. Another alternative, and if children are of the same sex: use of the other parent's surname as a middle name. There would be a feeling of continuity, a connection, with both parents." (Mary Jonston; cited in Margaret Mason 1983, *Washington Post*, August 8)

"When asked why she had dropped her surname and retained her first two given names, Margaret Sandra stated that a 'surname' was intended as an indication of the 'sire' and was so closely linked socially with the ownership of women that there was no 'surname' that she found acceptable." (Dale Spender 1980, 35)

As a verb, to name is to designate by a particular combination of sounds an individual person, place, thing, animal, or concept; or to make reference to an individual person or general class of persons, places, etc. To name is to evoke things; to change them. "Possessing the creative word and thereby being enabled to call things by their proper names means acting upon their original ideas and literally *evoking* them; it means exercising the most awesome magic power for good or evil; it means changing things in their very nature. Calling goods and demons by their proper names means subjecting them to one's will; calling the dead by their proper names means pulling the dead back from their free dissolution; calling any creatures by their correct names means forcing them to appear in their true nature. . . . Name is equal to substance. . . . In the Indo-European nature religion, the goddess *Vac* is that first, inscrutable word which evokes the eternal ideas themselves. Therefore, she is said to be 'surrounded by pictures of all creation of the deepest, very deepest abyss.' When Goethe understood the original word 'mothers' in this sense, he said . . . that he could not help a strange shudder." (Helen Diner 1973, 7-8)

To *call someone out of their name* is to use naming to insult them. This may involve addressing someone not by her name but by a generic designation, often with a demeaning or insulting result: *stewardess, waitress, doll, hey lady*. It may also take the form of a direct insult: *four-eyes, fatso, bitch,* etc. Though speaker and addressee may disagree upon what is appropriate or acceptable, to call someone out of her name involves going beyond what she has given permission to be called. (John Langston Gwaltney 1980; Bernice Reagon 1984)

NAMING

Fundamental process for identifying, defining, and conceptualizing experience. "Women have had the power of naming stolen from us. We have not been free to use our own power to name ourselves, the world, our God. . . . The evolving spiritual consciousness of women is . . . a reclaiming of the right to name." Reclaiming naming involves, for Daly, both the creation of new words and the use of old, often 'obsolete,' words in new semantic contexts that arise from qualitatively new experiences. (Mary Daly 1973, 8)

> (See AUTHORITY, DICTIONARY, EPONYM, HURRICANE, MATRONYMY, NAME, NEW NAMING, PATRONYMY)

"What we name must answer to us; we can shape it if not control it." (Starhawk 1982, 23)

"Might be considered a process rather than a fait accompli. . . . I want other women to name themselves to me so we can exchange experiences and understandings about our loving, anger, work, naming, and living processes." (Ida VSW Red 1981, 65, 71)

In the Bible, "a mythological account of a profoundly important truth in the sociology of our contemporary knowledge. We live in Adam's world, for men socially constructed the reality which defined and controlled how people would perceive their world. If you doubt it has all been 'named' from a man's experience, ask yourself why a computer, when it's working, it's 'up' and, when it's not working, it's 'down.' " (Elizabeth Dodson Gray 1982, 48-9)

"I named the stars myself." (Jessamyn West 1979, 34)

NAIL POLISH

Liquid, often colored, which hardens on

finger and toe nails to form a protective or beautifying function. A minor interference with nature, it's not usually harmful to one's health or activities. Some feminists argue that such self-beautification invites being viewed as female sex object. Others argue that being aesthetically pleasing and being a sex object are not the same, and that polishing nails is quite different from binding one's feet so that walking is painful or constricting the waist with a corset. "As I see it, God Herself might polish Her nails." (Helen Heise 1984, 369) Many women who have little use for nail polish nevertheless find nail polish remover one of life's indispensable items.

NANA

Common term of address or reference for grandmother or godmother. In some Caribbean English Creoles, it refers to a nursemaid, foster mother, or other care-taker. This generic sense may derive from some African languages to which many Creoles are related) in which *nana* is the name given to tribal chiefs – not because they rule but because it is their responsibility to care for others. (Lito Valls 1981, 84)

NANNY'S-EYE-VIEW

A calm and ordered view of the world which knows at once what people ought to do in it. (Pamela Frankau 1970, 91)

NAPFRYING

Hair-straightening; refers to the process of applying heat to the curly ("nappy") hair of Black men and women to take out the curl. (John Langston Gwaltney 1980, 17)

NAPPIES

Baby underclothing for the containment of excreta. Nappy changing "is a central issue in establishing the boundaries of fathers' willingness to help in child-care." Women are assigned to a virtual monopoly in dealing with the human excreta of babies and of incontinent and handicapped adults. (Clare Ungerson 1983, 73) Mary Kelly's *Post-Partum Document* explores concrete and theoretical relations in child

development and motherhood and includes a detailed empirical three-month record of a child's diaper stains in relation to food intake. "An infant of seven months is only able to dispose of 13 per cent of food energy for growth, the rest being lost in excreta. The introduction of solid foods is a dramatic event in so far as putrefactive organisms are consequently introduced into the essentially sterile intestinal tract of the newborn infant. Hence, the exact character of the faeces of a normal infant will depend upon: (1) the kind of food and the completeness of digestion; (2) the amount of putrefaction or fermentation; (3) the amount of bile secreted; (4) the amount of fat and water remaining unabsorbed." Kelly concludes that infant care is "the last stronghold of the heterosexual imperative.... Certain tasks such as bathing, changing and attending in the night remain almost exclusively female. Yet the specificity of this labour is essential to the reproduction of the relations of production, in so far as the monolithic mother-child relationship which it welds becomes the basic structure upon which adult socialisation is founded." (Mary Kelly 1983, 9, 1)

(See POST-PARTUM DOCUMENT)

NARCISSISM

In psychoanalysis, by reference to the myth of Narcissus, love directed toward the image of oneself. Havelock Ellis first invoked the myth of Narcissus in 1898 to help characterize a clinical case; commentary on the case by Paul Nacke in 1899 led to Freud's use of the term in 1911 and in his first paper on the topic "On Narcissism: An Introduction" in 1914. Originally conceived as a *stage* in psychic development, Freud came to postulate a kind of ongoing seesaw balance between the ego (the subject) and external objects as the object of sexual feelings. (J. Laplanche and J.-B. Pontalis 1973, 255) In U.S. psychoanalysis, this was a hotly debated concept in the development of a "psychology of women" (see, for example, Helene|Deutsch| [1944, 188] for a statement of the relationship between sexuality, ego, self-love, masochism, and narcissism); current feminist psychoanalytic theory has not emphasized this topic. The term is common in non-psychoanalytic feminist discussions; Audre Lorde, for example, writes that it "comes not out of self-love but out of self-hatred." (Audre Lorde 1979, rpt. 1984, 62)

NARCISSUS

Purple flower which figured prominently in Greek myths, one with Lesbian undertones – the story of Demeter and her daughter Persephone. (Judy Grahn 1984, 9)

NATIONALIST FEMINIST ARMED FORCES

NFAF proposes to represent the armed forces of the Nationalist Feminist Government. "The female sex needs self-defense, self-government, and self-employment. The female sex must be employed by the female sex. The first massive employer of womyn by womyn will be the NFAF, because only the NFAF is capable of such an economic policy. Wifism can not employ womyn as feminists only as Wifists, because Wifist policy agrees to a female population employed by the male sex." (Mia Albright 1983, 80)

(See WIFISM)

NATIVE AMERICAN LITERATURE

A label that is useful "if you have to begin to break things up into groups. It's better than talking about Group 1, Group 2, Group 3. . . . [But] there's also the danger of demeaning literature when you label certain books by saying this is Black, this is Native American, and then, this is just writing. That's what's going on now, and I don't like it." (Leslie Marmon Silko 1980, 21)

(See AUTHOR, EAGLE FEATHER POETRY)

NATURAL

"Along with 'normal' a word a feminist should use with extreme caution." (Sona Osman 1983, 30) "An ordinary little word, and yet it stands for so much in the mind of the public." It is often deduced from studies of "the lower animals" which are presumed to illustrate what human beings are "really" like – e.g., that males are "naturally dominant" and females "naturally subordinate." "It all comes from there being so few women scientists. Some woman scientist ought to start passing it around that males must be unnatural because they don't have cyclical changes during the month." (Ruth Herschberger 1948, 7-9)

NATURALLY

Term defining the moral requirement to behave in a certain way and threat of punishment for transgression. She who does not act "naturally" can be called crazy and deprived of adult status. Women who are unwilling to perform the tasks in society that are "naturally" theirs are often judged to be "abnormal" and identified by terms like "castrating bitch," "domineering," "aggressive," and "witch." Women who do not behave according to etiquette books, which instruct them on how to be "naturally" available, are "punished by deprivation of full female status." (Pamela Fishman 1983, 99)

(See DSM-III, MENTAL HEALTH)

NATURE OF MAN

Thought by men to be "whatever it shows itself to be, under various influences, environment, and modifying circumstances." (Catherine C. Osler 1913, 51-5)

NATURE OF WOMAN

Thought by men to be uniform, "recognizable, independently of race, period, and environment; and any divergence from this accepted and restricted type is regarded as abnormal, undesirable, and even dangerous." (Catherine C. Osler 1913, 51-5) Men's power to define has been a powerful weapon in the hands of anti-feminist males. During the nineteenth century, "scientific" accounts of women's "true nature" were ingeniously constructed and adapted to argue that women should not be permitted to pursue higher education. "As middle-class women increasingly sought access to colleges and universities, physicians, scientists, and other authorities argued that such intellectual over-stimulation could terminate their menstrual periods, cause atrophy and other damage to the reproductive organs, and produce unhealthy babies. Besides, their brains were different, rendering them incapable of abstract, objective, or original thought. Some argued that their brains were smaller, and softer. (This argument was flawed because the critical ratio of brain weight to body weight gave women proportionally the larger brain.) Others argued that the frontal lobes, then thought to be the location of the intellect, were more developed in men. (When at the turn of the century the experts situated the intellect in the parietal lobes, they decided women actually had larger frontal lobes.) Some scientists concluded that women showed greater variability (that is, deviation from physical and psychological norms) and were thus more unstable, inferior creatures. (After Darwin argued that variation from the norm was linked to evolutionary progress, biologists and anatomy experts began to suggest that males actually showed more variation from the norm.) Such 'scientific' declarations bolstered arguments that women's intellectual and scholarly aspirations were probably dangerous and certainly futile. Black women were subjected to racial as well as sexual mythologies; according to prevailing stereotypes, they were, as [Bettina Aptheker 1982b, 96] has put it, 'allegedly approaching extinction and possessing the mental capacity of an anthropoid ape.' " (Paula A. Treichler, in press c).

(See ESSENTIALISM, NATURAL, REPRESENTATION)

NAWSA

National American Woman Suffrage Association. Formed in the 1890s when two distinct suffrage organizations (the National and the American) merged, NAWSA's banner and slogan VOTES FOR WOMEN symbolized the common denominator that united a broad coalition of women across the U.S. (Edith P. Mayo 1981)

NECKTIE
(See BEAUTY)

NECROPHILIA
Male attraction or need for female energy " – not in the sense of love for actual corpses, but of love for those victimized into a state of living death." (Mary Daly 1978, 59)

NEEDED WORDS
A word for the deception many women must practice to survive psychologically, a word which doesn't blame the victim. (Renate Duelli Klein 1983, 101)

A word for the fact that whatever a woman does, it is all her fault. Mothering, for example, "is a no-win arrangement nowadays: if you devote yourself entirely to the child, you are failing yourself in your duties to self-development, damaging your husband's frail ego, and probably 'over-mothering – or spoiling' – your child. If you do not so devote yourself you are depriving your child of her/his emotional needs. Either way you are isolated and either way, whatever happens, it is *all your fault*." (Sara Maitland 1980, 88)

A positive word for the condition of not having two breasts: thousands of women each year have breast surgery which removes one or both breasts partially or in their entirety.

A positive word for the decision not to have children and for the state of not having children.

A word or phrase to introduce and describe partners and other relationships without using the possessive "my": my wife, my lover, my daughter, my friend. (Renate Duelli Klein 1983, correspondence)

A positive and active verb to express female sexual activity. "I know no non-degraded English verb for the activity of sexual expression that would allow a construction parallel to, for example, 'I am working,' a phrase that could apply to nearly any activity. This fact of language may reflect and contribute to the process of obscuring sexuality's pervasiveness in social life. Nor is there *any* active verb meaning 'to act sexually' that specifically envisions a woman's action." (Catharine A. MacKinnon 1982a, 517)

(See NUTTING)

A word to designate something which is too masculine. "Never has it occurred to the androcentric mind to conceive of such a thing as being *too* masculine. There is no such word! It is odd to notice that whichever way the woman is placed, she is supposed to exert this degrading influence; if the teacher, she effeminises her pupils; if the pupil, she effeminises her teachers." "We can readily see, that had women always written the books, no men either writing or reading them, that would have surely 'feminised' our literature; but we have not in our minds the concept, much less the word, for an over-masculised influence." (Charlotte Perkins Gilman 1911, 155, 92)

(See MACHO, MACHISMO)

Words that can be pronounced and will still be respected by physicians so that women can have reasonable discussions with doctors and participate in the negotiation of diagnosis and treatment.

A word that means women are damned if they do, damned if they don't. The test for witches: If they sink (and drown) they are innocent; if they float they are witches and must be killed. Catch 23?

A word to describe the strategy through which women workers and professionals are "re-sexualized" to keep them in their place. "I came up to a group of men at an academic conference and one of them said, 'Here she is! Isn't she beautiful!' I want a word for that!" (Caller on 1982 radio talk show about *A Feminist Dictionary*)

(See SEXUAL HARASSMENT)

A word to describe the strategy of complimenting a woman on her traditional skills ("I'd be glad to cook dinner but you do it so much better than I") to keep her in her traditional place. (Cheris Kramarae 1981, 8)

A word for a woman that connotes an individual, autonomous human being rather than a qualifying term that calls attention to the woman/man division. (Dale Spender 1977; cited in Cheris Kramarae 1981, 8)

A word for a man who takes a woman's No to mean Yes and appears to think this is clever. (Cheris Kramarae 1981, 8)

A word for a woman who is not flattered by male propositions. (Julia Stanley 1974; cited in Cheris Kramarae 1981, 8)

A positive word to take the place of the phrase "not sexist." (Dale Spender; cited in Cheris Kramarae 1981, 8)

(See INCLUSIVE LANGUAGE)

A word for a fussy old man who is now frequently said to be "acting like an old lady."

A word to express love for old times' sake.

A term for an older male friend who is not a "boyfriend."

A word for women like "castration." "Why is there no equivalent term for women who have been deprived of their full stature?" (Dale Spender 1980, 183)

Affectionate terms for female genitalia.

(See RUBYFRUIT JUNGLE)

A term to describe the fact that many women have to prove that their children are not solely the children of their father. A particular problem when children living with their mother in one country have a father of another nationality elsewhere.

A word other than "lover" to name the other partner in a lesbian relationship.

A word other than "husband" or "wife" to name the other partner in any relationship.

(See FRIEND, PARTNER, POSSLQ)

A word to describe women's foolishness in order to please their menfolk. "It's the penalty of belonging to the parasite class." (Elizabeth Robins 1907, 122)

A word for the "problem that had no name." "The problem lay buried, unspoken, for many years in the minds of American women. It was a strange stirring, a sense of dissatisfaction, a yearning that women suffered in the middle of the twentieth century United States. Each suburban wife struggled with it alone. As she made the beds, shopped for groceries, matched slipcover material, ate peanut butter sandwiches with her children, chauffeured Cub Scouts and Brownies, lay beside her husband at night – she was afraid to ask even the silent question – 'Is this all?' " (Betty Friedan 1963, 11)

(See FEMININE MYSTIQUE)

Words that represent the "development of a 'good/female' vocabulary ('Wow, has that ever got Womb . . . ') or, preferably, the development of a vocabulary that can treat [literary] structures made of words as though they are exactly that, not biological entities possessed of sexual organs." (Margaret Atwood 1982, 198)

(See BALLS)

A word for the erasure – inadvertent or systematic – of women from history.

(See ANDROCENTRISM, DE-BIOGRAPHER, HERSTORY)

A word for the displacement and invisibility of Native Americans.

A word for women's strength.

NEEDLEWORK

Form of creative expression and bonding among women. "I am sure that just as I pour my heart into my needlework, so did slave women doing quilts in their cabins from the little pieces of material they got from their white masters, turning them into quilts for everyday use, pouring their sadness, their creativity into their work, just as they did into the spirituals. It's part of our creative history, showing that we have always been here, and doing these things all the time." (Beverly Smith 1982, 8)

(See ART, SEWING, WORK)

Once occupied nearly the whole time of a girl's school days. Mary Smith remembered that in the 1820s in North Oxfordshire "a girl's education . . . consisted principally of needlework of various descriptions, from plain sewing to all manner of fancy work and embroidery, including muslin and net, on which we worked, or flowered squares for the shoulders, veils, caps, collars and borders; likewise a multitude of things not in wear now, but then considered very necessary." (Mary Smith 1892; quoted in Carol Dyhouse 1981, 85)

"Sight-Murder." (An Indignant Woman 1883, *Women's Union Journal* 8:89 [June], 50)

NEGRO

"The 'Negro,' that is the color black, was both a negation of African and a unity of opposition to white. The construct of Negro, unlike the older terms African, Moor or Ethiope, suggested no situatedness in time, that is history, or space, that is ethno- or politico-geography. The Negro had no civilization, no cultures, no religions, no history, no place and finally, no humanity which might command consideration. The Negro constituted a marginally human group, a collection of things of convenience for use and/or eradication. Obviously no historical political tradition could be associated with such beings." According to Cedric Robinson, the first task of Black intellectuals in the 19th century was to destroy "the Negro" in order to reassert the historical tradition of African peoples. (Cedric Robinson 1981, 367)

(See BLACK)

NERVOUS BREAKDOWN

Considered to be a result of women's physical weakness. "It occurs among men, but that is always accounted for on quite other grounds." "If the breakdown occurs in the home, it is then alleged to be due to the pressure of 'outside interests' conflicting with the 'natural' domestic ones; if it happens to a young woman, with no domestic cares as yet, it is credited to 'overstudy'; the only puzzling instance, from this point of view, is when the wholly domestic and maternal farmer's wife gives way. That she does, and frequently, is known to her friends, but as this woman lives in the privacy of the home and in rural seclusion, does not appear in public, or belong to clubs, and is seldom literary, her case is not prominent." (Charlotte Perkins Gilman 1916e, 202-3)

(See MENTAL HEALTH, YELLOW WALLPAPER)

NETWORK

Network as a verb is a word coined and used by women. (As a noun, it is an entry in Samuel Johnson's 1755 dictionary famous for enacting itself in an impenetrable network of interlocking words.) To network is to establish good connections with other women and provide for each other information, concrete help, and personal or professional support. (*Women and Language News* 1980, 5:2 [Winter] 1)

The "interconnectedness between seemingly disparate phenomena," "cosmic tapestries," a coherence made possible by "deep hearing by sisters." "It is this hearing which makes it possible to spin, to weave The Network. The Network which Spinsters spin, alone and together, can break our fall at those times when the ground opens up *right under us*. Like an acrobat's net, The Network catches us and springs us into new space, transforming our movement into ever more transcendent Spinning . . ." (Mary Daly 1978, 412-13)

NEVER BORN

"We who never weary,
We who were never sad,
Bless ye who never bore us
To woes such as ye have had . . .
We, who have felt no burden,
We, neither sad nor worn,
Bless ye who never bore us, –
We who were never born!"
(A. B. C. Sterrett 1919)

NEW NAMING

Term which distinguishes between name changing and naming anew. "Participating in a ritual of the new naming brings women's experiences and visions out into the open and through sharing transforms them from private into public reality" (Carol Christ 1980, 128). "American and Canadian cultures provide no structures for new naming. Ontario law prohibits a child from using the mother's last name even when she is sole supporter, while Quebec law requires a woman to retain her maiden name after marriage. But nowhere is a woman encouraged (or often allowed) to take a new first or last name. At best, American statutes regulating name changes *grant* a woman naming rights. . . . No one grants men naming rights; they are assumed. New naming, however, is not encouraged by law or custom for men *or* women." (Valerie Alia 1984)

NEW RIGHT

Political movement which is the enemy of feminism and feminist goals. "Until left liberals and leftists recognize that New Right politics is fundamentally about the familial and sexual structuring of society, they will remain ineffective in the politics of the 1980s. It will be feminists who will have to 'Fight the Right.'" (Zillah Eisenstein 1982, 569-70) The New Right "is 'pro-life,' but not anti-death. It means to save 'unborn babies,' but militaristic, it shrugs off the murder of persons born – it favors a 'tough' American foreign policy and opposes gun control legislation. It is pro-Israel, but anti-semitic. It professes the Christianity of Jesus the Lamb, but values wealth and power. It stands for 'families,' but opposes AFDE (Aid for Families of Dependent Children), shelters for battered wives and mothers, and child abuse legislation. It denounces violence and prepares for all out war." (Sheila Ruth 1983, 346)

NEWS

"Is written according to a set of news values which, with some exceptions, headlines those matters over which ordinary people feel they have least influence. Magazines present life in a very different way and at a pace which is closer to the rhythm of people's lives." (Angela Phillips 1983, 124)

NEWSPAPERS

Accounts of events and presentations of ideas which "as a rule are written for men's reading, and present for the most part a masculine point-of-view. This is taken for granted, and is so much a matter of course that any journal which attempts to give a woman's point of view is immediately and quite honestly accused of bias." ("Problems of the Day" 1914, *The Englishwoman*, 21:63 [March], 261) Newspapers provide "pages and pictures and floods of words about some murder, unsavory divorce case, or the like ... furnished as *entertainment*, to please the reader, to secure subscribers. The news involved is merely 'At 12:30, last night, at 41 Misery Street, John Smith fatally shot his wife Mary.' The 'particulars' belong to the police gazette, to special study by criminologists. What the people need to know about Murder is how much of it there is among us, does it increase or decrease, how can it be prevented.... For one man to own and dominate a great paper or group of papers is more insidiously dangerous than to have him dominate railroads, churches, or armed men." (Charlotte Perkins Gilman 1916g, 315)

NEWSPEAK

The official language of the thought-policed society described by George Orwell in his novel *Nineteen Eighty-four*. Newspeak was designed to make nonconforming ideas literally unthinkable; its objective was "not to extend but to *diminish* the range of thought" (304). Newspeak's linguistic devices included the invention of new words, the elimination of "undesirable" words like *peace* and *freedom*, the redefinition of remaining words, and the collapsing of words into a kind of telegraphic jargon that short-circuited or reversed their previous meaning. Chaucer, Milton, and Shakespeare were translated into Newspeak in such a way that the originals were "not merely changed into something different, but actually changed into something contradictory of what they used to be" (53). (George Orwell 1949, rpt. 1971)

NEW WOMAN

A creation of newspapers, fashion papers, and other media. "Members of literary clubs write papers about her; debating societies discuss her; conservative men and women rail against her; easy-going people accept her with a smile; collectively she is everywhere, and individually she is nowhere to be found. Who is she? Where is she? In woman suffrage leagues? The leaders in that movement are elderly now.... Most of them are grandmothers; not one can be considered as a representative 'New Woman.' Is she the woman editor, author or contributor? Evidently not, for the editorials, stories and articles which women give to the public, express as various views of the Woman Question as do those written by men. Is she the club woman? If she is, she is not a distinct type at all, for the clubs of our country are for every purpose and embrace in their membership women of every shade of opinion. Is she the college girl? College girls come from all sorts of homes, and have all sorts of futures before them ... Is she the bicyclist? ... But all kinds of women ride.... The woman who earns her own living and orders her own life as seems best to her? [Some of these women] have a daily life removed from the mass of the people who toil and struggle.... The woman who avails herself of these advantages [freedom to work, to educate self, to be healthy, to remain single without stigma if she chooses] is the New Woman.... All women to-day whose natures have not been atrophied by frivolity or luxury, by vice or destitution, are New Women, and it is just as unfair to hold them collectively responsible for the various idiosyncrasies of individuals of their sex as it is to judge American manhood by the annals of the police-court." (Mabel Ellery Adams 1898, 319)

"Nothing can be more preposterous than the talk of courage, self-reliance, and the power to take the initiative in important action as characteristic of 'new' women. Powerful individualities of our sex have always existed and developed themselves." ("Were These 'New

Women'?" 1896, *The Woman's Signal*, April 16, 247)

As she existed in the dictionary, the New Woman was a woman of "advanced" views who generated the terms *new-womandom* and *new-womanish*. "Both the cow-woman and the scum-woman are well within the range of the comprehension of the Bawling Brotherhood, but the new woman is a little above him." (Sarah Grand 1894; cited in the *Oxford English Dictionary*)

A "social and literary phenomenon. . . . Originally modelled after the 1860's generation of feminist crusaders, the New Woman herself surpassed them in many ways. Whereas her predecessors had remained cautious in their challenges to such cherished traditions as chastity, marriage, and motherhood, the so-called New Woman had, by the 1890s, become thoroughly unconventional, inside and out. As such, she represented . . . a composite figure, a type rather than a person; she was the embodiment of ideological extremes, and she came across as sometimes a positive and sometimes a negative figure, depending upon the bias of the person describing her." (Kathleen Hickok 1984, 159)

The New Woman is a contemporary myth as well. "More and more women every day are going out to work. A myth has grown around them: the myth of the 'new woman.' It celebrates the woman executive. It defines her look (a suit), and her drink (Dewar's or perhaps a fine white wine). It puts her 'in charge.' But it neglects to say whom she is in charge of – probably other women." (Karen Kenyon 1982, 15)

NIGGERIZATION

"The result of oppression – and it doesn't just apply to black people. Old people, poor people, and students can also get niggerized. Sure, there are differences in degree, but we've got to stop comparing wounds and go after the system that does the wounding." (Florynce Kennedy 1973, in Gloria Steinem 1973, 89)

NIGHT CLEANING

Invisible work done by women working for men who have contracts with large offices. (London Women's Liberation Night-Cleaners' Collective 1971, 225)

NIMINI-PIMINI

Feminine affectations encouraged among upper-class women during an earlier period. Lady Emily, in General Burgoyne's *The Heiress* (1786), tells another female character to stand before a mirror and keep pronouncing *nimini-pimini*: "The lips cannot fail to take the right plie." (*Brewers' Dictionary of Phrase and Fable*) In Louisa May Alcott's *Little Women*, straightforward Jo dismisses girls like her sister Amy, who put on ladylike airs, as "niminy-piminy chits!" (1869, 13)

NIOBE

An Anatolian mountain-goddess whose worshippers were destroyed by patriarchal Hellenic tribes. Having killed Niobe's followers, "Greek writers pretended she was a woman too proud of her children, so the gods killed them to punish her hubris." Hellenic myth accordingly transformed her into a figure who embodies maternal sorrow: in the legends, Niobe was the wife of Amphion, King of Thebes, and was the mother of fourteen children; in her pride, she taunted Latona because she had only two – Diana and Apollo. Latona commanded her children to avenge the insult and they consequently destroyed Niobe's sons and daughters. Niobe, inconsolable, wept herself to death and was turned into a stone from which water incessantly ran. (Barbara G. Walker 1983, 729)

NO

Heroic monosyllable with which denial and resistance may originate. "Access to women . . . is one of the faces of Power. . . . Female denial of male access . . . substantially cuts off a flow of benefits, but it has also the form and full portent of assumption of power." (Marilyn Frye 1983, 103) "No struggle is unimportant when people say no to a situation that oppresses them." (Susan Sherman 1983, 137) Also can be a vocal form of contraception: "Anita . . . continued to counter the inevitable proposal in her own way. Sophisticated, intellectual reasoning, arguments founded in logical positivism, expoundings of the New Enlightenment, references to bourgeois beliefs, all were child's play to Anita. She simply listened, or appeared to listen, understood nothing and finally, simply, said No." (Pamela Frankau 1970, 31)

NOAH'S ARK SYNDROME
"Two by two is so deeply imbedded in middle-aged and older persons that only the rare liberated hostess will invite a single woman without a male partner." (Ruth Harriet Jacobs 1979, 36)

NOBEL PRIZE
Founded by Alfred Nobel to encourage those working for the cause of peace after a conversation with pacifist and suffragist Baroness von Suttner, in order to help finance her work. However, the distributors preferred to begin by honoring male pacifists; her award came later. (Rosika Schwimmer 1914)

NO-FAULT DIVORCE
A divorce statute (enacted in 1980 in California and later adopted by several other states) which states that marriages may be dissolved without proof that a spouse was guilty of any particular misconduct. There is no finding of guilt, no blame. However, it does mean that the husband "who tires of the obligation of wife and children can simply dissolve the marriage and reduce his [stated but in most cases unfulfilled] duties to writing a check once a month." (Barbara B. Hirsch 1973, 71-3)

"Eliminates the need to prove legal 'fault' to dissolve a marriage and eliminates punitive financial settlements to 'punish' guilty partners. . . . [Judges] often split all assets into two equal parts. This usually requires that the family home must be sold. The children, however, are still usually awarded to the mother . . .

the result of non-fault divorce has been to put women into an even worse financial situation than they were in previously. They are forced to sell their house but do not have the financial status to buy another one. They receive less in child-support payments and are required to pay expensive child-care services. On a theoretical level . . . no-fault divorce sounds so reasonable, so fair, so equal. In actual operation, it provides another illustration of the way in which treating people the same when the conditions are very different perpetuates inequality." (Mary Lou Kendrigan 1984, 84-5)

(See EQUALITY)

NOM DE LAIT
"Milk-name," given by French mothers to children when they nurse. (Barbara G. Walker 1983, 708)

NOM DE PLUME
(See PEN NAME)

NO-NO THEORY
Proposes that human language originated through communicative exchanges between mother and child. "Commenting on the assumption of philologists that the exchange of meaningful vocal sounds began among males as they worked and hunted together – hence the so-called 'yo-heave-ho' and 'bow-wow' theories of language origin – Ethel Strainchamps, a psycholinguist, notes that most philologists have in the past been men. Considering the importance to human survival of communication between mother and child when open fires, venomous reptiles, and other hazards were everywhere, 'it might have occurred to a woman that a "no-no" theory was more likely,' Strainchamps says. Perhaps her suggestion should be taken a step further: who knows that it was not the creative effort of women, striving to communicate with each new baby, calling it by a separate and distinguishing sound, that freed the primordial human mind from the prison of animal grunts and led in time to the

development of language?" (Casey Miller and Kate Swift 1976, 4)

NONSEXIST GUIDELINES

Guidelines prepared by many publishers, professional organizations, and educators to assist writers in the use of inclusive language which does not discriminate on the basis of sex (and sometimes race, age, ethnic group as well). Some guidelines offer clearly worded dos and dont's while others strive for a consciousness-raising function as well. Arguments for using nonsexist language include the following: (1) sexist language no longer reflects social reality and therefore distorts it, (2) nonsexist language is clearer and less ambiguous, (3) sexist language denies equal linguistic representation to both sexes and can have consequences for behaviour, (4) sexist communication can have a negative effect upon an audience (at the least, the speaker will be seen as outdated), (5) sexist language preserves stereotypes of both men and women and is thus insensitive to individual needs, (6) sexist language is imprecise in circumstances where precision may be essential, and finally (7) sexist language may have legal implications. People have won lawsuits when sexist communication has contributed to discriminatory practices. (From Bobbye D. Sorrels 1983, 2-3; for an overview of guidelines with bibliography, see Francine Frank and Frank Anshin 1983, 107-19)

NONSEXIST LANGUAGE

Also called inclusive, nondiscriminatory, enlightened, new, progressive. See entries above and below.

NONVIOLENCE

"In relation to [U.S.] political activism 'violence' and 'nonviolence' are two categories of tactics which stand together in opposition to passivity and inaction. A nonviolent action . . . is not passive. On the contrary, nonviolent actions are assertive, forceful, and often coercive." (Jane Meyerding 1984, 60)

(See ACTIONS)

NON-WHITE WOMEN

"For non-white women in this country, there is an 80% fatality rate from breast cancer; three times the number of unnecessary eventurations, hysterectomies and sterilizations as for white women; three times as many chances of being raped, murdered, or assaulted as exist for white women. These are statistical facts, not coincidences, nor paranoid fantasies." (Audre Lorde 1981b, 97)

NORMAL

For women it means "lobotomized and tame behavior which is in fact indoctrinated, artifactual, man-made femininity." (Mary Daly 1978, 287) The term *normalcy* has been defined as women's "adaptation to their own oppression. Or to the male standard for perpetuating his privilege in unequal relationships. Normalcy is the fucked up condition of women." (Jill Johnston 1973a, 167) The term *normally*, "in the biological sciences, means that a certain phenomenon is statistically common. This is all it should mean. If what happens to be most common, by benefit of a 51 percent majority, is called the normal, and by implication the solely desirable, then what is statistically uncommon will be called abnormal, and by implication suspicious, imperfect, even dangerous." (Ruth Herschberger 1948, 2)

(See NATURAL)

NORMAN CONQUEST

An invasion which created a new fascination with women, love, extensive terminology of chivalry, romantic love, and feminine beauty. An examination of the linguistic data indicates that the attitudes toward women introduced at this time left much to be desired. Many words for *woman*, such as *lady*, *maiden*, and *dame*, took on idealized connotations, while others, such as *mistress* and *courtesan*, were pejorated in a sexual sense. The stereotypes of the Fair Maiden and Dark Lady acquired a prominent place in the English language. (Elizabeth Judd, in press)

NORTH AMERICA

Formed, according to Iroquoian myth, when a pregnant woman fell from the sky-world to the primeval sea and was lowered gently by birds to the back of a swimming turtle. A dollop of mud was brought up from the bottom by an aquatic animal and expanded on the back of the turtle to make a land for her to live on. Thus Turtle Island [North America] was created. The woman (or her daughter) died in giving birth to the good and evil twins. From the breasts of her corpse grew the corn that nourishes and sustains us. (Jordan Paper 1983, 49)

NOUVEAU POOR

Women. Title of an essay in the tenth anniversary issue of *Ms.* (1982) which predicts that by the year 2000 more than 90 percent of America's poor will be women and their children.

NOVEL

"Has existed . . . in Europe for only two or three hundred years. Its existence is directly related to the history of the technology of printing and to the growth of a leisure class with time to read. Much of that leisure class was female and the novel in Western Europe – unlike the forms it has taken when it has been exported to Latin America and Africa in this century – has tended to reflect the preoccupations of the lives of leisured women." (Angela Carter 1983, 73)

(See ART, AUTHOR, AUTHORITY, ANONYMITY, PEN, REPRESEN-TATION, WRITING)

A fictional form claimed by male scholars to have originated with Daniel Defoe's *Robinson Crusoe*; the British feminist writer Aphra Behn, however, had written thirteen novels some thirty years earlier. Her novel *Oroonoko* contained the first popular portrayal of the horrors of slavery. Behn offers a case study in "how women's active existence in the world can be negated, and how the realms of creative and intellectual achievement are retained by and for men, when a woman demonstrates her own competence in their

terms." (Dale Spender 1982, 35) It is men who have thus given "lady novelists" a bad name. Woman novelist should be a descriptive, not a pejorative, label. "One should object to being described as a lady novelist, but only on grouds of terminology. There is nothing pejorative about being described as a woman novelist, for women have always been as good at the job as men." (Margaret Drabble 1983, 156)

"A story of probability in a recognizably realistic setting." U.S. women novelists and fiction writers in the 19th century "conceptualized authorship as a profession rather than a calling, as work and not art. Women authors tended not to think of themselves as artists or justify themselves in the language of art until the 1870s and after. This practical approach, along with their unclassic educations, had an inevitable effect on their work. It did not make the sorts of claims on its readers that 'art' does – the dimensions of formal self-consciousness, attachment to or quarrel with a grand tradition, esthetic serious-ness, are all missing. Often the women deliberately and even proudly disavowed membership in artistic fraternity. 'Mine is a story for the table and arm-chair under the reading lamp in the living-room, and not for the library shelves,' Marion Harland announced in her autobiogra-phy." Fanny Fern also painted a homely scene, adding, "For such an hour, for such an audience, was [my story] written. Should any *dictionary on legs* rap inopportunely at the door for admittance, send him away to the groaning shelves of some musty library, where 'literature' lies embalmed, with its stony eyes, fleshless joints, and ossified heart, in faultless preservation." (Nina Baym 1978, 32-3)

NOW

The National Organization for Women, founded in 1966 by Betty Friedan and others, whose purpose is to take action to bring women into full participation in the mainstream of American society now, assuming all the privileges and responsi-bilities thereof in full and equal partnership with men. "It was a midddle-class initiative, with a programme which many feminists today would describe as 'reformist' – but at the time, and when combined with the newly felt anger of radical women emerging from the civil rights and anti-war protests, its implications were revolutionary." (Anna Coote and Beatrix Campbell 1982, 13)

NUDE

"The male nude, as well as the human figure, first appeared in Greek art in approximately 800 B.C. Due to the phallocentric nature of Greek culture, the male, in art as well as life, was idealized and represented in the most heroic manner. Although the culture worshipped the notion of the perfect human body, women were thought to be both intellectually and physically inferior to men. The appearance of the female nude postdated the male by over 300 years. Considering these facts, comparisons of male and female figures in Greek art indicate the misogynist attitudes inherent in Greek culture. Whether a slave or triumphant victor, the male figure always maintained its dignity and heroic quality. The female, even when represented as a goddess, was most often portrayed as passive, somewhat embarrassed of her nudity, and quite antiheroic. When one considers how often throughout the course of history there has been a renewed interest in classical art and philosophy, it becomes all too obvious how the subtle messages of visual imagery can be transported and rekindled in another time period." (Barbara DeGenevieve 1982, 11)

(See ART, PORNOGRAPHY, REPRESENTATION)

As used in mass media, the word usually conjures up an image of an undressed woman. "Over the last two hundred years or so, most artists interested in the human body have been obsessed by the famale nude. . . . Over the centuries of Western civilization, the male nude has carried a much wider range of meanings, political, religious and moral, than the female. The male nude is typically public: he strides through city squares, guards public buildings, is worshipped in Church. . . . The female nude, on the other hand, comes into her own only when art is geared to the tastes and erotic fantasies of private consumers. Most characteristically the posture and movements of the male nude suggest potency, those of the female, passivity. A victorious Greek athlete raises his arms to crown himself; a Venus, with an almost identical gesture, adorns her naked body with a necklace." (Margaret Walters 1978, 7-8)

Now almost always means a female nude. "It was only with Raphael that the female nude began to predominate. . . . The exclusive identification of women with beauty occurred at the same time that men stopped being sex objects." (Shirley Morahan 1981, 91)

"The reappearance in art of the male nude in the past ten years can be seen as being quite political. Male nudes are used by gay men as an expression of their sexual identity and by primarily heterosexual women for reasons ranging from eroticism to retaliation. . . . The male nude is being used primarily by those most disenfranchised by the traditional code of both female and male cultural symbolism, those who have the least to lose by refusing to accept a system perpetuated by old stereotypes." (Barbara DeGenevieve 1982, 12)

NUN

From the Latin *nonna* (feminine of *nonnus* 'monk'), was originally a title given to elderly persons (from whence comes Italian *nonno, nonna* 'grandfather,' 'grandmother' and Sicilian and Sardinian variants). Now chiefly a woman committed to a religious life who has taken certain vows, usually including poverty, chastity, and obedience, and who lives in a convent or nunnery of a certain religious order. By the 18th century, had pejorated to mean 'courtesan': "An abbess, well known about town, with a smart little nun in her suite" (1799; cited in the *Oxford English Dictionary*).

(See ABBESS)

Historically, one of the few occupations

open to women outside marriage. Though the nun is still a heavily cloaked figure in history, "nuns of the middle ages . . . were remarkable business women. They were outstanding doctors and surgeons. They were great educators. They were feudal lords operating self-sustaining estates and directing the manifold activities involved in producing goods, settling controversies as lawyers and judges settle them today, governing and participating in all the arts of social living." Until many of their activities were denied them, the convent was a place where women could "spring into freedom." (Mary Ritter Beard 1942; cited in Ann J. Lane 1977, 223)

At present, nuns are not little sisters to their male counterparts; they "are having the same trouble communicating with their male colleagues as are women in other professions and institutions. . . They have been involved in the Women's Movement from its beginning, and, historically, nuns are among the first women who worked in the professions." (Mary Kay Blakely 1983, 56)

NUN-LIEUTENANT

Catalina de Erauso lived during the reign of Philip IV of Spain; unwanted by her father, she was cared for by nuns until she escaped the convent at the age of fifteen and, disguised as a male, tramped, sailed, duelled, fought battles, explored, and climbed the Andes – feats of endurance pronounced impossible for "the weaker sex." (Edith Palliser 1914)

NURSE

Is "a different verb than doctor." (Philip A. Kalisch, Beatrice J. Kalisch, and Margaret Scobey 1983, 123) "A nurse only extended her ordinary female life when she learned to be instantly awake at a call, on her feet and functioning for as long as she was needed, and instantly asleep as soon as she could lie down again. It had never kept nurses, or women of any kind, from listening respectfully as the physicians whined about the way their vast incomes were justified by

the fact that they were awakened during the night to see to patients. They would have said, 'It's not the same thing at all!' As of course it was not. Women had to get up much oftener, stay up longer, and were neither paid nor admired for doing it. Certainly it wasn't the same thing." (Suzette Haden Elgin 1984, 210-11)

NURSE PRACTITIONER

Relatively new health professional with greater responsibility and autonomy than Registered Nurses. The profession emerges from a rich history, at least part of which depends upon complementarity with the medical profession exemplified by the paradigm physician-authority/nurse-compliance. "The nurse clinician and the nurse practitioner represent movement toward greater autonomy and greater responsibility, authority and expertise . . . Movements in these directions may lead to competition, to threatening and assertive postures which result in defensive or combative postures in others." In their efforts to take on a new role, nurse practitioners may find themselves instead playing out roles of (1) maids, (2) mistresses, (3) victims of male control, or (4) omnipotent professionals. All are destructive to real professional growth. (Linda Alexander 1983, 32-3)

NURSERY NAMES

The belittling names given to babies and young children. Also "the names of girls in the college catalogues. While the boys all have dignified names, such as Alexander, Nicholas, Howard, and William, the girls appear as Kittie, Mamie, Rose, Fannie, and Lizzie, instead of Elizabeth, Frances, Catherine, and Margaret. . . . The little pet nursery names do not look well in a college catalogue, or as writers in a popular journal." (Elizabeth Cady Stanton 1898, 342-3)

NURSING

Has been called the oldest of the arts and the youngest of the professions. "The word 'nursing,' derived from the Latin *nutrio* (to nourish), had its origin in the mother-care of helpless infants. Gradually it came to be used also for the care of sick, injured, or infirm persons of all ages. 'Nurture,' which stems from the same root, has been associated more closely with education, especially the rearing, training, and general upbringing of the young. This accounts for the two kinds of helpers who appeared quite early in some households – child-nurses and sick-nurses. Sick-nurses became more closely associated with the healing arts and child-nurses with the teaching and training of children. Often, the two functions were combined." (Isabel M. Stewart and Anne L. Austin 1962, 4)

The word *nurse* derives from the Latin 'to nourish.' The metaphors that underlie the concept of nursing include (1) mothering, (2) class struggle, (3) equality, (4) conscience, (5) intimacy, and (6) sex. "Something like the sum of these images makes up the psychological milieu in which nurses live and work. Little wonder that they can make us as nurses and others uncomfortable." The authors offer their own metaphors: "We think of ourselves as Florence Nightingale – tough, canny, powerful, autonomous, and heroic." (Claire Fagin and Donna Diers 1983, 117)

In an effort to professionalize nursing, many nurses (though significantly not Florence Nightingale) moved to organize: "We nurses of all nations, sincerely believing that the best good of our Profession will be advanced by greater unity of thought, sympathy and purpose, do hereby band ourselves in a confederation to further the efficient care of the sick and to secure the honor and interests of the Nursing Profession." (Preamble to the constitution of the International Council of Nurses, 1900; quoted in Isabel M. Stewart and Anne L. Austin 1962, 170)

A profession always committed in some respects to self-government. "The essential spirit of the International Council of Nurses is that of self-government. Nurses who appreciate their profession and take themselves seriously begin to realize that the period of tutelage is past, and that women are now fitted to take up such positions in the world as are now held by many of those here present, and are also capable of governing themselves. We also realize that in professions as well as in individuals the highest and greatest point of perfection is only attained when we do govern ourselves." (Isla Stewart 1909; quoted in Isabel M. Stewart and Anne L. Austin 1962, 171)

According to myth, nursing is a caring profession open to women which gives them dignity and responsibility. "No woman is more identified with service work than black women. . . . The relationship between the black woman and nursing of other people's children and other people's husbands and wives, dates from before any National Health Service. . . . In the head of the black nurse from the Caribbean is the echo of slavery, in the head of the Asian nurse is the servitude to Sahib and Memsahib." (*Race Today* 1977; quoted in Valerie Amos and Pratibha Parmar 1981, 144)

"An arduous and exacting occupation, where long hours, rigid discipline, imperfect security of tenure, and low rates of payment are unbalanced by those opportunities of attaining distinction which compensate the artist or the literary man. . . . Regarded strictly as a profession and not a philanthropic occupation, nursing offers singularly little inducement to any woman wishing to make herself independent." ("Problems of the Day" 1913, *The Englishwoman*, 18:53, 128-9)

"We might like to say nursing is a profession but most of us know that nurses, even senior nurses, are just servants as far as doctors are concerned." (A nurse quoted in Amrit Wilson; in Marsha Rowe 1982, 201)

Treated as a nurturing, supporting job, not one of authority. The madonna/whore dichotomy for women in the general culture is expressed in the nursing field in mythologies about the angel of mercy and the battle-axe nurse. (Hilary Callan 1978, 211)

NUTTING

"The companion act of screwing." (Midge Lennert and Norma Willson, eds, 1973, 9)

NWP

National Woman's Party. Established by Alice Paul and Lucy Burns, who had worked in the British suffrage movement, the NWP was more militant than the mainstream NAWSA and hence more committed to rhetoric which challenged women's traditional roles. (Edith P. Mayo 1981)

OAKLEY, ANNIE

Complimentary ticket for a performance, meal, or train trip. From Annie Oakley, expert American sharpshooter (1860-1926) who starred in Buffalo Bill's Wild West Show and, using a playing card as a target, fired a shot through each of the pips. This made the card look like a punched ticket. (*Brewer's Dictionary of Phrase and Fable*) The American musical "Annie Get Your Gun" is an androcentric version of Annie Oakley's life; among its memorable tunes is the famous "You Can't Get a Man With a Gun" – i.e., by competing with him or by demonstrating proficiency at a "masculine" skill.

OBEDIENCE

"That sad word a breeding ground for authoritarianism." (Liz Holmes c.1980, 11)

OBESITY

A disease for which there is no known cause and no known cure, which is political and social as much as it is medical, and which particularly affects women. "Obesity is a major problem . . . and it is primarily a problem for women. After skin color, excess body fat is probably the most stigmatized physical feature, but, unlike color, weight is thought to be under voluntary control. Efforts to lose weight consume an enormous amount of energy, interest, time, and money of women in all social classes and of all ages. For many women, concern with weight leads to a virtual collapse of self-esteem and sense of effectiveness. This is a result not only of a failure to achieve slenderness but the interpretation placed on failing. Unfortunately, most women struggle to comprehend their experience armed with a mass of misinformation. Experts in the field of obesity have failed to convey the simple truth in terms that make it understandable: there is *no known cause* of obesity and, with the exception of treatments more dangerous than obesity itself, *no known cure*. Overweight people do little if anything out of the ordinary to cause them to be fat, and once fat, only the most extraordinary behavior will enable them to become and remain thin. . . . A few feminists and other writers . . . have begun to articulate some of the important political implications of these facts." These include the need to treat obesity and fat as social and political rather than medical problems; and the need for new attitudes and treatments; these treatments should incorporate successful strategies from the feminist movement including a respect for the client's autonomy, a respect for the choice to remain heavy, and a continual challenging of the premise that "successful" treatment requires the client's adjustment to an unrealistic physical and social norm. (Susan C. Wooley and Orland W. Wooley, in press)

(See FAT)

OBEY

Most controversial word in the Christian marriage ceremony. "Some of the early women reformers put up a pitched battle to omit the word 'obey.' Sometimes the husband joined in the protest; the early 'marriage contracts' entered into by men and women who wished to found their marriage on a mutual concept of human dignity are eloquent not only of their aspiration, but of the conditions against which they rebelled." (Eleanor Flexner 1968, 63-4)

OBJECTIFICATION

"The primary process of subjection of women. It unites act with word, construction with expression, perception with enforcement, myth with reality." (Catharine A. MacKinnon 1982a, 541)

(See RACISM, REALITY, OBJECTIVITY, TRUE LOVE)

OBJECTIVITY

Is a mode "of knowing, analysis, interpretation, understanding" which is opposed to the "values of subjective knowledge, understanding, art, communion, craft, and experience." (Barbara Du Bois 1983, 111). For many feminists, it exemplifies "the methodological stance of which objectification is the social process" (Catharine A. MacKinnon 1982a, 541); a process whereby "the male condition is taken to be the human condition, so that, when any man speaks . . . he speaks *objectively* – that is, as someone who has, by definition, no special bone to pick, no special investment which would slant his view; he is somehow an embodiment of the norm" (Andrea Dworkin 1976, 51); "the reification of white-male thought. What could be less objective than the totally white-male studies which are still considered 'knowledge' " (Gloria T. Hull and Barbara Smith 1983, 27). It is "the name men give to their subjective attitudes" (Adrienne Rich 1979, 14).

In questioning the assumption of objectivity, feminism "does not see its view as subjective, partial, or undetermined but as a critique of the purported generality, disinterestedness, and universality of prior accounts" (Catharine A. MacKinnon 1982a, 537). Thus Ruth Herschberger contrasts the usual "patriarchal" account of biological development with a "matriarchal" account "for the purpose of illustrating the emotional connotations of

words thought by science to be objective and unprejudiced":

PATRIARCHAL ACCOUNT. "Nature has provided . . . an aggressive and active male cell. Each sperm manufactured in the complex tissues of the testes is composed of very rich and highly specialized material, and is equipped with a fine wriggling tail which gives it the power of self-locomotion. No less than 225,000,000 cells are emitted from the man's body with each ejaculation – and every cell is a human being!"

MATRIARCHAL ACCOUNT. "The male sperm is produced in superfluously great numbers since the survival of any one sperm or its contact with an egg is so hazardous, and indeed improbable. The egg being more resilient, and endowed with solidity, toughness, and endurance, can be produced singly and yet affect reproduction." (Ruth Herschberger 1948, 78, 75, 82)

OBSERVATION

Spy system by which telephone company management in the U.S. monitors and compares the work performance of its (mostly women) operators by secretly listening in on their calls. According to one supervisor, "observation was begun in 1924 and . . . although the company had tried other methods of measuring service, none had proved equally satisfactory." (Elinor Langer 1970, rpt 1972, 329)

OBSOLETE

In linguistics, said of a word no longer in current use. Marghanita Laski, a journalist and book reviewer who contributed work to the *Oxford English Dictionary Supplement*, often rescued words the Oxford staff thought were obsolete by including them in her own published writing and then submitting these citations as evidence of current usage. (Israel Shenker 1979)

OBSTETRICS

The field of medicine concerned with the care of women before, during, and after childbirth. The term comes from Latin *obstetrīx* 'midwife'; the literal translation was fervently disputed during the 19th century, with misogynistic medical men arguing that it means 'she who stands before' – i.e., who merely catches the baby. A stronger meaning is 'she who is present' or 'she who stands with.' Male physicians interested in appropriating the field of "women's diseases" for themselves were obviously interested in belittling their competition; the result was that they won the name for themselves. (Kate Campbell Hurd-Mead 1938)

> (See DOCTOR, DOCTORESS, MEDICA, NURSING, WOMEN'S HEALTH MOVEMENT)

OCCUPATIONAL TERMS

Includes such job titles as *politician, engineer, poet, pilot, taxidriver.* "In English, as in many other languages regardless of their typological structure, most occupational terms are understood to refer to males and will only occasionally include females . . . Very few titles are inherently feminine, and these usually denote occupations with low social status, as in the case of *maid, nurse, housewife,* or *prostitute.* In social areas where the presence of women is exceptional or regarded as inappropriate, speakers may feel the need to use feminine markers to identify female references. Thus, we get *woman pilot, female lawyer,* and *lady doctor.* Also, derivational morphemes are used to yield pairs such as *author/authoress, major/majorette,* or *governor/governess,* where the suffix often has a weakening, trivializing or even sexualizing effect on an occupational activity which for a man may carry connotations of power and prestige." (Marlis Hellinger in press)

An early twentieth-century writer discussed this phenomenon: despite the many words in English which are common to either gender (*cousin, baby, saint,* etc.), a stranger "would not be long in discovering a feature of our nomenclature which is not very eloquent of English chivalry – that this dual use of the same word applies, with very few exceptions, only to such terms as represent the undesirable or the inferior things in life, and that the discrimination between the sexes in all that is worth having or being is so unfairly partisan as almost to give the impression that the distribution of our English affixes is the outcome of a misogynist's spleen. For a woman, equally with a man, may be an imbecile, a convict, a liar, a thief, or a fool, without any terminological inexactitude. But when we come to the other side of the shield, she may not be a hero, a benefactor, an administrator, a prophet or a poet, because these things are masculine prerogatives, and the courage and ability of women must be otherwise expressed. We do not speak of a servantess, a drunkardess, an incendiarix, or a pauperine; these attributes are not worth claiming a preemption for. But everything denoting prominence or superiority must carefully distinguish between the real thing and its mere imitation. "Master" must not mean "mistress," nor "manager" include "manageress." There is a world of difference between "governor" and "governess," and between "adventurer" and "adventuress." One would think that heroism, like cowardice, would be the same in essence whether displayed by a woman or a man; but while this is tacitly admitted in the case of the vice, with the virtue it is otherwise. Cortez and Pizarro may be heroes; Joan of Arc is a heroine. If a woman conducts a paper, we call her an editress; if she writes a book she is dubbed 'authoress,' her best work thus receiving only that 'comparative respect which means an absolute scorn.' And, lastly, you may, if you feel so disposed, speak of a woman as a devil – one of Shakespeare's characters does so – but you cannot under any circumstances speak of her as a god. Only men can be gods. So that, to sum up, the shame and the dishonour of Adam may be shared by Eve, but in his honour and glory he must stand alone." (J. Beanland 1911, "The Sex War in Language," *The Vote*, Feb. 18, 207)

"Legislation enforcing equal job opportunities has helped to expose and eradicate employment terminology prejudicial to women. In one case a federal court found a major airline guilty of discrimination against its female flight attendants: by calling women 'stewardesses' and calling men performing the identical job 'pursers,' the company had camouflaged widely unequal pay and promotion schedules." (Casey Miller and Kate Swift 1976, 146)

Progress "in eliminating separate and unequal categorization was made when the United States Department of Labor revised its list of occupational classifications to drop sex-stereotyped job titles. For the most part the changes were accomplished by replacing the suffix -man with common gender terms such as operator or worker. Carmen R. Maymi, director of the Women's Bureau of the department, called the new job titles a welcome step toward ending sex discrimination in employment. 'It is not realistic to expect that women will apply for job openings advertised for foremen, salesmen or credit men,' she said, 'Nor will men apply for job vacancies calling for laundresses, maids, or airline stewardesses.' On the same grounds Mary M. Fuller, a management education specialist who advises government and private organizations, points out that the generic *he* covertly promotes economic discrimination and is inappropriate for use in job descriptions.... 'Categorizing ... by characteristics other than the ability to get the job done is now illegal as well as economically foolish for the total society.' " (Casey Miller and Kate Swift 1976, 145-6)

OEDIPUS

"Mythical king of Thebes at a point in time when kings were beginning to oppose matriarchal rule. Oedipus killed his father/predecessor and married his mother/queen in the conventional way, but he caused the Goddess's image (the Sphinx) to be thrown from a cliff and broken. His mother/queen was Jocasta ... who apparently called down the wrath of the Goddess on her consort. Some said he

was banished from Thebes, others said he was slain by the Goddess's Furies in her sacred grove. Most stories agree that he was blinded by a 'clasp' taken from Jocasta's garment. Jocasta's 'clasp' may have been a euphemism for the castrating moon-sickle. Herodotus said the women of Athens killed a man with their 'clasps,' but a new patriarchal law afterward forbade women to carry such weapons. Blindness was a common mythic symbol of castration.... The allegedly incestuous marriage between Oedipus and his mother/queen was no more than the conventional alternation of sacred kings, each one chosen by the queen and declared the 'son' or reincarnation of his slain predecessor. Oedipus's 'father' bore the name of Laius, not a name at all but simply a title: 'the king.' " (Barbara G. Walker 1983, 737)

OEDIPUS COMPLEX

In classical psychoanalysis, an "organised body of loving and hostile wishes the child experiences towards its parents.... The Oedipus complex plays a fundamental part in the structuring of the personality, and in the orientation of human desire. Psychoanalysis makes it the major axis of reference for psychopathology, and attempts to identify the particular modes of its presentation and resolution which characterise each pathological type. Psycho-analytical anthropology seeks to uncover the triangular structure of the Oedipus complex, which it holds to be universal, in the most varied cultures, including those where the conjugal family is not predominant." (J. Laplanche and J.-B. Pontalis 1973, 282-3)

"Both boys and girls have feminine and masculine attitudes, both share the identifications and attachments of the pre-Oedipal phase, both have masculine and feminine Oedipal complexes, but in the latter situation the key question is, which wins the day? Here the boy has learnt not to abandon his love for his mother by accepting an identification with her and the girl has to do precisely that; in other words the boy has to repudiate the possibilities of femininity and the girl has to embrace them. If we see then the Oedipus complex not, as it is popularly perceived, as a symmetrical structure, but as an asymmetrical situation, we can get to the heart of the problem." (Juliet Mitchell 1974, 229-30)

OFFICE OF SECRET INVESTIGATION

Unit of the U.S. armed services charged with identifying "dikes" (particularly independent, outspoken Lesbians) as part of a mass arrest, interrogation, and purge at the end of World War II and at regular intervals thereafter. The WWII purge was initiated by General Douglas MacArthur himself, the U.S. command-ing general, who, watching women soldiers disembarking in Japan, is reported to have said to his officers, "I don't care how you do it, but get those dikes out of here." Many servicewomen were accordingly "arrested and charged with the crime of Lesbianism. These women were humili-ated, disgraced, isolated from society, turned against each other in vicious police tactics of extracting 'confessions' and proof of guilt from their sister GIs, and bounced out of the army they had served with loyalty and trust." Actions of the OSI (the officers dressed in FBI-type trench coats) included "opening women's mail to search for innuendoes of too much affection, searching rooms for letters or photographs of friends inscribed 'with love,' training women to act as spies against each other, and conducting interrogations with no lawyers or hint of prisoner's rights in an ongoing war against women that no one talks about." (Judy Grahn 1984, 175, 176)

(See DYKE, LESBIAN, PURGE)

OGLE-IN

At the place where men classically "ogle" women – the construction site – New York City women in 1970 held an Ogle-In. Sponsored by *Bitch*, a New York women's liberation group, the Ogle-In included not only looking at men but touching them, calling out to them, passing out literature, and carrying signs.

The purpose was to demonstrate the degrading nature of flattery.

(See ACTION)

OLD MAID

A dreadful name "which yet none but Fools would reproach her with, nor any wise Woman be afraid of; to avoid this terrible Mormo, and the Scoffs that are thrown on superannuated Virgins, she flies to some dishonorable Match as her last, tho' much mistaken Refuge." (Mary Astell 1694, 111)

OLD TESTAMENT

"Is a volume of war." (Annie Laurie Gaylor 1981, 26)

OLD WIVES' TALE

"Related to gossip ... it presents a series of myth warnings within which forbidden subjects can be contained. This satisfies curiosity and restrains young girls from wandering out of the protected territory of dependent womanhood." (Sheila Rowbotham 1983, 11)

OLD WOMAN

Wise woman, sometimes old in chrono-logical age, always old in spiritual know-ledge. Scorned by patriarchs, honored by witches, she is often seen as the symbol of the Goddess, and consequently as a threat to male dominance. (Ann Forfreedom 1983, correspondence)

Many cultures make provision for the sharing of wisdom and perspective by elders. The Lakota Indians make no important decisions unless old ones, women, men, and children are present. In these decision-making gatherings, it is usually an old woman who admonishes the decision makers to take into account the effects of their actions for seven generations into the future. (Michel Avery et al. 1981, 49)

OLIVIA RECORDS

Record company formed by Ginny Berson and Meg Christian, Washington, D.C., in 1973, as a women's institution with a strong economic base, national impact, and ability to support, through jobs, working class women without the resources and leisure to contribute to and be heard within the mostly white, mostly middle-class feminist circles that predominated in the women's movement. In addition, the company would enable Lesbians to record their own music and poetry without tailoring it to the specifications of a white male management (when Meg Christian's Lesbian friends went to hear her sing in nightclubs, they would hide in the back to keep her from being fired for "attracting the wrong clientele"). In 1982, Olivia celebrated its tenth anniversary with a huge Carnegie Hall concert which sold out both shows months in advance. (Judy Grahn 1984, 189-91)

OM
Universal word of creation, "spoken by the Oriental Great Goddess upon her bringing forth the world of material existences; an invocation of her own pregnant belly. *Om* was called the Mother of Mantras (*Matrikamantra*), the supreme word." (Barbara G. Walker 1983, 738)

ONE O'CLOCK CLUB
A playground and meeting place for mothers with small children. Working-class women meeting in the Peckham Rye [south London] formed themselves into the One O'Clock Club, one of the first women's liberation groups in the country. (Anna Coote and Beatrix Campbell 1982, 16)

ONE OF THE BOYS
Means NOT one of the girls.

OPEN ADMISSIONS
"The first stage of Open Admissions involves *openly admitting* that education has failed for too many students." (Mina Shaughnessy 1972; cited in Adrienne Rich 1979, 61)

OPEN-MINDED
"A liberal phrase that justifies noncommittal and wishy-washy thinking. If you are open-minded, things tend to fall out – particularly those principles and convictions by which you define yourself." (Sue Yarber 1985, conversation)

OPPRESSION
Term used almost universally in feminist writing to designate the conditions and experience of subordination and injustice. Feminists differ in their use of the term – how they analyze the causes, nature, and primacy of women's oppression, what sort of experiences they apply the word to, how they believe it relates to other struggles for change, and what they think the steps toward change consist of. *Oppress* comes from Latin *opprimere* 'to press on, to press against.' Meanings include: to press against, press or bear down; to put down, crush, overwhelm; to fall upon, take by surprise; to suppress, conceal; and by late Latin, it meant the forcible violation of a woman. *Oppression* is the condition of being pressed down, crushed, overwhelmed; the exercise of wrongful authority or power in a burdensome, harsh, or wrongful manner; unjust or cruel treatment of subjects, inferiors; the imposition of unreasonable or unjust burdens. Comments by feminists include these:

"Oppression has at least four dimensions: The personal or psychological – like when you yourself believe that you're a big zero because society keeps telling you so. The private – like when some employer tries to make out with you when you ask for a job. The public – like when the government takes the money you need for child-care centers and uses it to kill people in Indochina. And the cultural – like when the history books attribute everything we did and invented to some guy we worked for." (Florynce R. Kennedy; quoted in Gloria Steinem 1973, 55)

"No other people is so entirely captured, so entirely conquered, so destitute of any memory of freedom, so dreadfully robbed of identity and culture, so absolutely slandered as a group, so demeaned and humiliated as a function of daily life. And yet, we go on, blind, and we ask over and over again, 'What can we do for them?' It is time to ask, 'What must they do now for us?' " (Andrea Dworkin 1976, 70)

"Refers to something arbitrary, to a *political* explanation and a *political* situation," rather than a natural condition. "The notion of a political, that is, social cause is an integral part of the concept of oppression." It provides "the base, the point of departure of any feminist study, as of any feminist approach." (Christine Delphy 1981, 69-70)

Oppression involves "a system of inter-related barriers and forces which reduce, immobilize and mold people who belong to a certain group, and effect their subordination to another group (individually to individuals of the other group, and as a group, to that group)." (Marilyn Frye 1983, 33)

"The oppression of women is like a typhoid epidemic. In the middle of the epidemic we must do three things: we must inform victims of their symptoms (consciousness-raising); we must treat the victim (alternate institutions, in part); and we must find the poisoned water supply and clean it up (changing society's institutions). Unless we get to the water supply, we will be fighting a losing battle." (Naomi Weisstein and Heather Booth 1975, 6)

"The experience of oppression offers one possible conceptualization of a given situation; and this particular conceptualization can only originate from one standpoint, that is, from a precise place in this situation: that of the oppressed." (Christine Delphy 1981, 75)

"To deny that you are oppressed is to collaborate in your oppression. To collaborate in your oppression is a way of denying that you're oppressed – particularly when the price of refusing to collaborate is execution." (Robin Morgan ed. 1970, xviii)

"Rape, battery, economic exploitation, and reproductive exploitation are the basic crimes committed against women in the sex-class system in which they are devalued because they are women." (Andrea Dworkin 1983, 23)

"Knowing oneself to be in the wrong, by definition, before one even begins to do anything, is a daily reality for many women." (Dale Spender 1982b, 31)

The oppression of women is impossible to analyze in isolation. It "knows no ethnic or racial boundaries, true, but that does not mean it is identical within those boundaries. . . . To deal with one without even alluding to the other is to distort our commonality as well as our differences." (Audre Lorde 1981b, 97)

"The assumption that we can divorce the issue of race from sex, or sex from race, has so clouded the vision of American thinkers and writers on the 'woman' question that most discussions of sexism, sexist oppression, or woman's place in society are distorted, biased, and inaccurate." (bell hooks 1981, 12)

"Black women in South Africa have a triple yoke of oppression. They suffer all the degradation of White racism. They are exploited as workers and peasants and they are females in a clearly patriarchal structure, where traditionally precedence is given to males in both public and private life." (Zanele Dhlamini 1972, 42)

"The danger lies in ranking the oppressions. *The danger lies in failing to acknowledge the specificity of the oppression.* The danger lies in attempting to deal with oppression from a purely theoretical base. Without an emotional, heartfelt grappling with the source of our own oppression, without naming the enemy within ourselves and outside of us, no authentic, non-hierarchical connection among oppressed groups can take place." (Cherríe Moraga 1981, 29)

"The relationship of man to woman is like no other relationship of oppressor to oppressed. It is far more delicate, far more complex. After all, very often the two love one another. It is a rather gentle tyranny. We are subdued at the moment of intimacy." (Sheila Rowbotham; quoted in Gloria I. Joseph and Jill Lewis 1981, 259)

On the term itself: "It seems to me to be abusive of language in the extreme when women speak, in the generation after Auschwitz, of the 'oppression' of women." (Cynthia Ozick 1972a, 66)

"Exploitation speaks to the economic reality of capitalist class relations for men and women. . . . Oppression is inclusive of exploitation but reflects a more complex reality. Power – or the converse, oppression – derives from sex, race, and class, and this is manifested through both the material and ideological dimensions of patriarchy, racism, and capitalism." (Zillah R. Eisenstein 1979b, 22-3)

"Trying to help an oppressed person is like trying to put your arm around somebody with a sunburn." (Florynce R. Kennedy; quoted in Gloria Steinem 1973, 55)

OPPRESSOR

"The person[s] who takes away your freedom. This means the person may be of the same class as you (your husband, your parents, your neighbors, strangers); the same race as you (your husband, your parents, your neighbors, strangers); even the same sex as you (a racist or class exploiter). The identity of the oppressors we face in our day-to-day lives is fluid and constantly changes. We may all oppress someone. Refusing to name persons as oppressors but instead using a remote concept means that people don't really have to be responsible for what they do, that any negative action is excusable because it's really the system's fault anyway." (Barbara Smith 1979a, 126)

ORGASM

"Feeling of intense sexual pleasure as the vagina goes into rhythmic muscular contractions which move down from the top of the uterus. . . . Lasts from five to 14 seconds in the male but may be prolonged and repeated indefinitely in the female. It is centered in the male in his penis but is a total body experience for the woman." (Midge Lennert and Norma Willson eds 1973, 9) Orgasm "originates not in the head but in the clitoris." (A Redstockings Sister, c.1969) "Necessarily takes place in ⋅he sexual organ equipped for sexual

climax – the clitoris." Yet the recognition of the clitoral orgasm "would threaten the heterosexual *institution*. For it would indicate that sexual pleasure was obtainable from either men *or* women, thus making heterosexuality not an absolute, but an option." (Anne Koedt 1970, 199, 206) "Is there a vaginal orgasm? The answer to that is: Since there is orgasm every other inch of the body, why not there?" (Muriel Rukeyser 1974, xiii)

(See CLITORIS, MASTURBATION, MYTH OF THE VAGINAL ORGASM, SEXUAL INTER-COURSE)

ORIENTAL

"is a color, a culture, a language, a
  tradition
oriental is often a role – high. low.
  middle.
i am me . . .
oriental is our history
     and history is not just the present –
        without a past
     i am not our history
     i am my present with a past.
     When is oriental?"

  (Beverly Lee 1971, 18)
  (See ASIAN-AMERICAN)

ORIGINAL

Political term used by gatekeepers to exclude women from the prestigious records of our society (other such terms are *innovative, creative, first rank, excellent*). "There is something about women who try to engage in intellectual, scholarly and creative work which elicits from many of their biographers a sense of obligation to comment negatively on the quality and originality of their contributions." All work has predecessors which means that no work is "original" as the term is often used. (Berenice A. Carroll 1981) Originality is often denied women because "if they followed the men's lead, they were imitators – and probably second-rate ones, at that; if they did not ape men, then they are historically unimportant because no one knows about them." (Dorothy P. Ludlow 1978, 343)

ORPHAN

Printing term for single word or incomplete line of type that has to be carried over by itself onto the next page. Nonsexist substitute for *widow*, devised by a feminist printing firm. (Frank Y. Gladney 1984, correspondence)

OSHÁANA

(See MENSTRUATION)

OTHER

Topic of Simone de Beauvoir's *The Second Sex*. "The thesis is that woman has always been defined by man as the Other, the inessential, while man himself is defined as the One, the Subject, the being capable of transcendence – of free, independent, and creative activity. The paradigm human, in other words, is conceived as male, and the female as a deviation from this norm. . . . The concept of the Other is a Hegelian one, and it is central to the existential philosophy of Sartre and de Beauvoir. It is, in de Beauvoir's words, 'a fundamental category of human thought,' 'as primordial as consciousness itself.' To be conscious is to be aware of oneself as a subject, as the One, which in turn is necessarily to be aware of *other* subjects, though not necessarily *as* subjects. . . . This tendency to objectify others, other individuals and other groups, can be overcome; reciprocity, the mutual recognition of one another as free beings, is possible and to some extent present among *men* (of the same nation, race, village, etc.,). But when men say 'we,' when they think of themselves as peers who are in some sense equal, they do not include women in this 'we'; woman remains 'the absolute Other, without reciprocity.' " (Mary Anne Warren 1980, 107-8) Margaret A. Simons (1983) describes how the editing and translating of Beauvoir's book made it known primarily as a book about *women* rather than a philosophical exploration of consciousness. Current critical theory focuses on the dynamic of the One and the Other in language, while feminists in many areas have sought to account for women's seemingly universal representation as Other ("Does Otherness stem from Motherness?" asks Elizabeth Janeway, 1980, 309)

OUTSIDERS' SOCIETY

"Has the same ends as your educated [men's] society – freedom, equality, peace; but it seeks to achieve them by the means that a different sex, a different tradition, a different education, and the different values which result from those differences have placed within our reach. . . . Whereas you will make use of the means provided by your position – leagues, conferences, campaigns, great names, and all such public measures as your wealth and political influence place within your reach – we, remaining outside, will experiment not with public means in public but with private means in private . . . we can best help you to prevent war not by repeating your words and following your methods but by finding new words and creating new methods." (Virginia Woolf 1938, 113, 143)

OVARIMONY

The act of giving witness; making statements. "I protest the use of the word 'testimony' when referring to a woman's statement, because its root is 'testes' which has nothing to do with being a female. Why not use 'ovarimony'? Think it sounds funny? Think it sounds funnier than 'testimony'?" (Rachel W. Evans 1978, letter to the editor, *Ms.* 6:11 [May] 15)

OVULAR

Significant, as of a contribution. "In her ovular work, Michelle Rosaldo indicated the importance of the value which attaches to [the public and to the private] sphere." (Linda Imray and Audrey Middleton 1983, 12) Also a new name for a seminar: "our ovular on H.D. was exciting today."

(See GERMINAL)

OWL

The bird of wisdom which "used to embody the wisdom of the Goddess.

Certain medieval magic charms apparently sought to use the bird's oracular power against its former mistress, woman. If an owl could be slain and its heart pulled out and laid on the left breast of a sleeping woman, the woman would talk in her sleep and reveal all her secrets. This seems to have been a basis of the expression 'heart-to-heart talk,' which meant a woman's secret conversation with her familiar." (Barbara G. Walker 1983, 754-5)

OXFORD ENGLISH DICTIONARY

Germinal work of linguistic scholarship which treated English as a serious language worthy of study rather than as a common vernacular. Commonly known as the OED, the dictionary, which sought to document historical as well as contemporary word usage, was initiated as a project in 1857; in 1878, James Murray was hired as editor to complete the dictionary, a project that took him until the end of his life. The final volume appeared in 1928 (a recent supplement contains words omitted from the original volumes). Murray's plan was to provide the history of every word in English with its range of meanings. Though documentation was to rely on the usages found in actual quotations identified by readers all over the world, Murray was alive to the problem of setting written evidence as the absolute criterion for inclusion in the dictionary; he remained obsessed for 70 years with the question of what "the English language" *was*. Though the dictionary claimed to include all of English ("a National Portrait Gallery, not only of the worthies, but of all the members, of the race of English words"), Murray himself recognized the project's shortcomings. In the end, meanings were largely culled from the "best" (and almost exclusively male) authors. On the grounds of sex, race, place, and class chauvinism (among others), the dictionary can be charged with bias. Nevertheless, it broke with tradition by using modern methods of lexicography to trace word etymologies and by attempting to include "what *is*" rather than what might have been or what ought to be. (K. M. Elisabeth Murray 1977, 137) As Raymond Williams notes in his preface to *Keywords*, if read with its editorial biases in mind, the OED is an incomparably useful research tool. A feminist OED has yet to be written.

(See AUTHORITY, DICTIONARY, ENGLISH)

PANDORA

A woman who, like Eve, made information available to the human race. (Jessie Sheridan 1974, quoted in the *Chicago Sun-Times* January 17) "A woman who made a fuss by opening her box and unleashing havoc which destroyed the world. (More precisely the masculine status quo)." (Judith Finlayson 1984, 19). Pandora Press is named for this woman.

(See EVE)

She is also one personification of the Earth-goddess Rhea, the "All-giver," and "the first woman in an anti-feminist fable by Hesiod, who tried to blame war, death, disease, and all other ills on women. Pandora's vessel was not a box but a honey-vase, *pithos*, from which she poured out blessings: a womb-symbol like the Cornucopia, anciently used as a vessel of death and rebirth. Pandora's Vase became Pandora's Box only in the late medieval period, when Erasmus mistakenly translated *pithos* as *pyxis*." (Barbara G. Walker 1983, 767)

PANSY

One of the many words which link gay men to flowers or fruit, in contrast to the words which link straight men to meat. Gay men call the display of their genitals under tight clothing their "basket" – something used to contain flowers or fruit. Also is one of many purple flowers, along with violets, narcissus, hyacinth, and amaranth, that are associated with homosexual rituals, wordplay, relationships, and love. (Judy Grahn 1984)

PANTS

Evolved from the flowing trousers worn by the stock character Pantaloon in Italian *commedia* whose name came down from an artificially created saint, St Panteleone, in medieval mystery plays. (Barbara G. Walker 1983, 768)

PAPER BAG

The square paper bag, universally used as a container for storing and carrying items such as groceries, was invented by Margaret E. Knight who received the decoration of the Royal Legion of Honor in 1871 from the Queen of England. (*New York Times*, Oct. 19, 1913; rpt. Elizabeth Janeway ed. 1973, 55)

PAPER PLATES

Disposable holders for food. They are not a solution to the dishwashing problem, however, since there are no paper pots, pans, spatulas and mixing bowls. (Maxine Hong Kingston 1980, 127)

PARADES

Occasions for organized spectacles on behalf of women's suffrage. "All along Fifth Avenue from Washington Square, where the parade formed, to 57th Street, where it disbanded, were gathered thousands of men and women of New York. They blocked every cross street on the line of march. Many were inclined to laugh and jeer, but none did. The sight of the impressive column of women striding five abreast up the middle of the street stifled all thought of ridicule. They were typical, womanly American women . . . women doctors, women lawyers, splendid in their array of academic robes; women architects, women artists, actresses and sculptors; women waitresses, domestics; a huge division of industrial workers; women of the seven suffrage states in the Union; a big delegation from New Jersey; another from Connecticut . . . all marched with an intensity and purpose that astonished the crowds that lined the streets." (Newspaper report 1912; cited in Eleanor Flexner 1968, 259)

PARADISE
A living garden where the tree of life bears the fruit of immortality. Paradise, in much religious writing, symbolizes both a natural garden and the female body. "Primitive notions of paradise as land flowing with milk and honey were clearly representative of the mother's body in the earliest memories. . . . Western culture made this paradise – the birthright of every primitive child – a paradise lost." (Barbara G. Walker 1983, 769)

Pleasure park. "The walls of the Patriarchal Pleasure Park represent the condition of being perpetually parked, locked into the parking lot of the past. A basic meaning of *park* is a 'game preserve' . . . an arena where the wildness of nature and of women's Selves is domesticated, preserved . . . Patriarchal Paradise is the arena of games, the place where the pleas of women are silenced, where the law is: Please the Patrons . . . Breaking through . . . the Playboys' Playground means letting out the bunnies, the bitches, the beavers, the squirrels, the chicks, the pussycats, the cows, the nags, the foxy ladies, the old bats, and biddies, so that they can at last begin naming themselves." (Mary Daly 1978, 7)

PARANOIA
"Far from a debilitating 'mental disease,' this is strengthening and realistic dis-ease in a polluted and destructive environment. Derived from the Greek terms *para*, meaning beyond, outside of, and *nous*, meaning mind, the term *paranoia* is appropriate to describe movement beyond, outside of, the patriarchal mind-set. It is

the State of Positively Revolting Hags." (Mary Daly 1978, 316)
(See HAG, MENTAL HEALTH)

PARAPHILIA
The paraphilias include exhibitionism, voyeurism, age-inappropriate sex, cross-dressing, fetishism, and sadomasochism. They should not be dismissed as "deviance" but given serious attention as we seek to better understand the nature of sexuality and desire. (Carole S. Vance 1983, 384)

PARASITISM
The condition of the unemployed modern female. The female of the dominant race or class feeds on unearned wealth (which is preceded by the subjugation of large numbers of other human beings), coming to exist "purely through the passive performances of her sexual functions." (Olive Schreiner 1911, 229)

The typical relationship between males and females in which it is generally "the strength, energy, inspiration, and nurturance of women that keeps men going, and not the strength, aggression, spirituality, and hunting of men that keeps women going." (Marilyn Frye 1983, 98-9)
(See NO)

PARENTHOOD
A condition which often brings dramatic changes to new mothers – "loss of job, income, and status; severing of networks and social contacts; and adjustments to being a 'housewife.' Most new fathers do not report similar social dislocations. (Lorna McKee and Margaret O'Brien 1983, 154)

PARIAH
In Hindu society, a person born outside of the castes dictated by scripture (thus an outcast) and assigned to do society's dirtiest work; an Untouchable. Outlawed in contemporary Indian society but perpetuated by custom nevertheless.

PARTHENOGENESIS
Virgin birth; reproduction of organisms

without conjunction of gametes of opposite sexes. Involves "the production of young by the mother without fertilisation . . . is quite common in some species. . . . It has been discovered recently . . . that the start of the process can occur in humans. Since all offspring of this form of cloning are female, it is obviously of use to animal breeders, but not, one would think, of much interest to most scientists in relation to humans!" (Diana Leonard 1984, 47) Is a recurrent element in female utopian writings (see Elizabeth Gould Davis 1971). From Charlotte Perkins Gilman's novel *Herland*: "For five or ten years they worked together, growing stronger and wider and more and more mutually attached, and then the miracle happened – one of these young women bore a child. Of course they all thought there must be a man somewhere, but none was found. Then they decided it must be a direct gift from the gods, and placed the proud mother in the Temple of Maaia – their Goddess of Motherhood – under strict watch. And there, as years passed, this wonder-woman bore child after child, five of them – all girls. . . . There you have the start of Herland! One family, all descended from one mother! She lived to be a hundred years old; lived to see her hundred and twenty-five great-grand-daughters born; lived as Queen-Priestess-Mother of them all; and died with a nobler pride and a fuller joy than perhaps any human soul has ever known – she alone had founded a new race!" (Charlotte Perkins Gilman 1915, 56-7)

PARTICIPATORY DEMOCRACY

Espoused ideal for organizational structure among New Left groups in the U.S. during the 1960s. "Often led to a lack of structure and clear responsibility, which only intensified the tendency toward informal, male leadership groups. At Harvard [according to Barbara Easton] this meant that 'all of the decisions got made in Adams House, which was where all the men lived. They'd get together at two o'clock in the morning and make decisions and then we'd all read about it the next morning in the *Crimson*.' As a result women were excluded, not necessarily by design, but thoroughly nonetheless." (Sara Evans 1980, 116)

PARTICULARIZATION

One device among many that people use to deny, resist, or ignore the reality of the sexual caste system; involves the narrowing of gynocide to one issue without seeing connections to other issues and contexts. "Since it is precisely the act of seeing the context that is terrifying, the choice to focus upon a single issue can even function as an excuse for not-seeing the context. Since feminism then becomes reduced to some particular issue, it becomes easy to dismiss as not sufficiently compelling or meaningful." (Mary Daly 1984, 323)

PARTNER, PARTNER OF LONG STANDING

Persons of any sex with whom one makes a life: shares a home, shares intellectual interests, talks over the day, has and/or raises children, tries to make ends meet.
(See FRIEND, HUSBAND, LOVER, NEEDED WORDS, POSSLQ, UM, WIFE)

PARTY, POLITICAL

An organization that "tends to stifle honesty and individuality. It substitutes numerical strength for sound reasoning, power for justice, organized machinery for the labour of conversion; the machine takes the place of the mind." (Teresa Billington-Greig 1911a, 693)

PASSAGE

"Also maze, riddle, labyrinth, and birth canal . . . all symbolize the mysteries of life, death, and rebirth." (Morneen Kamiki 1982, 15)

PASSING

Getting by in a male world by pretending to be a conventionally proper woman rather than a feminist. Long used by Blacks and gays. (Liz Stanley 1983, correspondence) For Jewish women, means passing as non-Jewish by changing looks (e.g., having 'nose jobs'), changing names, changing speech, and the like. (Evelyn Torton Beck 1982, xxx) "In the Jewish resistance, women did much of the courier, weapon-gathering, smuggling, communication, and guide work – in part because they could pass more surely than the men, who might be asked at any moment to drop their pants." (Melanie Kaye 1982, 33-4) Passing may also refer to lesbians who pass for straight or to lesbians "who look like men to the straight world. They wear men's clothes and work at men's jobs (e.g., driving taxis or clerking in stock rooms). Language, however, is inadequate here. Neither 'passing' nor 'transvestism' adequately explains the experience of the passing woman. Only she can. In other places I use 'passing' to mean disguising a deep identity for societal acceptance. 'Passing' in all its meanings is a central issue in Lesbian culture and deserves its own analysis." (Joan Nestle 1981a, 24) For many women, their color and poverty make it difficult to pass.

PASSIVITY

"*The* index to a woman's proper behavior as a role playing feminine counterpart to the aggressor. Passivity is *the* dragon that every woman has to murder in her quest for independence." (Jill Johnston 1973a, 154) "The male is psychically passive. He hates his passivity, so he projects it onto women, defines the male as active, then sets out to prove that he is ('prove he's a Man') . . . Since he's attempting to prove an error, he must 'prove' it again and again." (Valerie Solanas 1968, rpt. 1983, 3)

PASSOVER

Passover, or Pesach, commemorates Israel's deliverance from enslavement in Egypt more than 3,000 years ago as recounted in Exodus. On the first night of Passover, a *seder* is held, combining family banquet with deeply significant religious rituals, which tells the story of the Jews' flight from Egypt and arrival at Mount

Sinai. The *Haggadah*, the narrative read at the *seder*, uses the present tense to emphasize the recreation of a living experience and to link the present for all Jewish people with their history. The patriarchal language of some versions of the *Haggadah* ("This is the bread of affliction that our fathers ate in the land of Egypt. . . . Now we are slaves: in the year ahead may we be free men") has been changed to include women; if older versions are used, women at the *seder* may insert themselves ("This is the bread of affliction that our fathers and mothers ate in the land of Egypt") as the service progresses, often provoking lively discussions among participants.

PATERNITY

"Essentially a feminine attribute ultimately acquired by the human male in his attempt to keep his mastery of the female more secure and less disquieting in the light of periodic demonstrations of female superiority by way of having children." (G. Zillboorg 1974, 127)

PATRIARCH

"Dry-eyed, the inveterate patriarch
Raised his men of skin and bone,
Barbs on the crown of gilded wire,
Thorns on the bloody rose-stem."

(Sylvia Plath 1958, 106)

PATRIARCHAL FAMILY

"*Motherhood* is the institution which enforces the functions of childbearing and service to others (children); *marriage* is the institution whicn enforces the service to others (men) and sexual object function; *prostitution* is the institution which enforces the sexual object function. The patriarchal family (in which the institutions of marriage and motherhood are combined) is the institutionalization of all three functions." (Barbara Mehrhof and Sheila Cronan 1969, 4)

PATRIARCHAL IMPERATIVE

That men "*must have access* to women. . . . Access is one of the faces of Power. . . .

Female denial of male access to females substantially cuts off a flow of benefits, but it has also the form and full portent of assumption of power." (Marilyn Frye 1983, 103)

PATRIARCHY

An important term used in a variety of ways to characterize abstractly the structures and social arrangements within which women's oppression is elaborated. Means an ideology which arose out of men's power to exchange women between kinship groups; as a symbolic male principle; as the power of the father; to express men's control over women's sexuality and fertility; to describe the institutional structure of male domination. (Sheila Rowbotham 1979, 72) The following statements add to a definition of patriarchy as it is used in current feminist writings.

"A system originating in the household wherein the father dominates, the structure then reproduced throughout the society in gender relations." (Catharine A. MacKinnon 1982a, 528-9) "Patriarchy's chief institution is the family." (Kate Millett 1971, 55) Involves "not simply the tracing of descent through the father, which anthropologists seem to agree is a relatively late phenomenon, but any kind of group organization in which males hold dominant power and determine what part females shall and shall not play, and in which capabilities assigned to women are relegated generally to the mystical and aesthetic and excluded from the practical and political realms." (Adrienne Rich 1972, rpt. 1979, 78)

"Has been described as a way of structuring reality in terms of good/evil, redemption/guilt, authority/obedience, reward/punishment, power/powerless, haves/havenots, master/slave. The first in each opposite was assigned to the patriarchal father, or the patriarch's Father God, frequently indistinguishable from one another. The second, to women as 'the other' and in time to all 'others' who could be exploited. The father did the naming, the owning, the controlling,

the ordering, the forgiving, the giving, considering himself capable of making best decisions for all." (Nelle Morton n.d., 5)

"The prevailing religion of the entire planet, and its essential message is necrophilia." Women are "the real objects under attack in patriarchy." "Appears to be 'everywhere.' Even outer space and the future have been colonized . . . Nor does this colonization exist simply 'outside' women's minds, securely fastened into institutions we can physically leave behind. Rather, it is also internalized, festering inside women's heads, even feminist heads." (Mary Daly 1978, 39, 1)

"Radical feminists use patriarchy to refer to a social system characterized by male domination over women." It is constituted by "a set of social relations between men, which have a material base, and which, though hierarchical, establish or create interdependence and solidarity among men that enable them to dominate women. Though patriarchy is hierarchical and men of different classes, races, or ethnic groups have different places in the patriarchy, they also are united in their shared relationship of dominance over their women; they are dependent on each other to maintain that domination." "*Patriarchy is not simply hierarchical organization*, but hierarchy in which particular people fill *particular* places." (Heidi Hartmann 1979, 14, 15, 18)

"Our society . . . is a patriarchy. The fact is evident at once if one recalls that the military, industry, technology, universities, science, political offices, finances – in short, every avenue of power within the society, including the coercive force of the police, is entirely in male hands." (Kate Millett 1971, 25)

"Living under Capitalist Patriarchy, what is true for the man . . . is, to a great extent, true for the Chicano. He, too . . . wants to be able to determine how, when, and with whom his women – mother, wife, and daughter – are sexual. For without male imposed social and legal control of our reproductive function . . . Chicanas might very freely 'choose' to do otherwise, including being sexually independent from and/or with men." (Cherríe Moraga 1983, 110-11)

It implies a universal and historical form of oppression which returns us to biology – and thus it obscures the need to recognize not only biological difference, but also the multiplicity of ways in which societies have defined gender.... 'Patriarchy' implies a structure which is fixed, rather than the kaleidoscope of forms within which women and men have encountered one another.... 'Patriarchy' suggests a fatalistic submission which allows no space for the complexities of women's defiance." (Sheila Rowbotham 1979; in Rowbotham 1983, 208-9)

"A sexual system of power in which the male possesses superior power and economic privilege. Patriarchy is the male hierarchical ordering of society.... The patriarchal system is preserved, via marriage and the family, through the sexual division of labor and society. Patriarchy is rooted in biology rather than in economics or history." (Zillah Eisenstein 1979a, 17)

Used in the South as a defence of slavery: a beautiful patriarchal institution. (Linda Brent; cited in Adrienne Rich 1979, 238n)

At one time, "women alone held the monopoly on agriculture, and the male believed them impregnated by the gods. From the moment he discovered at once his two capacities as farmer and procreator, he instituted . . . 'the great reversal' to his own advantage. Having taken possession of the land, thus of *productivity* (later of industry) and of woman's body (thus of *reproduction*), it was natural that the overexploitation of both of these would end in this threatening and parallel menace: overpopulation, surplus births, and destruction of environment, surplus production." (Françoise d'Eaubonne 1974, 66-7)

Shares the same political goals all over the world: to assure female dependence and subservience by any and all means. In Africa, this involved first "economic control by denying women education and modern tools. Next, segregation by excluding women from the public sphere and all decisions. And finally physical control – violence, rape, sexual assault, excision, and infibulation. Some or all of these 'measures' are present in all patriarchal societies." (Fran Hosken 1981, 13)

PATRIOTISM

Love of country. Within Black U.S. culture, is equated with a sense of collective responsibility within the Black community (John Langston Gwaltney 1980). In modern times, "we seem to be teaching love of war" under the name of patriotism; "we seem to be teaching a lesson of retaliation. The war cry at Manila was 'Remember the Maine!' not 'Remember starving Cuba!' " (Mary Wood Allen 1898, 206). Patriotism is sometimes experienced more intensely by people when they are visiting a country other than their own – which they may associate with discrimination and repression. "I know that the Fourth of July happened! I say 'happened' because that's how I feel about it. To have one's National Holiday roll around when one is in a strange land and can't speak the language is an experience never to be forgotten. A homesickness more poignant and aching than anything I can ever imagine held me in its grip. All day long I did not see or speak to a single one of my compatriots . . . nor did I even hear a word of English spoken. There is this marvelous thing about my being here in France. A strange new patriotism has sprung up in me since I've been here in France . . . there are times that I'd give half of my remaining years to hear the 'Star Spangled Banner' played. And yet as I feel that way I know that it has nothing to do with the same 'home' feeling I have when I see crowds of American white people jostling each other about the American Express." (Gwendolyn Bennett 1925, journal entry Sunday, July 26; Bennett papers, Schomburg Center for the Study of Black Culture. See also Woolf 1938, 109)

PATRONYMY

Practice in which a person's name derived from the name of a father or paternal ancestor, especially one formed through affixes (Johnson-son of John). In 1804, a Jewish Statute was passed in Russia, requiring Jews to take patronymic last names, against their own custom and in keeping with gentile practices. Before that point, "Jews of Eastern Europe had used Hebrew names . . . distinctions between two Jews of the same given name were made through common sense – nicknames, street where you lived, your wife's or husband's name – not through patronyms." (Melanie Kaye 1982, 31, 42). A *patronymic* is a form of naming in which "only males are assured permanent surnames they can pass on to their children. Women are said to 'marry into' families, and families are said to 'die out' if an all-female generation occurs." (Casey Miller and Kate Swift 1976, 8)

PATTERN

A method designed in 1864 by Betsy Ann Stearns (b. 1830) to simplify and improve dressmaking for herself and her daughters.

PDOF

"Potential Dyke on Faculty." Name assigned to a professor by lesbian students at Vassar. (Sarah Lucia Hoagland 1980, 147)

PEACE

Under patriarchy, "never seems to mean peaceful cooperation, but only more arms and armies and undertakings to go to war." (H. M. Swanwick 1935, 475)

"Arise, then, women of this day! . . . Our husbands shall not come to us reeking with carnage, for caresses and applause. Our sons shall not be taken from us to unlearn all that we have been able to teach them of charity, mercy, and patience." This call in 1872 was from Julia Ward Howe who in her less pacifist younger days wrote the words to the Battle Hymn of the Republic." (Julia Ward Howe 1872; cited in Barbara Brotman 1983, 18)

PEACETIME

May "bring disaster to large numbers of women" as armies of men are disbanded from the armed services and throw women out of work. (A. B. T. 1919, 114)

PEDESTAL

Though *pedestal* means an architectural support or foundation – upon which a structure rests – its meaning for women has been that of an idealized position where she may be removed from the cares of everyday life and ostensibly adored. The following definitions suggest how women have experienced and analyzed this position.

A pedestal is "a cold, lonely place." (Midge Lennert and Norma Willson eds, 1973, 9) It is a form of entrapment. "Laws which disable women from full participation in the political, business and economic arenas are often characterized as 'protective' and beneficial. Those same laws applied to racial or ethnic minorities would readily be recognized as invidious and impermissible. The pedestal upon which women have been placed has all too often, upon closer inspection, been revealed as a cage." (J. Peters 1971, in the California Supreme Court case of *Sail'er Inn, Inc., v. Kirby, Pacific Reporter*; cited in Patricia A. Stringer and Irene Thompson 1982, ix)

In the South, a myth and legend that "is relevant to women of all races, although in different ways. For white women, it has represented a subtle kind of imprisonment under the guise of protection, and it has taken a terrible toll on those women who wanted to be strong within a system that required them to feign a special weakness. For black women, most of whom have been denied the luxury of protection and adulation, the myth has often typified an unattainable ideal with which they were and still are unfavorably compared." (Irene Thompson and Patricia A. Stringer 1982, 2-3)

"Antebellum Southern civilization was built upon the white woman's untouchable image. In order to keep her footing on the pedestal men had erected for her, she had to be aloof, aristocratic, and haughty. These qualities have always been required of women in societies based upon vast, entailed estates, but they were especially necessary in the South. They enabled the white woman to maintain her sanity when she saw light-skinned slave children, who were the very spit of Old Massa, running around the plantation. By being sufficiently frosty and above it all, she was able to ignore and endure the evidence of intercaste sexuality that surrounded her. . . . Southern men have actually been known to drink a toast to women's sexual coldness. The best of these florid paeans has been recorded by Carl Carmer in *Stars Fell on Alabama*: 'To Woman, lovely woman of the Southland, as pure and chaste as this sparkling water, as cold as this gleaming ice, we lift this cup, and we pledge our hearts and our lives to the protection of her virtue and chastity.' Southernese loses a great deal in translation. Here's what the toast really means: 'To Woman, without whose purity and chastity we could never have justified slavery and segregation, without whose coldness we wouldn't have had the excuse we needed for messing around down in the slave cabins and getting plenty of poontang. We pledge our hearts and our lives to the protection of her virtue and chastity because they are the best political leverage we ever did see.' " (Florence King 1975, 37-8)

A mythological point to which woman, in some patriarchal societies, is elevated. An illusory source of woman's power through preferential treatment where "indulgence is given her as a substitute for justice." "While woman's intellect is confined, her morals crushed, her health ruined, her weaknesses encouraged, and her strength punished, she is told that her lot is cast in the paradise of women: and there is no country in the world where there is so much boasting of the 'chivalrous' treatment she enjoys. That is to say – she has the best place in stage-coaches: when there are not chairs enough for everybody, the gentlemen stand: she hears oratorical flourishes on public occasions about wives and home, and apostrophes to women: . . . she has liberty to get her brain turned by religious excitements,

that her attention may be diverted from morals, politics, and philosophy; and, especially, her morals are guarded by the strictest observance of propriety in her presence." (Harriet Martineau 1837; in Alice Rossi ed. 1973, 125)

However idealized and oppressive, a pedestal is not a source of oppression which every woman has been privileged to experience: "While white feminists have tried to climb off the illusionary pedestal that has held them back, black women have never even had the illusion of a pedestal." (Kathryn Christensen 1975, 19)

PEN

Writing implement that stands, symbolically and metaphorically, for the ability and opportunity to author one's own words. For women, writing has been a more accessible way of earning a living creatively since it is not economically draining and can be conducted with some degree of anonymity. "Hannah Adams" is described as "the very first American woman who fought life with her pen" (Mrs. Charlotte Conrad 1891, 528). Sandra Gilbert and Susan Gubar (1982) posit the pen as a symbolic penis for male authors and speculate on its counterpart for women writers. Nélida Piñon (1982) speaks of the pen as a weapon in women's struggle. As a sharp object that a woman can legally carry with her, it has also been seen as a literal weapon against a rapist (*The Fourth World* 1971). The pen gives voice to silenced women. "I did not complain, or cry out. My pen did the speaking in words the ear could not hear." (Jessamyn West 1979, 220)

"You may rest assured that in my manners I shall observe simplicity and decorum, although I feel that with my pen I should like to break down a Chinese wall." (Carla Winckelbach; quoted in Margarethe Muller 1908, 209)

"My Sex forbids, I should my Silence break,
I lose my Jest, cause Women must not speak.

Mysteries must not be, with my search
Prophan'd,
My Closet not with Books, but Sweat-
meats cram'd . . .
My Pen if ever us'd imploy'd must be,
In lofty Themes of useful Houswifery . . .
But I can't here, write my *Probatum est.*
My darling Pen, will bolder sallies make,
And like my self, an uncheck'd freedom
take . . ."

(Sarah Fyge 1703, quoted in Jeslyn
Medoff 1982, 164)

PENCIL PICTURE DICTIONARY

An illustrated dictionary by Jenny R.
Snider (1973). The inside front cover
reads: "I was told to write clearly. I was
told to look it up. I was told I could not
draw. So here I am. For Jeff and for
Women – that we may help each other
with our own definitions."

PENETRATION

Envelopment; insight. Male metaphor for
keen perception. From Latin *penetrāre*,
from *penitus* 'deeply,' from *penus*, 'interior
of a house.' In some radical feminist
writings, an expendable aspect of sexual
pleasure. In her classic essay "The Myth
of the Vaginal Orgasm," Anne Koedt
(1970) used Masters and Johnson's findings that the clitoris rather than the
vagina figured crucially in bringing about
orgasm to suggest that vaginal penetration
was irrelevant to female pleasure and that
men might therefore be "sexually expendable." "Initially, in the context of a rising
tide of women's activities, Koedt's work
suggested possibilities for a female-
controlled sexuality. Her ideas, however
limited, helped women to decrease their
dependence on men, increase their sexual
autonomy, improve the odds that they
would obtain pleasure from sex, and find
through that pleasure not a new level of
subjugation but an affirmation of identity
and power. With these gains, however,
came losses, stemming from the movement's tendency to make law out of
necessity . . . [Some   writings],   for
example, did not appear to see the

interest of a caress or an erotic connection
of any kind – let alone of penetration.
Indeed . . . virtually no grounds remained
for desiring sexual intercourse – other
than, perhaps, that passivity had its
delights, that a lover other than the self
added an element of surprise, that a
second body warmed the sheets. Certainly,
it was very difficult for a feminist to admit
that she found penetration pleasurable or
orgasmic; later, in the face of lesbian-
feminist ideology, it became almost impossible to explain theoretically, anatomically,
or socially why any woman might want to
go to bed with a man." (Ann Snitow,
Christine Stansell, and Sharon Thompson
eds 1983, 27-8) The word *penetration*
"implies that it only takes the participation
of one force (the active) to fulfill the
act . . . [yet actually] a woman can be
understood to 'engulf' the man, actually
consuming him entirely in the act of
loving; making him the overwhelmed!"
But both terms leave out the reciprocal
nature of the act. (Adelaida Del Castillo
1978, 145)

(See PENIS, SEXUAL INTER-
COURSE)

PENILE HUMOR

"The ultimate in stand-up comedy; based
on a hierarchical power structure of the
put-down." (Kate Clinton 1982b, 42)

PENIS

From Latin *penis*, 'tail.' According to
traditional dictionaries, the male sex
organ for sexual intercourse and urination.
In feminist writing, it has several additional meanings. Some of these follow.

(See ERECTION, MALE MIND,
MYTH OF THE VAGINAL
ORGASM, PENETRATION, PENIS
ENVY, SEXUALITY, PLEASURE,
WOMB ENVY)

The Latin word from which *penis*
derives commences *pen-* yet was rendered
into English with a strong vowel *e*. "Now
pen- is not the same as the Latin *poen-*,
which takes a strong vowel, *e*, as in penal
(Alcatraz). *Pen-* is like *penicillus*, which
became the word *pencil*. In fact, *penicillus*

was originally the diminutive of *penis*, suggesting that the latter should receive the soft vowel *e*. Could it be, we ask incredulously, that scholars [invented] a strong vowel for the male . . . ? . . . One likes to envisage the difficulty Freud might have run into if he had had to prove the universal existence of something called *pennis envy*. An organ with so undistinguished a title as this would have had difficulty commanding attention at all, much less earning the jealousy of little girls." (Ruth Herschberger 1948, 37)

The penis is "held more sacred, i.e., harder to say publicly than 'vagina'" (Judith Kazantzis 1983, 29); "a dildo substitute" (Nomadic Sisters 1976, 9); "badge of the male's superior status in both preliterate and civilized patriarchies, [the penis] is given the most crucial significance, the subject both of endless boasting and endless anxiety" (Kate Millett 1971, 74); "a vestigial clitoris which has lost much of its sensitivity" (Ruth Herschberger 1948, 80); "the male genital organ so exposed that it must be protected from outside attack. [Traditional] Rod, shaft, peter, dick, ding-a-ling, thingamabob, it, stick, weenie, pee-pee, prick, cock, joint, pud" (Midge Lennert and Norma Willson, eds 1973, 10); an awkward appendage that dangles in front "instead of being neatly fitted into the whole structure" (Beata Bishop 1977, 37). "I wonder why men can get serious at all. They have this delicate long thing hanging outside their bodies, which goes up and down by its own will. . . . If I were a man I would always be laughing at myself." (Yoko Ono 1967; in Elaine Partnow 1977, 370)

The penis symbolizes male power. "The culture consents to believe the possession of the male indicator, the testes, penis, and scrotum, in itself characterizes the aggressive impulse, and even vulgarly celebrates it in such encomiums as 'that guy has balls.'" (Kate Millett 1971, 53-4)

The penis can be a source of pleasure and desire. In response to a panel on pornography in 1981, Joan Nestle wrote a memoir about her mother who put up with abuse from men but continued to enjoy them all her life. "My mother liked sex and let me know throughout the years both the punishments and rewards she earned because she dared to be clear about enjoying fucking." Writing about her experiences and passions, her mother wrote: "I SENSED THE SEXUAL ORDER OF LIFE," concluding her narrative "with a sexual credo, that she would not let [the ugliness of rape and other experiences] take away her right to sexual freedom, her enjoyment of 'the penis and the vagina.' . . . She was a working woman who liked to fuck, who believed she had the right to have a penis inside of her if she liked it and who sought deeply for love but knew that was much harder to find." Concluding, Nestle hears her mother responding to the anti-pornography equation of the penis with violence against women: "Don't scream penis at me but help to change the world so no woman feels shame or fear because she likes to fuck." (Joan Nestle 1981b, 468, 469, 470)

PENIS ENVY

In classical psychoanalysis, a fundamental element in female sexuality and the root of its development. According to Freud (who first mentioned the concept in a 1908 essay), "penis envy originates in the discovery of the anatomical distinction between the sexes: the little girl feels deprived in relation to the boy and wishes to possess a penis as he does (castration complex). Subsequently, in the course of the Oedipal phase, this penis envy takes on two secondary forms: first, the wish to acquire a penis within oneself (principally in the shape of the desire to have a child) and, secondly, the wish to enjoy the penis in coitus." (J. Laplanche and J.-B. Pontalis 1973, 302-3)

The concept of penis envy has seemed to some feminists a good reason to reject the psychoanalytic account of development. Feminists who have continued to work within a psychoanalytic framework have suggested various elaborations of and revisions to the classical conception. For some, penis envy "involves some presumptions which – as has been pointed out by critics like Karen Horney – are androcentric and implausible. Why, for example, should the small girl automatically suppose that having a penis (and no womb or vagina) is vastly preferable to having both a clitoris and a womb? Since she has experienced the phallic sensitivity of her clitoris, why should she not consider it quite adequate, and its compactness a virtue rather than a deprivation? As Horney and Mead have pointed out, Freud ignores motherhood except as 'substitute' for the possession of a penis; but mightn't the truth be closer to the reverse, at least in societies where motherhood is highly valued?" (Mary Anne Warren 1980, 171-2) Another view of the significance of penis envy is given by Maria Torok. In contrast to Freud's emphasis on women's wish for what they lack. Torok interprets penis envy as a "displacement of the frustrations in the close tie to the mother. This interpretation is much more positive and constructive [signifying] a symbol for another wish: *women do not want to be men, as Freud claims, but to separate themselves from the omnipotent mother and become whole and autonomous women.*" (Helle Thorning 1981, 5)

For other feminists, psychoanalysis remains a complex and ambitious theoretical attempt to explain how sexual difference is constructed in the first place; accordingly, penis envy and the castration complex play a key role in understanding this account and are not to be discarded solely on the grounds that they appear to reinforce asymmetry pervasive in western patriarchal culture. According to Juliet Mitchell, penis envy as the stimulus for the castration complex and thus the development of female sexuality is not founded upon the actual anatomical reality of the little girl's body. "For Freud the absence of the penis in women is significant only in that it makes meaningful the father's prohibition on incestuous desires. In and of itself, the female body neither indicates nor initiates anything . . .

Freud's intention was to establish [the historical or symbolic dimension] as the *sine qua non* of the construction of the human subject." (Juliet Mitchell 1982; in Juliet Mitchell and Jacqueline Rose, eds, 1982, 17)

PENIS-VAGINA FIXATION

A misconception about female pleasure. A belief in "the efficacy of the penis-vagina combination for producing orgasm for a woman," a notion repudiated by, among many others, Dr. Helena Wright in 1947. (Anna Coote and Beatrix Campbell 1982, 217)

(See PENETRATION, PENIS)

PEN NAMES

A social and economic necessity for many women. "So conscious is she it is *his* game she is trying her hand at, that she is prone to borrow his very name to set upon her title-page . . . Here is something quite in your line, she implies; for lo! my name is 'George.' " (Elizabeth Robins 1913, 6)

(See ANDROCENTRISM,
ANONYMOUS, NAMING)

Common among women journalists in the 19th century, including "Grace Greenwood" (Sara Jane Clarke) "Gail Hamilton" and "Cunctare" (Mary Abigail Dodge), "Penelope Penfeather" (Sally Joy), "Jennie June" (Jane Cunningham Croly), "Nellie Bly" (Elizabeth Cochran), "Iola" (Ida B. Wells-Barnett), "Bert Islew" (Lillian Alberta Lewis), and "Annie Laurie" (Winifred Black Bonfils). (Marion Tuttle Marzolf 1977)

PEOP

Pronounced peep. Singular form of *people*, a person. Also used as a suffix, e.g., *garbage peop*. In common usage in Worcester, Massachusetts, ten years ago; has since spread. (Ed Mary Rose Anthes 1983, correspondence)

PEOPLE

"*Humanity, human being, humankind, people, the thinking animal, the talking species,* or just plain *folks.* (Other possibilities for address include compounds such as *gentlefolk* and *gentlepeople*, both of which, perhaps, reflect a less realistic view of our nature than we are accustomed to, hence our discomfort with them.)" (Julia Penelope Stanley 1981b)

A concept of persons which sometimes includes women, but in some contexts refers only to enfranchised sources of power or to political institutions which exclude women. Semantically, " 'people' stands for 'man.' " (Marielouise Janssen-Jurreit 1982, 298)

A concept which includes women. "We've begun doing something revolutionary; we've begun to think of women as the people." (Ain't I A Woman Collective 1970; *Ain't I A Woman*, 9 October, 8)

"Black Is Beautiful is the direct antecedent to Women Are People." (Celestine Ware 1970, 11)

PER

Third person singular pronoun for either sex in Marge Piercy's novel *Woman on the Edge of Time*; it is derived from *person* used as a noun for a specific individual of either sex: "We could tell person intended to speak to more of you. . . . At first we were trying to save per." (Marge Piercy 1976, 315)

PERIODICALS

The publications mentioned here (some of which are occasional rather than periodical) are not the same as the so-called "women's journals" which have usually been journals published by men to be sold to women. We list below some of the irregular women's periodicals written by women for women. That is a revolutionary difference which is often reflected in their titles. Some of the initial dates and places are included. Many of the periodicals are no longer published; there are undoubtedly many more irregular titles published. (Please send a note about your favorite titles and their places of publication.) We have not included the names of feminist publishing houses, another rich source of viewy names.

Several journal titles call out clearly the labels that, in a patriarchy, are not to be voiced, and actions that are not to be taken, by women. Some announce the focus, bonding, and vision of women deliberately confronting homophobia and its vocabulary. *Lesbenfront, Lavender Vision, Lesbian Tide, Le'sBeinformed*. Others take action (*Leaping Lesbian*) or have fun with homophobic stereotypes (*Killer Dyke*). These journal titles recognize the importance of challenging those labels of deviancy, and assert our ability to create new worlds in part by calling explicit attention to the categories of the old.

The anti-female labels receive pro-female status when the namer is a woman talking about what men have wanted put down. Mary Daly (1978) writes about how women are calling attention to the labels: "We play games to end their games. Those who have been called bitches bark; pussies purr; cows moo; old bats squeal; squirrels chatter; nags whinny; chicks chirp; cats growl; old crows screech." So we have witchy journals with titles like *Cauldron* (Australia 1974), *Revolting Women* (Canada, feminist and anarchist connection), *Sinister Wisdom* (lesbian/feminist journal 1976), *Broomstick* (a periodical by, for, and about women over forty – "The menopause that refreshes" is a sample title), and *Spinning Off*. Witches are dangerous, in part because they are asexual, and do not rely on men for power and wisdom.

Other "nasty" women are also honored with titles; *Bitch* (Milwaukee), *Shrew* (London, and Brisbane, Australia), *Harpies Bizarre* (London), *Battleacts* (New York 1971), and *Bitches, Witches & Dykes* (New Zealand). All these journals promise trouble as does *Heresies* (feminist publication on art and politics 1977).

Other titles invite recognition of the various labels men have devised to evaluate women according to their sexual activity, labels which have been used to threaten women. By using the very words designed by men to punish women, women break convention, and debunk standard stereotypes about women in order to create subversive alternatives to men's views: *Shameless Hussy Review* (Berkeley, California 1969), *Scarlet Women, Scarlet Letter* (Australia, Council for the Single Mother and Her Child 1969), *Catcall* (G.B. feminist discussion periodical), *Other Woman* (1972), *Siren* (journal of Anarcho-Feminism, Chicago), *Coyote Howls* (The Intermittent Journal of Loose Women's Organization); and *Broadside* (Houston NOW). Far from being self-deprecating humor, these titles call attention to, and reject, men's stereotypes and labelling of women, and provide a wonderful sense of freedom from the older order of patriarchy. Anne Beatts writes: "The only way to de-fuse language that's been used against us is to acknowledge and laugh at it. It's as important for us as it was for Blacks in the '60s to use the word 'nigger' openly. You take the weapon out of the enemy's hands by using it yourself" (quoted in Kathleen Fury 1980, 166). The titles serve, as does much feminist humor, to isolate prejudices.

Titles which at the same time recognize men's attempts to domesticate women and suggest an alternative include *Velvet Fist, Velvet Glove, Wildflowers,* and *I used to be Sweet and a Little Sour but now I'm Sour and a Little Sweet* (Women's Correctional Institute Arts Workshop 1977). Several others confer a new status on old, odd ideas: *Just Like a Woman, Trouble and Strife* (national Radical Feminist magazine, Leeds, with title from cockney rhyming slang for *wife*), and *Hysteria* (Cambridge and Ontario). Cleveland women turned men's pseudo-question into their own statement with *What She Wants.* The existence and value of women's networks is recognized in *Grapevine* (newsletter of the Lesbian Mothers' Defense Fund, Ontario), *Gossip,* and *Telewoman* (newsletter from San Francisco Bay Area women).

Some of the titles call attention to the words men have used to try to define women as more earthy (more nature than culture) than men are, as well as to suggest that many women are interested in being on good terms with their environment, their bodies, and their productive possibilities: *Earth's Daughters* (feminist arts periodical 1971), *Mother, Mother Lode, Motherroot, Mom's Apple Pie* (Lesbian Mothers' National Defense Fund, Seattle), *MAW* (Magazine of Appalachian Women), and *The Monthly Extract: An Irregular Women's Periodical.*

Several journals refer to the combination of sexual and political activity of the women's movement: *Long Time Coming* and *Women Come Together* (Swansea). *Second Coming* is rich with allusions. The *Collective Lesbian International Terrors* published articles with the signature C.L.I.T. Others include *Lip* (arts and media journal 1977) and *The Opening.*

off our backs (1971) both announces a break in women's traditional sexual position and a demand for freedom; so does *Up From Under* (New York 1970). One of the 1968 liberation journals was *No More Fun and Games. Turn of the Screwed* was another early publication in the current feminist resurgence.

Other journals which call for changes in an unhealthy, oppressive society announce their firm, final rejection of male social traditions through titles like *Enough* (Bristol 1970), *Goodbye to All That, Paid my Dues* (journal of women and music), *A Change is Gonna Come: Moving Out* (literary and arts journal), *Frontiers: Branching Out* (1973), *On the Way,* and *The Mushroom Affect. Tooth & Nail Journal* and *Upstream* (Canada) suggest determination as well as the difficulty of this work for change. *Fireweed* (literary and cultural journal) foretells flourishing new growth in what have been inhospitable environments.

The following feminist journals make explicit reference in title to collective action: *Sisters: Daughters of Bilitis* (San Francisco 1970), *Sister Courage* (Maine), *Women in Struggle* (Wisconsin 1970). Others point out the potential strength of the bonding: *Vocal Majority* (Washington, D.C.), *Fifty-One Per Cent News* (news and literary magazine), and *Women's News . . . For a Change* (Chicago).

Several journals call upon the power of myth, moon, stars, and night: *13th Moon* (literary magazine, New York), *Woman-spirit* (journal of equinoxes and solstices 1974), *Lady-Unique-Inclination-of-the-Night*, and *Noga* (published in Hebrew – *Noga* means morning star or Venus). *Maenad* (literary journal 1980) was a female attendant of Bacchus; she's now defined in traditional dictionaries as a mad, raging woman. *The Furies* (lesbian feminist analytic paper, Washington, D.C., 1972) are avenging deities. Minerva's *Aegis* (magazine on ending violence against women) was her shield or breastplate. These plays on, and enriching of, myths contradict or alter the stories of patriarchal society.

Calling upon historical sisters are *Sappho* (lesbian/feminist voice, G.B. 1972-82), *Eve News*, *Lilith* (Jewish women's magazine 1976). The wife of Socrates, proverbially a shrew, speaks now to us as *Xanthippe* (feminist literary magazine). *Spare Rib* (G.B. 1972) is another name for Eve; that title and journal confronts patriarchy's myths about women's place in the creation of things and men's rewriting of biology which has a man giving birth to a woman. *Aphra* (feminist literary magazine) is the namesake of Aphra Behn, English dramatist and first novelist; the journal is the source of some aphra-isms. The words and intent of Sojourner Truth, a nineteenth-century feminist activist, gives drive to *Ain't I A Woman* (Iowa City), *Sojourner* (New England women's journal of news, opinions, and the arts), *Sojourner* (Third World women's research newsletter, Detroit), *Sojourner* (Ohio State Univ. Women's Studies Program) and *Truth* (Association of Black Women Historians newsletter, Univ. of Maryland).

These journal titles confront stereotypes, parody stereotypes, and offer new possibilities. The naming is playing – for keeps. The naming is, like much of feminist humor, "a humor which recognizes common oppression, notices its sources and the roles it requires, [and] identifies the agents of that oppression." (Naomi Weisstein; quoted in Alice Sheppard 1980, manuscript)

(See APHRA-ISM, AIN'T I A

WOMAN, CURSE, GODDESS, NAMING, RECLAMATION, ROCK AND ROLL, WOMEN'S MAGAZINES)

PERIODICALS AND POLITICS

"The cultural feminist takeover shows up both in periodicals from 1974 or later and in earlier, long-lasting ones. Consider, for example, the trend beginning around 1972 of giving publications mythological names: *The Furies*, *Amazon Quarterly*, *Hera*, *13th Moon*, *Pandora*, *The Full Moon*, *Siren*, etc., and compare these with earlier titles: *off our backs*, *Up From Under*, *Women: A Journal of Liberation*, *The Second Wave*, *A Journal of Female Liberation – No More Fun and Games*, *Ain't I A Women*, *Tooth 'n' Nail*, *It Ain't Me Babe*, *Women's Press*, etc. Graphics have changed, too – while pre-1972 issues were likely to feature photos of actions and demonstrations, current cover art is usually either goddess pictures or photos of a woman or two just *being*, or, if they are doing anything, it has no connection with movement activity. Hardly a periodical now isn't loaded with goddess articles, and many use the dyke separatist spellings for woman/women: womon, womyn, womin, wimmin, womben, womun, wommin, wymyn, etc." (Brooke 1980, 70)

(See CULTURAL FEMINISM, FEMINISM)

PERIODS

"Are still things most of us are vaguely ashamed of and secretive about, looking anxiously for stains on sheets or clothes, peering down the toilet to make sure the tampax has flushed away, and concealing soiled sanitary towels and knickers even from our nearest and dearest. For centuries menstruating women of all cultures have been treated in special, generally negative, ways [see for example Leviticus 15:19-24]." (Gillian Lacey; cited in Bristol Women's Study Group 1979, 98)

(See CURSE, MENSTRUATION, PULLING OUR OWN STRINGS, TAMPON)

PERSON

Word or suffix which provides an important alternative to *man*. "*Person* is a perfectly legitimate word, with its roots in Latin, and it has the advantage of referring to either sex. Thus, it serves as a fine substitute for *man* in compounds referring to either a man or a woman" as in *chairperson*. "Resistance to allowing the ending *-person* to take the place of *man* in compounds has its basis in the same resistance to change that has regularly negated attempts to bring sex equality to communication." (Bobbye D. Sorrels 1983, 27)

(See HUMAN, MAN, PEOPLE, PER, PHALLIC IDENTITY)

A male human being. The word has historically been interpreted to mean males only and thus is not intrinsically a safeguard of sexual equity. Common usage, legal decisions, and philosophical discussions indicate that a female human being is not a *person* in all meanings given the term. The word usually designates a being with certain legal and moral rights and responsibilities who is entitled to be treated in a special manner; this being is distinguished from a lowly thing. Female humans, however, are often defined as objects, as beings who lack the characteristics (including maleness) that would allow them to be recognized as persons. The Right to Life movement, ironically, urges the recognition of fetuses (of either sex) as *persons* (and thus the equation of abortion with murder) while refusing to advocate adoption of an equal rights amendment which would define women as persons under the law.

When women physicians were needed during World War I, they were permitted to enlist – but the Army refused to commission them on the same basis as their male colleagues on the grounds that the word *persons* in the Army statutes referred to males only. This definition was not enlarged to include women until World War II. (Mary Roth Walsh 1977, 225-30)

"Prior to 1860 married women were considered 'in the eye of the law, civilly dead' (*Declaration of Sentiments* Seneca Falls Women's Rights Convention, July 1858). They were chattels; indeed, the laws pertaining to slaves drew their precedents from the position of women. The feminist movement changed this. It won for women the legal status of *person*." (Naomi Weisstein and Heather Booth 1975, 1)

THE PERSONAL IS THE POLITICAL

A major slogan of feminist theory and politics which argues that personal and intimate experience is not isolated, individual, or undetermined, but rather is social, political, and systemic. As Michele Russell claims: "No life-area is too trivial for political analysis" (1979, 101). Catharine A. MacKinnon recently summarized its unique contribution to feminist theory: "Relinquishing all instinctual, natural, transcendental and divine authority, this concept grounds women's sexuality on purely relational terrain, anchoring women's power and accounting for women's discontent in the same world they stand against." "The personal as political is not a simile, not a metaphor, and not an analogy. . . . It means that women's distinctive experience as women occurs within that sphere that has been socially lived as the personal – private, emotional, interiorized, particular, individuated, intimate – so that what it is to *know* the *politics* of women's situation is to know women's lives." In other words: "to feminism, the personal is epistemologically the political, and its epistemology is its politics." (Catharine A. MacKinnon 1982a, 534, 535)

In the 1960s the "failure to recognize feminism as a political movement is the novelty of the idea that discontent with social roles is the stuff of politics. . . . For women, self-assertion is a political act. They have already become aware that privatism is a trap. Salvation through personal relationships, family and/or religious experience will not change the constraining nature of the sociological identity of women. It still leaves each generation of women to fight as best it can the oppressive roles, character traits and abilities assigned women before they can begin to live in their own reality." (Celestine Ware 1970, 18)

Comments on the phrase itself: it is a "brilliant insight" that tells us our personal failings are "not due to some secret stigma but to a society which denies us our humanity at every turn, a society which keeps us powerless, dependent and frightened." (Naomi Weisstein and Heather Booth 1975, 4) It "means that political power cannot be conceived just as a matter of running for office or even about seizing power. It is about power as it manifests itself in society. Resistance within these relationships cannot then be postponed until our candidate wins or until after the revolution. . . . We need to find ways of living and relating which begin to develop alternative possibilities." (Sheila Rowbotham 1983, 147) It was the dictum of the Radical Feminists. "The personal is political. . . . What seem to be 'personal' problems of women have their roots in the political system which oppresses women." (Rosario Morales 1973, 199) It means that "there is no private domain of a person's life that is not political and there is no political issue that is not personal." (Charlotte Bunch; quoted in Lydia Sargent 1981b, xix) It captures important connections, for "without an emotional, heartfelt grappling with the source of our own oppression, without naming the enemy within ourselves and outside of us, no authentic, non-hierarchical connection among oppressed groups can take place." (Cherríe Moraga 1981, 29) "I say woman overturns the 'personal,' for if, by means of laws, lies, blackmail, and marriage, her right to herself has been extorted at the same time as her name, she has been able, through the very movement of mortal alienation, to see more closely the inanity of 'propriety,' the reductive stinginess of the masculine-conjugal subjective economy, which she doubly resists." (Hélène Cixous 1975b, 259) But for some, "the personal is not political enough" (Elizabeth Fox-Genovese 1979).

PERSONALITY DISORDERS

Seem to be stacked against women in part because of the *DSM-III*, the manual used to diagnose and treat mental health problems. Psychologist Marcie Kaplan made this point by inventing two fictitious personality disorders based on stereotypically male traits:

Independent Personality Disorder – puts work and career above personal relationships, travels a lot and works long hours, makes career decisions without considering others' needs, is unable to express emotions.

Restricted Personality Disorder – appears to be self-assured, shows limited emotional expression, resists answering others' emotional needs, is stoic.

But these male behaviors would not be diagnosed as "disorders." Masculinity is not clinically suspect; femininity is. (Marcie Kaplan 1983, 791)

(See MENTAL HEALTH, NORMAL, YELLOW WALLPAPER)

PERVERSION

"The wish to have a vagina smell like a strawberry." (Midge Lennert and Norma Willson eds 1973, 10)

PETITION

Important strategy for women's equality through legislative action. Ernestine Rose, responsible for the 1836 petition in New York for a Married Woman's Property Law, described the difficulties of the petition process: "After a good deal of trouble I obtained five signatures. Some of the ladies said the gentlemen would laugh at them; others, that they had rights enough; and the men said the women had too many rights already. . . . I continued sending petitions with increased numbers of signatures until 1848 and '49, when the Legislature enacted the law which granted woman the right to keep what was her own. But no sooner did it become legal than all the women said: 'Oh! That is right! We ought always to have had that!'" (Ernestine Rose 1881; cited in Eleanor Flexner 1968, 65)

PF
Post-feminism. (Michelene Wandor 1980, 134)

PHALLIC IDENTITY
Where male identity is centered. "A man's identity is located in his conception of himself as the possessor of a phallus; a man's worth is located in his *pride* in phallic identity. The main characteristic of phallic identity is that *worth* is entirely contingent on the possession of a phallus. . . . Women, then, by definition, have no claim to the rights and responsibilities of personhood." Is the source of "all personal, psychological, social, and institutionalized domination on this earth . . . As nonphallic beings, women are defined as submissive, passive, virtually inert. For all of patriarchal history, we have been defined by law, custom, and habit as inferior because of our nonphallic bodies. Our sexual definition is one of 'masochistic passivity': 'masochistic' because even men recognize their systematic sadism against us; 'passivity' not because we are naturally passive, but because our chains are very heavy and as a result, we cannot move." (Andrea Dworkin 1976, 46, 47)

PHALLIC MORALITY
Expressed through "The Most Unholy Trinity: Rape, Genocide, and War." (Mary Daly 1973)

PHALLISM
A form of humanism. "It is an assumption of superiority, with accompanying rights and duties, that is seen as not requiring justification by personal virtue or individual merit and is taken to justify a contemptuous or patronizing attitude toward certain others. The phallist, confusing *Man* and *man*, meets women with humanist contempt and patronage." (Marilyn Frye 1983, 44)

PHALLOCENTRISM
Male-centeredness which places the male-identified subject at the center of intellect, perception, experience, values, and language. In 1916, Ernest Jones identified literal phallocentrism in works on sexual symbolism by other psychoanalysts ("There are probably more symbols of the male organ itself than all other symbols put together. . . . This is a totally unexpected finding, and is so difficult to reconcile with our sense of proportion that it needs an effort to refuse the easy escape of simply denying the facts"); when he presented his first paper on female sexuality in 1927, he began by remarking that "there is a healthy suspicion growing that men analysts have been led to adopt an unduly phallocentric view . . . the importance of the female organs being correspondingly underestimated." (Ernest Jones 1948, 103, 438; cited in Jane Gallop 1982, 16-18). Commenting on Jones' language, Jane Gallop writes that "the male analyst's view is 'unduly phallo-centric.' 'Unduly,' according to the dictionary, means '1. Excessively, immoderately. 2. In disregard of a legal or moral precept.' Phallocentrism seems wrong to Jones: that is, immoral by virtue of being 'excessive, immoderate,' which is to say, unreconcilable with a 'sense of proportion.' The phallic disproportion brings him . . . to champion the claims of an 'underestimated' female sexuality to a more balanced, more proportionate estimate. His 'sense of proportion,' his spirit of fair play, will be sufficiently scandalized to provoke his only major departure from Freud's theory . . . [Yet] if feminism is to change a phallocentric world, phallocentrism must be dealt with and not denied. If Jones, through his outraged spirit of fairness, appears as woman's ally, we should beware his faith in the harmonious relation between the sexes. Of what use is that faith when it wants nothing more than to cover over the disharmony from which feminism arises and which it would change." (Jane Gallop 1982, 16, 18)
(See PHALLOLOGOCENTRISM, PHALLUS)

PHALLOCRACY
The "social, political, ideological system that spawns racism and genocide as well

335

as rapism and gynocide." (Mary Daly 1984, 5n) "We've never been in a democracy; we've always been in a phallocracy." (Françoise Parturier 1968; cited in Elaine Partnow 1977, 240)

PHALLOGOCENTRISM

"The current tradition that constitutes a signifying system organized around gender. By 'gender,' I refer to a binary concept of a relation that assumes such dichotomies as male presence/female absence, male word principle (*verbs*)/female verbal object, male center/female margin . . . [it] regulates a set of systems that maintain the male identified subject at the center of words." (Namascar Shaktini 1982, 29-30)

(See LANGUAGE, PHALLUS, SEXUAL DIFFERENCE, SUBJECTIVITY)

Asserts the complicity between logocentrism and phallocentrism. As developed by Jacques Derrida and others, the term suggests that the continuing logic of the west, its model of truth and sense of identity, is centered on the symbolism of the phallus. "It is one and the same system: the erection of a paternal logos . . . and of the phallus as 'privileged signifier' . . . In both cases there is a transcendental authority and point of reference: truth, reason, the phallus, 'man.'" (Jacques Derrida, cited in Jonathan Culler 1982, 172). "In combating the hierarchical oppositions of phallocentrism, feminists confront in immediately practical terms a problem endemic to deconstruction: the relationship between arguments conducted in logocentric terms and attempts to escape the system of logocentrism. For feminists this takes the form of an urgent question: to minimize or to exalt sexual differentiation? Does one concentrate on a range of attempts to challenge, neutralize, or transcend the opposition between 'male' and 'female,' from demonstrating women's proficiency at 'male' activities, to tracing the historical evolution of the distinction, to challenging the very notion of an oppositional sexual identity? Or does one, on the contrary,

accept the opposition between male and female and celebrate the feminine, demonstrating its power and independence, its superiority to 'male' modes of thought and behavior?" (Jonathan Culler 1982, 172)

Male sexual model. "Based on a polarization of humankind into man/woman, master/slave, aggressor/victim, active/passive . . . the very identity of men, their civil and economic power, the forms of government that they have developed, the wars they wage, are tied *irrevocably* together. . . . All forms of dominance and submission . . . are tied irrevocably to the sexual identities of men." (Andrea Dworkin 1976, 12) "Phallic myth and language generate, legitimate, and mask the material pollution that threatens to terminate all sentient life on this planet." (Mary Daly 1978, 9)

PHALLOLOGOCENTRISM

"Lately, in particular, linguistically minded critics and philosophers have increasingly called attention to the indeterminacy of the terms through which we think we know the world, while psychoanalytic theorists have increasingly emphasized the inexorable psychological forces that determine the apparently logical terms in which we think. Inevitably, therefore, schools of 'phallologocentrists,' 'anti-phallologocentrists,' 'anti-phallo-theo-logo-centrists,' and what we might call 'vulvalogocentrists' have arisen to mediate on the sexuality of linguistics and the linguistics of sexuality. For if language is a process of cultural artifice that both distances and defines nature, then it would seem that its words and workings might well embody the bodily differences through which each human being first confronts the fundamental sexuality of his or her own nature." (Sandra M. Gilbert and Susan Gubar 1982, 1)

PHALLOPANACEA

The notion – the inevitable consequence of phallocentrism – "that all a woman needs to fulfill her every desire is a good

husband." (Michèle Le Doeuff 1977, 6)
(See PHALLOCENTRISM)

PHALLUS

"Represents abstract paternal power; it is almost by definition political. In however sophisticated and disguised form, phallic imagery remains the basis of present-day religious and political attitudes. It is worth noting that we have no female equivalent to 'phallic,' no word which sums up the symbolic power of the mother and of female sexuality." (Margaret Walters 1978, 8)

(See LANGUAGE, PENIS, PHALLOCENTRISM, SEXUAL DIFFERENCE)

"May be regarded as the organizing principle for all standard systems including that of law, since at this time – though, we can hope, not forever – no legal communication can entirely ignore its referential order." (Namascar Shaktini 1982, 29-30)

"Lacan makes the distinction between the 'function of the father' and a particular father who embodies this function. In the same way, he makes a radical distinction between the penis and the 'phallus,' between organ and information. The phallus is a set of meanings conferred upon the penis. . . . The phallus is, as it were, a distinctive feature differentiating 'castrated' and 'noncastrated.' The presence or absence of the phallus carries the differences between two sexual statuses, 'man' and 'woman . . .' Since these are not equal, the phallus also carries a meaning of the dominance of men over women, and it may be inferred that 'penis envy' is a recognition thereof. . . . We still live in a 'phallic' culture." (Gayle Rubin 1975, 190-1)

"The question of whether one can separate 'phallus' from 'penis' rejoins the question of whether one can separate psychoanalysis from politics. The penis is what men have and women do not; the phallus is the attribute of power which neither men nor women have. But as long as the attribute of power is a phallus which refers to and can be confused (in the imaginary register?) with a penis, this confusion will support a structure in which it seems reasonable that men have power and women do not. And as long as psychoanalysts maintain the separability of 'phallus' from 'penis,' they can hold on to their 'phallus' in the belief that their discourse has no relation to sexual inequality, no relation to politics." (Jane Gallop 1982, 97)

PHANTOM ELITE

For a given group, a presumed elite leadership who are responsible for policy and decision-making but who are never actually present in any given gathering of the group's members. (Berkeley Women's Liberation Archive 1969; Northwestern University Collection, Evanston, Illinois)

PHILOSOPHICAL FEMINISTS

Those who prized women's intellect and temperament which "they believed inhered in women's nature and comprised a female culture. They gave these traits an overriding social import and considered women to be more democratic, more moral, more sensitive to those in distress, and respectful of human life than men. Women were thus regarded as civilizers. Philosophical feminism was broad enough to include secular rationalists, religious believers, and men from all shades of the political spectrum. It emerged as the mainstream of male feminism . . . well into the twentieth century. . . . The philosophical feminists did not discount conditioning as significant in sex role definitions . . . [but] they believed that conditioning accounted for the more superficial personality traits." (Sylvia Strauss 1982, xi-xii)

PHOTOGRAPHY

"Can convey many things in women's lives which are not usually seen. . . . Photographs can be a stepping stone to enlarging our experience, introducing new ways of seeing." "As women in a patriarchal culture, it is crucial that we think critically about the interconnections between photographic imagery and life experience. It is crucial to understand our underlying assumptions, motives and attitudes as photographers. It is crucial that we realize our power in being able to make our own images." (Susan Iversen 1983, 1)

"During my coming out as a lesbian I began to see the process of self-reflection in quite a different light. I was just starting to use a camera at that time, and found that photography offered a means of exploring and integrating the new aspect of myself. The images I created from my emerging lesbian sensibility are important records of my growing self-acceptance." (Greacian Goeke 1982, 80)

Social worker who works with battered women: "I have turned to photography as a way of communicating to others what I have seen and felt. The women whom I have photographed have been courageous in allowing their most personal and painful emotions to be revealed and recorded on film in the hope that others may succeed where their own steps have faltered. In some cases, bruises or scars have been recorded, but these are secondary. When I look into the eyes of the women I have photographed, I believe that is where the real story is told. I hope the images I have created will disturb others as I have been disturbed." (Nancy Rees 1982, 25)

Complicates the issue of sexuality in art. "Prior to 1839, sexual imagery had a completely different character. After the invention of photography, any kind of photographically derived sexual imagery, including pornography, could no longer be interpreted as a manifestation of the artist's fantasy or imagination. Now the fantasy had the added proof of human flesh." (Barbara DeGenevieve 1982, 12)

PHRASE BOOK FOR THE FOREIGN COUNTRY OF FEMINISM

In an open letter to male colleagues, Joanna Russ suggests why a given man's attempts to be a "goodguy" often fail. "As tourists in a foreign country are given a phrase book so that without actually learning the language they can still complain . . . so I am going to give you a phrase book for the foreign country of feminism. There'll be a difference, though – this book translates what *you* say. It translates what you say into what you mean:

WHAT YOU SAY	WHAT YOU MEAN
I'm all for women's liberation, but . . .	I'm scared
It was only a joke.	I find jokes about you funny. Why don't *you* find jokes about you funny?
I asked my wife (secretary) about women's liberation and she said . . .	I asked my maid about Black Power and she said . . .
Gee, there's a woman jockey (elephant trainer, engineer, carpenter) out in Indianapolis. What won't they think of next?	Freak.
We're hiring a woman. What do you think of that!	Kiss me. I'm a goodguy.
You can't expect change to come overnight.	And if we're lucky, never."

(Joanna Russ 1974, 40-2, excerpts)

PHYLLIS BRADY

Prison name for Olive Beamish, a suffragist who was arrested on suspicion of militancy in 1913 and forcibly fed in Holloway Prison. She was one of the first women to be released under the Cat and Mouse Act, then lived underground, committing further militant acts, and was rearrested in 1914. In 1929 she did considerable work on behalf of Republican Spain. (*Calling All Women* February 1966, 4)

PIE

A food for all classes but the ingredients differ depending upon circumstances. "Rabbiting, if he went rabbiting, we'd have a rabbit pie. . . . And eel pie. No end of eel pie. Once I had to skin four dozen of them. . . . Sparrow pie. I've plucked hundreds." (Alice Rushmer; cited in Mary Chamberlain 1983, 79-80)

PIE

In linguistics, stands for Proto-Indo-European, the hypothesized and reconstructed language to which the Indo-European languages (of which English is one) are traced. One approach used to reconstruct PIE is to compare parallel words, or 'cognates,' from different languages and figure out what the 'common ancestor' must have been to yield those forms. Another approach is to look at changes internal to a single language and reconstruct what must have existed to bring about those changes. Dictionaries which list the cognates of a given word show differences and similarities in both sound and meaning. In some cases the reconstructed PIE form is given as well, always marked with an *asterisk to show it is reconstructed rather than attested (usually through written documents). The *American Heritage Dictionary* provides an appendix of Indo-European roots clearly and accessibly. A feminist approach to linguistic reconstruction is provided by Susan Wolfe and Julia Penelope Stanley (1980) and discussed in Dennis Baron (forthcoming).

PIGS

"Men who send other men into jungles, farmlands, cities, and campus parking lots to kill people and destroy land." (Pat Wainoch n.d.)

(See MALE CHAUVINIST PIG, PINK PIG AWARD)

PILL, THE

Oral contraceptive. "Originally the brainchild of a feminist – Margaret Sanger, founder of the American organization Planned Parenthood and protagonist of women's rights. At the age of 88, Margaret Sanger was introduced to Gregory Pincus, a reproductive scientist; she subsequently raised $150,000 to fund Pincus to carry out research on a 'simple, cheap, safe contraceptive to be used in poverty-stricken slums and jungles and among the most ignorant people.' " (Barbara Seaman and Gideon Seaman; quoted in Ann Oakley 1982, 193). Is "an imperfect drug, which brought with it a range of unpleasant side effects, it nevertheless enabled women to choose with some certainty when to have children." (Anna Coote and Beatrix Campbell 1982, 12). "Gives the women, as well as the men, some control. Simple as that" (Toni Cade 1969, 164). "Made millions for the drug companies, made guinea pigs of us, and made us all the more 'available' as sexual objects" (Robin Morgan ed. 1970, xxxv).

PINK PIG AWARD

Is given by the Equal Opportunities commission for Northern Ireland to the advertisers who are responsible for the worst example of sexist advertising. (*Irish News* 1981, October 8)

(See PIGS, MALE CHAUVINIST PIG)

PIN MONEY

Allowance for personal expenditures given by a husband to his wife. "Though the law gave husbands [in eighteenth-century England] almost unlimited power, public opinion usually restrained them from flagrantly abusing their wives or denying them money to spend in proportion to the fortune they had brought into the marriage. In the upper class, marriage settlements assured a wife 400 or 500 pounds a year spending money (called pin money) while her husband lived, and a jointure if he died. And courts became increasingly ready to intervene to enforce such provisions (for those who could afford a lawsuit)." (Priscilla Diaz Dorr 1984, correspondence; see also Katharine M. Rogers 1982).

(See MAD MONEY, PUSHKE)

PIONEER

Not only blond, blue-eyed Swedish people but also "Black people who came north after Reconstruction to settle the Great Plains territories, to homestead and break the sod and in many cases establish all-Black towns on the frontier." (Sandy Boucher 1984, 5) Included women doctors, who often "risked their lives on the open prairie to minister more than herbs and common sense. The description of a pioneer nurse/doctor, attending to a dying friend while defending the cabin from wolves attracted by the sick woman's odor, is chilling. "One got his head in between the door casing and as he was trying to wriggle through, mother struck him in the head with an axe and killed him. I shot one coming through the window. . . . Their howling was awful. We fought those wolves five nights in succession." (Joanna L. Stratton; cited in Joan Patchen 1981, review of *Pioneer Women* in *Louisville Courier-Journal*, April 12)

PITCH

A paralinguistic feature of a speech sound which depends on relative acoustic frequency. Women's speech is generally said to have higher pitch than men's, a characteristic sometimes attributed to their smaller, narrower vocal tracts but more probably the result of learned linguistic conventions and androcentric hearing practices. Pitch is a feature often exaggerated by female impersonators and others imitating women's speech. (See Sally McConnell-Ginet 1978b)

"I would suggest that high pitch and its undesirability is based on the sex of the speaker and not the speech itself. I think it would be perfectly possible for a woman

to be speaking in an electronically registered lower pitch than a man and for her to be classified as having a high-pitched, shrill and whining voice while the male's higher pitch could be classified as pleasing and acceptable." (Dale Spender 1980, 41)

PLACE

National identity. Like sex, race, class, age, ethnicity, and sexual preference, a potential source of difference and marginalization. "It is now conventional for feminist essays to begin by questioning the place from which one speaks; it has also long been customary for Australian essays to pose the question of speaking of place. To speak about Australia in other countries is, usually, to start with stories and descriptions; to speak about Australia in Australia is to begin half-deafened by the din of conflicting and variously invested discourses on place, space, movement, distance, identity and difference – wild histories of the mapping of a *terra incognita*." (Meaghan Morris 1984, 42)

PLACENTA

Organ which develops in female mammals during pregnancy, lining the uterine wall and partially circling the fetus to which it is attached by the umbilical cord. "The placenta performs an at present irreplaceable function in providing nutrients to the fetus in the womb. It certainly seems that the time when babies can be artificially incubated, as in *Brave New World*, *Woman on the Edge of Time*, and *The Dialectic of Sex*, is a long way off. However, womb-envy continues. A French geneticist, addressing a conference on In Vitro Fertilisation in May 1983, speculated that it might be possible one day for men to give birth via Caesarean section, to babies artificially nurtured in the abdomen." (Diana Leonard 1984, 49)

PLAY

"Making a mess, molding mud into pies and sculptures, tearing up bits of paper and reassembling them in patterns, mixing water paints and splashing them around, digging for treasures, fishing, exploring unknown places, finding out how things work, exploring the bodies of other children." Play is something women are encouraged "to give up at puberty in exchange for dedication to the needs of others." (Michele Roberts 1983, 65)

PLAYING DOLLS

A game of real dolls and fantasy families which girls, primarily, play; early experiments with women-raised children. (Sara Ruddick 1980, 252). Is a pastime avoided by some little girls like the plague.

(See DOLLANITY,
SOCIALIZATION, TOMBOY)

PLAYTHING

How women sometimes see themselves in the eyes of men. "We Wren officers used to call ourselves the Playthings – sometimes we were taken off our shelf and dusted and looked at, but then we were always put back again." (Barbara Pym 1952, 114)

PLEASURE

One current issue in feminism involves the exploration of pleasure: how does it develop, how is it experienced, who gets it, who gives it, what does it mean, how is it linked to patriarchal reality.

"Till women are led to exercise their understandings, they should not be satirized for their attachment to rakes; or even for being rakes at heart, when it appears to be the inevitable consequence of their education. They who live to please – must find their enjoyments, their happiness in pleasure!" (Mary Wollstonecraft 1792; cited in Cora Kaplan 1984, 15)

"The notion of women *taking* pleasure is a novel one, in contrast to giving and receiving pleasure. Taking pleasure implies some autonomous activity." (*Diary of a Conference* 1982, 32-3)

"The walls and doors of the women's toilets at the University of Sussex library were, and are, covered with women's writing. From this lowest seat of high learning a polylogic testament to women's entry into discourse can be read in the

round. There is, inevitably, a euphoric temptation to read too much out of these expressive inscriptions. For if young women can shit *and* write, not for some patriarchal pedant, but for each other's eyes only, what vestiges of Victorian constraints remain? It is true, of course, that the vast majority of contributors to this particular public/private debate are young, white and middle-class, but not all women's loos so decorated are quite so class and race bound. In the smallest rooms of this academy politics and intellectual matters are informally debated, but sex as the preferred topic wins hands down. 'How do I get an orgasm?' prompted a booth-full of replies and commentary in the early mid-seventies, showing the range and ingenuity of women's sexual practices and theories. Advice included detailed instructions to be relayed to a male partner as well as the succinct, laconic recommendation to 'Try Women.' There was an address for suppliers of vibrators and an illustration, definitely not erotic, to help one find the elusive clitoris. In the wide variety of responses one was noticeably absent – no contributor contested the importance of the question. No one queries the centrality of orgasm for women's sexual practice or the importance of sexual pleasure itself. No anachronistic bluestocking suggested that intellectual and sensual pursuits were incompatible. No devout Christian was moved to tell her sisters to wait until marriage. Only now, from a different time and place in the feminist debate over sexuality, does that apparently unanimous agreement among young educated women that sexual pleasure, however achieved, was an unproblematic desire seem curious. About the means of arriving at pleasure there was plenty of disagreement; if anything that cubicle was a telling reminder that there has never been a single femininity, and that within feminism sexuality and the meaning of pleasure have most frequently been the site of anger, contradiction and confusion, too often illuminating class, cultural and racial division between women. Now, when female sexuality is indisputably centre-stage in feminist debates but pleasure is too rarely its subject and eros rampant is more likely to conjure up a snuff movie than multiple orgasm, that loo wall remains with me as an important event in the history of feminism, a moment whose appearance and significance we must work to understand." (Cora Kaplan 1984, 33-4)

PLURALISM

Diversity. The only critical stance consistent with the multiplicity of the women's movement. (Annette Kolodny 1981, 40)
(See OBJECTIVITY, REALITY, THEORY)

P.M.

Post Marriage. As reflected in newspaper stories, one of the two great stages in a woman's life, the other being Ante Marriage. (Jean Ward 1980, 38)
(See A.M.)

PMS

(See PREMENSTRUAL SYNDROME)

PMT

(See PREMENSTRUAL SYNDROME)

PMZ

Postmenopausal zest. Term used by Margaret Mead for midlife change, growth, and creativity. (Rachel Josefowitz Siegel 1983, 95)

POETIC TRADITION

Much of it consists "of the ceaseless outcry of the male for the female, which is by no means so overwhelming a feature of human life as he imagines it." (Charlotte Perkins Gilman 1911, 87) It's also a notion which props up the idea of poetry "as a magical art, which must be performed by elite beings-apart." A notion which "is a very real indication of the problem facing high art in a capitalist society – how its practice is tied into and legitimized by society precisely because in

its hierarchical and elite nature it *reinforces* the ideological hierarchy of aspiration and remains the property of the few." (Wendy Mulford 1983, 35)

POETRY

"A poem is pure energy
horizontally contained
between the mind
of the poet and the ear of the reader"
(Nikki Giovanni 1975)

POINT OF VIEW

A relative matter. Some points of view: "Power to create the world from one's point of view is power in its male form." (Catharine A. MacKinnon 1982a, 538) "My point is that women and men see and hear and feel differently, and truth has many sides." (H. M. Swanwick 1935, 234) "The culture assumes in general, that male films are objective and female films are subjective; male subjectivity is still perceived as *the objective point of view* on all things, in particular women." (Michelle Citron 1978, 104) Raphaelesque: "the superficial point of view of the outsider, the person who has no actual experience of the subject." (Cicely Hamilton 1909, 113) "If I'm singing a man's song that's talking from a man's point of view to a woman, I'd still say it that way." (Marianne Faithfull 1980, 62) "Euro-Americans perceive the development of their culture as a mastery of the natural world, a prime example of the progress from primitive to civilized society. They seem to believe that culture is either immune to ecological disasters, or clever enough to survive them. This is racism, founded on the precarious conception of the technological and mental superiority of the consumer-producer system." (Winona LaDuke 1983, 56)
(See MALE CHAUVINISM, PHALLOCENTRISM, POWER, SEXISM, SUBJECTIVITY)

POLE-BENDERS

"Female competitors in a rodeo-like event, much like the ski slalom, in which horses are run in between and around poles stuck in the ground. Usually this event takes place outside the formal rodeo competition; the only formal event in which females can run is the barrel race." (Rayna Green 1984, 314)

POLEMIC

Feminist speech or writing which articulates too bluntly its unwelcome political perspective: thus Virginia Woolf's *A Room of One's Own* is considered a literary masterpiece but *Three Guineas* is a polemic.

POLITENESS

"Consists in a special way of treating people, saying and doing things in such a way as to take into account the other person's feelings. On the whole that means that what one says politely will be less straightforward or more complicated than what one would say if one wasn't taking the other's feelings into account . . . Three factors seem to be involved in deciding whether or not to take the trouble to be polite: (1) One tends to be more polite to people who are socially superior to oneself, or socially important: one's boss, the vicar, the doctor, the president. (2) One also tends to be more polite to people one doesn't know, people who are somehow socially distant: strangers, persons from very different walks of life. (3) A third factor is that kinds of acts in a society come ranked as more or less imposing, and hence more or less face threatening, and the more face threatening, the more polite one is likely to be." (Penelope Brown 1980, 114-15) The theory of politeness evolved by Penelope Brown (1980) and Stephen C. Levinson (1978) is significant in accounting for "how certain language choices relate to communicative goals and strategies for achieving them. They explain why, e.g., certain types of linguistic devices play similar roles cross-culturally in conversational politeness. . . . They do this by using a general theory of social relations . . . in combination with a detailed analysis of speech actions – of linguistic forms and their uses. . . . Principles exist to link aims with language

use." (Sally McConnell-Ginet 1983, 386) The fact therefore that women are said to be more polite and to have more politeness strategies is related both to rational strategies on the part of speakers and to the social and cultural contexts in which these strategies occur and have meaning.

POLITICS

"Is the machine; it concerns itself with the things that are immediately practicable and possible, the products of compromise, of buying and selling, of weighing and measuring, the safe things, the accepted things, the things that are orthodox." (Teresa Billington-Greig 1911a, 693)

"Power-structured relationships, arrangements whereby one group of persons is controlled by another." (Kate Millett 1971, 43)

"A male invention that emphasizes conflict and confrontation." (Tom Peterson 1984; cited in Laura Langston 1984, 25)

"An inadequate channel of expression for feminist desires." (Teresa Billington-Greig 1911a, 695)

"Is defined in such a manner as to have little to no meaning for [women]. One study found that although masculine people expressed more interest in the generic term 'politics,' feminine people showed more interest in issues such as women as candidates and public officials, abortion, and the equal rights amendment." (Mary Lou Kendrigan 1984, 12)

"We may suspect that the ultra-Right and the extreme Left stretch not along a straight line but curve, rather, into one circle, meeting each other in an apocalyptic blur, just as we may suspect that the Middle is not a place of safety and rationality but of an emptiness that runs as smoothly as Disney World." (Robin Morgan 1982, 5)

"Much of what is narrowly termed 'politics' seems to rest on a longing for certainty even at the cost of honesty, for an analysis which, once given, need not be reexamined. Such is the deadendedness – for women – of Marxism in our time." (Adrienne Rich 1979, 193)

"Listen   listen with care   class and

color and sex do not define people do not define politics   a class society defines people by class   a racist society defines people by color   We   feminist socialists   radicals   define people by their struggles against the racism sexism   classism   that they harbor that surrounds them." (Rosario Morales 1981, 92–3)

Practical politics: "The art of organizing and handling men in large numbers, manipulating votes, and especially, appropriating public wealth." (Charlotte Perkins Gilman 1911, 217)

POPULAR CULTURE

Feminists have approached popular culture from at least four perspectives. The now familiar concept, *images of women*, was the concern of the earliest critiques of the 1960s, when feminists began looking at what kind of images are present in popular culture and what they reveal about women's position in the culture, whom the images serve, and the consequences of those images. The *reception* approach has come out of an interpretive approach to popular culture that feminists have adapted to better understand the experiences of the woman audience member and the meaning she derives from cultural products. A third perspective, *recovery* and *reappraisal*, has attempted to reconstruct a lost history of women's creativity, looking at how women have managed to express themselves in a male-dominated culture, why women's creativity has been overlooked and undervalued, and how men's and women's creativity differ. Finally, some feminists have critiqued popular culture from a *social structure* approach, where women's relationship to popular culture is seen as part of a larger question about men's and women's differing worlds of social experience, resulting from economic, institutional, and sociological structures that create gender. A primary question from this perspective is whether two different cultural worlds are desirable and what changes can and should occur. (Lana Rakow 1984, correspondence)

"The study of women in popular culture is a stdy of political process whereby individual women attempt to subvert the group mentality that would keep their identities subject to the desire and fears of the collective imagination." (Katherine Fishburn 1982, 4)

PORNOCRACY

Governance by prostitutes or harlots; used contemptuously to indicate government corruption.

THE PORNOGRAPHIC AS POTENTIALLY DISTINGUISHABLE FROM THE EROTIC

The erotic: "a mutually pleasurable, sexual expression between people who have enough power to be there by positive choice." The pornographic: "its message is violence, dominance, and conquest." "Perhaps one could simply say that erotica is about sexuality, but pornography is about power and sex-as-weapon – in the same way we have come to understand that rape is about violence, and not really about sexuality at all." (Gloria Steinem 1980, 37–8) "Maybe Gloria Steinem can tell the difference between pornography and erotica at a single glance. I can't." (Joanna Russ 1982, 55) " 'Erotica' became the code word for stimulation appropriate to a feminist consciousness, while 'pornography' was defined as exclusively male and therefore 'naturally' devoid of distinctions between sex and violence. . . . The implications of this neat dichotomization and sex-typing of desire reflect, unchanged, the Victorian ideology of innate differences in the nature of male and female libido and fantasy. Men, we are to presume, because of their 'excessive' drive, prefer the hard edge of pornography. Women, less driven by the 'beast,' find erotica just their cup of tea." (Paula Webster 1981, 49) "In practice, attempts to sort out good erotica from bad porn inevitably come down to What turns me on is erotica; what turns you on is pornographic.' " (Ellen Willis 1981, 222)

PORNOGRAPHY

Originally, a description of prostitutes or

of prostitution, for the purposes (according to a 19th century medical dictionary) of public hygiene; description of the life, manners, and practices of prostitutes and their patrons; hence, by extension, the expression or suggestion of unchaste or unclean subjects in literature or art. Currently, pornography is discussed by feminists in relation to violence against women, patriarchy, and female sexuality, and is the subject of intense debate. Some of these views follow.

(See EROTICA, OBJECTIFI-CATION, PLEASURE, PROSTITUTION, RAPE, REPRESENTATION, SEXISM, SEXUALITY, VIOLENCE AGAINST WOMEN)

"Literally, 'writing about female slavery.' The preaching of woman hatred. Is a major way in which violence and dominance are taught and legitimized." "Comes from the Greek root *porné* (harlot, prostitute, or female captive) and *graphos* (writing about or description of). Thus, it means a description of either the purchase of sex, which implies an imbalance of power in itself, or sexual slavery." (Gloria Steinem 1983, 159, 221)

Is defined by Catharine A. MacKinnon and Andrea Dworkin (who proposed an amendment on pornography for the Minneapolis, Minn., City Council) as the sexually explicit subordination of women, graphically depicted, whether in pictures or in words, that also includes the presentation of women in one or more of the following ways:

a. as dehumanized sexual objects, things, or commodities;
b. as sexual objects who enjoy pain or humiliation;
c. as sexual objects who experience sexual pleasure in being raped;
d. as sexual objects tied up or cut up or mutilated or bruised or physically hurt;
e. in postures of sexual submission or sexual servility, including inviting penetration;
f. women's body parts – including but

not limited to vaginas, breasts, and buttocks – are exhibited, such that women are reduced to those parts;
g. as whores by nature;
h. being penetrated by objects or animals;
i. in scenarios of degradation, injury, torture, shown as filthy or inferior, bleeding, bruised, or hurt in a context that makes these conditions sexual.

The use of men, children, or transsexuals in the place of women is pornography for the purposes of this statute. (Jeanne Barkey 1983, *off our backs* 2, [Feb.], 1)

"*American Heritage Dictionary*:

pornography: written, graphic, or other forms of communication intended to excite lascivious feelings. From Greek *porno-graphos*, writing about prostitutes.
lascivious: of or characterized by lust, lewd, lecherous.
prostitute: one who sells his abilities or name to an unworthy cause [def. 2].

Therefore *pornography*: written or graphic form of communication by a lewd and lustful one who sells *his* abilities or name to the insult of un*wanting* women." (Lee Smith 1984)

For many feminists, pornography is the theory and rape is the practice. "Rape, battery, economic exploitation, and reproductive exploitation are the basic crimes committed against women in the sex-class system in which they are devalued because they are women. . . . [Pornography] is the ideology that is the source of all the rest; it truly defines what women are in this system – and how women are treated issues from what women *are*. Pornography is not a metaphor for what women are; it is what women are in theory and practice. Prostitution is the outer wall, symbolically the mirror reflection of the pornography, metaphorically built out of brick, concrete, stone, to keep women in – in the sex class. Prostitution is the all-encompassing condition, the body trapped in barter, the body imprisoned as commodity. They are crimes committed against women as women." (Andrea Dworkin 1983, 223)

Pornography is not about "mutual love, or love at all, but domination and violence against women. . . . [The root *graphos*] puts still more distance between subject and object, and replaces a spontaneous yearning for closeness with objectification and voyeurism." (Gloria Steinem 1980, 37); "is a male invention, designed to dehumanize women, to reduce the female to an object of sexual access, not to free sensuality from moralistic or parental inhibition." (Susan Brownmiller 1975, 32); "is verbal or pictorial material which represents or describes sexual behavior that is degrading or abusive to one or more of the participants *in such a way as to endorse the degradation*." (Helen Longino 1980, 43); "is an expression of man's desire to have the effect on women that he knows he does not, in reality, have." (Helen Buckingham, prostitute; quoted in Deirdre English 1980, 49); is based on degrading representations of the female body. "The staple of porn will always be the naked female body, breasts and genitals exposed, because as man devised it, her naked body is the female's 'shame,' her private parts the private property of man, while his are the ancient, holy, universal, patriarchal instrument of his power, his rule by force over her." (Susan Brownmiller 1975, 32)

Some writing attempts to characterize pornography, and identify the nature of its incompatibility with feminism. "Over the past fifteen years pornography, like the rest of society, has shown an increasing obsession with the female orgasm. Progress in pornography is of the two-steps-forward, one-step-back variety, though, since men in porn tend to remain sadly uninformed about how to pursue the female climax, a compulsive 'try-harder' approach flourishes, emphasizing penile length, strength and endurance, and often extra partners to relieve fatigued males as the new sexual woman swoons on from one climax to the next. As the performance pressures on men intensify, porn answers with increasing force and sadism, as if to literally *make* women climax." (Deirdre English 1980, 49)

Pornography is not definable according to its content alone. "There are . . . problems with the idea of a scale of increasingly explicit representation of the body, where representation is thought essentially as a transparent medium giving more or less access to its object. This might seem unexceptional insofar as we can all recognize pornography 'on sight.' But let us not mistake recognisability for a simple givenness of content. Recognisability does not depend just upon what and how much is shown – otherwise we would not be able to distinguish between pornographic, artistic, medical representations of sexual acts and naked bodies (indeed, if it is the extreme which is the test of the pornographic, then medical textbooks or biological cross-sections would be definitive)." "What makes pornography recognisable are its *non*-transparent features, the elements which constitute it as a distinctive representational genre – a certain rhetoric of the body, forms of narration, placing and wording of captions and titles, stylisations and postures, a repertoire of milieux and costume, lighting techniques, etc. Even where the distinctness of the genre is acknowledged – . . . [e.g., as shallow and trashy] – it is given a secondary status in identifying the pornographic, merely representation's rather nasty shade or colouring or, alternatively, a 'knowledge' that something is pornographic. These features are, however, an important element in feminism's objections to pornography." (Beverly Brown 1981, 6-7)

"Not so much an art form as . . . an ideology and an ideology which, like the ideology of racism, *requires* the creation of another, a not-I, an enemy." (Susan Griffin 1982, 643)

Is contradictory, "like most other mass media in our culture. . . . It can be sexist, misogynous, misanthropic, upsetting; it can be titillating, thrilling, life-affirming, *fun*. Its potential for any of these variations is nearly infinite, and its effect differs from person to person, as does sexuality itself. Pornography, in its graphic depiction of sex of all stripes, can undermine the often unspoken taboo against open sexuality that our society rests on. At the same time, it can display and reflect the most sexually oppressive and alienated tendencies of our society." (Barbara O'Dair 1983, 12)

Is not separate and different from the rest of life but rather "a genre of expression fully in harmony with any culture in which it flourishes. . . . [It] functions to perpetuate male supremacy and crimes of violence against women because it conditions, trains, educates, and inspires men to despise women, to use women, to hurt women. Pornography exists because men despise women, and men despise women in part because pornography exists." (Andrea Dworkin 1978, 289)

Is an overdetermined and rigidly codified genre which "in constructing certain representations of women . . . codes *woman* in a general way as sign, as an object, that is, of (implicitly male) looking." (Annette Kuhn 1982, 114)

Pornography "is the cultural scenario of male/female . . . the collective scenario of master/slave" (Andrea Dworkin 1974, 53); is the "eroticization of dominance and submission." (Catharine A. MacKinnon 1983, correspondence).

Is a means for the silencing of women. "By its systematic distortion of female sexuality and insult to our intelligence, [pornography] denies all women the right to speak." (Feminist Coalition Against Pornography in Montreal 1982; cited in *off our backs* 1983, April, 4)

Is primarily about sexuality. Because the anti-pornography movement focuses on victimization rather than on our subjectivity and self-definition, "we tend to embrace our sexually deprived condition and begin to police the borders of the double standard that has been used to effectively silence us. It is not in the interests of feminism to circumvent the vast area of sexual repression. And pornography is primarily about sexuality." (Paula Webster 1981, 50)

Is propaganda for heterosexuality. "If pornography is propaganda, and I do believe that it is, it is not promoting the violation and degradation of women, but traditional heterosexual intercourse and gender relations." "Perhaps it is premature to call for a truly radical feminist pornography-erotica. But to speak of our own desires and to organize for our own and our collective sexual pleasure would be a beginning. . . . It is precisely in the private, secret, and 'shameful' realm of our own sexuality that we have feared to take responsibility for being subjects. We easily talk about denying men pornographic pleasure, but this does not bring us closer to gaining our own." (Paula Webster 1981, 49, 51)

Is not proof of the violent rule of the penis over women. In response to a panel on pornography in 1981, Joan Nestle, in a piece about her mother's enjoyment of sex, "takes to task several of the panelists for denouncing pornography as proof of the violent rule of the penis over women. Nestle's mother was shameless, a word our shame-ridden culture still uses as a term of abuse, and she seems rarely to have found a penis overwhelming." (Joan Nestle 1981b, 468, intro.)

Constitutes a legal battleground and profound dilemma. "The classic dilemma around pornography is . . . a balancing of extreme harms of doubtful direct connection with pornography against the harms censorship offers not only to traditionally conceived freedoms of the individual but now to feminist interests as well. But this anxious irresolution is not the essence of feminism's problem with pornography. It is merely a symptom of the more general lack of fit between feminist politics and liberalism's central terms of reference: individual/society, harms, intervention." Rather the problem can be seen instead in terms of notions of public viewing and private space: "Surely the insistence that the personal is political, that sexuality is not innately private, involves both locating just this sort of 'public' configuration and making it an object of 'political' reform." This enables us to begin "to think about a relation between protocols of everyday conduct and organisations of visibility. As an opening proviso, any notion of a single public/private distinction would have to be jettisoned." (Beverly Brown 1981, 12, 15, 16)

There have been classically two sides to the pornography issue: the conservative approach, which argues that pornography is immoral because it exposes the human body; and the liberal approach, which presented pornography as just one more aspect of our ever-expanding human sexuality. [There is now] a third and feminist perspective: pornography is the ideology of a culture which promotes and condones rape, woman-battering, and other crimes of violence against women." (Laura Lederer 1980, 19-20)

"The basic purpose of obscenity laws is and always has been to reinforce cultural taboos on sexuality and suppress feminism, homosexuality, and other forms of sexual dissidence. No pornographer has ever been punished for being a woman hater, but not too long ago information about female sexuality, contraception, and abortion was presumed to be obscene. In a male supremacist society the only obscenity law that will not be used against women is no law at all." Pornography may be a key for exploring female sexuality and desire. "A woman who is raped is a victim; a woman who enjoys pornography (even if that means enjoying a rape fantasy) is in a sense a rebel, insisting on an aspect of her sexuality that has been defined as a male preserve. Insofar as pornography glorifies male supremacy and sexual alienation, it is deeply reactionary. But in rejecting sexual repression and hypocrisy – which have inflicted even more damage on women than on men – it expresses a radical impulse." (Ellen Willis 1981, 226, 223)

"I suspect that some of the emotional horror feminists and other women feel towards sexist pornography (which I share) is not simply that they think it encourages men to rape and objectify women (there is no evidence they need pornography for that), but that it is obnoxious because it both degrades and titillates us. And that is *not* a connection which we like. It feels as though the connection is thrust upon us from outside, by pornography itself, which if removed would sever the connection. But it is not unusual for feelings we dislike to come from somewhere else, when in fact they are buried inside us as well as reflected in the social world which shaped them to begin with." (Lynne Segal 1983, 43)

PORNOGRAPHY, MORAL

Used to critique current relationships between the sexes. "The moral pornographer would be an artist who uses pornographic material as part of the acceptance of the logic of a world of absolute sexual license for all the genders, and projects a model of the way such a world might work. A moral pornographer might use pornography as a critique of current relationships of the flesh and the subsequent revelation, through the infinite modulations of the sexual act, of the real relations of man and his kind. Such a pornographer would not be the enemy of women, perhaps because he might begin to penetrate to the heart of the contempt for women that distorts our culture even as he entered the realm of true obscenity as he describes it." (Angela Carter 1978, 19-20)

PORTNOY'S COMPLAINT

The title of a novel by Phillip Roth, now a term to refer to storytelling "in which the ostensible object of irony is the male character while the real butt of its sexual irony is the female." (Irving Weinman 1983, 139)

(See PORTNOY'S MOTHER'S COMPLAINT)

PORTNOY'S MOTHER'S COMPLAINT

An essay by sociologist Pauline Bart (1971) unmasking the sexism in Roth's novel *Portnoy's Complaint* and reflecting upon the stereotypical cultural positioning of mothers and middle-aged women in literature and society that leads to de-

P

pression and other problems.
(See PORTNOY'S COMPLAINT)

POSITIVISM
"Philosophical doctrine contending that sense perceptions are the only admissible basis of human knowledge and precise thought [and] the application of this doctrine in logic, epistemology, and ethics." From Latin *positivus* 'arbitrarily laid down, dogmatic.' (*American Heritage Dictionary*)

POSSESSIVE
Linguistic feature with social repercussions. Among the Mundurucu of central Brazil, women and men have different ideas about who is head of household and thus how the possessive form should be used. "Through their wives or mothers, the men are considered to belong to one or another household, and the males frequently refer to a house as being under the direction of the senior male. Thus, if the senior couple in a house are named José and María, following Brazilian usage, the men will refer to the dwelling as 'José's house.' The women, however, look upon this as just one more male pretension and will be quite emphatic in saying that the house is María's. After all, they point out, it is María who lives in it and directs its activities, and not José, who just comes there for sex and water (men live in a village men's house). Faced with this objection, most of the male informants back off and admit that the house probably is the woman's but qualify the concession by saying that the distinction is not very important." (Yolanda Murphy and Robert Murphy 1974, 116)

POSSLQ
Person of Opposite Sex Sharing Living Quarters. Pronounced POSSelkew, the acronym was coined by census-takers for the 1980 U.S. census to designate the unmarried live-in partner of many heads of households.

POSTCARDS
Form of feminist political expression, advertising, organizing, and fundraising.

POST-PARTUM DEPRESSION
A "whole area of disturbance, not clearly understood, is usually loosely labelled 'post(after)-partum(birth)   depression.' Yet it may not necessarily take place in the immediate post-partum period, nor take the form of depression, nor include feelings of aggression towards the baby, as is often supposed. . . . The most usual explanation for post-partum depression is 'hormone imbalance' but reports of depression in fathers and adoptive mothers indicate that the causes are not purely physical. . . . It is also argued that it might be the state of anxiety and depression which 'unbalances' the hormones, in the same way that anxiety is known to disturb the menstrual cycle. In any case, it is absurd that so little research has been done." (Catherine Ballard and Hilary Hackett 1976; in Marsha Rowe ed. 1982, 384-6)

Sane response to the difficulties of adjusting to small babies who are demanding, annoying, or boring. Traditional definitions of "Baby Blues" can and do prevent women from coming to face the realities of motherhood. "It is still important to society that we should consent to be nuclear family mothers, and enjoy it. If we are failing to enjoy it, it is easier to say we are poor sick things and some nice drugs will make us feel better, than face up to the fact that mothering is an impossible and treacherous job in our society." (Sara Maitland 1980, 88)

POST-PARTUM DOCUMENT
Art installation by Mary Kelly exhibited in sections in England during the mid-1970s and published as a series of photographs, graphic representations, and texts in various publications and finally in book form (1983). Kelly's project draws upon language and theoretical conceptions from Lacanian psychoanalysis, marxism, linguistics, and the feminist movement to document a child's linguistic and social development, the relationship between mother and son, and

the construction of motherhood through psychic processes and social practices. The *Document* includes detailed records of language learning, the mother's narrative commentary, theoretical interpretation, and concrete objects such as stained diapers. The child's language is presented on dark slate tablets resembling the Rosetta Stone. These memorabilia and their interpretive framework challenge, parody, appropriate, and transform the male monopoly on theory.

(See ART, AUTHORITY, MOTHER, NAPPIES, PHALLUS, REPRESENTATION, THEORY)

"Traditionally, the ability to produce children and the emotional relationship that ensues has been held up as the reason for women's lack of creativity. Now, with the women's movement, it is beginning to be possible to bring motherhood, with all the deeply traumatic emotions and unrecognized elements involved, into the kind of examination it desperately needs. Mary Kelly's exhibition *Post-Partum Document* is a crucial contribution to this. As an artist she forces into public view the unacceptable combination of roles mother/artist – a slap in the face for old guard concepts of the artist as freewheeling genius; as a feminist she focuses on the contradictory emotions that necessarily come with motherhood, which have been almost taboo as a subject for art in male-dominated culture. It is quite clear from the attention Mary Kelly's exhibition has received in the establishment press that it was a direct provocation to conventional concepts of 'art.' It is the form of the exhibition, its emphasis on work rather than art-object-for-critical-evaluation, that causes so much outrage. A painting of a mother changing her baby's nappy would be easily overlooked as kitsch, but not so with dirty nappy liners annotated and placed within a discourse that needs work to be unravelled, and refuses to place the figure of the mother on view." (Laura Mulvey 1976; in Mary Kelly 1983, 201)

Art critics were appalled by the *Document*. "A painting of a mother looking at her naked baby is one thing (*pace* a million Madonnas), infant shit on the wall something else indeed." (Ann Oakley 1982, 322)

POTS AND PANS

Instruments of protest. The banging of pots and pans has been used by women of all classes as part of their protest movement – for example in Chile in 1983.

POTTER

Useful word as in "I'll have a potter while you're gone." Is "sufficiently vague as to be unchallengeable." They can't come home and in righteous indignation say: "You haven't finished the pottering! You said you'd potter my jumper and you haven't even started." (Anna Livia 1983, 69)

POVERTY

Quality or condition of being poor or in need. "While for a man, poverty means starvation, for a woman, it invariably also involves rape and a myriad of forms of sexual exploitation." (Manushi Collective 1980, 8) "There is a fundamental difference between male and female poverty: for men, poverty is often the consequence of unemployment and a job is generally an effective remedy, while female poverty often exists even when a woman works full-time." (Karin Stallard, Barbara Ehrenreich and Holly Sklar 1983, 9)

(See FEMINIZATION OF POVERTY)

"With its attendant problem of malnutrition, is the greatest health problem in the nation." (Boston Women's Health Book Collective 1976, 338)

"In this country, lesbianism is a poverty – as is being brown, as is being a woman, as is being just plain poor." (Cherríe Moraga 1981, 29)

"That spreading disease which grows with our social growth and shows most horribly when and where we are most proud, keeping step, as it were, with private wealth." (Charlotte Perkins Gilman 1911, 269)

"Radicals look at reservation Indians

and get very upset about their poverty conditions. But poverty to us is not the same thing as poverty is to you. Our poverty is that we can't be who we are. We can't hunt or fish or grow our food because our basic resources and the right to use them in traditional ways are denied us. In order to live well, we must be able to provide for ourselves in such a way that we can continue living as we always have. We still don't believe in being slaves to the 'domineering' culture systems." (Carol Lee Sanchez 1983b, 152)

POWER

Ability to get things done. From Old French and Middle English forms meaning "to be able." Standard meanings include: (1) ability to act or perform effectively, (2) ability to command resources, (3) quality of being perceived as performing effectively and/or commanding resources, (4) ability or authority to exercise control, (5) political or military might, (6) influence over others. In communication studies, power is being reconceived not as something participants "have," or "bring to" the interaction (like a briefcase), but at least in part as a set of relations constructed within and through the interaction itself: thus power asymmetry between men and women need not be taken as an a priori assumption but rather explored in terms of how it unfolds in actual interaction. The notion of power, however, remains inextricably connected to real inequities in material and social circumstances.

(See ACTION, AUTHORITY, CLASS, LANGUAGE, MARXISM, POWERLESSNESS, SEXISM)

"Is the number of people you can reach with your message." (Donna Allen; cited in Patricia Bathurst 1977, 31)

Men's position of superiority and privilege based not "for [our] want of natural capacity, or merit, but for want of an equal spirit of violence, shameless injustice, and lawless oppression, with theirs." (Sophia 1739, 36)

"Can call itself scientific, objective, benevolent and so on, without ever revealing its own self-interests . . . Holding power means that a specific reality is being presented . . . the men who hold power are considered 'objective' and 'sane,' while the qualities traditionally associated with women, namely introspection and emotionality, are ridiculed. . . . Language is the guardian of the patriarchy . . . it supports an elite, while inhibiting the definition of radical alternatives." (Andrea E. Goldsmith 1980, 180-1)

"A daily presence in the asymmetrical nuclear family." (Ann Oakley 1982, 101)

Conceptualized by men as assertion and aggression, by women as nurturance. (David McClelland 1975; in Carol Gilligan 1982, 167-8)

"The process of growing up, for a girl, is one of being curbed and tamed: of losing power." (Patricia Meyer Spacks; in Juliann E. Fleenor 1979, 38)

POWERLESSNESS

"Not biology, but ignorance of our selves, has been the key to our powerlessness." (Adrienne Rich 1979, 240)

"Is a dirty word." (Florynce R. Kennedy; quoted in Gloria Steinem 1973, 89)

"To understand the workings of power as a relationship one must also consider the situation of the weak, the other, second, member of the process by which society at once exists and changes. And women are the oldest, largest, and most central group of human creatures in the wide category of the weak and the ruled." (Elizabeth Janeway 1980, 4)

Powers of the allegedly powerless: (1) disintegrative power, (2) inertial power, (3) innovative power, norm-creating power, (4) legitimizing, integrative, or socializing power, (5) expressive power, (6) explosive power, (7) power of resistance, (8) cooperative, collective power, (9) migratory power, population power. (Berenice A. Carroll 1972)

Powers of the weak: as women struggled to understand and challenge existing power relations (intimate and worldwide), they have passed through three stages: (1) disbelief, in which they began to question the world-definitions of the powerful, (2) bonding together ("the first taste of liberation came with the discovery that other women felt as they did: it was liberation from the doubts about their own health and sanity," 169); and (3) organizing for action. "These are all ordinary human responses that lie within reach of ordinary people." (Elizabeth Janeway 1980, 161-82)

POWER, RETHINKING

"I can not say that I think you very generous to the Ladies, for whilst you are proclaiming peace and good will to Men, Emancipating all Nations, you insist upon retaining absolute power over Wives. But you must remember that Absolute power is like most other things which are very hard, very liable to be broken – and notwithstanding all your wise Laws and Maxims we have it in our power not only to free ourselves but to subdue our Masters, and without violence throw both your nature and legal authority at our feet." (Abigail Adams 1776b; in Alice Rossi ed. 1973, 13)

"As every man is woman born, she has slow but sure means of redress, yet the sooner a general justness of thought makes smooth the path, the better." (Margaret Fuller 1843; in Alice Rossi ed. 1973, 168)

"Those caught in the myths that were meant to keep us exploited and oppressed are frightened, yet enchanted by the white world of male gods. We hold tight to the little capital (clothes, furniture, and bank account), lest its loss would symbolize that we are 'nothing' again. We are terrified of that gargantuan phallus – that big Dick, the war machine. But how we laud its power at the same time." (Pat Robinson and Group 1969, 199)

"A redefinition of power would involve a transformation in the social conditions surrounding women's fertility. It would also involve not only a redistribution of tasks and activities between men and women but also a change in the balance of power involved in the significance given to how we organize the care of children and dependents and how we produce wherewithal and wealth." (Sheila Rowbotham 1983, 154)

"Women have at least three kinds of power: Dollar Power, to boycott with; Vote Power, to take over structures with, and maybe even get somebody elected; and Body Power, to get out and support our friends and make a damned nuisance of ourselves with everybody else." (Florynce Kennedy, in Gloria Steinem 1973, 89)

"Power fascinates us as much as it fascinates men, except that we don't have any." "Accepting the role of slave is exactly the same as accepting the role of master." (Denise le Dantec 1976, 119)

"Resorting to ridicule when other strategies fail, our opposition ultimately reveals a deep fear, a fear of what would happen to male power and what kind of society would result if we could establish a social order free from sexual exploitation and violence. They are not afraid of what we are *against*. They are afraid of what we are *for*. What we are for is so much more powerful than what we are against." (Kathleen Barry 1980, 312)

"Anytime we think of power as being simply a possession of the powerful we are thinking inaccurately." (Elizabeth Janeway 1980, 17)

Of the erotic: "When we begin to live from within outward, in touch with the power of the erotic within ourselves, and allowing that power to inform and illuminate our actions upon the world around us, then we begin to be responsible to ourselves in the deepest sense." (Audre Lorde 1980b, 299)

PRACTICAL

"I have learned that practical means something that can be done while keeping everything else the same." (Catharine A. MacKinnon 1983b)

PRAYER

Earnest request, plea, discussion, supplication, usually to god. "That night I prayed earnestly to God to make the dear King better and let him live. The fact that he actually did recover established in me a touching faith in the efficacy of prayer, which superstitiously survived until the Great War proved to me, once and for all, that there was nothing in it." (Vera Brittain 1933, 23)

Communication usually couched in male language. "As the worship progresses through prayers, creeds, and sermon, the same language forms keeps recurring – always the masculine when referring to people; always the masculine when referring to God. While I sing and during prayer I change the word 'men' to 'people,' 'mankind' to 'humankind,' 'sons' to 'children,' 'Father' to 'Parent,' but I feel as though I am outshouted by the rest of the congregation. My words are swallowed up by theirs. . . . I feel as though I am eavesdropping on a conversation labeled 'For Men Only.' " (Sharon Neufer Emswiler; in Sharon Neufer Emswiler and Thomas Neufer Emswiler 1984, 2-3)

Lord's Prayer: "Jesus did not say that we were to pray the Lord's Prayer at every worship service. He said instead that we are to pray 'like this.' We feel he was inviting new prayers based on his prayer. We wonder if he really feels honored that we repeat the same words over and over again at each service. Our first recommendation is therefore to consider eliminating [such] liturgical texts or other habitually used sexist texts from the worship service. If such elimination is not deemed wise, then two other alternatives are possible. First, you may want to use the texts as they are and announce or publish a statement in the bulletin that these texts represent a particular time in history when people were not aware of concerns for inclusive language. Second, you may want to devise alternatives using some of the same ideas . . . but different and inclusive words." Example:

The Lord's Prayer

Original	Alternative
Our Father, who art in heaven,	Our Mother/ Father, who is everywhere,
Hallowed be Thy name.	Holy be your names.
Thy kingdom come,	May your new age come
Thy will be done,	May your will be done
On earth, as it is in heaven.	In this and in every time and place
Give us this day our daily bread,	Meet our needs each day and
And forgive us our debts	Forgive our failure to love
As we forgive our debtors.	As we forgive this same failure in others.
And lead us not into temptation,	Save us in hard times, and
But deliver us from evil.	Lead us into the ways of love.
For Thine is the kingdom, and the power, and the glory, forever.	For yours is the wholeness, and the power, and the loving, forever.
Amen.	Amen

(Sharon Neufer Emswiler and Thomas Neufer Emswiler 1984, 90, 92)

Can be a very personal form of communication. "My mother was a woman who prayed. She believed in prayers. Three times a day you'd see her on her knees talkin' to God. She made an impression upon me especially. . . . I know she was following the right way. She tried to get [my father] to quit that kind of life and come home - help her with the children. He didn't do it. She'd been prayin' and prayin' and prayin'. God talked to my mother. He told her to tell my father if he didn't come home and take care of his children as he ought to that He was going to send him to the pen the next time. Mama tried to tell my father what the Lord had told her. They had a fight. My mother, she bein' a hard working woman, she was able to cope with it. I seen him pull out his razor and say, 'I'll cut your so-and-so throat.' She hit him in his arm and knocked the razor out of his hand and kicked it under the bed. When court started that year, in the spring, he was a prisoner. If he had listened when the Word of God spoke to him, he could have been a free man all his life." (Lillian Caro b.1889, Clarksville, Texas; oral history collected by Priscilla Diaz Dorr 1984)

PRAYER-MEETING

Important social event and meeting place during the nineteenth and early twentieth centuries that also afforded opportunities for public speaking as "scenes" that became village legend. Women spoke out at these gatherings as well as men, often in memorable ways: "One evening Aunt Atossa bounced up. She didn't either pray or preach. Instead, she lit into everybody else in the church and gave them a fearful ranking down, calling them right out by name and telling them how they all had behaved, and casting up all the quarrels and scandals of the past ten years. Finally she wound up by saying that she was disgusted with Spencervale church and she never meant to darken its door again, and she hoped a fearful judgment would come upon it. Then she sat down out of breath, and the minister, who [was deaf and] hadn't heard a word she said, immediately remarked, in a very devout voice, 'Amen! The Lord grant our dear sister's prayer!'" (L. M. Montgomery 1915, 111)

PREACHING

Until recently, a male occupation in many churches. "Denied the right to preach, [women] organized the Women's Christian Temperance Union and developed their skills in ministry through its multiple programs." (Anne Firor Scott 1984, 330)

"The Lord is pleased, when he mentions his Church, to call her by the name of *Woman*. . . . Thus much [Scripture] may prove that the Church of Christ is a Woman, and those that speak against the Woman's speaking, speak against the Church of Christ . . . that is to say, Those that speak against the Power of the Lord, and the Spirit of the Lord speaking in a Woman, simply, by reason of her Sex, or because she is a Woman, not regarding the Seed, and Spirit, and Power that speaks in her; such speak against Christ, and his Church, and are of the Seed of the Serpent, wherein lodgeth the enmity." (Margaret Fell 1666, rpt 1980)

PREFACE

In Manglish texts, the place where (male) authors give thanks to (male) colleagues for ideas and substantive intellectual contributions and to (female) secretaries, editors, helpers, and relatives (especially wives) for typing, proofreading, indexing, holding the world at bay, and providing limitless encouragement. In feminist texts, the place where women and men are thanked for contributions of thought, intelligence, and care, and where the world of the text is often offered to the reader on behalf of all women. Some examples follow.

(See ACKNOWLEDGMENTS, AUTHORITY, CLASS SYSTEM OF THE INTELLECT, ORIGINAL)

"Didn't she even do the index or the proof-reading for one of his books? You know what it often says in a preface or dedication – 'To my wife, who undertook the arduous duty of proofreading' or 'making the index.'" (Barbara Pym 1952, 94)

"I have but one thing more to add, that this Present, worthless as it is, is the humble Tribute of a Female; the First, I imagine, of the kind that hath been offer'd to Your Royal Highness." (Elizabeth Elstob 1715, Preface to her book on Anglo-Saxon grammar dedicated to Her Royal Highness, the Princess of Wales)

"My first thanks go to those women from and with whom I have learned what feminist practice is, what feminist theory should be, and more rarely but far more delightfully, what the two can be together." (Teresa De Lauretis 1984, ix)

"But most of all, I must thank my husband. . . . Perhaps the quality of his 'sacrifice' might best be measured by totaling the hours he has spent on a Saturday afternoon in the sticky darkness of a movie theater with Walt Disney and two boisterous little boys – so that I might write." (Cynthia Griffin Wolff 1977, viii)

"While we are both committed to creating a state of affairs where husbands are thanked as frequently as wives on the acknowledgements page, I am very glad that I have a husband whose actions match his beliefs." (Margery W. Davies 1982, x)

"And I am grateful to Benjamin Uroff, who agreed not to read the manuscript and helped in every other way too." (Margaret Dickie Uroff 1974, xi)

PREGNANCY

Defined by the medical profession as a pathological condition, by many organizations as a medical disability, by some employers as a disqualification for employment, and by universities as a high risk factor in admissions and employment of female applicants. Women's diverse experiences of and views about pregnancy are currently finding fuller expression. The women's health movement, for example, seeks to redefine pregnancy as a normal and often joyous life process, and to regain control for women over how it is defined and experienced. Has historically been the province of women healers. (Fran Leeper Buss 1980; Michelle Harrison 1982; Sandra L. Chaff et al. eds 1978; Gena Corea 1977; Bettina Aptheker 1982a)

Though U.S. middle-class women are fighting for a more "natural" approach to pregnancy, at other periods and in other countries and cultures, pregnancy has been a critical health hazard. One example is the experience of many Black women under slavery: "Many African women were pregnant prior to their capture or purchase.They were forced to endure pregnancy without any care given to their diet, without any exercise, and without any assistance during the labor. In their own communities African women had been accustomed to much pampering and care during pregnancy, so the barbaric nature of childbearing on the slave ship was both physically harmful and psychologically demoralizing. Annals of history record that the American slave ship Pongas carried 250 women, many of them pregnant, who were squeezed into a compartment of 16 by 18 feet. The women who survived the initial stages of pregnancy gave birth aboard ship with

their bodies exposed to either the scorching sun or the freezing cold. The numbers of black women who died during childbirth or the number of stillborn children will never be known." (bell hooks 1981, 18-19)

A complex and various experience: *lawida*, 'to be pregnant'; *lalewida* 'joyfully,' *loda* 'wearily,' *lewidan* 'for the first time,' *widazhad* 'late in term and eager for the end.' (Suzette Haden Elgin 1983, 10)

(See LÁADAN for pronunciation)

PREHISTORY

"I prefer the power of the term *Prehistory* to name the prior importance of the interconnected significant events of women's living and dying. *Her-story*, I think, shortcircuits the intent of radical feminism by implying a desire to parallel the record of men's achievement." (Mary Daly 1978, 24n)

(See HERSTORY)

PREJUDICE

"Sometimes when I hear the word 'prejudice,' the first thing that pops into our minds is Black and white. But it's not always Black and white. My boss, he wouldn't care if you're pink, brown, blue. He's just prejudiced. He's sick. Prejudice is a sickness. Like cancer. You might contract cancer in one part of the body but eventually it spreads out over the whole body." (Members of District 1199 [AFL-CIO Hospital and Health Care Union] 1982, 24)

PREMENSTRUAL SYNDROME

A medically-named phenomenon which on the one hand gives "scientific" legitimacy to women's own reports of premenstrual changes and thus encourages research on an area of women's experience previously dismissed as psychosomatic, caused by overprotective mothers, or simply "female problems" not worthy of serious attention; on the other hand, the identification of a "syndrome" emphasizes sexual difference and provides potential evidence for anti-feminist arguments that women are regularly "disabled" and hence "unfit" to work, write, etc. (See Hilary Allen 1984.)

(See AUTHORITY, MENSTRU-
ATION, MENTAL HEALTH,
NAMING, WOMEN'S HEALTH
MOVEMENT)

"Thus it happened in the summer of 1982 that premenstrual syndrome, or PMS, arrived. A disease that thousands of women had been told didn't exist suddenly became almost a media event. News-weeklies, talk shows, style pages, book-stores – all had something to offer on PMS. There was no news, no cure, not even a better idea of its cause. What happened was less tangible: PMS acquired medical legitimacy. After years of telling women their problems were 'all in the head,' the proportion of doctors who accepted PMS as a real disease reached critical mass. . . . In all the hoopla . . . one fact has been almost overlooked. Not one of the treatments being offered has ever been proven to work." (Nancy Heneson 1984, 67)

"The best cure [for premenstrual tension] is to stop calling it premenstrual tension. Call it PME – premenstrual energy – instead. 'Tension' implies sickness. 'Energy' suggests a gift. . . . 'Tension' implies that you're stuck with it. 'Energy' suggests it can *be* released, and in creative fashion at that." (M. Grace Melucci 1982, *Ms.*, September, 5)

PRESCRIPTIVE GRAMMAR
(See PRESCRIPTIVISM)

PRESCRIPTIVE *HE*
More accurate label for what is often called "generic *he*" as recommended in prescriptive grammars. In speech and writing, people use the prescriptive *he* only when referring to predominantly male antecedents (e.g., doctor, lawyer), not when referring to predominantly female antecedents (e.g., nurse, secretary). (Donald MacKay, 1983, 39)

(See GENERIC ASSUMPTION, HE, HE/MAN)

PRESCRIPTIVISM
A system of linguistic policing pervasive in textbooks, grammar books, literary magazines, classrooms, television talk shows, and some dictionaries, based on the myth that there exists an absolute standard of correctness for language use. This belief "is thought to be so clear that any educated man [sic] should compre-hend it immediately. Any failure to conform is evidence of poor education, bad taste, stupidity, or seditious intent to destroy English. In theory this norm is enshrined in the dictionaries and gram-mars. The author or editor of any such work, of course, is expected to have a fine feel for this standard. His [sic] objective must be to provide guidance for the less sensitive. To fail in this is to betray a public trust" (H. A. Gleason Jr., 1965, 8). Each new edition of prestigious diction-aries like Webster's is attacked for sup-posedly endorsing barbarous usage (the inclusion of *ain't* as a sample of actual even if nonstandard usage is the quint-essential litmus test). Linguists, and many lexicographers attempting to use linguistic principles, claim to reject pre-scriptivism in favor of the accurate description of what *is* – i.e., how language is actually used – yet have repeatedly resisted acknowledging and documenting nonsexist usage and other feminist inno-vations. Thus "pure description" also polices the language, guarding entrenched claims and excluding new ones.

(See AUTHORITY, DICTIONARY, LINGUISTICS, M.A.L.E., NON-SEXIST LANGUAGE, PRONOUN, PRONOUN ENVY)

PRE-WOMEN'S MOVEMENT
"Emotional and intellectual Purdah." (June Levine 1982, 136)

PRIDE
Along with "poverty, and beauty, are ill advisers, ill suited to conduct safely through a world like this, where the temptations without are sufficient dangers, without the seducers within the mind." (Mrs Montague; in R. Brimley Johnson 1926, 74)

(See SIN)

PRIESTS

"Pope Paul VI declared that priests must be correct physical images of Jesus. I guess that means semitic, dark haired, brown eyed, bearded, and under 35 years old. Fine. That ought to reduce the surplice population." (Joann Haugerud 1978, 19)

"I'm a priest, not priestess. . . . 'Priest-ess' implies mumbo jumbo and all sorts of pagan goings-on. Those who oppose us would love to call us priestesses." (Carter Heyward; in Elaine Partnow 1977, 494)

PRIMITIVES

Not the most telling term for the early women who launched the professions of medicine, nursing, obstetrics, domestic science, budgeting, and cooking. (Mary Ritter Beard 1939; in Ann J. Lane ed. 1977, 193)

PRINCESS

One of the early French words that entered English with the Norman invasion of the 11th century which (along with *countess, duchess, lioness, sorceress,* and others) provided the model for the feminine gender suffix *-ess*; this then began to be added to native English words to form feminine-gender compounds like *shepherdess* and *goddess*. Means: a female sovereign or ruler, a queen. Also may mean a prince's wife, a sovereign's daughter or grand-daughter, or a female member of a royal family. Like other words designating female nobility (such as *queen, dame,* and *madam*), and unlike their male counter-parts (*king, lord, sir*), it has acquired derogatory connotations. Miller and Swift quote a teacher talking about describing one of her most capable female students: "I found myself saying 'She's really a prince.' Appalled as I was at my own pro-masculine description, I just couldn't say that she was a *princess* because princess connotes someone who is fussy and spoiled and accustomed to living in the lap of luxury." (Casey Miller and Kate Swift 1976, 48, 65)

(See -ESS, GENDER, SEMANTIC DEROGATION)

PRINCESS, INDIAN

"The title 'Indian Princess' is greatly abused in present days when it is bestowed indiscriminately on young girls who may have accomplished nothing but look pretty, or dance well, or be pictured incongruously wearing a war bonnet, but time was when there were really red women rulers in many tribes – women who had the power of life or death, who decided on war or were able to persuade their warriors from making war. The fact that descent and distribution of property had always come through the women had added hugely to their prestige, not only among the Indians, but in later years when available oil lands were being leased or sold to white men, the courts always ruled in favor of owners who claimed inheritance under the female line." (Carolyn Thomas Foreman 1954, 13-14)

PRINCESS, JEWISH

"Judith, who saved the Jewish people; she flirted with the attacking general, drank him under the table; then she and her maid (whose name is not in the story) whacked off his head, stuck it in a picnic basket and escaped back to the Jewish camp. They staked his head high over the gate, so that when his soldiers charged the camp, they were met by their general's bloody head, looming; and ran away as fast as their goyishe little feet could run. Then Judith set her maid free, and all the women danced in her honor. That's a Jewish princess." (Melanie Kaye 1982, 39)

PRINT

Communicative medium off limits to blind people except in the form of Braille. At the same time, printed captions added to television and films make electronic media accessible to people with hearing disabilities. Disabled women have experienced special problems in getting materials adapted to their concerns and interests; the Womyn's Braille Press started because national organizations for the blind were unresponsive to the needs expressed by blind women for tapes and Braille editions of feminist and lesbian writings.

PRINTING PRESS

Operated by women as well as by men. A printing press accompanied the Reverend Jose Glover of England and his wife and family when they sailed for America; he died before the ship reached port, so it was Mistress Glover who set up the first printing press in North America in 1638. (Marion Tuttle Marzolf 1977, 1-2)

PRISON GUARD

Model of permissable female behavior who acts on behalf of Male Supremacy to keep women in their place. (Pat Wainoch, n.d.)

PRISON NAME

Jane Warton was the prison name taken by Constance Lytton, suffragette, who disguised herself as a woman of the working class to prove that she had received preferential treatment when she had earlier been imprisoned as a recognizable aristocrat. Arrested a second time (at a protest meeting outside a Liverpool prison where other suffragettes were confined), she was forcibly fed three times (her mouth forced open and a four-foot rubber hose pushed down her throat). Her health was permanently affected. (Karen Payne 1983, 198)

PRIVACY

"Everything women as women have never been allowed to be or to have; at the same time . . . everything women have been equated with and defined in terms of men's ability to have." (Catharine A. MacKinnon 1983a, 657)

PRIVILEGE

"privilege is simple:
going for a pleasant stroll after dark,
not checking the back of your car as you get in, sleeping soundly,
speaking without interruption, and not remembering
dreams of rape that follow you all day,

that wake you up crying, and privilege is not seeing your stripped, humiliated body
plastered in celebration across every magazine rack"

(*Together: UCLA Women's Newsmagazine* 1983, Summer, 7)

PROBLEMS

"For many scientists, are things to be 'attacked,' 'licked,' or 'conquered.' If more subtle means fail, then one resorts to 'brute force,' to the 'hammer and tongs' approach. In the effort to 'master' nature, to 'storm her strongholds and castles,' science can come to sound like a battle-field. Sometimes, such imagery becomes quite extreme, exceeding even the conventional imagery of war." (Evelyn Fox Keller 1983, 20)

Are often turned back on women. Women in the public aid system, for example, often find that "their husband's violence becomes 'their problem,' i.e., is turned back upon them, by all the relevant departments of the state. . . . [Thus the problem] is individualized, the direction of violence is ignored, and the ideology supporting male dominance is confirmed." (Jalna Hanmer 1981, 38)

PROBLEM THAT HAS NO NAME

Defined by Simone De Beauvoir (1953) and Betty Friedan (1963). Sexism, "the problem that has no name," makes women into cultural, social, and economic non-persons and robs them of their histories and their names. "It was a strange stirring, a sense of dissatisfaction, a yearning that women suffered in the middle of the twentieth century in the United States. Each suburban wife struggled with it alone. As she made the beds, shopped for groceries, matched slip cover material, ate peanut butter sandwiches, chauffeured Cub Scouts and Brownies, lay beside her husband at night, she was afraid to ask even of herself the silent question: 'Is this all?' " (Betty Friedan 1963, 11)

PRO-CHOICE

Favoring or advocating the right of women to choose abortion. "People who believe abortion should be legal and available call themselves *pro-choice*. They like this phrase because it means they do not believe in telling anyone she should have an abortion, but that everyone should have the choice to have one if necessary. Thus, they believe in *reproductive freedom*. This includes access to birth control" (Beverly Stephen 1980, "Reading the Labels," *New York Daily News*, 12 June). Coined in 1978 to distinguish the position from *pro-abortion*, which dates (like *pro-life*) from 1972. (*Barnhart Dictionary Companion* 1982, 1:3, 43). The term is an example of language activism, replacing *pro-abortion*, which was "a media-created term that implied women were advocating abortion as something more than a last resort." (Gloria Steinem 1980b, 19)

PROFANE

"The term *profane* is derived from the Latin *pro* (before) and *fanum* (temple). Feminist profanity is the wild realm of the sacred as it was/is before being caged into the temple of Father Time. . . . Since it is not confined within the walls of any spatial or temporal temple, it transcends the 'accepted' dichotomies between the sacred and the profane." (Mary Daly 1978, 48)

PROFESSIONAL

"A person who *has* status but who does not necessarily *seek* status; the arrogance that accompanies status-seeking is pro-fessional*ism*." (Sally Miller Gearhart 1983, 12)

A person with a certain degree of autonomy and self-sufficiency in her work who seeks to define and carry out her tasks accurately and effectively with a minimum of self-indulgence and ca-priciousness.

PROFESSIONALISM

A word that "covers such a multitude of sins. I always cringe when I hear *anyone* describe herself as 'professional,' because what usually follows is an excuse for inaction, an excuse for ethical irresponsi-bility." (Barbara Smith 1979b, 50)

PROFESSIONS

Institutions in which women remain "the hewers of wood and drawers of water." (A.B.T. 1919, 115) Commonly refers to those occupations that require advanced formal training, usually involving mental, technical, or administrative – as opposed to manual – labor. Sometimes connotes allegiance to an organization, discipline, or system.

"Seem to be as blood thirsty as the profession of arms itself. They make the people who practice them possessive, jealous of any infringement of their rights, and highly combative if anyone dares dispute them. . . . In another century or so if we [women] practise the professions in the same way, shall we not be just as possessive, just as jealous, just as pug-nacious, just as positive as to the verdict of God, Nature, Law and property as these gentlemen are now?" (Virginia Woolf 1938, 63, 66)

PROFESSORED

Made or encouraged to play the role of professor. "I hate being 'professored'; the mantle falls and the role must be played. This is a holiday from all our roles!" (May Sarton 1961, 146)

PROGRESS

"Almost the same daughters ask almost the same brothers for almost the same privileges. Almost the same gentlemen intone almost the same refusals for almost the same reasons. It seems as if there were no progress in the human race, but only repetition." (Virginia Woolf 1938, 66) "If it has any meaning it applies only to men." (Dale Spender 1982b, 30) "White" progress is connected to centuries of unpaid labor of slaves. (Alice Walker 1973, rpt. 1983, 163) " 'Progress' affects few. Only revolution can affect many." (Alice Walker 1979, rpt. 1983, 371)

PROLETARIAT

The word from the French *means* 'those who breed.' In fact, proletarian women are the *proletariat in the proletariat.*" (Catherine Henry 1971, 200)

PRONOUN

Stands for, refers to, or replaces a noun. "The male authors of [the] earliest English grammars wrote for male readers in an age when few women were literate. The masculine-gender pronouns they used in grammatical examples and generalizations did not reflect a belief that masculine pronouns could refer to both sexes. They reflected the reality of male cultural dominance and the male-centered world view that resulted." (Casey Miller and Kate Swift 1980, 35-6) Pronouns are the major linguistic expression of gender in modern English and have received much attention from feminists. Dennis Baron (forthcoming) summarizes the history of language scholarship on pronouns and charts chronologically the many proposals for pronoun reform as well as the continuing search for an "epicene" pronoun (i.e., a single form for either sex). Wendy Martyna (1983) provides arguments including experimental evidence for the necessity of nonsexist usage. Many other experimental and linguistic studies of pronouns are summarized in Barrie Thorne, Cheris Kramarae, and Nancy Henley eds. (1983). Only a few comments and examples are given here.

(See ANDROCENTRISM, GENERIC ASSUMPTION, HE, HE/MAN, LINGUISTIC SEXISM, PREFACE, PRESCRIPTIVISM, PRONOUN ENVY)

First person: "As Monique Wittig has shown, the pronoun *I* conceals the sexual identity of the speaker/writer. The *I* makes the speaker/writer deceptively feel at home in a male-controlled language. . . . The fact is that the female saying 'I' is alien at every moment to her own speaking and writing. She is broken by the fact that she must enter this language in order to speak or to write." (Mary Daly 1978, 19)

Third person: " 'He' deserves to live out its days doing what it has always done best – referring to 'he' and not 'she.' " (Wendy Martyna; quoted in Casey Miller and Kate Swift 1980, 38) "The use of *they* as a singular pronoun slips out in response to a healthy democratic instinct to include women when general references are made to people." (Casey Miller and Kate Swift 1976, 122) "For a boy, internalizing the generic interpretation of masculine pronouns is part of a continuum. He becomes aware that a symbol which applies to him is reflected throughout the animate world; a link is strengthened between his own sense of being and all other living things. For a young girl, no such continuum exists." (Casey Miller and Kate Swift 1976, 27) "A ship, a city, any entity that we half-seriously personify, is called 'she.' 'She' designates the borderline between the inanimate and the conscious." (Dorothy Dinnerstein 1976, 100) "When speaking of a person whose gender is unidentified, we use 'he or she' in odd-numbered chapters, and 'she or he' in even-numbered chapters. Our intention is to avoid confusion while attempting to use the two variations equally; if one version appears more than the other, it is accidental." (Michel Avery et al. 1981, xi) "Throughout this book I refer to teachers, researchers and other professionals as 'she' unless the context is masculine. As the teaching profession is overwhelmingly female and I am a female researcher it seems a perverse form of false consciousness to use 'he' except where absolutely necessary." (Sara Delamont 1976, 6)

Inclusive pronouns: "First-person plural pronouns ('we,' 'us,' and 'our') are used only when referring specifically to the authors. When speaking of 'everyone,' or 'most people in this society,' third person ('they') is used. This distinction is made to avoid confusion, not to set the authors apart from the readers. When we say, 'People in this culture learn to hide their emotions,' for example, we mean to include ourselves in the generalization." (Michel Avery et al. 1981, 96)

In detective stories, the convention of using *he* and *man* generically has always been challenged so as to emphasize the fact that the murder suspect could be anybody:

" 'Well,' said the Bishop indulgently [referring to a clue prepared by the murderer], 'he had a difficult task.' 'He or she,' said Henry." (Patricia Moyes 1983, 18)

Pronouns as an index to social change: "When referring to transsexuals, I have chosen to emphasize the pronoun *he* . . . to reinforce the fact that the majority of transsexuals are men [and that] transsexualism is originated, supported, institutionalized, and perpetuated primarily by males." (Janice G. Raymond 1979, 14) Marge Piercy in *Woman on the Edge of Time* derives *com* from companion or partner and *per* from person: "We could tell person intended to speak to more of you. . . . At first we were trying to save per." (Marge Piercy 1976, 315)

PRONOUN ENVY

In the early 1970s, graduate students in Harvard's linguistics department requested a ban on *man*, masculine pronouns, and other non-generic usage. Seventeen members of the faculty responded that "the fact that the masculine is the unmarked gender in English (or that the feminine is unmarked in the language of the Tunica Indians) is simply a feature of grammar . . . There is really no cause for anxiety or pronoun-envy on the part of those seeking such changes." (Quoted in Casey Miller and Kate Swift 1976, 76)

(See AUTHORITY, M.A.L.E., PRESCRIPTIVISM)

PROPAGANDA

"We have to keep in the back of our minds at all times that we wouldn't have to use the denigrated word 'propaganda' for what is, in fact, *education*, if it weren't consistently used against us. 'Quality' in art, like 'objectivity' and 'neutrality,' belong to *them*. The only way to combat the 'normal' taken-for-granted propaganda that surrounds us daily is to question *their* version of the truth as publicly and clearly as possible. . . . Feminism has potentially changed the terms of propaganda as art by being unashamed of its obsessions and political needs, and by confirming the bonds between individual and social experience." (Lucy R. Lippard 1980, 35, 36)

PROPERTY

"The thing authority regards as more sacred than human life." (Jessie Stephen 1905; cited in Anna Coote and Beatrix Campbell 1982, 10)

PROSTHESIS

Substitute for part of the body that's absent or lost through birth, illness, or accident. Some people may joke about prosthetic devices (e.g., as "bionic"), others may feel shy and awkward about them; still others may forsake prostheses, as Audre Lorde did after breast surgery: "I cannot wear a prosthesis right now because it feels like a lie more than merely a costume. . . . Prosthesis offers the empty comfort of 'Nobody will know the difference.' But it is that very difference which I wish to affirm, because I have lived it, and survived it, and wish to share that strength with other women. If we are to translate the silence surrounding breast cancer into language and action against this scourge, then the first step is that women with mastectomies must become visible to each other. For silence and invisibility go hand in hand with powerlessness." (Audre Lorde 1980a, 61)

PROSTITUTE

As used by feminists, often not clearly distinct from *woman*, *lady*, and other terms for female; used metaphorically to suggest the exchange value of women as commodities and the ultimate economic dependence of women on men. Semantically, a very large number of words designating females eventually come to include a connotative meaning of prostitute (*abbess*, *queen*, etc.).

(See ABBESS, MARRIAGE,

PROSTITUTION, SEMANTIC DEROGATION, SEXUALITY, TRAFFIC IN WOMEN)

"Sirs, you cannot hold us in honour so long as you drag our sisters in the mire. As you are unjust and cruel to them, you will become unjust and cruel to us." (Josephine Butler c.1875; in Judith R. Walkowitz 1983, 422)

"A prostitute hides beneath the skin of every lady. It is apparent in the way they slowly cross their legs, rubbing themselves lightly with the silky insides of their thighs. It is apparent in the way they get bored with men, they don't know what we go through, plagued by the same man for the rest of our lives. It is apparent in the way they jump from man to man in the tips of their eyelashes, hiding a swarm of green and blue lights in the depths of their vaginas." "Each prostitute is a potential lady, drowned in the nostalgia of a white house like a dove that will never be held, of that house with a balcony of silver amphoras and plaster fruit garlands hanging over the doors, drowned in the nostalgia of the sound of china when invisible hands set the table." (Rosario Ferre; in Margarite Fernandez Olmos 1982, 46)

Difficult to define in such a way that excludes wives, "who also exchange sexual services in return for support. *The difference between prostitutes and wives lies not within the women, but within the men,* and the role played by men is not and has not been open to investigation or indictment, while men have been in control." (Dale Spender 1982b, 341)

Is patriarchy's sexual slave. Prostitutes "are not respected or protected by society; they are used and abused. The prostitute model contributes to the HIStoric battle of the sexes by serving as a prototype for the 'other woman' of the double sexual standard. The prostitute role relieves men of responsibility for their sexual behavior (they were seduced), and dehuman- izes . . . womyn and sexuality." (Letter to the editor 1983, *off our backs*, April, 23)

For the woman it means "the carnal annihilation of will and choice, but for the man . . . signifies an increase in power, pure, and simple." (Andrea Dworkin 1974. 60-1)

"The ultimate results of male sexism – the sale of female flesh." (Midge Lennert and Norma Willson eds, 1973, 10)

"Promiscuity controlled by economics." (Ursula K. LeGuin; in Susan Wood ed. 1979, 166)

Spends more time as a counselor, giving listening and helping services. (Margo St James; cited in Elise Boulding 1976, 760)

Prostitutes "are the only people who have previous convictions used against them in court. (NB Men accused of rape *don't.*)" (Victoria Green 1977; in Marsha Rowe ed. 1982, 227)

PROSTITUTES' NAMES

"The literature abounds with an interest- ing initiation rite in which all new prosti- tutes changed their name as they entered a brothel. Perhaps the change of name helped to insure further privacy from family. Or, perhaps women simply chose to adopt more flamboyant names appro- priate to their trade, such as 'Violet' or 'Sugarplum.' Yet the strong emphasis on the entire initiation suggests something more important: for the novice, as well as for the initiated, the change of name was a means of bonding to a subculture considered deviant and degraded by the dominant culture. When one prostitute entered a brothel, for example, she repeatedly found all the 'girls bustling with suggestions for her new name.' It was as if a new name (as in a nunnery) made a new claim on the individual's loyalties to her past through the purpose- ful elimination of an older identity. Interestingly, the new name never included a surname; prostitutes simply became known as 'Lulu' or 'Buttercup.' In effect, they ceased to belong to any previous father or husband. . . . Was this need for a new name a way of dealing with internalized guilt from social and familial stigma? Was it a way of becoming integrated into a deviant and stigmatized subculture? Explanations can be only speculative. Perhaps the rite of name initiation helped transform whatever individual or collective worthlessness women experienced as a stigmatized group into a more positive sense of self-esteem." (Ruth Rosen 1982, 102-4)

(See ACRONYMS, BATTLE NAMES, NAMES, TESTOSTERONE POISONING)

PROSTITUTION

Though offers a means for women to survive and in some cases earn a better livelihood than they might otherwise obtain, prostitution is a high risk occupation in terms of exposure to physical risk, health problems, and emotional strain.

"A livelihood; the profession of the wife and mother is not. A woman can support her children by prostitution; she cannot do so by performing the duties ordinarily associated with motherhood." (Cicely Hamilton 1909, 68)

Throughout recorded history "has been the terrifying alternative to marriage. Men created marriage in part to provide each male with his own sexual object. They created prostitution to ensure the availability of women for sexual service at all times; to remind the male constantly of his role as sexual subject; and to keep us aware of our role as sexual object. We have been given the choice of being private property and serving one master in marriage or being public property and serving many masters outside of marriage." (Barbara Mehrhof and Sheila Cronan 1969, 5-6)

In Victorian society, "middle-class women were dominantly defined as asexual; prostitutes (and often working class women in general) were seen as sexual and thereby aberrant, sometimes conceived of as atavists – biological throwbacks to an earlier evolutionary stage (akin to the promiscuity 'of primitives'). The prostitute was 'needed' to keep the middle-class home and its female homemaker unsullied and pure." (Lucy Bland 1983, 10, paraphrasing a physician of 1896)

"Is a crime, gentlemen, but it is not victimless. There is a victim, and that is the woman." (Susan Brownmiller 1971, rpt. 1973, 72)

"The radical feminist attack on commercial sex is old-fashioned; it has its roots in earlier feminist campaigns against male vice and the double standard. . . . Past generations of feminists attacked prostitution, pornography, white slavery, and homosexuality as manifestations of undifferentiated male lust. These campaigns were brilliant organizing drives that stimulated grass-roots organizations and mobilized women not previously brought into the political arena. . . . By demanding women's right to protect their own persons against male sexual abuse and ultimately extending their critique of sexual violence to the 'private' sphere of the family, they achieved some permanent gains for women. Nonetheless, judging by the goals stated by feminists themselves – to protect and empower women – these campaigns were often self-defeating. A libertarian defense of prostitutes found no place in the social purity struggle; all too often prostitutes were objects of purity attack. Feminists started a discourse on sex, mobilized an offensive against male vice, but they lost control of the movement as it diversified. In part this outcome was the result of certain contradictions in these feminists' attitudes; in part it reflected their impotence in their effort to reshape the world according to their own image." (Judith R. Walkowitz 1983, 421)

"It was difficult for abolitionists to discuss the rape of black women for fear of offending audiences, so they concentrated on the theme of prostitution. But the use of the word prostitution to describe mass sexual exploitation of enslaved black women by white men not only deflected attention away from the prevalence of forced sexual assault, it lent further credibility to the myth that black females were inherently wanton and therefore responsible for rape." (bell hooks 1981, 34)

"Prostitution itself exemplified the intrusion of market values into one of the most private areas of human existence.

Although prostitution had always been a commercial transaction, the striking changes in the *scale* of its commercialization just before the turn of the century made it seem especially dehumanizing and most flagrantly immoral. It had evolved from a small-scale, informal operation to a highly organized business that reaped vast profits and maintained connections with numerous third-party agents, including liquor interests, landlords, police, and politicians. Brothels were opened 'much as grocery or hardware stores were opened in legitimate trade.' As one reformer put it, prostitution had developed into a 'man's business,' with 'business methods, bookkeeping, and cash registers and checks.' Commercialized vice had become the underworld analogue of the faceless trusts and monopolies of the legitimate business world; both robber barons and profiteers of prostitution had successfully consolidated, rationalized, and formalized their businesses. Furthermore, both were associated with crime, exploitation, and corruption; and both were politically protected and economically invisible. The connection between anxiety over prostitution and anxiety over the transition to monopolistic corporate capitalism is most clearly shown by Progressives' exaggerated portrayals of prostitution rings as invisible, conspiratorial syndicates of national, or even international, proportions." (Ruth Rosen 1982, 42)

Exemplifies the male sexual double standard. In the 1940s, a well-publicized study of dominance and subordination in male-female chimpanzee pairs concluded that "in the picture of behavior which is characteristic of femininity in the chimpanzee, the biological basis of prostitution of sexual function stands revealed. The mature and sexually experienced female trades upon her ability to satisfy the sexual urge of the male" (Yerkes 1943). Ruth Herschberger analyzes the androcentric naming practices of this study and of science in general: the male and female display identical behaviors "but by the time it gets down on paper, it has one name when [the male] does it, and

another [when the female does it]." Displaying "sexual invitation," the male was said to be "sexually impulsive," the female to illustrate the biological basis for prostitution. (Ruth Herschberger 1948, 5-14 and 212-13)

Important subculture in literature and society. "The new prostitute . . . became integrated into the subculture of prostitution by forming close relationships with other prostitutes and madams. The late anthropologist Michelle Rosaldo suggested that women in deviant roles such as witches or prostitutes may develop bases of female solidarity denied other women: 'The very symbolic and social conceptions that appear to set women apart and to circumscribe their activities may be used by women as a basis for female solidarity and worth.' Within the brothel, in particular, such solidarity seemed to be prevalent. Despite petty jealousies and competition, the women who lived and worked in the same houses and trade seem to have experienced a continuous bonding." (Ruth Rosen 1982, 104)

PROTECTED GROUPS

Groups officially designated as protected by affirmative action and equal opportunity programs. Usually includes women, specified ethnic and racial minorities, veterans, and handicapped people.

PROTECTIVE LEGISLATION

Laws passed supposedly to protect women from physically difficult work. Actually what "was being 'protected' was not women or weaker people. It was certain job slots that were now available only to men, however weak or strong they might be." (Elizabeth Kamarck Minnich 1982, 2)

PRO-WOMAN LINE

A theoretical position within U.S. second wave feminism developed by the group Redstockings: "We identify with . all women. We define our best . interest as that of the poorest, most brutally exploited woman. . . . In fighting for our liberation we will always take the side of women against their oppressors. We will not ask what is 'revolutionary' or 'reformist,' only what is good for women." (Redstockings Manifesto 1970, 535)

"What it says basically is that women are really neat people. The bad things that are said about us as women are either myths (women are stupid), tactics women use to struggle individually (women are bitches), or are actually things that we want to carry into the new society and want men to share too (women are sensitive, emotional). Women as oppressed people act out of necessity (act dumb in the presence of men), not out of choice. Women have developed great shuffling techniques for their own survival (look pretty and giggle to get or keep a job or man) which should be used when necessary until such time as the power of unity can take its place." (Carol Hanisch 1969, 204)

PRUDE

"Is derived from the French *prudefemme*, meaning wise or good woman, and is rooted in the Old French *prode*, meaning good, capable, brave. Prude has the same origins as *proud*. It makes sense that within the Lecherous State the name *Prude* is used disparagingly of women, for women who are wise, good, capable, brave, and – especially – Proud Women threaten the phallic lusters, thrusters." (Mary Daly 1984, 14)

PSEUDONYME

Name taken by a woman for purpose of disguise. "[My friend] turned deadly pale when I informed him of my intention to disguise myself as a man, and to enter the army on exactly the same footing as other combatants. . . . He was convinced, however, that I really meant business, when he saw the trunk with my military *pseudonyme* upon it, the male garments which the tailor had just sent home, and the accoutrements I had purchased within the past two or three days." (Loreta Janeta Velasquez 1876, 62)

PSYCHOANALYSIS

"Contains a unique set of concepts for understanding men, women, and sexuality. It is a theory of sexuality in human society. Most importantly, psychoanalysis provides a description of the mechanisms by which the sexes are divided and deformed, of how bisexual, androgynous infants are transformed into boys and girls. Psychoanalysis is a feminist theory *manque*." (Gayle Rubin 1975, 184-5)

"It is this history of the human subject in its generality (human history) and its particularity (the specific life of the individual) as it manifests itself in unconscious fantasy life that psychoanalysis traces. This immediately establishes the framework within which the whole question of female sexuality can be understood. As Freud put it: In conformity with its peculiar nature, psychoanalysis does not try to describe what a woman is – that would be a task it could scarcely perform – but sets about enquiring *how she comes into being*." (Juliet Mitchell 1966, rpt 1984, 252)

Has basically two tendencies of thought and analysis: blame the mother or the victim herself. (Mary Daly 1978, 265-6)

"Feminist preoccupation with Freud's patriarchal bias, with his failure to jump with alacrity right out of his male Victorian skin, seems to me wildly ungrateful. The conceptual tool he has put into our hands is a revolutionary one. If we are afraid to use it – and using it is frightening – we have only ourselves to blame." (Dorothy Dinnerstein 1976, xi)

Psychoanalytic theory "invariably finds women guilty for the failure of sexual intercourse. . . . As in the animistic thinking of primitive society, in which every bush, tree, and animal possesses a spirit of its own, psychoanalytic thought transforms sexual organs into bearers of independent will." (Marielouise Janssen-Jurreit 1982, 240)

PSYCHOLOGY

"Has always been used to substitute personal explanations of problems for political ones, and to disguise real material oppression as emotional disturbance." (A Redstockings Sister c.1969)

PUBLIC ENEMY NUMBER ONE

What Angela Y. Davis was named by the FBI for her work against prison slavery and for her commitment to George Jackson and the Soledad Brothers. She was subsequently acquitted. (Carole E. Gregory 1980, 17)

(See MATRIARCHY)

PUBLIC SPEAKING

Historically, an unwomanly thing. "Thirty-five years ago I read a graduating essay. I knew I was doing an unwomanly thing, and in order to preserve it I whispered the whole essay. I've quit that. Since I made up my mind to be heard, I have been heard." (Frances A. Griffin 1899; cited in Una Stannard 1977, 61)

Frances Wright, a Scotswoman and British subject, was the first woman to brave censure, contempt, and ridicule by lecturing in public to "mixed audiences." She lectured in Tennessee, Ohio, Pennsylvania, and New York in 1828. "She was attacked in the press and several times mobbed for her radical advocacy of free public education, atheism, and birth control." (Gerda Lerner 1972, 115)

Maria W. Stewart, a Black woman, was the first native-born American woman to speak publicly in the U.S. She gave a series of lectures in Boston in 1832. (Angela Y. Davis 1981, 253). Another Black woman speaker described her experience after one public speech: "While on my way to my seat after my essay, I was amused to overhear an audible comment by a white clergyman of prominence who ejaculated: 'Did you listen to that colored woman? Why, she speaks as good English as I do.' It recalled a criticism in the *New York Herald* by a reporter who had heard me some years before. He described me as a 'mustard colored girl in a chocolate frock,' adding, 'She spoke quite correctly.' " (Maritcha Rémond Lyons c.1920, 33)

Sarah Winnemucca, a Paiute Indian scout, interpreter, teacher, activist, and writer, was also a public speaker during the nineteenth century. Daughter of Chief Winnemucca, she spent many years mediating between the Paiutes and white soldiers and settlers. In 1879-80 and thereafter she travelled to the east coast to intercede with the government and to give public lectures on behalf of the Paiute tribe and other Indians. Her memoirs *Life Among the Paiutes: Their Wrongs, Their Claims* (1883) detailed the abuses committed by Indian agents. (Carolyn Thomas Foreman 1954, 50)

PUERTO RICAN WOMAN

"The Puerto Rican woman is too often pictured as a passive female, bending first to the will of her father, then of her husband – an obscure figure, shuffling to the needs of her children and the men in her family. . . . This image has become an excuse to justify her from full participation in the life of the United States." (Lourdes Miranda King 1979, 124)

PULLING OUR OWN STRINGS

Collection of feminist humor edited by Gloria Kaufman and Mary Kay Blakely (1980).

PUNISHMENT

"A special prerogative of the man. . . . Surely it is a strange doctrine that all power and honour should be given to that masculine force that makes for destruction, and nothing to that feminine energy which ministers to life." (Lady McLaren 1908, 9)

Is the main reliance in the rearing of children. " 'Spare the rod and spoil the child' remains in belief, unmodified by millions of children spoiled by the unspared rod. The breeders of race horses have learned better, but not the breeders of children." (Charlotte Perkins Gilman 1911, 204)

PURGE

Official action by organizations to expel intellectual, social, or sexual "deviants"; specific action, repeated at intervals, to eliminate Lesbians from the U.S. military. "Though ostensibly aimed at removing 'Lesbians,' the purges are actually for the purpose of getting rid of 'dikes,' that is, the more independent women who have pride, intense loyalties, and strong, often romantic feelings about each other." The mass arrest/interrogation program at the end of World War II was triggered by a command by General Douglas MacArthur to his officers to "get those dikes out of here." "So the 'dikes,' the ones who had been the first to break with women's traditional roles, the more short-haired, muscular, intense, aggressive, passionate, and woman-identified of the servicewomen were suddenly arrested and charged with the crime of Lesbianism. These women were humiliated, disgraced, isolated from society, turned against each other in vicious police tactics of extracting 'confessions' and proof of guilt from their sister GIs, and bounced out of the army they had served with loyalty and trust. They were left without benefits, self-esteem, jobs, and all too often with shattered family ties, since letters were sent to their parents telling of the charges against them. Suicide, psychosis, fear of sex, great mistrust of other women, lifelong terror and bitterness were the fruits of the general's seemingly so casual words 'get those dikes out of here.'" (Judy Grahn 1984, 175-6)

(See LESBIAN, LESBIAN POLITICS OF NAMING, OFFICE OF SECRET INVESTIGATION)

PURIM

In Jewish culture, the Feast of Lots, commemorating the rescue through the heroism of Esther of the Jews of Persia from Haman's plot to exterminate them. But though Esther saved her people by giving herself to the king, Vashti was the disobedient one who had refused to be shown off. Little girls on Purim dress up as Esther – but Vashti is perhaps the truer feminist heroine.

PURITANISM

Or neo-puritanism. A label "frequently leveled at feminists and lesbian/feminists, as if any revaluation or critique of heterosexual relations were by definition asexual, antipleasure, and repressive." (Adrienne Rich 1979, 69)

PURPLE

The traditional color of homosexual culture, passed down historically through myths, customs, costumes, celebrations, folklore, and language. Also a color associated with royalty and with male military power. Despite much that has been lost, the knowledge that purple is the "Gay color" is known in all strata of contemporary society, "whether upper-class Gay people or lower-class, urban or rural, religious or pagan or atheist, professional or blue collar, secretary or street person, bohemian artist or business executive." (Judy Grahn 1984, 12)

The Color Purple: title of a novel by Alice Walker about the transformation in consciousness of the protagonist Celie in part through her love of and friendship with Shug Avery. Talking about God, Shug tells Celie that God wants the feelings people have and other good things of the world to be loved and admired; not that God is vain, "just wanting to share a good thing. I think it pisses God off if you walk by the color purple in a field somewhere and don't notice it." The color purple is a metaphor for the treasures the world has to offer, including love and sexual enjoyment between women. (Alice Walker 1982, 178)

PUSHKE

Yiddish: a small can or container kept in Jewish homes, often in the kitchen, in which money is to be donated to charity is collected. Jewish women often put some money into the *pushke* on Friday evening before lighting the Sabbath candles. Often set out on the kitchen windowsill, the cans were labelled for various charities: for orphans, widows, the blind, a trip to the holy land, a new library wing for the *yeshiva*, etc. There is no Hebrew or Yiddish word for charity: the word used for charity – *tzedaka* – means justice.

Charity is considered a duty and necessity, not a choice. Also means the money saved up by a married woman out of the household funds given her by her husband; a nest-egg earned through careful money management available for personal uses. Often the *pushke* (or *knippl*) was the family's only fund for medical emergencies and other crises. (Leo Rosten 1968, 301-2)

(See MAD MONEY, PIN MONEY)

QUALIFIED

Is a word used "mainly for 'out' groups, as if white men were intrinsically *qualified*" by their birth. (Gloria Steinem 1980b, 23)

QUALIFIER

A problem in empirical research on women and language. "As with tag questions there is some difficulty associated with defining a qualifier, which generally speaking is 'a term which qualifies' and, presumably because female speech was believed to be more tentative and hesitant – and qualified – it was hypothesized that females used more qualifiers. [Maryann] Hartman stated that in her study females did use more qualifiers, but she adds an extra bit of information as well. She claims that men used more absolutes. I envy her such assurance and confidence for it seems to me that the use of the same term could be interpreted as a qualifier if used by females and an absolute if used by males; for example:

Perhaps you have misinterpreted me.
Maybe you should do it again.

I think the determining factor is more often the sex of the speaker rather than the speech, so that when females use *perhaps* or *maybe* it is interpreted as a qualifier; when males use the same terms the interpretation is that they are using absolutes." (Dale Spender 1980, 35)

QUARANTINE

A popular remedy for the disease of feminism. "If I had had cholera, hydrophobia, smallpox, or any malignant disease," wrote Harriot Hunt, a feminist physician who became increasingly radical, "I could not have been more avoided than I was." (Harriot K. Hunt 1856; cited in Mary Roth Walsh 1977, 2)

QUEEN

"Old Norse *kvaen*, Old English *cwene* meant 'owner,' specifically applied to female owners of the land in the days of the matriarchate. Ancient writers described many barbarian societies as nations of 'queens.' " (Barbara G. Walker 1983, 836)

"Originally a title of the goddess, this term came to be applied to Her earthly representative, the female ruler of the people, the leader of the priestesses. The famous Cleopatra of Egypt, for example, was a Queen in the ancient matriarchal Egyptian tradition, serving as Isis-in-the-flesh. In patriarchal cultures, the Queen came to be less powerful, finally serving as a figurehead for males and their institutions." (Ann Forfreedom 1983, correspondence)

"Word used to describe a Gay man who is into really anything, like Leather Queen is a man who goes in drag wearing leather. . . . *Queen* has a much broader meaning; a flaming faggot is just an outrageous, obviously Gay man. It doesn't mean the same as a *drag queen*." (Tede Matthews, quoted in Judy Grahn 1984, 89-90) "Queens are oracular as a rule, loquacious, helpful people as a rule, though also with a reputation for sharp-tongued, shrewish self-defense. Their usual character of speech is a spewing of a running stream of advice, predictions, protection, commentary, gossip, 'truth-saying.' " (Judy Grahn 1984, 87) Lesbian Queens: "Everywhere I went within the Gay underground culture I found that the men had queens to look to and admire or despise . . . I often wondered where the Lesbian queens might be; why do we not call each other 'queen'? Of course, Sweden had a Lesbian queen, Queen Christina in the 1600s, who, raised as a boy by her father, abdicated rather than marry a man and who apparently loved a certain countess, her lady-in-waiting. And of course, the Amazons had many queens, and Lesbians are closely connected to the female warrior tradition and often identify with it." (Judy Grahn 1984, 91)

QUEEN IN HER HOME

Euphemism for the occupation "house-wife" which receives no remuneration. A woman may work all day at her "calling" and still have to ask her husband for pocket money. (Carol Lee Bacchi 1983, 16)
   (See PIN MONEY)

QUEEN OF FAIRY

"The modern Queen of Fairy is a male in flaming female attire, airy gestures, swiveling hips, and distinct lisp. The queen, especially the older queen, is frequently a social focal point among Gay men, an organizer and a doer, a person to go to for advice and aid, the one who knows about people and events." (Judy Grahn 1984, 87)
   (See QUEEN)

QUEEN OF WANDS

Collection of poems by Judy Grahn inspired by tales of stolen queens, especially Helen, Queen of Sparta, and incorporating many threads of language research and folklore. "In investigating Helen's story I found an astonishingly worldwide myth of a female god of beauty, fire, love, light, thought and weaving. She is a figure of many forms and names and countries, and she is the Queen of Wands." (Judy Grahn 1982, xii)

QUEER

Perhaps from German *quer*, "crosswise" in the original sense of "crooked," "not straight," to modern English via Scots beggars' cant. Means singular, strange, odd, differing from what is "ordinary." Generic slang term used depreciatively and appreciatively to mean homosexual (also means "counterfeit" as in *queer as a two-dollar bill*). "One of the ways to understand better [what heterosexism is] . . . is to 'think queer,' no matter what your sexuality. By 'think queer,' I mean imagine life as a lesbian for a week. Announce to everyone – family, room-mate, on the job, everywhere you go – that you are a lesbian. Walk in the street and go out only with women, especially at night. Imagine your life, economically and emotionally, with women instead of men. For a whole week, experience life as if you were a lesbian, and you will learn quickly what heterosexual privileges and assumptions are, and how they function to keep male supremacy working." (Charlotte Bunch 1976; rpt. in Sheila Ruth 1980, 555)

QUESTION

Crucial way of inquiring into the nature of the female condition, but also a traditional interrogation of and about women, as though they were solely responsible for the analysis of women's oppression. "But what *do* we want? That's what they always ask us, as if they expected us, like tidy housekeepers, to come up in five short years with the magic remedy cleanser that will wipe clean the unbelievable mess men have created from their position of power during the past five thousand years." (Robin Morgan ed. 1970, xxxv) Also means a continuing issue: "The great question": Will women receive "equal pay for equal work?" (A. H. M. Fairbanks 1919, 3) Mode of exploration we need to formulate for ourselves: "The questions – such as Why? If? When? Where? How? How come? Why not? – have been frozen. . . . Males have posed the questions; they have *placed* the questions, tagged and labeled, into the glass cases of mental museums. They have hidden the questions. The task for feminists now is con-questioning, con-questing for the deep sources of the questions, seeking a permanently altering state of consciousness." (Mary Daly 1978, 345) Questioning strategies are also an important feature of interpersonal interaction in the study of women's and men's communication.

QUILT

Bedcover made by stitching together in a pattern two pieces of cloth with a soft layer in between; often the top cloth is itself made of bits and strips of cloth stitched together. Art form in which women have excelled. "That most anonymous of women's art, rarely dated or signed, summarizes more than any other form the major themes in a woman's life – its beginnings, endings, and celebrations retold in bits of colored cloth. In quilts a woman said everything she knew about art and life." (Mirra Bank 1979, 11) "Southern black women, incorporating features of African textile arts, have evolved a quilt-making style that contrasts sharply with the Euro-American aesthetic, which is rigid and uniform in pattern and highly predictable in design. . . . Enslaved women who created the Afro-American style of African textile aesthetics [simultaneously served the requirements as well as that quilts be made, preserved a cultural memory]. This memory lives today in the work of contemporary quilters." (Nancy Faires Conklin, Brenda McCalum, and Marcia Wade 1983, 49)

(See ART, DINNER PARTY,
FORMS OF EXPRESSION,
SAMPLER)

"[That quilt] took me more than twenty years, nearly twenty-five, I reckon, in the evenings after supper when the children were all put to bed. My whole life is in that quilt. It scares me sometimes when I look at it. All my joys and all my sorrows are stitched into those little pieces. . . . And John, too. He was stitched into that quilt and all the thirty years we were married. Sometimes I loved him and sometimes I sat there hating him as I pieced the patches together. So they are all in that quilt, my hopes and fears, my joys and sorrows, my loves and hates. I tremble sometimes when I remember what that quilt knows about me." (Margaret Ickis, quoting her great-grandmother; in Mirra Bank 1979, 94)

Art form exhibited to accompany "The Dinner Party," by Judy Chicago and colleagues. Women from around the country created quilts for the event. The "Honor Quilt," from Rochester, N.Y., for example, was created by 40 women artists to honor individual women and groups of women (including anonymous women). Using a variety of media ranging from clay, paper, glass, cloth, and needlepoint, the quilt in its entirety celebrates a long neglected tradition of women's art in fiber and needlework.

Star Quilt. "Developed by Native women from sewing methods and became uniquely Indian in the Northern Plains. Major ceremonial items in give-aways [community ceremonials held to honor someone in which the honoree's family gives away a variety of goods], these quilts feature one bright-colored central star with six points. They are often used as blankets by men undergoing vision quests." (Rayna Green 1984, 315)

QUILTING

Process of making art with an important social function. "Thus the day was spent in friendly gossip as they quilted and rolled and talked and laughed. . . . Serious matrons commented on the cake, and told each other high and particular secrets in the culinary art, which they drew from remote family archives. One might have learned in that instructive assembly how best to keep moths out of blankets; how to make fritters of Indian corn indistinguishable from oysters; how to bring up babies by hand; how to mend a cracked teapot; how to take grease from a brocade; how to reconcile absolute decrees with free will; how to make five yards of cloth answer the purpose of six; and how to put down the Democratic party." (Harriet Beecher Stowe 1895; in Mirra Bank 1979, 63)

Describing an oral history project: "As the quilters talked about quilts they were constantly reminded of some other parts of their lives, a story about pioneering times, an anecdote about a family member, or some technical detail of quilting. The quilts seemed to be the format in which they had condensed much of personal, family, and community history." (Patricia Cooper and Norma Bradley Buferd 1978, 18-19)

"My boy Jim, and some other of them old men, always find out where we're quilting. And at dinnertime here come their faces. They sit around poking fun, but we pay 'em no mind. Jim's wife still can't understand why he wants to come eat at his momma's with a bunch of old hens. We just grin." (Quilter, in Patricia Cooper and Norma Bradley Buferd 1978, 139)

Is "like livin' a life." (Aunt Jane of Kentucky, c.1900; in Mirra Bank 1979, 76)

Is a form of self-definition. "The cloth stands for personal definition and distance, boundaries and contact. The quilts, in the end, consciously became a speculum through which I finally came to love myself and accept my sexuality, my need for warmth and protective embraces coming first and foremost. In the initial fragmentation of the pieces of cloth, I also encountered my anger, which always precedes my surrender to others. The interactive quality of cloth as a visual, sensual, and social given became the bridge for me to receive what I had missed as a child." (Radka Donnell 1981, 87)

QUILTING BEES

"Were called for the purpose of assisting an individual woman in the actual 'quilting,' the tedious work of stitching together the designed 'top' – which she had already made – to the padding and lining. Even the design of the stitches was chosen in advance by the quiltmaker, who only invited the most expert needlewomen to assist her. In return, she would help them to do their quilting. These quilting bees were the only opportunity women had to get together in small groups and say what they would, out of earshot of men. And although these events have been characterized as an exchange of gossip and recipes, there was some serious business going on, too: Susan B. Anthony made her first speech, in Cleveland, to women at a church quilting bee, and the great age of quiltmaking (and quilting bees) coincided exactly with the Seneca Falls Conference of 1848 and the rise of organized feminism in America." (Patricia Mainardi 1973, 59-60)

"In the fall of 1974 we attended a quilting bee in West Texas. Early in the morning we arrived at the house of a woman whose quilts were exceptionally impressive. She pieced designs of unusual originality. We had been told her husband was also a quilter. . . . [He] was badly crippled from arthritis but could 'still push a needle right smart.' He had been a farmer until his retirement. We looked at the quilting both had done and were unable to distinguish between their stitches. He explained carefully that he didn't take part in the design, choice of pattern, or color composition of the quilts. He just helped by carefully sewing along the chalk marks his wife had drafted. Later as I started out the door he took my arm and explained again, 'I only do the quilting. She's the artist. She's the one that makes the light shine.' " (Patricia Cooper and Norma Bradley Bufferd 1978, 19)

QUILTING FOR THE PUBLIC
Making quilts to sell.

QUOTATION
Rich source of definitions and commentary for a feminist dictionary. Definitions for most standard dictionaries are constructed from the usages reflected in quotations and citations from the canon of "good authors" and other mainstream

printed sources; with few exceptions (the *Oxford English Dictionary* is a historic and notable example), these dictionaries derive definitions from usage, omitting the actual citations themselves. This dictionary is subtitled *In Our Own Words* because it is based on feminist quotations and because whenever possible it reproduces those words verbatim.

(See DICTIONARY, OXFORD ENGLISH DICTIONARY)

QPP

"The QPP
The quietly pacifist peaceful
always die
to make room for men
who shout"
    (Alice Walker 1971, 49)

RACE

From Spanish *la raza*, has come to have several meanings: (1) persons connected by common descent or origin; (2) offspring or descendants of a person, used almost always for males only ("race of Adam" but not "race of Eve"); (3) persons within a given kinship group, tribe or nation assumed to be descended from common stock; (4) a local geographic or global human population distinguished as a more or less distinct group by genetically transmitted physical characteristics; (5) [rare] division of humankind into sexes (female race).

"Ample evidence indicates that relations between the races have a long and important history which cannot be exclusively reduced to an analysis limited to sex or class. Blacks respond to the sociopolitical reality of a social structure in which Blacks are systematically dominated, exploited, and oppressed." (Gloria I. Joseph; in Gloria I. Joseph and Jill Lewis 1981, 80)

Is immutable. "It is possible for women to change their class and/or their class identification, but not their race. Often this difference between race and class can distort discussions of them." (Beverly Fisher-Manick 1977; rpt. 1981, 150)

RACISM

Institutionalized discrimination, prejudice, and oppression based on race; specifically oppression by white people of people of color. A crucial issue for feminism because any analysis of oppression needs to include intersecting oppressions, because any analysis of women's situation needs to engage with the specificities of different women's conditions (thus the assumption of a notion of "women" based primarily on white middle-class American women is glaringly insufficient), because white women themselves partake of the privilege afforded white people in many Western societies, and because racism within the women's movement itself needs to be addressed if solidarity among women is to be fostered. It is a co-responsibility: "It is inappropriate for progressive liberal white people to expect warriors in brown armor to eradicate racism. There must be co-responsibility from people of color and white people to equally work on this issue. It is not just my responsibility to point out and educate about racist activities and beliefs." (Barbara Cameron 1981, 51) Some definitions of and comments on racism follow.

(See ANGER, BLACK, CIVIL RIGHTS, COLOR, COLOR-STRUCK, FEMINISM, JEW-HATING, MATRIARCHY, THIRD WORLD)

"Black women have felt they had to make a choice – either fight their oppression as a race or fight as women. We have to ask, can we fight racism and women's oppression at the same time? Both the black and women's liberation movement are alike in that they are fighting a master-slave relationship. But there always has to be a consciousness that racism is THE issue in the U.S. That black women's and men's problems are not the same as white's. That consciousness has been lost at times in our history.

It was lost in 1920. The suffragists weren't aware of race as a key to their movement. Therefore as soon as the vote was won the movement died. If it had been linked to class and to race it could have continued and not been just a middle class thing." (*The Fourth World* 1971, 1)

Racism is "the practice of objectification [which] stands between all Black people and full human identity under the white supremacist system: racism requires that Black people be thought different from white; and this difference is usually translated as less than." (Michelle Cliff 1982, 35) Is "the belief in the inherent superiority of one race over all others and thereby the right to dominance, manifest and implied." (Audre Lorde 1981c, 7) Is "a pus, an ooze, a crust, a sore, a fever, a malaise, an unease, a disease." (Rosario Morales 1982, 5) Its key element is harm: racism "is not about isolated incidents but about continuing patterns, deeply entrenched ways of reacting, that cut people off from something vital – jobs, housing, education, due process of law, public accommodations, psychological health... Special interest groups (including everything from the Chinese Merchants Association to the Black Dragon Motorcycle Club) can boost their members' income and pride without injuring anyone else. Racist individuals and groups cannot." (Betty De Ramus 1982)

"We will define racism, borrowing from Albert Memmi, as 'the generalized and final assigning of values to real or imaginary differences, to the accuser's benefit and at his victim's expense, in order to justify the former's own privilege or aggression.' Memmi's definition has the advantage of calling attention to the *uses* to which racism is put. Just as the logic of sexism leads to rape, so the logic of racism leads to violence and exploitation." (Albert Memmi; in Robert Stam and Louise Spence 1983, 4)

An ideology. "Everyone is capable of being racist whatever their color and condition. Only some of us are liable to racist attack." (Rosario Morales 1981, 91)

A lived reality for those who suffer racial oppression. "For those of you who are tired of hearing about racism, imagine how much more tired *we* are of constantly experiencing it, second by literal second, how much more exhausted we are to see it constantly in your eyes." (Barbara Smith 1979b, 48) "Racism affects all of our lives, but it is only white women who can 'afford' to remain oblivious to these effects. The rest of us have had it breathing or bleeding down our necks." (Cherríe Moraga and Gloria Anzaldúa eds 1981, 62) "Sexist discrimination has prevented white women from assuming the dominant role in the perpetuation of white racial imperialism, but it has not prevented white women from absorbing, supporting, and advocating racist ideology or acting individually as racist oppressors in various spheres of American life." (bell hooks 1981, 124)

A problematic word. "The absence of language to talk about our own racism contributes to the difficulty and is in itself part of the problem. Only one term, 'racism,' exists to describe the range of behavior from subtle, nonverbal daily experience to murders by the Ku Klux Klan. 'Racism' covers individual acts and institutional patterns. But this stumbling block of language presents another theme to explore, not a reason to give up." (Tia Cross et al. 1982, 66)

"The word 'racism' is too simplistic, too general, too easy. You can use the word and not say that much, unless the term is explained or clarified. Once that happens, racism looks more like a psychological problem (or pathological aberration) than an issue of skin color." (doris davenport 1981, 85, 86)

"I thought of trying to claim another tongue in which to describe, specifically, the white woman's problem in encountering the black woman; the differences that have divided black and white women; the misnaming or denial of those differences in everyday life. But I am convinced that we must go on using that sharp, sibilant word; not to paralyze ourselves and each other with repetitious, stagnant doses of guilt, but to break it down into its elements, comprehend it as a *female* experience, and also to understand its inextricable connections with gynephobia." (Adrienne Rich 1979, 304)

A joint responsibility. "I do not hold any individual American woman responsible for the roots of this ignorance about other cultures [which is one basis for racist oppression] . . . I do hold every woman responsible for the *transformation* of this ignorance." (Judit Moschkovich 1981, 79) "The onus isn't on me to process out the racism in white women, any more than the onus is on white women to apologize to me for the history of oppression of black people by whites. . . . What I want is for all of us to love ourselves as who we are. That's difficult." (Sandra Lowe, Committee for the Visibility of the Other Black Women [CVOBM] to a reporter from *Gay Community News*; cited in Jill Clark 1981, 14) "While it is in no way racist for any author to write a book exclusively about white women, it is fundamentally racist for books to be published that focus solely on the American white woman's experience in which that experience is assumed to be *the* American women's experience." (bell hooks 1981, 137)

Crucial area for work and change. "I assume that I/we do not have to be *nonracist* in order to be *antiracist*. . . For me, this has been a crucial realization." (Elly Bulkin 1980; in Terry Wolverton 1983, 191) "There are certain political dogmas that are excellent in their 'analysis' of racism and how it feeds the capitalist system. To intellectually understand that it is wrong or politically incorrect to be racist leaves me cold. . . My personal attempts at eliminating my racism have to start at the base level of those mindsets that inhibit my relationships with people." (Barbara Cameron 1981, 49) "White women don't work on racism to do a favor for someone else, solely to benefit Third World women. You have to comprehend how racism distorts and lessens your own lives as white women – that racism affects your chances for survival, too, and that it is very definitely your issue." (Barbara Smith 1979b, 49)

"Understanding the racist ideology – where and how it penetrates – is what is important for the feminist movement, not 'including' women of color or talking about 'including' men. *Guilt* is a fact for us all, white and colored: an identification with the oppressor and oppressive ideology." (Rosario Morales 1981, 91)

"Man, like all the other animals, fears and is repelled by that which he does not understand, and mere difference is apt to connote something malign." (Alice Walker ed. 1979, 169)

"Women responding to racism means women responding to anger, the anger of exclusion, of unquestioned privilege, or racial distortions, of silence, ill-use, stereotyping, defensiveness, misnaming, betrayal, and coopting." (Audre Lorde 1981c, 7)

For the white person who wants to know how to be my friend:

"The first thing you do is to forget that i'm Black. Second, you must never forget that i'm Black.

You should be able to dig Aretha, but don't play her every time i come over. And if you decide to play Beethoven – don't tell me his life story. They made us take music appreciation too.

Eat soul food if you like it, but don't expect me to locate your restaurants or cook it for you.

And if some Black person insults you, mugs you, rapes your sister, rapes you, rips your house or is just being an ass – please, do not apologize to me for wanting to do them bodily harm. It makes me wonder if you're foolish.

And even if you really believe Blacks are better lovers than whites – don't tell me. I start thinking of charging stud fees.

In other words – if you really want to be my friend – don't make a labor of it. I'm lazy. Remember."

(Pat Parker 1982, 59)

Issue that has historically divided women. In 1903, the issue of racism arose in the Brooklyn branch of the Young Women's Christian Association and some Black women wished to form a separate branch. Asserting the presence of racism yet speaking against separatism, Maritcha Rémond Lyons addressed an assembly of one hundred women of color: "Don't give us a color line in the Young Women's Christian Association. . . White women think we are the subordinate race, and that we are weaker intellectually and every other way. I want to say to you that the black man is the one man that has looked the white man in the face and looked up straight. Don't try and foist upon us something we don't want. We have traitors among us. There should be a mass meeting of colored women to protest this thing. If the traitors won't come from under cover we can't help it. Let it be understood we see the color line whether the white women see it. Separation and segregation have been the great barriers against the progress of our race in the past. We are determined to administer justice." (1903 undated newspaper account, Williamson/Lyons papers, Schomburg Center for the Study of Black Culture)

"The location of white women in America as the *benefactors* of racism has enabled them to ignore their whiteness. The location of Black women in American society as the *objects* of racism has precluded the possibility that they might have their womanness as their sole identity. White women must realize that as womanness circumscribes their whiteness (they are not white males), so their whiteness circumscribes their womanness. White feminists must come to terms with the circumscribing nature of their whiteness." (Pat Armstrong 1972; in Gloria I. Joseph and Jill Lewis 1981, 102)

"White people, white women in particular, should not fight racism simply because they want to help those of us who are hurt by it. The vast majority of people in this country, and especially the masses of women, stand to benefit from the most militant, the most assertive, challenge to racism. . . Racism historically in this country has been demonstrated to be the most devastating, the most murderous tool to prevent the emergence of the kind of united movement that will allow us to move forward in general." (Angela Davis 1982, 8)

"True rebellion is something that, with each step we take, cuts us further off from identification with racist patriarchy, which has rewarded us for our loyalty and which will punish us for becoming disloyal. It does not matter how we change our names or what music we listen to, or whether we celebrate Christmas or Chanukah or the Solstice, or how many books by women we teach – so long as we can identify only with white women, we are still connected to that system of objectification and callousness and cruelty called racism." (Adrienne Rich 1981a, 5)

A continuing reality. "The problem of the 21st Century will still be the problem of the color line, not only 'of the relation of the darker [to the lighter] races of men in Asia and Africa, in America and the islands of the sea,' but of the relations between the darker and the lighter people of the same races, and of the women who represent both dark and light within each race. It is our 'familial' relations with each other in America that we need to scrutinize. And it is the whole family, rather than the dark or the light, that must be affirmed." (Alice Walker 1982b, 59)

RADICAL

"The dictionary says radical means root, coming from the Latin word for root. And that is what we meant by calling ourselves radicals. We were interested in getting to the roots of the problems in society. You might say we wanted to pull up weeds in the garden by their roots, not just pick off the leaves at the top to make things look good momentarily. Women's Liberation was started by women who considered themselves radicals in this sense." (Kathie Sarachild 1973, 144)

RADICAL FEMINISM

"What distinguishes radical feminism from all other feminist theories is its insistence that the oppression of women is fundamental. This claim can be interpreted in several different ways. It may mean: (1) that women were, historically, the first oppressed group; (2) that women's oppression is the most widespread, existing in virtually every known society; (3) that women's oppression is the deepest in that it is the hardest form of oppression to eradicate and cannot be removed by other social changes such as the abolition of class society; (4) that women's oppression causes the most suffering to its victims, qualitatively as well as quantitatively, although this suffering may often go unrecognized because of the sexist prejudices of both the oppressors and the victims; (5) that women's oppression, as [Shulamith] Firestone claims, provides a conceptual model for understanding all other forms of oppression. Different radical feminists emphasize different aspects of the fundamental nature of women's oppression but all agree at least on the first three claims listed above." (Alison M. Jaggar and Paula S. Rothenberg 1984, 86)

(See DIALECTIC OF SEX,
LIBERAL FEMINIST, MARXIST
FEMINIST, REDSTOCKINGS)

Holds that "it is not just capitalism, but the patriarchal family – which precedes capitalism historically and can survive its demise – which accounts for the oppression and inferior social status of women. [Radical feminists] therefore call not only for the end of capitalism and the legal, educational and occupational inequality of the sexes, but for the elimination of the biological family, at least as an economic and childrearing institution; they also demand the elimination of the sexual taboos which operate to preserve the biological family. . . There are also lesbian separatist feminists, who add to these radical feminist demands the rejection of heterosexuality as a valid life style for any free woman." (Mary Anne Warren 1980, 152)

"To Radical Feminists sex-class is the basic division in the world. All women are our natural allies (whether they know it or not), all men are our enemy." (Radical Feminists 1972, n.p.)

"Recognizes the oppression of women as a fundamental political oppression wherein women are categorized as an inferior class based upon their sex. It is the aim of radical feminism to organize politically to destroy this sex class system." Recognizes "that we are engaged in a power struggle with man, and that the agent of our oppression is man insofar as he identifies with and carries out the supremacy privileges of the male role." (New York Radical Feminists 1969, 379)

Recognizes "that no single element of our society has evolved free from male definition, so that to practice radical feminism means to question every single aspect of our lives that we have previously accepted as normal/given/standard/acceptable and to find new ways of doing things where necessary – which is most places." Recognizes "that theory follows from practice and is impossible to develop in the absence of practice, because our theory is that practicing our practice is our theory." (Gail Chester 1979, 68, 69)

"The belief with the radical left that capitalism must be dismantled (that reform of the system is not enough) and, more importantly, the belief with cultural feminism that the biopsychological dimension of oppression (sexism and patriarchy) and not the economic one (the class society) is fundamental." (Sally Miller Gearhart 1983, 3)

Term used initially to distinguish radicals (out of the New Left) who had also become feminists. "Radical feminists believe that feminism is the only truly radical political cause now in existence. They have a strong case for this belief. To achieve the elimination of dominance in human relationships, sex roles, i.e., stereotyped male and female identities, would have to be eradicated. Our economy would have to extend so that everybody – women, minority groups, homosexuals, and all religions and castes

– could have equal opportunities to be hired and advanced. Hierarchical systems would have to wither away. Radical feminists would replace them with systems in industry, government, the home and the military in which decision-making power would be widely diffused. Radical feminists advocate only those systems in which everyone has equal rights. They would sharply reduce the gaps between the most and least powerful groups in society. Radical feminists advocate social, economical, political, psychological (role-playing) experimentation: They wish us to invent a future in which it is possible for each individual to be self-regulating while striving to activate all personal capacities. The restrictions would be that no one could trespass on the freedom of others." (Celestine Ware 1970, 107-8)

"In the States 'radical feminist' has a very loose, wide meaning, so that it comes to include everyone that's not Left or Right. Therefore, it includes positions that are close to neo-femininity. As far as theory is concerned, as far as political vision is concerned, all the neo-femininity – represented . . . in the United States by the spiritualists, the mother goddess cults and other celebrations of femaleness – all of this is just bailing out, withdrawing from political action and justifying that withdrawal." (Christine Delphy 1984a, 25)

RADICALTEACHER

"First used in 1975, as two words, when a magazine of that name appeared, edited by a group of dissident college teachers of English. By 1982, small groups of academics throughout the United States and England thought of themselves as radicalteachers and began a process of self-examination on this issue. By the year 1982, it was written in its present form as one word and was synonymous with (the archaic) 'teacher.'" Meanings include these: one who provides a student-rather than teacher-centered classroom; nonauthoritarian; one who shares rather than transmits information; one who respects students; one with commitments

and awareness; one who listens well; one who combines theory with practice and is concerned with process as much as product; one for whom scholarship, teaching, service, and institutional need are not separable activities; one who understands the power of language; one who teaches holistically, not separating mind from body, male from female, one color from another, thought from experience; one who works to discover, name, and change sexism, racism, classism, and hetero-sexism; one who demands critical thinking from students. Radicalteachers do not assume they know it all. (Pamela Annas 1982, *Radical Teacher* 22, back cover)

(See CLASSROOM INTERACTION)

RAGE

"Is required as a positive creative force, making possible a breakthrough, encountering the blockages of inauthentic structures." Through anger and rage women can "trigger and sustain movement from the experience of nothingness to recognition of participation in being." (Mary Daly 1975, 43) "An appropriate and necessary reaction to oppression which blocks our need for safety, mastery, and self-actualization. It's about living not just surviving." (Yvonne A. Flowers 1979, 32)

(See ANGER)

RANDOM HOUSE DICTIONARY

Edited by Jess Stein (1967), was financed in-house by a publishing corporation interested in profit. Though dictionary-making in the U.S. has always been competitive and motivated by economics as well as scholarship, the *Random House Dictionary* embodies some of the consequences of purely commercial lexicography. (James Sledd 1972)

RAP

A Black speech event in which a male approaches a female and implicitly or explicitly indicates a sexual interest in her. "The purpose and motivation of rapping varies little. Men rap to women in the hope of getting sex. Sometimes men rap to exercise their verbal ability: sharpen their line or their wit or, as one black man remarked, to 'deposit their image,' to try to prove that they could 'score' if they wanted to. The topical content of raps can vary. But it is not unusual for men to delare their sexual interest and desires openly, comment directly on the sexually attractive features of females, or brag about their own sexual ability... Black women's role and pattern of response to the rapping of black men is active and forceful, for in black culture traits like independence, aggressiveness, and sexual assertiveness are seen to be common to both males *and* females. Likewise, women are free to express their own sexual interest in men. But of course a woman is not obliged to have such an interest in a man rapping·to her simply because he proposes that she should." (Thomas Kochman 1981, 76-7)

(See CAP)

RAPE

A common criminal sexual offense, committed primarily by males against females. Until recently, rape was generally thought to be a pathological act on the part of a small population of men who were unable to control their powerful sexual urges; at the same time it was assumed that females often provoked rape (thus that they were "asking for it" and "deserved it"). Some feminists had offered alternative analyses – e.g., of rape as a "mirror-image of our ordinary sex folkways. Two basic beliefs in these folkways are the natural aggressiveness of man, and man's natural physical superiority over women. Put these two beliefs together, set up a competition for masculine prowess such as we have today, and no one should be surprised by the incidence of rape." (Ruth Herschberger 1948; cited in Betty Roszak and Theodore Roszak, eds, 1969, 123) – but it was in the late 1960s and 1970s that feminists argued with increasing urgency that rape should be redefined "as a social institution which functions to maintain male

supremacy." (Mary Anne Warren 1980, 385). Susan Brownmiller (1975a) documented the prevalence of rape throughout history and analyzed the practice as "a conscious form of intimidation by which *all men* keep *all women* in a state of fear" (5). Subsequent studies have documented rape in greater historical detail. By the 1690s, for example, we know that Massachusetts law clearly defined rape in accordance with common law. To "ravish" a woman was to gain "carnal knowledge of any woman above the age of ten years against her will and of a woman child under the age of 20 years with or against her will"; conviction carried a mandatory death sentence (Barbara S. Lindemann 1984, 64). Further, it seems historically to have been viewed as a crime not against the rape victim but against her father or husband, thus equating women with property under male ownership (Susan Brownmiller 1975a; Barbara S. Lindemann 1984): rape is "an act of violence against a woman's body [which] has existed historically in all male dominated (Patriarchal) societies, long before men decided to define it as a crime. As the laws on rape continue to evolve they have never shaken free of their original concept – that the violation was first and foremost a violation of male rights of possession, based on male requirements of virginity, chastity, and consent to private access, all of which aim to secure patrilineal descent. A 'crime' against a woman's body is thus a crime against male property." (*Zero Anarchist/Anarca-feminist Monthly* 1977 (August), 1). Throughout U.S. history, however, "rape meant, by definition, rape of white women, for no such crime as rape of a black woman existed as law. Even when a black man sexually attacked a black woman, he could only be punished by his master; no way existed to bring him to trial or to convict him if so brought." (Eugene Genovese; cited in bell hooks 1981, 35)

Some feminists link rape with pervasive misogyny in patriarchal culture: rape is "not a special isolated act. It is not an aberration, a deviation from the norms ... [it] is simply at the end of the continuum of male-aggressive, female-passive patterns" (Andra Medea and Kathleen Thompson 1974, 11) and encompasses "any involuntary sexual intimacy" (Dana Densmore 1971, 12). Rape "occurs every time a man forces a woman to perform a sexual act against her will" (Frederique Delacoste and Felice Newman 1981, 71). Andrea Dworkin goes further to argue that rape "precedes marriage, engagement, betrothal, and courtship as sanctioned social behaviour"; it is a "direct consequence of our polar definitions of men and women ... it embodies sexuality as the culture defines it." (1976, 26, 45-6) Rape, no longer a private experience, becomes for feminists a "political act" (Kathleen Barry 1979, 11), an "act of political terrorism" (Andrea Dworkin 1983, 196), a "daily nightmare" (Julia Lesage 1982, lecture at University of Illinois at Urbana-Champaign), like pornography an element "of the ideology of the Patriarchy" (Ruth Wallsgrove 1977; in Marsha Rowe 1982, 452), an "assault with a deadly weapon" (1983 graffiti on bathroom door of Undergraduate Library, University of Illinois at Urbana-Champaign), and "the hatred, contempt, and oppression of women in this society concentrated in one act" (Andra Medea and Kathleen Thompson 1974, 11).

Though feminists are united in defining rape as a violent crime against women, some strongly resist the identification of rape with "normal" heterosexual relationships in the culture. "I find it absurd to assume that all coitus is rape. By saying that, one agrees to the masculine myth that a man's sex is a sword, a weapon. The real problem is to find new sexual relationships which will not be oppressive." (Simone de Beauvoir 1972, 254) "While sexual violence, coercion, and harassment have always been feminist issues, earlier feminist analyses tended to regard physical force as one of several ways that men insure women's com-

pliance to a sexist system, and in particular to their subordinate wife-and-mother role. The main function of sexual coercion, in this view, is to curb women's freedom, including their sexual freedom. Rape and the tacit social tolerance of it convey the message that simply by being sexual, women are 'provocative' and deserve punishment, especially if they step out of their place (the home) or transgress society's definition of the 'good' (inhibited) woman... [In contrast,] the current feminist preoccupation with male violence has a very different focus. Rape and pornography, redefined as a form of rape, are regarded not as aspects of a large sexist system but as the foundation and essence of sexism, while sexual victimization is seen as the central fact of women's oppression. Just as male violence against women is equated with male supremacy, freedom from violence is equated with women's liberation. From this standpoint the positive aspect of freedom – freedom for women to *act* – is at best a secondary concern, and freedom for women to assert an active genital sexuality is, by the logic of neo-Victorianism, a contradiction in terms." (Ellen Willis 1982, 8-9)

Many women of color, particularly within the historical context of slavery in the United States, are reluctant to join the contemporary feminist anti-rape movement on the grounds that (1) "the fraudulent rape charge stands out as one of the most formidable artifices invented by racism. The myth of the Black rapist has been methodically conjured up whenever recurrent waves of violence and terror against the Black community have required convincing justifications"; and (2) as rape victims themselves, Black women have often been shown little sympathy by the police, the courts, and even the mainstream feminist movement. "The historical knot binding Black women – systematically abused and violated by white men – to Black men – maimed and murdered because of the racist manipulation of the rape charge – has just begun to be acknowledged [in feminist analysis] to any significant extent. . . . That Black women have not joined the anti-rape movement en masse does not, therefore, mean that they oppose anti-rape measures in general. Before the end of the nineteenth century pioneering Black clubwomen conducted one of the very first organized public protests against sexual abuse. Their eighty-year-old tradition of organized struggle against rape reflects the extensive and exaggerated ways Black women have suffered the threat of sexual violence. One of racism's salient historical features has always been the assumption that white men – especially those who wield economic power – possess an incontestable right of access to Black women's bodies." (Angela Y. Davis 1981, 173, 175)

Increased discussion, research, and analysis add additional evidence to the view that rape is a crime of violence against women, not primarily sexual in nature, and that rapists are not uniquely distinguishable from the category "normal men." In a number of ways, sexist ideology continues to work within the culture to justify rape by promoting a view of rape as (1) arising from the overwhelming male sex urge and/or need for violence which, since "natural," is dangerous to tamper with; (2) arising from female provocation, conscious or unconscious; (3) arising from the frustration of the male sex urge and/or etc.; (4) arising from the view that males are members of an oppressed class who have been hurt or psychologically defeated and thus feel understandable hostility toward society; and (5) arising from pathology – i.e., the rapist is crazy. (Barbara Mehrhof and Pamela Kearon 1971, 230-1) Feminist analysis involves identifying such ideology as well as "exposing the sexist biases which have distorted the way in which the legal system has treated rapists and rape victims, and advising women as to how best to resist rape." (Mary Anne Warren 1980, 385)

(See MARITAL RAPE, VIOLENCE AGAINST WOMEN)

An example of women's silence in language. Often used metaphorically in common, even academic, conversation (rape of the land, rape of the text), the word *rape*, as Muriel Schulz (1975a) notes, though a four-letter word, is strangely not taboo. Unlike many other terms in English designated as "dirty words," "it is ironic [writes Schulz] that the most vicious sexual act of all is not among them. We have no four letter word for the act of taking women sexually by force"; rather rape is a "remarkably innocuous term" given the violent nature of the act (65). "It seems that there is a form of neutrality about the word *rape*. This apparent incongruity demands some explanation. Starting with the evidence which is irrefutable, we can state that there are at least two individuals involved in rape, the rapist and the rape victim. Their roles are sufficiently different for it to be impossible to encompass the meanings within one name. The experience of being the rapist could not match with the experience of being the rapist's victim; if these two dissimilar events are to be accurately represented in the language, then the minimum requirement would be two very dissimilar names. But there is only one name for this event, and therefore only one question to ask: whose name is it? Whose meanings are encompassed in the seemingly neutral word, *rape*?" (Dale Spender 1980, 178-9) Schulz suggests that the pervasive male belief that the only women who get raped are those who ask for it generates a different set of images associated with the word *rape* than the "frightening reality" it represents for women. For women, writes Spender, it "is an event which cannot be readily symbolized in our language, for the only name which is available names the experience as males see it, as it pertains to them, and there is a huge discrepancy between the male and female experience of this event. The meanings of the dominant group are sufficiently inadequate for females as to be completely false. Because there is no name which represents the trauma of being taken by force, the horror for the rape victim can be compounded. When an act cannot be accurately named it cannot be readily verified, to oneself, or to others. A woman who has been attacked in this way has no other name except *rape* to describe the event, but with the inbuilt neutrality of meaning, *rape* is precisely what she does *not* mean... Women need a word which renames male violence and misogyny and which asserts their blameless nature, a word which places the responsibility for rape where it belongs – on the dominant group." (Dale Spender 1980, 178-80)

"Until recently, rape was considered to be a crime committed by black men against white women; and black men have been lynched, castrated, tortured, and imprisoned for the suspicion of such a crime. The long history of legitimized rape of black women by white men, of white women by white men, of women – black and white – by their husbands and lovers, daughters by their fathers, sisters by their brothers, has only recently, with the emergence of a militant women's consciousness, begun to be documented." (Adrienne Rich 1979, 109)

"We hear and read of the great peril surrounding the white women and young girls of the South. Do the race agitators ever once raise their voice in behalf of the black women and young girls of the South, who are a constant prey of the lust of the white man? Every year hundreds of these respectable women and young girls are ruined by white men. The protection of the law does not reach these poor unfortunates. You don't need to go South, either, to find such a condition: it exists here in New York and Brooklyn. A neatly appearing colored woman is not safe on the streets, unescorted, from the insults of chivalrous white gentlemen." (H. Albro Williamson 1905, letter to the editor, *Evening Post*, March 24, Brooklyn, N.Y.; Williamson/Lyons papers, Schomburg Center for the Study of Black Culture)

"The dirtiest four-letter word in the English language." (Andrea Dworkin 1976, 25)

RAPE FANTASY

"The rape myth suggests that the erect penis is the source of ecstasy for a struggling yet willing female victim; the rape fantasy is the means through which the woman transforms her state of powerlessness into control... Used as a female initiation rite in many novels by women ... [which] allows the young woman to enter her society in a role of power, not powerlessness. In addition, I would suggest that the rape fantasy delineates the female consciousness, one of evasion and irony." (Juliann E. Fleenor 1979, 36)

"to have named rape love
is a heinous crime,
a tearing and twisting
of my mothertongue."
    (Cyndia Cole 1980, 69)

RAPSCALLIONS

"Even at the risk of static from family and friends PROTECT YO KITCH'N. it's hard though. sometimes look like in spite of all you do and as careful as you try to be a rapscallion will slip right in your kitchen. i can't stand rapscallions. among other things they are insensitive. you ask them 'may i offer you something' 'some coffee tea juice water milk juice or maybe an alcoholic beverage.' they always answer 'nah nutin for me' or else they say 'i'll have tea if you got tea bags' or 'coffee if it is instant i don't want to put you through no trouble.' check that out! talking about not going to any trouble. hell they already in your house and that is trouble and personal. what the rapscallions are really saying is dont go to any trouble for me cause i wouldnt go to none for you ... rapscallions love to talk about culture but their actions prove they aint got none. they don't understand that it is about more than the coffee tea or drink of water. it is about extending yourself." (Verta Mae Smart-Grosvenor 1970, 122-3)

RATIONALS

Another name for bloomers; they

constituted a "rational costume" for women in the nineteenth and early twentieth centuries. "Miss E. M. Vance was at one time an official of the Rational Dress League, which was formed about 1890. Lady Harberton, president, was refused lunch in the coffee-room at the Hartboy Hotel, Ockham . . . but offered it in the bar-parlour, which she refused, in pride of her bloomers." A printed circular invited "Supporters of the Rational Costume to attend a Gathering at Oxford [in 1897] . . . 'Only one condition will be enforced, namely: that all ladies must wear Rational Dress. Skirts will not be tolerated under any circumstances.' " (Kuklos 1938, "First Woman Cyclist," *Daily Herald* September 17)

(See BLOOMERS)

RAVE

Crush (British schoolgirl slang). "Little girls of eleven. They have 'raves.' . . . They swoon if Madame Lefèvre says a kind word to them." (Josephine Tey 1947, 27)

READERS

Are very often female. But the word *reader*, like *scholar*, *critic*, and *philosopher*, assumes a masculine sex in most academic writing.

(See DEAR READER)

READING

"Is just as creative an activity as writing. . . Most intellectual development depends upon new readings of old texts." (Angela Carter 1983, 69)

READY MADE

Made outside the home. A good or bad thing depending upon the item, the time period, and circumstances. "Men, for the most part, all but a wealthy and fastidious minority, buy their clothes 'ready made.' No one has ever suggested that ready-made clothes would disrupt the home. But when women buy 'ready made' dishes at the delicatessen store, press and pulpit proclaim the danger." (Charlotte Perkins Gilman 1916a, 23)

REALITY

"A set of statements a culture develops when some group agrees that a particular shared set of statements – its consensus set – represents the *real world*. Our current American set contains statements like the following: Ronald Reagan was a movie actor; Mountains are higher than plains; The gods don't give you three chances; Nobody cares about straight seams anymore. And so on. . . I will refer to the set of statements which constitutes consensus reality as C. . . All that a medium [e.g., television, film, print] has to do to preserve a given reality is to *present no alternatives*. . . In this context, the question 'What do women really want?' ceases to be a catch phrase. It may not be a question that can be answered within ordinary frames of reference. A woman can only express what she really wants in the form of statements of the language that she uses; and then you must imagine what those statements could be true of. And, at the moment, although a woman may have the feeling that there's something very wrong with the reality she's got, and may be able to express in crucifying detail every aspect of that reality, that does not necessarily help her answer the question. She would have to be able to tell you what it was that she would prefer in *place* of the reality she's got. . . Science fiction, including SF fantasy, has offered women an extraordinary opportunity – the potential to present alternative models of reality for other women to examine. . . Up to now, women have used science fiction for this purpose in two ways. First, they have described an alternative reality, M, a matriarchy. C says 'Women are subordinate to men.' M says 'Women are *not* subordinate to men; men are subordinate to women.' Formally, the feature +[male] is rewritten as the feature +[female] in the context of power. Second, women have presented androgyny (Reality A) as an alternative reality. A says 'Women are not subordinate to men, and men are not subordinate to women; they are equal.'

Formally, the set of features +[male] and +[female] is rewritten as null in the context of power... The women who have been exploring M and A have been making one *small* change, as a way of exploring what might happen. And it may very well be that other women, reading those models, reading those descriptions of alternative realities, will say 'Aha! *That* is what I always wanted, and I never knew it until now!' I am not putting down either of those alternatives. But there's a third alternative (which is, of course, nameless), which I will call Reality O [X, Y, Z, Q, W, and R are the male variables; let's use O this time]. O says 'Women are neither subordinate to men nor superior to men, nor equal to men; they are radically *different* from men.' That's O, the strange reality of the third kind, which so far as I know has never been done in science fiction or anywhere else." (Suzette Haden Elgin 1982, 30-1)

What we perceive by way of the senses and the intellect offer forms of reality. "There is another: the experience of a co-existing world/landscape where past and future dance in an eternal present. I can *call* this 'the unconscious'; 'the feminine'; 'God'; 'the irrational'; or I can *explore* it through writing poetry and novels." (Michele Roberts 1983, 68)

"There is always more reality around than we allow for; and there are always more ways to structure it than we use." (Elizabeth Janeway 1980, 34)

"REAL WOMAN"

"A 'real woman' is, in the end, one who wants to please men . . . (never a woman) or possibly an old maid (a failed woman) or if young enough, a tomboy (not yet a woman). A 'real woman' who finds the 'job' of pleasing men unsatisfying is a hysteric. So much for us from where they sit." (Radical Feminists 1972, n.p.)

REASON

Principles of observation. "It has been said that women . . . are never governed by what is called 'reason.' This observa-tion is not correct. Women are not

governed, it is true, by the reason (and experience) of men; they are governed by their own reason (and experience)." (Dr Alice Drysdale Vickery 1907, 7)

(See AUTHORITY, REALITY, THEORY)

Helps determine what is valid and what is not. Reason has been "perplexed and involved in error" because it is confined to male experience and "built on partial experience" and on "narrow views." (Mary Wollstonecraft 1792; quoted in Miriam Kramnick 1978)

REBELLION

"Remember the Ladies, and be more generous and favourable to them than your ancestors. Do not put such unlimited power into the hands of the Husbands. Remember all Men would be tyrants if they could. If particular care and atten-tion is not paid to the Ladies we are determined to foment a Rebellion, and will not hold ourselves bound by any Laws in which we have no voice, or Representation." (Abigail Adams 1776a, letter to her husband John Adams; in Alice Rossi ed. 1973, 10-11)

(See ACTION, REVOLUTION)

"The social system has put us into so many holes that it has no right to ask us [all] to obey the same rules." (Rebecca West 1913, *The Clarion*, November 28)

"Unless woman is going to make trouble she had better not seek her emancipation." (Rebecca West 1912, *Daily Herald*, September 5)

In June 1982, the Grassroots Group of Second Class Citizens, a group of women based mainly in Champaign, Illinois, organized A DAY OF REBELLION at the State Capitol in Springfield to mark and protest the failure of the Equal Rights Amendment to be ratified (Illinois was one of the crucial states in the ratification process). The rebellion took the form of a month-long act of civil disobedience at the capitol in which the women sat in, wore chains to protest the enslavement of women, sang, and took part in individual actions. The simultaneous vigil of another group of women took the form of a hunger strike to symbolize women's hunger for justice. Both groups received wide media coverage and suggest the potential strength of such dramatic campaigns as effective strategies for rebellion.

RECESSION

A time of economic crisis when nurseries are closed down, maternity rights are curtailed, and more women than men become unsalaried. (Anna Coote and Beatrix Campbell 1982, 152)

RECIDIVISM

A return to criminal behavior. A "reversion, by the mass media, to criminal attitudes towards women, towards the dispossessed, towards the powerless. This cultural recidivism warns us that those who would question the standing social order will henceforth be quarantined for shrill and disorderly conduct. . . [It] tells us we 'women's libbers' have changed things enough, and anyway, we can't change things any more than we have." (Naomi Weisstein and Heather Booth 1975, 2)

RECIPE

A form of creation at which women have excelled. "In the past in the Iberian world, [recipes] were poetry, very beautiful; recipes had 'volutas' like a chapel, and beautiful names. Food was a construction, it was like raising a cathedral for them, very modest, but that was what a woman could do. 'Dulces' and 'membrillos' – incredible; a kind of literary product. Like diaries, recipes were 'a primitive form of creation' – 'very fragile, but reflecting some kind of hidden aspiration of women.'" (Nélida Piñon 1982, 71-2)

No substitute for money. Susan Benjamin, editor at Big Mama Rag and mother of two handicapped sons, wrote to President Ronald Reagan to protest budget cuts in education funds for disabled children. The White House responded: with two large, glossy photos of the President, a form letter on volunteerism, and a recipe for crabmeat casserole. (Matrix 1982, July, 3)

RECLAIM THE NIGHT

Yearly demonstrations to protest men's control of streets at night. On November 23, 1977, in Leeds 130 women sang protest songs in City Square; 400 marched in Manchester, 100 marched with torches in Newcastle, 80 marched in York, hundreds invaded Soho in London. Similar marches were held throughout the U.S. (called Take Back the Night marches). These organized protests developed into large, more explicitly political campaigns such as Women Against Violence Against Women. (Anna Coote and Beatrix Campbell 1982, 44-5)

(See TAKE BACK THE NIGHT)

RECLAMATION

Feminist linguistic process in which individual words and concepts, given negative meanings through patriarchal traditions and writings, are identified, examined, redefined, and thus reclaimed. Mary Daly's work illustrates this strategy, as do the titles of many feminist periodicals (Shrew, Sappho, Telewoman) and other feminist writings. "Mother (Jewish or not) is still unclaimed, charged with negativity, though on its way to more positive ground; it shows up as a positive word/concept more in our art than in our conversations. In a class I taught jointly with Paula King, we had the group list every bad word we could think of about women; the assignment was then to pick one and reclaim it."

"As women and as lesbians we have learned to reclaim names like

dyke
bitch
manhater
golddigger
shrew
harpy
whore
cunt
amazon
(even) lesbian
even woman had first to be reclaimed from
    a place of squeamishness

As Jewish women and Jewish lesbians, we

need to reclaim words like

pushy
loud
politico
power trippy
cheap
dominating
garish
sexy
emotional
always screaming
bossy
scary temper
difficult style
(and, of course) Jewish mother
(and) Jewish princess." (Melanie Kaye
    1982, 44, 38)

(See AMAZON, FEMINIST
DICTIONARY, PERIODICALS,
PRINCESS, SHREW, WITCH)

RE-CONSIDER

"For women to re-consider our earlier
paternally prescribed tendencies, deceptively mis-named 'decisions,' is nothing
less than daring to see, name, and reach
for the stars." (Mary Daly 1978, 55)

RED

Is the description chosen by many North
American Indians to describe collectively
the native Indian people of North
America, whatever their Tribe or color
(there are some 200 officially identified
Tribes at present). For example, Women
of All Red Nations (WARN) is an activist
group of American Indian women who
focus on issues affecting the Indian
community.

(See ASIAN-AMERICAN, BLACK,
WHITE)

Red is also chosen by others as a name.
"Why 'Red' for my woman name?
Because red has always been my favorite
color? Because it is simple, primary,
strong? Because the single red geranium
my grandmother grew was my favorite
flower, vibrant life in a closed house?"
Other associations: a child's red rubber
ball, a glowing fire, Virginia creepers,
anger. (Ida VSW Red 1981, 67-8)

RED DIAPER BABIES

Young people whose parents had been at
one time in or associated with the
Communist Party; they, like other
children of parents from radical traditions
(socialists; labor, religious, and peace
activists; left-wing Zionists) made up a
large proportion of the early New Left in
the U.S. (Sara Evans 1980, 120)

(See RED DIAPER FEMINISTS)

RED DIAPER FEMINISTS

The daughters of U.S. radical families
emerged as leading figures in the revival
of the "woman question" in the 1960s;
"they had a tradition out of which they
could name oppression, and growing up
with the role models of politically active
mothers, they drew strength from the
sense of participating in an activist heritage... Again and again, when a voice
was raised within the new left pointing
out male domination at Chicago, at
Harvard, at Wellesley, at Swarthmore, at
Michigan, it came from one of these
women – these 'red diaper feminists.' "
(Sara Evans 1980, 120, 124)

(See RED DIAPER BABIES,
WOMAN QUESTION)

REDSTOCKINGS

Radical Feminist group of New York
which stated in its principles: "'We do not
ask what is radical, revolutionary, reformist, or moral – we ask: Is it good for
women or bad for women?" Originally
called Group One, the later name
Redstockings (coined by Shulamith
Firestone in 1969) "was intended to
represent a synthesis of two traditions:
that of the earlier feminist theoreticians
and writers who were insultingly called
Bluestockings in the 19th century and the
militant political tradition of radicals –
the red of revolution." (Kathie Sarachild
1975a, 30, 1975b, 55)

(See BLUESTOCKINGS,
PRO-WOMAN LINE, RADICAL
FEMINISM, RED DIAPER
FEMINISTS)

"Two constructs seem to underlie Redstockings; sisterhood and consciousness-

raising. Some members of Redstockings developed the language and psychology of sisterhood, which is basic to modern feminism. This is not to say that the word sister [is not used] or feminine solidarity is not practiced by other groups of women in other cities, but Redstockings has the most strongly verbalized pro-woman line of all the groups." The group gained national public consciousness when they disrupted the New York legislature's 1969 abortion hearings; among other actions, they organized a public consciousness-raising session in which women testified about their experiences with abortion. (Celestine Ware 1970, 38-9)

REFORM
"When the oppressed are worn out in the game of chasing the elusive shadow of Success, some 'successes' are permitted to occur – 'victories' which can easily be withdrawn when the victim's energies have been restored. Subsequently, women are lured into repeating efforts to regain the hard-won apparent gains... Because the 'changes' that are achieved are victories in a vacuum, that is, in a totally oppressive social context, they do not essentially free the Female Self but instead function to hide both the fact of continuing oppression and the possibilities for better options and for more radical freedom." (Mary Daly 1978, 375)

REFORMATION
Anti-feminist upheaval. "Where it did not sweep the convent away altogether, it narrowed its scope and sapped its influence; and, being anti-feminist, evolved no new system to take the place of that which it had swept away." (Cicely Hamilton 1909, 87-8)

REFORMING MEN
"It is a mistake to see men as pitiable victims or vessels to be 'saved' through female self-sacrifice. However possessed males may be within patriarchy, it is *their* order; it is they who feed on women's stolen energy. It is a trap to imagine that women should 'save' men from the

dynamics of demonic possession; and to attempt this is to fall deeper into the pit of patriarchal possession." (Mary Daly 1978, 2)

RE-FUSING
"Is essential to the process of the Self's re-membering, re-fusing." (Mary Daly 1978, 67)

RELATIONSHIP BETWEEN THE SEXES
"Through all the ages of the world's history the more powerful sex has been liable to use their power carelessly, not for protection only, but for pain." (Josephine Butler 1868, 12)

RELIGION
"The ideological reflection of... sexual domination and subjugation" (Rosemary Radford Ruether 1974, 9) and long a focus of feminist reform and revolutionary struggle.

(See BIBLE, CHRISTIANITY, JUDAISM, NONSEXIST LANGUAGE, PRAYER, SPIRITUALITY)

Practices of divinity whose functions are confined to males, "to attract some of them at least to those duties they have such a general apathy for." (Sophia 1739, 46)

"Word has come from Rome commanding a radical change in the music of the Roman Catholic church, by removal of women singers from the choirs. The American bishops refer to this papal order as a measure for the reform of 'an abuse' in the church – the services." ("Poor Woman!" 1904, editorial, *The Liberal Review*, 1:4, 186)

"Sets standards ahead of human conduct." Developed by man who "pictured his early gods as like to himself, and they behaved in accordance with his ideals." (Charlotte Perkins Gilman 1911, 138, 141)

"Can a woman be ordained to the priesthood? Is she allowed to teach in the church? Can she become a pope? Can she celebrate the sacraments? Can she give absolution, or expound the word of God?

Is she the peer of man in this divine and infallible church? Is she not, on the contrary, nearly a nonentity as far as the sacred privileges of the church are concerned? She is not even allowed to sing in church." (Editorial 1905, *The Liberal Review* 2:2, 80)

"While Western religions have traditionally portrayed the spiritual nature of human beings and their relation to God in male terms, sexuality is portrayed as female, the embodiment of sin, forever distracting men from godliness: sons of God but daughters of Eve. Catalysts in a cosmic struggle between evil and good, women are defined as extremes of the sexuality men experience – whore or virgin, agent of Satan or mother of God." (Casey Miller and Kate Swift 1976, 67)

"Once after a church service the missionaries asked for a collection as they always did. The Kiowas had always given what they could and didn't say anything, but the religion was new to them and they didn't quite understand how it worked. One old Kiowa man stood up and pulled some change from his pocket and looked at it long and hard. He seemed reluctant to give up his last bit of money. Old Mokeen stood there and squared his shoulders and spoke to one of the missionaries in broken English. 'Whatza matter this Jesus – He all time broke'" (Ethel C. Krepps 1979, 155)

REPRESENTATION

A term used to refer to the way women are presented which implies that images do not simply reflect social conditions but are themselves selected, constructed, and purveyed within specific social and ideological settings. The issue of how women are portrayed, written about, and constructed in a variety of mediums (fiction, nonfiction, scholarship, newspapers, magazines, films, radio, television, advertising, etc.) has consistently engaged feminist attention. Analysis has moved from an earlier concern with the nature of images of women (number, content, stereotyping) to an exploration of the structures (social, corporate, economic),

mechanisms, motives, personnel, audiences, and traditions involved in the construction, perception, and study of representations. Questions include: Do portrayals of women accurately reflect the population portrayed? Are images of women affected by the sex of their creators? Who controls the production of certain representations? Who benefits? Do representations reflect and reproduce prevailing social values? Or do they play a part in creating these values? How does the audience (reader, viewer, hearer) figure in the representation process? What artistic or aesthetic traditions are brought into play?

(See ADVERTISING, ART, MEANING, MISS AMERICA PROTEST, PHALLUS, POPULAR CULTURE, PORNOGRAPHY, POST-PARTUM DOCUMENT)

"How does representation work? What is the difference between a newspaper account of a rape and a fictionalized account of a rape; a porno account of a rape and our fantasy about a rape?" (*Diary of a Conference* 1982, 18)

In advertisements, "women tend to be represented as housewives and/or sex objects. Clearly there have been some changes in the representations over the past ten years or so, but women are still depicted in a limited array of roles... Women are written about, or depicted, in stereotypical ways and ... these are different from the ways in which men are written about and depicted. Great emphasis is placed on the woman's role as sex object, housewife and mother and little emphasis is placed on women's role as wage-earners... Little attention is paid to women as independent beings – independent, that is, from men or from the family." (Veronica Beechey with Richard Allen 1982, 34)

"To those who still ask, 'What do women want?' the cinema seems to provide no answer. For the cinema, in its alignment with the fantasies of the voyeur, has historically articulated its stories through a conflation of its central axis of seeing/being seen with the opposition male/female. . . Cinematic images of woman have been so consistently oppressive and repressive that the very idea of a feminist filmmaking practice seems an impossibility. The simple gesture of directing a camera toward a woman has become equivalent to a terrorist act. This state of affairs – the result of a history which inscribes woman as subordinate – is not simply to be overturned by a contemporary practice that is more aware, more self-conscious. The impasse confronting feminist filmmakers today is linked to the force of a certain theoretical discourse which denies the neutrality of the cinematic apparatus itself. A machine for the production of images and sounds, the cinema generates and guarantees pleasure by a corroboration of the spectator's identity. Because that identity is bound up with that of the voyeur and the fetishist, because it requires for its support the attributes of the 'noncastrated,' the potential for illusory mastery of the signifier, it is not accessible to the female spectator, who, in buying her ticket, must deny her sex. There are no images either *for* her or *of* her. . . If the female body is not necessarily always excluded within this problematic, it must always be placed within quotation marks. For it is precisely the massive reading, writing, filming of the female body which constructs and maintains a hierarchy along the lines of a sexual difference assumed as natural. The ideological complicity of the concept of the natural dictates the impossibility of a nostalgic return to an unwritten body. Thus, contemporary filmmaking addresses itself to the activity of uncoding, de-coding, deconstructing the given images. It is a project of de-familiarization whose aim is not necessarily that of seeing the female body differently, but of exposing the habitual meanings/values attached to femininity as cultural constructions." (Mary Ann Doane 1981, 23-4)

REPRODUCTION

"Not the essential aim of existence for either half of the human race. . . Every faculty bestowed by the Creator upon the creature, is bestowed for reverent use, not for irreverent and selfish abuse, and the reproductive faculty, like every other, is subject to the control of reason and morality. The faculties of reason and conscience are the signs of the *human* nature, and of the right of the human being to voluntary and responsible self-government." "The point of view [that a woman is 'eminently, essentially, and primarily a child-begetting animal' reduces her to the level of a cow." (Josephine Butler 1874a, 18)

One of the elements that must be transformed if women are to achieve liberation. "Women's absence from the critical sector of production historically . . . has been caused not just by their physical weakness in a context of coercion – but also by their role in reproduction. Maternity necessitates periodic withdrawals from work, but this is not a decisive phenomenon. It is rather women's role in reproduction which has become, in capitalist society at least, the spiritual 'complement' of men's role in production. Bearing children, bringing them up, and maintaining the home – these form the core of woman's natural vocation, in this ideology. . . Reproduction, it has been stressed, is a seemingly constant atemporal phenomenon – part of biology rather than history. In fact, this is an illusion. What is true is that the 'mode of reproduction' does not vary with the 'mode of production'; it can remain effectively the same through a number of different modes of production. For it has been defined till now, by its uncontrollable, natural character. To this extent, it has been an unmodified biological fact. . . . [because of which] women were effectively doomed to social exploitation. In any sense, they were not masters of a large part of their lives." (Juliet Mitchell 1966, rpt. 1984, 30-2)

"Women's reproductive lives are integrative because they reproduce children, a value in society. Men, who can not participate in the whole process of reproductive labor, are alienated and they have

needed to seek other kinds of creativity –
such as abstract thought and political life
– to create a continuity of their own. They
also have appropriated reproduction
through their physical and legal control of
women and children." (Mary O'Brien
1981, 116-39)

"It is noticeable that those who urge
women to breed, are men, or
imperialistically-minded women, to whom
consciously or unconsciously more babies
are but material in the great game of
personal or national aggrandizement."
(B. Liber 1919, 7)

"Women are not oppressed because of
the biological fact of reproduction, but are
oppressed by men who define this reproductive capacity as a function. 'The truth
is that childbearing isn't the function of
women. The function of childbearing is
the function of men oppressing women.'"
(Ti Grace Atkinson 1974; in Zillah
R. Eisenstein 1979c, 44)

Tends to be seen by women and by
physicians from radically different perspectives – that is, in terms of "competing
ideologies." (Hilary Graham and Ann
Oakley 1981, 50)

REPRODUCTIVE FREEDOM

A basic human right introduced as a
phrase by feminists in the 1970s and
defined to include safe contraception and
abortion, freedom from forced sterilization, and health care during pregnancy
and birth. Discussion of this issue previously went under the heading of
"population control," a term which
implied authoritarian power directed at
some races and economic groups more
than others. (Gloria Steinem 1980, 15)
"*Reproductive freedom* stated the right of the
individual to decide to have or not to
have a child. Though obviously a right
that is more important to women, it also
protects men." (Gloria Steinem 1983,
151-2)

REPRODUCTIVE IDEOLOGY

A view of women as being totally defined
by their bodies and "as more reproductive
than men." (B. Ettore 1980, 8)

REPUTATION

Is "vested in men." (Elizabeth Robins
1913, 6) For a woman, often a necessary
possession for contracting a suitable marriage; a woman who had "lost" her
reputation was "damaged goods."

RESEARCH

Is supposed to be disinterested. Claudine
Hermann, as many other feminists have
suggested, argues that the "work that
appears to be the most disinterested is
nothing but an empire being created with
a new master, and to construct his new
pyramids each man must find his own
slaves." (Claudine Hermann 1976b, 88)
"Is formalized curiosity. It is poking and
prying with purpose." (Zora Neale
Hurston 1942, 49) Has often been conducted at women's expense. "If you laugh
at women your laboratory will lie."
(Cynthia Ozick 1972a, 66)

(See METHOD, OBJECTIVITY,
REALITY, THEORY)

RESEARCH ESTABLISHMENT

"Is the last and best-protected residence
of patriarchal hegemony. It defines
'correct ideas' and 'correct ways of thinking.' It does not tolerate criticism. . .
Childbirth is by doctors, divorce by
lawyers, and teaching by tenured educators. Knowledge, in this contemporary
social order, comes from 'researchers'"
(Hugh Drummond 1983, 46)

RESISTANCE

To feminism: "They are not afraid of
what we are *against*. They are afraid of
what we are *for*. What we are for is so
much more powerful than what we are
against." (Kathleen Barry 1980, 312)

RESISTANCE TACTICS OF SECRETARIES

Willingness to go on dumb errands
laziness
taking extra time in the ladies' room
misfiling important letters
'forgetting' to correct typos
   (Judith Ann 1970, 86-100)

RE-VISION

"Re-vision – the act of looking back, of seeing with fresh eyes, of entering an old text from a new critical direction – is for women more than a chapter in cultural history: it is an act of survival." (Adrienne Rich 1979, 35)

REVOLUTION

Literally, movement, as of a body in an orbit or circle; drastic change, in which one government, structure, or paradigm is overthrown and another takes its place. "For many of us, the word 'revolution' itself has become not only a dead relic of Leftism, but a key to the deadendedness of male politics: the 'revolution' of a wheel which returns in the end to the same place; the 'revolving door' of a politics which has 'liberated' women only to use them, and only within the limits of male tolerance. When we speak of *transformation* we speak more accurately out of the vision of a process which will leave neither surfaces nor depths unchanged, which enters society at the most essential level of the subjugation of women and nature by men." (Adrienne Rich 1979, 248)

"Women must come together and become politically powerful to prevent relapses in the revolution. They struggle in the revolution, they fight colonialism and fight for national independence, and afterwards they ought to participate in the government as half of society. They ought to have the same rights as men. But this does not happen because women lack political power." (Nawal el Saadawi 1980a, 3)

"The Longest Revolution": an essay by Juliet Mitchell which attempts to describe woman's condition in terms of its separate structures "which together form a complex – not a simple – unity. This will mean rejecting the idea that woman's condition can be deduced derivatively from the economy or equated symbolically with society... Because the unity of woman's condition at any one time is the product of several structures, it is always 'overdetermined.' The key structures can

be listed as follows: Production, Reproduction, Sex and Socialisation of Children." For Mitchell, revolution requires change in all four structures. (Juliet Mitchell 1966, rpt. 1984, 26)

"Is a spark from two girls combing each other's hair." (Vistoria Redel 1981, 12)

"To die for the revolution is a one-shot deal; to live for the revolution means taking on the more difficult commitment of changing our day-to-day life patterns." (Frances Beale 1970, 99)

"I used to dream militant
dreams . . .
I used to dream radical dreams . . .
I even used to think i'd be the one
to stop the riot and negotiate the peace
then i awoke and dug
that if i dreamed natural
dreams of being a natural
woman doing what a woman
does when she's natural
i would have a revolution"
(Nikki Giovanni 1970, "Revolution" n.p.)

"It's not that women have more to gain; it's that they have nothing to lose." (Haydee Santamaria, Cuban Revolutionary leader; interview in Margaret Randall 1974, 318)

"*The real revolution is always concerned with the least glamorous stuff.* With raising a reading level from second grade to third. With simplifying history and writing it down (or reciting it) for the old folks. With helping illiterates fill out food-stamp forms – for they must eat, revolution or not." (Alice Walker 1971, 135)

"Furious women know that patriarchy is itself a continual resurrection of the past, a series of processions. No social revolution, however 'radical,' that falls short of metapatriarchal movement can break the circles of repetition." (Mary Daly 1978, 42)

"*A revolution capable of healing our wounds.* If we're the ones who can imagine it, if we're the ones who dream about it, if we're the ones who need it most, then no one else can do it. *We're the ones.*" (Aurora Levins Morales 1981, 56)

RHYTHM METHOD

Form of reproductive control practiced by women in many cultures, often because (especially in Catholic countries) other forms are neither easily nor safely available. Sometimes ridiculed as ineffectual:

– What do you call two people who use the rhythm method?
– Parents.

(Graffiti cited by Rachel Bartlett 1982)

RIGHT HONOURABLE

The term "as applied to certain persons must be taken ironically, as when an opponent cheers his enemy." (Mary Lowndes 1913a, 256)

RIGHTS

"It is not enough to win rights. One must be able to keep them." (A. Afetnan; cited in Naila Minai 1981, 162)
(See EQUAL RIGHTS)

RING

Golden signifier of attachment, usually to a husband: "It was the ring on the left hand that people at the Old Girls' Reunion looked for. Often, in fact nearly always, it was an uninteresting ring, sometimes no more than the plain gold band or the very smallest and dimmest of diamonds. Perhaps the husband was also of this variety, but as he was not seen at this female gathering he could only be imagined." (Barbara Pym 1952, 112) Feminist rings often signify love between women, militant struggle, or matriarchal culture.

RIPENING

The growth and unfolding of the "continuous woman" linked biologically, historically, and spiritually to other generations of women, through struggle and survival. (Meridel LeSueur 1982) "I don't admit age. I call it ripening. Like all of Nature, we are transformed into future seed. Ripening has distinct advantages for women – they have a chance to regain their full identity as a person." (Meridel LeSueur 1984, 34)

RIVALIZE

To portray women as rivals, thus defining their relationship to each other only in reference to the person or object for which they are presumed to be competing. In *The Waterfall*, Margaret Drabble makes "an attempt not to rivalize women." (Gayatri Chakravorty Spivak, in press)

ROCK AND ROLL

Until the present, rock and roll had the most influential presence of women in its history during the period 1958-65. Those were the years of the Girl Groups: young, all-female, and often black groups of singers who were brought together and produced by white, male producers, although Motown also had a few girl groups. They sang songs by contracted songwriters, about love and romance, "the boy." Their names, which were often also produced for them, reflect the yielding, diminutive, but sexy image these groups were meant to convey: the Chantels, the Shirelles, Kathy Young and the Innocents, the Marvelettes, the Angels, Darlene Love and the Crystals, the Cookies, Ronnie and the Ronettes, the Dixie Cups, the Jelly Beans, the Toys, the Chiffons, the Shangri-Las, Little Eva, and the Jaynettes. The names are edible or ethereal, always infantilizing or idealizing.

The next wave of women's prominence in rock and roll is the current (1976-present) period, with after-punk music being made by all-female bands. These groups exploded in the wake of such influential figures in punk as Patti Smith, Poly Styrene of X-Ray Spex, and the Slits and the Raincoats, the last two being the first punk all-women groups. Like the Girl Group era, the image these women convey is made explicit in their names. Unlike the Cookies or the Toys, these groups of women formed, discovered, and named themselves. Some names are ironic plays on the history of naming girl groups, others are departures calculated to shock, or to disrupt gender reference: the Real Insects, the Nancy Boys, Ministry of Marriage, the Androids of

Mu, Sisterhood of Spit, the Waitresses, Poison Girls, Au Pairs, Inflatable Boy Clams, Unknown Gender, Mydolls, the Bloods, ESG-Extra Sensory Girls, the Weather Girls, Killer Pussy, Catholic Girls, Blood and Lipstick, the Mo-dettes, Neo Boys, the Belle Stars, Die Hausfrauen (a German band "the house-wives"), Lora Logic, Kleenex (who when sued by the maker of Kleenex changed their name to Lilliput), the Marine Girls, the L.A. Girls, the Skirts, the Screaming Sirens, Butch, Sin 34, Lost Cherrees, Hot Food to Go, Amy and the Angels, and I.U.D. (Sally Green 1984, correspondence)

(See NAMES, PERIODICALS, POPULAR CULTURE, REPRESENTATION)

An industry which has depended economically upon a female teenage audience. A repeatedly stereotyped, parodied, and demeaned group, adolescent women rock fans in fact represent a diverse population. "The basic Rock Writer's Irritating Generalizations about Teenage Female Fans can be summarized as follows": (1) female fantasies consist of wanting to fuck rock stars; (2) teenage female interest in rock consists in wanting to fuck rock stars; (3) teenage females long to be their idol's groupies; (4) girls who like wimpy, soft pop don't daydream about sex. As a corrective to these generalizations, the following cross-cultural perspectives are offered: (1) Not all girls dream about rock stars; (2) some of the blandest girls, with the blandest musical tastes, are among the most perversely horny; (3) even with the New Sexual Openness, lots of girls really don't know what it's about (even intense desire can have surrealistically innocent overtones); (4) some females couldn't care less about the people making music on their records, or the music scene it came out of; (5) many rock star-crazed girls have a wide variety of interests; (6) women don't automatically condone the morals, drug intake, or male chauvinism of the rock star they worship; (7) a desire for sex shouldn't be confused with a desire to get fucked (teenage girls'

daydreams about sex rarely involved anonymous quickies with people who don't care about them; for every girl who daydreams about being a groupie, there must be at least 100 who daydream about being writers, musicians, photographers, costume designers, or poets); (8) desire for male attention isn't the same as sexual desire (many girls' fantasies are of friendship or working partners); (9) some fantasies are of the 'I wish I was my favorite star' type. In fact, probably more girls have daydreamed about being Mick Jagger than of being Bebe Buell, Britt Ekland, and Anita Pallenberg combined; (10) lots of females who love rock music never go to big concerts. "Ultimately, the female rock audience can no more be defined than can the male rock audience." (Lori Twersky 1983, 27-9)

A symbol of rebellion, even if compromised or poorly understood. "Women identified with youth culture as the only alternative to our parents' uptight and unhappy way of life. We linked up with rock and never saw how it fucked us over. Partly this was because we had no sense of being women together with other women. Partly because it was impossible to think of ourselves as performing as exhibitionists in macho sex roles, so we didn't wonder why there weren't more of us on stage. Partly because we identified with the men and not the other women when we heard the lyrics that put women down." (*RAT* 1970, 17)

"Listening to most rock-and-roll was like walking down the street at night, automatically checking out the men in my vicinity: this one's okay; that one could be trouble, watch out. Listening to most feminist music was like taking a warm bath." (Ellen Willis 1977, 99)

A symbol of women's continuing oppression in the face of apparently increasing freedom. "We must be strong enough to realize that even if we are free to smoke dope, speak hip and seem free as part of the hip scene, if we do not have complete control over our lives, our time, our bodies, our images we are still ripped off, even if we're surrounded by pretty colors, rock music, and waves of smoke." (The Women's Center, Philadelphia, 1971, 10)

A legitimate form of expression for women in which their creativity, artistry, and emotional commitments are almost wholly appropriated by men. "Watching men groove on Janis [Joplin], I began to appreciate the resentment many black people feel towards whites who are blues freaks. Janis sang out of her pain as a woman, and men dug it. Yet it was the men who caused the pain... In a way their adulation was the cruelest insult of all." (Ellen Willis 1976, 64)

"A frenzied celebration of masculine supremacy." (Toni Carabillo 1974; cited in Elaine Partnow 1977, 294)

"Rock remains a machismo cult, a rebellion of young men against old. Its sexual content reproduces and caricatures existing values.... As elsewhere, rock shows women as idealized, unreal male-fantasy people: the all-understanding women, the dependable women, the women who won't come up with the sexual goods and so on." (Lindsay Cooper 1978, 11)

Is a potential vehicle for feminist politics which can transform rather than reproduce cultural stereotypes about gender. "Women and men should be playing in groups together, women playing the instruments, writing the material. And not just having a 'chick' sex object singer, in a male group. There's nothing new about that. But women playing drums or electric guitar is somehow very threatening to our images of what is feminine and masculine." (Arlene Brown 1970, 26)

"The band is just a great form of propaganda because it's not intellectual and it's not theoretical and it's not formal and it's not [something that is just] some person who is an expert talking to somebody who needs to have their consciousness raised. It's a group of people being together in a way that's creative and which other people can participate in by listening and dancing. You have given your whole body and your whole senses instead of some tiny part of your brain." (*RAT* 1971, 9)

"Implicit in the formal language of mass art is the possibility that given the right sort of social conditions, it can act as a catalyst that transforms its mass audience into an oppositional community. This is precisely what rock-and-roll did." (Ellen Willis 1981, xvii)

"I had on my gold Elvis Presley-type suit, jumping around and doing some rockabilly numbers, and this girl came up to me aftc: the show and said, 'Well there's some interesting conversations about you going around in the audience.' I said, 'Oh yeah? Tell me about it.' She said, 'Well, those guys in back of me were having an argument about whether you were a transsexual or not.' I said, 'Holy shit, really? Why would they think that?' And she said, 'Well, these guys around here, they've never seen a girl look like you before.'" (Pearl E. Gates 1980, 31)

"I'm a woman and do what I do, and of course my sexuality has a lot to do with what I do, because it's *rock and roll*." (Ellen Foley 1980, 33)

"There is no bullshit going down with rock and roll. It's an honest form, and one of the most open. It goes beyond color, gender, anything." (Patti Smith 1982, poster)

ROLE

"A prison." (Virginia Woolf; cited in Midge Lennert and Norma Willson eds 1973, 10) "The notion of 'role' focuses attention more on individuals than on social structure, and implies that 'the female role' and 'the male role' are complementary (separate or different but equal). The terms are depoliticizing: they strip experience from its historical and political context and neglect questions of power and conflict. It is significant that sociologists do not speak of 'class roles' or 'race roles.'" (Judith Stacey and Barrie Thorne 1984)

(See SEX ROLE)

ROLE MODEL

"I dislike the term 'role model' partly

because of the context in which I first heard it." "It was explained to me that, for role-modelhood, even at a university, scholarship was not the only requirement. One also had to be punctual, clean behind the ears, a good mother, well dressed, and socially presentable. I'm afraid I'm a bad role model, but then, I long ago decided that I could be either a good role model or a writer, and for better or worse I chose writing." (Margaret Atwood 1982, 217, 330)

ROMANCE

Something the media are obsessed with, not unrelated to "commercial pressures to buy romance objects (engagement rings, mementoes, wedding dresses and so on)" and heterosexual sex. "Romance doesn't magically just happen. Rather, it's the result of unconscious choices, social pressures, and girls' and women's attempts to escape the boredom of everyday life." "Women and girls are faced with dull uninteresting jobs, with little chance of good training, never mind promotion, and rarely if ever are they encouraged into the kinds of *collective* activity necessary to change this situation. It is not surprising, then, that most girls opt for the most easily available *individual* solution. Boy, romance, sports car, lazy weekend." "Girls and women can use romance to transform the more crudely *sexual* relationship offered to them by boys and men and make them more palatable for female consumption. That is, romance stresses all-over sensuality and gentleness rather than straightforward genital sex, it demands softness rather than aggression, sensitivity rather than 'screwing.' " (Myra Connell et al. 1981, 165-6)

"For centuries has been the sweetener – artificial at that – of a woman's virtual serfdom within a monogamous relationship." (Carol Cassel 1984, 119)

"If there is to be any romance in marriage women must be given every chance to earn a decent living at other occupations. Otherwise no man can be sure that he is loved for himself alone, and that his wife did not come to the Registry Office because she had had no luck at the Labour Exchange." (Rebecca West 1912, *Manchester Daily Dispatch*, November 26)

"Like the rabbit at the dog track, is the illusive, fake and never attained reward which for the benefit and amusement of our masters keeps us running and thinking in safe circles." (Beverly Jones 1970, 59)

"A rosy glow which blinds adolescent girls to the realities of the labour market." (Sara Delamont 1980, 70)

ROMANCES

A controversial form of popular culture; they are written almost exclusively for women readers, are enormously successful in economic terms, give pleasure and a sense of adventure to large numbers of women readers, make some feminists uncomfortable who perceive them in ideological support of a feminist backlash, and are themselves increasingly self-conscious about their own status and mission. "If placed end to end, Harlequin books sold in 1981 could run along both sides of the Nile, both sides of the Amazon, and one side of the Rio Grande. If all the words of all the Harlequin books sold in 1981 were laid end to end, they would stretch 1000 times around the earth and 93 times to the moon." (Harlequin publicity release, quoted in Margaret Ann Jensen 1984, 15) Romances, which make up more than half the book sales in the U.S., have been seen as a mass market form in which women's lives are important. In updated versions, "the heroines now have well-paying jobs and independent lives, and the hero is a partner, not a reason for being. Even the required happy ending is not always sacred. Given their limitations – mostly heterosexual, mostly white middle class – current romances do show a positive view of the world, encouraging women to be active in pursuing work and pleasure. The 'cold bitch other woman' has been dropped, and women in current romances are much more apt to be warm and supportive friends." (Emily Toth 1984,

12-13) Another point of view is that "Harlequins, in addition to stabilizing the authority relationship, eroticize it and are, in fact, a form of feminine pornography." (Janet Patterson 1981, 33)

(See GOTHIC NOVEL, HARLEQUIN ROMANCES)

A scene from a romance novel mocks male criticism of the genre:

"Historical dramas and love stories?" he queried. . . "Do many women read that junk?"

Kyla gave him a level glance. "What do *you* read for relaxation, Mr. Nathan? The *Encyclopedia Britannica*?"

His mouth quirked a little in acknowledgement of her sarcasm. "Actually, I like a good thriller, and occasionally I read a Western. Which leaves me wide open, I suppose?"

"Yes, doesn't it?" Kyla agreed pleasantly. "If your fantasies run to mayhem and murder and the occasional smoking six-gun, do you think you can afford to criticize women for preferring to read about romantic encounters with Regency gentlemen or desert sheiks? Surely theirs is a less harmful kind of fantasy than the violent kind that men seem to indulge in?" (Daphne Clair, *The Loving Trap*; in Margaret Ann Jensen 1984, 27-8)

ROMANTICISM

"Is largely responsible for keeping people in ignorance about sex and maintaining many of our most oppressive myths. Women have tolerated miserable sexual relationships, faked orgasms, and generally kept quiet about their needs, all in the name of Romantic Love." (Eleanor Stephens 1975; in Marsha Rowe 1982, 324)

ROOM OF ONE'S OWN

In *A Room of One's Own* (1929), Virginia Woolf argued that a "woman must have money and a room of her own if she is to write fiction" (4) – something few women writers have had. The book, originally delivered as a lecture to women students, exemplifies Woolf's attempt to replace the pedantic male lecture format, which she hated, with what Jane Marcus has called a "trialogue" between female author, female audience, and female readers. A major source of ideas for the modern women's movement and especially for feminist literary criticism, *A Room of One's Own* touches on, among other things, economic oppression, male scholarship, feminist scholarship, traditions in women's writings, authority, women's relationships with women, and women's discourse. Sandra Gilbert and Susan Gubar's collection of essays on women poets, *Shakespeare's Sisters*, takes its title from Woolf's piece. (Sandra M. Gilbert and Susan Gubar eds 1979.)

Not something all women can count on. "Forget the room of one's own – write in the kitchen, lock yourself up in the bathroom. Write on the bus or the welfare line, on the job or during meals, between sleeping or waking. I write while sitting on the john. No long stretches at the typewriter unless you're wealthy or have a patron – you may not even own a typewriter. While you wash the floor or clothes listen to the words chanting in your body. When you're depressed, angry, hurt, when compassion and love possess you. When you cannot help but write." (Gloria Anzaldúa 1981a, 170)

"Not many women get to live out the daydream of women – to have a room, even a section of a room." (Maxine Hong Kingston 1975, 72)

ROSH HASHANAH

Jewish High Holiday which begins the Jewish year; "the time when God opens the Book of Life and judges each individual's deeds of the past year over a ten-day period of repentance which culminates in Yom Kippur. Thus Jews wish each other a good inscription for the coming year as a new year's greeting" (Evelyn Torton Beck ed. 1982, 283). A time when, according to the Yerushalmi *Talmud*, "Jews should not appear depressed and in somber clothes, as suppliants before a human judge, but joyous, dressed in festive white, betokening a cheerful and

confident spirit." (Leo Rosten 1968, 504)
(See ROSH HODESH)

ROSH HODESH

The first day of the Hebrew month, or New Moon; traditionally a Jewish women's holiday, feminists have revived it as an important ritual because, though a "minor" holiday, it is the only women's holiday that has been preserved. (Some women feel its unimportance was what enabled it to survive patriarchal gate-keeping.)

ROSIE THE RIVETER

Song written during World War II to glamorize working women. Its popularity died when the boys came marching home and the wartime Rosies were given pink slips (Lorraine Sorrel 1981, 25). Virtually all women were affected: women physicians took out a full page newspaper ad headed DOCTORS WANTED: NO WOMEN NEED APPLY to dramatize their situation (Mary Roth Walsh 1977). "Rosie the Riveter" became a film, frequently shown to feminist gatherings, courses, and film festivals.

ROYALTY

"For centuries a certain family has been segregated; bred with a care only lavished upon race-horses; splendidly housed, clothed, and fed; abnormally stimulated in some ways, suppressed in others; worshipped, stared at, and kept shut up, as lions and tigers are kept, in a beautiful brightly lit room behind bars. The psychological effect upon them must be profound; and the effect upon us is as remarkable. Sane men and women as we are, we cannot rid ourselves of the superstition that there is something miraculous about these people shut up in their cage." (Virginia Woolf 1934; in Michèle Barrett 1979, 193-4)

RUBBISH

Garbage put out by men!

RUBYFRUIT JUNGLE

"When I make love to women I think of their genitals as a, as a ruby fruit jungle . . . women are thick and rich and full of hidden treasures and besides that, they taste good." (Rita Mae Brown 1973, 203)

RULERS

Are made to fit those who rule. If women made rulers, "we might make it an 11-inch 'foot' ruler or a 13-inch 'foot' ruler and middle-aged white men might not fit. They might not meet the new criteria. They might be short on or lacking in spirit or humility, be overconfident and/or poor managers. Look around our world. What a mess they have made." (Yvonne A. Flowers 1979, 32)
(See OBJECTIVITY, POINT OF VIEW, REALITY, THEORY)

RUTHLESS

"A man has to be Joe McCarthy to be called ruthless. All a woman has to do is put you on hold." (Marlo Thomas; quoted in Suzanne Levine and Harriet Lyons, eds. 1980, 39)

SABBATH
(See RELIGION)

SACCHARIN
(See FORMS OF ADDRESS, COOKIES)

SADISM AND MASOCHISM (S&M)
"A consensual activity that involves polarized roles and intense sensations. . . The key word to understanding S/M is *fantasy*. . . A sadomasochist is well aware that a role adopted during a scene is not appropriate during other interactions and that a fantasy role is not the sum total of her being. . . [S/M] focuses on whatever feelings or actions are forbidden, and searches for a way to obtain pleasure from the forbidden. It is the quintessence of nonreproductive sex." (Pat Califia 1981, 31, 32)
(See SEXUALITY)

"A consensual minority sexual practice. Sadomasochists achieve sexual pleasure by fantasizing and/or acting out dominant and submissive roles as part of a sexual scenario. . . Sadomasochists come from all walks of life, from all races, social classes, sexual orientations." (Suzann Gage 1983)

The S&M debate has been more prominent in the States and "has now outlived its usefulness" in the UK. (Jayne Egerton 1983, 28)

"Sensual and Mutual (the basics)." Aunt Sadie 1981, 147)

"As much an irreducible condition of society as it is an individual 'sexual preference' or lifestyle: indeed, sadomasochism reflects the power

asymmetries embedded in most of our social relationships. . . For women and other oppressed peoples, the historical and pragmatic significance of oppression is that it is always a received rather than chosen condition. Indeed, it is difficult to imagine even having the *option* to embrace the conditions of oppression." (Robin Ruth Linden 1982, 5, 7)

"A leftist insurgency against feminism and the newest threat to feminist anti-rape and anti-pornography activism. . . Whatever your 'feelings' or 'desires' are, because you are a woman, a lesbian, a feminist, does not legitimize asserting them as a *political* right." (Kathleen Barry 1982, 77, 87)

SADOSOCIETY
The "sum of places/times where the beliefs and practices of sadomasochism are the Rule. It is formed/framed by statues of studs, decrees of droves, canons of cocks, fixations of fixers, precepts of prickers, regulations of rakes and rippers. It is bore-ocracy." (Mary Daly 1984, 35)

SAGE
A man who we are to think is wise, but who is often a "dotard." His words are often quoted in textbooks. "Care has been taken to hand down to us the best of [sages'] sentences, many of which nevertheless are weak enough: But had the same care been taken to register all their absurdities, how great a share of their present applause wou'd they have lost!" (Sophia 1739, 34)
(See KNOWLEDGE, WICCA)

SAINT

When female, she is one who is declared by the Church to be a virgin, "from Mary the virgin through Maria Goretti the virgin martyr, to all the virgin nuns who reach the sainthood... Every woman [is supposed to be] a virgin mother or a silent nun... Having dutifully produced like animals, we must go and be cleansed in sacramental ritual." (*Banshee: Journal of Irishwomen United* c.1980, 1:2, 12)

SALLY

Generic name for women factory workers. "I became suddenly conscious of a complete change in his manner from the easy familiarity of the morning before. Instead of the generic name of 'Sally,' or the Christian name which on better acquaintance he applied to the other girls, he had politely prefixed 'Miss' to my surname." (Dorothy Richardson 1905, 255)

(See MARY)

SALON

"An intellectual, political, and social [institution which] was a powerful phase of women's force previous to the rise of the democratic public forum." These drawing room assemblies for intellectual conversation became, in Britain, Germany and France, the centers of intellectual, political, and social influence. The salon existed in America also; two powerful salons were those of Alice Roosevelt and Mrs J. Borden Harriman. (Mary Ritter Beard 1942; in Ann J. Lane 1977, 223)

(See BLUESTOCKINGS)

SALVATION ARMY

"The only form of Christianity which is a living force." (Olive Schreiner; quoted in *The Woman's Journal* 1898, 29:21 (May 21), 163)

SAMPLER

From the Old French *examplaire* or *essamplaire*, "exemplers" or "samplers" of embroidery provided examples of designs and stitches women could make and exchange. Pattern books were first published in 1523, and the sampler gradually became an educational exercise for young girls. Samplers, often creative and beautiful, were a form of expression that ordinary women could adopt to order and decorate their world.

(See ART, FORMS OF EXPRESSION, SEWING)

By the eighteenth century, "to work a sampler was no longer an exercise of skill, it had become instead a display of 'femininity.'" (Rozsika Parker and Griselda Pollock 1981, 65) "As objects, samplers are often beautiful, and we rightly admire the use of colour, texture, the designs of stitches and the distinction of motifs. But they also represent a female childhood structured around the acquisition of prescribed feminine characteristics. Patience, submissiveness, service, obedience and modesty were taught both by the concentrated technical exercises as well as by the pious, self-denying verses and prayers which the samplers carried." (Rozsika Parker and Griselda Pollock 1981, 66)

"In the beginning was the Sampler. Its form was no accident of mere embellishment. Alphabet, numerals and humble rhyme illuminated with carefully stitched decorative motifs, embodied and codified the elements of a virtuous life: literacy, piety and needle wisdom. The smallest girl-child began to unravel the mysteries of hornbook and catechism while starting her first sampler." (Mirra Bank 1979, 10)

"Consists of fear melted down and poured into socially useful shapes." (Sheila Ortiz Taylor 1982, 2)

SAPPHO

Director of a girls' school on the island of Lesbos; widely known poet of her time, in what is now called the classical period of Greek culture. She was one of the "nine terrestrial muses"; others included Erinna, called by the ancients the equal of Homer, and Corinna of Boetia, Pindar's teacher who won five times over him in a poetic competition. (Elise Boulding 1976, 262)

(See LESBOS)

SATELLITE COMMUNICATION

"The communication system of the future. With every setback we must redouble our efforts to be a part of this new communication." (Statement by Women's Institute for Freedom of the Press, *Media Report to Women* July 1, 1978)

(See TECHNOLOGY)

"Makes a dream technically possible. We foresee the day when women can gather in simultaneous conferences on each continent to participate themselves in a World Conference of Women." (Statement issued by the first annual conference on planning a national and international communication system for women; in Cheris Kramarae and Paula A. Treichler 1982)

(See COMMUNICATION
REVOLUTION)

SATIRE

A speaking and writing style out of bounds for women. We are taught that "men are satirical – it is clever; women are nasty or bitchy – which is a reflection of their temperament." (Dale Spender 1982, 43)

SAWN LADY

The lady sawn in half by a magician; thus, fishy, a trick. "There's a strong aroma of sawn lady about this." (Josephine Tey 1950, 98)

SCARLET HARLETS

British feminist theatre company who have toured their shows in England and on the continent.

(See HARLOT)

SCHIZOPHRENIA

"Since patriarchy is the State of Schizophrenia, it is to be expected that those who show signs of integrity will be called 'schizophrenic.' " (Mary Daly 1978, 394)

(See ILLNESS, MENTAL HEALTH)

SCHLEPPER SEX, The

Women, the carriers. "In modern society as in ancient cultures, noticing who schleps and carries tells us a lot about

who is usually left holding the bag." (Letty Cottin Pogrebin 1983a, 18Y)

(See IN-CASES)

SCHOLARS

Usually applied to males, to lovers of antiquity who "may know perfectly the Sense of the learned Dead. . . But engage them in a Discourse that concerns the present Times, and their Native Country and they hardly speak the Language of it, and know so little of the affairs of it, that as much might reasonably be expected from an animated Egyptian mummy." (A Lady 1721, 25)

(See EXPERT)

SCHOLARSHIP

Excellence in study. Too often " 'excellence' is a set of mannerisms, external appearances, flashy skills, glibness, superficial fluency – all having no necessary relevance to imagination, originality, or even to intelligence." (Naomi Weisstein et al. 1975, 20)

Traditional: "The acceptable/unexceptional circular reasonings of academics . . . caricatures of motion. The 'products' are more often than not a set of distorted mirrors, made to seem plausible through the mechanisms of male bonding." Feminist: "Amazon expeditions into the male-controlled 'fields' [which] are necessary in order to leave the fathers' caves and live in the sun." (Mary Daly 1978, 23, 8)

SCIENCE

"A human construct that came about under a particular set of historical conditions when *men's* domination of nature seemed a positive and worthy goal. The conditions have changed and we know now that the path we are travelling is more likely to destroy nature than to explain or improve it. Women have recognized more often than men that we are part of nature and that its fate is in human hands that have not cared for it well." (Ruth Hubbard, Mary Sue Henifin, and Barbara Fried, eds 1979, 209)

(See EUTHENICS, OBJECTIVITY)

"A feminist resource." (Donna J. Haraway 1981, 478)

"Is seen as a fairy-tale enterprise in pursuit of the impossible dream... But the reality at Harvard and everywhere else is that science is firmly in the hands of men, while women, along with the poor and the black, are much more likely to be researched than be researchers." (Hugh Drummond 1983, 46)

"Science, it would seem, is not sexless; she is a man, a father, and infected too." (Virginia Woolf 1938, 139)

Tends "to serve and reinforce dominant social values and conceptions of reality – as much as and often more than they serve to challenge them." (Barbara Du Bois 1983, 105)

"White science studies dead things and creates poisonous substances to kill and maim the creatures as well as the humans. You call that progress. Indians call it insanity. Our science studies living things; how they interact and how they maintain a balanced existence. Your science disregards – even denies – the spirit world: ours believes in it and remains connected to it." (Carol Lee Sanchez 1983b, 152)

SCIENTIFIC METHOD

"Is no more than the systematic application of a few common sense principles which we all use in everyday life. These principles do not free us of bias... Anyone with a little common sense can spot poor scientific work *provided* the work is explained clearly, and *provided* enough information is given to base an evaluation on. Most reports of scientific work made by the mass media do not meet these criteria; instead, they list conclusions and speculations by scientists who support the status quo." (Judith Johnson 1984, 8)

SCIENTIST

A researcher who considers problems as "things to be 'attacked,' 'licked' or 'conquered.' If more subtle means fail, then one resorts to 'brutal force,' to the 'hammer and tongs' approach. In the

effort to 'master' nature, to 'storm her strongholds and castles,' science can come to sound like a battlefield. Sometimes, such imagery becomes quite extreme, exceeding even the conventional imagery of war." June Goodfield suggests that, for pursuing scientific research "the best analogy is always love." She says, "If you really want to understand about a tumor, you've got to *be* a tumor." The view of science as "putting nature on the rack and torturing the answers out of her" is a form of rape. (Evelyn Fox Keller 1983, 20)

(See FOOTBALL, RAPE)

SCUM MANIFESTO

SCUM stands for "Society for Cutting Up Men." The Manifesto by Valerie Solanas (known as one of the most radical feminists of the late 1960s) is the case for the elimination of males in order to eliminate male domination. Her (non-fatal) shooting of Andy Warhol dramatized her argument. (Mary Anne Warren 1980, 434)

"Is not a sober, reasonably argued programme for political change. It's a racy, hot-tempered outburst of rage against men... [It] marked a radical departure in feminist thought: it contains many valuable insights which were to be developed and elaborated on when the second wave of feminism truly took off." (Jayne Egerton 1984, 21)

SEAMSTRESS

A woman who is expert at sewing, especially one who makes her living by sewing. From the Middle English *seamestre*, man or woman who sews. The Indo-European root is *su-* to sew. The word demonstrates not only the formal feminine marker *-ess* but a semantic shift from the Middle English term which applied to both men and women.

(See -ESS, SEWING, WEAVING)

SEAT BELTS FOR AUTOMOBILES

Safety devices with shoulder straps designed for human beings without breasts. There is "disparate impact on women of the so-called 'shoulder belts,' more accurately described as 'chest belts.' Whether the heightened degree of discomfort suffered by those of us with breasts amounts to de jure (intentional) or de facto (unintentional) discrimination, it is a problem that deserves, finally, to be addressed in the light of . . . [new laws] requiring the use of seat belts. Perhaps they can be modified so that they are truly 'shoulder belts' with two straps coming down from behind in harnesslike fashion, over each shoulder, under each armpit and fastened on each side of the body. This suggestion is so simple and seems so obvious; I can only speculate that there was very little, if any, female input into the modeling of the current seatbelt." (Madeline Kochen 1985; letter to the *New York Times*, January 12)

(See ESCALATOR)

SECOND SEX

Title of germinal feminist work by Simone de Beauvoir.

SECOND WAVE

The name given sometimes to the 1960s revitalization of the feminist movement in Europe and the Americas. In fact, there have been many waves of the movement through the centuries.

(See FIRST WAVE)

On August 26, 1970, a group of women calling themselves the Emma Goldman Brigade marched down Fifth Avenue in New York City with many other feminists, chanting: "Emma said it in 1910/ Now we're going to say it again." (Christie V. McDonald 1982, 68)

SECRECY

Ability to keep a secret, an essential skill for women. "We must still hide what we are doing and thinking. . . The necessity for this, in certain circumstances, is not hard to discover. When salaries are low . . . and jobs are hard to get and keep . . . it is, 'to say the least, rather tactless,' as the newspaper puts it, to criticize your master." (Virginia Woolf 1938, 120)

SECRETARY

A professional without the label of professional. "I have been called Administrative, Clerical, Production, and even Other [on office memoranda]. The old-fashioned term is secretary, obviously a profession with no professional status. . . If I'm not a professional, am I an amateur?. . . As the scribbled and illegible memoranda cross my desk, I ponder once again, then switch on the Selectric, and my professional skills produce the expected quality. Tell me, who are the professionals?" (Ann E. Jones 1983; letter to editor, *Spring*, September, 14)

(See CLERK)

Ninety-nine per cent of these office workers are women. According to one management consultancy firm "the typical secretary spends only two percent of her time typing, the rest being occupied with a range of tasks and diversions, including talk, fetching-and-carrying, making coffee and waiting for work." (Anna Coote and Beatrix Campbell 1982, 51, 72)

A female (usually) whose job "has been changed from that of the clerical administrator to the glorified 'shorthand tea-lady,' over the past century or so. . . Secretarial work is a very cushy way of getting absolutely nowhere." (Zoe Pitt 1980, 25)

The title of the person, almost always female, whose tasks include technical skills such as typing and shorthand and who is also "expected to make coffee, run personal errands, water plants, organize leaving/wedding/birthday presents, and even sew on buttons for the boss. She is expected to be caring, tactful, sensitive to *his* moods, patient, protective and tidy – in short she is there to make his life easy and comfortable, protect him from unwanted visitors, lie to cover for his mistakes and make him feel important. Of course, these duties may be, and often are, a break in the routine of typing and can be used to leave the office for half an hour, but at the same time they clearly reinforce the woman's subservient role and act as a direct slap in the face for those women who go into secretarial work with the expectation of a challenging career." (Hazel Downing 1981, 90)

A job which "can be interesting and rewarding; it's cleaner and pays better than factory or shop work; it can end at the dot of five with no responsibility; it has some perks – and it's easy. But too often it's unbearably boring, there's overwork with no overtime pay, there's responsibility for mistakes but no credit, and there are conditions and pay scales no man would accept... The terrible thing about secretaryism is that for too many women *there is no alternative*... She does the follow-up work: typing letters, filing records, making appointments, etc. So there's a horizontal division: he takes the top half, she the bottom. Hers is a dead-end job, characteristic of the business world where men get trained to advance in the executive or specialist level and women may get as far as the nebulous 'personal assistant,' but rarely further... This division of labour has existed since women entered the office world – barely seventy-odd years ago! Shorthand in the nineteenth century was a male concern... It's not a career; it's marking time." (Clare Cherrington 1978; in Marsha Rowe 1982, 182, 179)

SELECTIVE REALITY (SR) SYNDROME

A complex hearing problem "known to have its roots in a socially conditioned contempt for women. Paradoxically, observers of this male disorder report that these men exhibit an unrelenting desire for attention of any kind from women. A large percentage are actually unaware that women do not exist only to meet their needs. The SR syndrome cripples the ability of these men to communicate. The same issues and questions may arise again and again, and the answers will go unheard. Total confusion may cause them to resort to inappropriate, tactile means of communication." (Elizabeth 1983, dot productions, Vancouver, B.C.; printed in *Heresies* #16, 93)

SELF-CONFIDENCE

"The beginning of all power. The recognition of self as valuable for being what it is can be a strong basis for solidarity among the oppressed whether black in a white society, female in a male dominated society or Muslim in a Hindu society." (Devaki Jain 1978, 12)

SELF-DEFENSE

Disobedience. "It means raising your voice and making a stink about the guy hassling you on the street or the creep rubbing you on the bus. It means embarrassing others and making scenes when we've been taught, even at our own expense, not to do so... Self-defense means learning how to effectively hurt others, how to fight dirty to cause pain, blood and broken body parts. It means being nasty, mean, ugly, loud – all the things that are not part of 'sugar and spice and everything nice.' " (Kathy Hopwood 1980, 58)

(See STREET REMARKS)

Action based on Sound Judgment. Meechee Dojo, a woman's self-defense school in Minneapolis, offered two defense classes. The first was called "Laws"; its purpose was to explore the nature of aggression and seek modes of resistance. "We look at a myriad of Feminine Images and search for the power and the weakness in each. We set up imaginative situations of verbal sparring. . . ." The second course was called "Justice" – "to see how we can aid Justice as she works in the world." A woman involved in the courses said, "We do not believe in the current physical self-defense courses that throw out a bunch of techniques to women, but do not explain the possible ramifications of each technique. We believe that Sound Judgment is the most important aspect of self-defense." (Susan Rennie and Kirsten Grimstad 1975, 219)

SELF-HELP

Taking charge of one's own health concerns and challenging the social control of women's sexuality and reproduction through techniques such as self-examination and information-sharing. "Is not an alternative to confronting the medical system with the demands for reform of existing institutions. Self-help, or more generally, self-knowledge, is critical to that confrontation." (Barbara Ehrenreich and Deirdre English; in Jill Rakusen 1982, 24)

(See CAESAREAN/C-SECTION, HEALTH SYSTEM)

"Is women relating to ourselves in order to demystify health care, the professionals and our own bodies; it involves being able to make personal choices based on our own valid experiences and knowledge... Self-help is a political act. It is deeply challenging to the existing health care center." (Women's Community Health Center, Cambridge, Massachusetts; in Boston Women's Health Book Collective 1976, 367)

SELF-HELP MOVEMENT

International activities through which we are liberated from "the oppression of misconceptions and misinformation. We learned that the structure of the cervix is beautifully simple. And by observing ourselves and each other on a regular basis, we learned that the medical definition of 'the range of normal' is impossibly narrow and restrictive. Such notions as 'tipped uteruses,' 'eroded cervixes,' 'irregular menstruation,' and 'vaginal discharge,' all considered 'health problems' by our doctors, became obviously absurd. We found that everyone's uterus is 'tipped' some way or other and that this term has no medical significance whatsoever... The first technology self-helpers gained was the ability to perform safe, early abortions in a procedure we called 'menstrual extraction.'" The movement encompasses the work of the clinics in the Federation of Feminist Women's Health Centers (FFWHC), which began with activities of the Los Angeles Feminist Women's Health Center in 1973 and similar clinics. "All of these clinics are collectively woman-controlled and provide woman-centered abortion care (including later abortions), birth control (including cervical caps), and ongoing weekly Self-Help Clinics. At times, different clinics have offered lesbian health groups, birth programs and the Los Angeles FFWHC started a donor insemination program in 1979." (Carol Downer 1984, 419-20)

SELF-INSEMINATION

"Self-insemination is very straightforward. The semen is placed inside the vagina near the mouth of the cervix (or not even that far up) . . . where it would usually be deposited during intercourse. It is as simple as putting a tampon or a finger inside your vagina. We used a needleless syringe, which can be obtained at a chemist, but on occasions one woman just tipped the sperm into her vagina. One woman in our group told a friend of her plans – 'But it's supposed to be painful, isn't it?' her friend said. This is completely untrue." (Feminist Self Insemination Group 1980; quoted in Rita Arditti, Renate Duelli Klein and Shelley Minden 1984, 383-4)

SELF-SACRIFICE

"Is the dearest vice of the virtuous. It is a violation of nature, and of nature's laws. It is a tare that grows and flourishes upon the fertile soil of some feminine natures until it chokes the fair and gracious flower of self-respect. It is a murderer, for it stifles character; not only in those who ignorantly practise it, but in those who accept, and are morally enervated by it. It bestows gifts, and the giving rends the heart of the giver, while failing to benefit the receiver." (Beatrice Lewis 1899, 183)

SEMANTIC DEROGATION OF WOMEN

Title of an article by Muriel Schulz which traces the process of debasement for terms which describe women. Any term for the female sex is pejorated over time. (Muriel Schulz 1975b)

(See SPINSTER)

SEMANTICS

The study of words and the ways they are

used. An important skill for women which "is not mere quibbling over the definitions of words [but an effort to] uncover buried facts and alter the interpretation of evidence." (Ruth Herschberger 1948, 6-7)

"Those who define semantics as 'the study of meaning' constitute a majority of past and contemporary linguists... We propose that linguists stop defining semantics as 'the study of meaning'... [We use] *semantics* to refer to those features that determine the internal relationships of lexical items in a language, and *meaning* to refer to the possible readings, or interpretations, that are the result of surface structure position (word order). The widespread error of identifying 'possible readings' with 'semantic structures' has led linguists to make false claims about our ability to describe language, and it has turned so-called 'formal' theories of language into hastily-constructed patchworks that account for nothing by trying to account for everything... Semantics will prove to be relatively more stable over time than meaning, and will, therefore, be more predictable, while meaning, although describable, is not always predictable." (Julia Penelope Stanley and Susan J. Wolfe 1979)

Can mean a study of how meanings are negotiated in discourse uses, including the ways that male-centered perspectives come to be considered "conventional" thought. "Discourse circumstances [including frequent interruptions by males] limit what speakers can try to mean by affecting the perceptions they have of consensus in the speech community. Those with less advantageous positions as speakers will be less able to assume their outlooks are shared and thus are more restricted in what they can mean... In other words, success as a discourse participant can lead in both direct and indirect ways to success in influence and perhaps to success in furthering one's line of thought." (Sally McConnell-Ginet, in press)

SEMANTIC SPACE

"The semantic space of English is neatly divided in accordance with social sex-role stereotypes; women are fragile, passive and dishonest, all negative attributes, whereas men are strong, bold, honest, and forthright, all positive attributes." Our space is small and "contains such labels as *prostitute, housewife, mother, nurse,* and *secretary*; the remainder of English semantic space, including those terms called "generics," belongs to the male sex. It would appear that the explicit semantic markers [+female] and [+male], are only the most obvious and superficial indicators of the way in which English semantic space, our cognitive space, reflects male dominance." (Julia [Penelope] Stanley 1975, 102, 97)

(See FALSE GENERICS)

SEMINAL

(See GERMINAL)

SEMINAR

(See OVULAR)

SENECA FALLS

The town in New York where women held a convention in July, 1848, to discuss their social, civil, and religious condition and rights. The Declaration of Sentiments passed at the convention included the line: "We hold these truths to be self-evident: that all men and women are created equal..." In recent years Seneca Falls has been the site of women's peace camps.

SENTENCE

A linguistic unit, a group of words, which is said by some to be used somewhat differently by a male and a female. Virginia Woolf describing the writing of Dorothy Richardson: "She has invented... a sentence... of a more elastic fibre than the old, capable of stretching to the extreme, of suspending the frailest particles, of enveloping the vaguest shapes... It is a woman's sentence, but only in the sense that it is used to describe a woman's mind by a writer who is neither proud nor afraid of anything she may discover in the psychology of her sex." (Virginia Woolf 1923; in Gillian E. Hanscombe 1983, 40)

SEPARATISM
A political stance of withdrawal and exclusion.

(See COALITION)

"Obviously 'separatist' is a volatile word, and can mean and has meant many different things... Yet the word does have a history. It goes back to when Black activists claimed the Civil Rights movement to themselves, inviting whites out. In the late 1960s, most radical feminists (many of them heterosexual) often called themselves separatists in that they didn't work politically with men. Since then, just within the women's movement, separatism has been called for in terms of class, age, whether one is single or not, a mother or not, etc. Most recently, it has been used to mean a lesbian who won't associate with men and/or heterosexual women and/or lesbians with male children." (Jane Ordway 1982, 17 fn)

A necessity in the 1960s because "one could not organize against male power with men right in the room... Generally speaking, whether the early [in this wave] women's liberation spokeswomen took a liberal therapeutic view or a radical political view of the solution to their problems as women, separatism was seen only as a necessary strategy. The purpose was always integration with equality." (Barbara Leon 1975, 153)

A situation needed by those who have been racially oppressed "to explore the meaning of their experiences – to heal themselves, to gather their energies, their strength, to develop their own voices, to build their armies." (Mirtha Quintanales 1981, 153)

"For a group of people whose history is one of negative identity, it is probably a necessary first step toward self-respect and self-comprehension." (Julia [Penelope] Stanley 1978a, 121)

A theme which "is there in everything from divorce to exclusive lesbian separatist communities, from shelters for battered women to witch covens, from women's studies programs to women's bars, from expansion of daycare to abortion on demand. The presence of this theme is vigorously obscured, trivialized, mystified, and outright denied by many feminist apologists, who seem to find it embarrassing, while it is embraced, explored, expanded, and ramified by most of the more inspiring theorists and activists." (Marilyn Frye 1983, 96)

"It's good for forging identity and gathering strength, but I do feel that the strongest politics are coalition politics that cover a broad base of issues." (Barbara Smith and Beverly Smith 1981, 126)

"The woman-only meeting is a fundamental challenge to the structure of power. It is always the privilege of the master to enter the slave's hut. The slave who decides to exclude the master from her hut is declaring herself not a slave. The exclusion of men from the meeting not only deprives them of certain benefits (which they might survive without); it is a controlling of access, hence an assumption of power. It is not only mean, it is arrogant." (Marilyn Frye 1983, 104)

"Will not do the trick of revolution. *Autonomy*, however, is *not* separatism. We recognize the right and necessity of colonized peoples throughout the world, including Third World Women in the U.S., forming independent movements toward self-government. But ultimately we must struggle together." (Gloria Anzaldúa; in Cherríe Moraga and Gloria Anzaldúa ed. 1981, 196)

"Is not a viable political analysis or strategy for us. It leaves out far too much and far too many people, particularly Black men, women, and children... Lesbian separatism completely denies any but the sexual sources of women's oppression, negating the facts of class and race." (Combahee River Collective 1979, rpt. 1981, 214)

"Doesn't fit my real life, or indeed, the

real life of any Indian lesbian I know.
When one is a member of the smallest
minority in existence (Native American),
one is hardly comfortable separating
oneself from all that one HAS. . . Separatism doesn't encompass my roots – it
simply cannot." (Chrystos 1982, 24)

Feminist: "Feminist separation is, of
course, separation of various sorts or
modes from men and from institutions,
relationships, roles, and activities which
are male-defined, male-dominated, and
operating for the benefit of males and the
maintenance of male privilege – this
separation being initiated or maintained,
at will, *by women*." (Marilyn Frye 1983,
96)

Feminist: To practice separatism. "Not
to need men for sex or love could as
easily blunt one's rage and pain and
therefore one's militance." (Ellen Willis
1981, 97)

Lesbian: "Not a way of promoting
exclusively lesbian concerns, or a way of
protecting lesbians from heterosexism in
political groups, but a possibility of
prioritizing feminism. . . As separatists
we choose to oppose men rather than try
to reform them, not out of a belief that
men can't change but out of a belief that
they won't change until they understand
that they have to. . . . We might fight
alongside (we do not say *with*) men in
certain situations . . . but in these situations we insist on our political independence." (Katharine Hess, Jean Langford
and Kathy Ross 1981, 59)

SEPARATIST

It is a label men apply to autonomous
women, but not to autonomous men.
(Renate Duelli Klein 1983, 420)

(See SEPARATISM)

SERVANTS

"Are the counterparts in the market
economy of housewives – ubiquitous and
essential, but working in the coerced
silence of a double oppression as women
and as secret agents maintaining the all-
important cultural boundary between

personal and public life." (Ann Oakley
1982, 182)

SERVICE

Is related to love and doing good, which
are all "side issues in a male world.
Service and love and doing good are the
spirit of motherhood and the essence of
human life." (Charlotte Perkins Gilman
1911, 209)

Domestic: Care of family and home. A
necessity of life from which the man has a
"charter of immunity" because he is
otherwise engaged. (Mary Lowndes 1919,
110-11)

SEWING

Women's work, and thus devalued. Sewing, often learned by middle-class girls
along with reading and writing and by
working-class girls as a means of support,
has utilitarian, artistic, and social dimensions. From the lines of seamstresses in
factories to the sewing circle with its
opportunities for conversation, women
have used sewing to symbolize their
femininity, their industriousness, and
their exploitation.

(See ART, NEEDLEWORK)

A way of connecting the fabric of life:
"I was not over fond of sewing, but I
thought it best to begin mine early. So I
collected a few squares of calico, and
undertook to put them together in my
usual independent way, without asking
direction. I liked assorting those little
figured bits of cotton cloth, for they were
scraps of gowns I had seen worn, and
they reminded me of the persons who
wore them." (Lucy Larcom 1889; in
Mirra Bank 1979, 20)

A skill expected of women, who are the
home hand stitchers and the factory
machine stitchers. "I lifted my head from
my father's heels to his head, and mused:
'How tall he is! And how long his coat
looks! and how many thousand, thousand
stitches there must be in his coat and
pantaloons! And I suppose I have to grow
up and have a husband, and put all those
little stitches into his coat and pantaloons.
Oh, I never, never can do it!' " (Lucy

Larcom 1889; by Mirra Bank 1979, 23)

A skill expected of women no matter her training or her career. "In surgery, there was a resident who was a real nice guy, but he was also the product of his background. The first day of surgery he said to me, 'Well, you know your stitches, don't you, Vanessa?' – just assuming that since I'm a woman I know about sewing. I said, 'Got the wrong person. Look, in order to pass home economics in either grade my mother had to finish my skirt.' " (Vanessa Gamble in Regina Markell Morantz, Cynthia Stodola Pomerleau, and Carol Hansen Fenichel, eds 1982, 255)

A peaceful activity. "When I feel self doubt or dried-up creatively, I turn to sewing. It's peaceful and seems to give me back self-confidence. There is comfort in the cloth itself. Sewing is subconscious, it flows, there are many stitches and much of it is images. Sewing is a safe area for women; I have always felt comfortable doing it. Art for women has been relegated to this area." (bülbül 1983, 19)

A women's industry in which a series of battles for equality were waged.

"A lull in the struggle,
A truce in the fight,
The whirr of machines
And dearly bought right,
Just to labor for bread,
Just to work and be fed."
(Mary O'Reilly, "After the Strike" 1911; cited by N. Sue Weiler, in Joan M. Jensen and Sue Davidson, eds, 1984, 114)

SEWING MACHINE

A technology hotly debated by women between 1820 and 1880. The editors of *Godey's Lady's Book and Magazine* wrote in 1855: "A friend of ours from Chester County, lately visited Philadelphia for the purpose of securing a sewing-machine. . . She herself calculated to do up her year's sewing in a week, and then have plenty of time for mental culture, for society, and general recreation, privileges from which women are often excluded solely by the never ending labors of the needle." In contrast, Caroline H. Dall wrote in 1859: "Nor would I have the sewing done with machines, unless those of the highest cost could be procured, able and super-intended. The best machine is as yet a poor substitute for the supple, human hand; and many practical inconveniences must result from its use. It requires more skill and intelligence to manage man's simplest machine, than to control with a thought that complicated network of nerve, bone, and fibre which we have been accustomed to use." (Ava Baron and Susan E. Klepp, in Joan M. Jensen and Sue Davidson, eds, 1984)

SEX

A three-letter word which problematically entwines the biological with the socially-constructed and to which current writings attach a diversity of meanings. The *American Heritage Dictionary* cites (1a) the property or quality by which organisms are classified according to their reproductive functions; (1b) either of two divisions, designated *male* and *female*, of this classification; (2) males or females collectively; (3) the condition or character of being male or female; the physiological, functional, and psychological differences that distinguish the male from the female; (4) the sexual urge or instinct as it manifests itself in behavior; and (5) sexual intercourse. In most male literature *sex* (5) has meant heterosexual, genital contact, male erection, penetration, and male satisfaction as necessary conditions or aims. Some feminist writers use *gender* instead of *sex* to emphasize the social or cultural nature of the process by which individuals are assigned to different sex groups. Some writers pointedly use the word *sex* to emphasize (4) and (5) and avoid confusion both with *gender* and with *sexuality*. Other meanings of *sex* quite commonly found in feminist writings include (6) hard work, (7) a system of oppressor/oppressee, (8) desire, (9) women's only asset, (11) common currency.

(See GENDER, SEX-GENDER SYSTEMS)

"Sex, which ought to be an incident of life, is the obsession of the well-fed world." (Rebecca West, *The Clarion* November 29, 1912)

"Is derived from the Latin verb *Secare*, to cut. It signifies the cutting or division of one into two or many parts. The female is termed *the* Sex, the organism which possesses the power of self-division, of self-diremption [sic] or self-separation, of multiplying itself *ad libitum* and *ad infinitum*." (Frances Swiney 1918, 36)

"It's pitch, sex is. Once you touch it, it clings to you." (Margery Allingham 1938, 60)

A word which does not provide needed distinctions for women. " 'Well,' we say, 'either a woman experiences pleasure or she does not experience pleasure. We do not demand names for those minute and complex degrees between pleasure and non-pleasure. Surely the language could provide some thought on this subject, if society provided some interest." (Ruth Herschberger 1948, 125)

"As the power dynamic between men and women, its primary form sado-masochism, is what we know now. Sex as community between humans, our shared humanity, is the world we must build." (Andrea Dworkin 1974, 63)

"For me sex is biological, whereas gender is sociological." So, a person can be biologically a woman, but sociologically a man. Such a person "has adopted stereotypic male qualities in order to be accepted by those she governs." (Susan Osman 1983, *Sunday Times*, January 23, 37)

"Has always been part of the question of freedom. The freedom to want passionately. To live it out in the body of the poem, in the body of the woman. So when I feel a movement inside of me and it is a fresh drawing in of new life that I want to breathe into my work, I also feel empowered and long to be a lover like youth." (Cherríe Moraga 1983, v)

The anatomical, physiological and sociological characteristics which distinguish females and males. "One of the basic determinants of life experience and therefore of behavior and even of values. From the moment of birth to the moment of death women experience life differently from men, they think about it differently, they deal with it differently – and since this is true, it follows that their influence in families, communities and ultimately in the whole society is different from the influence of men, and both must be understood if we are to adequately describe the social dynamics of any particular situation." (Anne Firor Scott 1984, 368)

In Western cultures sex as in heterosexual sexual intercourse is "by its very physical nature the most seductive, private, intrusive, direct, and possessing way to exert power and control. For this reason and because it lends itself so well to the combination of intimacy, psychological seduction, and physical strength, sex is potentially the most effective and abusive way to control women psychologically, physically, or through degradation and humiliation, and to maintain individual women's subjection to a particular man and collective women's social and political subjection." (Ruth Bleier 1984, 181)

Babble about sex: "Usually in the case of man implies special rights and privileges, and in the case of women burdens and obligations." (M.M.W. 1913, 245-6)

SEX, THE

With the definite article, *sex* has been used by men to mean (1) women and (2) bad women, i.e., prostitutes.

SEX, THE FIRST

Women. "The first males were mutants, freaks produced by some damage to the genes caused perhaps by disease or a radiation bombardment from the sun. . . The male sex represents a degeration and deformity of the female." (Elizabeth Gould Davis 1971, 35)

SEX DIFFERENCES

"We have no language at present that does not reflect a Cartesian nature/

nurture dichotomy for discussing sex differences. It is difficult to resist the urge to ask, 'But what, *underneath it all*, really *are* the differences between men and women.' *What we must begin to give voice to as scientists and feminists is that there is no such thing, or place, as underneath it all*. Literally, empirically, physiologically, anatomically, neurologically . . . the only accurate locus for research about us who speak to each other is the changing, moving, complex web of our interactions, in light of the language, power structures, natural environments (internal and external), and beliefs that weave it in time." (Susan Leigh Star 1979, 116)

SEX DIFFERENCES RESEARCH

The findings which result when *similarities* are ignored, distorted, or suppressed. Research on sex differences has been critiqued for emphasizing differences between women and men in the face of similarities, for drawing arbitrarily on "scientific" evidence to support stereotyped views of women, and for frequently confusing biological variables with socially and culturally-constructed ones. Research findings which point to differences between women and men are disseminated more widely than those which find no differences.

"Research on sex differences takes place within a gender-stratified society. That is, we are born into a sexual caste system and are heavily indoctrinated from birth with its values; this system is stratified . . . by virtue of the male-defined hegemony over money, power, and language. . . Given that sexual politics permeate all human interactions, including those within scientific laboratories, there is no way to 'control' for this variable." (Susan Leigh Star 1979, 115)

SEX DISCRIMINATION

Sounds like this: "If we wanted to pay that much, we'd hire a man." (Eve Merriam 1964, 61)

SEX/GENDER SYSTEMS

Are composed of interrelated components of gender divisions, sexual divisons of labor, and sexualities, which vary by culture and across time. This term or the terms *sex* and *gender* usefully suggests the complex interactions of biology and culture and suggests that sexuality is intricately related to gender. (Gayle Rubin 1975) "The set of arrangements by which a society transforms biological sexuality into products of human activity"; the process by which the penis, an organ with no inherent social character, is transformed into the phallus, an organ that symbolizes and indicates male authority, dominance, and social power; "the part of social life which is the locus of the oppression of women, of sexual minorities, and of certain aspects of human personality within individuals." (Gayle Rubin 1975, 159)

(See PENIS)

SEX HORMONES

"The so-called sex hormones are progestins, androgens, and estrogens produced by the ovaries, testes, and adrenal glands, in different quantities in females and males of all species." (Ruth Bleier 1984, 84)

(See CYCLICITY, ESTROGEN)

SEX-INEQUALITY

Discrimination, a social condition which "depends much more upon custom than upon law." (Teresa Billington-Greig 1911a, 698-9)

SEXISM

"A social relationship in which males have authority over females." (Linda Phelps 1975; rpt. 1981, 164) The word was evidently coined by Vanauken in a paper called "Freedom for Movement Girls – Now" (1968). (*No More Fun and Games* February 1969, 2, 31) It is an illustration of a concept, central to women's lives, which was wordless for many years.

Behavior, policy, language, or other action of men or women which expresses the institutionalized, systematic, comprehensive, or consistent view that women are inferior.

are waging at this moment on our own sex. A term "coined during the feminist renaissance of the Sixties, probably by analogy with the term *racism*. Both terms reflect a rising social awareness of the oppression suffered in our culture by those who are not white males. Sexism and racism [discriminate, and define] individuals as inferior, limits their options, and subjects them to exploitation and demeaning treatment, on the basis of their membership in some general class (e.g. women or blacks)." (Mary Anne Warren 1980, 424)

"Is stereotyping people by sex; just as racism is stereotyping people by race." (Sara Delamont 1980, 3)

A way of ordering life by gender "that robs people of their humanness and aborts the Spirit moving in the communities of which we are a part." (Nelle Morton n.d., 1)

"The oldest form of institutionalized oppression." (Betsy Warrior 1969a, 1)

Is an unconscious philosophy based on the premise that men must have first choice in everything. (Susan Sands 1970, 16)

"Seems to have arisen with class-divided societies, reaching its awful peak in slavery and feudalism." (Barbara Sinclair Deckard 1979, 119)

"The name of a dangerous disease." (Jennifer Fleming 1979; quoted in Victoria R. Garnier Barshis 1983, 391)

"Virulent social disease." (Marie Shear 1984 correspondence)

"Can never be seen in isolation. It has to be placed in the context of its interconnections with racism, and especially with class exploitation." (Angela Davis 1982, 6)

"Is no bias which can be eliminated but [is] the foundation stone of learning and education in our male controlled society." (Dale Spender 1982a, 37)

"Is the name of the problem addressed by feminism." (Liz Stanley and Sue Wise 1983, 18)

"The polite term" for the war on women. It is "the model for racism, classism, ageism – all the other wars we

Wrongful discrimination on the basis of soil against our own people." (Sonia Johnson 1984, 6)

SEXISM IN LANGUAGE/SEXIST LANGUAGE

The portrayal of male dominance in language structure and language usage. "One of the most powerful means of perpetrating masculinist interpretations of the world, including the view that wimin are inferior, passive, and, by definition, subordinate to males." (Julia Penelope Stanley 1979) See discussions of this social problem throughout this volume. For suggestions of repair see this volume, and the many guidelines and guidebooks listed in Cheris Kramarae, Barrie Thorne and Nancy Henley, eds 1983.

SEXOLOGY

A scientific tool, a social activity, used increasingly to mystify, inspire fear, and "swallow up" women in male definitions. (Kathy Overfield 1979) A word which can be used to define much of men's research about women which assumes that women are unable to define themselves.

SEX PREJUDICE

The term used in 1922 to describe the cause of lower salary, and lower ranked positions of women in U.S. government bureaux and offices. ("Capital Women Protest" *New York Times*, November 11)

SEX ROLE

A label for which there would be no concept if there were not sexism. *Sex role* (like *race role*) refers to proper or customary behavior from a person because of their assigned part in a play whose script was written by others.

"Let's talk straight facts. Boys have pee-pee tails; girls have woo-woos. When they grow up, the boys want to stick their pee-pee tails in the girls' woo-woos, and the girls let them. There is nothing else in this life you need to know. Everything that takes place upon the world's stage emanates from this irrefutable fact." (Susie Day 1984b)

SEXT

A text marked for sex; writing which bears the imprint of feminine sexuality. [Note: according to the *Oxford English Dictionary*, the word *sex* was commonly used in error for *sects*; phonologically, this would be similar to *sexts*.]

(See l'ÉCRITURE FEMININE)

"Text: my body – shot through with streams of song." "Let the priests tremble, we're going to show them our sexts!" (Hélène Cixous 1975b, 252, 255)

SEX TYPING IMAGERY

Process by which the media weigh, sift, and headline "raw news" into sex-typed categories from the perspective of white, middle-class, middle-aged men. "Thus you have a newspaper which calls prominent women 'lib chieftess' or 'libber' no matter what field she is specializing in, and which editorializes about the vindictiveness and general hysterical quality of the 'women's movement.' " (Kathy Kolkhorst 1975)

SEXUAL ATTRACTION

Considered women's economic base in this male defined world. (Charlotte Perkins Gilman 1899)

SEXUAL CASTE SYSTEM

Oppression of women based on their membership in a group which is predetermined and beyond their control. Not only is their labor different from that of men, it is considered inferior labor and they are considered inferior beings. Alternative analyses of women's oppression are based on class and family. (Naomi Weisstein 1970)

SEXUAL HARASSMENT

"Sexual harassment . . . refers to the unwanted imposition of sexual requirements in the context of a relationship of unequal power. Central to the concept is the use of power derived from one social sphere to lever benefits or impose deprivations in another. . . When one is sexual, the other material, the cumulative sanction is particularly potent." (Catharine A. MacKinnon 1979, 1) The only legal term defined by women. A collectively coined word by women working on Carmita Wood's case in Ithaca, NY, 1974. Working Women United Institute (now at 593 Park Avenue, New York, NY 10021) used these words in connection with the Wood case in 1975. The concept was also used and developed by the Alliance Against Sexual Coercion (P.O. Box 1, Cambridge, MA 02139). The term was used by Catharine A. MacKinnon (instead of, for example, *sexual coercion*) when she wrote the legal argument that became the basis of finding sexual harassment a form of sex discrimination. (Catharine A. MacKinnon 1979, 250; 1983 correspondence)

Male behavior at the workplace which made women uncomfortable "required a name, and *sexual harassment* seemed to come about as close to symbolizing the problem as the language would permit." (Lin Farley 1978, xi)

A major event in the history of sexual harassment was a 1976 survey conducted by *Redbook* magazine in which 88% of the 9,000 respondents said that they received unwanted sexual attention on the job. (Wendy Sanford, ed. 1979; rpt. 1981)

In many situations includes economically enforced sexual exploitation. In the academic context the fundamental element is the imposition of sexual advances by an instructor or other officer who is in a position to determine a student's grade or otherwise affect the student's academic performance or professional future.

Attacks, disturbances caused by the Georgie Porgies with a sledge hammer approach or The Boys with a dripping tap approach. (Sue Wise and Liz Stanley in press) A few years ago this was just called *life*. (Gloria Steinem 1983, 149)

SEXUAL-INSTINCT

Understood by men as a kind of innate impulse governing "every action performed by women, from the buttoning of boots to the swallowing of cough drops."

(Cicely Hamilton 1909, 99) "The first axiom of Feminism [is] that the majority of human attributes are not sexual." (Beatrice Forbes-Robertson Hale 1914, 19)

SEXUAL INTERCOURSE

"Sexual intercourse is thought by many to be an activity that involves (or ought to) both male and female equally. But female arousal and satisfaction, although they may be concomitant events occasionally, are not even constituents of sexual intercourse. Our language mirrors this confusion. Grammatically, polite expressions for sexual intercourse tend to be symmetric, giving the impression that what A does to B, B likewise does to A. Yet their definitions give a different picture. Although both male and female genitals are mentioned, the activity is characterized solely in terms of the *male* responses that constitute it." For example, *Webster's Third* defines intercourse as *coitus* which it defines as "the act of conveying the male semen to the female reproductive tract involving insertion of the penis in the vaginal orifice followed by ejaculation." *Ejaculation* is defined as "the sudden or spontaneous discharging of a fluid (as semen in orgasm) from a duct"; *orgasm* is "the climax of sexual excitement typically occurring toward the end of coitus." "According to these definitions the male orgasm is a necessary condition for sexual intercourse (coitus)." (Janice Moulton 1981, 184-5)

(See GREENS)

SEXUALITY

"A technicolor spectrum of biology, experience, psychology, behavior, society, ideation. The spectrum starts with the more social, shades imperceptibly into the psychological, and lastly becomes biological: gender role, sexual activity, sensuality, sexual orientation, choice of partner, sexual ideology, fantasy, pleasure, desire, gender identity, reproduction. In individuals, according to sexologists John Money and Anke Ehrhardt (1972), there are at least 12

important and distinct dimensions to sexuality: chromosomes; fetal gonads; fetal hormones; genital dimorphism; neurological dimorphism, observed behavior; body image, juvenile and adult gender identity; and pubertal hormones, erotics, and morphology. The individual variability in genitals, secondary sex characteristics, and gender psychology reported by social psychologists Suzanne Kessler and Wendy McKenna (1979) suggests that adult gender variation is 'polymorphic' rather than 'dimorphic'; that is, there are perhaps many genders rather than only two. And gender variation, or its lack, is culturally shaped; as anthropologist Gayle Rubin (1975) conceptualizes it, sexuality is most inclusively structured by a sex/gender system." (Muriel Dimen 1981, 66)

(See SEX, SEX/GENDER SYSTEM)

"Can be a dreadful trap. There are women who become frigid – but that's not the worst thing that can happen to them. The worst thing is for women to find so much happiness in sexuality that they become more or less slaves of men and that strengthens the chain that binds them to their oppressor... The idea should be the capacity to love a woman as well as a man, one or the other, a human being, without feeling fear or constraint or obligation." (Simone de Beauvoir 1976, 152)

(See FRIGIDITY)

"It seems feminism is the last rock of conservatism. It will not be sexualized. It's *prudish* in that way... Well, I won't give my sexuality up and I won't *not* be a feminist." (Amber Hollibaugh and Cherríe Moraga 1981, 62)

(See PRUDE)

Much of contemporary radical-feminism has been concerned with the negative consequences of male-centered sexuality and the intricate linking between sexuality and violence against women in this society, i.e., domestic abuse, incest, rape, forced sterilization. Consequently there has been a neglect of positive exploration and discussion of female sexuality. Paula Webster writes:

"Our pleasure, as it is constituted inside and out of heterosexuality and patriarchy, never got center stage." (Paula Webster 1981, 48)

"Poses a challenge to feminist scholarship, since it is an intersection of the political, social, economic, historical, personal, and experiential, linking behavior and thought, fantasy and action." (Carole S. Vance 1982, 39)

Jacqueline Rose has argued throughout her work that in psychoanalysis as well as in our culture women have come to represent *the difficulty inherent in sexuality itself*. She also stresses the relation of sexuality to the unconscious: "Reopening the debate on feminine sexuality must start, therefore, with the link between sexuality and the unconscious. No account of Lacan's work which attempts to separate the two can make sense. For Lacan, the unconscious undermines the subject from any position of certainty, from any relation of knowledge to his or her psychic processes and history, and *simultaneously* reveals the fictional nature of the sexual category to which every human subject is none the less assigned. In Lacan's account, sexual identity operates as a law – it is something enjoined on the subject. For him, the fact that individuals must line up according to an opposition (having or not having the phallus) makes that clear. But it is the constant difficulty, or even impossibility, of that process which Lacan emphasized. . . Exposure of that difficulty within psychoanalysis and for feminism is, therefore, part of one and the same project." (Jacqueline Rose; in Juliet Mitchell and Jacqueline Rose 1982, 29)

"In discussing sexuality there is a fine line between theorizing and setting norms." (*Diary of a Conference* 1982, 11)

"If human beings are multisexed, then all forms of sexual interaction which are directly rooted in the multisexual nature of people must be part of the fabric of human life, accepted into the lexicon of human possibilities, integrated into the forms of human community." (Andrea Dworkin 1974, 183)

"The half-swooning sense of flux which overtakes the spirit in their eternal moment at the apex of rapture sweeps into its flaming tides the whole essence of the man and woman, and as it were, the heat of the contact vaporizes their consciousness so that it fills the whole of cosmic space." (Marie Stopes 1918; in Barbara G. Walker 1983, 917)

Barbara G. Walker believes that countries which have retained the image of the Goddess have broader ideas of sexuality, and for these cultures sexuality as the pursuit of the male orgasm seems ludicrous and impoverished (1983, 910-20)

"It is depressing to have to insist that sex is not an unnecessary, morally dubious self-indulgence but a basic human need, no less for women than for men." (Ellen Willis 1981, 209)

Men's: "Is the product of a repressive society, which can be altered only by the elimination of sexism and the increase in women's freedom." (*Diary of a Conference* 1982, 18)

Sexual characteristics which come in a wide variety, mixed and matched with various ideologies. "Whether a woman defines herself as a traditional wife in a monogamous marriage, a lesbian, a celibate, a polygamous wife or a single woman, those decisions in and of themselves tell us very little about her political aspirations or political commitments or ideology." (Gloria I. Joseph; in Gloria I. Joseph and Jill Lewis 1981, 228)

A concept refined by Bessie Smith who made an historical contribution to the sexual lives of Black women. Michele Russell writes: "In a deliberate inversion of the Puritanism of the Protestant ethic, she articulated . . . how fundamental sexuality was to survival. Where work was often the death of us, sex brought us back to life. It was better than food, and sometimes a necessary substitute." (Michele Russell 1977; in Gloria I. Joseph; in Gloria I. Joseph and Jill Lewis 1981, 183)

SEXUAL LIBERATION

"Political opposition to restrictive sexual

mores. Is ultimately based on the premise that a gratifying sexual life is a human need whose denial causes unnecessary and unjustified suffering. Certainly, establishing people's right to pursue sexual happiness with a consenting partner is a precondition for ending that suffering. Yet as most of us have had occasion to discover, it is entirely possible to 'freely' participate in a sexual act and feel frustrated, indifferent, or even repelled. From a radical standpoint, then, sexual liberation involves not only the abolition of restrictions but the positive presence of social and psychological conditions that foster satisfying sexual relations." (Ellen Willis 1982, 10)

Not a new approach but more of the same old. "The most insidious device of all for brainwashing females is the contemporary demand for people to 'let go of their defenses,' to 'relax,' 'stop being uptight,' to 'groove.'. . . No responsible black leader would tell black people to throw off their old defenses without providing new ones that will work better." (Roxanne Dunbar 1969)

SEXUALLY TRANSMITTED DISEASES (STD)

Include about 25 diseases known to be transmitted sexually; STDs include old-fashioned venereal diseases like syphilis and gonorrhea, newly-identified diseases like AIDS, and previously familiar diseases like hepatitis B that are now recognized to be frequently transmitted sexually. With the exception of AIDS, whose main victims to date have been homosexual males, STDs often have the worst impact on women and children. Chlamydia, for example, causes a simple infection in both sexes but, untreated, can lead to infertility in women. Because STDs are affecting increasing numbers of people and effective vaccines do not yet exist, some clinicians and researchers advocate a change in sexual practices as the only means of prevention. (*Newsweek* 1985, February 4, 72-3)

(See AIDS, VENEREAL DISEASE)

SEXUAL RADICALISM

"Can mean many things. For some women it can mean acknowledging desire in the first place. For others it can mean talking about it. For still others it can mean taking risks to find out what gives pleasure. . . For feminists, it is not a time for reaction nor a politics of despair. It is time to relinquish the status of victim and to take *back* sex, in all its variety." (Barbara O'Dair 1983, 17)

SEXUAL REVOLUTION

Just as Susan B. Anthony called free love "man-vision," so some feminist writers see the "sexual revolution" as a male-created term to glorify and dignify a change in women's sexual behavior which serves men's interests at the expense of women's. The term is used to refer specifically to the increases in women's sexual activity which accessible methods of birth control have supposedly encouraged and, more broadly, to the increased freedom offered to both females and males over the past two decades to discuss and experience sexual behavior and to pursue sexual satisfaction. The term is often used ironically, to suggest that fundamentally what is happening is neither sexual nor a revolution but just the same old "man-vision."

Seemingly a new tolerance for unconventionality, but a "tragic farce" for women. (Karen Lindsey 1980, 246)

"A nonfeminist phrase of the 1960s that simply meant women's increased availability on men's terms." (Gloria Steinem 1980b, 17)

"The so-called 'sexual revolution' should not be confused with actual sexual liberation. True sexual freedom will be possible only when we break the connection between sex and power, when there is no power component in sexual interactions. The sexual revolution has never revolted against patterns of power between women and men." (Sally Roesch Wagner 1982, 30)

SEXUAL SLAVERY

Refers to international traffic in women

and forced street prostitution. Also the private practice by husbands and fathers who use battery and sexual abuse as a personal measure of their power over their wives and/or daughters. "Female sexual slavery is present in ALL situations where women or girls cannot change the immediate conditions of their existence; where regardless of how they got into those conditions they cannot get out; and where they are subject to sexual violence and exploitation." (Kathleen Barry 1979, 7, 39-40)

(See SLAVERY, WHITE SLAVERY)

SEX WAR
A combative situation created by men to maintain women's subordinate social status. It includes hypocritical "endless talk of chivalry, protection, and honour, of which we hear so much and see so little." (Dr Schrirmacher; in K. Douglas Smith 1912, 922)

(See CHIVALRY)

SHAKESPEARE'S SISTER
Is a figure imagined by Virginia Woolf (1929) as she pondered the differences between men's and women's creative achievements. William Shakespeare (1564-1616) is often held up as an example of greatness whom no woman has matched. "So there hasn't been a female Shakespeare . . . (a) So what . . . (b) There hasn't been a *male* Shakespeare since Shakespeare, dammit. (c) . . . One cannot, in reason, ask a shoeless peasant in the Upper Volta to write songs like Schubert's; the opportunity to do so has never existed." (Angela Carter 1983, 76). Woolf's Judith Shakespeare, though herself unsupported and tragic, made it possible for generations of future female poets to exist: Woolf emphasizes cultural continuity and a female intellectual community as important features of women's artistic production.

(See JUDITH)

SHE
(See GENERICS, HE-MAN, PRONOUN)

S/HE
"Replacement term for the third person singular generic 'he.' " (Midge Lennert and Norma Willson eds 1973, 10)

(See SHEY/SHEM/SHEIR)

SHEILASPEAK
Australian language and slang of women and girls. (Nancy Keesing 1982)

(See LILY ON THE DUSTBIN)

SHE-ROE
Female hero. "How important it is for us to recognize and celebrate our heroes and she-roes." (Maya Angelou, cited in Chris Orr 1983, 15)

(See HERA)

SHEY/SHEM/SHEIR
Gender-neutral substitutes for third person English pronouns: Everyone knows SHEY must examine SHEIR feelings about how sexist language effects SHEM. (Mary Jane Hawley 1982)

SHIFTING SEMANTICS
A game played with words defining women. The following sentence offers a lesson in shifting semantics: "WOMEN WHO REALLY WANT TO BE WOMEN WILL ACT LIKE WOMEN." This short declarative sentence – which sums up the message to women from much of society – depends on three definitions of the word *women*. "This first Women is all of us, you and I, your wife, sister, and mother. It is the individual woman with all her fears and hopes and imperfections. WOMEN – but this second women only includes normal women. If you aren't a normal woman, please raise your right hand, stand up and be counted (don't you *want* to be a woman?). WOMEN – this last and final women is our White House of femininity, the ideal woman. This is the woman that men love, cherish, and protect, that they take home to mother and buy only the best for. This third WOMEN is the woman women wish they were. It is also the one we suspect we aren't. By a semantical sleight-of-hand and the con-

stant switching of decks under the table, women are never quite sure when they are being average, normal, ideal, or even desirable." (Ruth Herschberger 1948, 164)

SHOULD MARRIED WOMEN WORK?

The question in the air and in the media during years when the nations are in relative peace and women are not thought vital in the defense industry or to fill in other jobs that men traditionally have. The question is really "Should married women work *outside the home as well as within?*" The answer: "Certainly, every one that has a sound mind and two hands should do her share of the work of the world. . . The wife, in a majority of the homes of the working and middle classes [is] overworked." (Elizabeth Cady Stanton 1898, *The Woman's Journal* October 29, 350)

(See WORK)

SHOUTING

"There can be little doubt that shouting is a survival of the African 'possession' by the gods. In Africa it is sacred to the priesthood or acolytes, in America it has become generalized. . . Broadly speaking, shouting is an emotional explosion, responsive to rhythm. It is called forth by: (1) sung rhythm; (2) spoken rhythm; (3) humming rhythm; (the foot-patting or hand-clapping that imitates very closely the tom-tom. . . Shouting is a community thing. It thrives in concert. It is the first shout that is difficult for the preacher to rouse. After that one they are likely to sweep like fire over the church. . . Women shout more frequently than men. This is not surprising since it is generally conceded that women are more emotional than men." (Zora Neale Hurston 1981, 91-2) "A lä lä lä lä lä" (from the Hidatsa Indian language): A cry of triumph by women; made by curling the tip of the tongue backward and vibrating it against the roof of the mouth. (Waheenee 1927, 177)

(See TREMOLO)

SHREW

Those who are quick to see connecting links and who are sharp in practical matters. A label associated with women.

A militant publication put out by the London Women's Liberation Workshop in 1970s. Cost: "6d. for women and 9d. for men until equal pay." (June Levine 1982, 149)

"I'd rather be a shrew than a piece of dough." (Janice Mirikitani; quoted in Elaine H. Kim 1982, 253)

SICK

(See HEALTH, ILLNESS, YELLOW WALLPAPER)

SIGMA

Poland's feminist group organized in late November 1980. (*Connexions: An International Women's Quarterly* 1981, May, 7)

SIGN OF THE CROSS

A prayer in sign language, touching forehead, chest or stomach, left shoulder and right shoulder. "The cross actually may be the tree of life or the crossroads of life, instead of a cross of crucifixion. . . The opening and closing positions for the sign of the cross is to raise the hands palm to palm. This is the same position used to pay homage to the Rice Mother after each meal in Thailand. . . A practice still found in Europe is to make the sign of the cross over bread before baking it. In the case of hot cross buns it is made on the bread. The latter custom definitely pre-dates Christianity." (Rose-Ellen Hope 1982, 9-10)

(See CHRISTIANITY, RELIGION)

SILENCE

Is not golden.

(See CONVERSATION, INEXPRESSIVE MALE, OPPRESSION, SPEAKING, SUPPRESSION OF WOMEN'S WRITING)

Below are some definitions and observations on the muffling of women's voices – from women who have managed to publish their words. While this dictionary as a whole recognizes many words, definitions and authors ignored or muffled by white male culture, we cannot hear the erased voices nor recreate the unrecorded voices of the past. (In the rare cases when the words of minority and working-class women are recorded, the names of the writers or speakers are often omitted, and we have only "Domestic workers 1915".) We can, however, comment on the causes, and meanings, of the silence and the silencing. (See Introduction.) Silence which is imposed is sometimes mistaken for passivity. However, women's culture has been very active through the centuries through our writing and, in particular, our telling our stories to each other.

"In a world where language and naming are power, silence is oppression, is violence." (Adrienne Rich 1976; rpt. 1979, 204)

"That willfully selfish tyranny . . . evolved by a crafty old ostrich of a world for its own well-being and comfort." (Radclyffe Hall 1928, 135)

Is not protection. "My silence has not protected me. Your silence will not protect you. . . In the cause of silence, each of us draws the face of her own fear – fear of contempt, of censure, of some judgment, of recognition, of challenge, of annihilation. But most of all, I think, we fear the very visibility without which we also cannot truly live." (Audre Lorde 1980a, 20, 21)

"There is no agony like bearing an untold story inside you." (Zora Neale Hurston 1942, rpt. 1979, 71)

"Let no one tell me that silence gives consent, because whoever is silent dissents." (Maria Isabel Barreno, Maria Teresa Horta, Maria Velho da Costa 1975; excerpted in *Ms.* January 1975, 87)

"The unnamed should not be mistaken for the nonexistent." (Catharine A. MacKinnon 1979, 28)

"Silence *is* like starvation. Don't be fooled. It's nothing short of that, and felt most sharply when one has had a full belly most of her life. When we are not physically starving, we have the luxury to realize psychic and emotional starv-

ation." (Cherríe Moraga; in Cherríe Moraga and Gloria Anzaldúa eds 1981, 29)

Is a rebellious wrap:

The night asks who am I?
   I am its secret – anxious, black, profound
I am its rebellious silence
I have veiled my nature, with silence,
wrapped my heart in doubt
and, solemn, remained here
gazing, while the ages ask me,
              who am I?
(Nazik al-Mala'ikah 1974, 244)

Is a concealing wrap. In her Book of Unspoken Thoughts, the narrator lists her husband's virtues:

1. *Jake is generous.*
2. *Jake is not jealous.*
3. *Jake is hard-working and successful.*
4. *Jake is clean and tidy.*
5. *Jake does not drink or gamble.*
6. *Jake is a faithful husband.*

"All these, written in my book, *were* thoughts never spoken. They weren't spoken because each one was only one-half of a sentence. The whole sentence would have been: 'Even though Jake put Pussy's kittens in a gunnysack and killed them by shooting into the sack with a shotgun, he is generous, faithful, clean, hard-working, etc." (Jessamyn West 1979, 210)

Is an oppression often enforced through rules and regulations. Women inmates at the Bedford Hills (New York) Women's Prison are given the following explanations when their letters are returned unsent:

"You did not sign properly
You did not fill out stub properly
Name of addressee has not been approved
Letters addressed to General Delivery not permitted
It contains Criminal or Prison News
Begging for packages or money not allowed
You are not permitted to receive the articles requested

The article requested can only be received new from dealer

Correspondence with newspapers or newspaper employees not permitted

You cannot have a visit with the person named in your letter unless approved by the Superintendent

Inmate who wrote letter for you did not sign his [sic] name

Special Letters must be submitted Saturday, Sunday or Holidays

You did not stick to your subject

You have no stamps on deposit."

(*No More Cages*, Winter 1982, 16)

SIN

"Come[s] from the contagion of Masculine serpent." (Ester Sowernam 1617, 48) *Sin* is a label more likely to be given to an offense if committed by a woman. "If a man abuse a Maide and get her with child, no matter is made of it, but as a trick of youth; but it made so heinous an offence in the maiden, that she is disparaged and utterly undone by it." (Ester Sowernam 1617, 24)

"Any act of self-denial which prevents one from questing for self-fulfillment." (Pam Salela 1985, correspondence)

Deadly Sins of the Fathers: Mary Daly's renaming of "the traditional Seven Deadly Sins, adding to the beginning of the list (which now totals eight) the most crucial one, which the fathers, of course, omit." These are:

Processions	(deception)
Professions	(pride)
Possession	(avarice)
Aggression	(anger)
Obsession	(lust)
Assimilation	(gluttony)
Elimination	(envy)
Fragmentation	(sloth)

(Mary Daly 1983, x)

The Greatest: For men, pride; for women, the negation of self. (Valerie Goldstein 1960; cited in Patricia D. Highby 1984, 8-9)

Radical: "The radical 'sin' is remembering the Goddess in the full sense, that is, recognizing that the attempt to murder her – mythically and existentially – is radically wrong, and demonstrating through our own be-ing that this deed is not final/irrevocable." (Mary Daly 1978, 111)

SINGING THE EGGS DOWN

A monthly premenstrual rite. (Sally Gearhart 1978)

SINISTER WISDOM

A journal whose title "was taken from a line in *The Female Man*, a novel by lesbian science-fiction/fantasy writer Joanna Russ, and was chosen to indicate the left side of wisdom, symbolizing a turning 'on the side' of patriarchal values. Sinister, meaning 'left side,' also represented 'the left', meaning revolution: in this case, a revolution to destroy the patriarchal, rational 'right' side and free the creative 'left.' Harriet Desmoines [co-founder] explained that the name was chosen because it represented a reversal, the underside, in praise of the 'left' wildness and creativity of women that the 'right,' logical, rational side (often viewed as masculine) had sought to confine or destroy." (Joy Parks 1984, 14)

SISTER

A term of affiliation used among girls and women. A term of address in letters written to Elizabeth Cady Stanton in 1880: "My sisters, my cousins, and my aunts [petition] man that he give back [our] *natural* and *indisputable*, birthright – 'The Ballot'" (Laura Rodeuau); "sister women" (Mary E. Taylor); and "noble band of sisters" (Mary E. Pritt). (From letters to Elizabeth Cady Stanton 1880, Chicago Historical Society library)

(See SSISTER

"A kind of kinship shorthand for a woman member of a community of owners of the means of production: an equal, an adult among adults, a decision maker." (Karen Sacks 1982, 6)

One of the main food crops. Before North American Iroquois Society was drastically transformed by reservation life, it was a matrilineal organization and the three main crops grown by women (corns, beans, and squash) were called the "Three Sisters," "Our Mothers," and "Our Supporters." (Cyndy Baskin 1982, 43-6)

Those who have special relationships and rights. *Fahu* (lit. 'above the law') is a relationship common to the Tonga islands of Polynesia which gives privilege to Tongan women in their roles as sisters. Fahu rights and benefits are seen as emanating from the mother and include a sister's call on her brother, his household, and his descendants. (Christine Ward Gailey 1980)

Ally. (Jeannie Wells 1969)

"To women, everywhere: we are all sisters. The time has come to break down the barriers separating us. To begin to talk. To smash the stereotypes when they oppress and stifle us. To fulfil our potential on every level. To see other women not as competitors, but as sisters whose problems are our problems. To support and cherish each other, and to be free." (Berkeley Women's Liberation New Monday Night Group 1969, Northwestern University Archives)

"Don't call us 'dear' or 'honey'
Or 'little lady,' sonny.
We're women free with dignity,
No cutie playboy bunny.
But neither are we men,
So listen once again:
If you call us 'brother,'
We'll call you 'mothah' –
Sister is the name!"

(Words by Woody Gurthrie; additional lyrics by Fanchon Lewis and Rebecca Mills, *Virgo Rising: The Once and Future Woman* record cover, 1973 Mollie Gregory Productions)

SISTERHOOD

"More than a word. It is a responsibility. It will become more important than status, color, or money." (Vann 1970)

"The word *sisterhood* no longer means a subordinate mini-brotherhood, but an authentic bonding of women on a wide scale for our own liberation." (Mary Daly 1973, 8)

Female solidarity, an idealist principle which invited "us to enter into an imaginary paradise and thus conceal the problem of class struggle and women's role within it." (LACW Collective 1977, 10-11)

A discovery of shared oppression. "We discover oppression in learning to speak of it as such, not as something which is peculiar to yourself, not as something which is an inner weakness, nor as estrangement from yourself, but as something which is indeed imposed upon you by the society and which is experienced in common with others. Whatever else sisterhood means, it means this opportunity. But what it also means is the discovery of women as your own people . . . as my people . . . as the people I stand with . . . as the people whose part I take." (Dorothy E. Smith 1977, 10-11)

"The word comes easily to most of us. Sisterhood. What holds us to that word is our commonness as Indians – as women. We come from different Nations. Our stories are not the same. Our dress is not the same. Our color is not the same. *Yet, we are the same.*" (Beth Brant 1983, 7)

Is a joining threatened by pollution from "the two 'ideals' of feminine fulfillment, namely 'unselfconscious inclusion' (tokenism) and feminine self-sacrifice." (Mary Daly 1978, 375)

"Cannot be forged by the mere saying of words. It is the outcome of continued growth and change. It is a goal to be reached, a process of becoming." (bell hooks 1981, 157)

Has different meanings for Black and white women. "I can remember being at women's conferences where the slogan 'Sisterhood is powerful' was used a lot. White women would address the audience with the word 'sisters.' Somehow I did not feel comfortable with the term because I knew when I used it I meant women of African descent. Some white women challenged me one day and demanded to know why I could not call them sisters. So I told them. When my ancestors were stolen from Africa and brought to Amerika as slaves, families were divided. Some because of health were dropped in the Caribbean. We were bred, traded, bought, and rarely knew where to find one another, so when we were so-called 'freed' most of us did not know where our relatives were. I have 'family' throughout the Third World, in Brazil, Cuba, the West Indies, etc. So when I meet someone who says that I remind them of someone else that they know, or I meet someone who reminds me of someone else that I know, I automatically think that somehow we are all 'slave-ancestor-relatives.' Therefore, the words 'sister' and 'brother' have very significant roots. I understand very well why I could not call a white woman my sister. They can be 'cousins' only." (Sylvia Witts Vitale 1982, 21)

Is "the mainspring of women's liberation . . . the positive assertion and creation of new relationships between women. . . ." "The first flush of sisterhood is no more. . . Sisterhood has bloomed and it has also taken a knocking, and not only from men. . . We, the feminists I mean, are not the pure embodiment of everything that is not tainted by the evil of masculinity." (Sheila Rowbotham 1983, 83, 351-2)

In the early 1970s, sisterhood "was like falling in love. In fact for many women it was falling in love. The love affair was sadly brief but it provided an atmosphere of total trust in which to learn how to think and how to act." (Angela Phillips 1983, 120)

SISTERHOOD IS POWERFUL

Sisterhood is Powerful. The title of a groundbreaking book in second-wave radical feminism, edited by Robin Morgan, 1970. A phrase which expresses women's new sense of solidarity. (Anna Coote and Beatrix Campbell 1982, 14)

A phrase coined by Kathie Sarachild. "As she herself said recently upon hearing the opening words to the Helen Reddy song, 'I am Woman' ('I am woman, hear me roar in numbers too big to ignore . . .') 'That's what sisterhood is powerful really meant!'. . . Today hardly anybody uses it that way. It has been changed from a means to power to a means to control women, to keep them worried about how they relate to each other – looking for approval again rather than figuring out what can be done to eliminate male supremacy." (Carol Hanisch 1973, 166)

SISTERHOOD OF POOR SPINNERS

A group which in 1788 drew up a petition pointing out the threat from mass production processes to hand-spinning because "this employment above all is suited to the condition of the *Female Poor*; inasmuch as not only single women, but married ones also, can be employed in it consistently with the cares of their families." (Quoted in B. L. Hutchins 1915, 271)

(See SPINSTER)

SISTERLY THESAURAL DICTIONARY

Title of a section of Madeline Gins's 1984 book *What the President Will Say and Do* (93-9). This is not a "dictionary" and is not exactly "sisterly" but reproduces some examples of feminist arguments about language: "Woman is the host. Man, the guest (ghestess?), But the host has been too amiable for too long. Look at what we have bred. We have acquiesced to such a degree that in our own homes we now speak their language instead of ours." (91)

SISTERSHIP

A reward to one woman for serving another woman well. A queen would typically reward a loyal lady-in-waiting by enabling her to retire to a sistership post of a hospital in the country. (Kate Campbell Hurd-Mead 1938, 212)

SIT ON/MAKE WAR ON

Sanctioned ways of disciplining individual men for errant behavior in some areas of Africa. "To 'sit on' or 'make war on' a man involved gathering at his compound at a previously agreed-upon time, dancing, singing scurrilous songs detailing the women's grievances against him (and often insulting him along the way by calling his manhood into question), banging on his hut with the pestles used for pounding yams, and in extreme cases, tearing up his hut (which usually meant pulling the roof off)." (Judith Van Allen 1976, 61-2)

SKIRT

An item of clothing which swings from the waist down and covers much or all of the legs, worn in the middle ages by both sexes as a sign of rank, but still worn by women as a mark of sex and a symbol of helplessness which would never have been submitted to by any class of beings who had the right to bodily freedom. (Beatrice Forbes-Robertson Hale 1914, 139)

A problematic item of clothing. "You can't do many things in them. You can't run or climb, because you have to wear special shoes with skirts, you can't just wear plimsolls. Skirts blow around in the playground, and the boys are always lifting them up. In trousers you can sit more comfortably on the floor. Your legs are protected when you fall over. You are generally much freer." In some schools skirts are required for girls – but not for boys. (Junior school girls, quoted by Susan Hemmings 1979; in Marsha Rowe 1982, 248)

SLANG

Has traditionally been assumed to be the linguistic province of males: "It seems quite evident that the sexual slang terms are coinages of our forefathers, not our foremothers. Indeed, the overwhelming preponderance of all slang is apparently the invention of males. Its roughness, its occasional savagery, its assertiveness – all suggest masculine origin. In addition, women in general are less inclined to use slang than are men and those women who use it extensively have over the years been considered unfeminine. This masculinity of slang can be explained . . . [by] the concept of the closed group. By the nature of their work in the world, men tend to constitute a closed group or at least to

belong to sub-groups. Women lead more isolated lives. If they participate in the working world at all, they are for the most part virtually substitute members of the male group. There is . . . some female slang, but it tends to be restricted to a few female physical characteristics and to a sparse number of items connected with the home and feminine decor." (Theodore M. Bernstein 1970; introduction to J. S. Farmer and W. E. Henley 1890-1904) The women's movement in both the nineteenth and twentieth centuries generated slang, however; and it seems likely that many women's communities have also produced slang. As in other instances, numerous factors influence the identification and preservation of women's words. Nancy Keesing (1982), for example, has demonstrated a wealth of slang terms among Australian girls and women, and it seems likely that female investigators elsewhere – committed to the importance of women's words and well-placed to discover them – will do the same.

(See ANDROCENTRISM, ENGLISH, GREENS, LILY ON THE DUSTBIN, MENSTRUATION, TESTOSTERONE POISONING)

SLAVE

The white term for a person who is held, bought and sold as property. Brenda Verner suggests a term is needed that indicts those who "own" these persons. We might better understand U.S. and world history by speaking of "enslaved Americans" or "Africans under slavery" rather than "slaves." (*Women and Language News* 7:1 (Spring 1983), 1)

(See SISTER)

"I frequently work from fourteen to sixteen hours a day. I am compelled to sleep in the house. I am allowed to go home to my children, the oldest of whom is a girl of 18 years, only once in two weeks. I lead a treadmill life and see my own children only when they happen to see me on the streets. You might as well say that I'm on duty all the time, from sunrise to sunrise, every day in the week.

I am the slave, body and soul of this family." (Black domestic worker 1915; cited in Barbara Mikulski 1976)

"From the first dawn of Life, unto the Grave,
Poor Womankind's in every State, a Slave.
The Nurse, the Mistress, Parent and the Swain,
For Love she must, there's none escape that Pain;
Then comes the last, the fatal Slavery,
The Husband with insulting Tyranny
Can have ill Manners justify'd by Law;
For Men all join to keep the Wife in awe."
(Sarah Fyge 1703; quoted in Jeslyn Medoff 1982, 169)

SLAVE NARRATIVES

The basis of literary tradition for Black writers. "Where escape for the body and freedom for the soul went hand in hand." (Alice Walker 1980, 152)

SLAVE OF A SLAVE

"The worker is the slave of capitalist society; the female worker is the slave of that slave." (James Connolly, Irish revolutionary, in Berkeley Women's Liberation newsletter 1969)

SLAVERY

Complete subjection of a person by another. A legalized or otherwise approved institution in which some person holds others as property. In the U.S. whites held Blacks in permanent servitude. Some use the word as synonymous with *patriarchy*. "The present position of women in Britain and other quarters of the civilised world is intimately connected with the history and practice of slavery and serfdom among the dominant races of mankind." (Mary Lowndes 1913b, 241) Others disagree. "Theoretically, the white woman's legal status under patriarchy may have been that of 'property,' but she was in no way subjected to the de-humanization and brutal oppression that was the lot of the

slave. When white reformers made synonymous the impact of sexism on their lives, they were not revealing an awareness of or sensitivity to the slave's lot; they were simply appropriating the horror of the slave experience to enhance their own cause." (bell hooks 1981, 126)
(See WHITE SLAVERY)

SLEEPING BEAUTY

"Generally said of a companion lover who is forgetful of her clitoris. She falls into a kind of somnolence whose motive she does not know. She may remain in that state an indeterminate lapse of time. One particularly solitary beauty has been widely known because that sleeping state overtook her in the middle of a wood. One hundred years passed before one of her companion lovers found her in the course of a long walk. That state of somnolence ends for the beauty when a companion lover tactfully reminds her that she has a clitoris." (Monique Wittig and Sande Zeig 1976, 143)
(See CINDERELLA)

SLIMMING

(See BEAUTY, CELLULITE, FAT)

SLOGAN

Short statements in support of, in the women's movement, large issues. E.g. "Keep my body off your ads." (Sticker from [U.K.] Women's Media Action 1980s)
(See BUTTONS, MISS WORLD PROTEST)
Mostly half truths "at best and so concentrated that truth – which is not simple – does not reside in them." (H. M. Swanwick 1935, 269)

SMILING

A facial expression required for many "women's jobs." "Your secretaries do not smile at you because they like you but because it is part of their job to be pleasant." (Joanna Russ 1974, 42)
Smiling strike: Action "of department store cashiers in Bagnoli (Napoli) in which cashiers refused to smile or be

'pleasing' to customers." (Women in Italy 1972, 87)

Habitual behavior for females. "I notice often, now, that when I'm angry, I smile; the corners of my mouth turn up instinctively. Though I'm furious, I keep the same smile that was plastered across the faces of my dolls. Even if I threw them across the room, or left them out in the cold all night, the dolls still smiled." (Beth Bagley 1984, 42)

SMOKING

Drawing in and puffing out smoke, an activity dangerous to health and to femininity. Woman college student talking to another in a fictional account: "Something really nice girls don't do." (Lynn Montross and Lois Syster Montross 1923, 245)

SNOOLS

Would-be preventers, ghosts/ghouls, that want the movement towards and retrieval of gynergy dead. "The noun *snool* means (Scottish) 'a cringing person.' I mean also 'a tame, abject, or mean-spirited person' (O.E.D.). In sadosociety, snools rule, and snools are the rule. The dual personalities of these personae . . . are unmasked by definitions of the verb *snool*. This means, on the one hand, 'to reduce to submission: COW, BULLY,' and on the other hand, 'CRINGE, COWER.' Snools are sadism and masochism combined, the stereotypic saints and heroes of the sado-state." (Mary Daly 1984, 20-1)

SOAP OPERA

Daytime television dramas which picture men who are more open and available for intimacy than real men, but "the men on the soaps don't work at ordinary jobs, doing ordinary things, for eight, ten, twelve hours a day. They're engaged either in some heroic, life-saving, glamour job to which working-class viewers can't relate or, worse yet, work seems to be one long coffee break during which they talk about their problems." (Lillian Rubin 1976, 121)

(See HARLEQUIN ROMANCES,

ROMANCES)

Continuing radio and TV stories with contradictory messages. In these stories women are trapped in their relationships, yet derive great pleasure from these relationships. The shows usually have a villainess who manipulates others and serves as a focus for women's anger. The discussions include small ups and downs, secrets and confessions as well as occasional life-threatening situations. (Tania Modleski 1982)

"The kitchenette version of the 'adult' horse opera." (Alice Embree 1970, 182)

SOB SISTERS

Women journalists who covered sensational crimes, writing stories with emotional intensity specifically designed, by the editor, for the female reader.

(See WOMEN'S PAGE)

SOCIALISM

A theory of social organization which argues that placing ownership and control of the means of production, capital, and land in the community as a whole will solve many social problems. However, it will not "resolve political conflicts that do not spring solely from an economic root. It may provide an atmosphere in which these situations can be criticized and worked upon, but it does not appear to contain the answers to or an analysis of phenomena which are based more directly in relations other than the economic."

(See CAPITALISM)

A theory which has "failed to get to grips with heterosexism and compulsory heterosexuality and [is] therefore failing to support lesbian political prisoners in other countries as well as assuming the continuation of lesbian oppression in future 'socialist' societies." (Jayne Egerton 1983, 30)

SOCIALIST-FEMINIST

A person who believes that "The System's the Problem." Includes those people associated with the following labels: Equal Rights, Traditional Marxist, Althusserian, Eurocommunist, Humanist,

Unaligned Socialist, Wages for Housework. Usually distinguished from the Radical Feminists associated with the following labels: Feministes Revolutionaires, Redstockings, Firestone, Cultural Feminist, Matriarchist, Female Supremacist, who believe that "Men are the Problem." (Amanda Sebestyen 1979, back cover chart)

"Barbara Ehrenreich has defined a socialist feminist as a socialist who goes to twice as many meetings." (Iris Young 1981, 64)

(See FEMINISM, MARXIST-FEMINIST)

SOCIALIZATION

A social science term used to avoid issues of power and inequality. A label given to the fact that "Little girls are taught very early that the main thing they are supposed to do is 'please' the menfolk, and they grow up to spend their lives at this thankless and impossible quest." (Ana Audilia Moreira 1980, 70)

For the Black woman, "socialization processes have determined: (1) her defining herself, her existence, in relationship to Black men (2) while simultaneously seeing herself as an independent being. This duality may seem incongruous, but only if 'womanhood' in Black mothers and daughters is compared to White patterns of 'womanhood,' marriage and relationships with men." (Gloria Joseph; in Gloria Joseph and Jill Lewis 1981, 123)

SOCIAL SYSTEM

Our s.s. is based on men's insistence that woman "is essentially an adjunct of some male person." This fallacy is "a rock of offense in every path of progress." (A.B.T. 1919, 116)

SOCIETY

"The child-game [a woman] has been allowed to entertain herself with; that poor simulacrum of real social life, in which people decorate themselves and madly crowd together, chattering, for what is called 'entertainment.'" (Charlotte Perkins Gilman 1911, 43)

SOCIOBIOLOGY

An androcentric science which persistently depicts males as the norm while defining females in relation to them, naming females passive and inferior. "Scientists often describe female sexual behavior in the passive voice, creating the impression that whatever occurs, *happens* to us." The syntactic and semantic features of scientific language "about wimmin and females in general force the unsuspecting reader to agree to stereotypic hypotheses which the scientist never openly defends." (Sarah Lucia Hoagland 1980a, 293, 285)

(See ANDROCENTRISM)

SOCIOLOGY

A study of social organization organized by its founding fathers as "a male profession." (Ann Oakley; quoted in Liz Stanley and Sue Wise 1983, 13)

Degree: "Three years of middle class men's class analysis." (Kate Monster 1984, letter to editor, *Trouble and Strife*, 3 [Summer], 3)

SOFT FEMINISTS

Women in the 19th century who perceived and welcomed subtle changes in the church and society but who accepted the view of woman that women had a special nurturing nature. This *soft feminism* did bring many women into social action but by emphasizing woman's space kept most women from obtaining more room. (Beverly Wildung Harrison 1974; in Barbara Brown Zikmund 1979, 208)

(See CLAPPING MILITANTS)

SOLDIER

A military person who "is rewarded not only with money, but also with honour; the mother receives neither. And yet, compare for one moment the services that these two render to the State! Men are called upon very occasionally to defend their country; women are called upon daily to replenish its citizens." (Lady McLaren 1908, 9)

(See WAR)

SOLICITATION

Asking someone to do something. Something "wrong" or "immoral" for example. Usually a charge leveled at women as it "is a rare thing for one man to appear [in court] for annoying women. Yet . . . constantly is this offense committed." (Teresa Billington-Greig 1911b, 48)

SOLIDARITY

A collective activity which "need not be against something but just *for* something." (Devaki Jain 1978, 15)
(See SISTERHOOD)

Action between Third World and First World women which "must be exercised on the basis of a clear understanding of what is going on in the underdeveloped countries, lest it be used to serve other purposes diametrically opposed to the cause of equality and freedom for all peoples." (Nawal el Saadawi 1980, viii)

SOMETWO

A useful term and concept. "Some*one* does not have to take care of the children, some*two* will share them." (Jane O'Reilly 1972, 19)

SONG

(See BLUES, MUSIC)

SOROMUNDI

Asteroid 2682, discovered in 1979 by planetary scientist Eleanor Helin, "who named it Soromundi (sisters of the world) in honor of the Los Angeles YWCA." (Report by Nancy Gula 1983, *Ms.* Aug., 20)

SOUL-SEARCHING

Contemplation which is "another privilege of the already privileged white middle-and-upper-class male." (Marcia Holly 1975, 39)

SPACE

Area, room. Men have a lot more space in this world than do women who have difficulty finding space. "I wanted to be alone, and what better place to choose than the sink, where neither of the men would follow me?" (Barbara Pym 1952, 161)
(See SPARKING)

The spatial elite not only own more space "but they own the most *desirable* spatial positions, too, whether they be the beachfront home or the seat on the 50-yard line, the farm with fertile land or the hotel suite with a fantastic view. Even in such seeming trivia as positions at the dining table, elaborate protocol determines that VIPs will sit in varying positions of privilege determined by their relative rank." (Nancy Henley 1977, 31)

SPARE RIB

A feminist magazine which began publication in 1972, in England, and since 1973 has been produced by a feminist collective. Like its forerunners, the earlier British feminist magazines, *Spare Rib* deals with many social issues. For example, "*The Common Cause*, put out by the giant National Union of Women's Suffrage Societies numbering 100,000 members . . . concentrated especially on education and propaganda. They linked the vote to a whole lot of problems we're still up against today, like the inequities of marriage or the difficulties of breaking into male-dominated professions. . . The suffragists inherited areas of concern from earlier feminists many of whom like Florence Nightingale felt 'There are evils which press more hardly on women than the want of the suffrage' – the Contagious Diseases Acts, for instance, which aimed to set up a legalised brothel system and which deprived suspected prostitutes of all civil rights. Feminists fought back after 1870 with their paper, *The Shield*. Today we're still fighting the arrogance of the medical profession. The feminist press has been with us since *The Englishwoman's Journal*, founded in 1858 well before the struggle for the vote; although it's worth remembering that in the U.K. the first women's suffrage bill was presented, together with a massive petition, in 1866." Other earlier feminist periodicals: *Women's Suffrage Journal*, *Shafts* ("a magazine for women and the working class" was anti-vivisection, vegetarian, and Theosophist as well as pro-universal suffrage), *The Victoria Magazine* (produced entirely by women), *Women at Work, Link* (publicised birth control information in 1877), *Votes for Women* (published by the militant Women's Social and Political Union), *The Freewoman* (included discussions of unmarried motherhood, lesbianism, and the female orgasm), Sylvia Pankhurst's *Woman's Dreadnought* (presented child-care as a central problem) and The Women's Freedom League's *The Vote* (opposed oppression everywhere, advocated clothing reforms, and guerilla action for militants). (*Spare Rib*, August 1978)

(See PERIODICALS,
SINISTER WISDOM)

SPARKING

"Is Speaking with tongues of fire. Sparking is igniting the divine Spark in women... Sparking is creating a room of one's own, a moving time/spaceship of one's own, in which the Self can expand, in which the Self can join with other Self-centering Selves." (Mary Daly 1978, 319)

SPEAKING

"When Black women 'speak,' 'give a reading,' or 'sound' a situation, a whole history of using language as a weapon is invoked. Rooted in slave folk wisdom which says: 'Don't say no more with your mouth than your back can stand,' our vocalizing is directly linked to a willingness to meet hostilities head-on and persevere." (Michele Russell 1979, 101)

(See CONVERSATION, SILENCE, TALK)

A skill females learn at an early age and continue to excell at during their lives, to maintain relationships and to work on creating a world where more people have a chance to have their say. Mrs Ben Hooper, lobbying for women's suffrage in Wisconsin: "I traveled over a good deal of distance talking the question out with politically prominent men... Some days I got up at 5:30 ... and did not get home until midnight." (in Dorothy Uris 1975, 18)

Giving voice. A vital activity. "The machine will try to grind you into dust anyway, whether or not we speak. We can sit in our corners mute forever while our sisters and our selves are wasted, while our children are distorted and destroyed, while our earth is poisoned, we can sit in our safe corners mute as bottles, and we still will be no less afraid." (Audre Lorde 1980a, 22)

SPEAKING SUBJECT

Meaghan Morris quotes Monique Wittig: "The 'I' (*Je*) who writes is alien to her own writing at every word because this 'I' (*Je*) uses a language alien to her; this 'I' (*Je*) experiences what is alien to her since this 'I' (*Je*) cannot be '*un* ecrivain'...Je poses the ideological and historic question of feminine subjects." Morris comments: " '*un* ecrivain' is 'a writer' (masculine, understood);...it is grammatically 'incorrect' in French to say '*une* ecrivain' – 'a writer, feminine understood.' So in writing the sentence '*Je suis un ecrivain*: I am a (masculine understood) writer,' the WOMAN writer in French is, as Wittig says, 'silenced/split by the babble of grammatical usage.' Hence Wittig's use of the split 'I' – *J/e*." (Meaghan Morris 1982, 89)

SPECULUM

A metal or plastic tool used for vaginal examination, including self-examinations. Has been a liberating device for many women: "On April 7, 1971, a group of women met in a small women's bookstore in Venice, California. I had acquired a plastic vaginal speculum and wanted to share what I had seen with the group. After I demonstrated its use, several other women also took off their pants, climbed up on the table and inserted a speculum. In one amazing instant, each of us had liberated a part of our bodies which had formerly been the sole province of our gynecologists. Afterwards, in a consciousness-raising discussion, we observed that in this supportive, nonsexist setting, feelings of shame fell away and we acknowledged the beginnings of feelings of power from being able to look into our own vaginas and see where our menstrual blood, secretions and babies came from." (Carol Downer 1984, 419)

(See DOWN THERE, SELF-HELP MOVEMENT)

SPEECH

Our voices, which can be heard by men if we express "anger in masculine terms: aggro, smashing things up." Not heard as often if the speech invites "an audience to listen, to open up, to take images inside." (Michele Roberts 1983, 62-3)

(See SPEAKING)

SPERM BANK

Repositories of sperm. The U.S. sperm banks for humans have "become the ultimate bastions of exclusivity and elitism, based on race, class and education." (Joanne Tsai 1983; letter to editor *Mother Jones* 8:9 (November), 3)

(See SELF INSEMINATION)

SPIDER

Is derived from OE *spinnan* "to spin." "Who is the spider and who the spinster? Deity/insect? Female/male? Benevolent/malevolent? Exalted/despicable? The answers depend upon culture and time." (Marta Weigle 1982, 2)

(See SPINNING, SPINSTER)

SPINDLE

The spindle is the pin on which the thread is wound from the spinning-wheel. The lozenge shape in heraldry, which is used to depict a woman's armorial bearings instead of the shield on which a man's are depicted, is thought to have originally been a spindle. Alfred the Great, in his will, calls the female part of his family the *spindle side* (as opposed to the *spear-side*). (*Brewer's Dictionary* 1962, 856-7)

A spinning tool which in some cultures is owned and used by women, in others by men. "At sunrise on spinning day [as part of the marriage ceremony] the custodian of each kiva [the underground ceremonial chamber of the Hopi and other Pueblo people] went early to clean up his kiva and start the fire and get it warm . . . each man went to his kiva, taking his spindle (every adult male owns one). [The bridegroom's] uncle came around early to deliver to each kiva the carded cotton to be spun. . . Soon all spindles were humming away." (Helen Sekaquaptewa 1980, 33)

SPINNING

"Glasgow 1856.
Back against a quieted loom, the spinner shifts –
then shuts her eyes against the hands of the supervisor –
submits –
her own hands grasp the frame –
plait a pattern in the dangling threads –
left over from another woman's shift:
an art work of necessity."

(emphasis ours; Michelle Cliff 1980, 39)

SPINSTER

A member of the "sisterhood" of unmarried women. "In Bible times, it is my belief that Miriam belonged to the ancient and honorable fraternity. It is quite likely that Dorcas did and Phoebe – else how could Dorcas have found time for the alms-deeds that she did, and how could Phoebe have gone to visit the church in Cenchrea?" (Frances Willard 1896, *The Woman's Signal*, Feb. 20 119)

Originally meaning a person who tended the spinning wheel. Like most terms connected with women, it became a euphemism for *mistress* or *prostitute*. (Muriel Schulz 1975b)

(See SEMANTIC DEROGATION OF WOMEN)

"The unmarried woman of a certain age (generally understood to be thirty) . . . in many ways as much a social outcast as the whore" in the nineteenth century. "While her legal rights were greater than those of married women, her opportunities for employment and for social contact were, especially early in the century, extremely limited. . . By the close of the century, the popular image of the 'old maid' pretty much gave way to the less pitiable and more controversial figure of the 'New Woman'." (Kathleen Hickok, 1984, 117)

(See NEW WOMAN)

In Navajo tradition, Spider Woman and Spider Man are involved with weaving the creation of the universe. Spider Woman instructed the Navajo women how to weave on a loom which Spider Man told them how to make. Spider Man said: When a baby girl is born to your tribe you shall go and find a spider web which is woven at the mouth of some hole; you must take it and rub it on the baby's hand and arm. Thus, when she grows up she will weave, and her fingers and arms will not tire from the weaving." (Aileen O'Bryan 1956; in Marta Weigle 1982, 5)

(See SPIDER)

An unmarried woman. The fleece brought home by the Anglo-Saxons in summer was spun and woven into clothing by the female family members during the winter. King Edward the Elder commanded his daughters to be instructed in the use of the distaff. It was generally believed that no young woman was fit to be a wife till she had spun for herself a set of linen. Hence the maiden was termed a spinner or spinster. (*Brewer's Dictionary* 1962, 856-7)

Unmarried women who "have been so circumscribed by habit, prejudice, and economic dependence that their various talents, untraded with and under-developed, have been wrapped away in the decent napkin of feminine seclusion." (Mary Lowndes 1914b, 134)

Figures of fun and ridicule to those men who see themselves as essential to a woman's existence. There are almost no positive images of the single woman in "malestream" literature. "It is a dangerous image and therefore one which I think should be actively encouraged." (Dale Spender 1982, 299)

(See COMPLETION COMPLEX, NEW WOMAN)

Of the leisured-class: "Unemployed, unpropertied, unendowed, uneducated, economically dependent on others." (Constance Lytton 1908; in Karen Payne 1983, 197)

"Spiders appear as powerful male and female symbols in myths, poems, images, dreams, popular beliefs, and tales. By extension, those who spin and weave – *spinsters* – are also viewed as persons with or in need of special powers, benevolent and/or malevolent. Only in Western tradition has the role spinster acquired so many derogatory, negative overtones, and the wizened, barren old maid must be recelebrated as a wise, creative spinner-weaver, a task in which she ought to be joined by brother as well as sister spinsters." (Marta Weigle 1982, viii)

"She who has chosen her Self, who defines her Self, by choice, neither in relation to children nor to men, who is Self-identified, as a Spinster, a whirling dervish, spinning in a new time/space." (Mary Daly 1978, 3-4)

"Is a word which has almost disappeared. It is a good fifteen or sixteen years since the Lord Chancellor issued a directive saying no woman need be described as 'spinster' on any document. I remember because about the same time I established with my (woman) lawyer, that I did not have to be labelled on a contract [as] 'widow,' as if all I was was my husband's relict." (Mary Stott 1984)

SPIRITUALITY, FEMINIST/WOMEN'S

"Refers to that segment of the women's movement which is concerned with the development of an explicitly feminist religious awareness. Spiritual feminism is not an entirely new phenomenon; some of the earliest defenders of women's rights were religious women who interpreted the spirit (if not the letter) of the Gospels as requiring, not prohibiting, a greater degree of equality between the sexes [e.g., the 1895 commentary on Old and New Testament passages in *The Woman's Bible*, edited by Elizabeth Cady Stanton]. Recently there have been more radical feminist challenges to patriarchal religious traditions, including sharp and scholarly interest in evidence for the existence of early goddess-worshipping, matrilineal, and woman-centered societies. Some feminists have investigated and revived rituals of ancient and medieval mystery religions and witchcraft traditions. Others work within churches to increase the involvement of women and to alter antifemale teachings." (Mary Anne Warren 1980, 441-2)

Feminist spirituality: "Ways of exploring and expressing spiritual connections within the universe through female-centered rituals, female leadership, and issues regarding women's rights." (Ann Forfreedom 1983, correspondence)

"The womenspirit movement is a necessity, not a luxury. Without it, we are operating with only half our potential tools and power. What we think we want is based on what we think is possible; one of womanspirit's most important functions is to create and implement a feminist vision. We need tools such as meditation, personal mythology, natural healing, dreamwork, study of matriarchal history and mythology, and ritual to reach beyond the possibility laid out for us by the patriarchy. We cannot wait until after the revolution for the new order to rise up, phoenix-like, out of the ashes of the old." (Hallie Iglehart 1978, 413)

SPRING-CLEANING

Potentially the enemy of herstory. Many records of women's lives go into the rubbish-bin.

(See DIARY)

SSISTER

The spelling used [rather than *sisters*] by Grace Shinell in the Great Goddess Issue of *Heresies*, and by Barbara Deming in her poem "A Song for Gorgons":

"Ssisters, ssisters – of course they dread us
Theirs is the kingdom
But it is built upon lies and more lies.
The truth-hissing wide-open-eyed rude
Glare of our faces –

If there were enough of us –
Could show their powers and their glories
To be what they merely are and
Bring their death-dealing kingdom
Down."
(Barbara Deming 1982, 43)
(See SISTER)

STANDARD ENGLISH

"What passes for standard, so-called correct English is not what is spoken by millions of people, Black or white, but what a small group of often unprincipled people speak. One can find some interesting linguistic contradictions in this group and speech forms that depart from the textbook descriptions of standard English. There seems to be a wide diversity of acceptance and practice among the standard English linguistic pacesetters. While they can be heard using such incorrect grammatical constructions as 'between you and I,' their range of standard English does not include speech forms used by Black (or white) working class people, with the possible exception of those idioms borrowed from the hipster segment of the masses." (Geneva Smitherman 1983, 21-2)

(See ENGLISH/CORRECT)

STARVATION

"Far from being a fact of life, starvation is a fact of man" as evidenced by the marketing of artificial milk for babies in the Third World. (Liz Butterworth 1983, 99)

(See FOOD)

STAR WARS

A show of intergalactic macho. (Phyllis Deutsch 1983, 15)

STATUE OF LIBERTY

A large statue in New York Harbor which portrays a woman holding a torch of freedom. On Oct. 28, 1886, the first day it was opened to the public, except for the two wives of the statue's creators, no women were invited to the ceremonies. (Tom Higgins 1983, correspondence; from Ripley's Believe It or Not)

STENOGRAPHER

Has an alternative name given by executives as "the girl who works for me." She often does much of the work of the office for which others get credit. She often possesses "a degree of intelligence and ability equal to that of the department head under whom [she works]." (Ruth Burns 1931, 105)

  (See CLERK, SECRETARY)

STEP GIRLS

Young women employed in Victorian England on Saturdays to clean other people's steps. (Mrs Layton 1931, 9)

STERILIZATION

America's new way of controlling people. (Ain't I A Woman Collective 1970a, 7)

  Sterilization has been promoted to help solve the supposed problems of over-population, although to the women it has been promoted as a "therapeutic, health-related procedure." A study in Puerto Rico [where more than 35 percent of women of childbearing age have been sterilized], as well as studies on Chicana, Black [estimated 32 percent have been sterilized], and American Indian women [estimated 25 percent have been sterilized] in the United States, has indicated that many poor and working-class women are sterilized after delivery when the physician's influence is the greatest and many times the women are under the influence of drugs. It has also been shown that the women are forcefully sterilized by bribes from county hospitals regarding their welfare and medicare aid. The women are further not told the consequences of sterilization. As a result of protests, guidelines have been established although the abuse of sterilization continues. (EPICA Task Force 1976, 62-5) [Sterilization of women in the United States has increased 300 percent since 1970.] (bracketed information above comes from Judy Barlow 1978; in Adrienne Rich 1979, 266)

STEWARDESS

"I don't think of myself as a sex symbol or a servant. I think of myself as somebody who knows how to open the door of a 747 in the dark, upside down, and under water." (a 12-year stewardess for TWA; in Lindsy Van Gelder 1973, 87)

STRAIGHT WOMAN

"The definition of a 'straight woman' is directly proportional to the extent of the prick in her head." (*off our backs*, 8, July 1974)

  Can also be upright in her life if she is straightforward in her questioning, listening, thinking.

STRANGERS

Unknowns who, if male, are not to be trusted. Knowns are not to be trusted either. "Police and court data indicate that women are much more likely to be seriously assaulted or murdered by men known to them." (R.E. Dobash and R. Dobash 1980; in Jalna Hanmer and Sheila Saunders 1983, 32)

STRATEGIES

Planning and action necessary for desirable change. "We must be able to threaten governments, to make them fall if necessary. But to just talk and write, that won't get us anywhere. Throughout history, no group of people has ever obtained their rights by begging peacefully; they have snatched it from the hands of the authorities. There is no other way for women to win." (Nawal el Saadawi 1980, 3)

  (See ACTION)

STRATIFICATION

Social: According to a hairdressing day-release class, using the criteria of cash and respect:

The Queen
pop singers (various grades)
employers
principal of college
vice-principal of college
teacher
hairdressing students
mothers
  (Sheila Rowbotham 1983, 21)

STREET HARASSMENT

"Is a linguistic and social phenomenon in which a woman is subject to free and evaluative commentary from unknown men about her appearance. Women are not at liberty to retaliate or to return similar commentary to men. There is no parallel linguistic behavior toward men, but men of all ages, races, and occupations are free to address any woman who walks alone, or 'alone' with other women, in public places. Street remarks are a daily reminder of women's 'proper' role in society. Every time a woman walks alone in a public place, she must constantly be aware of herself: her posture, her clothing, her walk, her countenance, and her social interactions, because everything she does or says is under scrutiny. She must beware of whom she greets, when she smiles, and whom she looks at. She must be prepared to stare straight ahead and ignore unsolicited comments. This ensures that a woman can never feel at ease, will remember her role as a sexual being available to men, and will never forget that she does not belong in public life." (Elizabeth Kissling 1984, manuscript)
(See SEXUAL HARASSMENT)

STRENGTH

"Usually, when people talk about the 'strength' of black women they are referring to the way in which they perceive black women coping with oppression. They ignore the reality that to be strong in the face of oppression is not the same as overcoming oppression, that endurance is not to be confused with transformation." (bell hooks 1981, 6)

STRESS

Physical and mental pressures usually resulting from bad work and living conditions. "Stress . . . which may cause tension, digestive disorders, depression, and heart disease, occurs at high rates in women under pressure from two jobs: one paid and one unpaid." (Women and Work Hazards Group 1979; in Marsha Rowe 1982, 189)

STRETCH

The opposite of SHRINK. A feminist psychotherapist. (Terry Dalsemer in conversation with Elizabeth Snyder 1982, University of Illinois, Urbana-Champaign)

STRIKE

A form of resistance. "In Malaysia in an electronics factory a woman sees a spirit in her microscope – another woman's face. Along the line she alerts the other workers – there is excitement: their mothers' likenesses have come to disrupt production. The owners call this a 'subconscious wildcat strike.' " (Michelle Cliff 1980, 40)

STRIPPER

Women (usually) who dress down. Presented by the media as bad and/or as powerless. However: "The thrill I got from stripping was power. I was seen as powerful. Alive and free, I reveled in my body, my beauty, the dance, the drama, my own glorious energy. My whole being was totally engaged; I was radiant. . . I think our culture discourages simple freedom of movement even more than sexuality. How many places can you go to exercise anything but your mouth without being labeled odd? As a stripper, I was getting a taste of what it would be like to be a woman in a society that honors the animal vitality in us all, instead of despising it." (Seph Weene 1981, 36)

STRUCTURELESSNESS

"An intrinsic and accepted part of women's liberation ideology . . . based on trust, sharing, nurturing of the individual while working for the good of all." Usually results in "barneys about who [is] taking on leadership, being elitist, doing things without proper consultation with the group." (June Levine 1982, 152)
(See ELITE, ELITISTS,
HORIZONTAL HOSTILITY,
PHANTOM ELITE)

STRUGGLE

Can I say "she struggled to make ends

meet" and have the words mean anything at all? For *struggle* in that house was a constant thing, a cohabiting monster, a river that flowed over the stone of Esther, hourly, daily, monthly, just as hard to escape, and causing erosion just as sure and permanent." (Mary Jo McConahay 1978, 203)

"The struggle against oppression is to disrupt and dislocate the very terms on which that oppression feeds, not to change bits of it or to be absorbed into it or to coexist with it." (Jill Lewis 1981c, 146)

STUDYS
Rooms usually owned by men. "I don't wonder that men have studys which . . . I imagine to be only an excuse for making themselves comfortable and being out of the bustle and confusion of . . . house-keeping . . . and children." (*E.G.C. Thomas Diary*, Dec. 31, 1863; quoted in Anne Firor Scott 1984, 179)
(See WRITER)

STUNT GIRLS
Women reporters in the early twentieth century who went to great lengths, often in disguise, to get a story. Winifred Black Bonfils, whose pen name was "Annie Laurie," dressed in shabby clothing and faked an accident in order to write a personal experience story about the bad treatment women got at the hospital. She also wrote an inside story about a leper colony, stowed away on a presidential train to get an exclusive interview with President Benjamin Harrison, and disguised herself as a boy to cover a flood in Galveston, Texas. (Marion Marzolf 1977, 33-4)

SUBORDINATION
Women's: More than a convenience, the subordination of women is a necessity in patriarchy, a culture whose driving ethos is an embodiment of masculist ideals and practices. (Sheila Ruth 1980)

SUB-PROFESSIONALS
The official label used in 1920s and 1930s to designate nurses, dietitians and social workers in Government Hospitals and Regional Offices of the Veterans Bureau (all of whom were women). A Brief prepared under the auspices of the American Nurses' Association, representing in 1930 more than 86,000 graduate nurses stated: "The fact that the word 'sub-professional' as used by the Government has a technical meaning which does not connote 'non-professional' has little bearing on the situation, because the number of individuals who recognize this fact are few, and would have little influence on the general acceptance of the meaning 'less than professional.' " (in Clara D. Noyes 1931, 144)

SUBURBS
Neither town nor country. The well-to-do suburbs breed "selfishness, boredom, and disruption of family ties." ("Problems of the Day" 1913, *The Englishwoman*, 20:60 (December), 249-56)

SUFFRAGE MOVEMENT
Women's: An organized struggle for more than 70 years in English-speaking countries. The movement included concerns with many aspects of women's lives in addition to voting rights. It was based on "a refusal to respect any old piece of foolishness merely because some man happens to like it." (Robert F. Cholmeley 1912, 143)

In the U.K. it had as one of its mottos: "Let Justice be done though the Heavens fall." "This was the answer that during the early years of this century the Suffragette Movement gave to all the many reasons that the Government of the day put forward for not putting this principle into practice by extending the Franchise to women." (Lady Pethick-Lawrence 1951, 2)

SUFFRAGETTE
Word coined by the *Daily Mail* to belittle the acts of militancy by women fighting for the vote in Great Britain. It was converted to a proud label by a militant group of women and the newspaper

edited by Christabel Pankhurst was called *The Suffragette*. She edited it from exile in Paris (while her mother was repeatedly imprisoned and force fed in England) after 1913.

"Very well. . . Suffragettes if you like. To get an abuse listened to is the first thing; to get it understood is the next. Rather than not have our cause stand out clear and unmistakable before a pre-occupied, careless world, we accept the clumsy label; we wear it proudly. And it won't be the first time in history that a name given in derision has become a badge of honour!" (A public speaker in Elizabeth Robins novel 1907, 89)

One of the dreamers who thinks "that they could take by force what they could not keep by force." (H.M. Swanwick 1915, 177)

One of "those women who fought gallantly for women's right to vote and 'who carried the torch for themselves and got first degree burns.' " (Carolyn Kizer; in Midge Lennert and Norma Willson eds 1973, 12)

SUFFRAGETTISM

The name given by a man to the activities of the suffragettes. He wrote "I think there can be no question that the cause of suffragettism is the disuse of whipping as a punishment for girls in schools and families. I venture to assert that not one of those who recently appeared before the magistrates experienced the birch when in her teens; and the great majority of the suffragettes are young women for the simple reason that the birch was not so completely disused when the elder women were educated. . . As a rule political women can always be cured by a vigorous application of the birch." (Cited in *The Englishwoman* 1:1 (February), 40.

(See WIFE-BEATING)

SUPERMOM

"A do-it-all woman: male chauvinist approved; takes care of the kids and manages the house and brings home an income too; is clever, organized, efficient, concerned, considerate of others; good at

everything; a nervous wreck, an obnoxious and guilt ridden person." (Madelon Bedell; in Midge Lennert and Norma Willson eds 1973, 12)

(See SUPERWOMAN)

SUPERSISTER INTERNATIONAL

The leader which the media has been trying to find. The search and the accompanying patriarchal paradigm has had an impact on women who have been continually told that there is one truth. Instead of valuing and celebrating our differences and transforming our diversity into our strength, we often declare each other "falsely conscious." (Renate Duelli Klein 1983, correspondence)

(See ELITISTS, HORIZONTAL HOSTILITY)

SUPERSISTERS

"A feminist answer to baseball cards. Each of the 72 cards in the set features a photograph of a contemporary woman on one side, and information about her achievements on the other." (*Supersisters* Advertisement, *MS.*, October 1982, 82)

SUPERWOMAN

Tries to be all things to all people except herself.

(See SUPERMOM)

SUPPRESSION OF WOMEN'S WRITING

Methods and strategies include: "Informal prohibitions (including discouragement and the inaccessibility of materials and training), denying the authorship of the work in question (this ploy ranges from simple misattribution to psychological subtleties that make the head spin), belittlement of the work itself in various ways, isolation of the work from the tradition to which it belongs and its consequent presentation as anomalous, assertions that the work indicates the author's bad character and hence is of primarily scandalous interest or ought not to have been done at all (this did not end with the nineteenth century), and simply ignoring the works, the workers, and the whole tradition, the most commonly employed technique and the hardest to combat." (Joanna Russ 1983, 5)

(See STUDYS, WRITER)

SURFACE LABELING

"Refers to the careless use of terms, regardless of whether the lack of care is deliberate or unthinking. For example, the term 'women's libber' has been applied to an enormously wide spectrum of women. These range from a woman who is totally 'apolitical' and who is sexually and racially biased, but happens not to wear a bra (or is flashily successful in the White male professional world), to a serious, progressive-minded woman who is presenting a well-documented thesis on sexual politics and who engages in political struggles to change the social conditions of women's lives." (Gloria Joseph; in Gloria Joseph and Jill Lewis 1981, 42)

(See WOMEN'S LIB, WOMEN'S LIBERATION MOVEMENT)

SURGEON

A young man and his father are in an auto accident; the father is killed, and the young man is rushed to the emergency room of a nearby hospital. The surgeon, on entering the room and seeing the patient, exclaims, "Oh, my god, I can't operate – it's my son!" How is this to be explained? The answer to this riddle of the 1970s is that the surgeon is the young man's mother. The crux of the riddle lies in the expectation that the listener's conception of *surgeon* does not include the feature [+ female]. Linda Coleman and Paul Kay (1981) argue that this is not a linguistic issue but a social one, based on the minority of the category *surgeons* who are female. In the history of organized medicine, however, we find consistent reluctance to authorize sentences constructed as "the surgeon . . . she". This has involved social enforcement (protection of the profession from the intrusion of females); but it has also involved the explicit legal definition of *doctor* and related terms as male (see Mary Roth Walsh 1977) as well as the creation of

auxiliary terms for women doctors, surgeons, etc., including *doctress, woman doctor, gal surgeon*, and others. Coleman and Kay's distinction between typicality (most surgeons are male) and proto-typicality (surgeons are male) founders when definitions are protected and legislated by those whose authority permits it.

(See DOCTOR, DOCTORESS, PERSON)

SURNAME

(See MAIDEN NAME, NAME, NAMING, TITLE)

SURVIVAL

"*Is not an academic skill*. It is learning how to stand alone, unpopular and sometimes reviled, and how to make common cause with those other identified as outside the structures, in order to define and seek a world in which we can all flourish. It is learning how to take our differences and make them strengths." (Audre Lorde 1981a, 99)

"For to survive in the mouth of this dragon we call America, we have had to learn this first and most vital lesson – that we were never meant to survive." (Audre Lorde 1980, 21)

SURVIVOR

One who recovers from male sexual and/or physical abuse. (Elizabeth Stanko 1984)

(See SURVIVAL)

SUSAN B. ANTHONY AMENDMENT

"The right of citizens of the United States to vote shall not be denied or abridged by the United States or by any state on account of sex."

SWEEDLING

Sweet wheedling. "Val was at her sweedling best." (Margery Allingham, 1938, 59)

SWIM

A water activity which "calls into exercise muscles which the usual feminine occupations – such as sewing and the lighter kinds of manual labour – leave for the most part at rest, and spares many of those muscles which are commonly overworked. Thus, for instance, the extensors of the fingers and hands are stiffened, and in constant use in swimming, while the corresponding flexors, the slaves of the needle, are relaxed." (Mrs F. Hoggan, M.D. 1885, *Women's Union Journal*, 10:112 [May], 39)

SWOONING

Fainting. It ranked for a time along with dancing and wool-work as a womanly accomplishment. "It survives (that accommodating desire to be as feeble as men may require) in the readiness with which a girl will subdue her physical strength, and allow herself to be helped . . . to mount a stile; or to cross a brook." (Elizabeth Robins 1913, 113)

SWORDSWOMAN

Recurrent figure in traditional Chinese cinema who is without counterpart in Western films. "The Chinese swordswoman has a mission. Typically, her duty is to avenge her dead parents or family. Or she may take part in a rebellion against corruption and oppression. She may help villagers being bullied by bandits or corrupt soldiers, or rescue a maiden from attack. Or she may be a champion of the weak, helping the poor and helpless. When thanked, she may simply reply that it is her duty to help others and quietly disappear." (Lily Tom 1971, 44)

SYMBOL

  (See BANNERS, BUTTONS, COLOR, ICONOGRAPHY, LANGUAGE, SLOGAN)

SYMBOLIC ANNIHILATION OF WOMEN

The representational death sentence.

"Consider the symbolic representation of women in the mass media. Relatively few women are portrayed there, although women are fifty-one percent of the population and are well over forty percent of the labor force. Those working women who are portrayed are condemned. Others are trivialized: they are symbolized as child-like adornments who need to be protected or they are dismissed to the protective confines of the home. In sum, they are subject to *symbolic annihilation*." (Gaye Tuchman 1978, 8)

SYNTACTIC EUPHEMISM

Exemplified in a statement that a Take Back the Night march is "to make the streets safe from sexual assault." In this statement "the victims of sexual assault are as invisible as the men who are guilty of the crime of rape. Such sentences, the result of fear of naming the agents, go beyond Dickinson's suggestion to 'tell the truth, but tell it slant.' " An example of syntactic euphemism from the *powerful* which detaches the actor from the realities of the action: "The occupied Eastern territories are to become free of Jews" (Letter from Himmler to an SS official, c. 1942). (Julia Penelope 1983)

SYNTAX

"The compound-complex structure of sentences, with its main and dependent clauses carefully balanced, the logical tendency of our linear directed language that makes it impossible to think across structures of main and subordinate intention, categories of negative/positive and binary logic." (Wendy Mulford 1983, 34)
  (See LOGIC)

TAB
(See TEMPORARILY
ABLE-BODIED)

TABLE RULES

"When Father started to school he could
not speak English, so Grandfather
decided that it would be best for the
children if they spoke only English at
mealtime. This would encourage them to
learn polite table manners and get them
used to conversing in the English language. The first time it was tried, Great-
greatgrandmother was there and she was
not too happy about the new table rules.
She knew broken English but preferred to
speak in Kiowa. Great-greatgrandmother
used a lot of salt on her food and never
began eating until she had salted everything down. That day she thought and
thought, wondering how to ask for her
favorite seasoning. Then obviously
pleased with herself she said, 'Come here,
salt!' " (Ethel C. Krepps 1979, 156-7)

TAILORING

A trade invented by women who "monopolized it for ages; now men have taken
it from them and have virtually forbidden
them even to learn the occupation which
was once theirs." (Carrie Chapman Catt
1909, 13)

TAKE BACK THE NIGHT

A slogan "first used in the United States
as a theme for a national protest march
down San Francisco's pornography strip.
The march took place at night and was in
the spirit of many similar events taking
place all over the world. Take Back the

Night was a profound symbolic statement
of our commitment to stopping the tide of
violence against women in all arenas, and
our demand that the perpetrators of such
violence – from rapists to batterers to
pornographers – be held responsible for
their actions and made to change."
(Laura J. Lederer 1980, 19) "We have to
take back the night every night, or the
night will never be ours. And once we
have conquered the dark, we have to
reach for the light, to take the day and
make it ours. This is our choice, and this
is our necessity. It is a revolutionary
choice, and it is a revolutionary necessity.
For us, the two are indivisible, as we must
be indivisible in our fight for freedom."
(Andrea Dworkin 1978, 290-1)
(See ACTION, RECLAIM THE
NIGHT, VIOLENCE AGAINST
WOMEN)

TALK

Probably from Anglo-Saxon *talian* "to
reckon," means many kinds of communication, usually spoken (but one can "talk
in signs" or "talk with the eyes"). A
wealth of idioms reflect the importance of
talk in everyday life: *talk at, talk big, talk
down to, talk to death, talk out, talk up*. In
communication studies, usually means
conversation (in contrast to technical
language, public speaking, etc.).
Women's talk has become an important
focus for research, in part because it is so
important in women's lives. The following
stories and descriptions reveal something
about women's relationship to talk.
(See ACTION, BASKETRY,
CONSCIOUSNESS-RAISING,

CONVERSATION, FORMS OF
EXPRESSION, GOSSIP,
QUILTING, QUILTING BEES,
WOMEN AND LANGUAGE
RESEARCH, WOMEN'S
LANGUAGE)

A Nootka Indian grandmother describes talk among the Indian women
(women warriors) of her own and her
mother's generations: "A woman warrior
recognized the face of the enemy and was
prepared to do whatever was necessary to
defeat it. Sometimes the women warriors
would meet without the men, to sit in a
circle and talk women talk, and if a
woman had somethin' botherin' her, or
puzzlin' her, or scarin' her, or makin' her
feel uneasy, she'd say what it was. She
could take all the time she needed to talk
about it, but it was expected she'd have
put some of her own time into findin' the
words and not talk in circles, endlessly,
takin' up everyone else's time. Then the
other women in the circle who had maybe
had somethin' the same happen in their
lives would talk about it, and about what
they'd done, or hadn't done, or should
have done, and sometimes out of it would
come an answer for the sister with
problems. And even if not, sometimes it
was enough to just have been heard and
given love. It was expected that besides
just talkin' about what was botherin' you,
you'd do somethin' about it. Usually it's
better to do almost anythin' than let
things continue if they're botherin' you.
But sometimes the best thing you can do
is nothin'. Sometimes you have to wait for
the right Time before you can do. A
woman would come to the circle as often
as she needed, but the circle wasn't there
to encourage a woman to only talk about
her problems. The first three times you
came with the same story, the women
would listen and try to help. But if you
showed up a fourth time, and it was the
same old tired thing, the others in the
circle would just get up and move and reform the circle somewhere else. They
didn't say the problem wasn't important,
they just said, by movin', that it was *your*
problem and it was time you did some-

thin' about it, you'd taken up all the time
in other people's lives as was goin' to be
given to you, and it was time to stop
talkin' and *do* somethin'. A woman might
not know what was botherin' her. And it
was fine to go to the circle, or even to ask
to have one formed, and just sit with
women, and listen and maybe get
strength from smiles and cuddles and just
bein' with women you knew loved you."
(Anne Cameron 1981, 133-4)

"Be careful what you say. It comes
true. It comes true." (Maxine Hong
Kingston 1975, 237)

"Meridian, no matter what she was
saying to you, no matter what you were
saying to her, seemed to be thinking of
something else, another conversation perhaps, an earlier one, that continued on a
parallel track. Or of a future one that was
running an identical course." (Alice
Walker 1976, 139)

"Their conversation is like a gently
wicked dance; sound meets sound, curt-
sies, shimmies, and retires. Another
sound enters but is upstaged by still
another: the two circle each other and
stop. Sometimes their words move in lofty
spirals: other times they take strident
leaps, and all of it is punctuated with
warm-pulsed laughter – like the throb of a
heart made of jelly. The edge, the curl,
the thrust of their emotions is always
clear to Freida and me. We do not,
cannot, know the meanings of all their
words, for we are nine- and ten-years-old.
So we watch their faces, their hands, their
feet, and listen for truth in timbre." (Toni
Morrison 1970, 16)

This Swampy Cree Indian narrative
poem tells how a young Indian woman
was given the name "Many Talks":

"This girl did not give up baskets easily.
She sewed many, and also traded for
   them
in this village
and all over, in other villages.
The baskets sat in rows on the ground,
each filled with talk. You see,
she put something important to her
in each basket. Something from her life.

Then you could pick one out
for her to talk about,
just by lifting the cover!

That way you let the talk out.

This is how she had many mouths
sitting in rows on the ground.

The time I picked one it had
a catfish skull in it!
She told about catching this fish
who was GRINNING under some rocks
when she caught it.
It was the first fish she ever caught.

She grinned all through
the telling."
(Cree Indian narrative; Howard A.
Norman 1976, 61)

A passage from *The Well of Loneliness*
describes how Stephen, the protagonist,
feels different from other girls because she
cannot seem to join in their seemingly
easy forms of talk: "She would try to
appear quite at ease with her companions, as she joined in their light-hearted
conversation. . . As long as they refrained
from too intimate details, she would
fondly imagine that her interest passed
muster. . . . At such moments she longed
to be like them. It would suddenly strike
her that they seemed very happy, very
sure of themselves as they gossiped
together. There was something so secure
in their feminine conclaves, a secure sense
of oneness, of mutual understanding; each
in turn understood the other's ambitions.
They might have their jealousies, their
quarrels even, but always she discerned,
underneath, that sense of oneness."
(Radclyffe Hall 1928, 81-2)

Alice Roosevelt, daughter of U.S.
President Theodore Roosevelt, was the
darling of the country during her years in
the White House and inspiration for the
popular song "Alice Blue Gown." She
was also famous and feared for her witty
tongue and enjoyment of a good gossip:
"If you can't say something nice about
somebody," she would say, "Sit by me."

(Blanche Wiesen Cook 1982; lecture,
University of Illinois, Urbana)

TALKATIVE
What women are, according to male
perception and myth, despite research
findings to the contrary. "The concept of
women as the talkative sex involves a
comparison: they must talk too much
against some sort of standard or yardstick
and we have erroneously assumed that
the measurement of women as talkers is
in comparison to men. But this appears
not to be the case. The talkativeness of
women has been gauged in comparison
not with men but with *silence*. Women
have not been judged on the grounds of
whether they talk more than men, but of
whether they talk more than silent
women. When silence is the desired state
for women (and I suggest that it is in a
patriarchal order, as do numerous other
feminists) then any talk in which a
woman engages can be too much. . . In a
male supremacist society where women
are devalued, their language is devalued
to such an extent that they are required to
be silent. Within this framework it
becomes 'logical' to have one rule for
women's talk and another for men
because it is the sex – and not just the
talk – which is, significant. Cheris
Kramarae has summed this up when she
suggested: 'Perhaps a talkative woman is
one who does talk as much as a man.' It
is possible to go even further and to
suggest that when people are supposed to
be quiet, a talkative woman is one who
talks at all." (Dale Spender 1980, 42-3)
(See AUTHORITY, LANGUAGE,
MEANING, WOMEN AND
LANGUAGE RESEARCH)

TALKING CURE
Phrase used to describe the psychothera-
peutic technique in which people are
encouraged to talk about the origin of
their symptoms in order to be cured of
them. Coined by Bertha Pappenheim
(known in psychoanalytic literature as
Anna O), the term was adopted by Freud
as a description of his technique. In the

year that Freud and a colleague published her case history, Pappenheim began her career as a feminist pioneer and social reformer and throughout her life championed progressive social and political causes.

(See PSYCHOANALYSIS)

TALKIN GENDER NEUTRAL BLUES

Well I was walkin down the street one
    day
Readin the signs that passed my way
And after awhile I started to see
That none of those words referred to
    me . . .
"Good will toward men . . ." "All men are
    created equal . . ."
"Praise Him . . ."

Well I asked some friends if they agreed
That they felt left out in the things they
    read;
They told me yes and added some more
And soon we all felt pretty sore. . .
Congressman . . . businessman . . .
    sideman . . .
But I sure never heard of a house-
    husband!

Well some men came by and a fight
    began to grow;
"You girls are so dumb you just don't
    know –
These here are called generic words;
They're meant to include both the bees
    and the birds."
Well gee fellas, how am I supposed to
    know?
I certainly don't feel included!

Well then okay, said I, if that's so true,
I'll just use "woman" to cover the two.
"It don't make a difference to us," they
    said,
"If you wanna use 'woman,' go right
    ahead."
I said, thanks, that's real sisterly of you;
Glad to see you believe in sportswoman-
    ship.

"Now hold your horses," they started to
    cry.

"I think I'll hold my mares," said I.
"You're leavin all of us guys behind!"
Why no! We're all part of womankind!
So don't fret, friends . . . take it like a
    woman . . .
You'll get used to it, just like we all did!
    (Kristin Lems 1978, from the album *Oh
    Mama!* on Carolsdatter Productions,
    copyright Kleine Ding Music)

TALKS FOR GIRLS

Were what Virginia Woolf called her talks to young women which were designed to subvert the standard male lecture format.

(See ROOM OF ONE'S OWN)

TALK-STORY

"Night after night my mother would talk-story until we fell asleep. I couldn't tell where the stories left off and the dreams began, her voice, the voice of the heroines in my sleep... At last I saw that I too had been in the presence of great power, my mother talking-story." (Maxine Hong Kingston 1975, 24)

TAMPON

A modern word for an ancient object. Often associated with health care by and for women, the tampon has been traced at least as far back as ancient Egypt where rolls or bundles of cloth, sometimes treated with herbs or medicines, were inserted into the vagina to stem menstrual flow, prevent conception, and treat a variety of health problems. "Make a suppository as large as your little finger and put it in her privy member. . . . These suppositories should be fastened with a thread bound round one of her thighs, in case the suppositories should be drawn completely into the uterus." (Fifteenth century women's health manual, Beryl Rowland 1981, 69) The word *tampon* (from French *tapon*, a piece of cloth to stop a hole) seems to have entered English as a medical term around the Civil War and referred both to a rolled bandage to control hemorrhage in a puncture wound and to a vaginal insertion. "Tampons are pear-shaped with a thread attached to the lower end." (*Oxford English Dictionary* 1896) The word also refers to the piece of wood shaped to fit the bore of a gun to ram the charge home, and to the small wooden tapper used to print an engraved stone. Tampons were first manufactured commercially in the U.S. in the 1930s after a nurse suggested to her husband, a manufacturer, that many women would prefer the convenience they offered. Literature throughout the 1940s and 1950s argued the advantages and disadvantages of tampons. Questions were raised again in the 1970s with feminist and consumer charges that tampons were potentially carcinogenic, hemotropic (causing more blood to flow thus requiring purchase of more tampons), and directly responsible for Toxic Shock Syndrome. Feminist photographer Barbara DeGenevieve titled one photograph of tampons "nine small white objects purported to have carcinogenic and hemotropic properties found casually arranged in a vacant lot near some cactus." (Barbara DeGenevieve, Small White Objects Series, n.d.)

(See MENSTRUATION,
MAGAZINE MENSTRUATION,
TOXIC SHOCK SYNDROME,
WOMEN'S HEALTH MOVEMENT)

TANGLE TITS
(See TITS)

TATTOOS
Often given to young women among the California [Native American] tribes when they reach the age of puberty. (Rayna Green 1984, 316)

TEACHING
Originally, "to show." Later came to mean "to conduct, to guide, to show the way" and "to show by way of information or instruction."

(See CALL AND RESPONSE,
CLASSROOM INTERACTION,
RADICALTEACHER)

"So much of what passes for teaching is merely a pointing out of what items to want." (Alice Walker 1976, 192)

"Woman's work, man's promotion." (Judith Summers 1980, 33)

For many feminists, an open-ended and non-authoritarian exchange that helps translate feminist thinking into classroom practices. Feminist teaching practices are best typified in women's studies: "The double purpose of women's studies – to expose and redress the oppression of women – was reflected in widespread attempts to restructure the classroom experience of students and faculty. Circular arrangements of chairs, periodic small-group sessions, use of first names for instructors as well as students, assignments that required journal keeping, 'reflection papers,' cooperative projects, and collective modes of teaching with student participation all sought to transfer to women's studies the contemporary feminist criticism of authority and the validation of every woman's experience. These techniques borrowed from the women's movement also were designed to combat the institutional hierarchy and professional exclusiveness that had been used to shut out women." (Marilyn J. Boxer 1982, 667)

TEAM PLAYING
"The notion that women aren't successful in the workplace because we didn't play football when we were twelve has a hidden 'blame-the-victim' message. It's not that we don't know how to play on teams. It's just very hard to play on a team that doesn't want you on it." (Rosabeth Moss Kanter 1979, 64)

TECHNOLOGY
Practical and applied products of science and invention whose history and control have been largely controlled by men. Contributions by and for women in these fields have often been overlooked or belittled. "Not only have women inventors and the impact of technological change on women's work and lives been ignored, but feminist questions, based on feminist values, about the nature and direction of our technology have also found no place... The title of my book,

Machina Ex Dea, and that of this essay, 'The Goddess and the Machine,' are a play on historian Lynn White's *Machina Ex Deo*, which reversed the *deus ex machina* phrase from ancient Greek drama. Instead of the god from the machine' that produced an actor on stage with a mechanical device, a human being with god-like powers now produces the machine, i.e., technology. Although White and others have sought to deal with possible tensions between technology and spirit and the human role, the unconscious use of the *deo* form and male pronouns throughout such philosophical discussions as well as almost all other writings on technology underscores the male cast of such thought. Such language also masks the power element of technology, limiting and distorting discussions of the relationship between technology and power." (Joan Rothschild 1984, 3)

"With the impetus of an oil shortage, it is no surprise to find communications systems touted as a non-polluting, energy efficient alternative to transportation. As these telecommunications services proliferate, fostered by the twin forces of increased computing power and decreased commuting power, women may find themselves once again prisoners of gilded suburban cages, their feet bound by copper cable, optical fiber, and the invisible chains of electromagnetic waves." "New technologies – computers, communication networks, energy production, genetic engineering – have the potential for improving women's lives if, and only if, women gain political and financial control over the development and implementation of these inventions. Without such control, women will find themselves replaying a familiar scenario in which new technologies serve to reinforce old values." Their traditional roles: to provide high quality work at low pay, to provide unpaid labor in the home, to consume goods, and to serve as the object of social violence. "New technologies which promise liberation may offer women only these same roles to play in the social drama of tomorrow." (Jan Zimmerman 1981, 355, 356, 361)

"I see technology as neither liberating nor subjugating; only politics can be liberating, and until women organize themselves as the majority they are, men will continue to exploit them as they always have. Men with liberated/feminist/democratic consciousness can help to a certain extent, but it would be rash for women to trust us – alliances yes, dependency no!" (Ernest Callenbach 1981, 161)

"Technology is power, and power accrues to those who are already in control of a society's resources. Therefore, introducing technological advances into a culture simply adds to the competency of the controlling group; and in all systems that group is male." (Letty Cottin Pogrebin 1981, 166)

Each morning at a large insurance company, several hundred word processing operators brought their terminals up to find the following words on the screen: "GOOD MORNING! HAPPINESS IS A SUNNY DAY!" One morning, they find the message reprogrammed: "GOOD MORNING! HAPPINESS IS A GOOD FUCK!" There is much laughter, but management soon arrives to shut down the computer system until an analyst can "repair" the program. (Cited in Cheris Kramarae and Paula A. Treichler 1982, 4)

TECHNOSEXISM

Reproduction of sexist cultural stereotypes through the synthetized electronic speech used in such mechanical objects as computers, clocks, elevators, automobiles, vending machines and bathroom scales. "These talking machines are associating females with low-level service jobs, while associating males with tasks that are broader in range and higher in status. Male voices are used in most speech synthesis applications, ranging from calculators and computers to automobiles and emergency calling devices. Female voices, in contrast, are used predominantly in only three low-status applications: supermarket checkout scanners, telephone information systems and vending machines." (Steven Leveen 1983, "Technosexism," *New York Times*, November 12).

TELEPHONE

A communications technology associated with women, who served as operators from its earliest days and who, according to research as well as popular culture, talk on the telephone more frequently and for longer periods than do men. For women isolated in homes by childrearing and other responsibilities, the telephone has long been a means to link them with others.

Despite the fact that the vast U.S. telephone industry was maternalistically nicknamed "Ma Bell," few companies showed greater paternalism toward its customers and employees. Operators were trained to be pleasant at all times (company observers could tap into their lines at will to monitor their manners) and learned to control their reactions if they wished to retain their jobs. A female telephone clerk reported her frustrations in 1910: "The other subscribers in trouble kept on jiggling their receivers up and down. If I could only have screamed at them to wait a minute. But I had to take one at a time. I kept telling myself not to lose my head. But I felt as if I should at any moment. I pictured myself uttering a roar of rage, disconnecting all my cords, and hurling my stool at the Chief Operator." (Barbara Peters and Victoria Samuels, eds, 1976, 49)

In 1924, Bell Telephone management in the U.S. established an observation system whereby management could monitor and evaluate the work performance of its women operators by secretly listening in on their calls. One manager noted that "although the company had tried other methods of measuring service, none had proved equally satisfactory. Specifically, he said, other methods failed to provide an accurate measure of the work performance of one unit as opposed to another." (Elinor Langer 1970, 329)

TELEVISION

In the late 1940s, television was spreading across the U.S. rapidly and was hailed, like other communications "revolutions," as an expanding industry that would open challenging new jobs for women in decision-making roles. But despite the terrific growth in stations and audience, it soon became clear that the top jobs for women were to be limited to local women's programs. (Marion Tuttle Marzolf 1977) Represents "a selection and interpretation of life as seen or imagined by programme makers. . . Until women's voices can be heard in the way programs are made, and what they should be about, we shall continue to see what men *think* women are, not what women *know* they are." (Carmel Koerber 1977, 124, 143)

TELEWOMAN

"What are the three fastest means of communication?"

"Telephone, telegraph, and tell a woman." From this old joke came the name of the feminist journal *Telewoman*.

TELLING OF THE NAME

"To say the name is to begin the story." Characteristic structure of narrative poems of the Cree Indians, among whom names, stories, and significance are inextricably connected. (Howard A. Norman 1976, 49)

(See NAMING)

TEMPERAMENT

"Formation of human personality along stereotyped lines of sex category . . . based on needs and values of the dominant group and dictated by what its members cherish in themselves and find convenient in subordinates: aggression, intelligence, force, and efficacy in the male; passivity, ignorance, docility, 'virtue,' and ineffectuality in the female." (Kate Millett 1971, 46-7)

TEMPORARILY ABLE-BODIED (TAB)

A term that originated among disabled people and has more recently been used by some U.S. feminists to refer to people who used to be called "able-bodied." "Disabilities are an issue for all, not just because many will (for instance) lose our hearing and our mobility if we live long enough, but because notions of having to have 'perfect' bodies disable us all." (Sona Osman 1983, 29)

TENDING
(See CARING, MOTHERING)

TERRORISM
A phenomenon that, as modern women move into new roles and positions, seems is structurally related to an identification with potential sites of power. "The large number of women in terrorist groups (Palestinian commandos, the Baader-Meinhof Gang, Red Brigades, etc.) . . . is the inevitable product of what we have called a denial of the sociosymbolic contract and its counterinvestment as the only means of self-defense in the struggle to safeguard an identity. . . When a subject is too brutally excluded from this sociosymbolic stratum; when, for example, a woman feels her affective life as a woman or her condition as a social being too brutally ignored by existing discourse or power (from her family to social institutions); she may, by counter-investing the violence she has endured, make of herself a 'possessed' agent of this violence in order to combat what was experienced as frustration – with arms which may seem disproportional, but which are not so in comparison with the subjective or more precisely narcissistic suffering from which they originate. . . Are women more apt than other social categories . . . to invest in this implacable machine of terrorism? No categorical response, either positive or negative, can currently be given to this question. It must be pointed out, however, that since the dawn of feminism, and certainly before, the political activity of exceptional women, and thus in a certain sense of liberated women, has taken the form of murder, conspiracy, and crime." (Julia Kristeva 1981, 28, 29)

TERRORISM, SEXUAL
"Sexual violence, by definition, constitutes acts of excess that are unlimited in potential, scope, and depth and that are therefore terrifying to both victims and nonvictims alike. Terrorism goes beyond one woman's experience of sexual violence. It creates a state of existence that captures the hearts and minds of all those who may be potentially touched by it. . . Sexual terrorism has become a way of life for women." (Kathleen Barry 1979, 42, 43)

TESTERIA
From Latin *testes*, "testicles," "balls." Inability to respond emotionally. Crippling condition found in males, sometimes dangerously pathological. "Accounts in part for the ability of the male ruling class to efficiently, calmly, and maturely carry out planetary catastrophe. Male inventions like war, capitalism, totalitarianism, industrialism, and other atrocities are only possible if millions of efficient, calm, mature male people are diligently repressing their healthy human emotions. Since the turn of the century, over 50 million human beings have been slaughtered in war by psychiatrically normal male people." (Juli Loesch 1972-3)
(See HYSTERIA, TESTOSTERONE POISONING, WAR)

TESTICULAR INSUFFICIENCY
Infertility in males; the male counterpart to "ovarian insufficiency" in women following menopause. (Ruth Herschberger 1948, 70)

TESTOSTERONE POISONING
Hormonal imbalance suffered by many normal males. "Until now it has been thought that the level of testosterone in men is normal simply because they have it. But if you consider how abnormal their *behavior* is, then you are led to the hypothesis that almost all men are suffering from *testosterone poisoning*. The symptoms are easy to spot. Sufferers are reported to show an early preference (while still in the crib) for geometric

shapes. Later, they become obsessed with machinery and objects to the exclusion of human values. They have an intense need to rank everything, and are obsessed with size. (At some point in his life, nearly every male measures his penis.). . . The pathological violence of most men hardly needs to be mentioned. They are responsible for more wars than any other leading sex. Testosterone poisoning is particularly cruel because its sufferers usually don't know they have it." (Alan Alda 1975, 15)

TESTOSTERONE POISONING STRIKES AGAIN

This dictionary emphasizes women's words about women rather than stereotypical or traditional men's words. This entry includes a few exceptions as a reminder that testosterone poisoning is a tenacious disease.

The "Church Father" Tertullian castigated midwives and women physicians who provided gynecological care for women as follows: "If a child is extracted dead it verily was once alive. It is your tubes, your speculums, your dilators and hooks that are to blame for causing this destruction of the fruit of the womb." (in Kate Campbell Hurd-Mead 1938, 88)

"Women are not bound to their names with any strong bond. When they marry they give up their own name and assume that of their husband without any sense of loss. . . The fundamental namelessness of the woman is simply a sign of her undifferentiated personality." (Austrian philosopher Otto Weininger 1906; in Casey Miller and Kate Swift 1976, 12-13)

"MAN, see also PERSON; PERSON, see also HUMAN BEING, MAN. WOMAN, see also WIFE; WIFE, see also ADULTERESS, MARRIAGE, WOMAN, PERSONS, see also MEN, PEOPLE." (Stith Thompson 1955; in Susan Schibanoff 1983, 475)

A linguist, writing on the supposed non-creativity of prostitutes, in contrast to other underworld subcultures, at coining words and idioms: "This is hardly the type of mind which produces the subtle, flickering, humorous metaphors which characterize the lingoes of other criminal professions. It requires a sprightliness of mind, a kind of creative imagination, if you will, to toy so adeptly with language, to take so obvious a pleasure in the nuances of euphemism in a minor key." (David W. Maurer 1939, 116)

"Terrill Clark Williams, a 42-year-old writer from Fresno, had his name legally changed to God. 'It's something I've wanted to do for a long, long time,' he said." (*Ms.*, September 1982, 10)

"We will fly women into space and use them the same way we use them on earth − for the same purpose." (Former U.S. astronaut James Lovell, quoted in Jan Zimmerman 1981, 355)

TEXTILE

"The Latin term *textere*, meaning to weave, is the origin and root both for *textile* and for *text*. It is important for women to note the irony in this split of meanings. . . . 'Texts' are the kingdom of males; they are the realm of the reified word, of condensed spirit." (Mary Daly 1978, 4-5)

TEXTILE INDUSTRY

"Spinning and weaving, scraping and tanning, dyeing and embroidering, tailoring and designing" − all branches originated by women. "They created meshes and stitches, netting, looping, braiding, puckering, gathering, inserting of gores, tacking and all the rest of the operations essential to the making of garments, sheets, draperies, and comforts generally." (Mary Beard 1931, 339)

(See DINNER PARTY, QUILT, SAMPLER)

THANKSGIVING

Feast celebrating white men's imperialism. (Minot [North Dakota] Women's Collective 1971)

THANKSGIVING RECIPE

"Fucked-Up Turkey

Prepare stuffing:

6 cups cubed sponge marinated in
1 cup vinegar

1/2 cup ground glass
1 cup mashed garlic
sprinkle of pubic hair
Mix all ingredients thoroughly with 1/2 bottle Elmer's glue.

Stuff body cavity lightly (stuffing expands in cooking). Cap opening with diaphragm. Truss drumsticks and wings with sturdy rubber bands (they melt in heat).

Rub bird with orthogynol jelly and salt peter, place breast side up in shallow pan (bed pan, oil pan, etc.), and bake 25 min/lb in 350 oven. Spray occasionally with vaginal deodorant to prevent fowl odor.

Serve to men only garnished with poison mushroom caps, gall & kidney stones, nuts (any kind), ear wax, belly button cheese, and toe jam for extra flavor." (Minot [North Dakota] Women's Collective 1971)

THEATRE

"Has always been a sort of exclusive [drama] club." "In England, actresses appeared around 1600. . . . However, they did not manage the companies or write or direct the plays. With few exceptions [e.g., Aphra Behn], that was the reality of the theatre until only a hundred years ago." Playwrighting continues to be primarily a man's occupation. (Corinne Jacker 1981, 25, 26, 29)

THEORY

Originally, and most broadly, meant "a looking at, a viewing, a contemplation." The *Oxford English Dictionary* documents several meanings over the past several centuries: (1) a speculation, a sight, a spectacle; (2) a mental view; (3) a conception or scheme of something to be done, or of a method; (4) a systematic statement of rules or principles; a scheme or system of ideas or statements used to account for facts or phenomena; a hypothesis supported or confirmed by observation or experiment; a statement of general laws, principles or causes; (5) abstractions which contrast with practice; (6) speculations, conjectures, ideas, and individual views or notions. The term *feminist theory* is variously used in ways that draw upon all these meanings, sometimes referring to general principles that attempt to account for the universal oppression of women, sometimes to a particular body of coherent theoretical work like psychoanalysis, and sometimes to formulations which are simply abstract and not transparently factual or practical. In feminist writing, theory often examines the interlocking oppressions based on sex, gender, race, class, sexual preference, national origin, and ethnicity; tries to demystify; values subjective knowledge; and potentially tries to encompass the experience of each and every woman. Feminist resistance to theory is often a skepticism about Received Male Theory and not a denial that general statements about women's experience can be made. "Feminist theory, emphasizing the importance of women's individual and shared experience and their political struggle in the world, seeks to build general accounts of experience from particularities. We are still discovering the nature and scope of these particularities and exploring what kind of theory we are able to create." (Paula A. Treichler in press a)

(See IDEA, METHOD, OBJECTIVITY, REALITY)

"Of all the theories currently concerning women, none is more curious than the theory that it is needful to make a theory about them. That a woman is a Domestic, a Social, or a Political creature; that she is a Goddess, or a Doll; the 'Angel in the house,' or a Drudge. . . . But as nobody ever yet sat down and constructed analogous hypotheses about the other half of the human race, we are driven to conclude, both that a woman is a more mysterious creature than a man, and also that it is the general impression that she is made of some more plastic material, which can be advantageously manipulated to fit our theory about her nature and office." (Frances Power Cobbe 1869, 1)

"Feminist theorizing about science is of

a piece with feminist theoretical production. Unlike the alienated abstract knowledge of science, feminist methodology seeks to bring together subjective and objective ways of knowing the world. It begins with and constantly returns to the shared experience of oppression." (Hilary Rose 1983, 87-8)

A proposed pattern – true to our feelings and experiences – to understand the world by. "Theory cuts off its roots, loses its connection to reality when it ignores feeling; feeling needs structuring, a means of evaluating between conflicting feelings. . . . Mystification of theory prevents its organic development; anti-individualism prevents users of mystified theory from matching it to their own experience. Theory is for *us*, not the other way around." (May Stevens 1980, 41)

Attempts to identify and take into account all aspects of women's oppression. "Consider a birdcage. If you look closely at just one wire in the cage, you cannot see the other wires. If your conception of what is before you is determined by this myopic focus, you could look at that one wire, up and down the length of it, and be unable to see why a bird would not just fly around the wire any time it wanted to go somewhere." Feminist theory attempts "to take a macroscopic view of the whole cage." (Marilyn Frye 1983, 4, 5)

"Not only is theory implicit in our conception of the world, but our conception of the world is itself a political choice. . . . For feminists, theory is the articulation of what our practical activity has already appropriated in reality. The role of theory, then, is to articulate for us what we know from our practical activity; to bring out and make conscious the philosophy embedded in our lives." (Nancy Hartsock 1979, 57, 64, 65)

A form of policing. "Feminist [literary] theory addresses an audience of prestigious male academics and attempts to win its respect. It succeeds, so far as I can see, only when it ignores or dismisses the earlier paths of feminist literary study as 'naive' and grounds its own theories in those currently in vogue with the men who make theory: deconstruction, for example, or Marxism. These grounding theories manifest more than indifference to women's writing; issuing from a patriarchal discourse, they exude misogyny. Mainly, feminist theorists excoriate their deviating sisters. Feminism has always been bifurcated by contention between pluralists and legalists. Pluralists anticipate the unexpected, encourage diversity; legalists locate the correct position and marshall women within the ranks. Theory is, by nature, legalistic; infractions – the wrong theory, theoretical errors, or insouciant disregard for theoretical implications – are crimes; theory is a form of policing." (Nina Baym 1984, 45)

A dubious project, when feminists build their theory using "the master's tools": "What does it mean when the tools of a racist patriarchy are used to examine the fruits of that same patriarchy? It means that only the most narrow perimeters of change are possible and allowable." (Audre Lorde 1981a, 98)

THEORY IN THE FLESH
"Means one where the physical realities of our lives – our skin color, the land or concrete we grew up on, our sexual longings – all fuse to create a politic born out of necessity." (Cherríe Moraga and Gloria Anzaldúa eds. 1981, 23) "The materialism in this book lives in the flesh of these women's lives: the exhaustion we feel in our bones at the end of the day, the fire we feel in our hearts when we are insulated, the knife we feel in our backs when we are betrayed, the nausea we feel in our bellies when we are afraid, even the hunger we feel between our hips when we long to be touched." (Cherríe Moraga; in Cherríe Moraga and Gloria Anzaldúa eds 1981, xviii)

THERAPIST
The/Rapist. (Mary Daly 1978, 24n)

THERE'S ALWAYS BREAD AND JELLY
Common saying of Ellen Theresa Kunold

(1892-1981), a Black woman born and raised in Washington, D.C. (Pat Logan 1983, correspondence)

THEY

Third person pronoun, plural; optional use in singular for sex-indefinite references. "Before the zealous practices of the nineteenth-century prescriptive grammarians, the common usage was to use *they* for sex-indeterminable references. It still is common usage, even though 'grammatically incorrect.'. . . Then – and now – when the sex of a person is unknown, speakers may use *they*, rather than the supposedly correct *he* in their reference. To the grammarians, however, this was incorrect and intolerable. When the sex is unknown the speaker should use *he* – because it is the more comprehensive term. It is also, of course, the term which makes males visible, and this is not just a coincidence. Users of a language are, however, sometimes reluctant to make changes which are decreed from above . . . and it is interesting to note just how much effort has been expended on trying to coerce speakers into using *he/man* as generic terms. As Ann Bodine (1975) has noted, using *they* as a singular is still alive and well, 'despite almost two centuries of vigorous attempts to analyze and regulate it out of existence' on the ostensible grounds that it is incorrect. And what agencies the dominant group has been able to mobilize in this task! Bodine goes on to say that the survival of *they* as a singular 'is all the more remarkable considering the weight of virtually the entire educational and publishing establishment has been behind the attempt to eradicate it' (131)." (Dale Spender 1980, 149)

(See PRONOUN)

THINK PINK

Compilation of Broadway songs and contemporary feminist writings by the Little Women Theatre Group. (*Spare Rib* 1982, September, 31)

THINKING

"Has no sex." (Doris Fleeson, cited in Marion Tuttle Marzolf 1977, 57) "Is difficult when the words are not your own. Borrowed concepts are like passed-down clothes: they fit badly and do not give confidence; we lumber awkwardly about in them." (Sheila Rowbotham 1973a, 4) Is "a pre-eminently uncomfortable process; it brings to the individual far more suffering than happiness in a semi-civilised world which still goes to war, still encourages the production of unwanted . . . children by exhausted mothers, and still compels married partners who hate one another to live together in the name of morality." (Vera Brittain 1933, 40)

THIRD WORLD

In common economic and political writing, the industrialized west is the first world, the Eastern-European countries are the second world, and the "underdeveloped" and indigenous populations form the third world. There are many problems with this terminology. "The definition of the 'Third World' flows logically out of [a] prior definition of colonialism, for the 'Third World' refers to the historical victims of this process – to the colonised, neo-colonised, or de-colonised nations of the world whose economic and political structures have been shaped and deformed within the colonial process. The colonial relation has to do with *structural* domination rather than with crude economic ('the poor'), racial ('the non-white'), cultural ('the backward'), or geographical categories." (Robert Stam and Louise Spence 1983, 4)

"The phrase Third World has its roots in the post-World War II economic policies of the United Nations, but today it is a euphemism. We use it knowing it implies people of color, non-white and, most of all, 'other.' Third World women are *other* than the majority and the power-holding class, and we have concerns *other* than those of white feminists, white artists, and men." (Editorial Statement, *Heresies*, 2:4 [Issue 8], 1979, 1)

"Domestically speaking, Third World means minority people united against their common oppression." (Chris Choy; interviewed by Valerie Harris 1979a, 25)

A number of speakers at a 1983 conference titled Common Differences: Third World Women and Feminist Perspectives expressed dissatisfaction with the label "third world." Motlalepula Chabaku, from South Africa, reminded people at the conference that historically she belongs to the First World, not the Third. Winona LaDuke, a Lakota Indian, uses the term the Host World. (*Women and Language News* 1983, 7:1 (Spring), 1) "To native peoples, there is no such thing as the first, second, and third worlds; there is only an exploiting world . . . whether its technological system is capitalist or communist . . . and a host world. Native peoples, who occupy more land, make up the host world." (Winona LaDuke 1983, 55)

THIRD WORLD WOMAN

Third world women are "those who, by virtue of their race or class are deprived of basic human rights which many of us take for granted. we have become convinced that in order to get beyond a third world reality, we must move beyond a third world mentality and recognize that the issue is not the underprivileged, as we have been led to believe by those who wage wars on poverty, but that the issue is privilege. until wars are waged on privilege in this country and in the world, we all will be powerless to make the changes that are necessary to provide quality – and equality – of life to all humans." (Donna M. Hawxhurst and Susan L. Rodekohr, c.1984)

The figure of the Third World Woman is in some sense a construction of Euro-American scholarship and theoretical writing: in this writing, she is poor, uneducated, largely ignorant of her civil and legal rights, sometimes locked in revolutionary struggle of which she understands little, and oppressed by structures and institutions (e.g., the veil in Arab countries) beyond her control.

This familiar image is largely the product of "experts" with whom the definitional process has resided: colonial and imperialist western governments, western-trained cultural anthropologists, and western-trained experts in economic development. The Third World Woman thus becomes known to us as among the groups who, in Marx's words, "cannot represent themselves – they must be represented." A false universalization hides the specificities (historical and contextual particularities) through which the situations, experiences, and oppressions of women in various parts of the world can begin to be studied and understood. (Chandra Talpade Mohanty 1984)

"Several of my San Francisco Asian-American women friends and I eagerly approached other Asian women as 'Third World sisters,' an identity we naively brought with us to the international gathering [International Women's Year Tribune, Mexico City, July 1975]. To our shock and dismay, our Asian sisters could not identify with us; we were 'part of the enemy: rich capitalist Americans'! In addition, a gulf had arisen over time, and transplantation had created cultural barriers which could not be bridged for the short duration of the conference. We were acutely and painfully aware of the different perception of feminist priorities we had in contrast to our overseas sisters." (Liang Ho 1982, 60)

THE THREE M'S

Marriage, Motherhood, and Monotony. (Eveyln Tension 1978, 85)

THRUST

One of many "masculine" words in English. (Susan Brownmiller 1984b, 9A) A second opinion: "I don't consider 'thrust' a 'masculine' word: *I* thrust!" (Woman participant 1983, classroom discussion, Marxism and the Interpretation of Culture, University of Illinois at Urbana-Champaign)

TIME

A commodity needed but rarely obtained

by women. "*Time* is an important consideration in any discussion of men's and women's writing, for writing takes time, and women in our society do not usually have as much of it as men. It takes sustained and uninterrupted time to work at writing, and with the sexual division of labour we have been 'blessed' with, women have been required to produce time – for men! Women have produced time for men to write and in the process they have reduced their own amount of time in which to write. Another variation on 'the art of conversation,' another development of male words at the expense of their own, another form of *shitwork*." (Dale Spender 1980, 218-19)

"I have no time for time, and so I break time into little pieces, like dog biscuits and lumps of sugar, and keep them in my pocket. All day long I nibble on hours, half hours, and their crumbs – the brittle minutes between one activity or person and the next. This diet gives me emergency energy, but I can't write poetry in it – my mind wanders. I fantasize constantly about real time-food: a home-cured day, a spring-fed weekend, the feast of a succulent month simmered in solitude." (Judith Thurman 1977; quoted in *Ms.* 5:7, January, 48)

TIPPING

"A fantasy that allows our society to justify less than minimum wages for waitresses." (Midge Lennert and Norma Willson, eds, 1973, 12)

TITLES

(See FORMS OF ADDRESS, JOB TITLES, NAMES, OCCUPATIONAL TITLES)

TIT

From 'teat,' now male slang for 'breast.' "The speakers of Gay male slang may be the only group in America who really admire the female breast as a powerful characteristic. In Gay slang *tits* means courage, unmitigated gall, 'the tits' means excellent. To 'tangle tits' means to do battle, and 'nit tits' are micro-

scopic breasts." (Judy Grahn, 1984, 231)
  (See BREAST)

TITTER

Laughter one is seeking to suppress, commonly said of women's but not of men's laughter. Not what "liberated women" do. "Self-loathing ladies titter; Hags and Harpies roar. Fembots titter at themselves when Daddy turns the switch. They titter when he pulls the string. They titter especially at the spinning of Spinsters, whom they have been trained to see as dizzy dames. Daddy's little Titterers try to intimidate women struggling to greatness. This is what they are made for and paid for. There is only one taboo for titterers: they must never laugh seriously at Father – only at his jokes." (Mary Daly 1978, 17)
  (See GIGGLE, LAUGHTER)

T OF L

T[ime] of L[ife]. Menopause. (Virginia Woolf; quoted in Paula Weideger 1977, 4)

TOGETHERNESS

"An obscenity taught to young women in the 1950s." (Midge Lennert and Norma Willson, eds., 1973, 12)

TOILET

Reason given why women should not be allowed to join in activities men have reserved for themselves, as in "The Board Room [Law School, Surgeons' Lounge, Stock Exchange, Moon] has no ladies' toilet."

Water closets whose labels and locations can tell us quite a lot about institutions. For example: "In the new House [of Commons], rebuilt after the Second World War, there is just one space in the House which is used by all women members irrespective of party, and *only* by women, and that is the toilet just outside the Chamber. There are in addition two sets of rooms, each marked 'PRIVATE, LADY MEMBERS ONLY'; one set of these is used by women members of the political left and the other by women of the political right. Men's toilets are simply marked 'MEMBERS ONLY'. . . . There would seem to be an implicit assumption, even though the House was rebuilt at a time when women were eligible for election to membership, that members are men." (Linda Imray and Audrey Middleton 1983, 19)

"The word 'toilet' used to be considered a dreadful genteelism by Australians with pretensions to plain usage; they preferred lavatory, which is itself a euphemism. 'Toilet' won and became universal, though it is considered very 'in' in some circles to revert to words like 'dunny' and 'sh'ouse' (from 'shit-house'), or to adopt overseas terms such as 'loo' or 'john.' 'Going to Mary's room' or 'going to visit Mary' or 'aunty' are examples of a range of euphemisms used by some women – the proper names vary widely. 'The little girls' room' is still heard of. 'To have a leak' or 'to make water' seem to be exclusively male usages." (Nancy Keesing 1982, 48-9)

TOKEN

From the root *deik* "to point, show"; also "betoken, symbolize." A member of an underrepresented group is permitted into the territory of the dominant group in order to be pointed to or shown, and in order to betoken or symbolize change. Some comments on token women and token feminists follow.

(See MRS GODBLESS)

A token woman is "an honorary man." (Elizabeth Wilson 1975, 14) Token women "have been allowed into pieces of patriarchal territory as a *show of female presence*. They are understood to represent the female 'half of the human species' in male terrain. The hidden agenda of their role includes thinking 'like a man,' that is, with the set limitations of patriarchal thought as prescribed for each situation, while at the same time behaving according to the feminine stereotype." (Mary Daly 1978, 334) "Kate would sometimes picture her tombstone with 'The Token Woman' engraved in the marble. Above the inscription, androgynous angels

would indifferently float." (Amanda Cross 1982, 4) "White females are the tokens among women in the society, in that they have the titles but not the power, while black women have neither." (Kay Lindsay, in Black Women's Action Committee 1972, 84)

The token feminist is "a triply compounded product of patriarchal ingenuity. . . . It is she who can best play the role which Robin Morgan has identified as 'the ultimate weapon in the hands of the boys.' " (Mary Daly 1978, 335) The token torturer is "the woman who often unwittingly pleases her masters by selling out her own kind. She increases their pleasure by performing the acts which are less than gentlemanly, thus obscuring their role." (Mary Daly 1978, 336)

TOKENISM

"A means of acknowledging and then forgetting oppression and discrimination." (Juliet Mitchell and Ann Oakley 1976, 8)

TOLERANCE

"The valuing of all contributions equally should not be confused with the male defined meaning of *tolerance*. Tolerance can only be exercised by those who are in power and it is often nothing but another means of protecting that power. Tolerance does not eradicate the distinction between right and wrong, it simply makes being in the wrong slightly less offensive. It is not tolerance which characterizes the women who are handling the inherent contradictions of existence within feminism . . . but a reconceptualization, a new classification of the objects and events of the world. Out of the understanding that the personal is political has grown the realization that the explanations of others are appropriate for their circumstances equally well as one's own." (Dale Spender 1980, 104)

(See REALITY, THEORY, TRUTH)

TOM

Lesbian; British slang.

(See TOMBOY)

TOMBOY

Girls who are "allowed to play a prominent part in an adventure, even to take over the leadership for part of the time, to be tough, resourceful, and to make decisions. They also openly attack the female role that outside people like parents and relations expect them to play." A tomboy may give "free rein to . . . fantasies of adventure, but at the same time she is sternly contrasted with the real girls . . . she is not totally accepted by the boys." The roles are not reversed; there are no janegirls. (Camilla Nightingale 1974; in Marsha Rowe ed. 1982, 37, 38) Traditionally defined as a syndrome in which girls display an aversion to conventional girls' activities and to girls as playmates and instead seek companionship in boys and boys' activities. "The term 'tomboyish' is based on a traditional conservative view of male-female behavior." (Lesley J. Rogers 1983, 1110-11)

"I was a tomboy, of course. It is no exaggeration to say that in general women who become dykes were known as tomboys when they were children. Of course, many aggressive, athletic, rambunctious tomboys never become Lesbians, and many Lesbians were never tomboys. Nevertheless, having once been a tomboy is a major theme in the life stories of a great majority of Gay women, especially those designated in Gay culture as dikes, and especially those dikes who are particularly butch. In England, a slang word for Lesbian is *tom*. *Tomboy* is also an old and perhaps spirit-based word, for one of the witches persecuted in England during the thirteenth century was accused by the authorities of having an imp, or spirit, in the form of a grey cat whose name was Tomboy." (Judy Grahn 1984, 147-8)

TOMBSTONE

In ancient Greece and Rome, tombstones erected by patients and families in memory of women healers preserve the feminine endings in *medica*, *obstetrix*, and *nutrix*, enabling us to establish that there were physicians, nurses, and other healers who were women. One tablet reads *MAGISTRA IN MEDICINA*, suggesting high professional attainment. Even when evidence is scant, "by every law of probability, if we have the tombstone of one, there were scores of others whose gravestones have not yet been discovered, or who never had stones erected to them at all." (Kate Campbell Hurd-Mead 1938, 66)

"A long time ago when people wanted to settle in a town they would go to the cemetery and look at the tombstones. If there weren't many recent dates or many small children's graves they would know that the water was safe to drink and that the town was a fairly safe place to live." (Ethel C. Krepps 1979, 157)

"All that is left of a married woman to be marked on her gravestone is that she was the wife of somebody who had owned her." (Lucy Stone 1850; in Una Stannard 1977, cover)

"I saw a woman looking at my cartoon of a woman in her grave holding up a sign that reads, 'My name was Helen,' while overhead the gravestone reads 'Mrs. Henry Smith.' The woman looking at the cartoon laughed; then she said, 'Oooohh, that hurts, that's me.' " (bülbül 1984, 18)

A tombstone is no substitute for earthly justice. "In the distant future, it may be, centuries and centuries hence, a monument of brass or stone will be erected to the Old Black Mammies of the South, but what we need is present help, present sympathy, better wages, better hours, more protection, and a chance to breathe for once while alive as free women." (Black nurse 1912, writing in the *Independent*; cited in bell hooks 1981, 58)

"I'm here against my better judgment. That would be a good thing for them to cut on my tombstone." (Dorothy Parker; in John Keats 1970, 207)

TONGUE

A metaphor for the freedom to speak, a freedom not always considered "ladylike" to exercise. " 'Oh, my tongue, my abominable tongue! Why can't I learn to keep it quiet?' groaned Jo [the 'tomboy' in *Little Women*], remembering words which had been her undoing." (Louisa May Alcott 1869, 343) "I have had to bury my father to set my tongue free." (Francine Du Plessix Gray 1982, 46)

(See MOTHER TONGUE)

TONGUERSOME

Adjective for those cumbersome nonsexist words some people claim will ruin the English language. "We have all been longing, I am sure, for a simple, yet suitably dignified suffix to replace the awkward and tonguersome *person*, as in *chairperson.* . . . In its place may I suggest the petite yet compelling, and completely association-free, peep." (Shelly Mintier, letter to the editor, *Ms.* 3:11, May 1975, 4)

TORAH

In Jewish history and scripture, the Five Books of Moses; essentially canonized against change in the 5th century B.C., it became customary to have an interpreter in the synogogue to explain and interpret the particularly complex, obscure, or difficult passages. This hermeneutic activity, called *Midrash* ("exposition"), was passed on by way of an increasingly scholarly oral tradition called *Mishnah* and, later, a continuation of *Torah* interpretation called *Gemara*. The shift to a written form of interpretation became necessary as a result of massive repression, dispersal, and murder of the Jews in the sixth century A.D., when it was feared that the interpretive tradition would be lost; over the next 200 years, scholars wrote down these interpretations, interpolations, and insights, a body of work that evolved into the *Talmud*. The synogogue was seen as the domain of men, as was the House of Study, the Talmudic academies, and other forms of Jewish leadership (Elyse Goldstein 1983, 26). Comments below suggest how feminists today are seeking to reverse the historical exclusion of women from these activities in a variety of ways.

(See JEWISH WOMEN, TSENA URENA, VULVIC KNOWLEDGE)

"Nearly three thousand years have passed since Sinai, three thousand years since our ancestors received Torah as a way of life. From the beginning there were words. We know that our fathers of the past decided to transmit revelation and all subsequent events by word of mouth: first came the oral tradition, only later to be recorded as the written law. And so we moved through history, remembering and transmitting the past in the experience of our lives. And yet some of us remain at the beginning, the word still to be formed, waiting patiently to be revealed, to rise out of the white spaces between the letters in the Torah and be received. I am speaking of the tradition of our mothers, our sister-wives, the secret women of the past. How would they have spoken of their own religious experiences if they had been given a space to record their stories? How would they have transmitted the written word? Would their ceremonies, rituals, and customs have been the same?" (Lynn Gottlieb 1976, in Susannah Heschel 1983, 273)

There is evidence that feminist perceptions of the world might have influenced the Torah "at the very moment when patriarchal power was defeating the ancient matriarchies" by being smuggled in, around, and under its patriarchal surface by certain ancient matriarchs. Now is the time to rediscover and strengthen those insights: "It is as if the voice of modern feminism woke a Sleeping Beauty in the Torah, a wisdom that recognized her daughter's voice." But "if Torah once bore within herself a secret feminist guerrilla victory smuggled into an obvious public patriarchal triumph, then the victory has oozed away. The feminism must be made explicit and public." (Arthur I. Waskow; in Susannah Heschel, ed., 270–1)

"My attraction to the idea of reading the Torah in public had to do both with my newly serious interest in Judaism and with my commitment to feminism. . . . Raised in an observant home, I found meaning and satisfaction in the ritual; yet for some years I found it actually painful to attend traditional synogogue services solely as passive consumer, barred by my gender from assuming any public role. . . . [After four class sessions on learning to chant the Torah, I agreed to participate in the Shabbat services.] The previous evening I had had one of my few glances into a Torah. It was intimidating. When the scroll is opened, one views a literal sea of words. The Torah is handwritten in columns several inches wide. There are no commas, no periods, few divisions of any kind – and no vowels at all!. . . The reading began, and I was told to come forward. . . . I faltered a few times, but the words came out and it all happened fairly quickly. . . . As I finished, I encircled my fellow students with one arm in exaltation. We were four women standing before everyone." (Arleen Stern; in Susannah Heschel, ed., 1983, 182-4)

TORONTO WOMEN'S LITERARY SOCIETY

Ostensibly a society, established in 1877, for the development of women's intellectual interests, it was really a front for suffrage activity. In 1883, it dropped its disguising name and became Canada's first national suffrage association (Carol Lee Bacchi 1983, 30). Many other women's groups are disguised in similar ways, a fact played upon by the makers of the t-shirts with the label "Ladies Sewing Circle and Terrorist Society."

TORVALDS

"Those who would address their wives (as does Torvald Helmer in Ibsen's play *A Doll's House*): 'Before all else you are a wife and a mother.' " (The Princess Bariatinsky 1911; *Votes for Women*, December 15, 177)

TOTAL RESPONSIBILITY THEORY (TRT)

The doctrine in heterosexual relationships that the man is totally responsible for the presence or absence of sexual satisfaction in either party. "A most unrealistic dogma." (Ruth Herschberger 1948, 96)

TOTAL WOMAN

The "Total Woman [Marabel Morgan, *The Total Woman*] makes blasphemous sexuality into a home art, redomesticating what prostitutes have marketed as forbidden." (Catharine A. MacKinnon 1982a, 530)

TOWER OF BABEL

"The erection of phallocracy. The voices and silences of Babel pierce all of our senses. They are the invasive extensions of the enemy of women's hearing, dreaming, creating. *Babel* is said to be derived from an Assyrian-Babylonian word meaning 'gate of god.' When women break through this multiple barrier composed of deceptions ejaculated by 'god' we can begin to glimpse the true gateways to our depths, which are the Gates of the Goddess." (Mary Daly 1978, 4)

TOXIC SHOCK SYNDROME (TSS)

A rare but serious disease that mainly strikes menstruating women under 30. Though the number of women is small, a few have died. TSS, which came to public attention in 1980, is a syndrome or group of symptoms. At present, only those people who have all the symptoms listed are officially counted as having TSS; however, reports indicate that many others may have milder forms of the disease. The symptoms are a high fever (usually over 102), vomiting, diarrhea, sudden drop in blood pressure which can lead to shock, and sunburn-like rash. (Boston Women's Health Book Collective 1984, letter to women consumers, August)
  (See TAMPON, UMBRELLY, WOMEN'S HEALTH MOVEMENT)
  The acronym TSS also stands for TOUGH SHIT, SWEETIE: both to protest the lack of research on the safety of tampons and other "feminine" products and to comment on the often cavalier attitude of corporations and government agencies toward women's health issues.

TRADE UNIONS

"Sites of patriarchal bonding which serve to make public space for men to gather as *men* in order to maintain and perpetuate the boundary between the public and private spheres." (Linda Imray and Audrey Middleton 1983, 17)

TRAFFIC IN WOMEN

Essay by Gayle Rubin (1975) that explores the social arrangements within which women acquire their status as commodities and introduces the notion of the sex/gender system, "the set of arrangements by which a society transforms biological sexuality into products of human activity, and in which these transformed sexual needs are satisfied."

(See MARXIST FEMINIST, SEX/ GENDER SYSTEM)

TRAGIC WOMAN

A neglected or misunderstood literary type. "To oversimplify, the tragic man acts before he thinks; the tragic woman thinks and knows she cannot act." (Carolyn Heilbrun and Catharine Stimpson 1975, 68)

TRANSCRIPTION

Incomplete representation on paper of spoken words. "No matter how accurate a transcription, words seem flatter on the page than they do in your ears. Some things get lost. For example, we were constantly reinforcing each other's remarks by saying 'right' or 'yeah' or 'un-hunh' while the other was speaking. We also laughed and this is undoubtedly the non-verbal element I most wish it were possible to recreate. It seemed like such an integral part of what we were saying, because so often it was the laughter of recognition." (Barbara Smith; quoted in Cenen and Barbara Smith 1983, 31)

TRANSFERENCE

In psychoanalysis, the process by which a wish (desire) is actualized through specific relationships, usually in the analytic situation itself (i.e., between the analyst and the analysand). In the pro-cess, childhood structures and feelings reemerge and are experienced with great immediacy. In classical psychoanalysis, "the transference is acknowledged to be the terrain on which all the basic problems of a given analysis play themselves out: the establishment, modalities, interpretation and resolution of the transference are in fact what define the cure." (J. Laplanche and J.-B. Pontalis 1973, 455)

In an essay analyzing the history of access to philosophy and the basic philosophical assumptions latent in discourse about women, Michèle Le Doeuff argues that women philosophers, historically consigned to marginal and amateur status, have been subject to a "curious form of transference." "It is only through the mediation of a man that woman could gain access to theoretical discourse." Lacking the institutional identity that allows men eventually to break such personal relationships, women's "transference relationships have only opened up to them the field of their idol's own philosophy." "This theoretical devotion of a woman is very comforting for someone experiencing his own lack." Thus philosophers have had something to gain by maintaining this kind of transference, a "confusion of amorous and didactic relationships." (Michèle Le Doeuff 1977)

TRANSFORMATION

"Requires a lot of heat. It requires both the alchemist and the welder, the magician and the laborer, the witch and the warrior, myth-smasher and the myth-maker. Hand in Hand, we brew and forge a revolution." (Gloria Anzaldúa; in Cherríe Moraga and Gloria Anzaldúa eds 1981, 196)

TRANSLATION

"Any woman who has moved from the playing fields of male discourse into the realm where women are developing our own descriptions of the world knows the extraordinary sense of shedding, as it were, the encumbrance of someone else's baggage, of ceasing to translate." (Adrienne Rich 1976b, 208)

TRANSVESTITISM

Is related to *travesty*, "caricature," and means literally "cross-dress," from *trans-* + *vestire* "to clothe." *Transvest* was once a verb: "How often did shee please her fancy with the imagination of transvesting herself, and by the help of a Man's disguise deceiving the eyes of those that watched her deportments?" (1652 citation, *Oxford English Dictionary*). (See Judy Grahn 1984, 228)

TRASHING

Is "a particularly vicious form of character assassination which amounts to psychological rape. It is manipulative, dishonest, and excessive. It is occasionally disguised by the rhetoric of honest conflict, or covered up by denying that any disapproval exists at all. But it is not done to expose disagreements or resolve differences. It is done to disparage and destroy." (Joreen 1976, 49)

TREMOLO

Vibrating high-pitched sound made by Ogalala Sioux women to men in battle; this reminds the men that it is the women whom the men are fighting for. According to Black Elk, the sound of the tremolo inspired the men to greater bravery in battle: it is then that they really fought with great courage. (Priscilla Diaz Dorr 1984, correspondence)
(See SHOUTING)

"A woman is making the tremolo into the wind
No longer is it the song she once made
For her husband and sons in battle
Now she sings it for herself . . .
And her tremolo is a new song
She sings in a voice of rolling thunder
Saying,
Listen, women! The new word for *strong*
is '*Woman-hearted!*'
(Joan Shaddox Isom, "Tremolo"; in Beth Brant ed. 1983, 209)

TRIAL MARRIAGE

Test of satisfaction with a partner, usually heterosexual. In 1906, Dr Elsie Clews Parsons, sociologist, wrote, "It would seem well to encourage early trial marriages, the relation to be entered into with a view to permanency, but with the privilege of breaking it, if it proves unsuccessful, without suffering any great degree of public condemnation." (Quoted in Elizabeth Janeway 1973, 30)

TRIANGLES

"Many gay people have taken up [a] Nazi symbol – the pink triangle that homosexuals were forced to wear in concentration camps. . . . It has come to be used as a symbol of gay defiance in the face of persecution, repression and annihilation. It was uncovered [in England] in 1971 by a man in the Gay Liberation Front, Alan Wakeman, who read in a Jewish library about the whole elaborate system the Nazis worked out with interlocking triangles to signify all they persecuted – Jews, Communists, gypsies, gays, people with disabilities and so on. Although he wrote about it, and although a wreath in the shape of a triangle was placed on the Cenotaph on Remembrance Day, to commemorate homosexuals killed in war – it didn't take off as a symbol until the Gay Activists Alliance produced a 'Gays Against Fascism' badge incorporating the pink triangle to counter the National Front in its rise in 1977." "Politically (as a reminder both that homosexuals died . . . in concentration camps, and that the struggle of gays can't be separated from a wider struggle) and aesthetically (reclaiming pink!) [the pink triangle is] very satisfying." It is sometimes used with the apex pointing down or (deliberately to reverse Nazi practice) up. (Ruth Wallsgrove 1982, 10)

TRIANGLE SHIRTWAIST COMPANY

In 1909 fired female shirt-waist makers who had joined a union; in protest, during 1909-10, women workers carried out a prolonged strike against the company. "During the strike this firm is said to have caused the arrest of more than 300 pickets and strikers. It was charged with hiring prostitutes to annoy the striking girls, besides employing thugs to attack them." In 1911, a terrible fire broke out at the company in which more than 140 workers, mostly women and girls, were either burned to death or died in jumping from the top floors. Investigation proved the building to be a fire-trap, with a single fire-escape that was wholly inadequate; furthermore, the doors of the shops opened inward and were kept locked. The company's name became synonymous with corrupt practices in the garment industry and fueled the movements for unionization and women's suffrage. (A.S.B. 1911, *The Woman's Journal*, April 11)

(See GARMENT INDUSTRY)

TRIBADISM

"The term for two women rubbing clitorises and mounds together with their thighs locked between each other's legs... the title of the woman who performs it is 'Tribas.'" (Judy Grahn 1984, 236) This (from the Greek word meaning "to rub") is one Lesbian sexword which suggests a vocabulary of women's love-making. (It is also one which was evidently academic enough to be included in the *Oxford English Dictionary*, which defines *tribade* as "a woman who practices unnatural vice with other women.")

TRIBE

"The basic teachings in every Tribe that exists today as a Tribe in the western hemisphere are based on respect for all the things our Mother gave us." "There are approximately 130 different Indian languages still spoken in North America of the some 300 spoken at contact; 180 different Tribes [are] incorporated and recognized by the Federal Government of the approximately 280 that once existed, with an additional 15 to 25 unrecognized Tribes that are lumped together on a reservation with other Tribes. We still have Women's Societies and there are at least 30 active women-centered Mother-Rite Cultures existing and practicing their everyday life in that manner, on this continent. We have been displaced, relocated, removed, terminated, educated, acculturated and in our hearts and minds we will always 'go back to the blanket' as long as we are still connected to our families, our Tribes and our land." (Carol Lee Sanchez 1983b, 152, 151)

TRICK

To have sex with a complete stranger. Both gay men and female prostitutes "call what they do 'tricking.' Some flaming queens brag of having sex with one thousand men in a one-year period. In *City of Night*, John Rechy's novel about the urban Gay underground of the early 1960s, Rechy described exuberantly one special night of his life, a night spent standing with his back to a tree having sex with seven different men, all of it happening outdoors in a park. *That* is what I mean by tricking. Even when two men have a long-term relationship with each other, tenderly living together as lovers, often they will trick outside the marriage.... As a rule, Lesbians... do not turn tricks. With rare exception, they do not pick strange women up on the street by displaying themselves sexually for the sole purpose of ten or fifteen minutes of genital sex; they do not perform cunnilingus or tribadism on total strangers in movie houses, restrooms, parks, alleys, tearooms, or baths, nor do they count these places as in any way having to do with themselves. Lesbians sometimes use the word *trick* when they really mean 'one-night stand,' that is, going to a bar or party, meeting someone, and going home with her to spend the night and have sex or at least hug and kiss and be in each other's arms. That isn't tricking.... I am not going through this definition as a means of making a moral judgment. I think there have been serious misunderstandings between Gay men and Gay women concerning tricking – with the men trying to assume that Lesbians operate exactly as they themselves do, and with the women trying to assume moral superiority because no, we don't. Our institutions and our precedents are different." (Judy Grahn 1984, 209-10)

TRIFLES

Name of a play by Susan Glaspell, American writer, in which a murder mystery is solved by women's attention to ordinary objects in a woman's kitchen and to details which are dismissed as "trifles" by the sheriff and attorney. (*Trivia: A Journal of Ideas* 1983, 1:1)

TRIVIA

"Deriving from 'trivium' (crossroads), was one of the names of the Triple Goddess. As such, it describes the matrix of our creative power, the gatherings of wise women in which our ideas originate and continue to live. . . . As we conceive it, [the journal] *Trivia* is the place where our friendships and our ideas assume their original power and significance." (Anne G. Dellenbaugh and Lise Weil eds. 1982)

TROPISMS

Are "those extremely quick movements that pass through our minds on the border of consciousness"; "everything that happens within us which is not spoken by the interior monologue." In author Nathalie Sarraute's work, a term devised for her attempt to record experience as it is felt before it passes through the filter of language. (Nathalie Sarraute; quoted by Le Anne Schreiber 1984, *New York Times*, March 30)

TROT

(See TROTULA)

TROTULA

The many handbooks on women's health which have come into English through a variety of routes are known collectively as "the English Trotula." Named for the legendary physician at the medical school in Salerno, Italy (eleventh century AD) who specialized in the study of women's health and wrote on gynecology and obstetrics. Both her name and work went through hundreds of manuscript permu-

tations as they were copied by different writers in many countries over many centuries. (Kate Campbell Hurd-Mead 1938, 127-42) Medieval scholar Beryl Rowland writes that though Trotula's authorship has never been wholly established, her name has left a permanent legacy in English: "the many connotations of *trot*, already proverbial in the Middle Ages, are too suggestive to be ignored. A *trot* was a *vieille*. She trotted for a living. Deprived of physical attractions by age, she had the wisdom of a sorceress, and in her business as a procuress, she taught her protegees the tricks of the trade. . . . To the medieval misogynist, she was the repulsive creature that the promiscuous, proud, and desirable young woman inevitably became." (Beryl Rowland 1981, 4)

(See DOCTOR, MEDICA, MEDICINE, SEMANTIC DEROGATION OF WOMEN)

TROUBLE AND STRIFE

Cockney rhyming slang for wife. "We chose this name because it acknowledges the reality of conflict in relations between women and men. As radical feminists, our politics come directly from this tension between men's power and women's resistance." (*Trouble & Strife*, a radical feminist magazine founded at Leeds, U.K., 1983)

TROUSERS

A serious piece of clothing. "It's easier to be taken seriously if you wear jeans, it's become a kind of tradition – that in the past women who were to be taken seriously wore jeans or trousers." (Lene Lovich 1980, 29) "I wear men's suits because I feel it makes everyone in the audience more comfortable. They know for sure that I'm not out there to prance around in a real sexual manner." (Pearl E. Gates, rock and roll performer, 1980, 31)

TRUE LOVE

"Is no less tyrannical than the classic 'male' objectification of Women as Tits-n-Ass. . . . Since it is always easier to see others' problems, we as feminists become obsessed with Tits-n-Ass objectification by men, without seeing our own objectification patterns." (J. Lee Lehman 1981, 81)

(See OBJECTIFICATION)

TRUTH

Freedom to devise and make use of available terms for communicating experiences. Space to make statements of existence. Relation of experiencing. Access to the means of expression. Respect for differentiation in communications. Unclassification. (Carole Walley 1983, correspondence) "There is no 'the truth,' 'a truth' – truth is not one thing, or even a system. It is an increasing complexity. The pattern of the carpet is a surface. When we look closely, or when we become weavers, we learn of the tiny multiple threads unseen in the overall pattern, the knots on the underside of the carpet." (Adrienne Rich 1979a, 187) "The universe is made of stories, not of atoms." (Muriel Rukeyser, quoted in Siew Hwa Beh 1981, 121) "Is [truth] the mere crowing of the cock? . . . And must it be told with such shrill scolding intonation . . . ?" Men's platitudes tend "to depress the spirits of half the human race and to embitter its relations with the other half." (H. M. Swanwick 1935, 168) "Finding truth in all the distortion is a feminist miracle." (Diane F. Germain 1983, 156)

TSENA URENA (TSENO-URENO)

The most widely read and influential work of all Yiddish literature, the *Tsena Urena* (which means "Come and See") by the Polish Jew Jacob ben Isaac Ashkenazi appeared in the seventeenth century; a unique mosaic of commentary, legend, allegory, epigram, and ethical observation, the book became a kind of "woman's bible" which "came to be used primarily by women in the East European Jewish community, who were not taught to read the Torah and its commentaries in Hebrew." (Susannah Heschel, ed., 1983, 287). According to another source,

it "has been the source of Jewish knowledge for generations of mothers, who, Sabbath after Sabbath, have absorbed its Cabala-flavored philosophy of life." (Leo Rosten 1970, 521)

TSHIWILA

Rite performed by women of the Tutshokwe, a matrilineal people now living in Angola, Zambia and Zaire. A short day-long ceremony, "*tshiwila* is only for women with some experience of life; usually only married women, widows or mature unmarried women already initiated . . . are accepted. The rite is for the brave women who are determined to assert their identity and their dignity vis-à-vis men, by facing and overcoming difficulties usually confronting the latter." Recommendations during the ritual rest on the basic idea that a woman must not define herself solely in relation to men for she is above all "a woman among women." (Maria Rosa Cutrufelli 1983, 158)

TUNNELING

Process discovered and described by Virginia Woolf while writing *Mrs. Dalloway* of feeling and seeing at the same moment *how it was* and *how it is*. She would simultaneously feel like a young child and a grown woman, and could consider her past as well as her future.

TU/VOUS (T/V)

Refers to the distinction in French between *tu*, the familiar or intimate form of the pronoun 'you,' and *vous*, the more formal form. T/V operates in many languages, though not English, and has important social functions in usage. Called by Roger Brown and Roger Gilman (1960) "the pronouns of power and solidarity," T and V are a sensitive index to relations between speaker and hearer with regard to age, class, social role, etc. Sally McConnell-Ginet (1978a), noting that Brown and Gilman ignore sex as a variable, suggests not only that the choice between T and V could be affected by sex but that in English forms of address have much the same social function (e.g., Jane, Sister, Mrs Smith, and Hey You would likely send quite different signals).

TWO REFRIGERATORS PRINCIPLE

In August 1984, Democratic Vice-Presidential candidate Geraldine Ferraro held a news conference to discuss her financial affairs. She contended that since entering public life she had kept her finances separate from her husband's real estate business and that she was therefore entitled to an exemption from the requirement that financial information of both candidate and spouse be completely disclosed. If *she* were not entitled to this exemption, she contended, few couples would be eligible for it – only those, in fact, who had so segregated their finances that they even used separate refrigerators. Her argument, which "added a phrase to the political lexicon," pointed to a double standard in disclosure laws aimed primarily at men seeking to conceal their earnings and business dealings under the wife's name; the wife is not expected to be a business person in her own right. (*Newsweek* 1984, September 3, 21)

TWO-SARIS-TOGETHER

The title of a fictional rendering of a true relationship between an American Lesbian and a South Indian woman in 1978. Married, mother of two children, and citizen of a country where Lesbians have little opportunity for open expression, the Indian woman "is unlikely to be easily singled out for recognition as a lesbian by a Western observer or anthropologist; indeed, she would not be recognized as such by the majority of Western Lesbians. Perhaps this is because she is not a 'Lesbian,' and certainly not a dike, not a wick or a fricatrice or a marimacha or a 'manly-hearted-woman.' In her own terms, she is a *two-saris-together*." (Judy Grahn 1984, 110)

TYPEWRITER

Technological innovation which in the post-Civil War era was "far and away the most important of the new office machines" and which, because it was not immediately sex-typed as masculine (as other machines were) "probably facilitated or eased the entrance of women into offices." "Rather than causing change, the typewriter followed in the wake of basic alterations in capitalism. Nonetheless, the typewriter did facilitate certain changes in office work ... [it] aided in the development of more rigid hierarchical structures within the office and in the diminution of what upward mobility existed in clerical work. Since the typewriter was most efficiently operated by a trained typist, the establishment of the job category 'typist' followed almost immediately upon the typewriter itself." "Woman's place at the typewriter must be explored within a dual structure that takes into account patriarchal social relations and such political-economic forces as the expansion of capitalist firms and the increased demand for clerical labor. Patriarchy and political economy may be separated for analytic purposes, but this does not mean that they operate independently. ... The issue ... is how 'woman's place' is determined by the interaction between them." (Margery W. Davies 1982, 4, 31, 55, 33, 38)

"CHRISTMAS PRESENT
for a boy or girl
And the benevolent can, by the gift of a 'Type-Writer' to a poor, deserving young woman, put her at once in the way of earning a good living as a copyist or corresponding clerk. No invention has opened for women so broad and easy an avenue to profitable and suitable employment as the 'Type-Writer,' and it merits the careful consideration of all thoughtful and charitable persons interested in the subject of work for women. Mere girls are now earning from $10 to $20 per week with the 'Type-Writer,' and we can at once secure good situations for one hundred expert writers on it in courtrooms in this city. The public is cordially invited to call and inspect the working of the machine, and obtain all information at our showrooms."

(Ad for the Remington typewriter 1875,

the *Nation*; cited in Margery W. Davies 1982, 54)

"Is seen as a woman's thing. Soon after its inception it became associated with doubly-subordinate female labour and has taken on woman's low status." This is in contrast to the linotype machine which "in spite of being basically a keyboard, had a certain mechanical mystique to it" and became a man's thing. (Cynthia Cockburn 1982, 14)

Also originally meant *typist*, usually a woman: "Situation wanted – by lady, rapid stenographer and typewriter." (*New York Herald*, Oct. 27, 1884) "The marriage of the type-writer and her employer is so frequent that it has passed into a joke." (1895 citation, *Oxford English Dictionary*)

TYRANT

"None can be Tyrants but Cowards. For nothing makes one Party slavishly depress another, but their Fear that they may, at one time or other, become strong, or courageous enough to make themselves equal, if not superior to, their Masters." (A Lady 1721, 18)

U AND NON-U

Elitist shorthand for differences in British English between upperclass and non-upperclass speech made famous by the writer Nancy Mitford. Professor Alan S. C. Ross sent a scholarly article on the subject to Mitford who included his findings with her own commentary in an article she was writing for *Encounter* on aristocracy. "It fascinated the public and the newspapers and *Encounter* sold out in no time at all. For a few days Nancy's interpretation of Professor Ross's research pushed murders and rapes to the back pages. Perhaps I exaggerate, but it certainly got a lot of publicity in unexpected places." (Diana Mitford; in Richard Buckle, ed., 1978, 1) Ross and Mitford then collaborated on *Noblesse Oblige* (1956), a fuller treatment of the topic. Different usages are supposed to mark not merely one's class but one's relationship to the entrenched British aristocracy; for Mitford, the entire exercise was somewhat tongue-in-cheek. The more well-known examples include

Non-U	U
bye-bye (or ta-ta)	goodbye
corsets	stays
escort	male companion
expecting	pregnant
give me a tinkle	ring me
handbag	bag
ill (has vomited)	sick
mirror	looking-glass
phone	telephone
the States	America
toilet	lavatory, loo

ULTRA-MANNISH

Blind to or ignorant of the presence and contributions of women. (Mary Ritter Beard 1942, 220)

ULYSSES

"Absentee father; mother heads single-parent household." (Eve Merriam 1975, 11)

UM

Lover or partner whose name is not known to speaker, who says "And please be sure to bring your um."

UMBRELLY

Satiric creation of the women's health movement; has been described in a variety of places. The following is from a "scientific abstract" which circulated during the 1970s. (See also Dawn Bracey 1980; in Marsha Rowe ed. 1982, 374-5)

Trade name for the intrapenal device (IPD), a breakthrough male contraceptive developed during the 1970s and unveiled at the American Women's Surgical Symposium by Dr. Sophia Merkin. The IPD resembles a tiny folded umbrella which is inserted through the head of the penis and pushed into the scrotum with a plunger-like instrument. Occasional perforation of the scrotum can be disregarded since it is known that the male has few nerve endings in this area of the body. The underside of the umbrella contains a spermicidal jelly, hence the name "umbrelly." Experiments on a thousand white whales from the Continental Shelf (whose sexual apparatus is said to be closest to man's) proved the umbrelly to be 100% effective in preventing the production of sperm, and eminently satisfactory to the female whale since it doesn't interfere with her rutting pleasure. Preliminary findings of a study conducted on 763 unsuspecting male graduate students at a large midwestern university suggest that the umbrelly is statistically safe for the human male. Of the 763 grad students, only 2 died of scrotal infection, only 20 experiencd swelling of the tissues, 3 developed cancer of the testicles, and 13 were too depressed to have an erection. Common complaints ranged from cramping to bleeding to acute abdominal pain. It is thought that these symptoms merely indicate that the man's body has not yet adjusted to the device and that they should disappear within a year. Other complications, including massive scrotal infection necessitating surgical removal of the testicles, are "too rare to be statistically significant." Members of the Women's College of Surgeons agree that the benefits far outweigh the risks to any individual man. (Belita H. Cowan, "New Device Tested," mimeograph, c.1972)

UN-

Prefix that women have sometimes employed to suggest their silence or the experience of being silenced: the protagonist of *The Life I Really Lived* keeps a "Book of Unspoken Thoughts" secret from her husband (Jessamyn West 1979); the short story "Unmailed, Unwritten Letters" paradoxically consists of a woman's letters written to her husband, her lover, her lover's daughter, her parents (Joyce Carol Oates 1970a); a female character in Barbara Pym (1982) speaks of "un-being."

UNCONSCIOUS

Central concept in psychoanalysis. "The unconscious contains all that has been repressed from consciousness, but it is not co-terminous with this. There is an evident lack of continuity in conscious psychic life – psychoanalysis concerns itself with the gaps. Freud's contribution was to demonstrate that these gaps constitute a system that is entirely different from that of consciousness: the unconscious. The unconscious is governed by its own laws, its images do not follow each other as in the sequential logic of consciousness but by condensing only each other or by being displaced onto something else. Because it is *unconscious*, direct access to it is impossible but its manifestations are apparent most notably in dreams, everyday slips, jokes, the 'normal' splits and divisions within the human subject and in psychotic and neurotic behavior." (Juliet Mitchell; in Juliet Mitchell and Jacqueline Rose eds 1982, 2-3)

UNDERDOG

"The dog that in all societies is most definitely 'under' is always the woman. But it does not occur even to the careful analysers of social trends to record her lot." (Teresa Billington-Greig c. 1949-60)

UNDERGROUND

In disguise. All women are, it is an act of survival. "Each sister wearing masks of Revlonclairolplaytex does it to survive." (Robin Morgan ed. 1970, xlii)

UNDERSTANDING MAN

"A figure who often appears in women's novels; a love affair with the Understanding Man will seemingly solve all problems." (Joanna Russ 1981, 82)

UNDERSTANDING MEN

"The verbal support of men in all-male institutions, groups, or cliques of power for mild feminist reform has no value in the world of real, substantive change for women: it is the all-male structure itself that must be subverted and destroyed. ... The antifeminism in exclusively male enclaves is not made humane through gestures; it is immune to modification through diplomatic goodwill. As long as a road is closed to women, it is closed to women; and that means that women cannot take that road, however nicely the men on it suggest they would not mind." (Andrea Dworkin 1983, 214)

UNDERWEAR

Garment worn underneath other garments in public, except in advertisements where it appears mostly on women "posed inanely, or looking in their mirrors." Women's underwear seems to scream "Sex" to men but male underwear does not have the same effect on a woman: "she has washed it; the trim socks mere sloppy rags in her hands, the impressive union suit a long wet rope, the shirts a labor of some magnitude to 'do up.' Also she has sewed buttons on it, darned it, patched it." For men obsessed with women's underwear, "a course of washing, ironing, and mending is recommended." (Charlotte Perkins Gilman 1916b, February, 54-5)

Symbolizes sexual adventure. In one Australian country family "someone voicing mock displeasure would say, 'Ahrrr, give me my hat and pants!' The phrase derived from a story often told by one of their aunts in warning tones – aunty plainly missed the point of the joke. A girl who was displeased by her boyfriend's importunate behaviour in a park at night exclaimed, 'Give me my hat and pants, I'm going home.'" (Nancy Keesing 1982, 40)

Is a metaphor for femininity. "I imagine women dressing and undressing – together in their white eyelet cotton camisoles, helping each other undo the ribbons. Perhaps napping during the afternoon of a nineteenth-century house party – lying side by side on large pillows, briefly released. Perhaps touching; stroking the ribcage bruised by stays; applying a hanky dipped in bay rum to the temples of another. Perhaps kissing her forehead after the application is done – perhaps taking her hand. Head on another's shoulder, drifting. To be waked too soon. I like to think of women making soft underclothes for their comfort; as they comfort each other." (Michelle Cliff 1980, 36)

UNFEMININE

A term used as an ancient weapon against women when they express what they are thinking, feeling, and experiencing. The reflex "She is unfeminine" seems indestructible. "Men – and many women, said that the suffragettes were defeminised, masculine, brutalised." (Doris Lessing 1962, preface)

UNFIT

"While many people would consider certain menial, laborious jobs as being 'unfit' for women, they fail to notice if Black women hold them. The jobs may be unfit for women, but not for Black women." (Gloria I. Joseph; in Gloria I. Joseph and Jill Lewis 1981, 27-8)

UNIVERSALIZATION

One of many devices used to deny, resist, or ignore the sexual caste system. Typically found in the context of questions such as "Isn't the real problem *human* liberation?" "One form is the notion that women must take on the responsibility for saving the 'human race.' This is actually a very old patriarchal line, and it always implies an agenda of female acceptance of male leadership ('mystical,' moral, political). Implicit in this ideology is the assumption that women are 'equally' (meaning primarily) to blame for every horror perpetrated by males. Another variation is 'as long as anyone (or any woman) is oppressed, all (or all women) are oppressed.' Such statements are not without a core of truth, which is the fact of common bonds among women. . . . The fallacy lies in the implications . . . that there is something wrong or selfish about being joyful, healthy, productive, and creative so long as 'any woman' is still oppressed. Such a political dogma implies a grim and worse than puritanical ethic of joylessness, demanding self-denial and hatred of Spinning." (Mary Daly 1984, 324-5) Universalization also occurs in language: "Most of the time when 'universal' is used, it is just a euphemism for 'white'; white themes, white significance, white culture. And denying minority groups their rightful place and time in U.S. history is simply racist." (Merle Woo 1981, 144)

UNMANLY

Used by men to define work done by men when the pay is low. (Eve Merriam 1958, rpt 1964, 169)

UNMARRIED

"A positive rather than a negative state." (Barbara Pym 1952, 190)
  (See SPINSTER)

UNMORAL

Describes the condition of woman "when she is just the wife-and-mother-and-nothing-else, the domestic animal. . . . Whether she did good or evil was not, as far as her own individuality went, of very much account since the standard set up for her was not of her own setting up." (Cicely Hamilton 1909, 57)

UNSCIENTIFIC

A judgment which is usually not a statement about science "but a charge of heresy." (Barbara Du Bois 1983, 106)

URANIUM

Radioactive chemical element found in ore and important in the production of nuclear energy; serious health hazard and an important issue for Indian women. "Two-thirds of all North American uranium is located on or adjacent to Indian reservations. In aboriginal Australia, the figures are the same. Millions of acres of Canadian reserves are under lease for mining exploration. . . . Radiation poisoning is fast becoming the main food of native peoples. And . . . in the name of economic and military security . . . control, occupation, and guns are the butter on the bread of oppression required to maintain uranium production." (Winona LaDuke 1983, 54)

USE

"Use is the Judge, the Law, and Rule of Speech." (Quoted in Elizabeth Elstob 1715, xxiv)

UTERUS

Womb; from Latin *uterus*. The Indo-european root means 'abdomen,' 'womb,' 'stomach.' Related forms yield the words *ventriloquism* and *hysteria*.
  (See BIRTHING, HYSTERIA, MATRIX, PREGNANCY, TESTOTERONE POISONING STRIKES AGAIN, WOMEN'S HEALTH MOVEMENT)

UTOPIA

Visionary plan or system for an ideal social order. "Our utopian potential – as women, as feminists – lies not in the reclaiming of our 'nature,' not in adopting a fictitious position 'outside,' but in our ability to change within the structures attempting to define us. As we deconstruct these structures by resisting appropriation within their categories, we engage in the process of continual transformation which can be our only true 'utopia.' " (Angelika Bammer 1981, 14)

"All the surrendering devotion our women have put into their private families, these women [of the feminist utopia *Herland*] put into their country and race. All the loyalty and service men expect of wives, they gave, not singly to men, but collectively to one another." (Charlotte Perkins Gilman 1915, 95)

"For men, utopia is the ideal state; for most women, utopia is statelessness and the overcoming of hierarchy and the traditional splits between human beings and nature, subject and other, man and woman, parent and child." (Elaine Hoffman Baruch 1984, xii)

UZR

Islamic ritual for airing discontent. "The *uzr* allows the rebel to engage in basically harmless antisocial behavior, such as uttering nonsense, showing disrespect for superiors, neglecting housework and children, losing consciousness, getting depressed, weeping for no apparent reasons, trembling, complaining of dizziness, stomachache, or headache. Since such a person is considered to be possessed by a spirit, she is not held responsible for any of her bizarre actions. When the husband has had enough, he organizes a *zar* ceremony to exorcise the spirit. The priest tries to establish communication with the spirit. . . . She finally speaks in a strange voice, and everyone strains to listen. It is the spirit talking. It will leave the patient's body only on certain conditions, all of which happen to be favorable to the afflicted. When the spirit's wishes are granted and it leaves, a lamb is sacrificed for a thanksgiving party, with the patient, in fancy clothes and jewelry, the guest of honor." (Naila Minai 1981, 181)

VAGINA

From Latin *vāgīna*, "sheath." Traditional dictionary definitions: "a sheath or sheathlike structure," "the canal leading from the vulva to the uterus." Compare definitions for *penis* as the "organ of copulation." According to psychoanalytic and medical literature of the first half of the twentieth century, the vagina was the site of orgasm for "mature" women, and the vaginal orgasm was yoked to maternal instinct, marital fidelity, domesticity, and theories of female masochism. There was evidence to the contrary: Alfred Kinsey's research, for example, "declared that the clitoris was the chief organ of female sexual pleasure [and that] . . . female masturbatory and lesbian practices showed the relative unimportance of penile penetration to female orgasm. . . . But despite the clinical, physiological, anatomical and sociological evidence, not to mention the possibilities of personal observation, mid-century doctors and psychiatrists had struggled manfully against the persistent appearance of the clitoris in female sexual activity. Until women themselves began to take apart the edifice of sexual masochism, the wealth of evidence was simply ignored." (Barbara Ehrenreich and Deirdre English 1979, 296)

  (See CLITORIS, MYTH OF THE VAGINAL ORGASM, PENETRATION, PENIS, PLEASURE, SEXUALITY, VAGINAL ORGASM)

"A famous poet told me, 'Vagina's ugly.' Meaning, of course, the *sound* of it. In poems.

Meanwhile, he inserts his penis frequently into his verse, calling it seriously, 'My Penis.' It *is* short, I know, and dignified. I mean of course the sound of it. In poems . . ."
  (Joan Larkin 1975, 59)

VAGINA DENTATA

Image of a "toothed vagina" is "the classic symbol of men's fear of sex." Barbara G. Walker draws evidence from many historical periods and cultures to suggest that the image may actually be of the vagina as a mouth with teeth. *Mouth*, coming from the same root as *mother*, seems deeply threatening to men (women's mouths, that is – though identical, men's mouths seem not to have inspired equivalent fear); there is also a confusion of sex with death, the vagina with the death of the penis, and other recurrent images. (Barbara G. Walker 1983, 1034-7) An "impulse – often acted upon by the nursling – is to hurt the mother by biting her. The archtypal 'vagina dentata' myth embodies the sensible anxiety that she will bite back." (Dorothy Dinnerstein 1976, 58)

VAGINAL ORGASM

"A man's penis and a woman's vagina are obviously different. Male orgasm is analogous to clitoral orgasm. Where, then, does vaginal orgasm come from? People say it's learned. And by God you'd better learn it, lady, especially if you're with a liberal man. . . ." "The theory of vaginal orgasm was the concoction of a man Freud, whose theories generally place women in an inhumane and exploited role. His theory of vaginal orgasm reaches the apex of these. The theory was inspired by his confrontations with women who were sick to death of the female role, and it adjusted women back into this female role by conning them that it was in a woman's interest *by her very nature* (i.e., it is in the interest of her vagina) to be dehumanized and exploited." (Ti-Grace Atkinson, quoted in Susan Rennie and Kirsten Grimstad 1975, 57)

VALENTINES

Are sweet, passionate, or satirical cards sent or exchanged on Valentine's Day which usually embody sexual stereotypes in the extreme. "He sent me a valentine he painted himself, and it is a big red heart with an arrow stuck through it, and one of my school friends says he is very fond of me, but I don't see much sense in the arrow." (Catherine Elizabeth Havens 1850; in Mirra Bank 1979, 48)
(See VALENTINE'S DAY)

VALENTINE'S DAY

"The celebration of double standards." (*Women's Voice: Women's Magazine of the Socialist Workers Party* 1982, February, cover)
Valentine's Day, February 14, "is celebrated by many Black Americans as the birthdate of Frederick Douglass, leading Black opponent of slavery before the Civil War. Since he was born a slave, Douglass was denied an official birthdate so his mother picked this date to mark the birth of the son she called her little Valentine. That small historic detail remains known today primarily because of the work of Carter Woodson, a Harvard-trained historian who founded the Association for the Study of Negro Life and History in 1915. Woodson established an annual black history week to coincide with Douglas' birthday, to set right the historic record he felt had been distorted or ignored. Black history week was officially extended to a month in 1976." (MacNeill/Lehrer NewsHour 1984, transcript, 14 February)

VALIUM

Tranquillizer taken by large numbers of men and women for varying reasons and with varying results. For some, it is undeniably a useful drug, which they feel enables them to carry out their daily functions; for others, the drug itself seems to compound distress and disability and side effects during withdrawal can be dangerous and even life-threatening. (Barbara Gordon 1979). Politically and economically, the drug depends on women as an exploited class. Advertising campaigns during the 1960s and 1970s aimed at women consumers were sharply criticized for their sexism: Valium prescribed for women, they suggested, would benefit men by keeping their rebellious, depressed, or emotional females on the job (at home or office). The drug thus serves male interests (Roisin Boyd c.1982), and its potential usefulness in combatting depression and suicide is compromised by this crucial conflict of interest within a capitalist economy.

VALSPEAK

Media label for the speech style of adolescent girls in the San Fernando Valley in California in the early 1980s: "Like it's so *totally* grody! It's like, you know, everybody's *pair-runce* have had it to the max, fer sher." Many parents have become sufficiently disgusted with the slang and inappropriate inflections of 'Valspeak' to haul their teen-aged daughters to see Lilian Glass, a Beverly Hills speech pathologist, for therapy. "Dr. Glass said last week that the whining, monotonously nasal speech . . . is actually a national phenomenon. The sales of 'Valley Girls,' a hit record parodying the speech style of 'Vals,' suggests she is right. In any case, Dr. Glass said, it's 'like an addiction' whose victims 'simply can't stop prefixing every thought with 'like' or using mind-numbing superlatives like 'to the max' or 'totally.' As a Val might put it, 'Well *gag* me with a *spoon*.' " (*New York Times* 1982, August 29)

VEIL

Material covering worn over the face. In some countries it is required women's wear. In other countries it is considered the mark of a demure female. "The closely drawn veil has a deadening as well as a beclouding effect, and the face of the speaker is not concealed, which is always a mistake, but her voice becomes inaudible." (Mary A. Livermore 1898, 1)

(See CLOTHING, SILENCE, THIRD WORLD WOMAN)

The *mousharabieh* is a kind of shutter in the veils Arab women wear which enables them to see what is going on without being seen themselves. "Men have no access at all to the women's world, but women, protected by the veil, hidden behind the *mousharabiehs*, can slip through public places without being recognized, can overhear men's conversations in the courtyards or in the rooms next to the kitchens. The only condition is that they should pass unnoticed and unrecognized. . . . In many areas, the practice of veiling women spread as the traditional structure was modified and the urban way of life became the recognized pattern. The phenomenon gradually affected every social category which could imitate the urban bourgeoisie. In the meantime, of course, the women of the bourgeoisie, who were in contact with the West, began to question not only the veil but their confined lifestyle and even the basic principles of Koranic law. In the face of such 'decadence,' the veil gained additional importance as a means for many poor families to defend the traditional Islamic values against Western incursions, cultural depersonalization and the supposed or real moral laxity of Westernized women." (Juliette Minces 1982, 40, 50)

"In the area [of Tunisia] where I was, the women wore veils that were not self-closing – to close the veils, they had to hold them in their teeth, so that the very design of the costume would ensure that they wouldn't speak. I found that terrifying: what we are dealing with is so old." (Marsha Norman 1983; quoted in *Ms.*, July, 59)

VENDIDA

"The potential accusation of 'traitor' or 'vendida' is what hangs over the heads and beats in the hearts of most Chicanas seeking to develop our own autonomous sense of ourselves, particularly through sexuality . . . the concept of betraying one's race through sex and sexual politics is as common as corn." (Cherríe Moraga 1983, 103)

(See MALINCHE)

VENEREAL DISEASE

The word *venereal*, from *Venus*, means "having to do with sexual love or intercourse," but is most commonly used to mean "transmitted by way of sex or intercourse with an infected person," as in *venereal disease*; perhaps the term has undergone pejoration like other words linked to women. Gender issues have marked the history of VD: prostitutes, thought to be the main "cause" of VD, were stigmatized as an "infected population" and set in opposition to the "innocent" wives who were the victims of their husbands' indiscretions. The wife was "protected" from knowledge of her condition by the prudish silence of society on this indelicate subject and, often, by collusion between the male husband and physician (problems explored in Henrik Ibsen's play *The Wild Duck*); this view of the woman as innocent victim (and nonsexual being) meant that laws requiring premarriage examinations were directed at men only. Today, the more neutral term *sexually transmitted diseases* (STD) has generally replaced VD, though the same split between "the infected" and "the innocent" colors discussions about AIDS. (For discussion, see Allan M. Brandt in press; Judith R. Walkowitz 1983)

(See AIDS, SEMANTIC DEROGATION OF WOMEN,

SEXUALLY TRANSMITTED DISEASES)

"When first I had to nurse a case of venereal disease – which I had hitherto seen referred to in the Press only under the mysterious title of 'the hidden plague' – I did not know exactly what it was; I was fully enlightened only in 1917, when in a Malta hospital I watched a syphilitic orderly die in convulsions after an injection of salvarsan." (Vera Brittain 1933, 49)

VENUS SYMBOL

"The first and still most widely used women's liberation symbol is a combination of a sign for the Roman goddess/planet Venus and a clenched fist. The Venus sign came, via astrology, to be used by biologists and psychologists to stand for females. In itself it's not very radical – Venus was the goddess of love, and supposedly the symbol is of a mirror – but after 13 years of use as a feminist sign it has gained quite different connotations. The fist reveals the early links of the US feminist movement with Black Power and the left. The combination fist and women's sign was taken up in [England] in 1969, right at the beginning of the women's liberation movement. . . . The women's sign on its own without the fist has been very useful, especially in more complicated poster and publication design. The use of two interlocking women's signs probably originated in an early Gay Liberation Front badge, a weird combination of the women's sign and the corresponding sign for men, of Mars, who was the Roman god of war. That was invented by Chicago GLF and taken up by the early GLF here in 1970. As many of the women broke away from GLF, the two women's signs too assumed a separate existence. But in 1972 a group of London feminists decided that two interlocking signs should stand for sisterhood – women together – and *three* should mean lesbianism. Three women's signs together are still used sometimes. . . . To add to the confusion, in the States some feminists use two to represent lesbianism

and three for sisterhood." (Ruth Wallsgrove 1982, 10)

VESTIGIAL

Word used by patriarchal biologists for "any organ in the female which is similar to an organ in the male but not quite like it." (Ruth Herschberger 1948, 72)
    (See OBJECTIVITY)

VICTIMISM

"Creating the role and status of the victim. . . . The status of 'victim' creates a mind set eliciting pity and sorrow. Victimism denies the woman the integrity of her humanity through the whole experience, and it creates a framework for others to know her not as a person but as a victim, someone to whom violence was done. . . . More than victims, women who have been raped or sexually enslaved are *survivors*. Surviving is the other side of being a victim. It involves will, action, initiative on the victim's part. . . . To be defined as victim in the context of victimism is to deny that identity is ongoing and changing; it is to deny whole parts of our active self in the experience of surviving the assault or slavery; it is to deny that women construct ways of coping and dealing with that violence in its aftermath." (Kathleen Barry 1979, 44-7)

VICTIMIZATION

Imposed physical and/or sexual abuse and suffering, particularly at the hands of men, mistakenly believed to be caused by the woman herself. Commonly associated with incestuous assault, rape, battering, and sexual harassment. (Elizabeth A. Stanko 1984)

VICTORY

"Each victory, however small, is hard won; no victory is ever secure; the struggle for change must be a reward in itself – educating and motivating women to recognize their own strengths." (Members of the Women's Studies College, State University of New York at Buffalo 1978 (1983), 59)

VIEWY

Holding strong and forceful views. Helaine Victoria Press (Martinsville, Indiana) note regularly in their catalogue that "we are indebted to Sarah Cleghorn (1876-1959) for our title, *Viewy News*. The New England poet was also a prose author, feminist, pacifist, vegetarian, and lifelong activist for her causes. The protagonist of her autobiographical novel, *The Spinster*, is often called 'viewy' or even 'too viewy' by other characters. That is, she has too many decided opinions and points of view for a proper young lady. Good for her. We hope you will enjoy this catalogue of our viewy postcards."

VIGILANCE

Remains crucial. Women's "political successes are not yet so secure that those who profit by them can afford to dispense with the few acknowledged feminists who are still vigilant, and still walk warily along once forbidden paths." (Vera Brittain 1933, 59)

(See WATCHERS)

VILDE CHAYES

(See WILD BEASTS)

VINDICATION OF THE RIGHTS OF WOMEN

Title of Mary Wollstonecraft's 1789 treatise which argues that femininity is an artificial construct, an imposition of patriarchal culture. Initiated a tradition of liberal feminism, with its origins in the social contract theories of the sixteenth and seventeenth centuries. "Wollstonecraft set the direction for later liberal feminism by arguing that physical sex alone was not a relevant ground for denying equal rights to women. As the possession of rationality was then considered the proper basis for the attribution of rights, Wollstonecraft argued that women's capacity to reason was equal with that of men. She claimed that the apparent inferiority of women's intellects was due to women's inferior education; women's apparent inferiority thus should be interpreted as the *result* of unequal

opportunities rather than as a *justification* for them." (Alison M. Jaggar and Paula S. Rothenberg 1984, 84)

VIOLENCE

(See NONVIOLENCE)

VIOLENCE AGAINST WOMEN

"The policing power of patriarchy which demands that male power be respected and never seriously challenged, threatening to explode if women are not pleasing and passive." (Sally Roesch Wagner 1982, 24)

Is symbolic as well as physical: the worst forms of aggression include the universe of thought, language, and behavior. "These symbolic universes are all present in each concrete violent act of aggression." (Mary Daly 1978, 357)

Affects all women, but especially Black women.

"Dead black women haunt the black maled streets
paying the cities' secret and familiar tithe of blood burn blood beat blood cut blood
seven year old child rape victim blood blood
of a sodomized grandmother blood blood
on the hands of my brother blood
and his blood clotting in the teeth of a stranger
as women we were meant to bleed
but not this useless blood . . ."
(Audre Lorde 1979, 112)

Can be met with nonviolence: "As women, nonviolence must begin for us in the refusal to be violated, in the refusal to be victimized. . . . The refusal to be a victim does not originate in any act of resistance as male-derived as killing. The refusal of which I speak is a revolutionary refusal to be a victim, any time, any place, for friend or foe. . . . Our nonviolent project is to find the social, sexual, political, and cultural forms which repudiate our programmed submissive behaviors, so that male aggression can find no dead flesh on which to feast." (Andrea Dworkin 1976, 71-2)

VIRAGO

A reclaimed feminist word. Typically defined as "a loud overbearing woman," the word also means "a woman of great stature, strength and courage; one possessing supposedly masculine qualities of body and mind." Viragos are Amazons, possessing the great stature, strength, and courage that are essentially female qualities of body and mind. Virago Modern Classics Press was founded in Great Britain by Carmen Calill in 1978 with the goal of publishing a range of less-known and well-known women novelists. "The name Virago, which in my two dictionaries is defined as 'a noisy, domineering woman' and 'a shrew', was chosen because of its original meaning, 'a heroic woman,' and because the founders knew it would shock a little." (Adrianne Blue 1984, 27)

VIRGIN

"One definition of the adjective *virgin* is 'never captured: UNSUBDUED.' Wild Virgins assume this definition of your (our?) Selves." (Mary Daly 1984, 13)

VIRGINIAWOOLF

"In real-estate parlance, a single room." (Eve Merriam 1980, 175) After "the British writer who knew and wrote about invisibility before Ellison or Baldwin, whose 'Room of One's Own' was a place where an integral self could remain detached and whole." (Midge Lennert and Norma Willson, eds, 1973, 13)
(See ANGEL IN THE HOUSE, ROOM OF ONE'S OWN)

VIRGINITY

Mental or physical, it is "more an obsession created by and for the use of men than an actual feminine state of being." (Adelaida R. Del Castillo 1978, 144)

VIRGINITY TESTS

Are gynecologic examinations performed by a physician or other expert supposedly to determine whether a woman is a "virgin" or not; have been used to police women's behavior in many cultures and historical periods. During the 1970s they were routinely performed by the U.K. immigration service on Indian women and other women of color seeking to immigrate to Great Britain. It is "an outrage that women of color should be treated by different standards than white female immigrants" and that "the British government should decide what is proper sexual behavior for us." The tests functioned to restrict immigration as well as to humiliate women. (Rekha Basu 1981, 72) Virginity tests are also carried out in many countries to determine whether a young woman is acceptable for marriage. (Nawal el Saadawi 1982)

VIRTUES

Conventional feminine: "meekness, courtesy, obedience to husbands, a sober demeanour and a reticent tongue." (M. G. May 1913, 52)

VISION

"Begins to happen in such a life
as if a woman quietly walked away
from the argument and jargon in a room
and sitting down in the kitchen, began
    turning in her lap
bits of yarn, calico and velvet scraps,
laying them out absently on the scrubbed
    boards . . ."
(Adrienne Rich 1977b, 76-7)

VISITATION

The right of a parent who doesn't have custody to see the children. "The zoos, museums, and miniature golf courses are filled every weekend with bored men trying to prove to themselves and the world that they are good fathers after all." (Barbara B. Hirsch 1973, 124)

VISUAL PLEASURE AND NARRATIVE CINEMA

Title of influential article by Laura Mulvey which argued that women's alienation and subordination within mainstream Hollywood narrative cinema was not primarily a matter of content (the "images of women" portrayed in these films) but more profoundly structured into the way in which films are made and viewed. Feminist film theory must therefore intervene in the relationship and set of conventions that exist between filmmaking practices and viewer satisfaction. (Laura Mulvey 1975)

VITRIFRAGISTS

People who break glass windows to call attention to their grievances. It was a term used by the British newspaper the *Globe* to describe the women who, in March 1912, broke a large number of London's business and institutional windows, with damage amounting to thousands of pounds, to express their indignation at the government's treatment of the Suffrage question. More than 200 vitrifragists were arrested. (*Votes for Women* 1912, March 3, 351, 354)

VOICEOVERS

The male voices in television commercials that tell women to do things, to buy things, and to shape up. Not only does this assume that women need men to tell them how to live, it also deprives women actors of jobs.

VOICES

In the space of this dictionary, we hope that the voices of many women will be heard. Traditionally, women's voices have been expected to be soft and low, and this may be "an excellent thing in its place. But if you are being robbed, or if you are drowning and you say 'help' who is to blame if nobody notices? If your child is perishing in a burning house, the woman who stops to think what the man in the street will think of the timbre of her voice is a poor creature and a guilty mother." (Charlotte Perkins Gilman 1911, 31) The women in this book have learned the virtues of speaking out.

VOID

A space women have long inhabited. "Physical or mental, man's space is a space of domination, hierarchy, and conquest, a sprawling, showy space, a *full*

space. Woman, on the other hand, has long since learned to respect not only the physical and mental space of others, but space for its own sake, *empty* space. It is because she needs to maintain a protective distance between herself and the men she has not chosen. As for those she may have chosen, there too, in order to avoid total annihilation, to escape man's habitual urge to colonize, she must conserve some space for herself, a sort of *no man's land*, which constitutes precisely what men fail to understand of her and often attribute to stupidity because she cannot express its substances in her inevitably alienated language. The *void* is for her, then a respectable value." (Claudine Hermann 1976a, 169)

"Is part of every woman. . . . We begin out of the void, out of darkness and emptiness. It is part of the cycle understood by the old pagan religions, that materialism denies. Out of death, rebirth; out of nothing, something. The void is the creatrix, the matrix. It is not mere hollowness and anarchy." (Adrienne Rich 1979, 191)

VOLUNTARY ASSOCIATIONS

"Community institutions [created by women] to carry out things they wanted to accomplish. Shut out, as they usually were, from traditional social structures – the bench, the bar, the medical profession, the ministry, and higher education – women created their own social organizations that they themselves could run. . . . The voluntary association was their principal tool, and with it they changed and shaped nineteenth-century America and in the process changed and emancipated themselves." (Anne Firor Scott 1984, 330-1)

VOLUNTEER

"Most often, 'volunteer' has meant female, free labor, and such labor has gone unrewarded. This is true of Christian and secular humanitarian volunteers as well as Jewish volunteers. Few historians adequately document and credit women's volunteer work in churches, hospitals, orphanages, and settlement houses." (June Sochen 1981, 47)

VOLUNTEERISM

"The deeply rooted American tradition which encourages non-paid community services as the most acceptable activity for women away from home. Feminists are opposed to this re-enforcement of the feminine mystique as non-beneficial for women." (Pat McCormick; cited in Midge Lennert and Norma Willson, eds. 1973, 12)

VOODOO

Is a set of religious beliefs and practices, originating in Africa and now practiced in the Caribbean and other parts of the world including the Southern U.S. (the name is African). Women as well as men can be voodoo sorcerers (the term *voodoo-ienne* is sometimes used). The writer and anthropologist Zora Neale Hurston collected material on voodoo in Haiti (see Hurston 1981); as word of her investigations passed around, she came down suddenly with violent gastric disturbances and thought she might die. She remained convinced that her illness and her voodoo explorations were related.

VOTES FOR WOMEN

The single most common and unifying slogan in the British and U.S. suffrage movements. The phrase created "instant recognition of an entire movement with its shared cluster of images, associations, and meanings to those inside and outside of the cause." Used in the U.S. on buttons, banners, flyers, posters, pins, postcards, the familiar phrase "was calculated to appeal to the lowest common denominator – a broad middle-class consensus – the single unifying factor in the myriad groups of reformist women" who came together in the suffrage movement. (Edith P. Mayo 1981, 7-8)

VULVA

"The hands held in the shape of a vulva (women's genitals) have come in as a second all-purpose women's liberation symbol. It may have been invented twice. In 1973 there was a badge of two hands, sideways so that you couldn't see the separate fingers, with a flame-clitoral symbol between them. It's a clever symbol, but actually it's a hard gesture to make without looking like a prayer, and it didn't really take off. Then in 1977 *Spare Rib* workers noticed that other European women were making the same gesture in demonstrations, this time with their fingers outstretched. They used a photograph of the hands of Laura Margolis – the *Spare Rib* designer at the time – on the cover of the 5th Birthday issue, dramatic in yellow black. The SR image took off. It's amazing the places that Laura's hands have been copied, even in jewellery. Some of us tried very hard to get the gesture taken up in demonstrations to counteract male lefty fists, but it seems to have faded away – perhaps because feminists don't want to represent themselves as genitalia." (Ruth Wallsgrove 1982, 10)

(See SYMBOL, VENUS)

An 1819 British lampoon of women's struggle for equality shows a woman holding her hands to form this symbol. (Trevor Lloyd 1971, 4) Women have used the same symbol in demonstrations in many parts of the world.

"It is often said of the vulva, that it is a mouth. Mouths and vulvas are the two most sensitive zones in a state of love, one often going joined with the other." (Monique Wittig and Sande Zeig 1976, 109)

VULVIC KNOWLEDGE

In Carolee Schneemann's performance "Interior Scroll" (1975), a scroll is extracted from the vagina: "the serpentine manifestation of vulvic knowledge can be associated at several symbolic levels. Among these: ticker tape, rainbow, torah in the ark, chalice, choir loft, bell tower, umbilicus and tongue." (*Heresies* 1982, 2:1, issue 5, 2nd ed. 128)

WAGES FOR HOUSEWORK

A movement to win wages for the productive but unpaid work women perform for the State. (Amanda Sebestyen 1979) "The Wages for Housework Movement originated in Italy, where its first public demonstration took place in March, 1974. Addressing the crowd assembled in the city of Mestre, one of the speakers proclaimed: 'Half the world's population is unpaid – this is the biggest class contradiction of all! And this is our struggle for wages for housework. It is *the* strategic demand; at this moment it is the most revolutionary demand for the whole working class. If we win, the class wins, if we lose, the class loses.' According to this movement's strategy, wages contain the key to the emancipation of housewives, and the demand itself is represented as the central focus of the campaign for women's liberation in general. Moreover, the housewife's struggle for wages is projected as the pivotal issue of the entire working-class movement. . . . The demand that housewives be paid is based on the assumption that they produce a commodity as important and as valuable as the commodities their husbands produce on the job." (Angela Y. Davis 1981, 232-4)

(See HOUSEWORK)

WAITRESS

"One of the acceptable jobs for women." (Midge Lennert and Norma Willson eds 1973, 12) A vulnerable worker in food service. "We make most of our salary in tips. . . . We really work for our money. We run miles every day. . . . Waitresses are always called 'girls' no matter what our ages. . . . A lot of people think that if you're a waitress you're automatically stupid, and they treat us like children." (Joyce Betries 1973; in Marsha Rowe 1982 ed., 1969-73) "The social definition of a waitress is the archetype of its definition of a woman. . . . Every woman spends time as a waitress: nurses, secretaries, stewardesses, teachers, housewives – and all women who have related to men." (The Fourth World 1971, 7)

WAITRESSING

A physically and mentally difficult restaurant job in which women facilitate the decisions of men. (Susan Wood 1979b, 84)

WANDERGROUND

Title of Sally Miller Gearhart's 1978 science fiction novel. The Wanderground is the wilderness where the Hill Women live; in telepathic communication with each other, with animals, trees, water and stone, they are in partnership with the world. Metaphorically, it envisions a future in which women have expanded their ability to communicate with each other and have discarded patriarchal models of relationships. (Sally Miller Gearhart 1978)

WAR

A senseless brutality that causes many men to "forswear their culture, their humanity, their intellectual efforts, their fruitful labours, to wallow in the joys of regimentation, brainlessness, the abandonment of the will, the primitive delights of destruction!" (H. M. Swanwick 1935, 241)

(See AGGRESSIVITY, MACHO, PEACE, VIOLENCE AGAINST WOMEN, WAR BETWEEN THE SEXES, WARFARE, WOMEN'S WAR)

Is the "ultimate grisly tragedy . . . the spectacle of young men who could have loved each other, blasting each other out of existence with guns." (Noel Greig 1983, 79)

Is a series of anti-social convulsions that do not result in improvements in the situation of women. Any temporary improvements come from the selfishness of governments seeking additional workers for short-term and unconstructive ends. (Vera Brittain 1953, 195)

Is an "insupportable horror for anyone who has nourished and appreciated growing lives." (Sara Ruddick 1980, 266)

Has become a "calculated, unemotional, intellectual product of the machine." (Dora Russell 1983, 207)

Is "the male's normal method of compensation for not being female, namely, getting his Big Gun off, is grossly inadequate, as he can get it off only a very limited number of times; so he gets it off on a really massive scale, and proves to the entire world that he's a Man." (Valerie Solanas 1968, 6)

Is "a male institution – as are all other institutions in the society – and war is simply an extension of the colonial policy of the subjection of the female culture and 'weaker' male cultures, i.e., 'weaker' national cultures." (Barbara Burris 1971, 326)

Embodies "the unknown male world: the extremes of chaos and fear." (Pamela Frankau 1970, 53)

Is "a social disease, freely admitted to be most characteristic of the male. It is the instinct of sex-combat, overdeveloped and misused." (Charlotte Perkins Gilman 1912; cited in Ronald W. Hogeland and Aileen S. Kraditor eds. 1973, 133)

Represented, by men, as a separate and special department of human conduct. ("Our Lost Illusions" 1914, *The Englishwoman* 24:72)

Is a product of men in power, only possible if supported by admiring women "trying, after all, to be what men said they wanted them to be." Is a "silly bloody game of massacring the sons of women." "I do wish men would leave off protecting me! I should feel so much safer." (H. M. Swanwick 1935, 246, 247, 306)

"There's no mother or wife in England nor Germany that would give their loved one to be killed." (Mrs. Wrigley 1931, 65)

Is a time when "the saving of a gun is of infinitely more importance [to man] than the saving of many women." (Fanny Smart 1915, 76)

"What connection is there between the sartorial splendours of the educated man and the photograph of ruined houses and dead bodies? Obviously, the connection between dress and war is not far to seek; your finest clothes are those that you wear as soldiers." (Virginia Woolf 1938, 21)

"Always has a special tendency to highlight paradoxes in the position of women." (Ann Oakley 1982, 18)

Is "the only appropriate word for women's lives. More than 2,000 women are raped in this country every day, 50 per cent of women are beaten by the men they live with, sometimes beaten to death, incest is an epidemic – one out of four females will be incestuously assaulted before age 18. Thousands of Black and Hispanic women are sterilized every year against their will. Not only physical violence but economic violence against women is woven implacably into the fabric of our society. Eighty-nine per cent of Americans living in poverty are women and our children; by the year 2000 we will comprise the entire poverty population. To be born female on a patriarchal planet is to be born behind enemy lines. Sexism [is] the polite term for this war." (Sonia Johnson 1983, 6)

Is an aggression waged as a violation of women. "The primordial, universal object of attack in all phallocratic wars is the Self in every woman. . . . Indeed, the War State requires women for the recreation of its warriors. This is true not only in the obvious sense that mothers produce sons who will be soldiers. It is true also on a deep psychic level: the psychic sapping of women in patriarchy functions continually to re-create its warriors. . . . Clearly, the primary and essential object of aggression is not the 'opposing' military force. The members of the opposing teams share the same values and play the same war games. The secret bond that binds the warriors together, energizing them is the violation of women, acted out physically and constantly re-played on the level of language and of shared fantasies." The War State's identity is that of the "State of Rapism, in which all invasions, occupations, destructions of 'enemy territory' are elaborations upon the theme of rape/gynocide." (Mary Daly 1978, 355-7, 361)

WAR BETWEEN THE SEXES

Ancient battle that women always lose. "Women hardly notice this fact because they take 'losing' for granted just as men take 'winning' for granted. . . . What is new, however, is the desire to either end the war or turn the 'losers' into 'winners.' " (Phyllis Chesler 1972a, 297)

WARFARE

"Maleness in its absurdest extremes. Here is to be studied the whole gamut of basic masculinity, from the initial instinct of combat, through every form of glorious ostentation, with the loudest accompaniment of noise." (Charlotte Perkins Gilman 1911, 219)

WARRIOR-WOMAN

"The warrior-woman, using sexuality as a weapon, is a masculinist construct, the true counterpart of the macho male." (Seph Weene 1981, 37)

WASHING

A heavy household chore. "To do the washing you first had to save everything that would burn to stoke up the stone copper or stone and cast-iron copper. My mother-in-law remembered that her mother was friendly with the owners of

the corner shop who would give her wood in the shape of boxes. Once you had your fuel, you had to fill your copper by hand and when the water was hot you ladled it out into a tin bath where you would use a rubbing board and blocks of soap. Once all the washing had been rubbed it went back into the refilled copper together with bleaching soda and ordinary soda and would be left to boil for twenty minutes. It was a steaming job pushing down every so often with a copper stick. . . . When the wash had finished boiling it would be lifted out into a bath of clean water to be rinsed and 'whites' would be 'blued' with Reckitt's bluebag or starched and finally it would all be wrung out through a hand-operated mangle. After the wash had been dried it would be ironed on the kitchen table. . . . The irons would be hot irons heated by the fire." (Marilyn Clark's interview with her mother-in-law, cited in Sheila Rowbotham 1983, 184)

WATCHERS

"In order to survive, those of us for whom oppression is as American as apple pie have always had to be watchers, to become familiar with the language and manners of the oppressor, even sometimes adopting them for some illusion of protection." (Audre Lorde 1980, rpt 1984, 114)
   (See VIGILANCE)

W.C.T.U.

Women's Christian Temperance Union, founded in 1874 and led for many years by Frances E. Willard. Inextricably connected to the feminist movement in the U.S., its motto was "Do everything." Until her death in 1898, Willard campaigned actively for women's suffrage, for temperance in the use of alcohol, and for other social reforms. She believed the woman's vote would help "the nation to put away the liquor traffic and its accompanying abominations." (Frances E. Willard 1898, March 5, 1)

WE

"Often means *men*." (Elizabeth Robins 1913, 112) In feminist texts, strives to create a common bond among all women in sentences like "Women must struggle to break our chains" that a few years ago would have been written "Women must struggle to break their chains." This usage is problematic because it assumes inclusion and obscures differences. In feminist texts, for example, "we" often means white women. To explore this usage, the Commission on the Status of Women in the Profession of the Modern Language Association organized a series of programs in 1984 entitled "Who are the 'We'? Opening the Terms of Feminist Discourse." In a preface which also described the use of nonsexist language, the authors of a recent workbook attempted to reduce the ambiguity of "we": "First-person plural pronouns ('we,' 'us,' and 'our') are used only when referring specifically to the authors. When speaking of 'everyone,' or 'most people in this society,' third person ('they') is used. This distinction is made to avoid confusion, not to set the authors apart from the readers. When we say, 'People in this culture learn to hide their emotions,' for example, we mean to include ourselves in the generalization.' " (Michel Avery et al. 1981, xi)

Acronym for Women Employed, an organization of working women in Chicago that grew out of conversations among activists in the Chicago Women's Liberation Union. "The success of such organizing revealed dramatic changes in consciousness among clerical workers who realized that their treatment on the job reflected their position as women. When a legal secretary was fired for refusing to make coffee, Women Employed instigated a nationally televised demonstration to protest the stereotypic assumptions involved. The woman – who announced that she made coffee at home in the mornings and had no intention of doing it again at work – was quickly rehired." A Boston group, 9 to 5, was organized with similar aims. (Sara Evans 1980, 230)

WEARING THE COLORS

Meant dressing for suffrage parades and other public events in the colors that symbolized the suffrage movement.

(See COLORS, ICONOGRAPHY)

WEAVING

Long an art and occupation of women. The weaving of the women of the Laymi Indians of the central Bolivian highlands illustrates their relation to symbolic discourse: "while men knit highly-intricate patterns into their *ch'ulus*, or woollen caps, women are responsible for the vast outpouring of motifs, of densely-composed bands of design, particularly on the carrying-cloths, belts and bags woven by them. What must be borne in mind is not only the degree of artistic investment that these weavings represent, but also that they are key elements in the code by which ethnic groups in the Andes differentiate themselves. Thus it is women's symbolization, handed from mother to daughter, and shared as a professional skill among all women, that is a major repository of ethnic identity." (Olivia Harris 1980, 74)

(See ART, QUEEN OF WANDS, WEBSTER, WIFE)

WEBSTER

"Is a word that formerly meant 'female weaver,' the '-ster' ending indicating a female ancestor, or female possession of the word. The word-weavers of recent centuries who have given us the oration of Daniel Webster and the dictionary listings of Merriam-Webster stem from English family names that once descended through the female line. Some great-great grandmother gave them her last name, *Webster*, she-who-weaves. In this story of the Queen of Wands, webster is a spider/spirit. . . . If the webster of dictionary fame comes first to your mind when you see Spider Webster's name, remember that she gave the surname to him, as well as giving the words. For language is a form of weaving too, a clothing our ideas wear, a glowing flesh they are made of, a heart that beats in them." (Judy Grahn 1982, xiii)

(See QUEEN OF WANDS)

WEBSTER'S

Generic name for any traditional dictionary, after Noah Webster, who produced the most well-known of nineteenth-century American dictionaries.

(See WEBSTER)

WEBSTER'S THIRD

Is shorthand for *Webster's Third New International Dictionary* (Philip Babcock Gove ed. 1961) which created a furor among usage critics, writers, and others because it tried to put into practice the principle of descriptive linguistics that language as it is *used* is right – hence the dictionary's function is to *de*scribe rather than *pre*scribe. Though *Webster's Third* usually indicates what is "standard" or "preferred" usage, it enraged critics by labelling words like *ain't* as "variants" rather than as the unacceptable and substandard mistakes of ignoramuses. It was accused of trying to "democratize" that which is "naturally" hierarchical and elitist (Sheridan Baker 1972, 147) and thus hastening the end of civilization as we know it (James Sledd and Wilma R. Ebbitt 1962; Rulon A. Wells 1973) – accusations that are alive and well today in reaction to feminist proposals for language change.

(See AUTHOR, AUTHORITY, DICTIONARY, M.A.L.E., PRESCRIPTIVISM)

WEDDING

A virtually universal ritual event. Common ceremony at which the civil death of the woman is celebrated and she becomes one with the man to whom she is joined. (Marlene Dixon and Joreen 1970, 17) Ritual with fine dresses. Sad from the observer's view "because of . . . knowing how empty it all is mostly, seeing how unhappy they often turn out after, and I thought the burial service was much the best and to be coveted." (Hannah Cullwick; in Liz Stanley ed. 1984, 233) "Matriarchal totalitarian event, in which men have no more relevance than the elevator operator on a self-service elevator. . . . Rampant female chauvinism?

It would certainly seem so, this exaltation of women, dismissal of men. But on closer examination, the truth becomes clear. The bride is the central figure because the real change in status is *hers*. She changes her name to her husband's, prepares to have children, follows him wherever he goeth because his work is assumed paramount. He continues his growthful journey through the real world as before, with the addition of a new appendage, a wife; she is transferred from economically dependent child to economically dependent 'adult.' " (Marcia Seligson 1973, 102-4)

(See MARRIAGE)

WEDDING RING

Is worn by women more frequently than by men, with greater and more varying importance. For example, "before the Second World War, when many authorities would not employ married women teachers, a wedding ring would have been a disabling stigma. Now society expects everyone to marry, the absence of the ring is a stigma." (Sara Delamont 1976, 79)

WEED

Metaphor for women in patriarchal society, helped along by descriptions like the following from the *New Garden Encyclopedia* (ed. E. L. D. Seymour): "Weeding means the removal, from among crops, of obnoxious plants, that is, undesired plants growing in competition with desired ones. However, the term weed is a relative one because many plants may be useful, beautiful or interesting where they are wanted, but pernicious elsewhere." Similarly, from *Weeds of the North Central States* (Circular 718 of the University of Illinois Agricultural Experiment Station): "The seeds of many weeds remain dormant in the soil for years and then germinate when conditions are favorable. Some weeds have extensive root systems and underground stems that help the weed to spread and persist. Perennial weeds store reserve foods in their root systems and continue to sprout again and again after the tops are destroyed. These characteristics of weeds make control a problem." (Quoted in *Weeds: Women's Week Magazine* 1974, University of Illinois at Urbana-Champaign) In Edith Summers Kelley's "lost" novel *Weeds*, the word serves as a metaphor for farming (Edith Summers Kelley 1923).

(See FARMER, FIREWEED)

WELFARE

Invented for women. "Welfare's like a traffic accident. It can happen to anybody, but especially it happens to women. . . . In fact, welfare was invented mostly for women. To be eligible, you had to be female, you had to be a mother, you had to be 'worthy.' 'Worthy' meant were your kids 'legitimate,' was your home 'suitable,' were you 'proper'?" (Johnnie Tillmas 1972; quoted in Suzanne Levine and Harriet Lyons eds. 1980, 49)

"One of our society's attempts to preserve the traditional role of women as childbearer, socializer, and homemaker . . . [in which] domination by a husband was replaced with control over every aspect of a woman's life by the welfare agency . . . [who] like a jealous husband, doesn't want to see any men around who might threaten its place as provider and authority." (Carol Glassman 1970, 102-3)

From the social worker's point of view, a hard job to carry out. "Nothing's as bad as working for Welfare. Do you know what they really mean by social investigator? A spy. Someone whose dirty job it is to snoop into the corners of the lives of the poor and make their poverty more vivid by taking from them the last shred of privacy." (Social worker; in Paule Marshall 1962, 30)

WELFARE QUEENS

Women who through persistence and ingenuity have learned to operate efficiently within the welfare system and are therefore often assumed to be "cheating" it. "There's lots of discussions of welfare queens. No juicy word for businessmen who cheat the government of thousands of dollars." (Julia Lesage 1982, lecture at University of Illinois at Urbana-Champaign, October 5)

WENCH

"*Wench* derives from *wenchel*, and means originally a child of either sex, though it also has the meanings 'servant, slave, or whore.' [Etymologist C. T.] Onions and the *Oxford English Dictionary* derive it ultimately from Old English *wancol*, 'unsteady, inconstant, wavering,' an association with young rather than femininity, and the *American Heritage Dictionary* sees its Indo-European root as **went-*, 'bend, curve.' But many etymologists have allowed their ideas about women's nature to influence their derivations. For example, Skeat (1910), who thinks of women as wavering and bendable, is not surprised by the shift in reference for *wench* from sex-neutral to sex-specific: 'As the word also implied "weak" or "tender," it was naturally soon restricted to the weaker sex.' . . . Only partly in jest, Junius (1743) offers to derive *wench* from English *wince*, likening *wenches* to horses: 'Girls shrink from a touch the way unbroken steeds whinny and shy away when their grooms rub their chests and stomachs.' " (Dennis Baron forthcoming)

WET/DRY

Alternative computerese: a terminal is "wet" instead of "up" when it's working and "dry" instead of "down" when it's crashed. (Pauline B. Bart 1983, correspondence)

WG

White Girl. Term used by Latinas and Blacks to describe White women. (Lourdes Torres 1984, correspondence)

(See MISS ANNE)

WHITE

"A major ethnic division [which] stems from the early enslavement of African and Indian peoples by the European colonists and from the fear which arose from the increasing numbers of Blacks after 1720, as Africans began to constitute the majority of the [South Carolina] colony's population. 'White' emerged as the cover term for those colonists who could claim land and accumulate property; old world distinctions between Welsh, Scots, English, Germans, French, and Sephardic Jews which might have been important in another time and place were virtually forgotten in the economic sphere. New world distinctions between the Siouan, Iroquoian, and Muskogean nations disappeared also, as native Americans died of disease and war or moved [or were moved] to frontier areas – the few remaining [in the area] becoming assimilated into either the Black or white ethnic group. . . . Gone also are the distinctions between African cultural groups from Senegambia, Nigeria, and Angola, even though these groups formed the majority of the colony's population for much of its early history." (Patricia Nichols 1984)

(See ASIAN-AMERICAN, BLACK, EURO-AMERICAN WOMEN, RED, THIRD WORLD WOMAN, WOMEN OF COLOR)

Often implicitly included within the designation WOMAN or WOMEN. "It was breathtaking to discover that in the culture I was born and reared in, the word 'woman' means *white woman*, just as we discovered before that the word 'man' means *male man*." (Marilyn Frye 1983, 117)

A political as well as an ethnic category. "It is true that being white-skinned means that everything I do will be wrong – at the least an exercise of unwarranted privilege – and I will encounter the reasonable anger of women of color at every turn. But 'white' also designates a political category, a sort of political fraternity. Membership in it is not in the same sense 'fated' or 'natural.' It can be resisted." (Marilyn Frye 1983, 126)

Symbol in U.S. white middle-class culture of innocence, young, joy, and leisure. "Wedding dresses tend to be not just white but lustrous and shiny. This connection of white and light suggests a radiance and spirituality in the bride, a radiance that comes from her inner happiness, tranquility, and purity of

heart. She, as maker and physical symbol of the home, will provide a home which is a refuge and retreat from the depressing, corrupt, and hurried world of work for her husband and children." (Diana Leonard 1982, 133)

Has come to designate a certain set of cultural values and activities, deemed by "liberal" males and females to be undesirable: "When asked to talk about our white culture, many of us could only speak derisively of ourselves as the products of hot dogs, pop tarts, dippity-do, uptightness, racism. We felt shame about being white, or vagueness about whether we had any culture at all. We had judgments about other white people and did not want to be identified with them. One of us finally suggested that we make a rule that we could only speak positively about our cultures. This dumbfounded us; we believed we had nothing to say." (Terry Wolverton 1983, 196)

WHITE FEMINISTS

Have the potential to confront racism as well as sexism. "As White feminists learn not to make, from a position of racial privilege, misleading generalizations and incorrect parallels into the sexual and social experiences of Black men and women, as well as those of men and women of different classes and other Third World cultures, we also have to confront the racist fabric of the sexism fought by feminism, and the racist perspectives of that feminism itself. The political framework evolved by the Women's Liberation Movement . . . provides a landscape of political imagination for engaging with struggles against racism, racial inequality, and White dominance at all levels. This is, for Whites, unprecedented." (Jill Lewis; in Gloria I. Joseph and Jill Lewis 1981, 271)

"It is incumbent upon White women to understand that this is both a sexist and a racist society and that, as social beings, they too participate in inhumane conditions. White women's position in the United States society as the benefactors of racism has allowed them to ignore their

Whiteness." (Gloria I. Joseph; in Gloria I. Joseph and Jill Lewis 1981, 41)

WHITE LIES

One strategy for dealing with single parenthood. "He got the Dodge and I got two kids in diapers. . . . Sundays were too long. I decided to make them shorter. Around 4 p.m. – sometimes even 3:30 – I would pull down the shades, start yawning, and snuggle the kids into their cribs. If I could get past Josh, I was home free. 'Time for nighty-night, angel,' I would croon. 'Wasn't that a good dinner?' 'What dinner?' 'Don't you remember? You had tomato juice, lamb chops, french fries, and chocolate ice cream. Wasn't that good? Aren't you full?' (Always use imagery.) 'Uh huh, thanks, Mom,' my trusting little boy would reply vaguely and go off to sleep. Six-month-old Gregg needed no further proof. If his brother was sleeping, it had to be nighttime. . . . I think you can get away with a few off-white lies." (Joan Gelman 1983; *New York Times*, July 14)

WHITE MEN

"*Are* the ruling class, the ruling class *are* white men. It is true that not all white men are capitalists or possess extreme class privilege, but it is safe to assume that 99.44% of them are racists and sexists. It is not just rich and powerful capitalists who inhibit and destroy life. Rapists, murderers, lynchers, and ordinary bigots do too and exercise very real and violent power because of their white-male privilege." (Barbara Smith 1979a, 125-6)

WHITE SLAVERY

Prostitution trade dealing in white women and children. "Following the abolition of black slavery in the British Empire in 1833, white slavery seemed a natural enough metaphor [for overwork of females by employers]. . . . Finally in the 1870s white slavery and its continental counterparts, *traite des blanches* and *Madchenhandel*, became firmly associated with prostitution. . . . By the end of the 1870s the term changed connotation . . . [and]

white slavery decisively took on the suggestion of recruitment to prostitution by force or fraud." (Edward J. Bristow 1982, 36-7) Became an important concern of nineteenth and early twentieth century feminists and social reformers. "White Slavery exists because thousands upon thousands of ordinary men want it to exist, and are willing to pay to keep it going. . . . Intelligent women are revolted by men's commerce with white slaves. It makes them regard men as inferiors. . . . The disparity between the moral standards of men and women is more and more destroying women's respect and regard for men. Men have a simple remedy for this state of things. They can alter their way of life." (Christabel Pankhurst 1913, 7, 11)

(See SLAVERY)

WHITE SOLIPSISM

"Snow-blindness. White solipsism: to think, imagine, and speak as if whiteness described the world. . . . Not the consciously held *belief* that one race is inherently superior to all others, but a tunnel-vision which simply does not see nonwhite experience or existence as precious or significant, unless in spasmodic, impotent guilt-reflexes, which have little or no long-term, continuing momentum or political usefulness." A form of passive collusion. (Adrienne Rich 1979, 299, 306)

WHITE WOMEN

"The myth was that white wimmin were the most envied, most desired (and beautiful), most powerful (controlling white boys) wimmin in existence. The truth is that Black people saw white wimmin as some of the least enviable, ugliest, most despised and least respected people, period. From our 'close encounters' (i.e., slavery, 'domestic workers,' etc.) with them, white people increasingly did seem like beasts or subnormal people. In short, I grew up with a certain kind of knowledge that all black folk, expecially wimmin, had access to." (doris davenport 1981, 87)

(See WHITE, WHITE FEMINISTS)

WHORE

"The derivations of *whore* often reveal more about the attitudes of the etymologists than they do about the nature of the word. Twentieth-century etymologists are generally agreed that the word *whore* comes ultimately from an Indo-European root, **ka-* according to the *American Heritage Dictionary*, which means 'like, desire,' and which produces such cognates as *care, caress,* and *cherish* as well as *whore*." Proposed derivations by earlier etymologists, however, link *whore* to words that mean 'to hire,' 'for sale,' 'venereal sport,' 'wife,' 'to conduct business,' 'excrement,' 'pregnant,' 'fornication,' 'filthy,' and 'to pour out, urinate.' '(Dennis Baron forthcoming)

> (See PROSTITUTE, PROSTITUTION, SEMANTIC DEROGATION OF WOMEN, TESTOSTERONE POISONING STRIKES AGAIN)

WHORE/VIRGIN

The polarity used by generations of men to label women. (Sheila Ruth 1980) Less common in Judaism, where "the polemic of woman as 'whore/virgin' is very rare indeed. Although there are a few examples of woman as temptress in the Midrash, these are not seen as mainstream views." (Elyse Goldstein 1983, 26)

> (See EVE, TORAH)

WICCA, WICCE

Derived from the Anglo-Saxon word meaning 'bend, shape,' is the practice of witchcraft within a framework of female spiritual identity and theism. Women's covens preserved the ancient knowledge and power of women, despite periods throughout history of intense persecution and destruction. Also linked to healing. (See Starhawk 1979, Z. Budapest 1979, 1980, Carol Ochs 1979, and Charlene Spretnak ed. 1982) The Old English singular, masculine, meant "a male witch, or a man who bends or shapes reality, or a wise man. Today, usually used as a name for the entire religion of witchcraft. Originally pronounced 'Witch-ah.' Now

usually 'Wick-ah.' " (*The Wise Woman* 1983, 4:2, June 21, 7) Wise women healers. Women who performed abortions and helped women bear children less painfully were known as wicca or wise women, Anglo-Saxon for witch. The Church tortured and killed an estimated nine million of these women. (Eileen Fairweather 1979, 26) *Dianic Wicce* "focuses primarily on deity as the Great Goddess." (Ann Forfreedom 1983, correspondence) *Wicca* is a contemporary Irish feminist magazine.

> (See ABORTION, SPIRITUALITY, TESTOSTERONE POISONING, WICKEDARY, WITCH, WITCH PERSECUTIONS)

WICCAN

Old English plural, today also an adjective: female and male witches, or wise people, or people trained in the techniques and rituals of witchcraft. (*The Wise Woman* 1983, 4:2, June 21, 7)

WICCE

(See WICCA)

WICKEDARY

"Archaic: a wicked/wiccan dictionary. *Webster's First New Intergalactic Wickedary of the English Language*. The adjective *wicked* can be traced to the same Indo-European root (*weik-*) as wicce, the Old English word meaning witch. . . . The adjective *wiccen* is here constructed from the noun *wicce*. A *Wickedary* is a dictionary for Wicked/Wiccan Women." (Mary Daly 1983, 37; and see 1984, 1)

WICKING

Process by which the string on the Dalkon Shield intrauterine device (IUD) acts like the wick of a kerosene lamp and allows bacteria from the vagina to creep up and enter the uterus, potentially causing infection, blood poisoning, and even death. Protests against the Dalkon Shield eventually caused it to be publicly withdrawn (though some women remain unaware of its dangers) and caused a class action suit on behalf of all wearers to be filed against the manufacturer (which had detailed the dangers of "wicking" in its own internal memos long before the case became public). (in Claudia Dreifus ed. 1977, 95)

WIDDERSHINS

Sacred left-handed dance performed by witches. (*Heresies* 1982, 2:1, issue 5, 131). By extension, means going around anything from left to right, i.e., by any strange or unconventional route.

WIDOW

A harsh and hurtful word. "It comes from the Sanskrit and it means 'empty.' . . . I resent what the term has come to mean. I am alive. I am part of the world." (Lynn Caine; in Mary Daly 1978, 113) Ideal state in which the freedom of the unmarried is coupled with the respectability of the married. "If you're married your husband bosses you and if you aren't married people call you an old maid. Oh, to be a widow!" (Lucy M. Montgomery 1915, 190–1) Resurrection of "miraculous maidenhood." (Sylvia Plath 1952, 175)

(See ORPHAN)

WIDOWER

Later formation than widow; one of the few cases in which the male term developed later than its supposed female counterpart possibly because the female's loss of male economic support was more worthy of being named than the male's loss of female companionship.

WIDOWHOOD

A lonely state. "All the couple friends sort of disappeared because they were doing things in couples. Not at first. There were a few social occasions, but somehow or other, I got the feeling that husband and wife going to the movies with another couple is one way of socializing, and it doesn't work with a couple plus one." (Ruth Powell, describing her experience after her husband died; quoted in Mary Clare Powell 1981, 7)

WIFE

"Muse, momma, agent, promoter, domestic, peacemaker, and brow-mopper.'" (Paula Weideger 1980, 209) "The Old English word *wif* [long *i*] is descended from the Indo-European vocabulary, and it retained its original meaning, 'female human being,' well into the Old English period. . . . Eventually it came to mean only 'female attached to a male.' Perhaps as a consequence of the narrower semantic range accorded to the word *wif*, the compound *wifman* came to be used more and more frequently to mean 'female human being.' The companion term for *wif* in Old English was *wer* cognate with Latin *vir*. That is, *wer* referred to 'male human being' as *wif* referred to 'female human being.' During the same period the term *man*, once a true generic in the Germanic languages, began to develop its current specialized meaning, 'male human being.' *Wer* became obsolete, and it occurs now only in the compound *werewolf*." Lost were terms which designated female participation in social activities outside the home: *locbore* (free woman), *qucwena* (battle woman), *maedenheap* (band of female warriors). In the midst of this lexical turmoil, the compound *wifman* appeared as a new compound for 'female human being.' Variant spellings of *wifman* and *wymman* co-existed until the fourteenth century. (Julia Penelope and Cynthia McGowan 1979)

(See AMAZON, ETYMOLOGY, FEMALE, GIRL, MARRIAGE, PRONOUN, WEAVE, WENCH, WHORE, WOMAN)

"Does not, in our opinion, simply mean . . . 'a woman that has a husband,' for some women have husbands and good ones too, who are not wives according to our understanding of the term – WIFE does not mean, a woman, not a lady only, not a slave, not a mistress, a mother, not a nurse, a teacher, not a companion, a tool, not a plaything; but she is all these things, united together, in one beautiful and harmonious whole. In society she is a woman, in the parlor a lady, in the nursery a slave, in the dining room a mistress, and in her chamber a mother." (Elizabeth Cady Stanton 1852, *The Lily* 4:1, 3)

A harem of one. (Charlotte Perkins Gilman 1911, 43)

Wives are similar to mothers and widows in that "their status and conditions in these relations have been wholly made by men, and are unjust to women." (Teresa Billington-Greig 1911b, 19)

WIFE BATTERING

"The violent victimization of women by the men to whom they are married or with whom they share a marriagelike relationship. . . . Recently, battering has been 'discovered' as a social problem. It is now becoming publicly illegitimate to batter one's wife, and victims are now seen as requiring advocacy and redress. Pervasive abuse [of wives, however,] is reflected in media images of sexually vulnerable females and in everyday social life, with its repertoire of jokes about nagging wives inviting their just desserts." (Dorie Klein 1982, 83, 85)

WIFE-BEATING

A by-product of the Christian view of woman as man's property. (Barbara G. Walker 1983, 593)

WIFE RAPE

(See MARITAL RAPE)

WIFISM

The opposite of Nationalist Feminism. "The wifist wants womyn united with men and the Nationalist Feminist doesn't because the wifist assumes that womyn can be independent of men as individuals without being independent on men as a group and the Nationalist Feminist knows that is impossible: that if womyn are not independent of men as a group we are not independent of men as individuals." (Mia Albright in progress, 38)

(See NATIONALIST FEMINIST ARMED FORCES)

WIFIST

(See WIFISM)

WIG

A transforming element of costume. Describing her experience of working at the New York Telephone Company, Elinor Langer noted that many women working there were "fascinated by wigs. Most women have several wigs and are in some cases unrecognizable from day to day, creating the effect of a continually changing work force. The essence of wiggery is escapism: the kaleidoscopic transformation of oneself while everything else remains the same. Anyone who has ever worn a wig knows the embarrassing truth: it *is* transforming. . . . I think they are a kind of tax, a tribute enacted by the social pressures of the work-place. For the preservation of their own egos against each other and against the system, they had to feel confident of their appearance on each and every day. Outside work they needed it too: to keep up, to keep their men, not to fall behind." (Elinor Langer 1970, 338-9)

WILD

Means " 'great in extent, size, quantity or intensity: EXTREME, PRODIGIOUS.' It means (of a playing card): 'having a denomination determined by the will of the holder.' " "*Wild* is the name of the Self in women, of the enspiriting Sister Self. The wildness of our Selves is visible to wild-eyes, to the inner eyes which ask the deepest 'whys,' the interconnected 'whys' that have not been fragmented by the fathers' 'mother tongues,' nor by their seductive images or -ologies. These are the 'whys' undreamt of in their philosophies, but which lie sleeping, sometimes half-awake, in the wild minds of women. These are the *whys* of untamed wisdom." (Mary Daly 1978, 344) "Wild women don't have the blues." (Ida Cox c.1950s, 278)

WILD BEASTS

Is what Jewish mothers sometimes call their daughters when they don't comb their hair or otherwise act like proper little girls; *Di Vilde Chayes*, literally 'the wild beasts,' is the name taken by a U.S. Jewish Lesbian feminist group who remember the label from their own childhoods and wish to retain and celebrate their identity as disobedient daughters.

WILL

Legal document that until the mid-nineteenth cenutry in the U.S. subordinated a married woman to her husband. "David has signed my will and I have sealed it up and put it away. It excited my towering indignation to think it was necessary for him to sign it. . . . I was indignant for womankind made chattels personal from the beginning of time, perpetually insulted by literature, law, and custom. The very phrases used with regard to us are abominable. 'Dead in the law.' 'Femme couverte.' How I detest such language!" (Lydia Maria Child 1883; in Eleanor Flexner 1968, 62-3)

WILLY WAGGLING
(See SEXUAL HARASSMENT)

WIMMIN
"We have spelt it this way because we are not wo*men* neither are we fe*male*. . . . You may find it trivial – it's just another part of the deep, very deep rooted sexist attitudes." (*This Magazine Is For, About, and By Young Wimmin* 1979, August, 1)

WISEWOMAN
(See WICCA)

WITCH
Female magician, sorceress, sage, soothsayer, wise woman skilled in occult arts and beneficient charms. Only later, a woman in league with evil spirits. From *wic*, to bend or shape, thus one who shapes or influences reality. (Shekhinah Mountainwater 1983, 5) From Old English *wiccian* 'to practice witchcraft,' *wigle* 'divination,' *viglian* 'to divine,' *wig* 'idol image'; and from Old Norse *ve* 'temple,' same root as victim. Also related to Anglo-Saxon *wis* 'wise' from which

comes wizard, witchcraft, vouchsafe, vessel, wish. Also connected by root to wicker, from Danish *viger* 'willow'; Swedish *vika* 'to bend'; hence pliant branches capable of being woven as in wicker basketry. All from Indo-European base *weig* 'violent strength.' (*Heresies* Great Goddess Collective 1982, 131) "A priestess or priest of *Wiccecraft* ('witchcraft'); a wise woman or wise man; a person skilled in healing and psychic work and occult magic; a person able to bend or reshape universal energies; a woman accused by the patriarchy of being too independent, uppity, powerful, or outrageous; a woman learning techniques to overcome the patriarchy." (*The Wise Woman* 1983, 4:2, June 21, 7) In Western superstitious lore, a witch is an unattractive, old person who has made a compact with the devil. "The belief in witchcraft is considerably older than Christianity, and prior to the thirteenth century it was opposed by the Church as a heresy. Yet between the twelfth and seventeenth centuries perhaps as many as nine million persons, most of them women, were tortured and killed as witches, with the approval of the Catholic and later the Protestant Churches. . . . It can be argued . . . that the very concept of witchcraft represents the epitome of misogynism, and must be understood in these terms. Some recent feminist writers have looked upon the legends and rituals of witchcraft as a part of women's spiritual heritage, and have found in the witch an inspiring image of female strength." (Mary Anne Warren 1980, 489-90)
(See HEALING, RECLAMATION, WICCA, WITCH PERSECUTIONS)
Witches "were scientists and healers of the people." (Ann Oakley 1982, 326; also see Barbara Ehrenreich and Deirdre English 1973)
"Is really all women; it names the natural state of women." (Morene 1982; quoted in Karen Payne 1983, 392)
Formed as the "action wing" of New York Radical Women around 1968. WITCH originally stood for Women's International Terrorist Conspiracy from

Hell but was taken over by other groups and transformed into: Women Incensed at Telephone Company Harassment; Women Indentured to Traveler's Corporate Hell (a coven who worked at an insurance company); Women Intent on Toppling Consumer Holidays; Women's Independent Taxpayers, Consumers, and Homemakers; Women Infuriated at Taking Care of Hoodlums; and Women Inspired to Commit Herstory. (Robin Morgan 1978, 72; Ann Oakley 1982, 327)

WITCH BURNING
(See WITCH PERSECUTIONS)

WITCHCRAFT
The "usual Old English spelling was *Wiccecraeft*, meaning 'bending craft' or 'shaping craft'; the act of doing magic, or magical skill. Also, the Goddess-oriented, Nature-loving religion that pre-dates Judaism and Christianity." (*The Wise Woman* 1983, 4:2, June 21, 7)

"Witchcraft was hung, in History,
But History and I
Find all the Witchcraft that we need
Around us, every Day –"
(Emily Dickinson 1890, 208)

"Though traveling by broom is a pleasant idea, it seems that in reality witches could move without transportation, as described in the writings of Maria Feiticeira (*Acts of the Witches*, Iberia, Iron Age). According to her, witches knew how to reach a state which permitted them to go to the sabbath, and, at the same time, remain materially in their prisons. From which came the expressions 'second sight' and 'second state.'" (Monique Wittig and Sande Zeig 1976, 22)

An ancient craft for women. "Historically, the source of this female power was rooted in a sisterly network or coven of women whose knowledge of herbs and potions, words and poisons gave them power over others. The image was essentially domestic – women in dark smocks with brooms and pots of bubbling brews." (Diana M. Meehan 1983, 95)

WITCH CRAZE
(See WITCH PERSECUTIONS)

WITCH HUNTS
(See WITCH PERSECUTIONS)

WITCH PERSECUTIONS
Of the fourteenth through the seventeenth centuries "involved one of the great historic struggles – a class struggle and a struggle for knowledge – between the illiterate but practiced female healer and the beginnings of an aristocratic nouveau science, between the powerful patriarchal Church and enormous numbers of peasant women, between the pragmatic experience of the wisewoman and the superstitious practices of the early male medical profession." (Adrienne Rich 1979, 135)

Have "so much in common with the customary masculine policy of repressing, at any cost, all deviations from the type of wife-and-mother-and-nothing-else, that one cannot help the suspicion that it was more or less unconsciously inspired by that [witch-burning] policy." (Cicely Hamilton 1909, 88)

Were possibly provoked by male fear of women's sexuality. "The suggestion that the witchcraft craze was in large part a result of male paranoia about female sexuality gains considerable support from the words of the *Malleus Maleficarum* (i.e. *Hammer Against Witches*). This document was published in 1486 by two Dominican inquisitors, with the authorization of Pope Innocent VIII, and it became the witch hunters' Bible during the height of the Inquisition. The *Malleus* ascribes the preponderance of female witches to women's excessive sexuality." (Mary Anne Warren 1980, 490)

Possibly took place in relationship to the revolution in scientific knowledge of the sixteenth and seventeenth centuries. "The revolution in scientific and particularly medical thought that characterized the late Renaissance, and which has heretofore been thought to be fundamentally inimical to a belief in witches, actually proved the intellectual basis, indeed the mainspring of witch hunting in the two centuries when the craze and the 'new science' flourished together so extravagantly. . . . It might be worthwhile to look at how such a hunt for the witch disease might plausibly proceed. . . . A peculiar illness might be the work of almost anyone in the village. However, it has been well demonstrated that only a small class of people were normally openly accused. . . . The rich, the powerful, the well-connected and those well situated within a large group of kin, could and probably would retaliate if they were accused of witchcraft. Such accusations would have been pushed only in unusual circumstances. But against those who were more or less incapable of retaliation, the old, the poor and especially women, and those who had already alienated the community by their lewd, immoral or quarrelsome behavior, accusations could be brought with relative impunity. . . . In this model of the craze the stereotype of the witch did not precede the hunts, but was the result of the hunts themselves. Put another way, it was the witch craze that produced the witch and not, as has been traditionally argued, the figure of the witch that stimulated hunting." (Leland L. Estes 1984, 271, 277)

Witch-hunts attempt to eliminate women who live outside the patriarchal family, who subvert a masculine version of society. (Mary Daly 1978)

"The stakes in the square one afternoon
  in Augsburg
were so thick it seemed to be a forest: We
  are still
learning to recognize what we see.
Traces erased. Details removed.
Letters sewn into quilts – or burned.
Self-portraits hidden in trunks – or
  burned.
The perishable nature of so many of our
  artifacts.
Shrines erected over shrines.
The line replaces the circle.
If we do these things to remember witches
If in our remembrance we find the depth
  of our history

Will we opt for description only
or choose to ignite the fuse of our
  knowledge?"
(Michelle Cliff 1980, 42)

WITZ

A seminar-discussion group in Toronto for Women's Independent Thoughtz. "An alternative to the University. An alternative to the bars. An alternative to the political network (but not, of course, an absence of political or any other line of analysis). An alternative way to meet women." (Vera Tarman 1984, 6)

WLM

Women's Liberation Movement. An inclusive term for the multiple organizations, theoretical positions, and strategies whose overall goal is to struggle against the oppression of women everywhere. When the name was appropriated in the form of a legal patent by one French feminist group, other women's groups argued that the term was generic and could not be the "property" of any single group. (*Spare Rib* 1981, July, 19-21)

WOMAGE

To take charge, to "manage." *Womager* is the woman who does this. (From the Pagoda Women's Resort in St Augustine, Florida; zana 1983, correspondence)

WOMAN

Subject of this dictionary. Some notes and comments toward the meanings of *woman* follow. "I had better, at the outset, define the word 'woman' as I understand and use it, since it is apt to convey two distinct and differing impressions, according to the sex of the hearer. My conception of woman is inevitably the feminine conception; a thing so entirely unlike the masculine conception of woman that it is eminently needful to define the term and make my meaning clear; lest, when I speak of woman in my own tongue, my reader, being male, translate the expression, with confusion as the result. By a

489

woman, then, I understand an individual human being whose life is her own concern; whose worth, in my eyes (worth being an entirely personal matter) is in no way advanced or detracted from by the accident of marriage; who does not rise in my estimation by reason of a purely physical capacity for bearing children, or sink in my estimation through a lack of that capacity." (Cicely Hamilton 1909, 19-20)

(See AMAZON, ETYMOLOGY, GIRL, LADY, LESBIAN, MAN, MATRIARCHY, OBJECTIVITY, REPRESENTATION, SEMANTIC DEROGATION OF WOMEN, WIFE, WOMAN-IDENTIFIED WOMAN, WOMANLY, WOMANIST, WOMEN, WOMEN OF COLOR, WOMON, and all entries above and below)

The Old English singular form was *wifman* (*wif* 'woman' + *mon(n)* *man(n)*) 'human being' the plural *wifmen*. Both nouns proliferated into a myriad of inflected forms in Old and Middle English (offering some precedent for variant spellings of the words today). Singular forms included wifman, wifmon, wimman, wim(m)on, wyman, wymman, wymmon, wyfman, wummon, wumman, womman, wommon, voman, vomman, woman(n)e, wommane, whoman, wooman, woman, oman, owman, o'man, uman, 'ooman, umman; plural forms included wifmen, wimmen, wymmen, wyfmen, wimen, wemmen, wymen, vymmen, ymen, wummen, wommen, womene, vommen, woymen, woemen, women, vemene, women, wemyn, whemen, weymen, weomen, vemen, weemen, weamen. The historical results of these variants linger on in the many dialect differences of England, Scotland, Ireland, and Wales.

The English word *woman* is peculiar to English among the Indoeuropean languages and relatively recent, the ancient word being *wif*. The evolution to modern English was "regular," following the pattern of many other words. The standard ME descendants of the OE forms were wifman/men and wimman/wimmen, which continued in use until the fifteenth century. By 1200, the rounding of the vowel [wi] in speech to [wu] in the sg. had occurred, with the written form *womman* first appearing in late 13th century texts and the corresponding plural *wommen* in the late 14th. Until the early modern period, the first syllables of the singular and the plural were clearly differentiated; the singular was marked *wo* and the plural *we*, giving rise to the puns "woe-man" and "we-men" which are still around today. From about 1400 *woman* and *women* became regular spellings, for by then they were seen as proper parallels with *man/men*; but pronunciation diverged, evidently following the pattern of sg./pl. pairs like *foot/feet*.

The *Oxford English Dictionary* cites Mrs Wheeler 1790 "What is cum among Wimmen an Lasses E this Parish?" Derogatory citations begin early, around 1400 (e.g., "a womans tounge," 1515). But also *woman* meant "one's own woman," mistress of oneself, independent. The citation of a "young woman of colour" is from Lyell, 1849.

Compounds include gentlewoman, charwoman, horsewoman. There is a 1382 citation (Wyclif) to "a woman-widowe" and 1400 to a "woman gossyb," words that later became semantically marked for gender and dropped "woman" as an adjective. Dryden refers to "a Woman-Grammarian, who corrects her husband for speaking false Latin." *Woman-* remained a productive compound: *woman-palaver* became a colonialist product to signify illicit commerce with a woman or women. The compound form often doubled to place women in active or passive roles: *woman-actor* meant both (1) a female actor and (2) male actor who takes women's roles; *woman-physician* meant both (1) a doctor of women's diseases and (2) a doctor who is a woman. As a verb, *to woman* meant to address someone as "woman," or in a style in which you would address a woman.

"Proposed spelling changes [in modern English]: womn or wom'n instead of woman (second spelling is awkward if saying 'wom'ns); womnn in place of women. When the vowels are changed to i or y (womin, womyn) the words feel different and strange, but when the a or e is just omitted, the reader can scan the words without feeling a jolt every time, and can figure out which is plural more easily." (Cherie Lyn 1984, correspondence)

"The word *woman*, and its etymological companion, *wife*, have together received from the English etymologists an astonishing number of interpretations, most of them based on the presumed sexual or domestic function of women." These include derivations from *womb-man* ("in our toung the feminyne creature also hath as wee see, the name of man, but more aptly in that it is for due distinction composed with womb, shee beeing that kynde of man that is wombed, or hath the womb of conception" – seventeenth century etymologist quoted in Dennis Baron forthcoming), from *wifman* meaning female person,' and folk derivations like 'woe to man.' Many etymologists also pursued a connection between the word *wife* and *weaving*, waging many arguments over the logic by which the first derived from the second; more recently these have been replaced by a connection of *wife* to the root for 'tremble' or 'vibrate.' "The proponents of 'woe-to-man' did not hesitate to prove their argument by pointing to the trouble caused by women, and the advocates of 'womb-man' were quick to point out that women were physiologically equipped with wombs. Similarly, those who favored 'weaver' were certain that attending to cloth was what Indo-European women did best. While none of the advocates of 'vibrator' go so far as to say the derivation is attractive to them because women are wavering, or irresolute, as cognates of this supposed root suggest, or even good at vibrating – although Partridge does find this last notion somehow *basic* to women – it seems clear that they find the etymology

semantically compelling. Man, the etymologizing animal, cannot rest until he explains woman to his satisfaction." (Dennis Baron forthcoming)

According to at least one feminist interpretation, the connection of *wife* to *waver* is not unappealing: "Now, 'to waver' is not to be irresolute in any negative sense; rather 'waver' derives from Old Norse *vabra* 'to vibrate, to hover about' and from Danish *viger* 'willow' from which also derive wicca, weave, and wiles and guiles, i.e., sorcery. In other words, pliancy is the value, the pliancy of wicker work. In confirmation, the Indo-European root WEIP has a basic sense of 'to twist or turn,' which again supports the old popular notion of a wife as a weaver, or should we say – a spinster – a word that continues to mean 'without man.' " This writer notes that "modern English (and most likely every other language) contains women's heritage of social and cultural eminence. Through a study and propagation of English, we can regain/retain a true sense of that entirely natural eminence. Moreover reclaiming, rather than the arduous task of undoing, is far more likely to succeed. This radical approach to the creation of a feminist language not only puts us in touch with our past, it also makes worldwide connections." (Grace Shinell 1983, correspondence)

"What is a woman you ask.... Una mujer? ... Are you like me, are you proud, brown, bilingual, confused and anxious? ... The voices of our culture – our mothers and grandmothers – filter through the cracks of our personal feminism.... Independence. We want to be our mothers ... crochet like our grandmothers – abuelita – and write reports and analytical studies." (Gladys Benavides Corbit 1984; "What is a Woman You Ask," *Women of Color News* (April), 25)

"Although it might first appear that woman, lady, and girl are interchangeable terms – one's choice of words reflecting habit rather than attitude – people are indeed cognizant (at least unconsciously) that *only the term woman has sexual and aggressive implications and connotes reproductive functioning....* As linguists have noted, the term lady functions as a euphemism, in that it removes the sexual and reproductive implications inherent in the word woman ... [it] denotes an absence of aggressive impulses in the female sex.... The term girl not only serves to avoid certain anxiety-arousing connotations inherent in the word woman regarding aggression, sexuality, and reproduction, it also serves to impart a tone of frivolousness and lack of seriousness to ambitious, intellectual, and competitive strivings that women may pursue." (Harriet E. Lerner 1976a, 295-6)

In language, "a possibility everyone tends to forget." "Consider the congressman. He is a man of the people. To prove that he's the best man for the job, he takes his case to the man in the street. He is a champion of the workingman. He speaks up for the little man. He has not forgotten the forgotten man. And he firmly believes: one man, one vote. Consider the policeman or fireman, the postman or milkman, the clergyman or businessman. Whatever else he may be, he is by title a man, and if his employer feels that he is 'our kind of man,' he may become 'our man in the home office' or 'our man in Algiers.' " (Shirley Morahan 1981, 63)

Is "a generic term used to encompass all of homosapiens, since it includes 'man' within it. Example: 'Traces of early woman were found at Olduvai Gorge. Contrasts with *womon*." (zana 1983, correspondence)

"If you are willing to grant that language and literature *are* important, why is it irrelevant to you that wimmin are called 'girls' until we die? Why is it irrelevant that female address terms (Miss, Mrs.) serve to indicate whether or not a woman is sexually available ('on the market') while the male Mr. does not?" (Julia Penelope 1978, 6)

Is a "slave who has chains to break." (Margaret Fuller 1843; in Alice Rossi ed. 1973, 169)

Is "in her sufferings bound hand and foot, unprotected by the law or public sentiment, dumb alike in Church, State, and at the domestic hearth." (Susan B. Anthony 1852, 1)

"Is what she is because she has lived as she has. And no estimate of her character, no effort to fix the limits of her activities, can carry weight that ignores the totally different relations toward society that have artificially grown up, dividing so sharply the life of woman from that of man." (Ellen Glasgow 1913; rpt in Elizabeth Janeway ed. 1973a, 14)

"From father's house to husband's house to a grave that still might not be her own, a woman acquiesces to male authority in order to gain some protection from male violence. She conforms, in order to be as safe as she can be." (Andrea Dworkin 1983, 14)

"As we know her to-day, is largely a manufactured product." (Cicely Hamilton 1909, 121)

Is considered by man to be "a dangerous animal, and in order to compete with her, man must be protected by the whole machinery of the State." (Lady McLaren 1908, 14)

Is economically invisible. "To the androcentric mind she does not exist – women are females, and that's all." (Charlotte Perkins Gilman 1911, 245)

Is the signifier of an uneasy and perhaps meaningless identity. Implies universality rather than diversity. "There are only women, who, to begin with, are divided, as men are divided, by differences of race, creed, class, training, inherited character; who may, indeed, 'like the Colonel's lady and Judy O'Grady,' be 'sisters under their skins,' but whose sisterhood in nowise justifies those sweeping generalisations that come so readily from the tongue of the average Englishman." (Sidney Pickering 1912, 293)

"When I say 'woman,' I'm speaking of woman in her inevitable struggle against conventional man; and of a universal woman subject who must bring women to their sense and to their meaning in history. . . . There is, at this time, no general woman, no one typical woman. What they have *in common* I will say. But what strikes me is the infinite richness of their individual constitutions: you can't talk about *a* female sexuality, uniform, homogeneous, classifiable into codes – any more than you can talk about one unconscious resembling another. Women's imaginary is inexhaustible, like music, painting, writing: their stream of phantasms is incredible." (Hélène Cixous 1975b, 245-6)

Identity imposed, not "natural." Woman "is concretely – not mythologically – woman only for the sake of the few hours of childbirth. . . . But imagine a lucky and healthful land where a human being is likely to live peaceably until 80. Imagine one who has experienced childbirth only twice, with the event lasting each time about six hours. For the sake of 12 hours out of a life 700, 800 hours long, this person is called 'woman'. . . . This person is thrust into an ethos which enjoins rigid duties on her, almost none of them rationally related to the two six-hour events of childbirth." (Cynthia Ozick 1972b, 151)

Regarded by men "as a breeding-machine and the necessary adjunct to a frying-pan." (Cicely Hamilton 1909, 50)

As used by men, holds no recognition of women, young and old, rich and poor, gifted or dull – no individuals – a label with very restricted meaning. (Beatrice Forbes-Robertson Hale 1914; in Cheris Kramarae 1981, 44)

Identity constructed for strategic purposes. "The belief that 'one is a woman' is almost as absurd and obscurantist as the belief that 'one is a man.' I say 'almost' because there are still many goals which women can achieve: freedom of abortion and contraception, day-care centers for children, equality on the job, etc. Therefore, we must use 'we are women' as an advertisement or slogan for our demands. On a deeper level, however, a woman cannot 'be!'; it is something which does not even belong in the order of *being*. . . . In 'woman' I see something that cannot

be represented, something that is not said, something above and beyond nomenclatures and ideologies." (Julia Kristeva 1974, 137)

"Has just about come to signify to me straight woman. . . . It's probably been happening gradually, over years, in bitter confusion, as 'the women's liberation movement' in the U.S. turned into 'the women's movement' turned into 'women's development' and 'women's culture' and left/liberal coalition politics." (Harriet Ellenberger 1984, 43)

Are human beings noted for patience and endurance.

"Jill-of-all-trades
Lover, mother, housewife, friend, bread-winner
Heart and spade
A woman is a ritual
A house that must accommodate
A house that must endure
Generation after generation . . ."
  (Genny Lim 1981, 26)

"A woman, unless she submits,
is neither a mule
nor a queen
though like a mule she may suffer
and like a queen pace the floor."
  (Alice Walker 1975, 7)

Will be different in the future. "The future woman must have a life work and economic independence. She must have knowledge. She must have the right of motherhood at her own discretion. The mincing horror at free womanhood must pass if we are ever to be rid of the bestiality of free manhood; not by guarding the weak in weakness do we gain strength, but by making weakness free and strong." (W. E. B. DuBois "The Damnation of Women," cited in Frederica Y. Daly 1978, 62)

"At the beginning of our history, woman was a sun, a real human being. Now, woman is a moon, pale, like a sick person, given life by others and illuminated by others' light. We must take back our hidden sun, right now!" (Hiratsuka Raicho 1911)

Has been "obsolete since the beginning

of the Glorious Age. Considered by many companion lovers as the most infamous designation. This word once applied to being fallen in an absolute state of servitude. Its meaning was, 'one who belongs to another.' " (Monique Wittig and Sande Zeig 1976, 165)

Real woman: "A 'real woman' is, in the end, one who wants to please men . . . (never a woman) or possibly an old maid (a failed woman) or if young enough, a tomboy (not yet a woman). A 'real woman' who finds the 'job' of pleasing men unsatisfying is a hysteric. So much for us from where they sit." (Radical Feminists 1972)

Straight woman: "The definition of a 'straight woman' is directly proportional to the extent of the prick in her head." (*off our backs* 1984, July, 8))

WOMAN, NEW

(See NEW WOMAN)

WO/MAN

"Generic term. Replacement term for generic 'man'; 'wolman' includes both 'man' and 'woman.' " (Midge Lennert and Norma Willson, eds, 1973, 13)

WOMAN AND LABOUR

"To Olive Schreiner's *Woman and Labour* – that 'Bible of the Woman's Movement' which sounded to the world of 1911 as insistent and inspiring as a trumpet-call summoning the faithful to a vital crusade – was due my final acceptance of feminism." (Vera Brittain 1933, 41)

WOMAN IDENTIFICATION

(See WOMAN-IDENTIFIED WOMAN, WOMANIST, WOMANLY)

WOMAN-IDENTIFIED WOMAN

Title of influential essay by the group Radicalesbians which offered a political analysis of the category "lesbian" in relation to the category "woman" and in relation to male homosexuals. "Lesbianism, like male homosexuality, is a category of behavior possible only in a sexist society characterized by rigid sex roles and dominated by male supremacy. . . . But lesbianism is also different from male homosexuality, and serves a different function in society. . . . Lesbian is the word, the label, the condition that holds women in line. When a woman hears this word tossed her way, she knows she is stepping out of line." "Lesbian" was thus redefined not strictly in terms of sexual orientation but in terms of "the primacy of women relating to women, of women creating a new consciousness of and with each other, which is at the heart of women's liberation." This was an important and useful step in opening up the terms of discussion and making it possible to address homophobia within the women's movement more directly. (Radicalesbians 1970, 241, 245)

(See LESBIAN, WOMAN, WOMEN'S LIBERATION MOVEMENT)

"A woman committed to herself and I mean by that the woman as combined image of mother daughter and sister was absolutely at odds with society which has been in the modern western world organized around the principle of heterosexuality which in effect means the prime commitment of woman to man who is committed to himself." (Jill Johnston 1973a, 90)

"Seems to me to have become a euphemism for lesbians, rather than the attempt it originally was to locate the strategic significance of lesbians with regard to a movement against male dominance." (Harriet Ellenberger 1984, 43)

"The lesbian peoples who appeared just about everywhere had no difficulty in speaking a single language. Each companion lover loved another who, loving her in turn, began to speak a language familiar to them all. This very ancient and rediscovered tongue is called the lesbian language." (Monique Wittig and Sande Zeig 1976, 17)

WOMANIFESTO

Strong political statement by women for

women: for example Jill Johnston's "Comingest Womanifesto." (Jill Johnston 1973c, 89)

WOMANISH

(See WOMANISM, WOMANIST, WOMANLY)

WOMANISM

Black feminism. "Feminism (all colors) definitely teaches women they are capable, one reason for its universal appeal. In addition to this, womanist (i.e., black feminist) tradition *assumes*, because of our experiences during slavery, that black women already *are* capable. . . . I don't choose womanism because it is 'better' than feminism. . . . Since womanism *means* black feminism, this would be a nonsensical distinction. I choose it because I prefer the sound, the feel, the fit of it; because I cherish the spirit of the women (like Sojourner) the word calls to mind, and because I share the old ethnic-American habit of offering society a new word when the old word it is using fails to describe behavior and change that only a new word can help it more fully see." (Alice Walker 1984, *New York Times Magazine*, February 12)

(See AUTHOR, AUTHORITY, WOMANIST)

WOMANIST

1. From *womanish* (opposite of *girlish*, i.e., frivolous, irresponsible, not serious). A black feminist or feminist of color. From the black folk expression of mothers to female children, "You acting womanish," i.e., like a woman. Usually referring to outrageous, audacious, courageous, or *willful* behavior. Wanting to know more and in greater depth than is considered "good" for one. Interested in grown-up doing. Acting grown-up. Being grown-up. Interchangeable with another black folk expression: "You trying to be grown." Responsible. In charge. *Serious.*
2. *Also*: A woman who loves other women, sexually and/or nonsexually.

Appreciates and prefers women's culture, women's emotional flexibility (values tears as natural counterbalance of laughter), and women's strength. Committed to survival and wholeness of entire people, male *and* female. Not a separatist, except periodically, for health. Traditionally universalist, as in: "Mama, why are we brown, pink, and yellow, and our cousins are white, beige, and black?" Ans: "Well, you know the colored race is just like a flower garden, with every color flower represented." Traditionally capable, as in: "Mama, I'm walking to Canada and I'm taking you and a bunch of other slaves with me." Reply: "It wouldn't be the first time."
3. Loves music. Loves dance. Loves the moon. *Loves* the Spirit. Loves love and food and roundness. Loves struggle. *Loves* the Folk. Loves herself. *Regardless.*
4. Womanist is to feminist as purple is to lavender. (Alice Walker 1983, xi)

WOMANITY

The supposed disposition of womankind. "I will be secret beyond womanity, if you are frank beyond discretion." (Elizabeth Barrett Browning 1843, cited in the *Oxford English Dictionary*)

WOMANLINESS

"Female potency: a feeling of psychological wholeness, dependency upon no one but a willingness to touch and be mutually affected by others." (Midge Lennert and Norma Willson eds 1973, 13) "In the past was very much a matter of coercion." (Teresa Billington-Greig c.1908, 5)

WOMANLY

Means taking the woman's part, though in men's dictionaries means the opposite. "I am ready to go to the polls at the next election. Of course this is not at all proper, and is exceedingly womanish – or womanly, as some people misuse that blessed word. Nevertheless, this is how the arrest of Miss Anthony has affected one woman." (R. R., letter to *The Woman's*

Journal 1873, January 18, 24) "It is 'womanly' to be meek, patient, tactful, modest. It is manly to be strong, brave, honourable. We make here . . . an initial mistake, or, at least, over-statement, apt to damage the morality of both man and woman. To be meek, patient, tactful, modest, honourable, brave, is not to be either manly or womanly; it is to be humane, to have social virtue." (Jane Ellen Harrison 1912, 5)

WOMAN OF COLOR
(See WOMEN OF COLOR)

WOMAN QUESTION
Is how classical marxists referred to the question of women's historical status and role within current social arrangements. "The woman question has never been the 'feminist question.' The feminist question is directed at the causes of sexual inequality between women and men, of male dominance over women. Most marxist analyses of women's position take as their question the relationship of women to the economic system, rather than that of women to men, apparently assuming the latter will be explained in their discussion of the former." (Heidi Hartmann 1979, 3-4)
(See MARXIST FEMINIST, RED DIAPER FEMINISTS)

WOMAN'S ISSUE, THE
Employment, Peace, Black, Progress, Security, Recession, Legislation, Red, Nutrition, White, Africa, Sexuality, Brown, Children, Environment, Happiness, Politics, Yellow, Prosperity, Ecology, Legislation, Equality, Peace. . . . (Jo Haugerud ed. 1982)

WOMANSPIRIT
The power of women's wisdom, the synthesis of feminism and spirituality. (Hallie Iglehart 1983, xii)

WOMAN'S PLACE
"(1) [Traditional] Women's role defined by male religious, educational, legal, societal institutions – i.e., the kitchen, the bedroom, the vegetable garden. (2) The world." (Midge Lennert and Norma Willson eds 1973, 13)

WOMAN'S RIGHTER
Media label for feminist, c.1885.
(See WOMEN'S LIBBER)

WOMAN'S WORK
"Is never done . . . by men" (Grafitti, in Rachel Bartlett comp. 1982)
"The kind of work which man prefers not to do." (Cicely Hamilton 1909, 69)
"Is defined as inferior work, and inferior work tends to be defined as work for women." (Catharine A. MacKinnon 1979, 11)

" 'Don't any men work in this place except the foreman?' I asked Mrs. Mooney, who had toiled a long time in the [garment factory] and knew everything.
'Love of Mary!' she exclaimed indignantly; 'and d'ye think any white man that called hisself a whiteman would work in sich a place as this . . . ?'
'But we work here,' I argued.
'Well, we be wimmin,' she declared, drawing a pinch of snuff into her nostrils in a manner that indicated finality.
'But if it isn't good enough for a man, it isn't good enough for us, even if we are women!' I persisted.
She looked at me half in astonishment, half in suspicion at my daring to question the time-honored order of things. Economics could make no appeal to her intelligence, and shooting a glance out of her hard old black eyes, she replied with a logic that permitted no gainsaying.
'Love of Mary! if yez don't like yer job, ye can git out. Sure and we don't take on no airs around here!' " (Dorothy Richardson 1905, 243-4)

"The definition of woman's work is shitwork." (Gloria Steinem 1974; quoted in Elaine Partnow 1977, 389)

WOMB
From Old English *wamb, womb*. In the earliest citations listed in the OED, the

word had a variety of meanings: the abdomen (of both women and men), 825; the stomach, receptacle of food, 950; the bowels, from 1000; the uterus, from 825; a hollow space or cavity, from 969; and (figuratively), a place or medium of conception and development. *Womb-cake* was the placenta; *womb-stones* were calcified fibroid tumors of the uterus. The word was also a verb, meaning to enclose as in a womb: "Wombed within our walles" (1557).

(See ABORTION, ANATOMY IS DESTINY, MATRIX, OBJECTIVITY, WOMAN)

"Men have every right to be envious of the womb. I'm envious of it myself, and I have one." (Alice Walker 1979, 368)

"The myth that women's sexuality ceases on the stroke of the menopause is based on several erroneous assumptions, among them the view of the womb as the ideal center of women's sexuality; the loss of function suffered by the uterus at menopause is thought to have an extinguishing influence on the entire sex life." (Ruth Herschberger 1948, 63)

WOMEN

Are the subject of this dictionary. See all entries above and below. Some feminist conceptualizations of women follow.

Are "recognized as individual by the State for the purposes of taxation and punishment. When powers, rights, or privileges, are conferred, women are regarded as non-existent." (Teresa Billington-Greig 1911b, 18)

Are sometimes called the "opposite sex" – "though why 'opposite' I do not know; what is the 'neighboring sex'? . . . The fundamental thing is that women are more like men than anything else in the world. They are human beings. *Vir* is male and *Femina* is female: but *homo* is male and female. This is the equality claimed and the fact that is persistently evaded and denied. No matter what arguments are used, the discussion is vitiated from the start, because Man is always dealt with as both *Homo* and *Vir*, but Woman only as *Femina*." (Dorothy L. Sayers 1947; in Betty Roszak and Theodore Roszak eds 1969, 117)

Are the adults who carry babies, groceries, household supplies, laundry, baby bags, and packages of assorted necessities because their garments have skimpy pockets and because men are elsewhere doing other things with their hands. (Letty Cottin Pogrebin 1983a, 18Y)

Are lesbians. "It's impossible to separate our oppression as women from our oppression as lesbians. All women are lesbians." (Jill Johnston 1973a, 90)

"Are born Slaves, and live Prisoners all their Lives." (A Lady 1721, 19)

"Are a spare resource for employers in times of expansion; they are also a spare resource for politicians to call upon in times of recession. When it ceases to be convenient to spend money on public services, responsibility is handed back to those two euphemisms for unpaid female labour, 'the community' and 'the family.' " (Anna Coote and Beatrix Campbell 1982, 81)

As a class "are the dulled conformists, the orthodox believers, the obedient followers, the disciples of unwavering faith. To waver, whatever the creed of the men around them, is tantamount to rebellion; it is dangerous." (Andrea Dworkin 1983, 14)

"Are cast as mere 'resting places' of the family's honour, morality, and dignity, as defined by men in their role as heads of the family hierarchy." (LACW Collective 1977, 84)

Though "embedded in the heart, factory, and kitchen of culture, are treated as though we are peripheral to it; and many of us feel like exiles." (Michele Roberts 1983, 65)

Are returning "from afar, from always: from 'without,' from the heath where witches are kept alive; from below, from beyond 'culture'; from their childhood which men have been trying desperately to make them forget. . . . What an effort it takes – there's no end to it – for the sex cops to bar their threatening return. Such a display of forces on both sides that the struggle has for centuries been immobilized in the trembling equilibrium of a deadlock." (Hélène Cixous 1975b, 247)

WOMEN AND LANGUAGE [NEWS]

Title of interdisciplinary research newsletter started in 1976 by Pat Nichols, Barrie Thorne, Pam Tiedt, and others and published at Stanford University 1976-81, (ed. Sharon Veach). Since 1981 it's been edited by Cheris Kramarae and Paula A. Treichler and published at the University of Illinois at Urbana-Champaign.

WOMEN AND LANGUAGE RESEARCH

Growing field of investigation across many academic disciplines. In their comprehensive annotated bibliography of the field (an update of Barrie Thorne and Nancy Henley eds. 1975), Barrie Thorne, Cheris Kramarae, and Nancy Henley eds. (1983) categorize current research as follows: gender marking and sex bias in language structure and content; stereotypes and perceptions of language use; sex differences and similiarities in language use – linguistic components; conversational interaction; genre and style; children and language; language varieties; and nonverbal aspects of communication. Whatever its theoretical or disciplinary base, most work in the field assumes close relationships between language and society, and seeks to explore the interaction between linguistic structures, social structures, and sex.

(See INTRODUCTION, DICTIONARY, ETYMOLOGY, FEMINIST DICTIONARY, ENGLISH, LINGUISTIC SEXISM, MEANING, SEMANTICS)

"Studies of the interaction of language and gender/sex systems have flourished during the past decade, becoming increasingly sophisticated and subtle. . . . The primary motivation of much of the best such work has not been curiosity about language, but rather feminist concern to understand the nature and persistence of male dominance of women. Unless the implications of these studies for our understanding of language itself are made explicit, only linguists who happen also to be concerned with feminist issues will find them of interest. Insofar as gender/sex distinctions have been considered by people who also have a major interest in language as such . . . they have all too often been analyzed in terms of theories of psychology and social life which are ill-suited to deal with the realities of women's experience – or more generally, with the complex interactions of language, mind, and society. Excellent descriptive and theoretical work is being done by anthropologists, psychologists, sociologists, philosophers, and other contributors (including some linguists) to recent feminist scholarship. Some of this work deals directly with the role of language and linguistic communication of women's lives; some provides a useful re-examination of general social and psychological theories to account for both women's and men's perspectives. However . . . the value of much feminist research on language is lessened by investigators' unfamiliarity with linguistic categories and principles. Comparability of different studies of speech could be facilitated, for example, by including detailed descriptions of the linguistic structures actually used by the people being observed. In addition, the interest of such studies for linguistics is much more likely to emerge when their results can be interpreted within some general theory of language." The benefits of continued work on these questions can "gain for feminist scholarship on language the benefits to be found in increased attention to linguistic theory and practice" and "gain for linguistics itself new perspectives required to make sense of observations that focus on gender/sex distinctions." (Sally McConnell-Ginet 1983, 373-4)

One crucial assumption underlying research in sociolinguistics is that language both reflects and recreates non-linguistic structural arrangements. Specific to research on language and gender is that symptoms of the oppression of women are ubiquitous, and certainly revealed in language interaction. If these two premises are accepted, then there are several possible purposes for research on language use and the sexes: to document and explain sex differences in verbal interaction so that we will better understand the problematic or oppressive features of communicative events; to analyze particular areas of inequitable language use in order to encourage change and create a more equitable social order. But the relationship between micro interactions and structural arrangements is complicated: equal participation in language use will not alone bring about changes in structure (features of production, distribution, property, knowledge, social organization, etc.). (Carole Edelsky 1983, *Women and Language News* 7:1, Spring, 4-5)

WOMEN OF COLOR

A positive term designating women of many different ethnic and racial heritages (including Black, Native American, Chicana, Puerto Rican, Filipino, Hispanic, and Asian) and emphasizing commonalities, sisterhood, and shared oppressions. The term deliberately invokes the language used historically for populations who were "colored" in contrast to the population of the dominant white culture.

"We are women from all kinds of childhood streets: the farms of Puerto Rico, the downtown streets of Chinatown, the barrio, city-Bronx streets, quiet suburban sidewalks, the plains, and the reservation." (Cherríe Moraga and Gloria Anzaldúa eds 1981, 5)

"Have grown up [in America] within a symphony of anguish at being silenced, at being unchosen, at knowing that when we survive, it is in spite of a whole world out there that takes for granted our lack of humanness, that hates our very existence, outside of its service. And I say 'symphony' rather than 'cacophony,' because we have had to learn to orchestrate those furies so that they do not tear us apart." (Audre Lorde 1981c, 9)

"For us, the 'radical women of color,' who have been disenfranchised, locked

out of this society, the question not only is 'to be or not to be . . .,' but *who* to be, *how* to be, *what* to be, or even *when* to be in a culture that is extremely hostile to our existence – our survival. This culture is so full of racist, sexist, and classist landmines and hidden traps that all of us carry scars. Some of us are more maimed than others, some of us dead." (Deborah Aslan Jamieson 1982, 6)

Some women suggest that it obscures diversity and specificity and lumps all racial and ethnic groups together, thus facilitating the tendency in language to universalize (Commission on the Status of Women forum 1984; Modern Language Association, New York).

WOMEN'S

A descriptive put in front of words such as "center or newspaper, network or rock band. Indicates a positive choice. Ten years ago, it was a put-down." (Gloria Steinem 1983, 149)

WOMEN'S AILMENTS

Term used in the late nineteenth century for women's health problems and concerns.

WOMEN'S BURDEN

"Take up the Women's Burden!
She's waiting to be freed,
From the tyranny of priestcraft,
from court and rite and creed,
Your dogmatism cast aside,
Remember human ties;
Unbind the Woman's Burden,
And let the victim rise."
(Harriet M. Close 1904, 415)

WOMEN'S HEALTH MOVEMENT

Activist tradition thousands of years old of women caring for women, often risking insult, attack, disease, and death to do so. The modern movement began in the late 1960s; though it takes different forms and focuses on different problems in different parts of the world, the worldwide movement shares a grassroots organizational structure, critique of economic systems not geared toward women's interests, challenge to the "doctrine of female expendability" (Claudia Dreifus; in Claudia Dreifus ed. 1977) in policy and experimentation, concern for women's health within an overall economic context, and a commitment to preventive medicine and education. In the U.S., the women's health movement critiques the capitalist for profit health care system with its privileging of male experts, and stresses the development of alternative structures of health care delivery, self-help and the validity of personal experience, reproductive freedom, and feminist involvement in health care planning and delivery. Specific issues include right to reproductive freedom including access to contraception and abortion; diagnosis, treatment, and research on women's health concerns including menstruation, menopause, breast cancer; critique of medical practice with regard to surgical procedures including caesarian section, hysterectomy, and mastectomy; the differential treatment including involuntary sterilization of poor women and women of color; health care costs; childbirth; mental health; the provision of drugs to women in the U.S. and in third world countries; and research, information, and ethical issues involved in modern biotechnological developments (*in vitro* fertilization, etc.). (Claudia Dreifus 1977; Michelle Harrison 1982; Judith Walzer Leavitt ed. 1984; Helen Roberts ed. 1981; Shelly Romalis ed. 1981)

(See ABORTION, BIRTHING, CONTRACEPTION, DOCTOR, HEALING, MEDICINE, MIDWIFE, NURSING, NURSE PRACTITIONER, SELF-HELP, TAMPON, TOXIC SHOCK SYNDROME, WICKING, WOMEN'S VOCABULARY)

WOMEN'S LANGUAGE

Stereotyped and often parodied, so-called "women's language" in speech is said to consist of a number of lexical, structural, stylistic, and paralinguistic features which, interpreted negatively (as they usually are), function to weaken or trivialize the female speaker and to keep her in her place (Robin Lakoff 1975). These include "feminine" words and particles (*adorable, oh, dear*), intensifiers (*simply, truly*), tag questions ("Women don't really use more tag questions, do they?"), "ladylike" lexical items and euphemisms (*little girls' room*), lexical terms for colors, cooking, sewing, and so on (*mauve*), repetition, questions rather than statements, less assertive, and greater marking of intonation. Language and gender research over the past 15 years has failed to substantiate the existence of these features in women's speech; rather they seem to occur in anyone's speech depending on audience, circumstances, intention, and purpose (Sally McConnell-Ginet 1983). In writing, women are supposed to be more wordy, more "flowery," and emphasize content concerned with home, "feminine" pursuits and responsibilities, religion, art, and personal relationships. In theoretical writing, particularly in France, the term "women's language" (*l'écriture feminine*) more frequently designates the experimental writing of a number of specific feminist authors including Hélène Cixous (1975b), Luce Irigaray (1977, 1983), and Michèle Montrelay (1980). In the U.S., numerous empirical studies attempting to determine whether "women's language" "really exists" have yielded contradictory responses. Taken as a whole, however, they seem to suggest that the stereotype is very consistent; that in certain contexts communication patterns emerge which are more characteristic of women than of men; that in other contexts no differences between men and women are apparent; that what has been called "women's language" is in some cases the function of powerlessness and subordination rather than gender alone; that whatever women do is more likely to be given a negative interpretation; that certain features of "women's language" (for example, support through head nods and ongoing responses like "Mm Hm" or "Yeah") of the talk of others have positive consequences for maintaining conversations;

and that much of the research in this area, derived from male paradigms and interpreted by male criteria (for example, the definition of what an "interruption" is), will not yield fruitful or interesting results. (Cheris Kramarae 1981; Sally McConnell-Ginet, Ruth Borker, and Nelly Furman eds 1980; Barrie Thorne, Cheris Kramarae, and Nancy Henley eds. 1983)

(See CONVERSATION, TALK, LANGUAGE AND WOMAN'S PLACE, LANGUAGE AND BLACK WOMAN'S PLACE, MEANING, MEN'S LANGUAGE, POLITENESS, WOMEN AND LANGUAGE RESEARCH, WOMEN'S VOCABULARY)

WOMEN'S LIB

A trivializing term. Its use has diminished but has not disappeared. (Gloria Steinem 1983, 155) "It would appear that the substitution of lib for liberation is more an attempt at diminution rather than abbreviation, a lessening rather than a shortening." (Jane Lafferty 1970, 6) Is an insult, "as if liberation is just another catch phrase to be abbreviated." (Ain't I A Woman Collective 1970; *Ain't I A Woman*, September 25, 9) "We have been talking about Women's Lib for some time now, as shorthand for Women's Liberation, and would like to argue strongly for our stopping use of the term and using the fullword – Liberation. . . . Those unsympathetic or simply ignorant of Women's Liberation almost always use 'lib' in a way that ends up degrading and making light of our cause. . . . Also, use of 'lib' reflects our own tendency as women not to take ourselves seriously, and our liberation seriously." (Jenny Bull 1971, 7) Is a defense against a threat. "When you are threatened, you use any means of defense at hand. . . . [Men] diminish the threat by shortening that enormous concept of Liberation to little Lib. . . . Imagine the movements for Nationalism referred to as Nash . . . Axiom: women will not become liberated so long as they tolerate – let along use among themselves

– the expression women's lib." (Eve Merriam 1974, 23, n.p.) A name created by the male dominated left. (Robin Morgan 1970, 6) "The fact that feminists are called 'women's libbers' and the Women's Liberation Movement is referred to as 'Women's Lib' is another example of language reflecting unconscious anxiety about aggression and power in women. No other liberation movement in the history of the world has similarly been given a 'cute' nickname that so undermines its spirit and seriousness of purpose." (Harriet E. Lerner 1976a, 297) Contrasts with women's liberation. "Middle-class women's lib is a trend; working women's liberation is a necessity." (Donna Redmond 1973, 183)

(See FEMINISM, SURFACE LABELLING, WOMEN'S LIBERATION, WOMEN'S LIBERATION MOVEMENT)

WOMEN'S LIBBER

"Just as the terms 'black libbers' or 'Palestine libbers' are not used, the term 'women's libbers' should not be used. The women's movement should be reported as seriously as any other civil rights movement; it should not be made fun of, ridiculed, or belittled." ("Media Reform Committee" 1981, *Women's Media Action-Bulletin* September)

(See WOMEN'S LIB)

WOMEN'S LIBERATION

A household word.

(See FEMINISM, WOMEN'S LIB, WOMEN'S MOVEMENT)

Title given by women to U.S. feminist groups in the late 1960s. Advocates of the term argued that the problem "was not one of women, but of women's liberation and the best way to get people to think of the problem in those terms was to label it as such from the very beginning." (Jo Freeman 1975, 108-9)

The phrase "came from activists in the Student Non-Violent Coordinating Committee in 1964 at a workshop during its Waveland staff conference in Mississippi at which Ruby Doris Smith Robinson and others challenged the position of women in the organization." (Kathie Sarachild 1975a, 17)

"Realizing that this is a social problem of national significance not at all confined to our struggle for personal liberation within the Movement, we must approach it in a political manner. Therefore it is incumbent on us, as women, to organize a movement for women's liberation." ("To the Women of the Left" 1967; in Sara Evans 1980, 193, 200)

No rigid principles exist. Some early principles which are still important include the following:

"– All women share a common oppression. . . . Men do not share that oppression with women, rather they benefit from it. . . .
- Consciousness-raising cannot be outgrown: it must remain the basis of all our theory and practice. . . .
- No change is so trivial or so fundamental that it must wait till after The Revolution.
- But we also know that the political is not personal: there can be no one liberated woman. . . .
- We have been divided so long, sisterly solidarity is important especially in relation to men. . . . It means recognizing that when women do things which maintain their oppression, we are not collaborating or being stupid, but just trying to get by as best we may in the given situation. . . .
- We reject hierarchy and the 'star' system. No one person or group can speak for the movement. . . ."
(Collective for Radical Feminist meeting 1979, 2-3)

Takes somewhat different forms in different places at different times. "One characteristic which has distinguished the British from the American women's movement is the strength of the organized left. In Britain there has been a mass-based Labour Party in government and a trade union movement which constitutes the biggest working-class assembly in the country. British feminism has always

been more socialist than its American counterpart." (Anna Coote and Beatrix Campbell 1982, 31)

WOMEN'S LIBERATION MOVEMENT

"A repudiation of the obligation to follow a certain pattern if you are a woman. It is much more fundamental than suffragism. And, on the whole, I am with it." (Rebecca West 1972; in Linda Charlton 1983)

"Is not a united and unanimous monolith, with a 10-story H.Q. address and telephone number. It is multi-faceted, dynamic (still!), beyond doctrinaire definitions – and it would be counterproductive, destructive indeed, to try to limit feminist writing and research to one point-of-view, tendency, or 'line.' " (Ailbhe Smyth 1983)

WOMEN'S MAGAZINES

Periodicals which "are about more than women and womanly things, they are about femininity itself – as a state, a condition, a craft, and an art form which comprise a set of practices and beliefs. In this they present a paradox, for they are specialist periodicals yet concern themselves with a general audience: everyone born female is a candidate for their services and sacraments." There are no men's magazines in the same generic sense. "Men's magazines are aimed at particular groups of males and cater for parts of a man's life – his business, hobby or sporting interests – not for the totality of his masculinity, nor his male role as such." They constitute "a social institution which serves to foster and maintain a cult of femininity. This cult is manifested both as a social group to which all those born female can belong, and as a set of practices and beliefs; rites and rituals, sacrifices and ceremonies, whose periodic performance reaffirms a common femininity and shared group membership. In promoting a cult of femininity these journals are not merely reflecting the female role in society; they are also supplying one source [of] definitions of, and socialization into, that role. . . . The cumulative and covert meaning of the cult's messages is not only that sex is the ultimate dividing line. Rather, biological determinism is the manifest and latent ideology of women's magazines: only females can qualify for membership. Thus is this cult made conscious of itself." (Marjorie Ferguson 1983, 1-2, 184, 186)

(See ADVERTISING, REPRESENTATION, ROMANCES)

Exhibit "a discourse of friendliness, reassuring and relocating women in an identity of oppression and a position of exploitation." (Joy Leman 1980, 65)

Are shaped by "a few businessmen with limited social and less journalistic experience [who] are in a position to impose their view of what women want on an enormous mass market through the instrumentality and talent of other women." (Carolyn Faulder 1977, 192)

Exist "not to serve the housewife but to keep her servile.... Keep her barefoot, keep her pregnant, and keep her subscribing." (Eve Merriam 1958, rpt 1964, 37)

WOMEN'S MOVEMENT

"There's always been a woman's movement." (Dale Spender 1983a)

(See FEMINISM, WOMEN'S LIB, WOMEN'S LIBERATION MOVEMENT)

More generic term for women's struggle for equality. Though often used interchangeably with *feminist movement* and *Women's Liberation Movement*, the general term does not have the *feminist movement*'s theoretical orientation toward "feminism" and does not invoke the specific "liberation" movement that grew out of 1960s leftist politics.

"Our woman's movement is woman's movement in that it is led and directed by women for the good of women and men, for the benefit of *all* humanity, which is more than any one branch or section of it. We want, we ask the active interest of our men, and, too, we are not drawing the color line; we are women, American women, as intensely interested in all that pertains to us as such as all other American women; we are not alienating

or withdrawing, we are only coming to the front, willing to join any others in the same work and cordially inviting and welcoming any others to join us." (Josephine St Pierre Ruffin 1895, addressing representatives of Negro Women's Clubs; cited in Eleanor Flexner 1968, 190)

Is "the first radical movement to base its politics – in fact, create its politics – out of concrete personal experiences." (Robin Morgan ed. 1970, xviii)

Offers life memberships. (Anna Livia 1983, 65)

"Demanded a transformation of society, a revolution, a change in the American social structure.... Yet ... they revealed that they had not changed, had not undone the sexist and racist brainwashing that had taught them to regard women unlike themselves as Others. Consequently, the Sisterhood they talked about has not become a reality.... Instead, the hierarchical pattern of race and sex relationships already established in American society merely took a different form under 'feminism.'" (bell hooks 1981, 121)

WOMEN'S PAGE

Said to be the creation of Jane Cunningham Croly, whose 1859 column for the *New York Dispatch* was called the first newspaper column in the U.S. devoted exclusively to women. A nineteenth century journalist who wrote about fashion, food, and home decoration in articles syndicated around the U.S., Croly said "There's no sex in labor." Conscious of her influence, she wrote, "I have never done anything that was not helpful to women, so far as it lay in my power." She helped found the Sorosis Club, a forum for women journalists, since the Press Club forbade their participation. She wrote under the name Jennie June. (Marion Tuttle Marzolf 1977, 20-2) Is a section of a newspaper "dealing with face-powder, frilled nightgowns, and anchovy toast." (Cicely Hamilton 1909, 85) "A disaster for women [journalists] who can write about other than dedicated 'women's subjects.' Their work is 'shoved in there, in company with antimacassars and lip-stick and -bead mats." (H. M. Swanwick 1935, 234)

WOMEN'S POSITION
"A cultural product that can be altered." (Michelle Zimbalist Rosaldo and Louise Lamphere eds 1974, 14)

WOMEN'S RIGHTS
"Man seems to start up in alarm at the bare mention of Women's Rights. He seems to think that there is a fixed number of rights for the whole human family, laid down in some great reservoir, and that in proportion as you increase claimants, you must decrease the hoard of those already in possession." (Elizabeth Cady Stanton 1851, 82)

WOMEN'S STATUS
"According to UN statistics, two out of every three illiterates in the world are women. Though women account for one-third of the labor force, they put in two-thirds of the work hours, earn about one-tenth of the world's income and own less than one percent of the property." (*Time* 1980, August 4, 52)

WOMEN'S STUDIES
Men's studies modified. (Dale Spender ed. 1981). "From a radical feminist perspective, a women's studies program is responsible for providing students with an education first in radicalism, and second in the patriarchal/capitalist tools which will enable them to function in society as feminist professionals." (Sally Miller Gearhart 1983, 11) "The question now facing Women's Studies, it seems to me, is the extent to which she has, in the past decade, matured into the dutiful daughter of the white, patriarchal university – a daughter who threw tantrums and played the tomboy when she was younger but who has now learned to wear a dress and speak almost as nicely as Daddy wants her to." (Adrienne Rich 1981a, 4-5)

(See ACADEMIA, CLASSROOM INTERACTION, MAINSTREAMING, RADICAL TEACHER, THEORY)

WOMEN'S WAR
Events that occurred in Calabar and Owerri provinces in Nigeria in 1929 were termed "Aba Riots" by the British, but the Igbo term *Ogu Umunwanyi* means "Women's War." This term, in contrast to the British term, retains women's presence and significance: the word "war" is derived from the pidgin English expression "making war," an institutionalized form of punishment employed by women on a man which included gathering at his compound, dancing, detailing the grievances against him in song, and tearing up his hut. " 'Women's War' thus conveys an action by women that is also an extension of their traditional method for settling grievances with men who had acted badly towards them." (Judith Van Allen 1976, 61-2) In the Women's War of 1929, "an estimated 10,000 Ibo and Ibibio women sustained the only widespread rebellion against British authority to occur in the 15 years following the formal extension of indirect rule to Southern Nigeria in 1914." (Susan G. Rogers 1980, 22)

(See ANLU, MIKIRI, WAR)

WOMEN'S VOCABULARY
A long established training program for Sudanese village midwives draws its vocabulary from the realities of women's everyday lives. To encourage village women to seek and understand the value of antenatal care, for example, the midwives created the following metaphor: "When a cooking pot is on the fire, is the food allowed to burn and spoil, or is it usual to inspect the contents occasionally?" Because it made sense to the women that you would keep your eye on a pot, they accepted the parallel value of pelvic examination; the term *gabana* (coffee pot) 'pot inspection' became the recognized term for antenatal care, also used in the teaching hospital. One harmful practice among Sudanese village women is the custom, following child-

birth, of remaining in a horizontal position for many weeks, promoting the development of infection. Again, the midwives reasoned that after washing a coffee pot you would turn it upside down to drain. (Hassan Bella and David Morley 1983, 639-40)

WOMEN WHO WORK

"As if women who worked were the exceptions!" (R.J. 1884, *The Women's Union Journal*, 9:100 [May], 44)

WOMON

In contrast to the generic term *woman*, *womon* is used as the "non-generic term, meaning only the stronger sex (also the fairer, in both senses of the word)." Can be used to generate forms like *womontic*, 'passionate, loverly, sentimental' as in "Isn't this a womontic night!" (zana 1983, correspondence)

" 'Woman' is derived from the old english word 'wif,' and 'man.' 'Wif' meant woman, without any implications of a relationship to any man. The combined form of 'wifman,' from which comes 'woman,' explicitly connects an entity called 'woman' to 'man.' I deny the necessity and/or the desirability of such a connection, and use the spellings 'womon/wimmin' as one way of removing man and men from the picture." (Debbie Alicen 1983, 6)

WOMYN'S BRAILLE PRESS

Started in the early 1980s by Edwina Franchild and others who felt that national U.S. organizations for the blind had little sensitivity to feminist and lesbian interests and concerns and that if materials were to be provided for blind and other disabled women, "we would have to do it ourselves." The press makes available feminist and lesbian books and periodicals on tape and is presently exploring computer programs that would produce Braille. The women of WBP feel strongly that women with disabilities have been disenfranchised from the women's movement and that, like all minority women, they are not seen as "women." This is an issue of concern to all feminists, not simply those who happen to be disabled.

WONDER WOMAN
(See AMAZON)

WOODSTOCK NATION

"A country where no self-respecting feminist would feel at home." (Marion Meade 1970, 24)

WORD

"The axiom of the living word stands imperturbably, beginning with the sublime limits of metaphysical speculation, through all the strata of the soul, to the practices of witches and medicine men, in all the more gifted races of the five continents and in all realistic times. Word creation is equated with world creation, evocation of form. At the same time, it is a spell and an incantation, and as such, it is necromancy and poetry."

(See A, LANGUAGE, MA,
MOTHER, NAME, SPIRITUALITY,
WICCE, WORDS, WRITING, and all
other entries above and below)

"May God keep you safe until the word of your life is spoken." (Margaret Fuller, cited in *Women and Language News* 1983, 7:2/3, 5)

Nineteenth-century U.S. reading primers linked stereotypical qualities of boys and girls with language, even individual words:

"*Shan't* and *Won't* were two sturdy
brothers,
Angry and sullen and gruff;
Try and *Will* are dear little sisters,
One scarcely can love them enough."
(Carol Adams 1982, 48)

"A broken bone can heal, but the wound a word opens can fester forever." (Jessamyn West 1979, 32)

WORD GAMES

Verbal play at which women excel. "When it came to word games, the gentlemen discovered they had met a master [in Dorothy Parker]. Challenged to use the word 'horticulture' in a sentence, Mrs. Parker immediately replied, 'You can lead a horticulture, but you can't make her think." (Dorothy Parker, cited in John Keats 1970, 46)

WORD PROCESSING

Electronically-based word production, usually tied to electronic typewriters or computer-based systems. Elizabeth Nickles and Laura Ashcraft in *The Coming Matriarchy* (1981) posit a brave new world of matriarchal management in which word processing is one of women's central power domains. This will be possible, in part, because many men believe word processing is "just typing" and do not understand that the word processing supervisor may be building an empire (158).

(See COMMUNICATIONS REVOLUTION, TECHNOLOGY)

An attempt to squeeze out the minutes and hours of labour power lost in the personal relations and contacts among secretaries. "The effect of automation in the office will be to remove skills and knowledge (which provide workers with control over their movements and pace of work) by fragmenting operations in much the same sort of way as has already happened in factories." (Juliet Lozenby 1982, 21)

WORDS

"Although they are
Only breath, words
which I command
are immortal"
　　(Sappho, sixth century, 9)

"Enter [the earhole] like personal messengers, selected to fit the unique spirals and curlicues of your individual hearing passages; and to go from there into the brain's storehouse, where they fire memories and imaginings that have long been waiting." (Jessamyn West 1979)

Can be made accessible. A midwife wrote her seventeenth-century midwifery guide in easy language. "It is not hard words that perform the work – words are but the shell that we oftimes break our Teeth with them to come at the kernel. I mean our braines to know what is the meaning of them." (Mrs Jane Sharp 1671; in Kate Campbell Hurd-Mead 1938, 396)

Are potentially explosive. "Sentences like 'I loved my father very much' were loaded with words like hidden landmines." (Mary Gordon 1978, 161)

Are signals that can please or displease. "I was just as ladylike as could be about words myself. I never said belly for stomach, butt for bottom, or puke for throw up. True, there were quite a few words I didn't know were bad, and these, like pussy, I used freely. . . . My plan was to please my husband. If there were words he didn't like, I would find others. There are thousands of words in the dictionary." (Jessamyn West 1979, 204)

"Have, along with a semiotic usage, a symbolic or metaphoric usage. They also have a sound – a fact that the linguistic positivists take no interest in. A sentence or paragraph is like a chord or harmonic sequence in music: its meaning may be more clearly understood by the attentive ear, even though it is read in silence, than by the attentive intellect." (Ursula K. LeGuin; in Susan Wood ed. 1979a, 195)

"Are a war to me
They threaten my family.
To gain the word
to describe the loss
I risk losing everything."
　　(Cherríe Moraga; in Cherríe Moraga
　　and Gloria Anzaldúa eds 1981, 166)

"Funny how white folks use words. I have always liked words – they seem like a good way to tell people what you want and what you don't want. There are other ways, but I just have this weakness for words. I never understood why a soldier was not called a murderer, though; or why science is not considered antisocial; or why bail isn't called ransom; or why Clairol doesn't ask, 'Is she or isn't she?' I never understood why." (Nikki Giovanni 1969, 132-3)

WORDS FAIL ME

"Dear Sirs. man to man. manpower. craftsman. working men. the thinking man. the man in the street. fellow countrymen. the history of mankind. one-man show. man in his wisdom. statesman. forefathers. masterful. masterpiece. old masters. the brotherhood of man. Liberty Equality Fraternity. sons of free men. faith of our fathers. god the father. god the son. yours fraternally. amen. words fail me." (Stephanie Dowrick 1981; Words Fail Me postcard, The Women's Press, London)

WORDS NOT NEEDED

Husband-swapping, bunny boys, char-gentlemen, bit of trouser, boy Friday, guy Friday, man doctor, man astro-physicist. . . .
   (See NEEDED WORDS)

WORK

What all women do, whether inside the home or outside it. Provides practical education and key to women's independence. "A practical education, which a profession or business career gives to a woman, only helps to arouse and develop her intellectual faculties. It opens her mind which has too long been kept under lock and key; it teaches her to think for herself; it enables her to know men better; and above all, it gives her the assurance of self-support – an assurance which increases her independence without which she cannot command the respect of the laws. . . . If you have an educated man, you only have an educated man, but when you have an educated woman, you have an educated family." (Editorial, *The Liberal Review* 1904, 1:1, 5)
   (See WAGES FOR HOUSEWORK, WOMAN'S WORK, WORKING GIRL, WORKING WOMAN)
   "Proportionately, more Black women have always worked outside their homes than have their white sisters. The enormous space that work occupies in Black women's lives today follows a pattern established during the very earliest days of slavery. As slaves, compulsory labor

overshadowed every other aspect of women's existence. . . . The starting point for any exploration of Black women's lives under slavery would be an appraisal of their role as workers." (Angela Y. Davis 1981, 5)
   Is an active verb, different from "being worked." "Not having learned to work, either at school or at home, [the working girl] goes to the factory, to the workshop, or to the store, crude, incompetent, and worst of all, with an instinctive antagonism toward her task. *She cannot work, and she does not work. She is simply 'worked.'* And there is all the difference in the world between 'working' and 'being worked.' To work is a privilege and a boon to either man or woman, and, properly regulated, it ought to be a pleasure. To be worked is degrading. To work is dignified and ennobling, for to work means the exercise of the mental quite as much as the physical self." (Dorothy Richardson 1905, 278)
   " 'Do you work?' we women ask one another, knowing full well by now that we're all working like crazy. . . . Behind the question reverberate profound tensions and anxieties. . . . Are you earning your own living? Are you haunted by that dreadful dependency on a man's wage? Are you somebody? or are you 'just a housewife'? Do you have self-confidence? Can you stand on your own two feet? Are your children adequately cared for? Does your work have more status than mine?" (Ann Martin-Leff 1983, 2)
   "Implicit in the assertion that work was the key to women's liberation was a refusal to acknowledge the reality that, for masses of American working class women, working for pay neither liberated them from sexist oppression nor allowed them to gain any measure of economic independence." (bell hooks 1981, 145)
   What women have always done. "Since women have always worked in patriarchal societies . . . the issue here is not labor but economic reward." (Kate Millett 1971, 64)
   Underpaid and undervalued. "Being a mother and a housewife not only means

having kids and looking after them, so that one day they can be workers. It also means keeping men clean and fed and emotionally supported – in other words keeping them in working order, fit for the factory or the office or the dole queue. This maintenance work is unpaid and undervalued. If all women went on strike, our society would grind to a halt." (Hackney Flashers Collective 1980, 89)

Maternal work: is a form of creativity. It takes place in a context of the possibility of illness, accident, physical and mental damage, supplemented by cruelty, bigotry, and violence. "War can destroy, in an instant, years of maternal love and hope. Ideological division, moral recalcitrance and political purity can unravel a fabric of family and community life which is largely the creation of mother-artists." (Sara Ruddick 1980, 268-9)

An activity which for at least some sectors of the white population in the U.S. is separated "from convictions, family, politics, art, friends, from 'hobbies,' play and exercise activities, and from children." (Bettina Escudero 1984, 6)

WORKBRICKLE

Able to work hard – e.g., "Most women are workbrickle." (Pearl Patterson b. 1910, Oklahoma; reported by Priscilla Diaz Dorr 1984, correspondence)

WORKER

Is "anyone who *has* to work for a living as opposed to those who don't. All women are workers." (Carol Hanisch 1969, 204)

WORKING GIRL

"In the happy future, the working girl will no longer be content to be merely 'worked.' Then she will have learned to work. She will have learned to work intelligently, and, working thus, she will begin to think – to think about herself and all those things which most vitally concern her as a woman and as a wage-earner. And then, you may depend upon it, she will settle the question to please herself, and she will settle it in the right way." (Dorothy Richardson 1905, 303)

(See MENSTRUAL STRIKE, TYPEWRITER)

WORKING MOTHER

A redundancy. "The sexual definition of woman as mother either keeps her in the home doing unpaid labor or enables her to be hired at a lower wage because of her defined sexual inferiority. . . . The sexual division of labor and society remains intact even with women in the paid economy. Ideology adjusts to this by defining women as working mothers. And the two jobs get done for less than the price of one." (Zillah Eisenstein 1979b, 29)

(See CHILD CARE, MOTHER, MOTHERHOOD)

WORKING WOMAN

A new product: "In this country she is hardly three generations old." (Dorothy Richardson 1905, 279) "When the '70s began, work was largely defined as what men did, and a *working woman* was someone who labored outside the home and got paid for it, masculine style. By the end of the '70s, the term *working woman* was identified as inaccurate and a put-down: a way of excluding (and thus not rewarding with either money or respect) all the homemaking and human-support services that women have traditionally done at home. We began to speak carefully of work *inside the home*, work *outside the home*." (Gloria Steinem, in Suzanne Levine and Harriet Lyons eds 1980, 19)

(See HOUSEWIFE, WORK)

WORLD

Is in a chaotic condition. "It is old-fashioned, running into ruts. . . . Perhaps one of the chief reasons for the present chaotic condition of things is that the world has been trying to get along with only half of itself. Everywhere we see running to waste [a] woman-force that should be utilized in making the world a more decent home for humanity." (Helen Keller 1915; quoted in Karen Payne 1983, 152)

WORTH

"Let us learn to pride our ſelves in ſomething more excellent than the invention of a Faſion; And not entertain ſuch a degrading thought of our own worth, as to imagine that our Souls were given us only for the ſervice of our Bodies, and that the beſt improvement we can make of theſe, is to attract the Eyes of Men. We value *them* too much, and our ſelves too little, if we place any part of our deſert in their Opinion; and don't think our ſelves capable of Nobler Things than the pitiful Conqueſt of ſome worthleſs heart." (Mary Astell 1694, 13)

WRINKLES

"Facial ridges or furrows in women that provide a lucrative business to cosmetic plastic surgeons but, in fact, are proud, overt, earned symbols of adventure and experience." (Midge Lennert and Norma Willson eds 1973, 14)

WRITER

"I, a woman, cannot be exempt from the malice and aspersions of spiteful tongues, which they cast upon my poor writings, some denying me to be the true authoress of them; for your Grace remembers well, that these books I put out first to the judgement of this censorious age were accounted not to be written by a woman, but that somebody else had writ and published them in my name." (Margaret, Duchess of Newcastle, 1667, in a letter to her husband; quoted in Alison Adburgham 1972, 22) Male: often just called writer. "Men have got to come out as *men*. This will alter their prose." (Michele Roberts 1983, 63)

WRITE-SPEAK

"It is not clear whether write-speak is a language invented by women's magazine journalists, but the richness of its imagery and the fluency of its grammar have surely been perfected by them. In a medium which conveys a sense of belonging and group membership as a second order message of all content, the written word strives to evoke the intimacy of the spoken. So pervasive is this sense of talking to the audience that it carries over unconsciously into the language of the production process. An art editor asks of a cover transparency 'Does it talk to the reader?' The editor asks a knitting editor of a pull-over, 'What does it say?' Novice journalists learn the craft of writing speech within this chatty communication context. . . . Write-speak also lends itself to 'personalising,' a technique used to inject familiarity, directness and intimacy into the tone of voice and what it is talking about." (Marjorie Ferguson 1983, 166)

WRITING

"In the development of modern Western civilization, writing was the first of the arts, before painting, music, composing, and sculpting, which it was possible for women to practice; and it was the fourth of the job categories, after prostitution, domestic service and the stage, and before wide-scale factory work, nursing, secretarial work, telephone operating and school teaching, at which it was possible for them to make any money. The reason for both is the same: writing as a physical activity is private." (Margaret Atwood 1982, 193) "In our common struggle and in our writing we reclaim our tongues. We wield a pen as a tool, a weapon, a means of survival, a magic wand that will attract power, that will draw self-love into our bodies. . . . The act of writing is the act of making soul, alchemy. It is the quest for the self, for the center of the self, which we women of color have come to think as 'other' – the dark, the feminine. . . . The writing is a tool for piercing that mystery but it also shields us, gives a margin of distance, helps us survive." "Is dangerous because we are afraid of what the writing reveals: the fears, the angers, the strengths of a woman under a triple or quadruple oppression." (Gloria Anzaldúa; in Cherríe Moraga and Gloria Anzaldúa eds 1981, 163, 169, 171)

(See FARKSOO, LÁDAAN, LANGUAGE, PEN, POWER,

SUPPRESSION OF WOMEN'S WRITING, WORDS)

"By writing her self, woman will return to the body which has been more than confiscated from her, which has been turned into the uncanny stranger on display. . . . Censor the body and you censor breath and speech at the same time." (Hélène Cixous 1975b, 250)

Is often an enthralling process very early. The writer and feminist Vera Brittain wrote five "novels" before she was eleven "on special books patiently constructed for me by a devoted and intelligent governess out of thick waste paper from the mills"; she also created a mythical community whose exciting adventures she would tell her brother in the nursery when they were supposed to be sleeping. "I was always the inventor and he the recipient of these enthralling communications, which must have begun when I was about six, and continued until I reached the mature age of eleven and went to school." (Vera Brittain 1933, 27)

Is terrifying.

"What is writing a novel like?
1. The beginning: A ride through a spring wood.
2. The middle: The Gobi Desert.
3. The end: A night with a lover.
I am in the Gobi Desert."
(Edith Wharton 1934; in Cynthia Griffin Wolf 1977, 406)

"Woman's place in literary life, if she survives to write at all, has been a place from which men grant her leave to write about either love or religion." (Louise Berkinow ed. 1974, 6)

"I write all the things *I should have been able to read.*" (Alice Walker 1976, 13)

"We must make of the breaches in the language our weapons, our woman's text. . . . You must know who is the object and who is the subject of a sentence in order to know if you are the object or the subject of history. If you can't control a sentence you don't know how to put yourself into history, to trace your own origin in the country, to vocalize, to use voices." (Nélida Piñon 1982, 71, 74)

Women's writing "is part of the slow process of decolonialising our language and our basic habits of thought. . . . With the creation of a means of expression for an infinitely greater variety of experience than has been possible heretofore, [it will become possible] to say things for which no language previously existed." (Angela Carter 1983, 75)

"Is Re-naming." (Shirley Morahan 1981, 16)

Old-fashioned rule of thumb for: "Never write a line you would be ashamed to read at your own funeral." (L. M. Montgomery 1915, 282)

WRITING THE BODY
(See L'ÉCRITURE FEMININE)

WUSBAND
Ex-husband. (Belle Shalom, via Ruth Mountaingrove, via zana 1983; correspondence)

X

Tale of a child (X) whose parents do not reveal its sex to other children, school officials, or anyone else. The experiment is successful: X has an X-cellent childhood. (Lois Gould 1978)

Last name of U.S. feminist Laura X. Signifies the anonymity of women's history. Malcolm X claimed that since slaves were often given the last names of their masters, most Black Americans still carried the mark of their oppression generations later. Laura X contended that a woman who has either her father's or her husband's name is burdened in like manner with an emblem of patriarchal ownership. In September 1984, Laura X celebrated the 15th anniversary of her name and reflected on reactions to it during that period. "I'm not going to deal with anyone who's anonymous," she is told. "*I'm* not anonymous," she replies, "Women's history is anonymous." The only recurrent problem she has encountered is in the making of collect telephone calls, in which the operator's request to "Spell that name, please" inevitably requires a full explanation. (Laura X, Women's History Research Center flyer 1980; *Ms.* 1982, April 23; correspondence 1984)

"The female sex chromosome, also still the unknown quantity." (Eve Merriam 1975, 11)

XANTHIPPE

Wife of Socrates, fifth century B.C.; stimulated him to develop the Socratic method.

XENOGENESIS

Spontaneous generation; from 'stranger' + 'creation.' Production of an individual completely different from either of its parents.

X FACTOR

Keeps women invisible, subordinate, undervalued, overworked. (Anne Firor Scott 1984, 299-300)

(See ACHIEVEMENT)

X-O

Metaphor used "to understand group dynamics in mixed groups, especially when there are newcomers, outsiders, strangers, or 'deviants.' . . . It provides a new, less emotion-laden language, which blames neither the X's nor the O's for what occurs. It makes it possible for everyone to look to the *situation* – and not to the problems of specific individuals – as the source of any awkwardness that might arise or any difficulty the O might encounter." (Rosabeth Moss Kanter with Barry A. Stein 1980, 213)

Y

"The male sex chromosome, also part of a mathemetical formulation as in $X=Y$." (Eve Merriam 1980, 175)

YANAN LANGUAGES

Are spoken by the Yahi people of Northern California and by others; they contain a number of sex-exclusive markers, including differences in pronunciation, kinship terms, and noun and verb forms. Whereas most sex-linked formal markers depend on the sex of the speaker, the Yana forms are linked to both sex of speaker and of the person spoken to. These different forms occur often and make it possible to differentiate female and male speech. Edward Sapir's early study (1939; in Sapir 1949) is followed up in Ann Bodine's discussion (1975) of sex differentiation: "for languages which differentiate on the basis of the sex of both members of the conversational interaction it is not strictly accurate, as Sapir pointed out, to speak of 'women's speech' or 'men's speech'" (142); rather the nature of the dyad (female-female, female-male, male-female, or male-male) determines the linguistic form to be used.

YELLOW RIBBON

During the 1876 U.S. Centennial women wore yellow ribbons as a sign of their struggle for women's rights. A poem "The Yellow Ribbon," written by Marie le Baron and to be sung to the tune of the Irish ballad "The Wearing of the Green," ends, "We boast our land of freedom, the unshackling of the slave; We point with proud, though bleeding hearts, to myriads of graves. They tell the story of a war that ended Slavery's night; And still women struggle for our Liberty, our Right." (In 1981 the Homemakers' Equal Rights Association launched another yellow ribbon campaign.) (Paula Kassell 1981, 1, 10) The *Yellow Ribbon Speaker* is a book of "Equal Rights Readings and Recitations, in Prose and Verse, compiled by Rev. Anna H. Shaw, Alice Stone Blackwell, and Lucy E. Anthony," sold in the U.S. in the 1890's.

(See COLORS, ICONOGRAPHY, PUBLIC SPEAKING)

YELLOW WALLPAPER

Metaphor for women's condition and madness in a patriarchal society, based on a short story by Charlotte Perkins Gilman published in 1892. A woman, suffering from an unstated "condition," is taken by her physician-husband to an isolated country estate for a "rest cure." Confined to a single room which contains little more than a bed and is decorated with yellow wallpaper that the woman perceives as hideous, she gradually goes mad. Gilman intended the story as an attack on the rest cure treatment for neurasthenia developed by the neurologist Weir Mitchell and as a more general critique of the patriarchal treatment of women which makes it difficult or impossible for them to carry out active, useful, creative work and instead enforces passive domesticity. (Paula A. Treichler in press b)

YIDDISH
Language derived from High German dialects with additional vocabulary from Hebrew and Slavic languages; spoken in eastern European Jewish communities and throughout the world. In contrast to Hebrew, was learned and spoken by women.
(See MAMA-LOSHEN)

YIN
"Feminine life force, a Chinese cognate of 'yoni'; usually represented as a fluid emanating from a female 'Grotto of the White Tiger' (genitals). According to the doctrines of *Tao*, the power of *yin* was stronger than any male power; therefore men had to learn to take feminine fluids into themselves, to gain wisdom and health." (Barbara G. Walker 1983, 1097)

YONI
" 'Vulva,' the primary Tantric object of worship, symbolized variously by a triangle, fish, double-pointed oval, horseshoe, egg, fruits, etc." (Barbara G. Walker 1983, 1097)

YOU
"*Ye* and *you* in Old English were plural pronouns only, the singular forms being *thou* and *thee*. In the late thirteenth century *you* began to be used as the 'polite' singular in addressing someone of superior social status or age. . . . The respectful singular *you* soon came to be used by the English gentry when speaking to one another, thus marking a recognition of equality. *Thou* was used, with some inconsistency, both as the form of address for God and between intimates, on the one hand, and for peasants, servants, and children, on the other. In the latter usage, *thou* marked the socially inferior rank of the person spoken to. When the Quakers, who wished to emphasize the natural equality of all human beings, began to use *thou* and *thee* for everyone, they did not foresee that standard English was moving the other way. In response to the revolutionary spirit of the eighteenth century, the respectful and democratic *you* was extended downward to the masses, and all English-speaking people were able thereafter to address one another as equals. *They* as a singular illustrates once again that in spite of studied efforts to hold it back, our remarkably sensitive tongue is capable of responding to its speakers' longing for equality." (Casey Miller and Kate Swift 1976, 136)
(See PRONOUNS, TU/VOUS)

YOUNG LADY
Flaubert's *Dictionary of Accepted Ideas* summarized clichés about "young ladies" as follows: "Utter these words with diffidence. All young ladies are pale, frail, and always pure. Prohibit, for their good, every kind of reading, all visits to museums, theaters, and especially to the monkey house at the zoo." (Gustave Flaubert 1881, 92)
(See DICTIONARY OF ACCEPTED IDEAS)

YOU'VE COME A LONG WAY, BABY
Controversial advertising slogan for Virginia Slims cigarettes. "Perhaps one of the most horrifying [commerical messages] for women interested in *real* women's liberation, not liberation to desire more products." (Alice Embree 1970, 188)

Z

ZAMANI SOWETO SISTERS

Umbrella women's organization in South Africa. "The Zamani sisters are women of Soweto – a huge complex outside Johannesburg where two million Black people live ... The Zamani Soweto sisters came together through a common need to build a better life for themselves and their families. They act as an umbrella organization to many small self-help groups throughout Soweto. ... Their work takes the form of patchwork quilts, clothing, fabric collage, and textile crafts such as crochet and appliqué. ... The message portrayed by the bold and beautiful work is not in keeping with the often servile position of women in African history. The cushions depict scenes of the lives of these women and their sisters – desperate women employed by Soweto council to sweep and clean the streets, and earn frustrating wages." ("Patchwork of our Lives" 1982, *Spare Rib*, August, 7)

(See ARPILLERAS, BASKETRY, QUILTS)

ZEITGEIST

"Spirit of liberty, equality, sorority." (Eve Merriam 1975, 11)

ZUGASSENT

Term used by George Noyes Miller (1845-1904) for the male continence practiced at Oneida, New York, a utopian community in which members regularly analyzed sex roles and discussed their utopian visions of sex and class equality. (Sylvia Strauss 1982, 116)

Bibliography

AARON, Dorothy. 1975. *About Face, Towards a Positive Image of Women in Advertising.* Toronto, Canada: Ontario Status of Women Council.

ABBOTT, Sidney and Barbara J. Love. 1972. *Sappho Was a Right-On Woman: A Liberated View of Lesbianism.* New York: Stein & Day.

A.B.T. 1919. "Woman's Place." *The Englishwoman,* 41:123, 113-17.

ACROBATEAU, Red. 1978. "Susie Q." In *True to Life Adventure Stories.* Ed. Judy Grahn. Vol. 1. Trumansburg, New York: The Crossing Press, 102-32.

ACWORTH, Evelyn. 1965. *The New Matriarchy.* London: Gollancz.

ADAMS, Abigail. 1776a. "Letter to John Adams, Braintree, March 31, 1776." In *The Adams Papers, Series II, Adams Family Correspondence.* Ed. L. H. Butterfield. Cambridge, Massachusetts: Harvard University Press, 1963, 76-402. Rpt. in *The Feminist Papers: From Adams to de Beauvoir.* Ed. Alice Rossi. New York: Bantam, 1973, 10-11.

ADAMS, Abigail. 1776b. "Letter to John Adams, Braintree, May 7, 1776." In *The Adams Papers, Series II, Adams Family Correspondence.* Ed. L. H. Butterfield. Cambridge, Massachusetts: Harvard University Press, 1963, 76-402. Rpt. in *The Feminist Papers: From Adams to de Beauvoir.* Ed. Alice Rossi. New York: Bantam, 1973, 13.

ADAMS, Carol. 1982. *Ordinary Lives.* London: Virago.

ADAMS, Mabel Ellery. 1898. "The New Woman." *The Woman's Journal,* 29:40 (1 October), 318-19.

ADBURGHAM, Alison. 1972. *Women in Print. Writing Women and Women's Magazines From the Restoration to the Accession of Victorian.* London: Allen & Unwin.

ADLER, Margot. 1979. "Meanings of Matriarchy." In *The Politics of Women's Spirituality.* Ed. Charlene Spretnak. Garden City, New York: Anchor Press, 1982, 127-37.

AKERS, Elizabeth. 1891. "A Farmer's Wife." *The Homemaker,* 5:4, 490.

AL-HIBRI, Azizah. 1981. "Capitalism is an Advanced Stage of Patriarchy: But Marxism is not Feminism." In *Women and Revolution.* Ed. Lydia Sargent. Boston: South End Press, 165-93.

AL-MALA'IKAH, Nazik. 1974. "Who Am I?" In *An Anthology of Modern Arabic Poetry.* Ed. Mounah A. Khouri and Hamid Algar. University of California Press, 1974. Rpt. in *Middle Eastern Muslim Women Speak.* Ed. Elizabeth Warnock Fernea and Basima Qattan Bezirgan. Austin: University of Texas Press, 1977, 244.

AL-SAMMAN, Ghadah. 1970. "Al-Thawrah al-Jinsiyah wa-al-Thawrah al Shamilah." Interview in *Mawaqif,* 2:12, 68-73. Trans. Elizabeth Warnock Fernea and Basima Qattan Bezirgan. Rpt. in *Middle Eastern Muslim Women Speak.* Ed. Elizabeth Warnock Fernea and Basima Qattan Bezirgan. Austin: University of Texas Press, 1977, 392-99.

ALBRIGHT, Mia. 1978. *Feminist Versus Malist Sexual-Political Philosophy*. Manuscript.

ALBRIGHT, Mia. 1980. "Transcendent Politics: Feminist Apocalypse Versus Malist Holocaust." Addition to Section XVIII of *Feminist Versus Malist Sexual-Political Philosophy*, 1978. Manuscript.

ALBRIGHT, Mia. 1983. "Revolution as Economy." In *The Nationalist Feminist Education*. Manuscript.

ALBRIGHT, Mia. In progress. *Strategies for the Nationalist Feminist Leader*.

ALCOTT, Louisa May. 1869. *Little Women*. Rpt. New York: Collier Books, 1962.

ALDA, Alan. 1975. "What Every Woman Should Know About Men." *Ms.*, 4:4 (October), 15-16.

aldridge, adele. 1972. "NOTPOEMS." *Black Maria*, 1:1.

ALEXANDER, Sally and Barbara Taylor. 1980. "In Defense of 'Patriarchy.' " *New Statesman*, 1 February. Rpt. in *No Turning Back: Writings from the Women's Liberation Movement 1975-80*. Ed. Feminist Anthology Collective. London: The Women's Press, 1981, 79-81.

ALIA, Valerie. 1984a. "Women, Names, and Power: Toward a Politics of Naming." Political Linguistics Conference, York University, Toronto. April.

ALIA, Valerie. 1984b. "Ethnography and Literature: Women and the Politics of Naming." 20th Annual Conference. Canadian Association for American Studies, University of Ottawa. October.

ALICEN, Debbie. 1983. "Intertextuality: The Language of Lesbian Relationships." *Trivia*, 3 (Fall), 6-26.

ALLEN, Donna. 1970. "Why Can't Men Listen to Women?" *No More Fun and Games: A Journal of Female Liberation*, 4 (April). Mimeograph. Northwestern University Library, Evanston, Illinois.

ALLEN, Hilary. 1984. "At the Mercy of Her Hormones: Premenstrual Tension and the Law." *m/f*, 9, 19-44.

ALLEN, Mary Wood. 1898. "Teaching Patriotism." *The Woman's Journal*, 29:26 (25 June), 206.

ALLEN, Paula Gunn, ed. 1983. *Studies in American Indian Literature: Critical Essays and Course Designs*. New York: Modern Language Association.

ALLINGHAM, Margery. 1938. *The Fashion in Shrouds*. Rpt. New York: Manor Books, 1969.

"The All-American Complaint: 'If I Only Had the Time. . . .' " 1977. *Ms.*, 5:7 (January), 48-9, 84.

AMOS, Valerie and Pratibha Parmar. 1981. "Resistances and Responses: The Experiences of Black Girls in Britain." In *Feminism for Girls*. Ed. Angela McRobbie and Trisha McCabe. London: Routledge & Kegan Paul, 129-48.

ANDREWS, Lynn V. 1981. *Medicine Woman*. New York: Harper & Row.

ANGELOS, Constantine. "Teacher Creates New Non-Sexist Pronouns." *Seattle Times*, 19 March.

ANTHONY, Susan B. 1852. "Address to the State Temperance Convention." *The Lily*, 4:7, 1.

ANTONIUS, Soraya. 1983. "Fighting on Two Fronts: Conversations with Palestinian Women." In *Third World/Second Sex*. Ed. Miranda Davies. London: Zed Press, 63-77.

ANZALDÚA, Gloria. 1981a. "Speaking in Tongues: A Letter to Third World Women Writers." In *This Bridge Called My Back: Writings by Radical Women of Color*. Ed. Cherríe Moraga and Gloria Anzaldúa. Watertown, Massachusetts: Persephone Press, 165-74.

ANZALDÚA, Gloria. 1981b. "La Prieta." In *This Bridge Called My Back: Writings by Radical Women of Color*. Ed. Cherríe Moraga and Gloria Anzaldúa. Watertown, Massachusetts: Persephone Press, 198-209.

"Aphra Behn: Novelist, Spy, Libertine." 1973. *Ms.*, 1:8 (February), 16-18.

APRESJAN, Ju.D., I. A. Mel'cuk, and A. K. Zholkovsky. 1969. "Semantics and Lexicography: Towards a New Type of Unilingual Dictionary." Ed. F. P. Kiefer. Dordrecht: Reidel, 1-33.

APTHEKER, Bettina. 1982. *Women's Legacy: Essays on Race, Sex, and Class in American History*. Amherst: University of Massachusetts.

ARATI. 1983. "Racism: Black to Black." *Spare Rib*, November, 17-18.

ARDENER, Shirley. 1977. "Sexual Insult and Female Militancy." In *Perceiving Women*. Ed. Shirley Ardener. London: Malaby Press, 29-51.

ARDENER, Shirley. 1978. "The Nature of Women in Society." Introduction to *Defining Females: The Nature of Women in Society*. Ed. Shirley Ardener. New York: John Wiley, 9-48.

ARDITTI, Rita, Renate Duelli Klein, and Shelley Minden, eds. 1984. *Test-Tube Women: What Future for Motherhood?* London: Pandora Press.

ARDNOFF, Mark. 1980. "Contextuals." *Language*, 56:4, 744-58.

ASHTON-WARNER, Sylvia. 1970. *Three*. Quoted in *The Quotable Woman*. Ed. Elaine Partnow. Vol. II. Los Angeles: Pinnacle Books, 1977, 119.

ASPHODEL. 1982. "Feminist Spirituality." *Women's Studies International Forum*, 5:1, 103-8.

ASPINALL, Sue. 1983. "One Way – or Another?" *Screen*, 24:2 (April), 74-7.

ASTELL, Mary (A Lover of her Sex, Pseudonym). 1694. *A Serious Proposal to the Ladies for the Advancement of Their True and Greatest Interest*. London: R. Wilkin. Excerpt in *Before Their Time: Six Women Writers of the Eighteenth Century*. Ed. M. Rogers. New York: Frederick Ungar, 1979, 28-38.

ATKINSON, Paul. 1978. "Fitness, Feminism, and Schooling." In *The Nineteenth-Century Woman: Her Cultural and Physical World*. Ed. Sara Delamont and Lorna Duffin. London: Croom Helm, 92-133.

ATTIK, Mririda N'ait. 1972. Recorded from her oral recital by Rene Euloge. From *Les Chants de la Tassaout*. Casablanc: Maroc Editions. In *Women's Songs from the Berber Mountains*. Trans. Elizabeth Warnock Fernea. In *Middle Eastern Muslim Women Speak*. Ed. Elizabeth Warnock Fernea and Basima Qattan Bezirgan. Austin: University of Texas Press, 1977, 127-34.

ATWOOD, Margaret. 1977. "Giving Birth." In *Dancing Girls and Other Stories*. New York: Simon and Schuster, 225-40.

ATWOOD, Margaret. 1982. *Second Words*. Boston: Beacon Press.

ATWOOD, Margaret. 1984. "Wondering What It's Like to Be a Woman." *New York Times Book Review*, 13 May, 1, 40.

AUNT SADIE (Pseud.). 1981. "Dear Aunt Sadie." From regular columns of SAMOIS Newsletter. Rpt. in *Coming to Power: Writings and Graphics On Lesbian S/M*. Ed. SAMOIS, a lesbian/feminist S/M organization. Boston: Alyson Publications, 1982, 146-50.

AUSTEN, Jane. 1813. *Pride and Prejudice*. Rpt. New York: Vintage, 1976.

AUSTEN, Jane. 1818. *Persuasion*. Rpt. Baltimore: Penguin, 1967.

AUSTIN, Gertrude. 1914. "The Unmarried Mother in France." *The Englishwoman*, 23:68, 138-51.

AUSTIN, Mary S. 1984. "Portraits of Myself." *Matrix*, April, 11.

AVELING, Eleanor Marx and Edward Aveling. 1886. "The Woman Question: From a Socialist Point of View." *Westminster Review*, 207-22.

AVERY, Michel, Brian Auvine, Barbara Streibel, and Lonnie Weiss. 1981. *Building United Judgment: A Handbook for Consensus Decision Making*. Madison, Wisconsin: The Center for Conflict Resolution.

BABCOCK, Emma W. 1891. *The Homemaker*, 5:4, 459.

BACCHI, Carol Lee. 1983. *Liberation Deferred? The Ideas of the English-Canadian Suffragists, 1877-1918.* Toronto: University of Toronto Press.

BAGLEY, Beth. 1984. "Silences." *Women's Studies Quarterly,* 12:1 (Spring), 42-3.

BAILEY, Kathie. 1979. "I Hate Christmas." *Lesbian Connection,* 4:7 (November).

BAKER, Sheridan. 1972. "The Sociology of Dictionaries and the Sociology of Words." In *New Aspects of Lexicography: Literary Criticism, Intellectual History, and Social Change.* Ed. Howard D. Weinbrot. Carbondale and Edwardsville: Southern Illinois University Press, 138-51.

BAMMER, Angelika. 1981. "Utopian Futures and Cultural Myopia." *Alternative Futures,* 4:2/3 (Spring/Summer), 1-16.

BANDARAGE, Asoka. 1983. "Toward International Feminism." *Brandeis Review,* 3:3 (Summer), 6-11.

BANK, Mirra. 1979. *Anonymous Was a Woman.* New York: St Martin's Press.

BARLOW, Judy. 1978. "Sterilization of Native American Women." *Big Mama Rag,* 6:5 (May).

BARNHART, Clarence L. 1980. *Second Barnhart Dictionary of New English.* New York: Harper & Row.

Barnhart Dictionary Companion. 1982. 1:3. Ed. Clarence L. Barnhart. Cold Spring, New York: Clarence L. Barnhart.

BARON, Dennis. 1982. *Grammar and Good Taste: Reforming the American Language.* New Haven: Yale University Press.

BARON, Dennis. 1984. "Is It [mIs] or [mIz]?" *Verbatim,* 11:2 (Autumn), 10.

BARON, Dennis. Forthcoming. *Eve's Rib: Grammar and Gender.* New Haven: Yale University Press.

BARRENO, Maria Isabel, Maria Teresa Horta, and Maria Velho da Costa. 1975. *The Three Marias' New Portuguese Letters.* Trans. Helen R. Lane. New York: Doubleday. Excerpt in *Ms.,* 8:7 (January), 86-7.

BARRETT, Michèle, compiler. 1979. *Virginia Woolf: Women & Writing.* London: The Women's Press.

BARRETT, Michèle. 1980. *Women's Oppression Today: Problems in Marxist Feminist Analysis.* London: Verso.

BARRY, Kathleen. 1979. *Female Sexual Slavery.* New York: Avon.

BARRY, Kathleen. 1980. "Beyond Pornography: From Defensive Politics to Creating a Vision." In *Take Back the Night.* Ed. Laura J. Lederer. New York: William Morrow, 307-12.

BARRY, Kathleen. 1982. " 'Sadomasochism': The New Backlash to Feminism." *Trivia: A Journal of Ideas,* 1:1 (Fall), 77-92.

BARSHIS, Victoria. 1983. "The Question of Marital Rape." *Women's Studies International Forum,* 6:4, 383-93.

BART, Pauline. 1971. "Depression in Middle-Aged Women." Originally titled "Portnoy's Mother's Complaint." In *Woman in Sexist Society.* Ed. Vivian Gornick and Barbara K. Moran. New York: Basic Books, 99-117.

BART, Pauline. 1981. "Seizing the Means of Reproduction: An Illegal Feminist Abortion Collective – How and Why it Worked." In *Women, Health, and Reproduction.* Ed. Helen Roberts. London: Routledge & Kegan Paul, 109-28.

BART, Pauline. In press. "Being a Feminist Academic: What a Nice Feminist Like Me is Doing in a Place Like This." In *For Alma Mater: Theory and Practice in Feminist Scholarship.* Ed. Paula A. Treichler, Cheris Kramarae, and Beth Stafford. Urbana, Illinois: University of Illinois Press.

BARTKY, Sandra Lee. 1975. "Toward a Phenomenology of Feminist Consciousness." *Social Theory and Practice,* 3:4 (Fall), 425-39. Rpt. in *Feminism and Philosophy.* Ed. Mary Vetterling-Braggin, Frederick A. Elliston, and Jane English. Totowa, New Jersey:

Rowman & Littlefield, 1977, 22-34.

BARTLETT, Rachel, compiler. 1982. *Off The Wall: A Collection of Feminist Graffiti.* New York: Proteus Books.

BARUCH, Elaine Hoffman. 1984. "The Quest and the Questions." Introduction to *Women in Search of Utopia: Mavericks and Mythmakers.* New York: Schocken Books, xi-xv.

BASKIN, Cyndy. 1982. "Women in Iroquois Society.'" *Canadian Woman Studies/les cahiers de la femme,* 4:2 (Winter), 43-6.

BASU, Rekha. 1981. "Sexual Imperialism: The Case of Indian Women in Britain." *Heresies,* 3:4 (Issue 12), 71-3.

BATHURST, Patricia. 1977. "Facts, Actions, Ideas, Philosophy. It's All There in Media Report." *Matrix,* 62:4 (Summer), 26-7, 31.

BAUER, Laurie. 1983. *English Word Formation.* Cambridge: Cambridge University Press.

BAUGH, Albert C. 1957. *A History of the English Language.* 2nd edition. New York: Appleton-Century-Crofts.

BAUM, Charlotte, Paula Hyman and Sonya Michel. 1976. *The Jewish Woman in America.* New York: New American Library.

BAYM, Nina. 1978. *Woman's Fiction: A Guide to Novels by and about Women in America, 1820-1870.* Ithaca: Cornell University Press.

BAYM, Nina. 1984. "The Madwoman and her Languages: Why I Don't Do Feminist Literary Theory." *Tulsa Studies in Women's Literature,* 3:1/2 (Spring/Fall), 45-59.

BEALE, Frances. 1970. "Double Jeopardy: To be Black and Female," In *The Black Woman: An Anthology.* Ed. Toni Cade. New York: New American Library, 90-100.

BEANLAND, J. 1911. "The Sex War In Language." *The Vote,* 18 February, 207-8.

BEARD, Mary. 1931. "Women at the Crossroads." *Independent Woman,* 10:8 (August), 339, 374-5.

BEARD, Mary Ritter. 1942. In *Mary Ritter Beard: A Sourcebook.* Ed. Ann J. Lane. New York: Schocken Books, 1977.

BEARD, Mary Ritter. 1946. *Women as Force in History: A Study in Traditions and Realities.* New York: Macmillan.

BEAUVOIR, Simone de. 1953. *The Second Sex.* Trans. and ed. H. M. Parshley. New York: Knopf.

BEAUVOIR, Simone de. 1972. Interview by Alice Schwarzer. Trans. Helen Eustis. Rpt. in *The First Ms. Reader.* Ed. Francine Klagsbrun. New York: Warner Communications, 250-60.

BEAUVOIR, Simone de. 1976. Interview by Alice Schwarzer. From *Marie-Claire,* October. In *New French Feminisms.* Trans. Elaine Marks. Ed. Elaine Marks and Isabelle de Courtivron. New York: Schocken, 1981, 150-3.

BEAUVOIR, Simone de. 1981. Interview by Hazel Rowley and Ranate Reisman. *Hecate,* 7:2, 90-6.

BECK, Evelyn Torton, ed. 1982. *Nice Jewish Girls: A Lesbian Anthology.* Watertown, Massachusetts: Persephone Press.

BECK, Evelyn Torton. 1983. " 'No More Masks': Anti-Semitism as Jew-Hating." *Women's Studies Quarterly,* 11:3 (Fall), 11-14.

BECK, Evelyn Torton. 1984. "Yentl's Daughters." *The Women's Review of Books,* 2:2 (November), 10-11.

BECKER, Susan D. 1981. *The Origins of the Equal Rights Amendment: American Feminism Between the Wars.* Westport, Connecticut: Greenwood Press.

BEECHEY, Veronica with Richard Allen. 1982. *The Woman Question.* Unit 1 in The Changing Experience of Women. Milton Keynes: The Open University Press.

BEETON, Mrs. Isabella. 1861. *The Book of Household Management.* London: Ward, Lock, and Tyler.

BEH, Siew Hwa. 1981. "Growing Up with Legends of the Chinese Swordswomen." In *The Politics of Women's Spirituality*. Ed. Charlene Spretnak Garden City, New York: Anchor-Doubleday, 1982, 121-6.

BELKIN, Madeline. 1970. "Drowning in the Steno Pool." *Up from Under*, May/June, 11-13.

BELL, Diane. 1980. "Desert Politics: Choices in the 'Marriage Market.' " In *Women and Colonization: Anthropological Perspectives*. Ed. Mona Etienne and Eleanor Leacock. New York: Praeger, 239-69.

BELLA, Hassan and David Morley. 1983. "The Use of Women's Vocabulary in Teaching Primary Health Care." *The Lancet*, 19 March, 639-40.

BEM, Sandra L. 1974. "The Measurement of Psychological Androgyny." *Journal of Consulting and Clinical Psychology*, 42:12, 155-62.

BENGIS, Ingrid. n.d. *A Woman's New World Dictionary*. Special Collections, Northwestern University, Evanston, Illinois.

BENNETT, Gwendolyn. Collected papers. SCM 82-70. Schomburg Center for Research in Black Culture. New York Public Library.

BENSTON, Margaret Lowe. 1984. "The Myth of Computer Literacy." *Canadian Woman Studies/les cahiers de la femme*, 5:4 (Summer), 20-2.

BERGIN, Ann. c.1979. "Feminists Prefer Legend of Lilith to Scheming Eve." *Arizona Republic*.

BERGMAN, Arlene Eisen. 1975. *Women of Vietnam*. San Francisco: People's Press.

Berkeley Women's Liberation (New Monday Night Group). 1969. "Women's Liberation." *The Free You*, June, 6. Northwestern University Library Archives, Evanston, Illinois.

BERMÚDEZ, María Elvira. 1955. *La vida familiar del mexicano*. México y lo Mexicano, Vol. 20. México: Antigua Librería Robredo.

BERNARD, Jessie. 1964. *Academic Women*. New York: New American Library.

BERNARD, Jessie. 1971. "The Paradox of the Happy Marriage." In *Woman in Sexist Society: Studies in Power and Powerlessness*. Ed. Vivian Gornick and Barbara K. Moran. New York: Basic Books, 145-62.

BERNIKOW, Louise, ed. 1974. *The World Split Open: Four Centuries of Women Poets in England and America, 1552-1950*. New York: Random House.

BERNSTEIN, Richard. 1983. "Swagmen and Other Australians Finally Get a 'Webster' of their Very Own." *New York Times*, 17 March.

BERRY, Donna. 1980. Letter to the editor. *WomanSpirit*, 6:24 (May), 35.

BETHEL, Lorraine. 1982. " 'This Infinity of Conscious Pain': Zora Neale Hurston and the Black Female Literary Tradition." In *But Some of Us Are Brave*. Ed. Gloria T. Hull, Patricia Bell Scott, and Barbara Smith. Old Westbury, New York: The Feminist Press, 176-88.

BIERCE, Ambrose. 1911. *The Devil's Dictionary*. Rpt. New York: Dover,1958.

BILLINGTON-GREIG, Teresa. 1908a. "The Storm Center of the Woman Suffrage Movement." *The International*, September, 109-13.

BILLINGTON-GREIG, Teresa. c.1908b. "Suffragist Tactics Past and Present." London: Women's Freedom League Pamphlet. Fawcett Library, London.

BILLINGTON-GREIG, Teresa. 1911a. "Feminism and Politics." *The Contemporary Review*, November, 693-703.

BILLINGTON-GREIG, Teresa. 1911b. *Towards Woman's Liberty*. London: Women's Freedom League.

BILLINGTON-GREIG, Teresa. c.1949-60. Collection of Quotations (on Status of Woman). Fawcett Library, London.

BIRD, Caroline. 1983. "Growing Up to Be A 'Salty Old Woman.' " *Ms.*, August, 102.

BIRKBY, Phyllis, Bertha Harris, Jill Johnston, Esther Newton, and Jane O'Wyatt, eds. 1973. *Amazon Expedition: A Lesbianfeminist Anthology*. Albion, California: Times Change Press.

BISHOP, Beata with Pat McNeill. 1977. *Below the Belt: An Irreverent Analysis of the Male Ego*. London: Coventure.

BLACKHOUSE, Helen. 1984. "Not Another 'Ism'?" *Working With Girls*, 19 (December), 4, 5.

BLACKWELL, Elizabeth. 1895. *Pioneer Work in Opening the Medical Profession to Women*. Rpt. New York: Schocken, 1977.

Black Women's Action Committee, Black Unity and Freedom Party. 1971. Rpt. in *The Body Politic: Women's Liberation in Britain*. Ed. Michelene Wandor. London: stage 1, 1978, 82-9.

BLAKELY, Mary Kay. 1980. "Dear Gloria." In *Pulling Our Own Strings*. Ed. Gloria Kaufman and Mary Kay Blakely, 9-13. Bloomington, Indiana, Indiana University Press.

BLAKELY, Mary Kay. 1983. "The Nun's Revolt." *Ms.*, September, 545, 56, 102, 103.

BLAND, Lucy. 1983. "Purity, Motherhood, Pleasure, or Threat? Definitions of Female Sexuality 1900-1970s." In *Sex and Love, New Thoughts on Old Contradictions*. Ed. Sue Cartledge and Joanna Ryan. London: The Women's Press, 8-29.

blasing, anne. 1982. "the lavender kimono." *off our backs*, March, 6.

BLEASE, W. Lyon. 1913a. "The Emancipation of the Heroine." *The Englishwoman*, 20:59 (November), 198-209.

BLEASE, W. Lyon. 1913b. "Equal Divorce." *The Englishwoman*, 17:50 (February), 143-53.

BLEIER, Ruth. 1984. *Science and Gender: A Critique of Biology and Its Theories on Women*. New York: Pergamon Press.

BLUE, Adrianne. 1984. "Virago Modern Classics – Bedtime Reading for a Lifetime." *Ms.*, April, 27-30.

BLUH, Bonnie Charles. 1974. *Woman to Woman: European Feminists*. New York: Starogubski Press.

BODICHON, Barbara. 1857. *Women and Work*. Pamphlet. Fawcett Library, London.

BODINE, Ann. 1975. "Sex Differentiation in Language." In *Language and Sex: Difference and Dominance*. Ed. Barrie Thorne and Nancy Henley. Rowley, Massachusetts: Newbury House, 130-51.

BOMBECK, Erma. 1984. "Bombeck on Bombeck." *Family Circle*, January 3, 14, 21.

BOND, Jean Carey and Patricia Peery. 1969. "Is the Black Male Castrated?" *Liberator*, 9:5 (May). Rpt. in *The Black Woman: An Anthology*. Ed. Toni Cade. New York: New American Library, 1970, 113-18.

BONDFIELD, Margaret C. c.1910. "Shop Workers and the Vote." People's Suffrage Federation. Pamphlet. Fawcett Library, London.

BOOTH [Luce], Clare. 1937. *The Women*. New York: Random House.

BORKER, Ruth. 1980. "Anthropology: Social and Cultural Perspectives." In *Women and Language in Literature and Society*. Ed. Sally McConnell-Ginet, Ruth Borker, and Nelly Furman. New York: Praeger, 26-44.

BOSMAJIAN, Haig. 1977. "Sexism in the Language of Legislatures and Courts." In *Sexism and Language*. Ed. Alleen Pace Nilsen, Haig Bosmajian, H. Lee Gershuny, and Julia P. Stanley. Urbana, Illinois: National Council of Teachers of English, 77-104.

Boston Women's Health Book Collective. 1971 [1976]. *Our Bodies, Ourselves*. New York: Simon & Schuster.

Boston Women's Health Book Collective. 1983. *Our Bodies, Ourselves*. New York: Simon & Schuster.

Boston Women's Health Book Collective. 1984. "Report on Toxic Shock Syndrome." Boston: Boston Women's Health Book Collective, August.

BOSTON WOMEN UNITED. 1971. Advertisement for *The Digging Stick* Periodical. *Ain't I A Woman*, 2 April, 9.

BOTTOMORE, Tom, ed. 1983. *A Dictionary of Marxist Thought*. Cambridge: Harvard University Press.

BOUCHER, Sandy. 1984. "Hype Versus Reality." *Plexus*, March, 5.

BOULDING, Elise. 1976. *The Underside of History: A View of Women Through Time*. Boulder, Colorado: Westview Press.

BOXER, Marilyn J. 1982. "For and About Women: The Theory and Practice of Women's Studies in the United States." *Signs*, 7:3 (Spring), 661-95.

BOYD, Roisin. c.1982. "Depression." *Wicca: 'Wise Woman' Irish Feminist Magazine*, No. 9, 6-7.

BRADBERRY, Elsie. 1970. "an open letter to all secretaries." *Everywoman*, 21 August, 2.

BRANDT, Allan M. In press. *No Magic Bullet: A Social History of Venereal Disease in the U.S. since 1880*. Oxford: Oxford University Press.

BRANT, Beth. 1983. "A Gathering of Spirit." *Sinister Wisdom*, 22/23, 5-9. Special Issue: on North American Indian Women. Ed. Beth Brant.

BRAUDE, Beatrice. 1973. "Marguerite Durand: Journalistic Mother-of-Us-All." *Ms.*, 1:9 (March), 33-5.

BRAUDY, Susan. 1977. "A Day in the Life of Joan Didion." *Ms.*, 5:8 (February), 65-8, 108-9.

BREARLY, Vera. 1982. Letter. *Women's Voice*, 64 (June), 23.

BREEZE, Nancy. 1984. "Who's Going to Rock the Petri Dish?" *Trivia*, 4 (Spring), 43-8.

BRETT, Sally. 1982. "A Different Kind of Being." In *Stepping Off the Pedestal: Academic Women in the South*. Ed. Patricia A. Stringer and Irene Thompson. New York: Modern Language Association of America, 13-22.

Brewer's Dictionary of Phrase and Fable. 1962. London: Cassell.

Brewer's Dictionary of Phrase and Fable. 1970. New York: Harper & Row.

BRIGHT, Clare. 1982. "Essay on NWSA." *National Women's Studies Association Newsletter*, 1:1, 2-3.

Bristol Women's Studies Group, eds. 1979. *Half the Sky*. London: Virago.

BRISTOW, Edward J. 1982. *Prostitution and Prejudice: The Jewish Fight Against White Slavery 1870-1939*. Oxford: Clarendon Press.

BRITTAIN, Vera. 1933. *Testament of Youth*. London: Victor Gollancz. Rpt. London: Virago, 1978.

BRITTAIN, Vera. 1953. *Lady into Woman: A History of Women from Victoria to Elizabeth II*. London: Andrew Dakers.

BRODINE, Karen. 1980. "Journal Entries: Always the Ideas Carry Themselves Forward." *Heresies*, 3:1 (Issue 9), 48.

BRONSTEIN, Audrey. 1982. *The Triple Struggle: Latin American Peasant Women*. London: WOW Campaigns Ltd.

BROOKE. 1980. "The Chador of Women's Liberation: Cultural Feminism and the Movement Press." *Heresies*, 3:1 (Issue 9), 70-4.

BROOKS, Betty Willis and Sharon L. Sievers. 1983. "The New Right Challenges Women's Studies: The Long Beach Women's Studies Program." In *Learning Our Way*. Ed. Charlotte Bunch and Sandra Pollack. Trumansburg, New York: The Crossing Press, 78-88.

BROSSARD, Nicole. 1984. "From Radical to Integral." Trans. Miranda Hay and Lise Weil. *Trivia*, Fall, 6-15.

BROTMAN, Barbara. 1983. "Mother's Day Marchers to Make a Cry for Peace." *Chicago Tribune*, 8 May, Sec. 1, 18.

BROWN, Arlene. 1970. "Grateful Dead." *RAT*, 4-18 April, 26.

BROWN, Beverly. 1981. "A Feminist Interest in Pornography – Some Modest Proposals." *m/f*, 5/6, 5-18.

BROWN, Clair (Vickery). 1982. "Home Production for Use in a Market Economy." In *Rethinking the Family: Some Feminist Questions*. Ed. Barrie Thorne with Marilyn Yalom. New York: Longman, 151-67.

BROWN, Lawrence. Personal papers. Schomburg Center for Research in Black Culture. New York Public Library.

BROWN, Penelope. 1980. "How and Why Are Women More Polite: Some Evidence from a Mayan Community." In *Women and Language in Literature and Society*. Ed. Sally McConnell-Ginet, Ruth Borker, and Nelly Furman. New York: Praeger, 111-36.

BROWN, Penelope and Stephen Levinson. 1978. "Universals of Language Usage: Politeness Phenomena." In *Questions and Politeness: Strategies in Social Interaction*. Cambridge Papers in Social Anthropology 8. Ed. Esther Goody. Cambridge: Cambridge University Press, 56-311.

BROWN, Rita Mae. 1973. *Rubyfruit Jungle*. New York: Daughters Publishing.

BROWN, Rita Mae. 1976. *A Plain Brown Rapper*. Oakland, California: Diana Press.

BROWN, Roger and Alfred Gilman. 1960. "The Pronouns of Power and Solidarity." In *Style in Language*. Ed. Thomas Sebeok. Cambridge: MIT Press, 253-76.

BROWNLEE, W. E. and M. Brownlee. 1976. *Women in The American Economy: A Documentary History, 1675-1929*. New Haven: Yale University Press.

BROWNMILLER, Susan. 1971. "Speaking Out on Prostitution." In *Radical Feminism*. Ed. Anne Koedt, Ellen Levine, and Anita Rapone. New York: Quadrangle, 1973, 72-7.

BROWNMILLER, Susan. 1975a. *Against Our Will: Men, Women, and Rape*. New York: Simon & Schuster.

BROWNMILLER, Susan. 1975b. Excerpt on Pornography from *Against Our Will: Men, Women, and Rape*. In *Take Back the Night*. Ed. Laura J. Lederer. New York: William Morrow, 1980, 30-4.

BROWNMILLER, Susan. 1984a. *Femininity*. New York: Linden Press/Simon & Schuster.

BROWNMILLER, Susan. 1984b. "Femininity." *USA Today*, 31 January, 9A.

BROYARD, Anatole. 1982. "Women and Heroines." *New York Times Book Review*, 31 October, 39.

BRULEY, Sue. 1976. "Women Awake, The Experience of Consciousness-raising." Pamphlet. Rpt. in *No Turning Back: Writings from the Women's Liberation Movement 1975-80*. Ed. Feminist Anthology Collective. London: The Women's Press, 1981, 60-6.

BRUMBERG, Joan Jacobs. 1983. " 'Fasting Girls': Reflections on Writing the History of Anorexia Nervosa." Society for Research on Child Development Conference.

BRUMBLE, H. David III. 1981. *An Annotated Bibliography of American Indian and Eskimo Autobiographies*. Lincoln: University of Nebraska Press.

BRUNER, Edward M. and Jane Paige Kelso. 1980. "Gender Differences in Graffiti: A Semiotic Perspective." In *The Voices and Words of Women and Men*. Ed. Cheris Kramarae. Oxford: Pergamon Press, 239-52. Also in *Women's Studies International Quarterly*, 2/3, 239-52.

BRYANT, Dorothy. 1976. *The Kin of Ata are Waiting for You*. New York: Random House. Originally published as *The Comforter*. Moon Books, 1971.

BUCHANAN, Mary. 1980. "Domestic Science." *Women and Education*, 20 (Autumn), 23-5.

BUCKLE, Richard, ed. 1978. *U and Non-U Revisited*. New York: Viking.

BUDAPEST, Z. 1979, 1980. *The Holy Book of Women's Mysteries*. Vols I and II. Los Angeles: Susan B. Anthony Coven No. 1.

BUDGE, E. A. Wallis. 1960. *The Book of the Dead*. New Hyde Park: University Books.

BUESING, Natalie. 1970. "Women in Advertising: Convenient, Charming, Disposable." Manuscript. Northwestern University Library, Evanston, Illinois.

bülbül. 1984. Interview by leah halper. *off our backs*, July, 18-19.

BULL, Jenny. 1971. In *Awake and Move* (Philadelphia Women's Liberation Center), March.

BUNCH, Charlotte. 1975. "Not for Lesbians Only." *Quest: A Feminist Quarterly*, 2:2 (Fall). Rpt. in *Building Feminist Theory: Essays for Quest*. New York: Longman, 1981, 67-73.

BUNCH, Charlotte. 1978. "An Introduction." *Quest*, 4:2 (Winter), 4-8.

BUNCH, Charlotte. 1983. "Not by Degrees: Feminist Theory and Education." In *Learning Our Way*. Ed. Charlotte Bunch and Sandra Pollack. Trumansburg, New York: The Crossing Press, 248-60.

BUNCH, Charlotte and Sandra Pollack, eds. 1983. *Learning Our Way: Essays in Feminist Education*. Trumansburg, New York: The Crossing Press.

BURKE, Barbara. 1984. "Infanticide." *Science 84*, 5:4 (May), 26-31.

BURLEIGH, Celia. 1873. *The Woman's Journal*, 8 March.

BURNS, Ruth. 1931. "The Executive Invisible." *Independent Woman*, March, 105, 134-5.

BURRIS, Barbara. 1971. "The Fourth World Manifesto." In *Radical Feminism*. Ed. Anne Koedt, Ellen Levine, and Anita Rapone. New York: Quadrangle Books, 1973, 322-52.

BUSFIELD, Joan. 1983. "Gender, Mental Illness, and Psychiatry." In *Sexual Divisions: Patterns and Processes*. Ed. Mary Evans and Clare Ungerson. London: Tavistock Publications, 106-35.

BUSS, Fran Leeper. 1980. *La Partera: Story of a Midwife*. Ann Arbor: University of Michigan Press.

BUTLER, Josephine. 1868. *Education and the Employment of Women*. London: Macmillan.

BUTLER, Josephine. 1869. *Women's Work and Women's Culture*. London: Macmillan.

BUTLER, Josephine. 1870. "An Appeal to the Mothers of England."

BUTLER, Josephine, 1871a. *The Constitution Violated*. Edinburgh: Edmonston and Douglas.

BUTLER, Josephine. 1871b. *Sursum Corda: Annual Address to the Ladies National Association*. Liverpool: T. Brakell.

BUTLER, Josephine. 1872. *An Address to Truehearted Women*.

BUTLER, Josephine. 1874a. Legislative Restrictions on the Industry of Women, Considered from the Women's Point of View. London.

BUTLER, Josephine. 1874b. *Some Thoughts on the Present Aspect of the Crusade Against the State Regulation of Vice*. Liverpool: T. Brakell.

BUTLER, Josephine. 1888. *Social Purity: An Address*. London.

BUTLER, Matilda and William Paisley. 1980. *Women and the Mass Media, Sourcebook for Research and Action*. New York: Human Sciences Press.

BUTRUILLE, Susan G. 1981. "Feminism's Heritage: Suffragist Grandmas Had it Tougher Than Their ERA Granddaughters." *Christian Science Monitor*, 17 September, B15-16.

BUTTERWORTH, Liz. 1983. "Thought for Food." In *Reclaim the Earth: Women Speak Out for Life on Earth*. Ed. Léonie Caldecott and Stephanie Leland. London: The Women's Press, 91-100.

BYNUM, Caroline Walker. 1982. *Jesus as Mother: Studies in the Spirituality of the High Middle Ages*. Berkeley: University of California at Berkeley Press.

BYRNE, Eileen M. 1978. *Women and Education*. London: Tavistock.

BYRNE, Josefa Heifetz. 1974. *Mrs. Byrne's Dictionary*. New York: Pocket Books, 1984.

BYRON, B. 1984. "US PROS Introduce Services for Prostitutes." *Plexus*, May, 3.

CADE, Toni. 1969. "On the Issue of Roles." Excerpt from *The Scattered Sopranoes*.

Lecture. Livingston College Black Woman's Seminar, December. Rpt. in *The Black Woman: An Anthology*. Ed. Toni Cade. New York: New American Library (Signet), 1970, 101-10.

CAIRD, Mona. 1910. "The Lot of Women." Pamphlet. Fawcett Library, London.

CALDICOTT, Helen. 1984. *Missile Envy*. New York: William Morrow.

CALIFIA, Pat. 1981. "Feminism and Sadomasochism." *Heresies*, 3:4 (Issue 12), 30-4.

CALIFIA, Pat. 1982. "A Personal View of the History of the Lesbian S/M Community and Movement in San Francisco." In *Coming to Power: Writings and Graphics on Lesbian S/M*. Ed. SAMOIS, a lesbian/feminist S/M organization. Boston: Alyson Publications, 243-87.

CALLAN, Hilary.1978. "Harems and Overlords: Biosocial Models and the Female." In *Defining Females: The Nature of Women in Society*. Ed. Shirley Ardener. New York: John Wiley.

CALLENBACH, Ernest. 1981. Statement in "AF Symposium on Women and the Future." *Alternative Futures*, 4:2/3 (Spring/Summer), 157-83.

CAMERON, Anne. 1981. *The Daughters of Copper Woman*. Vancouver, B.C.: Press Gang Publishers.

CAMERON, Barbara. 1981. "Gee, You Don't Seem Like an Indian from the Reservation." In *This Bridge Called My Back: Writings by Radical Women of Color*. Ed. Cherríe Moraga and Gloria Anzaldúa. Watertown, Massachusetts: Persephone Press, 46-52.

CANAAN, Andrea. 1981. "Brownness." In *This Bridge Called My Back: Writings by Radical Women of Color*. Ed. Cherríe Moraga and Gloria Anzaldúa. Watertown, Massachusetts: Persephone Press, 232-7.

CARABILLO, Toni. 1965. "Womanpower and the Media." Address to the National Association of Broadcasters. Quoted in *The Quotable Woman*. Ed. Elaine Partnow. Vol. II. Los Angeles: Pinnacle Books, 1977, 294.

CARROLL, Berenice. 1972. "Peace Research: The Cult of Power." *Journal of Conflict Resolution*, 4, 587-616.

CARROLL, Berenice. 1981. "The Politics of 'Originality': Women Scholars and Intellectuals." Berkshire Conference on Women's History, Vassar College, 17 June. Revised as "The Politics of 'Originality': Women and the Class System of the Intellect." Unit for Criticism and Interpretive Theory Colloquium. University of Illinois at Urbana-Champaign, April, 1984.

CARTER, Angela. 1978. *The Sadeian Woman and the Ideology of Pornography*. New York: Pantheon Books.

CARTER, Angela. 1983. "Notes From the Front Line." In *On Gender and Writing*. Ed. Michelene Wandor. London: Pandora Press, 69-77.

CASSELL, Carol. 1984. *Swept Away: Why Women Fear Their Own Sexuality*. New York: Simon & Schuster.

CATT, Carrie Chapman. 1909. "Presidential Address for the National Union of Women's Suffrage Societies." Pamphlet. Fawcett Library, London.

CAVENDISH, Ruth. 1982. *Women on the Line*. London: Routledge & Kegan Paul.

Cell 16. November 1970. Letter. Mimeograph. Northwestern University Library, Evanston, Illinois.

CENEN, and Barbara Smith. 1983. "The Blood – Yes, the Blood: A Conversation." In *Home Girls: A Black Feminist Anthology*. Ed. Barbara Smith. New York: Kitchen Table: Women of Color Press, 31-51.

CHABRÁN, Myrtha. 1979. "Visit to the Dentist: Dialectics." *Heresies*, 2:4 (Issue 8), 106.

CHAFF, Sandra, Ruth Haimbach, Carol Fenichel, and Nina Woodside, eds. 1978. *Women in Medicine: An Annotated Bibliography of the Literature on Women Physicians*.

Metuchen, New Jersey: The Scarecrow Press.

CHAMBERLAIN, Mary. 1983. *Fenwomen: A Portrait of Women in an English Village*. London: Routledge & Kegan Paul.

CHAPMAN, Gwynneth. c.1912. "Vote for Women and the New Militancy." League of Justice. Pamphlet. Fawcett Library, London.

CHARLTON, Linda. 1983. "Dame Rebecca West Dies in London." *New York Times*, 16 March, n.p.

CHARREN, Peggy. 1983. "Color the Boardroom White." *USA Today*, 23 September.

CHENG, Lucie. 1984. "Asian American Women and Feminism." *Sojourner*, October, 11.

CHERNIN, Kim. 1981. *The Obsession: Reflections on the Tyranny of Slenderness*. New York: Harper & Row.

CHESEBRO, James W., ed. 1981. *Gayspeak: Gay Male and Lesbian Communication*. New York: The Pilgrim Press.

CHESLER, Phyllis. 1972. *Women and Madness*. New York: Doubleday.

CHESLER, Phyllis. 1976a. *Women, Money, and Power*. New York: Bantam.

CHESLER, Phyllis. 1976b. "The Amazon Legacy." Rpt. in *The Politics of Women's Spirituality*. Ed. Charlene Spretnak. Garden City, New York: Anchor Press/Doubleday, 1982, 97-113.

CHESS, Stella and Jane Whitbread. 1979. *Daughters: From Infancy to Independence*. New York: New American Library.

CHESTER, Gail. 1979. "Feminist Practice: Notes from the Tenth Year." Theory Press Pamphlet. Rpt. in *Not Turning Back: Writings from the Women's Liberation Movement 1975-80*. Ed. Feminist Anthology Collective. London: The Women's Press, 1981, 67-71.

CHICAGO, Judy. 1979. *The Dinner Party: A Symbol of Our Heritage*. New York: Anchor Press/Doubleday.

CHICAGO, Judy with Susan Hill. 1980. *Embroidering Our Heritage: The Dinner Party Needlework*. Garden City, New York: Anchor Books.

Chicago Women's Liberation Union. 1975. Introduction to *Blazing Star*, 1:3 (May), 1.

CHILD, Mrs. 1932. *Frugal Housewife: Dedicated to Those Who Are Not Ashamed of Economy*. 8th Edition. London: Thomas Tegg.

CHOLMELEY, Robert F. 1908. "The Women's Anti-Suffrage Movement." Pamphlet. London: National Union of Women's Suffrage Societies. Fawcett Library, London.

CHOLMELEY, Robert F. 1912. " 'Man Overboard!' " *The Englishwoman*, 14:41 (May), 139-47.

CHOPIN, Kate. 1899. *The Awakening*. Rpt. New York: Capricorn, 1964.

CHRIST, Carol P. 1980. *Diving Deep and Surfacing: Woman Writers on Spiritual Quest*. Boston: Beacon Press.

CHRIST, Carol P. 1982. "Why Women Need the Goddess." *Heresies*, 2:1 (Issue 5), revised ed., 8-13.

CHRISTENSEN, Kathryn. 1975. "Black Women Battle Double Prejudice." *Chicago Daily News*, January, 19.

CHRYSTOS. 1981. "No Rock Scorns Me as Whore." In *This Bridge Called My Back: Writings by Radical Women of Color*. Ed. Cherríe Moraga and Gloria Anzaldúa. Watertown, Massachusetts: Persephone Press, 243-5.

CHRYSTOS. 1982. "Nidisenok (Sisters)." *Maenad*, 2:2 (Winter), 23-32.

CITRON, Michelle. 1978. "Women and Film: A Discussion of Feminist Aesthetics." *New German Critique*, 13 (Winter), 104.

CIXOUS, Hélène. 1975a. "Sorties." From "Sorties" in *La jeune née* [The Newly Born Woman]. Union Generale d'editions, 10/18. In *New French Feminisms*. Trans. Ann Liddle. Ed. Elaine Marks and Isabelle de Courtivron. New York: Schocken, 1981, 90-8.

CIXOUS, Hélène. 1975b. "Laugh of the Medusa." "Le rire de la Méduse." *L'arc*, 39-54. In *New French Feminisms*. Trans. Keith Cohen and Paula Cohen. Ed. Elaine Marks and Isabelle de Courtivron. New York: Schocken, 1981, 245-64.

CLANCY, Marilyn D. 1984. "Mothers, Miracles, Rebirth." *Chicago Tribune*, 13 May, 9. Based on a 1976 Mother's Day sermon.

CLARK, Eve V. 1983. "Meanings and Concepts." In *Manual of Child Psychology, V. 3, Cognitive Development*. Ed. J. H. Flavell and E. M. Markham. New York: Wiley, 787-840.

CLARK, Herbert H. and Eve V. Clark. 1979. "When Nouns Surface as Verbs." *Language*, 55:4, 767-811.

clark, jill. 1981. "becoming visible: black lesbian conference in New York City." *off our backs*, March, 14.

CLARK, Joanna. 1970. "Motherhood." In *The Black Woman: An Anthology*. Ed. Toni Cade. New York: New American Library (Signet), 63-72.

CLARK, Linda, Marian Ronan, and Eleanor Walker. 1981. *Image-breaking/Image-building*. New York: The Pilgrim Press.

CLARK, Mary Stetson, comp. n.d. "The First Feminist Movement." *Women's Rights in the United States*. Jackdaw No. A 20. Northwestern University Library, Evanston, Illinois.

CLARKE, Cheryl. 1981. "Lesbianism: An Act of Resistance." In *This Bridge Called My Back: Writings by Radical Women of Color*. Ed. Cherríe Moraga and Gloria Anzaldúa. Watertown, Massachusetts: Persephone Press, 128-37.

CLARKE, Cheryl, Jewelle Gomez, Evelynn Hammonds, Bonnie Johnson, and Linda Powell. 1983. "Black Women on Black Women Writers: Conversations and Questions." *Conditions: Nine*, 88-137.

CLARKE, Robert. 1973. *Ellen Swallow: The Woman Who Founded Ecology*. Chicago: Follett Publishing.

clay, rebecca. 1982. "rolling stones." *off our backs*, February, 7.

CLÉMENT, Catherine. 1975. "Enclave esclave" [Enslaved enclave]. From *L'Arc*, No. 61. In *New French Feminisms*. Trans. Marilyn R. Schuster. Ed. Elaine Marks and Isabelle de Courtivron. New York: Schocken, 1981, 130-6.

CLEYRE, Voltairine de. 1914a. "In Defense of Emma Goldman." In *Selected Works of Voltairine de Cleyre, 1866-1912*. Ed. Alexander Berkman. New York: Mother Earth Publishing Association, 205-19.

CLEYRE, Voltairine de. 1914b. "Sexual Slavery." In *Selected Works of Voltairine de Cleyre, 1866-1912*. Ed. Alexander Berkman. New York: Mother Earth Publishing Association, 342-58.

CLIFF, Michelle. 1979. "Against Granite." *Heresies*, 2:4 (Issue 8), 49.

CLIFF, Michelle. 1980. *Claiming an Identity They Taught Me to Despise*. Watertown, Massachusetts: Persephone Press.

CLIFF, Michelle. 1982. "Object Into Subject: Some Thoughts on the Work of Black Women Artists." *Heresies*, 4:3 (Issue 15), 34-40.

CLINTON, Kate. 1982a. *Making Light!* Whyscrack Records, a Division of Making Light Productions.

CLINTON, Kate. 1982b. "Making Light: Another Dimension. Some Notes on Feminist Humor." *Trivia*, 1 (Fall), 37-42.

CLOSE, Hariet M. 1904. "The Woman's Burden." *The Lily*, 1:7, 415.

COBBE, Frances Power. 1861. "Social Science Congresses and Women's Part in Them." *Macmillan's Magazine*, 81-94.

COBBE, Frances Power. 1868. "Criminals, Idiots, Women, and Minors." *Fraser's Magazine*, 777-94.

COBBE, Frances Power. 1869. "The Final Cause of Woman." In *Woman's Work and*

Woman's Culture. London: Macmillan, 1-26.

COCKBURN, Cynthia. 1982. "Women and Printing . . . Sharing the Toys with the Boys." *Scarlet Women: Journal of the Socialist Feminist Current of the Women's Movement*, 14 (January), 14-17.

COHEN, Nancy Wainer and Lois J. Estner. 1983. *Silent Knife: Caesarean Prevention and Vaginal Birth After Caesarean*. South Hadley, Massachusetts: Bergin and Garvey.

COLE, Cyndia. 1980. "No Rape. No." *Room of One's Own*, 5:4, 69-71.

COLEMAN, Linda and Paul Kay. 1981. "Prototype Semantics: The English Verb *lie*." *Language*, 57:1, 26-44.

Collective for Radical Feminist meeting. 1979. *Feminist Practice: Notes from the Tenth Year!* Ed. Organizing Collective for the one-day Radical Feminist meeting, London, 8 April. London: In Theory Press, 1-3.

COLLINS, Sheila. 1975. "Adam's Illusion." Summer. Women Committed to Women Collection. Northwestern University Library, Evanston, Illinois.

Combahee River Collective. 1977. "A Black Feminist Statement." Rpt. in *This Bridge Called My Back: Writings by Radical Women of Color*. Ed. Cherríe Moraga and Gloria Anzaldúa. Watertown, Massachusetts: Persephone Press, 1981, 210-18.

CONABLE, Charlotte Williams. 1977. *Women at Cornell: The Myth of Equal Education*. Ithaca: Cornell University Press.

CONKLIN, Nancy Faires, Brenda McCallum, and Marcia Wade. 1983. *The Culture of Southern Black Women: Approaches and Materials*. University of Alabama: Archive of American Minority Cultures and Women Studies Program of the University of Alabama.

CONNELL, Myra, Tricia Davis, Sue McIntosh, and Mandy Root. "Romance and Sexuality: Between the Devil and the Deep Blue Sea?" In *Feminism for Girls*. Ed. Angela McRobbie and Trisha McCabe. London: Routledge & Kegan Paul, 155-77.

CONRAD, Mrs. Charlotte. 1891. "Our Literary Foremother." *The Homemaker*, 5:4, 528-34.

CONRAD, Susan. 1976. *Perish the Thought: Intellectual Women in Romantic America, 1830-1860*. Oxford: Oxford University Press.

COOPER, Baba. 1981. "The Voice of Women's Spirituality in Futurism." In *The Politics of Women's Spirituality*. Ed. Charlene Spretnak. Garden City, New York: Anchor Press-Doubleday, 1982, 496-509.

COOPER, Lindsay. 1978. "Rock Around The Cock." *The Leveller*, 19 October, 10-12.

COOPER, Patricia and Norma Bradley Buferd. 1978. *The Quilters: Women and Domestic Art, An Oral History*. Garden City, New York: Anchor/Doubleday.

COOTE, Anna and Beatrix Campbell. 1982. *Sweet Freedom: The Struggle for Women's Liberation*. London: Pan Books.

COPJEC, Joan. 1983. "Seduction, Sedition, and the Dictionary." *m/f*, 8, 67-78.

CORDOVA, Jeanne. 1974. "What's in a Name." *The Tide: A Feminist Lesbian Publication, Written By and For the Rising Tide of Women Today*, June, 21-3.

CORDOVA, Jeanne. 1981. "Trauma in the Heterosexual Zone." In *The Lesbian Path*. Ed. Margaret Cruikshank. Tallahassee, Florida: The Naiad Press, 74-9.

COREA, Gena. 1977. *The Hidden Malpractice: How American Medicine Treats Women as Patients and Professionals*. New York: William Morrow.

"Corporate Success: You Don't Have to Play by *Their* Rules. A Conversation with Rosabeth Moss Kanter." 1979. *Ms.*, 8:4 (October), 63-4, 107-9.

COTT, Nancy. 1977. *The Bonds of Womanhood: 'Woman's Sphere' in New England, 1780-1835*. New Haven: Yale University Press.

COURTOT, Martha. 1982. "A Spoiled Identity." *Sinister Wisdom*, 20, 10-15.

COWAN, Ruth Schwartz. 1979. "From Virginia Dare to Virginia Slims: Women and

Technology in American Life." In *Dynamos and Virgins Revisited: Women and Technological Change in Society*. Ed. Martha Moore Trescott. Metuchen, New Jersey: The Scarecrow Press, 30-44.

COWARD, Rosalind. 1982. "Sexual Politics and Psychoanalysis: Some Notes on Their Relation." In *Feminism, Culture, and Politics*. Ed. Rosalind Brunt and Caroline Rowan. London: Lawrence and Wishart, 171-87.

COWARD, Rosalind. 1983. *Patriarchal Precedents: Sexuality and Social Relations*. London: Routledge & Kegan Paul.

COX, Ida. c.1950s. "Wild Women Blues." In *The World Split Open: Four Centuries of Women Poets in England and America, 1552-1950*. Ed. Louise Bernikow. New York: Random House, 1974, 278.

CRAIK, Dinah Maria (Mulock). 1858. *A Woman's Thoughts About Women*. Columbus: Follett, Foster & Company.

CROCKER, Phyllis. 1983. "An Analysis of University Definitions of Sexual Harassment." *Signs*, 8:4 (Summer), 696-707.

CROSS, Amanda. 1982. *Death in a Tenured Position*. New York: Ballantine Books.

CROSS, Tia, Freada Klein, Barbara Smith, and Beverly Smith. 1982. "Face-To-Face Day-To-Day Racism CR." In *All the Women are White, All the Blacks are Men, But Some of Us Are Brave*. Ed. Gloria T. Hull, Patricia Bell Scott, and Barbara Smith. Old Westbury, New York: The Feminist Press. Rpt. in *Heresies*, 4:3 (Issue 15), 66-7.

CRUIKSHANK, Margaret, ed. 1982a. *Lesbian Studies: Present and Future*. Old Westbury, New York: Feminist Press.

CRUIKSHANK, Margaret. 1982b. Introduction to *Lesbian Studies: Present and Future*. Old Westbury, New York: Feminist Press, ix-xviii.

CRYSTAL, David. 1971. *Linguistics*. Baltimore, Maryland: Penguin.

CUDDON, J. A. 1977. *A Dictionary of Literary Terms*. Garden City, New York: Doubleday.

CULLER, Jonathan. 1982. *On Deconstruction: Theory and Criticism After Structuralism*. Ithaca: Cornell University Press.

CUTRUFELLI, Maria Rosa. 1983. *Women of Africa: Roots of Oppression*. London: Zed Press.

D'ABREU, Brook. 1980. In *Why Children?* Ed. Stephanie Dowrick and Sibyl Grundberg. London: The Women's Press, 93-103.

DALY, Frederica Y. 1978. "Comments on 'Science and Racism.'" In *Genes and Gender*. Ed. Ethel Tobach and Betty Rosoff. Staten Island, New York: Gordian Press, 61-2.

DALY, Mary.1973. *Beyond God the Father*. Boston, Massachusetts: Beacon Press.

DALY, Mary. 1978. *Gyn/Ecology: The Metaethics of Radical Feminism*. Boston: Beacon Press.

DALY, Mary.1983. "On Lust and the Lusty." *Trivia*, 3 (Fall), 47-69.

DALY, Mary. 1984. *Pure Lust*. Boston: Beacon Press.

DANTEC, Denise le. 1976. Interview by Elaine Marks. In *New French Feminisms*. Ed. Elaine Marks and Isabelle de Courtivron. New York: Schocken, 1981, 119.

DARSHINI, Priya. 1984. "Bombay Doctors Do Brisk Trade in Hymenoplasty." *Committee on South Asian Women Bulletin*, 2:4 (Fall), 9.

DAUZAT, Albert. 1908. *La Langue française d'aujourd'hui*. Paris: Librairie Armand Colin.

davenport, doris. 1981. "The Pathology of Racism: A Conversation with Third World Wimmin." In *This Bridge Called My Back: Writings by Radical Women of Color*. Ed. Cherrié Moraga and Gloria Anzaldúa. Watertown, Massachusetts: Persephone Press, 85-90.

DAVIDSON, Osha. 1984. "How feminism rescued desperate single father." *Des Moines Register*, 16 November, 11A.

DAVIES, Margaret Llewelyn, ed. 1978. *Maternity: Letters from Working-Women*. New York: W. W. Norton.

DAVIES, Margery W. 1982. *Woman's Place Is at the Typewriter: Office Work and Office Workers 1870-1930*. Philadelphia: Temple University Press.

DAVIS, Angela. 1971. "Reflections on the Black Woman's Role in the Community of Slaves." *The Black Scholar*, December. Excerpts rpt. as "The Myth of the Black Matriarch." In *The First Ms. Reader*. Ed. Francine Klagsbrun. New York: Warner Communications, 241-9.

DAVIS, Angela Y. 1981. *Women, Race, and Class*. New York: Random House.

DAVIS, Angela. 1982. "Women, Race, and Class: An Activist Perspective." National Women's Studies Association Convention, Humboldt State University, California. 17 June. In *Women's Studies Quarterly*, 10:4 (Winter), 5-9.

DAVIS, Elizabeth Gould. 1971. *The First Sex*. Baltimore: Penguin, 1972.

DAWSON, Sarah Ida Fowler (Morgan). Second half 19th century. "Comment on the Role of Women as Childbearers." Manuscript. Duke University Library, Durham, N.C.

DAY, Susie. 1984a. "An Open Letter to Our President." *Gay Community News*, 13 October.

DAY, Susie. 1984b. "Pee-pee tails and woo-woos." *Equal Time*, 22 August.

DEBO, Angie. 1951. *The Five Civilized Tribes of Oklahoma: Report on Social and Economic Conditions*. Philadelphia: Indian Rights Association.

DECARNIN, Camilla. 1981. "Interview with Five Faghagging Women." *Heresies*, 3:4 (Issue 12), 10-14.

DECKARD, Barbara Sinclair. 1979. *The Women's Movement: Political, Socioeconomic, Psychological Issues*. New York and London: Harper & Row.

DEEM, Rosemary. 1978. *Women and Schooling*. London: Routledge & Kegan Paul.

De GENEVIEVE, Barbara. 1982. "An Essay on Photography and Gender." *Image*, 11-12.

DEITRICH, Sheila C. 1980. "An Introduction to Women in Anglo-Saxon Society (c. 600-1066)." In *The Women of England: From Anglo-Saxon Times to the Present*. Ed. Barbara Kanner. London: Mansell, 32-56.

DELACOSTE, Frederique and Felice Newman, eds. 1981. *Fight Back! Feminist Resistance to Male Violence*. Minneapolis, Minnesota: Cleis Press.

DELAMONT, Sara. 1976. *Interaction in the Classroom*. London: Methuen.

DELAMONT, Sara. 1978. "The Contradictions in Ladies' Education." In *The Nineteenth-Century Woman: Her Cultural and Physical World*. Ed. Sara Delamont and Lorna Duffin. London: Croom Helm, 134-63.

DELAMONT, SARA. 1980. *Sex Roles and the School*. London: Methuen.

DELANEY, Janice, Mary Jane Lupton, and Emily Toth. 1977. *The Curse: A Cultural History of Menstruation*. New York: New American Library.

DELAPLAINE, Jo. 1978. "Mujeres y la Comunidad Latina/Women and the Latin Community." *Quest*, 4:4 (April), 6-14.

DELBRIDGE, Arthur, ed. 1981. *The Macquarie Dictionary*. Sidney, Australia: Macquarie Library.

De LAURETIS, Teresa. 1984. *Alice Doesn't: Feminism, Semiotics, Cinema*. Bloomington: Indiana University Press.

Del CASTILLO, Adelaida R. 1978. "Malintzin Tenepal: A Preliminary Look into a New Perspective." In *Essays on La Mujer*. Ed. Rosaura Sánchez and Rosa Martínez Cruz. Los Angeles: Chicano Studies Center Publications, UCLA, 124-49.

DELLENBAUGH, Anne G. 1982. "She Who Is and Is Not Yet: An Essay on Parthenogenesis." *Trivia: A Journal of Ideas*, 1:1 (Fall), 43-63.

DELLENBAUGH, Anne G. and Lise Weil, eds. 1982. Preface to *Trivia: A Journal of*

Ideas, 1:1 (Fall).

DELPHY, Christine. 1981. "For a Materialist Feminism." *Feminist Issues*, 1:2 (Winter), 69-76.

DELPHY, Christine. 1984a. "Christine Delphy: French Feminist." Interview by Laura Cottingham. *off our backs*, March, 10-11, 24-5.

DELPHY, Christine. 1984b. *Close to Home: A Materialist Analysis of Women's Oppression*. Trans. and ed. Diana Leonard. Amherst: University of Massachusetts Press.

DEMING, Barbara. 1977. "Remembering Who We Are: An Open Letter to Susan Saxe." *Quest*, 4:1 (Summer), 52-74.

DEMING, Barbara. 1982. "A Song for Gorgons." In *Reweaving the Web of Life: Feminism and Nonviolence*. Ed. Pam McAllister. Philadelphia, Pennsylvania: New Society Publishers.

DENNETT, Mary Ware. 1919. *The Birth Control Review*, 3:6 (June), 20.

DENNY, Elizabeth. 1984. "Daughters of Harpalyce: Incest and Myth." *Trivia*, 4 (Spring), 49-58.

DENSMORE, Dana. 1971. "The Dating Freud." *No More Fun and Games: A Journal of Female Liberation*, 5 (July), 4-15.

De RAMUS. 1982. "Real racism cuts deep and leaves scars." *Detroit Free Press*, 11 December.

DEUTSCH, Helene. 1944. *Psychology of Women*. Vol. 1. New York: Grune & Stratton.

DEUTSCH, Phyllis. 1983. "There's No Space Like Home." *Womanews*, 4:9 (October), 15.

DHLAMINI, Zanele. 1972. "Women's Liberation: A Black South African Woman's View." *Sechaba*, September. Rpt. in *Women in the Struggle for Liberation*. Ed. World Student Christian Federation. Book Series, 3:2/3, 1973, 39-44.

DIAMOND, Arlyn and Lee R. Edwards, eds. 1977. *The Authority of Experience: Essays in Feminist Criticism*. Amherst: University of Massachusetts Press.

Diary of a Conference on Sexuality. 1982. Memphis: Faculty Press.

Dictionaries of the World. 1982. New York: Pergamon Press.

Dictionary of the Vulgar Tongue. 1811. Foreword by Robert Cromie. Northfield, Illinois: Digest Books.

DIMEN, Muriel. 1979. "Theory from the Inside Out, or Process is Our Most Important Product." The Second Sex – Thirty Years Later Conference, New York University.

DIMEN, Muriel. 1981. "Variety Is the Spice of Life." *Heresies*, 3:4 (Issue 12), 66-70.

DINER, Helen. 1973. *Mothers and Amazons*. New York: Anchor Press.

DINNERSTEIN, Dorothy. 1976. *The Mermaid and the Minotaur*. New York: Harper & Row.

DIXON, Marlene. c.1970. *It Ain't Me Babe*, 7 April, 8.

DIXON, Marlene. 1976. *Things Which Are Done In Secret*. Montreal: Black Rose Books.

DIXON, Marlene, and Joreen. 1970. "A Dictionary of Women's Liberation." In *Everywoman*, 21 August, 16-17.

DOANE, Mary Ann. 1981. "Woman's Stake: Filming the Female Body." *October*, 17, 23-36.

DOBASH, R. E. and R. Dobash. *Violence Against Wives: A Case Against the Patriarchy*. Shepton Mallet, Somerset: Open Books.

Doctor X. 1965. *Intern*. New York: Harper & Row/Perennial.

DONNELL, Radka. 1981. "Confessions of a Quiltist." *Heresies*, 3:4 (Issue 12), 85-7.

DONNELLY, Susan. 1982. "Eve Names The Animals." In *Saturday's Women*. Ed. Charlotte Mandel, Maxine Silverman, and Rachel Hadas. Upper Montclair, New York: Saturday Press, 28-9.

DONOVAN, Josephine. 1978. Review of *Feminology*. *Signs*, 3:4, 916.

DONOVAN, Josephine. 1981. "A New Direction." In *Feminist Literary Criticism*. Research Triangle Park, North Carolina: National Humanities Center, 83-9.

DORR, Priscilla Diaz. 1984. *Pot of Gold*. Unpublished oral history and creative writing manuscript.

DORR, Rheta Childe. 1931. "Let Women Settle In." *Independent Woman*, 10:11 (December), 483, 526-7.

DOWNER, Carol. 1984. "Through the Speculum." In *Test-Tube Women: What Future for Motherhood?* Ed. Rita Arditti, Renate Duelli Klein and Shelley Minden. London: Pandora Press, 419-26.

DOWNING, Christine. 1984. *The Goddess: Mythological Images of the Feminine*. New York: Crossroad.

DOWNING, Hazel. 1981. " 'They Call Me a Life-size Meccano Set': Super-secretary or Super-slave." In *Feminism for Girls*. Ed. Angela McRobbie and Trisha McCabe. London: Routledge & Kegan Paul, 80-100.

DOWRICK, Stephanie. 1980. In *Why Children?* Ed. Stephanie Dowrick and Sibyl Grundberg. London: The Women's Press, 67-76.

DRABBLE, Margaret. 1975. *The Realms of Gold*. New York: Knopf. Rpt. New York: Bantam, 1982.

DRABBLE, Margaret. 1983. "A Woman Writer." In *On Gender and Writing*. Ed. Michelene Wandor. London: Pandora Press, 156-9.

DRAMNICK, Miriam, ed. 1978. *Wollstonecraft: Vindication of the Rights of Woman*. Harmondsworth: Penguin.

DREIFUS, Claudia, ed. 1978. *Seizing Our Bodies: The Politics of Women's Health*. New York: Vintage.

DRUMMOND, Hugh. 1983. "Insignificant Others." *Mother Jones*, September/October, 46, 49, 50.

DUBLIN, Thomas, ed. 1981. *Farm to Factory: Women's Letters, 1830-1860*. New York: Columbia University Press.

DU BOIS, Barbara. 1983. "Passionate Scholarship: Notes on Values, Knowing, and Method in Feminist Social Science." In *Theories of Women's Studies*. Ed. Gloria Bowles and Renate Duelli Klein. London: Routledge & Kegan Paul, 105-16.

DUCROT, Oswald and Tzvetan Todorov. 1979. *Encyclopedic Dictionary of the Sciences of Language*. Trans. Catherine Porter. Baltimore: The Johns Hopkins University Press. First published in France by Editions du Seuil, 1972.

DUFFIN, Lorna. 1978. "Prisoners of Progress: Women and Evolution." In *The Nineteenth-Century Woman: Her Cultural and Physical World*. Ed. Sara Delamont and Lorna Duffin. London: Croom Helm, 57-91.

DUNBAR, Roxanne. 1969. "Sexual Liberation – More of the Same." *No More Fun and Games: A Journal of Female Liberation*, 3 (November). Mimeograph. Northwestern University Library, Evanston, Illinois.

DUNTON, John. 1694. *The Ladies Dictionary Being a General Entertainment for the Fair Sex*. London: Raven in the Poultry.

DURAS, Marguerite. 1973. "Smothered Creativity." Interview in *La création étouffée* [Smothered Creativity]. Ed. Suzanne Horer and Jeanne Socquet. Horay. In *New French Feminisms*. Trans. Virginia Hules. Ed. Elaine Marks and Isabelle de Courtivron. New York: Schocken, 1981, 111-13.

DWORKIN, Andrea. 1974. *Woman Hating*. New York: E. P. Dutton.

DWORKIN, Andrea. 1976. *Our Blood: Prophecies and Discourses on Sexual Politics*. New York: Harper & Row. Rpt. New York: Perigree Books, 1981.

DWORKIN, Andrea. 1978. "Pornography and Grief: Feminist Perspectives on Pornography Conference, San Francisco." In *Take Back the Night*. Ed. Laura J.

Lederer. New York: William Morrow, 1980, 286-91.

DWORKIN, Andrea. 1980. "Why So-Called Radical Men Love and Need Pornography." In *Take Back the Night*. Ed. Laura J. Lederer. New York: William Morrow, 148-54.

DWORKIN, Andrea. 1981. *Pornography: Men Possessing Women*. New York: Perigree Books.

DWORKIN, Andrea. 1983. *Right-wing Women*. New York: Perigree Books.

DWORKIN, Susan. 1978. "Notes on Carter's Family Policy – How It Got That Way." *Ms.*, 7:3 (September), 61-3, 94-6.

DYHOUSE, Carol. 1981. *Girls Growing Up in Late Victorian and Edwardian England*. London: Routledge & Kegan Paul.

EASTMAN, Max. 1914. "Woman Suffrage and Sentiment." New York: National Woman Suffrage Publishing Company. Pamphlet. Fawcett Library, London.

d'EAUBONNE, Françoise. 1974. "Feminism or Death." From *Le Feminisme ou la mort* (Feminism or Death). Horay. In *New French Feminisms*. Trans. Betty Schmitz. Ed. Elaine Marks and Isabelle de Courtivron. New York: Schocken, 1981, 64-7.

E.C. 1919. "Impressions in a Workshop." *The Englishwoman*, 42:124, 22-7.

ECHOLS, Alice. 1983. "The New Feminism of Yin and Yang." In *Powers of Desire*. Ed. Ann Snitow, Christine Stansell, and Sharon Thompson. New York: Monthly Review Press, 439-59.

ECO, Umberto.1984. "Metaphor, Dictionary, Encyclopedia." *New Literary History*, 15:2 (Winter), 255-71.

EDELSKY, Carole. 1982. "Who's Got the Floor?" *Language in Society*, 10, 383-421.

EGERTON, Jayne. 1983. "A Sense of Possibility." *Trouble and Strife*, 1 (Winter), 28-31.

EGERTON, Jayne. 1984. "For 'thrill-seeking females' only." *Trouble and Strife*, 2 (Spring), 21-3.

EHRENREICH, Barbara and Deirdre English. 1973. *Witches, Midwives, and Nurses: A History of Women Healers*. London: Writers and Readers Publishing Co-operative.

EHRENREICH, Barbara and Deirdre English. 1979. *For Her Own Good: 150 Years of the Experts' Advice to Women*. New York: Anchor Books.

EHRLICH, Carol. 1981. "The Unhappy Marriage of Marxism and Feminism: Can it be Saved?" In *Women and Revolution*. Ed. Lydia Sargent. Boston: South End Press, 109-33.

EICHLER, Margrit and Hilda Scott. 1981. Editorial. *Women's Studies International Quarterly*, 4:1, v. Special Issue: Women in Future Research. Ed. Margrit Eichler and Hilda Scott.

EISENSTEIN, Hester. 1980. Introduction to *The Future of Difference*. Ed. Hester Eisenstein and Alice Jardine, Barnard College Women's Center. Boston: G. K. Hall, xv-xxiv.

EISENSTEIN, Zillah R., ed. 1979a. *Capitalist Patriarchy and the Case for Socialist Feminism*. New York and London: Monthly Review Press.

EISENSTEIN, Zillah R. 1979b. "Developing a Theory of Capitalist Patriarchy and Socialist Feminism. Ed. Zillah Eisenstein. New York and London: Monthly Review Press, 5-40.

EISENSTEIN, Zillah R. 1979c. "Some Notes on the Relations of Capitalist Patriarchy." In *Capitalist Patriarchy and the Case for Socialist Feminism*. Ed. Zillah Eisenstein. New York and London: Monthly Review Press, 41-55.

EISENSTEIN, Zillah R. 1981. *The Radical Future of Liberal Feminism*. New York and London: Longman.

EISENSTEIN, Zillah R. 1982. "The Sexual Politics of the New Right: Understanding the 'Crisis of Liberalism' for the 1980's." *Signs*, 7:3 (Spring), 567-88.

ELGIN, Suzette Haden. 1981. "Some Proposed Additions to the Glossary of Needed

Lexical Items for the Expression of Women's Perceptions." *The Lonesome Node*, 1:1 (September/October), 2-3.

ELGIN, Suzette Haden. 1982. "Why a Woman Is Not Like a Physicist." *Aurora: Speculative Feminism*, 8:1 (Issue 21, Summer), 30-4.

ELGIN, Suzette Haden. 1983. *A First Dictionary of Láadan*. Huntsville, Arkansas (Route 4, Box 192-E): The Láadan Group.

ELGIN, Suzette Haden. 1984. *Native Tongue*. New York: DAW.

ELLENBERGER, Harriet. 1984. "The Dream is the Bridge: In Search of Lesbian Theatre." *Trivia: A Journal of Ideas*, 5 (Fall), 17-59.

ELLIAS, Marian. 1974. "oPRESSion." In *Rooms with No View*. Ed. Ethel Strainchamps. Comp. Media Women's Association. New York: Harper & Row, 235-45.

ELLMANN, Mary. 1968. *Thinking About Women*. New York: Harcourt Brace Jovanovich.

ELSEY, Cy. 1982. "Holy Spirit's Female, Visitor Tells Oshawa." *Shekinah*, 3:4 (October-December), 23.

ELSTOB, Elizabeth. 1715. *The Rudiments of Grammar for the English-Saxon Tongue, First Given in English: With an Apology for the Study of Northern Antiquities*. London: W. Bowyer.

EMBREE, Alice. 1970. "Media Images I: Madison Avenue Brainwashing – The Facts." In *Sisterhood is Powerful*. Ed. Robin Morgan. New York: Random House, 175-91.

EMSWILER, Sharon Neufer and Thomas Neufer Emswiler. 1984. *Women and Worship: A Guide to Nonsexist Hymns, Prayers, and Liturgies*. Rev. and expanded ed. San Francisco: Harper & Row.

ENGLAND, Jean. 1974. "Is 'Riffraff' an Adjective?" *Ms.*, 3:4 (October), 119.

ENGLISH, Deirdre. 1980. "The Politics of Porn, Can Feminists Walk the Line?" *Mother Jones*, April, 20-50.

EPHRON, Nora. 1983. *Heartburn*. New York: Pocket Books.

EPICA (Ecumenical Program for Interamerican Communication and Action), PRISA (National Ecumenical Movement in Puerto Rico), and AFSC (American Friends Service Committee). 1976. *Puerto Rico: A People Challenging Colonialism*. Washington, D.C.: EPICA Task Force.

ESCUDERO, Bettina. 1984. Editorial statement. *Bearing Witness/Sobreviviendo: An Anthology of Native American/Latina Art and Literature*. Special issue of *Calyx: A Journal of Art and Literature by Women*, 8:2 (Spring), 6.

ESTES, Leland L. 1984. "The Medical Origins of the European Witch Craze: A Hypothesis." *Journal of Social History*, 17:2, 271-84.

ETTORE, E. M. 1980. *Lesbians, Women, and Society*. London: Routledge & Kegan Paul.

EVANS, Mary. 1983a. "In Praise of Theory: The Case for Women's Studies." In *Theories of Women's Studies*. Ed. Gloria Bowles and Renate Duelli Klein. London, Boston, and Melbourne: Routledge & Kegan Paul, 219-28.

EVANS, Mary. 1983b. Introduction to *Sexual Divisions: Patterns and Processes*. Ed. Mary Evans and Clare Ungerson. London: Tavistock Publications, 1-14.

EVANS, Sara. 1980. *Personal Politics: The Roots of Women's Liberation in the Civil Rights Movement and the New Left*. New York: Vintage/Random.

EVERYWOMAN COLLECTIVE. 1970. "Ogling." *Everywoman*, 19 June, 3.

FAGIN, Claire and Donna Diers. 1983. "Nursing as Metaphor." *New England Journal of Medicine*, 309:2 (14 July), 116-17.

FAIRBAIRNS, Zoë. 1979. *Benefits*. London: Virago.

FAIRBANKS, A. H. M. 1919. "Women's Position in Industry." *The Englishwoman*, 41:121, 1-3.

FAIRWEATHER, Eileen. 1979. "The Feelings Behind the Slogans." *Spare Rib*, 87 (October). Rpt. in *No Turning Back: Writings from the Women's Liberation Movement 1975-*

80. Ed. Feminist Anthology Collective. London: The Women's Press, 1981, 25-35.

FAIRWEATHER, Eileen. 1983. "Looking for Daddy." In *Fathers: Reflections by Daughters.* Ed. Ursula Owen. London: Virago Press, 188-96.

FAITHFUL, Marianne. 1980. Interview by Toby Goldstein. *Cream,* May, 36-8, 62.

FALLACI, Oriana. 1975. *Letter to a Child Never Born.* New York: Simon & Schuster. Rpt. New York: Washington Square Books, 1982.

"The Family of Woman: Growing Toward the Light." 1982. *Ms.,* 10:7 (January), 56-59.

FARLEY, Harriet. 1850. Letter to Mrs C. H. Dall, 14 May. Rpt. in *Common Sense: A Newsletter for Columbia History Students.* Special Issue, n.d. Northwestern University Library, Evanston, Illinois.

FARLEY, Lin. 1978. *Sexual Shakedown: The Sexual Harassment of Women on the Job.* New York: McGraw-Hill.

FARMER, J. S. AND W. E. Henley. 1890-1904. *Slang and Its Analogues.* Rpt. with an introduction by Theodore M. Bernstein. New York: Arno Press, 1970.

FARNHAM, Margot. 1983. "Slimming: Conquering the Nature in Our Bodies." *Trouble and Strife,* 1 (Winter), 17-22.

FARRUKHZAD, Furugh. 1970. "Another Birth (Tavalludi Digar)." From *Tavalludi Digar.* Tehran: Murvarid. In *Middle Eastern Muslim Women Speak.* Trans. Michael C. Hillman. Ed. Elizabeth Warnock Fernea and Basima Qattan Bezirgan. Austin: University of Texas Press, 1977, 305.

FAULDER, Carolyn. 1977. "Women's Magazines." In *Is This Your Life? Images of Women in the Media.* Ed. Josephine King and Mary Stott. London: Virago, 173-94.

FAWCETT, Millicent Garrett. 1878. "The Future of Englishwomen: A Reply." *Nineteenth Century,* 4, 347-57.

FAWCETT, Millicent. 1905. "Speech for the Women's Local Government Society, November 29." Pamphlet. Fawcett Library, London.

Federation of Feminist Women's Health Centers. 1981. *A New View of a Woman's Body.* New York: Touchstone.

FELL, Margaret. 1666. "Women's Speaking Justified, Proved and Allowed of by the Scriptures." London. Rpt. Amherst, Massachusetts: Mosher Book and Tract Committee, New England Yearly Meeting of Friends, 1980.

FEMINIST ANTHOLOGY COLLECTIVE, ed. 1981. *No Turning Back: Writings from the Women's Liberation Movement 1975-80.* London: The Women's Press.

FEMINISTS, The. 1970. Collective statement. *Rat,* 5-19 June. Rpt. in *Ain't I A Woman,* 1:2 (10 July), 1970, 8.

FERGUSON, Heather M. 1982. "Matriarchy: Patriarchal Myth of Economic and Social Oppression." *Canadian Woman Studies/les cahiers de la femme,* 3:4 (Summer), 60-1.

FERGUSON, Marjorie. 1983. *Forever Feminine.* London: Heinemann.

FERN, Fanny. 1853 [1881]. "Aunt Hetty on Matrimony." *Fern Leaves from Fanny's Port Folio.* New York: Arundel Printing and Publishing.

FERNEA, Elizabeth Warnock and Basima Qattan Bezirgan, eds. 1977a. *Middle Eastern Muslim Women Speak.* Austin: University of Texas Press.

FERNEA, Elizabeth Warnock and Basima Qattan Bezirgan. 1977b. "Huda Sh'arawi, Founder of the Egyptian Women's Movement." In *Middle Eastern Muslim Women Speak.* Ed. Elizabeth Warnock Fernea and Basima Qattan Bezirgan. Austin: University of Texas Press, 193-200.

FIGES, Eva. 1971. *Patriarchal Attitudes.* Greenwich, Connecticut: Fawcett Publications.

FILLMORE, Charles J. 1975. "An Alternative to Checklist Theories of Meaning." *Proceedings of the First Annual Meeting of the Berkeley Linguistic Society,* 123-31.

FINKELSTEIN, Joanne and Patricia Clough. 1983. "Foetal Politics and the Birth of an Industry." *Women's Studies International Forum,* 6:4, 395-400.

FINLAYSON, Judith. 1984. "Vive la Fuss." *Canadian Woman Studies/les cahiers de la femme*, 5:4 (Summer), 19.

FIRESTONE, Shulamith. 1969. Coinage of Redstockings. Rpt. in *Feminist Revolution.* Ed. Kathie Sarachild. New York: Random House, 1975, 55.

FIRESTONE, Shulamith. 1970. *The Dialectic of Sex, The Case for Feminist Revolution.* New York: William Morrow.

FISHBURN, Katherine. 1982. *Women in Popular Culture: A Reference Guide.* Westport, Connecticut: Greenwood Press.

FISHER, Berenice. 1980. "Who Needs Woman Heroes?" *Heresies*, 3:1 (Issue 9), 10-13.

FISHER, Dexter, ed.1980. *The Third Woman: Minority Women Writers of the United States.* Boston: Houghton-Mifflin.

FISHER-MANICK, Beverly. 1977. "Race and Class: Beyond Personal Politics." Rpt. in *Building Feminist Theory: Essays from Quest.* Ed. The Quest Staff. New York: Longman, 1981, 149-60.

FISHER, Sue and Alexandra Dundas Todd. 1983. "Introduction: Communication and Social Context – Toward Broader Definitions." In *The Social Organization of Doctor-Patient Communication.* Ed. Sue Fisher and Alexandra Dundas Todd. Washington, D.C.: Center for Applied Linguistics, 3-17.

FISHMAN, Pamela. 1977. "Interactional Shitwork." *Heresies*, 2 (May), 99-101.

FISHMAN, Pamela. 1983. "Interaction: The Work Women Do." In *Language, Gender and Society.* Ed. Barrie Thorne, Cheris Kramarae, and Nancy Henley. Rowley, Massachusetts: Newbury House, 89-101.

FLAUBERT, Gustave. 1881. *Dictionary of Accepted Ideas.* Rpt. with trans. by Jacques Barzun. New York: New Directions, 1967.

FLEENOR, Juliann E. 1979. "Rape Fantasies as Initiation Rite: Female Imagination in the 'Lives of Girls and Women.' " *Room of One's Own*, 4:4, 35-49.

FLEISCHER, Manfred P. 1981. " 'Are Women Human?' – The Debate of 1595 Between Valens Acidalius and Simon Gediccus." *The Sixteenth Century Journal*, 12:2 (Summer), 107-20.

FLEMING, Margaret B. 1983. "Women as Purveyors of the English Curriculum: Speculations on the Genesis and Destiny of Miss Fidditch." *English Journal*, February, 30-4.

FLEXNER, Eleanor. 1968. *Century of Struggle: The Woman's Rights Movement in the United States.* New York: Atheneum.

FLOWERS, Yvonne A. 1979. "On Never Quite Being Good Enough: Legal Institutional Racism, Sexism, and Elitism." *Heresies*, 2:4 (Issue 8), 31-32.

FLYNN, Edith Elisabeth. 1982. "Women as Criminal Justice Professionals: A Challenge to Change Tradition." In *Judge Lawyer Victim Thief: Women, Gender Roles, and Criminal Justice.* Ed. Nicole Hahn Rafter and Elizabeth A. Stanko. Boston: Northwestern University Press, 305-40.

FOGLIA, Gina and Dorit Wolffberg. 1981. "Spiritual Dimensions of Feminist Anti-Nuclear Activism." In *The Politics of Women's Spirituality.* Ed. Charlene Spretnak. Garden City, New York: Anchor Press/Doubleday, 1982, 446-61.

FOLEY, Ellen. 1980. Interview by Mark J. Norton. *Creem*, May, 33.

FOREMAN, Carolyn Thomas. 1954. *Indian Women Chiefs.* Muskogee, Oklahoma: Star Printery.

FORFREEDOM, Ann. 1970. "First L.A. Ogle-In." *Everywoman*, 1:7 (11 September), 9.

Fourth World. 1971. "Dialog on Black Women." *The Fourth World*, 1:2, 1. Rpt. courtesy of *News and Letters Pamphlet on Minorities.*

Fourth World. 1971. "hey, waitress. . . ." *The Fourth World*, 1:1 (22 June), 7.

Fourth World. 1971. "Self Defense and the Liberation of the Body." *The Fourth World*, 1:1 (22 June), 6.

FOWLER, H. W. 1927. *A Dictionary of Modern English Usage*. Oxford: Clarendon Press.

FOX-GENOVESE, Elizabeth. 1979. "The Personal Is Not Political Enough." *Marxist Perspectives*, 2 (Summer).

FRANK, Francine Wattman. 1978. "Grammatical Gender and Social Change." Manuscript.

FRANK, Francine and Frank Anshen. 1983. *Language and the Sexes*. Albany: State University of New York Press.

FRANKAU, Pamela. 1970. *Colonel Blessington*. New York: Dell.

FRANKLIN, J. E. 1977. *Black Girl From Genesis to Revelations*. Washington, D.C.: Howard University Press.

FRANKLIN, Phyllis, Helene Moglen, Phyllis Zatlin-Boring, and Ruth Angress. 1981. *Sexual and Gender Harassment in the Academy*. New York: Modern Language Association.

FRAZIER, N. and M. Sadker. 1978. *Sexism in School and Society*. New York: Harper & Row.

FREEMAN, Jo. 1975. *The Politics of Women's Liberation: A Case Study of an Emerging Social Movement and Its Relation to the Policy Process*. New York: David McKay.

FREEMAN, Jo. 1979. "The Feminist Scholar." *Quest*, 5:1 (Summer), 26-36.

FRIEDAN, Betty. 1963. *The Feminine Mystique*. New York: W. W. Norton.

FRIEDAN, Betty. 1977. *It Changed My Life: Writings on the Women's Movement*. New York: Dell.

FRIEND, Beverly. 1982. Course proposal on Women in Science Fiction, citing "The Stepford Wives," film by Ira Levin, 1972. *Media Report to Women*, 10:3 (1 March), 1,6.

FRITH, Gill. 1981. "Little Women, Good Wives: Is English Good for Girls?" In *Feminism for Girls*. Ed. Angela McRobbie and Trisha McCabe. London: Routledge and Kegan Paul, 27-49.

FRYE, Marilyn. 1980. "Assignment – Bloomington – 1980: Speak on Lesbian Perspectives on Women's Studies." *Sinister Wisdom*, 14, 3-7.

FRYE, Marilyn. 1983. *The Politics of Reality: Essays in Feminist Theory*. Trumansburg, New York: The Crossing Press.

FULLER, Margaret. 1843. "The Great Lawsuit. Man Versus Men. Woman versus Women." *The Dial*, 4:1 (July), 1-47. Rpt. in *The Feminist Papers: From Adams to de Beauvoir*. Ed. Alice Rossi. New York: Bantam, 1973, 158-82.

FURY, Ann. c.1970. "Ideological Myths in Women's Liberation." Manuscript. Northwestern University Library, Evanston, Illinois.

FURY, Kathleen. 1980. "Okay, Ladies, What's the Joke?" *Redbook*, June, 163-6.

GAGE, Suzann (Coordinator of "Women on the Sexual Fringe" [Los Angeles]). 1983. Statement at National Women's Studies Association Convention, Columbus, Ohio, June.

GAILEY, Christine Ward. 1980. "Putting Down Sisters and Wives: Tongan Women and Colonization." *Women and Colonizaton: Anthropological Perspectives*. Ed. Mona Etienne and Eleanor Leacock. New York: Praeger, 294-322.

GALLOP, Jane. 1982. *The Daughter's Seduction*. New York: Cornell University Press.

GARCIA-BAHNE, Betty. 1978. "La Chicana and the Chicano Family." In *Essays on La Mujer*. Ed. Rosaura Sánchez and Rosa Martínez Cruz. Los Angeles: Chicano Studies Center Publications, UCLA, 30-47.

GARDNER, Gerald H. F. April 1969. "Want-ads Tomorrow: Neutral with Respect to Sex." Pittsburgh, Pennsylvania: KNOW, Inc.

GARDNER, Nanette B. 1873. *The Woman's Journal*, 8 February.

GARY-HARRIS, Faye. 1982. "Racial Myths and Attitudes Among White Female Students at the University of Florida." In *Stepping Off the Pedestal: Academic Women in the South*. Ed. Patricia A. Stringer and Irene Thompson. New York: Modern Language Association of America, 99-108.

GATES, Pearl E. 1980. Interview by Dave DiMartino. *Creem*, May, 31.

GAUTHIER, Xavière. 1974. "Existe-ti-il une écriture de femme?" [Is there such a thing as women's writing?]. From *Tel Quel*, Summer. In *New French Feminisms*. Trans. Marilyn A. August. Ed. Elaine Marks and Isabelle de Courtivron. New York: Schocken, 1981, 161-4.

GAYLOR, Annie Laurie. 1981. *Woe to the Women – The Bible Tells Me So: The Bible, Female Sexuality and the Law*. Madison, Wisconsin: Freedom From Religion Foundation.

GEARHART, Sally. 1974. "Cultural Feminist." *The Tide: A Feminist Lesbian Publication, Written By and For the Rising Tide of Women Today*, June, 3, 25, 26.

GEARHART, Sally Miller. 1978. *The Wanderground: Stories of the Hill Women*. Watertown, Massachusetts: Persephone Press.

GEARHART, Sally Miller. 1983. "If the Mortarboard Fits . . . Radical Feminism in Academia." In *Learning Our Way*. Ed. Charlotte Bunch and Sandra Pollack. Trumansburg, New York: The Crossing Press, 2-18.

GELPI, Barbara Charlesworth and Albert Gelpi, eds. 1975. *Adrienne Rich's Poetry*. New York: Norton.

GENTILE, Mary C. 1982. "Adrienne Rich and Separatism: The Language of Multiple Realities." *Maenad*, 2:2 (Winter), 136-46.

GERMAIN, Diane F. "Feminist Art and Education at Califia: My Personal Experience." In *Learning Our Way*. Ed. Charlotte Bunch and Sandra Pollack. Trumansburg, New York: The Crossing Press, 154-9.

GERSHUNY, H. Lee. 1973. Sexist Semantics: An Investigation of Masculine and Feminine Nouns and Pronouns in Dictionary Sentences that Illustrate Word Usage as a Reflection of Sex-Role. Dissertation, New York University.

GERSHUNY, H. Lee. 1974. "Sexist Semantics in the Dictionary." *A Review of General Semantics*, 31:2 (June), 159-69.

GERSHUNY, H. Lee. 1977. "Sexism in the Language of Literature." In *Sexism and Language*. Ed. Alleen Pace Nilsen, Haig Bosmajian, H. Lee Gershuny, and Julia P. Stanley. Urbana, Illinois: National Council of Teachers of English, 107-29.

GIBSON, Guadalupe. 1983. "Hispanic Women: Stress and Mental Health Issues." In *Women Changing Therapy*. Ed. Joan Hamerman Robbins and Rachel Josefowitz Siegel. New York: The Haworth Press, 113-33.

GILBERT, Sandra M. and Susan Gubar. 1979. *The Madwoman in the Attic*. New Haven: Yale University Press.

GILBERT, Sandra M. and Susan Gubar. 1982. "Alphabet Soup: Women, Language, Sexuality." Manuscript.

GILBERT, Sandra M. and Susan Gubar, eds. 1979. *Shakespeare's Sisters: Feminist Essays on Women Poets*. Bloomington: Indiana University Press.

GILLIGAN, Carol. 1982. *In A Different Voice*. Cambridge, Massachusetts: Harvard University Press.

GILMAN, Charlotte Perkins. 1899. *Women and Economics: The Economic Factor Between Men and Women as a Factor in Social Revolution*. Boston, Massachusetts: Small Maynard.

GILMAN, Charlotte Perkins. 1904. *The Home: Its Work and Influence*. London: William Heinemann.

GILMAN, Charlotte Perkins. 1911. *The Man-Made Word or Our Androcentric Culture*. London: T. Fisher Unwin.

GILMAN, Charlotte Perkins. 1915. *Herland*. Serialized in *The Forerunner*. Rpt. New York: Pantheon, 1979.

GILMAN, Charlotte Perkins. 1916a. "Some Un-Familiar Ways of Living." *The Forerunner*, 7:1 (January), 20-4.

GILMAN, Charlotte Perkins. 1916b. "The Nude in Advertising." *The Forerunner*, 7:23

(February), 54-5.

GILMAN, Charlotte Perkins. 1916c. "Femina: A Magazine for Thinking Women." *The Forerunner*, 7:6 (June), 168.

GILMAN, Charlotte Perkins. 1916d. "The Football Theory." *The Forerunner*, 7:10 (October), 269. Reprint edition. New York: Greenwood Reprint Corporation, 1968.

GILMAN, Charlotte Perkins. 1916e. "The 'Nervous Breakdown' of Women." *The Forerunner*, 7:7 (July), 202-6.

GILMAN, Charlotte Perkins. 1916f. "A Summary of Purpose." *The Forerunner*, 7:11 (November), 286-90.

GILMAN, Charlotte Perkins. 1916g. "Newspapers and Democracy II." *The Forerunner*, 7:12 (December), 314-18.

GINS, Madeline. 1984. *What the President Will Say and Do!!* Barrytown, New York: Station Hill.

GIOVANNI, Nikki. 1969. "I Fell Off the Roof One Day (A View of the Black University)." In *The Black Woman: An Anthology*. Ed. Toni Cade. New York: New American Library (Signet), 1970, 132-6.

GIOVANNI, Nikki. 1970a. "Revolution." In *The Women and the Men*. New York: William Morrow, 1975, n.p.

GIOVANNI, Nikki. 1970b. "Housecleaning." In *The Women and the Men*. New York: William Morrow, 1975, n.p.

GIOVANNI, Nikki. 1975a. "Poem for a Lady Whose Voice I Like." In *The Women and the Men*. New York: William Morrow, n.p.

GIOVANNI, Nikki. 1975b. "Poem for Flora." In *The Women and the Men*. New York: William Morrow, n.p.

GIOVANNI, Nikki. 1975c. "Poetry." In *The Women and the Men*. New York: William Morrow, n.p.

GLASSMAN, Carol. 1970. "Women and the Welfare System." In *Sisterhood is Powerful*. Ed. Robin Morgan. New York: Vintage, 102-15.

GLEASON, H. A., Jr. 1965. *Linguistics and English Grammar*. New York: Holt, Rinehart, and Winston.

GOEKE, Greacian. 1982. *The Blatant Image*, No. 12, 80.

GOLD, Joel. 1982. " 'Buried Alive': Charlotte Forman in Grub Street." *Eighteenth Century Life*, 8:1 (October), 28-45.

GOLDBERG, Marilyn. n.d. *On Misandrism*. Pittsburgh, Pennsylvania: KNOW, Inc.

GOLDEN, Eunice. 1981. "The Male Nude in Women's Art: Dialectics of a Feminist Iconography." *Heresies*, 3:4 (Issue 12), 40-2.

GOLDEN, Judith. 1984. "You're Just in Menopause." *Canadian Woman Studies/les cahiers de la femme*, 5:3 (Spring), 74-6.

GOLDENBERG, Naomi. 1979. *Changing of the Gods: Feminism and the End of Traditional Religions*. Boston: Beacon Press.

GOLDFIELD, Bina. 1983. *The Efemcipated English Handbook*. New York: Westover Press.

GOLDSMITH, Andrea E. 1980. "Notes on the Tyranny of Language Usage." In *The Voices and Words of Women and Men*. Ed. Cheris Kramarae. Oxford: Pergamon Press, 179-91. Also in *Women's Studies International Quarterly*, 2/3 179-91.

GOLDSTEIN, Elyse. 1983. "Judaism's View of Women." *Canadian Woman Studies/les cahiers de la femme*, 5:2 (Winter), 25-6.

GÓMEZ, Alma, Cherríe Moraga, and Mariana Romo-Carmona, eds. 1983. *Cuentos: Stories by Latinas*. New York: Kitchen Table: Women of Color Press.

GOODFIELD, June. 1981. *An Imagined World: A Story of Scientific Discovery*. New York: Harper & Row.

GOODISON, Lucy. 1980. In *Why Children?* Ed. Stephanie Dowrick and Sibyl

Grundberg. London: The Women's Press, 30-41.

GOODISON, Lucy. 1983. "Really Being in Love Means Wanting to Live in a Different World." In *Sex and Love, New Thoughts on Old Contradictions*. Ed. Sue Cartledge and Joanna Ryan. London: The Women's Press Limited, 48-66.

GORDIMER, Nadine. 1965. "Not for Publication." In *Not for Publication*. Quoted in *The Quotable Woman*. Ed. Elaine Partnow. Vol. II. Los Angeles: Pinnacle Books, 1977, 274.

GORDON, Ann D. and Mari Jo Buhle. 1976. "Sex and Class in Colonial and Nineteenth-Century America." In *Liberating Women's History*. Ed. Berenice Carroll. Urbana, Illinois: University of Illinois Press, 278-300.

GORDON, Barbara. 1979. *I'm Dancing as Fast as I Can*. New York: Bantam, 1980.

GORDON, Linda. 1976. *Woman's Body, Woman's Right: A Social History of Birth Control in America*. New York: Viking Grossman.

GORDON, Mary. 1978. *Final Payments*. New York: Ballantine.

GORDON, Rebecca. 1983. Book review. *Calyx*, 8:1 (Fall), 70-2.

GORNICK, Vivian. 1983. *Women in Science: Portraits From a World in Transition*. New York: Simon & Schuster.

GOSSETT, Hattie. 1981. "into 10 takes: a satire." *Heresies*, 3:4 (Issue 12), 15-18.

GOTTLIEB, Alma. 1982. "Sex, Fertility, and Menstruation Among the Beng of the Ivory Coast: A Symbolic Analysis." *Africa*, 52:4, 34-47.

GOULD, Lois. 1978. *X: A Fabulous Child's Story*. New York: Daughters.

GOULIANOS, Joan, ed. 1973. *By A Woman Writt: Literature from Six Centuries By and About Women*. Baltimore: Penguin.

GRAHAM, Alma. 1973. "How to Make Trouble: The Making of a Nonsexist Dictionary." *Ms.*, December, 16.

GRAHAM, Alma. 1975. "The Making of a Nonsexist Dictionary." In *Language and Sex: Difference and Dominance*. Ed. Barrie Thorne and Nancy Henley. Rowley, Massachusetts: Newbury House, 57-63.

GRAHAM, Hilary and Ann Oakley. 1981. "Competing Ideologies of Reproduction: Medical and Maternal Perspectives on Pregnancy." In *Women, Health, and Reproduction*. Ed. Helen Roberts. London: Routledge & Kegan Paul, 50-74.

GRAHAM, Virginia. 1949. *Say Please*. Quoted in *The Quotable Woman*. Ed. Elaine Partnow. Vol. II. Los Angeles: Pinnacle Books, 1977, 162.

GRAHN, Judy. 1977. *A Woman Is Talking To Death*. Oakland: Diana Press.

GRAHN, Judy. 1978a. *The Work of a Common Woman: The Collected Poetry of Judy Grahn, 1964-1977*. New York: St Martin's Press.

GRAHN, Judy, ed. 1978b. *True to Life Adventure Stories*. Vol. I. Trumansburg, New York: The Crossing Press.

GRAHN, Judy. 1978c. "Murdering the King's English." Introduction to *True to Life Adventure Stories*. Ed. Judy Grahn. Vol. I. Trumansburg, New York: The Crossing Press, 6-14.

GRAHN, Judy. 1982. *The Queen of Wands*. Trumansburg, New York: The Crossing Press.

GRAHN, Judy. 1984. *Another Mother Tongue: Gay Words, Gay Worlds*. Boston: Beacon.

GRANDCOURT, Genevieve. 1919. "Selling 'The Review' on Broadway." *The Birth Control Review*, 3:1 (January), 7.

GRANFORS, Malanie. n.d. Account of the Lucy Stone League. *her-self*, 3:3, 17.

GRAY, Elizabeth Dodson. 1982. *Patriarchy as a Conceptual Trap*. Wellesley, Massachusetts: Roundtable Press.

GRAY, Francine Du Plessix. 1982. "The Making of a Writer." *New York Times Book Review*, 12 September, 46.

GREEN, Nancy. 1978. "Masks and Mirrors." In *True to Life Adventure Stories*. Ed. Judy

Grahn. Vol. I. Trumansburg, New York: The Crossing Press, 184-92.

GREEN, Rayna, ed. 1984. *That's What She Said: Contemporary Poetry and Fiction by Native American Women*. Bloomington: Indiana University Press.

Greenham Common Peace Camp. 1983. *The Greenham Factor*. Pamphlet. London: Greenham Print Prop.

GREER, Germaine. 1970. *The Female Eunuch*. New York: Bantam Books, Inc.

GREER, Germaine. 1982. "The Tulsa Center for the Study of Women's Literature: What We Are Doing and Why We Are Doing It." *Tulsa Studies in Women's Literature*, 1:1, 5-26.

GREER, Germaine. 1983. Interview by Joseph Kestner. In *Women Writers Talking*. Ed. Janet Todd. New York: Holmes & Meier, 136-58.

GREGORY, Carole E. 1980. "Black Activists." *Heresies*, 3:1 (Issue 9), 14-17.

GREIG, Noel. 1983. "Writing in a Context." In *On Gender and Writing*. Ed. Michelene Wandor. London: Pandora Press, 78-86.

GRIEVE, Norma. 1981. "Beyond Sexual Stereotypes. Androgyny: A Model or An Ideal?" In *Australian Women: Feminist Perspectives*. Ed. Norma Grieve and Patricia Grimshaw. Melbourne: Oxford University Press, 247-57.

GRIFFIN, Susan. 1982. "The Way of All Ideology." *Signs*, 7:3 (Spring), 641-60.

GRIMSTAD, Kirsten and Susan Rennie, eds. 1975. *The New Woman's Survival Sourcebook*. New York: Alfred A. Knopf.

GROSSMAN, Marilyn and Pauline B. Bart. 1979. "Taking the Men out of Menopause." In *Women Look at Biology Looking at Women*. Ed. Ruth Hubbard, Mary Sue Henifin, and Barbara Fried. Cambridge, Massachusetts: Schenkman, 163-85.

groupo de acao lesbico-feminista. 1982. "brazilian lesbian statement." *off our backs*, March, 2.

GUILLAUMIN, Colette. 1981. "The Practice of Power and Belief in Nature, Part I: The Appropriation of Woman . . ." *Feminist Issues*, 1:2 (Winter), 3-28.

GUILLAUMIN, Colette. 1982. "The Question of Difference." *Feminist Issues*, 2:1 (Spring), 33-52.

GWALTNEY, John Langston. 1980. *Drylongso: A Self-Portrait of Black Americans*. New York: Random House.

HACKER, Marilyn. 1982. "Part of a True Story." *13th Moon*, 6:1/2, 64-6.

Hackney Flashers Collective. 1980. "Who's Holding the Baby?" *Heresies*, 3:1 (Issue 9), 88-9.

HAILE, Berard. 1981. *Women Versus Men: A Conflict of Navajo Emergence*. Lincoln: University of Nebraska Press.

HAIMAN, John. 1980. "Dictionaries and Encyclopedias." *Lingua*, 50, 329-57.

HALE, Beatrice Forbes-Robertson. 1914. *What Women Want: An Interpretation of The Feminist Movement*. New York: Frederick A. Stokes.

HALL, Radclyffe. 1928. *The Well of Loneliness*. New York: Covici Friede.

HALL, Roberta M. with the assistance of Bernice Sandler. 1982. "The Classroom Climate: A Chilly One for Women." Project on the Status and Education of Women. Washington, D.C.: Association of American Colleges.

HALLECK, Dee Dee. 1983. "Ladies Home Channels." *Heresies*, Issue 16, 26-9.

HAMBLIN, Angela. 1983. "Is a Feminist Heterosexuality Possible?" In *Sex and Love, New Thoughts on Old Contradictions*. Ed. Sue Cartledge and Joanna Ryan. London: The Women's Press, 105-23.

HAMILTON, Annette. 1981. "A Complex Strategical Situation: Gender and Power in Aboriginal Australia." In *Australian Women: Feminist Perspectives*. Ed. Norma Grieve and Patricia Grimshaw. Melbourne: Oxford University Press, 69-85.

HAMILTON, Cicely. 1909. *Marriage as a Trade*. Rpt. London: The Women's Press, 1981.

HAMILTON, Cicely. 1911. "The Spirit of the Movement: Miss Cicely Hamilton's Speech at the Bijou Theatre on Jan. 3." *The Vote*, 3 (14 January), 140-1.

HAMILTON, Sylvia. 1982. "Our Mothers Grand and Great: Black Women of Nova Scotia." *Canadian Woman Studies/les cahiers de la femme*, 4:2 (Winter), 33-7.

HAMLIN, Margaret. 1931. "What Chance Back on the Farm." *Independent Woman*, 10:4 (April), 152-4, 174, 188.

HAMMOND, L. H. 1917. *Southern Women and Racial Adjustment*. Pamphlet. University of Illinois-Chicago Circle Archives.

HAMPSTEN, Elizabeth. 1982. *Read This Only to Yourself: The Private Writings of Midwestern Women, 1880-1910*. Bloomington, Indiana: Indiana University Press.

HANISCH, Carol. 1968. "What Can be Learned: A Critique of the Miss America Protest." 27 November. Mimeograph. Northwestern University Library, Evanston, Illinois.

HANISCH, Carol. 1969. "The Personal is Political." In *Feminist Revolution*. Ed. Redstockings. New York: Random House, 1975, 204-5.

HANISCH, Carol. 1973. "The Liberal Takeover of Women's Liberation." In *Feminist Revolution*. Ed. Redstockings. New York: Random House, 1975. 163-7.

HANMER, Jalna. 1981. "Violence and the Social Control of Women." *Feminist Issues*, 1:2 (Winter), 29-46.

HANMER, Jalna and Sheila Saunders. 1983. "Blowing the Cover of the Protective Male: A Community Study of Violence to Women." In *The Public and the Private*. Ed. Eva Gamarnikow, David H. J. Morgan, June Purvis, and Daphne Taylorson. London: Heinemann, 28-46.

HANSCOMBE, Gillian E. 1983. *The Art of Life: Dorothy Richardson and the Development of Feminist Consciousness*. Athens, Ohio: Ohio University Press.

HARAWAY, Donna J. 1981. "In the Beginning was the Word: The Genesis of Biological Theory." *Signs: Journal of Women in Culture and Society*, 6:3, 469-81.

HARNE, Lynne. 1984. "Lesbian Custody and the New Myth of the Father." *Trouble and Strife*, 3 (Summer), 12-15.

HARRIS, Barbara J. 1978. *Beyond Her Sphere: Women and the Professions in American History*. Westport, Connecticut: Greenwood Press.

HARRIS, Olivia. 1980. "The Power of Signs: Gender, Culture, and the Wild in the Bolivian Andes." *Nature, Culture, and Gender*. Ed. Carol MacCormack and Marilyn Strathern. Cambridge: Cambridge University Press, 70-94.

HARRIS, Suzanne. 1980. Quotation as past editor. *Heresies*, 3:1 (Issue 9), 3.

HARRIS, Valerie. 1979a. "Power Exchange 1: Chris Choy." In *Heresies*, 2:4 (Issue 8), 24-7.

HARRIS, Valerie. 1979b. "Power Exchange 2: Barbara Ann Teer." *Heresies*, 2:4 (Issue 8), 42-4.

HARRISON, Jane Ellen. 1910. "Heresy and Humanity." *The Englishwoman*, 6:16 (May), 10-18.

HARRISON, Jane Ellen. 1912. '*Homo Sum.*' New York: National College Equal Suffrage League.

HARRISON, Michelle. 1982. *A Woman in Residence: A Doctor's Personal and Professional Battles Against an Insensitive Medical System*. New York: Random House. Rpt. New York: Penguin, 1983.

HARTMAN, Joan E. and Ellen Messer-Davidow, eds. 1982. *Women in Print I: Opportunities for Women's Studies Research in Language and Literature*. New York: The Modern Language Association.

HARTMANN, Heidi. 1979. "The Unhappy Marriage of Marxism and Feminism." *Capital and Class*, Summer. Revision in *Women and Revolution*. Ed. Lydia Sargent. Boston: South End Press, 1981, 1-41.

HARTSOCK, Nancy. 1976-7. "Fundamental Feminism: Process and Perspective." Rpt. in *Building Feminist Theory: Essays from Quest*. Ed. The Quest Staff. New York: Longman, 1981, 32-43.

HARTSOCK, Nancy. 1979. "Feminist Theory and the Development of Revolutionary Strategy." In *Capitalist Patriarchy and the Case for Socialist Feminism*. Ed. Zillah Eisenstein. New York and London: Monthly Review Press, 56-82.

HASLAM, James. 1912. "The Work of Our Lady Factory Inspectors." *The Englishwoman*, 15:44 (August), 135-45.

HATEM, Mervat. 1984. "The Roots of Prejudice." *The Women's Review of Books*, 2:2 (November), 5-6.

HAUGERUD, Joann. 1978. *Flame Cartoons*. Seattle: Coalition on Women and Religion.

HAUGERUD, Jo, ed. 1982. *The Flame* (Newsletter of the Coalition on Women and Religion), December.

HAWXHURST, Donna M. and Susan L. Rodekohr. c.1984. *Fourth World: Empowerment Advocates*. Pamphlet. Temple, Arizona.

HEIDE, Wilma Scott. 1976. "Why Don't We . . . ?" *Ms.*, 4:12 (June), 88-9.

HEILBRUN, Carolyn G. 1980. "Androgyny and the Psychology of Sex Differences." In *The Future of Difference*. Ed. Hester Eisenstein and Alice Jardine, Barnard College Women's Center. Boston: G. K. Hall, 258-66.

HEILBRUN, Carolyn and Catharine Stimpson. 1975. "Theories of Feminist Criticism: A Dialogue." In *Feminist Literary Criticism: Exploration in Theory*. Lexington, Kentucky: University of Kentucky Press.

HEISE, Helen. 1984. "Eyeshadow, Aesthetics, and Morality." *Women's Studies International Forum*, 7:5, 365-73.

HELD, Sue. 1980. "Another Name for 'Down There'." In *Pulling Our Own Strings: Feminist Humor and Satire*. Ed. Gloria Kaufman and Mary Kay Blakely. Bloomington, Indiana: Indiana University Press, 184.

HELLINGER, Marlis. 1984. "Effecting Social Change Through Group Action: Feminine Occupational Titles in Transition." In *Language and Power*. Ed. Cheris Kramarae, Muriel Schulz, and William M. O'Barr. Beverly Hills, California: Sage, 136-53.

HENESON, Nancy. 1984. "The Selling of P.M.S." *Science 84*, 5:4 (May), 67-71.

HENLEY, Nancy M. 1977. *Body Politics*. Englewood Cliffs, New Jersey: Prentice-Hall.

HENLEY, Nancy M. 1980. "Gender Hype." In *The Voices and Words of Women and Men*. Ed. Cheris Kramarae. Oxford: Pergamon Press, 305-12. Also in *Women's Studies International Quarterly*, 2/3, 305-12.

HENRY, Catherine. 1971. *Red Women's Detachment*. Quoted in *Feminist Revolution*. Ed. Redstockings. New York: Random House, 1975, 200.

HERESIES GREAT GODDESS COLLECTIVE. 1982. Glossary of Great Goddess Issue. *Heresies*, 2:1 (Issue 5), 128-31.

HERMANN, Claudine. 1976a. "Women in Space and Time." From "Les coordonnées feminines: espace et temps" [Women in space and time]. In *Les voleuses de langue* [The tongue snatchers]. des femmes. In *New French Feminisms*. Trans. Marilyn R. Schuster. Ed. Elaine Marks and Isabelle de Courtivron. New York: Schocken, 1981, 168-73.

HERMANN, Claudine. 1976b. "The Virile System." From "Le systeme viril" (The virile system). In *Les voleuses de langue* [The tongue snatchers]. des femmes. In *New French Feminisms*. Trans. Marilyn R. Schuster. Ed. Elaine Marks and Isabelle de Courtivron. New York: Schocken, 1981, 87-9.

HERRING, John W. 1931. "The Matriarchate of These Prosperous States." *Independent Woman*, 10:4 (April), 150-1, 182-3.

HERSCHBERGER, Ruth. 1948. *Adam's Rib*. New York: Pellegrini and Cudahy. Rpt. New York: Harper & Row, 1970.

HESCHEL, Susannah, ed. 1983. *On Being a Jewish Feminist: A Reader*. New York: Schocken.

HESS, Katharine, Jean Langford, and Kathy Ross. 1981. *Feminismo Primero/Feminism First*. Translated/Traducio por Helen Weber and Fabiola Rodriguez. Seattle, Washington: Tsunami Press.

HEYWARD, Carter. 1974. Quoted in "Who's Afraid of Women Priests?" Malcolm Boyd. Quoted in *The Quotable Woman*. Ed. Elaine Partnow. Los Angeles: Pinnacle Books, 1977, 494.

HICKOK, Kathleen. 1984. *Representation of Women: Nineteenth-Century British Women's Poetry*. Westport, Connecticut: Greenwood Press.

HICKS, Emily. 1981. "Cultural Marxism: Nonsynchrony and Feminist Practice." In *Women and Revolution*. Ed. Lydia Sargent. Boston: South End Press, 219-37.

HIGGINSON. Thomas Wentworth. 1900. *Women and the Alphabet*. Boston and New York: Houghton Mifflin. Rpt. Arno Press, 1972.

HIGHBY, Patricia D. 1984. "The Effects of Conversion to Feminism." *Broomstick*, 6:1 (January-February), 8-10.

HINDING, Andrea, ed. (in association with the University of Minnesota). 1980. *Women's History Sources: A Guide to Archives and Manuscript Collections in the United States*, 2 volumes.

HIRSCH, Barbara B. 1973. *Divorce: What A Woman Needs to Know*. Chicago: Henry Regnery.

HIRSCH, Susan F. 1984. "Defining Incest: A Synchronic and Diachronic Approach to Substantive Law." Department of Anthropology, Duke University.

HITE, Shere. 1976. *The Hite Report: A Nationwide Study of Female Sexuality*. New York: Macmillan. Rpt. New York: Dell, 1977.

HO, Liang. 1982. "Asian-American Women: Identity and Role in the Women's Movement." *Feminist International No. 2: Asian Women '80*. Rpt. in *Heresies*, 4:3 (Issue 15), 60-1.

HOAGLAND, Sarah Lucia. 1980a. "Coming Home." In *The Coming Out Stories*. Ed. Julia Penelope Stanley and Susan J. Wolfe. Watertown, Massachusetts: Persephone Press, 146-8.

HOAGLAND, Sarah Lucia. 1980b. "Androcentric Rhetoric in Sociobiology." In *The Voices and Words of Women and Men*. Ed. Cheris Kramarae. Oxford: Pergamon Press, 285-93. Also in *Women's Studies International Quarterly*, 2/3, 285-93.

HOCHSCHILD, Arlie Russell. 1983a. *The Managed Heart: Commercialization of Human Feeling*. Berkeley: University of California Press.

HOCHSCHILD, Arlie Russell. 1983b. "Smile Wars." *Mother Jones*, 8:10 (December), 34-42.

HODGE, Bob. 1979. "Birth and the Community." In *Language and Control*. Ed. Roger Fowler, Bob Hodge, Gunther Kress, and Tony Trew. London: Routledge & Kegan Paul, 175-84.

HOFFMAN, Nancy. 1981. *Woman's "True" Profession: Voices from the History of Teaching*. Old Westbury, New York: The Feminist Press.

HOGELAND, Ronald W. and Aileen S. Kraditor, eds. 1973. *Women and Womanhood in America*. Lexington, Massachusetts: D. C. Heath, 133-5.

HOLLIBAUGH, Amber and Cherríe Moraga. 1981. "What We're Rollin Around in Bed With." *Heresies*, 3:4 (Issue 12), 58-62.

HOLLY, Marcia. 1975. "Consciousness and Authenticity: Toward a Feminist Aesthetic." In *Feminist Literary Criticism: Exploration in Theory*. Lexington, Kentucky: University of Kentucky Press.

"Hollywood Mobilizes for the ERA." *Ms.*, 6:12 (June), 53-7, 76.

HOLM, John A. and Alison Watt Shilling. 1982. *The Dictionary of Bahamian English*.

Cold Spring, New York: Lexik House.

HOLMES, Liz. c.1980. "Give Me the Child." *Wicca: 'Wise Woman' Irish Feminist Magazine*, 4, 10-11.

hooks, bell. 1981. *Ain't I A Woman: Black Women and Feminism*. Boston: South End Press.

HOPE, Rose-Ellen. 1982. "Feminine Origin of Many Religious Symbols and Rituals." *The Flame*, 10:1 (March), 4-16.

HOPWOOD, Kathy. 1980. "I teach disobedience." *Feminary*, 11:1/2, 58.

HORMEL, Olive Deane. 1926. *Co-Ed*. New York: Charles Scribner's Sons.

HORNEY, Karen. 1967. *Feminine Psychology*. Ed. Harold Kalman. New York: W. W. Norton.

HOSKEN, Fran P. 1981. "Female Genital Mutilation and Human Rights." *Feminist Issues*, 1:3 (Summer), 3-24.

house, seamoon. 1981. "a radical feminist model of psychological disability." *off our backs*, May, 34.

HOWE, Florence and Ellen Bass, eds. 1973. *No More Masks! An Anthology of Poems by Women*. Garden City, New York: Anchor/Doubleday.

HUBBARD, Ruth and Marian Lowe, eds. 1979. *Genes and Gender, Vol. 2: Pitfalls in Research on Sex and Gender*. Staten Island, New York: Gordian Press.

HUBBARD, Ruth, Mary Sue Henifin, and Barbara Fried, eds. 1979. *Women Look at Biology Looking at Women: A Collection of Feminist Critiques*. Cambridge, Massachusetts: Schenkman.

HUGHES, Diane. 1984. "Earrings as Signs in the Italian Renaissance City." *The Committee for Gender Research*, 4 (Fall), 1, 5-6.

HULL, Gloria T., Patricia Bell Scott, and Barbara Smith, eds. 1982. *All the Women are White, All the Blacks are Men, BUT SOME OF US ARE BRAVE*. Old Westbury, New York: The Feminist Press.

HULL, Gloria T. and Barbara Smith. 1983. "The Politics of Black Women's Studies." In *Learning Our Way*. Ed. Charlotte Bunch and Sandra Pollack. Trumansburg, New York: The Crossing Press, 19-33. Originally the Introduction to *But Some of Us are Brave*. Ed. Gloria T. Hull, Patricia Bell Scott, and Barbara Smith. Old Westbury, New York: The Feminist Press, 1982, xvii-xxxii.

HUNT, Cecil. 1949. *Word Origins: The Romance of Language*. New York Philosophical Library, 1962.

HURD-MEAD, Kate Campbell. 1938. *A History of Women in Medicine From the Earliest Times to the Beginning of the Nineteenth Century*. Haddam, Connecticut: Haddam Press.

"Hurricane Alice." 1983. *Hurricane Alice*, 1 (Spring), 3.

HURSTON, Zora Neale. 1937. *Their Eyes Were Watching God*. Rpt. Urbana, Illinois: University of Illinois Press, 1978.

HURSTON, Zora Neale. 1942. *Dust Tracks on a Road*. Rpt. in *I Love Myself When I Am Laughing*. Ed. Alice Walker. Old Westbury, New York: The Feminist Press, 1979, 127-81.

HURSTON, Zora Neale. 1981. *The Sanctified Church*. Berkeley: Turtle Island.

HUTCHINS, B. L. 1915. *Women in Modern Industry*. London: G. Bell.

HUXLEY, Elspeth. 1938. *Murder on Safari*. Harmondsworth, England: Penguin, 1957.

HUXLEY, Elspeth. 1959. *The Flame Trees of Thika: Memories of an African Childhood*. New York: Penguin, 1962.

HYMES, Dell H. 1981. "Reading Clackamas Texts." In *Traditional Literatures of the American Indian*. Ed. and comp. Karl Kroeber. Lincoln: University of Nebraska Press, 117-59.

HYMES, Dell. 1984. Response to Symposium on Sexist Language, Linguistic Society of America. Baltimore, December.

IGLEHART, Hallie. 1978. "The Unnatural Divorce of Spirituality and Politics." In

The Politics of Women's Spirituality. Ed. Charlene Spretnak. Garden City, New York: Anchor Press/Doubleday, 1982, 404-14.

IGLEHART, Hallie. 1983. *Womanspirit. A Guide to Women's Wisdom*. San Francisco: Harper & Row.

IMRAY, Linda and Audrey Middleton. 1983. "Public and Private: Marking the Boundaries." In *The Public and the Private*. Ed. Eva Gamarnikow, David H. J. Morgan, June Purvis, and Daphne Taylorson. London: Heinemann, 12-27.

IRIGARAY, Luce. 1977. "Women's Exile: Interview with Luce Irigaray." Trans. Couze Venn. *Ideology and Consciousness*, 1, 62-76.

IRIGARAY, Luce. 1983. "Veiled Lips." Trans. Sara Speidel. *Mississippi Review*, 33, 93-131.

IRVINE, Jacqueline Jordan. 1982. "The Black Female Academic: Doubly Burdened or Doubly Blessed?" In *Stepping Off the Pedestal: Academic Women in the South*. Ed. Patricia A. Stringer and Irene Thompson. New York: Modern Language Association of America, 109-17.

ISASI-DIAZ, A. M. 1982. "The Motherhood of God in Japan." *Shekinah*, 3:4 (October-December), 3.

IVERSEN, Susan. 1983. "A Challenge to Feminists." *The Blatant Image*, No. 3, 1.

JACKER, Corinne. 1981. "Better than a Shriveled Husk: New Forms for the Theatre." In *Toward the Second Decade: The Impact of the Women's Movement on American Institutions*. Ed. Betty Justice and Renate Pore. Westport, Connecticut: Greenwood Press.

JACKSON, Stevi. 1983. "The Desire for Freud: Psychoanalysis and Feminism." *Trouble and Strife*, 1 (Winter), 32-43.

JACOBI, Mary Putnam. 1877. *The Question of Rest for Women During Menstruation*. New York: Putnam's.

JACOBS, Ruth Harriet. 1979. *Life After Youth: Female, Forty, What Next?* Boston: Beacon Press.

JACOBS, Sue-Ellen. 1977. "Berdache: A Brief Review of the Literature." *Colorado Anthropology*, 1, 235-40.

JAGET, Claude, ed. 1980. *Prostitutes – Our Life*. Bristol, England: Falling Wall Press. First published in France as *Une Vie de putain*. Les Presses d'aujourd'hui, 1975.

JAGGER, Alison and Paula S. Rothenberg. 1984. *Feminist Frameworks: Alternative Theoretical Accounts of the Relations Between Women and Men*. 2nd ed. New York: McGraw-Hill.

JAIN, Devaki. 1978. "Can Feminism be a Global Ideology?" *Quest: A Feminist Quarterly*, 4:2 (Winter), 9-15.

JAMIESON, Deborah Aslan. 1982. Review of *This Bridge Called My Back: Writings by Radical Women of Color*, ed. Cherríe Moraga and Gloria Anzaldúa. *off our backs*, April, 6, 11.

Jane. 1973. "Jane." *Voices*, June-November.

JANEWAY, Elizabeth. 1971. *Man's World, Woman's Place*. New York: Dell.

JANEWAY, Elizabeth, ed. 1973a. *Women: Their Changing Roles*. New York: Arno Press.

JANEWAY, Elizabeth. 1973b. Women: Their Changing Roles. Quoted in *The Quotable Woman*. Ed. Elaine Partnow. Vol. II. Los Angeles: Pinnacle Books, 1977, 175.

JANEWAY, Elizabeth. 1980. *Powers of the Weak*. New York: Alfred A. Knopf.

JANSSEN-JURREIT, Marie Louise. 1982. *Sexism: The Male Monopoly on History and Thought*. Trans. Verne Moberg. London: Pluto Press.

JARDINE, Alice. 1979. Interview with Simone de Beauvoir. *Signs*, 5:2, 224-36.

jas. 1983. "wimmin's fire brigade bombs porn." *off our backs*, April, 4.

JEFFERSON, Margo. 1983. "Cynthia Ozick, Moral Minority." *Village Voice Literary Supplement*, 13 September, 13.

JENSEN, Joan M. and Sue Davidson, eds. 1984. *A Needle, A Bobbin, A Strike: Women Needleworkers in America.* Philadelphia: Temple University Press.

JENSEN, Margaret Ann. 1984. *Love's Sweet Return: The Harlequin Story.* Toronto: Women's Educational Press.

JESPERSEN, Otto. 1922. *Language: Its Nature, Development, and Origin.* London: Allen & Unwin.

JOAN, Polly and Andrea Chesman. 1978. *Guide to Women's Publishing.* Paradise, California: Dustbooks.

JOFFE, Natalie F. 1948. "The Vernacular of Menstruation." *Word*, 4:3, 181-6.

JOHNSON, Buffie and Tracy Boyd. 1982. "The Eternal Weaver." *Heresies*, 2:1 (Issue 5), revised ed., 64-9.

JOHNSON, George Douglas. 1918. "The Heart of a Woman." In *The World Split Open: Four Centuries of Women Poets in England and America 1552-1950.* Ed. Louise Bernikow. New York: Random House, 1974, 263.

JOHNSON, Judith. 1984. "Feminism and Science: Dissecting the Bias." *Broadside*, 6:1 (October), 8, 9, 14.

JOHNSON, R. Brimley, ed. 1926. *Bluestocking Letters.* London: John Lane.

JOHNSON, Samuel. 1755. *Dictionary of the English Language: In which the Words Are Deduced from Their Originals and Illustrated in Their Different Significations by Examples from the Best Writers.* 2 vols. New York: Adler, 1968.

JOHNSON, Sonia. 1984. Campaign Announcement. Rpt. in *Trivia: A Journal of Ideas*, 4 (Spring), 5-10.

JOHNSTON, Jill. 1973. *Lesbian Nation: The Feminist Solution.* New York: Simon & Schuster.

JOHNSTON, Jill. 1973c. "The Comingest Womanifesto." In *Amazon Expedition: A Lesbianfeminist Anthology.* Ed. Phyllis Birkby et al. Albion, California: Times Change Press.

JONES, Beverly. 1970. "The Dynamics of Marriage and Motherhood." In *Sisterhood is Powerful.* Ed. Robin Morgan. New York: Vintage, 46-61.

JONES, Deborah. 1980. "Gossip: Notes of Women's Oral Culture." In *The Voices and Words of Women and Men.* Ed. Cheris Kramarae. Oxford: Pergamon Press, 193-8. Also in *Women's Studies International Quarterly*, 2/3, 193-8.

JONG, Erica. 1972. "The Housewife as Artist." *Ms.*, December. Rpt. in *The First Ms. Reader.* Ed. Francine Klagsbrun. New York: Warner Books, 1973, 111-22.

JONG, Erica. 1975. *Here Comes and Other Poems.* New York: New American Library.

JOOS, Martin. 1961. *The Five Clocks: A Linguistic Excursion into the Five Styles of English Usage.* New York: Harbinger, 1967.

JOREEN. c. 1970. "The Bitch Manifesto." Pittsburgh: KNOW, Inc.

JOREEN, 1976. "Trashing: The Dark Side of Sisterhood." *Ms.*, April, 49-51, 92-8.

JOSEPH, Albert. 1983. In *The English Journal.* December, 14.

JOSEPH, Gloria. 1981. "The Incompatible Ménage À Trois: Marxism, Feminism, and Racism." In *Women and Revolution.* Ed. Lydia Sargent. Boston: South End Press, 91-107.

JOSEPH, Gloria I. 1983. Review of *Woman, Race and Class*, by Angela Y. Davis. *Signs: Journal of Women in Culture and Society*, 9:1, 134-6.

JOSEPH, Gloria I. and Jill Lewis. 1981. *Common Differences: Conflicts in Black and White Feminist Perspectives.* Garden City, New York: Anchor/Doubleday.

JUDD, Elizabeth. In press. "Fair Maiden and Dark Lady: The Impact of Courtly Love on Sexual Stereotypes in Modern English." In *Sprachwandel und Feministische Sprachpolitik* (Linguistic Change and Feminist Language Policy). Ed. Marlis Hellinger. Frankfurt: Fischer Taschenbuch Verlag.

Judith Ann. 1970. "The Secretarial Proletariat." In *Sisterhood is Powerful*. Ed. Robin Morgan. New York: Vintage, 86-100.

JUNE, Jennie [Jane Cunningham Croly]. 1864. *Jennie Juneiana: Talks on Women's Topics*. Boston: Lee and Shepard.

JUNE, Jennie. 1891. "Why Should All Women Marry?" *The Homemaker*, 5:4, 540.

JUSTIN, Dena. 1973. "From Mother Goddess to Dishwasher." *Natural History*, February. Quoted in *The Quotable Woman*. Ed. Elaine Partnow. Vol. II. Los Angeles: Pinnacle Books, 1977, 163.

JUSTUS, Carol F. 1983. "Indo-Europeanization of Myth and Syntax in Anatolian Hittite: Dating of Texts as an Index." *Journal of Indo-European Studies*, 11, 59-103.

KAHN, Kathy. 1973. *Hillbilly Women*. New York: Doubleday.

KALLAWAY, Sheryn. n.d. "Organizational Structure or Relationships Within Women's Liberation." Mimeograph. Berkeley Women's Liberation Papers. Northwestern University Library, Evanston, Illinois.

KALISCH, Philip A., Beatrice J. Kalisch, and Margaret Scobey. 1983. *Images of Nurses on Television*. New York: Springer.

KAMIKI, Morneen. 1982. "The Earth is Our Sacred Mother." *WomanSpirit*, 8:31, 14-15.

KANTARIS, Sylvia. 1983. Letter to the editor. *Times Literary Supplement*, 19 August, 882.

KANTER, Rosabeth Moss. 1979. "Corporate Success: You Don't Have to Play by *Their* Rules. A Conversation with Rosabeth Moss Kanter." *Ms.*, 8:4 (October), 63-4, 107-9.

KANTER, Rosabeth Moss, with Barry A. Stein. 1980. *A Tale of "O."* Ill. Booth Simpson Designers. New York: Harper & Row.

KANTROWITZ, Joanne Spencer. 1981. "Paying Your Dues, Part-Time." In *Rocking the Boat: Academic Women and Academic Processes*. Ed. Gloria DeSole and Leonore Hoffmann. New York: The Modern Language Association of America, 15-36.

KAPLAN, Cora. 1984. "Wild Nights: Pleasure/Sexuality/Feminism." *Formations of Pleasure*. London: Routledge & Kegan Paul, 15-35.

KAPLAN, Marcie. 1983. "A Woman's View of DSM-III." *American Psychologist*, July, 786-92.

KASSELL, Paula. 1981. In *New Directions for Women*, 10:5 (September/October), 1, 10.

KAUFMAN, Gloria and Mary Kay Blakely, eds. 1980. *Pulling Our Own Strings: Feminist Humor and Satire*. Bloomington, Indiana: Indiana University Press.

KAYE, Melanie. 1982. "Some Notes on Jewish Lesbian Identity." In *Nice Jewish Girls*. Ed. Evelyn Torton Beck. Watertown, Massachusetts: Persephone, 28-44.

KAZANTZIS, Judith. 1983. "The Errant Unicorn." In *On Gender and Writing*. Ed. Michelene Wandor. London: Pandora Press, 24-30.

KEATS, John. 1970. *You Might As Well Live: The Life and Times of Dorothy Parker*. New York: Simon & Schuster.

KEESING, Nancy. 1982. *Lily on the Dustbin: Slang of Australian Women and Families*. Ringwood, Victoria: Penguin Books.

KELLER, Evelyn Fox. 1983. "Feminism as an Analytic Tool for the Study of Science." *Academe*, 69:5 (September/October), 15-21.

KELLEY, Edith Summers. 1923. *Weeds*. New York: Harcourt, Brace. Rpt. New York: Popular Library, 1972.

KELLOR, Frances A. 1918. "Americanization of Women: A Discussion of an Emergency Created by Granting the Vote to Women in New York State." Lecture. New York State Woman's Suffrage Party, New York. 17 January. Northwestern University Library, Evanston, Illinois.

KELLY, Joan. 1982. "Early Feminist Theory and the *Querelle des Femmes*, 1400-1789."

Signs, 8:1 (Autumn), 4-28.

KELLY, Liz. 1984. " 'Sharing a particular pain.' " *Trouble and Strife*, 3 (Summer), 16-20.

KELLY, Mary.1983. *Post-Partum Document*. London: Routledge & Kegan Paul.

KEMPTON, Sally. 1970. "Cutting Loose." *Esquire*, July. Quoted in *The Quotable Woman*. Ed. Elaine Partnow. Vol. II. Los Angeles: Pinnacle Books, 1977, 475.

KENDRIGAN, Mary Lou. 1984. *Political Equality in a Democratic Society: Women in the United States*. Westport, Connecticut: Greenwood Press.

KENNEDY, Mopsy Strange. 1976. "The Sexual Revolution Just Keeps on Coming." *Mother Jones*, December, 25-9.

KENT, Corita. 1974. Quoted in "A Time of Transition for Corita Kent." Lucie Kay Scheuer. *Los Angeles Times*, 11 July. Quoted in *The Quotable Woman*. Ed. Elaine Partnow. Vol. II. Los Angeles: Pinnacle Books, 1977, 224.

KENYON, Karen. 1982. "A Pink-Collar Worker's Blues." *Newsweek*, 4 October, 15.

KESSLER, Suzanne and Wendy McKenna. 1978. *Gender: An Ethnomethodological Approach*. New York: Wiley.

KEY, Mary Ritchie. 1975. *Male/Female Language*. Metuchen, New Jersey: The Scarecrow Press.

KICKNOSWAY, Faye. 1974. *A Man is a Hook. Trouble*. Santa Barbara: Capra Press.

KIM, Elaine H. 1982. *Asian American Literature: An Introduction to the Writings and Their Social Context*. Philadelphia: Temple University Press.

KING, Florence. 1975. *Southern Ladies and Gentlemen*. New York: Stein & Day.

KING, Lourdes Miranda. 1979. "Puertorriqueñas in the United States: The Impact of Double Discrimination." In *The Puerto Rican Woman*. Ed. Edna Acosta-Belén with collaboration of Elia Hidalgo Christensen. New York: Praeger, 124-33.

KINGSTON, Maxine Hong. 1975. *The Woman Warrior, Memoirs of a Girlhood Among Ghosts*. New York: Random House.

KINGSTON, Maxine Hong. 1980. "Dishwashing and Suicide." In *Pulling Our Own Strings*. Ed. Gloria Kaufman and Mary Kay Blakely. Bloomington, Indiana: Indiana University Press, 127-9.

KISSLING, Elizabeth. 1984. "Verbal Abuse in the Streets." Manuscript. University of Illinois.

KITT. 1981. "Taking the Sting out of S/M." In *Coming to Power: Writings and Graphics on Lesbian S/M*. Ed. SAMOIS, a lesbian/feminist S/M organization. Boston: Alyson Publications, 1982, 60-3.

KLAGSBRUN, Francine, ed. 1973. *The First Ms. Reader*. New York: Warner.

klef, deborah van. 1982. "ladies against women." *off our backs*, April, 16.

KLEIN, Dorie. 1982. "The Dark side of Marriage: *Battered Wives and the Domination of Women*." In *Judge Lawyer Victim Thief: Women, Gender Roles, and Criminal Justice*. Ed. Nicole Hahn Rafter and Elizabeth A. Stanko. Boston: Northeastern University Press, 83-107.

KLEIN, Renate Duelli. 1983a. "How To Do What We Want To Do: Thoughts About Feminist Methodology." In *Theories of Women's Studies*. Ed. Gloria Bowles and Renate Duelli Klein. London: Routledge & Kegan Paul, 88-104.

KLEIN, Renate Duelli. 1983b. "The 'Men-Problem' in Women's Studies: The Expert, The Ignoramus, and The Poor Dear." *Women's Studies International Forum*, 6:4, 413-21.

KLEIN, Renate Duelli. 1984. "Doing It Ourselves: Self Insemination." In *Test-Tube Women: What Future for Motherhood?* Ed. Rita Arditti, Renate Duelli Klein, and Shelley Minden. London: Pandora Press, 382-90.

KLEPFISZ, Irena. 1980. In *Why Children?* Ed. Stephanie Dowrick and Sibyl Grundberg. London: The Women's Press, 15-28.

KNIGHT, Isabel. 1981. "The Feminist Scholar and the Future of Gender." *Alternative*

Futures, 4:2/3 (Spring/Summer), 17-35.

KOCHMAN, Thomas. 1981. *Black and White Styles in Conflict*. Chicago: University of Chicago Press.

KOEDT, Anne. 1970. "The Myth of the Vaginal Orgasm." *Notes From the Second Year*. Rpt. *Radical Feminism*. Ed. Anne Koedt, Ellen Levine, and Anita Rapone. New York: Quadrangle/New York Times, 1973, 198-207.

KOEDT, Anne. 1971. "Lesbianism and Feminism." *Notes From the Third Year*. Rpt. *Radical Feminism*. Ed. Anne Koedt, Ellen Levine, and Anita Rapone. New York: Quadrangle/New York Times, 1973, 246-58.

KOEDT, Anne, Ellen Levine, and Anita Rapone, eds. 1973. *Radical Feminism*. New York: Quadrangle/New York Times.

KOERBER, Carmel. 1977. "Television." In *Is This Your Life? Images of Women in the Media*. Ed. Josephine King and Mary Stott. London: Virago, 123-42.

KOLODNY, Annette. 1975. *The Lay of the Land: Metaphor as Experience and History in American Life and Letters*. Chapel Hill: University of North Carolina Press.

KOLODNY, Annette. 1978. " 'To Render Home a Paradise': Women on the New World Landscapes." In *Women's Language and Style*. Ed. Douglas Butturff and Edmund L. Epstein. *Studies in Contemporary Language #1*. Akron, Ohio: L & S Books, 36-46.

KOLODNY, Annette. 1979-80. "A Map for Rereading: Or, Gender and the Interpretation of Literary Texts." *New Literary History*, 11.

KOLODNY, Annette. 1981. "Dancing Through the Minefield: Some Observations on the Theory, Practice, and Politics of Feminist Literary Criticism." In *Men's Studies Modified: The Impact of Feminism on the Academic Disciplines*. Ed. Dale Spender. Oxford: Pergamon Press, 23-42.

KOMISAR, Lucy. 1971. "The Image of Woman in Advertising." In *Woman in Sexist Society*. Ed. Vivian Gornick and Barbara Moran. New York: Basic Books, 207-17.

KOPPELMAN, Susan. 1985. Introduction to *Between Mothers and Daughters: Stories Across a Generation*. Ed. Susan Koppelman. Old Westbury, New York: The Feminist Press, xv-xxxix.

KORNEGGER, Peggy.1979. "Anarchism: The Feminist Connection." In *Reinventing Anarchy*. Ed. Howard J. Ehrlich, Carol Ehrlich, David DeLeon, and Glenda Morris. London: Routledge & Kegan Paul, 237-49.

KRAMARAE, Cheris, ed. 1980. *The Voices and Words of Women and Men*. Oxford: Pergamon Press.

KRAMARAE, Cheris. 1981. *Women and Men Speaking*. Rowley, Massachusetts: Newbury House.

KRAMARAE, Cheris and Paula Treichler. 1982. "Women and Communication Technologies: The 'Revolution' Continues." Communication, Language, and Gender Conference, Athens, Ohio, 15-16 October.

KRAMARAE, Cheris, Barrie Thorne, and Nancy Henley. 1983. "Sex Similarities and Differences in Language, Speech, and Nonverbal Communication: An Annotated Bibliography." In *Language, Gender, and Society*. Ed. Barrie Thorne, Cheris Kramarae, and Nancy Henley. Rowley, Massachusetts: Newbury House, 151-331.

KRAMER, Cheris. 1975. "Sex-Linked Variations in Address Systems." *Anthropological Linguistics*, 17 (May), 198-210.

KREPPS, Ethel C. 1979. "A Strong Medicine Wind." *True West*, 26 (March-April), 7-10, 40-2. Rpt. in *Oklahoma Memories*. Ed. Anne Hodges Morgan and Rennard Strickland. Norman: University of Oklahoma Press, 1981, 145-61.

KREPS, Bonnie. 1977. "Lib Lives." *Homemakers Magazine*, September, 112.

KRISTEVA, Julia. 1974. "La femme, ce n'est jamais ça" [Woman can never be defined]. Interview by "Psychoanalysis and Politics." *Tel Quel*, Autumn. In *New*

French Feminisms. Trans. Marilyn A. August. Ed. Elaine Marks and Isabelle de Courtivron. New York: Schocken, 1981, 137-41.

KRISTEVA, Julia. 1980. "Motherhood According to Giovanni Bellini." In *Desire in Language: A Semiotic Approach to Literature and Art.* Ed. Leon S. Roudiez. Trans. Thomas Gora, Alice Jardine, and Leon S. Roudiez. Oxford: Basil Blackwell, 409-35. Rpt. as "The Maternal Body." *m/f,* 5 and 6, 1981,158-63.

KRISTEVA, Julia. 1981. "Women's Time." Trans. Alice Jardine and Harry Blake. *Signs: Journal of Women in Culture and Society.* 7:1 (Autumn), 13-35.

KUHN, Annette. 1982. *Women's Pictures: Feminism and Cinema.* London: Routledge & Kegan Paul.

kulp, denise. 1984. "expanding visions." *off our backs,* June, 16-17.

LABOV, William. 1972. *Sociolinguistic Patterns.* Philadelphia: University of Pennsylvania Press.

LACW (Latin American and Caribbean Women's Collective). 1977. *Slaves of Slaves: The Challenge of Latin American Women.* London: Zed Press.

LaDUKE, Winona. 1983. "They'll Always Come Back." Interview. *Sinister Wisdom,* 22/23, 52-7. Reprinted from *Science for the People.*

A Lady. 1721. *An Essay in Defense of the Female Sex.* 4th ed. London: S. Butler.

LAFFERTY, Jeanne. 1970. *The Female State.* Quoted in *Goodbye To All That,* 2 December, 6.

LAGACE, Martha. 1984. "Insiders vs. Outsiders: Who Should Define Images of Women in African Societies?" *Second Century Radcliffe News,* June, 1-4.

LAGUILLER, Arlette. 1975. Interview with Jacqueline Aubenas. *Les Cahiers du GRIF,* March. In *New French Feminisms.* Trans. Isabelle de Courtivron. Ed. Elaine Marks and Isabelle de Courtivron. New York: Schocken, 1981, 121-4.

LAKOFF, Robin. 1975. *Language and Woman's Place.* New York: Harper & Row.

LAMBDIN, William. 1979. *Doublespeak Dictionary.* Los Angeles, California: Pinnacle Books.

LANCASTER, Jane. 1975. *Primate Behavior and the Emergence of Human Culture.* New York: Holt, Rinehart & Winston.

LANDERS, Nedhera. 1980. "Black is Beautiful – Fat is Fine." *Catalyst,* 15 May, 6.

LANE, Ann J., ed. 1977. *Mary Ritter Beard: A Sourcebook.* New York: Schocken Books.

LANGER, Elinor. 1970. *Inside the New York Telephone Company.* Rpt. Chicago: Quadrangle, 1972.

LANGER, Suzanne. 1951. *Philosophy in a New Key.* New York: New American Library.

LANGSTON, Laura. 1984. "Changing the Ways to the Means." *HERizons,* 2:1 (April), 24-5.

LANSING, Marjorie. 1984. "The Outlook for the Gender Gap." *The Committee for Gender Research,* 4 (Fall), 3.

LAPLANCHE, J. and J.-B. Pontalis. 1973. *The Language of Psychoanalysis.* New York: W. W. Norton.

LARCOM, Lucy. 1889. *A New England Girlhood.* Quoted in *Anonymous Was A Woman.* Mirra Bank. New York: St Martin's Press, 1979, 23.

LARKIN, Joan. 1975. "Vagina Sonnet." *Amazon Quarterly,* 3:2, 59.

LAWRENCE, Barbara. 1973. "Dirty Words Can Harm You." *Redbook,* Vol. 143, 33.

LAWS, Judith Long. 1975. "The Psychology of Tokenism: An Analysis." *Sex Roles,* 1:1, 51-60.

LAYTON, Mrs. 1931. "Memories of Seventy Years." In *Life as We Have Known It: By Co-operative Working Women.* Ed. Margaret Llewelyn Davies. London: Hogarth Press. Rpt. London: Virago, 1982, 1-55.

"Learning To Be A Girl." 1980. *Women and Education,* 20 (Autumn), 4.

LEAVITT, Judith Walzer, ed. 1984. *Women and Health in America.* Madison: University of Wisconsin Press.

LeCLERC, Annie. 1974. "Woman's Word." From *Parole de femme*. Grasset. In *New French Feminisms*. Trans. Gillian C. Gill. Ed. Elaine Marks and Isabelle de Courtivron. New York: Schocken, 1981, 79-86.

LEDERER, Laura J., ed. 1980. *Take Back the Night*. New York: William Morrow.

Le DOEUFF, Michèle. 1977. "Women and Philosophy." *Radical Philosophy*, 17 (Summer), 2-11.

Le DOEUFF, Michèle. 1981. "The Public Employer." *Les Temps Modernes*. Rpt. *m/f*, 9, 1984, 3-17.

LEE, Beverly.1971. "to be oriental." In *Asian Women*. Ed. and published by Asian Women of University of California at Berkeley, 18.

Leech, Geoffrey. 1974. *Semantics*. Baltimore, Maryland: Penguin.

Leeds Revolutionary Feminist Group. 1981. "Political Lesbianism: The Case Against Heterosexuality." In *Love Your Enemy? The Debate Between Heterosexual Feminism and Political Lesbianism*. London: Onlywomen Press, 5-10.

LeGUIN, Ursula K. 1976. "Is Gender Necessary?" In *Aurora: Beyond Equality*. Ed. Vonda N. McIntyre and Susan Janice Anderson. Greenwich, Connecticut: Fawcett, 130-9.

LEHMAN, J. Lee. 1981. "Lust is Just a Four-Letter Word." *Heresies*, 3:4 (Issue 12), 80-1.

LEMAN, Joy. 1980. " 'The Advice of a Real Friend.' Codes of Intimacy and Oppression in Women's Magazines 1937-1955." In *Women and Media*. Ed. Helen Baehr. Oxford: Pergamon Press, 63-78.

LENNERT, Midge and Norma Willson, eds. 1973. *A Woman's New World Dictionary*. Lomita, California: 51% Publications. Pamphlet. Special Collections. Northwestern University Library, Evanston, Illinois.

LEO, John. 1984. "Journalese as a Second Tongue." *Time*, 6 February, 78.

LEON, Barbara. 1975. "Separate to Integrate." In *Feminist Revolution*. Ed. Redstockings. New York: Random House, 152-7.

LEONARD, Diana. 1982. *Sex and Generation: A Study of Courtship and Weddings*. London: Tavistock.

LEONARD, Diana. 1984. "Who's holding the test-tube?" *Trouble and Strife*, 3 (Summer), 44-9.

LERNER, Gerda. 1972. "So You Think You Know Women's History." *Ms.*, 1:3 (September), 32-3, 115.

LERNER, Gerda. 1977. *The Female Experience: An American Documentary*. Indianapolis, Indiana: Bobbs-Merrill Educational Publishing.

LERNER, Harriet E. 1976a. "Girls, Ladies, or Women? the Unconscious Dynamics of Language Choice." *Comprehensive Psychiatry*, 17:2 (March/April), 295-9.

LERNER, Harriet E. 1976b. "Parental Mislabeling of Female Genitals as a Determinant of Penis Envy and Learning Inhibitions in Women." *Journal of the Psychoanalytic Association*, 24:5, 269-83.

LESAGE, Julia. 1982. "Film as Politics." Lecture. University of Illinois, 5 October.

LESSING, Doris. 1962. *The Golden Notebook*. London: Michael Joseph.

LESTER, Tanya. 1984. "Reaching for a Feminist Workplace." *HERizons*, 2:1 (April), 26-8.

LeSUEUR, Meridel. 1982. *Ripening: Selected Work, 1927-1980*. Ed. Elaine Hedges. Old Westbury, New York: The Feminist Press.

LeSUEUR, Meridel. 1984. "Writer." *Psychology Today*, January, 34.

LEVINE, June. 1982. *Sisters*. Dublin: Ward River Press.

LEVINE, Suzanne and Harriet Lyons, eds. 1980. *The Decade of Women. A Ms. History of the Seventies in Words and Pictures*. New York: Putnam's.

LEVINSON, Leonard Louis. 1963. *The Left Handed Dictionary*. New York: Collier MacMillan.

LEWIN, Rebecca. 1983. "Truth-Telling Through Feminist Fiction." *Womanews*, 4:9 (October), 17.

LEWIS, Beatrice. 1899. "Self-Sacrifice: A False Ideal." *Womanhood*, February, 183-5.

LIBER, B. 1919. *The Birth Control Review*, 3:7 (July), 7.

LIFSHIN, Lyn, ed. 1982. *Ariadne's Thread: A Collection of Contemporary Women's Journals.* New York: Harper & Row.

LIM, Genny. 1981. "Wonder Woman." In *This Bridge Called My Back: Writings by Radical Women of Color*. Ed. Cherríe Moraga and Gloria Anzaldúa. Watertown, Massachusetts: Persephone Press, 25-6.

LINCOLN, Abbey. 1966. "Who Will Revere the Black Woman?" *Negro Digest*, Summer. Rpt. in *The Black Woman: An Anthology*. Ed. Toni Cade. New York: New American Library (Signet), 1970, 80-4.

LINDEMANN, Barbara S. 1984. " 'To Ravish and Carnally Know': Rape in Eighteenth Century Massachusetts." *Signs*, 10:1 (Autumn), 63-82.

LINDEN, Robin Ruth. 1982. Introduction to *Against Sadomasochism: A Radical Feminist Analysis*. Ed. Robin Ruth Linden, Darlene R. Pagano, Diana E. H. Russell, and Susan Leigh Star. East Palo Alto, California: Frog In The Well, 1-15.

LINDSEY, Karen. 1980. In *Why Children?* Ed. Stephanie Dowrick and Sibyl Grundberg. London: The Women's Press, 243-9.

LINDSEY, Karen. 1981. "The Woman in the Moon." *New Women's Times Feminist Review*, 15 (April/May), 15.

LINDSEY, Karen. 1982. "Women and the Draft." In *Reweaving the Web of Life: Feminism and Nonviolence*. Ed. Pam McAllister. Philadelphia, Pennsylvania: New Society Publishers, 322-5.

LINDSEY, Kay. 1970. "The Black Woman as a Woman." In *The Black Woman: An Anthology*. Ed. Toni Cade. New York: New American Library (Signet), 85-9.

LIPPARD, Lucy R. 1980. "Some Propaganda for Propaganda." *Heresies*, 3:1 (Issue 9), 35-9.

LIPPARD, Lucy. 1983. "Feminist Space: Reclaiming Territory." *The Village Voice*, 29 November, 120.

LIVERMORE, Mary A. 1898. "Talking Behind a Veil." *The Woman's Journal*, 29:31 (30 July), 1.

LIVIA, Anna. 1983. *Relatively Norma*. London: Onlywomen Press.

LLEWELLYN, Chris. 1978. "In Memoriam: Carolyn Johnson." In *True to Life Adventure Stories*. Ed. Judy Grahn. Vol. I. Trumansburg, New York: The Crossing Press, 97-101.

LLOYD, Trevor. 1971. *Suffragettes International: The World-wide Campaign for Women's Rights*. London: American Heritage Press.

LOESCH, Juli. 1972-3. "Testeria and Penisolence: A Scourge to Humanity." *Aphra: The Feminist Literary Magazine*, 4:1 (Winter), 43-5.

LOEWENBERG, Bert James and Ruth Bogin, eds. 1976. *Black Women in Nineteenth-Century American Life: Their Thoughts, Their Words, Their Feelings*. University Park, Pennsylvania: Pennsylvania State University Press.

London Women's Liberation Night-Cleaners' Collective. 1971. "The Night-Cleaners' Campaign." Rpt. in *The Body Politic: Women's Liberation in Britain*. Ed. Michelene Wandor. London: stage 1, 1978, 225-34.

LONGINO, Helen E. 1980. "Pornography, Oppression, and Freedom: A Closer Look." In *Take Back the Night*. Ed. Laura J. Lederer. New York: William Morrow, 40-54.

LORDE, Audre. 1978. *The Black Unicorn*. New York: W. W. Norton.

LORDE, Audre. 1979. "Need." *Heresies*, 2:4 (Issue 8), 112-13.

LORDE, Audre. 1980a. *The Cancer Journals*. Argyle, New York: Spinsters Ink.

LORDE, Audre. 1980b. "Uses of the Erotic: The Erotic as Power." In *Take Back the Night*. Ed. Laura J. Lederer. New York: William Morrow & Co., 295-300.

LORDE, Audre. 1981a. "The Master's Tools Will Never Dismantle the Master's House." In *This Bridge Called My Back: Writings by Radical Women of Color*. Ed. Cherríe Moraga and Gloria Anzaldúa. Watertown, Massachusetts: Persephone Press, 98-101.

LORDE, Audre. 1981b. "An Open Letter to Mary Daly." In *This Bridge Called My Back: Writings by Radical Women of Color*. Ed. Cherríe Moraga and Gloria Anzaldúa. Watertown, Massachusetts: Persephone Press, 94-7.

LORDE, Audre. 1981c. "The Uses of Anger." *Women's Studies Quarterly*, 9:3 (Fall), 7-10.

LORDE, Audre. 1982. "Sister Outsider." *Heresies*, 4:3 (Issue 15), 15-16.

LORDE, Audre. 1984. *Sister Outsider: Essays and Speeches*. Trumansburg, New York: Crossing Press.

LOUD, Pat with Nora Johnson. 1974. *Pat Loud: A Woman's Story*. Quoted in *The Quotable Woman*. Ed. Elaine Partnow. Vol. II. Los Angeles: Pinnacle Books, 1977, 304.

LOVICH, Lene. 1980. Interview by David DiMartino. *Creem*, May, 29.

LOWNDES, Mary. 1910. "On Banners and Banner-Making." *The Englishwoman*, 7:20 (September), 172-8.

LOWNDES, Mary. 1913a. "Honour and Dishonour." *The Englishwoman*, 17:51 (March), 250-6.

LOWNDES, Mary. 1913b. "Slavery." *The Englishwoman*, 19:57 (September), 241-53.

LOWNDES, Mary. 1914a. "A Christmas Book." *The Englishwoman*, 21:61 (January), 39-49.

LOWNDES, Mary. 1914b. "National Waste." *The Englishwoman*, 21:62 (February), 121-34.

LOWNDES, Mary. 1919. "Domestic Service." *The Englishwoman*, 41:123, 109-12.

LOZENBY, Juliet. 1982. "Is Even Patriarchy Not Sacred?" *Scarlet Women: Journal of the Socialist Feminist Current of the Women's Movement*, 14 (January), 19-22.

LUCERO-TRUJILLO, Marcela Christine. 1980a. "The Dilemma of the Modern Chicana Artist and Critic." In *The Third Woman: Minority Women Writers of the United States*. Ed. Dexter Fisher. Boston: Houghton-Mifflin, 324-31.

LUCERO-TRUJILLO, Marcela Christine. 1980b. " 'Machismo' is Part of Our Culture." In *The Third Woman: Minority Women Writers of the United States*. Ed. Dexter Fisher. Boston: Houghton-Mifflin, 401-2.

LUCY, Juicy. 1981. "If I Ask You to Tie Me Up, Will You Still Want to Love Me." In *Coming to Power: Writings and Graphics on Lesbian S/M*. Ed. SAMOIS, a lesbian/feminist S/M organizaton. Boston: Alyson Publications, 1982, 29-40.

LUDLOW, Dorothy P. 1978. " 'Arise and Be Doing': English 'Preaching' Women, 1640-1660." Diss. Indiana University.

LYONS, John. 1968. *Introduction to Theoretical Linguistics*. Cambridge: Cambridge University Press.

LYONS, John. 1977. *Semantics*. Vol. 1 Cambridge: Cambridge University Press.

LYONS, Maritcha Rémond. c.1920. *Memories of Yesterdays: All of Which I Saw and Part of Which I Was*. Typescript. Williamson/Lyons papers, Schomburg Center for Research in Black Culture. New York, New. York.

MACÍAS, Anna. 1982. *Against All Odds: The Feminist Movement in Mexico to 1940*. Westport, Connecticut: Greenwood Press.

MACKAY, Donald G. 1983. "Prescriptive Grammar and the Pronoun Problem." In *Language, Gender and Society*. Ed. Barrie Thorne, Cheris Kramarae, and Nancy Henley. Rowley, Massachusetts: Newbury House, 38-53.

MACKIE, Liz. 1984. "Career Woman." Excerpt from "Socialist Feminist Dictionary, 59th Edition." *Sourcream*, 4 and 5, 8-9.

MacKINNON, Catharine A. 1979. *The Sexual Harassment of Working Women*. New Haven: Yale University Press.

MacKINNON, Catharine A. 1982a. "Feminism, Marxism, Method, and the State: An Agenda for Theory." *Signs*, 7:3 (Spring), 515-44.

MacKINNON, Catharine. 1982b. "Women as Women in Law: On Exceptionality." University of Minnesota. October.

MacKINNON, Catharine A. 1983a. "Feminism, Marxism, Method, and the State: Toward Feminist Jurisprudence." *Signs*, 8:4, 635-58.

MacKINNON, Catharine. 1983b. "*Roe v. Wade*: A Retrospective." Persons, Morality and Abortion Conference, Hampshire College. January.

MacNAMARA, Mary. c.1978. "The Face that Fits the Fashion." *Wicca: 'Wise Woman' Irish Feminist Magazine*, 1-2.

MacNAMARA, Mary, c.1982. "What Is Feminism? Another View . . ." *Wicca: 'Wise Woman' Irish Feminist Magazine*, 12, 6-7.

MACROSTY, Edith. 1913. "The Municipal Step-Mother." *The Englishwoman*, 17:51 (March), 272-8.

MAHL, Mary R. and Helene Koon, eds. 1977. *The Female Spectator: English Women Writers Before 1800*. Bloomington: Indiana University Press, and Old Westbury, New York: The Feminist Press.

MAINARDI, Patricia. 1973. "Quilts: A Great American Art." *Ms.*, 2:6 (December), 58-63. 86.

MAITLAND, Sara. 1980. In *Why Children?* Ed. Stephanie Dowrick and Sibyl Grundberg. London: The Women's Press, 78-91.

MAITLAND, Sara. 1983. "A Feminist Writer's Progress." In *On Gender and Writing*. Ed. Michelene Wandor. London: Pandora Press, 17-23.

MALVEAUX, Julianne. 1979. "Three Views of Black Women – The Myths, the Statistics, and a Personal Statement." *Heresies*, 2:4 (Issue 8), 50-5.

MANLEY, Seon and Susan Belcher. 1972. *O, Those Extraordinary Women! Or the Joys of Literary Lib*. Philadelphia and Ontario: Chilton.

Manushi Collective. 1980. "Drought: 'God-Sent' or 'Man-Made' Disaster?" *Manushi*, 6 (July-August). Rpt. in *Third World/Second Sex*. Ed. Miranda Davies. London: Zed Press, 1983, 3-19.

MARCET, Jane. 1814. *Conversations on Chemistry*. New Haven: Sidney's Press.

MARCH, Kathryn S. and Rachelle Taqqu. 1982. "Women's Informal Associations and the Organizational Capacity For Development." *Cornell University Rural Development Committee Monograph Series*, MS 5, September.

MARIEDAUGHTER, Paula. 1982. "A Random Thought." *Heresies*, 2:1 (Issue 5), revised ed., 131.

MARKS, Elaine and Isabelle de Courtivron, eds. 1981. *New French Feminisms*. New York: Shocken.

MARLATT, Daphne. 1984. "Musing with Mothertongue." *Room of One's Own*, 8:4 (January), 53-6.

MARSDEN, Madonna. 1972. "Gentle Truths for Gentle Readers: The Fiction of Elizabeth Goudge." In *Images of Women in Fiction: Feminist Perspectives*. Ed. Susan Koppelman Cornillan. Bowling Green Ohio: Bowling Green University Popular Press.

MARCH, Margaret S. 1981. *Anarchist Women: 1870-1920*. Philadelphia: Temple University Press.

MARSHALL, Joan K. 1977. *On Equal Terms: A Thesaurus for Nonsexist Indexing and Cataloging*. New York: Neal-Schuman.

MARSHALL, Paule. 1962. "Reena." In *The Black Woman: An Anthology*. Ed. Toni Cade. New York: New American Library (Signet), 1970, 20-37.

MARTIN, Biddy. 1982. "Feminism, Criticism, and Foucault." *New German Critique*, 27 (Fall), 3-30.

MARTIN, Del and Phyllis Lyon. 1972. "Lesbian Love and Sexuality." In *Lesbian/Woman*. San Francisco: Bantam Books and Glide Publications. Rpt. In *The First Ms. Reader*. Ed. Francine Klagsbrun. New York: Warner Books, 1973, 135-44.

MARTIN, Jane Roland. 1981. "Sophie and Emile: A Case Study of Sex Bias in the History of Educational Thought." *Harvard Educational Review*, 51:3 (August), 357-72.

MARTINEAU, Harriet. 1837. *Society in America*. London: Saunders and Otley, Vol. III, 105-51. Rpt. in *The Feminist Papers: From Adams to de Beauvoir*. Ed. Alice Rossi. New York: Bantam, 1973, 125-43.

MARTIN-LEFF, Ann. 1983. "Do You Work." *New Directions for Women*, May/June, 2.

MARTYNA, Wendy. 1978. "What does 'he' mean? Use of the Generic Masculine." *Journal of Communication*, 28:1, 131-8.

MARTYNA, Wendy. 1983. "Beyond the He/Man Approach: The Case for Nonsexist Language." In *Language, Gender and Society*. Ed. Barrie Thorne, Cheris Kramarae, and Nancy Henley. Rowley, Massachusetts: Newbury House, 25-37.

MARZOLF, Marion Tuttle. 1977. *Up From the Footnote: A History of Women Journalists*. New York: Hastings House.

MAURER, David W. 1939. "Prostitutes and Criminal Argots." Rpt. in *Language of the Underworld*. David W. Maurer. Louisville: University of Kentucky Press, 1981, 111-18.

McALLISTER, Pam, ed. 1982. *Reweaving the Web of Life: Feminism and Nonviolence*. Philadelphia, Pennyslvania: New Society Publishers.

McCARTHY, Mary. 1954. *The Group*. Quoted in *The Quotable Woman*. Ed. Elaine Partnow. Vol. II. Los Angeles: Pinnacle Books, 1977, 166.

McCONAHAY, Mary Jo. 1978. "Turtle Voices." In *True to Life Adventure Stories*. Ed. Judy Grahn. Vol. I. Trumansburg, New York: The Crossing Press, 197-206.

McCONNELL-GINET, Sally. 1978a. "Address Forms in Sexual Politics." In *Women's Language and Style*. Ed. Douglas Butturff and Edmund L. Epstein. Akron, Ohio: L and S Books, 23-35.

McCONNELL-GINET, Sally. 1978b. "Intonation in a Man's World." *Signs: Journal of Women in Culture and Society*, 3:3, 541-59.

McCONNELL-GINET, Sally. 1979. "On the Deep (and Surface) Adjective 'Good.' " In *Contributions to Grammatical Studies*. Ed. Linda R. Waugh and Frans van Coetsem. Leiden: E. J. Brill, 132-50.

McCONNELL-GINET, Sally. 1980. "Linguistics and the Feminist Challenge." In *Women and Language in Literature and Society*. Ed. Sally McConnell-Ginet, Ruth Borker and Nelly Furman. New York: Praeger, 3-25.

McCONNELL-GINET, Sally. 1981. "The Origins of Sexist Language in Discourse." New York Academy of Sciences. New York, December. Rpt. in *Discourses in Reading and Linguistics: Proceedings of the New York Academy of Sciences*, in press.

McCONNELL-GINET, Sally. 1982. "The Sexual (Re)Production of Meaning: A Discourse-Based Theory." Manuscript.

McCONNELL-GINET, Sally. 1983. Review article on Language and Sex. *Language*, 59:2, 373-91.

McCONNELL-GINET, Sally. 1984. "On Saying and Meaning: Radical Pragmatics and the 'Sexist Language' Question." Symposium on Sexist Language, Linguistic Society of America. Baltimore, December.

McCURDY, Harold Grier, with Helen Follett. 1966. *Barbara: Unconscious Autobiography of a Child Genius*. Chapel Hill: University of North Carolina Press.

McDANIEL, Judith. 1982. "We Were Fired." *Sinister Wisdom*, 20, 30-43.

McDONALD, Christie V. 1982. "Choreographies [an exchange between Jacques Derrida and Christie V. McDonald]." *Diacritics*, 12 (Summer), 66-76.

McDONOUGH, Roisin and Rachel Harrison. 1978. "Patriarchy and Relations of Production." In *Materialism and Feminism*. Ed. Annette Kuhn and Ann Marie Wolpe. London, Boston, and Henley: Routledge & Kegan Paul, 2-41.

McDOWELL, Linda. 1983. "City and Home: Urban Housing and the Sexual Division of Space." In *Sexual Division: Patterns and Processes*. Ed. Mary Evans and Clare Ungerson. London: Tavistock Publications, 142-63.

McGEE, Micki. 1981. "Narcissism, Feminism, and Video Art." *Heresies*, 3:4 (Issue 12), 88-91.

McINTOSH, Peggy. 1983. "A Note on Terminology." *Women's Studies Quarterly*, 11:2 (Summer), 29-30.

McKEE, Lorna and Margaret O'Brien. 1983. "Interviewing Men: 'Taking Gender Seriously.' " In *The Public and the Private*. Ed. Eva Gamarnikow, David H. J. Morgan, June Purvis, and Daphne Taylorson. London: Heinemann, 147-59.

McLAREN, Lady. 1908. " 'Better and Happier': An Answer from the Ladies Gallery to the Speeches in Opposition to the Women's Suffrage Bill, February 28th, 1908." Sixth edition. London: T. Fisher Unwin.

McPHEE, Carol and Ann Fitzgerald, eds. 1979. *Feminist Quotations: Voices of Rebels, Reformers, and Visionaries*. New York: Thomas Y. Crowell.

McROBBIE, Angela. 1981. "Just Like a Jackie Story." In *Feminism for Girls*. Ed. Angela McRobbie and Trisha McCabe. London: Routledge & Kegan Paul, 113-28.

MAY, M. G. 1913. "Morals for Daughters." *The Englishwoman*, 20:58 (October), 47-58.

MAYO, Edith P. 1981. "Redemption and Reform: Iconography of the U.S. Suffrage Movement." Eighth Biennial Convention of the American Studies Association. October.

MAYS, Vickie M. 1981. "I Hear Voices But See No Faces: Reflections on Racism and Woman/Identified Relationships of Afro-American Women." *Heresies*, 3:4 (Issue 12), 74-6.

MEAD, Margaret. 1949. *Male and Female: A Study of the Sexes in a Changing World*. New York: Dell Publishing Company, 1971.

MEADE, Marion. 1970. "Women and Rock: Sexism Set to Music." *Women: A Journal of Liberation*, 1:2 (Fall), 24-6.

MECKING, P. R. 1981. "fried chicken and feminism." *New Women's Times Feminist Review*, No. 15, 18.

MEDEA, Andra and Kathleen Thompson. 1974. *Against Rape*. New York: Farrar, Straus & Giroux.

MEDIN, Douglas L. and Edward E. Smith. 1984. "Concepts and Concept Formation." *Annual Review of Psychology*, 35, 113-38.

MEDOFF, Jeslyn. 1982. "New Light on Sarah Fyge (Field, Egerton)." *Tulsa Studies in Women's Literature*, 1:2 (Fall), 155-75.

MEEHAN, Diana. 1983. *Ladies of the Evening: Women Characters of Prime-Time Television*. Metuchen, New Jersey: The Scarecrow Press.

MEHRHOF, Barbara and Sheila Cronan. 1969. "The Origins of Woman's Oppression: One View." Manuscript. Northwestern University Library, Evanston, Illinois.

MEHRHOF, Barbara and Pamela Kearon. 1971. "Rape: An Act of Terror." *Notes From the Third Year*. Rpt. in *Radical Feminism*. Ed. Anne Koedt, Ellen Levine, and Anita Rapone. New York: Quadrangle/New York Times, 1973, 228-33.

MEIER, August and Elliott Rudwick. 1966. *From Plantation to Ghetto*. New York: Hill & Wang.

MELNICK, Jane. 1980. In *Why Children?* Ed. Stephanie Dowrick and Sibyl Grundberg. London: The Women's Press, 181-95.

Members of District 1199 (AFL-CIO Hospital and Health Care Union). 1982. "Race? Sex? Class? Prejudice in the Workplace." *Heresies*, 4:3 (Issue 15), 24-6.

Members of the Women's Studies College, State University of New York at Buffalo. 1978. "All-Women Classes and the Struggle for Women's Liberation." In *Learning Our Way*. Ed. Charlotte Bunch and Sandra Pollack. Trumansburg, New York: The Crossing Press, 1983, 59-77.

MENCKEN, H. L. 1963. *The American Language*. Abridged and annotated by Raven I. McDavid, Jr. New York: Alfred A. Knopf.

MERRIAM, Eve. 1958. *After Nora Slammed the Door: American Women in the 1960s: The Unfinished Revolution*. Rpt. Cleveland, Ohio: The World Publishing Company, 1964.

MERRIAM, Eve. 1974. "Sex and Semantics: Some notes on BOMFOG." *New York University Education Quarterly*, 5:4 (Summer), 22-4. Rpt. Pittsburgh, Pennsylvania: KNOW, Inc.

MERRIAM, Eve. 1975. "A Feminist Alphabet." *Newsweek*, 2 August, 11.

MERRIAM, Eve. 1980. "A Feminist Dictionary." In *Pulling Our Own Strings*. Ed. Gloria Kaufman and Mary Kay Blakely. Bloomington, Indiana: Indiana University Press, 174-5.

MEYERDING, Jane. 1984. "In Response: On Nonviolence and Feminism." *Trivia*, 5 (Fall), 60-9.

MICHAELS, Leonard and Christopher Ricks, eds. 1980. *The State of the Language*. Berkeley: University of California Press.

MIKULSKI, Barbara. 1976. "The White Ethnic Catholic Woman." In *Dialogue on Diversity: A New Agenda for American Women*. Ed. Barbara Peters and Victoria Samuels. New York: Institute on Pluralism and Group Identity of the American Jewish Committee, 35-9.

MILES, Barbara. 1971. "Amazons and Battle Axes: Herstory." In *Everywoman*, 5 March, 5.

MILLER, Casey and Kate Swift. 1976. *Words and Women: New Language in New Times*. Garden City, New York: Doubleday.

MILLER, Casey and Kate Swift. 1980. *The Handbook of Nonsexist Writing For Writers, Editors, and Speakers*. New York: Lippencott & Crowell.

MILLER, Cheryl Regina. 1980. "Seven Letters." *Catalyst*, March, 5.

MILLER, Jean Baker. 1983. "The Necessity of Conflict." In *Women Changing Therapy: New Assessments, Values, and Strategies in Feminist Therapy*. Ed. Joan Hamerman Robbins and Rachel Josefowitz Siegel. New York: The Haworth Press, 3-9.

MILLETT, Kate. 1971. *Sexual Politics*. New York: Avon Books. Fourth Printing.

MILLETT, Kate. 1975. "The Shame is Over." *Ms.*, 3:7 (January), 26-9.

MILLS, Ernestine. 1919. "Mothers in Factories." *The Englishwoman*, 41:121 (January), 9-11.

MINAI, Naila. 1981. *Women in Islam: Tradition and Transition in the Middle East*. New York: Seaview Books.

MINCES, Juliette. 1982. *The House of Obedience: Women in Arab Society*. Trans. M. Pallis. London: Zed Press.

MINNICH, Elizabeth Kamarck. 1982. " 'Natural' and 'Unnatural' Woman." *Comment*, 13:2 (May), 1-2.

Minot Women's Collective. 1971. "Day by Day Women Will Unite" A calendar edited and designed by women. Minot, North Dakota.

MIRANDÉ, Alfredo and Evangelina Enríquez. 1979. *La Chicana: The Mexican-American Woman*. Chicago: University of Chicago Press.

MIRIAM, Selma. 1982a. "Anti-Semitism in the Lesbian Community: A Collage of

Mostly Bad News by One Jewish Dyke." *Sinister Wisdom*, 19, 50-60.

MIRIAM, Selma. 1982b. Letter. *Sinister Wisdom*, 21, 115-18.

MIRWALDT, Patricia. 1984. "Notions and Potions: Osteoporosis and Women." *HERizons*, 2:1 (April), 44.

"Miss World." 1972. Rpt. in *The Body Politic: Women's Liberation in Britain*. Ed. Michelene Wandor. London: stage 1, 1978, 249-60. Written by the women who took part in the demonstrations and were arrested.

"Miss Read" (pseud.), 1955. *Village School*. Rpt. London: Penguin, 1976.

MITCHELL, Juliet. 1966. "The Longest Revolution." Rpt. in *The Longest Revolution: On Feminism, Literature, and Psychoanalysis*. New York: Pantheon, 1984.

MITCHELL, Juliet. 1974. "On Freud and the Distinction Between the Sexes." In *Women and Analysis*. Ed. Jean Strouse. New York: Grossman, 27-36.

MITCHELL, Juliet. 1984. *The Longest Revolution: On Feminism, Literature, and Psychoanalysis*. New York: Pantheon.

MITCHELL, Juliet and Ann Oakley, eds. 1976. *The Rights and Wrongs of Women*. Harmondsworth, Middlesex: Penguin Books.

MITCHELL, Juliet and Jacqueline Rose, eds. 1982. *Feminine Sexuality: Jacques Lacan and the école freudienne*. Trans. Jacqueline Rose. New York: Norton, Pantheon.

MODLESKI, Tania. 1982. *Loving with a Vengeance: Mass Produced Fantasies for Women*. Hamden, Connecticut: Archon Books.

MOHANTY, Chandra Talpade. 1984. "Under Western Eyes: Feminist Discourse of Appropriation." Modern Language Association, Washington, D.C. December.

MOLLOY, Alice. c.1973. *In Other Words: Notes on the Politics and Morale of Survival*. Oakland: The Women's Press Collective.

MONCUR, Andrew. 1981. "Sexist Images are Cast Into Outer Darkness." *The Guardian*, 24 November.

MONEY, John and Anke A. Ehrhardt. 1972. *Man and Woman, Boy and Girl*. Baltimore: The Johns Hopkins University Press.

MONTINI, Graca Maria Aires. 1978. "O Homosexual Brasilero." Trans. Victor Harris. *Quest: A Feminist Quarterly*, 4:2 (Winter), 43-4.

MONTRELAY, Michèle. 1980. "The Story of Louise." In *Returning to Freud: Clinical Psychoanalysis in the School of Lacan*. Ed. and trans. Stuart Schneiderman. New Haven: Yale University Press, 75-93.

MONTROSS, Lynn and Lois Seyster Montross. 1923. *Town and Gown*. New York: George H. Doran.

MONTGOMERY, L. M. 1912. *Chronicles of Avonlea*. New York: Grosset & Dunlap.

MONTGOMERY, L. M. 1915. *Anne of the Island*. New York: Grosset & Dunlap.

MORAGA, Cherríe. 1981. "La Güera." In *This Bridge Called My Back: Writings by Radical Women of Color*. Ed. Cherríe Moraga and Gloria Anzaldúa. Watertown, Massachusetts: Persephone Press, 27-34.

MORAGA. Cherríe. 1983. *Loving in the War Years*. Boston: South End Press.

MORAGA, Cherríe and Gloria Anzaldúa, eds. 1981. *This Bridge Called My Back: Writings by Radical Women of Color*. Watertown, Massachusetts: Persephone Press.

MORAHAN, Shirley. 1981. *A Woman's Place: Rhetoric and Readings for Composing Yourself and Your Prose*. Albany, New York: State University of New York Press.

MORALES, Aurora Levins. 1981. ". . . And Even Fidel Can't Change That!" In *This Bridge Called My Back: Writings by Radical Women of Color*. Ed. Cherríe Moraga and Gloria Anzaldúa. Watertown, Massachusetts: Persephone Press, 53-7.

MORALES, Rosario. 1973. "Stop Leaving Women Out of the Proletariat." *Guardian*, 15 August. Rpt. in *Feminist Revolution*. Ed. Redstockings. New York: Random House, 1975, 199-201.

MORALES, Rosario. 1981. "We're All in the Same Boat." In *This Bridge Called My*

Back: Writings by Radical Women of Color. Ed. Cherríe Moraga and Gloria Anzaldúa. Watertown, Massachusetts: Persephone Press, 91-3.

MORALES, Rosario. 1982. "The Origins of Racism: A Story." *Heresies*, 4:3 (Issue 15), 1-5.

MORANTZ, Regina Markell, Cynthia Stodola Pomerleau, and Carol Hansen Fenichel, eds. 1982. *In Her Own Words: Oral Histories of Women Physicians.* Westport, Connecticut: Greenwood Press.

MOREAU, Noëlle Bisseret. 1984. "Power Relationships in Education." In *Language and Power.* Ed. Cheris Kramarae, Muriel Schulz, and William M. O'Barr. Beverly Hills, California: Sage.

MOREIRA, Ana Audilia. 1980. "Our National Inferiority Complex: A Cause for Violence?" In *Latin American Women: The Meek Speak Out.* Ed. June H. Turner. Silver Spring, Maryland: International Educational Development, 65-72.

MORGAN, Fidelis. 1981. *The Female Wits: Women Playwrights on the London Stage 1660-1720.* London: Virgo.

MORGAN, Robin, ed. 1970. *Sisterhood is Powerful.* New York: Vintage.

MORGAN, Robin. 1971. "Good-Bye To All That." In *Ain't I A Woman*, 25 September, 6-7.

MORGAN, Robin. 1978. *Going Too Far: The Personal Chronicle of a Feminist.* New York: Vintage.

MORGAN, Robin. 1982. *The Anatomy of Freedom: Feminism, Physics, and Global Politics.* Garden City, New York: Anchor Press/Doubleday.

MORISON, Stanley. 1932. *The English Newspaper, Some Account of the Physical Development of Journals Printed in London Between 1622 and the Present Day.* Cambridge, England: Cambridge University Press.

MORRIS, Meaghan. 1982. "A-Mazing Grace: Notes on Mary Daly's Poetics." *Intervention*, 16, 70-92.

MORRIS, Meaghan. 1984. "Identity Anecdotes." *Camera Obscura*, 12 (Summer), 41-65.

MORRIS, William, ed. 1969. *The American Heritage Dictionary of the English Language.* New York: American Heritage Publishing Company and Houghton Mifflin.

MORRIS, William and Mary Morris, eds. 1975. *Harper Dictionary of Contemporary Usage.* New York: Harper & Row.

MORRISON, Toni. 1970. *The Bluest Eye.* New York: Washington Square Press.

MORRISON, Toni. 1973. *Sula.* New York: New American Library.

MORRISON, Toni. 1981. *Tar Baby.* New York: New American Library.

MORTON, Nelle. n.d. "Toward a Whole Theology." Task Force on Women of the World Council of Churches. Typescript. Northwestern University Library, Evanston, Illinois.

MOSCHKOVICH, Judit. 1981. "– But I Know You, American Woman." In *This Bridge Called My Back: Writings by Radical Women of Color.* Ed. Cherríe Moraga and Gloria Anzaldúa. Watertown, Massachusetts: Persephone Press, 79-84.

MOULTON, Janice. 1981. "Sex and Reference." Rpt. in *Sexist Language: A Modern Philosophical Analysis.* Ed. Mary Vetterling-Braggin. Totowa, New Jersey: Littlefield, Adams.

MOULTON-BARRETT, Donalee. 1984. "Atlantic Women." *Fireweed, A Feminist Quarterly*, Winter/Spring, 8.

MOUNTAINWATER, Shekhinah. 1983. "Hallowe'en: Harmony with the Dead." *Matrix*, October, 5.

MOYES, Patricia. 1983. *A Six-Letter Word for Death.* New York: Holt, Rinehart & Winston.

MOZANS, H. J. (pseud.). 1913. "Woman's Long Struggle for Things of the Mind."

Introduction to *Woman in Science*. John Augustine Zahm. New York and London: D. Appleton and Company, 5.

Ms. 1973. "Ms. As A Form of Address." In *The First Ms. Reader*. Ed. Francine Klagsbrun. New York: Warner Books, 271-2.

MUHAMMAD, Zahrah. 1977. "Zahrah Muhammad, A Rural Woman of Morocco." Edited interview by Susan S. Davis. In *Middle Eastern Muslim Women Speak*. Ed. Elizabeth Warnock Fernea and Basima Qattan Bezirgan. Austin: University of Texas Press, 201-17.

MULFORD, Wendy. 1983. "Notes on Writing: A Marxist/Feminist Viewpoint." In *On Gender and Writing*. Ed. Michelene Wandor. London: Pandora Press, 31-41.

MÜLLER, Margarethe. 1908. *Carla Wenckelbach, Pioneer*. Boston and London: Ginn.

MULVEY, Laura. 1975. "Visual Pleasure and Narrative Cinema." *Screen*, 16:3, 6-18.

MURCOTT, Anne. 1983. " 'It's a pleasure to cook for him': Food, Mealtimes, and Gender in Some South Wales Households." In *The Public and the Private*. Ed. Eva Gamarnikow, David H. J. Morgan, June Purvis, and Daphne Taylorson. London: Heinemann, 78-90.

MURPHY, Gregory L. and Douglas L. Medin. In press. "The Role of Theories in Conceptual Coherence." *Psychology Review*.

MURPHY, Marilyn. 1983. "Califia Community." In *Learning Our Way*. Ed. Charlotte Bunch and Sandra Pollack. Trumansburg, New York: The Crossing Press, 138-53.

MURPHY, Yolanda and Robert Murphy. 1974. *Women of the Forest*. New York: Columbia University Press.

MURRAY, K. M. Elisabeth. 1977. *Caught in the Web of Words: James A. H. Murray and the Oxford English Dictionary*. Oxford: Oxford University Press, 1979.

NELSON, Sharon H. 1982. "Mad Women and Crazy Ladies." *Room of One's Own*, 7:1/2, 69-71.

NESTLE, Joan. 1981a. "Butch-Fem Relationships: Sexual Courage in the 1950's." *Heresies*, 3:4 (Issue 12), 21-4.

NESTLE, Joan. 1981b. "My Mother Liked to Fuck." In *Powers of Desires*. Ed. Ann Snitow, Christine Stansell, and Sharon Thompson. New York: Monthly Review Press, 1983, 468-70.

NEW YORK RADICAL FEMINISTS. 1969. "Politics of the Ego." In *Radical Feminism*. Ed. Anne Koedt, Ellen Levine, and Anita Rapone. New York: Quadrangle Books, 1973, 379-83.

NICHOLS, Patricia. 1976. "Black Women in the Rural South: Conservative and Innovative." In *The Sociology of the Languages of American Women*. Ed. Betty Lou Dubois and Isabel Crouch. Papers in Southwest English, 4. San Antonio: Trinity University Press, 103-14.

NICHOLS, Patricia. 1980. "Women in Their Speech Communities." In *Women and Language in Literature and Society*. Ed. Sally McConnell-Ginet, Ruth Borker, and Nelly Furman. New York: Praeger, 140-9.

NICHOLS, Patricia. 1984. "Networks and Hierarchies: Language and Social Stratification." In *Language and Power*. Ed. Cheris Kramarae, Muriel Schulz and William M. O'Barr. Beverly Hills, California: Sage.

NICKLES, Elizabeth with Laura Ashcraft. 1981. *The Coming Matriarchy*. New York: Seaview. Rpt. New York: Berkeley, 1982.

NIGHTINGALE, Florence. 1852, 1859. "Cassandra." In *The Cause: A Short History of the Women's Movement in Great Britain*. Ray Strachey. London: Virago, 1978.

NILSEN, Alleen Pace. 1977. "Sexism as Shown Through the English Vocabulary." In *Sexism and Language*. Ed. Alleen Pace Nilsen, Haig Bosmajian, H. Lee Gershuny, and Julia P. Stanley. Urbana, Illinois: National Council of Teachers of English, 27-41.

NILSEN, Alleen Pace, Haig Bosmajian, H. Lee Gershuny, and Julia P. Stanley, eds. 1977. *Sexism and Language*. Urbana, Illinois: National Council of Teachers of English.

NITTI, John J. 1978. "Computers and the Old Spanish Dictionary." *Computers in the Humanities*, 12, 43-52.

NOMADIC SISTERS. 1976. *Loving Women*. 2nd edition. Saratoga, California: Nomadic Sisters.

NORMAN, Howard A. 1976. *The Wishing Bone Cycle: Narrative Poems from the Swampy Creek Indians*. New York: Stonehill.

NOYES, Clara D. 1931. "Sub-Professionals – What Are They?" *Independent Woman*, 10:3 (March), 142, 144.

OAKLEY, Ann. 1976. *Women's Work: The Housewife, Past and Present*. New York: Random House, Vintage.

OAKLEY, Ann. 1982. *Subject Woman*. Glasgow: Fontana.

OATES, Joyce Carol. 1970a. *The Wheel of Love and Other Stories*. New York: Vanguard.

OATES, Joyce Carol. 1970b. "What is the Connection Between Men and Women?" *Mademoiselle*, February. Quoted in *The Quotable Woman*. Ed. Elaine Partnow. Vol. II. Los Angeles: Pinnacle Books, 1977, 425.

O'BRIEN, Mary. 1981. *The Politics of Reproduction*. London: Routledge & Kegan Paul.

OCHS, Carol. 1979. *Behind the Sex of God*. New York: Beacon/Harper & Row.

OCHSHORN, Judith. 1981. *The Female Experience and the Nature of the Divine*. Bloomington, Indiana: Indiana University Press..

O'DAIR, Barbara. 1983. "Sex, Love, Desire: Feminists Strugggle Over the Portrayal of Sex." *Alternative Media*, Spring, 12-17.

O'FAOLAIN, Julia. 1983. "Sean at Eighty." In *Fathers: Reflections by Daughters*. Ed. Ursula Owen. London: Virago Press, 120-31.

OKELY, Judith. 1978. " Privileged, Schooled, and Finished: Boarding Education for Girls." In *Defining Females: The Nature of Women in Society*. Ed. Shirley Ardener. New York: John Wiley.

O'LAURA, Eileen. c.1978. "The Circle Is . . ." *Wicca: 'Wise Woman' Irish Feminist Magazine*, 3-4.

OLMOS, Margarite Fernandez. 1982. "Sex, Color, and Class in Contemporary Puerto Rican Women Authors." *Heresies*, 4:3 (Issue 15), 46-7.

OLSEN, Tillie. 1979. *Silences*. New York: Delta.

ONIONS, C. T., ed. 1967. *The Oxford Dictionary of English Etymology*. New York: Oxford University Press.

ONO, Yoko. 1967. "On Film No. 4." In *Grapefruit*. Quoted in *The Quotable Woman*. Ed. Elaine Partnow. Vol. II. Los Angeles: Pinnacle Books, 1977, 370.

ORDWAY, Jane. 1982. "Ain't I A Feminist?" *Maenad*, 2:2 (Winter), 14-22.

O'REILLY, Jane. 1972. "The Housewife's Moment of Truth." *Ms.*, Spring. Rpt. in *The First Ms. Reader*. Ed. Francine Klagsbrun. New York: Warner Books, 1973, 11-22.

O'REILLY, Jane. 1976. "Do We Need a Divorce Ceremony?" *Ms.*, 4:7 (January), 38-40.

O'REILLY, Jane. 1977. "Clunk!" *Ms.*, 6:1 (July), 66-7.

ORR, Chris. 1983. "Moms and Whoopi: Pioneers of Black Theater." *Plexus*, November, 15.

ORWELL, George. 1949. *Nineteen Eighty-Four*. New York: Signet, 1971.

OSLER, Catherine C. 1913. "Tethered." *The Englishwoman*, 13:55 (July), 51-5.

OSMAN, Sona. 1983. "A to Z of Feminism." *Spare Rib*, November, 27-30. With help from Ruth Wallsgrove, Sue O'Sullivan, and Alice Henry.

OSTRIKER, Alicia. 1982. "The Thieves of Language: Women Poets and Revisionist Mythmaking." *Signs*, 8:1, 68-90.

OUGHTON, Libby. 1984. "And We Bleed...." *Fireweed, A Feminist Quarterly*, Winter/Spring, 38.

OVERFIELD, Kathy. 1979. Abstract. Feminist Summer School Program, September. WRRC and University of Bradford Women's Group.

OWEN, Ursula. 1983. Introduction to *Fathers: Reflections by Daughters*. Ed. Ursula Owen. London: Virago Press, 9-14.

Oxford English Dictionary. 1971. Ed. J. M. Murray. Compact ed. Originally published 1874-1928. Oxford: Oxford University Press.

OZICK, Cynthia. 1972a. "We are the Crazy Lady and Other Feisty Feminist Fables." *Ms.*, Spring. Rpt. in *The First Ms. Reader*. Ed. Francine Klagsbrun. New York: Warner Books, 1973, 60-72.

OZICK, Cynthia. 1972b. "The Hole/Birth Catalog." *Ms.*, October. Rpt. in *The First Ms. Reader*. Ed. Francine Klagsbrun. New York: Warner Books, 1973, 150-61.

OZICK, Cynthia. 1983. *Art and Ardor: Essays*. New York: E. P. Dutton. Rpt. Dutton Obelisk, 1984.

PACKWOOD, Marlene. 1983. "The Colonel's Lady and Judy O'Grady – Sisters Under the Skin?" *Trouble and Strife*, 1 (Winter), 7-12.

PALLISER, Edith. 1914. "Martial Heroines." *The Englishwoman*, 23:69, 273-8.

PALMER, Cynthia and Michael Horowitz, eds. 1982. *Shaman Lady, Mainline Lady: Women's Writings on the Drug Experience*. New York: Quill.

PALMER, Frank. 1971. *Grammar*. Baltimore: Penguin.

PANKHURST, Christabel. 1913. "The Government and White Slavery." Pamphlet. Rpt. in *The Suffragette*, 18 April & 25 April, 7-11. Quoted in *Female Sexual Slavery*. Kathleen Barry. New York: Avon, 1979, 36, 37.

PANKHURST, Emmeline. 1914. *My Own Story*. London: Eveleigh Nash.

PAPER, Jordan. 1983. "The Forgotten Grandmothers: Amerindian Women and Religion in Colonized North America." *Canadian Woman Studies/les cahiers de la femme*, 5:2 (Winter), 48-51.

PARKER, Dorothy. 1973. *The Portable Dorothy Parker*. New York: Viking.

PARKER, Pat. 1982. "For the White Person Who Wants to Know How to be My Friend." *Heresies*, 4:3 (Issue 15), 59.

PARKER, Rosie. 1982. Book Review. *Spare Rib*, 124 (October), 46.

PARKER, Rozsika and Griselda Pollock. 1981. *Old Mistresses: Women, Art, and Ideology*. New York: Pantheon. Orig. London: Routledge & Kegan Paul.

PARKER, Rozsika. 1983. "Art, Feminism, and Criticism." In *On Gender and Writing*. Ed. Michelene Wandor. London: Pandora Press, 87-95.

PARKS, Joy. 1984. "Sinister Wisdom: A Chronicle." *The Women's Review of Books*, 1:5 (February), 14-15.

PARSONS, Elsie Clews. 1913a. *The Old-Fashioned Woman: Primitive Fancies About the Sex*. New York: Putnam's.

PARSONS, Elsie Clews [published under the pseudonym John Main]. 1913b. *Religious Chastity: An Ethnological Study*. New York: Macaulay.

PARTNOW, Elaine, compiler and editor. 1977. *The Quotable Woman*. Volumes One and Two. Los Angeles, California: Pinnacle Books.

PARTRIDGE, Eric. 1959. *Origins: A Short Etymological Dictionary of Modern English*. New York: Macmillan.

PARTRIDGE, Eric. 1961. *A Dictionary of Slang and Unconventional English*. New York: Macmillan; London: Routledge & Kegan Paul. Revised and edited by Paul Beale, 1984.

PARTURIER, Françoise. 1968. From *Lettre ouverte aux hommes* [An open letter to men]. Albin Michel. In *New French Feminisms*. Trans. Elissa Gelfand. Ed. Elaine Marks and Isabelle de Courtivron. New York: Schocken, 1981, 59-63.

PASTAN, Linda. 1978. *The Five Stages of Grief.* New York: W. W. Norton.

PASTERNAK, Judith. 1983. "The Strangest Bedfellows: Lesbian-feminism and the Sexual Revolution." *Womanews*, 4:9 (October), 5.

PATTERSON, Janet. 1981. "Consuming Passion." *Fireweed*, 11, 19-33.

PAXTON, Susan. 1982. *Burning Times: A Study of Witchhunting.* London: Community Press.

PAYNE, Karen. 1983. *Between Ourselves: Letters Between Mothers and Daughters.* Boston: Houghton Mifflin.

PAZ, Juana María. 1982. "Statement to the Racism Workshop." *Heresies*, 4:3 (Issue 15), 64-5.

PEARSON, Karl. 1897. *The Chances of Death and Other Studies in Evolution.* London: Edward Arnold.

PEDRAZA, Pedro, Jr., John Attinasi, and Gerald Hoffman. 1980. *Rethinking Diglossia.* New York: Research Foundation of the City University of New York.

PENELOPE, Julia. 1978. "Language Change/Social Change: Systems and Power." *Iowa English Bulletin*, Spring, 5-9.

PENELOPE, Julia. 1979. "The Articulation of Bias: Hoof in Mouth Disease." National Council of Teachers of English, San Francisco. November.

PENELOPE, Julia. 1980. *The Articulation of Bias: Hoof in Mouth.* ERIC ED 179 998.

PENELOPE, Julia [Stanley]. 1981a. "John Simon and the 'Dragons of Eden.' " Manuscript. College Composition and Communication Conference, Minneapolis. April.

PENELOPE, Julia [Stanley]. 1981b. "Power and the Opposition to Feminist Proposals for Language Change; or, What Can We Learn from This?" English Department, University of Nebraska.

PENELOPE, Julia. 1983. "Syntactic Euphemism." *Quarterly Review of Doublespeak.*

PENELOPE, Julia and Cynthia McGowan. 1979. "*Woman* and *Wife*: Social/Semantic Shifts in English." Kentucky Foreign Language Conference. April.

PENELOPE (Stanley), Julia and Susan J. Wolfe. 1983. "Consciousness as Style: Style as Aesthetic." In *Language, Gender, and Society.* Ed. Barrie Thorne, Cheris Kramarae, and Nancy Henley. Rowley, Massachusetts: Newbury House, 125-39.

PENLEY, Constance. In press. "Teaching in Your Sleep: Feminism and Psychoanalysis." In *Theory in the Classroom.* Ed. Cary Nelson. Urbana: University of Illinois Press.

PERENYI, Eleanor. 1983. "Gertrude Jekyll, Garden Reformer." *New York Times*, 14 July.

PERRY, Suzanne C. 1983. "Sexual Harassment on the Campuses: Deciding Where to Draw the Line." *Chronicle of Higher Education*, 23 March, 21-2.

PETCHESKY, Rosalind. 1979. "Dissolving the Hyphen: A Report on Marxist-Feminist Groups 1-5." In *Capitalist Patriarchy and the Case for Socialist Feminism.* Ed. Zillah R. Eisenstein. New York and London: Monthly Review Press, 373-90.

PETERS, Barbara and Victoria Samuels, eds. 1976. *Dialogue on Diversity: A New Agenda for American Women.* New York: Institute on Pluralism and Group Identity of the American Jewish Committee.

PETERSEN, Karen and J. J. Wilson. 1976. *Women Artists: Recognition and Reappraisal from the Early Middle Ages to the Twentieth Century.* New York: New York University Press.

PETERSON, Virgilia. 1961. *A Matter of Life and Death.* Quoted in *The Quotable Woman.* Ed. Elaine Partnow. Vol. III. Los Angeles: Pinnacle Books, 1977, 66.

PETHICK-LAWRENCE, Lady. 1951. "Greetings." *Calling All Women*, February, 2.

PHELPS, Linda. 1975. "Patriarchy and Capitalism." Rpt. in *Building Feminist Theory: Essays from Quest.* Ed. The Quest Staff. New York: Longman, 1981, 161-73.

PHILIP, Marlene I. 1983. "The Absence of Writing or How I Almost Became a Spy." *Fireweed*, 17 (October), 20-6.

PHILLIPS, Angela. 1983. "Two Steps Forward, One Step Back?" In *On Gender and Writing*. Ed. Michelene Wandor. London: Pandora Press, 119-25.

PHILLIPS, John A. 1984. *Eve: The History of An Idea*. San Francisco: Harper & Row.

PHILLIPS, Mary T. C. 1971. Editorial. *Broadside*, 1:1 (October).

PHIPPS, Emily. 1919. "Impressions of the General Election." *The Englishwoman*, 41:121, 18-20.

PICKERING, Sidney. 1912. "Women and the Average Englishman." *The English-woman*, 16:48 (December), 293-303.

PIERCY, Marge. 1969. "The Grand Coolie Dam." *Leviathan*. Rpt. in *Sisterhood Is Powerful*. Ed. Robin Morgan. New York: Random House/Vintage, 1970, 421-38.

PIERCY, Marge. 1973. "A Shadow Play for Guilt." In *To Be Of Use*. Garden City, New York: Doubleday.

PIERCY, Marge. 1976. *Woman on the Edge of Time*. New York: Ballantine, 1983.

PIERCY, Marge. 1982. "For the Furies." *13th Moon*, 4:1/2, 7.

PIERCY, Marge. 1983. "Listening to a Speech." *13th Moon*, 7:1/2, 119.

PINDELL, Howardena. 1979. "Criticism/or/Between the Lines." *Heresies*, 2:4 (Issue 8), 2-4.

PING, Yang. 1973. *Fragment from a Lost Diary and Other Stories*. Quoted in *The Quotable Woman*. Ed. Elaine Partnow. Vol. II. Los Angeles: Pinnacle Books, 1977, 132.

PIÑON, Nélida. 1982. "La Contaminación de la Lenguaje." Interview by Catherine Tinker. *13th Moon*, 6:1/2, 71-5.

PITT, Zoe. 1980. "Secretarial Studies." *Women and Education*, 20 (Autumn), 25.

PLATH, Sylvia. 1952. "Stone Boy With Dolphin." In *Johnny Panic and the Bible of Dreams: Short Stories, Prose, and Diary Excerpts*. New York: Harper & Row, 1980, 173-95.

PLATH, Sylvia. 1981. *The Collected Poems*. Ed. Ted Hughes. New York: Harper & Row.

PLAZA, Monique. 1982. "The Mother/The Same: Hatred of the Mother in Psychoanalysis." *Feminist Issues*, 2:1, 75-100.

POGREBIN, Letty Cottin. 1981. Statement in "AF Symposium on Women and the Future." *Alternative Futures*, 4:2/3 (Spring/Summer), 157-83.

POGREBIN, Letty Cottin. 1983a. "One Traditional Role of Women is to Tote Things Around." *Chicago Tribune*, 15 September, 18Y.

POGREBIN, Letty Cottin. 1983b. "The Power of Beauty." *Ms.*, December, 73, 75, 76, 78, 109.

POLLAY, Richard W. 1984. "The Languishing of 'Lydiametrics': The Ineffectiveness of Econometric Research on Advertising Effects." *Journal of Communication*, 34:2 (Spring), 8-23.

POTEET, Lewis J. 1983. *The South Shore* [of Nova Scotia] *Phrase Book*. Hansport: Lancelot Press.

POTTS, Billie and River Lightwomoon. 1983. Brochure. Hecuba's Daughters.

POWELL, Linda C. 1983. "Black Macho and Feminism." In *Home Girls*. Ed. Barbara Smith. New York: Kitchen Table Press, 283-92.

POWELL, Mary Clare. 1981. *The Widow*. Washington, D.C.: Anaconda Press.

PRAGER, Emily. 1983. *A Visit from the Footbinder*. London: Chatto & Windus/The Hogarth Press.

PRITCHARD, Jack A. and Paul C. MacDonald. 1976, 1980. *Williams' Obstetrics*. New York: Appleton-Century-Crofts.

"Problems of the Day." 1913. *The Englishwoman*, 18:53 (May), 128-36.

PTASHKINA, Nelly. 1918. *The Diary of Nelly Ptashkina*. Quoted in *The Quotable Woman*. Ed. Elaine Partnow. Vol. II. Los Angeles: Pinnacle Books, 1977, 57.

PUTNAM, Emily James. 1910. *The Lady: Studies of Certain Significant Phases of Her History*. Rpt. Chicago, Illinois: University of Chicago Press, 1969.

PUTNAM, Hilary 1973. "Meaning and Reference." *Journal of Philosophy*, 70, 669-711.

PYM, Barbara. 1952. *Excellent Women*. Rpt. New York: Harper/Perennial, 1980.

PYM, Barbara. 1980. *A Few Green Leaves*. New York: Harper & Row/Perennial.

PYM, Barbara. 1982. *An Unsuitable Attachment*. New York: Harper & Row/Perennial.

Quest Staff, ed. 1981. *Building Feminist Theory, Essays from Quest*. New York and London: Longman.

Quiet Rumours: An Anarcha-Feminist Anthology. c.1983. London: Dark Star.

QUINN, Naomi. 1984. "American Marriage and the Folk Social Psychology of Need Fulfillment." Manuscript. Duke University and Institute for Advanced Study.

RACZ, Elizabeth. 1952. "The Women's Rights Movement in the French Revolution." *Science and Society*, 16:1 (Spring). Northwestern University Library, Evanston, Illinois.

Radical Feminists. 1972. "Thoughts on Feminism." London. Northwestern University Library, Evanston, Illinois.

RADICALESBIANS. 1970. *The Woman Identified Woman*. Pittsburgh, Pennsylvania: KNOW, Inc. Also in *Radical Feminism*. Ed. Anne Koedt, Ellen Levine, and Anita Rapone. New York: Quadrangle/New York Times, 1973, 240-5.

rae, arachne. 1981. "open letter to disabled lesbians." *off our backs*, May, 39.

RAHMAN, Shahana. 1984. "No End to Femicides." *Depthnews Women's*, 29 January. Rpt. in *Committee on South Asian Women Bulletin*, 2:2 (Spring), 7.

RAICHO, Hiratsuka. 1911. Declaration in *Seito* (Blue Stocking) Magazine. Reported by Yoko Akiyama in the International Socialist Review, March, 1974. Rpt. in *Feminist Revolution*. Ed. Kathie Sarachild. New York: Random House, 1975, 55.

RAKUSEN, Jill. 1982. "Feminism and the Politics of Health." *Medicine in Society*, 8:1, 17-25.

RAMIREZ, Judith. 1979. "Immigrant Domestics: Modern Day Slaves." *Wages for Housework Campaign Bulletin*, 4:2 (Winter), 1.

RANDALL, Margaret. 1974. *Cuban Women Now*. Toronto, Canada: The Women's Press/Dumont Press.

Random House Dictionary of the English Language. 1967. Ed. Jess Stein. New York: Random House.

RAT. 1970. "Out Of The Frying Pan And Into The Fire." *RAT*, 29 October-18 November, 17, 26.

RAT. 1971. "New Haven Women's Liberation Band." *RAT*, 3 May-1 June, 9.

RAVEN, Arlene. 1973. "Women's Art: The Development of a Theoretical Perspective." *Womanspace*, February/March. Quoted in *The Quotable Woman*. Ed. Elaine Partnow. Vol. II. Los Angeles: Pinnacle Books, 1977, 485.

RAYMOND, Janice G. 1979. *The Transsexual Empire: The Making of the She-Male*. Boston: Beacon Press.

RAYMOND, Janice G. 1982. "A Genealogy of Female Friendship." *Trivia*, 1:1 (Fall), 5-26.

RAYMOND, Jill and Janice Wilson. 1983. "Feminism – Healing the Patriarchal Disease." In *Reclaim the Earth: Women Speak Out for Life on Earth*. Ed. Léonie Caldecott and Stephanie Leland. London: The Women's Press, 59-65.

REAGON, Bernice Johnson. 1983. "Coalition Politics: Turning the Century." In *Home Girls: A Black Feminist Anthology*. Ed. Barbara Smith. New York: Kitchen Table: Women of Color Press, 356-69.

REAGON, Bernice. 1984. "We Are 'Girl,' 'Chile,' 'Lady,' That 'oman,' 'Hussy,' 'Heifer,' 'a Woman'; or, Naming That Imprisons and Naming That Sets You Free." Modern Language Association, Washington, D.C. December.

REBOLLEDO, Tey Diana. In press. "The Maturing of Chicana Poetry: The Quiet Revolution of the 1980s." In *For Alma Mater: Theory and Practice in Feminist Scholarship*. Ed. Paula A. Treichler, Cheris Kramarae, and Beth Stafford. Urbana: University of Illinois Press.

RED, Ida VSW. 1981. "Naming." In *The Lesbian Path*. Ed. Margaret Cruikshank. Tallahassee, Florida: The Naiad Press, 63-71.

REDEL, Vistoria. 1981. "For Chou Chin Ti." *The Second Wave*, 6:1, 12.

REDMOND, Donna. 1973. Interview. In *Hillbilly Women*. Kathy Kahn. New York: Doubleday, 1983.

Redstockings Manifesto. 1970. In *Sisterhood is Powerful*. Ed. Robin Morgan. New York: Vintage, 533-5.

Redstockings of the Women's Liberation Movement, eds. 1975. *Feminist Revolution*. New York: Random House.

Redstockings Sister. c.1969. "Brainwashing and Women." Mimeograph. Northwestern University Library, Evanston, Illinois.

REED, Helen Leah. 1891. *The Homemaker*, 5:4, 342.

REES, Nancy. 1982. "Battered Women." *The Blatant Image*, No. 2, 25.

RENNIE, Susan and Kirsten Grimstad. 1975. *The New Woman's Survival Sourcebook*. New York: Alfred A. Knopf.

RICH, Adrienne. 1974. "The Fact of a Doorframe." In *Adrienne Rich Poems: Selected and New, 1950-1974*. New York: W. W. Norton, 231-2.

RICH, Adrienne. 1976. *Of Woman Born: Motherhood as Experience and Institution*. New York: W. W. Norton.

RICH, Adrienne. 1977a. From "Natural Resources." In *The Dream of a Common Language (Poems 1974-1977)*. New York: W. W. Norton, 1978, 60-7.

RICH, Adrienne. 1977b. From "Transcendental Etude." In *The Dream of a Common Language (Poems 1974-1977)*. New York: W. W. Norton, 1978, 72-7.

RICH, Adrienne. 1979. *On Lies, Secrets, and Silence: Selected Prose 1966-1978*. New York: W. W. Norton.

RICH, Adrienne. 1980. "Compulsory Heterosexuality and Lesbian Existence." *Signs*, 5:4 (Summer), 631-60.

RICH, Adrienne. 1981a. "Disobedience is What NWSA is Potentially About." *Women's Studies Quarterly*, 9:3 (Fall), 4-6.

RICH, Adrienne. 1981b. "Notes for a Magazine: What Does Separatism Mean?" *Sinister Wisdom*, 18 (Fall), 83-91.

RICH, Adrienne. 1983. "Split at the Root." In *Fathers: Reflections by Daughters*. Ed. Ursula Owen. London: Virago Press, 170-86.

RICH, B. Ruby. 1980. "In the Name of Feminist Film Criticism." *Heresies*, 3:1 (Issue 9), 75-81.

RICHARDSON, Dorothy. 1905. *The Long Day: The Story of a New York Working Girl*. Rpt. Chicago: Quadrangle, 1972.

RICHON, Oliver. 1983. "Orientation." *Screen*, 24:2 (April), 81-9.

RIDDLE, Dorothy. 1981. "Politics, Spirituality, and Models of Change." In *The Politics of Women's Spirituality*. Ed. Charlene Spretnak. Garden City, New York: Anchor Press/Doubleday, 1982, 371-85.

RIVERS, Caryl. 1977. "Egalitarian Marriage: No More Ring Around the Collar." *Mother Jones*, November, 40-1.

ROACH, Dusty. 1979. *Patti Smith, Rock and Roll Madonna*. South Bend, Indiana: and books.

ROBERTS, Helen. 1981. "Male Hegemony in Family Planning." In *Women, Health, and Reproduction*. Ed. Helen Roberts. London: Routledge & Kegan Paul, 1-17.

ROBERTS, Helen, ed. 1981. *Women, Health, and Reproduction*. London: Routledge &

Kegan Paul.

ROBERTS, Katherine. 1910. *Pages From the Diary of a Militant Suffragette.* Letchworth and London: Garden City Press.

ROBERTS, Michele. 1983. "Questions and Answers." In *On Gender and Writing.* Ed. Michelene Wandor. London: Pandora Press, 62-8.

ROBERTSON, Jane. 1983. "Menopause." *Spare Rib,* 127 (February), 50-5.

ROBERTSON, Priscilla. 1982. *An Experience of Women.* Philadelphia, Pennsylvania: Temple University Press.

ROBINS, Elizabeth. 1907. *The Convert.* Introd. Jane Marcus. Rpt. London and New York: The Women's Press and The Feminist Press.

ROBINS, Elizabeth. 1913. *Way Stations.* London: Hodder & Stoughton.

ROBINS, Elizabeth [Anonymous]. 1924. *Ancilla's Share.* London: Hutchinson.

ROBINSON, Cedric. 1981. "Coming to Terms: The Third World and the Dialectic of Imperialism." *Race and Class,* 22:4, 363-86.

ROBINSON, Lillian. 1978. *Sex, Class, and Culture.* Bloomington: Indiana University Press.

ROBINSON, Marilynne. 1981. *Housekeeping.* New York: Bantam.

ROBINSON, Pat and Group. 1969. "A Historical and Critical Essay for Black Women in the Cities, June 1969." In *The Black Woman: An Anthology.* Ed. Toni Cade. New York: New American Library, 1970, 198-210.

ROBINSON, Paul. 1984. "Reanalyzing Anna a Century After the Talking Cure." *Psychology Today.* 18:6 (June), 8-9.

ROGERS, Katharine M. 1982. *Feminism in Eighteenth-Century England.* Urbana, Illinois: University of Illinois Press.

ROGERS, Lesley J. 1981. "Biology: Gender Differentiation and Sexual Variation." In *Australian Women: Feminist Perspectives.* Ed. Norma Grieve and Patricia Grimshaw. Melbourne: Oxford University Press, 44-57.

ROGERS, Lesley J. 1983. "Hormonal Theories for Sex Differences – Politics Disguised as Science." *Sex Roles,* 9:11, 1109-13.

ROGERS, Susan G. 1980. "Anti-Colonial Protest in Africa: A Female Strategy Reconsidered." *Heresies,* 3:1 (Issue 9), 22-5.

ROHRBAUGH, Joanna Bunker. 1979. *Women: Psychology's Puzzle.* New York: Basic Books.

ROMALIS, Shelly ed. 1981. *Childbirth: Alternatives to Medical Control.* Austin, Texas: University of Texas Press.

ROOT, Jane. 1983. "Harriet Harman: A Victory for Us All?" *Honey,* March, 74-5.

ROSALDO, Michelle Zimbalist and Louise Lamphere, eds. 1974. *Woman, Culture, and Society.* Stanford, California: Stanford University Press.

ROSE, Hilary. 1983. "Hand, Brain, and Heart: A Feminist Epistemology for the Natural Sciences." *Signs: Journal of Women in Culture and Society,* 9:1 (Autumn), 73-90.

ROSE, Jacqueline. 1983. "Femininity and its Discontents." *Feminist Review,* 14 (Summer), 5-21.

ROSEN, Ruth. 1982. *The Lost Sisterhood: Prostitution in America 1900-1918.* Baltimore: Johns Hopkins.

ROSENBERG, Carroll Smith. 1972. "The Hysterical Woman: Sex Roles and Conflict in Nineteenth-Century America." *Social Research,* 39, 652-78.

ROSENFELD, Deborah S. 1982. "The Politics of Bibliography: Women's Studies and the Literary Canon." In *Women in Print I: Opportunities for Women's Studies Research in Language and Literature.* Ed. Joan E. Hartman and Ellen Messer-Davidow. New York: Modern Language Association, 11-35.

ROSENFELD, Rita. 1979. "Apocrypha." *Room of One's Own,* 4:3, 66-7.

ROSS, Alan S. C. and Nancy Mitford. 1956. "U and Non-U." In *Noblesse Oblige.* Ed.

Nancy Mitford. New York: Harper.

ROSSI, Alice, ed. 1973. *The Feminist Papers: From Adams to de Beauvoir*. New York: Bantam.

ROSTEN, Leo. 1968. *The Joys of Yiddish*. New York: Pocket Books.

ROSZAK, Betty and Theordore Roszak, eds. 1969. *Masculine/Feminine: Readings in Sexual Mythology and the Liberation of Women*. New York: Harper & Row.

ROTHSCHILD, Joan. 1984. "The Goddess and the Machine: The Impact of Feminist Perspectives on Technology." *Revisions* [Office of Women's Studies Newsletter, University of Illinois at Urbana-Champaign], 2:1, 3.

ROWBOTHAM, Sheila. 1972. *Women, Resistance and Revolution*. New York: Pantheon Books.

ROWBOTHAM, Sheila. 1973a. *Woman's Consciousness, Man's World*. New York: Penguin.

ROWBOTHAM, Sheila. 1973b. "Women's Liberation and the New Politics." In *The Body Politic: Writings from the Women's Liberation Movement in Britain 1969-72*. Ed. Michelene Wandor. London: stage 1.

ROWBOTHAM, Sheila. 1979. "The Trouble with 'Patriarchy.'" *New Statesman*, 28 December. Rpt. in *No Turning Back: Writings from the Women's Liberation Movement 1975-80*. Ed. Feminist Anthology Collective. London: The Women's Press, 1981, 72-8.

ROWBOTHAM, Sheila. 1983. *Dreams and Dilemmas*. London: Virago.

ROWE, Marsha, ed. 1982. *Spare Rib Reader*. Harmondsworth, Middlesex: Penguin Books.

ROWLAND, Beryl, ed. 1981. *Medieval Woman's Guide to Health: The First English Gynecological Handbook*. Middle English Text with English Translation. Kent, Ohio: Kent State University Press.

ROWLAND, Robyn. 1982. "Women's Studies Courses: Pragmatic and Political Issues Concerning Their Establishment and Design." *Women's Studies International Forum*, 5:5, 487-96.

RUBIN, Gayle. 1975. "The Traffic in Women: Notes on the 'Political Economy' of Sex." In *Toward An Anthropology of Women*. Ed. Rayna R. Reiter. New York: Monthly Review Press, 157-210.

RUBIN, Gayle. 1981. "The Leather Menace: Comments on Politics and S/M." In *Coming to Power: Writings and Graphics on Lesbian S/M*. Ed. SAMOIS, a lesbian/feminist S/M organization. Boston: Alyson Publications, 1982, 192-227.

RUBIN, Lillian Breslow. 1976. *World of Pain: Life in the Working-class Family*. New York: Basic Books.

RUDDER, Joan. 1982. "All you ever wanted to know about Mary Daly but never dared to ask . . ." *Women's Voice*, 63 (May), 12-13.

RUDDICK, Sara. 1980. In *Why Children?* Ed. Stephanie Dowrick and Sibyl Grundberg. London: The Women's Press, 251-71.

RUETHER, Rosemary Radford, ed. 1974. *Religion and Sexism*. New York: Simon & Schuster.

RUKEYSER, Muriel. 1974. Preface to *The World Split Open: Four Centuries of Women Poets in England and America, 1552-1950*. Ed. Louise Bernikow. New York: Random House.

RUSH, Anne Kent and Anica Vesel Mander. 1974. *Feminism as Therapy*. New York: Random House.

RUSH, Florence. 1980a. "Child Pornography." In *Take Back the Night*. Ed. Laura Lederer. New York: William Morrow, 71-81.

RUSH, Florence. 1980b. *The Best Kept Secret: The Sexual Abuse of Children*. Englewood Cliffs, New Jersey: Prentice Hall.

RUSHIN, Donna Kate. 1981. "The Bridge Poem." In *This Bridge Called My Back:*

Writings by Radical Women of Color. Ed. Cherríe Moraga and Gloria Anzaldúa. Watertown, Massachusetts: Persephone Press, xxi-xxii.

RUSHTON, Peter. 1983. "Purification or Social Control? Ideologies of Reproduction and the Churching of Women After Childbirth." In *The Public and the Private.* Ed. Eva Gamarnikow, David H. J. Morgan, June Purvis, and Daphne Taylorson. London: Heinemann, 118-31.

RUSS, Joanna. 1974. "Dear Colleague: I Am Not An Honorary Male." *Colloquy,* 7:4 (April), 40-3. Rpt. Pittsburgh: KNOW, Inc. Also in *Pulling Our Own Strings: Feminist Humor and Satire.* Ed. Gloria Kaufman and Mary Kay Blakely. Bloomington: Indiana University Press, 1980, 179-83.

RUSS, Joanna. 1979. Review of *Gyn/Ecology: The Metaethics of Radical Feminism,* by Mary Daly. *Frontiers: A Journal of Women's Studies,* 4:1, 68-70.

RUSS, Joanna. 1981. "Recent Feminist Utopias." In *Future Females: A Critical Anthology.* Ed. Marleen S. Barr. Bowling Green, Ohio: Bowling Green State University Popular Press, 71-85.

RUSS, Joanna. 1982. "Being Against Pornography." *13th Moon,* 6:1/2, 55-61.

RUSS, Joanna. 1983. *How To Suppress Women's Writing.* Austin: University of Texas.

RUSSELL, Dawn. 1979. "Black Women and Work: My Experiences." *Heresies,* 2:4 (Issue 8), 72-5.

RUSSELL, Diana E. H. and Nicole Van de Ven, comp. and eds. 1984. *Crimes Against Women: Proceedings of the International Tribunal.* East Palo Alto, California: Frog in the Well.

RUSSELL, Dora. 1983. *The Religion of the Machine Age.* London: Routledge & Kegan Paul.

RUSSELL, Michele. 1979. "Black Eyed Blues Connections: From the Inside Out." *Heresies,* 2:4 (Issue 8), 99-105.

RUTENBERG, Taly. 1983. "Learning Women's Studies." In *Theories of Women's Studies.* Ed. Gloria Bowles and Renate Duelli Klein. London: Routledge & Kegan Paul, 72-8.

RUTH, Sheila. 1980. *Issues in Feminism: A First Course in Women's Studies.* Boston: Houghton Mifflin Company.

RUTH, Sheila. 1983. "A Feminist Analysis of the New Right." *Women's Studies International Forum,* 6:4, 345-51.

SAADAWI, Nawal el. 1980a. Interview. *Newsfront International,* October. Excerpted in *Connexions,* 1 May, 1981, 3.

SAADAWI, Nawal el. 1980b. *The Hidden Face of Eve: Women in the Arab World.* Trans. and ed. Dr. Sherif Hetata. London: Zed Press.

SAADAWI, Nawal el. 1982. *The Hidden Face of Eve.* Boston: Beacon.

SACKS, Karen. 1982. *Sisters and Wives: The Past and Future of Sexual Equality.* Urbana, Illinois: University of Illinois Press.

SAFIRE, William. 1980. *On Language.* New York: Avon.

ST JAMES, Margo. 1980. "What's a Girl Like You . . . ?" In *Prostitutes – Our Life.* Ed. Claude Jaget. Bristol: Falling Wall Press, 189-201. First published in France as *Une Vie de putain.* Les Presses d'aujourd'hui, 1975.

ST JOAN, Jackie. 1975. "The Ideas and the Realities: Sagaris, Session I." Rpt. in *Learning Our Way.* Ed. Charlotte Bunch and Sandra Pollack. Trumansburg, New York: The Crossing Press, 1983, 116-28. Originally appeared as "First Session Sagaris: What Happened" and "Sagaris: The End of a Love Affair." *Big Mama Rag,* IIIA:7.

ST JOHN, Christopher. 1914. "Woman on Her Own." *The Englishwoman,* 21:61 (January), 90-3.

SANCHEZ, Carol Lee. 1983a. "Racism: Power, Profit, Product – and Patriarchy." *Women's Studies Quarterly,* 11:3 (Fall), 14-16.

SANCHEZ, Carol Lee. 1983b. "Sex, Class, and Race Intersections: Visions of Women of Color." In *Sinister Wisdom: A Gathering of Spirit: North American Indian Women's Issue*, 22/23, 150-4.

SANCHEZ, Sonia. 1968. "Summary." In *Black Fire: An Anthology of Afro-American Writing*. Ed. Leroi Jones and Larry Neal. New York: William Morrow, 252.

SANDS, Susan. 1970. "The Art of Occidental Love." *Broadside*, October, 16.

SANFORD, Wendy, ed. 1979. *Fighting Sexual Harassment: An Advocacy Handbook*. 2nd ed. Boston, Massachusetts: Alyson Publications and Alliance Against Sexual Coercion, 1981.

SANGER, Margaret. 1919. "A Letter to the Women of America." *The Birth Control Review*, 3:4 (April), 20.

SANGER, Margaret. 1923. "Apostle of Birth Control Sees Cause Gaining Here." *New York Times*, 8 April. Rpt. in *Women: Their Changing Roles*. Ed. Elizabeth Janeway. New York: Arno Press, 1973, 123-4.

SAPIR, Edward. 1949. *Selected Writings in Language, Culture, and Personality*. Ed. David G. Mandelbaum. Berkeley: University of California Press.

SAPPHO. Sixth Century. *Sappho: A New Translation*. Trans. Mary Barnard. Berkeley: University of California Press, 1958.

SARACHILD, Kathie. 1973. "Consciousness-Raising: A Radical Weapon." First National Conference of Stewardesses for Women's Rights, New York City, 12 March. Rev. in *Feminist Revolution*. Ed. Redstockings. New York: Random House, 1975, 144-50.

SARACHILD, Kathie. 1974. "Psychological Terrorism . . ." Rpt. in *Feminist Revolution*. Ed. Redstockings. New York: Random House, 1975, 57-61.

SARACHILD, Kathie. 1975a. "The Power of History." In *Feminist Revolution*. Ed. Redstockings. New York: Random House, 12-42.

SARACHILD, Kathie. 1975b. "Who Are We? The Redstockings Position on Names." In *Feminist Revolution*. Ed. Redstockings. New York: Random House, 53-5.

SARAH, Elizabeth. 1982. "Toward a Reassessment of Feminist History." Editorial. *Women's Studies International Forum*, 5:6, 519-24.

SARGENT, Laurens and Stephen Potter. 1974. *Pedigree*. New York: Taplinger Publishing Company.

SARGENT, Lydia, ed. 1981a. *Women and Revolution: A Discussion of the Unhappy Marriage of Marxism and Feminism*. Boston, Massachusetts: South End Press.

SARGENT, Lydia. 1981b. "New Left Women and Men: The Honeymoon is Over." In *Women and Revolution*. Ed. Lydia Sargent. Boston, Massachusetts: South End Press, xi-xxxii.

SARTON, May. 1961. *The Small Room*. Rpt. New York: W. W. Norton, 1976.

SARTON, May. 1965. *Mrs. Stevens Hears the Mermaids Singing*. Quoted in *The Quotable Woman*. Ed. Elaine Partnow. Vol. II. Los Angeles: Pinnacle Books, 1977, 168

SARTON, May. 1982. Quoted in "The Family of Woman: Growing Toward the Light." *Ms.*, 60:7, 56-9.

SATTEL, Jack W. 1983. "Men, Inexpressiveness, and Power." In *Language, Gender and Society*. Ed. Barrie Thorne, Cheris Kramarae, and Nancy Henley. Rowley, Massachusetts; Newbury House, 119-24.

SAUNDERS, Lesley. 1983. "Sex and Childbirth." In *Sex and Love, New Thoughts on Old Contradictions*. Ed. Sue Cartledge and Joanna Ryan. London: The Women's Press Limited, 89-104.

SAYERS, Dorothy L. 1930. *Strong Poison*. Rpt. New York: Avon, 1967.

SAYERS, Dorothy L. 1936. *Gaudy Night*. Rpt. New York: Avon, 1968.

SAYERS, Jane. 1982. *Biological Politics: Feminist and Anti-Feminist Perspectives*. London: Tavistock.

SCHEMAN, Naomi. 1980. "Anger and the Politics of Naming." In *Women and Language in Literature and Society*. Ed. Sally McConnell-Ginet, Ruth Borker, and Nelly Furman. New York: Praeger, 174-87.

SCHIBANOFF, Susan. 1983. "Early Women Writers: In-Scribing, Or, Reading the Fine Print." *Women's Studies International Forum*, 6:5, 475-89.

SCHNORRENBERG, Barbara B. with Jean E. Hunter. 1980. "The Eighteenth-Century Englishwoman." In *The Women of England: From Anglo-Saxon Times to the Present*. Ed. Barbara Kanner. London: Mansell, 183-228.

SCHREINER, Olive. 1911. " . . . on Parasite Woman." *The Vote*, 4 March, 229-30.

SCHULZ, Muriel. 1975a. "Rape Is a Four-Letter Word." *E.T.C.*, June, 65-9.

SCHULZ, Muriel. 1975b. "The Semantic Derogation of Women." Rpt. in *Language and Sex: Difference and Dominance*. Ed. Barrie Thorne and Nancy Henley. Rowley, Massachusetts: Newbury House, 64-73.

SCHWARZ, Judith. 1982. *Radical Feminists of Heterodoxy: Greenwich Village 1912-1940*. Lebanon, New Hampshire: New Victoria Publishers.

SCHWIMMER, Rosika. 1914. "Baroness von Suttner." *The Englishwoman*, 23:68, 164-7.

SCOTT, Anne Firor. 1984. *Making the Invisible Woman Visible*. Champaign, Illinois: University of Illinois Press.

SCOTT, Diana, ed. 1982. *Bread and Roses: An Anthology of Nineteenth- and Twentieth-Century Poetry by Women Writers*. London: Virago.

SCOTT, Patricia Bell. 1974. "The English Language and Black Womanhood: a Low Blow at Self-Esteem." *Journal of Afro-American Issues*, 2, 218-24.

SCOTT, Sara. 1983. "Holding On to What We've Won." *Trouble and Strife*, 1 (Winter), 23-7.

SEAMAN, Barbara and Gideon Seaman. 1977. *Women and the Crisis in Sex Hormones*. New York: Bantam.

SEBESTYEN, Amanda. 1979. "Tendencies in the Women's Liberation Movement." In *Feminist Practice: Notes from the Tenth Year!* Ed. Organizing Collective for the one-day Radical Feminist meeting, London, 8 April. London: In Theory Press, chart attached to back cover.

SEGAL, Lynne. 1983. "Sensual Uncertainty, or Why the Clitoris is Not Enough." In *Sex and Love, New Thoughts on Old Contradictions*. Ed. Sue Cartledge and Joanna Ryan. London: The Women's Press Limited, 30-47.

SEGAL, Sondra. 1981. "The Babyman." *Heresies*, 3:4 (Issue 12), 9.

SEGREST, Mab. 1982. "Feminism and Disobedience: Conversations with Barbara Deming." In *Reweaving the Web of Life: Feminism and Nonviolence*. Ed. Pam McAllister. Philadelphia, Pennsylvania: New Society Publishers, 45-62.

SEKAQUAPTEWA, Helen. 1980. "Marriage." In *The Third Woman: Minority Women Writers of the United States*. Ed. Dexter Fisher. Boston: Houghton Mifflin, 31-7.

SELIGSON, Marcia. 1973. "Here Comes the Bride . . ." *Ms.*, 1:8 (February), 80-3, 102-4.

SENNETT, Mrs Arncliffe. n.d. "Make Way for the Prime Minister." Pamphlet. Fawcett Library, London.

SHAINWALD, Sybil. 1984. "A Right to Privacy." *The Network News* (The National Women's Health Network), November/December, 6.

SHAKTINI, Namascar. 1982. "Displacing the Phallic Subject: Wittig's Lesbian Writing." *Signs*, 8:1 (Autumn), 29-44.

SHAW, George Bernard. 1909. "The Unmentionable Case for Women's Suffrage." *The Englishwoman*, 1:2 (March), 112-21.

SHEARD, Sarah. "Version Quebec." *Broadside*, 5:6 (April), 6.

SHENKER, Israel. 1979. *Harmless Drudges: Wizards of Language – Ancient, Medieval, and Modern*. Bronxville, New York: Barnhart Books.

SHEPPARD, Alice. 1980. "Women's Humor: Its Relation to Sex Role, Status Constraints and Social Change." Manuscript.

SHEPPARD, Alice. In press. "Suffrage Cartoons." *Journal of American Culture*.

SHERMAN, Susan. 1983. "Women and Process: The Sagaris Split, Session II." In *Learning Our Way*. Ed. Charlotte Bunch and Sandra Pollack. Trumansburg, New York: The Crossing Press, 129-37.

SHERWOOD, Elizabeth J. 1931a. "For the Feminist Library." *Independent Woman*, 10:6 (June), 268.

SHERWOOD, Elizabeth J. 1931b. "For the Feminist Library." *Independent Woman*, 10:9 (September), 408.

SHIELDS, Laurie. 1981. *Displaced Homemakers, Organizing for a New Life*. New York: McGraw-Hill.

SHINELL, Grace. 1980. "To Hell and Back Again: Towards A Feminist Metaphysics." *Womanspirit*, 6:23 (Spring), 15-57.

SHINELL, Grace. 1981. "Women's Collective Spirit: Exemplified and Envisioned." In *The Politics of Women's Spirituality*. Ed. Charlene Spretnak. Garden City, New York: Anchor Press/Doubleday, 1982, 510-25.

SHINELL, Grace. 1982. "In These Pregnant Times: Lesbian Parturition." *Maenad*, 2:2, 108-11.

SHORE, Jane. 1971. "The Princess and the Pea." In *Eye Level*. Amherst, Massachusetts: University of Massachusetts Press, 28.

SHOWALTER, Elaine. 1979. "Towards a Feminist Poetics." In *Women Writing and Writing About Women*. Ed. Mary Jacobus. London: Croom Helm.

SIEGEL, Rachel Josefowitz. 1983. "Change and Creativity at Midlife." In *Women Changing Therapy*. Ed. Joan Hamerman Robbins and Rachel Josefowitz Siegel. New York: The Haworth Press, 95-102.

siegel, thyme. 1983. Letter. *off our backs*, October, 27.

SILKO, Leslie Marmon. 1980. "Stories and their Teller – A Conversation with Leslie Marmon Silko [1977]." In *The Third Woman: Minority Women Writers of the United States*. Ed. Dexter Fisher. Boston: Houghton-Mifflin, 18-23.

SILVA, Carmen. 1983. "Women of Color Califia." In *Learning Our Way*. Ed. Charlotte Bunch and Sandra Pollack. Trumansburg, New York: The Crossing Press, 160-8.

SILVEIRA, Jeanette. 1980. "Generic Masculine Words and Thinking." In *The Voices and Words of Women and Men*. Ed. Cheris Kramarae. Oxford: Pergamon Press, 165-78.

SIMMS, Marian. 1981. "The Australian Feminist Experience." In *Australian Women: Feminist Perspectives*. Ed. Norma Grieve and Patricia Grimshaw. Melbourne: Oxford University Press, 227-39.

SIMONS, Margaret A. 1983. "The Silencing of Simone de Beauvoir: Guess What's Missing from *The Second Sex*." *Women's Studies International Forum*, 6:5, 559-64.

SIMSON, Rennie. 1983. "The Afro-American Female: The Historical Context of the Construction of Sexual Identity." In *Powers of Desire: The Politics of Sexuality*. Ed. Ann Snitow, Christine Stansell, and Sharon Thompson. New York: Monthly Review Press, 229-35.

SINGER, Rochelle. 1980. *The Demeter Flower*. New York: St Martin's Press.

Siren. c.1983. "An Anarcho-Feminist Manifesto." *Quiet Rumours: An Anarcha-Feminist Anthology*. London: Dark Star, 4-5.

SLEDD, James. 1972. "Dollars and Dictionaries: The Limits of Commercial Lexicography." In *New Aspects of Lexicography: Literary Criticism, Intellectual History, and Social Change*. Ed. Howard D. Weinbrot. Carbondale: Southern Illinois University Press, 119-37.

SLEDD, James and Wilma R. Ebbitt. 1962. *Dictionaries and That Dictionary: A Case Book on the Aims of Lexicographers and the Targets of Reviewers*. Chicago: Scott Foresman.

SMART, Fanny. 1915. "Women and Defense." *The Englishwoman*, 25:73, 76-80.

SMART-GROSVENOR, Verta Mae. 1970. "The Kitchen Crisis." In *The Black Woman: An Anthology*. Ed. Toni Cade. New York: New American Library (Signet), 119-23.

SMITH, Barbara. 1979a. "Notes for Yet Another Paper on Black Feminism, Or Will the Real Enemy Please Stand Up?" *Conditions: 5 The Black Women's Issues*, 2:2 (Autumn), 123-32.

SMITH, Barbara. 1979b. "Racism and Women's Studies." In *But Some of Us are Brave*. Ed. Gloria T. Hull, Patricia Bell Scott, and Barbara Smith. Old Westbury, New York: The Feminist Press, 1982, 48-50.

SMITH, Barbara. 1982. "On Separatism." *Sinister Wisdom*, 20 (Spring), 100-4.

SMITH, Barbara, ed. 1983. *Home Girls: A Black Feminist Anthology*. New York: Kitchen Table: Women of Color Press.

SMITH, Barbara. 1983. Introduction to *Home Girls: A Black Feminist Anthology*. Ed. Barbara Smith. New York: Kitchen Table: Women of Color Press, xix-lvi.

SMITH, Barbara and Beverly Smith. 1981. "Across the Kitchen Table: A Sister-to-Sister Dialogue." In *This Bridge Called My Back: Writings by Radical Women of Color*. Ed. Cherríe Moraga and Gloria Anzaldúa. Watertown, Massachusetts: Persephone Press, 113-27.

SMITH, Beverly. 1982. "Beverly Smith in Conversation." Interview by Linda Bellos. *Spare Rib*, August, 8.

SMITH, Dorothy. 1977. *Feminism and Marxism*. Vancouver: New Star Books.

SMITH, Dorothy. 1978. "A Peculiar Eclipsing: Women's Exclusion from Man's Culture." *Women's Studies International Quarterly*, 1:4, 281-96.

SMITH, Eleanor. 1979. "And Black Women Made Music." *Heresies*, 2:4 (Issue 8), 58-64.

SMITH, Julia. 1876. *The Holy Bible; Containing the Old and New Testaments; Translated Literally from the Original Tongues*. Hartford: American Publishing Company.

SMITH, K. Douglas. 1912. "Women: The Riddle." *Votes for Women*, 5 January, 922.

SMITH, Lee. 1984. "Direct Action and Pornography: Women's Right to Fight Back Guaranteed by Our Sacred First Amendment." Feminist Forum Series, University of Illinois. 2 May.

SMITH, Mary Ann Yodelis. 1982. "Research Retrospective: Feminism and the Media." *Communication Research*, 9:2 (January), 145-60. Rpt. in *Mass Communication Review Yearbook*. Vol. 4. Ed. Ellen Wartella, A. Charles Whitney, and Sven Windahl. Beverly Hills: Sage.

SMITH, Patricia Clark. 1983. "Ain't Seen You Since: Dissent among Female Relatives in American Indian Women's Poetry." In *Studies in American Indian Literature*. Ed. Paula Gunn Allen. New York: Modern Language Association, 108-26.

SMITH, Patti. 1982. On poster. Atlanta: Art 101, Ltd.

SMITHERMAN, Geneva. 1983. "Language and Liberation." *The Journal of Negro Education*, 52:1 (Winter), 21-2.

SMYTH, Ailbhe. 1983. "Contemporary French Feminism: Bibliography." *Hecate*, 9:1/2, 203-36.

SNIDER, Jenny R. 1973. *The Pencil Picture Dictionary*. A Head Hand Heart and Tooth Publication.

SNITOW, Ann Barr. 1983. "Mass Market Romance Pornography for Women is Different." In *Powers of Desire*. Ed. Ann Snitow, Christine Stansell, and Sharon Thompson. New York: Monthly Review Press, 245-63.

SNITOW, Ann, Christine Stansel, and Sharon Thompson, eds. 1983. *Powers of Desire: The Politics of Sexuality*. New York: Monthly Review Press.

SNOWDEN, Ethel. 1913. *The Feminist Movement*. London and Glasgow: Collin's-Clean-Type-Press.

SOCHEN, June. 1981. *Consecrate Every Day: The Public Lives of Jewish American Women 1880-1980*. Albany: State University of New York Press.

SOLANAS, Valerie. 1968. *Scum Manifesto*. New York: Olympia Press. Rpt. London: The Matriarchy Study Group, 1983.

SONTAG, Susan. 1973. "The Third World of Women." *Partisan Review*, 40:2 180-206.

SONTAG, Susan. 1977. *Illness as Metaphor*. New York: Random House.

SOPHIA, A Person of Quality [thought to be the pseudonym of Lady Mary Wortley Montagu]. 1739. *Woman Not Inferior to Man or, A Short and Modest Vindication of the Natural Right of the Fair-Sex to a Perfect Equality of Power, Dignity, and Esteem, With the Men*. London: John Hawkins.

sorrel, lorraine. 1981. "the life and times of rosie the riveter." *off our backs*, June, 25.

SORRELS, Bobbye D. 1983. *The Nonsexist Communicator: Solving the Problems of Gender and Awkwardness in Modern English*. Englewood Cliffs, New Jersey: Prentice Hall.

SOUTH, Chris. 1980. "Collective Comments." *Feminary*, 11:1/2, 5.

Southern Female Rights Union. 1970. "Spies in Women's Liberation." *Everywoman*, 31 July.

SOWERNAM, Ester [pseud.], neither Maide, Wife nor Widdowe, yet really all, and therefore experienced to defend all. 1617. *An Answer To a Lewd Pamphlet entitled, The Arraignment of Women*. [Answer to Joseph Swetnam.] London: Nicholas Bourne.

SPENCER, Mickey and Polly Taylor. 1982. Preface to *BROOMSTICK, By, For, and About Women over Forty*, November-December, 2.

SPENDER, Dale. 1980. *Man Made Language*. London: Routledge & Kegan Paul.

SPENDER, Dale, ed. 1981. *Men's Studies Modified*. Oxford, England: Pergamon Press.

SPENDER, Dale. 1982a. *Invisible Women: The Schooling Scandal*. London: Writers and Readers Publishing.

SPENDER, Dale. 1982b. *Women of Ideas and What Men Have Done to Them: From Aphra Behn to Adrienne Rich*. London: Routledge & Kegan Paul.

SPENDER, Dale. 1983a. *There's Always Been a Women's Movement*. London: Routledge & Kegan Paul, Pandora Press.

SPENDER, Dale. 1983b. "Theorizing About Theorizing." In *Theories of Women's Studies*. Ed. Gloria Bowles and Renate Duelli Klein. London: Routledge & Kegan Paul, 27-31.

SPENDER, Dale and Lynne Spender. 1983. Editorial. *Women's Studies International Forum*, 6:5, 467.

SPINSTER, Sidney. 1982. "On Separatism." Letter. *Sinister Wisdom*, 20 (Spring), 104-5.

SPIVAK, Gayatri Chakravorty. In press. "Feminism and the Critical Condition." In *For Alma Mater: Theory and Practice in Feminist Scholarship*. Ed. Paula A. Treichler, Cheris Kramarae, and Beth Stafford. Urbana, Illinois: University of Illinois Press.

SPRETNAK, Charlene, ed. 1982. *The Politics of Women's Spirituality*. Garden City, New York: Anchor Press/Doubleday.

STACEY, Judith and Barrie Thorne. 1984. "The Missing Feminist Revolution in Sociology." American Sociological Association, San Antonio. August.

STACK, Carol B. 1974. *All Our Kin*. New York: Harper & Row.

STALEY, Alene. 1971. "Genesis Revisited." *Black Maria*, 1:1, 46-9.

STALLARD, Karin, Barbara Ehrenreich, and Holly Sklar. 1983. *Poverty in the American Dream: Women and Children First*. Boston: South End Press.

STAM, Robert and Louise Spence. 1983. "Colonialism, Racism, and Representation – An Introduction." *Screen*, 24:2 (April), 2-20.

STANBECK, Marsha Houston. In press. "Language and Black Woman's Place: Some Evidence from the Black Middle Class." In *For Alma Mater: Theory and Practice in Feminist Scholarship*. Ed. Paula A. Treichler, Cheris Kramarae, and Beth Stafford, Urbana: University of Illinois Press.

STANKO, Elizabeth A. 1984. *Intimate Intrusions: Women's Experiences of Male Violence.* London: Pandora Press.

STANLEY, Julia P. 1971. "Syntactic Exploitation: Passive Adjectives in English." Southwestern Conference on Linguistics, Atlanta, Georgia.

STANLEY, Julia P. 1973. " 'Correctness,' 'Appropriateness' and Uses of English." Manuscript.

STANLEY, Julia P. 1974. "The Stylistics of Belief." College Composition and Communication Conference, Anaheim, California.

STANLEY, Julia P. 1975. "Prescribed Passivity: The Language of Sexism." In *Views on Language.* Ed. Reza Ordoubadian and Wilburga Von-Raffler Engel. Murfreesboro, Tennessee: Inter-University Publishing.

STANLEY, Julia [Penelope]. 1976. "Fear of Flying?" *Sinister Wisdom*, 1:2 (December), 52-62.

STANLEY, Julia P. 1977a. "Gender-Marking in American English." In *Sexism and Language.* Ed. Alleen Pace Nilsen, Haig Bosmajian, H. Lee Gershuny, and Julia P. Stanley. Urbana, Illinois: National Council of Teachers of English, 43-74.

STANLEY, Julia P. 1977b. "Paradigmatic Woman: The Prostitute." In *Papers in Language Variation.* Ed. David L. Shores and Carole P. Hines. Birmingham, Alabama: University of Alabama Press, 303-21.

STANLEY, Julia [Penelope]. 1978a. "Lesbian Separatism: The Linguistic and Social Sources of Separatist Policies." In *The Gay Academic.* Ed. Louie Crew. Palm Springs, California: ETC Publications, 121-31.

STANLEY, Julia Penelope. 1978b. "The Sexist Tradition: Words and Meaning." *Iowa English Bulletin*, 27:2 (Spring), 5-9.

STANLEY, Julia Penelope. 1979. "Language Change/Social Change: Systems and Power." *Azimuth*, 1:1, 7-10.

STANLEY, Julia [Penelope] and Susan [Wolfe] Robbins. 1975. "Sexist Slang and the Gay Community." Modern Language Association Convention, New York. December.

STANLEY, Julia P. and Susan W. Robbins. 1976. "Truncated Passives: Some of Our Agents are Missing." *Linguistic Theory and the Real World*, 1:2 (September), 33-7.

STANLEY, Julia [Penelope] and Susan Robbins Wolfe. 1978. Response to William E. Coles, Jr. *College Composition and Communication*, December, 404-6.

STANLEY, Julia Penelope and Susan J. Wolfe. c.1979. "Style as Meaning." Manuscript.

STANLEY, Julia Penelope and Susan J. Wolfe. 1980. Introduction to *The Coming Out Stories.* Ed. Susan J. Wolfe and Julia Penelope Stanley. Watertown, Massachusetts: Persephone Press, xv-xxiv.

STANLEY, Julia Penelope and Susan J. Wolfe. 1983. "Consciousness as Style: Style as Aesthetic." In *Language, Gender, and Society.* Ed. Barrie Thorne, Cheris Kramarae and Nancy Henley. Rowley, Massachusetts: Newbury House, 125-39.

STANLEY, Liz, ed. 1984. *The Diaries of Hannah Cullwick, Victorian Maidservant.* London: Virago.

STANLEY, Liz and Sue Wise. 1983. *Breaking Out: Feminist Consciousness and Feminist Research.* London: Routledge & Kegan Paul.

STANNARD, Una. 1971. "The Mask of Beauty." In *Woman in Sexist Society.* Ed. Vivian Gornick and Barbara K. Moran. New York: Signet, 187-203.

STANNARD, Una. 1977. *Mrs. Man.* San Francisco: Germainbooks.

STANTON, Domna. 1983. "Inscriptions of the Feminist 'I' in Early-Modern French Poetry." *The Committee for Gender Research*, 3 (Spring), 1, 6, 7.

STANTON, Elizabeth Cady. 1850. "Man Superior – Intellectually – Morally – Physically." *The Lily*, 2:2 (February), 12.

STANTON, Elizabeth Cady. 1851. Letter from Mrs. Elizabeth Cady Stanton to the Worchester Convention. *The Lily*, 3:11, 82.

STANTON, Elizabeth Cady. 1891. "The Matriarchate, or Mother-Age." In *Transactions of the National Council of Women of the United States*. Philadelphia, 218-27. Excerpted in *Up From the Pedestal: Selected Writings in the History of American Feminism*. Ed. Aileen S. Kraditor. New York: Quadrangle, 1977, 140-7.

STANTON, Elizabeth Cady. 1895, 1898. *The Woman's Bible*. Rpt. *The Original Feminist Attack on the Bible*. New York: Arno Press, 1974.

STANTON, Elizabeth Cady. 1898a. Introduction to *The Woman's Bible: Comments on Genesis, Exodus, Leviticus, Numbers, and Deuteronomy*. New York: European Publishing. Rpt. Seattle: Coalition Task Force on Women and Religion, 1974.

STANTON, Elizabeth Cady. 1898b. "Nursery Names Unfit for Women." *The Woman's Journal*, 29:43 (22 October), 342-3.

STANTON, Elizabeth Cady and the Revising Committee. 1898. *The Woman's Bible*. New York: European Publishing Company. Rpt. Seattle: Coalition Task Force on Women and Religion, 1974.

STARHAWK. 1979. *The Spiral Dance*. San Francisco: Harper & Row.

STARHAWK. 1982. *Dreaming the Dark (Magic, Sex, and Politics)*. Boston: Beacon Press.

STEENSTRUP, Johannes C. H. R. 1968. *The Medieval Popular Ballad*. Seattle. University of Washington Press.

STEINEM, Gloria. 1972. "Marilyn – The Woman Who Died Too Soon." *Ms.*, August. Rpt. in *The First Ms. Reader*. Ed. Francine Klagsbrun. New York: Warner Books, 1973, 200-12.

STEINEM, Gloria. 1973. "The Verbal Karate of Florynce R. Kennedy, Esq." *Ms.*, 1:9 (March), 54-5, 89.

STEINEM, Gloria. 1979. "These are Not the Best Years of Your Life." *Ms.*, 8:3 (September), 64-8.

STEINEM, Gloria. 1980a. "Erotica and Pornography: A Clear and Present Difference." In *Take Back the Night*. Ed. Laura J. Lederer. New York: William Morrow, 35-9.

STEINEM, Gloria. 1980b. "The Way We Were – and Will Be." In *The Decade of Women*. Ed. Suzanne Levine and Harriet Lyons. New York: Paragon Books, 7-25.

STEINEM, Gloria. 1981. Foreword to *Building Feminist Theory: Essays from Quest*. New York: Longman.

STEINEM, Gloria. 1983. *Outrageous Acts and Everyday Rebellions*. New York: Holt, Rinehart & Winston.

STEINEM, Gloria. 1984. Foreword to *Goddesses in Everywoman*. Ed. Jean Shinoda Bolen. New York: Harper & Row, ix-xii.

STERRETT, A. B. C. 1919. "The Hymn of The Never-Existing." *The Birth Control Review*, 3:1.

STETSON, Charlotte Perkins. 1896. "Women to Men, Relatives and Otherwise." *The Woman's Column*, 9:5 (1 February).

STETSON, Erlene. 1979. "A Note on the Woman's Building and Black Exclusion." *Heresies*, 2:4 (Issue 8), 45-7.

STETSON, Erlene. 1982. "Black Women In and Out of Print." In *Women in Print I: Opportunities for Women's Studies Research in Language and Literature*. Ed. Joan E. Hartman and Ellen Messer-Davidow. New York: Modern Language Association, 87-107.

STEVENS, Evelyn P. 1973. "*Marianismo*: The Other Face of *Machismo* in Latin America." In *Female and Male in Latin America: Essays*. Ed. Ann Pescatello. Pittsburgh: University of Pittsburgh Press, 89-102.

STEVENS, May.1980. "Taking Art to the Revolution." *Heresies*, 3:1 (Issue 9), 40-3.

STEWART, Isabel M. and Anne L. Austin. 1962. *A History of Nursing*. New York: Putnam's.

STEWART, Marianne. 1984. "The Class War Called 'Crime.' " *No More Cages: Women's Prison Newsletter*, 5:3 (June-July), 20-3.

STIMPSON, Catharine R. 1979a. "The Power to Name: Some Reflections on the Avant-garde." In *The Prism of Sex: Essays on the Sociology of Knowledge*. Ed. J. Sherman and E. Beck. Madison: University of Wisconsin Press, 55-77.

STIMPSON, Catharine. 1979b. "I'm Not a Feminist But . . ." *Ms.*, 8:1 (July), 62-4, 86.

STIMPSON, Catharine. 1981. "Feminist Criticism and Feminist Critics." In *Feminist Literary Criticism*. Research Triangle Park, North Carolina: National Humanities Center, 57-63.

STOCK, Phyllis. 1978. *Better Than Rubies: A History of Women's Education*. New York: Capricorn/Putnam's.

STOLTENBERG, John. 1977. "Refusing to be a Man." In *For Men Against Sexism*. Ed. Jon Snodgrass. San Rafael, California: Times Change Press. Rpt. in *Women's Studies International Forum*, 7:1, 1984, 25-7.

STONE, Ruth. 1982. "Poetry." Quoted in "Alphabet Soup: Women, Language, Sexuality." Sandra M. Gilbert and Susan Gubar. Manuscript.

STOPES, Charlotte Carmichael. 1908. *The Sphere of 'Man' in Relation to That of 'Woman' in the Constitution*. London: T. Fisher Unwin.

STOTT, Mary. 1983. "Women in Newspapers." In *On Gender and Writing*. Ed. Michelene Wandor. London: Pandora Press, 126-32.

STOTT, Mary. 1984. "Why be sorry for spinsters?" *The Guardian*, 24 January.

STOWE, Harriet Beecher. 1859. *The Minister's Wooing*. Quoted in *Anonymous Was a Woman*. Mirra Bank. New York: St Martin's Press, 1979, 63.

STRAINCHAMPS, Ethel, ed. 1974. *Rooms with No View, A Woman's Guide to the Man's World of the Media*. Comp. Media Women's Association. New York: Harper & Row.

STRAUSS, Sylvia. 1982. *"Traitors to the Masculine Cause": The Men's Campaigns for Women's Rights*. Westport, Connecticut: Greenwood Press.

STRESHINSKY, Shirley. 1973. "Are You Safer With a Midwife?" *Ms.*, 7:4 (October), 24, 26-7.

SULLEROT, Evelyne. 1974. *Women on Love: Eight Centuries of Feminist Writing*. Trans. Helen R. Lane. London: Jill Norman, 1980.

SUMMERS, Judith. 1980. "Teaching – No 'Career' for Women." *Women and Education*, 20 (Autumn), 33-4.

SUNCIRCLE, Pat. 1981. "A Day's Growth." In *Lesbian Fiction*. Ed. Elly Bulkin. Watertown, Massachusetts: Persephone Press.

SUNDERLAND, Jane. 1978. " 'Lines Driven Deep': Radical Departures, or the Same Old Story, for Prichard's Women?" *Hecate*, 4:1 (February), 7-24.

SUTHERLAND, Brigitte. 1984. "Fundamental Families: Spawn of the Astronauts." *HERizons*, 2:1 (April), 34-5.

SWANWICK, H. M. 1915. "The Implications of the Women's Suffrage Movement – A Reply." *The Englishwoman*, 26:77, 175-8.

SWANWICK, H. M. 1935. *I Have Been Young*. London: Victor Gollancz.

SWINEY, Frances. 1918. *The Ancient Road or The Development of the Soul*. London: G. Bell.

TANNEN, Deborah and Cynthia Wallat. 1982. "A Sociolinguistic Analysis of Multiple Demands on the Pediatrician in Doctor/Mother/Child Interaction." In *Linguistics and the Professions: Proceedings of the Second Annual Delaware Symposium on Language Studies*. Ed. Robert J. Di Pietro. Norwood, New Jersey: Ablex Publishing, 39-50.

TANNER, Leslie B., ed. 1970. *Voices from Women's Liberation*. New York: New American Library.

TARMAN, Vera. 1984. "WITZ." *Broadside*, 6:1 (October), 6.

TASKIRAN, Tezer. 1976. *Women in Turkey*. Istanbul, Turkey: Redhouse Press.

TAYLOR, L. R. 1919. "Madame Bergman Osterberg." *The Englishwoman*, 41:121, 65-8.

TAYLOR, Sheila Ortiz. 1982. *Fault-Line*. Tallahassee, Florida: Naiad Press.

TENSION, Evelyn. 1978. "You Don't Need a Degree to Read the Writing on the Wall." *Catcall*, 7 January. Rpt. in *No Turning Back: Writings from the Women's Liberation Movement 1975-1980*. Ed. Feminist Anthology Collective. London: The Women's Press, 1981, 82-9.

TERRELL, John Upton and Donna M. Terrell. 1974. *Indian Women of the Western Morning: Their Life in Early America*. New York: The Dial Press.

Tessera Editorial Discussion. 1984. "SP/ELLE: Spelling Out the Reasons." *Room of One's Own*, 8:4 (January), 4-24.

TEY, Josephine. 1947. *Miss Pym Disposes*. Rpt. New York: Berkley, 1971.

TEY, Josephine. 1949. *The Franchise Affair*. Rpt. New York: Berkley Medallion, 1971.

TEY, Josephine. 1950. *To Love and be Wise*. Rpt. New York: Berkley Medallion, 1971.

THASS-THIENEMANN, Theodore. 1967. *The Subconscious Language*. New York: Washington Square Press.

THOMAS, Rosalind. 1982. "Anais Nin's Erotics: A Feminine Perspective." *Room of One's Own*, 7:4, 57-69.

THOMPSON, Irene and Patricia A. Stringer, eds. 1982. *Stepping Off the Pedestal: Academic Women in the South*. New York: Modern Language Association.

THOMPSON, Judith Jarvis. 1971. "A Defense of Abortion." *Philosophy and Public Affairs*, 1:1 (Fall). Rpt. in *Issues in Feminism*. Ed. Sheila Ruth. Boston: Houghton Mifflin, 1980, 287-99.

THOMPSON-PRICE, Louisa. 1910. "The Chivalrous Man." *The Vote*, 24 December, 107, 113.

THORNE, Barrie. 1982. "Feminist Rethinking of the Family: An Overview." In *Rethinking the Family: Some Feminist Questions*. Ed. Barrie Thorne with Marilyn Yalom. New York: Longman, 1-24.

THORNE, Barrie and Nancy Henley, eds. 1975. *Language and Sex: Difference and Dominance*. Rowley, Massachusetts: Newbury House.

THORNE, Barrie, Cheris Kramarae, and Nancy Henley, eds. 1983. *Language, Gender, and Society*. Rowley, Massachusetts: Newbury House.

THORNE, Barrie, Cheris Kramarae, and Nancy Henley. 1983. "Language, Gender, and Society: Opening a Second Decade of Research." In *Language, Gender, and Society*. Ed. Barrie Thorne, Cheris Kramarae, and Nancy Henley. Rowley, Massachusetts: Newbury House, 7-24.

THORNING, Helle. 1981. "The Mother-Daughter Relationship and Sexual Ambivalence." *Heresies*, 3:4 (Issue 12), 3-6.

TOBIAS, Lenore Keeshig. 1982. "My Grandmother is Visiting Me." *Canadian Woman Studies*, 4:1 (Fall), 9.

TODASCO, Ruth, ed. 1973. *An Intelligent Woman's Guide to Dirty Words*. Chicago: Loop Center YWCA.

TOLSCH, Adrienne. 1981. Comic. *Voice*, 9-15 September, 40.

TOM, Lily. 1971. "Swordswoman." In *Asian Women*. Ed. and published by Asian Women at Berkeley: University of California, 44-6.

TOMALIN, Claire. 1977. *The Life and Death of Mary Wollstonecraft*. Harmondsworth: Penguin.

TOTH, Emily. 1983. "Who'll Take Romance." *The Women's Review of Books*, 1:5 (February), 12-13.

TREICHLER, Paula A. 1981. "Verbal Subversions in Dorothy Parker: 'Trapped like a Trap in a Trap.' " *Language and Style*, 13:4 (Fall), 46-51.

TREICHLER, Paula A. 1983. "Words for a Feminist Dictionary: Barbara Newhall Follett and Farksoo." Modern Language Association Convention, New York. December.

TREICHLER, Paula A. 1984. "From Discourse to Dictionary: How Sexist Meanings Are Authorized." Symposium on Sexist Language, Linguistic Society of America. Baltimore, December.

TREICHLER, Paula A. In press a. "Teaching Feminist Theory." In *Theory in the Classroom*. Ed. Cary Nelson. Urbana: University of Illinois Press.

TREICHLER, Paula A. In press b. "Escaping the Sentence: Diagnosis and Discourse in 'The Yellow Wallpaper.' " *Tulsa Studies in Women's Literature*.

TREICHLER, Paula A. In press c. "Alma Mater's Sorority: Women at the University of Illinois, 1880-1925." In *For Alma Mater: Theory and Practice in Feminist Scholarship*. Ed. Paula A. Treichler, Cheris Kramarae, and Beth Stafford. Urbana: University of Illinois Press.

TREICHLER, Paula A. and Cheris Kramarae. 1983. "Women's Talk in the Ivory Tower." *Communication Quarterly*, 31:2 (Spring), 118-32.

TREICHLER, Paula A., Cheris Kramarae, and Beth Stafford, eds. In press. *For Alma Mater: Theory and Practice in Feminist Scholarship*. Urbana, Illinois: University of Illinois Press.

TRUJILLO, Marcella. 1979. "The Dilemma of the Modern Chicana Artist and Critic." *Heresies*, 2:4 (Issue 8), 5-10.

TUCHMAN, Gaye. 1978. "The Symbolic Annihilation of Women by the Mass Media." Introduction to *Hearth and Home: Images of Women in the Mass Media*. Ed. Gaye Tuchman, Arlene Kaplan Daniels, and James Benet. New York: Oxford University Press, 3-38.

TUCHMAN, Gaye, Arlene Kaplan Daniels, and James Benet, eds. 1978. *Hearth and Home: Images of Women in the Mass Media*. New York: Oxford University Press.

TUKE, Margaret J. 1919. "Women and the Civil Service." *The Englishwoman*, 43:127, 89-95.

TURNER, C. 1919. "Women and the Future of National Kitchens." *The Englishwoman*, 44:132, 161-9.

TURNER, G. W. 1973. *Stylistics*. Baltimore, Maryland: Penguin.

TWEEDIE, Jill. 1983. "Strange Places." In *One Gender and Writing*. Ed. Michelene Wandor. London: Pandora Press, 112-18.

TWEEDIE, Jill. 1984. "She must be tough – but she is not one of the boys." *The Guardian*, 28 February.

TWERSKY, Lori. 1983. "Devils or Angels? The Female Teenage Audience Examined." *Trouser Press*, April, 27-9.

UNGERSON, Clare. 1983. "Women and Caring: Skills, Tasks, and Taboos." In *The Public and the Private*. Ed. Eva Gamarnikow, David H. J. Morgan, June Purvis, and Daphne Taylorson. London: Heinemann, 62-77.

United Feminist Parties of France and Belgium. 1978. "A Feminist International." Trans. Nancy Hartsock and Dahlia Judovitz. *Quest: A Feminist Quarterly*, 4:2 (Winter), 51-4.

URBANOVIC, Jackie and Susie Day. 1982-3. *Mother Goddess Funnies*. Comics series.

URIS, Dorothy. 1975. *A Woman's Voice: A Handbook of Successful Private and Public Speaking*. New York: Barnes & Noble.

UROFF, M. D. 1974. *Hart Crane: The Patterns of His Poetry*. Urbana, Illinois: University of Illinois Press.

U.S. Commission on Civil Rights. 1977. *Window Dressing on the Set: Women and Minorities in Television*. Washington, D.C.: U.S. Government Printing Office.

U.S. Commission on Civil Rights. 1979. *Window Dressing on the Set: An Update*.

Washington, D.C.: U.S. Government Printing Office.

VALESKA, Lucia. 1975. "The Future of Female Separatism." Rpt. in *Building Feminist Theory: Essays from Quest*. Ed. The Quest Staff. New York: Longman, 1981, 20-31.

VALLS, Lito. 1981. *What a Pistarkle! A Dictionary/Glossary of Virgin Islands English Creole*. Cruz Bay, St John, Virgin Islands: Prestige Press.

VAN ALLEN, Judith. 1976. " 'Aba Riots' or Igbo 'Women's War'? Ideology, Stratification, and the Invisibility of Women." In *Women in Africa: Studies in Social and Economic Change*. Stanford: Stanford University Press, 59-86.

VANCE, Carole S. 1982. "Concept Paper: Towards a Politics of Sexuality." The Scholar and the Feminist Conference, Barnard College, 24 April. In *Diary of A Conference*. Memphis: Faculty Press, 38-40.

VANCE, Carole S. 1983. "Gender Systems, Ideology, and Sex Research." In *Powers of Desire*. Ed. Ann Snitow, Christine Stansell, and Sharon Thompson. New York: Monthly Review Press, 371-84.

VAN GELDER, Lindsy. 1973. "Coffee, Tea, or Fly Me." *Ms.*, 1:7 (January), 86-91, 105.

VAN GELDER, Lindsy. 1980. "The Great Person-hole Cover Debate." *Ms.*, April, 120.

VANN, 1970. Rebuttal to "Spies in Women's Liberation." *Everywoman*, 31 July, 1, 16.

VANN. 1976. "We *Are* the Revolution." *Everywoman*, 2 October.

Varda One. 1970-1. "Manglish." Columns in *Everywoman*.

Varda One. 1971. *Everywoman*. Pittsburgh, Pennsylvania: KNOW, Inc.

VELASQUEZ, Madame Loreta Janeta. 1876. *The Woman in Battle: A Narrative of the Exploits, Adventures, and Travels of Madame Loreta Janeta Velasquez, Otherwise known as Lieutenant Harry T. Buford*. Hartford: T. Belknap. Rpt. Arno Press.

VETTERLING-BRAGGIN, Mary, ed. 1981. *Sexist Language: A Modern Philosophical Analysis*. Totowa, New Jersey: Littlefield, Adams.

VICKERY, Dr Alice Drysdale. c.1907. "The Political Rights of Women." Pamphlet. Fawcett Library, London.

VINCENT, Madeleine. 1976. "A basic fact of our time." From "Une grande donnée de notre temps" [A Basic Fact of Our Time]. In *Femmes: quelle libération?* [Women: What Liberation?]. Editions Sociales. In *New French Feminisms*. Trans. Susan O'Leary. Ed. Elaine Marks and Isabelle de Courtivron. New York: Schocken, 1981, 125-9.

VITALE, Sylvia Witts. 1982. "Growing Up Negro, Soon to be Black." *Heresies*, 4:3 (Issue 15), 20-1.

W., M. M. 1913. "The Last Round." *The Englishwoman*, 17:51 (March), 241-9.

W. S. 1981. "Notes From Just Over the Edge: A New Lesbian Speaks Out." *The Second Wave*, 6:1 (Summer), 20-6.

WAGAR, W. Warren. 1981. Statement in "AF Symposium on Women and the Future." *Alternative Futures*, 4:2/3 (Spring/Summer), 157-83.

WAGNER, Sally Roesch. 1982. "Pornography and the Sexual Revolution: The Backlash of Sadomasochism." In *Against Sadomasochism: A Radical Feminist Analysis*. Ed. Robin Ruth Linden, Darlene R. Pagano, Diana E. H. Russell, and Susan Leigh Star. East Palo Alto, California: Frog In The Well, 23-44.

WAHEENEE, as told to Gilbert L. Wilson. 1927. *Waheenee: An Indian Girl's Story*. Webb Publishing Co. Rpt. Lincoln, Nebraska: University of Nebraska Press, 1981.

WAINOCH, Pat. n.d. "The Guard System." Mimeograph. Berkeley Women's Liberation Papers. Northwestern University Library, Evanston, Illinois.

WALKER, Alice. 1968. "The Diary of an African Nun." *Freedomways*, Summer. Rpt. in *The Black Woman: An Anthology*. Ed. Toni Cade. New York: New American Library (Signet), 1970, 38-41.

WALKER, Alice. 1971. *Revolutionary Petunias and Other Poems*. New York: Harcourt Brace Jovanovich.

WALKER, Alice. 1976. *Meridian*. New York: Harcourt Brace Jovanovich.

WALKER, Alice, ed. 1979. *I Love Myself When I am Laughing – A Zora Neale Hurston Reader*. New York: The Feminist Press.

WALKER, Alice. 1980a. "Saving the Life that Is Your Own: The Importance of Models in the Artist's Life." In *The Third Woman: Minority Women Writers of the United States*. Ed. Dexter Fisher. Boston: Houghton-Mifflin, 151-8.

WALKER, Alice. 1980b. "Coming Apart." In *Take Back the Night: Women on Pornography*. Ed. Laura Lederer. New York: William Morrow, 95-118.

WALKER, Alice. 1982a. "Only Justice Can Stop A Curse." In *Reweaving the Web of Life: Feminism and Nonviolence*. Ed. Pam McAllister. Philadelphia, Pennsylvania: New Society Publishers, 262-5.

WALKER, Alice. 1982b. "If the Present Looks Like the Past, What Does the Future Look Like?. . ." *Heresies*, 4:3 (Issue 15), 58-9.

WALKER, Alice. 1982c. *The Color Purple*. New York: Harcourt Brace Jovanovich.

WALKER, Alice. 1982d. *You Can't Keep a Good Woman Down*. New York: Harcourt Brace Jovanovich.

WALKER, Alice. 1983. *In Search of Our Mothers' Gardens, Womanist Prose*. New York: Harcourt Brace Jovanovich.

WALKER, Barbara G. 1983. *The Woman's Encyclopedia of Myths and Secrets*. New York: Harper & Row.

WALKER, Beverly. 1981. "Psychology and Feminism – If You Can't Beat Them, Join Them." In *Men's Studies Modified*. Ed. Dale Spender. London: Pergamon, 111-24.

WALKER, Fuller. 1873. "Woman in American Society." *The Woman's Journal*, 5 April.

WALKOWITZ, Judith R. 1983. "Male Vice and Female Virtue: Feminism and the Politics of Prostitution in Nineteenth-Century Britain." In *Powers of Desire*. Ed. Ann Snitow, Christine Stansell, and Sharon Thompson. New York: Monthly Review Press, 419-38.

WALLACE, Michele. 1975. "A Black Feminist's Search for Sisterhood." In *But Some of Us are Brave*. Ed. Gloria T. Hull, Patricia Bell Scott, and Barbara Smith. Old Westbury, New York: The Feminist Press, 1982, 5-12.

WALLACE, Michele. 1978. *Black Macho and the Myth of the Super-Woman*. New York: The Dial Press.

WALLACE, Michele. 1983. Review of *Black Women Writers at Work*, ed. Claudia Tate. *The Women's Review of Books*, 1:1, 7-8.

WALLECHINSKY, David and Irving Wallace. 1975. *The People's Almanac*. Garden City, New York: Doubleday.

WALLSGROVE, Ruth. 1982. "Signs of the Times." *Spare Rib*, 120 (July), 10.

WALSH, Elizabeth Miller. 1981. *Women in Western Civilization*. Cambridge, Massachusetts: Schenkman Publishing.

WALSH, Mary Roth. 1977. *Doctors Wanted: No Women Need Apply*. New Haven: Yale University Press.

WALTERS, Margaret. 1976. "The Rights and Wrongs of Women: Mary Wollstonecraft, Harriet Martineau, and Simone de Beauvoir." In *The Rights and Wrongs of Women*. Ed. Juliet Mitchell and Ann Oakley. Harmondsworth: Penguin.

WALTERS, Margaret. 1978. *The Nude Male: A New Perspective*. New York and London: Paddington Press.

WANDOR, Michelene. 1980. In *Why Children?* Ed. Stephanie Dowrick and Sibyl Grundberg. London: The Women's Press, 133-42.

WANDOR, Michelene. 1983. "Masks and Options." In *On Gender and Writing*. Ed. Michelene Wandor. London: Pandora Press, 1-9.

WARD, Jean. 1980. "Check Out Your Sexism: A Quiz for Journalists." *Columbia Journalism Review*, May/June, 38-9.

WARE, Celestine. 1970. *Woman Power: The Movement for Women's Liberation*. New York: Tower Publications.

WARENSKI, Marilyn. 1978. *Patriarchs and Politics: The Plight of the Mormon Woman*. New York: McGraw-Hill.

WARNER, Marina. 1982. *Joan of Arc: The Image of Female Heroism*. New York: Vintage Books.

WARREN, Mary Anne. 1980. *The Nature of Woman: An Encyclopedia and Guide to the Literature*. Inverness, California: Edgepress.

WARRIOR, Betsy. 1969a. Preface to *No More Fun and Games: A Journal of Female Liberation*, 3 (November), 1.

WARRIOR, Betsy. 1969b. "Man as an Obsolete Life Form." *No More Fun and Games: A Journal of Female Liberation*, 2 (February). Mimeograph. Northwestern University Library, Evanston, Illinois.

WARRIOR, Betsy. 1971. "Slavery or a Labor of Love?" *No More Fun and Games: A Journal of Female Liberation*, 5 (July), 29-41.

WARTELLA, Ellen, A. Charles Whiteney, and Sven Windahl, eds. 1983. *Mass Communications Review Yearbook*. Vol. IV, Part III. Beverly Hills: Sage.

"Watch Your Language: Non-Sexist Language: A Guide for NALGO Members." c.1980. Pamphlet. London: NALGO.

WATTLES, J. 1980. "Affirming Myself as a Whole and Beautiful Womon." *Womanspirit*, 26 (Winter Solstice), 19-20. Rpt. *The Blatant Image*, 1982, No. 2, 47.

WEBB, Marilyn Salzman. 1969. "America's Comic Culture." *The Guardian*, 12 April.

WEBSTER, Noah. 1817. Letter to John Pickering. Quoted in *Webster's Third New International Dictionary of the English Language*. Ed. Philip Babcock Gove. Springfield, Massachusetts: G. and C. Merriam, 1971, 2a.

WEBSTER, Paula. 1981. "Pornography and Pleasure." *Heresies*, 3:4 (Issue 12), 48-51.

WEBSTER, Paula and Esther Newton. 1972. Quoted in Margot Adler, "Meanings of Matriarchy," 1979. In *The Politics of Women's Spirituality*. Ed. Charlene Spretnak. Garden City, New York: Anchor Press, 1982, 131.

Webster's New World Dictionary of the American Language. 1958. Col. ed. Cleveland and New York: The World Publishing Company.

Webster's Third New International Dictionary of the English Language. 1971. Ed. Philip Babcock Gove. Springfield, Massachusetts: G. and C. Merriam.

WEENE, Seph. 1981. "Venus." *Heresies*, 3:4 (Issue 12), 36-7.

WEIDEGER, Paula. 1977. *Menstruation and Menopause*. New York: Delta.

WEIDEGER, Paula. 1980. In *Why Children?* Ed. Stephanie Dowrick and Sibyl Grundberg. London: The Woman's Press, 197-211.

WEIGLE, Marta. 1982. *Spiders and Spinsters: Women and Mythology*. Albuquerque: University of New Mexico Press.

WEIL, Simone. 1933. *Oppression and Liberty*. Quoted in *The Quotable Woman*. Ed. Elaine Partnow. Vol. II. Los Angeles: Pinnacle Books, 1977, 147.

WEIL, Simone. 1949. *The Need for Roots*. Quoted in *The Quotable Woman*. Ed. Elaine Partnow. Vol. II. Los Angeles: Pinnacle Books, 1977, 146.

WEINBROT, Howard D., ed. 1972. *New Aspects of Lexicography: Literary Criticism, Intellectual History, and Social Change*. Carbondale: Southern Illinois University Press.

WEINMAN, Irving. 1983. "On the Edge." In *On Gender and Writing*. Ed. Michelene Wandor. London: Pandora Press, 133-40.

WEISMAN, Leslie Kanes and Noel Phyllis Birkby. 1983. "The Women's School of Planning and Architecture." In *Learning Our Way*. Ed. Charlotte Bunch and Sandra Pollack. Trumansburg, New York: The Crossing Press, 224-45.

WEISSTEIN, Naomi. 1970. "The Sexual Caste System." *The Spark*, 3:3.

WEISSTEIN, Naomi. 1973. Introduction to *All She Needs*. Ellen Levine. Quoted in *The*

Quotable Woman. Ed. Elaine Partnow. Vol. II. Los Angeles: Pinnacle Books, 1977, 400.

WEISSTEIN, Naomi. 1981. "Abortion Rights: Taking the Offensive." *Ms.*, 10:3 (September), 36, 38.

WEISSTEIN, Naomi and Heather Booth. 1975. "Will the Women's Movement Survive?" *Sister*, 4:12 (December), 1-6.

WEISSTEIN, Naomi, Virginia Blaisdell, and Jesse Lemisch. 1975. *The Godfathers: Freudians, Marxists, and the Scientific and Political Protection Societies.* New Haven, Connecticut: Belladonna Publishing.

WELLS, Jeannie. 1969. "Notes on Women: Where It's At." *Speaking Out*, February. Northwestern University Library, Evanston, Illinois.

WELLS, Rulon A. 1973. *Dictionaries and the Authoritarian Tradition.* The Hague: Mouton.

WEST, Candace and Don H. Zimmerman. 1983. "Small Insults: A Study of Interruptions in Cross-Sex Conversations Between Unacquainted Persons." In *Language, Gender, and Society.* Ed. Barrie Thorne, Cheris Kramarae, and Nancy Henley. Rowley, Massachusetts: Newbury House, 102-17.

WEST, Jessamyn. 1979. *The Life I Really Lived.* New York: Penguin.

WEST, Rebecca. 1911-17. Selections of Rebecca West's Writings. In *The Young Rebecca.* Ed. Jane Marcus. London: MacMillan, 1982.

WHARTON, Edith. 1913. *The Customs of the Country.* New York: Scribner's.

WHARTON, Edith. 1934. Quoted in *A Feast of Words: The Triumph of Edith Wharton.* Cynthia Griffin Wolff. New York: Oxford University Press, 1977, 406.

WHEELER, Ethel Rolt. 1910a. " 'Fair Ladies in Revolt.' " *The Englishwoman*, 5:13 (February), 13-22.

WHEELER, Ethel Rolt. 1910b. *Famous Bluestockings.* London: Methuen.

WHISLER, Sandra M. 1981. "The Celibacy Letters." *Heresies*, 3:4 (Issue 12), 26-8.

WHITALL, Susan. 1980. "Women in Revolt!" *Creem*, May, 24.

WHITE, Julie Belle. 1980. "Sacred and Profane Metaphors About Women." Central States Speech Association Conference, Chicago. April.

WHITELEY, Opal. 1975. "The Story of Opal," ed. Jane Boulton. *Ms.*, 3:10 (April), 55-8.

WHITING, Pat. 1972. "Female Sexuality: Its Political Implications." In *The Body Politic: Women's Liberation in Britain.* Ed. Michelene Wandor. Rpt. London: stage 1, 1978, 189-213.

WIENER, Philip P. 1968. *Dictionary of the History of Ideas: Studies of Selected Pivotal Ideas.* New York: Scribner's.

WILLARD, Frances E. 1898. "Reasons for Woman's Enfranchisement." *The Woman's Journal*, 29:10 (5 March), 1.

WILLARD, Nancy. 1971. "The Poet Stumbles Upon the Astronomer's Orchard." *19 Masks for the Naked Poet.* Santa Cruz: Kayak Books, n.p.

WILLIAMS, Raymond. 1976. *Keywords: A Vocabulary of Culture and Society.* New York: Oxford University Press.

WILLIAMSON, Nancy. 1971. Untitled Poem. *The Second Wave*, 1:2 (Summer), 9.

WILLIS, Ellen. 1981. *Beginning to See the Light.* New York: Alfred A. Knopf.

WILLIS, Ellen. 1982. "Toward a Feminist Sexual Revolution." *Social Text*, 6, 3-21.

WILSON, Arthur L. 1981. "Why do Russians Defect? Their Language Tells Us." *Shipmate*, March, 25-6.

WILSON, Elizabeth. 1975. "An Opposing Image." *Red Rag*, 9. Rpt. in *No Turning Back: Writings From the Women's Liberation Movement 1975-80.* Ed. Feminist Anthology Collective. London: The Women's Press, 1981, 11-14.

WILSON, Elizabeth. 1980. *Only Halfway to Paradise: Women in Postwar Britain 1945-1968.* London: Tavistock.

WILSON, Emily Herring, narrative, and Susan Mullally, photographs. 1983. *Hope and Dignity: Older Black Women of the South*. Philadelphia: Temple University Press.

WINANT, Terry R. 1983. "How Ordinary (Sexist) Discourse Resists Radical (Feminist) Critique." *Women's Studies International Forum*, 6:6, 609-19.

WISE, Sue and Liz Stanley. In press. *Kiss the Girls and Make Them Cry*. London: Pandora Press.

WITT, Shirley Hill and Stan Steiner, eds. 1972. *The Way: An Anthology of American Indian Literature*. New York: Vintage.

WITTIG, Monique. 1976. *The Lesbian Body*. New York: Avon.

WITTIG, Monique. 1981. "One is Not Born a Woman." *Feminist Issues*, 1:2 (Winter), 47-54.

WITTIG, Monique. 1982. "The Category of Sex." *Feminist Issues*, 2:2 (Fall), 63-8.

WITTIG, Monique and Sande Zeig. 1976. *Lesbian Peoples: Material for a Dictionary*. New York: Avon, 1979.

WOLF, Christa. 1978. "Self Experiment: Appendix to a Report." Trans. Jeanette Clausen. *New German Critique*, 13, 113-31.

WOLFE, Ann. 1976. "The Jewish Woman." In *Dialogue on Diversity: A New Agenda for American Women*. Ed. Barbara Peters and Victoria Samuels. New York: Institute on Pluralism and Group Identity of the American Jewish Committee, 42-8.

WOLFE, Susan J. 1980. "Amazon Etymology: Rooting for the Matriarchy." *Sinister Wisdom*, 12 (Winter), 15-20.

WOLFE, SUSAN J. 1984. "The Codification of Sexist Language Usage." Symposium on Sexist Language, Linguistic Society of America. Baltimore, December.

WOLFE, Susan J. and Julia Penelope. 1980a. "Crooked and Straight in Academia." In *Pulling Our Own Strings*. Ed. Gloria Kaufman and Mary Kay Blakely. Bloomington: Indiana University Press, 119.

WOLFE, Susan J. and Julia Penelope Stanley. 1980b. "Linguistic Problems with Patriarchal Reconstructions of Indo-European Culture: A Little More than Kin, A Little Less than Kind." In *The Voices and Words of Women and Men*. Ed. Cheris Kramarae. Oxford: Pergamon Press, 227-37.

WOLFE, Susan J. and Julia Penelope Stanley, eds. 1980c. *The Coming Out Stories*. Watertown, Massachusetts: Persephone Press.

WOLFF, Cynthia Griffin. 1977. *A Feast of Words: The Triumph of Edith Wharton*. New York: Oxford University Press.

WOLFSON, Nessa. In press. "Pretty Is As Pretty Does: A Speech Act View of Sex Roles." In special issue of *Applied Linguistics*. Ed. Elite Olshtain and Shoshana Blum-Kulka.

WOLFSON, Nessa and Joan Manes. 1980. "Don't 'Dear' Me!" In *Women and Language in Literature and Society*. Ed. Sally McConnell-Ginet, Ruth Borker, and Nelly Furman. New York: Praeger, 79-92.

WOLLSTONECRAFT, Mary. 1789. "A Vindication of the Rights of Women." From *A Vindication of the Rights of Women*. Rpt. New York: W. W. Norton, 1967. Excerpt in *Feminist Papers*. Ed. Alice Rossi. New York: Bantam, 1973, 40-85.

WOLVERTON, Terry. 1983. "Unlearning Complicity, Remembering Resistance: White Women's Anti-Racism Education." In *Learning Our Way*. Ed. Charlotte Bunch and Sandra Pollack. Trumansburg, New York: The Crossing Press, 187-99.

A Woman's New World Dictionary. 1973. Pamphlet. Women's Collection, Northwestern University Library, Evanston, Illinois.

Woman's Center, The (Philadelphia). 1971. "Groupies (I'd rather be a hip oppressed woman than a straight oppressed woman)." In *Through the Looking Glass*, 1:1 (February), 10.

Women in the Publishing Industry. c.1980. *Non-Sexist Code of Practice for Book Publishing*.

Equal Opportunity Council Library, Manchester, England.

Women in Italy. 1972. "a few notes about the italian women's movement today." In *Women in Italy*. Rpt. in *Women in the Struggle for Liberation*. World Student Christian Federation Book Series, 3:2/3, 1973, 85-7.

Women of Europe. 1984. January-March. Brussels, Belgium: Commission of the European Communities.

WOO, Merle. 1981. "Letter to Ma." In *This Bridge Called My Back: Writings by Radical Women of Color*. Ed. Cherríe Moraga and Gloria Anzaldúa. Watertown, Massachusetts: Persephone Press, 140-7.

WOOD, Susan, ed. 1979a. *The Language of the Night: Essays on Fantasy and Science Fiction by Ursula K. LeGuin*. New York: Perigee Books.

WOOD, Susan. 1979b. "Waitressing: Taking Control of Our Work." *Quest*, 5:1 (Summer), 82-94.

WOOLEY, Susan C. and Orland W. Wooley. In press. "Women and Weight Obsession: Toward a Redefinition of the Underlying Problem." In *For Alma Mater: Theory and Practice in Feminist Scholarship*. Ed. Paula A Treichler, Cheris Kramarae, and Beth Stafford. Urbana, Illinois: University of Illinois Press.

WOOLF, Virginia. 1929. *A Room of One's Own*. New York: Harcourt, Brace & World.

WOOLF, Virginia. 1938. *Three Guineas*. New York: Harcourt Brace Jovanovich.

WOOLSTON, Florence Guy. 1919. "Marriage Customs and Taboo Among the Early Heterodites." *Scientific Monthly*. Rpt. in *Radical Feminists of Heterodoxy*. Judith Schwarz. Lebanon, New Hampshire: New Victoria Publishers, 1982, Appendix B, 95-6.

WORKMAN, Fanny and William Hunter Workman. n.d. *Two Summers in the Ice-Wilds of Eastern Karakoram*. New York: E. P. Dutton.

WRIGHT, Frances. 1829. "Of Free Enquiry." In *Course of Popular Lectures*. New York: Free Enquirer, Lecture II, 41-62. Rpt. in *The Feminist Papers: From Adams to de Beauvoir*. Ed. Alice Rossi. New York: Bantam, 1973, 108-17.

WRIGLEY, Mrs. 1931. "A Plate-Layer's Wife." In *Life as We Have Known It: By Co-operative Working Women*. Ed. Margaret Llewelyn Davies. Hogarth Press. Rpt. London: Virago, 1982, 56-66.

YOUNG, Iris. 1981. "Beyond the Unhappy Marriage: A Critique of the Dual Systems Theory." In *Women and Revolution*. Ed. Lydia Sargent. Boston: South End Press, 43-70.

YOUNG, Willa. 1984. "Gender Gap." *The Women's Studies Review*, 6:5 (September/ October), 4-5.

ZAJICEK, Mary. 1983. "Women and Computing." *Spare Rib*, June, 27.

zakre, sheila, 1984. "on disability – language and meaning." *off our backs*, January, 20.

ZGUSTA, Ladislav, ed. 1980. *Theory and Method in Lexicography: Western and Non-Western Perspectives*. Columbia, South Carolina: Hornbeam Press.

ZIKMUND, Barbara Brown. 1979. "The Feminist Thrust of Sectarian Christianity." In *Women of Spirit: Female Leadership in the Jewish and Christian Traditions*. New York: Simon & Schuster, 206-24.

ZILLBOORG, G. 1974. "Masculine and Feminine." In *Psychoanalysis and Women*. Ed. Jean Baker Miller. Harmondsworth: Pelican.

ZIMMERMAN, Bonnie. 1981. "What Has Never Been: An Overview of Lesbian Feminist Literary Criticism." *Feminist Studies*, 7:3 (Fall), 451-75.

ZIMMERMAN, Bonnie. 1982. "One Out of Thirty: Lesbianism in Women's Studies Textbooks." In *Lesbian Studies*. Ed. Margaret Cruikshank. Old Westbury, New York: The Feminist Press, 128-31.

ZIMMERMAN, Jan. 1981. "Technology and the Future of Women: Haven't We Met Somewhere Before?" *Women's Studies International Quarterly*, 4:3, 355-67.

ZITA, Jacqueline. 1981. "Historical Amnesia and the Lesbian Continuum." *Signs*, 7:1 (Autumn), 172-87.

ZIUKOVICH, Tania. 1971. "Prostitution-PROperty's inSTITUTION." *Battle Acts*, 1:5 (April/May), 8.

Comments and contributions will be welcomed by us
at: 244 Lincoln Hall
          University of Illinois
          702 South Wright Street
          Urbana
          Illinois 61801
          USA

or by our publishers at:
          Pandora Press
          14 Leicester Square
          London WC2H 7PH